A
Mary Shelley
Encyclopedia

A Mary Shelley Encyclopedia

Lucy Morrison and Staci Stone

GREENWOOD PRESS
Westport, Connecticut • London

Library of Congress Cataloging-in-Publication Data

Morrison, Lucy, 1971–
  A Mary Shelley encyclopedia / Lucy Morrison and Staci Stone.
    p. cm.
  Includes bibliographical references and index.
  ISBN 0–313–30159–X (alk. paper)
  1. Shelley, Mary Wollstonecraft, 1797–1851—Encyclopedias. 2. Authors, English—19th century—Biography—Encyclopedias. I. Stone, Staci, 1971– II. Feldman, Paula R. Mary Shelley encyclopedia. III. Title.
  PR5398.A2M67 2003
  823'.7—dc21   2002192784
  [B]

British Library Cataloguing in Publication Data is available.

Copyright © 2003 by Lucy Morrison and Staci Stone

All rights reserved. No portion of this book may be reproduced, by any process or technique, without the express written consent of the publisher.

Library of Congress Catalog Card Number: 2002192784
ISBN: 0–313–30159–X

First published in 2003

Greenwood Press, 88 Post Road West, Westport, CT 06881
An imprint of Greenwood Publishing Group, Inc.
www.greenwood.com

Printed in the United States of America

The paper used in this book complies with the Permanent Paper Standard issued by the National Information Standards Organization (Z39.48–1984).

10 9 8 7 6 5 4 3 2 1

For our Husbands and Families

And
In Memory Of

Kath Littlewood
1909–1999

Tom Metcalf Christine Metcalf
1911–1984 1912–2002

Albert Morrison
1922–2001

Ernest Stone Kitty Stone
1909–1989 1912–2000

Hershellene Peek McCurdy
1920–2003

Contents

Acknowledgments ix

Introduction xi

How to Use This Encyclopedia xiii

Shelley's Texts xv

Editions of Shelley's Texts Used xvii

Citations xix

A Mary Shelley Encyclopedia 1

Appendix I: Quotations Attributed to Their Authors 489

Appendix II: Unidentified Quotations 497

Bibliography 499

Index 517

Acknowledgments

We thank Paula R. Feldman for her early support of this project. We appreciate her belief in our ability, her assistance with negotiations and decisions, and, foremost, her interest in and enthusiasm for Shelley studies. We also appreciate the assistance of the friendly, helpful staff at the University of South Carolina's Thomas Cooper Library, especially those in the Interlibrary Loan Department and the Map Library, as well as staff at the Waterfield Library at Murray State University and Pennsylvania State University, Hazleton. We also thank the Departments of English and Continuing Education at the University of South Carolina, Deans Sandra Gleason and Diane Disney and Division Head Richard Kopley of the Commonwealth College, Director of Academic Affairs Monica Gregory, Campus Executive Officer John Madden, and Alan Price at Pennsylvania State University, Hazleton, Dean Sandra Jordan and Peter Murphy, Sarah Aguiar, Michael Cohen, and Kevin Binfield in the Department of English and Philosophy at Murray State University for their support. George Butler at Greenwood, Pelham Boyer, and Lori Ewen at Westchester Book Services were very helpful to us and to them we extend our gratitude. For research assistance, we thank Amber Cash, Siobhan Groitl, Alex Ingber, Jon Jones, William Jones, Michael Katner, Amanda Pettit, Laura di Prete, Sara Rashid, Tonya Wertz-Orbaugh, and Lisa Whitish. We are grateful for Lisa Vargo's and Arnold A. Markley's encouraging editing suggestions, insightful comments, and invaluable input; also, Arnold's textual generosity was crucial to a late stage of our work on this book. Jeanne Moskal and Charles E. Robinson gave helpful advice early in this project. Nora Crook was absolutely vital to this book's progression and eventual shape; we thank her for being the scholarly exemplar she is and for all her very generous help. Steven Morrison's dedicated efforts to respond to telephoned queries were inestimable; his commitment to

Acknowledgments

searching out obscure details helped and encouraged us greatly. We extend grateful appreciation and love to our families and friends, especially Ivan Young, Jason Walker, Darlene M. Pagán, Siobhan Brownson, Park Bucker, Virginia Hodges, Carol Osbourne, and Melissa Johnson.

Introduction

Only recently has Mary Shelley emerged from the shadows of her famous parents, Mary Wollstonecraft and William Godwin, and her husband, Percy Bysshe Shelley. Today, *Frankenstein* (1818, 1831) is one of the most popular classroom texts in high school and college, and in the 1990s her other works appeared in print again after over a century and a half. These other works reveal much about the Romantic literary period and Shelley's ongoing development as a writer. *The Last Man* (1826), with its dire, millennial visions of the end of the world, reveals Shelley's active participation in contemporary literary debates, as do her many reviews and articles. *Valperga* (1823) and *Perkin Warbeck* (1830) supplement our experience of the historical novel genre so popular in the early-nineteenth century, while her later works, *Lodore* (1835) and *Falkner* (1837), reflect larger movements of the 1830s—from the individual to society, from Romantic to Victorian. Shelley's many short stories, poems, dramas, novellas, and critical pieces reveal much about the difficulties of a shifting literary marketplace, one that opened many doors to women writers, while her travel writing, *History of a Six Weeks' Tour* (1817) and *Rambles in Germany and Italy* (1844), tells us perhaps the most about this woman's incredible mind and life. Similarly, her biographies for Dionysius Lardner (1830s) confirm the diligent research and crafted prose evident in all her work. *A Mary Shelley Encyclopedia* will assist and encourage readers to venture beyond her infamous science-fiction text into the realms of her other works, a worthy expedition.

Readers of Shelley's texts can use this encyclopedia to acquire more information about all of Shelley's works, as well as about her life, friends, relatives, residences, fictional characters, allusions, and much more. This book serves as an instant reference guide, containing textual footnotes to nearly all aspects of Shelley and her works. We have surveyed available informa-

Introduction

tion about Shelley's life and works, and we have included here many new discoveries that further understanding of her achievements. *A Mary Shelley Encyclopedia* will join ever-expanding scholarly material about Shelley, so that her canonical status will remain secure well into the twenty-first century.

How to Use This Encyclopedia

CONTENTS

We have annotated information within Shelley's drama, fiction, poetry, and travel writing as minutely as possible; for her articles, biographies, and reviews, we provide broader annotations. We have endeavored to include all published works known definitively to be Shelley's at the time of going to press (July 2002); we have not included unfinished works or extensive reference to her editions of, and annotations to, her husband's works. The order of works within an individual entry is dependent upon publication date except where a work remained unpublished until after her death, in which cases the works are inserted in chronological order of composition. Abbreviations and page numbers in brackets at the end of an entry indicate additional references within Shelley's works.

ABBREVIATIONS

Throughout, we refer to Mary Shelley as Shelley, Percy Bysshe Shelley as PBS, and Percy Florence Shelley as PFS. Consult the "Citations" for information regarding abbreviations of sources and "Shelley's Texts" for the abbreviations of her works.

CROSS REFERENCES

Bolded words within an entry (e.g., **Coliseum** within **Rome**) indicate a separate entry upon the term used. We also bold the adjectival forms of countries (e.g., **French** for **France**) and cities (e.g., **Lucchese** for **Lucca**); these variants direct readers to the main entries (**France**; **Lucca**). If Shelley refers to a work by its title (e.g., *The Italian*), the entry for that work can be found under its author's name (e.g., **Radcliffe, Ann**); thus *Italian, The* directs readers to its author.

xiii

How to Use This Encyclopedia

QUOTATIONS

"Appendix I: Quotations Attributed to Their Authors" gives a list of quotations Shelley uses from other works and directions to the entry in which we identify and contextualize these quotations; the same words from the quotation appear bolded in the main entry for easy identification. For example, "**Alack! what trouble**" directs readers to *The Tempest*; in the latter's entry, the same three words are bolded. "Appendix II: Unidentified Quotations" includes unidentified quotations and the contexts in which Shelley uses them. When Shelley quotes from a particular work two or more times (e.g., *Paradise Lost*), the work has its own entry. Exceptions to this principle are works by Beaumont and Fletcher, Byron, Samuel Taylor Coleridge, Dante, Milton, Shakespeare, and Percy Bysshe Shelley, since she repeatedly quotes these authors.

LOCATION OF ENTRIES

The entries are arranged in alphabetical order. Titled and noble figures are mostly listed under their names or countries (e.g., **Sibylla, Queen** and **Bavaria, Louis of**), including bishops, duchesses, dukes, earls, kings, lords, marquises, popes, princes, princesses, and queens. Geographical features in English are listed under place name (e.g., **Geneva, Lake**), while foreign geographical features are listed straightforwardly (e.g., **Mont Blanc**). Castles, cathedrals, churches, and convents with English names are principally listed by place-name (e.g., **Ballybeg, Abbey of**), and such places in a language other than English are listed straightforwardly (e.g., **Palazzo Pitti**). Fictional female characters are generally listed under their married names (Elizabeth Falkner and Elizabeth Lavenza are two exceptions to this rule), while people Shelley knew are generally listed under the names by which she would have known them. Works of art and literature in all languages are listed under their first noun (e.g., *Barbier de Paris, Le* and *Assumption, The*) rather than article. All hotels, universities, baths, and councils are listed under those words (e.g., **Hotel de la Ville, University of Berlin, Council of Basle**), while all Villas are listed under the family name (e.g., **Diodati, Villa**).

Shelley's Texts

The following list gives the citation abbreviations used for all of Shelley's works:

BMI	"Bride of Modern Italy"
Brother	"The Brother and Sister"
C	*Relation of the Death of the Family of the Cenci*
Ch	"The Choice"
D	"The Dream"
Death	"The Death of Love"
DefVel	"Defense of Velluti"
E	"Euphrasia: A Tale of Greece"
EC	"An Eighteenth Century Tale"
EE	"The Evil Eye"
ES	"The Elder Son"
F	*Falkner*
FE	"Ferdinando Eboli"
FL	*Lives of the Most Eminent Literary and Scientific Men of France*
FR	"The False Rhyme"
Fr1	*Frankenstein* (1818 ed.)
Fr3	*Frankenstein* (1831 ed.)
GV	"Giovanni Villani"
H	*History of a Six Weeks' Tour*
HM	"Heir of Mondolfo"
IG	"The Invisible Girl"
ISPL	*Lives of the Most Eminent Literary and Scientific Men of Italy, Spain and Portugal*
La Vida	"La Vida es Sueño"
L	*Lodore*
LM	*The Last Man*
M	*Matilda*
Mad d'H	"Madame d'Houtetôt"
Maurice	"Maurice; or, The Fisher's Cot; A Tale"
Midas	*Midas*
ModItRom	"Modern Italian Romances"
ModIt	"Modern Italy"
Mourner	"The Mourner"
On Ghosts	"On Ghosts"
On Reading	"On Reading Wordsworth's Lines on Peel Castle"
P	*Proserpine*
Par	"The Parvenue"
PW	*The Fortunes of Perkin Warbeck*

Shelley's Texts

R	*Rambles in Germany and Italy, 1840, 1842, and 1843*	*Stanzas: O come*	"Stanzas: O, come to me in dreams, my love!"
RD	"Roger Dodsworth: The Reanimated Englishman"	*Stanzas: The Tide*	"Stanzas: The Tide of Time Was at my Feet"
Rev1572	"Review of *1572 Chronique du Temps de Charles IX*"	*Stanzas: To Love*	"Stanzas: To love in solitude and mystery"
RevB	"Review of *The Bravo; a Venetian Story*"	*SA*	"The Sisters of Albano"
RevC	"Review of *Cloudesley; A Tale*"	*SP*	"The Swiss Peasant"
RevEng	"Review of *The English in Italy*"	*TJ*	"To Jane"
RevIll	"Illyrian Poems—Feudal Scenes"	*TP*	"A Tale of the Passions"
RevLoves	"Review of *The Loves of the Poets*"	*Tempo*	"Tempo è ben di Morire"
RI	"Recollections of Italy"	*Trans*	"Transformation"
S	"The Smuggler and His Family"	*Trial*	"The Trial of Love"
Stanzas: How like	"Stanzas: How like a star you rose upon my life"	*Un*	"Untitled: 'Fair Italy!'"
		V	*Valperga*
Stanzas: I must Forget	"Stanzas: I must forget thy dark eyes' love-fraught gaze"	*Val*	"Valerius the Reanimated Roman"
		Visit	"A Visit to Brighton"

Editions of Shelley's Texts Used

In preparing this *Encyclopedia*, we attempted to use editions of Shelley's works that we thought would be available to high school students and other readers. *The Novels and Selected Works of Mary Shelley*, under the general editorship of Nora Crook, have subsequently provided definitive texts; individual editors' annotations have proven invaluable to our work. In order to assist readers in locating citations, we used the following editions of Shelley's texts:

The Choice. A Poem on Shelley's Death by Mary Wollstonecraft Shelley. Ed. H. Buxton Forman. London: Privately printed, 1876.

Collected Tales and Stories. Ed. Charles E. Robinson. Baltimore: Johns Hopkins UP, 1990.

Falkner. A Novel. New York: Harper and Brothers, 1837.

The Fortunes of Perkin Warbeck, A Romance. 3 vols. London: Henry Colburn and Richard Bentley, 1830.

Frankenstein. 1818. Ed. D. L. Macdonald and Kathleen Scherf. Peterborough, ON: Broadview P, 1994.

Frankenstein. 1831. Ed. Johanna M. Smith. Case Studies in Contemporary Criticism Ser. Boston: Bedford, 1992.

History of a Six Weeks' Tour Through a Part of France, Switzerland, Germany, and Holland; with letters descriptive of a sail around the Lake of Geneva, and of the Glaciers of Chamouni. London: T. Hookham, 1817.

The Last Man. Ed. Morton D. Paley. World's Classics ed. Oxford: Oxford UP, 1994.

Lives of the Most Eminent Literary and Scientific Men of France. 2 vols. London: Longman, Rees, Orme, Brown, Green and Longmans, 1838–1839.

Lives of the Most Eminent Literary and Scientific Men of Italy, Spain and Portugal. 3 vols. London: Longman, Rees, Orme, Brown, Green and Longmans, 1835–1837.

Lodore. Ed. Fiona Stafford. London: Pickering, 1996. Vol. 6 of *The Novels and Selected Works of Mary Shelley*. Ed. Nora Crook. 9 vols. London: Pickering, 1996.

Matilda. Ed. Janet Todd. London: Penguin, 1992.

Maurice; or, The Fisher's Cot. Ed. Claire Tomalin. London: Viking, 1998.

Mythological Dramas: 'Proserpine' and 'Midas.' Bod MS. Shelley d.2. Ed. Charles E. Robinson. Vol. 10 of *The Bodleian Shelley Manuscripts*. Gen. ed. Donald H. Reiman. Fac-

Editions Used

simile ed. Garland Ser. New York: Garland, 1992.

Relation of the Death of the Family of the Cenci. Bodleian MS.Shelley adds.e.13. Trans. Mary Wollstonecraft Shelley. Ed. Betty T. Bennett. Vol. 10 of *The Bodleian Shelley Manuscripts.* Gen. ed. Donald H. Reiman. Facsimile ed. Garland Ser. New York: Garland, 1992.

Travel Writing. Ed. Jeanne Moskal. London: Pickering, 1996. Vol. 8 of *The Novels and Selected Works of Mary Shelley.* Ed. Nora Crook. 9 vols. London: Pickering, 1996.

Valperga: or, the Life and Adventures of Castruccio, Prince of Lucca. 3 vols. London: G. and W. B. Whittaker, 1823.

Consult individual entries for publication information of Shelley's poems and reviews.

Citations

Parenthetical citations in the *Encyclopedia* are to authors of texts listed in the bibliography, except in the cases of Shelley's works and some frequently cited critical works. "Crook 2" acknowledges personal communication with Nora Crook. Unless otherwise noted, all parenthetical citations to Robinson are to his edition of Shelley's *Tales and Stories*. We have used the following abbreviations throughout the text parenthetically as citations for works often used. Parenthetical remarks in the list below indicate how to locate the full reference in the bibliography; titles below without parentheticals are listed by their titles in the bibliography:

Artistic	*Artistic Guide to Florence and its Surroundings*
BAUS	*Baedeker's Austria* (see Baumgarten, Peter)
BCSR	*Baedeker's Czech/Slovak Republics* (see Baumgarten, Peter)
BGE	*Baedeker's Germany* (see Baumgarten, Peter)
BRH	*Baedeker's Rhine* (see Baumgarten, Monica)
BSW	*Switzerland and the Adjacent Portions of Italy, Savoy, and Tyrol: Handbook for Travellers* (see Baedeker)
CHP	*Childe Harold's Pilgrimage* (see Byron)
DBF	*Dictionnaire de Biographie Francaise* (see Balteau)
DIL	*Dictionary of Italian Literature* (see Bondanella)
DMIH	*Dictionary of Modern Italian History* (see Coppa)
DNB	*The Dictionary of National Biography*
Journals	*The Journals of Mary Shelley: 1814–1844* (see Shelley)
LCCL	*The Life of Castruccio Castracani of Lucca* (see Machiavelli)
Letters	*The Letters of Mary Wollstonecraft Shelley* (see Shelley)

Citations

Lives	*Plutarch's Lives: The Dryden Plutarch* (see Plutarch)	*MSGE*	*A Handbook for Travellers in Southern Germany*
MCIT	*A Handbook for Travellers in Central Italy*	*MSWI*	*A Handbook for Travellers in Switzerland*
MCON	*A Handbook for Travellers on the Continent*	*NGD*	*The New Grove Dictionary of Music and Musicians* (see Sadie)
MGRE	*Handbook for Travellers in Greece*	*OED*	*Oxford English Dictionary*
MIAU	*Michelin Tourist Guide: Austria*	*Phaidon*	*Phaidon Encyclopedia of Art and Artists*
MIIR	*Michelin Motoring Map: Ireland*		
MIIT	*Michelin Tourist Guide: Italy*	*SCGS*	*The Godwins and the Shelleys: The Biography of a Family* (see St. Clair)
MIPA	*Michelin Tourist Guide: Paris*		
MIRO	*Michelin Tourist Guide: Rome*	*SIDTC*	*Information and Directions for Travellers on the Continent* (see Starke)
MNIT	*A Handbook for Travellers in Northern Italy*		
MROM	*A Handbook of Rome and its Environs*	*STIE*	*Travels in Europe* (see Starke)

A
Mary Shelley
Encyclopedia

A

Aachen: German town forty-five miles southwest of **Cologne** (**Aix-la-Chapelle** in **French**). Shelley saw Aachen, **Charlemagne**'s favorite residence, but did not enter it June 1842 (*R* 1.166).

Abbot: Don Rodrigo Ponce de Leon's cousin, who raises **Hernan De Faro** in *Perkin Warbeck*.

Abel: See **Cain**.

Aberdeen: Scottish port (in Aberdeenshire) fifty-five miles northeast of **Dundee**. **James IV** leads **Richard of York** to the latter's wedding there (*PW* 2.240). **Gordon Castle** is in Aberdeenshire (*PW* 2.237).

Abon Hassan: See **Weber**.

Abruzzi: Central **Italian** region. **Euthanasia** and **Beatrice** pass through Abruzzi (*V* 1.202, 3.91). Shelley recounts **Ferdinand IV**'s possession of **Naples** when people fled to Abruzzi's mountains, and she notes rampant **Carbonarism** there (*R* 2.165, 2.177).

Absalom: Favorite son of the **biblical** king **David**, killed after rebelling against his father (2 Samuel 18). **Maurice** cries over David's sorrow after "Absalom revolted against him" (*Maurice* 75).

"Absence": Poem, beginning "Ah! he is gone—and I alone!—," first published in the 1831 *Keepsake* as "By the Author of **Frankenstein**" (39). In three quatrains, the poem's speaker mourns her isolation, comparing it to a dark night's sky. But she finds comfort in the "hope of dawn," asserting that "More welcome than the morning star / Is the dear thought—he will return!" (lines 9, 11–12).

Acarnania: Mountains on the Gulf of **Patras**'s northern shore and region south of **Epirus** (*MGRE* 116). **Dmitri** crosses "woods of Acarnania" (*EE* 103).

Accademia delle Belle Arti (Florence): "Academy of Fine Arts" museum founded 1350 and at San Marco since 1784 (*Florence* 160–167; *Artistic* 120). Shelley visited it January 1843 (*R* 2.156).

Accademia delle Belle Arti (Venice): On the **Grand Canal**, this "Academy of Fine Arts" displays 14th–18th century paintings (*MIIT* 246). Shelley visited it September 1842 (*R* 2.89–91).

Acroceraunia: **Albanian** mountain range opposite Corfu (*MGRE* 63). Shelley describes Acroceraunia "clos[ing] in the various prospects" of **Zitza** to the northwest (*EE* 110–111).

Acropolis: Fortified elevated part of ancient **Greek** cities; the most famous is in **Athens**. It is the omnipresent background to *The Last Man*'s Athens scenes (*LM* 170).

Actaeon: In **Greek** mythology, hunter Artemis turned into a stag; his own hounds subsequently tore him apart (Tripp 10–11). **Rupert Falkner** compares himself to Actaeon (*F* 19).

"Ad Sirmionem Peninsulum": See **Catullus**.

***Adalid*:** **Hernan De Faro**'s ship, which he took from **Algerines** and christened *Adalid*, **Spanish** for "champion," because "she embraced the true faith" (*PW* 2.64). Hernan uses the *Adalid* to serve **Richard of York** (*PW* 3.52–55, 3.66). Hernan sails for the **West Indies** on the *Adalid* near the novel's close (*PW* 3.344). [*PW* 2.87, 2.128, 2.177, 2.206, 3.82, 3.94–95, 3.172–173].

Adam: As Shelley frequently draws upon the myth of the Fall in the **biblical** book of **Genesis**, references to the first man, Adam, abound in her work. The **Creature** tells **Victor Frankenstein** " 'I ought to be thy Adam' " (*Fr1* 128; *Fr3* 90). **Matilda** compares **Woodville** to Adam (*M* 191). **Bindo** has "every prophecy that has been made since the time of Adam" and a lock of Adam's hair in his collection of strange relics (*V* 1.251–252). **Winzy**'s "habitual credence was, that I should meet the fate of all the children of Adam at my appointed time" (*MI* 226). Shelley notes a pretty girl and her ugly fiancé in **Baden-Baden** looking "at each other as Adam and **Eve** might have done when no other human creature existed" (*R* 1.39). [*Fr1* 157; *Fr3* 113; *R* 2.108]. See *As You Like It*.

Adams, Parson Abraham: See **Fielding**.

Adda: **Italian** river flowing from the **Alps** through **Lake Como** to **Lecco** and joining the **Po** near **Cremona**. Shelley describes traveling from **Splügen** to **Colico** on a road the Adda spoils July 1840 (*R* 1.61). [*R* 1.105].

Addison, Joseph (1672–1719): British dramatist, poet, and essayist known for his contributions to *The Tatler* and *The Spectator*. Shelley read Addison's *Cato* (1713) and was familiar with his contributions to *The Spectator* (*Letters* 1.122–123, 3.98–99). Viewing scenery near **Gmunden** September 1842, Shelley adapts a passage from *The Spectator* (25 October 1712): "should we not perceive that '**all the regions** of nature swarm with spirits' " (*R* 2.27; Moskal 241).

Adelchi: See **Manzoni**.

Adige: **Italian** river flowing through **Verona** and emptying into the **Adriatic** south of the **Brenta**. Shelley's September 1842 route from the **Eisach** followed Adige's valley to **Roveredo** (*R* 2.49, 2.62, 2.66–68).

Adimari, Antonio dei: **Euthanasia**'s father in *Valperga*; Shelley makes him the mouthpiece for her father **William Godwin**'s philosophy (Crook 2).

Adimari, Euthanasia dei: See **Euthanasia**.

Adimari, Fiammetta dei: **Euthanasia**'s close relative in *Valperga*.

Adimari, Lauretta dei: **Euthanasia**'s cousin in *Valperga*.

Adonis: In **Greek** mythology, **Aphrodite** loved this handsome **Asiatic** who died young; he was widely mourned (Tripp 13). **Lionel Verney** compares **Syrian** women's sorrow for Adonis to **Athenians** mourning over **Raymond**'s capture (*LM* 168).

Adoration of the Magi: See **Magi**.

Adoration of the Magi: See **Raphael**.

Adoration of the Magi, The: See **Ghirlandajo**.

Adrian: Last Earl of **Windsor** and last Protector of England in *The Last Man*. He represents the ideal gentle leader, inspiring loyalty with love rather than force, and is Shelley's tribute to **PBS**.

Adrian: See **Hadrian**.

Adriatic Sea: Arm of the **Mediterranean** separating Serbia and Croatia from **Italy**'s east coast. **Castruccio** views "gloomy Adriatic" en route from **Ancona** to **Este** (*V* 1.41). Bad weather forces **Lionel Verney**'s ship into the Adriatic when returning from **Greece**, and Verney is sole survivor of an Adriatic storm (*LM* 215, 445). [*R* 2.247].

Aegean Sea: Body of water between **Greece** and **Turkey**. *The Last Man*'s characters journey upon the Aegean during Greece's war with Turkey (*LM* 209).

Aegina: Island in and gulf between **Corinth** and **Athens**. **Cyril Ziani**'s home overlooks the gulf, and **Constans Ziani**'s parents sail across it to visit **Camaraz** (*EE* 103, 108).

Aegyptian day: Unlucky day named for **Egyptian** fortune-tellers (Crook 3.145). **Beatrice** predicts **Obizzo**'s return to **Ferrarra** as her opponents' Aegyptian day (*V* 2.66).

Aeneid: Between 29 and 19 B.C.E., **Virgil** composed this twelve-book, epic poem detailing **Rome**'s establishment and development. Shelley read it January 1818 and March 1820, as well as at other points in her life (*Journals* 191–195, 313–314, 317, 319). She draws on the *Aeneid* for descriptions of **Elysian fields** and the **Cumaean sibyl**'s cave; she notes "this was certainly the **Sibyl**'s Cave; not indeed exactly as Virgil describes it" (*LM* 3, 5, 37; Virgil 6.735–824). Shelley describes the **Irish** invading England with reference to Virgil's text: "details, proceeding from mouth to mouth, might, like Virgil's ever-growing Rumour, reach the heavens with her brow" (*LM* 298; Virgil 4.208–211). She says of reincarnation "that according to the theory explained by Virgil in his sixth *Aeneid,* every thousand years the dead return to life" (*RD* 48–49; Virgil 6.975–976, 988–993).

Africa: Shelley refers to explorations of the continent Africa. **Robert Walton** writes about traveling "by the most southern cape of Africa" (*Fr1* 55; *Fr3* 31). **Lionel Verney** hears of the sun's eclipse "from Africa" (*LM* 224). He later refers to the "swarthy African," a plague victim (*LM* 426). **Katusthius Ziani** recounts escaping from Africa (*EE* 102). **Hernan De Faro** makes numerous voyages around Africa (*PW* 1.146, 1.196). **Stephen Frion** was formerly a slave there (*PW* 1.150). Shelley compares **Ethel Villiers**'s loneliness to **Mungo Park**'s desolation in central Africa (*L* 2.284).

Agioli: See **Aziolo**.

Agli, Messer Giani dei: Weaver and minor character in "**A Tale of the Passions**."

Agnus Dei: Latin phrase for "Lamb of God" (Jesus), part of Roman Catholic liturgy said or sung between the Lord's Prayer and Communion; also, wax charms used to protect against **Satan** (McBrien 25, 748). *Valperga*'s Judgment of God trial is held in view of "a white standard with the words *Agnus Dei* embroidered on it" (*V* 2.58).

Agosto: **Castruccio** builds this thirty-towered fortification in **Lucca**'s section facing **Pisa**, forcing people who live there to relocate (*V* 3.110–11).

Agrippa von Nettesheim, Cornelius (1486–1535): Scientist and sorcerer, Christopher Marlowe's model for *Doctor Faustus* (1604). Agrippa learned about **Albertus**'s theories, dabbled in alchemy, and wanted to create gold, claiming by the time of his death to know the procedure (Nauert 10, 12, 24, 70, 72–73). Like Agrippa, **Victor Frankenstein** also attempts to understand the secrets of the **philosopher's stone** (*Fr1* 68–69; *Fr3* 44–45). Agrippa is an alchemist searching for the **Elixir of Immortality**, which he discovers, in "**The Mortal Immortal**."

Ahasuerus: See **Esther**.

Ahmed, Prince: See *Arabian Nights*.

Aigle Noire: French for "Black Eagle"; name of a **Liège** inn. Shelley stayed there June 1842 on **Murray**'s recommendation; robbers stole **PFS**'s money during the night (*R* 1.164–165).

Airolo: Swiss town on the **Ticino**, seven miles south of **Andermatt**. Shelley describes her son and his friends' dangerous September 1840 journey from **Milan** to **Lucerne**, when the road from **Faido** to Airolo was flooded (*R* 1.149, 1.151).

Aix-la-Chapelle: See **Aachen**.

Aladdin: See *Arabian Nights*.

Alastor; or, The Spirit of Solitude: Poem **PBS** wrote 1815, first published 1816 (*Journals* 104). Shelley paraphrases a line to describe **Servi di Maria**'s founders as "**generous, brave, and gentle**" (*R* 2.147; PBS line 58).

Albani, Cardinal Guiseppe (1750–1834): Shelley mentions this **Roman** nobleman and cardinal who led papal regiments against the **Carbonari** (*R* 2.253; Moskal 364).

Albania: Country bordering northwest **Greece**, under the **Ottoman Empire**'s control in Shelley's time. **Adrian**, **Clara**, and **Lionel Verney** are shipwrecked en route to Albania (*LM* 439). "**The Evil Eye**" is partially set there; Shelley asserts, "Albanians are characterized as despisers of women" (*EE* 100, 101). **Vasili** is an Albanian Greek (*F* 62). **Chief Constantine** and "a band of Albanians" fight in the Greek revolution (*E* 303). [*EE* 110].

Albano: Resort town and lake in the Alban Hills fifteen miles south of **Rome**. The Shelleys passed "over the beautiful hills of Albano" March 1819 (*Journals* 251). The narrator of "**The Sisters of Albano**" records traveling to the lake and breakfasting at Albano, where **Countess Atanasia D——** tells her story; the tale's events occur in and near Albano (*SA* 51–52).

Albaro: Hill east of **Genoa**. **Guido il Cortese** sells his "remaining estate near Albaro for half its worth" (*Trans* 123). Shelley's footnoted information on storms includes her experience with one that carried away the bridges on the **Bisagno** from Genoa to Albaro (*R* 1.58).

Albé: See **Byron, Lord George Gordon**.

Albergo Grande: Brentani family-operated hotel in **Cadenabbia**. Shelley stayed there summer 1840 (*R* 1.66).

Albert, Prince (1819–1861): Prince Consort of Britain's Queen Victoria. Shelley "saw nothing of **Gotha**," Prince Albert's "native-place," July 1840 (*R* 1.209).

Albert the Great (c. 1206–1280): German saint who taught **St. Thomas Aquinas** (Delaney 36–37). At the **Santa Maria Novella Church** January 1843, Shelley saw a painted tablet showing Albert the Great surrounded by disciples (*R* 2.146).

Alberti: Count of **Capraia** who attends **Euthanasia**'s court in *Valperga*.

Albertus Magnus (c. 1193–1280): Natural philosopher who taught at **Cologne** University, renowned as **Saint Thomas Aquinas**'s tutor. In addition to work on **Aristotle**, Albertus wrote treatises about magic; **Cornelius Agrippa** studied Albertus's *Speculum Astronomiae* (1260s), a text on natural philosophy and magic (Nauert 12, 224). **Victor Frankenstein** studies Albertus's writings (*Fr1* 68, 75; *Fr3* 44, 49).

Albigenses: Twelfth and 13th-century southern **French** Catharist heretic sect, taking its name from the city of Albi; the Crusades and the **Inquisition** exterminated it (*OED*). **Beatrice** mentions the "extirpation of the Albigenses" (*V* 3.11).

Albinois: Term used to refer to *Valperga*'s albino character, **Bindo**. Possibly Shelley's variant of **Italian** "albino" or of **French** "albinos."

Albion: Celtic name for England. **Lionel Verney** bids a sad farewell to his native Albion (*LM* 378).

Albion House: House on **Marlow**'s outskirts the Shelleys took 18 March 1817, with a twenty-one-year lease (*Journals* 165–166). **Clara Shelley** was born there, and it was the Shelleys' first home of their own; however, it proved very cold (Seymour 183–184). Rumors about **Claire Clairmont**'s position in the household intensified in **London** while the Shelleys sheltered her and her illegitimate child (Sunstein 133, 135–136). On 14 February 1818, the Shelleys moved back to London (*Journals* 191–192).

Alcala: Also called **Alcala-la-Real**; **Spanish** town twenty-five miles northwest of **Granada**. A kidnapper deposits young **Hernan De Faro** at Alcala's monastery, where he grows up (*PW* 1.205, 1.207). De Faro returns to live there with **Madeline, Monina De Faro**, and **Richard of York** (*PW* 1.207). [*PW* 1.208, 1.217, 1.323, 2.21].

Alcala-la-Real: See **Alcala**.

Alcalde: Sheriff of a **Spanish** or **Portuguese** town (*OED*). Injured **Richard of York** convalesces in the Alcalde's home near **Granada** (*PW* 1.235).

Alcibiades (c. 450–405 B.C.E.): **Athenian** noble and **Socrates**'s friend, who earned renown 420 B.C.E. as a military commander. The Athenians suffered defeat under his command 405 B.C.E. when they disregarded his good advice (Howatson 22). Shelley probably learned of Alcibiades from **Plutarch**'s *Lives* (1.290–326). Shelley remarks that **Richard Brinsley Sheridan** could have learned from Alcibiades' example that good advice is frequently ignored, thus avoiding his own disappointing career in **Parliament** (*RD* 49).

Alderigo: **Castruccio**'s "rich relation" residing in England in *Valperga*. Shelley adopts this character from **Tegrimi**'s accounts of Alderigo **Antelminelli**, "wealthy merchant at King Edward I's court" (Green 42, 44).

Aldiani: Italian class of peasants. An Aldiani man escorts **Euthanasia** to the boat when **Castruccio** sends her to **Sicily** (*V* 3.257).

Aldino: **Lucchese** senator whom **Castruccio** accuses of plotting his death in *Valperga*.

Alessandria: Italian city thirty-five miles northwest of **Genoa**. **Benedetto Pepi** heads toward Alessandria after leaving **Castruccio** (*V* 1.129–130).

Alexander the Great (356–323 B.C.E.): Legendary military conqueror who helped to spread **Greek** culture abroad as far as **India** (Kinder 1.65). **PBS** read an account of Alexander in **Plutarch**'s *Lives* November 1816 (*Journals* 147; *Lives* 2.463–530). Shelley uses Alexander as an example of conquerors who "have indulged the hope of subduing the world, and spreading by their triumphs refinement into its barbarous recesses" (*V* 1.49). **Raymond** wants to be a king and military leader as renowned as Alexander (*LM* 56, 194). The narrator of "**The Mourner**" describes **Virginia Water**, noting that its silence is broken by strains "more inspiring than the song of **Tiresias** which awoke Alexander" (*Mourner* 81). Shelley refers to John Dryden's "Alexander's Feast" (1697), mistaking Tiresias for Timotheus, whose music inspires Alexander to burn conquered Dersepolis 331 B.C.E. (Crook 2). Shelley recalls how Alexander, according to Plutarch, felt the lack of someone to record his story (*R* 2.7). She saw **Veronese**'s "*Family of Darius at the feet of Alexander*" October 1842 (*R* 2.120).

Alexandria: Egyptian seaport on the **Nile** delta at the **Mediterranean**. **Miss Jervis** and the **Cecils** arrive in Egypt there (*F* 73). [*R* 2.5].

Alexandria, Patriarch of: See **John II**.

Alfieri, Vittorio (1749–1803): Prolific **Italian** writer known principally for his tragedies (published in **Paris** collectively 1789), some of which Shelley read September 1818 (*Journals* 226; Seymour 125). **Matilda**'s admiration for *Myrrha* as "the best of Alfieri's tragedies" causes her father's frame to shake (*M* 165). Shelley translated *Myrrha* in preparation for writing **Proserpine** and **Midas** (Sunstein 155). She wrote Alfieri's biography for *Italian and Spanish Lives*, noting particularly the successes of *Philip*, for which she provides a plot summary, and of *Polinice* (*ISPL* 2.275; *Journals* 226). She highlights several works as having the "energy and conciseness [which] are the distinguishing marks of Alfieri's dramas" and asserts Alfieri's "inventive powers consisted in being able to conceive situations of passion and interest, and giving to his personages feelings and language at once natural, powerful, and pathetic" (*ISPL* 2.282, 2.284). Shelley calls *Saul* (first read October 1818) "the chef d'oeuvre of Alfieri" (*Journals* 228; *ISPL* 2.287). Shelley concludes that Alfieri "is a great tragedian: it is impossible to read his best dramas without being carried away by the eloquence and passion of the dialogue, and deeply interested by the situations of struggle or peril in which his personages are placed" (*ISPL* 2.295, 2.300). Describing **Gerard Neville**, Shelley notes: "Well has Alfieri said, '**There is no struggle** so vehement as when an upright but passionate heart is divided between inclination and duty,'" perhaps Shelley's imperfect recollection of a passage from Alfieri's critique (*Parere*) on *Saul* (*F* 242; Crook 2). Shelley describes Alfieri as "the writer who best knew how to echo the passions and hopes of his contemporaries" (*R* 2.193, 2.203).

Alfred: **Lionel Verney** and **Idris**'s eldest son in *The Last Man*.

Algerines: Algerian pirates. **Hernan de Faro** obtains the *Adalid* from Algerines (*PW* 2.64).

Alhambra: Moorish fortress near **Granada**, built 1238–1358. **Hernan De Faro** avoids seeing Granada fall, evidence of which would be a cross flying over Alhambra (*PW* 1.210).

Ali: See **Ali Pasha**.

Ali, Mohammed: Albanian, rebellious, despotic vassal of **Turkey**'s sultan, Ali was also **Egypt**'s governor (1805–49); Shelley also terms him **Mehemet Ali** (Dupuy 851; Crook 2). Shelley mentions that "several persons" thought her plan to travel through **France** "rash" due to "war with" Ali (*R* 1.139). She alludes to the Second Turko-Egyptian War (1839–41), when France broke ranks with other **European** powers to support Ali against the sultan (Dupuy 851; Crook 2).

Ali, Prince: See *Arabian Nights*.

Alighieri, Dante: See **Dante**.

Alison, Sir Archibald (1792–1867): British historian renowned for *History of Europe* (1829–42) (*DNB*). Shelley relies on his account of the **Tyrolese** uprising and quotes his description of **Hofer**'s dedication to Tyrolese people: " 'He would fight with them and for them, as a father for his children' " (*R* 2.57; Moskal 247; Alison 3.278). She also quotes **Napoleon**'s statement, that "the **Bavarians** did not know how to govern the Tyrolese, and were unworthy to reign over that noble country," from Alison (*R* 2.43; Alison 3.222; Moskal 250). She credits Alison as the source for her quoted description of the area near **Brenner**, but Moskal asserts the account comes from "an editorial footnote by the translator in the Introduction to Hormayer, *Memoirs*" (1820) (*R* 2.54; Moskal 256).

Allah: Muslim God. Characters view the plague's arrival in **Turkey** as Allah's "curse" (*LM* 191). **Monina De Faro** overhears "an exclamation in the name of Allah" (*PW* 1.231).

Allegra: See **Byron, Clara Allegra**.

Alleyn, Marcott: Giacomo de' Tolomei's seventeen-year-old British artist friend in "**The Bride of Modern Italy.**" Shelley based Marcott on **PBS**, who fell in love with **Emilia Viviani**; however, unlike the infatuated PBS, who attempted to have Emilia released from her convent, Marcott does not help **Clorinda Saviani** escape (*BMI* 38; *Journals* 593; Sunstein 254–255).

Allori, Alessandro (1535–1607): Michelangelo influenced this **Florentine** painter, renowned for *The Pearl Fishers* (c. 1570) (Chilvers 14). Shelley notes that Allori, "a good painter," has made several "admirable" copies of **Correggio**'s *Magdalen;* one is still at the **Gallery in Dresden** (*R* 1.237; Moskal 199).

Almack's: **London** assembly rooms used for public meetings, concerts, and readings, extremely popular with aristocrats until the mid-19th century (Bayne-Powell 58; Timbs, *Curiosities* 4). In June 1824, Shelley noted **Gioacchino Rossini**'s "concerts under the patronage of the ladies of Almacks [*sic*]" (*Letters* 1.426). She asserts, "love in a cottage is the dream of many a highborn girl, who is not allowed to dance with a younger brother at Almack's" (*L* 2.139–40). In **Italy**, the **Saville** sisters tell **Clorinda Saville** about Almack's (*L* 3.205). Shelley found **Kissingen**'s assembly room "as good a ball-room" as Almack's (*R* 1.190–191).

Almaviva: See **Mozart**.

Almeria: Mediterranean seaport seventy miles southeast of **Granada**. **Hernan De Faro** sails there when departing **Alcala** (*PW* 1.231, 1.240).

Alpha: Greek alphabet's first letter, often broadly suggesting "beginning"; **Omega**, the last letter, generally indicates "ending." On 26 October 1824, Shelley bemoaned her husband's death, calling her emotional upheaval "the alpha & omega of my tale—I can speak to none" (*Journals* 485). **Lionel Verney** declares that life "was the Alpha and Omega of the desires, the prayers, the prostrate ambition of human race" (*LM* 294).

Alpheus: In **Greek** mythology, a river and its god. Alpheus fell in love with **Arethusa**, who bathed in his waters; she fled and became a spring, and Alpheus followed and mingled their waters (Tripp 39). **PBS** authored verses detailing Arethusa's flight, which **Ino** relates for **Proserpine**'s entertainment (*P* 35, 65).

Alps: Largest mountain range in **Europe**, extending from southern **France** through **Switzerland**, **Italy**, **Germany**, **Austria**, Bosnia, Hercegovina, and **Albania**; the highest peak is **Mont Blanc**. Shelley first saw the Alps 1814 and records crossing them 1816 (*Journals* 114; *H* 94). **Victor Frankenstein** first encounters his **Creature** in the Alps's **Jura** range (*Fr1* 103, 123; *Fr3* 72, 86). When **Castruccio** meets **Galeazzo Visconti** in **Milan**, he finds his own name "had passed the Alps," gaining him a warm welcome (*V* 1.134). In "**The Choice**," Shelley notes her son **William** "dwelt beside the Alps" summer 1816 (*Ch* 71). Many of *The Last Man*'s scenes are set against the Alps, the plague survivors' destination (*LM* 216). The Alps cause **Lionel Verney** to be "carried away by wonder" (*LM* 419). **Horace Neville** recognizes other countries' beauty, "sublime in Alpine magnificence" (*Mourner* 83). **Clorinda Saville**'s fit of madness is a scene "such as an English person must cross Alps and **Apennines** to behold" (*L* 2.193). Shelley admired the mountains while in **Cadenabbia** and Milan 1840 (*R* 1.75, 1.118–119). Crossing the Alps October 1840, Shelley recorded "the scene in its summer appearance was sublime; abrupt precipices, majestic crags, and naked pinnacles.... There was a majestic simplicity that inspired awe; the naked bones of a gigantic world was here" (*R* 1.134–35). [*V* 1.102–103; *R* 2.47, 2.102].

Alsatian Hills: Hills along the **Rhine** in the Alsace region between **France** and **Germany**. Elizabeth Falkner recalls **Gerard Neville** "roving wildly among the Alsatian hills" (*F* 82).

Alstadt: See **Altstadt**.

Alt Markt: "Old market" section of **Dresden** south of the **Elbe** (Meras 154). Shelley stayed there August 1842 (*R* 1.235, 1.249).

Altdorf: **Swiss** town twenty miles southeast of **Lucerne**; Shelley spells it **Altorf** (*BSWI* 124). Shelley considered visiting Altdorf 1814 and eventually passed through it September 1840 (*H* 46; *R* 1.152).

Altissimo, Cristofano (di Papi) dell' (c.1552–1605): Italian painter whom Shelley calls **Cristofaro**. July 1552, **Cosimo I** sent Altissimo to copy **Paolo Giovio**'s portraits; Shelley mentions this event in *Rambles* (*R* 2.156; Turner 1.730).

Altissimo, Cristofaro dell': See **Altissimo, Cristofano dell'**.

Altopascio: Italian town ten miles southeast of **Lucca**. **Castruccio** defeats and captures **Raymond de Cardona** retreating near Altopascio. **Arrigo de Guinigi** dies during this battle, and Castruccio buries him at Altopascio (*V* 3.172–74).

Altorf: See **Altdorf**.

Altstadt: "Old City" of **Prague**. Shelley visited it September 1842 (*R* 2.4).

Alviani: Family exiled from **Lucca** in *Valperga*, not further identified.

Amadeo: Shelley traveled by carriage from **Baveno** to **Simplon** in October 1840 with driver Amadeo, a "civil, obliging fellow" from **Turin** (*R* 1.133).

Amadis: Hero of Garcia Rodriguez de Montalvo's **Spanish** romance, *Amadis de Gaula* (1508), whom **Don Quixote** admired. Amadis is an idealized chivalric figure; Shelley read Robert Southey's 1803 translation 1817 (*Journals* 677). **Henry Clerval** writes a play about Amadis (*Fr1* 66).

Amalfi: Italian town ten miles west of **Salerno**. Shelley describes her July 1843 "Excursion to Amalfi," giving Amalfi's history (*R* 2.280–96). She directs readers to the engraving accompanying "**Amalfi**" in **Samuel Rogers**'s *Italy* (*R* 2.285–86).

"Amalfi": See *Italy*.

Amalthea: In **Greek** mythology, goat or nymph that supplied **Zeus** with nourishment while he was hiding from Cronus; in some versions, one of the goat's horns was perpetually overflowing with food and drink (Tripp 605).

Lionel Verney reflects upon his childhood when "the horn of Amalthea contained no blessing unshowered upon us" (*LM* 258). Plague survivors head south to where "**Jove** has showered forth the contents of Amalthea's horn" (*LM* 323). **Ino** compares **Cere's** fields to Amalthea's horn (*P* 45).

Amari, Michele (1806–1889): Sicilian historian and **Carbonari** member during 1820 revolution; Shelley read his *Un Periodo delle storie Siciliane del XIII secolo* [*Episode of Thirteenth-Century Sicilian History*] (1839), summarizing and recommending it in *Rambles* (*R* 2.205, 2.209–210). She also footnotes that its publication in **Palermo** caused Amari's exile and calls a later version of the work *Guerra del Vespro Sicilianno* [*War of the Sicilian Vespers*] (*R* 2.210).

Amazon, The: Statue in **Rome**'s Museum of the **Capitol** (*MROM* 257). Shelley viewed it April 1843 (*R* 2.230).

Ambrosian Library: **Borromeo** founded the first **Italian** public library, **Milan**'s *Biblioteca Ambrosiana*, named for **St. Ambrose**, 1609. Shelley visited it September 1840 and was disappointed at the strict guard kept over literary relics, a caution that arose from the attempted theft and destruction of some **Petrarchan** texts (*R* 1.110–111).

America: **Robert Walton** thinks his travels may lead him to the continent of America (*Fr1* 55; *Fr3* 31). **Victor Frankenstein** suggests an overriding passion led to the speedy discovery and exploitation of the continent, while the **Creature** learns "the hapless fate of the original inhabitants" from **Volney**'s

Ruins of Empires (*Fr1* 84, 147; *Fr3* 57, 105). America appears more frequently in Shelley's works as the country now known as the United States. Shelley wrote November 1825 that "to the feelings of an English woman who has never dreamt of crossing the **Atlantic**, America appears cut off from human intercourse," and, July 1826, that "I should be *very* melancholy if I were going there—but I may be prejudiced, and ought to feel more kindly towards the overgrown daughter of England—but then she is hardly . . . out of her teens, and I do not like snipes in their teens" (*Letters* 1.494, 3.402). Shelley's prejudice against America is not so evident in her works, where the country figures principally as an alternative to **Europe**. **Lionel Verney** believes class distinctions and England's history are irreconcilable with "the democratic style of America" (*LM* 222). The arrival of the *Fortunatus* from America brings plague to England (*LM* 217). *Perkin Warbeck* opens "just previous to the discovery of America by **Columbus**" (*PW* 1.146). Much of *Lodore*'s first volume is set in **Illinois**, "the desert wilds of America," where **Lord Lodore** takes **Ethel Villiers** into exile with him (*L* 1.152). **Admiral Fitzhenry** fought in the **Revolutionary War**, Mrs. Greville's relatives were American royalists, and **Fanny Derham** finds "the very air of America" distasteful (*L* 1.4, 1.220, 1.224). **Lord Reginald Desborough** lends **Lawrence Cooper** five hundred pounds "to send him and his wife to America" (*Par* 273). As a child, **Gerard Neville** imagines **Alithea Neville** may have fled to America; toward *Falkner*'s close, America becomes central to the search for the truth about her (*F* 113). Shelley refers to American mercenaries in her discussion of **Franconia**'s history and also asserts that "**Germans** know how to give the glory of spirit-stirring names to their valleys and their forests, very different from the **Little Woman** or **Muddy Creek** of America" (*R* 1.45, 1.203–204). [*E* 301; *LM* 296, 426; *PW* 1.146; *L* 1.62, 1.276, 2.45, 2.76, 2.112, 3.140; *R* 1.144].

American war: See **Revolutionary War**.

Amiens: French city seventy-five miles north of **Paris**. Shelley refers to the Peace of Amiens (1802), a treaty that Britain, France, **Spain**, and **Holland** signed 27 March 1802, bringing a fourteen-month peace between the **French Revolutionary** wars and the **Napoleonic** wars (May 1803). France abandoned **Egypt**, and Napoleon focused on **Italy**, while England surrendered most of its colonies; Napoleon then made British tourists prisoners of war in 1803 (*R* 1.139; Kinder 2.25). Shelley compares the "fate of English travellers at the time of the peace of Amiens" to the danger she could be encountering by traveling while France is involved in conflict with **Mehemet Ali** (*R* 1.139). Shelley mistakenly guessed that the treaty was signed 1797 (*Letters* 1.388).

Ampezzo: **Alpine** pass near the border between **Austria** and **Italy**. Shelley mentions the pass as the "shortest road from **Insbruck** to **Venice**," but, wanting to see **Lago di Garda**, she took another route September 1842 (*R* 2.61).

Amphitrite: **Greek** mythological sea goddess who married Poseidon; also occasionally a reference for **Venice**

(Tripp 44–45; Moskal 294). Shelley describes her affinity for Venice, a "favourite of Amphitrite" (*R* 2.123).

Amstag: Swiss town on the **Reuss** twenty-five miles southeast of **Lucerne**. Shelley includes **PFS**'s friend's account of their dangerous September 1840 journey from **Milan** to Lucerne; they were relieved to arrive finally at Amstag (*R* 1.152).

Anchises: In **Greek** mythology, Anchises, with **Venus**, had son Aeneas, who carried his father on his back when Troy fell (Tripp 50). **Matilda**'s father compares his love for his daughter to Anchises's love for Aeneas, "if the sex had been changed" (*M* 179).

"Ancient Mariner": See "**Rime of the Ancient Mariner**."

Ancients: Ancient **Greek** and **Roman** artists. Shelley compares **Canova**'s *Hebe* to the Ancients' work in **Accademia delle Belle Arti (Venice)** (*R* 2.91).

Ancilla Dei: "Handmaid of the Lord," usually referring to **Mary** (Crook 2). **Beatrice** is called *Ancilla Dei* and wears a plate displaying the phrase (*V* 2.21, 2.23, 2.43, 2.46, 2.78).

Ancona: Eastern **Italian** port on the **Adriatic**. **Castruccio** and his parents travel there when exiled; **Ruggieri dei Antelminelli** dies there (*V* 1.10, 1.30, 1.37). **Lionel Verney**'s ship takes refuge from bad weather in Ancona (*LM* 215). Shelley discusses **French** occupation of Ancona 1832 at length (*R* 1.120, 2.252–258; Kinder 2.51). [*V* 1.17].

Andalusia: Southern region of **Spain** formerly under Muslim control. Part of *Perkin Warbeck* is set there, since **Hernan De Faro** "had chosen among the foldings of the mountains on the borders of Andalusia" a retreat for his family (*PW* 1.203). [*PW* 1.200–211, 1.240, 1.301, 2.21, 2.182, 2.238, 2.242, 2.266, 3.22, 3.38, 3.92, 3.246].

Andermatt: Swiss city near **Mont St. Gothard**, thirty miles southeast of **Lucerne**. Shelley includes **PFS**'s friend's account of their dangerous September 1840 journey from **Milan** to Lucerne, when they traveled to Andermatt (*R* 1.152–153).

Andes: Mountain range running north and south in western South America. **Victor Frankenstein** states violent antagonism toward the **Creature**: "I would have made a pilgrimage to the highest peak of the Andes, could I, when there, have precipitated him to their base" (*Fr1* 121; *Fr3* 84). **Gerard Neville** compares his anxiety to hear **Hoskins**'s story to his willingness to "walk barefoot to the summit of the Andes to have these questions answered" (*F* 134).

Andrea: **Maria** and **Anina**'s widowed father in "**The Sisters of Albano**."

Andrea del Sarto [Andrea d'Angelo di Francesca] (1486–1531): **Florentine** painter renowned for frescoes, whom **Vasari** criticized for his character and personal life; "del Sarto" means "tailor's son" (Chilvers 19; Vasari 3.296–298). Shelley mentions viewing Andrea's masterpiece at the **Tribune** January 1843, possibly referring to either *Madonna of the Harpies* (1517) or *Madonna of the Sack* (1525), both regarded as masterpieces (*R* 2.153; Berti 86). Shelley notes "*Andrea senza Errori*," meaning "praise that implies a want of elan," as the artist's alternative name (Vasari 3.299; *R* 2.153).

Andrea senza Errori: See **Andrea del Sarto**.

Andreuccio: One of *Valperga*'s *Uomini di Corte*. Shelley took this character's name from **Boccaccio**'s *The Decameron*, but Shelley's Andreuccio is an entertainer, not a horse dealer (Boccaccio 2.5).

Andrew of the Shawe: In *Perkin Warbeck*, **Irish** prophet who predicts that **Lady Katherine Gordon** will marry a king.

Andryane, Alexandre Philippe (1797–1863): **French** author of *Mémoires d'un prisonnier d'état au Spielberg* [*Memoirs of a Prisoner of Spielberg*] (1838) (Moskal 138). Shelley footnotes a reference to Andryane's account of his imprisonment at **Spielberg** (*R* 1.121).

Angel of Annunciation: See **Guido Reni**.

Angel of Fame: See **Carracci**.

Angelica: See **Ariosto**.

Angelico, Fra [Guido di Pietro] (c. 1400–1455): Also called **Fra Giovanni** of **Fiesole**, Benedictine monk and painter of the **Florentine** school. Shelley praises his work in Florence (*R* 2.144). Fra Angelico's painting of the *Deposition* (1445) was displayed in **Santa Trinita Church**'s sacristy in Shelley's day and is now exhibited in **Accademia delle Belle Arti** (Florence) (Vasari 2.38). Shelley supplements her history and opinion of Fra Angelico with those of **Vasari** and **Rio** (*R* 2.145–146).

Angeline: Character who endures separation from **Ippolito della Toretta** in "The Trial of Love." In "The Brother and Sister," **Flora Mancini**'s companion.

Angelo, Michel: See **Michelangelo**.

Angus, Earl of: See **Douglas, Archibald**.

Aniaschiadus: See **Athanasius**.

Anina: **Andrea**'s daughter and **Maria**'s younger sister in "The Sisters of Albano."

Anio: **Latin** name for Aniene River, rising near **Subiaco** and joining the **Tiber** north of **Rome**. "The Swiss Peasant's" frame narrator and **Ashburn** "jolted along a rough ravine, through which the river Anio sped" (*SP* 137).

Anspach, Margrave of: German nobleman. Shelley suggests *Kabale und Liebe*'s duke could be modeled on him (*R* 1.204).

Anstey, Christopher (1724–1805): British poet. Shelley notes that bells " 'salute mine ear' " in **Cadenabbia**; she may have taken this line from Anstey's "Ode on an Evening View of the Crescent at Bath" (1766) or from **Wilson** (*R* 1.103; Moskal 128; Anstey line 35).

Antaeus: See **Hercules**.

Antelminelli: In *Valperga*, **Castruccio**'s family name.

Antelminelli, Castruccio: See **Castruccio**.

Antelminelli, Dianora dei: **Castruccio**'s mother in *Valperga*.

Antelminelli, Ruggieri dei: **Antelminelli** family head and **Castruccio**'s father in *Valperga*.

Antigone: In **Greek** mythology, **Oedipus**'s loyal daughter who defied her uncle Creon to give her brother burial rites; she was subsequently imprisoned and killed herself. **Lionel Verney** imaginatively endows Antigone with **Perdita**'s "beauty and matchless excellences" (*LM* 78).

Antiparos: **Cycladean** island in the **Aegean** off **Greece**'s coast. **Matilda** compares rain on the night of her father's suicide to the action of water in a spectacular Antiparos grotto containing stalagmites and stalactites (Todd 216; *M* 184).

Antonello of Messina (c. 1430–1479): **Italian** painter from **Messina** rumored to have brought oil painting to **Venice** (Chilvers 24). Shelley asserts that **Giovanni Bellini** learned oil painting from Antonello (*R* 2.93).

Antoninus, Marcus (143–87 B.C.E.): **Roman** consul (99 B.C.E.) and **Mark Antony**'s grandfather, renowned as "one of the greatest orators of his day" (Howatson 41). Shelley suggests "the mild spirit of [**Charles James**] **Fox** would have been soothed by the recollection that he had played a worthy part as Marcus Antoninus" (*RD* 49).

Antoninus, Pius (86–161 C.E.): **Roman** emperor who earned "fame for his integrity" even before **Hadrian** appointed him as his successor 138; Antoninus's "reign was peaceful and orderly, without striking incident" (Howatson 41). **Isabell Harley** delights "to visit the baths of Antoninus," but there are no baths of this name in Rome (*Val* 340).

Antony and Cleopatra: **Shakespeare**'s tragedy, first performed 1607–1608 and printed 1623. Shakespeare drew historical background from **Plutarch**'s account of the love affair between **Cleopatra** (c. 69–30 B.C.E.), last and most famous **Egyptian** queen, and **Mark Antony** (c. 82–30 B.C.E.), **Roman** general under **Julius Caesar**; they married 36 B.C.E. (Kinder 1.93). Shelley first read the drama August 1817 (*Journals* 179). **Edmund Malville** remembers being on a gondola in **Venice** " 'matched only by that which bore Cleopatra to her Antony' " (*RI* 26). *The Last Man* opens with reference to the spectacle of Cleopatra's progress along the **Nile**, asserting the beautiful blue Bay of **Naples** would have been more suitable for Cleopatra's barge (*LM* 3; Shakespeare 2.2.201–229). **Lionel Verney** terms an eclipse that causes disturbances throughout the world "the convulsion which '**shook lions into** civil streets,' " a line Caesar speaks upon learning of Antony's death (*LM* 224; Shakespeare 5.1.14–17). Verney suggests the **Countess of Windsor** thinks like "**Octavius Caesar** and Mark Antony, '**We could not** stall together / In the whole world,' " lines Caesar speaks after learning of Antony's death (*LM* 332; Shakespeare 5.1.39–40). **Perdita** notes: " 'As well might Cleopatra have worn as an ornament the vinegar which contained her dissolved pearl, as I be content with the love that **Raymond** can now offer me' " (*LM* 144). **Pliny the Elder** records, in *Natural History* (after 79 C.E.), that Cleopatra contentedly dissolved a pearl which was "the largest in the whole of history" in vinegar and drank it, thus winning a bet with Antony about who could have the most expensive banquet (Pliny 9.58.119–121). Referencing Shakespeare's text, **Lady Katherine Gordon** is content to be with her husband en route from Scotland to **Ireland**: "Cleopatra, basking in sunny pomp, borne, the wonder of the world, in her gilded bark, amidst all the aroma of the east, upon the gently rippling **Cydnus**, felt neither the pride nor joy of Katherine" (*PW* 3.21). As epigraph to the chapter in which **Richard of York** lovingly parts from Katherine before proceeding to battle in **Cornwall**, Shelley quotes Antony's speech to Cleopatra as he leaves to battle Caesar: " '**Dost thou hear**, lady? / If from the field I shall return once more / To kiss these lips, I will appear in blood; / I and my sword will earn our chronicle; / There is hope in it yet' " (*PW* 3.85; Shakespeare 3.13.172–176). Shelley uses Enobarbus's description of Cleopatra's magnificent procession along the Cydnus to contrast **Ethel Villiers**'s meagre surroundings: Cleopatra is on the "bark which—'**Like a burnished** throne / burnt on the water' . . . borne along '**By purple sails** / . . . So perfumed, that / The winds were lovesick with them' " (*L* 2.276; Shakespeare 2.2.201–204). [*RI* 26; *PW* 3.21; *L* 2.197, 2.246, 3.1].

Antony, Mark: See *Julius Caesar* and *Antony and Cleopatra*.

Antwerp: Chief **Belgian** port on the **Scheldt**, fifty-five miles southeast of the **North Sea**. Shelley crossed to Antwerp June 1842 (*R* 1.156–157). She visited the 14th-century Gothic cathedral, the largest in Belgium, there to view **Rubens**'s *The Descent from the Cross* (*R* 1.159).

Apennines: Mountain range along the axis of the **Italian** Peninsula. The Shelleys crossed the Apennines repeatedly 1818–22. **Valperga** castle is situated in the Apennines (*V* 1.24). **Adrian**, **Clara**, and **Lionel Verney** watch the sun set behind the Apennines (*LM* 216, 439). Verney wanders "through their vallies, and over their bleak summits" when he returns to **Rome** as the plague's only survivor (*LM* 457). **Ludovico Mondolfo** enjoys hunting in the Apennines, and his wedding to **Viola Arnaldi** occurs in a chapel there (*HM* 311, 317). **Ferdinando Eboli** visits **Adalinda Spina** and her father at their villa near **Salerno** in these mountains; Adalinda later moves to a castle in the Apennines near **Arpino** (*FE* 66, 74, 78). **Count Fabian de' Tolomei** and **Flora Mancini** wander among the Apennines (*Brother* 186, 188). The **Villiers**es' carriage breaks down crossing the Apennines (*L* 2.170, 3.18). Shelley records an "unfavourable" crossing of the Apennines while traveling to **Florence** October 1842, but she enjoyed viewing the mountains November 1842 (*R* 2.133–134, 2.136). [*HM* 326].

Aphrodite: In Greek mythology, goddess of love to whom Paris awarded the golden apple for her beauty. She bore **Anchises** a son and was sometimes depicted as **Cupid**'s mother (Tripp 57–58). **Proserpine** asks **Ino** to entertain her with Aphrodite's myth, and Ino compares **Ceres**'s lands to Aphrodite's beauty (*P* 33, 45).

Apocrypha: Fourteen books of religious writings typically omitted from Protestant versions of the **Bible**. Shelley records reading Tobit and Wisdom of **Solomon** 1820 (*Journals* 312, 314). She also read **Maccabees** (*R* 2.220).

Apollo: Greek god of "youth, music, prophecy, archery, and healing," also known as **Phoebus**, the "bright one" (Tripp 61, 477). January 1837, Shelley wrote that her son "plays like Apollo on the flageolet—& like Apollo is self taught" (*Letters* 2.278). **Midas** admires Apollo's gold and subsequently judges **Pan** the winner of a musical contest between him and Apollo (*Midas* 95–105). Apollo takes revenge by giving the king ass's ears; Midas acknowledges finally that gold belongs to Apollo, who "is my bitterest enemy, / And what pertains to him he makes my bane" (*Midas* 151). Shelley uses the alternate name Phoebus in both *Proserpine* and *Midas* and also uses "Phoebus" to describe dawn (*V* 2.68). **James IV** pauses on the **Tweed**'s Scottish bank with "lips, proud as the Apollo's—[which] spoke of struggle and victory" (*PW* 2.294). In "**The Death of Love**," Shelley attributes the death of the personification of love to "The waning moon; by fickle Phoebus left" (line 15). **Proserpine** appeals to her mother to recount "how the **Python** fell beneath the dart / Of dread Apollo," and refers repeatedly to Apollo's arrows, comparing their swiftness and design to her own desires (*P* 29, 31, 33). **Gaspar de Vaudemont** disguises himself as **Dan Apollo** in "The Dream" (*D* 159).

Apollo Belvedere: Pope Julius II placed this statue of **Apollo** in the inner courtyard of the **Vatican**'s Belvedere Palace; Shelley spells it *Apollo Belvidere* (Levy 16, 19). **Raymond** compares himself favorably to the statue (*LM* 63). Shelley notes **Ghirlandajo**'s *Adoration of the Magi* "might (as the Apollo Belvidere is said to have done), create a passion in a woman's heart" (*R* 2.143). Shelley admired *Apollo Belvedere*'s "divine presence"—"[I]n some sort, this statue is the ideal of a youthful hero"—in **Rome** April 1843 (*R* 2.217).

Apollo Belvidere: See *Apollo Belvedere*.

Apulus, Guglielmus: See **Gibbon**.

Aquobuona: Fortified Apennine village that **Castruccio** takes as he expands his territories (*V* 1.174).

Arabia: In Shelley's time, the peninsula between the Red Sea and the Persian Gulf including modern-day Saudi Arabia and neighboring countries; also known as **Araby**. **Arabic** is the language spoken there. **Henry Clerval** learns Arabic and creates imaginative stories similar to those of Arabic literature (*Fr1* 97, 99; *Fr3* 67–68). The **Creature** watches Arabian **Safie** become part of the **De Lacey** family (*Fr1* 145; *Fr3* 103). **Matilda**'s father visits Arabia during his sixteen-year absence from Britain (*M* 161). **Monina De Faro** visits dying **Elizabeth Woodville**, appearing "at the monastery [as] a pilgrim, with relics collected in Araby" (*PW* 1.323). **Ethel Villiers** recounts that her first vision of her mother "stole, according to the Arabian image, beneath her lids, and smiled sweetly" (*L* 2.18). **San Marco**'s "strange Arab architecture . . . denotes its great antiquity" (*R* 2.121). Shelley records **Salerno**'s medical school reached the height of its fame in the 12th century, when "students went to study in Arabia" and returned with knowledge learned there (*R* 2.294). [*V* 3.206; *LM* 225].

Arabian Nights: *The Arabian Nights' Entertainment*, or *The Thousand and One Nights*, a collection of stories drawn from **Arabic**, **Persian**, and **Indian** sources, first translated into English 1704–17. **Scheherazade** frames the stories, saving herself from death by telling the sultan tales after marrying him; he had traditionally had new wives killed after their first night together. Shelley read Dom Chaves and M. Gazotte's English translation of the **French** version, *Arabian Tales; or, a Continuation of the Arabian Nights Entertainment* (1814), 1815 and 1817 (*Journals* 88, 641). In July 1827, Shelley recorded her son's "reading with great extacy [*sic*] the Arabian Nights" (*Letters* 1.555). The narrator of "**Recollections of Italy**" describes park grass near the **Thames** as "softer than the velvet on which the **Princess Badroulboudour** walked to **Aladdin**'s palace," a reference to Badroulboudour's bridal procession from her father's palace to Aladdin's in "Aladdin and the Wonderful Lamp" (Aladdin commands a genie to stretch a carpet between the palaces, so his bride will not be forced to walk upon the ground) (*RI* 25; Lane-Poole 410). **Raymond** proposes that "men were to be transported from place to place almost with the same facility as the Princes **Houssain**, **Ali**, and **Ahmed**"; in "Prince Ahmed and Fairy Paribanou," these sultan's sons fly on a magic carpet (*LM* 106; *Arabian Nights* 60–94). Attempting to use Scheherazade's craft, **Stephen Frion** begins a story about **El Zagal** and **Boabdil El Chico**'s quarrels and suggests continuing it en route to **Lille**, if **Richard of York** will serve as his guide (*PW* 1.159). Recounting her visit to **Green Vaults**, Shelley says "we need not go so far afield as the 'Arabian Nights' to imagine regal splendour" (*R* 1.253). Shelley describes meals in **Bohemia** as "a **Barmecide** feast," alluding to a tale about a prince who placed empty plates before a beggar and pretended they contained food; the word refers to "one who offers illusory delights" (*R* 2.17; *OED*).

Araby: See **Arabia**.

Aragon: Historic northeastern **Spanish** region; Shelley spells it **Arragon** and refers to **Sicily** when Aragon's kings ruled it (*V* 3.259). Shelley gives a brief account of **Conradin**'s execution, enacted "under the auspices of **Don Pedro**," king of Aragon (*R* 2.209–210).

Ararat: Mountain in eastern **Turkey**, near its borders with Iran and Armenia, said to be **Noah**'s ark's resting place after the great flood (Genesis 8.4). **Lionel Verney** bemoans the fact that humanity, "which, like a flood. . . . had come down clear and unimpeded from its primal mountain source in Ararat," has diminished to just eighty people (*LM* 412). See **Genesis**.

Arbesau: Shelley's itinerary for **Saxon Switzerland** includes Arbesau; not identified (*R* 1.260).

Arcadia: Mountainous interior region of the **Peloponnese**, which writers present as a peaceful paradise where nymphs and shepherds lived (Tripp 69). Both **Raymond** and **Lionel Verney** compare their happiness in **Windsor** forests to that of Arcadian shepherds (*LM* 131, 153). Shelley says of **Hythe**'s neighborhood that "Arcadia seems to breathe from the fertile landscape," and **Richard of York** later compares himself to an Arcadian shepherd (*PW* 2.161, 2.288).

Arch of Constantine: Facing the **Coliseum**, imposing **Roman** monument commemorating Constantine I the Great's 312 c.e. victory over Maxentius (*MROM* 54–55). **Valerius** sees "'the arch of Constantine at my feet'" (*Val* 336).

Arch Tempter: See **Satan**.

Archangel: **Russia**'s largest Arctic port, on the northern Dvina River near the Gulf of the White Sea. **Robert Walton** begins his voyage there (*Fr1* 52–55; *Fr3* 28–31).

Archduke: Ferdinand I's uncle, not further identified. Shelley saw *Chi dura Vince*, which played at the **Fenice** because of the Archduke's October 1842 visit to **Venice** (*R* 2.128–129).

Arcite: See **Palamon**.

Ardfinnin: Irish town fourteen miles south of Cashel. **Desmond** takes **Richard of York** to his Ardfinnin residence (*PW* 1.308). Richard later revisits Ardfinnin after escaping from England (*PW* 2.175).

Ardmore: Irish port five miles east of Youghal. 22 July 1497, **Richard of York**'s supporters proceed to **St. Declan**'s shrine there to pray for their expedition (*PW* 3.33–34). **Lady Katherine Gordon** remains praying at the tower there during the ensuing battle at **Waterford** (*PW* 3.49, 3.52).

"Arethusa": See **Pearson**.

Arethusa: Greek mythological nymph who bathed in **Alpheus**'s waters and then fled to an island near **Sicily**, where she became a spring (Tripp 39). She is the subject of the first of **PBS**'s verses in *Proserpine* and is **Proserpine**'s friend (*P* 35, 47). Arethusa recounts seeing **Pluto** snatching Proserpine, but Pluto prevents Arethusa from assisting her (*P* 61, 63). Shelley notes PBS's "song of '*Arethusa*,'" set to music by **Pearson**, is "light and fanciful" as well as "beautiful" (*R* 1.234).

Arezzo: Italian city forty-five miles southeast of **Florence** in the **Apennines**. **Beatrice** passes through Arezzo (*V* 2.191, 3.83).

Argoli, Professor: **Padua** University professor who predicted that **Wallenstein** would have a "great martial fame" (Mitchell 48). Shelley relates that Wallenstein "first heard from the Professor Argoli that the stars above echoed the cherished dreams of his own heart" (*R* 2.7).

Argus: See **Eusta**.

Argyro-Castro: Large town, region, and river in **Albania** (*MGRE* 394–395). Shelley accurately describes the river as flowing "among the savage mountains of the district between **Ioannina** and **Tepeleni**," and **Cyril Ziani** later wanders through its valley (*EE* 100, 112).

Argyropylo: Greek commander in chief in *The Last Man*. The name is based on that of Prince and Princess Argiropoulo, whom Shelley met 1821 (Sunstein 196). Princess Ralou Argiropoulo was **Mavrocordato**'s cousin, and Shelley enjoyed her company (*Journals* 341; *Letters* 1.188).

Ariadne: In **Greek** mythology, daughter of Minos, **Crete**'s king. She fell in love with **Theseus** and, with **Daedalus**'s assistance, helped Theseus escape the labyrinth after he killed the **minotaur**. **Castruccio** compares **Beatrice**'s beauty to **Guido**'s painting of "a Virgin or an Ariadne" (*V* 2.17). **Raymond** asserts that **Lionel Verney** cannot help **Adrian** in his "labyrinth" madness, since "some unkind Ariadne [**Evadne Zaimi**] has the clue"; love for Evadne drives Adrian temporarily insane (*LM* 70). Shelley records seeing "**Dannecker**'s *Ariadne*" (1803) at **Frankfurt** June 1842 (*R* 1.176).

Arians: Followers of Arius (c. 250–c. 336), who led a heretical group that believed Jesus was not God. The Council of Nicaea condemned this faction's doctrine 325, but it again became influential under Holy Roman Emperor Constantius (ruled 337–361). St. **Athanasius** consistently opposed Arianism until its 365 eradication in **Alexandria** (Bowker 87–88; Delaney 76). Shelley records visiting **St. Michael's Church**, where she toured "subterranean vaults" where Athanasius "hid from the persecution of the Arians" (*R* 1.206).

Ariosto, Ludovico Giovanni (1474–1533): **Italian** poet whose most famous work is the epic poem *Orlando Furioso* (1516), which continues the story of Orlando, a hero from the days of **Charlemagne**, as **Bojardo** recounts in the unfinished *Orlando Innamorato* (1483, 1495), extended by **Berni**. Orlando abandons his military duty to pursue his love, **Angelica**, who marries Medoro; Orlando goes insane. Shelley read Ariosto's poem 1818, writing she had "finished Ariosto . . . I think I shall like **Tasso** better than Ariosto. . . . [H]ow Ariosto runs on sometimes for stanza[s] with—nothing!" (*Journals* 211, 220; *Letters* 1.76). **Elizabeth Lavenza** compares **Justine Moritz** to Ariosto's Angelica (*Fr1* 94; *Fr3* 64). Shelley quotes Astolfo's lines relating Alcina's seduction of him in *Orlando Furioso*: " '**Pareamo aver qui** tutto il ben raccolto. / Che fra mortali in piu parte si rimembra' "; the lines translate to "The sum of all delights it seemed to be, / Such as no lovers in this world enjoy" (*LM* 92; de Palacio 31; Ariosto 6.47.2–3). Shelley uses Ariosto's line concerning Alcina's eyes to describe **Lord Lodore**'s; "**Pietosi a** riguardare, a mover parchi," which loosely translates to "compassionate in looking, delicate in movement" (*L* 1.18; Ariosto 7.12.3; Crook 2). **Lady Lodore** compares Edward Villiers's search for her in Wales to "Angelica [being] run after by the **Paladins**" or knights; Shelley alludes to the opening of Ariosto's text when Rinaldo and other Paladins pursue Angelica (*L* 3.302; Ariosto 1.32, 1.77). Shelley praises Ariosto as a great poet who abandoned himself to his mind's "genuine impulse" (*R* 2.191).

Aristides (c. 530–468 B.C.E.): Athenian general and statesman famed for benevolence and known as "the Just," ostracized by political rival **Themistocles** 483 B.C.E. (Kinder 1.57). **Lionel Verney** suggests that the **Countess of Windsor**'s death is the culmination of "the ancient state of things," including "the disputes of Themistocles and Aristides" (*LM* 416).

Aristotelian rules: Poetic rules Aristotle (384–322 B.C.E.) presented in *Poetics* (late-4th century B.C.E.). Shelley terms **Dante**, **Petrarch**, and **Ariosto** great poets for resisting these rules (*R* 2.191).

Armenia: Southwestern **Asian** country south of the **Caucasus** bordering **Georgia**, **Turkey**, Azerbaijan, and Iran; the **Ottoman Empire** controlled it in Shelley's lifetime. Armenians die in the Ottomans' service (*LM* 184).

Armenian Convent: Convent on San Lazzaro island near **Venice** (Moskal 283). Shelley visited it September 1842 (*R* 2.101).

Armida: See *Gerusalemme Liberata*.

Arnaldi, Viola: Peasant girl who weds **Ludovico Mondolfo** in "**The Heir of Mondolfo**."

***Arnaldo da Brescia*:** Niccolini's 1843 tragedy celebrating Arnold of Brescia (c. 1100–1155), a monk who rebelled against the pope; **Barbarossa** executed him (Moskal 336). Shelley quotes lines a **German** captain speaks, beginning "**O vedovate** da perpetuo gelo**,**" as the epigraph to *Rambles*; Moskal provides Theodosia Garrow's 1846 translation of this long passage (*R* 1.xv; Niccolini 4.4.17–22; Moskal 62). Shelley uses lines Ferondo speaks to Galgano (to convince him to stop supporting Arnold) to describe **Italians'** avoidance of heresy: "**Il gran peccato** è l'eresia! che gli altri / Pesan men d'una piuma, e se ne vanno / Con un segno di croce"; the lines translate to "Great sin is heresy! / Compared with which all else weigh less than down, / And banish all the signing of the cross" (*R* 2.242; Niccolini 3.5.41–43). Shelley quotes *Arnaldo* to describe corrupt Catholic leaders; Arnold speaks the passage beginning "**Ahi, la vedete**" to the public (*R* 2.245; Niccolini 1.3.32–50, 1.3.59–62). Further criticizing Catholicism, Shelley quotes another long passage beginning "**Nelle chiese**," in which Giordano tells Arnold he has lost people's support; Moskal translates these passages (*R* 2.259; Niccolini 3.2.26–35; Moskal 359, 367).

Arnaoot: See **Arnaout**.

Arnaout: **Turkish** word for **Albanians**; Shelley spells it **Arnaoot** (*MGRE* 48). Shelley refers to **Dmitri** as both Albanian and Arnaout (*EE* 101, 106).

Arno: Central **Italian** river flowing through **Florence** and **Pisa** to the Ligurian Sea. In May 1818, Shelley descended "along the vale of the Arno which is very beautiful," although she later wrote that "nothing was wanting to the beauty of the [vale of the Arno] but that the river should be capable of reflecting its banks but unfortunately it is too muddy"; the narrator of "Recollections of Italy" makes a similar observation (*Letters* 1.66; *RI* 25). The Shelleys lived on the Arno's banks in Pisa 1821 (*Journals* 208). **Monna de' Gegia Becari** recalls blood running in the Arno after the **Monte Aperto** battle, and **Cincolo de' Becari** later crosses the river bearing a package to **Corradino** (*TP* 4, 20). **Castruccio** travels to Florence to see the spectacle on the River Arno (*V* 1.20). **Lionel Verney** believes the Arno spreads plague through Italy (*LM* 269). **Count Fabian de' Tolomei** crosses the Arno before reaching the **Apennines**; **Flora Mancini** later follows the same path (*Brother* 186, 188). Visiting **Dresden**, Shelley noted the **Elbe**'s "waters have ebbed even as the Arno does" (*R* 1.246). [*R* 2.135–136].

Arona: Italian city near **Lago Maggiore**'s southern tip, forty miles northwest of **Milan**. Shelley slept there September 1840 (*R* 1.128).

Arpino: Italian **Apennine** town sixty-five miles northeast of **Naples**. **Adalinda Spina** retires to the family castle near Arpino (*FE* 74).

Arragon: See **Aragon**.

Arrivabene, Count Giovanni (1801–1874): **Mantuan** noble who donated money to charity and education efforts; he was imprisoned with **Pellico** but released (Pellico 122). While exiled from **Italy**, he wrote *Delle Società di Publica Beneficenza in Londra* [*London's Society of Public Benefit*] (Pellico 244). Shelley acknowledges Arrivabene's political contributions made *Il Conciliatore* a success (*R* 2.195).

Arsenal: See **Zeughaus**.

Arta: River flowing south from **Epirus**'s Pindus mountains to its gulf. **Cyril Ziani** and **Camaraz** sail "to the gulf of Arta" (*EE* 110).

Artemesia (d. c. 350 B.C.E.): Artemesia II ruled Caria c. 353–350 B.C.E. after her husband's and brother's deaths. As a tribute to them, Artemesia built a tomb, called the **Mausoleum**, at ancient Halicarnassus (now Bodrum, **Turkey**). This tomb was one of the Seven Wonders of the World (Howatson 64). **Edmund Malville** says **Rome** is a more impressive tribute to its past than Artemesia's Mausoleum (*RI* 28).

Arthur's Seat: Craggy ridge dominating **Edinburgh**'s eastern skyline (Catford 12–13). **Henry Clerval** and **Victor Frankenstein** see it (*Fr1* 189; *Fr3* 138).

Arthur Mervyn: See **Brown**.

Arthur, Prince of Wales (1486–1502): Eldest son of **Henry VII** of England and **Elizabeth of York**; he married Katharine of **Aragon** and died a few months later. Minor character in *Perkin Warbeck*.

Arti Minori: Collection of workers' guilds that constituted the **Florentine** guild system in the 13th century. In addition to functioning economically, the guilds had a social role; crests and colors were associated with them (Higson

115–119). **Monna Gegia de' Becari**'s green dress displays her *Arti Minori* membership (*TP* 2).

Arve: River flowing through **France** at the **Alps**'s base. Shelley suggests walking up **Mont Salève** would provide a rewarding view of the Arve (*H* 103). In their 1816 **European** journey, both Shelleys were struck by the river's beauty, and **PBS**'s "**Mont Blanc**" contemplates the scene (*Journals* 114–115). **Victor Frankenstein** says of the Arve: "the dashing of the waterfalls around spoke of a power mighty as Omnipotence" (*Fr1* 123; *Fr3* 86). English plague survivors follow the Arve to its source (*LM* 423–424).

Arveiron: See **Arvéron**.

Arvéron: River in the **French Alps**; Shelley spells it **Arveiron**. In July 1816, Shelley traced the river's source (*Journals* 116). **Victor Frankenstein** stands "beside the sources of the" Arvéron, admiring the "sublime and magnificent" Alpine scenery (*Fr1* 124; *Fr3* 87). **Lionel Verney** records following the same route (*LM* 425).

As You Like It: Shakespearean comedy first performed 1599 and printed 1623. Shelley first read it April 1815 (*Journals* 75). **Matilda** evokes Shakespeare's heroine **Rosalind** in her daydreams because Rosalind is courageous, adventurous, and defiant of convention (*M* 159). Shelley uses **Adam**'s speech to his master Orlando de Boys promising fidelity even in exile in noting that **Lady Lodore** "could not exactly say, like old Adam in the play, '**At seventeen years** many their fortunes seek, / But at fourscore it is too late a week'" (*L* 3.158; Shakespeare 2.3.73–76).

Ascalaphus: Greek mythological figure who reveals that **Proserpine** has eaten **pomegranate seeds** in the Underworld; thus, she must be confined there. Ascalaphus upholds **Jove**'s will in restricting Proserpine to the Underworld but cannot deny **Ceres**'s prayer to Jove to allow her daughter six months each year in the mortal world (*P* 71, 73).

Asdrubal: See **Hasdrubal**.

Ashburn: Painter and audience in "**The Swiss Peasant**."

Ashley, Mr.: In *Falkner*, the **Nevilles**' neighbor and a magistrate.

Asia: Continent the **Ottoman Empire** controlled during Shelley's lifetime; she calls its inhabitants **Asiatics**. The **Creature** gives an account of Asia based on **Safie**'s history and **Volney**'s *Ruins of Empires* (*Fr1* 147, 151; *Fr3* 105, 108; Volney 60–61). **Midas** celebrates his golden touch by comparing it to wealth and beauty of "Asia's utmost citadels" (*Midas* 129). **Beatrice** recalls "myriads whose bones are now bleached beneath the sun of Asia" as an example of God's animosity toward humanity (*V* 3.45). **Raymond** dreams of conquering Asia, since it is a powerful force in **Turkey**'s war with **Greece** (*LM* 57, 161). **Lionel Verney** reflects that even the "luxurious Asiatic . . . had been vanquished and destroyed" by plague (*LM* 189, 426). The plague begins in Asia, and Verney plans to sail there at *The Last Man*'s close (*LM* 175, 224, 426). [*Fr1* 229; *Fr3* 171; *Maurice* 78].

Asiatic: See **Asia**.

Asisa: See **Assisi**.

Aspern, Battle of: Napoleon lost this battle (May 1809), about six miles northeast of **Vienna** (Kinder 2.29). Shelley mentions it in her historical account of **Hofer** (*R* 2.49).

Asphalion: Courtier who wants **Zopyrion** to reveal the secret of the king's ears in *Midas*.

Assedio di Firenze, L': See **Guerazzi**.

Assisi: Italian town twenty-two miles northeast of **Spoleto**, renowned as St. Francis's native town; Shelley spells it **Asisa**. **Teresa de' Tolomei** tells **Eusta** that a written marriage proposal is an account of the Assisi miracle, probably a reference to Francis's vision of Christ (*BMI* 33; Delaney 234).

Assumption, The: See **Titian**.

Astley, John: Scribe who supported **Perkin Warbeck** in his attack on **Exeter** and sought refuge with him at **Beaulieu** 1497; he was formally pardoned later that year (Holinshed 3.518; Arthurson 189–191). He is a *Perkin Warbeck* character.

Astura: Western **Italian** port and tower twenty miles southwest of **Velletri**. A **Frangipani** man seizes **Corradino** at Astura after the **Battle of Tagliacozzo**; **Conradin** was attempting to sail from Astura when seized (*TP* 22; Runciman 114).

Astwood: **Tower** of **London** guard involved in **Perkin Warbeck**'s 1499 attempted escape; minor character in *Perkin Warbeck* (Holinshed 3.524).

Astwood, Thomas (d. 1499): Marton Abbey, **Yorkshire** steward arrested when **Robert Clifford** betrayed a **Yorkist** conspiracy 1495; pardoned just prior to his execution, he conspired (1499) to release **Perkin Warbeck** and the **Earl of Warwick** from the **Tower** (Arthurson 85, 217; Holinshed 3.507). He appears in *Perkin Warbeck*.

Atawel, Ethelbert: In *Valperga*, Englishman who escorts **Castruccio** to England and introduces him to **Edward II**.

Athanasius (c. 297–373): Bishop of **Alexandria** around 327; his opposition to the **Arians** resulted in exile to **Trèves**; he subsequently spent seventeen years alternately in hiding and in "on-and-off exile" before finally regaining his seat of authority in Alexandria 365 (Delaney 75–76). Shelley, visiting **Fulda**'s St. Michael's Church, was told of one "**Aniaschiadus**" [*sic*] who was said to have hidden in the church vaults for seven years (*R* 1.206; Crook 2).

Athens: **Greece**'s capital city, served by an important **Mediterranean** seaport, **Piraeus**. **Isabell Harley** compares **Valerius**'s situation to that of " 'a man of the age of **Pericles**' " reviving " 'in Athens' " (*Val* 342). **Beatrice** recalls that "the country about Athens was adorned by the most exquisite works man had ever produced," which **Philip of Macedon** subsequently destroyed in just three days (*V* 3.49–50). **Raymond**

Athol

is born in Athens, which "claimed him for her own" and mourns his capture; he is buried with a hero's funeral at Athens's outskirts (*LM* 161, 168, 170, 208). Shelley consistently characterizes Athenians as noble and portrays the city as a key possession in Greece's war with **Turkey**. **Clara**, **Lionel Verney**, and **Adrian** set sail for Athens, which Shelley depicts as a safe haven in *Falkner* too (*LM* 327, 439; *F* 56). **Chief Constantine** travels home to Athens only to find Turks have desecrated it and taken his sister **Euphrasia** prisoner (*E* 303). [*R* 1.219, 2.217].

Athol: Forest in northwest Scotland's **Grampian** mountains. **Lionel Verney** visits **Adrian** in the "romantic seclusion" of the **Duke of Athol**'s seat at **Dunkeld** (*LM* 55, 71).

Athol, Duke of: Minor character in *The Last Man*.

Athos, Mount: Mountain at Chalcidice Peninsula's eastern point in northeast **Greece**, known as "Holy Mountain" because of its numerous monasteries and chapels and famous for its ban on female visitors (*MGRE* 419; Crook 2). Ice for the Greek army is stored there, and **Lionel Verney** sees the sun set behind the mountain (*LM* 180, 190).

Atlantic Ocean: **Victor Frankenstein** fears he will drift into the Atlantic after disposing of the female creature's body (*Fr1* 198; *Fr3* 145). **Lionel Verney** worries that nature's apparent abandonment of humankind will result in England being cast loose upon the Atlantic (*LM* 230). **Clarice Eversham** calls the Atlantic "murderous" after her father drowns in it (*Mourner* 98). **Richard of York** hears tales of **Columbus**'s voyages "over the slant and boundless Atlantic" (*PW* 1.258, 1.260). **Lord Audley** is driven off course into the Atlantic en route from **Cork** to **Bristol**, and rough weather prevents **Monina De Faro** from crossing the Atlantic to the **West Indies** (*PW* 2.263, 3.53). The Atlantic divides **Lord Lodore** from his wife and home during his exile in **America**, for which reason Shelley refers frequently to the Atlantic (*L* 1.194). For **Gerard Neville**, the benefits of sailing the Atlantic outweigh the dangers (*F* 282).

Atlantis: Legendary island ruled by **Atlas**, supposedly destroyed by earthquake and sunk into the **Atlantic** west of Gibraltar. "Atlantis" derives from the **Greek** for "no place" and "good place"; it would have come to Shelley from many sources (Crook 2). Plague survivors read "poets of times so far gone by, that to read of them was as to read of Atlantis" (*LM* 431).

Atlas: In **Greek** mythology, half-divine **Titan** giant who supported the sky and kept it above earth. As plague spreads through England, **Lionel Verney** records the struggle to survive as an "Atlean weight" (*LM* 322).

Attica: Southeastern **Greek** region including **Athens**. **Lionel Verney** and **Perdita** travel through Attica (*LM* 208).

Aube: French river joining the **Seine** north of Romilly. Shelley viewed it August 1814 (*H* 28; *Journals* 14).

Auber, Daniel François Esprit (1782–1871): French operatic composer. His five-act *Masaniello*,

Shelley's name for *La Muette de Portici* [*The Dumb Girl of Portici*] (1828), was first performed in **Berlin** (Rosenthal 339). Shelley attended *Masaniello* in **Dresden** August 1842 (*R* 1.248).

Audenarde: Also spelled Oudenarde, **Belgian** town thirty-five miles west of **Brussels** (Crook 2). **Richard of York** resides there temporarily (*PW* 2.30).

Audley, Lord (c. 1465–1497): James Touchet, seventh Baron of Audley, led **Yorkist** supporters to **Blackheath**, where **Daubeney** defeated them and took Audley prisoner; he condemned and then beheaded Audley (*DNB*). Audley is a minor character in *Perkin Warbeck*.

Augustine: See **Erfurt**.

Aurelius, Marcus (121–180): **Roman** emperor from 161 (Howatson 81). His "bronze equestrian statue" is in Rome's Square of the **Capitol** (*MGRE* 244). Shelley saw it 1819 (*Journals* 252). **Valerius** resembles the statue (*Val* 332).

Aurora: Goddess of dawn in **Roman** mythology (Eos in **Greek**) (Tripp 127, 223, 267). Aurora appears at *Midas*'s beginning to set the scene and time (*Midas* 93). Shelley alludes to Aurora's "chariot" to designate dawn (*V* 2.68). **James IV** describes **Lady Katherine Gordon** as having eyes that a poet might dream about; having "kissed eyelids soft as those, when he came unawares on the repose of young Aurora, [the poet would] go mad ever after, because it was only a dream" (*PW* 2.210).

Ausonia: Land an ancient tribe inhabited in southern **Italy** (Tripp 127).

Ino claims that **Ceres**'s lands exceed Ausonia in beauty (*P* 45).

Austria: Central **European** country that, ruled by the **Habsburgs**, was a major power during Shelley's lifetime (Kinder 2.29). Shelley told **Leigh Hunt** that Austria and **Russia** both disapproved of the **Greeks'** revolt (*Letters* 1.189). Austria suppressed the 1821 **Italian** revolution in **Naples**; Shelley's sympathies were with Italy in its 1848 war with Austria (Sunstein 378). The **Countess of Windsor**, formerly an Austrian princess, plans to take **Idris** there to prevent her marriage to **Lionel Verney** (*LM* 10). The countess later returns alone to her brother's court there (*LM* 85–88). **Elizabeth Lavenza** has a valiant Italian father, but "whether he had died or still lingered in the dungeons of Austria was not known" (*Fr3* 41). Shelley records, "the life of a soldier in the Austrian service is so hard, ill-fed, and worse paid, that these poor wretches often hold out long; but they are forced, at last, to yield" (*R* 1.100). Shelley visited **Milan** September 1840 while it was under Austrian rule, noting that the "Milanese nobility live much among themselves, keeping their palaces sacred from the Austrian" (*R* 1.120–121, 1.126). Shelley expressed surprise at her easy admittance into Austria August 1842 and records her September 1842 impressions of the Austrian **Tyrol** (*R* 1.275, 2.41). [*Journals* 256; *TP* 21; *FE* 68; *PW* 1.315; *R* 1.275, 2.41].

Austria, Don John of (1547–1578): **Spanish** military commander who defeated **Turks** at the **Battle of Lepanto** (1571). Shelley relates that **Gabriel Ser-**

belloni fought with Don John at that battle (*R* 1.81).

Austria, Duke of: See **Frederick, Duke of Austria**.

Austria, Emperor of: See **Emperor Francis**.

Austria, Leopold of: See **Leopold I**.

Auxerre: French city ninety miles southeast of **Paris**; the Shelleys passed through it 1816 (*Journals* 132). **Lionel Verney** leads a party toward Auxerre, following the reverse of the Shelleys' route (*LM* 396, 401).

Ave Maria: First words, in **Latin**, of the "Hail Mary" prayer honoring the Incarnation. Closely associated with this prayer is the *Ave* or Angelus bell, rung during the prayer (Attwater 42). **Buzeccha** arrives at **Cincolo de' Becari**'s home shortly after the evening *Ave* bell (*Passions* 7). Shelley repeatedly refers to *Ave Maria* to signify the evening hour in *Valperga* and many of her short stories set in **Italy** (*V* 1.7, 1.288; *HM* 325; *SA* 56; *Tr* 124; *Brother* 188; *FE* 76; *L* 2.184; *R* 1.98).

Aventures de Télémaque, Les: See **Fénelon**.

Avenue des Champs Elysées: French for "Avenue of the **Elysian Fields**," broad **Parisian** street running about a mile from the Arc de Triomphe to the **Place de la Concorde**. Shelley probably saw Champs Elysées 1816, mentioning it by name in *Rambles* in stating her preference for **Hyde Park**'s grass over the Champs Elysées's gravel (*R* 1.7–8).

Avernus: Lake near **Naples**; Shelley visited it December 1818 (*Journals* 242). **Roman** poets believed the circular lake to be "an entrance to the Underworld" (Tripp 129). **Valerius** notes " 'Avernus is but a short distance' " from the **Elysian Fields** (*Val* 333). *The Last Man*'s frame narrator visits Avernus at the novel's start (*LM* 3).

Avignon: French city on the **Rhône**, forty miles north of the **Mediterranean**. Pope Clement V moved the papal seat from **Rome** to Avignon 1309, where it stayed until 1377 (Kinder 1.181). Promoted, **Marsilio** travels to Avignon to receive investiture (*V* 3.76). [*V* 2.54–55].

Avogadii: Lucchese family opposing **Castruccio**'s rule in *Valperga*. Shelley draws on the history of the aristocratic Lucchese family Avvocati, which Castruccio suppressed 1317–27 (Green 93).

Avogadii, Berta: Female member of the **Avogadii** family suspected of being involved in a plot to overthrow **Castruccio** in *Valperga*.

Avogadii, Nicola dei: Avogadii family member involved in a plot against **Castruccio** in *Valperga*. Shelley took this name from Nicolao degli Avvocati, killed 1317 defending the Avvocati commune from Castruccio (Green 93).

Avon: Southwestern English river flowing through **Bristol** and **Bath**. At

Perkin Warbeck's opening, defeated knights cross it near **Welford** (*PW* 1.2).

Awbeg: Blackwater tributary in southern **Ireland** also called **Mullagh**; **Richard of York** and **Keating** meet near it (*PW* 1.293).

Ayala, Don Pedro de: Shelley accurately places this **Spanish** ambassador in Scotland (visited 1496 and 1497) when **James IV** invades England in *Perkin Warbeck* (Arthurson 131–132, 142, 156).

Ayza, Sultana: Boabdil el Chico's mother in *Perkin Warbeck*.

Azeglio: See **d'Azeglio, Massimo Taparelli**.

Aziolo: Owl that is subject of **PBS**'s "The Aziolo" (1829) (Crook 3.108). **Castruccio** and **Euthanasia** hear Aziolo's "regular moan," and **Lionel Verney** enjoys the aziolo's "soft cooing" (*V* 1.266; *LM* 177). In "**The Choice**," Shelley states that the "aziolo's cry" breathes **PBS**'s spirit (lines 132–133).

B

B——, Lord: See **Byron**.

B——, Prince: In *Rambles*, Shelley mentions Prince B—— who, while in exile, said "the stage would be a sure resource" for himself if impoverished (*R* 1.91). Moskal suggests Shelley refers to Lucien Bonaparte (1775–1840), Prince of Canino; his brother **Napoleon** exiled him from **France** 1803 (122).

Babel: **Biblical** city on the Euphrates River where **Noah**'s descendants attempted to build a tower to reach heaven. Their attempt angered God, who confused them by changing their speech so that they spoke several languages and could no longer communicate (Genesis 11.1–9). In **Hebrew**, Babel derives from "to confuse." **Bindo** possesses "a brick of the tower of Babel" (*V* 1.252).

"Babes in the Wood": See *Reliques*.

Bacchus: In **Roman Mythology**, god of wine and vegetation, usually called Dionysus in **Greece**. Bacchus rewards **Midas** by granting his wish for a golden touch, finally allowing the king to wash away the power in **Pactolus** (*Midas* 125, 143). **Tripalda** swears in disgust "by the body of Bacchus," as do the convent's superior in "**The Bride of Modern Italy**" and **Prince Fernando Mondolfo** (*V* 3.210; *BMI* 35; *HM* 316). Bacchus attends the gods' feast at *Proserpine*'s opening (*P* 31).

Bacon, Lord Francis (1562–1626): English statesman and author best known for essays in which he outlines a system of philosophy based upon a scientific approach to nature. Shelley read his *Apophthegmes New and Old* (1625) and *Sylva Sylvarum: Or a Naturall Historie. In Ten Centuries* (1626) 1822 (*Journals* 411). Discussing natural science with **Lionel Verney**, **Raymond** draws a passage beginning "**The falling from** a discord to a concord" from *Sylva Sylvarum* (*LM* 66; Blumberg 54; *Sylva Sylvarum* 113). Verney later refers to the opening of Bacon's "Of Marriage and the Single Life" from *Essayes, or Counsels, Civill and Morall* (1597–1625), which states, "He that hath *Wife* and *Children,* hath given Hostages to Fortune" (*LM* 248; Bacon 36). From the same work, Shelley quotes "Of Friendship," suggesting that **Elizabeth of York** "had been 'the **cannibal of** her own heart,'" commenting in *Lodore* that "men become '**cannibals of their own hearts**'" when they suffer loneliness, and noting that **Rupert Falkner** became "the **cannibal of** his own heart" in prison (*PW* 3.311; *L* 1.21; *F* 258; Bacon 83). In *Perkin Warbeck*'s preface, Shelley states she has drawn from "the partial pages of Bacon" for her novel; Bacon's *The Historie of the Raigne of King Henry the Seventh* (1622) demonstrates that contemporaries believed historical **Perkin Warbeck** was indeed the lost **Richard of York** (*PW* vi). Shelley quotes from Bacon's poem beginning "The world's a bubble" as epigraph to the chapter in which **Lord** and **Lady Lodore** separate: "**Who then to frail** mortality shall trust, / But limns the water, or but writes in dust" (*L* 1.147; Bacon lines 7–8; Stafford 54). Shelley quotes Bacon's *The Advancement of Learning* (1605) in noting **Manzoni**'s and **Niccolini**'s concurrence with Bacon that letters should be "'**a rich storehouse** for the glory of the creator, and the relief of man's estate'" (*R* 2.194; Bacon 1.5.11).

Bad: German for "bath." Shelley's planned tour of **Bohemia** included reaching **Tatchen** and then stopping at the Bad (*R* 1.260). Both Tatchen and **Botenlaube** have bathhouses (*MSGE* 497).

Bad Gastein: Austrian town fifty miles south of **Salzburg** (*MIAU* 51). Shelley regrets not visiting this health resort (*R* 2.29).

Baden: See **Baden-Baden**.

Baden, Grand Duke of: Leopold of Hochburg, created duke 1830 (Moskal 92). Shelley criticizes a **Darmstadt** inn that was expecting him; all private dining rooms were reserved for his visit July 1840 (*R* 1.33).

Baden-Baden: Southwestern German city in the **Black Forest** and a leading cultural center in Shelley's time. Shelley traveled through Baden-Baden July 1840 and revisited 1846, taking the waters there (*Letters* 3.2, 3.289–298; Seymour 476). **Edward Villiers** looks for **Lady Lodore** in **London**, only to learn "she was still at **Baden**" (*L* 1.300). **Elizabeth Falkner** first meets **Gerard Neville** there (*F* 44). Shelley found it a cheerful, even "a gay place" 1840 (*R* 1.37, 1.40). [*L* 2.70].

Badroulboudour, Princess: See *Arabian Nights*.

Bagnères de Bigorre: Southwestern French village at the foot of the **Pyrennees,** 125 miles southeast of **Bordeaux**; **Charles Clairmont** visited it 1816 (Vargo 416). **Horatio Saville** describes it as "distant, secluded, situated in sublime and beautiful scenery, singularly cheap, and seldom visited by strangers" (*L* 3.239). [*L* 3.242].

Bagni di Lucca: Corsena mineral baths ten miles northeast of **Lucca** (Bratchel 188). The Shelleys moved there June 1818, and Shelley remembered time spent there (*Journals* 213; *R* 1.62). [*V* 1.179].

Baiae: In **Latin**, a coastal or bathing resort, the most renowned of which was at **Naples**; also bay within northwestern **Bay of Naples** (Crook 2). In Naples 1818, Shelley recorded "the Bay of Baiae is beautiful" (*Journals* 242). **Valerius** "perhaps thought of the days he had formerly spent at Baiae" (*Val* 339). **Euthanasia** envisions **Castruccio**'s exile on **Istria**, island in Baiae (*V* 3.205). *The Last Man*'s narrator crosses the Bay of Naples "to visit the antiquities which are scattered on the shores of Baiae" (*LM* 3). **Horatio Saville** recovers from his love for **Lady Lodore** when he looks over the Bay of Naples and feels "one universal love and adoration" (*L* 2.173). Shelley recalls an 1843 visit to **Capri**'s **Palace of Tiberius**, from which she describes a view including Naples's Baiae (*R* 2.270). [*L* 2.180; *R* 2.283; *TP* 22].

Bainbridge, Mrs.: Sir Peter Vernon's bad-tempered, widowed sister in "The Invisible Girl."

Baker, Mrs.: Landlady of the house in which **Elizabeth Falkner** becomes an orphan in *Falkner*.

Baldelli, Giovanni Battista (1766–1831): Italian writer; his name is used in error for **Bandello** in *Rambles* (*R* 2.76; Moskal 268).

Baldi, Domenico: Italian bandit who loves **Anina** in "The Sisters of Albano."

"Ballad of Jane Shore": See *Reliques*.

Ballahourah: Irish mountains northeast of **Buttevant**. **Desmond** meets **Macarthy of Muskerry** there (*PW* 1.301–302).

Ballybeg, Abbey of: Southern Irish abbey twenty-three miles north of Cashel. **Richard of York** hopes to find **Abbot of Kilmainham** at the abbey, where **Lord Barry** has offered the abbot asylum (*PW* 1.289).

Balmaine: See **Ramsay**.

Balmayne, Lord of: See **Ramsay**.

Baltic Sea: European body of water north of **Germany** and **Poland** and west of **Russia**. Shelley describes **Charlemagne** ruling "from the tepid waters of the **Mediterranean** to the frozen Baltic" (*V* 1.285).

Bandello, Matteo (1485–1561): Italian novelist whose four volumes of writings contain 214 stories similar in theme and structure to **Boccaccio**'s (*DIL* 28–30). Shelley claims **Francesco**'s story in *Valperga* is based on one by Bandello, but it may be Giovanni Fiorentino's (*V* 2.156; Crook 3.177). Shelley refers to **Baldelli**'s account of **Juliet** and the **Capulets**' tomb in *Rambles*; Moskal suggests Shelley's "Baldelli" is an error for "Bandello" (*R* 2.76; Moskal 268).

Banditti: Italian robbers. **Ferdinando Eboli** joins banditti, and **Domenico Baldi** leads banditti (*FE* 78–79; *SA* 55). Banditti fought **Carbonari** in **Naples** (*R* 2.170).

Bar-sur-Aube: French town twenty miles northwest of **Chaumont**; the

Shelleys stayed there August 1814 (*H* 28; *Journals* 14).

Barbadoes: See **Barbados**.

Barbados: Easternmost **West Indian** island, in Shelley's day a British colony, now an independent nation; Shelley spells it **Barbadoes** (Kinder 1.277, 2.305). **Lord** and **Clarice Eversham** visit his estates there (*Mourner* 92–93).

Barbarigo Palace: Venetian palace (where **Titian** died) on the **Grand Canal** renowned for its art collection; Shelley spells it **Barberigo** (Zorzi 314–321). She describes viewing Titian's *Maddalena Scapigliata* there October 1842 (*R* 2.120).

Barbarossa, Frederic [Frederick I] (c. 1152–1190): King of **Germany** (1152) who became Holy Roman Emperor 1155, called "Barbarossa" because of his red beard; his family inherited **Sicily** (Salvatorelli 181, 192, 233). **Benedetto Pepi** cites Barbarossa's quarrel with the pope as the reason why **Florence** flourishes as a republic (*V* 1.127). Old men at **Euthanasia's** court still remember "the death of the last unfortunate descendant of Frederic Barbarossa," who is **Corradino** (*V* 1.249).

Barbary: Large North **African** region, stretching from **Egypt** to the **Atlantic**. A Barbary pirate takes **Katusthius Ziani's** father's vessel (*EE* 102).

Barbatelli, Bernardino (c. 1542–1612): Florentine painter, also called **Poccetti**, who studied with **Ghirlandajo** (Williamson 1.80). Shelley praises Barbatelli's frescoes in Florence, especially the **Santissima Annunziata Convent** series depicting **Servi di Maria's** seven founders (*R* 2.147). Shelley thinks Barbatelli's best work is in a **Santa Maria degli Angioli Convent** cupola—a fresco of **Biblical** saints (c. 1568–69) (*R* 2.148).

Barberigo Palace: See **Barbarigo Palace**.

Barberini Palace: Largest palace in **Rome**, completed 1640, housing a library and "impressive" gallery (*MROM* 270–271). Shelley visited it April 1843 and especially noted *Fornarina* (*R* 2.223).

Barbier de Paris, Le: See **Kock**.

Barbiere di Siviglia: Opera about "The Barber of Seville"; **Rossini's** two-act version (1816) is based on Pierre Augustin Caron de Beaumarchais's comedy *Le Barbier de Séville* (1775) (Rosenthal 31). Shelley attended the *famiglia Vianesi's* performance of *Barbiere* in **Venice** October 1842 (*R* 2.127).

Barley, William: Robert Clifford's father-in-law, who "defected" from his **Lancastrian** stance in 1493 to support **Perkin Warbeck** (Arthurson 66, 88). He was arrested 1495 and pardoned 1498 and is a minor *Perkin Warbeck* character (Arthurson 200–201).

Barmecide: See *Arabian Nights*.

Barnes: London district nine miles southwest of the city's center. **Richard of York** passes through London "as high as Barnes" while escaping from the **Tower** (*PW* 3.270).

Barnet: Dame **Barnet**'s widower, a fisherman, and **Maurice**'s adopted guardian in "**Maurice**."

Barnet, Dame: Barnet's wife in "**Maurice**."

Barnet, Gregory: Torquay shopkeeper and **Barnet**'s brother in "**Maurice**."

Barretts: Important **Irish** family related to **Desmond** by marriage (*PW* 1.279, 1.304). Lord John Barrett was allied to Desmond through fealty or marriage (Arthurson 106).

Barrier: See **Barrière de l'Etoile**.

Barrière de l'Etoile: "Gate of the Star," another name for **Paris**'s central Place Charles de Gaulle, where twelve avenues intersect at the Arc de Triomphe (*MIPA* 90–92). Possibly this **barrier** is indicated when **Adrian** rides "slowly, to give time to all to join him at the Barrier," before directing followers to **Versailles** (*LM* 382; Crook 2). Shelley mentions the Barrière as part of the view from the **Tuilleries**'s terrace (*R* 1.8).

Barry, Lord: Irish noble known as Munster William, Lord Barry, who organized a Munster faction that includes the **Knight of Kerry** and **Desmond** (Arthurson 106). He is a *Perkin Warbeck* character and **Baron of Buttevant** (*PW* 1.229).

Barrymores: Irish family in *Perkin Warbeck*.

Barrys: Irish family in *Perkin Warbeck*.

Basilika: Small **Greek** village ten miles northwest of **Corinth**; Shelley calls it **Vasilico** (*MGRE* 242). **Katusthius Ziani** joins "**Arnaoots** lurking about" Basilika (*EE* 106).

Basle: Swiss city where the **Rhine** and **Rhône** meet; Catholic council meeting, **Council of Basle**, met there 1431–49 in response to the **Hussite** problem (McBrien 143). The Shelleys passed through Basle summer 1814 (Sunstein 87; *H* 59). **Elizabeth Falkner** and her father travel homeward through Basle (*F* 82). Shelley relates that before the **Reformation**, the church of **Bohemia** was uniquely permitted by the Council of Basle to offer the laity both wine and bread during mass (*R* 2.2; Crook 2).

Bassano, Jacopo (c. 1510–1592): Italian painter of the **Venetian** school. Shelley viewed Bassano's paintings at **Saints Giovanni's and Paolo's Church** September 1842 (*R* 1.98).

Bastei: See **Bastion**.

Bastille: Parisian prison razed early in the **French Revolution** (1789). Shelley refers to it when theorizing about misery just before **Richard of York**'s execution (*PW* 3.323).

Bastion: Land mass rising to 1,040 feet overlooking the **Elbe** about six miles west of Pirna in east central **Germany**. It is a popular tourist spot, which Shelley calls **Bastei** (Seltzer 172). Shelley visited it August 1842 (*R* 1.264–265).

Bateman, Captain: Captain of the *Owyhee*, upon which **Gerard Neville** plans to sail to **New York** in *Falkner*.

Bath: Southwestern English city on the river **Avon**, ten miles southeast of **Bristol**, renowned for its hot springs and **Roman** baths; it was a fashionable society gathering place in Shelley's day. In August 1816, to hide **Claire Clairmont**'s pregnancy from the **Godwins**, the Shelleys and Claire took lodgings in Bath (Seymour 165–166). Shelley composed portions of *Frankenstein* and learned of **Fanny Godwin**'s and **Harriet Shelley**'s suicides while there (*Journals* 134–156). **Lady Santerre** retires to Bath (*L* 1.106). **Mrs. Greville** lives in Bath close to the **Derham** family (*L* 1.220). [*L* 3.73].

Baths of Bohemia: Numerous mineral springs in the present Czech Republic supply an abundance of spas; **Karlsbad** is perhaps the most renowned. Shelley notes: "Except to visit **Prague**, and one or two of their Baths, no strangers enter" Bohemia (*R* 2.16).

Baths of Caracalla: Marcus Caracalla began these baths c. 217 in **Rome**; they could house 1,600 bathers. They fell into ruin in the 6th century (*MROM* 58–60). In March 1819, Shelley recorded a walk "to the baths of Caracalla," and she returned there to sketch April 1819 (*Journals* 252–253, 256). In December 1824, Shelley recalled "the deserted and solitary ruins of the Baths of Caracalla, [where] we enjoyed the spectacle of spring" (*Letters* 1.459). **Isabell Harley** and **Valerius** often seek isolation on the baths' walls (*Val* 343). The **Villiers**es take refuge from heat there (*L* 2.202). Mornings in April 1843, Shelley read among the Baths' ruins (*R* 2.225, 2.228).

Baths of Diocletian: Ancient **Roman** baths Diocletian began 302; they covered 150,000 square yards where the **Quirinal** and Viminal hills meet (*MROM* 60–61). Shelley viewed **Santa Maria degli Angeli's Church**, built with "remnants of the Baths of Diocletian" April 1843 (*R* 2.229).

Baths of Pfäfers: Resort fifty-seven miles east of **Lucerne**; Shelley terms it Baths of Pfeflers, regretting not visiting this resort (*R* 1.55).

Baths of Pfeflers: See **Baths of Pfäfers**.

Batistero: Baptistry of San Giovanni at **Florence**'s **Duomo** (Moskal 313). Shelley viewed it January 1843 (*R* 2.160).

Bauli: Villa on the southern edge of **Baiae**'s north headland (Headlam 119–20). "**Valerius the Reanimated Roman**" begins when "two strangers landed in the little bay formed by the extreme point of **Cape Miseno** and the promontory of Bauli" (*Val* 332).

Bavaria: Southeast **German** region famous for its mountains and castles, many of which **Louis of Bavaria** built. *Valperga* concludes during Louis's reign (*V* 3.263–264). Shelley traveled throughout Bavaria 1842, staying at various resorts (including **Kissingen** and **Brükenau**) and enjoying the "extreme tranquillity in these secluded spots in Bavaria" (*R* 1.200). Shelley also describes Bavarian dancing and gives a brief history of the **Tyrol** and Bavaria

Bavaria, Crown Prince of

under **Napoleonic** rule (*R* 2.39, 2.42–56).

Bavaria, Crown Prince of: See **Maximilian II**.

Bavaria, King of (1786–1868): Ludwig I ruled Bavaria 1825 until abdicating 1848 (Morby 140; Bolt 36). He was in **Kissingen** during Shelley's stay there July 1842, and he frequented **Brükenau**'s baths (*R* 1.192).

Bavaria, Louis of: See **Louis IV**.

Baveno: Italian town on **Lago Maggiore**'s western shore, twenty miles north of **Arona**. Shelley stayed there September 1840 (*R* 1.131).

Baxter, William Thomas: "Prosperous sailcloth manufacturer" who met **William Godwin** only once but had supported the latter with a "subscription for the Treason Trial defendants of 1794, and was the father-in-law of [Godwin's] friend **David Booth**" (Sunstein 56; Seymour 70). Baxter acted as Shelley's foster-father and host during her visits to Scotland 1812 and 1813–14, and she regarded him as "an indulgent uncle" (Sunstein 57). Shelley became friends with Baxter's daughters, Christina and **Isabel Baxter Booth**, while **Charles Clairmont** had previously been acquainted with Robert, Baxter's son, in **Edinburgh**. Although he shunned Shelley immediately following her elopement, Baxter visited the Shelleys at **Marlow** September 1817, and they, especially Mary Shelley, enjoyed his visit (*Journals* 179). Baxter was initially approving of **PBS**, arranging a meeting between him and David, but Baxter's friendship for the Shelleys declined toward the end of 1817 (184). See volume V of Kenneth Neill Cameron and Donald Reiman's *Shelley and His Circle* (1961–70).

Bayard: Pierre Terrail, Seigneur de Bayard (1473–1530), chivalric **French** military hero (Moskal 312). Shelley criticizes **Accademia delle Belle Arti (Florence)** for having "no picture such as would idealise" Bayard (*R* 2.157).

Baza: Spanish town fifty miles northeast of **Granada**. Ferdinand's army captured Baza fortress 1489 (Dupuy 469). **Richard of York** and **Edmund Plantagenet** fight against **Moors** in the siege of Baza (*PW* 1.212–216).

Bear: Constellation. **Ludovico Eboli** claims "'the descending Bear shows that midnight is past'" (*FE* 67).

Beatrice: William Godwin called this main character of *Valperga* "the jewel of the book" (qtd. in *Letters* 1.323). Shelley may have modeled Beatrice after **Madame De Staël**'s **Corinna** and Joanna Southcott, a religious zealot who died 1814 after claiming she was pregnant with the second Christ (Sunstein 53). Beatrice of **Dante**'s *Divine Comedy* may also have influenced Shelley's choice of name; Shelley refers to **Guido**'s painting of **Beatrice Cenci** (1577–99) in comparison with her character's beauty (*V* 2.17). *Blackwood's* severely criticized Beatrice's explanation to **Euthanasia** of her **Paterin** beliefs in *Valperga*'s "anathema scene" (Sunstein 253; Crook 2). Sunstein asserts "Beatrice represents unbridled passion, energy, and imagination," and her Paterin beliefs reflect Shelley's own pessimism following the deaths of her children, **Clara** and **William Shelley** (Sunstein 162, 169, 189).

Beatrice: **Dante**'s love interest; he expressed his love for Beatrice Portinari throughout his works; *Vita nuova* (1290–94) relates his emotional reaction and attachment to Beatrice, and he further glorified her in *Divine Comedy* (Ciardi xviii). Shelley describes **Giotto**'s portrait of Dante: "We see here the lover of Beatrice" (*R* 2.158).

Beauclerk, Aubrey William [Major] (1801–1854): Shelley's acquaintance and **George Beauclerk**'s brother who served in the British army and became a Member of **Parliament** 1832–37, gaining a reputation as a radical reformer (*Journals* 600–601; Seymour 412, 425). In 1834, he married Ida Goring, with whom he had several children before her 1838 death; he married **Rosa Robinson** 1841 (*Journals* 601; *Letters* 1.540). Aubrey used parliamentary privileges to assist Shelley with her postage, and she frequently dined with the Beauclerks in **London** (*Journals* 520). In July 1834, Shelley noted, "I have received one little note from AB. sole testimonial of his existence," which could be a reference to Aubrey; his first marriage may relate to a "frightful calamity" Shelley suffered August 1833 (*Journals* 539, 530; Crook 2). Shelley's *Journals* include a brief biographical sketch in Appendix III, in which Feldman and Scott-Kilvert suggest that "A" could refer to Aubrey; Shelley's references outline a close personal relationship with the unidentified figure (*Journals* 600–601). Shelley maintained a friendship with Aubrey for much of her life and was hurt by his second marriage; **Claire Clairmont** reported that Shelley, "much chagrined," delivered Aubrey's proposal of marriage because of his family's objections (*Clairmont Correspondence* 2.356–357; Seymour 426). Sunstein also discusses Aubrey and Shelley's relationship during the 1830s and 1840s in detail, suggesting they "began seeing each other" September 1839, and there are several extant letters from the 1840s that demonstrate Shelley's continued interest in him (Sunstein 316, 321–322, 347; *Letters* 3.84, 3.152).

Beauclerk, George Robert (1803–1871): Shelley's acquaintance. In the biographical sketch included in Appendix III of Shelley's *Journals*, Feldman and Scott-Kilvert note George and Shelley were "confidantes," and he wrote to her frequently with advice, including an 1834 personal letter regarding **PFS**'s schooling, which reveals George as "an intelligent, well-educated, widely read, and discriminating person who suffered from pretentiousness, a sense of self-importance, and bitterness about his unfulfilled artistic aspirations" (*Journals* 601–602). Shelley frequently dined with the Beauclerks in **London** during the 1830s and 1840s; she remained friends with George even during the latter's affair with Mary Anne Lewis at the end of the 1830s (*Journals* 520, 535, 540; *Letters* 3.177). George was also the author of "a well-received book, *Journey to Morocco*" (1828) (Sunstein 315).

Beauclerk, Rosa Matilda (d. 1878): Aubrey **Beauclerk**'s second wife, née Robinson; Shelley knew her and her family by 1827 (*Journals* 506–507). Rosa spent "some weeks" with Shelley 1833 and traveled to **Brussels**

with sister **Julia Robinson** December 1834 for a year; Rosa lived with Shelley from 1838 and seems to have become a financial burden (*Journals* 529, 541; Sunstein 319, 337, 340). Shelley took Rosa to one of **Samuel Rogers**'s breakfasts June 1838 and again February 1840 but was troubled by the expenses of Rosa's 1840 illness; Rosa returned to her father's house later that year (*Journals* 552; Sunstein 339, 347). Shelley was hurt to learn of Rosa and Aubrey's December 1841 marriage (Bennett notes the wedding as occurring 1840 in Shelley's *Letters*) but recognized that Rosa would thus no longer be poor or dependent upon her (*Journals* 601; Sunstein 352; *Letters* 1.540; Seymour 478–479). Rosa had two daughters (*Letters* 3.98). Shelley noted Rosa's "husband's family" disliking her September 1844 (*Letters* 3.152). She visited Rosa December 1844, and the two women seem to have renewed their acquaintance and maintained correspondence throughout the late 1840s (Sunstein 362; *Letters* 3.167, 3.373).

Beaufort: Alphonse Frankenstein's friend and **Caroline Frankenstein**'s father in *Frankenstein*.

Beaufort, Caroline: See **Frankenstein, Caroline**.

Beaulieu: English town seven miles southwest of **Southampton**; its famous abbey is west of the town. Shelley spells it **Bewley**. An old woman advises **Richard of York** to seek asylum at Beaulieu; he, **Skelton**, **Astley**, **O'Water**, and **Heron** arrive there, and Richard rests briefly before departing to meet **Henry VII** (*PW* 3.158, 3.173, 3.184–85).

Beaumont, Sir Francis (1584–1616): Prolific English Restoration dramatist who collaborated with **John Fletcher**. Shelley read Beaumont and Fletcher's *Works* August 1817 and August–October 1819 (*Journals* 178, 295–299). When her father's attitude toward her alters in **London**, **Matilda** quotes lines Leila speaks to her lover Julio when he presses his advances upon her in Beaumont and Fletcher's comedy *The Captain* (1613): "**for what should** I do here, / Like a decaying flower, still withering / Under his bitter words, whose kindly heat / Should give my poor heart life?" (*M* 165; *The Captain* 1.3.237–240). Shelley attributes epigraph lines from *The Tragedy of Thierry and Theodoret* to Beaumont and Fletcher in **Perkin Warbeck**, but this play was probably Fletcher's collaboration with Philip Massinger; the Shelleys read it May 1820 (*PW* 1.117; *Journals* 317). For her epigraph to the *Lodore* chapter in which **Lady Lodore** learns of her daughter's financial difficulties, Shelley quotes from Evadne's soliloquy in Beaumont and Fletcher's *The Maid's Tragedy* (1619), which **PBS** read aloud July 1818: "**O, where have** I been all this time? How 'friended / That I should lose myself thus desp'rately, / And none for pity show me how I wandered!" (*Journals* 218; *L* 3.108; *The Maid's Tragedy* 4.1.177–179). See *The Custom of the Country*.

Becari, Cincolo de': Monna Gegia de' Becari's **Ghibelline** husband and **Despina dei Elisei**'s foster-father in "**A Tale of the Passions**."

Becari, Monna Gegia de': In "A Tale of the Passions," Cincolo de' Becari's wife.

Beccaria, Cesare (1738–1794): Political writer who pushed for penal reform in his *Dei delitti e delle Pene* [*On Crimes and Punishment*] (1764) (*DIL* 40–42). Shelley points to Beccaria as the reason **Manzoni**'s wife (Beccaria's daughter) was "an accomplished and active-minded woman" (*R* 2.199).

Beckford, William (1759–1844): English author renowned for *Vathek: An Arabian Tale* (1786), a Gothic, oriental novel written in **French** but first published in Samuel Henley's English translation 1786; Shelley read "Caliph Vathek" 1815 (*Journals* 636; Crook 2). **Raymond** describes his dislike for concealing his feelings for **Evadne Zaimi** from **Perdita** with reference to *Vathek*'s beginning, when the protagonist erects a tower as a monument to his pride: "The veil must be thicker than that invented by **Turkish** jealousy; the wall higher than the unscaleable tower of Vathek, which should conceal from [Perdita's] view the secret of [Raymond's] actions" (*LM* 122; Beckford 7). Shelley quotes Beckford's description of **Tyrol**, beginning " 'the Tyrol, a country of picturesque wonders,' " from *Italy, with Sketches of Spain and Portugal* (1834) (*R* 2.40; Moskal 249; Beckford 202).

Beddoes, Thomas Lovell (1803–1849): British poet and playwright renowned for *The Brides' Tragedy* (1822) and *Death's Jest-Book* (1850). Beddoes greatly admired **PBS**, and, although they never met, Beddoes stood as a guarantor to the sale of *The Posthumous Poems*, which Shelley prepared 1824 (*Journals* 434). Beddoes was also Shelley's supportive friend and admirer after PBS's death. **Lionel Verney** adapts one of Hesperus's lines from *The Brides' Tragedy* to describe how **Raymond** cheers **Evadne Zaimi**: "he partook of her delirium. '**They built a wall** between them and the world' " (*LM* 116–117; Beddoes 4.3.67). Verney quotes with minor adjustments from another of Hesperus's speeches in describing **Idris** after **Evelyn**'s near-death: "**As one / In some** lone watch-tower on the deep, awakened / From soothing visions of the home he loves, / Trembling to hear the wrathful billows roar" (*LM* 292; Beddoes 5.4.16–19). Shelley quoted a version of these lines in her *Journals* (468). Verney later quotes Hesperus's opening speech, suggesting the number of plague survivors has diminished so much that they are "like a cloud . . . which, when the shepherd north has driven its companions '**to drink Antipodean** noon,' fades and dissolves in the clear ether" (*LM* 423; Beddoes 1.1.7–8).

Bedford, Duke of: Jasper Tudor (1431–1495), **Henry VII**'s **Lancastrian** half-brother (*DNB*). He defeats **Lovel**'s insurrection in *Perkin Warbeck*.

Beech Grove: Sir Richard Gray's family home in **Hampshire**, "spacious and elegant, and situated in an extensive park" (*ES* 247).

Belfast: Principal northern **Irish** coastal city. Irish people fleeing famine travel to Belfast before crossing to Scotland (*LM* 297).

Belgium: Northwest **European** country surrounded by **Holland, Germany,**

Belial

Luxembourg, **France**, and the **North Sea**; its capital is **Brussels**. Shelley traveled through Belgium June 1842, stopping only to see **Antwerp** and its cathedral (*R* 1.159).

Belial: See **Satan**.

Bell' Alma innamorata: See **Donizetti**.

Bell's and Lancaster's: Educational system developed by Andrew Bell (1753–1832) and Joseph Lancaster (1778–1858); students monitor and teach each other. Shelley notes that **Venetian** schools use this system (*R* 2.117).

Bellaggio: **Italian** town on the point between **Lake Como** and **Lake Lecco**. Shelley planned to stay there July 1840, but the steamer neglected to stop (*R* 1.62). Shelley later made several trips there, visiting **Villa Serbelloni** repeatedly August 1840 (*R* 1.77).

Belleforest: **Raby** family mansion in **Northumberland**, a "fine old Gothic building, adorned by the ruins of an ancient abbey" (*F* 148). [*F* 320].

Bellerive: See **Belrive**.

Bellerophon: In **Greek** mythology, the gods favored Bellerophon, but when he attempted to join them in heaven, they spurned him and he subsequently wandered the earth alone (Tripp 133–134). "His majesty's frigate" that rescues passengers from the burning *St. Mary* is *Bellerophon* (*Mourner* 90, 93). Shelley could be referring to the Royal Navy's *Bellerophon*, which brought **Napoleon** from **France** to Britain's southern coast 1815; from there, Napoleon was taken to exile (McLynn 632–636; Seymour 135–136).

Bellini, Gentile (1429–1507): **Giovanni Bellini**'s brother; **Venetian** painter who specialized in portraits (*Phaidon* 55). Shelley viewed Bellini's works at **Accademia delle Bella Arti (Venice)** September 1842 (*R* 2.91). Bellini's three-painting series on the *Legend of the True Cross* (1500) is there (*Phaidon* 55).

Bellini, Gian: See **Bellini, Giovanni**.

Bellini, Giovanni (c. 1430–1516): **Italian** painter of the **Venetian** school, considered the best artist of the Bellini family; Shelley calls him **Gian Bellini** (Chilvers 55). She saw Bellini's paintings at **Saints Giovanni's and Paolo's Church**, **Accademia delle Belle Arti (Venice)**, and **Santa Maria de' Frari's Church** September 1842, noting that he was **Giorgione**'s teacher (*R* 2.91, 2.93, 2.98, 2.119). These paintings are probably Bellini's *St. Vincent Ferrer* (mid-1470s) at the Saints' Church and his triptych (1460s–1470s) for Santa Maria Church (Honour 89; *Phaidon* 56). [*R* 2.85].

Bellini, Vincenzo (1801–1835): **Italian** opera composer. Shelley saw Bellini's *I Capuleti e I Montecchi* [*Capulets and Montagues*] (1830), calling it *Montecchi e Capuletti*, in **Venice** October 1842; its plot is based upon *Romeo and Juliet* (*R* 2.127, 2.129; *NGD*).

Bellinzona: **Swiss** city thirteen miles northeast of **Lugano**. Shelley includes **PFS**'s friend's account of their dangerous September 1840 journey, which included traveling a flooded road from Lugano to Bellinzona (*R* 1.148–49).

Bellona: **Roman** goddess of war. Shelley opines that "winter [was] Bellona's fitting mate" (*V* 3.109).

Belouk-Bashee: **Ottoman** town governor. **Katusthius Ziani** requests that **Sagori**'s Belouk-Bashee assist him against **Dmitri** (*EE* 112).

Belrive: Promontory near **Cologny** on **Lake Geneva**'s southern shore, where the Shelleys and **Byron** spent much of summer 1816, Byron having rented **Villa Diodati** there; Shelley spells it **Bellerive** (*Journals* 107; Crook 2). The **Frankenstein** family prefers the seclusion of their idyllic Belrive country house, spending most of their time there (*Fr3* 42). **Victor Frankenstein** observes there a storm that sparks his interest in electricity (*Fr1* 70; *Fr3* 45). Shelley describes viewing this area October 1840, seeing "scenes among which I had lived, when first I stepped out from childhood into life" (*R* 1.139). [*Fr1* 104, 120; *Fr3* 72, 83].

Belvidera: See **Otway**.

Ben Nevis: Highest Scottish mountain, five miles east of Loch Linnhe. Shelley describes ambushed **Stephen Frion** as "pale as the snow on Ben Nevis" (*PW* 3.12).

Benacus: See **Lago di Garda**.

Benevento: **Italian** city thirty-five miles northeast of **Naples**; **Charles of Anjou** defeated and killed **Manfred** there in 1266 (Kinder 1.173). A **Frangipani** man receives an estate near Benevento for handing over **Corradino** to Charles of Anjou (*TP* 22). **Clorinda Saviani**'s mother threatens to remove her to "a convent of **Carthusian** Nuns at Benevento" (*BMI* 40).

Bengal: **Indian** region surrounding Calcutta and bordering Bangladesh. **Rupert Falkner** recalls helping **Osborne** once when they were both stationed there (*F* 139).

Benson: Farmer in "**Maurice**."

Beppe: See **Bosticchi, Giuseppe de'**.

Beppo: Shelley's favorite **Venetian** gondolier (*R* 2.124).

Berchet, Giovanni (1783–1851): **Italian** writer whose earliest pieces were translations of Thomas Gray (1807), **Schiller** (1810), and **Goldsmith** (1810). Active in the **Italian** Romantic literary movement, he was involved with *Il Conciliatore* 1818–19. Shelley credits Italian Romantic literature's inception to Berchet's *Leonora of Burgher* (1816) (*R* 2.194). *Sul "Cacciatore feroce" e sulla "Eleonora" di Goffredo Augusto Burger: Lettera semiseria di Grisostomo al suo figliuolo* [*On the "Fierce Hunter" and "Leonora" of G. A. Burger: The Semiserious Letter from Chrysostom to His Son*] (1816) presents Berchet's stance that these **German** poems encouraged Romantic literature based on popular tradition, thus making poetry universal. Shelley also mentions Berchet's patriotic odes, written 1822–29 (*R* 2.195; *DIL* 48–50).

Berg Isel: Alpine hill near **Innsbruck** (also called **Mount Isel**) famous as the site of **Hofer**'s 1809 victories over **French** and **Bavarians** (*MSGE* 329). Shelley visited this site of "gallant exploits" September 1842 (*R* 2.46, 2.55).

Bergamino: In *Valperga*, entertainer who attends **Euthanasia**'s court.

Bergamo: **Italian** city thirty miles northeast of **Milan**. The first section of *Rambles*' "Letter X" bears the heading "Bergamo, 10th Sept. [1840]" (*R* 1.105). Shelley traveled from **Lecco** to Bergamo to hear **Marini** perform **Rossini**'s *Mosè* (*R* 1.108). She enjoyed the opera but detested her Bergamo lodgings and was too tired to enjoy the city's sights (*R* 1.107).

Berkeley: Family in attendance at **Lord Surrey**'s daughter's wedding feast in *Perkin Warbeck*.

Berkeley Square: Fashionable square in **London**'s Westminster district, close to **Piccadilly** and **Hyde Park**. **Lord Lodore** lives with his wife and her mother there (*L* 1.115, 1.158).

Berkeley, George [Bishop] (1685–1753): PBS read this influential 18th-century **Irish** philosopher's *Works* (1784) December 1817, which is probably how Shelley became familiar with Berkeley's theories (*Journals* 186–187). **Lionel Verney** studies Berkeley (*LM* 77).

Berkshire: County west of **London** in central England (abbreviated as "Berks"). Shelley set many of *The Last Man*'s important scenes there (*LM* 268). **Horace Neville** thinks "of riding across the country from **Shropshire** to Berks" to see **Ellen Burnet** (*Mourner* 95).

Berlin: **Germany**'s capital city, on the **Spree**. Shelley stayed in Berlin at the Hotel **Stadt Rom**, on the **Unter-den-Linden**, for three days July 1842, touring the city extensively (*R* 1.218–230). [*R* 2.96].

Bermondsey: Convent, formerly about a mile south of **London**'s center. **Henry VII** imprisons **Elizabeth Woodville** at Bermondsey; **Meiler Trangmar** and **Monina De Faro** visit her there (*PW* 1.127–128, 1.251, 1.331).

Bernardi: **Castruccio** banishes several powerful families, including the Bernardi, from **Lucca** (*V* 2.149). Shelley might be referring to the Bernardini, a 14th-century Lucchese family that Castruccio disliked (Green 86, 102).

Berncastel: See **Bernkastel**.

Berne: **Switzerland**'s capital, forty-three miles west of **Lucerne**. **Fanny Chaumont** is Bernese. Political upheaval threatening the **Marvilles** ends when the governor is invited to return to Berne, seat of the Swiss government (*SP* 150).

Berni, Francesco (c. 1497–1535): **Italian** author renowned for his rewriting of **Bojardo**'s *Orlando Innamorato* (1483, 1495). In her Berni biography for *Italian and Spanish Lives*, Shelley compares passages from Bojardo's and Berni's versions (*ISPL* 1.189–190). Shelley emphasizes that Berni's "earnest language" gives Bojardo's plot a "graceful wit" and asserts that **Ariosto**'s *Orlando Furioso* is a continuation of Berni's text (*ISPL* 1.191). Shelley found **Sorrento** scenery recalled "passages of Berni" (*R* 2.262).

Bernkastel: German town on the **Moselle**, twenty-three miles northeast of **Trèves**; Shelley spells it **Berncastel**. Shelley passed through it June 1840 (*R* 1.22–23).

Bertha: **Winzy**'s childhood playmate who later becomes his wife in "**The Mortal Immortal**."

Berthier, Louis Alexandre (1753–1815): **France**'s marshal and **Napoleon**'s chief of staff (*DBF*). Shelley records Berthier's statement that **Hofer**'s death "would cause great pain to Napoleon" (*R* 2.60).

Berwick: Most eastern Scottish border county, north of **Northumberland**. Scottish nobles offer **Richard of York** Berwick for a hundred thousand marks (*PW* 2.216).

Besançon: French town forty-four miles east of **Dijon**; the Shelleys passed through it 1814 (*H* 32; *Journals* 15).

Bess: Nickname given by **Henry VII** of England for **Elizabeth of York** (*PW* 3.103, 3.336).

Bessy, Aunt: **Ethel Villiers**'s familiar name for **Elizabeth Fitzhenry** (*L* 1.289, 2.15).

Bethlem: **London** priory and hospital established 1247; Shelley also calls it **Priory** (Weinreb 60). **Richard of York** follows **Heron** to Bethlem House to receive his last sacraments and to see **Lady Katherine Gordon** (*PW* 3.271).

Bethman, Mr.: See **Bethmann, Simon Moritz von**.

Bethmann, Simon Moritz von: Imperial **Russian** councillor and consul general who founded **Frankfurt**'s Bethmann Gallery in the early-19th century; Shelley spells his name **Bethman** (Bethmann 12). Shelley viewed **Dannecker**'s *Ariadne* there (*R* 1.176).

Betsy: In "**Maurice**," **Benson**'s daughter and sister of the countryman who tells **Maurice**'s father about **Barnet** (*Maurice* 64).

Beverem, Sire de: **Robert Clifford** is Beverem's page at **Lille**, where Beverem helps **Stephen Frion** attempt to capture **Richard of York** (*PW* 1.162–165, 1.170, 1.184, 1.189). Fischer notes that Beverem is probably either Corneille of **Burgundy** or **Charles the Bold**'s nephew Philippe (69).

Bewley: See **Beaulieu**.

Bewling: Village three miles from **Longfield**; **Lady Lodore**, **Dame Nixon**, and **Margaret** attend church there (*L* 3.253).

Bewling, Vale of: Valley three miles from **Longfield** and site of **Dame Nixon**'s cottage, where **Lady Lodore** lodges (*L* 2.231, 3.248, 3.257). **Elizabeth Fitzhenry** visits Cornelia there (*L* 3.264, 3.292).

Bianchi: Literally "whites" in **Italian**, faction that began as part of the **Guelph** political party. **Neri** ("blacks") and the Bianchi were branches of the

Pistoian Cancellieri family, which quarreled violently 1296–1300. The moderate Guelph Bianchi sided with **Ghibellines**, and thus "Bianchi" and "Ghibelline" are somewhat interchangeable (Sismondi 115–117). **Cincolo de' Becari** remembers watching Neri ride triumphantly through **Florence**'s streets (*TP* 4). At *Valperga*'s beginning, Shelley summarizes **Tuscany**'s Bianchi-Neri strife and records Pistoian Neri's 1301 expulsion of Bianchi from **Lucca**; **Castruccio**'s family is exiled with this group (*V* 1.2–3). Castruccio is Ghibelline, although his family is Bianchi (*V* 1.3).

Bianco, Carlo (b. 1785): Calabrian Carbonari founder; this exile's book about guerilla warfare impressed Mazzini (Moskal 317; Holt 83–84). Shelley (calling him **Capo Bianco**) notes his commitment to **Italy**'s reunification, how he led Carbonari in **Catanzaro**, and his execution (*R* 2.166–172).

Bible: Shelley refers to the Bible frequently in her writing, especially in connection with **Milton**'s retelling of the first three chapters of **Genesis** in *Paradise Lost*. **Matilda** compares "bitter anguish" in her heart to Isaiah's proclamation: "**as the waters** cover the sea," so the "earth shall be full of the knowledge of the Lord" (*M* 210; Isaiah 11.9). **Dame Barnet** teaches neighborhood children to read from the Bible (*Maurice* 62). **Beatrice** quotes the Bible to describe her humiliation: "**Oh, that my** head were water, and mine eyes a fountain of tears!" (*V* 3.73; Jeremiah 9.1). **Adrian** uses a passage from John, " '**there are many** mansions,' " to urge consideration of **Raymond**'s conduct (*LM* 150; John 14.2). **Lionel Verney** recalls death used to be " 'a **thief that comes** in the night,' " before plague's onset; Thessalonians records "the day of the Lord will come like a thief in the night" (*LM* 272; 1 Thessalonians 5.1–2). Shelley states "that as **Jehovah** hardened the heart of **Pharaoh** for his own destruction, so does he soften the heart of **Prince Metternich**" to improve **Lombardy** (*R* 2.116). "Jehovah" is an erroneous English transliteration of the Hebrew YHWH, for Yahweh or God; Shelley alludes to the account in Exodus of Ramses II, who allowed Moses to lead the Israelites out of **Egypt** (Browning 196, 292; Exodus 7–12). Shelley also records attending mass in **Milan**, where she heard a sermon on the Good **Samaritan**, a parable in Luke (*R* 1.112; Luke 10.30–35). She mentions that **Luther** spent ten months translating the Bible at the **Wartburg Castle**; she saw the Bible he found, which is kept at the convent in **Erfurt** (*R* 1.207, 1.209). Shelley paraphrases Ephesians to describe marriage: "**therefore shall a man leave his father and mother, and cleave unto his wife**" (*R* 2.108; Ephesians 5.31). [*Maurice* 66, 75]. See **Absalom, Ahaseuras, Apocrypha, Babel, David, Ecclesiastes, Gabriel, Gospel, Hebrew, Heliodorus, Job, Joseph, Maccabees, Magi, Noah, Philistines, Psalms, Samson, Solomon**.

Bindo: **Euthanasia**'s albino dwarf servant in *Valperga*, termed **Albinois**.

Birnam Hill: Scottish hill south of **Dunkeld** and northeast of Dunsinnan. **Lionel Verney** notes regrowth in Birnam Hill's forest, perhaps alluding to *Macbeth* (*LM* 71; *Macbeth* 4.1.92–94).

Biron, Louisa: Young **William Frankenstein**'s five-year-old "wife" in *Frankenstein*.

Bisagno: River in **Genoa**; Shelley spells it **Bisanzio**. Shelley's footnoted information on storms includes her experience with one that carried away Bisagno's bridges from Genoa to **Albaro** (R 1.58).

Bisanzio: See **Bisagno**.

Biscay, Bay of: Body of water bordering northern **Spain** and western **France**. **Robert Clifford** tells **Edmund Plantagenet** that **Richard of York**, en route to **Malaga** on the *Adalid*, is probably in the Bay of Biscay (PW 1.200). Later, a storm tosses the *St. George* into the bay (PW 1.259, 1.261).

Bishopsgate: Area on **London**'s western outskirts; in Shelley's time, **Bishopsgate Heath** was a large, open stretch of land beyond **Chapel Wood** and **Virginia Water** on the grounds of **Windsor** Castle. The Shelleys lived in Bishopsgate August 1815–May 1816, near "the eastern entrance to Windsor Great Park" (*Journals* 104–107; Seymour 139–140). **Perdita**'s cottage seems based upon the Shelleys' residence there, and many of *The Last Man*'s important scenes are set there (LM 257). **Raymond** detours through Bishopsgate Heath to visit Perdita at her cottage (LM 41, 67). **Horace Neville** and his cousins meet their carriage at Bishopsgate and "ride across Bishopsgate Heath" (*Mourner* 85, 86, 88, 97).

Bishopsgate Heath: See **Bishopsgate**.

Bissone: Swiss town five miles south of **Lugano** on **Lake Lugano**. Shelley includes **PFS**'s friend's account of their dangerous September 1840 journey, during which they left Bissone on a small raft during a storm (R 1.147).

Black Forest: The 2,320-square-mile southwestern **German** region where the **Danube** and **Neckar** Rivers begin. Schwarzwald in German (Shelley's spelling is **Swartzwald**), the forest is named for its dark pine trees and renowned for its beauty and mineral springs, such as **Baden-Baden**. In July 1840, Shelley traveled from **Freyberg** into the Black Forest; she enjoyed riding through **Hollenthal** (R 1.45–47). Shelley writes about the forest to **Everina Wollstonecraft** (*Letters* 3.2).

Black Spectre: Mysterious horseman dressed in black who follows plague survivors through **France**. Just before his death, he reveals that he is an isolated French noble who could not approach survivors for fear of infection and yet "could not resolve to lose sight of us, sole human beings who besides himself existed" (LM 411).

Black Sea: Almost landlocked body of water surrounded by **Russia**, **Turkey**, **Georgia**, Ukraine, Romania, and Bulgaria, flowing into the **Mediterranean** through the Bosporus Straits near **Istanbul** and **Marmora**. The **Creature** hides on a vessel sailing to the Black Sea (Fr1 227; Fr3 169). [R 2.49].

Blackfriars: Central **London** district on the **Thames**'s south bank. A large bridge over the Thames links the Blackfriars, City, and Southwark districts and provides a view of many famous London landmarks; **Ethel Villiers** and her husband walk together "over Blackfriars' Bridge" (Leigh 267; L 3.28). **Lady Katherine**

Blackheath

Gordon and **Elizabeth of York** travel along the Thames to Blackfriars to visit **Richard of York** in the **Tower** (*PW* 3.330).

Blackheath: London district and 1497 battle wherein **Lord Daubeney** defeated **Lord Audley**'s **Cornish** forces (Cannon 107). This defeat becomes a motivation for later violence on **James IV**'s part: "to avenge their losses at Blackheath" (*PW* 2.298, 3.65). [*PW* 3.102].

Blackwall: Eastern **London** district that in Shelley's day was notable for **East India Company** dockyards (Leigh 446). **Ethel Villiers**'s carriage passes through Blackwall into London (*L* 2.257).

Blackwater: Southern **Irish** river cutting across County **Cork** and emptying into **Youghal Bay**. Shelley accurately situates Youghal at the Blackwater's mouth (*PW* 3.33).

Blamire, Susanna (1747–1794): English poet best remembered for "Stoklewath; or, the Cumbrian Village" (c. 1780). Shelley quotes Blamire's "The Nabob" (1803), in which a traveler returns to Scotland after thirty years' absence and nostalgically laments changes found there, in *Valperga* and *Lodore* (Blamire lines 33–36). **Euthanasia** thinks about humans clinging to sorrows rather than "a **new-sprung race** of pleasures"; **Lord Lodore**'s focus shifts from himself to his daughter, since "a 'new-sprung race' [cannot] compensate for that, whose career we hoped to see run" (*V* 3.11; *L* 1.46).

Blewet, Abel: See **Blewit, Abel**.

Blewit, Abel: In *Perkin Warbeck*, dwarflike guard whom **Richard of York** bribes while in the **Tower**; he assists Richard's escape. Shelley's alternate spelling is **Blewet**.

Blondel: **Manzoni**'s wife's father. Shelley describes Henriette Manzoni (formerly Henriette Blondel) as "daughter of Blondel, a banker of **Geneva**" (*R* 2.200; *DIL* 312).

Blücher, Gebhard Leberecht von (1742–1819): **Prussian** soldier promoted to field marshal for his actions in the 1813 Battle of **Leipzig** and renowned for his important maneuvers at **Waterloo**. Shelley enumerates various associations with the **Rhine**, one of which is how "**German** soldiers, led by Blücher, and driving the proud fallen victor before them, beheld the river honoured by them" (*R* 1.27).

Boabdil El Chico (d. 1527): **Granada**'s sultan as Muhammad XI 1482–92, when **Ferdinand** and **Isabella I** defeated him. "El Chico" means "little king," a Castilian nickname occasioned by his mother **Sultana Ayza**'s involvement in his reign. **Stephen Frion** formerly advised Boabdil and relates tales of the "quarrels of **El Zagal** and El Chico" to **Richard of York** (*PW* 1.150, 1.159). While Richard is in **Spain**, Ferdinand demands Granada from Boabdil (*PW* 1.216).

"Boat on the Serchio, The": Unfinished poem **PBS** wrote 1821, first published 1824. As a second epigraph to the *Perkin Warbeck* chapter in which **Monina De Faro** nurses **Richard of York** after battle, Shelley quotes: "**The chain is loos'd, the sails are spread,** / **The living breath is fresh behind;** / **As**

with dews and sunrise fed, / Comes the laughing morning wind" (*PW* 1.222; PBS lines 88–91). Shelley quotes "**All rose to do** the task, he set to each / Who shaped us to his ends, and not our own" from the poem in *Lodore*; she quotes these same lines in *Perkin Warbeck* as well as two further lines: "**And many rose** / Whose woe was such, that fear became desire" (*L* 3.1; *PW* 3.311; PBS lines 30–31, 34–35).

Boccaccio, Giovanni di [da Certaldo] (1313–1375): **Italian** writer and humanist widely recognized for his importance as a formative author of narrative fiction. His best-known work is *The Decameron* (1349–51), a collection of tales told by a group of young people retreating from the 1348 plague in **Florence**. Shelley read Boccaccio May 1819 and again September 1820, calling him the "most delightful author"; Shelley possibly drew references to **Troilus** and **Cressida** from Boccaccio's *Il filostrato* (c. 1335), the basis of **Chaucer**'s version (*Journals* 263, 332; *Letters* 1.104). **Matilda** compares her grief following her father's declaration of incestuous desire to that of Boccaccio's description of "the intense and quiet grief of **Sigismunda** over the heart of **Guiscardo**" (*M* 174). Shelley alludes to *The Decameron*'s story detailing Tancred's possessive love for his only daughter Ghismonda; Todd notes Shelley's alteration of " 'Ghismonda' to 'Sigismunda,' " the name in John Dryden's *Fables Ancient and Modern* (1700) (Boccaccio 4.1; Todd 216). Shelley takes the names of *Uomini di Corte* members who entertain **Euthanasia**'s court, such as **Andreuccio** and **William Borsiere**, from *Decameron,* and she also alludes to Boccaccio's famous preface about plague in *The Last Man* (*LM* 267). Shelley wrote Boccaccio's biography for *Italian and Spanish Lives*, asserting his talent lies in narrative rather than poetry (*ISPL* 1.124). She finds that *Decameron* "bears the undoubted stamp of genius" (*ISPL* 1.128–129). Shelley concludes that "the tenderness, the passion, the enthusiasm, the pathos, and above all, the heartfelt nature of his best tales, raise [Boccaccio] to the highest rank of writers of any age or country" (*ISPL* 1.130). Shelley wants to explore scenes familiar to Boccaccio and compares **Roman** villages to those in *Decameron* (*R* 2.134, 2.241). [*Letters* 2.209].

Bodenlauben: See **Botenlaube**.

Bodmin: English town twenty-seven miles northwest of Plymouth. **Edmund Plantagenet** travels there (*PW* 3.63, 3.72, 3.77).

Boeotian: Shelley uses "Boeotian," a reference to a rural area of ancient **Greece** northwest of **Athens**, to describe a rough **Bavarian** dialect, meaning that it is "dull, stupid" (*R* 1.187; *OED*).

Bohemia: Ancient central **European** kingdom that became the Czech Republic's western region. Shelley names **Beatrice**'s mother "**Wilhelmina of Bohemia**," since she is supposedly the daughter of **Constance**, Queen of Bohemia (*V* 2.26, 3.35). **Richard of York**, **Monina De Faro**, and **Desmond** encounter a band of gypsies, or "Bohemians," when fleeing the **Tower** (*PW* 2.122). Shelley passed through Bohemia 1842 and describes Bohemian girls entertaining her by playing harps (*R*

1.35, 1.270, 1.273). Shelley visited **Prague**, capital of Bohemia, September 1842 and gives an account of the city's history (*R* 2.1–9). [*R* 2.13].

Boiardo, Matteo: See **Bojardo**.

Boieldieu, François-Adrien (1775–1834): French comic opera composer. He based *La Dame Blanche* [*The White Lady*] (1825) on **Sir Walter Scott**'s *Guy Mannering* (1815) and *The Monastery* (1820). Shelley records *La Dame Blanche* playing in **Dresden** as *Die weise Frau* [*The White Lady*] during summer 1842 (*R* 1.248).

Boileau-Despréaux, Nicholas (1636–1711): French author renowned for seven verse satires (1660–66). He focused in his works principally upon faults he perceived in his era's literature, satirizing them before laying out correct paths for authors in *L'Art poétique* [*Poetic Art*] (1674). Shelley wrote Boileau-Despréaux's biography for *French Lives*. She admires his *Lutrin* (1674) particularly, providing excerpts and asserting that it is the best of his works; however, she also felt that the severity of Boileau-Despréaux's criticisms harmed authors personally (*FL* 1.259).

Bojardo, Matteo Maria (1441–1494): Italian author about whom little is known; Shelley spells his name **Boiardo**. Shelley wrote Bojardo's biography for *Italian and Spanish Lives*, declaring that his "lyrical poetry is extremely beautiful, tender, and spirited, being characterised by that easy flow of thought and style peculiar to him" (*ISPL* 1.182). Bojardo's *Amorum libri* [*Love songs*] (1499) is a three-book collection of **Petrarchan** lyrics; Shelley asserts that his "great work," founded upon old romances, is *Orlando Innamorato* [*Orlando in Love*] (1483, 1495), continued in **Ariosto**'s *Orlando Furioso* (*ISPL* 1.183). She also discusses **Francesco Berni**'s rewriting of Bojardo's text (*ISPL* 1.187).

Bolingbroke: Reference to **Henry IV** in *Perkin Warbeck*.

Bologna: Italian city fifty miles northeast of **Florence**. The Shelleys passed through Bologna 1818 (*Journals* 208). **Castruccio** passes through Bologna, primarily a **Guelph** city in league with Florence, en route from **Ancona** to **Este** and also from **Ferrara** to **Lucca** (*V* 1.44, 1.118, 2.173). **Benedetto Pepi** voices disapproval of Bologna's liberty (*V* 1.124). Florentine troops under **Bondelmonti** reach **Valperga** castle via Bologna (*V* 2.249). **Flora Mancini** loses her way among wooded mountains near Bologna (*Brother* 188). **Camilla della Toretta** and her brother are from Bologna (*Trial* 233, 243). Shelley regretted not revisiting "galleries, and palaces, and churches of Bologna" (*R* 2.133, 2.162, 2.247, 2.257). [*V* 1.290].

Bologna, John of (c. 1524–1608): Flemish sculptor who worked in **Italy**, renowned for his bronze statue of **Mercury** (1580) (Gowing 257–258). Shelley saw it in **Florence**'s **Uffizi** January 1843 (*R* 2.155).

Bolter's Lock: Lock on the **Thames** north of **Windsor**. People leave a plague sufferer in a hut near Bolter's Lock (*LM* 258).

Bolvedro: Shelley mentions the Italian village of Bolvedro on **Lake**

Como's shore between **Tremezzo** and **Como** (*R* 1.66).

Bolzano: **Italian** city on the **Adige**, twenty miles southwest of **Brixen**; Shelley's **German** for it is "**Botzen**." Shelley passed through it September 1842 (*R* 2.62).

Bonaparte, Napoleon (1769–1821): **Corsican** who became **France**'s emperor 1804–14 and 1814–15; he married **Josephine** 1796, divorced her 1809 for not bearing a son, and married **Marie Louise** 1810; she had their son 1811. He commanded the French army fighting the **Austrians** for control of **Italy** 1796. Supporting Italian republicans, he also fought against Austria in Italy 1799–1800. As emperor, he warred against Austria, Britain, **Russia**, **Spain**, and **Portugal**; Shelley hated Napoleon "for his dictatorship and bloody imperial wars" (Sunstein 52). Finally overturned and exiled to **Elba** 1814, Napoleon returned to **Paris** 1815 (*Journals* 67, 72). British forces defeated him at **Waterloo**; he died in exile on St. Helena. In *History*, Shelley observes destruction and fear in one of the earliest reports about France after Napoleon's reign (*Journals* 11; Sunstein 86; *H* 12, 19–20, 24). She lists Napoleon's worst crimes as the deaths of **Hofer**, **l'Ouverture**, and **Duc d'Enghien** (*R* 1.43–44). She notes **Coblentz**'s monument memorializing Napoleon's defeat in his 1812–13 Russian campaign, mentions several Napoleonic battles, and details his invasion of the **Tyrol** (*R* 1.169, 2.40–44, 2.50–61). Shelley saw Napoleon's body, entombed in Paris's Les Invalides, December 1843 (Sunstein 351; *Letters* 3.19). [*H* 17; *LM* 56–57; *R* 1.175, 1.213, 1.215, 1.219, 1.225, 1.230, 1.253, 1.277, 2.113, 2.165, 2.167, 2.187].

Bonconti: In *Valperga*, **Pisan** noble respected as "a man of understanding and courage" (*V* 1.227–28).

Bondelmonti: **Guelph** family of **Florence** whose name was derived from a Montebuono fortress (Villani 100–199). Guelph and **Ghibelline** factions resulted from **Bondelmonte de' Bondelmonti**'s actions. Three brothers belonging to the Bondelmonti family attend **Euthanasia**'s court (*V* 1.256).

Bondelmonti, Bondelmonte de': **Florentine** commander of the **Guelph** faction; **Euthanasia**'s guardian is his descendant (*V* 1.256). **Villani** records that the historical figure was engaged to an Amidei daughter but ended the engagement to marry a **Donati** woman. Angered by this insult, the Amidei and their allies attacked and killed Bondelmonti near Ponte Vecchio 1215 (Villani 121–123). Those who sided with Bondelmonti became Guelph, and their enemies **Ghibelline**.

Bondelmonti, Francesco: Bondelmonte de' Bondelmonti's cousin in *Valperga*.

Bonifazio, Veronese (c. 1487–1553): **Italian** painter of the **Venetian** school. Shelley saw his paintings at Venice's **Saints Giovanni's and Paolo's Church** September 1842 (*R* 2.98). See **Veronese, Paul**.

Bonn: **German** city on the **Rhine**, fifteen miles southeast of **Cologne**. The Shelleys traveled from Bonn to Cologne 1814 (*H* 71; *Journals* 23).

Bonshaw, Laird of: In *Perkin Warbeck*, **Mary Boyd**'s father.

Booth, David (1776–1846): Married to Margaret Baxter when Shelley first met him in 1812. After his first wife's death, David married Margaret's younger sister and Shelley's close friend **Isabel Baxter Booth**, 1814, despite an age difference of twenty-seven years. David, "a wealthy retired brewer, brilliant lexicographer and scholar, autocratic and tough," was **William Godwin**'s friend (Sunstein 60; Seymour 70). David disapproved of Isabel's friendship with Shelley following her elopement with **PBS**, forbidding her to correspond with Shelley November 1814 (*Journals* 42). Writing to PBS September 1817, Shelley noted that **William Baxter** had asserted "Mr Booth is illtempered and jealous towards Isabell" (*Letters* 1.41). David moved to **London** and met PBS November 1817, an encounter Baxter arranged, but David did not like him and found reasons for discontinuing the acquaintance January 1818 (*Journals* 42, 184). In London, David "became superintendent for the press of the Society for the Diffusion of Useful Knowledge" and published several works demonstrating diverse interests. The most important of these books is *Analytical Dictionary of the English Language* (1822–35), which Shelley called "an excellent work" (*Journals* 42; *Letters* 3.196). Shelley renewed her friendship with Isabel March 1823 and frequently saw her and David in subsequent years (*Journals* 458). Isabel faithfully nursed David during his lingering illness and epileptic fits in the 1830s and 1840s, when they were nearly destitute (*Letters* 3.196–197). In 1845, Shelley unsuccessfully intervened with friends in an attempt to secure David money the government had promised him; **PFS** finally "obtained forty pounds from the Royal Literary Fund" (*Journals* 516; Sunstein 370; *Letters* 3.196–197). See volume five of Kenneth Neill Cameron and Donald Reiman's *Shelley and His Circle* (1961–70) (371–392).

Booth, Isabel Baxter (b. 1793): June 1812, Shelley went to Scotland to stay with the Baxters, who "became her second family, [and] with whom she would spend sixteen of the next twenty-two months" (Sunstein 57). Shelley formed a lifelong friendship with the youngest Baxter daughter, Isabel, who was four years older than Shelley: "the two girls studied together, and ranged the beach," and they also "delved into the occult with which Scottish culture abounded" (56–57, 60). They parted 1814, and later that year Isabel married **David Booth**, who was twenty-seven years her senior and the former husband of her deceased older sister; such a marriage was illegal under English law (Sunstein 61; *Journals* 42). In 1814, David informed Shelley that Isabel could no longer correspond with her, in view of her elopement with **PBS** and its affront to **William Godwin**; Shelley sadly noted receipt of this letter: "so all my hopes are over there—ah Isabel—I did not think you would act thus" (*Journals* 42). In 1818, Isabel's father told Shelley that David was poisoning his wife against the Shelleys and that Isabel "was wretched in her marriage" (Sunstein 148). Shelley planned to invite her friend to **Italy** to remove her from her husband. Following rumors about

PBS's relationship with **Claire Clairmont**, David "convinced Isabel they were lovers," and Isabel remained with him (Sunstein 148). They had a daughter, Catherine, and before Shelley's departure Isabel managed to see her. When Shelley returned to **London** 1823, she and Isabel reunited, but Shelley found her friend "melancholic after a breakdown from which she never entirely recovered" (Sunstein 243). Shelley told **Leigh Hunt** she had "now renewed my acquaintance with the friend of my girlish days—she has been ill a long time, even disturbed in her reason, and the remains of this still hang over her.... The great affection she displays for me endears her to me & the memory of early days," but Isabel declined in health and their contact was sporadic (*Letters* 1.380). In 1845, Isabel "was near destitution, nursing her aged, epileptic husband"; Shelley tried to get governmental support for David (Sunstein 369, 370). In 1847 and 1850, Shelley applied to the Royal Literary Fund on Isabel's behalf (Sunstein 376, 383). Isabel wanted to visit Shelley when she learned of her friend's illness, but **PFS** "told her not to make an unnecessary journey" (Sunstein 383). Shelley asked PFS to give her friend "fifty pounds a year and a mourning suit" following her death; Isabel "had a presentiment that day that she was dead" (Sunstein 383). PFS subsequently sent Isabel a lock of Shelley's hair (Sunstein 384). PBS's "**Rosalind and Helen**" is partly based on Shelley's friendship with Isabel, and "**A Night Scene**," attributed to Shelley, may also be a commentary on the two women's ties (*Journals* 516–517; *Letters* 1.41; White 1.535).

Bordeaux: Large port city on **France**'s southwestern coast, 170 miles southeast of **Nantes**. **Edmund Plantagenet** follows **Richard of York**'s route from Bordeaux to **Malaga** (*PW* 1.203). **Horatio Saville** hopes to locate **Lady Lodore** at **Bagnères de Bigorre**, "annual resort of the French from Bordeaux" (*L* 3.240). *Rambles* opens with a description of Shelley's journey from **Calais** to Bordeaux June 1840 (*R* 1.6).

Boreas: Greek god of the north wind. Shelley refers to Scotland as "this eyrie of Boreas" (*PW* 2.187).

Borghese Gardens: **Roman** gardens named after the Borghese family, prominent in **Italian** society 16th–19th centuries; Shelley enjoyed reading and sketching in the Borghese Gardens March 1819 (Sunstein 155; *Journals* 255). **Lionel Verney** reads "opposite the fair temple in the Borghese Gardens" (*LM* 465).

Borromeo: Noble **Italian** family possessing most of **Lake Como** during the 15th century (*BSWI* 480). Shelley visited the Borromean Islands, enjoying **Isola Madre** and **Isola Bella**; Borromeo family's mansion is on the latter (*R* 1.129).

Borromeo, Cardinal Carlo (1538–1584): Cardinal appointed **Milan**'s archbishop 1560 and later sainted; Shelley saw the large bronze **statue of San Carlo Borromeo** in **Arona** September 1840 (Roeder 33; *MIIT* 123; *R* 1.128). She mentions Borromeo as a personification of "the merits and uses of a pious clergy" **Manzoni** presents in *Promessi sposi* (*R* 2.199).

Borromeo, Federigo (1564–1631): Cardinal and archbishop of **Milan**; he founded the **Ambrosian Library** in 1609. Shelley mentions **Ripamonti**'s account of his "character and life" (*R* 2.198).

Borsiere, William: *Uomini di Corte* member in *Valperga*. Shelley named this character after a courtier mentioned in both **Dante**'s *Inferno* and **Boccaccio**'s *Decameron* (*Inferno* 16.70; *Decameron* 1.8).

Boscán Almugáver, Mosen Juan (c. 1500–1543): **Spanish** poet who experimented with **Italian** meters and initiated the era of great Spanish lyrics; Shelley wrote Boscán's biography for *Italian and Spanish Lives* but had difficulty obtaining necessary materials (*Letters* 2.289). Boscán translated Castiglione's *Libro del Cortigiano* [*The Book of the Courtier*] as *Los cuatro libros del Cortesano* [*The Four Books of the Courtier*] (1534) and wrote imitations of **Horace**; Shelley asserts that Boscán's "chief praise results from his coming forward as the reformer of Spanish poetry" (*ISPL* 3.33–34). She finds that Boscán's poetry "is all calm, earthly, unidealised, though not unimpassioned," while she feels "he cannot compress" and "his poetry wants concentration and energy" (*ISPL* 3.34–35).

Bosticchi, Giuseppe de': Minor character in "**A Tale of the Passions**," also called **Beppe**. Shelley named him after a 1015 **Guelph** family of **Florence** (Villani 82, 124).

Boston: **Hoskins** emigrates to this northeastern **American** city (*F* 138).

Bosworth Field: Battle twelve miles southwest of **Leicester**; **Lancastrians** defeated **Yorkists** in 1485, making **Henry VII** king. *Perkin Warbeck* opens immediately following this battle (*PW* 1.1, 1.61, 1.185).

Botenlaube: Castle ruins on a hill about a mile south of **Kissingen**; Shelley spells it **Bodenlauben** (*MSGE* 114). Shelley visited Botenlaube repeatedly 1842 (*R* 1.187). See **Bad**.

Bothwell, Lord: See **Ramsay, Sir John**.

Botta, Carlo Giuseppe Guglielmo (1766–1837): **Italian**-born **French** historian who supported **Napoleon** and is renowned for *History of Italy from 1789–1814* (1824) and *History of the War of the Independence of the United States* (1820–1821) (Moskal 337). Shelley lists his name with those of other Italian historians (*R* 2.205).

Botzen: See **Bolzano**.

Boularias: **Katusthius Ziani**'s rescue of **Dmitri** " 'from the savage **Kakovougnis** of Boularias' " establishes the **Pobratimo** bond between them (*EE* 102). Not further identified.

Boulevard: See **Corso**.

Boulevards: Main and outer streets encircling **Paris**, following the **Barrier**'s course. Shelley admired one of the outer boulevards June 1814 (*H* 11).

Boulogne: **French** city sixteen miles south of **Calais**. Shelley traveled from Calais to Boulogne 1814 (*H* 3, 8–9; *Journals* 8). **Lionel Verney** bids Britain farewell from Boulogne (*LM* 378). **Henry VII** of England lands at Calais in his invasion of France before proceeding to Boulogne (*PW* 1.314).

Bourbons: **France**'s ruling family 16th–18th centuries; also rulers of **Spain** in the 18th century and of various **Italian** principalities. **Adrian**'s party resides at **Versailles** "amidst the luxuries of the departed Bourbons" (*LM* 382). Discussing French possession of **Naples**, Shelley observes "[m]ore than the Bourbon who had persecuted them, [Neapolitans] hated the usurpation of the stranger" (*R* 2.166). She notes: "During and after the fall of **Murat** and the return of the Bourbon dynasty, **Carbonarism**, which had never been destroyed, spread" (*R* 2.174). Bourbons returned to the French throne 1815, ruling until 1848 (Kinder 2.19–21, 2.49).

Bournemouth: British coastal town twenty-seven miles southwest of **Southampton**. **PFS** bought Boscombe Manor near Bournemouth 1850 and lived there after 1851 (Sunstein 383–384, 388). **Jane Shelley** moved **Mary Wollstonecraft**'s and **William Godwin**'s graves from **St. Pancras** in **London** to St. Peter's Churchyard in Bournemouth and buried Shelley (according to her wishes) with them there 1851; the rector was nervous about having such figures in the churchyard, so Shelley was buried at night without religious ceremony (Sunstein 384–385). **PFS** was buried in the same grave (along with **PBS**'s heart) 1889 (Sunstein 395).

Boxhill: Beautiful hill on the Mole river in Surrey, southwest of **London**. Shelley compares **Schandau** inn's "secluded and peaceful" beauty to a **Burford Bridge** inn near Boxhill (*R* 1.267).

Boyd, Mary: **James IV**'s mistress in *Perkin Warbeck*; their illegitimate child is in **Fife**.

Brabant: Former western **European** duchy and part of **Belgium** since 1830. Shelley relates how **Gabriel Serbelloni** fought for **Charles V** there (*R* 1.80–81).

Bracknel: See **Bracknell**.

Bracknell: English town eight miles southwest of **Windsor**, where **PBS** was living when he visited the **Godwins** in **London** July 1813 (White 1.306, 1.327, 1.334–335; Holmes 226). Shelley sets many of *The Last Man*'s important scenes there, spelling it **Bracknel** (*LM* 262).

Brakenbury, Sir Robert: In *Perkin Warbeck*, he reputedly helps to murder **Edward V** in the **Tower**.

Brambilla, Teresa (1813–1895): One of many Brambilla sisters who were **Italian** opera singers (Rosenthal 61). Shelley describes hearing Teresa sing **Lucia**'s part "very tolerably" at **Como**'s Opera House August 1840 (*R* 1.90).

Brampton, Lady: Influential **Richard of York** supporter in *Perkin Warbeck*.

Brampton, Sir Edward: Lady Brampton's husband and **Yorkist** supporter in *Perkin Warbeck*.

Brandenburg Gate: Large gate at **Unter den Linden**'s western end. It opened 1791; the Quadriga—four horses pulling the chariot of the goddess of Victory—was added 1793 (Tucker 53). Shelley records seeing the monument July 1842 and recounts its history—how "**Napoleon** carried off the **car of Victory** which decorates the top; it was brought back after the battle of **Waterloo**" (*R* 1.218–219).

Brenner: Large **Alpine** mountain in western **Austria** and town about twenty miles south of **Innsbruck**. Shelley ascended the Brenner September 1842 to reach the town (*R* 2.48–49). Shelley also recounts historical battles fought in this area, such as one fought by **Hofer** in 1809 (*R* 2.52–55; *MSGE* 329).

Brenner Pass: In western **Austria**, lowest **Alpine** pass between **Germany** and **Switzerland** (*MSGE* 329). Shelley took the Brenner Pass September 1842 to view **Lago di Garda** (*R* 2.29).

Brennus: **Gallic** king who captured **Rome** c. 390 B.C.E. The Romans, forced to pay a gold ransom, caught the Gauls using false weights, whereupon Brennus tauntingly added his sword to the scales (Plutarch, *Lives* 1.212; Crook 2). Shelley compares the **Ghibelline** attack on the **Guelphs** in **Lucca** to Brennus's act: "the Ghibellines wishing, like Brennus, to throw the sword into the ascending scale, assailed the stronger party with arms in their hands" (*V* 1.4). In both cases, the aggressors were defeated and expelled (Crook 2).

Brenta: Northeastern **Italian** river; the Brenta Canal empties into **Venice**'s **Laguna**. Shelley rushed to Venice 1818 along the Brenta Canal with her sick daughter, but **Clara Shelley** died upon arrival (*Journals* 227). The narrator of "**Recollections of Italy**" deplores "'that dirty Brenta,'" and **Edmund Malville** agrees that it is unappealing (*RI* 25–26). **Lionel Verney**, **Adrian**, and **Clara** journey to Venice on the Brenta (*LM* 438). Shelley describes an 1842 trip: "the Brenta presented to me a moving scene; not a palace, not a tree of which I did not recognise, as marked and recorded, at a moment when life and death hung upon our speedy arrival at Venice" (*R* 2.77, 2.79).

Brentani: Shelley records that the Brentani brothers run **Cadenabbia**'s **Albergo Grande** inn, where she stayed summer 1840 (*R* 1.68). **Battista Brentani** was the inn's cook (*R* 1.69). **Bernardo Brentani** worked as an under-waiter and hoped to travel to England (*R* 1.69). **Giovanni Brentani** was the oldest brother; married to **Peppina Brentani**, he was "a tall stout man" who kept the accounts (*R* 1.68). Peppina "is of good parentage, but [orphaned].... [She] lost her all through the rascality of guardians during the troubled times of **Napoleon**'s wars and downfall. She waits on us; she is hard-working, good-humoured" (*R* 1.68). **Luigi Brentani**, second-oldest brother, was in charge of customer relations; Shelley describes him as the "beau of the establishment" (*R* 1.69). **Paolo Brentani**, also called **Piccol**, was a "handsome lad, who runs about, and does everything" at the inn (*R* 1.69).

Brentford: Village on **London**'s outskirts, fifteen miles east of **Windsor**.

Lionel Verney first notices plague there (*LM* 249).

Brera: Picture gallery established at **Milan** 1803; it houses one of **Italy**'s most extensive art collections (*MIIT* 141; Jackson 1.585–589). Shelley viewed the Brera's paintings September 1840, admiring **Raphael**'s *Marriage of the Virgin* especially (*R* 1.110, 1.123).

Brescia: **Italian** city fifty miles east of **Milan**. During the 14th century, it was occupied primarily by **Guelphs**. **Henry VII** of **Germany** began his siege of Brescia May 1311; it finally surrendered September 1311, after many deaths on both sides (Villani 403–405). **Castruccio** serves Henry during the siege; Shelley's account is historically correct (*V* 1.148, 1.157; Green 46).

Bressanone: See **Brixen**.

***Bride of Abydos, The: A Turkish Tale*:** Long poem **Byron** wrote and published 1813; it was "very successful" (Marchand 1.423–424). **Richard of York** describes **Lady Katherine Gordon** with a phrase from Byron's poem, feeling " 'music breathing from her face' " (*PW* 2.213; Byron line 179).

"Bride of Modern Italy, The": Story Shelley published anonymously in the April 1824 *London Magazine* (Robinson 376). It is based upon the Shelleys' acquaintance with **Emilia Viviani** (*Journals* 595). **Clorinda Saviani**, like Emilia, has been confined to a convent while her parents search for a suitable husband willing to accept a small dowry (*BMI* 34). She has formed several attachments to various men who have visited the **St. S—— Convent** (*BMI* 34). Her latest suitor is **Giacomo de' Tolomei**, brother of **Teresa de' Tolomei**, who also lives at the convent (*BMI* 33). When the Savianis reject Giacomo's marriage proposal, he discourages Clorinda from trying to escape and travels to **Siena** to obtain his father's assistance (*BMI* 36). His friend **Marcott Alleyn** visits the convent to comfort the girls, and Clorinda falls in love with him (*BMI* 38). When Clorinda requests that he help her escape and take her back to England, Marcott stops visiting (*BMI* 38–39). At their final meeting, Clorinda relates her detestable situation—her parents are forcing her to marry **Romani**—and begs Marcott to " 'bear me away to freedom and love, and let me not be sacrificed to this unknown bridegroom' " (*BMI* 40). Marcott ends his visits and does not act when Clorinda asks that he contact a past suitor who may still be willing to marry her (*BMI* 40). The story concludes with Clorinda and Romani's marriage.

***Brides' Tragedy, The*:** See **Beddoes**.

Bridesmaid: See **Weber**.

Bridge of Prague: Bridge connecting **Kleine Seite** with **Prague**. Shelley saw the **St. John Nepomuk** statue on the Charles Bridge September 1842 (*R* 2.6).

Bridget: See **St. Bridget**.

Bridgewater Collection: The second Duke of Bridgewater purchased an art collection from the **Duke of Orleans (Louis-Philippe)** 1792 and exhibited it in **London** 1798–99 (B. Arnold

121–122). Shelley notes that **Titian**'s original *The Three Ages of Man* is in the Bridgewater Collection; she spells it **Bridgwater** (*R* 2.157).

Bridgwater Collection: See **Bridgewater Collection**.

Brig: **Swiss** city on the **Rhône**, eighteen miles north of **Simplon**; Shelley spells it **Brigg**. Shelley reached Brig October 1840 (*R* 1.137).

Brigg: See **Brig**.

Brighton: Fashionable **Sussex** seaside resort. Shelley spent "a whole month of happiness" in Brighton with **Jane Williams** August–September 1826 (*Journals* 497). In August 1826, Shelley wrote: "read the papers about Brighton & you will hear that it is the gayest of places...but the hermitesses know nothing of this.... [S]uch as we are, solitary and quiet, Brighton is the worst place in the world" (*Letters* 1.529–530). Shelley visited Brighton again 1827 and 1836 for health reasons; she worked on *Falkner* during her recovery there 1836 (*Journals* 504, 549–550; Sunstein 334). Shelley also stayed at Brighton June 1840, prior to her **European** tour (*R* 1.1, 1.4). **Horatio Saville** visits **Lady Lodore** there after her mother's death (*L* 2.51). **Harry Valency** talks about friends traveling from Brighton during Christmas 1836 (*E* 295). Shelley describes the resort in "**A Visit to Brighton**."

Bristol: Large port city ten miles northwest of **Bath**. **Castruccio** crosses the **Irish** Sea from Bristol to **Cork** (*V* 1.79). **Lord Audley** is driven off course into the **Atlantic** en route from Cork to Bristol (*PW* 2.262). [*LM* 268].

Brittany: Northeastern **French** province on the **Bay of Biscay** and the **English Channel**. Several *Perkin Warbeck* characters visit Brittany: **Lord Lovel** is there when **Louis XI** dies (*PW* 1.4). **Richard of York** misses seeing the **Earl of Rivers** in **Spain** due to his return to Brittany (*PW* 1.211). Brittany becomes part of France upon **Anne of Brittany**'s marriage with **Charles VIII** (*PW* 1.242, 1.312). **Henry VII** of England had been exiled in Brittany, where he met **Meiler Trangmar** (*PW* 1.247).

Brittany, Anne of (1477–1514): Ruler of **Brittany** since 1488; when her marriage to **Austria**'s **Maximillian I** was annulled 1491, she married **Charles VIII** and became **France**'s queen, annexing Brittany to France. **Henry VII** of England resents his marriage to **Elizabeth of York**, because he wanted to marry "beautiful and spirited" Anne (*PW* 1.121).

Brixen: **Italian** city on the **Adige**, forty miles southeast of **Innsbruck**, also known as **Bressanone**. Shelley slept at the **Elephant** Inn there September 1842 (*R* 2.61).

Brixton: **London** district south of the **Thames**. The **Villiers**es stay in "a little inn near Brixton" to avoid bailiffs (*L* 3.51).

Brobdignagians: See **Swift**.

Brockedon, William (1787–1854): **British** painter who published several series of landscapes in various books;

in 1836, he wrote part of *Murray's Handbook for Switzerland* (Williamson 1.197–198; *DNB*). Shelley mentions viewing the **Simplon Pass**, which Brockedon depicted (*R* 1.134).

Brocklet: German town on the **Saale**, four miles north of **Kissingen**. Shelley relates her trip from Kissingen to Brocklet, which **Murray** recommends (*R* 1.195). Shelley quotes Murray's description and adds her opinion that the water in Brocklet tastes like ink (*R* 1.195).

Broke, Lord: In *Perkin Warbeck*, one of (English) **Henry VII**'s counselors who assemble at **Shene**.

Brook Street: Fashionable street leading into **Grosvenor Square** in **London**'s Westminster district, close to **Piccadilly** and **Hyde Park**. The **Villiers**es stay at a hotel there before taking "a furnished house in the same street for a short time" (*L* 2.207).

"Brother and Sister, The": Story Shelley published in the 1828 *Keepsake* as "By the author of 'Frankenstein'" (Robinson 386). Shelley made several revisions to her original, including altering the sister's name from **Angeline** to **Flora** to match the accompanying illustration, *Flora*, which Louisa Sharpe drew and Francis Engleheart engraved (*Brother* 187; Robinson 386). The story focuses on injuries resulting from a feud between **Sienese Mancini** and **Tolomei** families. As a result of their animosity, **Ugo Mancini** dies in exile and his children, **Lorenzo** and Flora, eventually return to Siena destitute. Lorenzo trains himself in the use of weapons, aspiring to reclaim the Mancini's station by destroying the Tolomei house. Lorenzo and Flora are very close; when **Count Fabian de' Tolomei** banishes Lorenzo from Siena, the separation is almost unbearable. In order to secure protection for Flora during his absence, Lorenzo persuades Fabian to be her guardian (*Brother* 174–175). About three years later, Fabian, injured by a fall from his horse, encounters Flora daily as she nurses him back to health (*Brother* 179–180). Fabian falls in love with Flora, who rejects him, her "brother's murderer" (*Brother* 181). In an effort to win Flora's love, Fabian enlists **Countess de' Tolomei**'s help, repeals Lorenzo's banishment, and restores the Mancini fortune and palace (*Brother* 183–184). He finally sets out to search for the exile, whom he finds suffering from fever in an **Apennine** inn (*Brother* 186). Almost simultaneously, Flora also attempts this strategy but loses her way to **Milan** and coincidentally finds herself at the same inn; Lorenzo gives the couple his blessing (*Brother* 189). "The Brother and Sister" shows Shelley's continuing interest in **Italian** politics, exile, bloodlines, and love, also prominent themes in "**A Tale of the Passions**," *Valperga*, and "**The Sisters of Albano**."

Broughton, Sir Thomas: In *Perkin Warbeck*, **Lord Lovel**'s **Yorkist** friend; Broughton dies at a battle fought near **Newark-upon-Trent**.

Brown, Charles Brockden (1771–1810): American Gothic novelist renowned for *Wieland; or, The Transformation* (1798), which Shelley read 1815; she read many of his novels (*Journals* 638; Seymour 124). She read Brown's *Arthur Mervyn: Memoirs of the Year*

Browne, Sir Thomas (1605–1682)

1793 (1799–1800), July 1817 (*Journals* 177). Brown's novel records Mervyn's first-person narrative of a yellow fever epidemic in **Philadelphia**. Shelley admired Brown's work and drew upon his depictions of illness for *The Last Man*. **Lionel Verney** reads Brown's work, admiring its vivid accounts of plague (*LM* 259).

Browne, Sir Thomas (1605–1682): Renowned as author of lively prose tracts on science and religion, Browne was a fervent British royalist and anti-Puritan. **Charles II** knighted him 1671. **PBS** read Browne's *Religio Medici* (1642) aloud to Shelley 1815 (*Journals* 69). **Lionel Verney** refers to Browne's *Hydriotaphia, Urne Buriall, or, A Discourse of the Sepulchrall Urnes Lately Found in Norfolk* (1658), in which Browne explores burial ceremonies and humanity's fragility, recalling Browne's statements that " '**Tis too late** to be ambitious. . . . **We cannot hope** to live so long in our names, as some have done in their persons, one face of *Janus* holds no proportion unto the other' " (Browne 308–309; *LM* 262). Verney also refers readers to Browne for an account of the plague; however, this would seem to be a reference to **Brown's** *Arthur Mervyn* (*LM* 267).

Bruce: See **Robert the Bruce**.

Brükenau: **German** town on the Sinn, eighteen miles south of **Fulda**. Shelley arrived in Brükenau July 1842 and visited Baths near there (*R* 1.199–203).

Brundisium: Ancient name for Brindisi, **Adriatic** seaport in southeastern **Italy** situated on the "heel" of the boot; Shelley spells it **Brundusium**. **Ludovico Mondolfo** travels there to sail to the **Holy Land** (*HM* 330–331). [*R* 1.xv].

Brundusium: See **Brundisium**.

Brunen: See **Brunnen**.

Brünn: German name of Brno, **Moravian** city 120 miles southeast of **Prague**. Shelley mentions **Colletta**'s imprisonment there (*R* 2.207–208).

Brunnen: City on **Lake Lucerne**'s eastern shore; Shelley spells it **Brunen**. The Shelleys sailed to Brunnen, staying overnight August 1814 (*Journals* 19; *H* 48–49). "**The Swiss Peasant**'s" frame narrator is visiting Brunnen (*SP* 136).

Brussels: **Belgium**'s capital city. Many *Perkin Warbeck* characters visit Brussels when the **Duchess of Burgundy** holds court there. **Richard of York** resides there; he makes a "brilliant figure," and "noble followers clustered around him" (*PW* 1.148, 2.14, 2.28). Richard's followers plan to return to England while at Brussels spring 1494 (*PW* 2.47–48). **Edward Villiers** hopes to obtain enough money to take himself and his wife to Brussels (*L* 3.16). Shelley boarded a train destined for Brussels in **Malines** June 1842 (*R* 1.163).

Brutus, Lucius Junius (c. 6th century B.C.E.): Founder of **Rome** who became consul 509 B.C.E.; after his brother's murder, he pretended to be an idiot and thus avoided the same fate (Howatson 101; Crook 3.306). Shelley terms **Battista Tripalda** a "self-named Brutus of modern **Italy**" (*V* 3.217).

Brutus, Marcus Junius (c. 85–42 B.C.E.): Roman senator famous for leading the 44 B.C.E. conspiracy resulting in **Julius Caesar**'s assassination. **Valerius** reminisces about how "the sons of my friends, Brutus, **Cassius**, were rising with the promise of equal virtue" (*Val* 336). Shelley notes **Stephen Frion** "looked not the man Caesar would have feared," referring to Brutus's betrayal (*PW* 1.151).

Bryan: Sire de Beverem's servant in *Perkin Warbeck*.

Bubbles of the Brunnens, The: See **Head**.

Buchan: In *Perkin Warbeck*, the **Earl of Huntley** joins in Buchan's plot against **Richard of York**.

Buckingham: Town eighteen miles northeast of **Oxford**. **Irish** invaders retreat from **London** to make their headquarters there (*LM* 300).

Buckingham, Duke of: In *Perkin Warbeck*, Shelley refers to two different Dukes of Buckingham without distinguishing them. The duke who opposes **Richard III** is Henry Stafford, second Duke of Buckingham (1455–83) (*PW* 1.32). The duke who counsels **Henry VII** is Edward Stafford, third Duke of Buckingham (1478–1521) (*PW* 1.122).

Buckinghamshire: English county northwest of **London** (abbreviated "Bucks"). The Shelleys made a home together there 1817 immediately after their marriage (Sunstein 133). *The Last Man*'s main characters live in Buckinghamshire; Shelley set many important scenes there (*LM* 268). The **Neville** family moves there after **Alithea Neville**'s disappearance (*F* 119). **Elizabeth Falkner** and **Gerard Neville** settle there at *Falkner*'s close (*F* 321). [EC 345].

Budweis: Czech city on the **Moldau**, forty-five miles north of **Linz**. Shelley arrived there September 1842 (*R* 2.17).

Buffon, Comte George-Louis Leclerc de (1702–1788): French scientist who translated Stephen Hales's *Vegetable Staticks* (1735) and Isaac Newton's *Fluxions* (1740). Buffon wrote a forty-four-volume *Histoire Naturelle* [*Natural History*] (1749–67), some of which Shelley read June–July 1817 (Fellows 15; *Journals* 658). **Victor Frankenstein** reads Buffon (*Fr1* 71).

Bulwer-Lytton, Edward George Earle Lytton (1803–1873): First Baron Lytton and popular British writer who published a wide variety of highly esteemed novels as well as plays, poetry, essays, and translations. He edited *The New Monthly Magazine* 1831–33, during which time he asked Shelley for information about **PBS**'s life and works; he subsequently served in **Parliament** and became a lord. Lytton sought an introduction to **William Godwin** in the late 1820s and became his friend, also befriending Shelley (Scymour 404–405). She read his *Devereux* (1829) 1829 and his *Paul Clifford* (1830) January 1831 "with encreased [*sic*] admiration," finding it to be "a wonderful, a sublime book" and feeling that its "magnificent writer" could become "the first Author of the age"

(*Journals* 517; *Letters* 2.80–81). Shelley refers to a letter *Paul Clifford*'s Sir William Brandon writes to Lord Mauleverer about his niece Lucy Brandon: **Edward Villiers** feels quite comfortable at **Longfield** and gives "orders to the servant, as if he had been at home," which Shelley relates to the "deep philosophy" of the observation that "'**Women**,' says the accomplished author of Paul Clifford, '**think that** they must always love a man whom they have seen in his night-cap'" (Lytton 185; *L* 2.129). Shelley wrote an unpublished review of Bulwer-Lytton's *Eugene Aram* (1831) 1832 and asked **Ollier** to send her Bulwer-Lytton's *The Last Days of Pompeii* (1834) 1834, noting, "you know I admire & delight in his novels beyond all others—There is none comparable to them" (*Letters* 2.151–155, 2.207). She came to dislike Bulwer-Lytton personally: in July 1834, she wrote "Bulwer[-Lytton] is a man of extraordinary & delightful talent—but spoilt by vanity disappointed ambition . . . and a certain vulgarity of fashion, not acknowledged by supreme *ton* [manners]," and she derided him for his disapprobation of her favorite country, **Italy** (*Letters* 2.210). Even though Shelley solicited Bulwer-Lytton's parliamentary aid for her son's interest 1839, she could not forgive him for harsh remarks about her husband's poetry in his introduction to the two-volume *Poems and Ballads of Schiller* (1844), writing January 1846 that Bulwer-Lytton "thinks to gain popularity by truckling to the times—& mistakes the spirit of the times, & casts an indelible stain on his own name" (*Letters* 3.275). In June 1843, Shelley, however, declared that Bulwer-Lytton's *The Last Days of Pompeii* "has peopled [**Pompeii**'s] silence"; she admired the work's "imagination" (*R* 2.279). Feldman and Scott-Kilvert give a brief biography of Bulwer-Lytton's friendship with Shelley in Appendix III of her *Journals,* while Sunstein also provides details of their relationship (*Journals* 604–605; Sunstein 316–317, 347, 374). See Michael Sadleir's *Bulwer and His Wife: a Panorama, 1803–1836* (1931).

Buoni Cugini: Italian for "good cousins," secret **Carbonari** name mentioned by Shelley (*R* 2.170).

Burano: One of two main outer islands in **Venice**'s **Laguna** northeast of **Lido** near **Mazzorbo** and **Torcello** (Littlewood 233; Honour 233). Shelley visited Burano September 1842 (*R* 2.101).

Burchiello (1404–1449): Little is known about this **Italian** author and barber, whose real name was Domenico di Giovanni and who purportedly lived in **Florence**; his sonnets remained unpublished until 1552. Shelley wrote Burchiello's necessarily brief biography for *Italian and Spanish Lives*. Shelley records that his "poems are a strange and capricious mixture of sayings, proverbs, and jokes," noting that Burchiello's name and works gave rise to the term "burlesque" (*ISPL* 1.180).

Burford Bridge: Bridge in Surrey "on the road to **Brighton**" (Moskal 214). Shelley compares **Schandau**'s bridge to Burford's (*R* 1.267).

Burgau, Margraf of: Habsberg prince, grandson of Ferdinand I; Shelley mentions **Wallenstein** was his page, probably in 1603 (*R* 2.47).

Burgh, Hubert: Lord Barry's foster-brother in *Perkin Warbeck*; he accompanies **Richard of York** to see **Keating** at **Buttevant**.

Burghersh, Lord (1784–1859): John Fane, known as Lord Burghersh until he became eleventh Earl of **Westmoreland** (1841), was **Berlin**'s resident minister 1841–51 (*DNB*). From **Bagni di Lucca** July 1818, Shelley wrote that Admiral Fremantle's family has "Lord and Lady Berghersh on a visit at their house." Lord Burghersh knew **Thomas Medwin** and **Edward John Trelawny** (*Letters* 1.76, 2.140; Seymour 420). Shelley mentions Lord Burghersh's house on the square in front of **Brandenburg Gate** (*R* 1.219).

Burgundy: South central **French** region; its capital is **Dijon**. Burgundian chronicler **Chastellain** authored *Perkin Warbeck*'s epigraph, and Shelley mentions the region repeatedly, since **Margaret of Burgundy** actively suppports **Richard of York** (*PW* 1.109, 2.17, 3.269). Shelley mentions that the **Serbelloni** family was originally Burgundian but left France during **Charles VI**'s reign (*R* 1.80).

Burgundy, Duchess of: See **Burgundy, Mary of**.

Burgundy, Duke of: John the Fearless (1371–1419); he arranged the **Duke of Orleans**'s (1372–1407) murder; **Guido il Cortese** is in **Paris** at this time (*Trans* 122–123).

Burgundy, Mary of (1457–1482): **Charles the Bold**'s daughter who became **Duchess of Burgundy** 1477; she married **Maximillian I** 1477. **Henry VII** of England resents his marriage to **Elizabeth of York** because he wanted to wed Mary instead (*PW* 1.121).

Burke, Edmund (1729–1797): **Irish** author and politician who championed civil justice and espoused the emancipation of **America**, **India**, and Ireland. His *A Philosophical Enquiry into the Origin of Our Ideas of the Sublime and the Beautiful* (1757) is widely acknowledged to be a central work of Romantic aesthetics. Shelley read Burke's *A Vindication of a Natural Society* (1756) 1815 (*Journals* 639). Burke's *Reflections on the Revolution in France* (1790) is a conservative response to the **French Revolution**. **Mary Wollstonecraft** composed her *Vindication of the Rights of Men* (1790) to combat Burke's ideas. **Adrian** quotes from Burke's *Reflections* verbatim in describing **Raymond**: " 'in all bodies, those who would lead, must also, in a considerable degree, follow' " (*LM* 162; Burke 8.91–92). **Lionel Verney** uses the phrase "**Corinthian capital** of polished society" to describe English nobility; Burke uses this phrase to describe nobility in his *Reflections* (*LM* 222; Burke 8.188). Verney also quotes a lengthy passage beginning "**the mode of existence**" from Burke's *Reflections* as he contemplates his son's **Eton** playmates (*LM* 228; Burke 8.84). Verney draws on the subsequent paragraph of Burke's *Reflections* as plague threatens humankind, which "**carried with it** an imposing and majestic aspect" (*LM* 412; Burke 8.85). Verney returns to **Windsor** with **Idris**, relieved to approach "the Castle, '**the proud Keep** of Windsor, rising in the majesty of proportion, girt with the double belt of its kindred and coeval towers,' " and he envies Idris's "enjoyment of '**the sad**

immunities of the grave' " (*LM* 356–357). Shelley takes these lines from Burke's "Letter to a Noble Lord" (1796) (Burke 9.147, 9.172). In the 1831 *Frankenstein*, Shelley describes **Polidori**'s effort at a ghost story as "some terrible idea about a skull-headed lady" who ends up in the **Capulets'** tomb, and, in **Verona** in September 1842, Shelley doubted a sarcophagus supposed to be **Juliet**'s tomb was truly "the **tomb of the Capulets**"; both references echo Burke's *Reflections* reference to the "family vault of 'all the Capulets' " (*Fr3* 21; *R* 2.76; Moskal 268; Burke 8.140).

Burnet, Ellen: Character in "The Mourner," also called **Clarice Eversham**.

Burns, Robert (1759–1796): Influential and popular 18th-century British poet who helped revive the ballad tradition and preserve traditional Scottish songs. **Lionel Verney** notes that plague survivors are "frailer than the '**snow fall** in river,' " a line adapted from Burns's "Tam O' Shanter. A Tale" (1791) (*LM* 428; Burns line 61). Shelley describes **James IV**'s attraction to **Lady Jane Kennedy** as due, in part, to her " '**bonny brent brow**,' " an echo, as Fischer notes, of Burns's "John Anderson My Jo" (*PW* 2.190; Burns line 4; Fischer 211). Shelley describes **Edward Villiers**'s misery at his imprisonment with a line from Burns's "For a' that and a' that" (1795), in which Burns expresses hope that all men will be brothers despite social differences: Edward "was manly enough to feel '**that a man's** a man for all that' " (*L* 3.142; Burns line 12). **Elizabeth Fitzhenry** returns home "in the chariot, '**nursing her wrath** to keep it warm,' " a line from "Tam O' Shanter" (*L* 3.281; Burns lines 10–12). Shelley uses part of the same line earlier in *Lodore* to describe how Elizabeth "brooded over her sorrow [at **Lord Lodore**'s death] '**to keep it warm**' " (*L* 1.285). **Gerard Neville** introduces **Elizabeth Falkner** to Burns's poetry (*F* 236).

Butler: Ormond family, important Anglo-Norman family that held its lordship 1185–1715 and controlled land between **Leinster** and **Munster** (Connolly 416; Fischer 117). Shelley mentions the Butlers when providing **Irish** history (*PW* 1.287, 1.306, 2.322, 3.30–31).

Butler, Lady Eleanor: In *Perkin Warbeck*, Shelley mentions **Edward IV**'s rumored marriage to Lady Butler (*PW* 1.52).

Butrinto: Small village on **Albania**'s west coast east of the island of Corfu; **Katusthius Ziani** sails there from **Corinth** (*EE* 103).

Buttevant: Irish town on the **Awbeg**, twenty-five miles northwest of **Cork**. Shelley mentions **Kilnemullagh** as the town's Irish name; **Richard of York** travels there to meet **Keating** (*PW* 1.229, 1.292, 1.305).

Buttevant, Baron of: See **Barry, Lord**.

Buttlar: German town twenty miles northeast of **Fulda**. Shelley stayed at Buttlar's "quiet, comfortable, country inn" July 1842 (*R* 1.206).

Buzeccha: Saracen chess player in "A Tale of the Passions."

Byron, Clara Allegra (1817–1822): Daughter of **Claire Clairmont**, who named her Alba upon her birth but baptized her Clara Allegra, "reputed daughter of Rt. Hon. George Gordon, Lord **Byron**" (*Journals* 197). The Shelleys called her **Allegra**. She first stayed with her mother and the Shelleys, but Byron placed her in a convent school at Bagnacavallo, **Italy**, 1821; she died of typhus there (Seymour 274, 292). Shelley mourns Allegra's death in "**The Choice**" (*Journals* 409; *Ch* 97–102). Byron was "deeply affected" by her death (Marchand 2.731–732, 3.993).

Byron, Lord George Gordon (1788–1824): British Romantic poet. Inheriting his title 1798, Byron was a profligate youth whose first works, *Poems on Various Occasions* (1807) and *Hours of Idleness* (1807) were savagely received; Byron responded with *English Bards and Scotch Reviewers* (1809), in which he satirically attacked many of his critics. Byron toured **Spain**, **Portugal**, and the eastern **Mediterranean** with **John Cam Hobhouse** in 1809. Upon returning to England, he published the first two cantos of *Childe Harold's Pilgrimage* (1812), which made him famous overnight. Among others of his works, *The Bride of Abydos* (1813) and *The Corsair* (1814) were also successful, as were his *Hebrew Melodies* (1815), which includes "**Stanzas for Music.**" Byron became a literary and social celebrity; Shelley first met him in **London** April 1816, and he began an affair with **Claire Clairmont** then (Sunstein 115). He had married Annabella Milbanke 1815, and they had a daughter, Ada, that year, but the couple then separated. Byron left Britain April 1816 after rumors spread about the brief marriage's difficulties; he never returned, but he remained apprised of events there and continued his literary career, sending his works back to **Murray** (Sunstein 115). Byron and the Shelleys reunited 1816, when they spent summer together on **Lake Geneva**'s shores, but the party broke up after rumors spread about Byron's relationships with both Shelley and Claire; Byron and Claire's daughter, **Clara Allegra Byron**, was born 1817 (Sunstein 119; *Journals* 154). At Lake Geneva, Byron wrote the third canto of *Childe Harold* and "**Prisoner of Chillon**," which Shelley copied for him (*Journals* 131). Shelley was clearly attracted to Byron and his celebrity while also repelled by his seemingly carefree relationships with women (*Journals* 197, 225). Byron moved to **Venice** 1817, where he wrote works including "**The Lament of Tasso**" (1817), the fourth canto of *Childe Harold* (1818), "**Mazeppa**" (1819), "**Ode on Venice**" (1819), began *Don Juan* (1819, 1821, 1823, 1824), and met and began his lasting affair with **Teresa Guiccioli**. Living outside **Ravenna**, Byron was involved with the **Carbonari** before moving with Teresa to **Pisa** 1821, where the Shelleys were also living; Byron befriended **Edward John Trelawny** there. By 1821, when he published (among other works) *Heaven and Earth, Sardanapalus,* and *The Two Foscari*, his reputation as a leading poet was established throughout **Europe**. Byron subsequently lived in **Leghorn** and **Genoa** and maintained a prodigious output. Allegra died 1822, and after **PBS**'s death that year, Byron was initially supportive of Shelley, intervening with **Sir Timothy Shelley** on her behalf and offering financial assistance; she affectionately termed him **Albé** (*Journals* 457). Shelley seems to have been reluctant to accept Byron's money, but she wrote to **Jane Williams** December 1822 that Byron "is to me as kind as ever. . . . [H]e is all profession & politeness. . . . [H]e is so truly generous that when he allows that part of him to be uppermost he must be liked" (*Letters* 1.295). However, Shelley was not always so complimentary, and their relationship grew strained over the issue of Claire's finances (*Journals* 457). Byron sailed to **Greece** 1823 to help Greeks struggling for independence and died from fever there. Byron's death was widely mourned; Shelley recorded, "Beauty sat on his countenance and power beamed from his eye—his faults being for the most part weaknesses induced one readily to pardon them. Albe—the dear capricious fascinating Albe has left this desart [*sic*] world" (*Journals* 478). Shelley read Byron's works throughout her life and frequently refers to them in her own, calling him **Lord B——** in *Rambles* (*Journals* 639–640; *R* 2.107, 2.201). Byron's amusing letters and journals are indicative of his personality; their editor, Leslie Marchand, also produced the biography, *Byron: A Biography* (1957). See **"On this day I complete"** and *Werner*.

Byzantine: In the style developed by the Byzantine Empire (395–1453), characterized by formal structure, rich color, and religious iconography. Shelley mentions "paintings of the Byzantine school" (*R* 2.141). [*R* 1.221].

C

C——, Lord: Catholic nobleman not otherwise identified. Shelley celebrates Lord C——'s actions during **Rome**'s 1837 cholera epidemic (*R* 2.240).

C——, Marquess of: Minor *Lodore* character.

***Cabal and Love*:** See **Schiller**.

Cadenabbia: Town on **Lake Como**, five miles northwest of **Como**. Shelley stayed there at **Grande Albergo** July 1840 (*R* 1.61–62, 1.64, 1.70–92). [*R* 2.68].

Cader Idris: Welsh for "Chair of Idris," mountain three miles south of **Dolgellau**; Shelley would have seen it June–August 1841 (Tomes 141; Sunstein 354). Shelley describes the **Alps** as "like Cader Idris, but on a larger scale" (*R* 2.32).

Cadiz: **Spanish** coastal city sixty-five miles southwest of Seville. **Don Rodrigo Ponce de Leon** is Marquess of Cadiz (*PW* 1.205).

Cadiz, Marquess of: See **Ponce de Leon**.

Cadmus, Dan: Legendary founder of Thebes (Radice 26). **Keating** compares **Richard of York** to Dan Cadmus (*PW* 3.29).

Caelian Hill: One of **Rome**'s **Seven Hills**, in southeastern Rome near **Lateran** Palace; Shelley calls it **Mount Caelius**. **Isabell Harley** refers to Rome's declining glory by mentioning Mount Caelius's neglected appearance (*Val* 340–341).

Caelius, Mount: See **Caelian Hill**.

Caen Wood: See **Kenwood**.

Caernarvon: See **Edward II**.

Caesar, Julius (c. 100–44 B.C.E.): **Roman** Empire's most renowned leader, whose family name became a title, equivalent after the end of the Republic to "emperor." **Marcus Brutus**

led a senatorial conspiracy that murdered Caesar March 44 B.C.E., events that **Shakespeare** depicted in *Julius Caesar* (1599) (Kinder 1.91). **Victor Frankenstein** believes "Caesar would have spared his country" if not ruled by a single-minded passion (*Fr1* 84; *Fr3* 57). **Valerius** declares that Caesar "'was distinguished only by the debauchery of his manners'" (*Val* 333). **Isabell Harley** refers to Caesar's 55 B.C.E. invasion of Britain (*Val* 338; Howatson 95). **Raymond** compares his ambition to be a king to that of Caesar, who "died in his attempt to become one" (*LM* 56). **Lionel Verney** admires Rome's "ponderous stone, which once made part of the palace of the Caesars" (*LM* 461). Shelley described **Trèves** as "a metropolis . . . before the time of Julius Caesar" (*R* 1.19). [*V* 2.160; *PW* 1.151].

Caesar, Octavius (63 B.C.E.–14 C.E.): Julius Caesar's great-nephew and adopted son; he became **Rome**'s first emperor (Howatson 387). The **Countess of Windsor** thinks like Octavius and will not be reconciled to her daughter's marriage (*LM* 332). See *Antony and Cleopatra*.

Cain: **Adam** and **Eve**'s son, who killed his younger brother **Abel**; he was condemned to wander the earth with a mark on his forehead (Genesis 4.1–16). **Matilda** declares herself another Cain (*M* 203). **Robert Clifford** resembles Cain after betraying **Richard of York**; "the Abel he had killed was his own fair fame" (*PW* 3.141). **Winzy** wants to test his immortality "without making another man a Cain" (*MI* 230).

Cain Slaying Abel: See **Titian**.

Calabria: Southwestern **Italian** region opposite **Sicily**. **Guielmo Lostendardo** retires to a convent by Calabria's shore (*TP* 23). **Viola Arnaldi** travels through Calabria (*HM* 327). **Lionel Verney** ultimately feels that he is the only human between Calabria and the **Alps** (*LM* 456, 469). **Villa Spina** looks down "over the plain of Calabria," and **Ferdinando Eboli** intends to be a robber among Calabria's hills (*FE* 66, 73–74, 78–79). **Katusthius Ziani** sails to Calabria (*EE* 102). Shelley noted that **Carbonari** hide in Calabria to escape persecution, and she admired **Colletta**'s "accounts of the earthquake in Calabria in 1783"; she viewed **Ravello** when visiting Calabria's "outskirts" (*R* 2.165–166, 2.208, 2.290).

Calais: **French** seaport closest to England, twenty-two miles east of **Dover**. A storm prolonged the Shelleys' June 1814 promised two-hour crossing to Calais, where they spent two days (*H* 2–4, 6). Shelley admitted "partiality for the people of Calais" April 1826 but added that "the place is ugly enough, perhaps dull" (*Letters* 1.515). Plague survivors cross from Dover to Calais (*LM* 373). **Lord Fitzwater** becomes ill en route to Calais, and **Robert Clifford** arranges for **Richard of York** to meet him at Calais after leaving **Sire de Beverem**'s residence (*PW* 1.163, 1.188). **Henry VII** of England lands at Calais in an invasion of France, and Fitzwater later arrives there as a prisoner (*PW* 1.314, 2.11, 2.53). **Clinton Gray** finds **Lady Caroline Hythe** there (*ES* 263). The **Villiers**es cross the **English Channel** from Calais upon returning from **Italy** (*L* 2.207). Shelley opens *Rambles* with her June 1840 crossing to Calais (*R* 1.5–6). [*LM* 248; *L* 3.239].

Calamas: See **Kalamas**.

Calderón de la Barca, Pedro (1600–1681): Spanish dramatist. **PBS** read Calderón August–September 1819, greatly admired his work, and translated some scenes from Calderón's *Magico Prodigioso* [*The Marvellous Magician*] (1637) into English; Crook points out parallels between a shipwreck scene in the latter work and "**Transformation**" (White 2.374; Crook 2). Shelley read Calderón December 1820; both Shelleys learned Spanish this way (*Journals* 296–297, 341; *Letters* 1.168). **Raymond** quotes princess Estrella's speech to her uncle, King Basilius, as prince Sigismund's forces threaten those of his father, from Calderón's *La Vida es Sueño* [*Life is a Dream*] (1635); the lines begin "**Cada piedra** un piramide levanta" and translate to "Each stone a mournful obelisk is here, / And every flower erects a monument; / And each house seems a grave, where life is gone— / Each soldier is a living skeleton" (*LM* 187; Calderón 3.2.45–48). **Lionel Verney**, presenting an excerpt from **Adrian**'s letter, quotes protagonist Don Fernando's speech—beginning "**Un dia llama** a otro dia"—reconciling himself to his position as a slave from Calderón's *El Príncipe Constante* [*The Constant Prince*] (1629); the lines mean, "One day follows on another, / And so sorrow follows sorrow, / Pains with miseries intertwine" (*LM* 46; Calderón 2.1.162–164). Verney later quotes another speech of Fernando, who suffers imprisonment and humiliation rather than relinquish his religion: "**la fortuna** / deidad barbara importuna, / oy cadavar y ayer flor, / no permanece jamas!"—meaning, "Bear with that whatever sorrow / Time or fortune makes you see; / For that fickle deity, / Now a flower, a corpse tomorrow, / Ever changing o'er and o'er—" (*LM* 258; Calderón 2.1.111–115). Again using Fernando's lines, Verney records the hope of respite from plague that winter's onset encompasses: "**Pisando la** tierra dura / de continuo el hombre està / y cada passo que dà / es sobre su sepultra"; the lines mean, "On the hard earth, year by year, / Man is treading, hopeful, brave, / But each step is on his grave" (*LM* 270; Calderón 3.2.313–315). Shelley wrote an accurate biography of Calderón for *Italian and Spanish Lives*, suggesting Calderón "is a master of the passions and the imagination" and noting *La Vida es Sueño* as one outstanding example of Calderón's "clothing in sensible and potent imagery, the thoughts of the brain, the feelings of the heart" (*ISPL* 3.283, 3.285). As a poet, she finds Calderón "diffuse and exaggerated at times, but he is highly imaginative" (*ISPL* 3.285, 3.287). Shelley also asserts Calderón is "master of comedy" and terms him one of "the master geniuses of the world" (*ISPL* 3.286–287).

Calmaldoli Convent: Italian convent near **Vallombrosa** (*STIE* 77). Shelley mentions that many travelers tour it (*R* 2.139).

Caloyer: A monk in the **Greek** church. **Cyril Ziani** "half envied the Caloyers their inert tranquility"; caloyers in a **Sagori** mountain monastery attempt unsuccessfully to shield **Constans Ziani** from **Dmitri** (*EE* 111–112).

Calvinist: Subscriber to 16th-century John Calvin's religious teachings (predestination, God's sovereignty, the **Bible**'s supreme authority). Shelley mentions the Calvinist **Elector Palatine**, who ruled **Bohemia** prior to **Ferdinand II**'s invasion (*R* 2.3).

Camaraz: Brave **Mainote** pirate who abducts **Zella Ziani** and raises her as his own child in "**The Evil Eye**."

Camberwell: Small town in **London**'s southwest outskirts, three miles west of **Greenwich**. **Ellen** visits **Sir Richard Gray** there (*ES* 264).

Cambridge: University city fifty miles northeast of **London**. Shelley planned to begin her **European** tour at the university term's end in mid-June 1840 so that **PFS** could accompany her (*R* 1.3). [*R* 1.25].

Camillus, Marcus Furius: Powerful early-4th-century B.C.E. **Roman** statesman and general who "founded a temple to Concord" at the foot of the **Capitoline** Hill, rebuilt 768 and excavated 1807 (Howatson 113; *MROM* 33). Shelley probably saw remains 1819 and learned about Camillus from **Plutarch** and **Livy** (*Journals* 259; Plutarch, *Lives* 1.191–225). **Valerius** views " 'columns that remain of the temple erected by Camillus' " and talks of how " 'during my life . . . men were again vivified by the sacred flame that burnt in the souls of Camillus and **Fabricius**' " (*Val* 335–336). **Isabell Harley** describes Rome's monuments " 'as planned and modified by Camillus' " (*Val* 340). **Lionel Verney** imagines Camillus in the **Forum** (*LM* 462).

Camoens, Luis Vaz de Diaresis (1524–1580): Portuguese epic poet renowned for his patriotic *Os Lusiadas* [*The Lusiads / Portuguese*] (1572). Shelley wrote an accurate biography of Camoens for *Italian and Spanish Lives* and admires his early poetry: "there never breathed a more genuine poet" (*ISPL* 3.304). Shelley considers *Lusiad* "full of beauties: stanzas that rise to sublimity, touch the heart by their pathos, or charm it by descriptive beauties" (*ISPL* 3.326, 3.333). Shelley wrote: "Camoens was more unfortunate than [**Cervantes**]—but does not *come home to you* in the same manner" (*Letters* 2.292–293). Viewing **Goethe** and **Schiller**'s tombs in **Weimar**, Shelley recalls Camoens's last words, beginning "**Lo! the vast scene**" (*R* 1.212). She provides a footnote: "Lord Holland possesses a copy of the first edition of the *Lusiad*, in which these words were written by the friar Josepe Judio, who left it in the convent of the barefooted Carmelites of Guadalaxara" (*ISPL* 3.329).

Campagna: District north of **Rome** with which Shelley would have been familiar from 1818–19 visits there (*MROM* 11; Rossington 418). **Beatrice** experiences "frightful wrongs" during **Battista Tripalda**'s imprisonment of her there (*V* 3.83, 3.120, 3.216). **Lionel Verney** hails "the wild Campagna," which Shelley finds "very beautiful" (*LM* 460; *R* 2.225).

Campanile: Bell tower **Giotto** designed; begun 1334, it is in **Florence**'s **Piazza del Duomo** (*STIE* 65); thereafter, any such free-standing bell tower. **Ricciardo de' Rossini** hears the Campanile sound "an hour of night" (*TP* 9).

Campbell, Thomas (1777–1844): Scottish poet chiefly remembered for songs of war. Campbell edited the *New Monthly Magazine* 1820–30 and was **William Godwin**'s friend. Shelley had limited correspondence with him but invited him to dinner 1839, and his death saddened her (*Letters* 2.325, 3.138). Shelley found Campbell's *Poetical Works* (1839) a "valuable present" which she "fell on... with extreme delight" upon receiving it; she probably drew on his poem, "The Last Man" (1824), for her novel of that name (*Letters* 2.314, 2.336). **Monina De Faro** and **Richard of York** support each other with hope even when "shadows of 'coming events' clouded their spirits," a phrase the wizard addresses to Lochiel in Campbell's "Lochiel's Warning" (1802) (*PW* 3.96; Campbell line 56). Shelley compares **Ethel Villiers**, "innocent and free," to **Gertrude**, motherless English protagonist of Campbell's "Gertrude of Wyoming; A Pennsylvanian Tale" (1809), raised in **America** and her father's sole comfort (*L* 1.210; Campbell 1–73).

Campidoglio: Tower atop **Rome**'s **Capitoline**, "from its height and central position," it provides a wonderful view of Rome, also known as **Tower of the Capitol** (*MRON* 10–11). Shelley visited it several times March 1819 (*Journals* 252). **Castruccio** bears the sword of state in the procession from Campidoglio to **St. Peter's** when **Louis of Bavaria** knights him (*V* 3.265). **Lionel Verney** looks up to Campidoglio from the **Forum** (*LM* 462–463). Shelley ascended Campidoglio April 1843 (*R* 2.227–230).

Campo Morto: Estate and farm in the **Maremma**, five miles inland from the Tyrrhenian Sea. Shelley describes a criminals' asylum "called Campo Morto" where fugitives hid before dying of malaria due to the climate (*R* 2.243).

Campo Vaccino: See **Forum**.

Canada: British colony that became a British Commonwealth member 1931. **Edward Villiers** travels alone to Canada's border (*L* 2.45).

Canal, Giovanni Antonio (1697–1768): **Venetian** painter whom Shelley terms **Cannaletti**, famous for picturesque views of Venice. Shelley omits describing **Piazza San Marco** because "numerous pictures by Cannaletti and his imitators... show all that can be shown" (*R* 2.84).

Canal Oriano: Channel of the **Venetian Laguna** near the **Lido** (Moskal 275). Shelley mentions that **Pozzi** and **Piombi** prisoners were drowned there (*R* 2.87).

Canale della Giudecca: Large canal separating **Venice** from Giudecca Island. Shelley describes it September 1842 as "almost a lagune" inconvenient "for common traffic" (*R* 2.100).

Canale Grande: See **Grand Canal**.

Candiano, Tommaso: Shelley cites Candiano as evidence of the **Venetian** nobility's descent from **Roman** families, claiming that he assisted in the construction of the **Rialto** 421 C.E. (*R* 2.114).

Cannae: Southeastern **Italian** town 105 miles east of **Naples**. The August

Cannaletti

216 B.C.E. battle nearby was "the worst **Roman** defeat in history"; **Hannibal** killed almost fifty thousand Romans by making the center of his army thinner than the wings, which enveloped Romans when they attacked (Kinder 1.81). Shelley compares **Castruccio**'s defeat of the **Florentine** army at **Montecatini** to the Roman loss at Cannae (*V* 1.212). **Machiavelli** describes Castruccio's use of a strategy similar to Hannibal's (*LCCL* 539).

Cannaletti: See **Canal, Giovanni Antonio**.

Canosa, Prince of (1768–1838): Antonio Capece Minutolo; he became police minister of **Naples** 1816 and actively opposed **Carbonarism** (Woolf 240; Moskal 338). Shelley refers to **Colletta**'s admirable characterization of, among others, the "infamous Canosa" (*R* 2.208; Crook 2).

Canova, Antonio (1757–1822): **Italian** sculptor who made several sculptures of *Cupid and Psyche* (c. 1790s), the most famous of which is now at **Paris**'s Louvre (Chilvers 100; *Phaidon* 108). Shelley mentions that **Villa Sommariva** owns a Canova *Cupid and Psyche* and confesses she is "not an admirer of Canova's women" (*R* 1.92). She criticized his *Hebe* (1796) in the **Accademia delle Belle Arti (Venice)** September 1842 (*R* 2.91).

Cantabs: Abbreviation of Cantabrigian, **Cambridge** University students (*OED*). At **l'Hotel de Trèves**, Shelley met two Cantabs who joined her party (*R* 1.18). One may have been **Robert Leslie Ellis** (Moskal 85).

Canterbury: English cathedral city fifteen miles northwest of **Dover**. **Monina De Faro** lives at Canterbury, where she meets **Astley** (*PW* 2.156). **Stephen Frion** visits her there and makes a list of **Yorkists** in the area before **Richard of York** arrives (*PW* 2.159–60).

Capaletti: See *Romeo and Juliet*.

Capitol: "Square of palaces" in **Rome** at the **Capitoline**'s top, consisting of three buildings, built to **Michelangelo**'s designs, that house art and architecture museums (*MROM* 244–260). Shelley visited the Capitol repeatedly 1819 and attended the "feast of the Capitol" (celebratory fireworks honoring the **Austrian** emperor) April 1819 (*Journals* 259). Shelley compares **Valerius**'s appearance to that of "the statue of **Marcus Aurelius** in the Square of the Capitol" (*Val* 332). Valerius recalls how he appealed to "'**Jupiter** of the Capitol'" and was disappointed to find "'temples of [Rome's] Capitol destroyed'" (*Val* 334, 336). Shelley revisited the Capitol April 1843 (*R* 2.227–230). [*LM* 463].

Capitoline: Smallest of **Seven Hills** of **Rome**, located near the city's center, sometimes termed the **Capitol** because of the palaces and **Campidoglio** at its summit. Shelley visited the area frequently 1819 (*Journals* 251–265). **Valerius** observes modern buildings that he believes defile the Capitoline (*Val* 341).

Capo Bianco: See **Bianco**.

Capo del Monte: Italian town between **Naples** and **Sorrento**. Shelley was there in June 1842 (*R* 2.266).

Capponi, Gino (1792–1876): Italian historian and politician instrumental in the **Risorgimento**; he had a **Florentine** salon (Petronio 1.574). Shelley mentions that Capponi wrote the preface to **Colletta**'s *History of the Kingdom of Naples*, and some commentators believe he authored the entire book (*R* 2.207, 2.209).

Capraia: Small island between **Italy** and **Corsica**, forty-five miles southwest of **Leghorn**. **Alberti**, Capraia's count, attends **Euthanasia**'s court (*V* 1.256).

Capri: Island and city off **Italy**'s western coast, ten miles southwest of **Sorrento**. Shelley visited it June 1843 (*R* 2.267). [*R* 2.207, 2.265–269].

Capuan: Inhabitant of Capua, southern **Italian** town nineteen miles north of **Naples**. Shelley describes statues she viewed in **Rome** portraying "a Capuan woman, **la Grazia**" (*R* 2.224).

Capuchin: Franciscan friar who takes vows of poverty. Shelley records that **Joseph Haspinger** was a Capuchin, and she describes **Amalfi**'s Capuchin convent (converted into a hotel) as "most beautifully situated near the sea" July 1843 (*R* 2.52, 2.284–285).

Capulets: See *Romeo and Juliet*.

Car of Victory: See **Brandenburg Gate**.

Caracalla, Marcus Aurelius Antonius (188–217): **Rome**'s emperor 211–217 (Kinder 1.99). **Isabell Harley** regards "'Caracalla and **Nero**...as the mere workmen'" of Rome's monuments (*Val* 340).

Caracci: See **Carracci**.

Carate: **Italian** town ten miles southeast of **Como**; Shelley spells it **Caratte**. PFS bought a boat from a builder there (*R* 1.66).

Caratte: See **Carate**.

Carbonari: Italian for "charcoal burners"; early-19th-century secret society that espoused patriotic and liberal ideas and advocated Italy's unification. Carbonari opposed **Joachim Murat** in **Naples** and helped to prepare for the **Risorgimento** movement. Shelley wanted to meet some Carbonari 1840 and relates this sect's history (*R* 1.120, 2.167–179).

Cardela: Probably in or near Seville, **Spain**, site of **Ponce de Leon**'s 1471 feuds with Guzmán (L. Harvey 266). **Hernan De Faro** was wounded at the 1471 "taking of Cardela" (*PW* 1.206).

Cardona, Raymond de: Florentine general whom **Castruccio** takes prisoner at **Altopascio** (*V* 3.172; Green 161, 173–175).

Carega: Family name of **Guido il Cortese** (*Trans* 124, 132).

Carlisle: Northwestern English town ten miles south of the Scottish border and setting for **Rupert Falkner**'s imprisonment and trial (*F* 239).

Carlsbad: See **Karlsbad**.

Carlsruhe: German city thirty miles southwest of **Heidelberg**. Shelley slept there July 1840 (*R* 1.36–37).

***Carmagnola*:** See **Manzoni**.

***Caroccio*:** Decorated **Italian** carriage. According to Shelley's *Valperga* footnote, it "was introduced after the tenth century[,] . . . a large car, painted red, adorned with numerous standards, the spoils of vanquished enemies, and surmounted by the banner of the *commune* to which it belonged. . . . Its loss was an indelible disgrace, and its capture the greatest of triumphs" (*V* 2.74). When **Obizzo** resumes power in **Ferrarra**, citizens celebrate with a *Caroccio*-led parade (*V* 2.74). At "'A Tale of the Passions'" celebration of the **Guelphs** of **Florence**, a "*Caroccio* was led through the principal streets" (*TP* 1).

Caroline, Queen (1782–1839): **Napoleon**'s sister who married **Murat** 1800, becoming Queen of **Naples** (Morby 103). **Adalinda Spina** gains support from Queen Caroline, who is instrumental in restoring **Ferdinando Eboli**'s property (*FE* 79).

Carracci, Annibale (1560–1609): **Bolognese** painter whose ceiling in **Rome**'s Farnese Gallery rivaled the **Sistine Chapel**'s; he is buried in the **Pantheon** (Chilvers 106). Shelley spells his name **Caracci**; she viewed his *Angel of Fame* (before 1606) at the **Gallery in Dresden** (*R* 1.242).

***Carraia*:** Bridge on the **Arno** in **Florence** constructed 1078–1220 (Villani 76, 126). Rebuilt 1269 after being destroyed by a flood, it was destroyed again 1304 (Villani 246). In *Valperga*, Shelley relies on **Villani**'s *Chronicle*'s discussion of events leading up to this second disaster; the bridge collapsed because "it was so burdened with people that it gave way in many places, and fell with the people which were upon it, wherefore many were killed and drowned, and many were maimed" (Villani 360–361; *V* 1.17–21). People were crowded on the bridge to observe the **Festa d'Inferno**, which fourteen-year-old **Castruccio** travels to Florence to see (*V* 1.17, 1.20).

Carrara: City near **Italy**'s northeast coast, fifteen miles southeast of **La Spezia** at the foot of the Apuan **Alps**, which yield the marble for which Carrara is known (*MCIT* 134; *STIE* 91). Shelley visited Carrara September 1821 (*Journals* 379). Castle **Valperga**'s staircase is Carraran marble (*V* 1.184).

Carse of Gowrie: Marshland on the Firth of **Tay**'s north bank stretching from **Dundee** westward to Inchyra. Shelley states that Scottish defiance against England "would be echoed in glad shouts from . . . the **Lothians** to the Carse of Gowrie" (*PW* 2.194).

Carter, Mr.: In *Falkner*, young **Gerard Neville**'s tutor.

Carthage: Ancient city on North **African** coast near what is now Tunis. **Lionel Verney** plans to journey past its site (*LM* 469).

Cartoons: See **Raphael**.

Casa Magni: House just outside **San Terenzo** that the Shelleys and **Williamses** shared April–September 1822 (*Journals* 410). Shelley describes it as "beautifully situated on the sea shore, under a woody hill"; see Angeli's de-

Casaregi, Radolfo di: Euthanasia's uncle in *Valperga* and first guest to arrive at **Valperga**'s court.

Cascine: Florentine public park (*STIE* 75). Shelley terms Cascine Florence's **Hyde Park** (*R* 2.134).

Casentino: Italian valley of the upper **Arno**. Shelley described this region November 1842 as vying "with **Switzerland** or the **Tyrol** in beauty" (*R* 2.138).

Cashmere: See **Kashmir**.

Caspian Sea: West **Asian** inland sea surrounded by **Georgia**, Iran, and Kazakhstan. Panic sets in after a solar eclipse reaches the Caspian Sea (*LM* 224).

Cassandra: In **Greek** mythology, **Apollo** wooed Priam and Hecuba's daughter and taught her the art of prophecy. When Cassandra rejected Apollo's amorous advances, he sought revenge by betraying her prophetic gift with a curse that her predictions would be disbelieved and ignored. Shelley compares **Viola Arnaldi** to Cassandra (*HM* 322).

Cassils, Earl of: David Kennedy (d. 1513), whom **James IV** created Earl of Cassils 1509 (Keay 569). **Lady Jane Kennedy**'s father in *Perkin Warbeck*.

Cassius, Gaius Longinus (d. 42 B.C.E.): **Roman** official who helped lead the 44 B.C.E. conspiracy against Julius Caesar (Howatson 118). **Valerius** says that in former times " 'the sons of my friends, [Marcus] **Brutus**, Cassius, were rising with the promise of equal virtue' " (*Val* 336).

Castel à Mare: See **Castelammarre**.

Castelammarre: Italian seaport eight miles northeast of **Sorrento**; Shelley spells it **Castel à Mare**. **Horatio Saville** promises to rent a house there for the **Villiers**es (*L* 2.196). PFS often sailed to Castelammarre 1843 (*R* 2.265, 2.295).

Castelbarco, Guglielmo da: Italian noble of the 13th and 14th centuries who was Val Lagarina's feudal lord (Moskal 262). Shelley mentions that he entertained **Dante** in exile at **Castello Lizzana** (after 1301) (*R* 2.66).

Castel Sant' Angelo: Papal fortress in **Rome Hadrian** built around 130, now called Castle of St. Angelo rather than Hadrian's Mausoleum; it also contains a prison (*MROM* 68–71). Shelley saw fireworks there April 1843 (*R* 2.232).

Castel Tealdo: **Ferrara** fortress and site of a military siege (*V* 2.73, 2.88–89).

Castellana: Italian for "mistress of a castle." **Euthanasia** inherits the title and castle of **Valperga** from her maternal line, since her mother was Castellana (*V* 1.10).

Castello Lizzana: Castelbarco's castle near **Lago di Garda** (Moskal 262). **Dante** stayed there after 1301 while exiled from **Florence** (*R* 2.66).

Castiglione, Giovanni da: General who commands **Castruccio**'s troops and warns him about **Florentine** invasion of **Val di Nievole** (*V* 2.202–203). The name comes from historical accounts of Castiglione, a **Lucchese** exile and, by 1311, **Lombardy**'s Proctor-General (Green 46). He controlled **Pisa** 1328 and apparently supported Castruccio (Green 235).

Castillejo, Cristóbal (c. 1492–1550): Minor **Spanish** poet. Shelley wrote Castillejo's brief biography for *Italian and Spanish Lives*, terming him a "great partisan of the old Castilian style, and the antagonist of **Boscán**" (*ISPL* 3.93). Castillejo eventually became a monk, but Shelley gives little further detail, noting only he is an "inferior poet" whose "lyrics are light, airy, graceful" (*ISPL* 3.94).

Castor: In **Greek** mythology, mortal twin renowned as a horse tamer; he sailed with the Argonauts and became immortal. Twin brother **Pollux**, an immortal with boxing skills, also sailed with the Argonauts (Tripp 211). Shelley must have known the *Colossal Equestrian Group* sculpture standing beside **Rome**'s **Monte Cavallo** obelisk and depicting "fine anatomy and action" of Castor and Pollux and horses (*MROM* 88). **Lionel Verney** admires a statue of the two brothers (*LM* 461). Shelley sailed on the *Castor* to Rome 1843 (*R* 2.213).

Castruccio, Castracani dei Antelminelli (1281–1328): Both a historical figure and major character in *Valperga*. In 1819, Shelley learned of Castruccio from **Sismondi**'s *Histoire* and based her novel's character on **Machiavelli**'s, Sismondi's, **Tegrimi**'s, and **Villani**'s various biographical accounts (*Journals* 268; Sunstein 162; *V* iii). She admits to altering events' dates, but her history of Castruccio is fairly accurate (*V* iv; *Journals* 329).

Catanzaro: Southern **Italian** town thirty miles southwest of Crotone. Shelley describes **Carbonari** action led by **Capo Bianco** near Catanzaro (*R* 2.170).

Caterina: "The Trial of Love" character who accompanies **Faustina Moncenigo** and **Angeline** when they travel from **Sant' Anna Convent** to **Villa Moncenigo**.

Catiline, Lucius Sergius (d. 62 B.C.E.): Disreputable **Roman** politician who, after **Cicero** defeated him for the consul position, rebelled against Rome 62 B.C.E. (Howatson 119). **Valerius** says he died " 'defending [his] country against Catiline' " (*Val* 333).

Cato, Marcus Porcius (95–46 B.C.E.): **Roman** statesman and Stoic who supported **Pompey** in the Roman Civil War. After fleeing to **Africa**, Cato committed suicide at Utica when **Julius Caesar** was victorious (Kinder 1.91; Howatson 120). Shelley probably learned about him from **Plutarch** (*Journals* 668; Plutarch, *Lives* 1.516–541). **Henry Clerval** remarks upon **Victor Frankenstein**'s mourning **William Frankenstein**'s death: "Even Cato wept over the dead body of his brother" (*Fr1* 102). **Valerius** recalls that he " 'gloried with an excessive joy to be the friend of . . . Cato' " and calls upon Cato to reawaken when he returns to Rome (*Val* 333–334, 336). **Eu-**

thanasia mourns Cato's death when she sees the **Tiber**'s beauty (*V* 1.202). **Lionel Verney** imagines Cato in the **Forum** (*LM* 462). Shelley comments upon **Roger Dodsworth** as one of those men "who did not follow Cato's advice as recorded in the **Pharsalia**" (*RD* 45). *Pharsalia* is **Lucan**'s epic poem about the Roman Civil War; in Book Nine Cato exhorts his men to have the courage to fight valiantly (Howatson 428, 328; Lucan 9.256–410; Crook 2).

Catullus, Gaius Valerius (c. 84–54 B.C.E.): **Roman** lyric poet renowned for his love poems to Clodia Metelli, whom he called "Lesbia" as a tribute to **Sappho**. Shelley footnotes his "**Ad Sirmionem Peninsulum**" ["On the Syrian Peninsula"] and provides **Leigh Hunt**'s translation to complement her description of **Lasise** (*R* 2.73; Moskal 266).

Caucasus, Mount: Mountain range stretching from the **Black Sea** to the **Caspian Sea**, separating **Europe** from **Asia**. In their room at **Mrs. Derham**'s, the **Villiers**es "might have been at the top of Mount Caucasus, instead of in the centre of **London**, so completely were they cut off from every thing except each other" (*L* 2.278).

Cava: Southern **Italian** town two miles northwest of **Salerno**. Shelley mentions "a very pretty hotel at Cava," perhaps Hôtel de Londres, which **Murray** notes (*R* 2.295; Moskal 385).

Cavalcanti, Guido (c. 1240–1300): Thirteenth-century **Italian** considered to be the best poet before **Dante**, who dedicated *Vita nuova* (1290–94) to him. Born into a **Guelph** family of **Florence**, Cavalcanti authored about fifty-two love poems and is considered father of the *dolce stil nuovo* (sweet new style) school (*DIL* 113–115). **Euthanasia** adores Cavalcanti's poetry, comparing her suitors' lyrics to his (*V* 1.170, 1.188).

Cecil, Lady Sophia: Sister, by his father's remarriage, and surrogate mother of **Gerard Neville** in *Falkner*.

Cecil, Lord: Lady Sophia Cecil's ineffectual husband in *Falkner*.

Cefalonia: **Ionian** island off **Greece**'s southwestern coast north of **Zante**. **Cyril Ziani** and **Camaraz** sail north of Cefalonia (*EE* 110). **Harry Valency** recovers from battle wounds there (*E* 307).

Celian Hill: See **Caelian Hill**.

Cellini, Benvenuto (1500–1571): **Florentine** sculptor whose masterpiece is *Perseus with the Head of Medusa* (1545–54); in **Greek** mythology, Perseus was **Zeus**'s son and slew **Gorgon** Medusa (*Phaidon* 115). Shelley viewed Cellini's *Perseus* at Florence's Loggia dei Lanzi January 1843; she thought his model of the statue, in the **Uffizi**, better than the full-size version (*R* 2.155).

Celt: Now meaning any person of Breton descent, including inhabitants of Britain, **Ireland**, and **France**, in Shelley's day it loosely meant inhabitants of northern **Europe** as distinct from southern **Mediterranean** races (Crook 2). **Lionel Verney** wishfully suggests that plague "never feasts on the pale-faced Celt" (*LM* 233).

Cenci; A Tragedy, in Five Acts, The

Cenci; A Tragedy, in Five Acts, The: Working from Shelley's translation *Relation of the Cenci*, **PBS** began this drama 1819; it was published 1820 but, because of its incestuous theme, was not staged privately until 1886 and publicly 1922 (White 2.96, 2.100). Shelley was closely involved with PBS's work. **Edmund Malville** quotes Orsino's line to describe visitors searching for and admiring the past: "those who pant to quit the **'painted scene** of this new world'—for the old world" (*RI* 26; PBS 5.1.78). **Raymond** asserts " **'broad and garish** day' is the element in which I live," which seems an allusion to Francesco Cenci's seeing "a garish, broad, and peering day" (*LM* 49; Blumberg 41; PBS 2.1.177). Writing *The Last Man*, **Lionel Verney** remembers "beauteous lips are silent, their **'crimson leaves**' faded," a phrase Bernardo Cenci speaks in farewell to his sister (*LM* 80; Blumberg 66; PBS 5.4.138). Verney watches over his ill son **Evelyn**, " **'Whose narrow fire** / Is shaken by the wind, and on whose edge / Devouring darkness hovers,'" lines Giacomo Cenci speaks while contemplating his father's imminent death (*LM* 291; PBS 3.2.9–11). As an epigraph to the *Perkin Warbeck* chapter in which traitorous **Robert Clifford** flees to **London**, Shelley quotes Orsino's lines beginning " **'Shall I be** the slave / Of—what? a word?'" (*PW* 2.72; PBS 5.1.98–104). As an epigraph to the chapter in which **Lady Katherine Gordon** is finally able to visit **Richard of York** in prison, Shelley quotes **Beatrice Cenci**'s lines beginning " **'So young** to go / Under the obscure, cold, rotting, wormy ground!'" (*PW* 3.328; PBS 5.4.49–55). **Edward Villiers** points out that he "was trained to **'high-born necessities**,'" a line Giacomo speaks (*L* 3.56; PBS 2.2.7–12).

Cenci, Beatrice (1577–1599): Francesco Cenci's youngest daughter in *Relation of the Cenci*, executed for patricide (Ricci 1.8, 2.207–13). Shelley viewed **Guido**'s painting of Beatrice at **Palazzo Colonna** April 1819 and subsequently asked **Amelia Curran** to paint a copy for her (*Journals* 259; *Letters* 1.159; *R* 2.223). Shelley refers to Guido's painting in *Valperga* in comparing **Dante**'s **Beatrice**'s beauty to Beatrice Cenci's (*V* 2.17).

Cenis, Mount: Alpine mountain and pass on **France**'s border with **Italy**. The Shelleys crossed the mountain March 1818 (*Journals* 202). Shelley wrote July 1823, "I was not so much delighted with the passage of Mont Cenis as I expected, but this was because I had formed a wrong idea of it"; she had not expected its lush vegetation and lack of snow (*Letters* 1.355, 1.360). **Felix De Lacey** leads **Safie** and her father along the same route the Shelleys followed; British plague survivors also make this journey (*Fr1* 152; *Fr3* 109; *LM* 428). The **Villiers**es follow "the beaten route of Mont Cenis" (*L* 2.207). Shelley observed that "one of the great evils of the division of Italy" is the neglect of the **Simplon Pass**, so that "travellers may be induced to prefer Cenis" (*R* 1.132). [*R* 2.45].

Centaur: In **Greek** mythology, creature that is half horse and half man. **Lionel Verney** compares accounts of **Irish** invaders' deeds to "strange and appalling accounts" of centaurs (*LM* 298).

Cerberus: In **Greek** mythology, **Hades**'s watchdog; it had at least three heads, delighted in spirits entering Hades, and ate spirits who tried to leave; Aeneas drugged him with a cake soaked in narcotics and honey ("sop to Cerberus"). Shelley recalls when "iron gates enclosing the plantations and **Virginia Water** were guarded by no Cerberus untamable by sops," setting "**The Mourner**'s" time frame during **George III**'s residence at **Windsor** (*Mourner* 83). Shelley compares **Lady Santerre**'s ability to do as she pleases to Cerberus's delight in preventing people from leaving Hades (*L* 1.206).

Ceres: In **Roman** mythology, fertility goddess presiding over earth's fields (Demeter in **Greece**) (Tripp 194–198). **Midas** celebrates "rich-haired Cere's" natural wealth and beauty (*Midas* 149). **Lionel Verney** terms northern England's unfruitful land "the hard-earned Ceres of the north," "Ceres" meaning both "corn" and "corn goddess" in **Latin** (*LM* 323). In *Proserpine*, Shelley presents Ceres as a distraught mother distressed by her daughter **Proserpine**'s kidnapping.

Cerigo: **Italian** name of **Greek** island of Cythera, south of the **Peloponnese**. **Cyril** and **Zella Ziani** sail around it (*EE* 108).

Cerito, Fanny (1817–1909): Italian choreographer and dancer (Moskal 131). Shelley saw her perform in **Bergamo** September 1840 (*R* 1.108).

Cervantes Saavedra, Miguel de (1547–1616): **Spanish** novelist and dramatist best known for his satirical romance *Don Quixote de la Mancha* (1605 and 1615), which Shelley read 1816 and 1820 (*Journals* 139, 341). Shelley wrote an accurate biography of Cervantes for *Italian and Spanish Lives*. She considers *Don Quixote*'s first part "perfect in all its parts" (*ISPL* 3.181). Shelley records the successful appearance of its second part and describes *Los trabajos de Persiles y Sigismunda* [*Persiles and Sigismunda's Trials*] (1617), which she first records reading May 1819 (*ISPL* 3.187; *Journals* 264–265). Reviewing Cervantes's life, Shelley is "struck by the equanimity of temper preserved throughout," and she wrote to **Leigh Hunt** that "writing of Cervantes so much reminded me of you that I thought it would please you" (*ISPL* 3.174; *Letters* 2.292). Outlining **Serbelloni**'s history, Shelley includes a reference to Cervantes's loss of his hand at the Battle of **Lepanto** (1571) (*R* 1.81).

Cerveaux: **French** village on the **Arve**, five miles west of **Chamonix**; Shelley sometimes spells it **Servox** or **Servoz**. The Shelleys climbed to Cerveaux July 1816 (*Journals* 114). **Victor Frankenstein** claims that Cerveaux's valley is more "beautiful and picturesque" than Chamonix's (*Fr1* 123; *Fr3* 86). Plague survivors "loitered along the lovely **Vale of Servox**" (*LM* 428). [*Fr1* 188; *Fr3* 137].

Cestius, Tomb of: First-century B.C.E. tomb in **Rome** housing the remains of tribune Caius Cestius, about whom little is known; it forms part of the Protestant cemetery's wall (*MROM* 67–68). The Shelleys visited it March 1819; **PBS** and **William Shelley** are buried near it (*Journals* 253). **Isabell Harley** takes **Valerius** to visit "the foot of the tomb of Cestius, that lovely spot" (*Val* 343). **Lionel Verney** reads there (*LM* 465). Shelley noted an April 1843 view from the **Coliseum** wherein "the tomb of Cestius, gleaming at a distance, is a resting-place for the eye" (*R* 2.226).

Chablais: French region south of **Lake Geneva**. Shelley locates **La Maurienne** between Chablais and **Mount Cenis** (*R* 2.45).

Chaldee: Chaldean; language and inhabitants of Chaldea, ancient Babylonian region on the **Persian** Gulf, now part of Iraq. The **Sibylline** leaves' discoverer notes that some written characters are "ancient Chaldee" (*LM* 5).

Chalons-sur-Marne: French city ninety miles east of **Paris**. Shelley passed through Chalons twice in 1840 (*R* 1.12, 1.144).

Chamber of Peers: Formerly, upper branch of **France**'s legislative body, consisting of hereditary nobles, established 1814 but reconstituted 1848 (Kinder 2.49, 2.55). Shelley quotes a comment **Soult** made in the Chamber of Peers (*R* 2.249).

Chamonix: Southeastern **French** town at the **Alps**'s foot, close to **Swiss** and **Italian** borders; Shelley spells it **Chamounix**. The Shelleys made a special trip to Chamonix July 1816, where they viewed **Mont Blanc** and **PBS** wrote his famous poem of that name. Shelley found the nearby glacier "the most desolate place in the world" (*Journals* 119). In PBS's "Introduction" to *History*, he acknowledges that "Mont Blanc" is by the same author as the letter from Chamonix published in his *Letters from Geneva* (*H* vi). When **Victor Frankenstein** needs to escape "sullen despair," he goes to the "valley of Chamounix," where he meets the **Creature** (*Fr1* 123; *Fr3* 86). Plague reaches even to Chamonix's glaciers (*LM* 424, 426). [*Fr1* 176, 188; *Fr3* 128, 137].

Chamounix: See **Chamonix**.

Champagnole: French village thirty-eight miles south of **Besançon**; Shelley spells it **Champagnolles**. She slept there May 1816 (*H* 88–89).

Champagnolles: See **Champagnole**.

Champlitte: French town thirty miles northeast of **Dijon**. The Shelleys dined there August 1814 (*Journals* 15; *H* 30).

Champs Elysées: See **Avenue des Champs Elysées**.

Chapel Wood: Part of **Windsor**'s park. **Lionel Verney** admires its beauty (*LM* 41). **Horace Neville** hid among trees there when he ran away from **Eton** (*Mourner* 87). "The Mourner" is set during **George III**'s reign, when the "mazy paths of Chapel Wood" were closed to the public (*Mourner* 83).

Characteristic Songs of Shelley: See **Pearson**.

Charenton: See **Charenton-le-Pont**.

Charenton-le-Pont: French town five miles southeast of **Paris**; Shelley terms it **Charenton**. The Shelleys arrived there August 1814 (*Journals* 11; *H* 15).

Charing Cross: At the **Strand**'s west end, long road adjoining Trafalgar Square in **London**'s Westminster district. **Ethel Villiers** journeys by coach to "**Union Club**, in Charing Cross" (*L* 2.259).

Charlemagne (742–814): King of the **Franks** 768–814 and first Holy Roman Emperor 800–814, also known as Charles the Great (Kinder 1.123). **Benedetto Pepi** defends his strange dress with a story about Charlemagne, who ridiculed well-dressed nobles in **Fugolano** (*V* 1.285–288). [*R* 2.197].

Charles I (1600–1649): England's king from 1625, also known as **Charles Stuart**; financial problems, rebellion, and disagreements with **Parliament** plagued his reign and resulted in the English Civil War (1642–48), after which Charles was tried and executed. Shelley read his *Letters* (1645) 1822 (Sunstein 104; *Journals* 408). She thought the king's tumultuous life and horrifying death would make good material for a literary project; **PBS** attempted to write a play on the subject, "**Charles the First**" (Sunstein 164; White 2.216). **Victor Frankenstein** and **Henry Clerval** visit historical sites connected to Charles (*Fr1* 186; *Fr3* 136). **Roger Dodsworth**'s father died during Charles's reign (*RD* 43, 46). Shelley viewed **Van Dyck**'s portrait of Charles in **Berlin**'s Royal Palace and quotes **Ben Jonson**'s response to a gift Charles sent him (*R* 1.225, 2.132).

Charles II (1630–1685): Raised in exile in **France**, **Charles Stuart** was crowned Charles II of Scotland (1651) after his father **Charles I**'s execution. He spent ten more years in exile until called to England's throne 1660 at the **Commonwealth**'s end (Kinder 1.267). When **Roger Dodsworth** died 1654, "Charles II was an outcast, a beggar, bankrupt even in hope"; Shelley's observation is historically accurate (*RD* 45).

Charles IV [French] (1294–1328): King of **France** 1322–28, also known as **Charles of Valois**, for the family that ruled France 1328–1498 (Sismondi 116; Kinder 1.191). Charles was actually a Capetian king, and the House of Valois did not assume the throne until his death. Charles intervenes in **Guelph** and **Ghibelline** strife in **Florence** (*V* 1.12). **Villani** records that Charles exiled Florentine **Bianchi** September 1301 (Villani 331–339).

Charles IV [German] (1316–1378): King of **Germany** and **Bohemia** 1346–78, also crowned Holy Roman Emperor 1355. Charles made his capital at **Prague**, began construction of several of Prague's Gothic buildings, and founded **Neustadt** 1348 (*BCSR* 294–295). Shelley credits Charles's contributions and recounts Prague's history; it was most prosperous during Charles's reign (*R* 1.280, 2.1).

Charles V (1500–1558): **Spain**'s king as Charles I 1516–56 and Holy Roman Emperor as Charles V 1519–57 (Morby 118, 123; Kinder 1.219). Charles banned **Martin Luther** at the **Diet of Worms** 1521 (Kinder 1.231). [*R* 1.79–80].

Charles VI (1368–1422): France's king 1380–1422; madness hindered his political decisions, and the royal family's rivalries incited civil war at the same time that **Henry V** of England attempted to claim France (Famiglietti xi). Shelley writes in "**Transformation**," "The poor king, Charles the Sixth, now sane, now mad, now a monarch, now an abject slave, was the very mockery of humanity" (*Trans* 122). Shelley gives a historical sketch of the **Serbelloni** family, one of whom served in Charles's army; other family members left France during Charles's reign (*R* 1.80, 1.82).

Charles VIII (1470–1498): France's king 1422–61. Shelley details Charles's attempt to control **Brittany** in *Perkin Warbeck* (*PW* 1.242, 1.308, 1.311–314). Shelley states that from 1494, when Charles first invaded **Italy**, until 1815, "Italy has been a battle-field" and not simply "a discontented province of **Austria**" (*R* 1.xiv).

Charles d'Anjou: See **Charles of Anjou**.

Charles of Anjou (1227–1285): **Naples**'s king 1266–82. With **Guelph** support, Charles became **Sicily**'s king (1266) and later defeated **Manfred** and **Conradin** to end **German** rule of southern **Italy**. Shelley's "**A Tale of the Passions**" takes place in **Florence** during Charles's reign (*TP* 1, 22). **Ethelbert Atawel** "accompanied Charles of Anjou to Italy" (*V* 1.60–61).

Charles of Valois: See **Charles IV** (1294–1328).

Charles the Bold (1433–1477): Final, great **Burgundian** duke allied to **Edward IV** through 1468 marriage to **Margaret of Burgundy**; he died trying to make Burgundy independent of **France**. Shelley refers to him as **Charles the Rash of Burgundy**. She relates of Charles's history that he commenced "his reign by combating and vanquishing" **Louis XI**, then "dying miserably at last by a traitor's hand, his armies cut to pieces" (*PW* 1.130, 1.149).

"Charles the First": Dramatic fragment that **PBS** started 1820, continued 1822, and first published 1824 (White 2.216, 2.334; *Journals* 409). As second epigraph to the *Perkin Warbeck* chapter in which **Richard of York** briefly reunites with his mother in **Spain**, Shelley quotes: " '**England, farewell!** thou, who hast been my cradle, / Shalt never be my dungeon or my grave!' " (*PW* 1.83; PBS 4.1–2). **Shelley** quotes "the **lilies glorious** as **Solomon**, / Who toil not, neither do they spin" from PBS's poem to describe **Vienna**'s "pleasure-seeking society" (*LM* 38; PBS 1.156–157).

Charles the Rash of Burgundy: See **Charles the Bold**.

Charlestown: In Shelley's time, northeastern **American** town that has since become part of **Boston**. **Osborne** takes the steamer to Charlestown (*F* 268).

Charlotte Sophia, Queen (1744–1818): **German** princess of Mecklenberg-Strelitz who married Britain's **George III** (1761) (J. Clarke 281). When the doctor feels that the lodger at **Dame Nixon**'s cottage "is more like the Queen of England in her looks and ways than anyone he ever saw," **Elizabeth Fitzhenry** mistakenly thinks this reference is to Queen Charlotte, "who had been the queen of the greater part of the good lady's life" (*L* 3.254).

Charon: In **Greek** mythology, boatman who ferries souls across **Styx** to **Hades**. **Guarino** sings of Charon refusing **Dante** passage in his descent to Hell (*V* 1.273–274; *Inferno* 3.82–99).

Charybdis: See **Scylla**.

Chastellain, Georges (c. 1415–1475): **French** chronicler and poet. Shelley used an excerpt beginning "J'ai veu filz d'Angleterre, Richard d'Yorc nommé" from an **Old French Chronicle** as *Perkin Warbeck*'s epigraph. Fischer provides Marcelle Thiébaux's translation: "I have seen the son of England, named **Richard of York** (who people in the world said was defeated and destroyed) undergo great suffering; and [yet] by his noble accomplishments live in great hope to become king of the English" (2–3). In her preface, Shelley notes the quote is from *Recollection des Merveilles, advenues en nostre temps, commencé par très élègant orateur, Messire Georges Chastellan, et continuèe par Maistre Jean Molinet* [*Recollection of Our Time's Marvels, begun by the very elegant speaker, Mr. Georges Chastellain, and continued by Monsieur Jean Molinet*] (wr. c. 1464–1466) (*PW* vii).

Chatham, Lord: See **Pitt**.

Chaucer, Geoffrey (c. 1343–1400): Influential English author renowned for *The Canterbury Tales* (c. 1387), which recounts the tales of pilgrims en route to **Canterbury**; Shelley read it 1815 (*Journals* 641). As an epigraph to the *Perkin Warbeck* chapter in which **Richard of York** discovers **Meiler Trangmar**'s treachery, Shelley quotes from Chaucer's "Prologue to the Summoner's Tale": "**This Friar boasteth** that he knoweth hell, / And God it wot that is but litel wonder; / Friars and fiends ben but litel asonder" (*PW* 1.255; Chaucer lines 8–10). **Gerard Neville** introduces **Elizabeth Falkner** to the joys of Chaucer's works (*F* 236). Shelley calls Chaucer "one of our greatest poets" (*R* 2.132).

Chaumont: **French** town fifty miles southeast of **Troyes**. The Shelleys dined there August 1814 (*Journals* 14; *H* 30).

Chaumont, Fanny: **Louis Chaumont**'s wife and "**The Swiss Peasant**'s" main character.

Chaumont, Louis: **Fanny Chaumont**'s husband in "**The Swiss Peasant**."

Cheapside: **London** street running approximately east-west from **St. Paul**'s to the Bank of England. **Ethel Villiers** endures a long journey until "at last, in Cheapside, [she] stopped jammed up by carts and coaches" (*L* 2.258).

Chelmsford: **London** district thirty miles northeast of the city's center. **Lord Lovel** departs London through it (*PW* 1.48).

Chelsea: **London** district on the **Thames**'s north bank south of **Hyde**

Park. **Castruccio** goes on a hawking expedition there (*V* 1.82).

Cheltenham: English city eight miles east of Gloucester. **Colonel Villiers** lives there (*L* 2.224).

Chêne: Large village in east **Geneva**. **Justine Moritz** says she was in Chêne at her aunt's house on the night of **William Frankenstein**'s murder (*Fr1* 111; *Fr3* 77).

Cheney, Lady: Minor character in *Perkin Warbeck*.

Cheney, Sir John: In *Perkin Warbeck*, **Henry VII**'s chamberlain who leads English troops against **Richard of York** at **Exeter**.

Chester: English city sixteen miles south of **Liverpool**. **Edward II** meets **Castruccio** and **Piers Gaveston** there (*V* 1.80).

"Chevy Chase": See *Reliques*.

Chi dura Vince: See **Ricci**.

Chiabrera, Gabbriello (1552–1638): Italian poet. Shelley wrote Chiabrera's biography for *Italian and Spanish Lives*, describing his work as "harmonious and dignified, fervent and spirited" (*ISPL* 2.165). She admires Chiabrera's canzoni especially, finding "his style ... more original and beautiful than his ideas," his works "models of lyrical composition," and observing that "a fairy-like colouring, and a thrilling sweetness, like the scent of flowers, invest them, and render them peculiar in their aerial vivacity and spirited flow" (*ISPL* 2.165–166). Shelley refers readers to **Wordsworth**'s translations of some of Chiabrera's elegiac poems.

Chiaja: Street in **Naples**, alternatively spelled Chiaia. The Shelleys lived there December 1818–February 1819 (*Journals* 242). **Clorinda Saville** finds that "one house in the Chiaja is worthy fifty **Pompeiis**" (*L* 2.184). In miserable lodgings in **London**, **Edward Villiers** recalls Chiaja (*L* 2.240).

Chiaro Oscuro: Italian for "light dark," referring to effects of shade and light in artwork, especially when strongly contrasted; also chiaroscuro. Shelley praises **Correggio**'s Chiaro Oscuro effects in his paintings at the **Gallery in Dresden** (*R* 1.237–238).

Chiavenna: Italian town thirteen miles north of **Colico**. Shelley arrived there July 1840 (*R* 1.60).

Childe Harold's Pilgrimage: **Byron**'s poem. The first two cantos, published 1812, made him famous overnight; Canto III appeared 1816 and Canto IV 1818. The poem records a character's experiences and journeys through **Europe** and his thoughts during this attempt to escape the monotony and dissipation of his previous debauched, pleasure-seeking life. Shelley made a fair copy of Canto III for Byron summer 1816, which Sunstein says Shelley "always cherished because it incorporated their summer experience"; McGann notes Shelley's contributions to Canto III (Sunstein 121; McGann 2.306). Shelley repeatedly references the poem. She read Canto III while traveling down the **Rhine** 1814

(*H* 68; Byron 3.406–571). Rereading this part of the poem May 1817 made Shelley "melancholy," as she notes "how very vividly does each verse of his poem recall some scene of this kind to my memory" (*Journals* 172). In both *Frankenstein* and *Rambles*, Shelley uses Byron's description of the **Alps**, "**palaces of nature**," to describe mountains (*Fr1* 102; *Fr3* 71; *R* 1.119; Byron 3.591). In *Matilda*, Shelley draws from Canto IV for her image "**as a rainbow** gleams upon a cataract" (*M* 166; Todd 216; Byron 4.631–648). **Lionel Verney** warns **Perdita** not to abandon **Raymond** despite his apparent neglect of her, because "irreparable change '**will move / In hearts** all rocky now, the late remorse of love'" (*LM* 169). With the same phrase in *Lodore*, Shelley describes how "'**the remorse of love**' awakened in" **Ethel Villiers**'s heart when she learned of **Lady Lodore**'s generosity, and, in *Falkner*, **Mrs. Raby**'s "'**late remorse** of love' was awakened" upon **Edwin Raby**'s death (*L* 3.237; *F* 241; Byron 4.1232–1233). As an epigraph to "**The Evil Eye**," Shelley quotes the following accurately: "**The wild Albanian** kirtled to his knee, / With shawl-girt head, and ornamented gun, / And gold-embroider'd garments, fair to see; / The crimson-scarfed man of Macedon" (*EE* 100; Byron 2.514–517). **Camaraz** and **Cyril Ziani** stop at "**monastic Zitza**," another phrase from Byron's poem (*EE* 110; Byron 2.424). Shelley quotes Byron to describe **James IV**'s approaching battle in England: "'**In his eye** / And nostril, beautiful disdain and might / And majesty flashed their full lightnings by'" (*PW* 2.294; Byron 4.1446–1448). **Lord Lodore** tries to hide emotional pain in **America**, "but this reserve was not natural to him, and it added to the misery which his state of banishment occasioned. '**Quiet to quick** bosoms is a hell'" (*L* 1.20; Byron 3.370). Shelley recalls verses from Canto III, noting that "these, as he brought them successively to us, clothed in all the light and harmony of poetry, seemed to stamp as divine the glories of heaven and earth" (*Fr3* 21). Shelley draws from Byron's description of "**castled crags** of Drachenfels" in her own description of "romantic hills of the glorious **Rhine**" (*R* 1.171; Byron 3.496). She also quotes Byron to describe **Soracte**, which "'**Heaves like** a long-swept wave, about to break, / And on the curl hangs pausing'" (*R* 2.227; Byron 4.668–669).

Children in the Wood: See *Reliques*.

Chillon: Swiss village on **Lake Geneva**'s eastern bank between **Clarens** and Villeneuve, renowned for its castle. **Byron** describes it in "**Prisoner of Chillon**" (1816). In *History*'s preface, Shelley includes Chillon in the list of **Swiss** towns on her route (*H* v).

China: Lionel Verney imagines the plague's spread through "crowded cities of China" and speculates about plague's power as he learns that "crowded abodes of the Chinese" are threatened "with utter ruin" (*LM* 225, 233). Shelley says of **Lady Lodore**: "pride had been the wall of China to shut up all her better qualities" (*L* 3.95).

Chiverton Park: Elizabeth Fitzhenry reads a newspaper announcement of a rumored marriage involving **Edward Villiers** of Chiverton Park (*L* 2.104). Nothing further about this property appears in *Lodore*.

"Choice, The": Long confessional poem Shelley wrote July 1823 while mourning (*Journals* 494). Shelley left the poem in **Italy** and later asked **Leigh Hunt** to send her the manuscript; he revised it, but Shelley accepted only some of his editorial suggestions (Forman 5). The title refers to Shelley's choice to disobey her father and to disregard social custom in order to unite with **PBS**. After confessing her attachment to and love for her deceased husband, Shelley recalls the time she spent in Italy and grieves for her children, **Clara** and **William Shelley**, who died and were buried there. She also mourns **Clara Allegra Byron**'s and **Edward Williams**'s deaths. The poem concludes with a description of the anxious wives (Shelley and **Jane Williams**) awaiting in vain their husbands' safe return (*Ch* 143–145). Shelley did not publish the poem in her lifetime. H. Buxton Forman first published "The Choice: A Poem on Shelley's Death by Mary Wollstonecraft Shelley" for private distribution 1876. It contains an additional final stanza not present in the 1825 copy Shelley made in her *Journals* (490–494).

"Christabel": Poem **Samuel Taylor Coleridge** wrote 1797–1800 and circulated in manuscript before its 1816 publication; the Shelleys read it August 1816 (*Journals* 131). When **Matilda** awakens after sleeping exhaustedly on the heath, Shelley quotes "**The moon is behind**, and at the full / And yet she looks both small and dull" from the opening of Coleridge's poem (*M* 206; Coleridge lines 18–19). As an epigraph to the *Perkin Warbeck* chapter detailing **Monina De Faro**'s visit with dying **Elizabeth Woodville** and **Robert Clifford**'s response, Shelley quotes: " '**She was most beautiful** to see, / Like a lady of a far countree' " (*PW* 1.326; Coleridge lines 224–225). **Lord Lodore** contemplates nature's beauties with a line detailing Coleridge's sleep: "tufted groves crowning the uplands, and '**the blue sky** bent over all' " (*L* 1.171; Coleridge lines 329–331).

***Chronicle of the Conquest of Granada*:** See **Irving**.

Chur: Swiss city thirty-five miles northeast of **Chiavenna**; Shelley uses the **French** name **Coire**. Shelley stayed there July 1840 (*R* 1.55).

Cicero, Marcus Tullius (106–43 B.C.E.): Roman prose writer widely respected as a statesman, rhetorician, and orator. Shelley read Conyers Middleton's *The History of the Life of Marcus Tullius Cicero* (1741) 1820 and Cicero's *Orations* (46 B.C.E.) July 1820 (*Journals* 326–327). A mile from Cicero's tomb in **Gaeta** lies **Villa di Cicerone**, the reputed ruins of Cicero's villa, where he was buried after soldiers caught him and executed him because of his political outspokenness in 43 B.C.E. (Howatson 128–134, 594). Shelley visited this site November 1818: "in the midst of the olive wood—It is a tower of two stories smaller at top than at bottom & overgrown with weeds. . . . [T]he ruins . . . overlook the sea" (*Journals* 241). Shelley requested a copy of Cicero's works from **Thomas Jefferson Hogg**, and, December 1824, recorded, "I have pondered for hours on Cicero's description of that power of virtue in the human mind w[hic]h renders man's frail being superior to fortune" (*Journals* 486). **Valerius** was Cicero's friend and calls upon Cicero to reawaken to aid his country (*Val* 333–334, 336). Valerius later claims " 'Cicero did not love his **Tullia**' " as he loves **Isabell Harley** (*Val* 339). **Euthanasia** reads Cicero's "polished language" to her father (*V* 1.28). **Lionel Verney** recreates Cicero's "glowing periods" in Rome (*LM* 462). The narrator of "**The Sisters of Albano**" mentions visiting Cicero's villa (*SA* 51). **Fanny Derham** enjoys reading Cicero's **Tusculan Questions**, a five-section book, *Tusculanae disputationes* [*Tusculan Disputations*] (44 B.C.E.), in which Cicero presents philosophical theories about "the conditions for happiness" in the "form of conversations between two characters indicated as M and A" (*L* 3.9, 3.326; Howatson 585). Both **Ethel Villiers** and Fanny "fostered a state of mind, '**lofty and magnificent**, fitted rather to command than to obey, not only suffering patiently, but even making light of all human cares' "; Shelley translates these lines from Cicero's *De Finibus Bonorum et Malorum* [*About the Ends of Good and Evil*] (45 B.C.E.), in which Cicero defines moral worth and reason in his Stoic's refutation of Epicurus's philosophies (*L* 3.40–41; Stafford 224; Cicero 2.46). **Clorinda Saville** dies at "the inn called the Villa di Cicerone, at the **Mola di Gaeta**" (*L* 3.213).

Cicerone, Villa di: See **Cicero**.

Cimmerian: **Homer** uses this term to describe mythical people variously located in **Greece** but in a "*strange Nation,* covered with Perpetual darkness, and unvisited by the Beams of the Sun" (T. Blackwell 236). Cimmerian, also spelled **Cymmerian**, has subsequently come to mean gloomy darkness. **Lionel Verney** calls on "Melancholy" to "quit thy Cimmerian solitude" and describes how "sadness, bred in Cimmerian caves, robed my soul in a mourning garb" (*LM* 437, 463). **Ino** fears **Proserpine** may have been taken to a "black Cymmerian cave" (*P* 53).

Cincinnatus, Lucius Quinctius (c. 519–438 B.C.E.): Statesman and general who became **Rome**'s dictator 458 B.C.E., to whom George Washington is often compared, since both men returned to private lives after serving their countries (Howatson 135; Crook 2). **Adrian** compares himself and **Lionel Verney** to Cincinnatus (*LM* 96).

Cinderella: Fairy tale's title character; her fairy godmother saves her from a life of drudgery by casting a spell and dressing her in gorgeous clothes so she can attend a ball. There the prince falls in love with her; when Cinderella flees at midnight just before the spell wears off, she leaves a small glass slipper behind. The prince traces her by finding the woman whose foot fits the shoe, and they live happily ever after; **French Charles Perrault (1628–1703)** first published this tale 1697 (first translated into English 1729). **Henry Vernon** finds "a slipper. Since Cinderella so tiny a slipper had never been seen" (*IG* 199). The **Villiers**es are happy to be reunited despite troubles with creditors: "had Cinderella's godmother transmuted their crazy vehicle for a golden coach, redolent of the perfumes of fairy land, they had scarcely been aware of the change" (*L* 3.50). Describing the seven sisters in the family that keeps **Riva**'s inn, Shelley observed "some . . . are the Cinderellas of the establishment; but all are lazy and negligent" (*R* 2.68).

"Cinque Maggio": See **Manzoni**.

Circassia: Beautiful **Caucasus** mountain region on the **Black Sea** in northwest **Georgia**. Shelley seems to have been aware of the declining traditional Circassian practice of selling women to **Turkish** harems, which Edmund Spencer describes in *Travels in Circassia* (1837) (2.372). **Lionel Verney** mourns the plague's destruction of Circassia and "the ruin of its favourite temple—the form of woman" (*LM* 234).

Circean Stye: Allusion to **Greek** mythology: Circe was a sorceress who transformed humans into beasts on the island of Aeaea, as she does in **Homer**'s *Odyssey* when she transforms Odysseus's men into swine and keeps them in a sty (*Odyssey* 10.252–268). Shelley discusses **Italy**'s political climate, where a man "either sinks into the Circean Stye, in which so many drag out a degraded existence, or he is irresistibly impelled to resist" (*R* 1.xii).

Cisalpine: **Alps**'s **Roman**, or south, side. Shelley recounts how **Charles of Anjou** led the **French** through the Alps, thereby introducing luxury into Cisalpine palaces (*TP* 6).

Cisalpine Gaul: See **Gauls**.

Civita Vecchia: **Italian** port city forty miles northwest of **Rome**. Shelley was detained there for three hours March 1843 (*R* 2.213).

Clairmont, Charles Gaulis (1795–1850): Mary Jane Clairmont **Godwin**'s eldest illegitimate child, from an affair with **Swiss** Karl Gaulis (*SCGS* 249–253). Charles studied the bookselling trade in **Edinburgh** 1812, where he met the **Baxters** (*SCGS* 297, 324). Charles was glad to welcome his half-sister **Claire Clairmont** and stepsister Shelley back from their 1814 **European** tour, and he was instrumental in Shelley's subsequent reconciliation with **William Godwin** (*SCGS* 372, 381–384; *Journals* 26, 41–43). Shelley seems to have felt affection for Charles, and they maintained a steady correspondence (*Letters* 2.149). Charles traveled in **Spain** for fifteen months before staying with the Shelleys in **Italy** for two months 1819 and then moving to **Vienna**, where he worked "as an English language teacher" (*Journals* 296, 369; *SCGS* 473). Claire (the two were close) visited him there 1822; in 1824, Charles married Antoine Ghislain d'Hembyze (1800–68), and they had six children (*Journals* 509; *Letters* 2.55, 3.356; Gittings 127). Charles and his family visited Britain briefly 1828–29 and borrowed money from Shelley to return to **Austria**, settling there permanently (*SCGS* 477; *Letters* 2.101). Shelley asked Claire to say to Charles "everything that is kind . . . & how glad I shall be to see him here" when Charles visited Britain 1845; she told Claire she hoped for "good tidings of [Charles's] recovery" 1848, but he died suddenly (*Letters* 3.198, 3.344). See Robert Gittings and Jo Manton's *Claire Clairmont and the Shelleys* (1992).

Clairmont, Claire [Jane] (1798–1879)

Clairmont, Claire [Jane] (1798–1879): Mary Jane Clairmont Godwin's illegitimate daughter; originally called Jane, she took the name Clara 1814, then became Clare 1816, and finally Claire 1819 (Sunstein 95, 115, 163; Gittings 23). Her mother's favorite, Claire "was troublesome from the beginning" in stepfather **William Godwin**'s household; she both admired and disliked Shelley, with whom she was always to have a complex relationship (Sunstein 35–36). Claire admired **PBS** greatly upon his first visits to the Godwin household, and the Shelleys took Claire with them upon eloping to **Europe**; Claire lived with them often in subsequent years and depended upon their financial support in **London** (White 1.384–385). Sunstein claims that Claire "fell in love with" PBS; her presence was consistently problematic for the Shelleys' relationship, since she flirted with PBS (Sunstein 95; Gittings 55). When the Shelleys moved to **Bishopsgate**, Claire traveled briefly to **Ireland** with her brother **Charles Clairmont** and then took lodgings in London, where she began an affair with **Byron** April 1816; Claire accompanied the Shelleys to **Geneva** that summer so as to continue the relationship, even though Byron's interest rapidly declined (Sunstein 114–118). In **Bath** January 1817, Claire gave birth to **Clara Allegra Byron** (Sunstein 129). She refused **Thomas Love Peacock**'s marriage proposal later that year, but he remained a valuable friend (Gittings 39). Claire accompanied the Shelleys to **Italy** 1818 and sent Allegra to Byron in **Venice** in April; PBS accompanied Claire when she went to visit Allegra in August. **Clara Everina Shelley** died en route to the city with Shelley; she surely thereafter resented Claire's demands on PBS, regarding Allegra as perhaps speeding her own daughter's demise (Sunstein 158). Claire wrangled with Byron about her daughter's care before Allegra's death (*Journals* 409; Gittings 58–61, 69–70). Claire refused **Henry Reveley**'s marriage proposal and, following increased friction with Shelley, lived with the Bojti family in **Florence** 1820–22, visiting the Shelleys often and returning to their household in **Pisa** April 1822 (Gittings 54, 62, 68; *Journals* 320). After PBS's death and having evaded **Edward John Trelawny**'s declarations of love (although they remained close and she cared for his daughter Zella), Claire joined Charles in **Vienna** and then traveled to **Russia** to work as a governess (Gittings 70–71, 83–89, 89–91; *Letters* 2.203). Claire's life was subsequently one of hard work and near poverty, alleviated by Shelley's assistance: Claire moved to **Germany**, visited London 1828–29 (where she renewed her friendship with **Jane Williams** and lived with Shelley at Shelley's expense), then worked in Germany, **France**, and Italy; she stayed with **Lady Margaret Mountcashel** in Pisa 1832 (Gittings 125–139, 143, 152; *Journals* 509, 545). Shelley maintained their correspondence, but their relationship was never easy. In May 1836, Shelley wrote, "Claire always harps upon my desertion of her—as if I could desert one I never clung to—we were never friends—Now, I would not go to Paradise, with her for a companion—she poisoned my life when young—that is over now—but as [I never] we never loved each other, why these eternal complaints to me of me. I respect her now much—& pity her deeply—but years ago my idea of [an agreable world] Heaven was a world without a Claire—of course these feelings are altered—but she still has the faculty of making me more uncomfortable than any human being—a faculty she, unconsciously perhaps, never fails to exert whenever I see her—" (*Letters* 2.271). Claire returned to England with her employers 1836, then moved in with her mother 1840; her brother's children often visited her (Gittings 168, 177). After her mother's and **Sir Timothy Shelley**'s deaths, which rendered Claire financially independent by virtue of PBS's bequest to her, Claire settled in **Paris** for several years (where Shelley visited her), and then returned to a house near **Regent's Park** 1847, before moving to **Brighton** (1848–49), Ramsgate (1852), and Surbiton (1857), and returning to and settling in Florence (1860) (Gittings 183, 201, 207, 217–218, 223). Claire visited her nephew in **Austria** 1871, having bought a farm there, but this purchase severely damaged her finances, and she returned to Florence 1872, where she lived with two nieces until her death (Gittings 231–232, 245). See Marion Kingston Stocking's *The Journals of Claire Clairmont* (1968), Robert Gittings and Jo Manton's *Claire Clairmont and the Shelleys* (1992), and Marion Kingston Stocking's *The Clairmont Correspondence: Letters of Claire Clairmont, Charles Clairmont, and Fanny Imlay Godwin* (1995).

Clan Cartie Reagh: Irish clan in *Perkin Warbeck*; **Desmond** and **Barry** plan to "take **Coollong** from Clan Cartie Reagh" (*PW* 1.306).

Clara: **Perdita** and **Raymond**'s only child in *The Last Man* (*LM* 92). Her name recalls the Shelleys' daughter, **Clara**, and **Claire Clairmont**'s daughter with **Byron**, **Allegra** Clara (*Journals* 227).

Clare: **Connaught** river in western **Ireland**. **Murrogh-en-Ranagh** conquered the country from Clare to **Munster** (*PW* 1.291).

Clarence, Duke of (1449–1478): George Plantagenet became Duke of Clarence 1461; **Edward IV**'s younger brother, he was executed for treason (*DNB*). **Lord Lovel** explains how Clarence's attainder excluded him from the throne but that **Richard III** proclaimed Clarence's son, the **Earl of Warwick**, heir (*PW* 1.24–25, 1.30). **Lambert Simnel**'s initial appearance in **Ireland** is due to Clarence's past popularity there (*PW* 1.115, 1.283). Clarence made **Long Roger** servitor in the **Tower**, which makes him loyal to Warwick (*PW* 3.286–87).

Clarens: Swiss village on **Lake Geneva**, three miles southeast of **Vevay** (*BSWI* 265). In *History*'s preface, Shelley lists Clarens as on her route (*H* v).

Claude Gellée Lorrain (1600–1682): Widely known **French** landscape painter (Grahame 14–54). Shelley attended an 1824 **London** exhibition "of fine old paintings.... The Claude's [*sic*] bring all **Italy** before [my] eyes" (*Letters* 1.427). **Perdita** decorates an alcove with her copies of Claude's paintings (*LM* 51).

Claudus: See **Earl of Desmond**.

Clayton, Lucy: See **Martin, Lucy**.

Clement IV, Pope (c. 1195–1268): Pope 1265–1268. He encouraged **Charles of Anjou** to fight **Manfred**, and after Manfred's death at **Battle of Benevento**, the pope banned **Conradin**, rightful heir, from rule. When Charles beheaded Conradin in **Naples**, Clement did nothing to prevent it (Kelly 196–197). Shelley calls Clement "murderer of Manfred" and describes Clement's encounter with Conradin at **Viterbo** (*TP* 14, 21).

Cleopatra: See *Antony and Cleopatra*.

Clermont: Clermont-en-Argonne is a **French** town thirty-five miles northeast of **Chalons-sur-Marne**. Shelley passed through it June 1840 (*R* 1.12).

Clerval, Henry: Victor **Frankenstein**'s childhood friend whom the **Creature** kills in *Frankenstein*. Some commentators assert **PBS** was the model for Clerval.

Cleveland, John (1613–1658): Political poet and satirist who opposed **Cromwell** and fought for Royalists during the English Civil War (1642–48). **Lionel Verney** closes *The Last Man*'s second volume by determining to leave England and quoting the opening lines of Cleveland's "An Elegie on the best of Men and meekest of Martyrs, Charles the I. &c.": "**Does not the sun** call in his light? and day / Like a thin exhalation melt away—/ Both wrapping up their beams in clouds to be / Themselves close mourners at this obsequie" (*LM* 314; Paley 477; Cleveland 86). When Verney leaves England forever, he quotes the final lines of Cleveland's "Chronostichon Decollationis Caroli Regis" ["The Chronicle of King Charles's Beheading"]: "Farewell, sad Isle, farewell, thy fatal glory / Is summed, cast up, and cancelled in this story" (*LM* 324; Paley 477; Cleveland 82). As Paley notes, neither poem is now thought to be Cleveland's (477).

Clêves: German town twelve miles southeast of **Nijmegen**. The Shelleys arrived there September 1814 (*Journals* 23; *H* 72–74). Shelley briefly refers to **Frederic the Great**'s meeting with **Voltaire**, which occurred near Clêves (*R* 1.227).

Clifford, Lady: In *Perkin Warbeck*, **Roger Clifford**'s dead wife.

Clifford, Robert: "Double agent" who alternately supported the **Yorkists** and **Lancastrians**; he conspired against **Henry VII** of England 1493 because he truly believed **Perkin Warbeck** to be **Richard of York** but later became disillusioned and an informer for both sides (Arthurson 62, 69, 74, 83–88). Major *Perkin Warbeck* character: he causes Richard's downfall, loves **Monina De Faro**, and dies fighting Richard.

Clifford, Sir Roger: In *Perkin Warbeck*, **Henry V**'s follower; **Yorkist** conspirators meet at Clifford's castle.

Clim of Tregothius: Commoner fighting for **Richard of York** in *Perkin Warbeck*; **Holinshed** records that Clim

Clorinda

injured the **Earl of Devon** at **Exeter** (Holinshed 3.518).

Clorinda: See *Gerusalemme Liberata*.

Clym of the Lyn: "Outlawed forester" who guides **Robert Clifford**, then **Richard of York**, in *Perkin Warbeck* (PW 3.148). Fischer notes that Shelley probably took the name from *Reliques'* "Adam Bell, Clym of the Clough, and William of Cloudelsey" and that a *lyn* is a waterfall (321).

Coblentz: German city on the **Rhine**, thirty-three miles northwest of **Weisbaden**; Shelley spells it **Koblentz**. Shelley stayed there July 1840 and reached Coblentz by boat June 1842 (R 1.26, 1.169).

Cochem: German city on the **Moselle**, twelve miles southwest of **Coblentz**; Shelley spells it **Kochheim**. Shelley stayed there June 1840 (R 1.24–25).

Cocumella: Large house, not quite a mile from **Sorrento**, transformed into a hotel (STIE 361). Shelley stayed there June 1843 (R 2.263–265, 2.296).

Codja-Bashee: "Elder," title given to a **Greek** holding a district governorship under **Ottoman** rule; alternatively spelled Cogia or Coda (Marchand 1.220). **Katusthius Ziani** learns **Cyril Ziani** "would be named Codja-Bashee" (EE 105).

Coire: See **Chur**.

Colchester: Essex city fifty miles northeast of **London**. **Sir Humphrey Stafford** plans to hide at **St. Mary's** near Colchester (PW 1.5). **Lord Lovel** arrives there safely with **Richard of York** two days after **Bosworth Field** (PW 1.42, 1.48).

Coleridge, Henry Nelson (1798–1843): English lawyer, author, and **Samuel Taylor Coleridge**'s nephew (married to his daughter, Sara Coleridge) (Barnhart 261). Shelley observes that "a delightful writer has described [**Ethel Villiers**] individually. '**She was in her nature** a superior being. Her majestic forehead, her dark, thoughtful eye, assured you that she had communed with herself'" (L 2.99). Shelley adapted this quotation from the "Trinidad" chapter of H. N. Coleridge's *Six Months in the West Indies, in 1825* (1826), wherein he describes **Spanish** ladies (H. N. Coleridge 70).

Coleridge, Samuel Taylor (1772–1834): Major Romantic poet and **William Godwin**'s friend; he frequently visited the Godwin home, and eight-year-old Shelley heard him recite *The Rime of the Ancient Mariner* there (Sunstein 40). Shelley frequently alludes to, and bases *Frankenstein*'s frame structure upon, this poem. Shelley knew many of Coleridge's poems by heart, and traces of his works are scattered throughout her own writings—she quotes Coleridge's translation of **Schiller**'s "**The Death of Wallenstein**," mentioning it in *Rambles* (Sunstein 111; LM 142, 265–266; R 2.7). With lines from Coleridge's "Kubla Khan: Or, a Vision in a Dream" (1798), which Shelley read August 1816, **Lionel Verney** records being happy in the **Alps**: "as we sat ... beside the waterfalls, near '—**Forests, ancient as the hills**, / And folding sunny spots of greenery,' where the chamois grazed . . . we were, in an empty world, happy" (*LM* 428; *Journals* 131; Coleridge lines 10–11). Shelley draws epigraphs from "**Fire, Famine, and Slaughter**" and "**Christabel**" in *Perkin Warbeck* and references "Christabel" in *Lodore* (*PW* 1.293, 1.326; *L* 1.171). **Gerard Neville** writes in a letter to **Lady Cecil**, " '**And hooting at** the glorious sun in Heaven, / Cries out, 'Where is it?' " lines taken from Coleridge's "Fears in Solitude . . . Written in April 1798, during the Alarm of an Invasion" (*F* 134; Coleridge lines 85–86). Expressing her belief that certain scenes are indelibly linked with a certain time of life, Shelley shares her memory of Coleridge's remark about **Wordsworth**'s "Her Eyes Are Wild" (*R* 2.78).

Colico: Italian town twenty-five miles northeast of **Como**. Shelley arrived there July 1840 (*R* 1.61).

Coligny: See **Cologny**.

Coliseum: Roman amphitheater started by **Vespasian** 72 C.E. and dedicated by **Titus Domitian** 80 C.E. (*MROM* 46). It housed gladiatorial contests and was also the site for public Christian persecutions; it was dedicated 1750 to the memory of Christian martyrs who perished there (*MROM* 46–47). When the Shelleys first visited Rome in November 1818, they visited the Coliseum each day; Shelley found it "is much finer than I expected—The whole of the ruins do not disappoint in grandeur & beauty but in quantity" (*Journals* 238). **Valerius** finds " 'the Coliseum was a stranger to me' "; he calls it " 'that noble relict of imperial greatness' " and feels it represents Rome (*Val* 335). He haunts the Coliseum, since only there can he find " 'the grandeur of my country' " (*Val* 336, 338). **Giacomo de' Tolomei** and **Marcott Alleyn** visit the Coliseum's highest part (*BMI* 39). **Lionel Verney** finds consolation in "the Coliseum, whose naked ruin is robed by nature in a verdurous and glowing veil" (*LM* 462). The narrator of "**The Sisters of Albano**" observes, "the Coliseum falls and the **Pantheon** decays—the very hills of Rome are perishing" (*SA* 51). The **Villiers**es visit the Coliseum at night, as did the Shelleys; in miserable lodgings in **London**, **Edward Villiers** recalls this visit with joy (*L* 2.202–203, 2.240). Shelley recorded her April 1843 visits there (*R* 2.225–226, 2.228).

Colletta, Pietro (1775–1831): Italian historian and soldier who fought in **Napoleonic** campaigns 1814–15. His *Memoria militare sulla campagna d'Italia dell'anno 1815* [*Military Memoir of the 1815 Italian Campaign*] and *Storia del reame di Napoli dal 1734 al 1825.* [*History of the Kingdom of Naples 1734–1825*] were published posthumously (1834) (Boia 392). Shelley names Colletta one of Italy's great historians and provides a brief biography, specifically referencing *Narrative of the Revolution of Naples in 1820* and *History of the Death of Murat* from the above works (*R* 2.205–209). [*R* 2.164, 2.253].

Colli di Fontanelle: Mountain two miles southeast of **Sorrento**; Shelley spells it **Conti delle Fontanelle** and describes its view of the **Italian** coastline (*R* 2.266).

Cologne: English spelling for **German** city **Köln**, on the **Rhine** fifteen miles northwest of **Bonn**. **Henry Clerval** and **Victor Frankenstein** pass through Cologne, as Shelley did in 1814 (*Fr1* 184; *Fr3* 134; *H* 67, 71). Shelley enjoyed Rhineland scenery between Cologne and **Coblentz** June 1842 (*R* 1.167). [*LM* 88].

Cologny: **Swiss** village on **Lake Geneva** on a hill between **Geneva** and **Belrive**. Shelley wrote *History*'s second letter while at **Maison Chapuis**, near Cologny, June 1816 (*H* 98).

Colonna Gallery: **Roman** art gallery housed in 15th-century **Colonna Palace** on the **Quirinal**, rebuilt 1730 (*MROM* 278–279). Shelley initially visited it November 1818 (*Journals* 238). **Lionel Verney** sleeps in Colonna Palace (*LM* 461, 464). Shelley notes **Raphael**'s *Madonna di Casa Colonna* at the **Berlin** Museum "was once the gem of the Colonna" (*R* 1.220).

Colonna Palace: See **Colonna Gallery**.

Colonna, Vittoria (1492–1547): **Italian** poet. Shelley wrote an accurate biography of Colonna for *Italian and Spanish Lives*. Married for seventeen years, Colonna consistently supported her husband in his military endeavors until he died from battle wounds 1525; Shelley records that "from that time this illustrious lady never ceased to spend every faculty of her soul in lamenting her lost husband" (*ISPL* 2.79). Colonna wrote sonnets in her husband's honor, *Canzoniere* [*Songbook*] (1544), as well as religious and moral sonnets "full of tenderness, of absorbing passion, of truth and life," although Shelley feels they "fail in poetic fancy" (*ISPL* 2.79). Colonna formed close friendships with cardinals and **Michelangelo**, and **Ariosto** addressed stanzas to her in *Orlando Furioso* (37.16–18).

Columbus, Christopher (1451–1506): **Italian** explorer said to have discovered **America** 1492 for **Spanish** rulers **Isabella I** and **Ferdinand**. Shelley refers to an "apocryphal story of Columbus and his egg" (*Fr3* 22). Upon Columbus's return to Spain from his first voyage, a dinner guest suggested that another Spaniard would have discovered the **West Indies** if Columbus had not. Columbus challenged his dinner companions to stand an egg on its end, but no one was able to do so. Columbus slammed an egg onto the table, breaking it but leaving it standing on one end, demonstrating that, once he had shown the way, the challenge became easy (**Irving** 165). Shelley compares **Hernan De Faro** to Columbus (*PW* 1.146, 1.258, 2.26).

Column of Antoninus: Column in **Rome** discovered 1709; its shaft was "a single piece of red granite 48 ft. high" (*MROM* 52). Dedicated to **Marcus Aurelius** 174 C.E., it broke when an attempt was made to lift it out of the ground (*MROM* 52–53). **Valerius** recalls he " 'paused beside the Column of Antoninus, which . . . impressed the idea of decay upon my mind' " (*Val* 335).

Colville, Mr.: *Falkner*'s unemotional but effective solicitor who helps **Rupert Falkner**.

Comasque: **Italian** dialect spoken in the region around **Como**. Shelley mentions hiring an **Italian** teacher for her traveling companions September 1840, but the man she employed lapsed from Italian into Comasque (*R* 1.97).

Combes, Colonel Michel (1787–1839): **French** military commander (*DBF*). Combes and **Captain Gallois** led French troops that defeated **Ancona** February 1832 (*R* 2.255–256).

Commonwealth: Following the English Civil War (1642–48), **Cromwell** established a Commonwealth in England; he was its Lord Protector 1649–58. Shelley refers to **William Godwin** suspending his "history of the Commonwealth he had just begun" (*RD* 43).

Como: Town on the tip of **Lake Como**'s eastern arm in northern **Italy**. The Shelleys visited Como for ten days April 1818 to look for a summer residence, and Shelley revisited the area August 1840 (*Journals* 204, 566). **Guelph** Como is one of many towns that "set up the standard of revolt against the emperor" (*V* 1.144). **Beatrice** flees **Milan** to Como's forest to hide in a leper's dwelling (*V* 2.35). While in **Cadenabbia** July–August 1840, Shelley went to Como for letters and money (*R* 1.64, 1.66–67). [*LM* 434–435; *R* 1.88–89, 2.155].

Como, Lake: Third-largest lake in **Italy**, north of **Milan** near the **Swiss** border. The Shelleys visited it April 1818 (*Journals* 204). **Alphonse** and **Caroline Frankenstein** stay a week there, where Caroline finds and adopts **Elizabeth Lavenza** (*Fr3* 40–41). **Victor Frankenstein** and Elizabeth set off to honeymoon at **Villa Lavenza**, on the lake's shores (*Fr3* 161). **Lionel Verney**, **Adrian**, **Clara**, and **Evelyn** spend summer at the lake and visit many of the sites the Shelleys saw (*LM* 432). Shelley revisited the lake July 1840; she always admired its beauty but feared for herself and **PFS** when sailing on it (*R* 1.77–78). [*R* 2.20].

Compagni, Dino (c. 1260–1324): Florentine historian, politically **Guelph**, who wrote *Cronaca delle cose occorenti ne' tempi suoi* [*Chronicle of Events Which Occurred During His Lifetime*] (1310–12) (*DIL* 258–259). Shelley lists Compagni as a notable **Italian** historian (*R* 2.205).

Comus: **Milton**'s dramatic poem, *Comus: A Masque Presented at Ludlow Castle* (1634). The poem's Lady resists deceptive Comus's entreaties to drink a magic potion that would transform her face into that of a wild beast. **PBS** read part of *Comus* aloud October 1814, and Shelley read it January 1817 (*Journals* 37, 154). **Matilda** evokes the Lady as a companion in her childhood daydreams (*M* 159). Shelley describes **Stephen Frion** as a "man of '**low-thoughted care**,'" a line taken from Thyrsis's speech at *Comus*'s opening (*PW* 2.237; Milton line 6). When the **Villiers**es are alone together in **London**, "there was, besides, '**A sacred and home-felt** delight, / **A sober certainty** of waking bliss,' which is the crown and fulfillment of perfect human happiness"; Shelley had previously used part of the above quotation to describe **Lord Lodore**'s early love for **Lady Lodore** (*L* 1.112, 2.270–271). Comus speaks these lines in response to the Lady's song (Milton lines 262–264).

Conciliatore, Il [The Conciliator]: Periodical started and published by a group of **Italian** Romantic writers 1818–20 (*DIL* 391). Shelley discusses **Italy**'s Romantic literary movement and praises *Il Conciliatore*, to which **Gioja**, **Manzoni**, **Grossi**, **Montani**, **Berchet**, and **Romagnosi** contributed (*R* 2.195–196).

Concressault, Lord of: Scottish Alexander of Menypeny held this title in 1487. **Charles VIII** appoints Concressault head of the guard protecting **Richard of York**, to whom Concressault becomes "warmly attached" (*PW* 1.312, 1.316, 2.256, 2.320).

Condorcet, Marquis Marie Jean Antoine Nicolas Caritat de (1744–1794): **French** figure whose genius was invested in exact sciences, especially mathematics, and produced the *Essai sur la calcul intégral* [*Essay on Integral Calculus*] (1765); it won him a seat in the French Academy of Sciences. He was a leading democratic politician during the **French Revolution**. Shelley wrote Condorcet's biography for *French Lives*. She especially admires his "most celebrated work," the historical sketch *Progrès de l'esprit humain* [*Progress of the Human Spirit*] (1794), which Condorcet wrote in hiding toward his life's end (*FL* 2.190).

Confalonieri, Federico (1785–1846): Count who led **Milanese Carbonari**; he advocated **Lombard** independence in **France** 1814; he was arrested and imprisoned 1824–36 at **Spielberg** with **Pellico** (Holt 58–59; Petronio 2.110–111). Shelley saw "the honoured and noble Confalonieri" return from Spielberg during her 1840 stay at **Como** (*R* 1.121). She mentions Confalonieri supported *Il Conciliatore* (*R* 2.195).

Connaught: Western **Irish** county. **Desmond** advises **Keating** to settle for Connaught rather than **Dublin** (*PW* 3.31).

Conradin (1252–1268): **Manfred**'s nephew and son of Conrad IV, king of **Germany** and **Sicily**; Shelley also calls him **Corradino**. With **Ghibelline** support, Conradin attempted to take Sicily from **Charles of Anjou**, who defeated and then executed him in **Naples** (Trevelyan 114–115). Shelley's "**A Tale of the Passions**" details events in **Florence** that led to Conradin's execution, focusing on **Despina Elisei**, Conradin's fictional staunch supporter (*TP* 22). **Beatrice** points to "the death of the innocent Conradin" as evidence that God is evil (*V* 3.45).

Constance: Mother of Arthur, Duke of Britain in **Shakespeare**'s *King John*. Constance grieves for her son throughout the play. **Matilda** compares herself to Constance when mourning her father and hopes she will not change with grief as Constance did, comparing Constance's binding and unbinding of her hair, an act of control, to her own thoughts of her father and desire to keep them (*M* 186–187; *King John* 4.2.122). Like Constance, Matilda resists madness and wills her own death as a release from the burden of guilt. Shelley notes "women nurse grief— dwell with it. Like poor Constance, they dress their past joys in mourning raiment, and so abide with them" (*PW* 2.138). While traveling the **Brenta** September 1842, Shelley recalled Queen Constance's "passionate grief" (*R* 2.78).

Constance: **Wilhelmina** of **Bohemia** claims to be daughter of Constance, queen of Bohemia (*V* 2.26). Shelley probably refers to 13th-century Constantina, married to Ottocar I and mother of Wenceslas III, both Bohemian kings (Runciman Table VI).

Constantine XI Palaiologos (1405–1453): Christian emperor of **Constantinople** and the Byzantine Empire 1448–53; he lost the empire and his life when **Ottomans** conquered the city (Nicol 70). **Lionel Verney** refers to Constantinople as "where Constantine had died" (*LM* 183).

Constantine, Chief: Greek forces' leader and elder brother of "**Euphrasia**'s" title character. Constantine is another example of Shelley's esteem for Greek bravery and nobility, which she also explores in *The Last Man*. Like **Raymond**, Constantine is to some extent a portrait of **Byron**.

Constantinople: **Turkish** port city south of the Bosporus Straits between the **Black Sea** and **Marmora Sea**, sometimes called **Golden City** in recognition of its magnificence, and now known as **Istanbul** (Coufopoulos 10). Reputedly established 658 B.C.E., several nations alternately besieged, occupied, and destroyed Constantinople in attempts to gain control of its important port; **Constantine I the Great** established the city 328 C.E. as the Byzantium Empire's capital, and the **Ottomans** conquered it 1453 (Coufopoulos 5–9, 18–19). The city comprises three distinct areas: **Stamboul** (the oldest section) and **Galatea-Pera** are on the **European** shore, divided by the **Golden Horn** from **Scutari** on the **Asian** shore (Coufopoulos 1). In Shelley's time, Constantinople was a focal city in the Ottoman Empire, and merchants there supported **Greece** in its war for independence. Shelley anxiously followed events in Constantinople and Turkish reprisals against Greeks (*Letters* 1.198–200). **Safie** travels from Constantinople to join her father in **Paris**, and he subsequently leaves **Leghorn** for Constantinople (*Fr1* 150, 154; *Fr3* 107, 110). **Euthanasia** pleads with **Castruccio** not to keep fighting, suggesting "purple-clad emperors of Constantinople may envy your state and power" if he can conquer his pride, ambition, and cruelty (*V* 2.161). **Raymond** declares " 'my first act when I become King of England, will be to unite with the Greeks, take Constantinople, and subdue all Asia,' " and much of Greece's war with Turkey detailed in *The Last Man*'s first volume hinges on Constantinople (*LM* 57). **Evadne Zaimi** lives there (*LM* 111). **Lionel Verney** joins Raymond and the Greek army in a siege of Constantinople despite **Perdita**'s fears about plague's rumored presence there; Raymond dies alone in Constantinople (*LM* 161, 175–177, 198–201, 206). **Ka-**

tusthius **Ziani** works in Constantinople after his escape from the **Barbary** pirate (*EE* 102). **Rupert Falkner** and **Elizabeth Falkner** spend winter there with **Miss Jervis** (*F* 33, 38, 43). Shelley observes treasures from Constantinople have disappeared from **Venice**'s **San Marco** (*R* 2.122). [*TP* 7; *LM* 183, 195, 202, 469; *R* 2.281].

Conti delle Fontanelle: See **Colli di Fontanelle**.

Cooke, Mr.: In "The Mourner," sexton of **Old Windsor**'s churchyard, where **Ellen Burnet** is buried.

Coollong: **Desmond** and **Barry** plan to "take Coollong from **Clan Cartie Reagh**" (*PW* 1.306). Shelley could be referring to the ruin Cúl Collainge, formerly a monastic community, about fifteen miles northwest of **Cork** (*MIIR*).

Cooper, James Fenimore (1789–1851): **American** novelist best known for *The Last of the Mohicans* (1826). Shelley read several of Cooper's works and identifies him as author of *The Spy* (1821) (Sunstein 266–267; *R* 2.266). Shelley's **Review of** *The Bravo; a Venetian Story* (1831) appeared in 16 January 1832 *Westminster Review*. Shelley characterizes Cooper's writing as "founded upon one plan.... [H]is best tales narrate an escape and a pursuit, either complicated or single" (*RevB* 184). Shelley elaborates upon her high opinion of **Sorrentines** by noting that Cooper also esteemed them; she footnotes a passage from his *Excursions in Italy* (1838) to strengthen her comparison of **Salerno** to **Switzerland** (*R* 2.274, 2.292).

Cooper, Lawrence: Minor character in "The Parvenue."

Copêt: See **Côppet**.

Côppet: **Swiss** village at **Lake Geneva**'s western end between Nyon and Versoix; Shelley spells it **Copêt**. **William Frankenstein**'s "funeral dirge" is a violent storm over Lake Geneva between **Belrive** and Côppet (*Fr1* 104; *Fr3* 72).

Corinna: Poet-heroine of **Madame de Staël**'s *Corinne, ou l'Italie* [*Corinne, or Italy*] (1807). Shelley read *Corinne* 1815, 1818, and 1820 (*Journals* 66–67, 243, 340). Mirroring a chapter in de Staël's novel in which Lord Oswald Nelvil hears Corinne speak before she ascends the **Capitol**'s steps to be crowned with myrtle in recognition of her poetic talents, **Lionel Verney** imagines "Corinna ascending the Capitol to be crowned" in **Rome** (*LM* 462; de Staël 30–32). Shelley asserts "the soul of our modern Corinna would have been purified and exalted by a consciousness that once it had given life to the form of **Sappho**" (*RD* 49).

Corinth: Ancient town where the eastern end of the **Peloponnese** connects to mainland **Greece**; the most elaborate of the three orders of Greek architecture is Corinthian, generally characterized by a fluted column and capital elegantly crafted with leaves. **Lionel Verney** prepares to leave England forever and bids farewell to "the fluted column with its capital, Corinthian, **Ionic**, or **Doric**" (*LM* 321). In

Rome, Verney sees "broken capitals—Corinthian and Ionic" (*LM* 461). A rich Corinthian merchant raises **Katusthius Ziani**, and **Cyril Ziani** is "beloved and respected" in Corinth, near which he makes his home and from where **Dmitri** abducts **Constans Ziani** (*EE* 102–103, 108). Shelley terms **Lord Lodore** "a Corinthian column" (*L* 1.27). See **Burke**.

Coriolanus, Gnaeus Marcius: Legendary 5th-century B.C.E. **Roman** soldier whom **Plutarch** describes in his *Lives*. After losing election to consul and being accused of treason, the tribunal banished Coriolanus from Rome. He then helped the Volscians attack Rome but later withdrew at his mother's request and died at the Volscians' hands (Plutarch, *Lives* 1.327–362). **Shakespeare** based *The Tragedy of Coriolanus* (1609–1608) on Plutarch's historical account; Shelley read this play July 1818 (*Journals* 218). **Guido il Cortese** plans to be "a new Coriolanus" when he returns from banishment to defeat **Marchese Torella** (*Trans* 126).

Cork: County and port on Cork Harbor in southern **Ireland** near St. George's Channel. **Castruccio** crosses from **Bristol** to Cork to reach **Dublin** (*V* 1.76, 1.79). **Richard of York** voyages to Cork several times in order to regroup and find additional support. Cork's mayors, **John O'Water** and **John Lavallan**, and **Baron of Buttevant**, are Richard's friends (*PW* 1.229, 1.278–280). Richard stays there until a **French** embassy invites him to **Paris** (*PW* 1.308). He returns after a disappointing defeat on **Kent**'s coast (*PW* 2.175, 2.178, 3.26).

Cornaro, Catherine (1454–1510): **Venetian** noble who was **Queen of Cyprus** 1472–89. Shelley admires a painting of the queen abdicating in the **Doge's Palace** (*R* 2.85).

Corneille, Pierre (1606–1684): Widely regarded as the father of **French** tragedy. He staged many successful dramas in **Paris**; *Le Menteur* [*The Liar*] (1642) ensured his high standing in the French comedic tradition. Perhaps his best-remembered work is *Le Cid* (1636), the success of which, with other works, resulted in his 1647 election to the French academy; Shelley first read it June 1818, when she also read Corneille's *Horace* (1639), *Cinna* (1639), and the tragedy *Polyeucte* (1640) (*Journals* 213). Shelley wrote Corneille's biography for *French Lives*. She notes a certain narrowness of taste in Corneille's work and provides an account of his many dramatic successes during his lifetime. She asserts that "Corneille, in heroic verse and majestic situation, impart[s] a dignity and simplicity to the French drama" (*FL* 1.40).

Cornish: See **Cornwall**.

Cornwall: Coastal county on England's southwestern tip; its people are Cornish. **Richard of York** learns of rebellion in Cornwall while at **James IV**'s court (*PW* 2.261–262). **Lord Audley** and **Monina De Faro** lead Cornish people toward **London**, but they are "defeated on **Blackheath**" (*PW* 2.297–298). **Hernan De Faro** subsequently helps Richard and his followers escape from Ireland to Cornwall, where Monina raises support for Richard's cause (*PW* 3.56, 3.62, 3.106, 3.120–121). The **Harding** family lives "at the extreme point of Cornwall" (*S* 203). **Rupert Falkner** arrives in Cornwall with the intention of killing himself (*F* 5). **Edward John Trelawny** was Cornish, and tales of his early life may have influenced Shelley's accounts. [*PW* 3.63, 3.73, 3.171].

Cornwall, Barry: See **Procter**.

Corradino: See **Conradin**.

Correggio, Allegri Antonio (c. 1489–1534): Greatest northern **Italian** painter of early 16th century (Turner 7.885). He painted *Io* (c. 1526–30), based on the **Greek** mythological daughter of Ianchus and Melia who was transformed into a cow (Tripp 319; Schmeckebier 515). Shelley saw this "most lovely picture" at **Berlin**'s **New Museum** 1842 (*R* 1.220). She also saw *Leda and the Swan* (c. 1526–30) and enjoyed his "charming *Madonna*" in the **Uffizi**; it is Correggio's *The Virgin Adoring the Child* (c. 1522) (Schmeckebier 515; *R* 1.220, 2.154). In August 1842, Shelley viewed Correggio's *La Notte* (1530), his famous painting of Jesus's birth (Vasari 3.30; *R* 1.244). See *The Magdalen*. [*PW* 1.8].

Corsair: A Tale, The: Poem **Byron** wrote 1813–14; it had "amazing success" upon its 1814 publication (Marchand 1.433). Shelley read it February 1818 (*Journals* 192). As the first epigraph to the *Perkin Warbeck* chapter in which **Stephen Frion** captures **Richard of York** in **Sire de Beverem**'s house, Shelley accurately quotes, "In the high chamber of his highest tower / Sate Conrad, fettered in the Pasha's power" (*PW* 1.158; Byron 2.366–367).

Corsica: French island in the **Mediterranean**, north of Sardinia, and **Napoleon**'s birthplace. **Genoa** ruled it 14th–18th centuries. Shelley heard that **PBS** and **Edward Williams**'s boat may "have been driven over to Corsica" when it disappeared 1822 (*Letters* 1.248). **Euthanasia**'s ship meets one from **Pisa** that warns of a Genoese squadron sailing off Corsica's shore (*V* 3.260). Shelley notes that there were **Carbonari** in Corsica (*R* 2.169). She viewed "the shadowy form of distant Corsica" from the *Castor* 1843 (*R* 2.213).

Corso: On the **Tiber**'s western bank, this "main street of **Rome**" is about a mile long and runs roughly north-south (*MROM* 2). Named for the Carnival "corse" or races that were run there, in Shelley's day it was a busy and fashionable **boulevard**. The Shelleys lived at **Palazzo Verosposi** on the Corso 1819 (*Journals* 251). **Valerius** passes "along the Corso" (*Val* 335). **Marcott Alleyn** chooses the Corso to "walk that he might get rid of" troubling thoughts (*BMI* 38, 41). **Lionel Verney** finds "the long extent of the Corso" astonishing (*LM* 460). Shelley compares the "wide drive on the walls of" **Milan** to Rome's Corso (*R* 1.118).

Cortona: Italian city fifteen miles southeast of **Arezzo**. Shelley mentions it as **Casentino**'s capital (*R* 2.138).

Cosimo I [de' Medici] (1519–1574): Named second duke of **Florence** 1537 and first grand duke of **Tuscany** 1569; Cosimo built the **Uffizi**. Shelley describes Uffizi's art and mentions portrait copies painted by **Cristofaro dell' Altissimo**, whom Cosimo hired (R 2.155–56).

Cossacks: People who settled on the **Russian** frontier and became a sort of border guard; Shelley spells it **Cossacs**. From the 15th and 16th centuries, Cossacks lived in military outposts and received special privileges in exchange for military service. Shelley guesses that, for revenge, Cossacks "entirely desolated" **Nogent** during the **Napoleonic** Wars: "perhaps they remembered **Moscow** and the destruction of the Russian villages" (H 19). Cossacks took all of **St. Aubin**'s cows, which prevented the Shelleys from procuring milk when they visited August 1814 (*Journals* 12; H 20). Shelley notes **Echemines**'s people would not rebuild their houses for fear that Cossacks would again destroy them (H 24).

Cossacs: See **Cossacks**.

Côte d'Or: Southwest-facing ridge beginning just southeast of **Paris** and crossing the **Jura** into **Switzerland**. The Shelleys returned to England on this route from Switzerland to Paris 1816 and found the scenery impressive (*Journals* 132). **Lionel Verney** leads a party of men from Paris, taking the Côte d'Or road (LM 396).

Council of Basle: See **Basle**.

Council of Ten: Established 1310 in **Venice** to defend the existing patrician political régime. Shelley describes the Council's room at the **Doge's Palace** as "peculiarly impressive in its aspect and decorations" (R 2.86).

Council of Trent: See **Trent**.

Count ——: Acquaintance Shelley made in **Venice** through Laura Galloni's introductory letter, not further identified (Moskal 270; *Letters* 3.40; Sunstein 358; R 2.79–80).

Coupar: See **Cupar**.

Courcy, de: Important **Irish** family related to **Desmond** by marriage in *Perkin Warbeck*. Lord James Courcy was allied to Desmond through fealty or marriage (Arthurson 106).

Courland: **Russia** captured this independent duchy 1795; it is now a western Latvian region (Kinder 1.163, 1.249, 2.131). **Lord Lodore** visited Courland as a youth (L 1.90–91).

Courtney, Sir John: **Heron**'s new name in *Perkin Warbeck*. Courtney defended **Exeter** against **Perkin Warbeck** (Fischer 295; Arthurson 185).

Courtney, William (d. 1512): Courtney defends **Exeter** against **Richard of York**, a historically accurate account (*PW* 3.102; Arthurson 185; Fischer 295).

Coutts' *lettre d'indication*: Financial credit letter, also termed circular note, that travelers commonly used; **Murray** recommends those that Coutts and Company offered (*MCON* xvi). Shelley used them during her travels (*R* 2.76).

Coventry: English city eighty miles northwest of **London**. "To send someone to Coventry" is to isolate them socially, a phrase originating from England's Civil War (1642–48) when royalists were sent to Coventry, a **Parliamentary** stronghold, for punishment. **Perdita** jokingly warns **Clara** she is not to interrupt happiness at **Windsor** by recalling the immediate past: " 'remember any one that mentions **London** is sent to Coventry for an hour' " (*LM* 138).

Cowper, William (1731–1800): British poet best known for "The Task" (1785). Many of his poems deal with the isolated individual in relation to God's mysterious ways; they express a love for nature and evince a gentle wit. **Matilda** discovers his poems in her aunt's library (*M* 158). See "**Essay on Man.**"

Craycroft: A gentleman at the opera informs **Lady Lodore** that "young Craycroft has seen [the **Villiers**es] riding together perpetually in **Richmond Park**" (*L* 2.120).

Creature: The being **Victor Frankenstein** creates (from human body parts found in charnel houses), brings to life, and then abandons (*Fr1* 82–83, 85, 87; *Fr3* 55–59). Victor refers to him as "creature," "wretch," "devil," "demon," "abortion," and "monster." He is Victor's double and acts out that part of himself that Victor represses. He is also, in some ways, Shelley's view of her own artistic creation, which she calls "my hideous progeny" (*Fr3* 23). In other ways, he represents those marginalized in society by race, gender, or economic status.

Crécy: French village fifty miles south of **Calais**; also reference to a battle of the Hundred Years' War in which **Edward III** defeated the French (1346) (Cannon 258–259). Shelley spells it **Cressy**. **Richard of York** inspires supporters by reminding them of how few English troops it took to defeat the French there (*PW* 3.17).

Crema: Italian town twenty-five miles southeast of **Milan**. It rebels against but later submits to **Henry VII** of **Germany** (*V* 1.144).

Cremona: Italian city forty miles southeast of **Milan**. **Benedetto Pepi** is from Cremona, which joins **Guelph** towns revolting against **Henry VII** of **Germany** (*V* 1.115, 1.122, 1.129, 1.144). Henry besieges Cremona until its surrender, 20 April 1311 (*V* 1.145; Villani 401). He punishes innocent citizens, razes the walls, and allows German mercenaries to plunder the city (*V* 1.145). Shelley is historically correct to place **Castruccio** in Cremona with Henry at this time (Green 46). Pepi wants to be Cremona's lord and reveals his plan to Castruccio, who is appalled, threatens Pepi, and leaves Cremona (*V* 2.106, 2.112). Pepi later dies attempting to aid **Cane della Scala**'s invasion of Cremona around 1317 (*V* 2.117, 2.120). [*V* 1.145–148, 1.278, 2.101, 2.105; *R* 1.79].

Cremona, Bishop of: See **Sforza**.

Cressenor, Thomas: Lord **Fitzwater**'s steward and **Yorkist** supporter, arrested at the 1493 conspiratorial meeting at **Robert Clifford**'s house (Arthurson 75; *PW* 2.50; Holinshed 3.507).

Cressida: See *Troilus and Cressida*.

Cressy: See **Crécy**.

Crete: Large **Mediterranean** island southeast of **Greece**. **Ino** suggests Crete cannot rival the beauty of **Ceres**'s lands (*P* 45). Shelley compares activity at **Amalfi**'s port to Crete's (*R* 2.289).

Cristo della Moneta: See **Titian**.

Cristofero, Father: See *Promessi Sposi*.

Critic, The: See **Sheridan**.

Cromwell, Oliver (1599–1658): **Parliamentary** army leader during the English Civil War (1642–48); his forces defeated the Royalists and executed **Charles I** 1649. Cromwell established a **Commonwealth** with himself as Lord Protector. Cromwell's régime was a strict Puritan dictatorship. It dissolved with his death, and the monarchy was restored (1660). **Raymond** compares his ambition to be king to that of "Cromwell, the puritan and king-killer, [who] aspired to regality" (*LM* 56). **Roger Dodsworth** "was lost to the world when Oliver Cromwell had arrived at the summit of his ambition" (*RD* 44–45).

Crook-back: See **Richard III**.

Cubières, General: See **Despans de Cubières**.

Cumaean Sibyl: In **Roman** mythology, **Apollo**'s prophetess, who gave the gods' prophecies in the form of riddles to those who sought them, "who acted as Aeneas' guide to the Underworld and, during her thousand years of life, wrote down the oracles contained in the **Sibylline** Books that were preserved in the Roman temple of **Capitoline Jupiter**" (Tripp 530). **PBS** read aloud from **Virgil**'s *Aeneid*, which recounts the myth, during 1820 (*Journals* 681; *Aeneid* 6.85–87). The Shelleys visited various sites near **Naples** December 1818 but did not go to the nearby subterranean temple at Cumae that was supposedly the sibyl's (*Journals* 242). *The Last Man*'s narrator does visit this temple, which Shelley imagines as a natural cave on **Avernus**'s banks; it contains the leaves on which is written the story told in the novel (*LM* 3).

Cumberland: See **Cumbria**.

Cumberland, Richard (1732–1811): British novelist and playwright renowned for sentimental comedies, such as *The Brothers* (1769), *The West Indian* (1771), and *The Wheel of Fortune* (1795). **Sheridan** caricatured him in *The Critic*. Shelley read Cumberland's *Memoirs of Richard Cumberland. Written by himself* (1806–1807) January 1817 (*Journals* 154). "**The Swiss Peasant**'s" narrator describes a dark cliff as "the turf stack or old wall that bounded Cumberland's view as he wrote the

'Wheel of Fortune' " (*SP* 136). Shelley's reference comes from Cumberland's memoirs: "With . . . nothing but the turf-stack to call off my attention, I took the character of an **Irishman** and **West Indian** for the heroes of my plot" (Cumberland 1.274). Cumberland describes his creative strategy for writing *The West Indian* (1771), not *The Wheel of Fortune* as Shelley states; however, Shelley's reference to this play is appropriate, because *The Wheel of Fortune* explores social problems similar to those in her story.

Cumbria: Northwestern English county bordering Scotland and including the Lake District and **Carlisle**, formerly called **Westmoreland** or **Cumberland**. **Victor Frankenstein** and **Henry Clerval** spend time there (*Fr1* 186, 188; *Fr3* 135, 137). **Lionel** and **Perdita Verney** grow up in Cumbria, where they first encounter **Adrian** (*LM* 11, 35). Lionel swears by " 'the fells of Cumberland' " and remembers his wild childhood there with great affection (*LM* 178). Cumberland is **Dromore**'s location, to which **Alithea Neville** retires (*F* 102). After meeting **Oswi Raby**, **Rupert Falkner** visits Cumbria's Lake District (*F* 153).

Cupar: Scottish riverport, seven miles inland from **St. Andrews**; Shelley spells it **Coupar**. **Henry Clerval** and **Victor Frankenstein** pass through it (*Fr1* 189; *Fr3* 138).

Cupid: **Aphrodite**'s son and **Roman** mythological archer whose arrows make people fall in love. Cupid himself loved **Psyche**, an earthly king's beautiful daughter. Claiming her in marriage, he refused to reveal his identity, recognizing his transgression in loving her; she promised not to look at him but eventually used a lamp to see him sleeping. She accidentally dropped oil upon him; after he awoke and departed, Psyche had to fulfill a series of tasks set by angry Aphrodite. The lovers eventually reunited, and Psyche became immortal. Shelley translated about half of an **Italian** copy of Lucius Apuleius's version of this tale in his *The Golden Ass* (2nd century C.E.) (*Journals* 169, 234). **Matilda** compares her initial delight in her idealized relationship with her father to that of the lovers prior to Psyche's discovery of Cupid's identity (*M* 163). A castle **Valperga** ceiling exhibits a scene of "**Venus** and her Cupids" (*V* 1.184). **Lionel Verney** "pressed the unconceiving marble" of a Cupid and Psyche statue (*LM* 465). In "**Stanzas: O, come to me in Dreams**," Shelley's speaker compares herself to Psyche and insists "gentle sleep shall veil my sight" so she will not see her lover and thus lose him as Psyche did (*Stanzas: O come* lines 9–10). Shelley admired **Canova**'s *Cupid and Psyche* at **Villa Sommariva** (*R* 1.92). She asserts that **Farnesina**'s "frescos of the history of Psyche" are fine examples of **Raphael**'s later work (*R* 2.223). [*PW* 2.6; *R* 2.230].

Cupid and Psyche: Sculpture displayed in the room containing *Venus of the Capitol* at **Rome**'s **Capitol**'s Museum (*MROM* 260). Shelley viewed it April 1842 (*R* 2.230).

Curious Traveller: See **Sterne**.

Curius Dentatus Manius (3rd century B.C.E.): Roman consul famous for severity; **Plutarch** describes him in "Life of **Marcus Cato**" (Plutarch, *Lives* 1.517; Howatson 162). Curius defeated the **Sabines** and Samnites 290 B.C.E.: "ambassadors of the Samnites, finding [Curius] boiling turnips . . . offered him a present of gold; but he sent them away" (Plutarch, *Lives* 1.517). **Lionel Verney** compares himself to Curius when **Adrian** and **Idris** visit him as he is "feasting on sorry fruits for supper; but they brought gifts richer than the golden bribes of the Sabines, nor could I refuse the invaluable store of friendship and delight which they bestowed" (*LM* 79).

Curran, Amelia (1775–1847): The Shelleys knew John Philpot Curran (1750–1817) through his friendship with **William Godwin** and had met Curran's daughter Amelia in **London** 1813 (Sunstein 58, 73–74; *Journals* 170). While living in **Rome** April 1819, the Shelleys moved next door to Amelia, who was living independently while studying art (Sunstein 166; *Journals* 261–265). Amelia and Shelley became intimate friends April–May 1819, during which time Amelia painted portraits of **Claire Clairmont**, both Shelleys, and **William Shelley** just before his sudden death (*Journals* 261; Sunstein 166; White 2.90–91). Shelley wrote to Amelia frequently, telling her, "I wish all the people that we depend upon were as good as you are" (*Letters* 1.106). Amelia planned to visit the Shelleys in **Pisa** May 1821, although Shelley subsequently excused herself from the obligation, fearing that Amelia's malaria could pass to **PBS**, but Shelley continued an intimate correspondence with Amelia 1819–25 (Sunstein 198; *Journals* 366; *Letters* 1.100, 1.461). Amelia sent PBS's portrait to Shelley September 1825; Shelley's *Letters* and *Journals* provide details of their continued correspondence. When Shelley returned to Rome March 1843, she stayed for two months at the house Amelia occupied 1819 (*Journals* 496–497; Sunstein 359; *Letters* 3.62).

Custine, Astolphe Marquis de (1790–1857): French nobleman whose most widely read book is *La Russie en 1839* [*Russia in 1839*] (1843) (France 216; Warner 127). Shelley compares **Italian** readers to British and French audiences; Custine describes the latter as " 'les concierges et les forcats' " ("gossips and convicted criminals"); Moskal believes the quotation comes from Custine's *Russia* (*R* 2.190; Moskal 328).

Custom of the Country, The: Drama **Beaumont** and **Fletcher** published 1647. Shelley quotes from Leopold's address to Hippolyta as an epigraph to *Lodore*'s chapter in which **Edward Villiers** falls in love with **Ethel Villiers**: "Excellent creature! whose perfections make / Even sorrow lovely!" (*L* 2.1; *Custom* 3.4.14–15). As an epigraph to the chapter in which the Villierses rejoice in each other's company, Shelley quotes from Zabulon's speech to Arnoldo: "**Do you not think** yourself truly happy? / You have the abstract of all sweetness by you, / The precious wealth youth labours to arrive at, / Nor is she less in honour than in beauty" (*L* 2.275; *Custom* 3.2.74–77).

Cybele

Cybele: **Roman** name for Rhea, mother of **Zeus** and other **Greek** mythological gods. In artistic representations, Cybele wears a crown "shaped like a turreted city wall" (Tripp 180). **Edmund Malville** describes **Venice** seen from **Fusina** as "crowning the sea with Cybele's diadem" (*RI* 26).

Cyclades: Group of **Greek** islands in the **Aegean**, south of the mainland. **Lionel Verney**, **Adrian**, and **Clara** plan to live "on one of the Cyclades" (*LM* 441). Sailing from **Rome**, Verney plans to pass through the Cyclades (*LM* 469).

Cyclopes: Mythological monster with an eye in the middle of its forehead who helped **Zeus** make thunderbolts in his war against the **Titans**; the term "Cyclopean" also applies to immense masonry (Tripp 181). **Midas** expects his golden touch to win "Cyclopean Powers" so he can compete with gods (*Midas* 129). **Edmund Malville** gently mocks travelers to **Italy** who naively expect " 'to find gorgeous temples and Cyclopean ruins in every street in **Florence**' " (*RI* 27). **Gerard Neville** sees mountains looming over the landscape of his mother's grave as Cyclopes's eyes (*F* 227). At an iron foundry Shelley visited in **Berlin**, she saw "diminuitive Cyclops pour the glowing living liquid from their cauldron" (*R* 1.229). See **Polyphemus**.

"Cyclops: A Satiric Drama, The": **PBS**'s 1819 translation of Euripides's **Greek** text (c. 5th century B.C.E.), which was a favorite of **PFS** (Holmes 612). **Lionel Verney** quotes a line the Chorus speaks as **Ulysses** prepares to meet **Bacchus** in PBS's text: " 'Speak!— What door is opened?' " (*LM* 37–38; PBS line 503). As the second epigraph to the *Perkin Warbeck* chapter in which **Richard of York** befriends **Robert Clifford**, Shelley quotes: "**And then, with you**, my friends, and the old man, / We'll load the hollow depth of our black ship, / And row with double strokes from this dread shore" (*PW* 1.179; PBS lines 466–468).

Cydnus: Southeastern **Asia** Minor river north of **Cyprus**, now part of eastern **Turkey**. Shelley notes that **Lady Katherine Gordon**'s contentment en route from Scotland to **Ireland** is similar to **Cleopatra**'s when she sailed the Cydnus (*PW* 3.21). Shelley compares "Cleopatra on the Cydnus" to **Ethel Villiers** (*L* 2.276; *Antony and Cleopatra* 2.2.196–97, 201). See *Antony and Cleopatra*.

Cymbeline: **Shakespeare**'s drama, first produced 1610 and published 1623; **PBS** read it aloud October 1818 (*Journals* 229). Looking across the **English Channel** from **Boulogne**, **Lionel Verney** quotes Imogen's line bemoaning her husband's scheme (which has resulted in her need to disguise herself and flee her native country) in observing that England "lay on the ocean plain, 'In the great pool a swan's nest.' Ruined the nest, alas!" (*LM* 378; *Cymbeline* 3.4.137–140).

Cymmerian: See **Cimmerian**.

Cyprus: Northeastern **Mediterranean** island reputed to be **Aphrodite**'s principal dwelling place. **Ranieri della Faggiuola** offers **Castruccio** a "cup of generous Cyprus" (wine) during a meal (*V* 1.224). **Proserpine** asks **Ino** to entertain her with a song of myths the goddess told in Cyprus (*P* 33).

Cyprus, Queen of: See **Cornaro**.

D

D——: A **Cantab**, identified only as D——, joined Shelley's party in **Cadenabbia** July 1840 for two to three weeks (*R* 1.76). Moskal suggests that D—— may be **Ellis** (113).

D——, Countess Atanasia: Narrator of "**The Sisters of Albano**."

D——, Earl of: **Lewis Elmore**'s father in "**The Mourner**." Minor *Lodore* character.

d'Aubigny, William: See **Daubeney, William**.

d'Ayala, Don Pedro: Shelley accurately places this **Spanish** ambassador in Scotland (visited 1496 and 1497) when **James IV** invades England in *Perkin Warbeck* (Arthurson 131–132, 142, 156).

d'Azeglio, Massimo Taparelli (1798–1866): Italian writer renowned for historical novels; Shelley calls him **Azeglio**. *Ettore Fieramosca o la sfida di Barletta* [*Ettore Fieramosca, or the Challenge of Barletta*] (1833) details the love affair between an Italian knight and Ginevra, a married woman. His second novel, ***Niccolò de' Lapi***: *ovvero, I Palleschi e I Piagnoni* [*Niccolò dei Lapi; or, The Last Days of the Florentine Republic*] (1841), describes the siege of **Florence** (*DIL* 155–157). Shelley ranks d'Azeglio as the highest romance writer imitating **Petrarch**, praising *Ettore Fieramosca* and *Niccolò de' Lapi* particularly (*R* 2.201).

d'Hilliers, Baraguay: **French** commander who led a six-thousand-man force against the **Tyrolese** 24 April 1809 (Alison 3.228). Shelley mentions he treated **Hofer** with courtesy and kindness at **Botzen** (*R* 2.58).

Dacre, Lord: Mentioned in *Perkin Warbeck* as **Randal of Dacre**'s brother. Lord Thomas Dacre supported **Perkin Warbeck** (Arthurson 134).

Dacre, Randal of: Richard of York's supporter in *Perkin Warbeck*; perhaps based on Ranulf, **Lord Dacre**'s brother (Arthurson 134).

Daedalus: **Athenian** inventor and artisan whom King Minos's wife, Pasiphae, commissioned to make a hollow cow, in which she hid to mate with a bull she loved. She gave birth to the **Minotaur**, and Daedalus then had to build a labyrinth to hide the beast and the king's shame. Daedalus helped **Ariadne** assist **Theseus** escape the labyrinth by tying the end of a thread to the entrance and paying it out along his route, so that it could be retraced. **Raymond** asserts: "Daedalus never wound so inextricable an error round Minotaur, as madness has woven about [**Adrian**'s] imprisoned reason" (*LM* 70).

Dalston: Hamlet two miles northeast of **London**; **Charles Lamb** lived there 1816, 1820, 1822, and 1823 (Prance 86). Shelley compares the **Terrace of Brühl** to Lamb's retreat there (*R* 1.246).

Damascus: **Syria**'s capital, famous for its steel and, particularly, sword blades (*OED*; Crook 2). **Lionel Verney** bids farewell to **London**, including "farewell to crowded senate . . . whose laws were keener than the sword blade tempered at Damascus!" (*LM* 321).

Dame Blanche, La: See **Boieldieu**.

Dan Apollo: See **Gaspar de Vaudemont**.

Dan Cadmus: See **Cadmus, Dan**.

Dandolo, Cenone: Member of **Venetian** noble family, also spelled **Daulo**. Shelley cites Dandolo's assistance constructing **Rivo Alto** 421 C.E. as evidence of Venetian nobility's descent from **Roman** families (*R* 2.114).

Dangle: See **Sheridan**.

Dannecker, Johann Heinrich von (1758–1841): **German** sculptor renowned for busts of **Goethe** and **Schiller** and for *Ariadne on a Panther* (1803) (Myers 2.209). Shelley admired *Ariadne* June 1842 at **Frankfurt**'s **Bethmann**'s **Gallery** (*R* 1.176).

Dante Alighieri (1265–1321): **Italian** poet whose most famous work is *Divina Commedia* [*Divine Comedy*] (first translated into English 1719), in three sections—the *Inferno*, *Purgatorio*, and *Paradiso*. **Victor Frankenstein** describes the **Creature**'s appearance as so hideous that "it became a thing such as even Dante could not have conceived" (*Fr1* 87; *Fr3* 59). Shelley was reading *Purgatorio* August 1819 as she started to write *Matilda*; female characters in both works share the same name, and Shelley quotes *Purgatorio* and *Paradiso* (*Journals* 294; *M* 158, 178, 198, 205). Shelley describes **Euthanasia**'s countenance with lines beginning " '**Quel, ch'ella** par quando un poco sorride,' " noting them as from Dante's *Vita Nuova* (1290–94), which she read 1821; **PBS** translated and adapted this verse 1815 (*V* 3.245; *Journals* 351–353). Shelley takes these lines from the conclusion of *Vita Nuova*'s twenty-first sonnet, beginning "Ne li occhi," which translates to "What Mary is when she a little smiles / I cannot even tell or call to mind, / It is a miracle, so new, so rare" (Crook 3.316; *Vita Nuova* lines 12–14). Shelley mentions *Vita Nuova* in her description of Dante's portrait (*R* 2.158). Shelley describes **Roger Dodsworth** as "a party, if to be of no party admits such a term, which Dante recommends us utterly to despise" (*RD* 45). **Edward Villiers** compares his poverty in **London** and Dante's characters, suggesting that "it is the present only which is so thorny, so worse than barren: like the souls of Dante, we have a fiery pass to get through before we reach our place of bliss" (*L* 2.240). In *Rambles*, Shelley refers to individual books of *Divina Commedia* and acknowledges that her affection for Italy is, in part, due to its being Dante's country; she states that Dante's work provided inspiration for **Florentine** painters (*R* 1.87, 2.91). At **Cadenabbia** September 1840, Shelley delighted to read Dante again (*R* 1.96). Shelley describes Dante as "greatest of all" Italian writers, and she viewed **Giotto**'s portrait of Dante in the **Tribune** 1843 (*R* 2.191, 2.158). Shelley notes **Manzoni** "read and admired Dante, with the deep-felt enthusiasm a poet naturally experiences for that sublime writer"; she also notes that **Raphael** "boldly placed Dante, with his laurel crown" in *Dispute of the Sacrament* (*R* 2.200, 2.220).

Dantzig, Duke of: See **Lefebvre**.

Danube: River flowing across central southeastern **Europe** from **Germany** to the **Black Sea**. Shelley viewed it upon entering **Linz** September 1842 (*R* 2.20).

Daphne: In **Greek** mythology, Daphne fled **Apollo**'s advances and prayed to earth goddess Ge for assistance; Ge turned her into a laurel tree, from which Apollo tore off a branch to wear on his head (Tripp 190). **Proserpine** asks her mother to tell her "of Daphne's change,—/ That coyest Grecian maid, whose pointed leaves / Now shade her lover's brow" (*P* 29, 31).

Daraxa: In *Perkin Warbeck*, **Richard of York**'s horse in **Spain**.

Darford: See **Dartford**.

Darmstadt: German city thirty-one miles north of **Heidelberg**. Shelley passed through Darmstadt July 1840 (*R* 1.33).

Dartford: Town (spelled **Darford** in the first edition of *The Last Man*) fifteen miles southeast of **London** on the main road to **Dover**; Shelley probably passed through it en route to **Italy** 1818. **Perdita** waits in Dartford to hear whether **Raymond** won election as Lord Protector (*LM* 103). Plague survivors leave England via Dartford (*LM* 353).

Darwin, Erasmus [Dr.] (1731–1802): English botanist and poet whose most famous work, *The Botanic Garden* (1791), set forth a heretical theory of creation and whose "Loves of the Plants," within that larger work, eroticized flora; his writings influenced **PBS** (White 1.147). His scientific botanical studies and his poems were widely read, but also criticized. PBS mentions "the event on which [*Frankenstein*] is founded has been supposed, by Dr.

Darwin, and some of the physiological writers of **Germany**, as not of impossible occurrence" (*Fr1* 47; *Fr3* 24). **Woodville** aligns himself with Darwin in refusing to adhere "to the objections of those petty cavillers and minor critics who wish to reduce all men to their own miserable level" (*M* 192).

Datchet: Village on the **Thames**, two miles east of **Eton**. **Lionel Verney** recounts the tale of an "aged grandmother of one of our servants" who goes to Datchet in search of food when all the village's inhabitants have died from plague (*LM* 287). **Lucy Martin** lives there (*LM* 362–364).

Daubeney, Giles (d. 1508): William Daubeney's son; he commanded the army at **Blackheath** 1497 (*DNB*). Called **Lord Dawbeny** in *Perkin Warbeck*, he advises **Henry VII** and is present at **Lord Stanley**'s interrogation.

Daubeney, William: Also referred to as **d'Aubigny**, supporter of **Earl of Warwick** arrested for attending the 1493 conspiratorial meeting at **Robert Clifford**'s house (*PW* 2.22, 2.50; Holinshed 3.507; Fischer 137).

Daubeny, Gilbert: In *Perkin Warbeck*, **Yorkist** conspirator who escapes to **Flanders** with **Sir Edward Lisle**.

Daulo, Cenone: See **Dandolo**.

Dauphin: Title given to king of **France**'s oldest son. The dauphin "neglects the miserable state of [his] country" after the **Duke of Orleans**'s (1372–1407) murder (*Trans* 123).

David: **Biblical** king and reputed author of the **Psalms**, succeeded by his son **Solomon** (2 Samuel 18). When her father is melancholic in **London**, **Matilda** compares herself, as she tries to soothe her father by singing, to David playing the harp to relieve Saul of an evil spirit. (*M* 165; 2 Samuel 1.23). **Maurice** cries over the story of David's sorrow after "**Absalom** revolted against him" (*Maurice* 75).

David: See **Donatello**.

David and Goliath: See **Titian**.

Davy, Sir Humphry (1778–1829): British scientist who discovered many chemical elements and compounds; he spent his last years in **Italy** and **Switzerland** (Knight 161, 168). Shelley read Davy's *Elements of Chemical Philosophy* (1812) 1816 (*Journals* 142–144). In September 1842, Shelley associated **Gmunden Lake** with Davy, who "visited during his last painful illness" (*R* 2.28).

Dawbeny, Lord: See **Daubeney, Giles**.

Dawlish: Small British coastal town twelve miles southeast of **Exeter**. Shelley locates fictional **Treby**, where *Falkner* opens, near Dawlish (*F* 5).

Dazio Grande: "Great Toll Road" threading the **Ticino** valley at Mont Piottino near the **Mount St. Gothard Pass** at **Switzerland**'s border with **Italy** (*MSWI* 101). **PFS**'s dangerous passage at St. Gothard included traversing the footpath above Dazio Grande (*R* 1.150–151).

De Courcy: Shelley identifies the De Courcy family as connected to the **Geraldines** by marriage (*PW* 1.279).

De Faro, Hernan: Madeline De Faro's husband and Monina De Faro's father in *Perkin Warbeck*.

De Faro, Madeline: Jahn Warbeck's sister, Hernan De Faro's wife, and Monina De Faro's mother in *Perkin Warbeck*.

De Faro, Monina: Hernan and Madeline De Faro's only child in *Perkin Warbeck*; she loves and supports Richard of York.

De Foe: See **Defoe**.

De Lacey: Blind, older man who is Felix and Agatha De Lacey's father in *Frankenstein*.

De Lacey, Agatha: De Lacey's daughter and Felix De Lacey's sister in *Frankenstein*.

De Lacey, Felix: De Lacey's son and Agatha De Lacey's brother in *Frankenstein*; he loves Safie.

***De Profundis*:** Latin for "out of the depths," drawn from Psalm 103, which begins, "Out of the depths have I called to thee, O Lord" and is often sung at funerals (McBrien 410). As **Cincolo de' Becari** awaits **Ricciardo de' Rossini**'s return, "a procession of monks passed, bearing a corpse and chaunting a solemn *De Profundis*" (*TP* 16–17).

"De Raptu Helenae": See **Gregory XIV**.

***Death of Abel*:** See **Titian**.

***Death of St. Francis*:** See **Ghirlandajo**.

***Death of St. Peter the Martyr*:** See **Titian**.

"Death of Wallenstein, The": Schiller's drama; Shelley was familiar with **Samuel Taylor Coleridge**'s 1799 translation. **Perdita** writes to **Raymond**, attempting to elucidate her feelings and behavior concerning their rupture, using **Wallenstein**'s lines lamenting the death of his friend and adopted son, Max Piccolomini: " '**For O, you stood** beside me, like my youth, / Transformed for me the real to a dream, / Cloathing the palpable and familiar / With golden exhalations of the dawn' " (*LM* 142; Paley 474; Coleridge 5.1.61–68). **Lionel Verney** later uses Wallenstein's speech to his sister-in-law Countess Tertsky to ask, "Were these warning voices, whose inarticulate and oracular sense forced belief upon me? '**Yet I would not** call *them* / Voices of warning, that announce to us / Only the inevitable. As the sun, / Ere it is risen, sometimes paints its image / In the atmosphere—so often do the spirits / Of great events stride on before the events, / And in to-day already walks to-morrow' "; Shelley also quotes these lines while discussing Wallenstein in *Rambles* (*LM* 265–266; *R* 2.7; Coleridge 5.1.93–102). As an epigraph to the *Perkin Warbeck* chapter in which **Richard of York** prepares to leave Scotland for **Ireland**, Shelley quotes Wallenstein's speech to Countess Tertsky about Isolani's desertion: " '**With / My fortune** and my seeming destiny, / He made the bond, and broke it not with me. / No human tie is snapped betwixt us two'" (*PW* 3.1; Coleridge 1.7.31–33, 41). As an epigraph to the chapter in which Richard battles **Henry VII** of England in **Devon**, Shelley quotes from the Duchess of Friedland's speech about her marriage to Wallenstein: "'**Oh, that stern** unbending man! / In this unhappy marriage what have I / Not suffered—not endured!'" (*PW* 3.98; Coleridge 1.3.18–20). Shelley notes "Coleridge's translation of Schiller's tragedy, giving the **German** poetry an English poetic form, causes [Wallenstein] to belong to both countries" (*R* 2.8). Shelley also quotes Countess Tertsky's line to Wallenstein, as they discuss dreams and premonitions, to express her own feeling of foreboding evil while awaiting a letter in **Milan**: "this shadow over my mind may be the forerunner; for often, as you know, '**in to-day already** walks to-morrow'" (*R* 1.115; Coleridge 5.1.102).

***Decameron*:** See **Boccaccio**.

***Defence of Poetry, A*:** Prose piece **PBS** wrote 1821 in response to **Peacock**'s essay identified in the subtitle, "or Remarks Suggested by an Essay Entitled 'The Four Ages of Poetry'"; PBS's essay was not published until 1840 (*Journals* 356; White 2.608). Highly influential on subsequent theories of poetry, it concludes with the famous claim, "poets are the unacknowledged legislators of the World" (PBS 508). Shelley praised **Dante**'s decision to write *Divine Comedy* in **Italian**, stating that he "**created a language**, in itself heroic and persuasive, out of a chaos of inharmonious barbarisms," a description adapted from **PBS**'s work (*R* 2.125; PBS 499).

"Defense of Velluti": Shelley's 11 June 1826 letter to *The Examiner*'s editor, Charles Cowden Clarke; it defends **Italian** castrato Giovanni-Battista Velluti (1781–1861), who sang at **King's Theatre**. After seeing Velluti perform in *The Crociato* (Shelley's name for **Meyerbeer**'s *Il Crociato in Egitto* [*The Crusader in Egypt*] [1824]), Shelley described him as "handsome graceful & with the exception of one or two peacock notes, his tones are sweet & clear, & his expression infinitely sweet" (*Letters* 1.520). Velluti's "effeminacy offended many English," but Shelley publicly defended him, stating, "Velluti has notes in his voice rare and perfect; his upper tones are sweet, clear, and true; some of his lower ones claim the same praise" (Sunstein 272–273; *DefVel* 372). Shelley signed her letter "Anglo-Italicus." She wrote a second defense, which she also sent to Clarke, but he did not publish it (*Letters* 1.523–524).

Deffell, George (1819–1895): **PFS**'s college friend who graduated from **Cambridge** with his B.A. 1842 and his M.A. 1845. He became a lawyer 1846 and was later a judge in Sydney, Australia (*Letters* 2.346). Deffell met Shelley and her son in **Paris** June 1840 and accompanied them on their travels through **Germany** to **Como**, as Shelley describes in *Rambles* (Sunstein 349). Deffell may have written the account of "the perilous journey" from **Milan** to **Lucerne** undertaken by PFS and his friends (*R* 1.146–152).

Defoe, Daniel (1660-1731)

Defoe, Daniel (1660-1731): British writer frequently credited as father of the novel, who produced over five hundred books and pamphlets during his lifetime; Shelley spells his name **De Foe**. **Lionel Verney** compares himself to **Robinson Crusoe**, protagonist of Defoe's *The Life and Strange Surprising Adventures of Robinson Crusoe, of York, Mariner* (1719), which Shelley read April–May 1820 (*Journals* 316–317; *LM* 448–49). Crusoe is shipwrecked on a desert island until his rescue twenty-eight years later. Shelley records she is "sunk ... in a state of loneliness no other human being ever before I beleive [*sic*] endured—Except Robinson Crusoe" October 1838 (*Journals* 555). Verney also "peruse[s] De Foe's account" of plague and suggests that the "pictures drawn in these books were so vivid, that we seemed to have experienced the results depicted by them" (*LM* 259). Verney later recommends reading Defoe for explicit details about the plague's daily deaths and accompanying rituals (*LM* 267). Verney alludes to Defoe's *A Journal of the Plague Year* (1722), which Shelley read May 1817 (*Journals* 171). Defoe uses a first-person narrator as witness to the plague in **London** 1664–65, and the vivid depictions of the plague's effects upon the city's inhabitants undoubtedly served as a source for Shelley's novel. Similar elements in these two works include questioning God, reading stars as forecasts of disaster, false prophets, the airborne spread of disease, and the effects of grief upon humanity.

***Dei delitti e delle Pene*:** See **Beccaria**.

Del Carretto, Marchese Francesco Saverio (1778–1861): Police director of the kingdom of **Naples**, known for his repression of the 1828 uprising there (Moskal 340). In a footnote, Shelley explains circumstances causing **Amari**'s exile, when Del Carretto, "influenced by some sinister, and, as is supposed, personal motive," terminated Amari's employment and ordered him to prison (*R* 2.211).

Delhi: Northeast **Indian** town. In Delhi after the sun's eclipse, streets "were strewed with pestilence-struck corpses" (*LM* 224).

Della Crusca Academy: Famous literary society **Cosimo I** founded 1587; it met at **Florence**'s National Library (*Florence* 23–24; *Artistic* 114). Shelley mentions the "fierce battle between the Della Crusca Academy and the authors of the '**Proposta**'" when the **Austrian** government ordered reformation of the **National Dictionary**, also alluded to in Shelley's biography of **Monti** (*R* 2.163; *ISPL* 2.334).

Delphi: See **Delphic oracle**.

Delphic oracle: **Apollo** patronized the Delphic oracle at **Delphi** on **Greece**'s Mount **Parnassus**; there, the **Pythian maid** uttered prophecies. Its "reputation for reliability extended throughout the **Mediterranean** world in quite early times," and it "figured prominently in innumerable myths" (Tripp 193). **Lionel Verney** wishes "for some Delphic oracle" to explain humanity's history (*LM* 426–427). **Monina De Faro**'s voice disturbs **Robert Clifford** with its power, "such as a prophetess of Delphi felt, when the oracular vapour rose up to fill her with sacred fury" (*PW* 2.26).

Demogorgon: God of Hell in **Milton**'s *Paradise Lost* (Milton 2.965). Also monstrous source of revolutionary power in **PBS**'s *Prometheus Unbound* (1820) who lives alone in the Underworld but rises to overthrow his wicked father **Jupiter** (PBS 3.2.53–61). **Fanny Derham** cries when **Ethel Villiers** moves, since their parting will return her to her former isolation: " 'I shall do my best to forget this brief interval, during which, I have no longer, like Demogorgon, lived alone in my own world' " (*L* 3.42).

Deo, Emanuel de (1774–1799): "Patriot" active at the 1799 revolution in **Naples**, when he was captured and executed (Moskal 338). Shelley mentions that **Colletta** knew Deo, whom he includes in his writings (*R* 2.208).

Deposition from the Cross: See **Titian**.

Derby: Capital of Derbyshire, a hundred miles northwest of **London**. **Henry Clerval** and **Victor Frankenstein** visit Derby (*Fr1* 188; *Fr3* 137). **Irish** invaders get to Derby before the English in London hear of their approach (*LM* 298). **Rupert Falkner** visits Derbyshire's "mountain scenery" (*F* 153).

Derham, Fanny: Francis **Derham**'s favorite daughter and **Ethel Villiers**'s best friend in *Lodore*. Sunstein suggests Shelley depicts certain elements of her youthful self in Fanny, including "self-sufficiency and aspiration" (Sunstein 49). Fanny's journey to **America** is partly caused by friction with her mother, just as Shelley's conflicted relationship with her stepmother led to her childhood absences from home. Sunstein finds Fanny "the most original" of *Lodore*'s female characters, "trained by a gentle **Godwinian** father, intellectual, asexual, confident, calm, and unswerving in dedication to justice" (Sunstein 320–321). Fanny's name evokes both **Mary Wollstonecraft**'s friend Fanny Blood and Wollstonecraft's daughter (also Shelley's half-sister) **Fanny Godwin** (Sunstein 48).

Derham, Francis: Lord **Lodore**'s childhood friend and **Fanny Derham**'s father in *Lodore*. Francis's system of education, while differing drastically from conventional early-19th-century beliefs in restrictive education for girls, is similar to the upbringing and beliefs that Shelley's parents and their works instilled in her. Sunstein calls Francis "a gentle **Godwinian** father" (Sunstein 321).

Derham, Mrs.: Francis **Derham**'s widow and **Fanny** and **Sarah Derham**'s mother in *Lodore*.

Derham, Sarah: Francis and Mrs. Derham's elder daughter in *Lodore*.

Derham, Sir Gilbert: In *Lodore*, Francis **Derham**'s father and head of the family.

Desborough, Lord Reginald: Orphaned aristocrat who rescues **Fanny** from a fire in "The Parvenue."

Descent from the Cross: See **Raphael** and **Rubens**.

Desdemona: See *Othello*.

Desies: Easternmost **Desmond** territory; Desmond plans to support **Richard of York** after "root[ing] out the Desies" (*PW* 1.306; Fischer 125).

Desmond, Countess of: Desmond's wife in *Perkin Warbeck*.

Desmond, Earl Maurice of: Maurice Bacach FitzGerald (1487–1520), tenth Earl of Desmond, 15th-century **Irishman** who ruled **Cork**, **Munster**, and lands from Wexford to **Kerry** (Arthurson 22–23; Cosgrove 977). Nicknamed **Claudus** (**Latin** for "limping") because he was lame, he supports **Richard of York** in *Perkin Warbeck*.

Despans de Cubières, General Anédée Louis (1786–1853): French minister of war (*DBF*). Shelley relates that Cubières, commander in chief of the 1832 French expedition to take **Ancona**, arrived in **Rome** to obtain **Pope Gregory XVI**'s consent for the mission after the city's defeat (*R* 2.255).

Dettingen: See **Dottingen**.

Deucalion: In **Greek** mythology, son of **Prometheus**, who warned him to build a boat. Deucalion and his wife Pyrrha thus survived a flood with which **Zeus** intended to end the human race; stones thrown over the shoulders of Deucalion and Pyrrha turned into people to reinhabit earth (Tripp 199). **Midas** admits that his kingly descent is no "More noble than Deucalion's stone-formed men" (*Midas* 95).

Devil's Bridge: Narrow bridge suspended seventy feet above the **Reuss** at **Mount St. Gothard Pass** (*MSWl* 97). **PFS**'s dangerous passage at St. Gothard included crossing Devil's Bridge October 1840 (*R* 1.152).

Devon, Earl of: **Heron**'s cousin in *Perkin Warbeck*.

Devonshire: Southwestern English county renowned for natural beauty; the Shelleys visited it June 1815 (Sunstein 99). "Maurice" is set there (*Maurice* 59, 74, 80, 84, 86). **Lord Audley** could not "rouze the rich and satisfied men of Devon, from their inglorious repose" to join his cause (*PW* 2.262, 3.106). Devon's beauty is evident in the **Cornwall** setting of *Falkner*'s opening (*F* 5).

Devonshire, Earl of: **Heron**'s father in *Perkin Warbeck*.

Devrient, Shroeder: See **Schröder-Devrient**.

Diana: Protagonist's idealized mother in *Matilda*. Diana dies a few days after **Matilda**'s birth, just as **Mary Wollstonecraft** died following Shelley's.

Diana: Virgin goddess of childbirth and living things in **Roman** mythology (Artemis in **Greek**); the moon symbolizes her chastity. **Viola Arnaldi** appears "Diana-like" (*HM* 328). **Ceres** says **Proserpine**'s presence in **Tartarus** will "shine as chaste as Diana's silver car" (*P* 85).

Diaz, Bartholomew (c. 1450–1500): **Portuguese** explorer who led the first expeditions around **Cape of Good Hope**. **Hernan De Faro** discovers the Cape with Diaz in *Perkin Warbeck* (*PW* 1.206).

Dick: Nickname for **Richard of York**.

Dickon: Nickname for **Richard of York**.

Dido: Queen and founder of **Carthage**, **Virgil** adapts the story of Dido, "legendary daughter of a king of Tyre," in his *Aeneid*; she burned herself to death when abandoned by Aeneas (Howatson 189; Virgil book 4). In "**The Death of Love**," Shelley asks if personified love died "in the terrors of lost Dido's pyre" (line 4).

Diego: Spanish soldier who dies in battle with the **Moors** (*PW* 1.219–220).

Dieppe: French coastal city fifty-five miles northeast of **Havre**. Shelley and **Isabel Robinson** visited Dieppe October 1827 (*Journals* 504). **Lionel Verney** crosses the **English Channel** from Dieppe to **Portsmouth** (*LM* 216). Shelley planned to cross to Dieppe but arrived at **Calais** instead June 1840 (*R* 1.3).

Diet of Worms: 1521 meeting at which **Luther** defended his religious beliefs. Shelley relates that the **Elector of Saxony** safely hid Luther in **Wartburg Castle** after the Diet (*R* 1.207).

Dietfurth: Bavarian colonel mortally wounded at the April 1809 **Brenner** battle (Alison 3.226). Shelley relates a story about the **Tyrolese** victory: as Dietfurth died, he claimed to have seen a man on a white horse, and it was accordingly rumored that **St. James** had protected the Tyrolese (an episode from **Alison**) (*R* 2.46).

Digby, Sir John: Tower lieutenant in *Perkin Warbeck*.

Dijon: French city forty-five miles northwest of **Besançon**. The Shelleys "entered Dijon on the third evening" after leaving **Paris** 1814 (*H* 87–88). They also spent a night there en route to **Italy** March 1818 (*Journals* 198). **Lionel Verney** leads a party of men from Paris through Dijon on **Côte d'Or** (*LM* 396). [*LM* 408, 411].

Dioclesian: See **Domitian**.

Diodati, Villa: Villa near **Belrive** on Lake Geneva; it was once **Milton**'s residence (1639) and **Byron**'s (summer 1816). The Shelleys spent many evenings there 1816, sometimes staying overnight; the legendary ghost-story competition that eventually produced *Frankenstein* took place there (*Journals* 108–109). Shelley again saw Diodati 1840 (*R* 1.139, 1.147).

Diorama: Invented by the **Frenchman** Louis J. M. Daguerre 1822, a type of scenic painting, partially translucent, that simulates a changing three-dimensional scene. The first diorama was displayed in **London**'s **Regent's Park** (Chilvers 163). Shelley mentions that her memories of certain **Italian** scenes have faded, "as a painting in the Diorama melts away, and another struggles into the changing canvas" (*R* 2.77).

"Dirge, A": Two versions of Shelley's three-stanza poem exist. Shelley first published it in the 1831 *Keepsake* as "By the Author of **Frankenstein**," and H. Buxton Forman republished that early version with "**The Choice**" 1876. Shelley published a revised version in the 1839 edition of *The Poetical Works of Percy Bysshe Shelley*. Consisting of three octaves, the poem recounts **PBS**'s death—the speaker will mourn this death forever. Shelley included the poem in a June 1835 letter, calling it "the best thing I ever wrote" (*Letters* 2.246–248). Both **William Godwin** and **Jane Williams**, however, criticized it; Sunstein attributes their reactions to personal repugnance at the Shelleys' relationship (Sunstein 328–329).

***Dispute of the Sacrament*:** See **Raphael**.

Divedro: Small **Italian** village between **Iselle** and **Domodossola** (*STIE* 40). Shelley noted her good fortune at avoiding being detained "in a wretched hovel at Divedro" October 1840 (*R* 1.137).

***Divina Commedia*:** See *Divine Comedy*.

***Divine Comedy*:** Italian terza rima, in Italian the *Divina Commedia*, **Dante**'s great epic, first translated into English 1719. It consists of three books, the *Inferno*, *Purgatorio*, and *Paradiso* and depicts in rich moral allegory one man's journey to God. Shelley refers to Dante's work throughout her corpus. She read a translation at various times 1817–22 and also the original Italian (*Journals* 643–644). While in **Venice** October 1842, Shelley remarks, "Dante himself hesitated whether to write his 'Divina Comedia' in **Latin** or **Venetian**, till fortunately he became aware that the talk of the common people of **Tuscany** possessed all the elements of expression," which he collected "with that life-giving power proper to genius" (*R* 2.125).

Dmitri: "The Evil Eye's" Albanian **Klepht** title character.

Doctor Gregory: See **Gregory, Doctor**.

Dodona: Mythical city in **Epirus** reputed to be an ancient center of **Zeus** worship; it was "famous for its oracles, interpreted from rustlings of old oak trees and other natural sounds" (Tripp 213). **Zitza** and Chercovista (village near **Ioannina**) have been suggested as modern locations of this mythical site (Eisler 217). **Dmitri** rides with **Constans Ziani** over **Sagori** mountains "clothed with old Dodona's oaks" (*EE* 113).

Dods, Mary Diana (c. 1791–c. 1830): Illegitimate daughter of the Scottish Earl of Morton, this "secret lesbian and sometimes transvestite" became a multifaceted author under the pseudonym **David Lyndsay**; Shelley read her *Dramas of the Ancient World* (1822) March 1822, finding them "works of considerable talent, and strength of poetry & expression" (Sunstein 273; *Journals* 406; *Letters* 1.232). Shelley first met Dods, affectionately called "Doddy," 1825, and they were friends by 1826, when Dods seemed to have formed "warmer feelings" for Shelley than simple friendship; Shelley does not seem to have returned the affection other than as a good friend (Sunstein 273). Dods went abroad October 1826, and Shelley acted as her literary agent during her absence (Sunstein 273). Dods seems to have entered willingly into Shelley's plan regarding **Isabel Robinson**; after Dods's father died July 1827, and having settled his affairs, Dods joined Shelley and Isabel at Arundel September 1827 as "Mr. Sholto Douglas" (Bennett, *Mary Diana Dods* 26; Sunstein 281, 283). Shelley's July–August 1827 letters detail their plan (Bennett, *Mary Diana Dods* 76–85; *Letters* 1.556–575, 2.7–8, 2.12–13). Dods and Isabel traveled to **Paris** as husband and wife and continued to play these roles for two years; Shelley visited them there summer 1828 and was disconcerted by Dods's engagement with the role of "disconsolate husband," which Sunstein terms "perverse" (Sunstein 287; Bennett, *Mary Diana Dods* 105–107). Writing to **Jane Williams** from **Hastings** June 1828, Shelley would not describe Doddy: "one only trusts that the diseased body acts on the diseased mind, & that both may be at rest ere long" (*Letters* 2.51). Isabel's flirtatious nature probably contributed to Dods's "severe mental and physical deterioration in 1828 and 1829"; Dods was imprisoned for debt toward the end of 1829 and died between November 1829 and November 1830, as Betty T. Bennett records in her *Mary Diana Dods, A Gentleman and a Scholar* (1991), which unearthed Lyndsay's true identity (230).

Dodsworth, Mr. Roger (1585–1654): Historically, "**York** Cathedral" registrar and antiquary (*DNB*). Protagonist's father in "**Roger Dodsworth**."

Dodsworth, Roger: Subject and title figure of "**Roger Dodsworth: The Reanimated Englishman**." Shelley draws upon facts available from the debate about the reanimation of this figure which appeared prior to her composing her article, correcting the date of his first death from 1660 to 1654; Dodsworth appeared in "various newspapers and magazines" in late 1826 (Robinson 377).

Dogana: Italian for customhouse; Shelley was detained at one near **Lago Maggiore** September 1840 (*R* 1.128).

Doge's Palace: Located on **Venice**'s **Piazza San Marco**, it housed a chapel, the residence of the doges (chief magistrates), council chambers, a court, torture chambers, and prisons. Shelley also calls it the **Ducal Palace**. Its construction took several centuries; the present form dates from the early 14th century (Honour 41–52). Shelley initially visited the Doge's Palace September 1818 and recorded subsequent visits there September 1842 (*Journals* 228; *R* 2.84–89).

Dolce, Carlo: See **Dolci, Carlo**.

Dolci, Carlo (1616–1687): Major 17th-century **Florentine** painter renowned for religious depictions of single figures and portraits (Turner 9.76). When the **Saville** family is at **Mola di Gaeta**, a man enters with a picture "he declared to be an original Carlo **Dolce**" (*L* 3.215–216).

Dôle: French city twenty-five miles southeast of **Dijon**. The Shelleys passed through Dôle 1814 (*H* 87–88). They also spent a night there on their return to England August 1816 (*Journals* 132). **Lionel Verney** leads a party

Dolgellau

of men from **Paris** through Dôle on Côte d'Or (*LM* 396).

Dolgellau: Town on Wales's west coast, seventy miles southwest of **Liverpool**; Shelley uses the English spelling **Dolgelly**. She stayed there from mid-June to August 1841 (Sunstein 354). Shelley compares **Florence**'s foggy mists to those at Dolgellau (*R* 2.135).

Dolgelly: See **Dolgellau**.

Domenichino (1581–1641): Bolognese painter; Shelley saw many of his works in Bologna November 1818 (*Journals* 236). She viewed Domenichino's *Last Communion of St. Jerome* (1614), which she calls *San Geronimo*, at the **Vatican** April 1843 (*R* 2.218).

Dominican: Religious order founded by Dominic de Guzman 1216 and characterized by traveling preachers and poverty (McBrien 428–429). Dominicans lead *Valperga*'s **Inquisition** (*V* 1.259, 2.27, 3.21). Shelley visited a **Venetian** Dominican convent September 1842 (*R* 2.97). A Dominican enjoyed showing Shelley **Fra Angelico**'s works in **Santa Maria Novella Church** January 1843 (*R* 2.146).

Domitian, Titus Flavius (51–96 c.e.): **Vespasian**'s younger son who became **Roman** emperor 81 c.e., renowned for a seven-year reign of terror before his assassination (Howatson 196, 499). Shelley speculates that if people could remember ten centuries ago, "would not several of our free thinking martyrs wonder to find that they had suffered as Christians under Domitian" (*RD* 49). Shelley compares **Francis I of** **Austria**'s torturous **Spielburg** prison to Domitian's (mistakenly writing **Dioclesian**) hobby of killing flies, mentioned in 1st-century c.e. Suetonius's *De Vita Caesarum* [*Lives of the Caesars*]; Shelley read it May 1817 (Moskal 275–276; *R* 2.88; *Journals* 171).

Domodossola: Italian city near the **Swiss**-Italian border west of **Lago Maggiore**; Shelley slept at the **Post** in "**Duomo d'Ossola**" October 1840 (*R* 1.133).

Don Giovanni: See **Mozart**.

Don Pedro II (1236–1285): King of **Aragon** 1276–1285, renowned for seizing **Naples** and **Sicily** from **Charles of Angou** in 1282. Shelley admires **Amari**'s account of Pedro II's final war and death (*R* 2.210).

Don Quixote: Main character of **Cervantes**'s *Don Quixote de la Mancha* (1605 and 1615). Don Quixote's disordered mind leads him to observe outdated chivalric traditions wholeheartedly, directing him into many absurd adventures. He travels on his horse Rosinante, accompanied by his squire **Sancho**, and loves a young woman named Aldonza Lorenzo, whom Don Quixote renames **Dulcinea** del Toboso (Cervantes 11–12). "**Quixotic**" now means impractical and idealistically chivalrous, recalling Don Quixote's behavior. **PBS** read *Don Quixote* aloud October–November 1816, and Shelley returned to it December 1820 (*Journals* 139, 341). In January 1817, Shelley wrote to PBS that "you were born to be a don Quixote [*sic*] and if that celebrated personage had ever existed except in the brain of Cervantes I should certainly form a theory of transmigration to prove that you lived in **Spain** some hundred years before" (*Letters* 1.27). While in **Grosbois** 1814, the Shelleys "ate our bread and fruit, and drank our wine, thinking of Don Quixote and Sancho" (*H* 16). Writing playfully to **Edward John Trelawny** March 1831, Shelley informs him of Elizabeth St. Aubyn's marriage and jokes he will be left without a Dulcinea (*Letters* 2.133). **Edward Villiers** perceives **Horatio Saville**'s proposed trip to **America** as a "Quixotic expedition," and Shelley also notes **Fanny Derham** "had something Quixotic in her nature" (*L* 2.42, 3.23). Edward jokingly compares adventures he has with his wife in avoiding bailiffs to "those of Don Quixote and the fair Dulcinea" (*L* 3.49). Shelley notes her "**Greek**" reply to the innkeeper's daughter after being robbed in a **Liège** hotel: " '**Welcome this evil**, so that it be the only one!' " which seems to be from *Don Quixote* rather than a Greek source (*R* 1.165; Moskal 160; Cervantes 2.55). [*F* 47, 135].

Don Ricardo: See **Richard of York**.

Don Rodrigo: See *Promessi Sposi*.

Donatello (c. 1386–1466): Florentine Renaissance sculptor, renowned for *David* (after 1433), "credited with being the first free-standing nude statue since antiquity," displayed at the Bargello in Florence (Chilvers 166). Shelley saw a Donatello *David* in the **Uffizi** January 1843 (*R* 2.155; Gowing 181–182).

Donati: Noble **Florentine** family, members of which attend **Euthanasia**'s court (*V* 1.240, 1.256). **Bondelmonte** de Bondelmonte's marriage with a Donati woman caused his murder and the formation of Florentine **Ghibelline** and **Guelph** political factions (Villani 121–122).

Donegans: **Irish** family related to **Desmond** (*PW* 1.304).

Doneratico, Count Gherardo: **Conradin**'s principal attendant in "**A Tale of the Passions**." Doneratico was executed in **Naples** with Conradin 1268 (Villani 241).

Donizetti, Gaetano (1797–1848): **Italian** composer who presented his first opera in **Venice** 1818; critics consider *Lucia di Lammermoor* (1835), a three-act opera based on **Scott**'s *The Bride of Lammermoor* (1819), one of his best works (D. Arnold 1.566; Orrey 210). Shelley attended a *Lucia* performance at the **Opera-house at Como**, calling **Marini** a good singer despite "having been of late confined to Donizetti"; **Teresa Brambilla** was singing the lead (*R* 1.88, 1.108). Shelley notes **Lake Como** boatmen sing *Lucia*'s song *Bell' Alma innamorata* (*R* 1.88). Shelley also attended a performance of *Elisir d'Amore* [*The Love Potion*]; Donizetti's two-act opera was first presented in **Milan** 1832 (Rosenthal 152). She saw *famiglia Vianesi* perform it in **Venice** October 1842 (*R* 2.127).

Donna Estatica: Shelley takes this phrase from **Muratori**, providing a translation connected with "inspired women" in a footnote; **Beatrice** is one (*V* 2.43).

Doric: One of the orders of **Greek** architecture, characterized by simple forms and heavy columns; also a Scottish dialect. **Lionel Verney** bids farewell to "the fluted column with its capital, **Corinthian**, **Ionic**, or Doric" (*LM* 321). Shelley records that Scottish companions on her journey from **Sesto Callende** have "as rich a Doric accent as the lowlands can produce," suggesting the accent encapsulates their rustic upbringing (*R* 1.127).

Dorset, Lord (1451–1501): Thomas Grey, first Marquis of Dorset 1475, John Grey (Shelley uses **Gray**) and **Elizabeth Woodville**'s son; English **Henry VII** confirmed his titles 1486 (*DNB*). Minor *Perkin Warbeck* character.

Dottingen: **Swiss** town six miles northeast of Constance; Shelley spells it **Dettingen**. The Shelleys stayed overnight there August 1814 (*Journals* 20–21; *H* 57).

Douai: French city sixty-five miles southeast of **Calais**. **Castruccio** travels to **Alberto Scoto**'s military camp near Douai (*V* 1.90).

Douglas, Archibald (c. 1449–1514): Fifth **Earl of Angus**, Scottish border chieftain, and **James IV**'s Lord High Chancellor; he was engaged to **Lady Katherine Gordon** as a boy and was alternately loyal to James and to **Henry VII** (*DNB*; Fischer 216). **Richard of York**'s supporter in *Perkin Warbeck*.

Dover: Southeastern English port known for the **White Cliffs** nearby overlooking the **English Channel**. It is the closest English land to **France** and thus a frequent departure point for English travelers to **Europe**. Shelley stayed for a month in Dover for financial reasons 1828 and spent August 1835 there recovering from illness (*Journals* 508; Sunstein 329). Shelley felt "refreshed by a sea-bath" in Dover after an 1814 journey from **London** (*H* 2). **Lionel Verney** notes how small the distance is between Dover and **Calais**; plague survivors rest in Dover castle before crossing to Europe (*LM* 248, 370). The undulating beauty of land around **Hythe** contrasts to the "cliffs, which at Dover beetle so fearfully over the tremendous deep" (*PW* 2.160). Dover is **Rupert Falkner** and **Elizabeth Falkner**'s departure port for Europe (*F* 33). *Rambles* opens with Shelley's June 1840 crossing from Dover to Calais (*R* 1.5–6, 1.157). [*L* 3.238].

Downs: Body of water off the mouth of the **Thames** near **Kent**. **Lewis Elmore** learns that the *Bellerophon* is "expected in the Downs" (*Mourner* 93–94).

Doxan: Perhaps Shelley's name for Doksy, Czech town thirty-two miles northeast of **Prague**. Shelley stopped there August 1840 (*R* 1.279).

Draco: Seventh-century B.C.E. **Athenian** legislator renowned for "notoriously harsh" laws (Howatson 197). **Lady Santerre** finds that "poverty is a tyrant, whose laws are more terrible than those of Draco" (*L* 1.106).

Dragon: **Robert Clifford**'s horse in *Perkin Warbeck*.

Drance: River entering **Lake Geneva** at a small delta on its southeastern side, between **Evian** and **Thonon**; Shelley spells it **Dranse**. On their honeymoon voyage along Lake Geneva, **Victor Frankenstein** and **Elizabeth Lavenza** see the Drance before arriving at Evian (*Fr1* 218; *Fr3* 162). In *Rambles*, Shelley refers to an 1818 flooding of the Drance, which threatened **Martigny** (*R* 1.138).

Dranse: See **Drance**.

"Dream, The": Short story first published in the 1832 *Keepsake* as by "the Author of **Frankenstein**," accompanied by an illustration titled *Constance*, depicting the story's heroine reading, which Louisa Sharpe painted and Charles Heath engraved (Robinson 383; *D* 154). At the beginning of **Henry IV**'s reign in **France**, heiress **Constance Villeneuve** mourns her brothers and father (*D* 153). She vowed to love **Gaspar de Vaudemont** while their families were alive but at odds (*D* 157). Members of the two families subsequently killed each other; Constance and Gaspar are the last of their lines (*D* 157). Torn between love for Gaspar and family loyalty, Constance tells him she will enter a convent; he plans to leave for **Palestine** (*D* 156–158). She then spends a night on **St. Catherine**'s couch, a ledge overhanging the **Loire**; according to legend, anyone who spends a night there will be visited by St. Catherine, who "deigns to direct her votaries in dreams" (*D* 158). Her sleep is at first peaceful, as she dreams of her father and brothers in paradise and of herself in a convent; then she dreams that St. Catherine takes her to Palestine and shows her Gaspar as a prisoner (*D* 164). Awakening suddenly, she would have tumbled off the ledge, but Gaspar had climbed the cliff and prevents her fall (*D* 164). The couple then marry in the chapel with Henry's blessing (*D* 164–65). "The Dream" is another of Shelley's fictional pieces that explore the supernatural.

Drei Linden: **Prague** hotel on the **Graben**. Shelley stayed there August 1842 (*R* 1.280).

Dresden: **German** city on the **Elbe**, sixty miles southeast of **Leipzig**. Shelley arrived there July 1842, planning to stay a month (*R* 1.231, 1.235). She went to the **Hôtel de Pologne**, which **Murray** recommended, but subsequently stayed in **Alt Markt** (*R* 1.232, 1.235). While there, warm weather bothered Shelley, so she did not tour the entire city (*R* 1.250). See **Gallery**, **Green Vaults**, **Grosse Garten**, **Neu Markt**, and **Terrace of Bruhl**. [*R* 2.10, 2.23, 2.28, 2.34, 2.278].

Dromore: Sir **Boyvill Neville**'s home "in a beautiful, but wild and thinly-inhabited part of **Cumbria**, on the verge of the plain that forms the coast" (*F* 105–106). **Gerard Neville** returns to Dromore to look for his mother after her disappearance; **Alithea Neville**'s grave is nearby.

Drum: **Irish** mountains between **Ardmore** and Dungarvan. **Lady Katherine Gordon** watches the "passes of the mountains of Drum" (*PW* 3.49).

Drummonds: **Irish** family feuding with the **Murrays** (*PW* 2.194).

Drury Lane Theatre: **London** theater erected during **James I**'s reign and named for the street upon which it stands. The existing building is of Shelley's day and was the fourth on that site; Benjamin Wyatt designed it (opened 1812) (Weinreb 861–862). Shelley visited Drury Lane Theatre many times (*Letters* 1.412, 2.68, 3.403). **Lionel Verney** watches part of **Shakespeare's** *Macbeth* there (*LM* 281).

Dublin: Ireland's capital city, on the Liffey River. Shelley's maternal aunts, Eliza and **Everina Wollstonecraft**, lived in Dublin, where they were schoolteachers, and **William Godwin** visited them there summer 1800 (Sunstein 25; *SCGS* 221). **PBS** visited Dublin for two months 1812; there he published and distributed "An Address to the Irish People," a pamphlet intended to assist Catholic emancipation (White 1.203–227; Holmes 117–132). **Castruccio** agrees to travel to Dublin secretly to deliver a message to **Piers Gaveston** (*V* 1.76–77, 1.79). **Ellen Gray**'s governess accompanies her to Dublin (*ES* 245). The **Earl of Warwick** appears in Dublin, where Irish enthusiasm "spread a glory round the imposter they supported" (*PW* 1.120, 1.132). **Keating** later proposes attacking Ireland and taking Dublin (*PW* 3.31–32).

Ducal Palace: See **Doge's Palace**.

Duc d'Enghien [Louis-Antoine-Henri de Bourbon-Condé] (1772–1804): French noble. **Napoleon** received a false report that connected the duke to a conspiracy and executed him. Shelley visited **Ettenheim**, where the duke had been seized; she cites this occurrence as "one of three crimes which cast a dark stain on Napoleon's name" (*R* 1.44).

Duke of ——: Minor character in *The Last Man*.

Duke Street: South of **Piccadilly** in **London**'s Westminster district, Duke Street turns into **St James's**. **Mrs. Derham**'s house is on Duke Street (*L* 2.257). [*L* 3.242].

Dulcinea: See **Don Quixote**.

Dumb Knight, The: See **Markham, Gervase**.

Dundee: Scottish port forty miles northeast of **Edinburgh**. Shelley stayed with the **Baxter** family there 1812 and 1813 (Sunstein 56, 59). Shelley drew upon Dundee's natural surroundings for Scottish scenes in *Matilda*. Shelley calls Dundee landscape "blank and dreary," but also "the eyry of freedom, and the pleasant region where unheeded I could commune with the creatures of my fancy" (*Fr3* 20).

Dungeons of Spielburg: Former **Brünn** castle that the **French** converted into a prison for political offenders; **Pellico** was imprisoned there 1822–30 (*MSGE* 529). In her account of Pellico, Shelley mentions his confinement there, where **Colletta** was also imprisoned (*R* 2.88, 2.208).

Dunkeld: Scottish town fifteen miles northwest of **Perth** and the **Duke of Athol**'s home; **Adrian** stays there when he secludes himself, and **Lionel Verney** visits him there (*LM* 55, 71).

Duomo (Florence): Cathedral begun 1296 (*MCIT* 236–241). **Euthanasia**

praises Florentines for their dedication to constructing beautiful buildings, even though the "men who have conceived the idea, and contributed their money toward the erection of the Duomo, will never see its completion" (*V* 2.4). [*V* 2.125].

Duomo (Milan): Gothic cathedral begun in 1386. Shelley attended mass there in September 1840 and describes the Duomo as "a pleasure never to be forgotten," with its "multitudinous and snow-white pinnacles" viewed from its square, **Piazza del Duomo** (*R* 1.112–113, 1.116–117).

Duomo d'Ossola: See **Domodossola**.

Durham, Bishop of: See **Fox, Bishop Richard**.

Dutch: Language spoken in **Holland**; **Richard of York** speaks it (*PW* 1.88).

Duvillard: Wealthy banker who marries **Manon Mansfield** in *Frankenstein*. See **Foggi, Elise**.

Dwarf: In "**Transformation**," **Guido il Cortese**'s antagonist.

Dwarf: Wooden figure (c. 1728) of Perkeo, court fool, housed in **Heidelberg Castle**'s basement (*BGER* 149). Shelley saw "the wax figure of the celebrated dwarf" at the castle (*R* 1.36).

E

East India Company: Britain established its rule in **India** 1757, and the East India Company carried out British colonial policy there 1600–1858 (Kinder 1.283, 2.89). **Rupert Falkner** trains at East Indian Military College and becomes an East India Company cavalry captain (*F* 26, 178). [*F* 139].

Easterlings: German traders from **Hans**. Shelley mentions Easterlings' 1493 riots, which **Henry VII** of England's ban on **Flemish** products caused, in *Perkin Warbeck* (*PW* 2.59–60; Holinshed 3.502).

Eastwell Place: Early-14th-century house near Ashford, **Kent** (McRae 184). **Sir Thomas Moyle**'s seat; **Elizabeth of York** and **Lady Katherine Gordon** stay there overnight (*PW* 3.340).

Eaton, Charlotte (1813–1859): British travel writer and novelist renowned for *At Home and Abroad* (1831). Shelley agrees with this "clever writer['s]" assessment of Catholicism's effects in *Rome in the Nineteenth Century* (1826): " 'Wherever the Catholic religion is established, I have uniformly observed indolence, with its concomitants, dirt and beggary, to prevail; and the more Catholic is the place, the more they abound' " (*R* 2.234; Eaton 3.294).

Ebensee: Austrian city near **Lake Gmunden**'s southern tip, thirty-two miles east of **Salzburg**. Shelley sailed there September 1842 (*R* 2.29).

Eboli, Count: Protagonist's father in "Ferdinando Eboli."

Eboli, Ferdinando: Count Eboli's legitimate son and **Adalinda Spina**'s fiancé in "Ferdinando Eboli."

Eboli, Ludovico: Count Eboli's illegitimate son and Ferdinando Eboli's older brother in "Ferdinando Eboli."

Ecclesiastes: Biblical book. **Lionel Verney** specifies his farewell to the arts with a paraphrased line: "**there is no work,** nor device, nor knowledge, nor wisdom in the grave, whither thou goest!" (*LM* 321; Ecclesiastes 9.10). When only four plague survivors remain, Verney quotes Ecclesiastes again, referencing a **Hebrew poet**: " 'the grasshopper is a burthen' " (*LM* 418; Ecclesiastes 12.5). Shelley uses " '**The silver cord** is loosed, and the pitcher broken at the fountain' " to describe **Elizabeth Woodville**'s death and to conclude **Lord Lodore**'s story (*PW* 1.325; *L* 3.304; Ecclesiastes 12.6).

Echemine: See **Echemines**.

Echemines: French village three miles northwest of **Pavillon-Ste-Julie**; Shelley spells it **Echemine**. The Shelleys rested there August 1814 (*H* 24).

Echo: In **Greek** mythology, nymph whom Hera punished for diverting attention while **Zeus** made advances toward other nymphs; subsequently, Echo could only repeat others' words and pined away for **Narcissus**, until she existed only as a voice (Tripp 217). Shelley refers to "Echo's voice" in "**A Dirge**" (line 19; *Letters* 2.247).

Eclogues: Ten pastoral poems **Virgil** wrote (42–37 B.C.E.) (Howatson 201). "Recollections of Italy's" narrator carries "the Eclogues of Virgil" and sits on the **Thames**'s bank "to read the Eclogue of **Silenus**," a reference to the sixth *Eclogue* (*RI* 24–25; Howatson 202). Shelley records **Edward Villiers** " 'also was an Arcadian,' and made one of the self-enthroned 'world' "; Stafford suggests Shelley draws from the seventh *Eclogue* in which Virgil describes Thyrsis and Corydon "in the bloom of life, Arcadians both" (*L* 2.208; Stafford 176; *Eclogues* 7.4).

Eden: Biblical garden God creates for **Adam** and **Eve**, casting them out when they sin by succumbing to the snake's temptation (Genesis 3). Shelley comments that seventeen-year-old "men look on women as living Edens which they dare not imagine they can ever enjoy" (*BMI* 38). **Horace Neville** finds **Virginia Water**'s landscape Edenic (*Mourner* 83–85). **Ethel Villiers**'s life with her father was "Eden"; "no Eden was required to enhance" the **Villiers**es' happiness upon reuniting (*L* 1.281, 2.271). **Gerard Neville** sees **Rupert Falkner** as the snake spoiling Eden's beauties; he cannot reconcile love for **Elizabeth Falkner** with Falkner's actions (*F* 221).

Edgware: **London** district nine miles northeast of the city's center. **Lord Lovel** and **Edmund Plantagenet** approach London from Edgware (*PW* 1.28).

Edinburgh: Scotland's capital city forty miles east of Glasgow, a thriving intellectual, cultural, and commercial center in Shelley's time; she probably visited it while staying with the **Baxters** 1813 (Sunstein 60). **Victor Frankenstein** and **Henry Clerval** stay there (*Fr1* 189; *Fr3* 138). As site of **James IV**'s court, Edinburgh is a principal *Perkin Warbeck* setting (*PW* 2.198, 2.254). "Scottish troops... encamped near Edinburgh" before invading England (*PW* 2.261). **Henry VII** of England has spies there, and James retreats from England to Edinburgh (*PW* 2.326, 2.319). Shelley describes a Scottish traveling companion as "acquainted with

Edinburgh Castle

good Edinburgh society" (*R* 1.127). [*M* 160].

Edinburgh Castle: Edinburgh's 7th-century fortress (Donaldson 67). **James IV** receives **Richard of York** there (*PW* 2.198).

Edward I (1239–1307): England's king 1272–1307; Edward conquered Wales and waged war in Scotland (Kinder 1.189). Edward had "known and loved" **Alderigo** (*V* 1.68–69).

Edward II (1284–1327): England's king 1307–27, called **Edward of Caernarvon** in *Valperga* (*V* 1.69). Barons restricted the king's powers when Edward made his lover, **Piers Gaveston**, an earl, and Edward was deposed, imprisoned, and probably murdered.

Edward III (1312–1377): England's king 1327–77; his descendants contested the throne until the **Wars of the Roses**. **Richard of York** is "lineal heir of Edward III" (*PW* 2.15). [*PW* 1.303, 2.187].

Edward IV (1442–1483): England's king 1461–70 and 1471–83. **Richard of York** and **Elizabeth of York**'s father and **Elizabeth Woodville**'s second husband in *Perkin Warbeck*. Also called **Duke of York**.

Edward VI: Reference to England's king after **Edward IV**; **Elizabeth Woodville** calls **Warwick** Edward VI, and **Lambert Simnel** claims to be Edward VI (*PW* 1.63, 1.133).

Edward of Caernarvon: See Edward II.

Edward, Prince (1453–1471): Son of **Henry VI** and **Margaret of Anjou**; he died trying to obtain the throne from **Edward IV**. **Elizabeth Woodville** refuses to disclose **Richard of York**'s location to **Sir William Stanley** in order to save her son from Edward's fate (*PW* 1.125).

Edwards, Dr.: Shelley footnotes information about **Venetian** nobility and attributes some of it to a Dr. Edwards, not further identified (*R* 2.114).

Egham: English town on the **Thames**, twenty miles west of **London**. **Lionel Verney** sometimes takes an indirect route to **Windsor** from London through Egham (*LM* 257, 354). **Edward Villiers** travels to Egham's "neighbourhood" for **Lord Maristow** (*L* 2.283). [*L* 2.287–291].

Egna: Italian town eighteen miles northeast of **Trent**. Shelley slept there September 1842 (*R* 2.63).

Egypt: Northeast **African** country where an early, highly cultured civilization once flourished. In Shelley's time, the **Ottoman Empire** ruled it, and Egypt fought against **Greece** in its 1820s war for independence (Kinder 2.45). Shelley considered traveling there 1843: "I should like to spend next winter—No clouds nor cold there" (*Letters* 3.69). Some writings on *The Last Man*'s **Sibylline** leaves are "Egyptian hieroglyphics" (*LM* 5). Trade ceases between England and Egypt with the onset of plague, and **Lionel Verney** worries about English survivors enduring "intolerable heats of a summer in Egypt" (*LM* 233, 383). Troops from Egypt intensify their campaign, so **Elizabeth Falkner** fears for **Rupert Falkner**'s well-being as he participates in the Greek war (*F* 63). Shelley discusses "**Napoleon**'s expedition to Egypt" in her **Carbonari** account (*R* 2.165). [*TP* 7; *F* 141].

Ehrenbreitstein: German fortress ["The Broad Stone of Honor"] opposite **Coblentz** on the **Rhine**; the **French** destroyed it 1801 (Untermeyer 72; McGann 2.305–306). Shelley saw it June 1842 (*R* 1.169).

"Eighteenth-Century Tale, An": Robinson considers Shelley's "Fragment" was "written before 1824," while Sunstein suggests she worked on it 1819 (Robinson 398; Sunstein 164). Shelley set it in a **Buckinghamshire** mansion's garden on the **Thames** between **Marlow** and **Henley**; each character agrees to relate an autobiographical tale for the others' amusement (*EC* 345). The only character who begins her tale is **Maria Langley Graham**, informing listeners that she was left an orphan at age ten and lived with an aunt in the country (*EC* 346). Shelley's narrative goes no farther.

Eisach: Small river in western **Austria** forming a waterfall near **Brenner** (*MSGE* 330). Shelley crossed it September 1842 (*R* 2.49, 2.62).

Eisenach: German city eighteen miles west of **Gotha**. Shelley dined there July 1842 (*R* 1.207).

Eisengieserei: Shelley uses this German word, "iron foundry," for **Berlin**'s first ironworks, built 1826 (Spritzer 165). Shelley visited it July 1842 (*R* 1.229).

El Muchacho: See **Richard of York**.

El Zagal: **Boabdil El Chico**'s brother who deposed Boabdil and later surrendered to **Spain** 1491; his name means "the valiant" (Fischer 69). **Stephen Frion** entertains **Richard of York** with tales of these brothers' quarrels (*PW* 1.159).

Elba: Island in the **Tyrrhenian Sea** off **Italy**'s western coast; **Napoleon** was exiled there 1814–15. **Ferdinando Eboli** is released from prison during Napoleon's exile (*FE* 80). Shelley mentions Elba in comparing Napoleon to **Hofer**, and she sailed past it March 1843 (*R* 2.213, 2.285).

Elbe: Central **European** river originating near the Czech border with **Poland** and flowing across **Germany** into the **North Sea**. Shelley mentions the Elbe several times; she crossed it July 1842 and followed its course from **Dresden** to **Rabenau** August 1842 (*R* 1.232, 1.246, 1.256). Shelley did not see the Elbe at its best, since it was dry season (*R* 1.274). The river's low level changed her plans to sail the Elbe to **Prague** (*Letters* 3.38; *R* 1.256).

"Elder Son, The": Story first published in *Heath's Book of Beauty* (1835) as by "Mrs. Shelley" (Robinson 392). The accompanying plate titled *Ellen*, which Henry Wyatt painted and J. Henry Robinson engraved, depicts the story's heroine asleep over a book (*ES* 259). The plot's concern with inheritance and estates is, partially, drawn from Shelley's dealings with her father-in-law, but Shelley carefully verified the fictional situation she creates. Around 1831–33, Shelley asked **Thomas Jefferson** Hogg for help with "a little *law*. I want (in a story I am writing) to make a Nobleman die having one daughter, whose eldest son is to inherit his title & possessions—meanwhile, till she has a son, his wealth goes to another branch of the family, & his title lies dormant—Is this compatible with any arrangement of succession or entail" (*Letters* 2.147). "The Elder Son's" plot does not adhere strictly to this outline. Shelley's story opens with **Ellen**, narrator and central protagonist, briefly recalling her upbringing and her parents' deaths (*ES* 244–245). Left with a fifty-thousand-pound fortune to ensure her independence, on condition she does not marry until age twenty-one, Ellen becomes the ward of her uncle **Sir Richard Gray** (*ES* 245–246). She lives in "monotonous quiet" at her uncle's country seat, **Beech Grove** in **Hampshire**, with only her youngest cousin, **Marianne Gray**, for company (*ES* 246–247). When Sir Richard's second son, **Vernon Gray**, arrives there, his declarations of love flatter Ellen, and she agrees to a secret betrothal, though she does not love him; Sir Richard then separates them (*ES* 246–251). A week later, Ellen meets her eldest cousin, **Clinton Gray**, and quickly falls in love with him (*ES* 254–255). Ellen reveals her secret betrothal, and Clinton declares he will not interfere with his younger brother's prior claim to her. When Vernon unexpectedly arrives and sees Ellen with Clinton, Vernon declares that Clinton is " 'a natural son,' " hoping to guarantee Ellen's love for himself as legitimate heir (*ES* 260). Ellen understands only after learning from Sir Richard that Clinton was born when his mother, **Matilda Towers**, was still Sir Richard's mistress; Matilda became **Lady Gray** only just before Vernon's birth, and so Vernon is the legitimate son (*ES* 261–262). Sir Richard's daughter, **Lady Caroline Hythe**, then helps Ellen reunite with Clinton (*ES* 263). Ellen lives with Caroline in **London** for two years, and they develop a sisterly relationship while Clinton enthusiastically follows his profession in the army (*ES* 263–264). Sir Richard exchanges his extravagant life for poverty and obscurity, managing to gain twenty thousand pounds for his eldest son's fortune (*ES* 264). Ellen marries Clinton happily when she is twenty-one years old, and Sir Richard lives with them for four months before his death (*ES* 264). At the story's close, Ellen records that she has not seen Vernon since that day at Beech Grove, although she hears that he is rich and prosperous. She and Clinton contentedly "live principally abroad," with frequent visits from **Lord** and **Lady Hythe** (*ES* 265). Sunstein suggests Ellen's opening description of her relationship with her father, "the unmarried widower . . . may well depict Mary [Shelley] and [**William**] Godwin's relations," and, as in *Matilda, Valperga, Lodore,* and *Falkner,* Ellen's worship of her father, even after his death, is partly autobiographical (33).

Elector of Saxony: German Frederick III, the Wise (1463–25). Shelley relates that he safely hid **Luther** in **Wartburg Castle** for ten months 1521 (*R* 1.207).

Elector Palatine: Frederick V (1596–1632), Elector Palatine of the

Rhine and **Bohemia**'s king as Frederick I, 1619–20. Shelley (using **Palatinate** for Elector Palatine) mentions that he was **Calvinist** (*R* 2.3).

Elephant: Brixen inn **Murray** recommends (*MSGE* 331). Shelley slept there September 1842 (*R* 2.61).

Eleusis: Ancient **Greek** town ten miles northeast of **Athens**. **Perdita** nurses **Raymond** back to health there (*LM* 173).

Elia: See **Lamb**.

Elias: **Greek** name for Elijah, biblical prophet whose story the books of 1 and 2 Kings record. About twenty-five miles northwest of **Yannina** lies "a monastery dedicated to St. Elias," which Shelley terms the monastery of prophet Elias (Hobhouse 1.64). **Dmitri** follows **Katusthius Ziani** there, standing "on an elevated peak of the mountains of **Sagori**, eight leagues from Yannina," where **caloyers** protect **Constans Ziani** (*EE* 112).

Elinor: Heiress's daughter whom **Woodville** loves in *Matilda*.

Elisei: Thirteenth-century **Ghibelline Florentine** family; also characters in "**A Tale of the Passions**" (Villani 81, 125).

Elisei, Arrigo dei: Despina dei Elisei's father, **Madonna Pia**'s husband, and **Cincolo de' Becari**'s patron in "**A Tale of the Passions**."

Elisei, Despina dei: Arrigo dei Elisei and **Madonna Pia**'s daughter and **Cincolo** and **Monna Gegia de' Becari**'s foster-daughter in "**A Tale of the Passions**"; she masquerades as **Ricciardo de' Rossini**.

Elisir d'Amore: See **Donizetti**.

Elixir of Immortality: Fifteenth- and 16th-century alchemists sought this mystical potion (also called **philosopher's stone**) that supposedly confers immortality on humans who drink it. In **William Godwin**'s *St. Leon* (1799), Reginald St. Leon partakes of an elixir that prolongs life. **Victor Frankenstein** becomes obsessed with finding the philosopher's stone (*Fr1* 69; *Fr3* 45). **Cornelius Agrippa** discovers the elixir; scholar-servant **Winzy** drinks half of it and narrates his tale 323 years later (*MI* 219, 222, 226).

Elizabeth, Countess: Elizabeth of **Bavaria** was **Conradin**'s mother; she raised him at the home of her second husband, Mainard, Count of Gorizia, until 1267, when Conradin departed for **Italy** (Runciman 31, 101, 105). **Ricciardo de' Rossini** carries a letter to **Guielmo Lostendardo** from Countess Elizabeth, who encourages **Despina dei Elisei** to visit Guielmo (*TP* 10, 21).

Elizabeth of England: Elizabeth Stuart (1596–1662); British princess who married Frederick V, the **Elector Palatine**. Shelley also refers to her as **Princess Elizabeth** when discussing **Heidelberg Castle**. Shelley mentions she "held a gay and chivalrous court in **Prague**" (*R* 2.3).

Elizabeth of York (1466–1503): **Edward IV** and **Elizabeth Woodville**'s oldest child; she married English

Elizabeth, Princess

Henry VII 1486, becoming queen (Cook 121–127). She is **Richard of York**'s sister in *Perkin Warbeck*.

Elizabeth, Princess: See **Elizabeth of England**.

Elizabeth, Queen (1533-1603): Elizabeth I, queen of England 1558-1603. Shelley cites the **Reformation** as cause for lack of charity in England, footnoting that it forced Queen Elizabeth to institute Poor Laws (*R* 2.234).

Ellen: Central protagonist and narrator of "The Elder Son."

Ellis, Robert Leslie (1817–1859): Scholar and essayist who attended **Cambridge** with **PFS** 1836–40 (*DNB*). He may have joined Shelley's traveling party at **Trèves** June 1840 or at **Cadenabbia** July 1840 (*R* 1.18, 1.76; Seymour 476, 482).

Elmore, Lewis: Earl of D——'s second son in "**The Mourner**"; he is one of the mourners of the story's title.

Elmore-park: Earl of D——'s and the **Elmore** family's country house, where **Horace Neville** befriends **Lewis Elmore** (*Mourner* 91).

Elster: Southeastern **German** river branching from the **Elbe** east of Wittenburg. Shelley viewed the place on it where **Poniatowski** was killed 1813 (*R* 1.215).

Elton, Charles Abraham [Sir] (1778–1853): Author and patron to **Lamb** and Tennyson, among others. Shelley quotes **Hesiod**, specifically citing Elton's translation, *The Remains of Hesiod, Translated from the Greek into English Verse; with a Preliminary Dissertation on the Life, Writings, and Aera, of Hesiod and Illustrative Notes* (1812) (*LM* 229, 315, 400). She draws from Hesiod's *Works and Days* and *Shield of Hercules* (*Journals* 651). **Lionel Verney** reflects upon plague's spread by quoting directly from Hesiod's description of **Zeus** enacting punishment for one man's wrongdoing by punishing communities that do not correct such misbehavior; the lines begin "**The God sends down** his angry plagues from high, / Famine and pestilence in heaps they die" (*LM* 229; Hesiod, *Works and Days* lines 321–322, 325–328). Verney later quotes Hesiod's description of Zeus's punishment of humankind, when Zeus avenged **Prometheus**'s theft of fire by unleashing "woes innumerous" upon humanity from **Pandora**'s Box; the lines begin "**With ills the land** is rife, with ills the sea, / Diseases haunt our frail humanity" (*LM* 315; Hesiod, *Works and Days* lines 138–142). As plague survivors journey to **Geneva**, Verney notes the commonplace sight of dead plague victims: " '**Through the flesh** that wastes away / Beneath the parching sun, the whitening bones / Start forth, and moulder in the sable dust' " (*LM* 400). Shelley notes these lines as "Elton's translation of Hesiod's '*Shield of Hercules*,' " taken from Hesiod's description of **Hercules**'s armor (*LM* 400; Hesiod, *Shield of Hercules* lines 206–208).

Ely: English city fifteen miles northeast of **Cambridge**. **John Morton** is Ely's bishop, and **O'Carroll** is its prince (*PW* 1.122, 1.291).

Ely, Bishop of: See **Morton**.

Ely, Prince of: See **O'Carrolls**.

Elysian Fields: Mythical **Elysium** is a blessed place that either the virtuous dead or "mortals made immortal through" gods' favor occupied (Tripp 221–222). Shelley visited the Elysian Fields near **Naples** 8 December 1818 (*Journals* 242). **Valerius** tells his tale there, noting that it is " 'much changed by the sacreligious hand of man' " and that the place " 'chosen by our antient [*sic*] and venerable religion, as that which best represented the idea oracles had given or diviners received of the seats of the happy after death' " (*Val* 332–333). Shelley often uses Elysium to describe beauty and happiness: **Ildone**'s song to **Euthanasia**'s guests and **Castruccio**'s voice to a hopelessly enamored **Beatrice** are like souls "wrapped in Elysium" (*V* 1.268, 2.282). When Beatrice first loves Castruccio, she feels "Elysian happiness" (*V* 2.69). The discoverer of **Lionel Verney**'s narrative travels through the Elysian Fields, and part of his narrative is set there (*LM* 3, 37). Shelley frequently contrasts the Elysian Fields to **Tartarus**'s depths (*P* 73, 75, 77, 81). From her father's descriptions of **Europe**, **Ethel Villiers** expects "a very Elysium of wonders and pleasures" and later finds a "very Elysium of delight" with **Edward Villiers** (*L* 1.273, 2.234). Shelley describes **Armida** gardens at **Tasso**'s **Sorrento** house in terms suggesting "the poet had been carried away by enchantment to an Elysium" (*R* 2.263). Shelley's 1842 journey to **Gmunden** "imparted a sense of peace and amenity that lapped me in Elysium" (*R* 2.23). [*L* 3.40, 3.58; *R* 2.91, 2.263].

Elysium: See **Elysian Fields**.

Embrun, Lady of: Also "Black Virgin"; her shrine is in Embrun, southeastern **France** (Fischer 244). **Stephen Frion** swears by her (*PW* 2.280).

Emms: See **Ems**.

Emperor Mathias: See **Matthias**.

Empoli: Italian city on the **Arno**, fifteen miles southeast of **Florence**. Shelley traveled there 1819 and 1820 (*Journals* 298, 307). **Castruccio** invades, burns, and wastes Florentine territory "as far as Empoli" 1320 (*V* 2.201).

Empson, Richard (d. 1510): Lawyer and tax collector whom **Henry VII** of England favored; **Henry VIII** executed him (*DNB*). **Robert Clifford** hears news from Empson through **Garthe** (*PW* 3.118).

Ems: German town forty-five miles northwest of **Frankfurt**; Shelley spells it **Emms**. Bad Ems is famous for alkaline springs and was a popular early-19th-century watering place (Hecht 168). **Lady Lodore** plans to stay there for a few months (*L* 3.172). [*Letters* 3.380].

Englefield Green: English village about half a mile west of **Egham** on the eastern edge of the **Great Park** at **Windsor**. **Raymond** travels through it to Windsor (*LM* 67).

English Channel: Arm of the **Atlantic** separating England and **France**, ranging from about twenty to a hundred miles wide. Shelley first crossed it with **PBS** July 1814 (*Journals* 6–7). She made the voyage several more times, including *Ramble*'s 1840 opening (*R* 1.3, 1.109).

English traveller: See **Hayward**.

Enna: Central **Sicilian** town thought by many to be the site of **Pluto**'s abduction of **Proserpine** and also **Ceres**'s "ancient cult center" (Tripp 270). Shelley sets *Proserpine* on "the plain of Enna" (*P* 27). Enna is the location of **Arethusa** and **Alpheus**'s mingled waters; it lies in **Mount Etna**'s shadow (*P* 35, 43).

Enniscorthy: Small **Irish** village twenty-eight miles northeast of **Waterford**. **Lewis Elmore** believes **Clarice Eversham** lives near it (*Mourner* 96).

Epictetus (c. 50 C.E.–c. 120) Roman Stoic philosopher who believed in Providence and equality (Howatson 215). **Lord Lodore** finds "Epictetus [could] calm, his soul" (*L* 1.25). **Fanny Derham** finds comfort for life's miseries in Epictetus's philosophy (*L* 3.9). [*L* 2.296].

Epicharis: Slave imprisoned for conspiring against **Nero**. Epicharis refuses to reveal conspirators' names despite horrific torture and hangs herself on the second day of torment, as **Tacitus** records in *Annals* (c. 115–117 C.E.) (15.57). **Lionel Verney** compares **Idris** to Epicharis when she reacts stoically to his illness from plague (*LM* 340).

Epirus: Once an ancient kingdom; the **Greek** word means "mainland." Greece's northwest region bordering southern **Albania**; it was part of southern Albania in Shelley's day. **Cyril Ziani** refuses to leave his wife alone during "a long wandering search among the pathless wilds of Epirus" (*EE* 107). **Camaraz** later accompanies Cyril on his search, and many of "The Evil Eye's" events take place there (*EE* 110).

"Epistle to a Lady": Alexander **Pope**'s 1735 poem, subtitled "Of the Characters of Women." **Lord Lodore** uses a line from Pope's text in describing his wife as "endowed with the usual feminine infirmities—'The love of pleasure, and the love of sway' " (*L* 1.130–131; Pope line 210). **Rupert Falkner** quotes Pope at discovering **Miss Jervis**'s chief virtue is "to be 'Content to dwell** in decencies for ever——' " (*F* 41; Pope line 164).

Eppan Castle: Eleventh-century castle overlooking **Bolzano** (*MSGE* 334). Shelley saw it September 1842 (*R* 2.63).

Eraclea: Italian town twenty miles northeast of **Venice**. Shelley notes that it became Venetian government's seat in the 9th century (*R* 2.114).

Ercilla y Zúñiga, Alonso de (1533–1594): Spanish author of an epic poem relating the conquest of Chile. Shelley is not the author of Ercilla's biography, included in *Italian and Spanish Lives*; the prominent use of endnotes is without parallel in her other known biographies (*ISPL* 3.103–119; Crook 2).

Erebus: Synonym for **Hades** or **Tartarus** and name for the Underworld's darkness (Tripp 228). Throughout *Proserpine*, Shelley refers to the Underworld as Erebus (*P* 69, 75, 77, 79).

Erfurt: German city twelve miles west of **Weimar**. Shelley dined there July 1842 and toured the **Augustine** convent where **Luther** once lived (*R* 1.209).

Erin: Nickname for **Ireland**; Shelley uses it in *Perkin Warbeck* (*PW* 1.280, 1.306, 3.30).

Ermengarda: See **Manzoni**.

Errol, Earl of: Perhaps William Hay (d. 1462), created earl 1452 (Donaldson 71). He escorts **Richard of York** to **Edinburgh** in *Perkin Warbeck*.

Erzherzog Carl: Salzburg hotel **Murray** recommends (*MSGE* 179). Shelley noted that it was "very good" but did not sleep there September 1842 (*R* 2.34).

Espinel, Vicente Martínez (1550–1624): Shelley includes Espinel in her brief discourse upon minor **Spanish** poets for *Italian and Spanish Lives*. She provides very little commentary, terming Espinel a "writer of the natural school" who "was a musician as well as a poet" (*ISPL* 3.240).

Essay on Criticism: Alexander **Pope**'s influential 1711 essay; Shelley read it May 1821 (*Journals* 368). Describing time in **Cadenabbia**, Shelley uses " 'drag a slow length along,' " a line adapted from Pope's work (*R* 1.88; Pope line 357). She later quotes " 'Drink deep, or taste not the Pierian spring' " from the same work (*R* 2.118; Pope line 216).

"Essay on Man": Alexander **Pope**'s influential 1734 poem. **Lionel Verney** characterizes **Alfred**'s intelligence with a line from Epistle Two of Pope's text: "talents and virtues, which would **'grow with his growth**, and strengthen with his strength' " (*LM* 226; Pope line 136). **Francis Derham** educates his daughter carefully, so **Fanny Derham** "could look down with calm superiority on the **'low ambition'** of the wealthy" (*L* 3.22). This line is in Pope's text as well as **Cowper**'s *Table Talk* (1782) (Pope line 2; Cowper lines 590–591). Shelley adapts the same passage (beginning "**All meaner things**") while describing how **Lady Katherine Gordon** desires only to be with **Richard of York**, and she also quotes it accurately in describing the King of **Sardinia**'s neglect of **Simplon** pass (*PW* 3.21; *R* 1.133; Pope lines 1–2).

Essex: County northeast of **London**. **Lord Lovel** leaves the **Earl of Lincoln**'s home to travel there (*PW* 1.44). Many of *Lodore*'s important scenes are set there: **Lord Lodore** is raised at **Longfield**; **Elizabeth Fitzhenry** lives there all her life; the **Villiers**es fall in love there (*L* 2.230). **Dame Nixon**'s cottage is in Essex's **Vale of Bewling** (*L* 3.250). [*L* 3.274, 3.276].

Este: Italian town on the **Euganean Hills**' edge, nineteen miles southwest of **Padua**. The 14th-century Este family constructed a castle there, with five hundred rooms surrounding fifteen courtyards (Johnston 48). The Shelleys had a house in Este 1818: "[T]he villa sat above Este Castle, where three-year-old **William [Shelley]** promptly devised a new game, shouting to make echoes against the walls" (Sunstein 158; *Letters* 1.79). Journeying from Este to **Venice** September 1818, **Clara Shel-**

Esther

ley became seriously ill. Shelley draws on her observation of Este's landscape in *Valperga*. Dying **Ruggieri dei Antelminelli** tells **Castruccio** to deliver a letter to **Francesco de Guinigi**, living in exile in Este (*V* 1.38, 1.44). Castruccio finds Guinigi in a cottage on a hill above Este and lives there with him; Guinigi thinks the area paradisiacal (*V* 1.44–45, 1.51). **Angeline** boards at Este's **Sant' Anna Convent**, where **Faustina Moncenigo** once lived; much of "The Trial of Love" takes place in and near the town (*Trial* 231–234, 238, 243). [*Ch* 78].

Esther: Jewish wife of **Ahasuerus**, biblical king; she successfully petitions Ahasuerus to rescue her relations (Esther 7.3–10). **Elizabeth of York** tells the **Earl of Warwick** that when she becomes England's queen, "Esther will claim a boon from Ahasuerus, and Warwick shall be chief noble in my train" (*PW* 1.56).

Etienne: See **Frion, Stephen Etienne**.

Etna, Mount: Volcano and mountain near **Sicily**'s east coast, overshadowing **Enna** plains upon which Shelley set *Proserpine* (*P* 29, 33, 43, 55, 57). Shelley criticizes superficial tourists, such as the young British man she met at **Bastei**'s inn: "he had done his sunrise on Mount Etna" (*R* 1.265). [*P* 63].

Eton: Prestigious British private secondary school founded by **Henry VI** 1440 on the **Thames** opposite **Windsor**. **PBS** attended Eton and received an excellent classical education there; however, Eton's conformity and its fagging system, which demanded that younger pupils obey older ones, tormented him (White 1.31–39). **Matilda**'s father attends Eton, as do **Oswi Raby**'s eldest grandson and **Maurice** (*M* 152; *F* 241; *Maurice* 85). **Alfred** attends Eton, and Shelley conveys the desolation caused by the plague with descriptions of the school deserted by its "youthful congregation of gallant-hearted boys" (*LM* 226–227, 310). **Horace Neville** calls the despicable fagging system at Eton "my woeful slavery"; he subsequently runs away from school (*Mourner* 86–87, 95). **Lord Lodore** attends Eton from age thirteen; he too runs away (*L* 1.75, 1.79–81). **Francis Derham** and **Edward Villiers** also attend Eton, and Edward helps **Ethel Villiers** visit the school, of which her father spoke fondly (*L* 2.5–8). [*L* 1.81–83].

Etruria: Ancient country that existed 8th–1st centuries B.C.E. in **Italy**'s west central region between the **Arno** and **Tiber**; its inhabitants, civilization, art, and language are **Etruscan**. **Euthanasia**'s favorite spring is covered by a portico of Etruscan marble columns (*V* 1.235). As Shelley notes, **Dante** lived there (*R* 2.262).

Ettenheim: German town seventeen miles north of **Freyberg**. Shelley stayed at a nearby inn July 1840 (*R* 1.42).

Ettore Fieramosca: See **d'Azeglio**.

Eufemio da Messina: See **Pellico**.

Euganean Hills: Hilly region north of **Este**. During the Shelleys' 1818 stay, **PBS** composed "Lines Written Among the Euganean Hills" (1819) (White 2.40–41). **Castruccio** joins **Francesco de Guinigi** at the latter's cottage there for a year (*V* 1.44, 3.173). The hills serve as

Matteo Visconti's retreat (*V* 1.98). **Edmund Malville** thinks Euganean Hills similar to British topography, but more colorful and inspirational; he praises **Foscolo**'s description of them in *Ultime lettere di Jacobo Ortis* (*RI* 28; Foscolo 76–77). These hills are "**The Trial of Love**'s" setting; **Villa Moncenigo** nestles among them (*Trial* 231). Shelley recrossed the **Venetian Lagune** September 1842 while "the sun sinks behind the Euganean hills" (*R* 1.62–63, 2.99).

Eumenides: Greek for "the kindly ones," euphemistic name for the Erinyes, "spirits of punishment avenging without pity wrongs done to kindred" (Howatson 240). **Lionel Verney** endows the heroines of all he reads with **Perdita**'s "beauty and matchless excellences," including "**Antigone**, when she guided the blind **Oedipus** to the grove of the Eumenides," a reference to the opening scene of Sophocles's *Oedipus at Colonus* (401 B.C.E.) (*LM* 78). Memories pursue **Meiler Trangmar** "like the hell-born Eumenides" (*PW* 1.249). **Henry Vernon** suffers from knowing about his father's unkind actions, recalling "that one whom he ought to revere was guilty of so dark a crime, haunted him, as of old the Eumenides tormented the souls of men" (*IG* 198). As **Elizabeth Falkner** weighs her feelings toward **Rupert Falkner** and **Gerard Neville**, Shelley suggests that "perhaps of all the scourges wielded by the dread Eumenides, there is none so torturing as the consciousness of the wilfulness of the act deplored" (*F* 212).

Eunoe: Nymph attending **Proserpine**; her name is also the river that "can restore recall of each good deed" in **Dante**'s **Eden** (Clemit 73; Alighieri, *Purgatorio* 28.129–131).

Euphrasia: Chief **Constantine**'s younger sister in "**Euphrasia: A Tale of Greece**."

"Euphrasia: A Tale of Greece": Short story first published in the 1839 *Keepsake* and signed "Mrs. Shelley" (Robinson 394). The accompanying illustration, titled *Constantine and Euphrasia,* depicts **Chief Constantine**'s rescue of **Euphrasia**; Edward Corbould drew and J. Henry Robinson engraved it (*E* 305). **Harry Valency** relates his experiences during the **Greek** revolution to entertain fellow passengers in a snow-trapped carriage during a Christmas 1836 journey from **Brighton** to **Lewes** (*E* 296). He relates his travel to Greece when eighteen and eager to fight in the 1824 Greek revolution (*E* 296–297). He quickly attached himself to a Greek band led by Constantine and fought with them against **Turks** during an ambush in which Greek forces suffered heavy losses (*E* 298–299). After the battle, only Valency and Constantine were left alive (*E* 299). Valency could not move, since he had lost much blood, but mortally wounded Constantine, who had saved Valency's life by shielding him from a shot, managed to fetch water for them both and then related his story (*E* 300–301). An adoptive father had taught Constantine to be a warrior and his sister, Euphrasia, a scholar (*E* 301–302). Their father died, and the siblings remained close even though Euphrasia stayed in **Athens** while Constantine joined a band of **Albanians** and fought in western Greece, where he quickly earned a reputation as a valiant warrior (*E* 302).

Worried when his sister's letters stopped, Constantine returned to Athens to learn that his home had been destroyed and Euphrasia imprisoned in the harem of the **pasha**'s son (*E* 303). With friends, Constantine attacked the palace where Euphrasia was imprisoned and set fire to it, escaping with her in his arms (*E* 303–304). But Euphrasia was shot as he carried her away; he held her as she died and left her body at a convent, looking forward to joining her in heaven (*E* 304–307). Valency awakened to voices heralding rescue and found that Constantine had died peacefully in the night (*E* 307). Valency recovered from his wound in **Cefalonia** and returned to England (*E* 307).

Europe: Shelley spent most of her years with **PBS** in Europe and generally enjoyed traveling there. She sets many important fictional scenes in Europe—much of *Frankenstein*'s action takes place in **Switzerland** and **France** (*Fr1* 175, 192; *Fr3* 127, 140). *Valperga* is set principally in **Italy**, although the characters travel widely; much of *The Last Man*'s plot involves the **Greek** war of independence (*LM* 189). Parts of *Perkin Warbeck* are set in **Flanders**, France, and **Spain**. **Lord Lodore** misses Europe while living in **America** and longs to return (*L* 1.234). **Rupert Falkner** and **Elizabeth Falkner** travel in Europe to escape painful memories in Britain (*F* 35). In *History* and *Rambles*, Shelley records her European travels (*R* 1.19, 1.50, 2.35, 2.37). [*Val* 332; *RD* 44–45; *FE* 65; *PW* 1.203, 1.242, 2.187, 3.320; *SP* 151; *L* 1.256, 3.140; *E* 301; *EE* 101–102, 105].

Eusta: Teresa de' Tolomei and Clorinda Saviani's chaperone in "The Bride of Modern Italy." Shelley also calls her **Argus**, referring to the mythical **Greek** man said to have a hundred eyes all over his body, but she is not like the watchful Greek character; Eusta knits a shawl while observing Clorinda and **Giacomo de' Tolomei** and mistakes the marriage contract for an account of **Asisa**'s miracle (Tripp 98; *BMI* 33).

Euterpe: **Greek** muse of music. **Euthanasia** describes her "pleasure in music" by alluding to Euterpe (*V* 3.58).

Euthanasia: Fictional main character and **Castruccio**'s love interest in *Valperga*. Shelley modeled **Euthanasia dei Adimari** on Beatrice and **Matilda**, 11th-century **Tuscan** countesses (Sunstein 189). Her name is **Greek** for "gentle and easy death," and her death by shipwreck eerily foreshadows **PBS**'s death; some critics suggest Shelley based Euthanasia on him (Sunstein 230, 437; *Letters* 1.323).

Eve: According to **Genesis**, first woman made by God. She and **Adam** succumb to temptation, and God forces them to leave **Eden**. The **Creature** appeals to **Victor Frankenstein** to create a female creature, arguing, " 'no Eve soothed my sorrows nor shared my thoughts' " (*Fr1* 159; *Fr3* 114). For his daughter's education, **Lord Lodore** draws "his chief ideas from **Milton**'s Eve" in *Paradise Lost* (*L* 1.38). **Ethel Villiers** listens to **Whitelock**'s appeals of love as "Eve listened to the serpent" (*L* 1.60). **Elizabeth Falkner** wanders **Zante**'s shores "as if a new Eve, watched over by angels, had been placed in the desecrated land" (*F* 62). While in **Baden-Baden**, Shelley saw a pretty girl and her ugly fiancé look "at each other as Adam and Eve might have done when no other human creature existed to observe them" (*R* 1.39).

Eversham, Clarice: Lord Eversham's daughter in "The Mourner"; she also uses the name **Ellen Burnet**.

Eversham, Lord: Elmore family's nearest neighbor and **Clarice Eversham**'s father in "The Mourner."

Evian: French town on **Lake Geneva**'s southern shore, twenty-eight miles northeast of **Geneva**. **Victor Frankenstein** and **Elizabeth Lavenza** marry and rest overnight there, where the **Creature** murders Elizabeth (*Fr1* 217; *Fr3* 161).

"Evil Eye, The": Short story first appearing in the 1830 *Keepsake* as by "the Author of **Frankenstein**" (Robinson 379). The accompanying plate entitled *Zella*, which Henry Corbould drew and Charles Heath engraved, depicts **Zella Ziani** waiting on the coast for her husband at the story's conclusion (*EE* 109). The **Albanian** setting of this story is unusual in Shelley's corpus, although she had formerly demonstrated her familiarity with **Greece**'s landscape and customs in *The Last Man*. Shelley draws from **Byron**'s description of Albania and its people in *Childe Harold's Pilgrimage* (Byron 2.424–268). Legends of "The Evil Eye" are commonplace in both **Italy** and Greece and are recorded in the **Bible**, **Virgil**, and **Plato**. Although there are variations, the basic myth is that a person with an Evil Eye brings evil upon a person falling under its gaze. Shelley would surely have seen amulets and charms worn in protection against the Evil Eye during residence in **Naples** 1818–19 (*Journals* 241–249). In her review "**Illyrian Poems—Feudal Scenes**," Shelley includes a translation of one of **Prosper Mérimée**'s poems about the Evil Eye legend, which probably inspired her story. Shelley opens her story recounting how **Katusthius Ziani** returned to **Corinth** to learn that his father had left all his property to a newly acknowledged son, **Cyril Ziani**. Even though Cyril willingly divided the inheritance equally, Katusthius wants it all (*EE* 103). Katusthius travels to **Korvo** to claim assistance from **Dmitri**, his **pobratimo**, whose gentle youthful demeanor altered when he returned to his **Sciote** home to find that **Mainotes** had murdered his wife **Helena** and stolen his child (*EE* 101). Dmitri spent three years searching for his child, earning "a deep gash across his eyebrow and cheek" during his struggles; "his mind became reckless, his countenance more dark; men trembled before his glance, women and children exclaimed in terror, 'The Evil Eye!' " (*EE* 101). He delights in this appellation and the fear it inspires. Katusthius returns to Corinth and persuades Cyril and Zella to accompany him toward **Napoli**, while Dmitri, who has already appeared as the Evil Eye twice at the Zianis' home, abducts **Constans Ziani** (*EE* 104–106). Katusthius and Dmitri meet at **Vasilico** and take Constans into Albania, while Cyril searches fruitlessly for his child for several days before taking Zella to safety at her father **Camaraz**'s house in **Maina** (*EE* 106–108). Zella waits in miserable solitude while Cyril and Camaraz sail to Albania and proceed to **Yannina** without finding any trace of Constans (*EE* 110–

111). According to **caloyers** at **Zitza**, Dmitri grew fond of Constans and frustrated Katusthius with consistent pleas for mercy on the child's behalf, until Katusthius stole the child away (*EE* 111). Dmitri followed and forced Katusthius to take refuge in **Elias**'s monastery, which Dmitri besieged while Katusthius went secretly to the nearest town to gain **Sagorian** assistance (*EE* 112). During Katusthius's absence, Dmitri storms the monastery, and caloyers are glad to let him leave with Constans when they see the child's affection for his deliverer (*EE* 113). Cyril and Camaraz follow Dmitri's trail into the mountains, and battle ensues (*EE* 113). When Dmitri learns that Constans's grandfather is Mainote, he nearly drops the child deliberately, but is forced to defend himself against Camaraz; Constans escapes into his father's arms (*EE* 114). Camaraz reveals that fifteen years ago he led the attack on Scio in which Helena died protecting her child; thus Zella is his adopted daughter and Constans is Dmitri's grandson (*EE* 115). Shelley provides no further information about Camaraz or Katusthius but adds a postscript paragraph recounting that Zella, having fallen asleep on the beach at Maina under an opiate's effect, awakes onboard ship to see Dmitri holding Constans (*EE* 116).

Evoe: Euripedes's drama *The Bacchae* (c. 405 B.C.E.) presents the cry "Evoe!" as part of frenzied female worship of **Bacchus**. Bacchus sees his foster-father returning surrounded by "priests and bacchant women" who cry " 'Bacchus! Evoe!' " (*Midas* 117).

Excursions in Italy: See **Cooper, James**.

Exeter: English city twenty-eight miles southwest of **Taunton**. **Maurice**'s father returns from business there to claim his son (*Maurice* 67–68). **Richard Fox**, Exeter's bishop, advises **Henry VII** during the **Lambert Simnel** controversy (*PW* 1.122). **Richard of York** plans to attack Exeter, and Henry allows the **Courtneys** to defend it (*PW* 3.75–76, 3.81, 3.83, 3.102; Holinshed 3.518). After **Cornish** insurgents unsuccessfully attack Exeter, Richard writes a letter to Henry superscribed "Exeter 1497" (*PW* 3.106, 3.113, 3.120).

Exeter, Bishop of: See **Fox, Bishop Richard**.

Ezzelin: See **Ezzelino**.

Ezzelino (d. 1260): Ghibelline ruler who "was the most cruel and redoubtable tyrant that ever was among Christians"; Shelley's variant is **Ezzelin** (Villani 168). He controlled **Padua** and was excessively violent, burning "at one time 11,000 Paduans" (Villani 167–168). **Francesco de Guinigi** mentions Ezzelino to illustrate war's horror, and **Beatrice** refers to Ezzelino's cruelties to demonstrate evil's presence in the world (*V* 1.52, 3.44). **Castruccio**'s tyranny, similar to Ezzelino's, depresses **Euthanasia** (*V* 3.14).

F——, Mr.: Shelley mentions Mr. and **Mrs. F——**, whom she met at **Cadenabbia**'s **Albergo Grande** July 1840; Mr. **F——** is a middle-aged, gentlemanly scholar who has been in **Italy** two years (*R* 1.73). He is not further identified, and Shelley may also refer to him as **Mr.——**.

F——, Mrs.: Shelley mentions Mrs. **F——**, whom she met at **Cadenabbia**'s **Albergo Grande** July 1840; she welcomes the company of this "dear, gentle, sensible, warm-hearted" woman, not further identified (*R* 1.73).

Fabii: Probably a reference to family of Quintus Fabius Maximus (275–203 B.C.E.), who joined the **Scipios** in opposing **Hannibal** and was dictator during the 216 B.C.E. battle of **Cannae**; the Scipios and Fabii were dynasties that represented the best **Roman** republican virtues (Kinder 1.81; Crook 2). **Euthanasia** praises the **Tiber**, remarking upon its waters "which flowed here when the Scipios and the Fabii lived on thy shores" (*V* 1.202).

Fabricius Luscinus Gaius: Twice **Rome**'s consul, Fabricius was renowned for "old-style virtues of austerity, high principle, and incorruptibility," especially during Rome's war with Pyrrhus 280–272 B.C.E. (Howatson 231). **Valerius** talks of how " 'during my life . . . men were again vivified by the sacred flame that burnt in the souls of **Camillus** and Fabricius' " (*Val* 336). **Isabell Harley** admires Rome's monuments, considering Fabricius "planned and modified" them (*Val* 340).

***Faerie Queen, The*:** Edmund Spenser's highly influential epic allegorical poem, books 1–3 published 1590, books 4–6 1596. Each book explores a different topic within the larger framework of Arthur's quest for Gloriana. The epic contains adventures of various knights, each representing a different virtue, and explores contemporary issues and larger thematic concerns, such as religious differences. **PBS** read aloud from it 1814, and Shelley read it 1815 and 1817 (*Journals* 48, 77–79, 167). **Matilda** reads aloud "the descent of **Sir Guyon** to the halls of Avarice," which recounts **Mammon**'s temptation of Sir Guyon, fictional knight representing temperance (*M* 167; Spenser 2.7). Matilda appeals to **Woodville** to join her in a suicide pact with a reference to Despair's temptation of Redcrosse, knight of Holiness: "**What if some** little payne the passage have / That makes frayle flesh to fear the bitter wave? / Is not short payne well borne that brings long ease, / And lays the soul to sleep in quiet grave?" (*M* 201; Spenser 1.40). Woodville says he will support Matilda by playing "the part of **Una**," representative of truth or unity of the Anglican church's true religion (*M* 202). As an epigraph to *Perkin Warbeck*'s opening chapter, in which **Edmund Plantagenet** learns of **Richard of York**'s existence, Shelley quotes a description, beginning "**He seemed breathless**, heartless, faint and wan," of Guyon's view of fallen Pyrochles (*PW* 1.1; Spenser 2.6.41). As the first epigraph to the chapter in which Richard briefly reunites with his mother, Shelley quotes from Guyon's speech, made while holding an orphan child: " '**Poor orphan!** in the wide world scattered, / As budding branch rent from the native tree' " (*PW* 1.83; Spenser 2.2.2). Shelley adapts a passage describing Archimago seeing Guyon as an epigraph to the chapter introducing **Lambert Simnel**, lines beginning "**Such when as Archimago** him did view, / He weened well to work some uncouth wile" (*PW* 1.108; Spenser 2.1.8). As an epigraph to the chapter in which Richard and followers arrive in **Cork**, Shelley quotes from the passage in which Paridell tells Britomart his ancestry: "**Then Paridell**, in whom a kindly pride / Of gracious speech, and skill his words to frame / Abounded, being glad of so fit tide / Him to commend to them, thus spake, of all well eyed" (*PW* 1.278; Spenser 3.9.32). As an epigraph to the chapter in which Richard apprehends treacherous **Sir John Ramsay** and delays punishment, Shelley quotes from Arthur's speech to Cymochles, lines beginning "**Traitor, what hast** thou done?" (*PW* 2.276; Spenser 2.8.46). As an epigraph to the chapter in which Richard successfully escapes **Robert Clifford**'s treachery, Shelley quotes from Arthur's address to Turpine, lines beginning "**Art thou he**, traitor! that with treason vile / Hast slain my men in this unmanly manner" (*PW* 3.130; Spenser 6.6.25). As an epigraph to the chapter in which **Henry VII** of England takes Richard prisoner at **Taunton**, Shelley quotes Spenser's lines beginning "**For, when Cymocles** saw the foul reproach," describing Cymocles's attack on Arthur (*PW* 3.182; Spenser 2.8.44). Shelley subsequently uses Spenser's description of Guyon with reference to Richard: "**A sweet regard** and aimiable grace, / Mixed with manly sternness did appear" (*PW* 3.186; Spenser 2.12.79). Describing Henry's attraction to **Lady Katherine Gordon**, Shelley draws from Spenser's description of Duessa leading Guyon astray: "**So easy is**, t'appease the stormy wind / Of malice, in the calm of pleasant womankind" (*PW* 3.208; Spenser 2.6.8). As an epigraph to the chapter in which Richard escapes betrayal, Shelley draws from Britomart's lines appealing to the sea, beginning

"**Thou, God** of winds" (*PW* 3.217; Spenser 3.4.10). As an epigraph to the chapter in which Katherine and Richard learn he will be executed, Shelley draws from Una's appeal to the dwarf to continue narrating his master's downfall: "**Tempestuous Fortune** hath spent all her spite, / And thrilling Sorrow thrown his utmost dart: / Thy sad tongue cannot tell more heavy plight / Than that I feel and harbour in my heart" (*PW* 3.311; Spenser 1.7.25). Shelley quotes Spenser's description of Britomart as an epigraph to the *Lodore* chapter in which **Ethel Villiers** awaits her husband's return anxiously, lines beginning "**She to a window** came, that opened west" (*L* 2.127; Spenser 5.6.7).

Faggiuola, Francesco della (d. 1315): Uguccione della Faggiuola's son, who gained control of **Lucca** June 1314; he reputedly stole papal treasure to fund his father's military campaign against **Florence** (Green 59–60; Rossington 400). Francesco is in charge of Lucca in *Valperga*, and Shelley accurately places Francesco in command during **Montecatini**'s siege, when he died in battle (*V* 2.210; Green 66–69).

Faggiuola, Ranieri della: Uguccione della Faggiuola's son controlled **Lucca** after **Francesco della Faggiuola**'s death (1315) (Green 71; Rossington 401). In *Valperga*, Ranieri courts **Euthanasia** and instigates a plot against **Castruccio** (*V* 1.175). Shelley takes this episode from **Machiavelli** (*LCCL* 540; Green 72–74). As Uguccione approaches Lucca to assist his son, he encounters rebellion in all the towns he controls and frees Castruccio in exchange for safe passage; Ranieri and Uguccione give Castruccio control of Lucca (Green 72–74; *V* 1.228–231). Shelley accurately relates these developments but fictionalizes the events causing the Faggiuola plot: "sources disagree as to [their] exact circumstances" (Green 72).

Faggiuola, Uguccione della (c. 1250–1319): Lord of **Pisa** from 1313, a revolution deprived him and his son **Ranieri della Faggiuola** of power over **Lucca** April 1316 and conferred power on **Castruccio** (Villani 437; Sismondi 132–133; *LCCL* 538–541; Rossington 390). Uguccione is a *Valperga* character.

Faido: Swiss town twenty-three miles northwest of **Bellinzona**. Shelley includes **PFS**'s friend's account of their dangerous September 1840 journey through Faido (*R* 1.149).

Fairfax, Lord Thomas (1560–1640): English noble who swore loyalty to **James I** upon his accession to England's throne (*DNB*). Fairfax served in the military under both **Queen Elizabeth** I and James, receiving a knighthood for service in **France** (1580s); **Charles I** created him "Baron Fairfax of Cameron in the peerage of Scotland" 1627 in recognition of lifetime service (*DNB*). He authored several military publications, and, "about 1635, [he] ... settled on [**Roger Dodsworth**] a pension of 50 [pounds] a year" (*DNB*). Dodsworth's father "received a salary from the republican general, Lord Fairfax, who was himself a great lover of antiquities" (*RD* 45).

Fairlight Bay: Beautiful inlet on **Kent**'s southern coast, five miles east of

Fairy

Hastings. **Lady Cecil**'s house overlooks it (*F* 87).

Fairy: See **Férrai**.

Fairy's Fountain: Place close to **Valperga** castle; **Castruccio** and **Euthanasia** frequented it as children (*V* 1.238).

Faliero, Alberto: Noble **Venetian** family member. Shelley cites Faliero as evidence of Venetian nobility's descent from **Roman** families; he assisted with **Rialto**'s 421 C.E construction (*R* 2.114).

Falkland, Second Viscount [Lucius Cary] (1610–1643): English political leader during **Charles I**'s reign who aligned himself with the king 1639; Charles's 1640 dismissal of **Parliament** turned Falkland against him. Despite his negative attitude toward Charles, Falkland became secretary of state 1642 and died in the king's service at **Newbury** (Carlton 253; Crook 2). **Victor Frankenstein** and **Henry Clerval** remember "amiable Falkland" while touring **Oxford** (*Fr1* 186; *Fr3* 136).

Falkner: Shelley's 7 June 1836 *Journals* entry reads: "I am now writing a novel '*Falkner*'—My best it will be—I believe" (548). She began writing late 1835, but 1836 was a difficult year. Her father died in April, she found herself alone and struggling financially in **London**, and "in October, before finishing the book, she gave out emotionally and physically in a minor breakdown" (Sunstein 334). She completed the book while recuperating at **Brighton**, and it appeared to generally favorable reviews 1837. Heroine **Elizabeth Falkner** is an orphan: **Edwin Raby**'s Catholic family disowned him for marrying a "portionless, low-born girl" who died soon after him and after the **Raby** family's refusal to help her (*F* 149). At her mother's grave, Elizabeth prevents a stranger from committing suicide. The stranger, **Rupert John Falkner**, adopts Elizabeth and takes her with him around **Europe**. Guilt haunts Falkner, and he will not reveal its cause to Elizabeth; nevertheless, their mutual affection grows. Elizabeth falls in love with **Gerard Neville**, who is determined to solve the mystery around his mother **Alithea Neville**'s disappearance and thus clear her name. Falkner reveals that he loved and abducted Alithea and that she drowned trying to return home—he is put in prison and charged with murder. Elizabeth refuses the advances of her blood family, proclaiming love for her adopted father and defying propriety in accompanying him to prison. Neville ultimately recognizes Falkner's gentlemanly honor and joins Elizabeth's effort to clear his name. Falkner is acquitted of the crime, and he and Neville reconcile. Elizabeth marries Neville, but her love for Falkner does not diminish.

Falkner, Elizabeth (born Raby): *Falkner*'s angelic orphan heroine. Her conduct is exemplary and, like young Shelley, she spends time at her mother's grave at the novel's beginning. She honors her adoptive father, **Rupert John Falkner**, above all others; she marries **Gerald Neville**.

Falkner, John: Rupert Falkner's uncle and minor character in *Falkner*.

Falkner, Rupert John: *Falkner*'s protagonist. His relationship with **Elizabeth Falkner** is an idealized depiction of love and loyalty between father and daughter. With his guilt and passion, Falkner is a **Byronic** hero.

Falls of the Rhine: Shelley approached this area, about two miles south of **Schaffhausen**, in "a rough canoe," viewing the falls from a cottage July 1840 (*R* 1.50–52). She wrote to **Everina Wollstonecraft** about the falls' sublimity (*Letters* 3.2).

"False Rhyme, The": Story first published in the 1830 *Keepsake* as by "the author of **Frankenstein**"; Shelley compresses substantial action into her brief anecdote of 16th-century **France** (Robinson 380). The accompanying illustration titled *Francis the First & His Sister*, which Richard Parkes Bonington painted and Charles Heath engraved, shows royal siblings looking at the window where **Francis I** has the rhyme engraved (*TFR* 118). **Navarre**'s **Queen Margaret** finds her brother, Francis, melancholy about a lady and consoling himself by engraving on a window a rhyme reproaching women for fickleness (*TFR* 117). Margaret asserts that her brother's insult could more equitably be applied to men, but Francis reminds her of her own respected maid of honor, **Emilie de Lagny**, who married **Sire Enguerrard de Lagny** (*TFR* 119). Francis imprisoned Enguerrard for supposedly "traitorously yielding to the emperor a fortress under his command"; Emilie then disappeared and was rumored to have left the country with page **Robinet Leroux** (*TFR* 119). The royal couple make a bet after Margaret asserts she can prove her maid's innocence. At the end of a fruitless month searching, Enguerrard's jailor visits Margaret, guaranteeing that she will win the bet if Enguerrard can leave prison to present his case (*TFR* 119). Francis, pleased by the return of a mysterious, brave knight with news of recent victory, agrees; and the royal siblings are together when the prisoner arrives and reveals that he is actually Emilie (*TFR* 120). Husband and wife exchanged garments when she visited prison, and Enguerrard rode to freedom with Robinet (*TFR* 120). Emilie reveals her husband is the brave knight who brought Francis news of recent victory, and Margaret asks (and is rewarded) pardon for the de Lagnys as her prize (*TFR* 120).

Falstaff: Character who disguises himself as Herne the hunter in **Shakespeare**'s *The Merry Wives of Windsor* (1600), which Shelley read April 1819 (*Journals* 257). According to legend, Herne was wounded by a stag, went insane, and hanged himself from an oak in **Windsor**'s **Little Park**; this oak is still commemorated in Windsor Castle's private grounds, although it was felled 1796 (Hedley 93). **Lionel Verney** observes the familiar "hollow oak tree ... to whose fanciful appearance, tricked out by the dusk into a resemblance of the human form, the children had given the name of Falstaff" (*LM* 362).

***Famiglia Vianesi*:** Shelley saw this singing group perform *Barbiere di Siviglia* and *Elisir d'Amore* in **Venice** October 1842; the group was composed of "about half a dozen children" who were the "most popular amusement" while the **Fenice** was closed (*R* 2.127).

Family of Darius at the Feet of Alexander: See **Veronese**.

Fanar: **Turkish** name for a country's administrative body (Kinder 1.209). **Katusthius** and **Cyril Ziani** discuss the Fanar's "intrigues" (*EE* 105).

Fanariote: **Turkish** name for an elite class from which successive generations of administrators were drawn (Kinder 1.209; Crook 2). **Katusthius Ziani** was formerly "on the point of marriage with a Fanariote beauty" in **Constantinople** (*EE* 102).

Fanny: First-person narrator of Shelley's "**The Parvenue**." Fanny concludes her tale as **Matilda** did hers—longing for death. Shelley probably drew her protagonist's name from **Fanny Godwin**.

Fantozzi, Federigo: **Italian** author of *Nuova Guida, ovvero descrizione storico artistico-critica della città e contorni di Firenze* [*A New Guidebook; or, an Historical, Artistic, and Critical Description of Florence and its Environs*] (1842), which Shelley calls *The Guide-Book of Florence* (Moskal 307; *R* 2.148). Shelley liked the "very complete" guide, except for its lack of an artist index (*R* 2.148).

Farinata (d. 1264): Farinata degli Uberti, "most eloquent orator and the ablest warrior in **Tuscany**," saved **Florence** (c. 1260) when Tuscan **Ghibellines** wanted to raze it; he "protested that he loved his country far better than his party" (Sismondi 85, 87). Shelley uses this historical account when **Benedetto Pepi** curses Farinata and attributes **Guelph** Florence's freedom, which he despises, to him (*V* 1.124).

Farnesina: Palace, built 1506, facing **Rome**'s Corsini Palace (*MROM* 286). Shelley describes **Raphael**'s frescoes of **Psyche** and of ***Galatea*** there (*R* 2.223).

Fates: See **Moirae**.

Father Piers: Religious man **Long Roger** mentions, not further identified (*PW* 3.302).

Father Rhine: Rhine reference Shelley takes from **Murray** (*R* 1.169; Moskal 162).

Faust: See **Goethe**.

Fénelon, François de Salignac de la Mothe (1651–1715): **French** Catholic priest and author of *Traité de l'éducation des filles* [*Treaty on Girls' Education*] (1678), from which **Rousseau** drew, and of fables and dialogues written as educator of **Burgundy**'s duke. *Explication des maximes des saints sur la vie intérieure* [*Discussion of Saints' Maxims About Interior Life*] (1697) caused public outcry; Fénelon's palace was burned and he renounced the work after the pope condemned it. Fénelon later became a **French** Academy member. Shelley read *Les aventures de Télémaque* [*Telemachus's Adventures*] (1699) 1822 (*Journals* 407). In Fénelon's biography for ***French Lives***, Shelley admires *Télémaque* as Fénelon's "great work," finds most of his works "essentially didactic," and applauds the fortitude and Christian principles of "his benevolence, generosity, and sublime elevation above all petty and self-interested views" (*FL* 1.337, 1.372,

1.368). Shelley describes the sea near **Salerno** as similar to images in *Télémaque* (R 2.289).

Fenice: **Venice**'s oldest theater, *Teatro La Fenice*, built 1790 (Honour 181). Shelley noted that the Fenice was "only open during carnival" but attended a performance of *Chi dura Vince* during the **Archduke**'s October 1842 visit (R 2.127–129).

Fenton: *Lodore* valet who serves as messenger between **Lord Lodore** and his wife after their separation.

Ferdinand (1452–1516): **Aragon**'s and **Castile**'s king from 1479 as Ferdinand V, jointly ruling with wife **Isabella I**. He campaigned against **Granada** from 1482, defeating the **Moors** 1492. During his reign, he unified the **Spanish** kingdoms into one nation. **Stephen Frion** meets several **French**men at Ferdinand and Isabella's court (*PW* 1.150). **Richard of York** and **Edmund Plantagenet** fight for Ferdinand's army in **Andalusia** (*PW* 1.212). **El Zagal** surrenders to Ferdinand, but **Boabdil el Chico** fights until defeated (*PW* 1.216).

Ferdinand and his queen: See **Ferdinand IV**.

Ferdinand II (1810–1859): King of **Naples** and King of the Two Sicilies 1830-1859. Shelley notes that his mother, Maria Teresa Isabella, visited **Amalfi** often (R 2.285; Moskal 380).

Ferdinand II, Emperor (1578–1637): Holy Roman Emperor 1619-1637; he was **Matthias**'s brother. Shelley refers to him in her account of Matthias's death, when Ferdinand became emperor (R 2.3; Moskal 229).

Ferdinand III (1769–1824): **Tuscany**'s grand duke (1790). Shelley judges his rule benign but torpid (R 2.110, 2.186–87; Crook 2).

Ferdinand IV (1751–1825): **Naples**'s and **Sicily**'s ruler 1759–1806 and King of the Two **Sicilies** as Ferdinand I 1816–1825 (Mobry 103). **Count Eboli**'s concerns over Eboli property "made him often regret that he had followed his legitimate but imbecil king to exile" in Sicily (*FE* 65). Ferdinand married **Austria**'s Maria Carolina (his queen). Shelley cites their opposition to change and "barbarous imprisonments" as the reasons **Neapolitans** welcomed the **French** 1798–99 (R 2.162, 2.164–165, 2.167; Moskal 316). Opposing French rule, Ferdinand supported **Carbonari** (R 2.170–173).

"Ferdinando Eboli: A Tale": Shelley's story first appeared in the 1829 *Keepsake* as by "the Author of **Frankenstein**"; Robinson conjectures that Shelley may have heard this tale in **Naples** 1818–19 (Robinson 378; *Journals* 241–249). The accompanying plate titled *Adalinda*, which Alfred E. Chalon drew and Charles Heath engraved, depicts **Adalinda Spina** disguised as a page (*FE* 77). Shelley sets "Ferdinando Eboli" in Naples during **Murat**'s reign (1808–15) (*FE* 65, 67). After the death of his father, **Count Eboli**, **Ferdinando Eboli** returns from **Sicily** to Naples, where he regains his family's lands, becomes engaged to Adalinda, and becomes a junior officer in Murat's forces (*FE* 65, 67). Before leaving for a northern **Italian** campaign, Ferdinando bids

Fermoy, Lord

farewell to **Marchese Spina** and Adalinda; a visit from someone she believes to be her fiancé startles Adalinda later that night (*FE* 66). This man takes a lock of Adalinda's hair, cutting himself on the left hand in the process (*FE* 67). In northern Italy, Ferdinando accepts a dangerous mission, but someone seizes and leaves him bound and gagged in a shepherd's cottage; a peasant girl and child later free him (*FE* 67–69). Stripped of his clothes and jewelry, Ferdinando believes himself the victim of **banditti** and hurries back to Murat's camp to explain the mission's failure (*FE* 69). Dressed in rags, Ferdinando is arrested upon giving the password at Murat's camp; he learns that another Ferdinando returned three hours earlier (*FE* 69). When Murat observes and questions the two Ebolis—one with "matted hair" and "torn and mean dress," the other exhibiting signs of nobility—he mistakenly exiles the real Ferdinando (*FE* 69–70). Ferdinando manages to reach Naples to seek Spina's aid, but "false Eboli" arrives at **Villa Spina** shortly thereafter (*FE* 70–71). Richly attired, "pretended Eboli" displays the lock of hair and his scar, so Adalinda chooses him, and Spina ejects the true Ferdinando from Villa Spina (*FE* 72). Ferdinando's situation only worsens when he is arrested for theft—he pockets a jeweled miniature of Count Eboli at Eboli Palace—and is tried, found guilty, and sentenced to life as a galley slave (*FE* 73). "False Eboli" approaches him in prison and offers him freedom for a signed confession, which Ferdinando refuses, and so Ferdinando works hard labor in **Calabria** (*FE* 74). At this prison meeting, "pretended Eboli" claims to have married Adalinda, but Spina's death postpones their marriage (*FE* 74). While imprisoned at the Spina castle in the **Apennines**, Adalinda realizes "false Eboli" is an impostor and escapes disguised as a page (*FE* 74–76). Lost in the mountains, Adalinda wanders into a cave, which is a hideout for a band of criminals Ferdinando joined, having escaped from prison (*FE* 78). Reunited, the couple plans to return to Naples, but banditti arrive with a kidnapped victim—"false Eboli"—who is actually **Ludovico Eboli**, Count Eboli's illegitimate elder son (*FE* 79). The story concludes with a description of the brothers' military escapades in **Russia**; Ludovico saves Ferdinando's life but later dies in Ferdinando's arms (*FE* 79–80). Shelley uses doubles in "Ferdinando Eboli" as she does in *Frankenstein* and "**Transformation**."

Fermoy, Lord: Desmond's **Roche** father-in-law; Fermoy meets Desmond in **Mallow** (*PW* 1.302).

Ferney: Small **French** village three miles north of **Geneva**, now called Ferney-**Voltaire** after its most famous inhabitant. Plague survivors pass through Ferney, encountering a young woman who attempts to keep playing **Haydn**'s "New-Created World" in the church there though she has the plague (*LM* 420).

Férrai: **Greek** village just west of **Hebrus**; Shelley spells it **Fairy** (*MGRE* 434). **Lionel Verney** and **Raymond** meet women returning to Férrai from **Rodosto** (*LM* 178).

Ferrara, Cieco da (d. c. 1505): Little is known about the life of this **Italian** author, originally Francesco

Bello, except that he was poor and blind and lived at **Ferrarra**. Shelley wrote his biography for *Italian and Spanish Lives*. She asserts Ferrara's best known work is "Mambriano," published posthumously, but the "poem is little read, and has never been translated" (*ISPL* 1.180). Shelley confesses to having seen only excerpts, from which "it is evident that he possessed ease of versification, and a considerable spring of poetic imagery and invention" (*ISPL* 1.180).

Ferrarra: Italian city twenty-five miles northeast of **Bologna**; Shelley visited it November 1818 and October 1842 (*Journals* 235; *R* 2.132). Referred to frequently in *Valperga*, **Beatrice** is from there, and **Castruccio** helps to restore **Obizzo** to power there (*V* 2.73, 2.88–89).

Ferruccini, Ferruccio: See **Ferruccio**.

Ferruccio, Francesco (1489–1530): Florentine captain and hero of **Guerrazzi**'s *L'Assedio di Firenze*; Shelley calls him **Ferruccio Ferruccini**. Shelley faults the **Accademia delle Belle Arti (Florence)** for having no pictures to idealize Ferruccio (*R* 2.157, 2.185).

Festa d'Inferno: Spectacle held 1 May 1304 on the **Arno** near **Carraia** bridge. **Florentine** inhabitants of **San Friano** "erected upon the Arno a stage upon boats and vessels, and thereupon they made the similitude and figure of hell, with fires and other pains and sufferings" like those **Dante**'s *Inferno* describes (Villani 360). **Castruccio** witnesses it (*V* 1.17–20, 1.41).

Ficino, Marsiglio (1433–1499): Italian scholar of **Latin** and philosophy renowned for *Theologica Platonica de Immortalitate Animarum* [*Platonic Theology: On the Soul's Immortality*] (comp. 1469; pub. 1485). Shelley wrote Ficino's biography for *Italian and Spanish Lives*. Ficino learned **Greek** and translated **Plato**'s works into Latin during a five-year residence near **Florence** before becoming a cleric; Shelley considers Ficino a "disinterested and blameless man: gentle and agreeable in his manners, no violent passions nor desires disturbed the calm of his mind" (*ISPL* 1.160).

Fielding, Henry (1707–1754): Leading 18th-century humorous novelist. Shelley read his *The History of the Adventures of Joseph Andrews and of his Friend Mr. Abraham Adams* (1742) and *Amelia* (1751) 1818 (*Journals* 235, 647). Shelley describes **Elizabeth Fitzhenry** as knowing "as much of the world as **Parson Adams**"; Fielding says of this *Joseph Andrews* character that "Simplicity was his Characteristic" (*L* 1.243; Fielding 22–23).

Fields of Fancy, The: Title of early draft of Shelley's novella published as *Matilda*; Elizabeth Nitchie first published it and presents drafts and their significance in *Studies in Philology* (1959).

Fiesole: Tuscan town five miles northeast of **Florence**. **Fra Angelico** is from there (*R* 2.145).

Fife: Eastern Scottish county on the **North Sea**. **Mary Boyd** and **James IV** hide their illegitimate offspring there (*PW* 2.189).

Figaro: See **Mozart**.

Filicaja, Vincenzo da (1642–1707): Italian author. Shelley wrote his biography for *Italian and Spanish Lives*. Filicaja wrote love poetry, which he burned when he dedicated "his genius to the celebration only of moral and sacred subjects" (*ISPL* 2.181). He relinquished his law career for writing, combining piety with contemporary anti-**Turkish** sentiments to produce "odes, which breathe a pure and elevated lyric spirit" (*ISPL* 2.181). Shelley finds he "revivified his poetic diction by transfusing into it many elevated and energetic modes of speech, hitherto reserved for prose only," while she feels "facility, dignity, and clearness are his characteristics; and the grandeur of his ideas gives force to the originality of his expressions" (*ISPL* 2.182).

Filippini: Family exiled from **Lucca** (*V* 2.149). A Filippini was senator when **Castruccio** was consul (Crook 3.174).

Fior di Ligi: **Mandragola**'s name when young (*V* 3.125).

"Fire, Famine, and Slaughter. A War Ecologue": Samuel Taylor **Coleridge**'s 1798 poem in which he dramatizes war in England and **France** through the dialogic voices of the sisters—fire, famine, and slaughter (Jackson 701). Shelley quotes lines she identifies from Coleridge's poem in describing how **Matilda**'s relations attempt to comfort her during illness: they "**Whispered so and so** / In dark hint soft and low" (*M* 186; Coleridge lines 17–18). As an epigraph to the *Perkin Warbeck* chapter in which **Richard of York** garners **Irish** support for his English invasion, Shelley quotes "**Sisters, I from** Ireland came" (*PW* 1.293; Coleridge line 46).

Firenze la Bella: See **Florence**.

Fitzgerald, Lord Edward (1763–1798): Glamorous **Irish** peer who served in the **Revolutionary War** and became an Irish Member of **Parliament** 1790. An admirer of the **French Revolution**, he was a prominent figure in Ireland's 1798 rebellion, in the cause of which he died (Foster 268). Shelley quotes accurately from a letter Fitzgerald wrote detailing his delight at traveling and in the simple life as an epigraph to the *Lodore* chapter in which **Ethel Villiers** celebrates her abode's necessary simplicity while **Edward Villiers** deplores it: "**Few people know** how little is necessary to live. What is called or thought hardship is nothing; one unhappy feeling is worse than a thousand years of it" (*L* 3.51; Stafford 228; Fitzgerald 115).

FitzGerald, Maurice: See **Desmond, Earl Maurice of**.

Fitzhenry: Family name of *Lodore*'s central characters; **George III** awards **Admiral Fitzhenry** a peerage and thus a title (**Lord Lodore**) for service during the **Revolutionary War** (*L* 1.258).

Fitzhenry, Admiral: Lord Lodore and **Elizabeth Fitzhenry**'s father in *Lodore*.

Fitzhenry, Elizabeth: Lord Lodore's sister, affectionately called **Aunt Bessy**, in *Lodore*.

Fitzhenry, Ethel: See **Villiers, Ethel**.

Fitzhenry, Henry: **Lord Lodore** is known as Henry Fitzhenry before inheriting his father's title in *Lodore*.

Fitzroy: Son of a royal person (*OED*). *Perkin Warbeck* characters call **Richard of York** "Fitzroy" (*PW* 1.266, 1.309).

Fitzwater, Lord John (d. 1496): **Yorkist** supporter arrested when **Robert Clifford** betrayed conspirators 1494, subsequently taken to **Calais** and beheaded for attempting escape (Holinshed 3.507; Hume 3.44, 3.46; Fischer 160). He is a *Perkin Warbeck* character.

Fitzwilliam: **Tower** guard in *Perkin Warbeck*.

Fiume Latte: Italian town across **Lake Lecco** from **Bellagio**. A 985-foot waterfall is there; Shelley enjoyed it August 1840 (*Guide Bleu* 62; *R* 1.93).

Flanders: Former county on the **North Sea** where **Belgium**, **France**, and **Holland** are located; its inhabitants are **Flemish** or **Fleming** (Kinder 1.125). Fleeing England, **Castruccio**'s boat arrives at Flanders's **Ostend** (*V* 1.85). Both Castruccio and **Benedetto Pepi** fight in wars in Flanders; Pepi observes that "Castruccio is a name which . . . Flemings tremble to hear"; Shelley's account is historically accurate—Flemings disliked Castruccio because under **Scoto**'s 1303 command he led a troop of **Italian** mercenaries against Flemish rebels at Therouanne (*V* 1.115, 1.126; Green 44–45). **Richard of York** lives for several years in Flanders disguised as **Perkin Warbeck**; **Mary of Burgundy** and **Robert Clifford** also reside there (*PW* 1.93, 1.100, 1.130, 1.182). A drunk messenger termed "a Fleming" tells Richard about **Swartz** and **German** mercenaries landing in England (*PW* 3.126–127). [*TP* 22; *R* 1.82].

Fleet: Underground river rising in **Kenwood** and flowing through **London** to the **Thames** (Weinreb 428). **Desmond**, **Richard of York**, and **Monina De Faro** follow it as they flee the **Tower** (*PW* 2.119).

Fleet Street: Street running east-west from the **Strand** to Ludgate Hill in **London**'s City district, with **Temple Bar** at its west end. **Ethel Villiers**'s route through London includes Fleet Street (*L* 2.258).

Fleming: See **Flanders**.

Flemish: See **Flanders**.

Fletcher, John (1579–1625): Prolific English Restoration dramatist who collaborated principally with **Sir Francis Beaumont**. Shelley read Beaumont and Fletcher's *Works* 1817 and 1819 (*Journals* 178, 295–299). **Matilda** compares herself to Leila in Beaumont and Fletcher's comedy *The Captain* (1613) when her father's attitude toward her alters in **London**: "**for what should** I do here, / Like a decaying flower, still withering / Under his bitter words, whose kindly heat / Should give my poor heart life?" (*M* 165; *The Captain* 1.3.237–240). Writing to his daughter, Matilda's father remarks, "**Better have loved** despair, & safer kissed her," a line from Fletcher's *A Wife for a Month*

Fleur-de-Luce

(1624), which Shelley read in August 1819 (*M* 179; *A Wife for a Month* 1.2.103; Crook 2; *Journals* 295). As an epigraph to the *Perkin Warbeck* chapter in which Shelley details the troubled marriage of **Henry VII** of England, Shelley quotes lines that Theodoret speaks to his mother in Fletcher and Philip Massinger's *The Tragedy of Thierry and Theodoret* (1620), a play the Shelleys read 1820: "**Within these ten** days take a monastery; / A most strict house where none may whisper, / Where no more light is known but what may make you / Believe there is a day; where no hope dwells, / Nor comfort but in tears" (*Journals* 317; *PW* 1.117; *Thierry and Theodoret* 1.1.179–183). Shelley also draws upon Fletcher's collaborative play with **Shakespeare**, *Two Noble Kinsmen*, for *Perkin Warbeck* epigraphs (*PW* 2.108, 3.197, 3.292). Shelley quotes Don Jamie's speech to his elder brother in Fletcher's *The Spanish Curate* (1647) as an epigraph to the *Lodore* chapter describing **Colonel Villiers** spending his son's inheritance: "**Alas! he knows** / The laws of Spain appoint me for his heir; / That all must come to me, if I outlive him, / Which sure I must do, by the course of nature" (*L* 2.91; *The Spanish Curate* 1.1.187–190). Shelley quotes Beaumont and Fletcher's *The Custom of the Country* (1647) for epigraphs to other *Lodore* chapters (*L* 2.1, 2.275). As an epigraph to the chapter in which the **Villiers**es meet **Clorinda Saville**, Shelley quotes Ronvere's speech to Martia, lines beginning "**Sad and troubled?**," from Fletcher's *The Double Marriage* (1647), which the Shelleys read aloud 1820 (*Journals* 330; *L* 2.178; Fletcher 4.2.124–128). As an epigraph to the chapter in which **Ethel Villiers** journeys to warn her husband of the danger of arrest, Shelley quotes Philippo's speech from Fletcher's *Love's Pilgrimage* (1647), which she read 1819: "**Think but whither** / Now you can go; what you can do to live; / How near you have barred all ports to your own succour. / Except this one that here I open, love" (*Journals* 301; *L* 3.36; *Love's Pilgrimage* 5.4.97–100). As an epigraph to the chapter in which the Villierses live apart, Shelley adapts Aecius's lines from Fletcher's *The Tragedy of Valentinian* (1647): "**It does much** trouble me to live without you: / Our loves and loving souls have been so used / To one household in us" (*L* 3.27; *Valentinian* 3.3.108–110). As an epigraph to the chapter in which **Lady Lodore** learns of her daughter's financial difficulties, Shelley quotes Beaumont and Fletcher's *The Maid's Tragedy* (1619), which **PBS** read aloud 1818: "**O, where have** I been all this time? How 'friended / That I should lose myself thus desp'rately, / And none for pity show me how I wandered!" (*Journals* 218; *L* 3.108; *The Maid's Tragedy* 4.1.177–179). See *Laws of Candy, The*.

Fleur-de-Luce: French for "flower of light," name of one of the **Staffords'** horses (*PW* 1.3).

Flodden Field: 1513 battle fought five miles south of the **Tweed**; English forces led by **Surrey** defeated **James IV** and his Scottish troops (Cannon 380). Shelley mentions James's defeat and death at Flodden Field (*PW* 2.188, 2.295).

Florence: Italian city on the **Arno**, forty-two miles southeast of **Pisa**, also known as **Firenze la Bella**. The Shelleys moved to Florence October 1819, and **PFS** was born there (*Journals* 298, 302). They left Florence January 1820, but Shelley returned 1842–43 to study painting; she enjoyed the galleries but criticized the weather (Sunstein 359; *Letters* 3.45–56). "**A Tale of the Passions**" opens with a **Guelph** festival in Florence's streets (*TP* 1). Guelph and **Ghibelline** families began fighting in Florence in 1215; at **Valperga**'s opening, Shelley notes that "Florence was at the head of the Guelphs," and the city figures prominently in her novel as **Euthanasia**'s hometown and **Castruccio**'s desired prize (*V* 1.2, 1.206–207). **Edmund Malville** gently mocks travelers to Italy who naively expect " 'to find gorgeous temples and **Cyclopean** ruins in every street in Florence' " (*RI* 27). **Ethel Villiers** "would willingly have lingered in Florence," but her husband is eager to reach **Naples** (*L* 2.170). Shelley wanted to go to Florence while in **Milan** September 1840; in 1842, she asserted **Dresden** "may be said in some degree to rival Florence in its pretensions to beauty" (*R* 1.117, 1.248). Shelley visited Florence November 1842–March 1843; she includes lengthy discourses about Florentine painting and **Carbonari** (*R* 2.140–180). [*LM* 269; *Trans* 122; *Brother* 167].

Florian: **Venetian** café at **Place of Saint Mark** (*Honour* 18). Shelley mentions that it subscribes to **Galignani**'s periodical, thus attracting English customers (*R* 2.105).

Florio: **Raymond**'s dog; **Clara** hears him howling in **Constantinople**'s ruins (*LM* 206). Shelley seems to draw this incident from **Byron**'s "Darkness" (1816) (lines 47–54).

Foggi, Elise (b. 1795)

Floyer, Adam: Sir Simon Mountford's chaplain in *Perkin Warbeck*.

Fluelen: **Swiss** town two miles north of **Altdorf**. Shelley includes **PFS**'s friend's account of their dangerous September 1840 journey; they were relieved to rest at Fleulen (*R* 1.152).

Foggi, Elise (b. 1795): Baptized Louise Duvillard but known as Elise, **Swiss** woman who joined the Shelley household June 1816 as **William Shelley**'s nurse. She returned to England with the family and then traveled back to **Italy**, meeting her own family at Chambéry en route to **Milan** March 1818 (Sunstein 150). Elise accompanied **Clara Allegra Byron** to **Venice** April 1818; Elise's summer 1818 letters to **Claire Clairmont** compelled her and **PBS** to travel to Venice and attempt to resolve matters with **Byron** concerning Allegra (*Journals* 207, 218, 223). Elise traveled with Shelley and the children to **Padua** October 1818 and to **Naples** November 1818; in August 1821, Shelley recounted Elise "formed an attachment with **Paolo** [**Foggi**] . . . without marrying . . . she was ill we sent for a doctor who said there was danger of a miscarriage—I wd [*sic*] not turn the girl on the world without in some degree binding her to this man—we had them married" (*Letters* 1.206; White 2.306–315). Elise left Shelley's service at the end of 1818, "turned catholic at **Rome**, married [Paolo] & then went to **Florence**"; Shelley believed Elise had no part in Paolo's plans to blackmail PBS (*Letters* 1.206; White 2.306–315). In March 1819, Shelley wrote "Venise [*sic*] quite spoiled [Elise] and she appears in the high road to be as Italian as any of them she has settled at Florence," and

Elise, then in the service of another Englishwoman, visited Shelley in Florence 1820 (*Letters* 1.89; *Journals* 306; Sunstein 177). Elise wrote to Shelley July 1821, relating her daughter's birth and requesting financial assistance (*Letters* 1.208–209). Claire met Elise in Florence February 1822, when she first learned of the Foggis' linking her name with PBS's (*Journals* 398). Shelley seems to have thought of Elise as foolish but without her husband's malice. Sunstein suggests *Frankenstein*'s **Monsieur Duvillard** was named "for Elise, whose father had been a modest clockmaker" (128).

Foggi, Paolo: Italian man the Shelleys hired June 1818. Shelley wrote that month: "if Paolo did not cheat us he would be a servant worth a treasure for he does everything cleanlily [sic] & exactly without teazing [sic] us in any way" (*Letters* 1.72). Paolo drove Shelley and her family from **Este** to **Rome** November 1818; when the Shelleys learned that Paolo had made **Elise Foggi** pregnant, the Shelleys compelled their marriage before dismissing them (*Letters* 1.83). Shelley wrote January 1819 about her relief at Paolo's departure, since "lately he has cheated us through thick and thin" (*Letters* 1.86). Before he left, Paolo learned of **Elena Adelaide Shelley**'s existence and subsequently tried to blackmail **PBS** with this information (Sunstein 163; White 2.306–315). Feldman and Scott-Kilvert provide extensive notes outlining Paolo's blackmail attempts in Shelley's *Journals*, and they also discuss her use of a symbol in conjunction with Paolo (*Journals* 249–250, 321–322, 579–581). Sunstein details how Paolo spread incest stories and rumors that PBS had fathered a child with **Claire Clairmont**, paining Shelley personally and damaging both Shelleys' reputations (Sunstein 181–183, 201–202). Writing June 1820, Shelley terms Paolo "a most superlative rascal—I hope we have done with him but I know not"; however, the following day the Shelleys' lawyer "ordered [Paolo] to quit **Leghorn** in four hours" (*Letters* 1.147, 1.155). Writing March 1822, Shelley recalls "we were alarmed by Paolo's attack" June 1820, but the Shelleys seem to have had no further contact with him after his forced departure (*Letters* 1.222).

Foligno: Italian city twenty-five miles north of **Terni**. **Beatrice** mentions passing through it (*V* 3.83).

Fondamenti Nuovi: Literally, "new foundation," street along the **laguna** separating **Venice** from the mainland; the street was "new" 1589 (Honour 171). Shelley enjoyed walking along it September 1842 (*R* 2.99).

Fondi, Ludovico de: Ghibelline count in *Valperga*.

Fontainebleau: Town thirty-five miles southeast of **Paris**, fashionable resort in Shelley's day, and site of a **French** palace. **Napoleon** was forced to abdicate there 1814. The Shelleys passed through Fontainebleau August 1816 and visited the palace (*Journals* 132). **Lionel Verney** plans to lead plague survivors there (*LM* 396, 401). While in **Naples** May 1843, Shelley considered staying at Fontainebleau for a month after leaving **Italy** (*Letters* 3.73).

Ford, John (1586–c. 1640): English playwright whose tragedies demonstrate a consistent interest in moral dilemmas and human suffering; he is best known for *The Broken Heart* (1633) and *'Tis Pity She's a Whore* (1633). **Lionel Verney** uses Ford's "**In Vagabond pursuit** of dreadful safety" from *The Broken Heart* to convey his feelings that England dies as its occupants leave her in an attempt to flee the plague (*LM* 326; Ford 5.2.115–117). Shelley draws from Ford's *Perkin Warbeck* several times in her *Perkin Warbeck*, and in *Lodore* she quotes *The Lover's Melancholy* (*PW* 1.311, 2.195, 2.254, 3.1, 3.72; *L* 3.221). Shelley also quotes the closing lines of *The Lady's Trial* (1638) as an epigraph to *Lodore*'s final chapter, in which she briefly presents major characters' fates: "**None, I trust**, / Repines at these delights, they are free and harmless: / After distress at sea, the dangers o'er, / Safety and welcomes better taste ashore" (*L* 3.304; *The Lady's Trial* 5.2.254–257).

Forli: Italian town twenty miles southwest of **Ravenna**. **Lionel Verney** recovers from illness there (*LM* 455–456).

Fornarina: Famous portrait in **Barberini** and also reference to **Raphael**'s mistress (Muntz 139, 223; Vasari 3.184). Shelley notes *The Transfiguration*'s "most prominent figure, is a portrait of the Fornarina, whose hard countenance is peculiarly odious" (*R* 1.223).

Fortunatus: Ship from **Philadelphia** thought to have brought plague to England (*LM* 217).

Fortunes of Perkin Warbeck, The: See *Perkin Warbeck*.

Forum: "[I]rregular quadrilateral space at the foot of the **Capitoline** and the **Palatine** hills" that became the heart of **Rome**'s legal, political, and religious business but by the early 19th century was called **Campo Vaccino**, **Italian** for "cow pasture" (*MROM* 20). **PBS** records visiting the Forum every day November 1818 (*Journals* 238). **Valerius** recalls past political activity meant he " 'lived in the Forum,' " but he is later appalled by its " 'shattered columns and ruined temples,' " which to him make it " 'degraded and debased' " (*Val* 333, 335). He questions **Isabell Harley** sadly: " 'when the columns of its Forum were broken, what could survive in Rome' "? (*Val* 341). **Lionel Verney** imagines historical scenes while standing "in the open space that was the Forum" (*LM* 461–462). In April 1843, Shelley noted "the Forum used to be, long, long ago, before I ever saw it, a broken space of ground, with an avenue through the Campo Vacino [*sic*] leading to the **Coliseum**, with triumphal arches and tall columns half-buried in the soil. Now the excavations are considerable" (*R* 2.226). [*BMI* 39].

Foscari, Jacopo (d. c. 1456): Francesco Foscari's son, banished from **Venice** (1445) for accepting bribes. Jacopo returned 1456 and was again banished, after saying goodbye to his parents (Avery 400). **Byron** based *Two Foscari* on this anecdote. Shelley uses Foscari as an example of one who prefers "destitution and danger" in his own city to banishment (*Brother* 166).

Foscarini

She describes a painting of "Foscari taking leave of his father" (*R* 2.120–21).

Foscarini: See **Niccolini**.

Foscolo, Ugo (1778–1827): Italian author of dramas, novels, and poetry. Epistolary novel *Ultime lettere di Jacobo Ortis* [*Last Letters of Jacobo Ortis*] (1802) is considered the first Romantic Italian novel; Shelley read it 1822 (*Journals* 412; *DIL* 216). **Edmund Malville** praises Foscolo's description of the **Euganean Hills** and criticizes "**Recollections of Italy**'s" narrator for not attempting an immersion in Italian literature, including Foscolo's works (*RI* 27–28; Foscolo 34, 76–79). Shelley wrote Foscolo's biography for *Italian and Spanish Lives*. She consistently remarks upon the conceit she discerns in his work: not only did he portray himself in *Jacobo Ortis*, but Shelley also feels "Foscolo's excessive vanity shines very apparent in this account of himself" in the "disguised account of the translator" that Foscolo fixed at the start of his translation of **Sterne**'s *Sentimental Journey* (1804) (*ISPL* 2.373). Shelley considers Foscolo's *Dei Sepolcri* [*On Sepulchres*] (1807) "the most perfect of his poems" (*ISPL* 2.376). She terms Foscolo "purely a didactic writer; but perhaps no modern poet ever displayed so much harmony, grace, and truth of description" (*ISPL* 2.382). Shelley concludes Foscolo "may be said to be a bad tragedian, and not a good novelist; but he was an elegant writer, conversant with the depths and the refinements of the human heart" (*ISPL* 2.394).

Fosdinovo: Italian town eight miles northeast of **Spezia**; Shelley spells it **Fosedenovo**. **Castruccio** controls Fosdinovo, part of "territory around **Lucca**" (*V* 2.174). Castruccio actually took Fosdinovo August 1317 (Green 125).

Fosedenovo: See **Fosdinovo**.

Foudray: See **Fouldrey, Pile of**.

Fouldrey, Pile of: In Morecambe Bay on England's west coast, small rocky island with good port and early-14th century castle fifteen miles west of **Lancaster**; **Lambert Simnel**'s 1487 invasion landed there (Fischer 58; Bagley 219; Baines 1.628–629). Shelley knew **Wordsworth**'s 1807 poem about the castle there, responding to it December 1825 with "**On Reading Wordsworth**'s **Lines on Peel Castle**" (*Journals* 494–495). **Martin Swartz** lands there (*PW* 1.134).

Fountain of Myrtles: Site for **Richard of York**'s battle with **Gomelez** (*PW* 1.226–27).

Fox, Bishop Richard (1448–1528): Advisor to **Henry VII**, this **Bishop of Durham** became Bishop of **Winchester** in 1501 (*DNB*; *PW* 2.83, 2.118).

Fox, Charles James (1749–1806): **Parliamentary** liberal statesman, renowned for speeches but "deficient in statesmanship" (*DNB*). Shelley suggests "the mild spirit of Fox would have been soothed by the recollection that he had played a worthy part as **Marcus Antoninus**" (*RD* 49).

France: The Shelleys traveled through France 1814, 1816, and 1818; Shelley delighted particularly in her first visit's "exotics," being among the first tourists there "after two decades of war" (Sunstein 85). *History*'s first section records the Shelleys' 1814 journey through France (*H* 5–39). **Elizabeth Lavenza** prefers **Swiss** lack of class distinction to France's prejudices (*Fr1* 94; *Fr3* 64). **Victor Frankenstein**'s parents travel in France immediately after his birth (*Fr3* 40). The **De Laceys** are "descended from a good family in France," and the **Creature** learns French from them (*Fr1* 150; *Fr3* 110). **Castruccio** visits France when forced to flee England and there joins **Scoto**'s forces, an event that actually occurred: Castruccio commanded **Italian** mercenaries assisting France's **Philip IV** against a **Flemish** rebellion (*V* 1.92; Green 43, 45). England's inhabitants really begin to fear plague when they learn of its arrival in southern France; subsequently, plague survivors travel through France toward warmer climates (*LM* 216, 235). **Richard of York** escapes from England to France and is raised in **Flanders** in **Madeline De Faro**'s cottage; Shelley set many of *Perkin Warbeck*'s important scenes in France (*PW* 1.72, 1.145). Several of the novel's characters, including **Stephen Frion**, are French, while Shelley contextualizes her novel with historical events, such as **Charles VIII**'s unification of France and **Brittany** by marrying princess **Anne of Brittany**; Richard spends time at Charles's court before losing the king's support (*PW* 1.148, 1.242, 1.308, 1.311–314, 1.317, 2.14, 2.218, 3.194). **Guido il Cortese** learns "the art of pleasing the soft heart of woman" in France, describing it as a "hapless country, then preyed on by freebooters and gangs of lawless soldiery, [which] offered a grateful refuge to a criminal like me" (*Trans* 124, 125). "**The Dream**" is set near **Nantes** during **Henry IV**'s reign (*D* 153, 156). **Winzy** and his wife "take refuge in a remote part of western France" until **Bertha**'s death there (*MI* 228). **Lord Lodore** desires to take his daughter to France and, toward *Lodore*'s close, **Horatio Saville** looks for **Lady Lodore** there (*L* 1.213, 3.238–240). **Rupert Falkner** verges on death in France, and **Elizabeth Falkner** renews her acquaintance with **Gerard Neville** there (*F* 74). Shelley wrote biographies of French figures for *French Lives*. She began her 1840 journey by going to its capital **Paris** and traveling through much of France (*R* 1.6–7). *Rambles*' second volume contains multiple references to France (*R* 2.52, 2.115). [*TP* 5–6, 14; *V* 1.78–79, 1.90; *BMI* 33; *FE* 65, 67; *SA* 55, 57; *TFR* 119; *Brother* 176, 179; *R* 1.141–142].

***Francesca da Rimini*:** See **Pellico**.

Francesca da Rimini: Guido da Polenta of **Ravenna**'s daughter and Giovanni Malatesta of **Rimini**'s wife. **Dante** relates Francesca's romantic liaison with her husband's brother Paolo in the *Inferno* (5.118–140). According to legend, Francesca married Malatesta 1275, then fell in love with his brother, who had been married since 1269. The two carried on an affair for many years, until sometime between 1283 and 1286, when Malatesta killed both of them upon discovering them in Francesca's bedroom; Shelley quotes from **Leigh Hunt**'s version of the tale, *The Story of Rimini* (1816), in *Frankenstein* (Ciardi 63–64). **Castruccio** passes through Rimini, ruled "by the husband of Francesca" (*V* 1.42). **Edward Villiers** sees his wife's companionship as com-

Francesco

forting, just as Francesca was comforted by the fact she and Paolo "are one in Hell, as we were above" (*L* 3.145; *Inferno* 5.102). Shelley mentions **Manzoni**'s version of the tale (*R* 2.195).

Francesco: Shelley alludes to a Francesco, stating he is a character in a **Bandello** tale; **Castruccio** calls Francesco "a monster" for torturing and murdering his wife but notes Francesco's later feelings of guilt (*V* 2.156). According to Palacio, the account in *Valperga* matches a tale in Giovanni Fiorentino's *Pecorone* (c. 1400) better than the nearest parallel in Bandello's *Novelle* (1554–73) (Palacio 67–68; Crook 3.177; Crook 2).

Franciort: See **Frankfurt**.

Francia, Francesco Raibolini (c. 1450–1517): Bolognese painter and goldsmith. Shelley viewed **Francia**'s *Virgin in Glory Worshipped by Six Saints* (1502) in **Berlin** July 1842 (*R* 1.220; Vasari 2.310).

Francis, Emperor (1768–1835): Francis II, Holy Roman Emperor 1792–1806 and **Austrian** emperor 1804–35. Shelley calls him "one of the most treacherous and wicked tyrants that ever disgraced humanity," but notes his support of **Hofer** (*R* 1.120, 2.57, 2.61).

Francis I (1494–1547): France's ruler 1515–47, renowned for patronizing the arts and for establishing the concordat separating church and state (A. Grant 13). His sister **Queen Margaret**'s "affection for Francis remained to the end romantic, passionate and almost beyond the love of a sister" (A. Grant 54). Francis established a brief peace with Charles V of **Spain** in 1538 when Francis "gave Charles a valuable diamond ring," but Francis resumed war against imperial territories 1542 (A. Grant 62). Shelley evidently drew upon historical details (including the diamond ring anecdote) for "**The False Rhyme**," in which Francis is a character.

Franciscan: Member of religious order that St. Francis of **Assisi** founded 1209, dedicated to charities, missions, and preaching. **Meilar Trangmar** masquerades in "Franciscan habit" (*PW* 1.250). [*R* 2.52, 2.284].

Franckfort: See **Frankfurt**.

Franconia: German medieval duchy located mostly in **Main**'s valley; "Franconia" now pertains to **Bavaria**'s northern section. Shelley observed Franconia's topography July 1842 (*R* 1.200).

Frangipani: Noble family living near **Astura** (*TP* 22). John Frangipane arrested **Conradin** at Astura (Runciman 114).

Frankenstein, Alphonse: Caroline Frankenstein's husband; **Victor**, **Ernest**, and **William Frankenstein**'s father; and **Elizabeth Lavenza**'s adoptive father in *Frankenstein*.

Frankenstein, Caroline, [née Beaufort]: Alphonse Frankenstein's wife; **Victor**, **Ernest**, and **William Frankenstein**'s mother; and **Elizabeth Lavenza**'s adoptive mother in *Frankenstein*. In the 1831 edition, Caroline is an idealized mother, so devoted to her husband and children that she sacrifices her life to care for Elizabeth when she contracts scarlet fever; in the 1818 edition, Caroline dies as a result of impulsiveness rather than self-sacrifice (Crook 2).

Frankenstein, Ernest: Alphonse and Caroline Frankenstein's middle son, Victor Frankenstein's brother, and a minor character in *Frankenstein*. In the 1818 edition, Elizabeth Lavenza thinks Ernest should become a farmer, while his father wants him to train as a lawyer (*Fr1* 92–93). In the 1831 edition, Ernest plans to undertake a military career overseas (*Fr3* 63).

Frankenstein, Victor: Title protagonist and Alphonse and Caroline Frankenstein's eldest son in *Frankenstein*; the novel's subtitle "The Modern Prometheus" refers to him. The name "Victor" has several sources, since it is "an eponym, a juvenile nom de plume of [PB] Shelley's, and the name of the Wild Boy of Aveyron—which relates the maker to his" Creature (Sunstein 123). Castle Frankenstein on the Rhine, which Shelley could have seen 1814, is a probable source of the name (Sunstein 123; Seymour 110; Crook 2). Victor is Shelley's version of the Byronic hero; his guilt and passion are destructive, and he suffers due to obsessive ambition.

Frankenstein, William: Alphonse and Caroline Frankenstein's youngest son and Victor's brother, whom the Creature kills, in *Frankenstein*. Shelley probably named this character after her own son, William Shelley, or her father and half-brother, William Godwin.

Frankenstein; or, The Modern Prometheus: Begun summer 1816, Shelley's first novel was published anonymously 1818. In the 1831 edition's introduction, Shelley describes how a tale, "Les Portraits de Famille," in translator J. B. B. Eyriès's ghost story collection *Fantasmagoriana* (1812), influenced her and how the collection inspired Byron to suggest that he, Shelley, Polidori, and PBS each write a ghost story (*Journals* 118; *Fr3* 20–21; Sunstein 121). Byron immediately created his story, printed at *Mazeppa*'s conclusion, while Polidori wrote *The Vampyre* (1819) (*Journals* 118). PBS also easily began a poetic piece based on his early life (*Fr3* 21; White 1.444). Shelley, however, labored for days until the night after Byron and PBS conversed about the principle of life, when she finally conceived an idea; in her 1831 introduction, she describes a dream that she developed into the novel: "I saw the pale student of unhallowed arts kneeling beside the thing he had put together. I saw the hideous phantasm of a man stretched out, and then, on the working of some powerful engine, show signs of life, and stir with an uneasy, half vital motion" (*Fr3* 22–23). She outlined the "grim terrors" of her dream, which began with a chapter opening: "It was on a dreary night of November" (*Fr1* 85; *Fr3* 23, 57). Touring the Alps around Chamonix July 1816, Shelley first records work on *Frankenstein* (*Journals* 118). PBS encouraged Shelley to transform her story into a novel, a task she undertook in Bath (Sunstein 124–125). Shelley consulted sources, such as Rousseau's *Émile* (1762), Sir Humphrey Davy's *Elements of Chemical Philosophy* (1812), and "other contributory works: *Para-*

dise Lost, Locke, **Shakespeare**, **Gibbon**, *Political Justice*" (Sunstein 126–127; *Journals* 142). During *Frankenstein's* composition, three successive tragedies confronted Shelley: **Fanny Godwin's** and **Harriet Shelley's** suicides and Chancery Court proceedings concerning **Charles** and **Ianthe Shelley's** custody. But Shelley nevertheless managed to create *Frankenstein*, considered to be her masterpiece. Frame character **Robert Walton** relates **Victor Frankenstein** and the **Creature's** stories after encountering them both during his voyage on the Arctic Ocean. When young, Victor, an ambitious scientist, makes a Creature and immediately abandons him, horrified by the Creature's appearance. Ostracized by humans, such as the **De Lacey** family, the Creature seeks revenge on his creator by murdering brother **William Frankenstein** and, indirectly, **Justine Moritz**. In the Alps, Victor hears the Creature's story (embedded in the novel) and reluctantly agrees to create his female counterpart. The Creature then kills Victor's friend **Henry Clerval** and bride **Elizabeth Lavenza** after Victor destroys his work on the female mate. Deprived of friends and family, Victor resolves to find the Creature and follows him into the Arctic region. While on board Walton's ship, Victor dies, and the Creature mourns his creator's death while predicting his own. Walton learns from both characters about the dangers of obsessive ambition and questing after knowledge. Shelley finished *Frankenstein* 14 May 1817. After PBS edited it and **Murray** and **Ollier** rejected it, Lackington published the novel 1818 (Sunstein 136; *Journals* 169, 174, 178). PBS's preface accompanied Shelley's text, well received upon publication, as reviews in *Blackwood's*, the *Quarterly Review*, and *La Belle Assemblée* reveal (*Fr3* 24–25; Sunstein 155–156; *Journals* 214; White 1.527). Because of its popularity and a highly successful stage adaptation, Richard Brinsley Peake's *Presumption; or, The Fate of Frankenstein* (1823), **William Godwin** had Whitaker print a second edition 1823 (*Journals* 468). It differs only slightly from the original and includes a title page bearing Shelley's name. A third revised edition, which Henry Colburn published 1831, differs more from the 1818 edition (Lyles 6). In the 1831 introduction, Shelley claims, "I have changed no portion of the story, nor introduced any new ideas or circumstances. I have mended the language where it was so bald as to interfere with the interest of the narrative; and these changes occur almost exclusively in the beginning of the first volume" (*Fr3* 24). However, in the 1831 edition, differences exist regarding Elizabeth's familial connection, **Ernest Frankenstein's** professional goals, and the journey to Chamonix. Translated into **French** 1821, *Frankenstein* has been translated into most languages, adapted for stage and screen, and continues to be popular today (Lyles 6; Sunstein 401). *Frankenstein* heralded the science fiction genre.

Frankfort: See **Frankfurt**.

Frankfurt: German city on the **Main**, twenty-three miles northeast of **Mainz**; Shelley spells it **Francfort**, **Frankfort**, and **Franckfort** (*R* 1.11, 1.30–31, 1.172). She stayed at **Hôtel de Russie** there July 1840 and returned to the city June 1842 (*R* 1.155, 1.176).

Franks: Ancient **German** tribe that reached the height of its power in the 9th century; in Shelley's day, the term was used in the Balkans with general application to Western **Europeans** (Kinder 1.125–126). **Cyril Ziani** observes that " 'Franks call [the "Evil Eye"] superstition; but let us beware' " (*EE* 104).

Frederic, Duke of Austria (d. 1268): Also known as Frederic of **Baden**, **Austria**'s heir through his mother (Runciman 101). Frederic was a staunch supporter during his distant cousin **Conradin**'s **Italian** campaign, fighting with him in the **Battle of Tagliacozzo** and then being tried and beheaded with him in **Naples** (Runciman 110–115). **Pope Clement IV** observes Conradin and **"Frederic of Austria"** parading on the plain near **Viterbo** and describes them as victims; subsequently Shelley mentions the Duke of Austria's execution (*TP* 21–22).

Frederic of Austria: See **Frederic, Duke of Austria**.

Frederic, king of the Romans: See **Frederick III**.

Frederick III (c. 1286–1330): Known as "the Fair," Frederick III became king of **Germany** and Holy Roman Emperor 1314, but **Louis of Bavaria** overthrew him in 1326; Shelley calls him **Frederic, king of the Romans**. Frederick III declares **Castruccio** to be **Tuscany**'s imperial vicar (*V* 2.201). This event actually occurred August 1315 (Green 61).

Frederic the Great (1744–1797): Frederick William II, **Prussia**'s king from 1786. Shelley remarks the king "excites no jot of interest" but that in the past he was greatly admired (*R* 1.214). She credits him with **Berlin**'s design; vendors there sell statuettes of him (*R* 1.228, 1.230). Shelley also describes a wax Frederick figure in Berlin's museum; it presents him in old age rather than as when he met **Voltaire** near **Clèves** (*R* 1.226–227). When they met, 11 September 1740, Frederick was suffering from fever (Orieux 148).

Frederics: Monna Gegia de' Becari exclaims, " 'Cursed may the race of the Frederics ever be!' " (*TP* 7). She calls house of **Hohenstaufen** the "race of Frederics" because there had been four noble Frederics: Frederic I of Hohenstaufen; Frederic, **Swabia**'s duke; Frederic II, King of **Sicily;** and **Frederic, Duke of Austria** (Runciman Table IV).

Freemasons: International fraternity with secret signs and passwords, believed to have originated in medieval stonemasons' guilds (Crook 2). Shelley compares **Carbonari** to them; **Colletta** considered the Carbonari to be derived from **German** Freemasons (*R* 2.164, 2.169).

Freischütz, Der: See **Weber**.

French Empire: **Napoleon** ruled **France**'s first empire (1804–15). Shelley refers to a **Serbelloni** general during "wars of the French Empire" (*R* 1.82).

French Lives: See *Lives of the Most Eminent Literary and Scientific Men of France*.

French Revolution: Revolution that overthrew the **Bourbon** monarchy, beginning 1789 and ending with **Napoleon**'s overthrow of the Directory 1797. Shelley set "**The Swiss Peasant**" at the French Revolution's beginning; it spreads to **Switzerland** in the story (*SP* 142, 144, 152). Shelley refers to the 1789 French Revolution in her historical account of **Trèves** and discusses **Italian** nobility's loss of titles due to it (*R* 1.19, 2.115). She also reflects on how it sparked a revolution in Italy (*R* 2.245–249). [*R* 2.164].

Freyberg: French name for Freiburg, **German** city fifty-five miles northwest of **Zurich**. Shelley dined and visited the 13th–16th century cathedral there in July 1840 (*R* 1.44; *BGER* 127).

Fries, Herr: A "tall, fair **German**" who ran **Kissingen**'s **Kurhaus** hotel; the police also employed him (*R* 1.181–182, 1.196).

Fries, Madame: Kissingen's **Kurhaus** hotel's landlady, an invalid (*R* 1.181).

Frion, Stephen Etienne: Important figure who alternately supports and betrays **Richard of York** in *Perkin Warbeck*. Shelley based this character on Frion, **Henry VII**'s secretary, who deserted and encouraged **Charles VIII** to support **Perkin Warbeck** (Hume 3.43; *PW* 1.121).

Friuli: Northeastern **Italian** region. Shelley saw mountains in Friuli from **Venice**'s **Fondamenti Nuovi** (*R* 2.100). **Benedetto Pepi** tells a story about **Charlemagne** at **Fugolano**, a place **Muratori** explained as Friuli (*V* 1.285; Crook 3.115).

Frogmore Gate: Queen Charlotte acquired Little Frogmore near **Windsor** castle 1790 and created a rural retreat at which she held fêtes for all social ranks (Hedley 156–158). In Shelley's day, a swing gate on the path connected **Little Park**'s grounds at its southern end with Frogmore's, but the two areas were joined and restricted for the monarchy's private use during the 1840s (Hedley 186–187). When **Lionel Verney** returns to Windsor with news of plague, he enters Little Park at Frogmore Gate (*LM* 239).

"From Moschus": Sonnet **PBS** translated from **Greek** 1816 (White 2.295–296). Little is known about Syracuse's pastoral poet Moschus (c. 150 B.C.E.) (Howatson 371). **Adrian** quotes the opening lines from "a translation of Moschus's poem" as he sets out for Greece: "**When winds** that move not its calm surface, sweep / The azure sea, I love the land no more; / The smiles of the serene and tranquil deep / Tempt my unquiet mind—"; **Lionel Verney** "would have added in continuation, '**But, when the roar** / Of ocean's gray abyss resounds, and foam / Gathers upon the sea, and vast waves burst—'" (*LM* 440; PBS lines 1–6). Shelley quotes lines from the same sonnet, "**Whose house** is some lone bark,—whose toil the sea, / Whose prey the wandering fish, an evil lot / Has chosen," as "**The Smuggler and his Family**'s" epigraph (*S* 203; PBS lines 10–12).

Fucecchio: Italian town twenty miles west of **Florence**. **Castruccio** forces it to submit to **Lucca**'s control (*V* 2.174). The Florentine army pitches tents on the **Guisciana** River near Fucecchio (*V* 2.248).

***Fuggitiva*:** See **Grossi**.

Fugolano: See **Friuli**.

Fulda: German city thirty miles northwest of **Kissingen**. In July 1842, Shelley dined and visited the cathedral (1704–12) there, where St. Boniface was buried (*R* 1.205–206; *BGER* 130).

Fulda, Prince-Bishops of: Fulda was site of a Benedictine abbey 744–1803, and Fulda's abbots became prince-Bishops 1752 (*BGER* 130). Shelley mentions prince-bishops discovered mineral springs at **Brükenau**; portraits of these men decorate the *kursaal* ("cure room") there (*R* 1.202).

Fusina: Small **Italian** town and beach five miles southwest of **Venice**. In Shelley's time, travelers embarked on gondolas at Fusina to cross the **laguna**. **Edmund Malville** fondly recalls " 'the first view of [Venice] from Fusina' " (*RI* 26). **Lionel Verney**, **Adrian**, and **Clara** find "wrecks of gondolas, and some few uninjured ones, were strewed on the beach at Fusina" (*LM* 438). Shelley recorded "at Fusina . . . I now beheld the domes and towers of [Venice] arise from the waves" (*R* 2.79).

G

G——, Countess of: Lady Lodore talks with "young and new-married Countess of G——" during an evening in **London** society (*L* 3.105).

G——, Earl of: Lord **Cecil**'s father in *Falkner*.

Gabriel: Biblical archangel, who announces John the Baptist's and Jesus's births (Luke 1.11–20, 1.26–38). **Wilhelmina** claims that, just as Gabriel announced Mary's immaculate conception, **Raphael** announced the "incarnation of the Holy Spirit" that became her daughter **Beatrice** (*V* 2.26).

Gaeta: Village halfway between **Naples** and **Rome** on **Italy**'s west coast; "**Mola di**" refers to the inn there. Shelley stayed there November 1818, admiring **Villa di Cicerone**'s ruins in the inn's gardens (*Journals* 241). Shelley stayed at Gaeta again March 1819 (*Journals* 250–251). **Lady Lodore** reads a **London** newspaper's report of **Clorinda Saville**'s death at Mola di Gaeta (*L* 3.182). [*L* 3.213–214].

Galatea: Greek myth records that this beautiful sea-nymph was one of fifty daughters of sea god Nereus and Oceanid Doris (Tripp 395, 488). Shelley notes that the blue of **Naples**'s **Baiae** was "such as Galatea might have skimmed in her car" (*LM* 3). Shelley asserts that "the youthful and nymph-like loveliness of the *Galatea*" is an example of **Raphael**'s excellence (*R* 2.223).

Galatea: See **Raphael**.

Galignani, Giovanni Antonio (1757–1821): In addition to establishing an English bookstore and circulating library in **Paris**, Galignani founded a newspaper, *Galignani's Messenger,* 1814. The Shelleys read it to keep up with British politics while abroad, and Shelley later assisted Cyrus Redding in writing **PBS**'s biographical note for Galignani's *Complete Poetical Works of Coleridge, Shelley, and Keats* (1829) (Sunstein 178, 298; White 2.397). Galignani also published editions of some of Shelley's works, including *The Last Man* in 1826 and *Lodore* in 1835, but Shelley herself does not seem to have been involved with these editions. **Edmund Malville** criticizes "**Recollections of Italy**'s" narrator for reading Galignani in **Italian** coffeehouses rather than Italian literature (*RI* 27–28). Shelley mentions that *Galignani* could be obtained at **Venice**'s **Florian** (*R* 2.105).

Galileo, Galilei (1564–1642): **Florentine** physicist, astronomer, philosopher, and inventor. The **Inquisition** declared Galileo's insistence on the Copernican idea of a heliocentric universe heretical; Galileo was tried 1633 and imprisoned under house arrest for life (R. Blackwell 53–54, 130). **Castruccio** encounters arrogant **Venetian** nobles who "would have pursued with excessive hatred any one who should have pointed out to them their true station in relation to their fellow-creatures," just as the Inquisition persecuted Galileo for "demonstrating the relative insignificance of our globe" by insisting on the sun-centered model of the universe (*V* 1.65–66).

Gallery in Dresden: Picture gallery founded 1722 and now housed in **New Markt**'s Albertinum Museum (Meras 155; Jackson 1.340–342). Shelley visited it August 1842 (*R* 1.242–245).

Gallois, Captain Thomas (1783–1840): **French** naval commander (*DBF*). Shelley describes the French 1832 defeat of **Ancona**, at which **Colonel Combes** and Captain Gallois led the French forces (*R* 2.255–56).

Gamba, Pietro (c. 1801–1827): **Teresa Guiccioli**'s younger brother; he adored his sister (Sunstein 237). Gamba was exiled from **Lucca** for **Carbonari** activities and moved to **Pisa** with his father and sister August 1821; Shelley met Gamba November 1821 (*Journals* 376, 382). Shelley "liked [Gamba] exceedingly," describing him, affectionately called Pierino, as "one of the most gentlemanly **Italians** I have met with" January 1822 (Sunstein 204; *Letters* 1.215). Gamba visited the Shelleys frequently in Pisa until departing for Lucca July 1822 and then went to **Greece** with **Byron** 1823 (*Journals* 413; Sunstein 237). After Byron's death, Gamba escorted his body to England 1824 and revealed his death's true circumstances, contrary to **Edward John Trelawny**'s version of events (Sunstein 261). Shelley recorded "the presence of Pierino, our talks of **Albe**, have rendered me even less melancholy" in September 1824; Gamba remained in **London** until February 1825 to see his *A Narrative of Lord Byron's Last Journey to Greece* published then (*Journals* 484). Gamba died of typhoid in Greece (Sunstein 277).

Ganges: **India**'s holy river, flowing through southern **Asia**. Guests at **Euthanasia**'s court enjoy "fire-eating, rope-dancing, and every prank that has been known from the shores of the Ganges" (*V* 1.268–269).

Ganymede: In **Greek** mythology, beautiful Trojan boy who became **Zeus**'s cupbearer (Tripp 248). **Ferdinando Eboli** finds **Adalinda Spina** " 'a being of another world ... a Ganymede' " (*FE* 78). **Ceres** emphasizes her tardiness by reference to Ganymede's having already poured the gods' nectar (*P* 31).

Garcilaso de la Vega (c. 1503–1536): Spanish poet. Shelley wrote his biography for *Italian and Spanish Lives*, but had difficulty obtaining necessary materials, writing to John Bowring July 1837 for translations (*Letters* 2.289, 2.290). Shelley drew from Jeremiah Holmes Wiffen's translation of *The Works of Garcilaso de la Vega* (1823) for the biography (*ISPL* 3.41). She ranks Garcilaso "high as an elegiac poet" and asserts that "the most perfect of his poems is his second eclogue" (*ISPL* 3.47). She provides extracts from Garcilaso's *Oda a la flor de Gnido* [*Ode to the Flower of Gnido*] (comp. 1533–36), which she considers "fanciful and airy, more original, yet more classic" (*ISPL* 3.53).

Gargalandi, Ubaldo de': Once a "great and powerful" **Ghibelline** family of **Florence**'s **Sesto** of Oltrarno; Ubaldo is briefly mentioned in "**A Tale of the Passions**" (Villani 82, 124; *TP* 18).

Garth: Cloister-surrounded court (Fischer 115). **John Lavallan** and **John O'Water** meet **Richard of York** "within the walls of the Garth" at **Cork** (*PW* 1.280).

Garthe, Thomas: English military captain who suppressed the 1487 **Munster** rebellion, defended **Waterford** 1491, and was present at the 1497 Scottish invasion (Cosgrove 615–616; Arthurson 23, 173). **Robert Clifford** gets information from Garthe (*PW* 3.118).

Gascon: Inhabitant of Gascony, former duchy in southwestern **France**. **Castruccio** and **Ghibellines** fight Gascon troops supporting the **Guelphs** (*V* 2.7, 2.46, 3.222).

Gaspar: Loyal steward in *Matilda*.

Gates of the Batistero: Eastern doors, which Lorenzo Ghiberti executed 1447–52, of the Baptistry of San Giovanni near **Florence**'s **Duomo**; they are composed of ten panels displaying Old Testament subjects (*Florence* 127). Shelley quotes **Michelangelo**'s description of the gates as "worthy of Paradise" (*R* 2.160; *Florence* 127). See **Batistero**.

Gauls: Inhabitants of the ancient region of Gaul, now **France**. Shelley wanted to remain at **Baden-Baden** partly from fear of revisiting **Italy**, describing her emotional state by drawing on **Livy**'s reference to Gauls frightened by "the open gates and silent wall of **Rome**" (*R* 1.38; Crook 2). The Gauls invaded Rome 387 B.C.E. (Kinder 1.77). Shelley mentions that **Dante** "belonged to **Etruria** and Cisalpine Gaul," the name given to the territory in northern Italy occupied by Gauls in the first century B.C.E. (*R* 2.262; Crook 2). [*R* 2.227].

Gaveston, Piers (d. 1312): Gascon knight who was **Edward II**'s favorite and lover. **Edward I** banished Gaveston from England 1307, but Edward II recalled him later that year, after Edward I's death, and made him Earl of **Cornwall**. English nobles insisted on Gaveston's exile 1308, but he was recalled again 1311 and beheaded 1312. Gaveston is a character in *Valperga*.

Gayland, Mr.: Edward Villiers's and **Lord Maristow**'s solicitor in *Lodore*.

Gazzaniga, Marietta (1824–1884): Italian soprano who first performed 1840 (Rosenthal 187). Shelley saw Gazzaniga as **Romeo** in *Montecchi e Capuletti* in **Venice** and in a seriocomic role in *Chi dura Vince* at the **Fenice** October 1842 (*R* 2.127, 2.129).

Geant: According to *Rambles*, of **Coblentz**'s hotels "the largest and enjoy[ing] the best reputation," but Shelley stayed at the **Hôtel Bellevue** (*R* 1.26).

Genesis: Shelley draws frequently from the **Bible**'s first book and upon **Milton**'s retelling of its first chapters in *Paradise Lost*. She had read "[t]he Bible as far as the **Psalms**" 1819 (*Journals* 304). *The Last Man*'s narrator finds in the **Cumaean Sibyl**'s cave a "pathway" with " 'dry land for the sole of the foot,' " a loose reference to the Genesis passage relating **Noah**'s dove's search for land after the flood (*LM* 3–4; Genesis 8.9; Blumberg 6). **Lucy Saville** informs the **Villiers**es about the change affecting **Horatio Saville** now that he is in love: "he saw that the 'creation was good,' " a reference to the world's creation (*L* 2.173; Genesis 1.10). Shelley described **Castel Sant' Angelo**'s fireworks as the "human imitation of the third verse of the first chapter of Genesis," which states, "God said 'Let there be light,' and there was light" (*R* 2.232; Genesis 1.3). See **Adam**, **Ararat**, **Babel**, **Cain**, **Eden**, **Eve**, and **Haydn**.

Geneva: City at **Lake Geneva**'s southwestern point where the **Rhône** leaves the lake. The Shelleys spent summer 1816 at **Cologny**, near Geneva (Sunstein 117). Geneva is the **Frankenstein** family's native town; **Victor Frankenstein** feels, "I am by birth a Genevese" (*Fr1* 63; *Fr3* 38). Most of *Frankenstein*'s violence—**Elizabeth Lavenza** and **William Frankenstein**'s murders and **Justine Moritz**'s execution—takes place in or near Geneva. **Lionel Verney** leads plague survivors from **Paris** to Geneva (*LM* 396, 399, 416, 420). Shelley wanted to visit Geneva again 1843 but decided the plan was not financially feasible (*Letters* 3.78). [*H* 99; *RD* 47; *SP* 144; *R* 1.139–141].

Geneva, Lake: Large **Alpine** lake on eastern **France**'s border with **Switzerland**, called **Lac Leman** in French. The Shelleys lived at **Maison Chapuis** on the lake's Swiss bank summer 1816 (*Journals* 107; Sunstein 117). Shelley describes it: "blue as the heavens which it reflects, and sparkling with golden beams" (*H* 94). The **Frankenstein**s live near Lake Geneva, and **Victor Frankenstein**'s and **Elizabeth Lavenza**'s ill-fated honeymoon voyage begins there (*Fr1* 63, 217; *Fr3* 38, 161). Shelley mentions the lake's "fierce unrest" in "**The Choice**" as she reminisces about boat outings that **William Shelley**, **PBS**, **Byron**, and she enthusiastically undertook summer 1816 (*Ch* 74). Plague survivors admire the **Jura**'s view of Lac Leman (*LM* 419). "**The Swiss Peasant**'s" frame narrator reads Byron's "**The Prisoner of Chillon**," relating its composition on Lake Geneva's shores (*SP* 136). Shelley briefly describes sailing across Lake Geneva from **Vevay** to **Geneva** (*R* 1.139). For Shelley, its shores October 1840 reminded her of deceased friends and relatives: "Was I the same person who had lived there, the companion of the dead? For all were gone" (*R* 1.140).

Genlis, Madame de (1746–1830): Félicité Ducrest de Saint-Aubin, **French** romance writer; Shelley read **Holcroft**'s 1783 translation of her *Les Veillées du château* [*Tales of the Castle*] (1782) January 1815, and several of her other novels 1816–1817; she disliked Genlis's *Mémoires; ou, Souvenirs et Anecdotes* [*Memoirs; or, Souvenirs and Anecdotes*] (1824–1826) (*Journals* 58, 118, 123, 129–30, 141, 154; *Letters* 2.48). Shelley seems to agree with Genlis's description of **Venice**: " '**Quelle triste** ville que Venise!' " which translates to "What a sad town is Venice," probably from Genlis's *Mémoires* (*R* 2.100). Shelley quotes the same remark in her **Goldoni** biography (Moskal 282; *ISPL* 2.219).

Genoa: Italian port city on the **Mediterranean**, forty-eight miles northwest of **Spezia**. Shelley moved to Genoa immediately after **PBS**'s death and "hated" the city, principally since it was there that she first fully experienced her loss (Sunstein 234). She returned to England from Genoa July 1823. **Ghibellines** in **Florence** welcome **Conradin** there (*TP* 6). The 1320 siege of Genoa by **Ghibellines** of **Lombardy** is the backdrop for much of **Castruccio**'s early military action; he returns from Genoa to stop the conspiracy planned at castle **Valperga** (*V* 1.157–158, 2.171, 2.196–197, 2.211; Green 127). Fear grows in England when plague is confirmed in Genoa (*LM* 235). Genoa is **Guido il Cortese**'s birthplace, but he forfeits his ancestral palace there and is later banished; he returns to regain **Juliet Torella** (*Trans* 121, 125–126, 131). **Elizabeth Falkner** and **Rupert Falkner** change vessels at Genoa (*F* 74). [*V* 3.96, 3.260; *R* 1.149].

Genzstein, John of: See **Jenzenstein, John II of**.

George: Minor character in *The Last Man* (*LM* 279).

George III (1738–1820): British king who married Princess **Charlotte** a year after coming to the throne 1760; he was the ruler when Britain recognized **America**'s independence (1783) and was generally favorably regarded despite periods of illness, which culminated in insanity (1810) (J. Clarke 277, 285). His eldest son, George IV, became **Regent**. George III rewards the **Fitzhenry** family with a title in recognition of **Admiral Fitzhenry**'s service during the **Revolutionary War**, implying an approximate time frame for *Lodore* (*L* 1.258). Shelley laments "the obstinacy of George III, who, exhausting the English levies," called in foreign mercenaries against America (*R* 1.203).

Georgia: Country on the **Black Sea** that used to be part of the Soviet Union; the name is also given to a **Caucasus** mountain region in the country's northwest. **Lionel Verney** mourns the barrenness of earth swept by plague, including Georgia and "the ruin of its favourite temple—the form of woman" (*LM* 234). [*Letters* 1.137–138, 2.372].

***Georgics*:** Virgil wrote this four-book didactic poem (36–29 B.C.E.) in imitation of **Hesiod**'s *Works and Days*. He promotes an **Italian** farmer's life as ideal, bringing humankind and nature together in a satisfying partnership (Howatson 248–249). Shelley read *Georgics* 1817–20 and again 1822 (*Journals* 681). In January 1819, Shelley wrote, "I have been reading also Virgil's Georgics, which is, in many respects, the most beautiful poem I ever read," and in April 1825, "I bask in the sun on the grass reading Virgil, that is, my beloved Georgics. . . . I begin to live again" (*Letters* 1.85, 1.476). **Valerius** and **Isabell Harley** read *Georgics* together (*Val* 343). **Edmund Malville** fondly recalls **Tuscan** peasants' " 'Virgilian threshing floors,' " an allusion to *Georgics* also used in *Valperga* (*RI* 29; *V* 1.56; *Georgics* 2.179–185). At **Lago di Garda** September 1842, one of Shelley's companions quoted Virgil's description of the lake, beginning "**teque, / Fluctibus**"; the passage translates to "and thee, Benacus, swelling with waves and roaring like the sea" (*R* 2.27; *Georgics* 2.159–160; Moskal 265).

Geraldine, Maurice: See **Desmond, Earl Maurice of**.

Geraldine, Thomas: Thomas de Desmond, **Desmond**'s brother (Arthurson 241). Leader of **Irish** band supporting **Lambert Simnel** at **Stoke** (*PW* 1.132–134).

Geraldines: Another name for the **FitzGerald** family, **Richard of York** supporters in *Perkin Warbeck*.

German Emperor: See **Charles V**.

German Ocean: See **North Sea**.

Germany: **European** country on the **North** and **Baltic** Seas; Shelley first visited it during her 1814 elopement with **PBS** and returned 1816 and 1842–43. Both of Shelley's travel books draw upon these experiences. While she admired the Germans' past nobility and cultural heritage, she found the country's contemporary reality unattractive. October 1842, Shelley wrote: "I do dislike the Germans—& never wish to visit Germany again—but I would not put this in print—for the surface is all I know—& that does not deserve commemoration and vituperation" (*Letters* 3.42). Shelley asserts that travelers in Germany note a contrast in cleanliness "between the protestant and catholic towns" (*H* 40–41). Traveling on the **Rhine**, Shelley enjoyed remaining on deck separate from the cabin that "the lower order of smoking, drinking Germans who travelled with us" occupied (*H* 68). **Victor Frankenstein**'s parents travel in Germany immediately after his birth, and **Elizabeth Lavenza**'s mother is German (*Fr3* 40–41). The **De Lacey** family takes refuge in a German cottage when exiled from **France**; the **Creature** observes them there (*Fr1* 153; *Fr3* 110). **Ghibellines** in **Florence** are anxious for **Corradino**'s arrival from Germany (*TP* 6). German money funded, German mercenaries fought, and **Henry VII** of Germany frequently began, wars throughout **Italy** (*V* 1.98, 1.104, 1.147–148). The **Countess of Windsor** welcomes "travellers from her native Germany," **Idris** fears being forcibly carried there, plague destroys it, and English plague survivors encounter "Germans from **Saxony**" in **Ferney** (*LM* 33, 85, 269, 421). **Mary of**

Burgundy gives the **Earl of Lincoln** "an aid of two thousand Germans, led by **Martin Swartz**"; troops land at **Pile of Fouldrey** for battle with **Henry VII** of England (*PW* 1.132, 1.134). These "German auxiliaries were veteran soldiers, who spared neither blows nor blood"; however, they lost the battle (*PW* 1.137). Mary later sends "two hundred German mercenaries" to support **Richard of York** (*PW* 2.256). While in the French army, **Louis Chaumont** is wounded in Germany (*SP* 152). **Lorenzo Mancini** loves **Sienna** so much that he "would not have exchanged his obscure and penurious abode within its walls to become the favored follower of the German emperor," and **Flora Mancini** later speculates that her brother may have traveled to Germany (*Brother* 169, 179). **Francis Derham** studies at Germany's **Jena** University (*L* 1.83, 1.90, 1.213). **Rupert Falkner** and **Elizabeth Falkner** travel through Germany and meet **Gerard Neville** for the first time in **Baden-Baden**; Neville teaches Elizabeth to become "a fine musician of the German school" (*F* 236). Shelley traveled through much of Germany 1840, observing that "German hotels are all conducted with great order and regularity, and are very clean, quiet, and good" and that "the education of the poor is far more attended to in Germany than with us," while noting her ignorance of the German language made traveling a challenge (*R* 1.26, 1.55, 1.121, 1.163). Returning to Germany 1842, Shelley considered Germans "a race that loves justice and truth—whose powers of thought are, if slow, yet profound, and, in their way, creative" (*R* 1.174). Shelley had little success trying to learn German at **Kissingen** July 1842 and thereafter revised her favorable opinions: "Germans are not, as far as I can judge, a cleanly people.... German beds ... are uncomfortable" (*R* 1.241, 1.264). *Rambles* contains multiple references to Germany (*R* 1.182, 1.194, 2.11). [*H* 70; *TP* 14; *V* 1.153, 2.110; *PW* 3.128; *FE* 68; *L* 1.155].

Germany, Emperor of: See **Henry VII** (c. 1269–1313).

Gertrude: See **Campbell**.

***Gerusalemme Liberata*:** Tasso completed his epic poem about the First Crusade, *Jerusalem Delivered*, 1575 and published it 1581 to great success. The poem details Godfrey's crusade to **Jerusalem** 1099 and relates the love stories of Tancred and **Clorinda**, **Rinaldo** and Armida, and Erminia and Tancred. Shelley read it August 1818, noting that "now I have read more than half his poem I do not know that I like so well as **Ariosto** [*sic*]" (*Journals* 220–229; *Letters* 1.77). In **Venice** October 1840, Shelley enjoyed gondoliers singing *Gerusalemme* stanzas about Clorinda's death (Tancred unknowingly kills her in battle); the singers probably used "Canta alla Barcariola," a Venetian version of Tasso, which **Byron** also heard (*R* 2.125; Moskal 295; Tasso 12.51–69). Shelley compares **Sorrento**'s beauty to the gardens of **Armida**, which Tasso describes in *Gerusalemme* (*R* 2.263; Moskal 368; Tasso 16.10–12).

Gex: **French** village ten miles south of **Les Rousses**. Shelley took a "circuitous and dangerous" road to Gex May 1816 because it was listed in her passport (*H* 92).

Ghent: Chief **Flanders** town, known for luxury textiles. **Edward Brampton** tells **Stephen Frion** that he will find no "men of Ghent" in **Ireland** (*PW* 2.196).

Ghibelline (also Ghibeline): Thirteenth- and 14th-century **Italian** pro-imperial political party that violently opposed the **Guelphs**. The factions began in 12th-century **Germany** but were most divisive in **Florence**. The Ghibellines were mostly feudal aristocrats and noblemen (Crook 2). The name derives from the German word "Waiblingen," the name of a castle owned by the Hohenstaufens (Guelph opponents) of **Swabia**. Ghibellines and the **Bianchi** support the emperor, and **Castruccio** is a member of both (*V* 1.2–4). *Valperga* explains the parties' history and struggle. [*R* 1.79; 2.244].

Ghirlandajo [Domenico Bigordi] (1449–1494): **Florentine** painter so-called because he invented "garlands," decorative head ornaments worn by young Florentine girls (Vasari 2.168). His numerous frescoes are located throughout Florence; he also worked on the **Sistine Chapel** c. 1481–82 (Schmeckebier 217). Shelley viewed Ghirlandajo's *The Adoration of the Magi* (1488) January 1843: "Led by the admiration which this picture excited, I visited every other in Florence by Ghirlandajo" (*R* 2.143). *Adoration* is housed in the chapel of *Spedale degli Innocenti* [the Foundling Hospital] in Florence's **Piazza della Annunziata** (*Florence* 167; Vasari 2.172). Shelley specifically mentions Ghirlandajo's fresco in **Santa Trinita Church**—*The Life of St. Francis* (1485)—ranking it his best next to *Adoration* (*R* 2.144; *Florence* 19).

The two-section fresco depicts five scenes in St. Francis's life: his banishment from his father's house, Honorius III confirming the rule of the order, St. Francis before **Syria**'s sultan, his reception of the stigmata at the **La Verna Convent**, and his death and funeral (*Florence* 20). Shelley specifically mentions the last scene, the *Death of St. Francis*, and quotes both **Vasari**'s and **Lanzi**'s opinions of it (*R* 2.144).

Gianfigliazi: **Florentine** family that sided with the **Guelph** faction from its 1215 beginning (Villani 123–124). This family is included on the guest list for **Euthanasia**'s court (*V* 1.256).

Gibbon, Edward (1737–1794): British historian renowned for *The History of the Decline and Fall of the Roman Empire* (1776–88), which Shelley read 1815–18 (*Journals* 648–649). She read his *Miscellaneous Works* (1796) 1815. Shelley takes descriptions of **Salerno** from Gibbon (*R* 2.283, 2.294). Gibbon repeatedly quotes **Guglielmus Apulus**, or **William of Apulia**, 11th-century warrior-poet, to describe ancient southern **Italy**. Shelley includes passages describing **Amalfi**, beginning "**Nulla magis** locuples argento" and "**Urbs Latii** non est hac delitiosor urbe," translated in Moskal (*R* 2.283, 2.294; Gibbon 10.105, 10.103; Moskal 378–379, 385).

Gibson, John (1790–1866): British sculptor who worked in his **Roman** studio on Via della Fontanella (*MROM* xlii). Shelley visited several studios in Rome April 1843, specifically mentioning "Mr. Gibson's" (*R* 2.224).

Gillows: **Oxford Street** store selling fashionable modern furniture made by

Gioacchino

the **Lancaster**-based Gillow family, associated since the 1730s with furniture making (Hall 341–342). **Dame Nixon**'s cottage's interior includes "a large easy chair of Gillows's manufacture" (*L* 3.269).

Gioacchino: See **Murat**.

Gioja, Melchiore (1767–1829): Italian author renowned for his 1796 dissertation about Italy's government; Shelley notes his contribution to *Il Conciliatore* (Petronio 3.116; *R* 2.195).

Giorgione da Castelfranco (c. 1478–1510): Venetian painter renowned for frescoes, such as ones on the **Rialto**, and for numerous portraits, many of which "were sent beyond the confines of **Italy**" (Vasari 3.8). Shelley reports viewing *Rebecca at the Well* "by Giorgione" in the **Gallery in Dresden** August 1842, but no Giorgione of that name has been traced (*R* 1.242; Crook 2). She may have been referring to *The Meeting of Jacob and Rachel* in the Gallery, then attributed to Giorgione (*MCON* 439; Moskal 202; Crook 2). Shelley describes Giorgione as **Titian**'s "contemporary, and rival[;] . . . richness and grandeur of colouring" make his **Palazzo Manfrin** paintings (c. 1500–1505) "wonderfully beautiful" (*R* 2.119).

Giornico: **Swiss** town on the **Ticino**, sixteen miles northwest of **Bellinzona**. Shelley includes **PFS**'s friend's account of their dangerous September 1840 journey along a flooded road to Giornico (*R* 1.149).

Giotto and Francesca and other Poems: See **Knox**.

Giotto di Bondone (c. 1267–1337): **Florentine** architect and painter credited with initiating Western-style painting; he worked on Florence's **Duomo** 1334–37 (Chilvers 227). Shelley viewed Giotto's **Dante** portrait at **Palace of the Podestà** January 1843 (*R* 2.158).

Giovane Italia, La: Usually spelled "*Giovine*," republican nationalist society founded in 1832 (Mosakl 322). Shelley notes that the **Carbonari** united with other sects, such as this one (*R* 2.178).

Giovanni da Procida: See **Niccolini**.

Giovanni, Fra: See **Angelico**.

"Giovanni Villani": Essay Shelley published in 30 July 1823 *Liberal* (*Journals* 431–432). Shelley joins the Classical / Romantic debate, which was "highly politicized in **Italy**," finding "excellence in both modes" but preferring the Romantic, as evidenced by her praise of the Romantic convention of authorial intrusion into a text (Sunstein 440, 235; *GV* 282–283). She offers such authors as **Milton**, **Montague**, **Rousseau**, and **Mary Wollstonecraft** as examples and appreciates the type of self-intrusion seen in **Villani**'s *Cronica* [*Chronicle*] (1537, 1554) of **Florentine** history. Shelley describes the volumes' appearance and contents, giving chapter titles and quoting several long passages from Villani, "who guides us through the unfinished streets and growing edifices of **Firenze la bella**, and who in short transports us back to the superstitions, party spirit, companionship, and wars of the thirteenth and fourteenth centuries" (*GV* 285).

Giovio, Conte: See **Giovio, Paolo**.

Giovio, Paolo (1483–1552): Italian bishop and historian who wrote the forty-five book *Historiae sui temporis* [*History of His Own Times*] (1551–52) and *Elegia doctorum virorumad avorum memoria* [*Italian Portrait Gallery*] (1548), a prose and verse work describing his villa's portraits; Shelley also calls him **Conte Giovio** and **Paul Jovius** (*DIL* 247). Shelley remarks upon Giovio's collection of portraits (*R* 2.156).

Gisborne, John (d. c. 1835): Married to **Maria Gisborne** 1800, John was "a retired businessman . . . himself quite ordinary" (Sunstein 154). They moved to **Italy** 1801 and lived there with their two daughters; the Shelleys first met them in **Leghorn** May 1819 (*Journals* 209). John lived in his wife's shadow, and Shelley found at first that John "is most dreadfully dull" August 1819; nonetheless, "his letters show him to have been quite otherwise, an intelligent and reasonable man, and a reliable ally" (*Letters* 1.104; Holmes 423). John was a good friend to both Shelleys, and Shelley came to appreciate his good sense and generosity; their friendship continued until his death (White 2.552).

Gisborne, Maria [James Reveley] (1770–1836): Raised by her father in **Constantinople** and **Rome**, Maria married William Reveley 1788, and the couple settled in **London** 1790, where Maria became good friends with **William Godwin** (*SCGS* 154). Maria took care of Shelley in the week following **Mary Wollstonecraft**'s death, and her son **Henry Reveley** played with **Fanny Godwin** (Sunstein 153). Widowed 1799, Maria refused Godwin's marriage proposal but accepted **John Gisborne**'s 1800 (*SCGS* 200; Sunstein 154). The Gisbornes then moved to **Italy** and settled there; the Shelleys first met them May 1819 and "Maria Gisborne founded an intimacy" with Shelley (Sunstein 153). In August 1819 Shelley noted, "I like Mrs. Gisborne very much indeed," and her relationship with the woman who "could have been her stepmother" was one of the most fulfilling of her life (*Letters* 1.104; Sunstein 153). Maria filled a motherly role for Shelley, offering guidance in her personal life and worldly matters; with the exception of a rift September 1820–August 1821, fueled by **Mary Jane Clairmont Godwin**'s antipathy toward the Shelleys, Maria and Shelley were correspondents and friends throughout the elder woman's life (*Journals* 334–335). See Shelley's *Letters* and *Journals* and Frederick L. Jones's *Maria Gisborne and Edward E. Williams, Shelley's Friends: Their Journals and Letters* (1951).

Gitani: **Spanish** for gypsies. **Richard of York**, **Monina De Faro**, and **Desmond** encounter gitani after escaping the **Tower** (*PW* 2.122).

Giudi, Count Guido Novello de': **Manfred**'s lieutenant, driven out of **Florence** November 1266 (Sismondi 97). Guidi is a minor character in "**A Tale of the Passions**."

Giulia, Villa: Villa on **Lake Lecco**'s western shore between **Bellagio** and Limonto (*BSWI* 490). Shelley visited it twice August 1840 (*R* 1.83, 1.92).

Giulietta: See **Zingarelli**.

Giuseppe, Padre: Priest in "**Valerius the Reanimated Roman**."

Glenfell, Lady: Miss **Jervis**'s former employer in *Falkner*.

Gloucester, Duke of (1391–1447): Protector of England while **Henry VI** was a child; Gloucester had one illegitimate son, Arthur (*DNB*). **Edmund Plantagenet**'s father in *Perkin Warbeck*.

Gloucester, Duke of: See **Richard III**.

Gmunden: Austrian city on **Gmunden Lake**, thirty-five miles northeast of **Salzburg**. Shelley arrived there September 1842 (*R* 2.25–26).

Gmunden Lake: Alpine lake in central **Austria** east of **Salzburg** between **Gmunden** and **Ebensee**; Shelley also calls it **Gmunden-see**. She sailed on it September 1842 (*R* 2.26).

Gmunden-see: See **Gmunden Lake**.

Godwin, Fanny [Imlay] (1794–1816): **Mary Wollstonecraft** and **Gilbert Imlay**'s only child and Shelley's half-sister. Fanny was a "sensitive, passive child who expected little" and was "melancholy"; certainly, her childhood was difficult in **William Godwin**'s household—she was a reminder of Wollstonecraft's life prior to her marriage to Godwin and was constantly considered secondary to Shelley (Sunstein 23–24, 114). Fanny formed a lifelong friendship with Shelley; they maintained a steady correspondence after Shelley's **European** elopement, but Fanny was subsequently placed in an awkward mediating position between Shelley and Godwin. Shelley received "a very alarming letter from Fanny" 9 October 1816 and later recorded, "Fanny died this night," calling her "Poor dear Fanny" December 1816 (*Journals* 139; *Letters* 1.24). Despairing of life at home in **London**, Fanny had killed herself in Swansea by overdosing on laudanum; both Godwin and **PBS** had followed her there but turned back when they realized she was already dead (*Letters* 1.25; White 1.470–474). Godwin wanted the suicide to be kept secret and so "left the body to be buried by the parish"; the circumstances of Fanny's death seem to have been well concealed (*Journals* 140; Sunstein 127).

Godwin, Mary Jane Clairmont (1768–1841): William **Godwin**'s second wife; they were **London** neighbors before marrying 21 December 1801 (*Letters* 1.3; *SCGS* 238). Little is known about her early life, but she had lived in **France** and had two illegitimate children—**Charles Clairmont** with a **Swiss**, Karl Gaulis, and **Claire Clairmont**, father unknown (*Letters* 1.3; *SCGS* 249–253). Mary Jane's pregnancy hastened the marriage with Godwin, but the male child born prematurely 1802 died; they did have a son, **William Godwin**, 1803 (*SCGS* 241–242). Mary Jane had translated works written in French and had written children's stories, encouraging her husband to open a bookshop with her 1805; the couple successfully published works for children, and Mary Jane was instrumental in acquiring works for their Juvenile Library to publish (*SCGS* 284–285).

Mary Jane left Godwin for a few weeks 1811, but the couple seemed happy through their long marriage, even though Mary Jane surely felt the difficulty of being compared to **Mary Wollstonecraft**, and she constantly "accused Godwin of preferring Mary [Shelley] to herself"; Sunstein asserts that Mary Jane was "morally beneath" Godwin, and many of his friends could not understand the attraction (*SCGS* 312–213; Sunstein 30, 29). Shelley resented her stepmother throughout her childhood, writing October 1814: "I detest Mrs G. she plagues my father out of his life" (*Letters* 1.3). The feeling seems to have been mutual; Mary Jane resented her stepdaughter and favored her own children, always feeling that Shelley had corrupted Mary Jane's children, especially Claire (*SCGS* 473). The two women came, however, to tolerate each other; Shelley eventually wrote to Mary Jane as "Mamma" (*Letters* 2.250). After Godwin's death, Mary Jane received money from the Royal Literary fund and the government and assisted Shelley with her father's biography: "[T]o the surprise of both, the two widows found that they had become friends" before Mary Jane's death (*SCGS* 489–491). See William St. Clair's *The Godwins and the Shelleys* (1989).

Godwin, Mary: See **Shelley, Mary**.

Godwin, Mr.: See **Godwin, William**.

Godwin, William (1756–1836): Philosopher, novelist, and Shelley's father. He was actively involved with radical **London** literary circles during the **French Revolution** and was an important figure in **Jacobin** politics in the early 1790s. His highly controversial philosophical *Enquiry Concerning Political Justice* (1793) established his fame; his novel *Things as They Are; or, The Adventures of Caleb Williams* (1794) fictionalizes many of its central ideas. Godwin attacked existing institutions, including the monarchy and religion, insisting upon the primacy of reason. Conservative governmental opposition to the French Revolution targeted his works and brought him close to arrest for treason; a younger generation of writers, such as **Wordsworth** and **Samuel Taylor Coleridge**, admired him. Godwin married **Mary Wollstonecraft** in 1797 (after she became pregnant), although they continued to maintain separate households; she died in childbirth that year (Sunstein 17–18). Godwin published his *Memoirs* (1798) of Wollstonecraft (including her letters to **Gilbert Imlay** and accounts of her suicide attempts) to share his love and respect for her with the world; however, his candid disclosures instead caused her reputation to sink. Godwin raised Wollstonecraft's illegitimate daughter, **Fanny Godwin**, as his own child. His second marriage (1801) to **Mary Jane Clairmont Godwin** brought Shelley "an obnoxious stepmother," two stepsiblings, **Claire** and **Charles Clairmont**, and a half-brother, **William Godwin**. Godwin's household was an educationally stimulating one; his mentorship gave Shelley an enlightened education, disciplined habits of study, a lifelong bent toward historical fiction and biography, and a persistent concern with the freedom of the will (Crook 2). In childhood, she idolized her father and wrote later in December

Godwin, William (1756–1838)

1822, "[U]ntil I knew [**PB**] **Shelley** I may justly say [Godwin] was my God— & I remember many childish instances of the excess of attachment I bore for him" (*Letters* 1.296). It was through Godwin that Shelley met PBS, who visited the Godwin home as an admirer and patron (the profits of Godwin's writings and his educational bookshop were insufficient to support him and his family); Godwin was furious when the couple eloped to **Europe** but continued to press PBS for money (*Journals* 26, 41–43; White 1.260; Crook 2). Father and daughter were reconciled after her marriage, but Godwin continued to assert a strong influence over Shelley's life. He could be extremely insensitive; for example, when **William Shelley** died (1819), Shelley noted "I have no consolation in any quarter for my misfortune has not altered the tone of my father's letters"; his persistent and uncaring financial demands upon the Shelleys drained their finances, strained their relationship, and led PBS to prevent his wife from seeing her father's letters for a time (*Letters* 1.106). Nevertheless, Shelley did all she could to support her father, giving him *Valperga*'s profits, and the two grew close again after her 1823 return to Britain. Having declared bankruptcy (1825), Godwin was freer to write, being relieved of worry about his debts (*SCGS* 475–476). He completed his four-volume *History of the Commonwealth of England* (1824–28), to which Shelley playfully refers in "**Roger Dodsworth**" (*RD* 43; *SCGS* 474). His *Thoughts on Man* (1831) shows Godwin modifying his earlier views somewhat (Crook 2). While Shelley never fully reconciled her feelings for her husband and for her father, she and Godwin shared a mutually beneficial and rewarding professional relationship, especially during the 1820s and 1830s. He helped her with research for *Perkin Warbeck* (1830), while she wrote a short "Memoir" (1831) for the re-issued *Caleb Williams* and gave him both encouragement and assistance in the later *Cloudesley* (1830; see "**Review of *Cloudesley*; A Tale**"), *Deloraine* (1833), and *Lives of the Necromancers* (1834) (Crook 2). On his death (June 1836) she recorded, "I have lost my dear darling father"; Godwin was buried with Wollstonecraft, and Shelley acted as her father's literary executor, beginning an unfinished *Life* of him shortly after his death but suppressing his atheistic *The Genius of Christianity Unveiled*, published 1873 as *Essays, Never Before Published* (*Journals* 549; Sunstein 331–332). She read and reread her father's works throughout her life; influences from Godwin's earlier novels—*Caleb Williams*, *St. Leon* (1799), *Fleetwood* (1805), and *Mandeville* (1817)—are frequently apparent, and she has been called a "Godwinian" novelist because of affinities of theme, structure, and ideological perspective (*Journals* 649–650; Crook 2). She represents her relationship with her father under many guises, consistently creating fictional daughters such as **Euthanasia**, **Ethel Villiers**, and **Elizabeth Falkner**, whose closest attachment is to their fathers; *Matilda* and "**The Mourner**" demonstrate her resentment of the sometimes troubled relationship with Godwin and her own guilt concerning it, while *Falkner* explores Shelley's difficulties resulting from dividing her love between her father and husband. See William St. Clair's *The Godwins and the Shelleys* (1989) and

Godwin, William (1803–1832): William Godwin and **Mary Jane Clairmont Godwin**'s only son and Shelley's half-brother. Mary Jane spoiled the "rough, unmanageable little boy," who attended schools in **London** and **Greenwich** as well as being tutored at home; as a child, Shelley resented him somewhat (Sunstein 36, 40, 131; *Journals* 158). William was "bedeviled by incapacity to live up to his illustrious name," but he became a likeable man, happily marrying Mary Louisa Eldred, called Emily, February 1830, and turning from his intended career in architecture to become a writer and **parliamentary** reporter for the *Morning Chronicle* (Sunstein 249; *Letters* 2.156; *Journals* 527). Shelley maintained correspondence with William and encouraged his writing career; in December 1822, she wrote that she had "hardly ever seen him during the last eight years," so her "wishes more than my affections are interested in him" (*Letters* 1.297). However, William visited the Shelleys at **Marlow** January 1818 and met Shelley upon her return from **Europe** August 1823 (Sunstein 249; *Journals* 191, 527). They were in company together frequently in the 1820s; for example, William accompanied Shelley to **Vincent Novello**'s November 1823 (*Letters* 1.396). William died from cholera, leaving a novel, *Transfusion*, in manuscript; Shelley edited and Godwin published it 1835 (*Journals* 527; Sunstein 327). Shelley wrote to **Ollier** about her half-brother's work: William's "talents are such that I have no doubt that he has been able to execute well the plan he had in view" (*Letters* 1.434–435). When Shelley inherited **Sir Timothy Shelley**'s money, she "allotted fifty pounds a year" to William's widow (Sunstein 364).

Goethe House: See **Goethe**.

Goethe, Johann Wolfgang von (1749–1832): German poet and dramatist renowned for poetic drama *Faust* (part I 1808, part II 1832); Shelley also spells his name **Götha** (*R* 1.211). Shelley wrote and thanked **Hayward** for a copy of his new translation December 1839 (*Letters* 3.420). Faust, on a quest for knowledge, forms a pact with Mephistopheles and seduces Gretchen and then Helen of **Troy** before his death; the play ends with Faust's salvation. **Victor Frankenstein** is a Faustian overreacher; Shelley would have known of *Faust* through **De Staël**'s *Of Germany* (1810) as early as 1815 (Sunstein 427; Crook 2). In *Frankenstein*, Shelley refers to Goethe's epistolary novel *Die Leiden des jungen Werthers* [*The Sorrows of Young Werther*] (1774); she read it 1815 and visited Goethe's **Weimar** grave on her 1842 **European** tour (Sunstein 106, 357). **Ashburn** admires Goethe as a poet " 'of the imagination' " (*SP* 137). Shelley noted Germany's renown as "land of **Schiller** and Goethe" and, June 1842, saw **Frankfurt**'s **Goethe House**, where Goethe lived from birth to 1765 (*R* 1.175–176; *BGER* 125). She criticizes both *Faust* and " '**Wilhelm Meister**' " as "fragment[s]," referring to Goethe's famous bildungsromans, *Wilhelm Meisters Lehrjarhre* [*William Meister's Apprenticeship*] (1795–96) and *Wilhelm Meisters Wanderjarhre* [*William Meister's Travels*] (1821–29) (*R* 1.211). At Weimar, Shelley saw the house where Goethe lived, noting that Goethe's "startling quality . . . is his insight into the secret depths of the human mind; his power of dissecting motives—of holding up the mirror to our most inmost sensations; and also in dramatic scenes of touching pathos, and passages of overflowing eloquence: but he wants completeness, and never achieves a whole" (*R* 1.211). Shelley loosely translates and combines ideas from a review by Goethe of **Manzoni**'s *Carmagnola* (1821) and an essay on *Adelchi* (1822), noting that Goethe speaks of Manzoni's works "as making '**a serious and profound** impression, such as great pictures of human nature must always create' "; she adds Goethe's direction: " '**Let the poet** continue to disdain the feeble and vulgar portions of human passion, and attempt only such high arguments as excite deep and generous emotions' " (*R* 2.196; Goethe, *Gedenkausgabe* 14.837).

Goffredo, Count: Euthanasia's great-grandfather in *Valperga*.

Golden City: See **Constantinople**.

Golden Coast: British colony in West **Africa** on the Gulf of Guinea, named for the gold to be found in its rivers. It became an independent British Commonwealth member, as Ghana, in 1957. **Lionel Verney** hears of the sun's worldwide eclipse, including "Africa as far west as the Golden Coast" (*LM* 224). **Hernan De Faro** pursues "his fortunes down the Golden Coast" (*PW* 1.146–147).

Golden Horn: Bay six miles long at the southern end of **Constantinople**; it separates **Pera** from **Stamboul** and links to the Bosporus. It derives its name "from the resemblance . . . to the shape of a ram's horn" (Coufopoulos 149). **Lionel Verney** joins **Raymond** in the siege of Constantinople, finding the army already in possession of the Golden Horn (*LM* 183).

Goldene Sonne: Budweis hotel. Shelley stayed there September 1842 and found "no reason to alter" **Murray**'s positive recommendation (*R* 2.17; *MSGE* 526).

Goldener Löwe: Linz hotel **Murray** recommends (*MSGE* 193). Shelley stayed there September 1842 (*R* 2.21).

Goldoni, Carlo (1707–1793): Italian dramatist. Shelley wrote Goldoni's biography for *Italian and Spanish Lives*. Goldoni's *Belisarius* "met with complete success" in **Venice** 1734 (*ISPL* 2.232). Goldoni wanted to reinvigorate Italian drama with "comedies of character," and Shelley admires his "perfect fidelity to nature, the ease of his dialogue, and the dramatic effect of his pieces, [which] can only be entirely appreciated in the representation. The best of them have only a slight plot, but the interest is kept alive by the variety of the dialogue" (*ISPL* 2.233, 2.238–239). Shelley recommends a list of dramas and finds that *Le Bourro Bienfaisant* [*The Well-Meaning Grouch*] (1771) managed to "instil the spirit of **French** dialogue and plot with great success" (*ISPL* 2.246). Goldoni wrote his *Mémoires* 1783–87; Shelley read them in John Black's 1814 translation March 1815 (*ISPL* 2.246; *Journals* 69).

Goldsmith, Oliver (c. 1730–74): Irish author renowned for *The Vicar of Wakefield* (1766). Shelley read Goldsmith's *The Citizen of the World* (1762) January 1817 and was familiar with much of his work (*Journals* 154). Writing January 1821, Shelley notes "The Vicar of Wakefield for many other years recorded no other migration than from the blue bed to the brown—mine is one of far greater importance since it purposes to narrate a migration from **Pisa** to **Lucca**," metaphorically referring to a move from wealth (blue) to poverty (brown) (*Letters* 1.175). Shelley quotes Goldsmith's "A Ballad" in an August 1832 letter (*Letters* 2.166–167). In *The Vicar of Wakefield*, title protagonist Dr. Primrose narrates his family's mishaps as they sink into abject poverty and then rise again to their original financial and social status. The vicar's eldest son, George, describes his failure to obtain a position teaching **Greek** at a **Dutch** university, recording the university principal's statement: "**I have ten** thousand florins a year without Greek; I eat heartily without Greek" (Goldsmith 166). **Henry Clerval** compares his father to that principal (*Fr1* 89; *Fr3* 60). **Dame Barnet** reads "**Goody Two-shoes**" to neighborhood children; this moralistic children's story has been attributed to Goldsmith (*Maurice* 62; F. Moore 213). **Lady Lodore** resolves " 'Man wants but little here below, / Nor wants that little long,' " lines from Goldsmith's "The Hermit" (1765) (*L* 3.292; Goldsmith lines 29–32).

Gomelez, Almoradi: In *Perkin Warbeck*, Muslim soldier whom **Richard of York** kills.

Gonfalonieri: See **Confalonieri**.

Góngora y Argote, Luis de (1561–1627): **Spanish** poet. Shelley wrote Góngora's biography for *Italian and Spanish Lives*. She finds that his "early poetry is peculiarly simple and plain," suggesting that disappointed ambition led him to attack leading authors of the day with "scurrility and abuse" despite the "honesty and integrity of his disposition" (*ISPL* 3.244–245). Góngora's poems in Spanish meters "have the same brilliancy of expression, warmth of emotion, and vivid colouring" as many of his personal satires (*ISPL* 3.247). Shelley asserts that "Góngora surpasses every other Spanish lyrist, in the brilliant colouring of his poetry, and the vivacity of his expression" (*ISPL* 3.247). Góngora became a leading critic and founded the "culto," or refined style, of poetry, which **Lope** attacked for its high **Latinate** aspects (*ISPL* 3.250–251). Shelley concludes that Góngora's *Fábula de Polifemo* [*Fable of* **Polyphemus**] (c. 1613) and *Solidades* [*Solitudes*] (c. 1613) are "poems written in his most exaggerated style" (*ISPL* 3.252, 3.254).

Good Hope, Cape of: Cape forming **Africa**'s southwest tip on the **Atlantic**. **Lionel Verney** records plague spreading throughout it (*LM* 234). **Hernan De Faro** was in "the crew that discovered the Cape" and pursues "his fortunes . . . as far as the Cape" shortly after his marriage (*PW* 1.206, 1.146–147).

"Goody Two-shoes": See **Goldsmith**.

Gordian knot: Gordius, king of Gordium of Phrygia, tied an inextricable knot that **Alexander the Great**, during his campaign to conquer **Asia**, cut through with his sword (*OED*). Shelley describes **James IV**'s troubles as a Gordian knot (*PW* 2.326).

Gordon Castle: Bog o'Gight castle in Moray, northwestern region of Grampian County, bordering Moray Firth in Scotland (Fenwick 216). **Richard of York** and **Lady Katherine Gordon** marry there (*PW* 2.237, 2.249).

Gordon, Lady Katherine: James IV's cousin and George, **Earl of Huntly**'s daughter; she married **Perkin Warbeck** January 1496 (Arthurson 88, 122–123; *Letters* 1.78). **Richard of York**'s wife in *Perkin Warbeck*.

Gorgon: Greek mythical monsters with snakes for hair whose hideous faces would turn people who saw them to stone. **Lionel Verney** states that rumors about **Irish** invaders are exaggerated, including the Gorgon as an example "of the strange and appalling accounts brought to **London**" (*LM* 298). Shelley describes **Richard of York**'s reaction to **Robert Clifford**'s betrayal with an aside: there is "no pang so great, as the discovery of treachery where we pictured truth[;] . . . with Gorgon countenance, [treachery] transforms the past" (*PW* 2.68).

Goring, Augusta: See **Trelawny, Augusta Goring**.

Goring, George (1608–1657): Earl of Norwich who commanded part of **Charles I**'s army in his 1645 campaign, when Charles suffered defeat. Prior to this event, Goring supported the queen, Henrietta Maria, and was accused of involvement in a 1640 conspiracy to seize **London** (Carlton 225). **Henry Clerval** and **Victor Frankenstein** remember "insolent Goring" while visiting **Oxford** (*Fr1* 186; *Fr3* 136).

Gospel: Christian teaching generally; the first four books of the New Testament—Matthew, Mark, Luke, and John—are known as the "Gospels." Krempe finds **Victor Frankenstein**'s progress at **Ingolstadt** university remarkable, since he formerly "believed in **Cornelius Agrippa** as firmly as in the Gospel" (*Fr1* 97; *Fr3* 66).

Gotha: German city fifteen miles west of **Erfurt**. Shelley slept there July 1842 and regretted not touring **Prince Albert**'s native city (*R* 1.209).

Götha: See **Goethe**.

Graben: German word for ditch and former name of Kolowratstrasse, major **Prague** thoroughfare lined by the best hotels during Shelley's 1842 visit (*R* 1.280). It was originally a ditch separating **Neustadt** from Old Town, until filled in and paved (*MSGE* 511).

Gracchi: Tiberius and Caius, **Italian** brothers of the 2nd century B.C.E., remembered for "radical reforms" of **Rome**. Wealthy landowners resented the Gracchi's principles, and the Gracchi lost power and died violently (Howatson 254–255). Shelley probably learned of them from **Plutarch**'s *Lives* (3.126–159). **Lionel Verney** imagines the Gracchi in the **Forum** (*LM* 462).

Graham, Maria Langley: Only character to begin her tale in "**An Eighteenth-Century Tale**."

Grampians: Central Scottish mountain range. **James IV** leads **Richard of York** through them (*PW* 2.240, 2.248). Shelley's affinity for mountains began when she "saw . . . snow-clad Grampians" 1812–13, as recounted in *Frankenstein*'s introduction (*R* 1.119).

Gran Parigi: Verona hotel **Murray** recommends (Moskal 267). Shelley stayed there September 1842 (*R* 2.75).

Granada: **Spanish** city sixty miles northeast of **Malaga**. Shelley directs readers to **Irving**'s *The Chronicle of the Conquest of Granada* for a description and history of Granada, where **Richard of York** fights for **Ferdinand** and **Isabella** (*PW* 1.203, 1.216–217, 1.223, 2.226). Although **Hernan De Faro** is Spanish and returns to his homeland, he quickly departs, because he does not wish to see Granada fall (which it did 1492) (*PW* 1.204, 1.206–207, 1.210). Subsequently, throughout *Perkin Warbeck*, various characters idealize memories of Granada (*PW* 1.290, 1.307, 2.5, 2.21, 2.274, 3.189). **Stephen Frion** lived there (*PW* 1.150, 1.153, 1.159).

Grand Canal: Widest and most central **Venetian** canal, **Canale Grande** in **Italian**. Shelley resided at a hotel on it October 1818 but "was more often disgusted with Venice's stench than enraptured at wonders along the Canal" (Sunstein 160). **Guinigi** reveals plans for **Castruccio**'s travel to England as they pass along the canal (*V* 1.62). **Edmund Malville** fondly recalls " 'palaces that rose from the Canale Grande' " (*RI* 26). **Lionel Verney**, **Clara**, and **Adrian** enter deserted Venice along Canale Grande (*LM* 438). In September 1842, Shelley stayed at **Hôtel d'Italia** "three oar-strokes from the Canale Grande," and she frequently refers to the Canale Grande in depicting Venice and its sites (*R* 2.80, 2.94).

Grand Old Bridge: Carlsbrücker [Charles Bridge] over the **Moldau** in **Prague** (Moskal 228). Shelley notes that **Charles IV** (1316–78) built it (*R* 2.2).

Grand Trianon: House in **Versailles**'s gardens that **French** royalty and their courts used for intimate gatherings (Nolhac 279–280). The Shelleys visited it September 1816 (*Journals* 133). **Adrian** and his family reside in apartments there (*LM* 382).

Grande Albergo: **Cadenabbia** hotel that the **Brentani** family operated; Shelley stayed there 1840 (*R* 1.62, 1.68).

Granville, Augustus Bozzi [Dr.] (1783–1872): British physician who published *The Spas of Germany* (1837); during 1840–68 he spent three months of each year at **Kissingen**, establishing the resort's reputation among the British (*DNB*). Shelley notes that Granville's book "extended our acquaintance with the spas of **Germany**" (*R* 1.184). He was practicing at Kissingen during Shelley's 1842 visit (*R* 1.192–193).

Gravesend: **Thames** port seven miles east of **Dartford**. The Shelleys returned there at their 1814 **European** tour's conclusion (*H* 81). **Henry Clerval** and **Victor Frankenstein** visit Gravesend (*Fr1* 184; *Fr3* 134).

Gray: French town twenty-five miles northeast of **Dijon**. The Shelleys stayed there August 1814 (*Journals* 15; *H* 30).

Gray, Clinton: Title figure in "**The Elder Son**" and **Sir Richard Gray**'s oldest son.

Gray, John (d. 1461): Elizabeth Woodville's first husband; he died at St. Albans fighting for Henry VI (Cook 107). Minor character in *Perkin Warbeck*.

Gray, Lady: Matilda Towers becomes Lady Gray upon marrying Sir Richard Gray in "The Elder Son."

Gray, Lady Elizabeth: See Woodville, Elizabeth.

Gray, Marianne: Sir Richard and Lady Gray's youngest surviving child in "The Elder Son."

Gray, Sir Richard: Lady Caroline Hythe, Clinton, Vernon, and Marianne Gray's father and elder brother of Ellen's father in "The Elder Son."

Gray, Thomas (1716–1771): Highly influential 18th-century poet whose works, such as *The Bard* (1757), demonstrate a movement away from Neoclassicism toward personal poetry of sensibility. Gerard Neville introduces Elizabeth Falkner to Gray's works (*F* 236).

Gray, Vernon: Sir Richard Gray's second son in "The Elder Son."

Grazia, La: See Capuan.

Great Park: Area of Windsor forest enclosed in the 11th century and reserved for the royal family's hunting. George III took great interest in its "drainage and cultivation" in the 1790s (Hedley 107, 153). In Shelley's time, British royals frequently drove through these grounds, and Shelley would surely have been familiar with the area from her residence in nearby Marlow. Perdita's cottage is on Great Park's edge, and after their marriage Perdita and Raymond live in a house he builds close to the cottage (*LM* 90). Many of *The Last Man*'s Windsor scenes involve explorations of Great Park.

Greece: European country called Hellas in ancient times. Throughout her life, Shelley studied and admired classical Greek texts, art, and culture; many of her works refer to classical Greece. Victor Frankenstein finds Oriental poetry soothing but very "different from the manly and heroical poetry of Greece" (*Fr1* 89, 97; *Fr3* 60, 67). The Creature learns of Grecians' "stupendous genius and mental activity" from Volney's *Ruins of Empires* (*Fr1* 147, 229; *Fr3* 105, 171). Greece is the setting for and source of the myths upon which Shelley draws for *Proserpine* and *Midas*. Shelley also refers frequently to contemporary events in Greece; during her lifetime Greeks fought for independence from the Ottoman Empire—from 1821 until victory in 1829. The British press reported their cause sympathetically, and many young Britons, Byron being perhaps the most famous, enlisted in what was perceived as a noble cause; Raymond's, Rupert Falkner's, and Chief Constantine's adventures in Greece are drawn from Byron's. Living in Pisa 1820, Shelley became good friends with Prince Alexander Mavrocordato and moved in a circle of exiled Greek aristocrats (Sunstein 192–193). Shelley sent reports about events in Greece to London for publication, and throughout her life she studied and admired Greek texts and culture. In April 1826, she wrote: "I take more than common interest in the affairs of Greece because I have known & even had an affection for Greeks" (*Letters* 1.514). Shelley's sympathies are always with the Greek cause in her fiction. Victor Frankenstein suggests that an abundance of passion led to Greek enslavement (*Fr1* 84; *Fr3* 57). "**Recollections of Italy**'s" narrator and **Edmund Malville** discuss "the Greek Revolution" (*RI* 25). **Viola Arnaldi** dresses in "the costume of a Greek maiden" (*HM* 328). The **Countess of Windsor** welcomes "Prince Zaimi, ambassador to England from the free states of Greece," and his daughter **Evadne Zaimi** to **Windsor**; at **Perdita**'s cottage, **Lionel Verney** reads histories of Greece (*LM* 33, 77). Raymond plans a national art gallery according to a Greek design that Evadne submits, and *The Last Man*'s first volume deals largely with the characters' engagement in Greece's war against **Turkey**, as Shelley reconstructs the war of independence taking place when she was writing (*LM* 107). Raymond "became the darling of this rising people," and Greece is the background to many of the novel's important scenes (*LM* 40). **Dmitri** marries a girl from "**Scio**, the most civilized of the Greek islands"; Shelley characterizes Greeks as superstitious in "**The Evil Eye**" (*EE* 101, 103, 110). **Ethel Villiers** finds **Fanny Derham** intent upon a book "in Greek characters" (*L* 2.293). Rupert Falkner voices Shelley's attitude toward the Greeks' "glorious cause," "that of liberty and Christianity against tyranny and an evil faith" (*F* 56, 144). Falkner risks his life fighting for the cause, and **Elizabeth Falkner** accompanies him there. While in Greece, Falkner composes the narrative that records his guilty secret and constitutes *Falkner*'s central portion (*F* 306). **Harry Valency** relates experiences fighting for Greece, showing Shelley's antipathy toward the "usurping Turk" (*E* 297). Shelley found **Canova**'s women inferior to "those of Grecian sculpture" (*R* 1.92, 1.90). On **Gmunden Lake**, Shelley felt "the beauty of the Greek mythology was awakened in me," and she later observed that **Florence**'s large galleries are superior to "Greek temples [which] had but small interior shrines" (*R* 2.27, 2.159). Discussing **Raphael**'s works, Shelley notes, "it is said that all the works of ancient Grecian sculpture bear the character of divine repose," but she posits *Apollo Belvedere* as comparable in beauty (*R* 2.217). [*Maurice* 78; *Fr1* 89, 229; *Fr3* 60, 171; *TP* 7; *EE* 114; *L* 2.185; *F* 292; *Stanzas: O come* lines 6, 10; *R* 1.90, 1.96, 1.174].

Green Chamber: Shelley's descriptive reference for Huldigungssaal, **Prague** Palace hall where kings were once crowned; later a council chamber (*MSGE* 514). Shelley mentions a 1618 incident (the "Defenestration of Prague") during which three of **Ferdinand II**'s commissioners were thrown out of the Green Chamber's windows but survived (*R* 2.4). Stone obelisks mark where the men landed (*MSGE* 514–515).

Green Vaults: Dresden museum founded 1723–24, called **Grüne Gewölbe** in **German** (Jackson 1.338). Shelley spent 18 July 1842 there (*R* 1.251).

Greenland: World's largest island, mostly north of the Arctic Circle, northeast of **Canada**. Robert Walton journeys there onboard a whaler (*Fr1* 51; *Fr3* 27).

Greenock: Scottish port twenty miles northwest of Glasgow. **Stephen Frion** attempts to kidnap **Richard of York** by leading him to Greenock with the false promise of supporters there (*PW* 2.329, 3.6, 3.8).

Greenwich: **London** borough on the **Thames**'s south bank near **St. Paul's**. **Henry Clerval** and **Victor Frankenstein** visit it (*Fr1* 184; *Fr3* 134). **Monina De Faro** and **Richard of York** depart the **Tower** for the *Adalid* at Greenwich (*PW* 2.86).

Gregory VII, Pope (c. 1020–1085): Pope 1073–85; he was involved in an extended conflict with **Henry IV** of **Germany** concerning lay investiture (Kelly 154–155). Shelley confuses Gregory with **Pope Leo IX** when **Lionel Verney** compares Henry's penance with the **Countess of Windsor**'s attempts to repent and earn **Adrian**'s love after **Idris**'s death (*LM* 385). Describing **Rome**, Shelley states the mile between the **Lateran** and the **Coliseum** "was the most magnificent quarter of the old city," but it was burned and leveled when Henry sacked Rome (March 1084) while it was under Gregory's control (*R* 2.228).

Gregory XIV, Pope (1535–1591): **Francesco Sfondrati**'s youngest son, Niccolò Sfondrati; pope December 1590–October 1591 (*R* 2.79; Kelly 273). Shelley mentions that he wrote "**De Raptu Helenae**, Poema Heroicum, libro tres" ["Of the Ravishing of Helen, an Heroic Poem in Three Books"] (1559) (*R* 1.80; Moskal 115).

Gregory XVI, Pope (1765–1846): Pope 1831–46 (Kelly 307). Shelley criticizes April 1843 **Holy Week** ceremonies because she preferred **Pius VII** to Gregory, who, "shutting his eyes as he is carried round **St. Peter's**, because the motion of the chair makes him sea-sick, by no means excites respect" (*R* 2.230).

Gregory, Doctor: Tentatively identified with George Gregory (1754–1808), British chaplain and author of *Letters on Literature, Taste and Composition* (1800) (*DNB;* Moskal 285; Crook 2). Shelley attributes to him the opinion that reading novels is preferable to not reading at all (*R* 2.105).

Gregory, Miss: Only "daughter of a wealthy commoner," who marries **Colonel Villiers** against her father's wishes in *Lodore* (*L* 2.157).

Greville, Mrs.: Minor character in *Lodore*.

Grimaldi: Debtor to **Benedetto Pepi** in *Valperga*. Shelley uses a **Genoese** family name found in **Boccaccio** (*Decameron* 1.8).

Gros Bois: See **Grosbois**.

Grosbois: Meaning "Big Woods," park twelve miles southeast of **Paris**'s center; Shelley calls it **Gros Bois** (*STIE* 483). The Shelleys stopped for refreshments there in August 1814 (*Journals* 11; *H* 16).

Grosse Garten: **Dresden**'s park, "Great Garden," designed 1698 (Giebel 139). Shelley visited it August 1842 (*R* 1.247).

Grosse Winterberg: Mountain twenty-five miles southeast of **Dresden**. Shelley describes the view from its inn, where she stayed August 1842 (*R* 1.271). Shelley corrects **Murray**'s negative assessment of this inn, enthusiastically recommending it (*R* 1.271–272).

Grossi, Tommaso (1790–1854): **Italian** novelist and poet renowned for his first novel *Ildegonda* (1820), epic poem *I lombardi alla prima crociata* [*Lombards in the First Crusade*] (1826), and historical novel *Marco Visconti* (1834) (*DIL* 264–265). Shelley includes Grossi in her account of **Italian** romance writers; she praises *Ildegonda, Marco Visconti,* and *Fuggitiva* (1816) and calls him **Manzoni**'s "rival" rather than his "pupil" (*R* 2.195, 2.202). She specifically mentions *Marco Visconti,* relating Grossi dedicated this "popular romance" to Manzoni (*R* 2.202). [*R* 1.105].

Grosvenor Square: Large square east of **Hyde Park** in **London**'s Westminster district; it has magnificent houses "and the shrubs and walks well arranged" (Leigh 261). Shelley moved there late 1837 (*Journals* 550). **Edmund Malville** gently mocks his companion's naive opinion of **Italy**, suggesting that " 'you fancied yourself in Grosvenor-square' " (*RI* 27). **Ethel Villiers** is delighted to receive her husband's letter marked "Grosvenor Square" (*L* 2.152).

Grotto Azzuro: Large circular cave on **Capri**'s shore, wherein the blue water makes the ceiling seem blue (*STIE* 374). Shelley visited it June 1843 (*R* 2.268).

Grüne Gewölbe: See **Green Vaults**.

Guard-house: Berlin's "Neue Wache," which Karl Friedrich Schinkel built 1816–18 on **Unter den Linden** opposite the **New Museum**, now a war memorial (Low 74; Tucker 56). Shelley saw it July 1840 (*R* 1.218).

Guarini, Battista (1538–1612): **Italian** poet who "preferred the distinction of a court to poetic fame" (*ISPL* 2.82). Shelley wrote Guarini's biography for *Italian and Spanish Lives*. He is remembered for pastoral *Il Pastor Fido* [*The Faithful Shepherd*] (1590), which **PBS** read April 1815 (*Journals* 74). Shelley provides a long excerpt and notes it as "the principal monument of Guarini's poetic genius" (*ISPL* 2.90). She outlines the complex plot and admires "the simplicity and clearness of its diction, the sweetness and tenderness of the sentiments, and the vivacity and passion that animate the whole" (*ISPL* 2.91). Shelley notes Guarini's tendency "to consider himself an ill-used man"; he died at **Venice** while engaged in lawsuits (*ISPL* 2.94).

Guarino: One of *Valperga*'s **Uomini di Corte** (*V* 1.273–274). Shelley may have taken the name from **Muratori** (Crook 3.101).

Gueldres, Duke Adolph of: Ruler of **Dutch** province also known as Gelderland. Shelley praises a **Rembrandt** portrait of the duke as "remarkable" (*R* 1.220, 2.96).

Guelph (also Guelf): Thirteenth- and 14th-century **Italian** political party that supported the pope and violently opposed **Ghibellines**. In **Florence**, Guelphs were mostly wealthy merchants; the faction split in **Pistoia** into the **Neri** and **Bianchi**. Guelph comes from "Welf," **German** dynasty that ruled **Bavaria** and opposed **Swabia**'s Hohenstaufens. *Valperga* opens with Guelph seizure of control of **Lucca** and Florence, after which **Castruccio**'s family is banished from Lucca (*V* 1.2–4). **Euthanasia** is Guelph, compounding her problems with Castruccio (*V* 1.187). [*R* 2.244].

Guerazzi, Francesco Domenico (1804–1873): Italian novelist and political activist. Shelley lists Guerazzi as a great Italian author, specifically mentioning *L'Assedio di Firenze* [*The Siege of Florence*] (published 1836 as by "Anselmo Gualandi") and *La Battaglia di Benevento* [*Manfred, or Battle of Benevento*] (1828) (*R* 2.202; *DIL* 270). Shelley offers *L'Assedio* as proof of Guerazzi's "almost frantic love of liberty" and notes *La Battaglia*'s popularity in Italy and its evidence of Guerazzi's patriotism (*R* 2.202). Guerazzi also published *Beatrice Cenci* (1854) (*DIL* 270).

Guerra del Vespro Siciliano: See **Amari**.

Guglielmus Apulus: See **Gibbon**.

Guicciardini, Francesco (1483–1540): Florentine historian and politician renowned as wise governor of a large part of northern **Italy**. Shelley wrote Guicciardini's biography for *Italian and Spanish Lives*. Little is known about his personal life, but Shelley recounts his political rise accurately; "prudence and firmness, and even severity" were characteristic of his administration (*ISPL* 2.67). Guicciardini led the pontifical army (1527) and assisted the second **Medici** restoration; "his name has thus received a taint never to be effaced. He became the abettor of tyrants, the oppressor of his fellow citizens" (*ISPL* 2.69). Guicciardini wrote a history of Italy in his own times, *Storia d'Italia* (1561–64), which Shelley finds "a fine monument of his genius and industry," even while she criticizes its "prolixity" (*ISPL* 2.72).

Guiccioli, Countess Teresa (c. 1800–1873): At age eighteen, this **Italian** married Count Alessandro, some forty years older. Teresa became **Byron**'s mistress a year later and continued their love affair until Byron's death (Marchand 2.773–775). Shelley first met Teresa and her brother **Pietro Gamba** September 1821 and found Teresa "a nice pretty girl, without pretensions, good-hearted and amiable," but she subsequently viewed Teresa as enslaving Byron (*Journals* 378; *Letters* 1.209). Shelley enjoyed Teresa's company, although she was occasionally shocked by her manners; affection for Byron was the foundation of their continued contact. When Teresa visited England 1832 and 1835, Shelley saw little of her; Teresa's "artless flouting of British proprieties had society agog" (Sunstein 317, 327). Teresa returned to her husband briefly 1826, but separated from him and engaged in a series of affairs before his death (1840) (Marchand 3.1243). She then married **French** Marquis de Boissy but continued her "Byron worship" throughout her life (Marchand 3.1243). See Leslie A. Marchand's *Byron: A Portrait* (1957) and Iris Origo's *The Last Attachment* (1949).

Guide-Book of Florence, The: See **Fantozzi**.

Guido il Cortese: Main character and narrator of "**Transformation**." His nickname, "il Cortese," is **Italian** for "the Courteous." Guido attempts to convince **Juliet Torella** to join him without her father's consent, much as **PBS** encouraged Shelley (*Trans* 125).

Guido Reni (1575–1642): Bolognese painter renowned for religious paintings of Madonna and other female saints. Shelley saw "a great many of Guido['s]" works in Bologna November 1818 (*Journals* 236). She wrote to **Leigh Hunt** April 1819 that, besides **Raphael**, "Guido would be a great favourite of yours" (*Letters* 1.90). The Shelleys saw **Beatrice Cenci**'s portrait in **Rome**'s **Colonna Palace** April 1819, then misattributed to Guido, as has been subsequently demonstrated (*Journals* 259). **Lionel Verney** compares **Perdita**'s appearance to that of "one of Guido's saints, with heaven in her heart and in her look" (*LM* 15). Shelley describes **Lady Katherine Gordon**'s face when she learns that she will see her husband: "an irradiation of love passed over her countenance; her form; something like it dwells in . . . Guido's *Angel of Annunciation*" (*PW* 3.256). This painting (c. 1610) is in the **Quirinal**, where Shelley probably viewed it 1819 (Cavalli 60; Fischer 365). Shelley saw the Beatrice Cenci portrait again April 1843 (*R* 2.223). [*PW* 3.256].

Guignes: Town twenty-six miles southeast of **Paris**, formerly known as **Guignes-Rabutin**. The Shelleys stayed there August 1814, sleeping in the same rooms and beds as **Napoleon** and his officers once did (*Journals* 11; *H* 17).

Guignes-Rabutin: See **Guignes**.

Guinigi: Leading banking and trading family powerful in 14th-century **Lucca** (Green 112). Three *Valperga* characters are from this family: **Arrigo**, **Francesco**, and **Leodino** (*V* 1.38, 1.46, 2.206–208).

Guinigi, Arrigo de: Francesco de Guinigi's son in *Valperga*, loosely based on Pagolo Guinigi, Francesco's son in **Machiavelli**'s *The Life of Castruccio* (*LCCL* 537, 554).

Guinigi, Francesco de: Ruggieri dei Antelminelli's Lucchese Ghibelline friend and **Castruccio**'s tutor in *Valperga*.

Guinigi, Leodino de: Young man of the House of **Guinigi** who marries **Lauretta dei Adimari** in *Valperga*.

Guiscard, Robert (c. 1015–1085): Norman who moved to **Italy** 1047 and became Duke of Apulia 1059 (Kinder 1.131, 1.147). Shelley relates that he rescued **Pope Gregory VII** when **Henry IV** invaded **Rome** March 1084 (*R* 2.228).

Guiscardo: See **Boccaccio**.

Guisciana: **Italian** river mentioned repeatedly in *Valperga* with reference to nearby battles (*V* 2.248–249, 3.172, 3.198). Now called the Usciana, it flows near **Fucecchio** (Crook 3.211).

Gulf of Salerno: Body of water south of **Naples**. Shelley notes **Conti delle Fontanelle**'s excellent view of it June 1843 (*R* 2.266).

Gulliver: See **Swift**.

Gustavus Adolphus (1594–1632): Sweden's ruler 1611–32. He involved Sweden in the Thirty Years' War 1630 and was mortally wounded in battle near Lutzen (Roeder 124). In July 1842 Shelley saw the spot where Adophus fell (*R* 1.214).

Guyon, Sir: See *The Faerie Queen*.

H

Habsburg: German family that ruled **Austria** and other **European** countries and regions 1282–1918; Shelley spells it **Hapsburgh**. Shelley records that Habsburg rule of **Tyrol** began in the 14th century and that **Venetian** nobles refused to petition Habsburg invaders for retention of their titles 1797 (*R* 2.41, 2.95).

Hades: See **Pluto**.

Hadrian [Publius Aelius Hadrianus] (76–138): **Roman** emperor 117–138; Shelley terms him **Adrian**. **Isabell Harley** calls him "mere" workman of Rome's monuments (*Val* 340).

Haemus: Mountain range, now called the Balkans, extending from northeast **Macedonia** east across central Bulgaria to the **Black Sea** (Tripp 259). **Lionel Verney** notes that **Constantinople**'s army stored "ice . . . on Haemus" (*LM* 189).

Hagar: Biblical **Sarah**'s slave; after wandering in the desert, she had a son, Ishmael, with Abraham (Genesis 16.1–4). Shelley mentions **la Grazia**, model for a statue of Hagar (*R* 2.224).

Hague, The: City and site of government and royal palace on **Holland**'s west coast about seventeen miles southwest of **Amsterdam**. Shelley found **Kissingen**'s "Conversationhaus" "as good a ball-room as that" in The Hague's palace (*R* 1.190–191).

Haidée: Greek pirate Lambro's beautiful daughter, who rules their island in the **Cyclades** in his absence in **Byron**'s *Don Juan* (1819–24). Don Juan falls in love with her when shipwrecked there, but Lambro returns, separates the lovers, and sends Don Juan to be sold as a slave in **Constantinople**. Haidée dies of grief (Cantos 2–4). **Lionel Verney** endows the heroines of all he reads with **Perdita**'s "beauty and matchless excellences," including Haidée (*LM* 78). Shelley compares **Ethel Villiers**'s youth in **America** to Haidée's on her isolated island (*L* 1.210).

187

Hal: See **Henry VII of England**.

Hall: Austrian center of salt mining at **Salzberg**'s foot (Moskal 251). Shelley mentions the 1809 **Tyrolese** battle against the **French** at Hall's Bridge (*R* 2.46).

Hall, Edward (c. 1498–1547): British historian and author of *The Union of the Noble and Illustre Families of Lancastre and York* (1542) (*DNB*). Shelley directs readers to Hall for a version of **Perkin Warbeck**'s tale (*PW* 1.iv).

Hall of Hercules: Hall at **Versailles**, containing Francis Lemoyne's ceiling painting (1729–36) of **Greek** gods receiving **Hercules** (Nolhac 76). Shelley saw it September 1816 (*Journals* 133). **Adrian** is held under protective guard there (*LM* 404).

Hall of Knights: Shelley's July 1840 tour of **Heidelberg Castle** included the Hall of Knights (*R* 1.36). Moskal suggests Shelley refers to central Heidelberg's Ritterzaal ruins; one wall still stands (94).

Hallstadt, Lake: Austrian lake eight miles south of Bad **Ischl**; the **Traun** empties into it. Shelley regretted not visiting it September 1842 (*R* 2.29).

Hamburg: German port city on the **Elbe**, 170 miles northwest of **Berlin**. **Matilda** receives her father's letter postmarked Hamburg (*M* 155). The **Countess of Windsor** delays returning to England by staying there (*LM* 293). **Rupert Falkner** and **Elizabeth Falkner** lose an attendant there (*F* 38).

Hamilton, Sir Patrick: Scottish knight who supports **Richard of York** in *Perkin Warbeck*.

Hamlet: **Shakespearean** tragedy first performed 1602 and published 1603. Claudius assumes the throne by marrying his sister-in-law, Gertrude, widow of Denmark's recently dead king. When Hamlet (deceased king's son) returns from university, he learns the circumstances of the murder from his father's ghost. The ghost asks for revenge, but Hamlet delays action, and the play explores his doubt before its bloody conclusion. Shelley read *Hamlet* March 1819 (*Journals* 255). Shelley describes reading "History of the Inconstant Lover," from J. B. B. Eyriès's translation *Fantasmagoriana* (1812), finding a "gigantic, shadowy form" similar to *Hamlet*'s ghost (*Fr3* 21). Describing **Clorinda Saviani**'s vacillating emotions, Shelley quotes loosely from Hamlet's speech immediately after the players' dumb show: " '**Marry, this is** miching Mallecho; it means mischief' " (*BMI* 38; *Hamlet* 3.2.135). **Lionel Verney** worries about **Adrian**'s mental health, using Hamlet's instruction to Guildenstern about playing a pipe: "[d]oes that voice no longer '**discourse excellent** music?' " (*LM* 43; *Hamlet* 3.2.358). Verney records that Adrian and **Idris**'s visits to his cottage "beautify and enlighten this '**sterile promontory**,' " a phrase Hamlet speaks (*LM* 79; *Hamlet* 2.2.300). Verney feels powerless against the plague: "We had called ourselves the '**paragon of animals**,' and, lo! we were a '**quintessence of dust**' "; Hamlet speaks these lines (*LM* 398; *Hamlet* 2.2.308–310). Shelley quotes loosely lines that *Hamlet*'s ghost speaks in describing **Richard of York**'s struggle with remembering **Meiler Trangmar**'s death: he was "precipitated... '**unhouseled, unanointed, unannealed**,' into the life-quenching waters" (*PW* 1.273; *Hamlet* 1.5.78). After recounting how **Monina De Faro** was rescued from her father's sinking ship, Shelley declares, " '**There's a divinity that shapes our ends, / Rough-hew them how we will**,' " Hamlet's observation (*PW* 2.266; *Hamlet* 5.2.10). Shelley describes **Ethel Villiers** in **America**: "there was an affectionateness of disposition kneaded up in the very texture of her soul, which gave it its '**very form and pressure**,' " a loose quotation from Hamlet's speech directing the players (*L* 1.30; *Hamlet* 3.2.23–24). **Lady Lodore** "had begun to think all things '**stale and unprofitable**,' " before meeting **Horatio Saville**; Shelley quotes loosely from Hamlet's speech about the Danish court's trivialities (*L* 2.32–33; *Hamlet* 1.2.133). Shelley compares **Elizabeth Fitzhenry**'s custom of sleeping after dinner to that of "the father of Hamlet," referring to his murder during unsuspecting sleep (*L* 2.131). Young Ethel is like many youths who believe "our lives are a mere blank, not worth a '**pin**'**s fee**,' " the value Hamlet places upon his life after seeing his father's ghost (*L* 2.160; *Hamlet* 1.4.65). **Gerard Neville** compares his dilemma with Hamlet's and concedes his choice is easier; Shelley points out "his face, usually '**more in sorrow** than in anger,' now expressed the latter emotion" (*F* 92–93; *Hamlet* 1.2.234). **Elizabeth Falkner** defends Neville's passion for clearing his mother's name by referring to Neville's earlier discussion of Shakespeare's play: "there are secrets in the moral, sentient world, of which we know nothing: such as brought Hamlet's father before his eyes" (*F* 142). Neville seeks Elizabeth toward *Falkner*'s end, wanting to see her and thus "purify the world of the '**blasts from hell**' which the bad passions I have so long contemplated spread around me" (*F* 274; *Hamlet* 1.4.41). Considering **Raphael**'s paintings in *Rambles*, Shelley mentions "**Wordsworth**'s theory, that we enter this world bringing with us '**airs from heaven**,' " a reference to Wordsworth's "Ode: Intimations of Immortality" (1807); Hamlet speaks this phrase upon seeing his father's ghost (*R* 1.223; Wordsworth lines 63–64; *Hamlet* 1.4.41). Describing her 1842 visit to **Venice**, Shelley recalled her 1818 journey there during which her daughter died: "with my '**mind's eye**' I saw those before me long departed"; Hamlet speaks this phrase in imagining his dead father (*R* 2.77; *Hamlet* 1.2.185). Shelley describes **John of Bologna**'s "glorious statue... which **Shakspeare** we might think had seen when he spoke of the '**herald Mercury**,' " a phrase Hamlet uses (*R* 2.155; *Hamlet* 3.4.59). Shelley describes the discrepancy between the lives of Britain's rich and poor as revealing " '**That there is** something rotten in the state,' " a paraphrase of Marcellus's line (*R* 2.271; *Hamlet* 1.4.90).

Hammelburg: German town on the **Saale**, ten miles southwest of **Kissingen**. Shelley described Kissingen upon descending from Hammelburg June 1842 (*R* 1.179).

Hammersley's Bank: London bank that failed 1840 (Hardcastle 447). Shelley met a British traveler at **Simplon** October 1840 who related its failure (*R* 1.136, 1.140).

Hampden, John (1594–1643): English politician and defender of property and liberty who opposed **Charles I**, especially when the king attempted to impeach Hampden for treason 1642 (Bowle 147, 210, 244). Shelley visited Hampden's tomb with her father October 1817 (*Journals* 181). **Henry Clerval** and **Victor Frankenstein** visit this monument, which memorializes Hampden's 1643 mortal fall from his horse near **Oxford** (*Fr1* 187; *Fr3* 136; *Journals* 181).

Hampshire: County on England's southern coast. **Sir Richard Gray**'s family mansion is there (*ES* 246). **Miss Jervis** resides with the **Cecil** family "at the **Earl of G——**'s seat in Hampshire" (*F* 73).

Hampstead: Now a Greater **London** district, Hampstead was a separate village five miles northwest of the city's center in Shelley's day. Shelley stayed with the **Hunts** there immediately before her December 1816 marriage (Sunstein 129). **Lady Lodore** "drove out . . . along the new road to Hampstead" (*L* 3.125).

Hampton: British village on **London**'s outskirts, six miles west of **Wimbledon** and a mile from the palace of **Hampton Court**, which Cardinal Wolsey built in the 16th century. **Lionel Verney** passes through Hampton with **Idris** to **Windsor** (*LM* 353). Shelley stayed at **Richmond**, visited "Hampton Court, and saw [**Raphael**'s] *Cartoons*" June 1840 (*R* 1.3).

Hampton Court: See **Hampton**.

Handel, George Frideric (1685–1759): Naturalized British composer born in **Germany**. Shelley acknowledged **Leigh Hunt**'s fondness for Handel and asked him "what that piece of Handel is of which you only know a few bars" (*Letters* 1.359, 1.409). Shelley was "greatly pleased" to hear Handel at **Vincent Novello**'s October 1823 (*Letters* 1.392). She compared **Santa Maria della Salute**'s perfection to "the effect of one of Handel's airs" September 1842 (*R* 2.95).

Hannibal (247–183 B.C.E.): Carthaginian general renowned for crossing the **Alps** 218 B.C.E. to invade **Italy** in the Second Punic War (Kinder 1.81). **Castruccio** passes the spot where Hannibal's brother **Hasdrubal** "was defeated and slain" (*V* 1.40).

Hanover: Former northwestern **German** province and independent kingdom established 1814. When George I came to the throne 1714, the house of Hanover ascended the throne of England, ruling Scotland and England throughout Shelley's lifetime. Hanoverian rule ended with Queen Victoria's death 1901 (Morby 133–134, 71). **Dr. Hotham** informs **Roger Dodsworth** that the throne is " 'now worthily occupied by the house of Hanover,' " a reference to George IV, direct Hanoverian descendant and king when Shelley wrote her story (*RD* 46). Shelley finds it better "to learn German of the rough **Boeotian** (**Bavarian**) sort, than the effeminate softness of **Saxony** and Hanover" (*R* 1.187).

Hans: Thirteenth–17th-century trading alliance of two hundred **German** towns (Cannon 453). See **Easterlings**.

Hapsburgh: See **Habsburg**.

Harding, Charles: Jem and Jane Harding's fourteen-year-old son in "The Smuggler and His Family."

Harding, Jane: Jem Harding's wife and Charles, Tommy, and Jenny Harding's mother in "The Smuggler and His Family." In her overprotective love and concern for Charles while at sea, Jane is to some extent Shelley's autobiographical portrait.

Harding, Jem: Title figure of "The Smuggler and His Family," Jane Harding's husband and Charles, Tommy, and Jenny Harding's father.

Harding, Jenny: Jem and Jane Harding's youngest child in "The Smuggler and His Family."

Harding, Tommy: Jem and Jane Harding's youngest son in "The Smuggler and His Family."

Harley, Isabell: Scottish wife of older **Lord Harley**, with whom she has a son, in "**Valerius the Reanimated Roman**"; she befriends **Valerius**. At the close of Isabell's narrative, Shelley intimates that Valerius's relationship with Isabell transgresses friendship alone, and certainly the relationship of adoptive father and daughter, in a foreshadowing of *Matilda*'s theme of incest.

Harley, Lord: Englishman "a good deal older" than his Scottish wife **Isabell Harley**, with whom he has one son (*Val* 338).

Harry (1491–1547): Second son of **Henry VII** of England and **Elizabeth of York**; he became King Henry VIII 1509 and is mentioned in *Perkin Warbeck* (*DNB*).

Harwich: Port on England's west coast, sixty-eight miles northeast of **London**. **Admiral Fitzhenry** was briefly "placed with a clergyman near Harwich" (*L* 1.3). After their father's death, **Elizabeth Fitzhenry** accompanies **Lord Lodore** to Harwich on his departure for **Europe** (*L* 1.88).

Hasdrubal (d. 221 B.C.E.): **Hannibal**'s younger brother; he ruled **Spain** until his death (Kinder 1.81). Shelley spells his name **Asdrubal**. **Castruccio** traverses the **Apennines**, where Hasdrubal "was defeated and slain" (*V* 1.40–41).

Haspinger, Joseph (d. 1858): Capuchin friar who led **Tyrolese** into battle against the **Bavarians** and **French** carrying only a cross (Alison 3.224, 3.230; Moskal 255). Shelley mentions that Haspinger led Tyrol peasants when **Hofer** failed to appear; they successfully defended the **Brenner** pass 1809 (*R* 2.52–54).

Hastings: British seaside resort forty miles southwest of **Dover**. Shelley recovered from smallpox there in June–July 1828, describing it as "interspersed with hill & dale and beautiful woods" (*Journals* 508; *Letters* 2.53). **Horatio Saville** meets **Lady Lodore** nearby (*L* 2.26). **Lady Cecil** takes a house there and invites **Elizabeth Falkner** to be her guest (*F* 86). Shelley set many of *Falkner*'s important scenes in this location's happy familial atmosphere. Shelley

"Hate"

stayed overnight at Hastings June 1840 (*R* 1.4).

"Hate": Shelley's story that has been lost (Sunstein 87). **PBS** recorded that Shelley wrote "Hate" while in **Maassluis** 11 September 1814 (*Journals* 24).

Hatfield, Mr.: American in *Lodore* who kills **Lord Lodore** in a duel.

Havre: French port at the **Seine**'s mouth on the **English Channel**, better known as Le Havre. **Fanny Godwin** was born there 1794 (Poston x). The Shelleys crossed the English Channel from Havre to **Portsmouth** September 1816 (*Journals* 134). **Alphonse** and **Victor Frankenstein** travel there from **Ireland** (*Fr1* 210; *Fr3* 154). **Lord Lodore** sails from Havre to **America** (*L* 1.176, 1.179, 1.189, 1.199–200). Shelley planned to stay in Havre following her **European** travels 1843 (*Letters* 3.79).

Haydn, Franz Joseph (1732–1809): **Austrian** composer whose oratorios and masses were instrumental in forming the Classical style (*NGD*). After experiencing **Handel**'s music in **London** 1797, Haydn was inspired to write the oratorio *Die Schopfung* [*The Creation*] (1797–98), based on the first two chapters of **Genesis** (*NGD*). The work was an instant and unprecedented success, first performed in Britain 1800. December 1823, Shelley wrote that **Vincent Novello** "has made me a convert to Haydn—Do you know the piece, 'A new healed world'—in his *Creation*; what a wonderful stream of sound it is" (*Letters* 1.408). **Lionel Verney** sees a young girl playing the organ in **Ferney**: "The air was Haydn's '**New-Created** World,'" taken from *The Creation* (*LM* 420; Haydn I).

Hayward, Abraham (1801–1884): **Caroline Norton**'s legal aide. He became friends with Shelley around 1838; she invited him to an 1840 dinner that **Alexander Mavrocordato** also attended (Sunstein 337, 347). Shelley corresponded with Hayward during her 1840 **European** tour and invited him to visit upon her return (Sunstein 352). He assisted Shelley in researching **German** history for *Rambles*; in a footnote, she includes his crossing of the **Splügen** 1834 (Sunstein 363; *Letters* 3.112, 3.115; *R* 1.58). Shelley calls him **English traveller**.

Head, Sir Francis Bond (1793–1875): English author of *Bubbles from the Brunnens of Nassau, by an Old Man* (1834), which interested English readers in **Brunnen**; Shelley calls it *The Bubbles of the Brunnens* (*R* 1.184; Moskal 170; *DNB*).

Heart of Midlothian, The: See **Scott**.

Heathenesse: Muslim lands (*OED*). **Richard of York** insults **Robert Clifford** by referring to Heathenesse (*PW* 3.144).

Heaven and Earth: A Mystery: Drama that **Byron** wrote 1821–22 and published 1823; the Shelleys read it December 1821 (Marchand 3.965–966, 3.1048; *Journals* 387). Shelley asks whether the **Villiers**es "love the less for not loving '**in sin and fear**?'" a line that mortal Anah speaks in contemplating the immorality of loving immortal Azaziel, who supplants God (*L* 2.272; Byron 1.1.67).

Hebe: In **Greek** mythology, **Zeus** and **Hera**'s daughter and the gods' cupbearer. **Henry Vernon** calls **Rosina** a "Hebe beauty" (*IG* 200). Shelley viewed **Canova**'s *Hebe* 1842 (*R* 2.91).

Hebe: See **Canova**.

Hebrew: Semitic language that Canaanites and Israelites spoke during **biblical** times; most of the Old Testament was written in Hebrew. **Henry Clerval** studies Hebrew (*Fr1* 97). Shelley mentions Hebrew tombstones near **Lido** and believes that *David* by **Donatello** is a Hebrew shepherd boy (*R* 2.98, 2.155).

Hebrew poet: See **Ecclesiastes**.

Hebrus: River west of **Thrace** forming **Greece**'s border with **Turkey**. Mythically, it is associated with a poet's death, since Orpheus's head and lyre floated down it after he was killed and dismembered (Tripp 261). **Raymond** vanishes from a battlefield; "his favorite horse was found grazing" by Hebrus (*LM* 164). [*LM* 175].

Hecate: In **Greek** mythology, Underworld goddess associated with the dead and sorcery; she rules spirits in **Shakespeare**'s *Macbeth*. When **Lionel Verney** watches part of this drama, he feels Hecate's entrance "and the wild music that followed . . . took us out of this world" (*LM* 282).

Heidelberg: **German** city ten miles southeast of **Mannheim**, famous for its castle, built during the reigns of Otto Heinrich (1556–59), Friedrich IV (1583–1610), and Friedrich V (1610–20). The **French** destroyed the castle 1689 and 1693, and it remains a ruin (*BGER* 148). Shelley visited it July 1840 (*R* 1.33–36).

"Heir of Lynne, The": See *Reliques*.

"Heir of Mondolfo, The": According to Robinson, Shelley composed this story prior to the mid-1820s, and Sunstein believes Shelley sent the manuscript to **Leigh Hunt** 1833 (Robinson 395; Sunstein 450). It was published 1877 in the January *Appletons' Journal* as "by Mary Wollstonecraft Shelley, Author of '**Frankenstein**,' etc." (Robinson 395). Set in southern **Italy** near **Sorrento**, the story begins by contrasting the beautiful, peaceful scene with antagonist **Prince Fernando Mondolfo**'s passionate, evil character. He has two sons: favored elder son **Olimpio Mondolfo**, with his first wife, a **Sicilian** princess, and detested younger son **Ludovico Mondolfo**, with his second wife, **Florentine Isabel** (*HM* 308). Ludovico's generous nature and his efforts to shield Isabel from his father's anger draw Fernando's hatred. Upon Isabel's death, Fernando treats Ludovico terribly, attempting to force his removal from **Mondolfo**. At age eighteen, Ludovico encounters an angelic peasant, **Viola Arnaldi**, living in a cabin in woods below Mondolfo; he pursues a friendly relationship with her (*HM* 312–314). Fernando knows about these visits, assumes the relationship is sexual, and alludes to it as he toasts the couple (*HM* 316). Angered by his father's suggestion, Ludovico leaves Mondolfo and confesses amorous feelings to Viola; the two wed secretly. Two years later, they have a son;

Olimpio dies at about the same time. When Fernando relates this death to Ludovico, his new heir, Ludovico corrects his father by revealing his legitimate son's existence—the actual new "Heir of Mondolfo" (*HM* 319–20). Fernando tricks Ludovico into keeping the marriage a secret for six months and going alone to **Naples**. During his son's absence, Fernando visits Viola, demanding that she renounce the marriage and remove to **Spain**, where she would receive a yearly stipend (*HM* 323). Upon Viola's refusal, Fernando's men kidnap her and her son, transport them to **Salerno**, and imprison them in a tower. Viola escapes and travels toward her husband in Naples. When Ludovico returns to Mondolfo two days later, he is alarmed by his wife's disappearance and accuses Fernando of murder. Disbelieving Fernando's story of kidnap and escape, Ludovico investigates the Salerno tower, becomes disheartened, and resolves to fight in the Crusades and die at **Jerusalem**. He travels toward **Brundusium** and finds Viola and their son asleep in a forest. The family returns to their cabin until penitent Fernando apologizes and persuades them to join him at Mondolfo (*HM* 330).

Helena: Dmitri's wife, born on **Scio** in "**The Evil Eye**."

Heliodorus: Biblical king **Seleucus**'s secretary of state, sent to **Jerusalem** to confiscate funds secured in the temple; God flogged but subsequently saved Heliodorus (2 Maccabees 3.7–40). Shelley praises **Raphael**'s painting of Heliodorus and relates his story from **Maccabees** (*R* 2.220–221).

Hellas: See **Greece**.

Hellas: A Lyrical Drama: PBS's drama (written 1821) based on Aeschylus's *The Persians* (produced 472 B.C.E.) (White 2.328–332). Dedicated to **Mavrocordato**, **Ollier** published it 1822 (Holmes 677–681). **Lionel Verney** records the tale of a mechanic who has lost his family to plague, leaving them in his house as " '**dead earth upon dead earth**,' " a line Hassan speaks (*LM* 263; PBS line 398). **Skelton** talks "incessantly, apparently to deafen himself to '**the small still voice**' " of fear, a phrase from *Hellas* and 1 Kings (*PW* 3.123; PBS line 728; 1 Kings 19.12).

Hellespont: Now known as Dardanelles, forty-mile-long straits connecting **Marmora** with the **Aegean** in western **Turkey**. Panic caused by the solar eclipse spreads all over the world, "from the Hellespont even to the sea of **Omar**" (*LM* 224).

Helvetia: See **Switzerland**.

Henley-on-Thames: Frequently called Henley, English town ten miles northwest of **Eton**. Shelley set "**An Eighteenth-Century Tale**" at a house "half way between **Marlow** and Henley" (*EC* 345). "**Recollections of Italy**'s" conversation takes place in countryside around Henley (*RI* 24).

Henry: Real name of "**Maurice**'s" protagonist; see **Maurice** (*Maurice* 83–84).

1 Henry IV: Shakespeare's historical drama first staged 1597 and published 1598; **PBS** read it aloud 1820 (*Journals*

306, 309–310). As an epigraph to the *Perkin Warbeck* chapter in which **Richard of York** travels from **Ireland** to Scotland, Shelley quotes from Hotspur's speech: " '**Why, it cannot** choose but be a noble plot: / And then the power of Scotland and of York / To join—/ In faith it is exceedingly well aimed!' " (*PW* 2.173; Shakespeare 1.3.277–280). Shelley draws lines from **Falstaff**'s speech in her second epigraph to the chapter in which **Edmund Plantagenet** meets **Monina De Faro** in **Cornwall**: " '**If I am** not ashamed of my soldiers, I am a soused gurnet' " (*PW* 3.62; Shakespeare 4.2.11–12).

*2 Henry IV***:** **Shakespeare**'s historical drama first acted 1598 and published 1600; **PBS** read it aloud 1820 (*Journals* 309–310). Shelley notes that **Jane Shore** finds the shame attached to love hard to bear, because her "heart was '**open as day** to melting charity,' " a line Shakespeare's Henry IV speaks about his son (*PW* 2.135; Shakespeare 4.4.32).

*2 Henry VI***:** **Shakespeare**'s historical drama first performed 1592 and published 1594; **PBS** read it aloud 1820, and Shelley probably drew on its historical figures for *Perkin Warbeck* (*Journals* 311). As an epigraph to the chapter in which **Edmund Plantagenet** finds **Richard of York** at the **De Faro**'s **Spanish** house, Shelley quotes from Shakespeare's Richard of York's soliloquy: "**A day will come** when York shall claim his own; / Then York be still awhile, till time do serve" (*PW* 1.202; Shakespeare 1.1.237, 246). As a second epigraph to the chapter in which Shelley outlines the downfall of many of Richard's followers due to **Robert Clifford**'s maneuverings, she quotes the speech Shakespeare's Duke of Suffolk makes to the Duke of Gloucester: " '**I do arrest ye** of high treason here!' " (*PW* 2.38; Shakespeare 3.1.97). Shelley draws the first epigraph to the chapter in which Plantagenet meets **Monina De Faro** in **Cornwall** from Shakespeare's Duke of York's speech: " '**From Ireland thus** comes York to claim his right' " (*PW* 3.62; Shakespeare 5.1.1).

*3 Henry VI***:** **Shakespeare**'s historical drama first performed 1592 and published 1595; **PBS** read it aloud 1820, and Shelley probably drew on its historical figures for *Perkin Warbeck* (*Journals* 311). **Lionel Verney** arrives at **Lucy Martin**'s inn to find "the snow lay high about the door. . . . '**What scene** of death has Roscius now to act?' "—Shakespeare's protagonist speaks this line in predicting his approaching death (*LM* 363; Shakespeare 5.6.8–10). Quintus Roscius Gallus was the 1st century B.C.E.'s "most famous comic actor" (Howatson 502). As an epigraph to the *Perkin Warbeck* chapter in which **Lady Brampton** and **Elizabeth Woodville** become friends, Shelley quotes the Earl of Warwick's speech in the play to Queen Margaret: "**My noble Queen**, let former grudges pass, / And henceforth I am thy true servitor" (*PW* 1.66; Shakespeare 3.3.195–196). For the chapter in which **Richard of York**'s supporters gather in **Brussels**, Shelley's epigraph is from the Duke of Gloucester's soliloquy, lines beginning " '**Like one lost** in a thorny wood' " (*PW* 2.16; Shakespeare 3.2.174–178). As an epigraph to the chapter in which Richard discovers **Robert Clifford**'s treachery, Shelley

Henry III

quotes from Shakespeare's Richard of York's appeal to Lord Clifford: " '**Oh, Clifford**, but bethink thee once again, / And in thy thought oerrun my former time, / And if thou can'st for blushing, view this face!' " (*PW* 2.52; Shakespeare 1.4.44–46).

Henry III: Shelley's mistaken reference for **Henry IV** (1050–1106) (*R* 2.228).

Henry IV [French] (1553–1610): **Bourbon** King of **Navarre** who became **France**'s king 1589. To overcome Catholic opposition, he converted to Catholicism 1593 and was crowned 1594 (Seward 16–17). Shelley situates "**The Dream**" at "the commencement of the reign of Henry IV. [*sic*] of France" (a character in the story), noting that tensions between Catholics and Protestants are only apparently settled (*D* 153).

Henry IV [German] (1050–1106): Emperor of Germany 1056–1106. **Pope Gregory VII** deposed and excommunicated Henry 1076, and again briefly 1080, but Henry became Holy Roman Emperor 1084 and established the pope's rule as beyond the monarchy's power; Henry was later forced to abdicate (Kinder 1.147–148; Kelly 154–155). **Lionel Verney** notes: "As Henry, Emperor of Germany, lay in the snow before **Pope Leo**'s gate for three winter days and nights, so did [the **Countess of Windsor**] in humility wait before the icy barriers of [**Adrian's**] closed heart"—Shelley mistakenly wrote Leo for Gregory (*LM* 385). Shelley states that the mile between Rome's **Lateran** and the **Coliseum** "was the most mag-nificent quarter of the old city," but it was burned and leveled when Henry sacked Rome 1084 (*R* 2.228).

Henry V (1387–1422): England's king 1413–22. The **Clifford**s' house was built "in **Henry the Fifth**'s time" (*PW* 2.18).

Henry V: **Shakespeare**'s historical drama acted before 1600, when it was first published; **PBS** read it aloud 1820 (*Journals* 310). As an epigraph to the *Perkin Warbeck* chapter in which **Richard of York** escapes battle in **Kent** and sails to **Ireland**, Shelley quotes Shakespeare's Duke of Exeter's address to the Earl of Salisbury: " '**Farewell, kind lord**, fight valiantly to-day. / And yet I do thee wrong to mind thee of it, / For thou art framed of the firm truth of valour' " (*PW* 2.148; Shakespeare 4.3.12–14). As an epigraph to the chapter in which Richard fights in **Devon**, Shelley uses Henry's speech to troops in **France**: " '**Once more unto** the breach, dear friends, once more, / Or close up the wall with our English dead!' " (*PW* 3.98; Shakespeare 3.1.1–2).

Henry VI (1421–1471): England's king 1422–61 and 1470–71. **Lord Lovel** fought in Henry VI's battles with **Edward IV** (*PW* 1.20).

Henry VII [English] (1457–1509): Also **Henry Tudor**, Earl of **Richmond**, and nicknamed **Hal**, England's king 1485–1509; the **Wars of the Roses** ended during his reign (*PW* 3.76). He defeated **Richard III** at **Bosworth Field** and married **Elizabeth of York** 1486 to secure his claim to the throne. Numerous **Yorkist** plots against him, such as those involving **Lambert Simnel** and **Perkin Warbeck**, failed. Henry is **Richard of York**'s antagonist in *Perkin Warbeck*.

Henry VII [German] (c. 1269–1313): **Germany**'s king from 1308 and Holy Roman Emperor from 1312. Planning to add **Italy** to his empire, he entered northern Italy 1310 and became King of **Lombardy** 1311, when **Piedmont** and Lombardy submitted to him. The **Guelphs** revolted, and Henry VII subdued many **Tuscan** towns, but not **Florence**. After attempting to seize **Siena** 1313, he died from illness and was buried at **Pisa**. *Valperga* (calling him **Henry of Luxemburgh** and **Emperor of Germany**) refers to Henry VII's advance into Italy, coronation at **Rome**, 1311 siege of **Brescia**, and death (*V* 1.101, 1.127–128, 1.144, 1.157–158). **Castruccio** fights in his army (*V* 1.157).

Henry, Emperor of Germany: See Henry IV (1050–1106).

Henry, Mary Ann: Maid who traveled with Shelley on her 1840 and 1842–43 **European** tours and to **France** 1849 (Sunstein 349, 357, 382). She was Shelley's maid until Shelley's death (Sunstein 383). Shelley and Henry traveled from **Italy** to **Switzerland** 1840 with three Scottish women; Shelley mentions sending **M——** to see if the women would be reputable companions before beginning the journey (Sunstein 350; *R* 1.125).

Henry of Luxemburgh: See **Henry VII** (c. 1269–1313).

Henry the Fifth: See **Henry V**.

Hercules: In **Greek** mythology, man legendary for strength, courage, battle skills, and virtue; he became a god after his heroic life and death. Shelley wrote about slow snow removal in **Brighton** January 1837: "Nature is more of a Hercules—she puts out a little finger in the shape of gentle thaw—& it recedes and disappears" (*Letters* 2.278). As penance for killing his wife and children in a fit of madness, Hercules exiled himself and performed twelve tasks King Eurystheus set for him (Tripp 275–295). As part of his penance, Hercules wore women's clothing and did women's work for a time. Shelley describes **Beatrice**'s love for **Castruccio** as "distaff of the spinning Hercules" (*V* 2.94). The tenth task required Hercules to travel through the Strait of Gibraltar, where "he set up pillars on both the **African** and **European** sides to show future travellers how far he had come" or "to bar sea-monsters from the **Mediterranean**" (Tripp 285). **Lionel Verney** proposes travel to "the pillars of Hercules" (*LM* 469). On his journey to perform his eleventh task, Hercules wrestled several times with mythological giant **Antaeus**—who regained strength from touching earth—finally defeating him by lifting him into the air and crushing him (Tripp 52–53, 287). Shelley alludes to Antaeus to describe **Richard of York**'s optimism at overcoming obstacles (*PW* 2.261). **Horatio Saville** notes "with what Herculean labour I have concealed [**Clorinda Saville**'s madness] so long" (*L* 2.194). Shelley describes **Donatello**'s *David*: "the youthful hero is neither **Mars** nor Hercules" (*R* 2.155).

"Hermit's Cell": **Wordsworth**'s poem published 1820, "Inscriptions Supposed to be Found In and Near a Hermit's Cell." Shelley uses lines as an epigraph to the *Lodore* chapter detailing **Admiral Fitzhenry**'s death and **Lord Lodore**'s subsequent **European** travels: "**What is youth?** a dancing billow, / Winds behind, and rocks before!" (*L* 1.82; Wordsworth lines 29–30). Shelley uses as an epigraph to the chapter outlining difficulties evident in Lord Lodore's marriage with the lines: "**Hopes, what are they?** beads of morning / Strung on slender blades of grass, / Or a spider's web adorning, / In a strait and treacherous pass" (*L* 1.111; Wordsworth lines 1–4). As an epigraph for the chapter in which Lord Lodore quarrels with **Casimir Lyzinski** and is forced to leave England, Shelley uses "**What are fears,** but voices airy / Whisp'ring harm, where harm is not? / And deluding the unwary, / Till the fatal bolt is shot?" (*L* 1.126; Wordsworth lines 5–8). Shelley adapts as an epigraph to the chapter in which **Mr. Hatfield** shoots Lord Lodore the lines: "**What is peace?** When life is over, / And love ceases to rebel, / Let the last faint sigh discover, / Which precedes the passing knell" (*L* 1.247; Wordsworth lines 33–36). Shelley alludes to Wordsworth's poem, using "**Fears! what are they?**" to describe frustration while waiting for letters (*R* 1.115; Wordsworth lines 5–8).

Hernitskretschen: See **Herrnskretshen**.

Heron: In *Perkin Warbeck*, **Exeter** mercer who supports **Richard of York**; **Holinshed** mentions him (3.518).

Herrera, Fernando de (1534–1597): **Spanish** ecclesiastic who devoted himself to literature. Shelley wrote Herrera's biography for *Italian and Spanish Lives*. She had difficulty obtaining necessary materials, writing to John Bowring July 1837 for translations (*Letters* 2.289). Herrera's reputation rests principally upon prose works, including *Anotaciones* [*Annotations*] (1580), *Tomás Moro* [*The Life and Martyrdom of Thomas More*] (1592), and commentaries upon **Garcilaso**. **Cervantes** admired Herrera's work, and Shelley feels that he "delighted in the grandiose and sonorous" and "endeavoured to make harmony between the thought and its oral expression" (*ISPL* 3.86). Shelley admires Herrera's odes, especially "the fervour of expression, the grandeur of the ideas, and the harmony of the versification," but notes, "it is the poetry of the head rather than the heart" (*ISPL* 3.86). She gives the Spanish version of Herrera's "Ode to Sleep" as example (*ISPL* 3.86).

Herrnskretschen: **German** for Czech town Hrensko, on the **Elbe** five miles southeast of Bad **Schandau**; Shelley spells it **Hirnisdretschen** and **Hernitskretschen**. Shelley reached it August 1842 (*R* 1.274).

Herz, Henri (1803–1888): **Austrian** composer whose piano pieces were popular prior to 1850 (*NGD*; Loesser 350). **Lady Cecil** asks **Elizabeth Falkner** to play Herz for **Sir Boyvill Neville**'s entertainment (*F* 98).

Hesiod (c. 700 B.C.E.): Poet and teacher renowned among **Greeks** for *The Theogony*, about the world's creation and gods, and *Works and Days*, which Hesiod wrote as advice to his miscreant brother. It attributes humankind's deterioration to declining morals, drawing upon **Zeus**'s punishment exacted upon humankind for **Prometheus**'s theft of fire from the gods, and suggests that humankind can improve its situation by learning the virtues of justice and work (Howatson 277). **PBS** read Hesiod's *Works* 1815 (*Journals* 651; White 2.541). Shelley refers to **Elton**'s translation of Hesiod's narrative poem *Shield of Hercules* and draws from Elton's translation of *Works and Days* (*LM* 229, 315, 400). **Adrian**'s frustrations shows when he asks, "how could I— '**Turn back** the tide of ills, relieving wrong / With mild accost of soothing eloquence?,'" lines adapted from *Theogony* (*LM* 162; Hesiod lines 131–132; Crook 2).

Hesperus: **Latin** name for the evening star, associated with **Aphrodite**. **Edmund Malville** fondly recalls "'Hesperus in his glowing palace of sunlight'" over **Tuscany**, and **Ludovico Mondolfo** rushes to declare his love for **Viola Arnaldi** as "Hesperus glowed in the west" (*RI* 29; *HM* 317). **Lionel Verney** suggests that rumors of **Irish** invasion of England are so exaggerated that **Virgil**'s Rumour could reach up and take Hesperus from the sky (*LM* 298). "**Stanzas: How like a star's**" speaker mourns losing her Hesperus (*Stanzas: How like* 9, 10).

Hesse Cassel, Duke of: William I, who ruled **German** electorate of Hesse-Cassel 1785–1821. After the post-Napoleonic settlement, Shelley notes, he succeeded the **Prince-Bishops of Fulda** to rule **Fulda**; she remarks that **Schiller**'s reference to "a petty German prince" in *Cabal and Love* (1784) could be to this duke's predecessor (*R* 1.200, 1.204; Crook 2).

Hesse Cassel, Prince of: William II, elector of Hesse Cassel (central western **German** territory 1567–1945) 1821–47. Shelley entered his "domains" July 1830 (*R* 1.202). See **Hessians**.

Hessians: **Germans** from Hesse Cassel. About seventeen thousand Hessian mercenaries fought for Britain in the **Revolutionary War**; Shelley quotes **Lord Chatham**'s criticism of their having done so (*R* 1.203). See **Prince of Hesse Cassel**.

Heywood, Thomas (c. 1574–1641): Prolific English playwright best known for domestic dramas, including *A Woman Killed With Kindness* (1607). Shelley misattributes to **Shakespeare** lines **Lionel Verney** recites from Heywood's "The Tale of Daedalus": "'**Oh! human wit**, thou can'st invent much ill, / Thou searchest strange arts: who would think by skill, / An heavy man like a light bird should stray, / And through the empty heavens find a way?'" (*LM* 71; Blumberg 59; "The Tale of Daedalus" lines 25–28). As an epigraph for *Lodore*'s chapter in which **Lord** and **Lady Lodore** part forever, Shelley quotes John Frankford's speech banishing his wife to the country as punishment for infidelity: "**And so farewell**; for we will henceforth be / As we had never seen, ne'er more shall see" (*L* 1.194; *A Woman Killed With Kindness* 13.179–180).

Highland: Scotland's mountainous northwestern district. Shelley compares **Bavarian** dancing to a Highland fling (*R* 2.39).

Hillary: *Falkner* agent whom **Rupert Falkner**'s solicitor dispatches to **America**.

Hinckley: English town twelve miles southwest of **Leicester**. Knights defeated at **Bosworth Field** travel near Hinckley (*PW* 1.2).

Hindostan: North **Indian** region. Plague destroys Hindostan's "fertile plains" (*LM* 233). **Rupert Falkner** thought about driving "merchant sovereigns from Hindostan" to gain advancement in the **East India Company** (*F* 184).

Hirnisdretschen: See **Herrnskretschen**.

Histoire des républiques italiennes du moyen âge: See **Sismondi**.

History: See *History of a Six Weeks' Tour*.

History of the House of Swabia: See **Niccolini**.

History of a Six Weeks' Tour: Lead item Shelley wrote, describing her 1814 elopement with **PBS** and **Claire Clairmont**, in the travel book Shelley produced with PBS, *History of a Six Weeks' Tour through a part of France, Switzerland, Germany, and Holland: With Letters descriptive of a sail round the Lake of Geneva, and of the Glaciers of Chamouni*. **Hookham** and **Ollier** published it anonymously in 1817 (Crook 2). Shelley reworked the couple's journal entries 28 July–13 September 1814, revising them August 1817 into "History of a Six Weeks' Tour" and also contributed two 1816 letters apparently written from the environs of **Geneva** (revised October 1817) (*Journals* 181; Crook 2). PBS contributed the book's preface, two letters to **Peacock**, and "**Mont Blanc**" (Sunstein 85; *Journals* 6, 178). In the book's first part, Shelley relates the 1814 tour's route and sites; the letters forming the second part briefly describe the same route, traveled 1816. These are interspersed with criticism of lodgings, people, and transportation; praise for landscapes; and interesting historical and cultural facts.

History of Europe: See **Alison**.

History of Scotland: See **Pinkerton**.

History of the Death of Murat: See **Colletta**.

History of the Kingdom of Naples 1734–1825: See **Colletta**.

Hobhouse, John Cam (1786–1869): Having met at **Cambridge**, Hobhouse became one of **Byron**'s closest friends (Marchand 1.131). Hobhouse published an account of their **European** travels, *A Journey through Albania and other provinces of Turkey in Europe and Asia, to Constantinople, during the years 1809–10* (1813), and he was Byron's best man at his wedding (Marchand 1.389, 2.505–506). The two were close friends throughout Byron's life; Hobhouse served as Byron's executor and destroyed his memoirs (Marchand

3.1245–1254). **PBS** first met Hobhouse August 1816, when Hobhouse was staying at **Villa Diodati** with Byron (Sunstein 125; *Journals* 131; White 1.461). Hobhouse anonymously published an article in the January 1824 *Westminster Review* against **Medwin**'s *Conversations,* after Shelley had confirmed Hobhouse's factual corrections, and Hobhouse assisted **Moore** when the latter wrote his Byron biography (*Letters* 1.454–456). In February 1825, Shelley asked Hobhouse, then a "radical" Member of **Parliament**, to arrange for her to visit Parliament to research scenes for *The Last Man* (Sunstein 263; *Letters* 1.466). See Leslie A. Marchand's *Byron: A Portrait* (1957).

Hobler: **Long Roger** claims Hobler (not further identified) helped murder the princes in the **Tower** (*PW* 3.301).

Hockstein: See **Hohnstein**.

Hofer, Andreas (1767–1810): Tyrolese military leader who fought against **Bavaria** and **France** in defense of Tyrolese liberties; Shelley spells his name **Hoffer**. He defeated the Bavarians at **Berg Isel** August 1809, but was captured and executed in **Mantua**. Shelley pronounces Hofer's death a crime "which cast a dark stain on **Napoleon**'s name" (*R* 1.44). She provides a detailed account of Hofer's accomplishments, heroism, and death (*R* 2.50–62).

Hoff: **Strasburgh** university student who shared the Shelleys' boat to **Mannheim** September 1814 (*Journals* 22; *H* 64).

Hoffer, Albert: Character who rivals **Winzy** for **Bertha** in "**The Mortal Immortal**."

Hoffer, Andreas: See **Hofer**.

Hogg, Jane: See **Williams, Jane**.

Hogg, Thomas Jefferson (1792–1862): British writer and **PBS**'s friend; they collaborated on a collection of burlesque poems, *Posthumous Fragments of Margaret Nicholson* (1810) (*Journals* 31; White 1.92–94). Hogg and PBS were both expelled from **Oxford** 1811 after PBS published a pamphlet on "The Necessity of Atheism," about which Hogg would not answer questions (White 1.114–115). Hogg's October 1811 attempt to seduce **Harriet Shelley** resulted in a temporary estrangement, but they became close again 1812. PBS recorded Hogg "was pleased with" Shelley after their first meeting November 1814, and Hogg was frequently in their company thereafter; Hogg declared love for Shelley January 1815 (*Journals* 45). They do not seem to have consummated their relationship; she found Hogg "so good & disinterested a creature," but did not care for him as she did for PBS (*Letters* 1.7). In October 1814, Shelley read Hogg's pseudonymous novel *Memoirs of Prince Alexy Haimatoff* (1813), from which his nickname "Alexy" came (*Journals* 31). Hogg comforted Shelley over her lost child March 1815, but by 1817 Shelley's affection for Hogg had declined; she wrote March 1817 "I do not like [Hogg] and I think he is more disagreeable than ever" (*Letters* 1.10–11, 1.35). Hogg became a lawyer 1817 and traveled to **Italy** 1825 and **Paris** 1826, living on a private fortune; in 1827, Shelley described him as "a man of talent—of wit—he has sensibility, and even romance in his disposition, but his exterior is composed, and, at a superficial glance, cold," although she considered him a "man of honour" (*Journals* 496, *Letters* 1.448, 1.544–545, 3.165). At his death, PBS left Hogg two thousand pounds, and Shelley asked Hogg for a loan 1827; that same year, Hogg's family disowned him after he began living with **Jane Williams**—they had two daughters (*Letters* 3.165, 1.570, 1.556–557). Hogg and Shelley remained in contact, and she asked his advice on several matters, including the publication of PBS's work (*Letters* 3.301). Hogg drew on his 1832–33 series of articles on PBS in the *New Monthly Magazine* for his *Life of Percy Bysshe Shelley* (1858); **Jane Shelley** and **PFS** had asked Hogg to write this biography, but these first two volumes, "ending before [PB]S's separation from Harriet," were "a vivid but facetious, self-servingly manipulated work," and Hogg never completed it (Sunstein 389; White 2.388). See Winifred Scott's *Jefferson Hogg* (1951).

Hohnstein: Town nineteen miles southeast of **Dresden**; Shelley spells it **Hockstein**. Shelley planned to pass through it en route from Dresden to **Arbesau** August 1842 (*R* 1.260).

Holborn: London district north of the **Thames** that now contains the British Museum and Oxford Street. Shelley grew up "in the commercial district of Holborn, surrounded by warehouses, tanners, cheese wholesalers, and second-rate shops," close to Newgate Prison and the Old Bailey (Sunstein 47). The Shelleys lived in Holborn January–March 1818, and Shelley was very familiar with it (*Journals* 192). **Lionel Verney** wanders through Holborn (*LM* 279). **Richard of York** escapes from the **Tower** to Holborn (*PW* 2.119).

Holcroft, Thomas (1745–1809): British novelist and playwright; English **Jacobinism** caused his 1794 arrest, after which his friend, **William Godwin**, published *Cursory Strictures* (1794) to help gain his release (*Journals* 173; Sunstein 18). Shelley read several Holcroft works: in 1815, *The Adventures of Hugh Trevor* (1794–97); in 1816, *Memoirs of Bryan Perdue: a novel* (1805), *Travels from Hamburg through Westphalia, Holland and the Netherlands, to Paris* (1804), and *Memoirs of the late Thomas Holcroft* (1816); and in 1817, *Anna St. Ives: a novel* (1792) (*Journals* 138, 141, 145, 170, 652). Shelley calls Holcroft "martyr to intense physical suffering" and recalls his ideas about emotional pain in returning to **Venice** September 1842 (*R* 2.78).

Holinshed, Raphael (d. c. 1580): Historian whose *Chronicles of England, Scotlande and Irelande* (1577) were the source for many of **Shakespeare**'s plays. Shelley directs readers to Holinshed for a version of **Perkin Warbeck**'s tale (*PW* 1.iv).

Holland: Northwest **European** country, also called the Netherlands, bounded by the **North Sea**, **Germany**, and **Belgium**. The Shelleys visited Holland September 1814 (*Journals* 24; *H* 74). **Henry Clerval** and **Victor Frankenstein** notice that the **Rhine** scenery loses its beauty upon entering Holland (*Fr1* 184; *Fr3* 134). **Castruccio** flees England on a ship sailing to Holland (*V*

1.83). **Hernan De Faro** meets his future wife **Madeline** on a voyage there, and **Trereife** remembers winning battles there (*PW* 1.146, 1.206, 3.80). Shelley mentions plans to make a comprehensive tour of Holland (*R* 1.159).

Hollenthal: German for "**Valley of Hell**," on the **Treisam** River, thirteen miles southeast of **Freyburg**. Shelley passed through it July 1840 (*R* 1.44–46).

Holy Land: Biblical **Canaan** or **Palestine**. **Ludovico Mondolfo** resolves to fight and die there (*HM* 330). **Flora Mancini** suspects that her exiled brother may have traveled there (*Brother* 179).

Holyhead: Port on the Isle of Anglesey off northwest Wales. **Victor** and **Alphonse Frankenstein** land there before proceeding to **Portsmouth** in the 1818 *Frankenstein* (*Fr1* 210).

Holyrood: Tower that **James IV** built adjoining **Edinburgh** Abbey and British monarchy's official Scottish residence, now a large castle (Donaldson 99). James's Holyrood court "vied with those of **Paris**, **London** and **Brussels**" (*PW* 2.186). [*PW* 2.188, 2.268].

Homer: Greek poet; both the *Iliad* and the *Odyssey* are attributed to him. These two epic poems are the oldest sources of Greek mythology, and Homer is variously dated from the 12th to the 8th centuries B.C.E. (Howatson 283–284). Shelley read Homer 1820 and 1821 (*Journals* 339, 377). **Robert Walton** aspires to be as great a poet as Homer (*Fr1* 51; *Fr3* 27). **Lionel Verney** remarks that the plague, "like the Calamity of Homer, trod our hearts," referring to PBS's translation of **Plato**'s *Symposium*, which quotes Homer's *Iliad* (*LM* 315; *Iliad* 19.92–93; Crook 2). Verney plans to take Homer's books when traveling the world (*LM* 469). **Lord Lodore** assuages loneliness on **America**'s frontier by reading Homer, whom he views as "a dear and revered friend" (*L* 1.25). [*PW* 1.179]. See **Charybdis**, **Polyphemus**, **Scylla**, **Syrens**, and **Ulysses**.

Homes: Irish family at peace with other families (*PW* 2.228).

Honeymoon, The: See **Tobin**.

Hookham, Thomas (1787–1867): PBS's first publisher, issuing *Queen Mab* (1813). Hookham was friends with both PBS and **Peacock**, but when PBS deserted **Harriet Shelley**, their relationship was strained, as Hookham took Harriet's side (*Journals* 38; White 1.352). Hookham reportedly told bailiffs where to find PBS in 1814, but subsequently provided funds to the Shelleys and continued the relationship (*Journals* 38, 40). Shelley first met Hookham upon returning from **Europe** 1814 but never really liked him; she noted October 1814: "that man comes strictly under the appelation of a *prig*" and called him a "nasty little man" December 1814 (*Journals* 37, 53). He published the Shelleys' *History* jointly with **Ollier** in December 1817 (Sunstein 145; *Journals* 178).

Hoppner, Isabella: Swiss Isabella May married **Richard Hoppner**. Shelley met Isabella in **Venice** October 1818, and the two women went shopping and visited the library as Shelley grieved **Clara Shelley**'s death (*Journals* 228; White 2.39). The Shelleys fre-

Hoppner, Richard Belgrave (1786–1872)

quently dined with the Hoppners, and the two women corresponded intermittently until **Elise Foggi** falsely informed Isabella 1819 that **Claire Clairmont** had had a child by **PBS** December 1818 (*Journals* 233–234, 240, 250). The Hoppners, with their "penchant for gossip," eagerly told **Byron** of these rumors, and in August 1820 he informed PBS of what the Hoppners had heard (Marchand 2.875–877, 2.921). Shelley received a letter from Isabella April 1820, and in August she wrote to Isabella (at PBS's request) to inform her that Elise's information was incorrect (*Journals* 316, 322). Shelley emphasizes her shock at learning of these rumors, especially those condemning her husband's treatment of her, urgently defends PBS, denies that he had had an intimate relationship with Claire, and assures Isabella that "Claire had no child—the rest must be false" (*Letters* 1.206–207). The two women do not seem to have remained in contact after this episode, and Isabella continued to believe Elise; Shelley's letter was found among Byron's papers after his death, so it is unclear whether Isabella ever received Shelley's account of events (*Letters* 1.209). Shelley met Isabella once more at a February 1843 **Florentine** ball; she later wrote to Claire, "I cut her completely" (*Letters* 3.58).

Hoppner, Richard Belgrave (1786–1872):

Amateur painter and British consul at **Venice** after 1814. **Byron** found him a useful friend when he lived in Venice 1817, "captivated by his graciousness and his eagerness to be of service"; Byron delighted in the noble company to which the Hoppners introduced him (Marchand 2.714, 2.719).

PBS first met Richard and **Isabella Hoppner** in 1818, when he and **Claire Clairmont** visited **Clara Allegra Byron**, then staying at the Hoppners' house at Byron's request, and he initially liked Richard (White 2.33). Shelley met the Hoppners October 1818, writing November 1818 she found Venice disagreeable just as the Hoppners did, adding "they have lived between four and five years here, and are heartily sick of it" (*Letters* 1.81). While the Shelleys and Hoppners dined together frequently 1818, the Hoppners, with their "penchant for gossip," eagerly believed **Elise Foggi**'s false rumors about Claire's relationship with PBS, and Richard informed Byron of the rumors when Byron expressed disgust for Claire 1820 (*Journals* 233–234; Marchand 2.875–877). Shelley wrote in May 1820: "the Hoppners have behaved shamefully, but it is useless to detail in a letter" (*Letters* 1.145). Byron informed PBS of rumors the Hoppners had heard, and Shelley subsequently wrote to Isabella August 1820 to assert the falsity of Elise's claims, but the Shelleys and Hoppners had no further contact (Marchand 2.921; *Letters* 1.204–209).

Horace, Quintus Horatius Flaccus (65–8 B.C.E.):

Roman poet particularly admired for *Odes* (c. 23 B.C.E.) and *Epistles* (c. 20–16 B.C.E.) (Howatson 287). Shelley read Horace's *Odes* 1816, 1818, and 1819 and *Epistles*, with **PBS**, 1820 and 1821 (*Journals* 653). **Isabell Harley** introduces **Valerius** to Horace's works (*Val* 343). **Lionel Verney** recalls "the verses of Horace" (*LM* 462). "**The Sisters of Albano**'s" narrator mentions visiting **Mosaic**, the remains of Horace's villa in Alban hills (*SA* 51; Mc-

Gann 2.260). **Lord Lodore** finds "Horace a pleasant companion" (*L* 1.25).

Hormayr, General (1782–1848): **Tyrolese** Baron who became governor but delegated authority to **Hofer** (Alison 3.224; Moskal 255). Shelley mentions that Hofer refused to retreat with Hormayr 1809 (*R* 2.51).

Hoskins, Gregory: Minor character from **Ravenglass** in *Falkner*.

Hotel at Liège: See **Aigle Noire**.

Hôtel Bellevue: One of **Coblentz**'s "three first-rate hotels"; Shelley slept there July 1840 and again in 1842 (*R* 1.26, 1.168).

Hôtel Chatham: Shelley stayed at this **Parisian** hotel at the beginning and conclusion of her 1840s travels (*R* 1.6, 1.146).

Hotel d'Italia: Also spelled **Hôtel d'Italie**; Shelley stayed at this **Venetian** hotel, "three oar-strokes from the **Canale Grande**," within a three-minute walk of **Piazza San Marco**, September–October 1842 (*R* 2.80, 2.131).

Hôtel d'Italie: See **Hotel d'Italia**.

Hôtel de la Ville: Shelley stayed at this "extensive" **Milan** hotel 1840 (*R* 1.109).

Hôtel de Pologne: Hotel near **Dresden**'s **New Markt**. Shelley criticizes **Murray**'s advice to stay there because mostly men traveling alone or with pupils stayed at Hôtel de Pologne (*R* 1.231–232).

Hôtel de Russie: Shelley stayed at this **Frankfurt** hotel, on **Murray**'s recommendation, July 1840 (*R* 1.30, 1.172).

Hôtel de Saxe: **Leipzig** hotel overlooking a historic **Elster** bridge; Shelley stayed there July 1840 (*R* 1.215–216).

Hôtel de Trèves: Shelley stayed at this **Trèves** hotel June 1840 (*R* 1.18).

Hôtel des Bergues: **Genevese** hotel on **Lake Geneva**; **Murray** calls it a "grand establishment" (*BSWI* 245; *MSWI* 130). Shelley found it "the best of these **Swiss** hotels, where every thing is arranged with cleanliness, order, and comfort," believing **Hôtel du Lac** to have been modeled on it (*R* 1.52).

Hôtel du Lac: **Swiss** hotel overlooking **Lake Zurich**. Shelley stayed there July 1840 (*R* 1.52–53).

Hotel of the Post: Shelley confirms **Murray**'s recommendation of this **Brükenau** hotel, but she did not stay there July 1842 (*R* 1.202).

Hotham, Dr.: Shelley credits **Northumberland**'s Dr. Hotham with the discovery of "**Roger Dodsworth**'s" protagonist. In his *Keats-Shelley Journal* article about Shelley's story, Robinson notes that he did not locate mention of Dr. James Hotham in initial **French** accounts of the Dodsworth tale, "in histories of the Hotham family, in matriculation registers, or in professional listings" (21).

Houris: Beautiful virgins waiting in paradise for faithful Muslims. **Buzeccha** declares that there is plenty of time to play chess: "my games never last more than a quarter of an hour; and then ... you shall dance a set into the bargain with a black-eyed Houri" (*TP* 8). **Giacomo de' Tolomei** shares with **Marcott Alleyn** the news of **Clorinda Saviani**'s marriage and bitterly encourages him to visit the convent: " 'Go by all means, and make the best of your good fortune among these Houris' " (*BMI* 42).

House of Commons: Lower division of Britain's two **parliamentary** houses, formerly called **St. Stephen's**. While writing and doing research for *The Last Man* in February 1825, Shelley asked **Hobhouse** to arrange for her "to be present at a debate in the House of Commons" (*Letters* 1.466). A week later, she emphasized her need to "form a correct idea of the geography & modes of going on" (*Letters* 1.470). In Shelley's day, visitors could enter the galleries and gain "admission when the house is sitting, by an order from a peer, or an application to the door-keepers" (Leigh 220–221). Shelley amalgamates the two parliamentary houses into one before *The Last Man*'s beginning (*LM* 58). Shelley draws upon her visit to the House of Commons for the setting of **Ethel Villiers**'s meeting with **Lady Lodore** in St. Stephen's gallery (*L* 2.210).

House of Lancaster: See **Lancaster**.

House of Lords: Also called **House of Peers**; upper branch of Britain's **Parliament**, made up principally of bishops and members of the aristocracy who gained seats by descent, royal appointment, or election; the process of dismantling this house began in 1999, and membership is no longer a hereditary privilege (Leigh 54). In Shelley's day, visitors could enter the galleries and view "seats for the peers [which] are fitted up with red cloth" only after obtaining a lord's permission or by applying to a doorman (Leigh 220–221). "[T]he amalgamation of the two houses of Lords and **Commons**" occurs before events *The Last Man* records (*LM* 58). **Ethel Villiers** "graced a red bench of the House of Lords on the prorogation of Parliament," a ceremony in which the ruling monarch assumes the throne and ends a parliamentary session (*L* 2.210). Ethel later recalls speaking to **Lady Lodore** for the first time in the gallery (*L* 3.167). The House of Lords can be convened as a court to try members of the aristocracy; **Sir Boyvill Neville** forces **Gerard Neville** to appear in the House of Lords to give evidence in Sir Boyvill's divorce case (*F* 123). Shelley quotes from **Lord Chatham**'s speech there (*R* 1.203).

House of Peers: See **House of Lords**.

House of York: See **York**.

Houssain, Prince: See *Arabian Nights*.

Howard, John (c. 1430–1485): First Duke of Norfolk of the Howard family and a minor *Perkin Warbeck* character (*DNB*).

Howard, Lady Anne (1475–1512): Daughter of Edward IV, King of Scotland, and a minor *Perkin Warbeck* character (*DNB*).

Howard of Effingham: William Howard (1510–1573), first Baron Howard of Effingham; probably Shelley's mistaken reference either for **John Howard**, Duke of Norfolk, or Thomas Howard, Earl of Surrey (Fischer 272; Arthurson 16, 84–85). **Robert Clifford** and **Stephen Frion** pretend that Howard and troops will meet and support **Richard of York** (*PW* 3.9–10).

Howards: British family established in Norfolk during the 10th century (Low 577). Shelley mentions them repeatedly, particularly **John Howard** and **Howard of Effingham**, in *Perkin Warbeck* (*PW* 2.140, 2.147, 2.314, 2.328, 3.9, 3.82).

Hradschin: Bohemian palace built in **Prague** 1353 (*MSGE* 514). Shelley describes it as "extensive" and also uses its name to refer to "the imperial hill" it sits atop (*R* 2.1, 2.8).

Hughes, Professor: Shelley mentions this British tutor living in **Dresden**; she followed his advice on touring **Saxon Switzerland** and found his "kindness has been of the greatest use to us" (*R* 1.256, 1.260). Not further identified.

Huguenots: French Protestants persecuted in 16th and 17th centuries. Shelley queries the causes of certain historical events, such as the French suppression of the Huguenots (*R* 2.9). Shelley's readers would have understood her reference to **Louis XIV**'s 1685 Revocation of the 1598 Edict of **Nantes**, which caused approximately half a million Huguenots to flee France (Kinder 1.261; Crook 2).

Huguenots, Les: See **Meyerbeer**.

Hume, David (1711–1776): Influential Scottish historian, essayist, and philosopher who wrote *The History of England* (1754–62), which **PBS** read aloud 1818 (*Journals* 215–223; Sunstein 155). Shelley read Hume's *Essays and Treatises on several subjects* (1753–56) 1817–18, *Four Dissertations* (1757) 1818, and *Works* 1821 (*Journals* 185–190, 363–364). Shelley expresses belief in **Perkin Warbeck**'s legend despite Hume's contradictory historical account (*PW* 1.v).

Humphries, Mr.: Elizabeth Fitzhenry's **London** solicitor in *Lodore*.

Humphries, Mrs.: Solicitor's wife in *Lodore*.

Hungary: Country west of **Austria** in central **Europe**; the **Hapsburg** dynasty ruled it after the 15th century. The **Ottoman Empire** ruled it in the 16th century, so both Austrian and **Turkish** influences shaped it (Kinder 1.219, 1.209). Danubian monarchy ruled Hungary during Shelley's lifetime (Kinder 1.287, 2.59). **Matilda** conjectures that her father traveled through Hungary (*M* 156). **Lord Lodore** introduces Hungarian agricultural practices to his **American** residence (*L* 1.14). **Rupert Falkner** and **Elizabeth Falkner** plan to visit Hungary (*F* 33). Shelley notes that **Gabriel Serbelloni** "fought against the Turks with reputation and success in Hungary" in the 16th century (*R* 1.80). [*R* 2.112].

Hunt, Leigh [James Henry] (1784–1859): British poet, essayist, critic, and co-owner and editor of the *Exam-*

Hunt, Marianne (1788–1857)

iner after 1808. His first book of poems appeared 1801, and he also wrote theater criticism; Shelley read *The Story of Rimini* (1816) 1816 (*Journals* 654). In 1809, Hunt married **Marianne Hunt**, with whom he had at least eight children. He is best remembered as a critic, introducing **Keats**'s and **PBS**'s work in a December 1816 *Examiner* article, "Young Poets" (Sunstein 133). The Shelleys and Hunts became friends December 1816; Shelley stayed with the Hunts in **Hampstead** 1817, and the Hunts later shared the Shelleys' **Marlow** house for four months; Hunt was also **Byron**'s friend (*Letters* 1.24; Sunstein 130; *Journals* 166; White 1.475–478). Hunt often requested financial assistance from his friends (Sunstein 133). The Hunts and Shelleys remained close, frequently visiting each other, and maintained steady correspondence after the Shelleys' departure to **Italy** (*Journals* 164–165, 174). PBS invited the Hunts to Italy to start a periodical, the *Liberal,* with him and Byron August 1821; the Hunts eventually arrived June 1822 (*Journals* 378, 412). PBS drowned upon returning from greeting them (*Journals* 413). The Hunts comforted Shelley and moved to **Genoa** with her October 1822; in March 1823, Shelley felt Hunt disliked her, but by July 1823 Shelley was writing, "Hunt is all kindness, consideration, and friendship" (*Journals* 429, 456; *Letters* 1.344). Hunt's *Lord Byron and Some of His Contemporaries* (1828) was "a vengeful attack on Byron" and also misleading about Shelley's early relationship with PBS; the book was critically attacked, but Hunt's later work, including a staged drama, allowed him to live by his pen (Sunstein 289). Shelley maintained contact with the Hunts; she consulted Hunt when editing her husband's prose for publication 1839 and continued to help him financially until he received a government pension 1846 (Sunstein 344–345, 376). Hunt's *Autobiography* (1850) is an entertaining account of Hunt's life and friendships (*Letters* 3.162). Shelley quotes Hunt's description of Paolo being formed from, in *The Story of Rimini,* the "**very poetry** of nature" to describe **Henry Clerval** (*Fr1* 183; *Fr3* 133; Hunt 2.47). As an epigraph to the *Lodore* chapter in which **Lady Lodore**'s relationship with **Horatio Saville** alters, Shelley excerpts the narrator's commentary upon Francesca and Giovanni's growing love in Hunt's text: "**Ah now**, ye gentle pair,—now think awhile, / Now, while ye still can think and still can smile. / . . . / So did they think / Only with graver thoughts, and smiles reduced" (*L* 2.34; Hunt 3.340–341, 3.346, 3.353). Shelley quotes lines from Hunt's "Catullus's Return Home to the Peninsula of Sirmio" (1808), Hunt's translation of **Catullus**'s lines describing **Sirmio**, beginning "**O best of** all the scattered spots that lie" (*R* 2.73; Moskal 266). See Edmund Blunden's *Leigh Hunt: A Biography* (1930) and Ann Blainey's *Immortal Boy: A Portrait of Leigh Hunt* (1985).

Hunt, Marianne (1788–1857):

Married to **Leigh Hunt** 1809, Marianne, affectionately called Polly, was Shelley's first female friend after she returned to England from her **European** elopement. Marianne's artistic hobbies included silhouettes in paper, and she and Leigh had at least eight children together; Shelley and Marianne's "strongest bond was a common sister problem," since Shelley had to endure **Claire Clairmont**'s constant presence and interaction with **PBS**, while Marianne's sister, Elizabeth Kent, frequently stayed with her and seemed to be in love with Leigh (*Letters* 1.25, 1.39–41; Sunstein 134). The Shelleys stayed with the Hunts February 1817 and maintained close contact throughout 1818; Marianne was Shelley's faithful correspondent while Shelley was in **Italy** 1819 (*Journals* 164–165, 195; Sunstein 168–169). The Hunts and Shelleys reunited in Italy 1822, Marianne disliking **Genoa** as Shelley did; Shelley wrote "Marianne is sick & goodtempered Motherly & industrious," and Marianne supported Shelley after PBS's death (*Letters* 1.299–300, 1.280; *Journals* 413). Shelley shared the Hunts' house at the beginning of 1823 and noted that Marianne's "disposition is free from any particle of meanness"; Shelley asssisted Marianne in childbirth before returning to England (*Journals* 458–459; *Letters* 1.322). Marianne had become an alcoholic by June 1828, but she and Shelley maintained contact until Shelley's death (*Letters* 2.51). See Ann Blainey's *Immortal Boy: A Portrait of Leigh Hunt* (1985).

Huntley, Earl of: See **Huntly**.

Huntly, Earl of (d. c. 1502): George Gordon, second Earl of Huntly 1498–1501, **Byron**'s **Irish** ancestor; Shelley spells it **Huntley** (*DNB*; *Letters* 1.78). In *Perkin Warbeck*, Huntly supports **Richard of York**, who marries Huntly's daughter, **Lady Katherine Gordon**.

Hurtado de Mendoza, Diego (1500–1575): Spanish author. Shelley wrote Mendoza's biography for *Italian and Spanish Lives* but had difficulty obtaining materials, writing to John Bowring July 1837 for translations (*Letters* 2.289). Shelley terms *La Guerra de Granada* [*Granada's War*] (pub. 1610; trans. 1776) "the most esteemed of his prose works," calling it "*History of the War of Moriscos in Granada*" and finding its style "exceedingly pure" (*ISPL* 3.65). Shelley asserts that Mendoza is "not an imaginative poet," directing readers to his poems principally to ascertain their author's character, but she admires "his short and simple poems" as "the sparkling emanations of the passions, expressed at the moment, with all the ardour of living emotion" (*ISPL* 3.68–69).

Huss, John (c. 1372–1415): Czech religious reformer, also called Jan Hus, who anticipated the **Lutheran Reformation** and was burned at the stake; his followers were known as **Hussites**. Shelley celebrates Huss as an early religious reformer (*R* 2.2). She mentions his death and hymns honoring him (*R* 2.5–6).

Hyacinth: **Greek** myth records that both Zephyrus and **Apollo** loved this beautiful youth; Zephyrus accidentally killed Hyacinth with a discus, and from Hyacinth's blood sprang a flower with petals marked "aiai," which can be interpreted as "alas, alas" (Howatson 290). **Lionel Verney** compares the hyacinth's markings to his own feeling of being marked with "SHE LIVES! SHE IS!" after having fallen in love with **Idris** (*LM* 62).

Hyde Park: Large public park in **London**'s Westminster district, the most fashionable London royal park in

Hymera

Shelley's time and now renowned for its public meetings on popular issues in which all are allowed a voice. *The Last Man*'s central protagonists have homes near there (*LM* 93, 331). **Ethel Villiers** is nervous about "a drive in Hyde Park," fearing meeting **Edward Villiers** (*L* 2.142, 2.156). **Lady Lodore** notes sadly: "the drive in Hyde Park was beginning to fill with carriages and equestrians, to be thronged with her friends whom she was never again to see" (*L* 3.175). **Gerard Neville** paces in the park at night while his father reads **Rupert Falkner**'s narrative (*F* 222). Shelley noted "gravel of the **Tuilleries** and the **Champs Elysées** is not half so inviting as the sward of Hyde Park" and later described **Cascine** as **Florence**'s Hyde Park (*R* 1.7, 2.134).

Hymera: Nymph of a stream in *Proserpine* to whom **Eunoe** appeals concerning **Proserpine**'s disappearance. Hymera claims that she was asleep all day.

Hymettus: Mountain range southeast of **Athens**, famous in ancient times for its honey (*MGRE* 203). **Byron** records its "honey'd wealth" in *Childe Harold's Pilgrimage* (2.822). **Perdita** explains **Raymond**'s wishes to be buried on Hymettus (*LM* 208). **Lionel Verney** describes the "sublime chasm['s]" ragged beauty, and Perdita begins to construct a cottage there (*LM* 208). Lionel commits Perdita's remains to **Palli**'s care "for the purpose of having them transported to Hymettus" to join Raymond in the tomb (*LM* 215).

"Hymn to Mercury": Poem **PBS** translated from **Greek** 1820 (White 2.207; Holmes 600). **Lionel Verney** wonders if "cold philosophy" can be "engaged '**In this dear work** of youthful revelry,' " a line **Apollo** speaks in amazement over Hermes's song (*LM* 38; PBS 77.6). Verney resists poaching at **Windsor**, quoting Mercury's lines: " '**Nathelesse, / I checked** my haughty will, and did not eat;' but supped upon sentiment, and dreamt vainly of '**such morsels sweet**,' as I might not waking attain" (*LM* 78; PBS 22.2–3, 5). As the first epigraph to the *Perkin Warbeck* chapter in which **Richard of York** befriends **Robert Clifford**, Shelley quotes: "—**It is thy merit** / To make all mortal business ebb and flow / By roguery" (*PW* 1.179; PBS 88.5–7).

Hythe: English port ten miles west of **Dover**. Shelley describes Hythe's surroundings and mentions that **Lord Audley**'s estate is nearby; **Richard of York**'s fleet lands there (*PW* 2.152, 2.160–164, 2.166).

Hythe, Lady Caroline: Sir Richard Gray's married daughter in "**The Elder Son**."

Hythe, Lord: Lady Caroline Hythe's husband in "**The Elder Son**."

I

Icarus: In **Greek** mythology, **Daedalus**, imprisoned with son Icarus after helping **Ariadne** and **Theseus** navigate the labyrinth, escaped **Crete** using wings made of wax and feathers, but Icarus ignored his father's warning and flew too close to the sun. The wax holding his wings together melted, and he fell into the **Aegean**. **Lionel Verney** compares himself to Icarus, concealing love for **Idris** rather than "playing the mad game of a fond, foolish Icarus" (*LM* 51).

Ida: West central **Cretan** mountain range housing a cave where nurses reared infant **Zeus** (Tripp 315). **Ferdinando Eboli** describes **Adalinda Spina** as "a **Ganymede**, escaped from his thrall above to his natal Ida" (*FE* 78).

Idris: **Adrian**'s sister and only daughter of *The Last Man*'s **Countess of Windsor** and England's former king; she marries **Lionel Verney**, and they have three sons.

Ildegonda: See **Grossi**.

Ildone: Singer who entertains **Euthanasia**'s court in *Valperga*.

Ilfracombe: English coastal village forty miles northwest of **Exeter**. **Dame Smithson** snatches **Maurice** from his parents' nurse there (*Maurice* 79). Her husband's family is from Ilfracombe, Maurice is raised there for about ten years, and Maurice's father reclaims him after meeting Dame Smithson there (*Maurice* 80–82).

Illinois: Large state in central northern **America**, first settled early 18th century and admitted to the United States 1818 (Brogan 198, 235). **Lord Lodore** exiles himself from Britain to "a settlement in the district of the Illinois," where he becomes a gentleman farmer until **Ethel Villiers** turns sixteen (*L* 1.12, 1.36, 1.209, 1.227–229). **Horatio Saville** and **Edward Villiers** later travel to Illinois in search of them (*L* 2.44). Ethel's isolated upbringing there prepares her well for subsequent difficulties in **London** (*L* 2.238). Ethel recalls Illinois fondly, frequently evoking it as peaceful paradise (*L* 2.84, 1.280, 2.240, 3.61).

"Illyrian Poems—Feudal Scenes": Shelley published a favorable review of **Prosper Mérimée's** *La Guzla, ou Choir de Poesies Illyriques recueillies dans la Dalmatie, la Vosnie, la Croatie et l' Hervegowine* [*Guzla, or Chorus of Illyrian Poems Collected in Dalmatia, Bosnia, Croatia, and Herzegovina*] (1827), which she drew on for "**The Evil Eye**," *La Jaquerie; Feudal Scenes; followed by the Family of Carvajal, a Drama* (1828), and *Le Théâtre de Clara Gazul, Comédienne Espagnole* [*Spanish Comedienne Clara Gazul's Theater*] (1825) in the January 1829 *Westminster Review*. Editor John Bowring paid her about £5 (*Letters* 2.45, 2.70). Shelley finds "the 'Comedies of Clara Gazul' ... in every way, striking and interesting" (*RevIll* 72). She praises *Guzla* and concludes the article discussing *Jaquerie,* comprising "a series of dramatic scenes, developing the history of an insurrection in **France**" (*RevIll* 78). Shelley mentions the appended drama, " 'Family of Carvajal,' " is "founded on the same story" as the Cenci (*RevIll* 80, 81).

Imlay, Gilbert (1754–1828): **American** radical and author of *A Topographical Description of the Western Territory of North America* (1792) and *The Emigrants* (1793) (*SCGS* 159). Imlay was living in **London** when **Mary Wollstonecraft** met and fell in love with him 1793; they traveled to **France,** and when war broke out, Wollstonecraft adopted "Mrs. Imlay" before the couple settled in **Havre**; there **Fanny Godwin** was born (*SCGS* 160; Sunstein 14; Seymour 15-16). Imlay soon returned to London and took an actress as mistress; Wollstonecraft's 1795 solo visit to Scandinavia in an attempt to assist Imlay in his business as Ohio's Scioto Land Company's agent resulted in her *Letters Written During a Short Residence in Sweden, Norway, and Denmark* (1796) (Sunstein 14; *SCGS* 159–160). Upon their London 1795 reunion, it was clear that Imlay wished to have no more to do with Wollstonecraft (*SCGS* 159–160). **William Godwin** published Wollstonecraft's letters to Imlay 1798; nothing is known of Imlay's later life (*SCGS* 181, 296).

India: Large southern **Asian** country east of the **Indus** and south of the Himalayas. The name also traditionally applies to a region extending east toward **China**, to include Bangladesh, Nepal, and Bhutan. It was under British control and termed the Indian Empire in Shelley's time; it gained independence 1947 but remains a British Commonwealth member. **Matilda**'s father passes through north India (*M* 161). **Midas** expects his golden touch to bring him powers such as those the British Empire exerted: "India shall be mine, / Its blooming beauties, gold-encrusted baths, / Its aromatic groves and palaces" (*Midas* 129). British trade with India stops as plague spreads and goods from India in east **London** warehouses rot (*LM* 233, 319). After his father's death, **Lucy Martin's** lover travels to India and becomes a prisoner of war; he returns to find Lucy married to another and dies from plague (*LM* 347–349). Shelley contextualizes *Perkin*

Warbeck with reference to **Portuguese** efforts to discover "a route to India," and **Hernan De Faro** undertakes such an expedition, searching "beyond the equator [for] a route to the spicy Indian land" (*PW* 1.146, 1.196). **Richard of York** hears of **Columbus**'s "quest of the western passage to India" (*PW* 1.258). **Henry Clerval** plans to visit India and enters into an Indian trade enterprise with London men (*Fr3* 135, 144). **Edward Villiers** promises his wife "letters as long as if they were to go to India" (*L* 3.33). **Rupert Falkner** rises to captain's rank during ten years served in the **East India Company**, earning **Osborne's** loyalty and respect there (*F* 28, 183). When Falkner buries **Alithea Neville**, he recalls "to hide the dead with speed from every eye was the Indian custom" (*F* 205). [*Absence* lines 3–4].

"Indian Girl's Song, The": Lyric **PBS** wrote 1820, first published as "Song, Written for an Indian Air" 1823 (Holmes 568). Regarding **Elizabeth Falkner**, Shelley notes, "'there was a spirit in her feet,'" echoing PBS's poem (*F* 89; PBS lines 6–7).

Indian Isles: See **West Indies**.

Indies of the West: See **West Indies**.

Indus: River originating in southwest Tibet, flowing through **India** and Pakistan into the **Arabian** Sea. **Lionel Verney** suggests that living with plague makes humankind forget former existence: "navies used to stem the giant ocean-waves betwixt Indus and the Pole for slight articles of luxury" (*LM* 316).

Inferno: First part of **Dante**'s *Divina Commedia*; it describes hell as a gradual, stepped funnel containing rings of sinners confined to different categories, which Dante passes through with guide **Virgil**. Shelley read it 1817–22 (*Journals* 643–644). She draws from *Inferno* frequently in *Valperga*: she refers readers to Dante for **Francesca da Rimini**'s tale, **Guarino** sings of **Charon** refusing Dante's passage into hell, people crowd **Carraia**'s bridge to view **Festa d'Inferno** or the representation of hell that Dante provides, and Shelley draws **William Borsiere**'s last name from that of a courtier in Dante's work (*V* 1.17–21, 1.42, 1.257, 1.273–74; *Inferno* 3.82–99, 5.116–138, 16.69). **Beatrice** describes her **Paterin** beliefs, declaring that God created love, "that mansion whose motto must ever be 'Lasciate ogni speranza voi che intrate,'" part of the inscription Dante reads over hell's gate, which translates to "Abandon hope all ye who enter here" (*V* 3.46; *Inferno* 3.9). Shelley uses Dante's description for **Monte San Giuliano**: "'Perchè i Pisan veder Lucca non ponno,'" meaning, "preventing **Pisans** from seeing **Lucca**" (*V* 1.229; *Inferno* 33.30; Crook 3.94). Shelley notes "there are finer passages in the *Inferno* than can be found in the two subsequent parts; but the subject is so painful and odious, that I always feel obliged to shut the book after a page or two" (*R* 1.96). She was disappointed at not seeing **Slovino di San Marco**, as described in *Inferno*, when crossing into **Italy** 1842; she quotes Dante's "**Per aver pace** co' seguaci sui," which translates "to which the **Po** together with the waters / that follow it descends to final rest," in her own discussion of the **Arno** (*R* 2.66, 2.135; *Inferno* 12.4–10, 5.98–99). Arriving at **Lago di Garda** September 1842, Shelley quotes Dante's description of it, beginning "**Suso in Italia**"; the lines mean "High up, in lovely Italy, beneath / the Alps that shut in Germany above / Tirolo, lies a lake known as Benaco. / A thousand springs and more, I think, must flow / out of the waters of that lake to bathe / Pennino, Garda, Val Camonica" (*R* 2.68; *Inferno* 20.61–66). Shelley also quotes lines beginning "**Li ruscelletti**" from *Inferno* upon arriving at **Vallombrosa**, applauding Dante's description of northern Italy "in poetry that brings the very spot before your eyes, adorned with graces missed by the prosaic eye"; she also includes "Dante's apostrophe" in her discussion of papal government (*R* 2.138–139; *Inferno* 30.64–66, 19.115–117). Shelley quotes Dante's description of the church's greed, lines beginning " '**Ahi, Costantin,**' ": "Ah, Constantine, what wickedness was born—/ and not from your conversion—from the dower / that you bestowed upon the first rich father!" (*R* 2.244; *Inferno* 19.115–117).

Ingolstadt: German city forty-five miles north of **Munich**, site of a university 1472–1800. **Victor Frankenstein** spends several years studying science there; Ingolstadt is site of the **Creature**'s "birth" (*Fr1* 71–72, 85; *Fr3* 46, 58). **De Staël** "identified [Ingolstadt] as the place where experimental scientific work was under way" (Sunstein 427).

"Inni Sacri": See **Manzoni**.

Innominato: See *Promessi Sposi*.

Innsbruck: **Austrian** city in **Tyrol**, eighty-five miles southwest of **Salzburg**; Shelley spells it **Inspruck**. Shelley visited it September 1842 (*R* 2.45–47).

Ino: Nymph attendant in *Proserpine*; Ino is **Bacchus**'s aunt in **Ovid**'s *Metamorphoses* (Clemit 73; *Metamorphoses* 4.416–562).

***Ino e Temisto*:** See **Niccolini**.

Inquisition: Catholic court instituted 1231 in **Italy** and **France** to combat heresy, witchcraft, and alchemy, and revived in **Rome** 1542 to combat Protestantism; it was suspended 1820 and abolished 1834 (Collinge 209). Inquisitors condemn **Beatrice** for her **Paterin** beliefs (*V* 3.96). Shelley notes the pope issued an edict continuing the Inquisition in 1831 (*R* 2.253).

Inspruck: See **Innsbruck**.

"Invisible Girl, The": Story first published in the 1833 *Keepsake* as by "the Author of **Frankenstein**" (Robinson 389). Shelley describes the accompanying illustration titled *Rosina*, which William Boxall painted and J. C. Edwards engraved, at length (*IG* 191). In both the story and as the illustration accompanying its reprint in the **American** *Keepsake* (1854), **Rosina**'s portrait is titled "The Invisible Girl." In a note accompanying the submitted manuscript sent to her publisher 26 July 1832, Shelley asserts that the story's "shortness must make it a little abrupt" (*Letters* 2.165–166). Set in the early 18th century, its narrator recounts discovering the "The Invisible Girl" portrait in a ruined tower, then relates the tale learned there from an old lady looking after the place (*IG* 190–192). **Sir Peter Vernon** raised his only son, **Henry Vernon,** and orphan Rosina without suspecting their growing love (*IG* 195). When "odious **Mrs. Bainbridge**" alerts him, Peter sends his son abroad and tries to make Rosina marry a neighborhood gentleman (*IG* 196). Peter and Bainbridge take Rosina to isolation in Wales; when they find her writing to Henry for assistance, they throw her out of the house (*IG* 196–197). Peter is full of remorse when Rosina cannot be found the following day, and Henry returns from abroad and searches for her body (*IG* 197–198). Taking refuge from a storm, Henry sees a light in a tower and learns of the "Invisible Girl," whom neighboring fishermen have seen twice and whose elusiveness and mystery compel them to give her this appellation (*IG* 198–199). Henry sees a light in the tower the following night and there finds Rosina (*IG* 200). Fearful of Peter's harsh invective, Rosina had lived for three months by hiding in nearby woods and sheltering in the tower (*IG* 201). After a long illness, Rosina recovers from her ordeal, marries Henry, and the couple happily reunites with Peter (*IG* 201). Henry causes a portrait of Rosina entitled "The Invisible Girl" to be hung in the tower, to which the couple return every year (*IG* 202). This is one of many stories in which Shelley's "relevant fictional heroines either are orphaned of their fathers before they fall in love, or oppose their fathers and lose their lovers" (Sunstein 174).

Io: See **Correggio**.

Ioannina: Main "town of **Epirus**," seventy-five miles southeast of **Tepellenè**; Shelley spells it **Yannina** (*MGRE* 382). **Cyril Ziani** and **Camaraz** travel separately to Ioannina searching for **Constans Ziani** (*EE* 110). Subsequently, they leave Ioannina in pursuit of **Dmitri**, who learns of "six or eight well-armed **Moreots**" approaching on the road from Ioannina (*EE* 112–13).

Ion: PBS's translation (c. 1818) of **Plato**'s dialogue; Shelley filled out PBS's fragmentary translation (published 1840) with her own translation from the **Greek** (Holmes 432; Crook 2). Shelley places inside quotation marks a passage (beginning "**that golden chain**") describing **Raphael**'s power to create inspirational art as divine; Moskal believes it may be adapted from PBS's text, specifically from **Socrates**'s long speech to Ion (*R* 2.219; Moskal 344).

Ionian Isles: Group of islands along **Greece**'s southwest coast, under British protection during Greece's war of independence. **Adrian** speaks freely and frequently "of his beloved Ionian," **Evadne Zaimi** (*LM* 35). **Elizabeth Falkner** resides on **Zante**, an Ionian island, while **Rupert Falkner** fights in mainland Greece (*F* 56). [*LM* 78].

Ionic: Order of **Greek** architecture characterized by scrolls on the capital. **Lionel Verney** bids farewell to "the fluted column with its capital, **Corinthian**, Ionic, or **Doric**" (*LM* 321). In **Rome**, Verney admires the streets "strewed with truncated columns, broken capitals—Corinthian and Ionic" (*LM* 461). Shelley describes **Richard of York**'s neck, supporting "his head as

Ireland

the Ionic flute rears its graceful capital" (*PW* 1.180).

Ireland: Large island country west of Britain. Britain swiftly defeated Ireland's 1798 rebellion, and the 1801 Act of Union joined Ireland to Britain (Kinder 2.31). **Mary Wollstonecraft** worked as a governess in Ireland, **PBS** was an active agitator in Irish affairs, and Shelley closely followed political events there (White 1.206–207). An 1829 **parliamentary** act alleviated the tax burden placed on the Irish somewhat, but famine devastated the country 1845–46, followed by a swiftly crushed rebellion 1848 (Kinder 2.48). In March 1846, Shelley reflected, "Poor Ireland! The English have done their best by them," but in March 1848, she wrote, "One half of Ireland detests the other half—nor have the Irish any political grievance (for they have not the burthen of our taxes) except that the Catholics are forced to support the Protestant Church" (*Letters* 3.281, 3.336). **Victor Frankenstein** is imprisoned there (*Fr1* 199, 208–209; *Fr3* 146, 154). **Edward II** makes **Piers Gaveston** Ireland's Lieutenant, and **Castruccio** carries messages to Gaveston there at Edward's request (*V* 1.72). **Lionel Verney** takes his family and **Perdita** to stay in Irish **Killarney** for several weeks (*LM* 156). **Americans** fleeing plague rampage through Ireland; the Irish follow them to England as a "conquering army, burning—laying waste—murdering" until reaching **London**'s outskirts (*LM* 298, 302). **Horace Neville** receives letters suggesting "he might be obliged to visit an estate in the north of Ireland" (*Mourner* 85). **Lewis Elmore** visits passengers from the *St. Mary* there, believing that **Clarice Eversham** "had crossed to Ireland," and subsequently receives a "letter from Ireland, which made him think that Miss Eversham was residing near **Enniscorthy**"; he and Neville begin but do not undertake the crossing there (*Mourner* 93, 95–96). The **Earl of Lincoln** suggests **Lambert Simnel** "should first appear in Ireland," and the Irish rally around him (*PW* 1.115, 1.132). Irish forces subsequently challenge **Henry VII** of England at **Foudray**, where, "half naked and ill-armed, [they] fought with desperate bravery" but are ultimately defeated (*PW* 1.132, 1.137). **Lord Barry** stirs support for **Richard of York**'s cause in Ireland, finding it "the dear land of promise to the weary exile" (*PW* 1.243, 1.273). Richard has many loyal Irish supporters and is recognized at **Cork** as "Lord of Ireland with one acclaim," so Ireland is a frequent setting in *Perkin Warbeck* (*PW* 1.285, 1.310, 2.173, 2.177, 2.323, 3.27, 3.34, 3.48, 3.278, 3.280). **Ellen**'s father lives in north Ireland, and **Clinton Gray** spends two years there with his regiment (*ES* 244, 264). **Lord Cecil** goes to Ireland to look after his estate there (*F* 86). "[S]ome merry Irish students" accompanied Shelley on the carriage exterior en route to **Paris** June 1840, and Shelley's maid in **Milan** mistakenly thinks three sisters Shelley is to travel toward **Geneva** with are Irish (*R* 1.6, 1.125). [*PW* 3.66, 3.106; *IG* 190].

Iris: In **Greek** myth, the rainbow and gods' messenger (Tripp 325). Iris carries **Jove**'s message about **Proserpine**'s fate to **Ceres** (*P* 69). Iris obeys Jove's commands but orchestrates the division of Proserpine's time between earth and hell.

Irish Channel: Body of water separating **Ireland** from Britain. Weather thwarts **Gerard Neville**'s attempt to cross to **America**; the *John Adams* struggles in the Irish Channel (*F* 281).

Irish Melodies: **Moore**'s successful series of patriotic and sentimental poetic songs, published in ten parts 1808–34. As "**The Mourner**'s" epigraph, Shelley quotes accurately from Moore's "As a Beam Over the Face of the Waters May Glow": "**One fatal remembrance**, one sorrow that throws / Its bleak shade alike o'er our joys and our woes, / To which life nothing darker or brighter can bring, / For which joy has no balm, and affliction no sting!" (*Mourner* 81; Moore lines 5–8). As an epigraph to the *Perkin Warbeck* chapter in which **Richard of York** escapes battle in **Ireland**, Shelley quotes the refrain from Moore's "Where is the slave": " '**Farewell, Erin**! farewell all / Who live to weep our fall!' " (*PW* 3.49; Moore lines 11–12). Shelley quotes from Moore's "As Slow our Ship" as epigraph to the chapter in which **Lady Lodore** and **Elizabeth Fitzhenry** reunite: "**So loth we part** from all we love, / From all the links that bind us; / So turn our hearts, where'er we rove, / To those we've left behind us" (*L* 3.264; Moore lines 4–8). **Gerard Neville** brings **Elizabeth Falkner** "the melodies of Moore, so '**married to immortal verse**,' " describing *Irish Melodies* with a line from **Milton**'s *L'Allegro* (*F* 236).

Irving, Washington (1783–1859): **American** author renowned for the tales "Rip Van Winkle" and "The Legend of Sleepy Hollow," published in *The Sketch Book* (1820). Shelley first met Irving July 1824 at John Gilbert Newton's art studio, where Irving was sitting for a portrait; she thought him a "delightful person" (Sunstein 260; *Letters* 1.505, 1.507; Seymour 351). Shelley wrote to Louisa Holcroft January 1825 inquiring whether she had seen Irving in **Paris** and asking her to "Remember [Shelley] to him & tell him I claim his promised Visit when he does come" to England (*Letters* 1.464). He met Shelley twice after their initial meeting—August 1824 at the Haymarket Theatre and June 1830, when he attended Shelley's tea party (*Letters* 1.465, 2.106; *Journals* 512; Sunstein 308, 448). Sunstein also mentions the two met at an April 1830 dinner party (448). **Payne** was friends with both Shelley and Irving; when Shelley rejected Payne as a suitor, he attempted to play matchmaker between Shelley and Irving, giving Shelley's letters to Irving (Sunstein 268; Seymour 371). Irving read these letters (addressed to Payne) August 1825; they included such sentiments as "as yet I am still faithful to W.I.!" and "Give my love, of course Platonic, to I." (*Letters* 1.486, 1.493–494, 1.500). No romance developed between Irving and Shelley. Shelley read Irving's *A Chronicle of the Conquest of Granada* (1829) 1829 and based *Perkin Warbeck*'s **Spanish** scenes on his descriptions (*Letters* 2.93; *PW* 1.203). She offered to review *Conquest* for *Westminster Review* January 1830 (*Letters* 2.99). See Franklin B. Sanborn's *The Romance of Mary W. Shelley, John Howard Payne and Washington Irving* (1907).

Isabeau of Bavaria (1371–1435): Isabeau became **France**'s queen when she married **Charles VI** 1385; from 1393, she played a dominant role in

Isabel, Queen

France due to Charles's insanity (Famiglietti 14). Shelley notes her involvement in royal family strife (calling her simply **Queen**) and her favoring the **Duke of Orleans** (1372–1407) over the **Duke of Burgundy**; Isabeau confines herself and the **Dauphin** after the Duke of Orleans's 23 November 1407 murder (*Trans* 122, 123; Famiglietti 40, 63).

Isabel, Queen: See **Isabella I**.

Isabella I (1451–1504): Castile's queen from 1474 and **Aragon's** from 1479; she ruled jointly with husband **Ferdinand**, whom she married 1469. Isabella appears in a *Perkin Warbeck* Spanish scene.

Ischia: Island twenty miles southwest of **Naples**; Shelley also spells it Istria. **Euthanasia** envisions **Castruccio's** exile there (*V* 3.206). **Ferdinando Eboli** bids **Adalinda Spina** farewell while the sun sinks behind Ischia (*FE* 66). Shelley viewed Ischia 1843 but declined to sail there from Naples (*R* 2.265, 2.283).

Ischl: Famous spa since 1820, Bad Ischl is at the convergence of the Ischl and **Traun** rivers in **Austria**, twenty-seven miles southeast of **Salzburg**; Shelley spells it **Ishl**. She arrived there September 1842 (*R* 2.30).

Isel, Mount: See **Berg Isel**.

Isella: See **Iselle**.

Iselle: Italian village in the **Alps**, eighteen miles northwest of **Domodossola**; Shelley spells it **Isella**. Shelley luckily avoided delay in Iselle while trying to cross **Simplon Pass** October 1840 (*R* 1.137).

Ishl: See **Ischl**.

Isis: River joining the **Thames** at **Oxford**. **Victor Frankenstein** admires it (*Fr1* 187; *Fr3* 136).

Islam: Term applying collectively to the Muslim religion and to all lands where it dominates. **Lionel Verney** describes a battle fought on **Hebrus's** banks "which was to decide the fate of Islam" (*LM* 163).

Isola Bella: Borromean island in **Lake Maggiore** named for 17th-century Isabella, Count Carlo Borromeo's wife; Borromeo palace is there (constructed 1632–70) (*Berkeley* 132). Shelley visited it September 1840 (*R* 1.129–130).

Isola Madre: Borromean island in **Lake Maggiore**; Shelley visited it September 1840 (*R* 1.129).

Ispahan: City in eastern Iran, formerly **Persia's** capital, now called Esfahan. Ispahan's streets "were strewed with pestilence-struck corpses" after the sun's eclipse (*LM* 224).

Istanbul: See **Constantinople**.

Isthmus of Corinth: Narrow strip of land connecting the **Peloponnese** with mainland **Greece**. **Adrian** proposes passing over it to **Athens** (*LM* 439).

Istria: See **Ischia**.

Italian and Spanish Lives: See *Lives of the Most Eminent Literary and Scientific Men of Italy, Spain and Portugal*.

Italian Opera in Berlin: Shelley refers to **Berlin**'s opera house, "Deutsche Staatsoper," as "Italian Opera," near the **Guard-house** opposite **New Museum** (*R* 1.218–219). It opened 1742 on **Unter-den-Linden** (Tucker 55).

Italian Song: See "Chi Dice Mal" and **Appendix II**.

Italian, The: See **Radcliffe, Ann**.

Italy: Southern **European** country extending into the **Adriatic** and **Mediterranean**. Shelley was always interested in the land and its culture, reading Italian in **Geneva** 1816 (*H* 96). The Shelleys moved to Italy with **Claire Clairmont** 1818. They lived in a variety of places, including **Leghorn** and **Pisa**, and Shelley "would crisscross the peninsula and gravitate toward the Italophilia for which she... was later noted" (Sunstein 151). Shelley loved the land and enjoyed Italian cultural freedoms, but life there was difficult; she lost two young children. Still, she made a lifelong friend in **Maria Gisborne**; the Shelleys also associated with **Byron** and the **Williamses** there. **PBS** died in waters off its coast. On leaving the country where she had spent her life's happiest and worst days, she wrote 26 April 1823: "Italy! Beloved Country!—Your **Alps** are high, but alas! they cannot hold me in—Your seas—that has made me the wretch I am" (*Journals* 462). She recorded in May 1823, "How beautiful these shores & this sea are—such is the scene—such the waves within which my sole beloved vanished from mortality—But he is still there" (*Journals* 464). In England, May 1824, Shelley wrote "Italy—dear Italy—murdress of those I love & of all my happiness" (*Journals* 476). Her attitude toward Italy was always one of conflicting emotions. **Felix De Lacey** helps **Safie** and her father escape from **Paris** to Leghorn, and Safie's father leaves Italy for **Constantinople** from there (*Fr1* 152–154; *Fr3* 109–110). **Valerius** regards Italians as people " 'who usurp the soil once trod by heroes' " or **Romans**; they fill him " 'with bitter disdain' " (*Val* 333). "**A Tale of the Passions**," set in Italy, briefly refers to many of the issues Shelley explores fully in *Valperga*, which describes **Guelph** and **Ghibelline** wars in 14th-century Italy (*TP* 1). Shelley calls Italy a tomb, recalling all she lost there; nevertheless she wishes to stay: "Tear me not hence—here let me live and die, / In my adopted land—my country—Italy" (*Ch* 6, 59–60). She remembers **William Shelley**'s childish wonder and death and burial in Rome (*Ch* 76–87, 122–23). **Edmund Malville** demonstrates "strange enthusiasm" for the country and recalls its beauties with fondness, much as Shelley herself did (*RI* 25). Shelley observes "Italians, male or female, are not great patronizers of truth" and later presents "the widely spread maxim in Italy, that dishonour attaches itself to the discovered not the concealed fault" (*BMI* 33, 34). Like *Valperga,* "**The Heir of Mondolfo**," "**Ferdinando Eboli**," "**The Sisters of Albano**," and "**The Brother and Sister**" are set in Italy (*HM* 308; *FE* 70; *SA* 55; *Brother* 166). ***The Last Man***'s framework is set in Italy in the cave where **Sibylline** leaves (some written in Italian) are located (*LM* 5). Plague destroys much of Italy, but **Adrian** proposes to **Lionel Verney** that they take **Clara** to Italy's "sunny plains" (*LM* 427). Verney explores Rome and leaves his narrative there (*LM* 468). **Stephen Frion** had visited Italy "and studied there the wiles and cruelties of the Italian lords," while **Charles VIII**'s plans to invade Italy lead him to conclude a hasty peace with **Henry VII** of England after Henry's invasion of **France** (*PW* 1.150, 1.314). Shelley compares **Richard of York**'s sad and anxious wait for **Lord Stanley**'s funeral knell to the pilgrims' wait in Italy, where, "for three days in Passion Week, the sound of every bell . . . is suspended" until they are all rung "on the noon of the day when the mystery of the Resurrection is solemnized" (*PW* 2.137–138). **Victor Frankenstein**'s parents move to Italy immediately after their marriage (*Fr3* 39–40). In **Milan**, they welcome orphaned **Elizabeth Lavenza** into their family; her father "was one of those Italians nursed in the memory of the antique glory of Italy . . . who exerted himself to obtain" Italy's liberty in its 18th-century war with **Austria** (*Fr3* 41). In "**The Swiss Peasant**," **Louis Chaumont** intends to go to Italy after his discharge from the French army (*SP* 152). The **Mancini** family are " 'the best blood in Italy' " in **Count Fabian de' Tolomei**'s opinion, and **Flora Mancini** feels her protector has Italy's " 'most generous heart' " (*Brother* 177, 189). When **Faustina Moncenigo** first meets **Ippolito della Toretta**, she fans him "with her large green fan, which Italian ladies carry to make use of as a parasol," and, after their marriage, the couple "spent two or three years in Paris and the south of Italy" (*Trial* 236, 243). **Vernon Gray** gives **Ellen** Italian lessons, and Ellen observes he is "jealous as an Italian" (*ES* 248, 250). **Lord Lodore** visits Italy in his youth, reads Italian, and talks longingly of traveling there with his daughter (*L* 1.84, 1.25, 1.251). After **Horatio Saville**'s marriage to **Clorinda** and the establishment of their residence in **Naples**, the **Villiers**es travel to "fair, joyous Italy" to visit them (*L* 2.170). The **Saville** family also travels there (*L* 2.222, 3.219). **Ethel Villiers** meditates "on the wondrous beauty and changeful but deep interest of" Italy (*L* 2.240, 3.62). Shelley published the first two volumes of *Italian and Spanish Lives*, concerned with Italian figures, 1835. **Rupert Falkner** and **Elizabeth Falkner** travel in Italy (*F* 40). Shelley returned there with **PFS** 1840 and 1842–43, publishing *Rambles*, a record of these tours, 1844, and noting even in the "Introduction" her belief that "no one can mingle with the Italians without becoming attached to them" (*R* 1.viii). Shelley emphasizes her longing to return to the country where she experienced so much happiness; she stayed at **Cadennabia** July–August 1840, as well as visiting major towns, such as Milan, during her 1842 journey (*R* 1.2). Shelley was initially fearful of returning to Italy, where familiar sights caused her "strange and indescribable emotions" (*R* 1.61). Ultimately, her affection for Italy is clear: "the more I see of the inhabitants of this country, the more I feel convinced that they are highly gifted with intellectual powers, and possess all the elements of greatness" (*R* 1.86). She revels in Italian literature and recounts histories of great Italian families, such as the **Sfondrati** and **Serbelloni** (*R* 1.79–82). Shelley loves Italians: "they are affectionate, simple, and earnestly desirous to please" (*R* 1.87). Much of *Rambles*'s second volume records Shelley's return: in September 1842, she entered by **Lago di Garda** and proceeded to **Venice**, **Florence**, **Tuscany**, Rome, **Sorrento**, **Pompeii**, and **Amalfi** (*R* 2.69, 2.72, 2.79, 2.131, 2.212, 2.279–280). She describes Italian art and history and asserts that Italy formerly led Europe in great literature and "if a revolutionary spark is lighted up any where in Europe, the fire bursts forth in Italy" (*R* 2.191, 2.249). [*Maurice* 78; *Val* 338; *LM* 216; *RD* 43, 45; *FE* 70; *L* 1.294, 2.13]. See "**Untitled: 'Fair Italy!'** "

***Italy*:** **Rogers** published this collection of poems and prose pieces 1822–28. The narrative poems, most with place titles, present a catalogue of sites in or near various locations, such as "**Geneva**," "**Como**," and "**Florence**." When the **Villierses** arrive there, Shelley quotes "**piece of heaven** dropped upon earth" from the "**Naples**" section of Rogers's poem (*L* 2.178; Rogers lines 1–2). Shelley dedicated *Rambles* to Rogers, "Author of *The Pleasures of Memory*, *Italy*, etc.," and alludes to his verse throughout her work (*R* 1.vi). For example, Shelley directs readers to view the "vignette" accompanying "**Amalfi**"; **Turner**'s engraving shows a gondola and a ship in front of Amalfi, a serene city amidst a mountainous landscape (Rogers 216). Shelley adapts " '**The day we** come to a place we have long heard and read of, is an era in our lives; from that moment the very name calls up a picture,' " from Rogers's essay "Foreign Travel," to describe **Prague** (*R* 2.9; Rogers 172). She also quotes "Amalfi" to describe southern Italy: " '**In all her** wildness, all her majesty, / As in that elder time, ere man was made' " (*R* 2.280; Rogers lines 22–23). Shelley also quotes "The Compagna of Florence" to describe Florentine history: "**For deeds of violence** / Done in broad day; and more than half redeemed / By many a great and generous sacrifice of self to others," continuing "**the unpledged bowl**, / The stab of the stiletto" (*R* 2.185; Rogers lines 255–259). Shelley quotes "**Venice**" to describe the city: it "[H]**as floated down**, amid a thousand wrecks / Uninjured, from the Old World to the New" (*R* 2.83; Rogers lines 131–132). Shelley also quotes accurately from Rogers's "Florence" to describe the **Uffizi**'s "glorious **Medicean** monuments": "**Where the gigantic** shapes of Night and Day, / Turned into stone, rest everlastingly; / Yet still are breathing" (*R* 2.154; Rogers lines 54–56).

Ithaca, King of: See **Ulysses**.

J

Jack of the Wynd: Soldier who ambushes **Richard of York** near **Yeovil**.

Jackson: Farmer for whom **Maurice** leaves the **Smithsons** in "**Maurice**."

Jacobins: Political group associated with the **French Revolution**. Shelley relates how numerous **Italian** nobles lost their titles 1797, partly due to Jacobins' destruction of archives (*R* 2.114).

Jaén: Andalusian city and province fifty miles northwest of **Granada**. **Hernan De Faro** grows up in **Alcala** there (*PW* 1.205). **Boabdil el Chico** invades Christian country near Jaén (*PW* 1.216).

Jaggernaut: Title given to Hindu god **Vishnou**. When worshippers pulled the god's idol along in religious processions, they would become so excited as to be crushed under its wheels; the Jaggernaut image thus suggests incredible sacrifice and blind devotion. **Adrian** compares plague to the Jaggernaut procession: " 'I have hung on the wheel of the chariot of plague; but she drags me along with it, while, like Jaggernaut, she proceeds crushing out the being of all who strew the high road of life' " (*LM* 396–397).

Jamaica: Island in the **West Indies**. British forces captured it from **Spain** 1655. A British colony in Shelley's day, it remains a British Commonwealth member (Kinder 1.267). **Horace Neville** suggests that **Eton**'s fagging system is worse than Jamaican slavery (*Mourner* 86).

James: Guard whom a thunderstorm frightens in *Perkin Warbeck*. Minor *Falkner* character who recalls **Alithea Neville**'s kindness.

James I (1566–1625): James VI of Scotland inherited England's throne 1603 and thus established the **Stuart** line in England. This Protestant king tried to unite his two kingdoms, but questioning of his "divine right" led to constant political struggles during his reign. Shelley asserts "the former experiences of **Alcibiades** or even of the emasculated **Steeny** of James I might have caused **Sheridan** to have refused to tread over again the same path of dazzling but fleeting brilliancy" (*RD* 49). Shelley visited **Heidelberg Castle**, built for James's daughter, **Princess Elizabeth** (*R* 1.35).

James III (1452–1488): King of Scotland 1460–1488 and **James IV**'s father. **Desmond** mentions James III's death to **John Digby** (*PW* 2.117). Shelley characterizes him as "a weak, unhappy man" who distrusts all princes, including his son, and whose reign was full of rebellion (*PW* 2.184).

James IV (1473–1513): Scotland's king, 1488–1513. He broke the peace with England 1495 by invading it in support of **Perkin Warbeck**. He married Margaret Tudor, English **Henry VII**'s eldest daughter, 1503 (*DNB*). He supports **Richard of York** in *Perkin Warbeck*.

James, Sir: See **Tirrel**.

Jameson, Anna Brownell (1794–1860): British novelist and travel writer; Shelley spells her name **Jamieson**. Shelley recommends her writing in "**Review of** *The Loves of the Poets*" and "**Review of** *The English in Italy*." Jameson learned from Maria Jane Jewsbury that Shelley was "bewitching" (*Journals* 512; Seymour 417). Shelley and Jameson met April 1841 (*Letters* 3.12, 3.15). Shelley approves of **Titian**'s *Cristo della Moneta*, which Jameson "eulogizes with much taste and judgment" in *Sketches of Art, Literature and Character* (1837) (*R* 1.243; Jameson 358).

Jamieson, Mrs.: See **Jameson**.

Janicular Hill: Also called **Janiculum**, **Roman** hill west of the **Tiber**. Shelley entered Rome via Janiculum April 1843 and mentions **Campidoglio**'s view of it (*R* 2.214, 2.227).

Janiculum: See **Janicular Hill**.

Janisaries: See **Janizaries**.

Janizaries: **Turkish** infantry body begun in the **Ottoman Empire** during Sultan Osman I's reign (1299–1326); Shelley spells it **Janisaries**. They formed the Sultan's bodyguard, were forbidden to marry, and were greatly feared as bloodthirsty and merciless warriors. Their military strength lent them increasing political power, until Sultan Mahmoud II dissolved them during a bloody 1826 massacre (Coufopoulos 121). **Lionel Verney** records "defenceless citizens" suffer through Janizaries' barbarity and also details some Janizaries' foiled but defiant escape attempt from **Constantinople** (*LM* 189, 191).

Janus: **Roman** god representing beginnings, often depicted with two faces looking to past and future. Janus's gateway in Rome's **Forum** stayed open in wartime and closed in peacetime (Tripp 328). Shelley visited Janus's Arch in March 1819 (*Journals* 253). **Lionel Verney** is pleased to return to **Windsor**, noting "peace through all the world; the temple of Universal Janus was shut" (*LM* 219). Burying the **Countess of Windsor**, Verney feels "Janus veiled his retrospective face; that which gazed on future generations had long lost its faculty" (*LM* 416). At *The Last Man*'s close, Verney marks time's passage by carving the date 2100 on a stone at **St. Peter's**, responding to an ancient tradition that marked the beginning of another year in peacetime: "the **Sovereign Pontiff** was used to go in solemn pomp, and mark the renewal of the year by driving a nail in" Janus's gate (*LM* 467). See **Browne**.

Japanese Palace: Augustus II's summer residence on the **Elbe**'s right bank in **New Markt** of **Dresden**, now a museum (*MCON* 447). Shelley was disappointed by the porcelain collection she saw there July 1842 (*R* 1.253).

Jehovah: See **Bible**.

Jena: Large **German** town on the **Saale**, eleven miles southeast of **Weimar** and center for German Romanticism in the late 18th century. **Lord Lodore** visits **Francis Derham**, who is studying modern languages at a university there, perhaps Friedrich-Schiller University (founded 1548) (*L* 1.84).

Jenzenstein, John II of (1348–1400): Also spelled Jenstein, third **archbishop of Prague**. Shelley refers to him as **John of Genzstein** when recounting the execution of **St. John Nepomuk**, who became John II's secretary 1374 (*R* 2.5). Shelley's reference to him as **Patriarch of Alexandria** is puzzling, since John II moved to **Rome**.

Jerusalem: Ancient city in the Middle East, Israel's capital since 1950, and principal holy place of Christianity, Islam, and Judaism. **Ludovico Mondolfo** plans to "fight and die beneath" Jerusalem's walls (*HM* 330–331).

Jervis, Miss: **Rupert Falkner** hires Miss Jervis as **Elizabeth Falkner**'s governess in *Falkner*. Shelley perhaps modeled Jervis on her own governess, Miss Maria Smith, "to whom [Shelley] was devoted" (Sunstein 35).

Jesuits, Church of: Church of Il Gesù in **Rome** (Moskal 352). Shelley attended mass there in April 1843 (*R* 2.232).

Joachim: According to **apocryphal** book Gospel of James, Joachim was St. Anne's husband and the Virgin **Mary**'s father (Elliott 57–60). **Beatrice** reads and interprets Joachim's writings (*V* 2.42).

Job: In this **biblical** book, God permits **Satan** to test loyal servant Job's faith by taking his wealth and lands away and finally killing all his family. Job falters but never denounces God. **Matilda** quotes Job immediately following her father's death: "**Where is now** my hope? For my hope who shall see it? They shall go down together to the bars of the pit, when our rest is in the dust" (*M* 185; Job 17.15–16). Shelley quotes Job to describe **Lady Isabel Mondolfo**, who seems "on the point of entering upon that only repose 'where the wicked cease from troubling and the weary are at rest'" (*HM* 308; Job 3.17).

Johanko von Pomuk: See **St. John Nepomuk**.

John Adams: Vessel upon which **Gerard Neville** embarks for **America**; bad weather forces its return to **Liverpool** (*F* 282).

John, Archduke (1782–1859): **Habsburg** prince of **Austria** who led **Tyrolese** unsuccessfully against **Napoleon** 1810 (*R* 2.44, 2.51; Moskal 250; McLynn 443; Connelly 267).

Johnson, Dr. Samuel (1709–1784): English writer renowned for his *Dictionary of the English Language* (1755). Shelley attributes the idea that "the aim of every man's desire" is to reach **Italy** or **Rome** to Johnson; Moskal points to his reported conversation to General Paoli in James Boswell's *Life of Johnson* (1791), which Shelley read in May 1820, as the source (*R* 2.212; Moskal 340; *Journals* 318-319).

Jonson, Ben (1572–1637): Prolific British playwright and poet who wrote masques for **James I**'s court and was a leading literary figure of his day. He is best known for comedies, such as *Volpone* (1605); Shelley read many of his works 1817–21 (*Journals* 655–656). As an epigraph to *Perkin Warbeck*'s chapter in which **Richard of York** enters England to view scenes of destruction left by the Scottish army, Shelley quotes from a speech that Catiline makes in Jonson's *Catiline His Conspiracy* (1611), which Shelley read 1817 and 1820: "'**Methinks I see** Death and the Furies waiting / What we will do, and all the Heaven at leisure / For the great spectacle. Draw then your swords!'" (*Journals* 180, 311–312; *PW* 2.291; Jonson 5.5.45–47). Shelley quotes from *The Sad Shepherd* (1640), which she read August 1819, as an epigraph to the chapter in which the **Villiers**es live apart to avoid bailiffs: "*Marian*. **Could you so** long be absent? / *Robin*. What a week? / Was that so long? / *Marian*. How long are lovers' weeks, / Do you think, Robin, when they are asunder? / Are they not pris'ners' years?" (*Journals* 656; *L* 3.12; Jonson 1.6.15–18). Shelley recorded her driver's avarice en route from **Venice** to **Florence** 1842 and gives the anecdote "'**Tell him his soul** lives in an alley,' said Ben Jonson, when **Charles I.** [sic] sent him a niggard gift'" (*R* 2.132). Charles I "neglected" Jonson "during the early years of his reign," but this anecdote's source has not been traced (Moskal 298).

Joseph: Biblical figure whose brothers sold him into slavery in **Egypt**, where he became a successful official (Genesis 37–50). **Maurice** cries over Joseph's distress at being sold (*Maurice* 75). Also biblical husband of **Mary** (Matthew 1.16). Shelley admired **Raphael**'s *Madonna di San Sisto*, in which "Madonna is not the lowly wife of Joseph the carpenter" (*R* 1.236).

Joseph II (1741–1790): Austrian ruler who became Holy Roman Emperor in 1765 and instituted educational and military reform, abolished serfdom, and emancipated Jews. Shelley compares **Ferdinand IV** to Joseph for planning legal reform (*R* 2.164).

Josephine [Marie-Josèphe Tascher de la Pagerie] (1763–1814): **Napoleon**'s first wife and **France**'s empress. She met and married Napoleon 1785; he divorced her 1809 for failing to bear a son. In August 1914, Shelley met an old woman in **Guignes** who talked about Josephine traveling through the town (*H* 17). Shelley

Jove

viewed portraits of Josephine in **Berlin**'s Royal **Palace** July 1842 (*R* 1.225–226).

Jove: **Roman** name for **Jupiter**; **Zeus** is the **Greek** name. This mythological god's weapon was the thunderbolt; he controlled weather and commanded all the gods (Tripp 332–333). **Midas** declares his golden powers rank him with gods, since "Great Jove / Transcends me but by lightning," but he later humbly acknowledges Jove's supremacy over "the grass, the sky, the trees, the flowers" (*Midas* 129, 149). **Lionel Verney** justifies the intention of plague survivors to head south, where "Jove has showered forth the contents of **Amalthea**'s horn, and the earth is a garden" (*LM* 323). Jove is **Proserpine**'s father (Shelley mixes the Roman and Greek names). **Ceres** appeals to him for mercy when she learns of Proserpine's confinement to **Tartarus**: "The Thunderer frowned, & heaven shook with dread" (*P* 69). Ceres defies Jove's rule, and he relents somewhat by dividing Proserpine's existence between the realms of hell and earth.

Jovius, Paul: See **Giovio**.

Julian Alps: Alps section in northwest Slovenia that Shelley saw from **Fondamenti Nuovi** of **Venice** September 1842 (*R* 2.100).

***Julian and Maddalo; a Conversation*:** Dialogic poem between Julian and Maddalo (representative, perhaps, of himself and **Byron**, respectively) **PBS** composed 1818–1819, first published 1824 (White 2.40–41, 2.574; Crook 2). Shelley quotes lines that Maddalo speaks to Julian about the happy child before them as an epigraph to *Lodore*'s chapter in which **Lord Lodore** decides to leave **America**: "**It is our will** / That thus enchains us to permitted ill" (*L* 1.234; PBS lines 170–171). Shelley frequently passed San Servolo, the **Venice** madhouse believed to be the original of " '**A windowless, deformed**, and dreary pile' " in PBS's poem (*R* 2.99; PBS line 101). Describing **Leghorn**'s view of the **Ligurian Alps**, Shelley quotes a passage beginning " '**Towards the North** appeared' " (*R* 2.213; PBS lines 68–70).

Juliet: Duke of L——'s daughter in *The Last Man*. **Horace Neville**'s younger cousin in "**The Mourner**."

Julius: One of the **Cecil** children in *Falkner*.

Julius II, Pope (1453–1513): Pope 1503–13, renowned for patronage of **Michelangelo** and **Raphael** (Kelly 256). Praising Raphael, Shelley specifically mentions his **Vatican** frescoes, which Julius ordered c. 1508–17 (*R* 2.219).

***Julius Caesar*:** **Shakespeare**'s tragedy, produced 1599 and published 1623. Drawing on historical accounts, including **Plutarch**'s, Shakespeare's drama details the conspiracy led by **Marcus Brutus** that culminated in **Julius Caesar**'s death (Plutarch, *Lives* 2.530–581). Shelley read it April 1819 (*Journals* 256). As he records the eagerness of plague survivors to leave **Paris**, **Lionel Verney** quotes conspirator Casca's line remarking strange events occurring the night before the planned attack in Shakespeare's play: "dire visions and evil auguries, if such things were, thickened around us, so that in vain might men say—'**These are their** reasons, they are natural' " (*LM* 394–95; Shakespeare 1.3.28–32).

Juliet: See *Romeo and Juliet*.

Juno: **Roman** goddess of marriage and childbirth (Tripp 332). Shelley described her beautiful guide at **Capri** as "Juno-looking" (*R* 2.271).

Jupiter: **Roman** name (meaning "Heavenly father") for **Zeus** (Tripp 332). **Valerius** exclaims to Jupiter: " 'thou who has beheld so many triumphs, still may thy temples exist, still may the victims be led to thy altars' " (*Val* 334). **Lionel Verney** characterizes **Paris**'s religious leader "as a patriarch, a prophet, nay a deity; such as of old among the post-diluvians were Jupiter the conqueror" (*LM* 386).

Jupiter Stator: Three "white marble" columns believed in Shelley's day to belong to the remains of **Jupiter**'s temple in **Rome**'s **Forum**, now believed to be from **Castor** and **Pollux**'s temple (*MROM* 44; Crook 2). **Lionel Verney** embraces "vast columns of the temple of Jupiter Stator" (*LM* 461).

Jura: Mountain range along **France**'s border with **Switzerland**. The Shelleys "exchanged the view of **Mont Blanc** and her snowy [points] for the dark frowning Jura" in **Geneva** 1816 (*Letters* 1.20). **Belrive** and Geneva, **Victor Frankenstein**'s native towns, are at the Jura's base; Victor characterizes the Jura as "black," in opposition to the snowy **Alps** (*Fr1* 70, 103, 217; *Fr3* 45, 72, 161). Plague survivors travel through the Jura (*LM* 396, 416). Shelley was disappointed that weather rendered the Jura unobservable 1840 (*R* 1.141).

K

K——: See **Knox**.

Kabale und Liebe: See **Schiller**.

Kakaboulia: Greek for "Evil counsel," "ferocious and cruel" inhabitants of southern Greece's inner **Maina** region, renowned for blood feuds, piracy, and robbery; Shelley's variant is **Kakovougnis** (*MGRE* 269, 270). **Katusthius Ziani** rescues **Dmitri** " 'from the savage Kakovougnis of **Boularias**' " (*EE* 102). Shelley describes Kakaboulia as "a dark suspicious race, of squat and stunted form" (*EE* 107). **Cyril Ziani** rescues future wife **Zella** when Kakaboulians siege **Camaraz**'s **Kardymla** fortress (*EE* 107).

Kakovougnis: See **Kakaboulia**.

Kalamas: River above which **Zitza** stands in northern **Epirus**; Shelley spells it **Calamas**. Shelley notes "the Calamas in the depth of the vale gives life" (*EE* 111).

Kamnitz: Stream joining the **Elbe** after flowing through **Saxon Switzerland** (*MCON* 458). Shelley saw it near **Herrnskretschen** August 1842 (*R* 1.274).

Karazza: Admiral of **Greece**'s marine and naval forces in **Constantinople** in *The Last Man*.

Kardamyla: Small coastal village in **Greece**'s southern **Maina** region, called Cardamyle in ancient times and now Skardamula. **Cyril Ziani** rescues future bride **Zella** from **Kakaboulia** besiegement in Kardamyla, which remains **Camaraz**'s home (*EE* 107). Camaraz and Cyril leave Kardamyla to search for **Constans Ziani** (*EE* 110, 115).

Karlsbad: German name (which Shelley spells **Carlsbad**) for Karlovy Vary, Czech city about sixty miles northwest of **Prague**; renowned for mineral springs, it was extremely popular during Shelley's time (*BCSR* 589–

591; *SIDTC* 552). Shelley found Karlsbad's water salty July 1842 (*R* 1.185).

Kashmir: North **Indian** (now partly Pakistani) region between Afghanistan and **China**; Shelley spells it **Cashmere**. **Lionel Verney** imagines "the voice of lamentation" filling Kashmir's valley (*LM* 225, 234).

Keating, James: Prior or **Abbot of Kilmainham** and **Richard of York**'s **Irish** supporter in *Perkin Warbeck*.

Keats, John (1795–1821): British Romantic poet respected for lyrical odes and sonnets. **PBS** met Keats February 1817 (White 1.500, 1.504–505). Though they never became close friends, PBS wrote *Adonais* (1821) in Keats's honor immediately after Keats's premature death (*Journals* 150). Shelley first met Keats February 1817, and he called on her in **London** several times 1817 (*Journals* 162, 185). PBS invited Keats to join them at **Pisa** 1820, and Keats consented, but his February 1821 death prevented their reunion. The Shelleys read and enjoyed Keats's 1820 volume of poems (*Journals* 335–336). Shelley wrote to **Leigh Hunt** April 1821: "We have been shocked to hear of Keats' death—and sorry that it was in no way permitted us to be of any use to him since his arrival in **Italy**" (*Letters* 1.189). PBS was buried in the same **Roman** cemetery as Keats and, after PBS's death, Shelley noted "Poor Keats I often think of him now" (*Letters* 1.400). **Lionel Verney** welcomes spring and sees "the tender growth of leaves—'**Lifts its sweet** head into the air, and feeds / A silent space with ever sprouting green,'" lines Shelley takes from Keats's "Sleep and Poetry" (1817); she had specifically requested Keats's volume containing this text from his publisher, **Ollier**, November 1825 (*LM* 274; Keats lines 248–251; *Letters* 1.504). See Robert Gittings's *John Keats* (1968).

***Keepsake*:** Successful British literary annual published 1828–57; it collected short stories, poems, and engravings designed to appeal to a female, middle-class readership. Shelley published most of her short stories and poems in it.

Kennedy, Lady Jane: Earl of Cassils's daughter and **James IV**'s mistress in *Perkin Warbeck*.

Kennington: **London** district south of the **Thames**, two miles southwest of the city's center. **Sarah Derham** lives there (*L* 2.290, 2.294).

Kent: Large southeastern English county closest to **France**. Shelley passed through Kent before crossing to **Europe** 1814 and 1818. **Lord Audley** is from Kent, and **Sir John Peachy** is Kent's sheriff; he successfully leads troops against **Richard of York**'s supporters (*PW* 2.152, 2.164). Lord Audley later unsuccessfully leads **Cornish** insurgents toward Kent (*PW* 2.266). [*L* 3.238].

Kenwood: Wooded area, now garden and grounds, of Kenwood house, Hampstead Lane, **London** (Weinreb 428). **Desmond**, **Richard of York**, and **Monina De Faro** hide in **Caen Wood** (Shelley's spelling) after escaping the **Tower** (*PW* 2.120).

Kern: Irish soldiers or troops (*OED*). **Desmond** and **Keating** plan to support **Richard of York** with "our Irish Kern" (*PW* 3.29).

Kerry, Knight of: Geraldine warrior who accompanies **Desmond** from **Ballahourah** to **Mallow** (*PW* 1.302). Sir Maurice le White was the Kerry knight allied with Desmond then; Kerry is now a southwestern **Irish** county (Arthurson 106).

Kesan: Small town at **Hebrus** Plain's eastern end in western **Turkey**; Shelley spells it **Kishan**. Lionel Verney first joins the **Greek** army there (*LM* 175). **Raymond** and Verney meet the army at Kesan, and women and children remain there (*LM* 177–178).

Khiyat Hanch: Stream feeding into **Golden Horn's** northwest end at a point called **Sweet Waters**; Shelley terms it **Kyat Kbanah** (Coufopoulos 149). **Lionel Verney** remarks upon the **Greek** army's blockade of **Constantinople** "from the river Kyat Kbanah, near the Sweet Waters, to the Tower of **Marmora**" (*LM* 183).

Kilbarry: Southwest **Waterford** district. **Richard of York's** opponents dam the river flowing from Kilbarry into the **Suir** to cut off the **Yorkist** camp (*PW* 3.40, 3.51).

Kildare, Earl of (d. 1513): Gerald Fitzgerald, eighth Earl of Kildare, arrested and imprisoned in the **Tower** 1494 for supporting **Yorkists** in **Ireland**, though he denied the allegations. **Henry VII** pardoned and appointed him Lord Deputy 1496 (*DNB*). **Richard of York** supporter in *Perkin Warbeck*.

Killarney: Irish town forty-five miles northwest of **Cork**. **Lionel Verney**, **Idris**, and **Perdita** stay there several weeks (*LM* 156).

Killing of Goliath by David: See **Titian**.

Kilmainham, Abbot of: See **Keating**.

Kilmainham, Prior of: See **Keating**.

Kilnemullagh: See **Buttevant**.

King John: Shakespeare's historical drama, written 1596–97 and first published 1623; Shelley read it 1819 and 1820 (*Journals* 256, 306). As an epigraph to *Perkin Warbeck's* chapter in which **Meiler Trangmar** befriends **Richard of York**, Shelley quotes a line **Constance** addresses to Shakespeare's King John: "To England if you will!" (*PW* 1.241; Shakespeare 3.4.68). As a second epigraph to the chapter in which Richard meets **Jane Shore**, Shelley quotes Shakespeare's Earl of Salisbury's speech: " 'Oh, it grieves my soul / That I must draw this metal from my side / To be a widow-maker' " (*PW* 2.130; Shakespeare 5.2.15–17). Shelley notes **Elizabeth Falkner's** enjoyment of nature with lines adapted from Shakespeare's drama: "it is the property of love to enhance all our enjoyments, 'to paint the lily, and add a perfume to the rose' " (*F* 157; Shakespeare 4.2.11–12).

King Log: Shelley twice refers to King Log in discussing a **German** driver and **Florentines**; Moskal asserts that Shelley alludes to Aesop's fable, "The Frogs Desiring a King," in which foolish frogs change their inactive king (a log) for a devouring stork (*R* 1.48, 2.185; Moskal 100; Crook 2).

King's Theatre: **London** Haymarket theater that was extremely fashionable during the 1820s and 1830s; principally opera was performed there (Leigh 421). After the original 1705 building burned 1789, it was rebuilt with a "handsome" exterior completed 1818–19; it was renamed the Opera House after Queen Victoria's 1837 accession to the throne (Leigh 241; Cunningham 607). Shelley often attended opera performances there; she asked **Payne**'s assistance in obtaining "an Opera box" several times 1829, complaining to him May 1831 that "the *tariffe* they put on the boxes" prevented her more frequent attendance (*Letters* 2.71, 2.73, 2.136). **Lord** and **Lady Lodore** make their first public appearance there after marrying; "Lord Lodore had always rented a box" (*L* 1.114). **Ethel Villiers** attends an opera there and, on another occasion, sees her mother there (*L* 2.13, 2.213).

Kirkup, Mr. Seymour Stocker (1788–1880): British artist who settled in **Italy**, where he attended **PBS**'s funeral; Kirkup lived in **Florence** and became **Edward John Trelawny**'s friend (White 2.383). 21 July 1840, he drew **Giotto**'s portrait of **Dante**, which Shelley finds "excellent" (*DNB*; *R* 2.158).

Kirwin: Irish magistrate who defends **Victor Frankenstein** in the murder case against him in *Frankenstein*; the case is dropped.

Kishan: See **Kesan**.

Kissingen: German resort town on the **Saale**, thirty miles southeast of **Fulda**, famous for mineral springs. Shelley stayed at Kissingen about a month in 1842 and sought the cure in **Pandur**, **Ragozzi**, and **Max Brunnen** springs; she disliked the restricted diet and the poor condition of her living quarters (*Letters* 3.32). She describes her initial view and relates her activities there (*R* 1.179). [*R* 1.179–198, 2.10, 2.27].

Kleine Seite: "Little Quarter" **Prague** section dating from 1257 (Soukup 23). Shelley crossed Charles Bridge, connecting Kleine Seite with Prague, whereon stands **St. John Nepomuk** statue (*R* 2.4). She saw **Wallenstein**'s castle there September 1842 (*R* 2.6).

Kleine Winterberg: Steep hill in **Saxon Switzerland** near **Kuhstall** (*MCON* 458). Delays in **Schandau** "obliged [Shelley] to give up the idea of viewing" Kleine Winterberg in August 1842 (*R* 1.269).

Klephts: Greek for "robbers," used in Shelley's day in reference to Greek and **Albanian** patriot bands resisting **Turkish** rule. **Dmitri** is **Korvo**'s "famous Klepht" (*EE* 100, 102, 112).

Knight of the Glen: In *Perkin Warbeck*, **Geraldine** warrior who accompanies **Desmond** from **Ballahourah** to **Mallow**.

Knights of Malta: Brotherhood founded in **Jerusalem** in the 11th century; it subsequently relocated to Rhodes before obtaining **Malta** 1530. Shelley notes **Gabriel Serbelloni** was a Knight (*R* 1.80).

Knowing Traveller: See **Sterne**.

Knox, Alexander Andrew (1818–1891): PFS's **Cambridge** classmate; he was an extrovert, a writer, and Shelley's favorite of her son's acquaintances (Sunstein 356). He married **Charles Clairmont**'s daughter, Clari, 1849 (*Journals* 572). Knox accompanied Shelley and PFS to **Europe** 1840; Shelley describes their travels, referring to Knox as **K——** (*R* 1.161, 1.168). Shelley footnotes a stanza beginning " '**Thy mountain** torrent and thy narrow vale' " from "Rabenau" in Knox's *Giotto and Francesca and other Poems* (1842); the passage describes the " '**valley of beauty**, sunny **Rabenau**' " (*R* 1.240; Knox lines 9–16, 24). Shelley planned to send **Leigh Hunt** a copy of Knox's text (Moskal 201; *Letters* 3.39). She refers to Knox repeatedly in her *Letters*.

Koblentz: See **Coblentz**.

Kochheim: See **Cochem**.

Kock, Charles-Paul de (1793–1871): Prolific and popular **French** novelist; some of Shelley's contemporaries considered his works risqué. In October 1835, Shelley recorded **Peacock**'s eldest daughter Mary Ellen reading "Paul de Kock's novels in all innocence" (*Letters* 2.258). De Kock's *Le Barbier de Paris* [*The Barber of Paris*] (1827) explores Blanche and Urbain's idyllic and ultimately tragic love. Shelley quotes from *Barbier*, "**Les deserts sont faits** pour les amants, mais l'amour ne se fait pas aux deserts," as an epigraph to the *Lodore* chapter in which **Whitelock** declares love for **Ethel Villiers**; the line translates to "deserts are made for lovers, but love is not made in deserts" (*L* 1.45).

Köln: See **Cologne**.

Korvo: Small village on **Mount Trebucci** in southern **Albania**. **Dmitri** is native to Korvo (*EE* 100, 103). **Camaraz** and **Cyril Ziani** trace Dmitri there (*EE* 112).

Krempe: Victor Frankenstein's natural philosophy professor at **Ingolstadt** University (*Fr1* 49–50; *Fr3* 49). His name perhaps comes from Carl Moritz's 1783 travel book *Reisen eines Deutschen in England im Jahr 1782* (1783), or *Travels, Chiefly on Foot, through Several Parts of England in 1782* (1795), which Shelley read 1816 (Sunstein 430; *Journals* 664).

Kuhstall: "Cow stall," natural rock arch southeast of **Dresden** in **Saxon Switzerland**, six miles from **Schandau** (*MCON* 458). Delays in Schandau prevented Shelley visiting it August 1842 (*R* 1.267–269).

Kurhaus: Main building near springs in resort towns frequented as health spas. **Baden-Baden**'s Kurhaus, which Weinbrenner built 1821–24, was Baden's "hub of fashionable life" (*BGER* 68). It housed the casino where Shelley observed gamblers play *Rouge* *et Noire* (*R* 1.37). In July 1842, Shelley stayed at **Kissingen**'s Kurhaus, which Max Littmann designed 1827 (*BGER* 165; *R* 1.180).

Kursaal: See **Kurhaus** and **Fulda, Prince-Bishops of.**

Kyat Kbanah: See **Khiyat Haneh**.

L

L——, Duke of: **Juliet**'s father in *The Last Man*.

***L'Hote, Madame*:** A **French** female innkeeper. Shelley mentions several she met during her travels (*Journals* 8–11; *H* 14; *R* 1.146).

l'Ouverture, François Dominique Toussaint (d. 1803): Ex-slave who led a Haitian revolt and then ruled Santo Domingo; **Napoleon** captured and imprisoned him (Moskal 98). Shelley lists his death as one of Napoleon's worst crimes (*R* 1.44).

***La Battaglia di Benevento*:** See **Guerazzi**.

La Fontaine, Jean de (1621–1695): **French** fabulist author of *Contes et Nouvelles en vers* [*Tales and Stories in Verse*] (1665). His *Fables choisies mises en vers* [*Selected Fables in Verse*] (1688) remains an outstanding example of his lively and original versification. Shelley wrote La Fontaine's biography for *French Lives*. She respects his works' "simple graces of expression and imagination," while acknowledging his dramas are below mediocrity (*FL* 1.150, 1.152). Shelley admires La Fontaine's heroic verse and his fables' "universal and ingenuous moral, picturesque simplicity, and easy graceful negligence," excusing his licentiousness as not intended to corrupt (*FL* 1.179).

La Fortune: "Very excellent" inn in **Offenberg** run by a man who had formerly lived in England; Shelley dined there July 1840 (*R* 1.42).

La Maurienne: Valley running to **Mount Cenis** at the **Alps**'s base in southeastern **France**. Plague survivors arrive there (*LM* 428). Shelley locates "Saint Jean le Maurienne" between **Chablais** and Mount Cenis (*R* 2.45).

La Motte Fouqué, Baron Friedrich Heinrich Karl (1777–1843): **German** Romantic writer renowned for *Undine, eine Erzählung* (1811), which

Shelley read in English in October 1819 (*Journals* 299). She also read his *Sintram und seine Gefährten* [*Sintram and his Companions*] (1814) in December 1820 (*Journals* 344). Shelley alludes to his *Der Zaubbering* [*The Magic Ring*] (1813) when presenting **Germany** as mysterious (*R* 1.175).

La Noue, Monsieur de: Early-19th-century **French** Secretary of Legation, according to Shelley, who mentions his criticism of **Niccolini**'s "Sicilian Vespers" (*R* 2.204).

La Place, Pierre Simon [Marquis de] (1749–1827): French mathematician and astronomer renowned for a "hypothesis of the nebular origin of the solar system" (Paley 476). **PBS** read La Place's *Exposition du Système du Monde* (1796), which J. Pond translated into English as *The System of the World* (1809) 1813 (Holmes 220). **Lionel Verney** finds **Merrival** to be as "learned as La Place" (*LM* 289).

La Rocca: Scaliger "castle" at **Riva** on **Lago di Garda**; one of Shelley's companions sketched it in September 1842 (*R* 2.69; Moskal 264).

La Rochefoucauld, Francois de Marsillac, Duc de (1613–1680): **French** author and courtier. His reputation rests upon *Réflexions, ou sentences et maximes morales* [*Reflections, or Moral Sentences and Maxims*] (1665), a collection of brief, lucid observations about human character. Shelley quoted one of La Rochefoucauld's maxims in a letter October 1825, evidence of familiarity with them by that time (*Letters* 1.503). She wrote La Rochefoucauld's biography for *French Lives*, describing La Rochefoucauld as "leader of a party, a soldier, a man of gallantry, and of fashion" and asserting that his literary reputation rests upon "the experience of a long life, spent for the most part in the very nucleus of the intrigues of party and the artifices of a court, reduced into sententious maxims, [that] affords food for curiosity, while it flatters our idleness" (*FL* 1.63).

La Scala: **Milan** theater considered **Europe**'s "most beautiful Opera-house" (*STIE* 44). Built 1776–78, La Scala is northwest of the **Duomo** (*MIIT* 141, 144). Shelley attended a performance of *Templario* there September 1840 (*R* 1.111).

La Spezia: Town and gulf on **Italy**'s northeast coast forty-five miles southeast of **Genoa**. The Shelleys moved into **Casa Magni** there April 1822 (*Journals* 409–410). Shelley describes her anxious watch of the Gulf of Spezia when the boat **PBS** and **Edward Williams** sailed disappeared July 1822 (*Journals* 415; *Ch* 145). Part of the plan to take **Lucca** from **Castruccio** involves **King Robert** of **Naples**'s soldiers, who would disembark in the gulf (*V* 3.198).

La Valais: Swiss **Alpine** region southeast of **Lake Geneva**. Henry Clerval compares the **Rhine**'s "fairy-land" beauty to La Valais's mountains, preferring the former (*Fr1* 182; *Fr3* 133).

La Valle: According to *Valperga*, fortified **Apennine** village that **Castruccio** takes when expanding his territory to **Aquobuono**, **Valdinera**, and castles beyond **Magra** (*V* 1.174).

La Verna Convent: Central **Italian** convent near **Vallombrosa**, fourteen miles from **Calmaldoli Convent**; Shelley spells it **Laverna** and mentions it in *Rambles* (*STIE* 77; *R* 2.139).

"La Vida es Sueño": Shelley's poem. Palacio published a three-stanza 1833 version, **"Stanzas: The Tide of Time Was at my Feet"** in 1969 (Palacio 634). In 1953, Nitchie published an 1834 version with two additional sextets, which importantly revise the earlier version (in which the speaker is left despairing in a desolate landscape) by suggesting that dreams can alleviate the burden of the present, albeit only momentarily; the title, "Life is a Dream," echoes that of **Calderón's** 1635 drama (Nitchie 233–234). In the poem, the speaker recounts misery at the tide's ebbing; "a dream of joy" provides only transitory relief before the flood begins and the speaker is again alone on the sand (line 22).

Lablache, Luigi (1794–1858): Italian bass who performed regularly in **Paris** and **London** and was Queen Victoria's singing instructor (Rosenthal 269). Shelley mentions that **Marini** is esteemed "next to Lablache" in singing ability, but she disagrees: "the distance is far between" (*R* 1.107).

Lackland: Ruler without land (*OED*). **Richard of York** is "Prince Lackland" (*PW* 2.216, 2.232, 2.317).

Lacon: Courtier in *Midas*.

Lagny, Emilie de: Queen Margaret of **Navarre**'s maid of honor in "The False Rhyme."

Lagny, Sire Enguerrard de: Emilie de **Lagny**'s husband in "The False Rhyme."

Lago di Garda: Northern **Italian** lake (also called **Benacus**) between **Verona** and **Brescia** (*R* 2.69, 2.72). Shelley's desire to see it dictated her September 1842 route from **Germany** to Italy; she gives **Dante**'s description of it (*R* 2.29, 2.35, 2.68). From **Riva**, Shelley traveled across it by steamboat to **Lasise** (*R* 2.72). See *Inferno*.

Lago di Massaciucuoli: Italian lake seven miles west of **Lucca**; Shelley spells it **Macciucoli**. **Castruccio** and **Euthanasia** view it (*V* 3.254).

Lago Maggiore: Large **Alpine** lake on **Italian-Swiss** border; location of **Isola Bella** and **Isola Madre**. Shelley visited it September 1840 (*R* 1.128–131).

Lago Scuro: **Italian** lake adjacent to the **Po**, ten miles north of **Ferrarra**. When the Shelleys traveled to Ferrarra November 1818, they probably passed it (*Journals* 235). Troops pass Lago Scuro in approaching Ferrarra from the north (*V* 2.67).

Laguna: Body of water between **Venice** and mainland **Italy**. In Shelley's time, travelers had to go by boat across it from **Fusina** to Venice. **Castruccio** and **Francesco de Guinigi** board a gondola on Laguna's shore (*V* 1.59). **Lionel Verney**, **Adrian**, and **Clara** cross the Laguna and enter Venice's **Grand Canal**; they sail out across it on their disastrous attempt to reach **Greece** (*LM* 438, 440).

Lalayne, Sir Roderick de: Shelley's *Perkin Warbeck* character based on Rodigue de Lalaing, illegitimate son of **Charles the Rash**'s chamberlain; the Lalaings (**Flemish** family) served **Margaret of Burgundy** during the 1470s, and Rodigue fought as **Maximilian I**'s military commander. Maximilian paid him and gave him feudal rights for supporting **Perkin Warbeck** (Arthurson 108).

Lalla Rookh: An Oriental Romance: **Moore**'s 1817 best-seller, four lengthy narrative poems connected by a prose tale. Shelley read it June 1817 (*Journals* 172). She quotes lines describing Hinda's secret love for her father's enemy, Gheber Hafed, from "The Fire-Worshippers" as an epigraph to *Lodore*'s chapter introducing the **Villiers**es happiness at **Longfield**: "**The pure, the open**, prosperous love, / That pledged on earth, and sealed above, / Grows in the world's approving eyes, / In friendship's smile and home's caress, / Collecting all the heart's sweet ties / Into one knot of happiness" (*L* 2.229; Moore 447). Shelley also uses a stanza Nourmahal sings to her husband Selim in a successful attempt to regain his love in "The Light of the Haram" as an epigraph to the chapter in which Shelley details the Villierses' love: "**There's a bliss** beyond all that the minstrel has told, / When two that are linked in one heavenly tie, / With heart never changing, and brow never cold, / Love on through all ills, and love on till they die" (*L* 3.66; Moore 475). Shelley quotes two further stanzas Nourmahal sings as an epigraph to the chapter forecasting **Horatio Saville**'s return from **Italy** and his consistent love for **Lady Lodore**: "**But if for me** thou dost forsake / Some other maid, and rudely break / Her worshipp'd image from its base, / To give to me the ruin'd place;—/ Then, fare-thee-well—I'd rather make / My bower upon some icy lake / When thawing suns begin to shine, / Than trust to love as false as thine!" (*L* 3.193; Moore 476). Shelley adapts lines Feramoz speaks in "Paradise and the Peri" to describe **Gerard Neville**'s determination to "meet [**Rupert Falkner**] in such encounter as must end in the death of one of the combatants—whichever that might be, '**Alas, for man!** said the pitying spirit, / Dearly you pay for your primal fall! / Some flowers of Eden you still inherit, / But the trail of the serpent is over them all' " (*F* 221; Moore 428).

Lamb, Charles (1775–1834): British author best known for *Essays of Elia* (1820–23, 1833), published in the *London Magazine*; **Elia** was Lamb's pseudonym. Throughout his life, Lamb cared for his sister Mary, who had killed their mother during a bout of insanity, an illness that also plagued Lamb (Sunstein 41–42). Lamb published several children's stories with **William Godwin** and knew Shelley as a child (Sunstein 25, 31, 58). Lamb shunned Shelley after her elopement with **PBS**, but he associated with her after she was legally wed (Sunstein 88, 135). On 1 February 1817, Shelley copied Lamb's poem "To T.L.H. a Child" (1815) into her *Journals,* and she discusses Lamb's letter to T.L.H. (Thornton Hunt) in an August 1823 letter (*Journals* 158–160; *Letters* 1.357–358). Shelley's *Letters* contain several additional descriptions of Lamb (1.378, 1.389–390, 1.476–477). When Shelley returned to England, Lamb introduced her to *London Magazine*'s editors, who paid her a guinea a sheet for her writing (Sunstein 247). Shelley visited the Lambs regularly at Islington, where she associated with **London** literati, such as **Samuel Taylor Coleridge** and **Dods** (Sunstein 252, 258, 267, 273; *Journals* 474). **Victor Frankenstein** uses the title of Lamb's 1798 poem, "**Old familiar faces**," to describe the friends he leaves behind in going to University (*Fr1* 74; *Fr3* 48). Shelley uses Lamb's " '**My heart is** fixt: / This is the sixt' " as "**The Bride of Modern Italy**'s" epigraph, attributed to Elia; the quotation is not further identified (*BMI* 32). **Lionel Verney** discusses **Perdita**'s love for **Raymond** with a line Margaret speaks about her husband, protagonist of Lamb's *John Woodvil: A Tragedy* (1802), terming Raymond " '**Her dear heart's confessor**—a heart within that heart' " (*LM* 165; Lamb 1.1). Shelley quotes Lamb in describing dried fields near the **Elbe** at **Dresden**: " '**Talk of green** fields . . . every one has green fields; I have drab-coloured fields' " (*R* 1.246–47). Lamb probably made the statement at one of his many breakfasts Shelley attended (*Letters* 1.398). She compares Lamb's "retreat at **Dalston**" with the **Terrace of Brühl** (*R* 1.246).

Lambach: **Austrian** city twenty-five miles southwest of **Linz**. Shelley changed trains there September 1842 (*R* 2.23).

"Lament of Tasso, The": Poem **Byron** wrote and published 1817 (Marchand 2.689–690, 2.706–707). Shelley paraphrases a line to describe **Richard of York**'s delight in viewing the sky " '**unclouded** by his dungeon roof' " (*PW* 3.222; Byron line 188). As an epigraph to the chapter in which **Lady Katherine Gordon** and Richard are arrested, Shelley quotes accurately: " '**And bare, at once**, Captivity displayed, / Stands scoffing through the never-opened gate; / Which nothing through its bars admits, save day / And tasteless food' " (*PW* 3.274; Byron lines 11–14).

Lamentations: Old Testament book; specifically, passages of **biblical** prophet Jeremiah traditionally sung on Thursday, Friday, and Saturday of Holy Week (Attwater 280). Shelley visited the **Sistine Chapel** April 1843 to hear the Lamentations, "solemn, pathetic, religious" (*R* 2.231).

Lancashire: Northwestern English county. **Sir Thomas Broughton** resides there, and the **Lambert Simnel** rebellion begins there (*PW* 1.84, 1.134).

Lancaster: English city forty-seven miles northwest of **Manchester**; also name for the **Plantagenet** house's branch, which had three 15th-century English kings prior to **York**'s defeat. Shelley intertwines history with fiction in detailing conflicts between the "long rival houses of" York and Lancaster, represented by **White** and **Red Roses** respectively (*PW* 1.55). **Henry VII**, known then as "heir of the **House of Lancaster**," defeated **Richard** [III of York] at **Bosworth Field** and founded the House of **Tudor**'s dynasty (Kinder 1.189). Henry's "first ruling feeling of his heart was hatred of the **House of York**," aware that "his right of succession, even through the House of Lancaster, was ill-founded"; he solidifies his claim to the throne by marrying

Elizabeth of York (*PW* 1.50–51, 1.60). References to Lancaster abound throughout *Perkin Warbeck*. Lancaster is close to **Dromore**: **Rupert Falkner** takes the road toward it when he captures **Alithea Neville**; he passes through it en route to **Liverpool** after Alithea's death; and **Gerard Neville** later tries to locate **Hoskins** there (*F* 106, 206).

Lanceston: See **Launceton**.

Landon, Letitia Elizabeth (1802–1838): Popular and prolific writer of her time, L.E.L. (initials under which she published) wrote several novels and volumes of poetry and contributed to and edited periodicals. Shelley loosely quotes "**Time and Change** together take their flight," from L.E.L.'s "The Ring: The German Minnesinger's Tale" in *The Golden Violet* (1826), as an epigraph to *Lodore*'s chapter in which **Lord Lodore** meets **Fanny Derham** in **New York** (*L* 1.208; Landon line 39).

Landor, Walter Savage (1775–1864): English author best known for *Imaginary Conversations of Literary Men and Statesmen* (1824–29). Shelley remarks, "Mr. Landor says the **Germans** possess nine-tenths of the thought that exists in the world" (*R* 1.212). This remark is untraced; it has been suggested that it might derive from Landor's conversation as reported by a common acquaintance, such as **Rogers** or **Rio** (Moskal 184; Crook 2).

Land's End: Britain's southernmost point, on **Cornwall**'s western coast at **White Sand Bay**'s southern tip. **Lady Katherine Gordon** awaits **Richard of York** at **Saint Michael's Mount**'s monastery, near Land's End (*PW* 3.173).

Lanfranchi: **Ghibelline** family of **Pisa**. **Cincolo de' Becari** travels to Pisa to deliver a packet to **Conradin** at Lanfranchi palace (*TP* 20). Palazzo Lanfranchi is on the **Arno** there (*STIE* 86).

Lanfranco, Padre: Confessor at the convent where **Beatrice** plans to live as a nun in *Valperga*. Shelley probably adapted Lanfranco from **Lanfranchi** (Green 104; Villani 280).

Langborne, Robert: Yorkist supporter arrested at the 1493 conspiratorial meeting at **Robert Clifford**'s house (*PW* 2.50; Holinshed 3.507).

Langres: **French** town twenty miles southeast of **Chaumont**. The Shelleys dined there 1814 (*Journals* 14; *H* 30).

Langusco: **Lombard** city not further identified; Langusco's lord submits to **Henry VII** of **Germany** (*V* 1.118).

Lanti, Duke of: **Italian** duke who sold **Raphael**'s *Madonna di Casa Colonna* to the **King of Prussia** (*R* 1.220).

Lanzi, Luigi Antonio (1732–1810): **Italian** art historian who wrote a 1782 guide to **Florentine** galleries and published *Storia pittorica dell'Italia inferiore* [*Pictorial History of Southern Italy*] (1792) (Petronio 3.331). For *Rambles*'s art history portions, Shelley relied on Lanzi, giving his opinion of **Veronese**, **Ghirlandajo**, and **Michelangelo** (*R* 2.90, 2.144). Shelley uses Lanzi's description of **Raphael**'s **Vatican** paintings as originating not from mythology "but the mysteries of the noblest science—the most august circumstances pertaining to religion, and military deeds whose result established peace and faith in the world" (*R* 2.219; Lanzi 2.68).

Lardner, Dionysius (1793–1859): Clergyman who devoted himself to scientific and literary work and was "elected to the chair of natural philosophy and astronomy at **London** University" 1827 (*Journals* 611). Lardner is chiefly remembered as editor of the *Cabinet Cyclopaedia*, founded 1829 and comprising 133 volumes by its completion (1849), to which many eminent writers of the day contributed. Shelley "contracted for a five-year project" for Lardner's *Cabinet Cyclopaedia* 1833, writing most of the *Italian and Spanish Lives* (1835, 1837) and all of the *French Lives* (1838, 1839) (Sunstein 323, 340, 344). Shelley attended a party at Lardner's house May 1835 and "began writing for Lardner's *Monthly Chronicle*" 1838 (*Journals* 612; Sunstein 328, 340). See Appendix III of Shelley's *Journals* (611–612).

Lario: Steamer named after Lake Lario, the southern end of **Lake Como**'s eastern arm, where the **Adda** leaves it. Shelley mentions an August 1840 outing on the *Lario* (*R* 1.88).

Larissa: Small **Greek** town in central eastern **Thessaly**, 135 miles northwest of **Athens**. **Raymond**'s funeral procession crosses the Larissean plain to Athens (*LM* 208). **Zella Ziani** fears that her husband is "prey of some **Thracian** witchcraft, such as still is practiced in the dread neighbourhood of Larissa" (*EE* 110).

Lasise: Italian town on **Lago di Garda**'s southeastern shore, fifteen miles northwest of **Verona**. Shelley disembarked from the steamboat from **Riva** there September 1842 (*R* 2.72).

Last Man, The: Shelley began her third novel early 1824 as she struggled with depression upon returning to England alone from **Italy**. On 14 May 1824, she recorded: "The last man! Yes I may well describe that solitary being's feelings, feeling myself as the last relic of a beloved race, my companions, extinct before me—" (*Journals* 476–477). She noted "I write—at times that pleases me" 3 September 1824 and completed the novel November 1825 (*Journals* 482–483). To **Ollier** November 1825 Shelley mentioned that "the title of my book is to be simply 'The Last Man, a Romance, by the Author of *Frankenstein*"; Henry Colburn first published it in three volumes 23 January 1826, in such haste that Shelley could not make "the revisions she knew it needed" (*Letters* 1.504; Sunstein 269). While Shelley earned three hundred pounds, it was not well received critically (Sunstein 269). Many works dealing with the world's end, most notably **Byron**'s "Darkness" (1816) and **Campbell**'s poem "The Last Man" (1824) had preceded Shelley's novel, so the notion of humanity's eradication and the plight of a sole survivor was no longer fresh. Shelley had researched the factual basis of her novel to complement its roman-à-clef aspects. She wrote to Ollier to request "a book which describes minutely the Environs of **Constantinople**," so that the second volume's key battle scenes would be accurate (*Letters* 1.431). She also asked **Hobhouse** for assistance in arranging a visit to the **House of Commons** to witness a debate, so she could be precise in the first volume's political scenes (*Letters* 1.466). Shelley's accounts of **plague** seem to be drawn from a variety of documents, several of which she refers to in the novel itself; her interest in plague is evinced in her reading beginning 1817. Direct references include the famous preface about plague in **Boccaccio**'s *Decameron*, **Defoe**'s *A Journal of the Plague Year*, and **Brown**'s *Arthur Mervyn*. Another source is John Wilson's "The City of the Plague" (1816). *The Times* reported cases of the plague in **India** 1818, and "the beginning of a great pandemic that by September 1823 had reached the" **Caspian Sea** area, so Shelley's work is topical despite its precedents (Paley xiii). The novel's frame recounts a visit to the **Cumaean Sibyl**'s cave at **Baiae**, where the narrator claims to have discovered the **sibylline leaves** from which the novel is reconstructed. This frame is dated 8 December 1818, the day upon which Shelley really did make this expedition outside **Naples** (*Journals* 242). The frame's autobiography extends throughout the novel; for example, many important scenes are set around **Windsor**, for which Shelley drew upon her residence at **Bishopsgate**—she revisited the area September 1825 to refresh her memory (Sunstein 101, 269). "[N]ovels with characters based on real people were the rage," and, following **PBS**'s (1822) and Byron's (1824) deaths, Shelley capitalized on her acknowledged intimate associations in fictional versions of both men (Sunstein 269). Set toward the 21st century's close, *The Last Man* depicts humanity's end. **Lionel Verney** narrates, providing the novel's background while chronicling his own life. With his sister **Perdita**, Lionel becomes associated with **Adrian** and his sister **Idris**, the last descendants of the family that formerly ruled England; the king stepped down from the throne as England elected a Protector and became a republic. The ambition of Adrian's mother, formerly **Countess of Windsor**, stifles Adrian's love for **Evadne Zaimi**, but Lionel and Idris fall in love and marry. Perdita and ambitious Lord **Raymond** also fall in love and marry, but after Raymond becomes Protector, they drift apart, and Raymond turns to Evadne for comfort. Raymond subsequently abdicates and fights for **Greece** in its battle for independence. Adrian follows Raymond to Greece for about a year. After Adrian's return to England, Lionel accompanies Perdita to Greece to find Raymond recovering from imprisonment. At this point, plague arises (*LM* 175). Raymond and Perdita reunite, and Raymond leads Greeks in their successful siege of Constantinople while Lionel buries Evadne, who died fighting for Raymond and her country. When Constantinople falls silent and troops are reluctant to enter the city due to plague rumors, Raymond enters alone: the city collapses, and Lionel finds Raymond's corpse. Lionel insists that Perdita accompany him back to England against her wishes; she jumps from the boat and drowns. Lionel returns to England to find fear growing as the plague spreads throughout the world. Adrian proves his nobility in agreeing to become Protector after **Ryland** flees the post, and thereafter leads England; Lionel becomes Adrian's second. Lionel survives the plague, but he loses Idris and their son **Alfred** to it. Adrian and Lionel eventually lead plague survivors through **Europe** to a better climate: England has been decimated by disease and **Irish** invasion. A religious faction splits and detains survivors in **Paris**, but Adrian and Lionel keep moving south, attempting to find other survivors and reestablish a community. The party declines successively as they travel, until the only survivors are Lionel, **Evelyn**, Adrian, and **Clara**. When Evelyn dies, the remaining three travel into **Italy**, where Adrian and Clara persuade Lionel to sail with them to Greece. A shipwreck leaves Lionel "the LAST MAN"; Shelley links the novel's title to Lionel several times (*LM* 446, 330, 470). He journeys to **Rome**, where he spends over a year writing the novel, before ending it with his intended travel route to search for other plague survivors. Shelley regarded this novel highly, writing April 1837 that "I own [*The Last Man*] is a favourite of mine—yet I can see its defects—I had a vivid conception of the story & wrote with great speed—It wanted afterwards I believe, a sort of softening in the tone & something to diversify the continual pressure on one topic" (*Letters* 2.285–286).

Lateran: Papal palace and district in **Rome**; Shelley probably visited it March 1819 (*Journals* 255). **Henry VII** of **Germany** is crowned emperor there because **Guelphs** control the **Vatican** (*V* 1.158). Shelley describes Rome's old city from the Lateran to the **Coliseum** (*R* 2.228).

Latin: Language ancient **Romans** spoke throughout their empire. Shelley began studying it as an adolescent and continued to perfect her understanding by reading such works as *Aeneid* in the original (Sunstein 49, 118; *Journals* 681). **Victor Frankenstein** and **Elizabeth Lavenza** learn Latin (*Fr1* 67). **Euthanasia** learns the older form of Latin that **Cicero** and **Virgil** used rather than "rude and barbarous Latin" her contemporaries know (*V* 1.28). Shelley explains how Latin replaced the ancient **Tuscan** language (*R* 2.125).

Latin Poet: See **Lucretius** and **Virgil**.

Latini, Brunetto (c. 1220–c. 1295): Florentine Guelph poet, diplomat, and scholar. He influenced **Dante** and **Cavalcanti** with his **French** encyclopedia, *Le Trésors* [*The Treasures*] (c. 1260), and unfinished allegorical poem *Tesoretto* [*Little Treasure*] (after 1282) (*DIL* 76–77). Dante encounters Latini in *Inferno* (15.30–122). Guests at **Euthanasia's** court enjoy hearing Florentines sing Latini's *Tesoretto* (*V* 1.265). Shelley explains **Tuscan** linguistic developments, whereby **Latin** replaced Latini's *lingua Toscana* (*R* 2.125).

Latona: Goddess Leto in **Roman** myth who, pregnant by **Zeus**, searched for somewhere to give birth; no one would give her shelter, since they were all afraid of Zeus's wife Hera's wrath; with Poseidon's assistance, she finally gave birth to twins **Apollo** and Artemis on Ortygia island (Tripp 344). **Lionel Verney** suggests that Latona's "glorious twins" were not more welcome on earth than **Adrian** and **Idris** were to his isolation in **Windsor's** cottage (*LM* 79).

Laufenburg: Swiss town on the **Rhine**, twenty-eight miles southeast of **Schaffhausen**; Shelley terms it **Loffen-**

burgh (*BSWI* 27). Shelley rode over Laufenburg's falls August 1814 (*H* 55, 57; *Journals* 21).

Launceston: English city thirty-five miles southwest of **Exeter**. Wounded **Edmund Plantagenet** travels there (*PW* 3.172).

Laurenzi Berg: Petrìn Hill, west of **Prague**'s Little Quarter; church of St. Lawrence (Laurenzi) is on it (Soukup 14, 141). Shelley mentions **Bohemian** religious sacrifices there (*R* 2.1).

Laurette: Pet name for Anna Laura Georgina (1809–80), **Tighe** and **Mountcashel**'s eldest daughter; Shelley dedicated "**Maurice**" to Laurette (*Maurice* 59).

Laurie: **Edward Villiers**'s servant in *Lodore*.

Lausanne: Swiss city on hills overlooking **Lake Geneva**'s northern shore. **Victor Frankenstein** spends two days there, where the beautiful natural environment calms him after **William Frankenstein**'s death (*Fr1* 102; *Fr3* 71).

Lavallan, John: **Cork**'s mayor in *Perkin Warbeck*.

Lavenza, Elizabeth: **Alphonse** and **Caroline Frankenstein**'s adopted daughter and "more than sister," later wife, to **Victor Frankenstein** (*Fr3* 41). In the 1818 edition, she is Victor's half-**Italian** cousin; in the 1831 edition, she is the orphan of a **German** mother and a "**Milanese** nobleman" (*Fr1* 65; *Fr3* 41).

Lavenza, Villa: Part of the inheritance the **Austrian** government restores to **Elizabeth Lavenza** in the 1831 *Frankenstein*. It is on **Lake Como** and is the unrealized destination of the fateful honeymoon voyage (*Fr3* 161).

Laverna Convent: See **La Verna Convent**.

Lawrence, Sir Thomas (1769–1830): English portrait painter and **William Godwin**'s friend (Chilvers 313; Sunstein 40). Shelley records his assessment of her preference for sculptures over paintings, from a discussion with him that may have occurred 1829, when she accompanied **Moore** to Lawrence's house (*R* 1.222; Sunstein 305; *Letters* 2.197, 2.232).

Laws of Candy, The: **Fletcher**'s drama co-authored with Philip Massinger (1583–1640), which **PBS** read aloud 1818 (*Journals* 219). As an epigraph to the *Lodore* chapter in which **Ethel Villiers** joins her husband in prison, Shelley quotes Fernando's speech: "**Herein / Shall my** captivity be made my happiness; / Since what I lose in freedom, I regain / With interest" (*L* 3.77; *Laws of Candy* 3.2.104–107). As an epigraph to the chapter in which **Lucy Saville** asks the **Villiers**es to persuade her brother to return to England, Shelley quotes lines (attributed to "**Old Play**") Annophel speaks to her father, Castiline, pleading with him to repent of anger against her brother and his son, Antinous: "**Let me / Awake** your love to my uncomforted brother" (*L* 3.77; *Laws of Candy* 3.3.184–185).

Lazzarini, Colonel: Shelley recounts the **French** assault on **Ancona** in February 1832, when a Colonel Lazzarini "was made prisoner in his bed be-

Lea

fore he awoke" (R 2.256). Not further identified.

Lea: English river joining the **Thames** in **London**. **Clifford** family's castle is nearby (PW 2.18).

Leander: Legendary youth who swam the Hellespont every night toward a light that Hero, **Aphrodite**'s priestess and Leander's beloved, lit to guide him; when a storm extinguished the light one night, Leander drowned; Hero subsequently committed suicide (Howatson 321). In "**The Death of Love**," Shelley asks if personified love died by being "strangled by the raging deep, / Which wrestled with Leander fatally" (lines 7–8).

Lebadea: Town on river Hercyna, just south of **Parnassus** in central eastern **Thessaly**; Shelley terms it **Livadia** (Tripp 588). **Raymond**'s funeral procession passes through Lebadea (LM 208).

Lebanon: Middle Eastern country bordering the **Mediterranean** west of **Syria** and a mountain range there; **Solomon**'s **biblical** Temple used great cedar trees growing on Lebanese mountains (Browning 225; 1 Kings 7.2–3). **Elizabeth Woodville** takes rosary beads "formed of the blessed wood of Lebanon" to **St. Paul's** (PW 1.101).

Lecco: Italian city at **Lake Lecco**'s southern point, seven miles east of **Como**. Shelley visited it September 1840 (R 1.105–106).

Lecco, Lake: Eastern arm of **Lake Como**. Shelley sailed there August 1840 (R 1.77, 1.85).

Leda and the Swan: See **Correggio**.

Lefebvre, General Pierre François Joseph (1755–1820): Napoleon appointed this **French** general an imperial marshal 1804; he subsequently became **Duke of Dantzig**. Shelley spells his name **Lefevre**. She records the **Tyrolese** revolt against Lefebvre's French and **Bavarian** troops 1809 (R 2.52–55). She describes the **Brenner** battle where Lefebvre ordered an advance of four thousand Bavarians that led to thousands of fatalities when the Tyrolese caused an avalanche (R 2.54).

Lefevre: See **Lefebvre**.

Leghorn: English name for Livorno, **Italian** coastal town fifty-five miles southeast of **La Spezia**. Both Shelleys disliked it upon arrival May 1818, but Shelley formed a lifelong friendship with **Maria Gisborne** there (Journals 209; White 2.15). Shelley suffered a breakdown in Leghorn, where she lived until October 1819, after **William Shelley**'s June 1819 death. The Shelleys had to return to Leghorn summer 1820 so **PBS** could consult his lawyer, and he frequently took trips to Leghorn to enquire about purchasing a boat. He sailed from Leghorn with **Edward Williams** 8 July 1822 intending to return home to **San Terenzo**, but both died at sea. Shelley rushed to Leghorn; the men's bodies did not wash up on shore until 18 July (Journals 413–416). **Felix De Lacey** helps **Safie** and her father escape from **Paris** to Leghorn, and Safie's father embarks for **Constantinople** there (Fr1 152; Fr3 109). Fear in England grows when plague is confirmed at Leghorn (LM 235). A "long and vexatious quarantine" detains **Rupert**

244

Falkner and **Elizabeth Falkner** there, where Elizabeth first makes **Lady Cecil**'s acquaintance (*F* 71). Shelley noted "the view from the sea near Leghorn is not sufficiently praised" March 1843 (*R* 2.213). [*R* 2.255].

Leicester: City in **Leicestershire** (eastern English county), ninety miles northwest of **London**. Knights defeated at **Bosworth Field** pass through Leicestershire, and **Edmund Plantagenet** tells **Lord Lovel** how **King Richard III**'s half-naked corpse was paraded through Leicester on a mule (*PW* 1.2, 1.17). According to **Holinshed**, prior to Bosworth Field, Richard passed through Leicester "with pompe and pride"; on his return, "the dead corps of king Richard was as shamefullie caried" (Holinshed 3.446).

Leinster: Irish mountain twenty-seven miles northeast of **Waterford**. **Hubert Burgh** discusses **Murrogh-en-Ranagh**, who conquered the country from **Clare** to Leinster (*PW* 1.291).

Leipsig: See **Leipzig**.

Leipzig: Eastern **German** town sixty-four miles northwest of **Dresden**; Shelley spells it **Leipsig**. She stayed there at **Hôtel de Saxe** for three days July 1842; she passed through again en route to Dresden at the month's end (*R* 1.216, 1.231).

Leith: Northeastern **Edinburgh** district on the Firth of Forth. **Richard of York** arrives in Scotland "off Leith" (*PW* 2.195).

Leman, Lac: See **Lake Geneva**.

Lennox: Scottish earldom held by the Stewart family. Shelley lists the Lennoxes as a feuding family that was peaceful during **James IV**'s reign (*PW* 2.228).

Lenzkirch: German village twenty miles southeast of **Freyberg**. Shelley described breakfast there July 1840 (*R* 1.47).

Leo IX, Pope (1002–1054): Pope 1049–54. See **Gregory VII, Pope**.

León, Luis de (1527–1591): Spanish monk and author. Shelley wrote León's biography for *Italian and Spanish Lives*. He became an Augustinian monk 1544, having written poems and translated **Virgil**'s *Eclogues* and part of *Georgics* in his youth. After he translated the **biblical** Song of Songs into Spanish from **Hebrew**, the **Inquisition** imprisoned him (1572) for four years. Shelley esteems his piety and endurance, considering León "pure and high-hearted, with the nobility of genius stamped on his brow, but with religious resignation calming his heart" (*ISPL* 3.71). Shelley admires his poetry: "purity and elegance of his style are unsurpassed. . . . [N]othing can exceed the harmony and flow of his verse, the grace and propriety of his ideas, and the truth and simplicity—the extreme ease and animation, of his style," presenting León's "Ode to Tranquil Life" ["Oda a la Vita Retirada"] (c. 1543) as "most perfect of his compositions" (*ISPL* 3.78).

Leonardo da Vinci (1452–1519): **Florentine** painter renowned for *Mona Lisa* (c. 1503–1506) and *The Last Supper* (c. 1495–1497), which Shelley viewed in

Leone Bianco

Milan September 1840 (Chilvers 319; Moskal 131). Shelley mentions da Vinci several times in her discussions of art and respects him, but she does not praise him as she does **Michelangelo**, **Raphael**, and others (*R* 1.109, 1.222, 2.153, 2.219).

Leone Bianco: Venetian hotel on the **Grand Canal** that **Murray** recommends (Moskal 270). Its high rates allowed Shelley only one night's stay there September 1842 (*R* 2.79, 2.81).

Leonora of Burgher: See **Berchet**.

Leopold I (1747–1792): **Tuscany**'s grand duke 1765–90 who, on the death of his brother **Joseph II**, became **Austria**'s emperor and (as Leopold II) Holy Roman Emperor 1790–92 (Crook 2). Shelley calls his reign **Florence**'s "golden age" and compares **Ferdinand IV** to Joseph II and Leopold I in planning legal reform; Leopold I abolished Tuscany's primogeniture law (*R* 2.161, 2.164, 2.182). She finds him "a good sovereign, a clever and liberal man" (*R* 2.186).

Leopold II (1797–1870): Leopold I's grandson and Grand Duke of **Tuscany** from 1824–1859 (when he was forced to abdicate); Shelley records his aversion to violence and capital punishment (*R* 2.187–188; Crook 2).

Lepanto: Italian name for Naupactus, small town on mainland **Greece**'s southern shore 108 miles northwest of **Athens**. Gulf of Lepanto, also known as Gulf of **Patras** (for the **Peloponnese** port seventy miles northwest of **Corinth**), was the site of a bloody naval battle 7 October 1571, in which **Spanish** forces were victorious over **Turks** (*MGRE* 91). **Byron** notes the battle in *Childe Harold's Pilgrimage* (2.356). At Patras, **Katusthius Ziani** boards a vessel "for the northern shores of the gulf of Lepanto" with abducted **Constans Ziani** (*EE* 106). Shelley details **Gabriel Serbelloni**'s participation in the 1571 battle, in which **Cervantes** lost his left hand (*R* 1.81).

Leroux, Robinet: Page who escapes **France** with (apparently) **Emilie de Lagny** in "The False Rhyme."

Les Rousses: **French** village two miles west of the **Swiss** border near **Lake Geneva**. The Shelleys passed through it May 1816 (*H* 91–92).

Lessey, Sir Richard: In *Perkin Warbeck*, **Edward IV**'s chaplain, arrested at the 1493 conspiratorial meeting at **Robert Clifford**'s house (Holinshed 3.507).

Lessey, Sir William: In *Perkin Warbeck*, **Yorkist** supporter arrested at the 1493 conspiratorial meeting at **Robert Clifford**'s house.

Lethe: In classical myth, those who drank from this Underworld river forgot their former lives upon entering the world of the dead (Tripp 344). Shelley's speaker desires "a draught of that Lethean wave," preferring death to forgetting her love (*Stanzas: I must forget* lines 21). **Jove** condemns **Proserpine** to live by the Lethe six months each year (*P* 81).

"Letter to Maria Gisborne": Verse letter **PBS** composed June 1820 while living in the **Gisbornes' Leghorn** house, first published 1824 (White 2.553, 2.208–210; Holmes 597–598). Shelley wrote "O Witch Memory" 15 December 1823, echoing her husband's poem (*Journals* 469; PBS line 132). Shelley quotes her husband's poem as an epigraph to *Lodore*'s chapter in which the **Villiers**es meet in **London** society: "You are now / In London, that great sea, whose ebb and flow, / At once is deaf and loud" (*L* 1.290; PBS lines 192–194).

***Letters Written During a Short Residence in Sweden, Norway, and Denmark* (1796):** Travel book about **Mary Wollstonecraft**'s 1795 summer journey through Scandinavia. It is based on twenty-five letters Wollstonecraft wrote to **Gilbert Imlay** in **London**, in which she describes the landscape and people of these countries, outlines several realistic problems travelers encounter (such as dealing with language barriers and being overcharged), and offers social criticism about the lives of people she observes, particularly women (Poston xi). Shelley records reading it 1814, 1820, and 1822 and gave a copy to **PFS** as he left for the **Baltic** 1847 (*Journals* 684; Sunstein 376). **PBS** read aloud Wollstonecraft's *Letters* en route from **Basle** to **Strasburgh** (*H* 62). Plague survivors pass through the **Alps**, " 'the bones of the world, waiting to be clothed with every thing necessary to give life and beauty' "; Shelley footnotes this quotation from Wollstonecraft's work (*LM* 424; Wollstonecraft 42).

Levant: Term literally meaning "rising," as of the sun, once used to refer to the **Mediterranean**'s eastern shore, comprising **Egypt**, **Greece**, Israel, **Lebanon**, **Turkey**, and **Syria**. **Castruccio**'s father dies from fever a ship brings to **Italy** from the Levant (*V* 1.37).

Lewes: Small village ten miles northeast of **Brighton**. In "**Euphrasia**'s" frame story, the snow-trapped carriage sends to Lewes for help (*E* 296).

Library of St. Mark: Venetian library begun 1468 (Zorzi 272–276). Shelley mentions Venetian annals written in the vernacular stored there (*R* 2.124).

Libya: North **African** country on the **Mediterranean**, which **Egypt** and Algeria border; Shelley also spells it **Lybia**. Shelley saw a vineyard between **Pavillon** and **Troyes**, which "appeared like one of those islands of verdure met with in the midst of the sands of Libya" (*H* 25–26). **Lionel Verney** intends to steer north from the **Nile** "till losing sight of . . . deserted Lybia" (*LM* 469).

Lido: Large sandbar separating **Venice** from the **Adriatic**; it offers several beaches and resorts. **Clara Shelley** was buried at Lido's Protestant cemetery 25 September 1818; Shelley terms her grave "bleak Lido" (*Journals* 227; *Ch* 64). **Edmund Malville** lists Venetian sights, including "the dusty line of Lido" (*RI* 26). **Lionel Verney**, **Adrian**, and **Clara** look out from Venice to "the blue immensity, seen beyond Lido" (*LM* 439). Shelley rowed to Lido upon returning to Venice 1842 (*R* 2.98–99).

Liège: Belgian city sixty-five miles southeast of **Antwerp**. Shelley arrived there June 1842 (*R* 1.163–166).

Life of Castruccio: See **Tegrimi**.

Life of Castruccio Castracani of Lucca, The: See **Machiavelli**.

Life of St. Francis, The: See **Ghirlandajo**.

Life of Wallenstein: See **Mitchell**.

"Lift not the painted veil": Opening of sonnet **PBS** wrote 1818, first published 1824 (White 2.51–53). Shelley uses the opening line's image in her *Journals*: in December 1822, she noted "the reality of things resumes its place in my mind & I leave to look on the 'painted veil called life,' " and October 1824 that PBS "had said Lift not the painted veil whch [*sic*] men call life—mine is not painted—dark & enshadowed it curtains out all of happiness—all of hope" (*Journals* 446, 485; PBS lines 1–2). After **Edward Villiers**'s marriage proposal, **Ethel Villiers** would not have to "tear at once the '**painted veil** of life,' delivering herself up to cheerless realities" (*L* 2.159). **Horatio Saville**, watching **Fanny Derham**, finds "she brought to his recollection his own feelings before experience had lifted 'the **painted veil** which those who live call life' " (*L* 3.223). Shelley describes **Monina De Faro** as one who "had not yet '**Lifted the painted** veil, which men call life' " (*PW* 1.253).

Ligi, Fior di: Italian for "flower of the lily," another name for **Mandragola** in *Valperga*.

Ligne, Prince de [Charles Joseph] (1735–1814): Belgian military officer and author of thirty-four volume *Mélanges militaires, littéraires et sentimentaires* [*Miscellaneous Military, Literary, and Sentimental Memoirs*] (1795–1811). Shelley notes his admiration for **Frederic the Great** (*R* 1.214).

Ligurian Alps: Alps in northwestern **Italy** near **Genoa**. Shelley applies *Julian and Maddalo* lines to mountains she viewed from the sea near **Leghorn** March 1842 (*R* 2.213).

Lille: French city fifty-seven miles southeast of **Calais**; Shelley spells it **Lisle**. **Stephen Frion** searches for **Richard of York** there (*PW* 1.149). Richard subsequently accompanies Frion to Lille, where he is imprisoned for the day at **Sire de Beverem**'s house (*PW* 1.163–165). **Robert Clifford** later calls Richard "hero of Lisle" (*PW* 2.10).

Lilliputian: See **Swift**.

Limone: Italian town on **Lago di Garda**'s western shore, twenty-seven miles northwest of **Verona**. Shelley relates **Hofer**'s route to execution in **Mantua**; he boarded a boat in Limone, mistakenly printed **Simone** in *Rambles* (*R* 2.59; Moskal 258).

Lincoln: English cathedral city fifteen miles northeast of **Newark-on-Trent**. **Henry VII** enjoys "the festival of Easter at Lincoln" (*PW* 1.67).

Lincoln, Earl of (c. 1464–1487): John de la Pole, Earl of Lincoln 1466, **Ireland**'s Lord Lieutenant 1484, and heir to **Richard III**'s throne; he died at **Stoke** (*DNB*). Major **Richard of York** supporter in *Perkin Warbeck*.

Linda: See **Weber**.

Linz: Austrian city on the **Danube**, fifty miles south of **Budweis**. Shelley arrived there September 1842 (*R* 2.20–23).

Lion: Lionel Verney and Adrian find a little girl and her dog, Lion, alone in **London** (*LM* 333). **Byron** owned "a huge Newfoundland called Lyon" (Marchand 3.1087, 3.1192).

Lion-Heart: Nickname for Richard I, king of England 1189–99. **Richard of York** refers to his "namesake and ancestor" (*PW* 3.139).

Lions: Common 19th-century term for a place's important sites. Shelley repeatedly uses this term in describing her **European** journeys but criticizes travelers who "visit the *lions* of the place now and then; but, really, to wander, and ramble, and discover new scenes does not form a portion of their amusements" (*R* 1.41).

Lisbon: **Portugal**'s capital, on the **Atlantic** about 320 miles southwest of **Madrid**. **Hernan De Faro** explores the seas for Portugal, after moving to Lisbon (*PW* 1.146, 1.206). Shelley notes that **Columbus** offered to explore the seas for Portugal, but ultimately sailed on **Spain's** behalf (*PW* 1.146). **Meilar Trangmar** follows **Lady Brampton** there to seize **Richard of York** (*PW* 1.230, 1.240, 1.251). **Monina De Faro** is buried there (*PW* 3.344).

Lisle: See **Lille**.

Lisle, Sir Edward: In *Perkin Warbeck*, **Yorkist** conspirator who escapes to **Flanders** with **Gilbert Daubeny**.

Lismore: Irish city twelve miles northwest of **Youghal**. **Desmond** rides there to recruit the **Knight of the Valley** for the **Waterford** battle (*PW* 3.51).

Little Island: **Suir** island, east of **Reginald's Tower** in **Waterford**. **Richard of York**'s fleet drops down to Little Island to avoid the cannon of Reginald's Tower's (*PW* 3.42).

Little Marlow: Small village ten miles northwest of **Windsor**. **Lionel Verney** recounts the personal history of **Martha**, who "ruled" Little Marlow (*LM* 271).

Little Park: King Edward III founded **Windsor**'s Little Park by enclosing land north of the castle 1368; subsequent monarchs increased the area, and it "remained a deer park until 1785"—the nearly five hundred acres were open to the public in Shelley's time (Hedley 44, 93, 185). It became known as Home Park during Victoria's reign (1837–1901) (Hedley 185–188). Many of *The Last Man*'s characters roam there, and **Lionel Verney** makes his return to Windsor through **Frogmore** gate at the park's south end (*LM* 239). Verney later notes the oak tree called **Falstaff** on his way through it (*LM* 362).

Little Woman: Probably a natural **American** landmark. Shelley compliments the **German** ability to give "the glory of spirit-stirring names to their valleys and their forests, very different from the Little Woman, or **Muddy Creek**, of America" (*R* 1.45).

Livadia: See **Lebadea**.

Liverpool: Large English port and industrial town thirty-eight miles west of **Manchester**. Plague spreads from all England's "more populous towns," including Liverpool (*LM* 268). Liverpool was *St. Mary*'s destination, so **Lewis Elmore** travels there to find **Clarice Eversham**; she stayed only briefly at a hotel there before disappearing (*Mourner* 90, 93–95). Many of *Falkner*'s characters use Liverpool as embarkation point on vessels destined to other parts of the country or **America** (*F* 266).

Lives: See **Plutarch**.

Lives of the Most Eminent Literary and Scientific Men of France: In 1833, Shelley made a contract to contribute to a project that was eventually to last for five years, **Lardner**'s *Cabinet Cyclopedia*, to which **Moore**, **Scott**, and **Sismondi** also contributed (Sunstein 323; Crook 2). Shelley composed the two volumes of French *Lives*, probably beginning work 1838 after completing Italian *Lives*, and concluding French *Lives* by July 1839; contemporary advertisements for the volumes raise doubts about whether Shelley was the sole author of each biography in both volumes (Sunstein 340, 344; Crook 2). Her work formed volumes 102 and 103 of Lardner's *Cabinet Cyclopedia*, and the first volume, published 1838, contains biographies of **Montaigne**, **Rabelais**, **Corneille**, **La Rochefoucauld**, **Molière**, **La Fontaine**, **Pascal**, **de Sévigné**, **Boileau-Despréaux**, **Racine**, and **Fénelon**, while the second volume, published 1839, contains biographies of **Voltaire**, **Rousseau**, **Condorcet**, **Mirabeau**, **Roland**, and **de Staël**. In an undated letter to **Leigh Hunt** written between December 1837 and March 1838, Shelley affirmed "I am now writing French lives—The **Spanish** ones interested me—these do not so much—yet it is pleasant writing enough—sparing one's imagination yet occupying one & supplying in some small degree the *needful* which is so very needful" (*Letters* 2.293). Shelley's motivation for undertaking *Lives* was clearly financial, but these volumes demonstrate wide knowledge and diligent research. Shelley draws upon all available sources and provides, for the most part, factually accurate and insightful accounts of these prominent French figures' lives, stating her commitment to this "series of biography whose intent is to give an account of the persons whose genius has adorned the world" (*FL* 1.214). Shelley's admiration for political figures and writers, as well as for outstanding qualities of women she unabashedly includes in volumes supposedly confined solely to men, reveals her sympathies. Shelley clearly shaped several individual *Lives* according to her own interests, and the biographies contain certain structural similarities; for example, she describes each subject physically toward the end of his or her entry.

Lives of the Most Eminent Literary and Scientific Men of Italy, Spain and Portugal: In 1833, Shelley made a contract to contribute to a project that was eventually to last for five years, **Lardner**'s *Cabinet Cyclopedia*, to which **Moore**, **Scott**, and **Sismondi** also contributed (Sunstein 323; Crook 2). Shelley wrote April 1834: "at this moment I am engaged writing for Dr Lardner & am very busy indeed," and

July 1834 that the composition "is a source of interest & pleasure" (*Letters* 2.201, 2.209). The first two volumes concerned Italian authors, and Shelley wrote February 1835 that the first, *Cabinet Cyclopedia*'s volume 86, appeared that month: "The lives of **Dante** & **Ariosto** are by the Omnipresent Mr Montgomery—the rest are mine" (*Letters* 2.222). "The rest" includes biographies of **Petrarch**, **Boccaccio**, **Medici**, **Ficino**, **Mirandola**, **Poliziano**, three **Pulci** brothers, **Ferrara**, **Burchiello**, **Bojardo**, **Berni**, and **Machiavelli**. Shelley then completed the second volume of *Italian Lives*, *Cabinet Cyclopedia*'s volume 87 in 1835, writing November 1835: "the life of Gallileo is by Sir David Brewster that of **Tasso** by Mr Montgomery—the rest are mine & so ends the Italian lives; for which I am sorry," especially since Shelley wanted to write Tasso's life: "I am vain enough to think I should have written it better than [Montgomery] has done" (*Letters* 2.260, 2.257). For this second volume of *Italian Lives*, Shelley had asked Gabriele Rossetti for information about **Alfieri** and **Monti** 1835, and she also wrote biographies of **Guicciardini**, **Colonna**, **Guarini**, **Chiabrera**, **Tassoni**, **Marini**, **Filicaja**, **Metastasio**, **Goldoni**, and **Foscolo** (*Journals* 515). Shelley recorded December 1834 that "my life & reason have been saved by these '*Lives*' "; the research and writing they demanded occupied her mind during this troubled period (*Journals* 543). The third volume, dealing with Spanish and Portuguese authors, presented more of a challenge. Shelley wrote October 1835: "I am now about to write a Volume of Spanish & Portugueeze [sic] Lives— This is an arduous task, from my own ignorance, & the difficulty of getting books & information," and again November 1835 that "the Spanish & Portugueeze will cost me more trouble [than the *Italian Lives*], if I can do them at all—There is no Spanish Circulating Library" (*Letters* 2.257, 2.260). Moore assisted Shelley with access to rare Spanish texts; she also wrote to Dr. John Bowring 1835 and several times 1837, asking for his advice on how to locate texts and obtain information about various authors: "the very thing which occasions the difficulty makes it interesting—namely—the treading in unknown paths & dragging out unknown things—I wish I could go to *Spain*" (*Journals* 533; *Letters* 2.254–255, 2.288–290). Shelley had difficulty obtaining authors' works, but, "after meticulous research," she completed the volume summer 1837; it was published as volume 88 of the *Cabinet Cyclopedia* 1837 (Sunstein 337). References in Shelley's letters demonstrate she was author of biographies of **Boscán**, **Garcilaso de la Vega**, **Mendoza**, **Herrera**, **Cervantes**, **Quevedo**, and **Camoens**, and she presumably also authored sections titled "Introduction" and "The Dramatists" and others of this volume's *Lives*, including **Léon**, **Montemayor**, **Castillejo**, **Lope de Vega**, **Espinel**, **Villegas**, **Góngora**, **Calderón**, and **Sa de Miranda**. Shelley probably authored biographies grouped under the heading "The Early Poets of Portugal," including **Ribeyra**, **Vicente**, and **Ferreira**, while **Ercilla**'s biography is probably not Shelley's (Sunstein 413). Shelley's motivation for undertaking the *Lives* was clearly financial, but her engagement with her subjects, as indicated in her *Letters*, also reveals she was comfortable in undertaking writing that did not rely solely upon her own creativity. These volumes demonstrate wide knowledge and diligent research; Shelley draws upon all available sources and provides, for the most part, factually accurate and insightful accounts of these prominent authors' lives. Her love of Italy is clear in her admiration of authors under consideration, and she similarly appreciates an "originality, an independence, an enthusiasm in the Spanish character that distinguishes them from every other people" (*ISPL* 3.1–2). Shelley's admiration for political figures and writers, as well as for outstanding qualities of women she unabashedly includes in volumes supposedly confined solely to men, reveals her sympathies. Clearly, Shelley shaped several individual *Lives* according to her own interests. The Italian, Spanish, and Portuguese biographies were more challenging than the subsequent *French Lives* and are occasionally much shorter.

Livy, Titus Livius (59 B.C.E.–c. 17 C.E.): Roman historian best known for a history of Rome from its beginnings until 9 B.C.E. Shelley asked **PBS** December 1816 to "try to procure a good Livy, for I wish very much to read it"; she did so methodically from mid-1818 onward (*Letters* 1.22; *Journals* 216). Livy's works are among those **Matilda** finds in her aunt's library (*M* 158). **Isabell Harley** introduces **Valerius** to Livy's works (*Val* 343).

Lobositz: See **Lovosice**.

Loch Katrine: Beautiful Scottish lake thirty miles north of Glasgow. Lionel **Verney** takes his family there (*LM* 156).

Loch Lomond: Scottish lake twenty miles northwest of Glasgow. Drawing upon her solitary teenage wanderings on the beach when staying with the **Baxters**, Shelley describes **Matilda** growing up on her aunt's isolated estate on Loch Lomond's shores; Matilda leaps from a boat on the loch into her father's arms upon his return (*M* 156). **Lionel Verney** takes **Perdita** to Loch Lomond (*LM* 156).

Lodi: Italian town eighteen miles southeast of **Milan**. **Tadeo della Ventura** notes Lodi's submission to **Henry VII** of **Germany**, but Lodi later joins the **Lombard** revolt (*V* 1.118, 1.144).

Lodore: In her *Journals* at 1832's end, Shelley records "I write my novel—of *Lodore*," and she wrote January 1833: "I am in all the tremor of fearing what I shall get for my novel, which is nearly finished.... I do not know whether you will like it—I cannot guess whether it will succeed—There is no writing interest—nothing wonderful, nor tragic"; she sent the first volume to her publisher Richard Bentley at January 1833's end (*Journals* 528; *Letters* 2.183, 2.185). Shelley submitted the second volume November 1833, noting "the whole is ready however.... I mean the title to be '*Lodore—a tale of the present time*'" (*Letters* 2.196). A portion of the proofs was lost in transit in April 1834, so Shelley was forced to rewrite sections, informing her publisher of completion 10 June 1834 (*Letters* 2.206). Dissatisfied with the subtitle in June 1834 and asking for a date when she could expect to see it in November, Shelley wrote to her publisher March 1835, "at length I see that poor *Lodore* is crawling into existence"; she received a hundred pounds when it was published April 1835 (*Letters* 2.206, 2.217, 2.237). *Lodore* was well received, "praised & noticed," and, October 1835, Shelley noted "the Bookseller wants me to write another Novel—*Lodore* having succeeded so well" (*Letters* 2.251, 2.257). Shelley recalled 1843 that *Lodore* was "written off hand" and was one of her works that "pleased me most" (*Letters* 3.96). Shelley also acknowledged the novel's autobiographical episodes, drawn from her October 1814 experiences when **PBS** had to leave their lodgings to avoid creditors, so that the Shelleys communicated by letter and met secretly; Shelley asked **Maria Gisborne** November 1835: "did you recognize any of [PBS's] & my early adventures—when we were in danger of being starved in **Switzerland**—& could get no dinner at an inn in **London**?" (*Journals* 38; *Letters* 2.261). Characters' financial concerns, detailed in *Lodore,* can be attributed to Shelley's consistent financial difficulties. Perhaps Shelley distributes "elements of her youthful self among" *Lodore*'s heroines, **Lady Lodore**, **Fanny Derham**, and, particularly, **Ethel Villiers**; and **Cornelia Santerre** at sixteen is "a partial stand-in for **Harriet Shelley**" (Sunstein 48, 320). Shelley informed her publisher that "a mother & Daughter are the heroines—The Mother who after [sacrificing] *all* to the world at first—afterwards makes sacrifises not less entire, for her child—finding all to be Vanity, except the genuine affections of the heart. In the daughter I have tried to pourtray [*sic*] in its simplicity, & all the beauty I could muster, the *devotion* of a young wife for the husband of her choice—The disasters she goes through being described—& their result in awakening her Mother's affection, bringing about the conclusion of the tale" (*Letters* 2.185). *Lodore* is unusual in Shelley's corpus since the heroine's mother is present throughout, although "the young mother seemed scarcely to remember that [her daughter] existed," while the strong father-daughter ties that Shelley explores in so much of her fiction are again central concerns (*L* 1.128). In the novel, **Lord Lodore**, raised to be proud, willfully roams **Europe**, where he engages in an affair with **Countess Theodora Lyzinski**. Returning to England disheartened at this affair's unhappy conclusion, he meets young and beautiful Cornelia and, despite an eighteen-year age difference, they marry. In London, **Lady Santerre** (whom White asserts is based on Harriet Shelley's sister, Eliza Westbrook) continues to push her daughter into society so that, despite Ethel's birth, the couple remain distanced and unhappy (2.679). When Lord Lodore insults **Casimir Lyzinski** at the **Russian** ambassador's dinner, he is unable to accept the challenge of a duel since Casimir is his illegitimate son; Lord Lodore determines to leave the country where he has lost honor. Cornelia refuses to accompany him, and Lord Lodore takes Ethel with him to **Illinois**. He raises Ethel in the isolated paradise where her "earliest feeling was love of her father," an idolization she retains throughout life (*L* 1.30). En route to England after learning of Lady Santerre's death, **Mr. Hatfield** kills Lord Lodore in a duel in **New York**, where Ethel first meets **Edward Villiers** in his capacity as her father's second. During her husband's absence from England, Cornelia attracts **Horatio Saville**'s affection. But, after learning of her husband's death, Cornelia protects her reputation and becomes cold toward Horatio, which drives him to **Italy**. Ethel returns to live with aunt **Elizabeth Fitzhenry** at **Longfield**, and they travel to London, where they meet Edward again; he and Ethel soon fall in love. Despite his debts, they marry and travel to **Naples** to visit Horatio and his **Neapolitan** bride **Clorinda Saville** (perhaps modeled upon **Emilia Viviani**) (White 2.605, 2.679). Returning to England, debt plagues Edward, and the Villierses live in poverty at **Mrs. Derham**'s lodgings, where Ethel becomes reacquainted with Fanny, **Francis Derham**'s daughter. The Villierses are forced to live apart while Edward avoids creditors, until he is finally imprisoned; Ethel joins him in jail. Fanny informs Cornelia of her daughter's sufferings, and Cornelia, driven by emotions she cannot name, devises a secret scheme by which she releases Edward from all debt, gives the couple her London house, and leaves London for poverty and obscurity. Horatio, having become heir to his father **Lord Maristow**'s title, is returning to England when his wife dies; Horatio returns with baby daughter **Clorinda** and joins the Villierses in London. At **Maristow Castle**, intrigued by **Mr. Gayland**'s hints, Horatio discovers Cornelia's generosity and sets out to **France** to find her, while Edward searches London. Cornelia has, in fact, falling ill en route to **Rhyaider Gowy**, traveled to **Dame Nixon**'s cottage to recover and to visit her husband's grave at nearby Longfield. Elizabeth learns of her presence there and reunites Cornelia with Ethel. Finally, the Villierses are happy together, as are Cornelia and Horatio, who become **Viscount** and **Viscountess Maristow**. References throughout *Lodore* demonstrate Shelley's careful structure; for example, references to the **Revolutionary War** determine Lord Lodore's age, and further textual references confirm that the novel's main events are set in the early 1830s, roughly corresponding with its time of composition. Ethel, like **Elizabeth Falkner**, honors duty toward her father above all else; Shelley's descriptions of Ethel's and Fanny's different educations serve as an interesting commentary upon Shelley's own parents' educational theories and methods.

Lodore, Lady Cornelia: See **Lodore, Lady**.

Lodore, Lady: **Sir John** and **Lady Santerre**'s only daughter in *Lodore*. Originally **Cornelia Santerre**, she becomes Lady Lodore upon marrying **Lord Lodore**, with whom she has a daughter, **Ethel Villiers**; she becomes **Viscountess Maristow** when she marries **Horatio Saville**.

Lodore, Lord: Born **Henry Fitzhenry**, **Lady Lodore**'s first husband and **Ethel Villiers** and **Casimir Lyzinski**'s father in *Lodore*. Lord Lodore inherits his title from his father, **Admiral Fitzhenry**.

Loffenburgh: See **Laufenburg**.

Lohmen: **German** town twelve miles southeast of **Dresden**. Shelley passed through it August 1842 (*R* 1.261).

Lohr: **German** town on the **Main**, forty miles southeast of **Frankfurt**. Shelley slept there June 1842 (*R* 1.179).

Loire: River rising in south **France** and flowing north through Orleans before turning west to St. Nazaire and entering the **Bay of Biscay**, now a popular tourist area renowned for beautiful chateaux lining its banks. **Chateau Villeneuve** is "on a rugged steep overlooking the Loire," and **St. Catherine**'s couch is "a narrow ledge overhanging the deep rapid Loire" (*D* 153, 160).

Lombardo-Veneto: **Austrians** created this northern **Italian** region 1815. Shelley accurately relates that this new kingdom was formed when northern Italy was ceded to Austria (*R* 2.113).

Lombardy: Northern **Italian** region. Shelley first traveled there 1818 (*Journals* 204). She calls Lombardy and **Tuscany** Italy's "most civilized districts" (*V* 1.2). When **Louis of Bavaria** invaded Italy 1327, "he marched through Lombardy, crossed the **Apennines** at **Parma**, and was met by **Castruccio** at **Pontremoli**" (*V* 3.264). **Edmund Malville** admires Lombardy as "beautiful in its kind" (*RI* 27). **Flora Mancini** travels toward Lombardy, and "The Trial of Love" is set in and near Lombardy's **Este** (*Brother* 184; *Trial* 231). Shelley described her September 1840 travels in Lombardy (staying in **Milan**) and her September 1842 visit there, finding "fertile" Lombardy "so refreshing, so new, so enchanting" (*R* 1.108, 2.74). Shelley details Lombard nobility's history and **Carbonarism** (*R* 2.113–116, 2.177–178).

Lombardy, Governor of: See **Serbelloni**.

Lombardy, Plains of: Central Lombard plain where several **Alpine** passes meet. Shelley describes beautiful hills she saw between the Alps and plain September 1840 (*R* 1.106).

London: Shelley's childhood home was at the commercial heart of Britain's capital city. Her mother was buried in **St. Pancras** Church's graveyard, then north of London. The London of Shelley's day was not the sprawling metropolis it has since become but a smaller grouping of distinct areas that conglomerated as London's population exploded in the mid-nineteenth century (Crook 2). Shelley thrived on London's social, intellectual, and cultural opportunities, yet following **PBS**'s death, financial worries made it necessary for her to live outside the city. *History* begins with "We left London July 28th, 1814" (*H* 1). In **Geneva**, Shelley was glad to have "escaped" London (*H* 53, 96). **Henry Clerval** and **Victor Frankenstein** determine "to remain several months in this wonderful and celebrated city" (*Fr1* 149, 181, 185; *Fr3* 26, 132, 134). **Matilda**'s feeling that "a great city is a frightful habitation to one sorrowing" directly reflects Shelley's emotion upon returning to London after PBS's death (*M* 160, 187). **Dame Smithson**'s husband directs her move from London to **Ilfracombe** (*Maurice* 81). **Alderigo**, "a rich merchant in London," introduces **Castruccio** at London's court (*V* 1.68, 1.134). London is a prominent setting for many scenes central to *The Last Man*, and several protagonists have houses there near **Hyde Park** (*LM* 11, 47, 93). Plague survivors leave London for their journey abroad (*LM* 91). **Lewis Elmore** travels to London to inquire about **Clarice Eversham** (*Mourner* 93, 95). References to London abound throughout *Perkin Warbeck*, since it is the site of **Henry VII**'s court as well as of the **Tower**—central scenes and characters are naturally situated in the capital city, and **Richard of York** is executed there (*PW* 1.34, 1.47, 1.57, 3.321–327). **Sir Richard Gray** promises to take **Ellen** to London, and **Clinton Gray** and **Lady Caroline Hythe** both reside there (*ES* 246, 251, 163). Many of *Lodore*'s characters live there: **Lord** and **Lady Lodore** have their first home together at **Berkeley Square**, while the **Villiers**es live in several areas there (*L* 1.115, 1.290, 2.207, 2.257). **Colonel Villiers** and **Miss Gregory**, as well as the Villierses, are married in London, and Lady Lodore consistently participates in London society (*L* 2.248, 2.166, 3.75). **Elizabeth Falkner**'s parents struggle financially in London but are happy together, and many of *Falkner*'s characters live in London: **Rupert Falkner** takes a house at **Wimbledon** with Elizabeth; **Gerard Neville** is called to testify in the **House of Lords** and eventually locates **Hoskins** in London; **Sir Boyvill Neville** has a house there (*F* 11, 83, 138, 187, 216). Shelley emphasizes "**Euphrasia**'s" frame's veracity by including the detail that "the king's courier was stopt by the drift [of Christmas 1836 snow] on his way to London" (*E* 295). Shelley found "gaiety, animation, life" in **Paris** June 1840 that could not be found in London, attributing part of the contrast to London's lack of fountains (*R* 1.8). In **Bergamo** September 1840, Shelley recorded with distaste: the "waiters are unwashed, uncouth animals, reminding one of a sort of human being to be met in the streets of London" (*R* 1.107). Before leaving for **Europe** in 1842, Shelley regretted having to prepare to depart in London; she gave a negative report of **Frankfurt**'s opera as being comparable to "the company we had in London" (*R* 1.156, 1.177). Shelley noted: the "good people of **Kissingen** will hail a second harvest when we hurry across the channel at the end of the London season" (*R* 1.193). [*Par* 270, 273].

London Bridge: Stone bridge crossing the **Thames** in **London**, begun 1176; executed criminals' heads were displayed on it beginning 1305 (Weinreb 468). **James III**'s "personal friends and adherents" were hanged over the bridge (*PW* 2.184, 3.229).

London Coffee House: Opened 5 January 1771 on Ludgate Hill, this "integral part of the social life of the times" was a meeting place for "wits and men of fashion, as well as for learned men, merchants, and politicians" (Cunningham 496; Kent 208). While the Shelleys arranged meetings to circumvent bailiffs 1814, Shelley met **PBS** at the London Coffee House 24

October, writing to him the following day to arrange another appointment "at the door of the coffee house at five oclock [sic] as it is disagreeable to go into these places" (*Journals* 38; *Letters* 1.1). **Hookham** later warned PBS not to return there, presumably because of bailiffs (*Journals* 40). **Ethel Villiers** gives **Saunders** a letter to take to her husband at the London Coffee House (*L* 3.4).

London, Tower of: See **Tower**.

Long Roger: Probably Roger Ray, **Yorkist** prisoner in the **Tower** (Anderson 204). In Shelley's version, Roger is a Tower guard who assists **Richard of York** (*PW* 3.286–91).

Long Walk: Name given to path **Charles II** planned to improve the view from **Windsor**. Planting began 1684, and Long Walk now stretches south into **Great Park** about three miles from Windsor Castle (Hedley 116). Many of *The Last Man*'s characters traverse Long Walk (*LM* 262, 312). Verney records leaving Windsor forever down "the dusky avenue of the Long Walk" (*LM* 329).

Longfield: Fictitious **Essex** village "distant eight miles from any market town," and **Lodore** family house, also known as "Great House," where **Elizabeth Fitzhenry** lives, four miles from the village (*L* 1.1–2, 1.85, 2.166, 3.256). The **Villiers**es visit Elizabeth there several times, and **Lady Lodore** lodges nearby (*L* 3.249). Shelley consistently contrasts Longfield's "tranquility and remoteness" favorably with **London**'s busy life; **Lord Lodore** is buried at Longfield (*L* 2.230, 3.175).

Lope de Vega, Carpio (1562–1635): Prolific **Spanish** writer renowned for drama and successful in most genres. Shelley wrote Lope's biography for *Italian and Spanish Lives*. He took part in the **Spanish Armada** (1588) and wrote many sonnets, published in *Rimas humanes* [*Human Poems*] (1602), in memory of his first wife. Lope's *La Dorotea* [*Dorotea*] (1632) "presents a vivid picture of Spanish manners" and is "a story told in dialogue ... much of which is spirited and natural, but much, very much, pedantic, and beyond expression tedious" in Shelley's opinion (*ISPL* 3.204, 3.207). While in the Armada, Lope wrote *La Hermosura de Angélica* [*Angelica's Beauty*] (1602), "a continuation of **Ariosto**'s poem" that "possesses little merit" (*ISPL* 3.210–211). Shelley notes that by 1605 Lope's theatrical works' "originality, novelty, vivacity, and adaptation to the Spanish taste, secured unparalleled success" (*ISPL* 3.217). Lope's "name passed into a proverb; it became a synonyme [sic] for the superlative degree"; Shelley notes that his works are too numerous to list completely; Lope was "the most prolific of writers, and the most facile" (*ISPL* 3.219, 3.221). She finds his dramas "original, fecund, national, universal, true and spirited" and concludes that he possessed "a richness of invention, a freshness and variety of ideas, and a vivacity of dialogue unsurpassed by any author" (*ISPL* 3.230, 3.232, 3.237).

Lorenzo: **Beatrice** correctly predicts this child's death (*V* 2.82).

Lostendardo, Guielmo: Guelph supporter and **Despina dei Elisei**'s suitor in "**A Tale of the Passions**."

Lothbury: Street north of the Bank of England in **London**'s City district. **Jahn Warbeck**'s residence is there (*PW* 1.44). Some **Longfield** residents see London after visiting "cousins in Lothbury," and **Ethel Villiers** travels through it to meet her husband (*L* 1.2, 2.257).

Lothians: Three Scottish counties, divided into West-, Mid-, and East-Lothian, surrounding **Edinburgh**. Scottish defiance against England "would be echoed in glad shouts from . . . the Lothians" (*PW* 2.194).

Lotus land: See **Ulysses**.

Louis IV (c. 1287–1347): Called Louis of **Bavaria**, crowned king of **Germany** 1314 and excommunicated by Pope John XXII. He invaded **Italy**, deposed the pope, and invested Peter of Corvara as Pope Nicholas V in 1327; Peter crowned Louis Holy Roman Emperor 1328 (Kinder 1.195). **Castruccio** joins Louis's Italian campaign and is knighted for his service (*V* 3.263–265).

Louis XI (1423–1483): King of **France** 1461–83. Shelley mentions Louis's attempt to take **Burgundy** from the **Duchess of Burgundy** (*PW* 1.130, 2.28). **Stephen Frion** worked for Louis (*PW* 1.149, 3.8). **Lord Lovel** visits **Brittany** at the time of Louis's death (*PW* 1.4).

Louis XIV (1638–1715): Bourbon King of **France** 1661–1715; he built Versailles (Mobry 78; Kinder 1.259–261). Shelley relates that Louis "laid waste" **Heidelberg Castle** in 1693 (*R* 1.35; *Cook's* 143).

Louis-Philippe (1773–1850): Duke of Orleans 1793–1830 and King of **France** 1830–48. Shelley relates that Louis's government "excited two unfortunate enslaved countries, **Poland** and **Italy**, to rebel" (*R* 2.249, 2.251).

Lovel, Lord Francis (1454–c. 1487): **Richard III**'s trusted friend; he fought at **Bosworth Field**, took sanctuary in **Colchester**, organized a revolt with **Staffords** in Worcestershire and Yorkshire, and supported **Lambert Simnel**. He supposedly died at **Stoke** (*DNB*). **Richard of York** supporter in *Perkin Warbeck*.

Lover's Melancholy, The: Ford's tragicomedy, first performed 1629. Shelley quotes Corax's speech concluding Ford's drama as an epigraph to each *Lodore* volume: "**In the turmoil** of our lives, / Men are like politic states, or troubled seas, / Tossed up and down with several storms and tempests, / Change and variety of wrecks and fortunes; / Till, laboring to the havens of our homes, / We struggle for the calm that crowns our ends" (Ford 5.1.4–9). Shelley also quotes Prince Palador's speech upon finding his lost beloved, Eroclea, as an epigraph to the chapter in which **Horatio Saville** aspires to reunite with **Lady Lodore**: "The music / Of man's fair composition best accords, / When 'tis in consort, not in single strains: / My heart has been untuned these many months, / Wanting her presence, in whose equal love / True harmony consisted" (*L* 3.221; Ford 4.3.50–55).

Lovosice: Czech village on the **Elbe**, fourteen miles northwest of **Prague**, Shelley's **Lobositz** (Moskal 219). Shelley slept there August 1842 (*R* 1.279).

Lowlands: Southern Scottish region bordering England. Shelley joined Scottish traveling companions in **Milan** September 1840; they had "as rich a **Doric** accent as the Lowlands can produce" (*R* 1.127).

Loxa: Spanish "city of great strength, at no great distance from" the **Alhambra** (Irving 34). **Ferdinand** laid siege to and conquered it 1482 (Irving 34–38). The **Earl of Rivers** fights at the siege of Loxa (*PW* 1.211).

Lucan, Marcus Annaeus (39–65 C.E.): Poet and **Seneca the Younger**'s nephew, educated at **Rome** and **Athens**. Only one work has survived: his uncompleted ten-book epic *De Bello Civili* [*Concerning the Civil War*], commonly known as *Pharsalia*, about the civil wars between **Caesar** and **Pompey** (Howatson 328, 428–429; Crook 2). Shelley read Lucan's work June–September 1819 (*Journals* 293). **Isabell Harley** introduces **Valerius** to Lucan's works (*Val* 343). Shelley describes **Roger Dodsworth** as "one of those men . . . who did not follow **Cato**'s advice as recorded in the Pharsalia," a reference to Lucan's ninth book (*RD* 45; Lucan 9.256–410; Crook 2).

Lucas, Louis: French naval commander **Charles VIII** sent to **Ireland** 1492 to invite **Perkin Warbeck** to France (Arthurson 2, 15, 50–51). Charles sends to **Cork** an embassy led by Lucas and others (*PW* 1.308).

Lucca: **Italian** city ten miles northeast of **Pisa**. Shelley visited it August 1820 to observe locations associated with **Castruccio** and to see the city's surrounding terrain; she saw an *improvisatore* there in January 1821 (*Journals* 328–329, 348–349; Sunstein 185). "**A Tale of the Passions**" details **Florentine** 13th-century political turmoil, as **Ghibellines** seek refuge in Lucca (*TP* 1). Fourteenth-century Lucca and its surroundings are *Valperga*'s primary settings, and Shelley details her exploration of places mentioned in *Valperga* in a letter (*Letters* 1.364; Green 14). Castruccio becomes Lucca's ruler around 1314, holding this powerful post until his death (*V* 1.171, 1.230, 3.269).

Lucerne: Swiss city where the **Reuss** connects to **Lake Lucerne**. The Shelleys arrived there August 1814 (*Journals* 19; *H* 46). Poverty-stricken **Beauforts** move to Lucerne, where **Alphonse Frankenstein** finds his future wife mourning her father's death (*Fr1* 63; *Fr3* 38).

Lucerne, Lake: Central **Swiss** lake connecting several smaller lakes and the **Reuss**. The Shelleys visited it 1814 (*Journals* 18; *H* 47). **Henry Clerval** states that Lake Lucerne's beauty pales in comparison to **Rhine** landscape (*Fr1* 182; *Fr3* 133). Shelley finds Lake Lucerne, "with its dark lofty precipices

Lucia

and verdant isles," more beautiful than **Lake Zurich** (*R* 1.53). She traveled by steamer on it October 1840 (*R* 1.152).

Lucia: See **Donizetti**.

Lucia: See *Promessi Sposi*.

Lucifer: The Devil; in **Roman** mythology, morning star (Tripp 348). **Lionel Verney** suggests that rumors about **Irish** invaders are so exaggerated that **Virgil**'s Rumour could reach and take Lucifer from the sky (*LM* 298). **Robert Clifford** denies repentance of his treachery with the oath, " 'As Lucifer in hell!' " (*PW* 3.145). The **dwarf** calls **Guido il Cortese** "cousin of Lucifer" after learning of Cortese's misdeeds (*Trans* 128).

Lucretius, Titus Carus (98–c. 55 B.C.E.): **Roman** poet, philosopher, and author of *De rerum natura* [*On the Nature of the Universe*] (c. mid-1st century B.C.E.), which outlines Epicurean philosophy; Shelley read it 1820 (*Journals* 324). At *The Last Man*'s opening, the narrator states: "I have often wondered at the subject of [the **Cumaean Sibyl**'s] verses, and at the English dress of the **Latin poet**," possibly a reference to Lucretius or **Virgil** (*LM* 6; Crook 2). **Gerard Neville** perceives in **Elizabeth Falkner** "that emanation, that shadow of the shape, which the Latin poet tells us flows from every object, that impalpable impress of her form and being, which the air took and then folded round him"; Blumberg identifies this reference to Lucretius and his work (*F* 91; Blumberg 84; *On Nature* 4.42–52).

Lucullus, Lucius Licinius (c. 114–57 B.C.E.): **Sulla**'s officer who supported his general's 88 B.C.E. march on **Rome** and subsequently held various political offices, including Governor of **Africa** 77 B.C.E. and Consul of Rome 74 B.C.E.; he also led successful campaigns against **Mithridates** 74 B.C.E. (Howatson 332). **Valerius** ponders, " 'how could I despair of my country while such men as **Cicero**, **Cato**, Lucullus . . . full of virtue and wisdom—who were my intimate and dearest friends—still existed' " (*Val* 333). Valerius " 'gloried with an excessive joy' " to be Lucullus's friend (*Val* 336).

Ludgate: **London** city gate in what is now the **Fleet Street** area; formerly, a prison was above it (Weinreb 486). **Lady Katherine Gordon** and **Elizabeth of York** visit **Richard of York** imprisoned there (*PW* 3.330).

Lugano: Large **Swiss** town on **Lake Lugano**, fifteen miles northwest of **Como**. Shelley includes a description of **PFS**'s friend's dangerous September 1840 journey; they arrived at Lugano about two o'clock one morning (*R* 1.147–148).

Lugano, Lake: **Swiss** lake between lakes **Maggiore** and **Como** in northern **Italy**. Shelley includes **PFS**'s friend's account of their dangerous September 1840 journey, during which they viewed Lake Lugano (*R* 1.147–148).

Luini, Bernardino (c. 1485–1532): **Milanese** painter who imitated **Leo-**

nardo da Vinci; several Bernardino pieces are in the **Brera** (Chilvers 333). Shelley viewed several "Luinis" in Milan September 1840, finding him "ever a pleasing artist" (*R* 1.110).

Lumbard's Marsh: Marshland five miles southeast of **Cork** (Fischer 282). For the **Waterford** attack, **Richard of York** is close to the marsh (*PW* 3.35).

Lungo l'Arno: Banks of the **Arno**; streets along it are called "Lungarno," as well as such other designations as "Nuovo" or "Corsini" (*Florence* 80, 238). Shelley mentions **Pisa**'s riverside streets and took apartments on **Florence**'s "Lungo l'Arno" October 1842 (*R* 2.111, 2.133).

Lunigiana: Italian province just north of **La Spezia**. **Louis of Bavaria** makes **Castruccio** duke of an area including Lunigiana (*V* 3.264–265). He actually conferred this title on Castruccio November 1327 (Green 221).

Luther, Martin (1483–1546): German monk and **biblical** scholar whose "Ninety-Five Theses" criticizing papal policy triggered the Protestant **Reformation**. He defended his beliefs at the **Diet of Worms** (1521). Shelley journeyed to "Luther's Germany" and visited **Wartburg Castle** July 1842, where Luther lived for ten months while translating the Bible, and **Erfurt**'s **Augustine** convent, where she saw Luther's cell and the church where he gave his first sermon (*R* 1.175, 1.207–209).

Luton: English town twenty-five miles northwest of **London**. **Adrian** and his troops spend the night there (*LM* 300).

Luttrel, Sir Hugh: British soldier in *Perkin Warbeck*.

Luxembourg: Small Western European country bordered by **Belgium**, **France**, and **Germany**; Shelley spells it **Luxemburgh**. Shelley repeatedly refers to the invasion of **Italy** by **Henry VII** of Germany; he was count of Luxembourg (*V* 1.101, 1.127).

Luxemburgh: See **Luxembourg**.

Lybia: See **Libya**.

Lycurgus: Semimythical 9th-century B.C.E. **Spartan** lawgiver. He established a senate and a military societal system based on essentiality (Plutarch, *Lives* 1.59–81). The **Creature** reads **Plutarch**'s description of Lycurgus and admires him (*Fr1* 156; *Fr3* 112).

Lydian: Ancient name given to **Asia** Minor's central western area, which the **Aegean** borders to the west; its music is characterized as gentle and sensual (Tripp 352–53). At **Versailles**, **Lionel Verney** finds his mind drifting until "the softest melody of Lydian flute" recalls him to present misery (*LM* 384).

Lyndsay, David: See **Dods**.

Lyons: French town on the **Rhône**, sixty-five miles southwest of **Geneva**. Shelley passed through it en route to **Italy** 1818 (*Letters* 1.62–63; Sunstein 150). **Felix De Lacey** helps **Safie** and her father escape via Lyons to Italy (*Fr1*

Lyzinski, Count Casimir

152; *Fr3* 109). The **Villiers**es return from **Naples** by "the beaten route of **Mont Cenis**, Lyons, and **Calais**" (*L* 2.207). **Horatio Saville** describes **Bagnères de Bigorre** as "annual resort" for Lyons's people (*L* 3.240). **Elizabeth Falkner** and **Rupert Falkner** journey up the Rhône from **Marseilles** to Lyons (*F* 77, 82). Shelley stayed there October 1840 (*R* 1.141, 1.144).

Lyzinski, Count Casimir: **Lord Lodore** and **Countess Theodora Lyzinski**'s illegitimate son in *Lodore*. **Ethel Villiers** never encounters her half-brother.

Lyzinski, Countess Theodora: **Lord Lodore**'s former lover and mother of their illegitimate son, **Casimir Lyzinski**, in *Lodore*.

M

M——: See **Henry, Mary Ann**.

Maasluis: Small **Dutch** port where Lek River enters the **North Sea**; Shelley also uses the **French** form, **Marsluys**. The Shelleys stayed there September 1814 (*H* 78; *Journals* 24).

Mac Swiney: Probably variant of MacSweeney, famous **Irish** military family in **Munster** (Connolly 339). **Desmond** is related to them by marriage (*PW* 1.279).

Macarthy of Muskerry: One of three **Irish MacCarthy** chiefs; Cormac led Muskerry Macarthys 1461–95 (Fischer 123). **Desmond** meets Macarthy on **Ballahourah** (*PW* 1.301–302).

Macarthy Reagh: Finghin Mac-Carthy Reagh, Lord of Carbery; he led Macarthy clan in southwest **Cork** county 1478–1505 (Fischer 124; Connolly 334). **Desmond**'s sister marries Reagh (*PW* 1.302).

Macbeth: Tragedy **Shakespeare** wrote 1606; Shelley read it October 1818 (*Journals* 233). It records Macbeth's unconquerable ambition after three "weird sisters" (witches) visit and predict his rise. Macbeth kills Scotland's King Duncan, tries to kill the king's son, **Malcolm** (who flees to England), and becomes a bloody tyrant. Suspicious of Macbeth's rise to power, **Macduff** goes to England to raise an army with Malcolm; there, **Rosse** informs him that Macbeth has murdered Macduff's family. Macduff finally kills Macbeth. **Lionel Verney** watches part of *Macbeth* at **Drury Lane Theatre**: "we forgot that Malcolm and Macduff were mere human beings, acted upon by such simple passions as warmed our own breasts" (*LM* 282). Verney leaves the performance echoing "the cry of Macduff" when he learns of his family's murder: " '**All my pretty** ones? / Did you say all?—O hell kite! All? / What! all my pretty chickens, and their dam, / At one fell swoop!' " (*LM* 282–283; *Macbeth* 4.3.217–220). Verney com-

Maccabees

pares the dramatic depiction of troubled Scotland to the plague's threat to England, noting the connection "when Rosse exclaimed, in answer to '**Stands Scotland where** it did?' " with lines beginning " '**Alas, poor country**; / Almost afraid to know itself!' " (*LM* 282–283; *Macbeth* 4.3.165–174). Shelley terms conspiring **Robert Clifford** and **Stephen Frion** " 'mousing owls,' " adopting a phrase the Old Man speaks to Rosse regarding supernatural events (*PW* 3.118; *Macbeth* 2.4.13). Shelley describes **Sir William Stanley**'s wait for death: "it is an awful emotion, when we feel that the '**very shoal of time**' on which we stand, is freighted with the good and ill of futurity," an allusion to Macbeth's soliloquy (*PW* 2.113; *Macbeth* 1.7.6). Shelley uses the same speech in describing **Huntley** as an "ambitious noble, '**overleaping**' himself" (*PW* 2.250; *Macbeth* 1.7.25–28). Shelley also quoted from this speech in February 1840 (*Letters* 3.337). Noting **Lady Lodore**'s "frequent show of frank cordiality" gains society's approval, Shelley quotes from Macbeth's speech rejecting his wife's suggestion of harming Duncan with reference to the fact that Duncan "Hath honored me of late, and I have bought / **Golden opinions** from all sorts of people" (*L* 2.70; *Macbeth* 1.7.33–34). Shelley adapts a line to describe **Devon** flowers in " '**every nook** and coign of vantage' " (*F* 5; Clemit 5; *Macbeth* 1.6.7). She describes **Elbe**'s ebbing waters as not in " '**its pride** of place,' " a line the old man speaks to Rosse (*R* 1.246; *Macbeth* 2.4.12).

Maccabees: Two **apocryphal** books of the **Bible** (Browning 237). Shelley gives **Heliodorus**'s story from Maccabees, quoting several passages beginning "**there was no** small agony," "**And all**, holding up their hands," and "**the Lord of** Spirits" (*R* 2.220; 2 Maccabees 3.7–40).

MacCarthys: **Munster** political dynasty that ruled as the kings of Desmond in Kerry county (Connolly 334). **Desmond** is related to MacCarthys by marriage; **Hubert Burgh** tells **Richard of York** about feuds between them and Desmond (*PW* 1.279, 1.290–291, 1.297). Desmond meets **MacCarthy of Muskerry** to discuss peace (*PW* 1.301–302). The MacCarthys support Richard at **Waterford** (*PW* 3.32; Arthurson 114).

Macciucoli, Lago di: See **Lago di Massaciucuoli**.

Macduff: See *Macbeth*.

Macedonia: Formerly, country north of ancient **Greece**, now a southern **European** region including parts of the Balkans, especially northern Greece. **Beatrice** mentions **Philip of Macedon**'s violence and destruction (*V* 3.50). Shelley set many of *The Last Man*'s scenes there during Greece's war with **Turkey**: Turks initially control Macedonia, but subsequently Greek supplies stored in Macedonia reveal Greek repossession of it (*LM* 161, 190). When the Greek army disbands, "whole battalions" travel toward Macedonia; **Lionel Verney** and **Perdita** follow them to **Athens** (*LM* 195, 208). Plague spreads in Macedonia (*LM* 220).

Machiavelli, Niccolo (1469–1527): **Florentine** politician who drew upon professional experience to write treatises, the most renowned of which is *Il*

Principe [*The Prince*] (1513). Shelley drew broadly from Machiavelli's historical and political writings, particularly *La vita di Castruccio Castracani da Lucca* [**The Life of Castruccio Castracani of Lucca**] (written 1520, published 1532), which she read March–April 1820 (*DIL* 533; *Journals* 313–314; *V* 1.iii). Despite Shelley's disclaimer in **Valperga**'s introduction, she drew much from Machiavelli's version: **Francesco Guinigi**, **Uguccione della Faggiuola**, and **Matteo Visconti** appear in both works, and Machiavelli's detailed battle scenes influenced her; **William Godwin** abridged many battle scenes prior to *Valperga*'s publication (*V* 1.212; Sunstein 235). Shelley also probably borrowed **Mandragola**'s name from Machiavelli (*V* 3.126; Crook 3.272). Shelley wrote Machiavelli's biography for **Italian and Spanish Lives**. In July 1834, Shelley noted being "now engaged on Macchiavelli—This takes up my time & is a source of interest & pleasure" (*Letters* 2.209). Shelley analyzes Machiavelli's mission to Cesare Borgia extensively to determine "whether [Machiavelli] sincerely recommended the detestable principles of government which he appears to advocate [in *Il Principe*], or used the weapons of irony and sarcasm to denounce a system of tyranny which then oppressed his native country"; she favors the latter opinion (*ISPL* 1.263). Shelley introduces the principal Machiavellian ideas, interspersing her lengthy account of Machiavelli's turbulent political career with brief references to some of his works, such as *Discorsi sopra la prima Deca di Tito Livio* [*Essays on Livy's First Decade*] (wr. 1513–17; pub. 1531), *Arta della Guerra* [*Art of War*] (1517–20), his life of Castruccio, and comedy *Novella di Belfagor arcidiavolo* [*Belfegor Archdevil's Novella*] (wr. by 1520) (*ISPL* 1.300). Shelley read Machiavelli's *Istorie Fiorentine* [*Florence's History*] (wr. 1525; pub. 1532) April 1822 (*Journals* 406–408). She wanted to explore towns and scenes familiar to Machiavelli November 1842 (*R* 2.134).

Machin: See **Markham, Gervase**.

Mackey, Sampson Arnold: Early-19th-century shoemaker and author who published works dealing with astrology and the zodiac. In **The Last Man**, **Merrival** discusses an earthly paradise and earthly purgatory in the future; Shelley footnotes his comments with reference to "The Mythological Astronomy of the Ancients Demonstrated, by restoring to their Fables & Symbols their Original Meanings. By Sampson Arnold Mackey, Shoe-maker," of which there were three editions during the 1820s (*LM* 221).

"Madame d'Houtetôt": Essay Shelley published in the 26 April 1823 *Liberal* (*Letters* 1.325). She relates the biography of Elisabeth-Sophie, comtesse d'Houdetôt (1730–1813), who was "object of [**Rousseau**'s] passionate love and the cause of so many of his misfortunes" (*Mad d'H* 67). The spelling "Houtetôt" is seemingly without precedent and may be due to a typesetter's misreading of Shelley's handwriting (Crook 2). Sunstein compares the love triangle Shelley presents—between Rousseau, d'Houdetôt, and Jean-François, Marquis de Saint-Lambert—to the relationship between **Hogg**, Shelley, and **PBS** (105, 232). Shelley also includes an account of the Rousseau-d'Houdetôt relationship in

Maddalena Scapigliata

her Rousseau biography (*FL* 2.141–144).

Maddalena Scapigliata: See **Titian**.

Madeira: In the North **Atlantic Ocean**, island belonging to **Portugal**; it was a port of call on trade routes between **Europe** and the New World, such as **Barbados** (Crook 2). **Clarice Eversham** "wrote home...from Madeira" (*Mourner* 92).

Madge: **Long Roger**'s wife in *Perkin Warbeck*.

Madonna: See **Mary**.

Madonna: See **Correggio**.

Madonna del Soccorso: Festival celebrating the miracle of the Virgin stopping a plague. Shelley was in **Como** September 1840 during it (*R* 1.102).

Madonna di Casa Colonna: See **Raphael**.

Madonna di Foligno: See **Raphael**.

Madonna di San Sisto: See **Raphael**.

Madre, Isola: **Borromean** island in **Lake Maggiore**; Shelley visited it September 1840 (*R* 1.129).

Magdalen, The: Shelley's name for small picture, *The Reading Magdalen*, on display at **Gallery in Dresden**. Shelley found it "wonderful" August 1842 (*R* 1.237). She notes that the original had been copied numerous times, attributing it to **Correggio**, but its artist is uncertain (*R* 1.237; Vasari 3.31).

Magireda: **Wilhelmina** of **Bohemia**'s female companion in *Valperga*.

Magi: Biblical wise men from the East who followed a star to Bethlehem to see baby Jesus (Matthew 2.1–12). Shelley describes a **Raphael** painting of "adoration of the Magi" in **Berlin**, but her description does not match any of Raphael's paintings (*R* 1.221; Moskal 190).

Magic Ring: See **La Motte Fouquè**.

Magna Grecia: Latin for "great **Greece**," referring to ancient Greek colonies on **Italy**'s southern coast. Shelley notes that it "was the mother of many philosophers" and describes the region's commercial success (*R* 2.280, 2.289).

Magni, Cieco: **Clorinda Saviani**'s former suitor in "**The Bride of Modern Italy**."

Magnus, Albertus: See **Albertus Magnus**.

Magra: Italian river between **La Spezia** and **Pontremoli**. Attacking **Genoa**, **Castruccio** "deluged the country" from **Lucca** to Magra "in blood" (*V* 2.171). He later controls, then moves beyond, the region around Magra (*V* 2.174, 2.178).

Mahmoud: See **Mehmed II**.

Mahomet: See **Muhammed**.

Mahometan: A Muslim, follower of **Muhammad**, thus one who practices **Islamic** religion. Shelley uses "Mahometan" to refer to **Safie**'s father (*Fr1* 150; *Fr3* 108). **Euphrasia** is a **Greek** Christian looking "forward eagerly to the day when Mahometanism should no longer contaminate her native land" (*E* 302). **Stephen Frion** becomes a "Mahometan master's" servant (*PW* 1.150). [*TP* 7].

Main: German river joining the **Rhine** at **Mainz**. Shelley traveled through Main's "beautiful" valley June 1840 (*R* 1.178).

Maina: Greek village thirty-five miles northwest of **Cerigo**; the surrounding region's inhabitants, **Mainotes**, have a "tranquil cast of countenance," are proud of "their descent from the ancient **Spartans**," and were formerly renowned for feuds with **Kakovougnis** (*EE* 107; *MGRE* 268, 270). **Dmitri** finds "his home ravaged by the Mainotes" (*EE* 100–101). **Camaraz** is Mainote, and **Zella Ziani** is assumed to be before Camaraz reveals her true parentage (*EE* 107, 114–115).

Mainz: German city, **Mayence** in French, at the confluence of the **Main** and **Rhine** rivers. The Shelleys passed through it September 1814 (*Journals* 22; *H* 66–67). **Victor Frankenstein** and **Henry Clerval** pass through Mainz (*Fr1* 182; *Fr3* 132). **Rupert Falkner** arranges for **Elizabeth Falkner** to meet him there (*F* 51). Shelley traveled "up the Rhine to Mayence" and slept there July 1840 (*R* 1.9, 1.27). She returned June 1842 when, due to illness, she stayed in the train station while her companions visited **Mayence Cathedral** (*R* 1.28–29, 1.172). [*H* 61].

Maison Chapuis: Cottage at **Montalègre** on **Lake Geneva**'s eastern shore, where the Shelleys stayed summer 1816, beginning early June (Sunstein 117; *Journals* 107–108). Shelley saw it from a steamer October 1840 (*R* 1.147).

Maison Neuve: French inn two miles south of **Nods**. The Shelleys' driver left them at Nods and traveled to Maison Neuve and then **Pontalier** searching for them August 1814 (*Journals* 15–16; *H* 36).

Makri: Thracian town on the **Aegean**, 165 miles west of **Istanbul**. **Raymond** leads the cavalry charge at the Battle of Makri (*LM* 163).

Malaga: Spanish Mediterranean port seventy-six miles southwest of **Granada**. **Hernan De Faro** plans to take **Richard of York** there (*PW* 1.198, 1.200). **Edmund Plantagenet** follows, and **Lord Barry** meets De Faro there later (*PW* 1.203, 1.230–231).

Malamocco: Port on **Lido**, four miles south of **Venice**. Shelley relates that the **Archduke** viewed "sea-wall buildings" there prior to departing Venice October 1842 (*R* 2.129).

Malcolm: See *Macbeth*.

Malespino, Calista de: Guest at **Euthanasia**'s court (*V* 1.264). "Malespino" is Shelley's variant of Malaspina, powerful family that opposed **Castruccio** (Green 14, 125).

Malespino, Maroello: Guest at **Euthanasia**'s court (*V* 1.255). "Malespino" is Shelley's variant of Malaspina, powerful family that opposed **Castruccio**; Maroello led half of **Pontremoli**'s inhabitants in rebellion against another faction (Green 14, 125). This feud allowed Castruccio to take Pontremoli without military action (Green 138–139).

Malines: Belgian city twelve miles south of **Antwerp**. Shelley changed carriages there June 1842 (*R* 1.163).

Mallow: Irish city seventeen miles northwest of **Cork**. **Keating** urges **Richard of York** to meet **Desmond** there (*PW* 1.301–302). **Lord Barry** meets Desmond en route and accompanies him (*PW* 1.305–307).

Malta: Mediterranean islands south of **Sicily**, British-owned since 1815 (Kinder 2.23–25, 2.39). **Lionel Verney** intends to sail "towards Malta" (*LM* 469). See **Knights of Malta**.

Malvezzi, Viscount di: Viscountess di Malvezzi's deceased husband and Marquess **Obizzo**'s "bitter and determined enemy" (*V* 2.20–21).

Malvezzi, Viscountess di: Madonna Marchesana's title (*V* 2.20–21).

Malville, Edmund: "Recollections of Italy's" main character. His description of a journey from **Pisa** to **Vico Pisano** is based on Shelley's September 1821 trip, when **PBS** and the **Williamses** accompanied her (*Journals* 380). Robinson asserts that "Malville presents the author's own recollections of Italy" (375).

Malvoglio: One of **Benedetto Pepi**'s debtors in *Valperga*.

Mamertine: Ancient prison for political prisoners beneath San Giuseppe dei Falegnami Church on **Rome**'s **Capitoline** (*MIRO* 101). Shelley visited it April 1843 (*R* 2.229).

Mammon: Fallen angel who worships gold and leads humankind to the same error in **Milton**'s *Paradise Lost*; his name is synonymous with evil riches (1.678–688). **Lady Santerre** is "dedicated to the vulgar worship of Mammon" (*L* 1.204). Shelley admired the interior richness of **San Marco**'s "tribute of Mammon to Heaven" October 1842 (*R* 2.122).

Manchester: English industrial city thirty-eight miles east of **Liverpool**. PBS responded to the August 1819 Manchester Peterloo Massacre in "**The Mask of Anarchy**" (*Journals* 298; White 2.105–107). Both Shelleys were troubled by the oppression of workers but never visited Manchester. Plague is rampant there (*LM* 268). When the **Irish** invade England, they proceed "as far as Manchester" before the English are aware of them (*LM* 298).

Mancini: Siennese family feuding with the **Tolomei** (*Brother* 167).

Mancini, Flora: **Ugo Mancini**'s daughter, **Lorenzo Mancini**'s sister, and a title character of "**The Brother and Sister**."

Mancini, Lorenzo: Ugo Mancini's son, **Flora Mancini**'s brother, and a title character of "**The Brother and Sister**."

Mancini, Ugo: Lorenzo and Flora Mancini's father in "**The Brother and Sister**."

Mandragola, Fior di: Witch, also called **Fior di Ligi**, who causes **Beatrice**'s death in *Valperga*.

Manelli, Messer Tommaso de': Baker for all of the **Sesto** near the **Arno** when **Count Guido Novello de' Guidi** is in office (*TP* 18).

Manfred (c. 1232–1266): Frederick II's illegitimate son who became **Sicily**'s regent 1250 (on behalf of **Conradin**); he ruled as Manfred II of Sicily from 1258 until his death; Manfred's daughter Constance became Sicily's queen (Kinder 1.173; Villani 151–152, 156–158). Shelley admired Manfred, as seen in "**A Tale of the Passions**," which details events occurring after Manfred's death and gives his brief history (*TP* 1, 10–16). Shelley also mentions Manfred in "**Giovanni Villani**" and attempted to write a drama based on him 1822 and 1824 (Crook 3.8). War with Manfred strengthens **Ruggieri dei Antelminelli**'s **Ghibelline** beliefs (*V* 1.3, 1.25). At **Euthanasia**'s court, **Guarino** sings about **Dante**'s encounter with Manfred (*V* 1.274; *Purgatorio* 3.103–145). When **Castruccio** sends Euthanasia to Sicily, it is under the **Aragon** family's control, "who inherited [it] from the daughter of Manfred" (*V* 3.259).

Manheim: See **Mannheim**.

Manhes, General (1777–1854): French general (*DBF*). Shelley mentions **Colletta**'s graphic description of Manhes's destruction of **Carbonari** (*R* 2.173).

Mannheim: German port on the **Rhine**, thirty-five miles southeast of **Mainz**; Shelley spells it **Manheim**. The Shelleys found it "strikingly neat and clean" September 1814 (*H* 65). **Henry Clerval** and **Victor Frankenstein** stay there overnight (*Fr1* 181; *Fr3* 132).

Manoir, Louis: One of **Victor Frankenstein** and **Henry Clerval**'s schoolmates in *Frankenstein*.

Manon: Constance Villeneuve's loyal servant in "**The Dream**."

Mansfield, Manon: Ugly Mansfield sister who marries **Duvillard** in *Frankenstein*.

Mansfield, Miss: Pretty Mansfield sister who plans to wed **John Melbourne** in *Frankenstein*.

Mantone: Italian river flowing through **Ravenna**. Feverish **Lionel Verney** follows its course (*LM* 453).

Mantua: Italian town twenty miles southwest of **Verona**. Shelley recounts **Hofer**'s execution there (*R* 2.59).

Manzoni, Alessandro (1785–1873): **Italian** writer. Shelley ranks Manzoni and **Niccolini** as the best Italian poets (*R* 1.x, 2.193). She finds Manzoni's "Inni Sacri" ["Sacred Hymns"] (1812–15) "distinguished for the exquisite finish and poetic fire that adorns the fervent piety which they breathe" (*R* 2.201). She praises *Il conte di Carmagnola* [*Carmagnola's Count*] (1819); Manzoni based this tragedy on 15th-century **Venetian** military commander Francesco Carmagnola's life (*R* 2.196; *DIL* 311–315). Shelley includes **Goethe**'s high opinion of *Carmagnola* and notes that "the audience are at a loss on whom to expend their sympathy" (*R* 2.196–197). She heard Manzoni's "**Ode on Napoleon**" (1821–22) August 1840, finding it "a glorious poem; the opening calls at once the attention; its rapid sketching of events is full of fire" (*R* 1.85–86). Manzoni wrote "Il **Cinque Maggio**" ["The Fifth of May"] about Napoleon's death (1821); Goethe translated it 1822 (*DIL* 311–315). Shelley mentions it as Manzoni's most famous ode outside Italy (*R* 2.198). She gives an extended description of I *promessi sposi* [*The Betrothed*] (1825–27) and also of *Adelchi* (1882), a tragedy based on **Charlemagne**'s 773–774 **Lombardy** invasion (*DIL* 313). Shelley asserts that *Adelchi* and *Carmagnola* were "hailed as national and romantic dramas; their fame spread into **Germany** and **France**" (*R* 2.196). She preferred *Adelchi*, since a reader "is most excited by **Ermengarda**," Adelchi's sister and Charlemagne's rejected wife, but Shelley also found her "entirely episodical" (*DIL* 313; *R* 2.197). [*R* 1.67, 1.86, 1.105]. See *Promessi sposi*.

Marathon: Small village twenty-two miles northeast of **Athens**; site of Battle of Marathon 490 B.C.E., where the Athenians stopped a **Persian** invasion of **Greece**. **Perdita** spends the night there (*LM* 208).

March, Ausias (1397–1459): **Spanish** nobleman and poet (Terry 1–6). Shelley uses a line from March's poem beginning "Aquelles mans que jamés perdonaren" ["Those who never forgive"] as an epigraph to the *Lodore* chapter describing **Ethel Villiers**'s loss after her father's death: "**En cor gentil,** amor per mort no passa"; the line means, "In a noble heart, Love does not undergo death" (*L* 1.271; March line 11).

March, Earl of: Edward **IV**'s title before becoming king of England (*DNB*). Shelley refers to Edward by this title (*PW* 1.265, 2.109).

Marches: Central **Italian** region containing **Ancona**. Shelley mentions its resistance to papal government (*R* 2.247, 2.258).

Marchesana, Madonna: Marsilio's sister, **Beatrice**'s follower and mother figure, and **Viscount di Malvezzi**'s wife in *Valperga*; Shelley also calls her **Viscountess di Malvezzi**.

Marco: Antonio dei Adimari's servant in *Valperga*. In *Rambles*, Shelley directs readers visiting **Venice** to use a gondolier named Marco, number 307, "proud of his scraps of bad **French**" (*R* 2.124).

Marco Visconti: See **Grossi**.

Mare Morto: Harbor of **Misenum**, near **Naples**, consisting of three basins; the inner one, Mare Morto, is an extinct volcano crater between Lake Fusano and the **Elysian Fields** (Headlam 122; Clement 276). **Valerius** and his companion sit beside it (*Val* 332).

Maremma: Italian coastal region south of **Leghorn**. Wreckage of **Euthanasia**'s ship washes up on Maremma beach (*V* 3.261, 3.266). Shelley described it March 1843 as "deadly in its influence on man, but in appearance, a wild, verdant, varied pasture land" (*R* 2.214). [*R* 1.43].

Margaret: Margaret Tudor (1489–1541), eldest daughter of **Henry VII** of England and **Elizabeth of York**; she became Scotland's queen by marrying **James IV** (*DNB*). She appears as a child in *Perkin Warbeck*. Also name of **Dame Nixon**'s granddaughter (*L* 3.249).

Margaret, Queen (1492–1549): Sister of **Francis I** of **France**; she became **Navarre**'s queen upon marrying Henry II of Albret (1527) and is remembered as author of *Heptaméron* (posthumously pub. 1558), modeled on **Boccaccio**'s *Decameron*. Her affection for Francis was "almost beyond the love of a sister" (A. Grant 43, 54). "**The False Rhyme**" is structured around these royal siblings' historical intimacy and playfulness.

Margaret of Anjou (1430–1482): British **Henry VI**'s wife and **Prince Edward**'s mother; she failed to obtain the crown for her son and was imprisoned 1471–75, when **Louis XI** paid her ransom (Fry 79). Margaret's fate haunts **Elizabeth Woodville** and **Lady Brampton** (*PW* 1.125, 1.202).

Margate: Popular seaside resort in **Kent**, eighteen miles northeast of **Canterbury**. Shelley visited it summer 1811 (Pollin 13). **Fanny**'s family moves there for her mother's health, and Fanny visits and ultimately lives there (*Par* 270–271, 273).

Margery, Mistress: Anne Mowbray's governess (*PW* 2.144).

Maria: **Andrea**'s daughter and **Anina**'s older sister in "**The Sisters of Albano**."

Marie Louise (1791–1847): **Napoleon**'s second wife; they married March 1810 and had a son, François Charles Joseph, March 1811. Shelley describes meeting an old woman in **Guignes** August 1840 who praised Marie Louise, who had passed through the town on the same road the Shelleys traveled (*H* 17). She later criticizes Marie as "one who might have been respected among women, but she lost her privilege," perhaps a reference to Marie's rule of **Parma**, where the citizens rebelled 1831 (*R* 2.31).

Marini, Giambattista (1569–1625): Italian poet; Shelley also spells his name **Marino**. Shelley wrote Marini's biography for *Italian and Spanish Lives*. Marini published songs "which acquired for him a great reputation" and facilitated his move to **Rome**, then to **Venice**, where he "published a volume of lyrical poetry, which established his fame" fully (*ISPL* 2.174–175). Marini considered his "poem on the Murder of the Innocents" [*La Strage degli Innocenti*] (1632) "his best production" (*ISPL* 2.176). Marini published *L'Adone* [*Adonis*] (1623) in **Paris**; Shel-

Marini, Ignazio (1811–1873)

ley notes that it achieved huge literary success and caused envy among literary circles. She provides a lengthy plot summary, considering *Adonis* "a work of great beauty and imagination: it wants sublimity, and deep pathos and masculine dignity; but its fancy, its descriptions, its didactic passages, are animated by the undeniable spirit of poetry" (*ISPL* 2.177).

Marini, Ignazio (1811–1873): Bergamo bass whose first performance was probably at **La Scala** 1832 (Rosenthal 308). Shelley enjoyed his performance in *Mosè* at Bergamo September 1840 (*R* 1.107–108).

Marino, Giambattista: See **Marini, Giambattista**.

Maristow Castle: Lord **Maristow**'s family home in *Lodore*; **Edward Villiers** and the **Savilles** grow up there (*L* 2.90). Shelley set much of *Lodore*'s third volume there (*L* 3.221, 3.235, 3.288). **Horatio Saville** settles there after his father's death (*L* 3.308).

Maristow, Lady: Lord **Maristow**'s wife and **Horatio**, **Sophia**, **Harriet**, **Lucy**, and **Mr. Saville**'s mother in *Lodore*, also called **Viscountess Maristow**.

Maristow, Lord: Also called **Viscount Maristow**; **Horatio**, **Harriet**, **Sophia**, **Lucy**, and **Mr. Saville**'s father, **Lady Maristow**'s husband, and **Edward Villiers**'s uncle (*L* 2.19).

Maristow, Viscount: See **Maristow, Lord**.

Maristow, Viscountess: See **Lady Maristow**. **Lady Lodore** assumes this title after marrying **Horatio Saville** (*L* 3.305).

Marius, Gaius (c. 157–86 B.C.E.): From 107 B.C.E., **Roman** consul who repeatedly vied with **Sulla** for control (Howatson 347). **Valerius** recalls, " 'Marius and Sulla had already taught us some of the miseries of tyranny' " and later that " 'a new spirit had arisen' " during his lifetime in Rome, whereas " 'some years before, the empire, torn by Marius and Sulla and unsupported by the virtue of any, seemed tottering on the edge of subjection' " (*Val* 333, 336). Valerius notes Marius's killing of his father (*Val* 333).

Markham, Captain: Minor *Lodore* character.

Markham, Gervase (c. 1568–1637): Coauthor, with Lewis **Machin**, of the comedy *The Dumb Knight* (1608), from which Shelley quoted in her *Journals* in February 1822 (*Journals* 396). She footnotes the drama as the source of a quotation in *Valperga*, using a section of the Duke of Epire's speech about confidence and calmness in planning, beginning "Roll on, the chariot wheels of my dear plots," in contrast with **Euthanasia**'s unease over her plan regarding **Castruccio** (*V* 3.204; *The Dumb Knight* Act 4).

Marlow: English village on the **Thames**, six miles northeast of **Henley**. The Shelleys leased **Albion House** there March 1817—February 1818 (*Journals* 165, 192). Shelley set "**An Eighteenth-Century Tale**" at a house "about half way between Marlow and Henley" (*EC* 345).

Marmara: See **Marmora**.

Marmora: **Turkey** surrounds this sea, which connects to the **Aegean** and **Black Seas**; Shelley spells it **Marmara** occasionally; its ancient name was the **Propontis**. In Shelley's day, Marmora was **Europe**'s unofficial border with the Orient. **Lionel Verney** admires it and notes the **Greek** siege of **Constantinople** there (*LM* 180, 183). Verney later notes Greece's fleet blockading Constantinople from **Sweet Waters** to a tower on Marmora at Constantinople's eastern end (*LM* 183, 197). [*LM* 191].

Marmora, Tower of: One of **Seven Towers** on **Constantinople**'s southeast wall (Coufopoulos 137). **Greek** forces lay siege to Constantinople "on land from the river **Kyat Kbanah**, near the **Sweet Waters**, to the Tower of Marmora" (*LM* 183).

Marriage at Cana: See **Veronese**.

Marriage of the Virgin: See **Raphael**.

Mars: Mythological **Roman** god of war and **Romulus**'s and Remus's father (Tripp 357). Shelley saw the statue of Mars in the main entrance to **Doge's Palace**'s courtyard; Jacopo Tatti Sansovino completed it 1567 (*R* 2.84; Honour 43).

Marseilles: **Rhône** estuary port on the **Mediterranean** on **France**'s south coast. Shelley intended her 1843 return route from **Sorrento** to be "by sea to Marseilles—traverse France to **Havre**" (*Letters* 3.80). Fear in England grows with plague's confirmation at Marseilles (*LM* 235). **Stephen Frion** is "seized by corsairs and carried to **Africa**" from Marseilles (*PW* 1.150). **Gerard Neville** assists **Elizabeth Falkner** in nursing **Rupert Falkner** there (*F* 76, 253). Shelley was uncomfortable on the carriage journey from **Chalons** to **Paris** with "three little boys" from Marseilles (*R* 1.145).

Marsilio: **Ferrara** bishop and **Beatrice**'s adoptive father in *Valperga*.

Marsluys: See **Maasluis**.

Marsyas: In **Greek** mythology, satyr who learned to play Athena's double flute and challenged **Apollo** to a musical contest. When Apollo won, he hung Marsyas in a tree, whipped him, and left his skin there (Tripp 357–358). When **Midas** chooses **Pan** as the musical contest's victor, Apollo reminds Midas of Marsyas's fate (*Midas* 105).

Martello: Name of a circular fort with thick walls, recalling an English attack on one in **Corsica** 1794. Many Martello towers were built around England's southeastern coast in the early 1800s to ward off the threat of **French** invasion. Shelley characterizes an Englishman building "a Martello tower of his home" (*F* 265).

Martha: Elderly **Little Marlow** resident in *The Last Man*.

Martigny: **Swiss** city at the convergence of the **Drance** and **Rhône** rivers twenty-seven miles southeast of Vevay. Shelley traveled through it October 1840 (*R* 1.138).

Martin: Guard whom a thunderstorm frightens in *Perkin Warbeck*.

Martin, Lucy [née Clayton]: Idealized character in *The Last Man* (*LM* 346–352). "[G]ood-humoured, social, and benevolent," she selflessly devotes "herself throughout to . . . nursing the sick, and attending the friendless" before dying of the disease herself (*LM* 347, 414).

Martyrdom of St. Mark: See **Veronese**.

Martyrdom of St. Peter the Hermit: See **Titian**.

Marvell, Andrew (1621–1678): English politician and writer, remembered for witty satires and lyrics as well as for political works in which he consistently opposes tyranny. Shelley identifies "**Snatching their pleasures with rough strife / Thorough** [sic] **the iron gates of life**," as Marvell's; the lines come from "To His Coy Mistress" (1681) (*LM* 285; Marvell lines 41–46). Shelley quotes from "The Second Chorus from Seneca's Tragedy of Thyestes" as an epigraph to the *Lodore* chapter in which **Lord Lodore** retires to **America**: "Settled in some secret nest, / In calm leisure let me rest; / And far off the public stage, / Pass away my silent age" (*L* 1.12; Marvell lines 4–7). See **Seneca the Younger**.

Marville, Henry de: **Monsieur** and **Madame de Marville**'s son and **Fanny Chaumont**'s childhood playmate in "**The Swiss Peasant**."

Marville, Madame de: Fanny **Chaumont**'s benefactress, **Monsieur de Marville**'s wife, and **Henry de Marville**'s mother in "**The Swiss Peasant**."

Marville, Monsieur de: Swiss **Madame de Marville**'s aristocratic husband and **Henry de Marville**'s father in "**The Swiss Peasant**."

Mary: Jesus's virgin mother in the **Bible**, also called **Madonna** and **Panagia** in Eastern Orthodox church (Matthew 1.16). **Hernan De Faro** wants St. **Mary**'s guidance, and **Skelton** wants St. Mary to save him (*PW* 2.265, 3.153). **Zella Ziani** "besought the Panagia with earnest prayers" to protect **Constans Ziani**, and **Dmitri** swears by her (*EE* 105, 111). Deliriously remembering his rescue of **Euphrasia**, **Chief Constantine** cries out " 'a shot—gracious Panagia, is this thy protection' " (*E* 304). Shelley describes numerous religious paintings featuring Mary that she viewed in **Europe** (*R* 1.219–224, 1.236–238).

Mary Visiting the Tomb of Jesus: See **Titian**.

Masaniello: See **Auber**.

"Mask of Anarchy, The": Subtitled "Written on the Occasion of the Massacre at **Manchester**," **PBS** wrote this poem September 1819 in response to the Peterloo Massacre, in which innocent demonstrators for **Parliamentary** reform were killed (White 2.105–107). Shelley copied and sent the poem to **Leigh Hunt**, but it was not published until 1832 because of its political stance (*Journals* 298). Shelley slightly alters PBS's description of hope's resurrection when **Lionel Verney** calls **Raymond** "'hero of unwritten story'" (*LM* 200; PBS lines 147–148). Verney records the tale of a mechanic who loses family to plague, leaving them in his house as "'**dead earth upon** dead earth,'" PBS's description of Anarchy (*LM* 263; PBS line 131). Describing **Cornish** miners' anger toward **Henry VII**, Shelley quotes "'**We are many**—they are few!'" (*PW* 3.99; PBS lines 155, 372). As an epigraph to the *Lodore* chapter that recounts **Lady Lodore**'s visit to her imprisoned daughter, Shelley quotes PBS's description of hope overcoming anarchy: "**As flowers beneath** May's footsteps waken / As stars from night's loose hair are shaken; / As waves arise when loud winds call, / Thoughts sprung where'er that step did fall" (*L* 3.115; PBS lines 122–125).

Mason, Mrs.: See **Mountcashel**.

Matapan, Cape: Middle southern **Peloponnese** peninsula, now called Cape Tainaron or **Taenarus**. **Camaraz** is a Matapan pirate; **Zella Ziani** passes the cape by ship (*EE* 114, 116).

Mathias, Emperor: See **Matthias**.

Matilda: Protagonist and first-person narrator of *Matilda*, sometimes spelled "Mathilda." The character's name probably comes from **Dante**'s *Purgatorio* (*Journals* 294).

Matilda (1046–1115): Also known as Matilda of Canossa and the Great Countess of **Tuscany**, she owned land from **Verona** to **Lucca**, supported the papacy, and is renowned for accompanying troops into battle (Parry 452; Villani 94; Sismondi 32). Shelley modeled **Euthanasia** on her, comparing them directly in *Valperga*; similarities, such as political connections and control of important lands, exist (*V* 1.176; Seymour 252; Sunstein 189).

Matilda: Shelley's novella, first published 1959 by Elizabeth Nitchie as *Mathilda*, following Shelley's fair copy, but elsewhere Shelley consistently used the spelling *Matilda* (Crook 2). Shelley first refers to *Matilda*'s composition 4 August 1819; her working title was *The Fields of Fancy* (*Journals* 294). Her speedy composition (August–12 September 1819) seems to have served a therapeutic purpose as she struggled with grief at **Clara** and **William Shelley**'s deaths and her own strained marriage. She sent the manuscript's only copy to **William Godwin** in **London** May 1820 for him to superintend its publication (Gisborne 27). Godwin thought its subject "disgusting and detestable" and unsuitable for publication, objecting principally to the incest theme; he refused to return the manuscript despite Shelley's 1822 repeated requests (Gisborne 44). **Matilda** narrates; like Shelley, she writes to express grief. Matilda relates her lonely upbringing by an aunt who cares for her following her mother **Diana**'s death just after Matilda's birth. Matilda's father was so overcome by grief that he left Britain for sixteen years. Upon his return, father and daughter delight in an idealized relationship until her father confesses to Matilda that his love for her involves incestuous desire. When Matilda runs from this confession in horror, her father rushes to take his own life. They do not physically consummate this illicit love, but Matilda is so overcome by grief and shame that she fakes her own death and secludes herself in northern England. She encounters poet **Woodville**, modeled on **PBS**; Matilda denies any feelings for him. Woodville overcomes grief over his beloved **Elinor**'s loss; a need to benefit humanity inspires him to keep writing. In her life's final months, Matilda directs her autobiographical composition to Woodville, hoping her narrative will explain her behavior. Gradually she wills her own death. Most critical evaluations of *Matilda* focus on its autobiographical elements.

Matlock: English city twenty miles northwest of **Derby**. **Henry Clerval** and **Victor Frankenstein** tour the caves there (*Fr1* 188; *Fr3* 137).

Matthias (1557–1619): Habsberg ruler and Holy Roman Emperor from 1612; he became **Bohemia**'s king 1611. Shelley mentions he first invaded Bohemia (*R* 2.3).

Maurice: "Maurice's" protagonist; his parents named him **Henry**.

Maurice: See **Desmond**.

Maurice, Earl of: See **Desmond**.

"Maurice, or the Fisher's Cot; A Tale": Shelley's short story, written summer 1820 for eleven-year-old **Laurette**, thought to be lost; Cristina Dazzi found it in her family archives 1997, and Claire Tomalin published a 1998 edition (Tomalin 7). The story, set in **Devon**, is in three parts. In the first, a traveler sees a funeral and learns the good character of the thirteen-year-old mourner, **Maurice**, who had lived with and cared for fisherman **Barnet** after **Dame Barnet**'s death (*Maurice* 59–67). In the story's second part, Shelley relates a traveler's meeting at Barnet's cottage with Maurice and the boy's goodness and hospitality as they talk (*Maurice* 69–76). In the third part, the traveler relates his own history and how his two-year-old son **Henry** was kidnapped at **Ilfracombe**; the traveler spends two months every year searching for his lost son (*Maurice* 77–80). **Dame Smithson** recently confessed to taking the traveler's son (*Maurice* 80–83). The traveler concludes his narration by asking Maurice to be his son; Maurice realizes he truly is the traveler's lost Henry (*Maurice* 84–85). Father and son reunite, and Henry subsequently attends **Eton** and delights in his loving parents' attention (*Maurice* 85–86). Henry persuades his father to purchase Barnet's cottage, which they visit every year for two months; Dame Smithson lives there the rest of the year, repentant and loving toward Henry (*Maurice* 85–86). Henry grows up and travels abroad, returning to the cottage many years after Dame Smithson's death to find it ruined: he builds a new house there for a poor fisherman and his family and often visits (*Maurice* 87–88).

Mavrocordato, Alexander (1791–1865): Born at **Constantinople** and inheriting the title of prince, Mavrocordato returned to his native **Greece** from **Italian** exile June 1821 and was proclaimed Greece's first president 1 January 1822 (*Journals* 584). Mavrocordato fought in Greece's war for independence and befriended **Byron**; subsequently, Mavrocordato rose through governmental ranks and became prime minister 1854–56 (*Journals* 584–585). **Francesco Pacchiani** introduced Shelley to Mavrocordato in **Pisa** December 1820; she enjoyed their subsequent friendship, finding him "spirited, cultivated, and handsome" and "very pleasant" (Sunstein 196; *Letters* 1.173; Seymour 264–266). Shelley taught Mavrocordato English, while he taught her Greek 1821; and **PBS** dedicated *Hellas* to Mavrocordato (Sunstein 198). After the prince's return to Greece, Shelley continued to follow "his part in the war with urgent concern and considerable pride" (White 2.245). Shelley and Mavrocordato corresponded, reuniting 1839 in **London**, which Mavrocordato visited as Greek envoy (Sunstein 347). Shelley's depictions of valiant Greeks in *The Last Man* are probably drawn from admiration of Mavrocordato. See Shelley's *Journals* and Herbert Huscher's "Alexander Mavrocordato, Friend of the Shelleys" (1965).

Max Brunnen: Brine spring on **Kissingen** gardens' north side (*BGER* 165). Shelley mentions it "resembling **Seidlitz** water, but without iron" (*R* 1.183).

Maximilian, Archduke: See **Maximilian I**.

Maximilian I (1459–1519): **Austria**'s archduke, **Germany**'s king, and Holy Roman Emperor 1493–1519; he gained the **Netherlands** 1477 by marrying **Charles the Rash**'s daughter Mary of **Burgundy**. He subsequently married **Anne of Brittany** 1490. He appears in *Perkin Warbeck*.

Maximilian II (1811–1864): Crown Prince of Bavaria and Ludwig I's oldest son; Maximilian ruled Bavaria 1848–64 (Morby 140; Bolt 36). Shelley mentions that the **King of Bavaria** is worried about his son **Otho** but that "[t]he Crown Prince of Bavaria is much respected, and has the reputation of being gifted with his father's talents, with judgment superadded" (*R* 1.192).

Mayence: See **Mainz**.

Mayence Cathedral: Six-towered cathedral, begun 975, standing in **Mainz**'s center (*BGER* 182). Shelley's traveling companions viewed it June 1842 (*R* 1.172).

Mayr, Simon (1763–1845): **German** composer of *Medea in Corinto* (1813), two-act opera first presented at **Naples** 1813. It retells the **Medea** story, and **Madame Pasta** favored the lead role (Orrey 229). Shelley praises Pasta's singing talent, stating that she was superb in *Medea* August 1840 (*R* 1.89–90).

Mazeppa: Protagonist of **Byron**'s poem of the same name, first published 1819; Shelley transcribed it September–October 1818 (*Journals* 228). Mazeppa tells a story of his early life: caught in intrigue, he was strapped naked to the back of a wild horse that galloped unceasingly until it reached Ukraine's plains, where it fell dead; a peasant maid rescued him (Byron lines 1–869). Shelley notes that Byron's entry in the summer 1816 ghost story competition was published at *Mazeppa*'s end (*Fr3* 21). **Rupert Falkner** rails against confinement, declaring, "If even, like Mazeppa, I might seek the wilds, and career along, though death was the bourn in view, I were happy!" (*F* 258).

Mazzorbo: Island in **Laguna** near **Burano** northeast of **Venice** (Honour 233). Shelley visited it September 1842 (*R* 2.101).

Meath: Central-eastern **Irish** county north of **Dublin**. **Bishop of Meath** crowns **Lambert Simnel** king there (*PW* 1.132).

Meath, Bishop of: **Irish** John Payne (d. 1506), friends with **Earl of Kildare**, crowned **Lambert Simnel** 1487 and was pardoned 1488 (*DNB*). *Perkin Warbeck* character (*PW* 1.132).

Mecca: Saudi Arabia's capital and **Mahomet**'s birthplace. Moslems travel there when plague spreads: "if they were to die, their bones might rest in earth made sacred by the relics of true believers" (*LM* 225).

Medea: In **Greek** mythology, witch who used magic for good and bad purposes; married to Jason (of Jason and the Argonauts); when he tried to marry another woman, Medea killed her own children by Jason and the other woman and fled. Medea's slaying of her own children associates her with pitilessness (Crook 2). **PBS** read Euripedes's *Medea* (431 B.C.E.) March 1819 (*Journals* 255). **Lionel Verney** records that **Adrian** grows stronger as "virtue, more potent than Medean alchemy, endued him with health and strength" (*LM* 303). After actually meeting **Lady Lodore**, **Ethel Villiers** revises her former opinion: "Her mother was no longer a semi-**gorgon**, hid behind a deceptive mask—a Medea, without a touch of human pity" (*L* 2.218). When Ethel surprises **Edward Villiers** at **Mrs. Derham**'s, his joyful face rewards her, and she "felt indeed that Medea, with all her potent herbs, was less of a magician" (*L* 2.269). Edward considers Lady Lodore "must be a Medea" (*L* 3.136).

Medea: See **Mayr**.

Medicean: See **Medici**.

Medici: **Florentine** family that dominated **Italian** politics 1434–1737 (Avery 615–617). Shelley wrote **Lorenzo de Medici**'s biography for *Italian and Spanish Lives*. She mentions **Medicean** merchants and one family member, a minister who falsely accused **Murat**'s cabinet of conspiring against him (*R* 2.182, 2.206). [*R* 2.154].

Medici, Lorenzo de (1449–1492): **Italian** politician and poet. Shelley wrote Medici's biography for *Italian and Spanish Lives*. She situates Medici as inferior to **Dante** and **Petrarch**, but remarks that "simplicity and vivacity adorn his verses," which reinspired interest in the Italian language (*ISPL* 1.154). Shelley considers William Roscoe's 1795 translations of Medici's sonnets inferior to the originals and admires Medici's love poems, specifying *La Nencia da Barbarino* [*Nencia from Barbarino*] (1474) as one of many "animated by glowing sensibility or lighthearted hilarity" (*ISPL* 1.157). Shelley asserts that Medici's carnival songs were contemporaneously popular in **Florence** and that he was "universally lamented" when he died young (*ISPL* 1.159).

Mediterranean Sea: **Atlantic** arm separating **Europe** from **Africa** and the Middle East, famous for its clear blue color and many resorts. **Victor Frankenstein** sees the **Creature** near it (*Fr1* 227, 229; *Fr3* 169, 171). **Valerius** and his companion view it from beside **Mare Morto** (*Val* 333). Shelley mentions the Mediterranean in describing **Charlemagne**'s extensive possessions (*V* 1.285). **Mondolfo** Castle overlooks the Mediterranean (*HM* 308). Plague reaches the "southern shores of the Mediterranean" (*LM* 225). **Lionel Verney** plans a voyage that includes its "beauteous shores and sunny promontories" (*LM* 469). **Villa Spina** overlooks it near **Salerno** (*FE* 66). In "**Sisters of Albano**'s" frame story, Shelley describes the **Tiber** as eternally feeding the "land-encircling Mediterranean" (*SA* 51, 53). **Guido il Cortese** meets the **dwarf** in a Mediterranean seaside cave (*Trans* 121, 127). [*L* 3.212].

Medusa: In **Greek** mythology, one of three immortal monsters collectively known as **Gorgons**. She evoked Athena's wrath by sleeping with Poseidon, and in retribution Athena turned Medusa's hair into serpents and made her face so ugly that seeing it "would turn men to stone" (Tripp 363–364). **Matilda** denies any feelings for **Woodville** by declaring she has been "hardened to stone by the Medusa head of Misery" (*M* 191).

Medwin, Thomas (1788–1869): British author and **PBS**'s second cousin; they played together as children (White 1.19, 2.54). Medwin studied law and then bought an army commission, serving in **India** 1813–18 before retiring on half-pay; he relinquished his commission 1831 (*Letters* 2.131). In September 1819, Medwin shared a **Geneva** house with **Edward Williams**, and he introduced the Williamses to the Shelleys in **Pisa** October 1820 (*Journals* 337). Medwin read some of his *Journal in India* (1821) aloud to the Shelleys November 1820, but Shelley wrote 1821 that "be one reading or writing [Medwin] insists upon interrupting one every moment" and that he "has no sympathy with our tastes or conversation—he is infinitely common place and is as silent as a fire-skreen [*sic*] but not half so useful" (*Journals* 339; *Letters* 1.178, 1.417; White 2.228–229). Medwin introduced the Shelleys to **Edward John Trelawny**, toured **Italy** before going back to Geneva, and then returned November 1821, when he "courted **Byron**" as he made notes for a planned biography (*Journals* 383, 391–393; Sunstein 196, 204, 209). Having known "Byron only four months," Medwin published *Conversations with Lord Byron* (1824); there were fifteen editions 1824–42, and it was highly controversial—Medwin appended a PBS "Memoir" that Shelley found "one mass of mistakes" (Sunstein 260; *Letters* 1.439, 1.455; Seymour 351–352). Shelley was angry with Medwin's derision of **Guiccioli** in this work but quickly forgave him and "wrote to congratulate him on his marriage" 1824 to Anna, Baroness Hamilton of Sweden, Countess of Starnford (1788–1868) (Sunstein 262; *Letters* 1.470). Shelley also read Medwin's *Ahasueras, The Wanderer: A Dramatic Legend* (1823) (*Letters* 1.418–419). Medwin dissipated his wife's fortunes, finding himself near financial ruin by mid-1828, and left his wife and children 1829 in **Florence** (where Trelawny provided them with funds); thereafter, he "wrote professionally," returning to England early 1831 (Sunstein 262, 318; *Letters* 2.52, 2.73, 2.132). Writing December

1829, Shelley noted, "I thought I had always disliked" Medwin (*Letters* 2.94, 2.132). Medwin published *The Shelley Papers: Memoir of Percy Bysshe Shelley* in periodical installments 1832, collected 1833; he settled in **Heidelberg** by February 1841 (*Letters* 2.169, 3.202). In May 1846, Shelley wrote to him, "I must therefore in the most earnest manner deprecate the publication of particulars and circumstances injurious to the living" upon learning of Medwin's plan to publish further details about PBS (*Letters* 3.284). Shelley told **Leigh Hunt** July 1847 that Medwin had said he would not publish if she paid him; she didn't, and *The Life of Percy Bysshe Shelley* appeared 1847, revealing much about the Shelleys' early life (*Letters* 3.319–320; Seymour 515–516). See Ernest J. Lovell's *Captain Medwin: Friend of Byron and Shelley* (1963).

Mehemet Ali: See **Ali, Mohammed**.

Mehmed II: **Ottoman** sultan 1451–81 who successfully laid siege to **Constantinople**; Shelley's variant is **Mahmoud** (Nicol 54–64). **Lionel Verney** and **Raymond** ride to **Top Kapou** "on which Mahmoud planted his standard, and first saw the city" (*LM* 183).

Meillerie: **French** village on **Lake Geneva**'s north shore, spelled **Mellerie** in *History*. Shelley planned to travel there 1814 (*H* v).

Melbourne, John, Esq.: Miss **Mansfield**'s English fiancé in *Frankenstein*.

Mellerie: See **Meillerie**.

Melzi, Villa: Renowned for its gardens and art collection, villa on **Lake Lecco**'s eastern bank half a mile south of **Bellagio** (*BSWI* 491). Shelley visited it August 1840 (*R* 1.83).

Menaggio: Italian town on **Lake Como** across from **Varenna**. Shelley relates that it is three miles from **Cadenabbia** and "the largest town in our vicinity, and properly our post-town" (*R* 1.66–67). She describes an August 1840 moonlit voyage there (*R* 1.85).

Mercato Nuovo: **Italian** for "New Market," formerly **Florence**'s location for exchanging money, now a straw market (Higson 121). **Monna Lisabetta** works there (*TP* 18).

Merceria: Stretching from the clock tower in the **Piazza San Marco** to the **Rialto**, busiest shopping street in **Venice**. Shelley mentions "passing through" it September 1842 (*R* 2.100).

Mercury: **Roman** god of commerce, trickery, and theft; a messenger god; and leader of dead souls in the Underworld. Hermes in **Greek** mythology. After apprehending **Richard of York**, **Henry VII** of England states, "it is no feathered shoe our Mercury wears this day" (*PW* 3.254). Shelley calls "a beer boy" who takes **Ethel Villiers** to her husband's lodgings "Mercury" (*L* 2.262).

Mérimée, Prosper (1803–1870): Prolific and popular 19th-century **French** author. Writing to **Isabel Baxter Booth** from **Paris** June 1828, Shelley recorded meeting "one of the cleverest men in France, young and a poet" (*Letters* 2.46; Sunstein 288). Mérimée admired Shelley; she returned his letter containing "sentiments which you will probably repent of later" May 1828, assuring him, "you ask for my friendship—it is yours," while negating possibilities of any relationship beyond that of friends (*Letters* 2.40). They maintained a correspondence July 1828–February 1829, revealing that they were close, but the friendship did not last (Sunstein 290; Seymour 392–394). He assisted with her research for *Perkin Warbeck* by recommending several historians, such as Phillipe de Comines and Baron de Barante (Fischer xiv, xvii). Shelley wrote "**Review of 1572 Chronique du Temps de Charles IX**" and "**Illyrian Poetry—Feudal Scenes**," briefly and favorably mentioning Mérimée's works she drew upon for "**The Evil Eye**" (*Journals* 508). See A. W. Raitt's *Prosper Mérimée* (1970).

Merlin: Sorcerer of Arthurian legend. Like Merlin, who could predict the future, **Galeazzo Visconti** predicts **Castruccio** will take **Florence** (*V* 2.10). As a child, **Beatrice** reads and explains Merlin's prophecies (*V* 2.42).

Merrival: Astronomer in *The Last Man*.

Messina: City near **Sicily**'s northeast tip. Shelley mentions **Amari** in describing the siege of Messina (*R* 2.210).

Mestre: **Italian** town seven miles northwest of **Venice**. Shelley mentions a railroad from **Padua** to it being constructed 1842 (*R* 2.77, 2.104).

Metastasio, Pietro (1698–1782): **Italian** librettist, lyric poet, and author of popular operas. Shelley first read Metastasio's *Works* 1819 (*Journals* 258–259). She quotes from Metastasio's libretto *Demetrio* (1732) as an epigraph to the *Lodore* chapter in which **Lady Lodore**'s pride causes her to lose **Horatio Saville**, lines beginning "**Ma la fede degli Amanti**," which Olinthus speaks to Mithranes: "See the boasted truth of lovers / Like the Arabian bird renown'd, / Vouch'd by all, but none discovers / Where the wonder may be found" (*L* 2.49; *Demetrio* 2.3.41–44). Shelley accurately quotes from Metastasio's *Temistocle* [*Themistocles*] (1736) as an epigraph to the chapter in which Lady Lodore realizes her life's emptiness, lines beginning "**Veggo pur troppo**," which mean "I see, unfortunately, / That life is a fable, / And my fable is not yet done" (*L* 3.92; *Temistocle* 2.1.11–13). Shelley misattributes these lines to **Petrarch**, a common mistake (Brunelli 1503; Petrarch, *Rime Sparse* 254, line 13). Shelley wrote Metastasio's biography for *Italian and Spanish Lives*. She notes "the singular perfection of [Metastasio's] style" and asserts his "command of language is singularly great, and he adapted poetic diction to dramatic dialogue with wonderful felicity" (*ISPL* 2.195–196, 2.200–201). She expresses admiration particularly for *Attilio Regulo* [*Attilius Regulus*] (1732), of which she gives a plot summary, noting it as Metastasio's favorite of his own works, while she also emphasizes the virtues of *La Clemenza di Tito* [*The Clemency of Titus*] (1732) and *Temistocle* (*ISPL* 2.202). Shelley provides excerpts from Metastasio's letters that "let us into the secrets of his heart" (*ISPL* 2.195).

Methodius (827–885): **Greek** Christian missionary to Slavs; he and younger brother Cyril devised the first Slavic alphabet and translated the **Bible** into it. **Beatrice** reads and interprets Methodius's writings (*V* 2.42).

Metropolitan Magazine: British periodical that ran 1831–1833 as *Metropolitan: A Monthly Journal of Literature, Science, and the Fine Arts* and as *Metropolitan Magazine* 1833–1850; first British magazine to run serial fiction in monthly issues. Shelley footnotes that **Reeve**'s "Sketches of Bohemia" appeared in volumes 18 and 19 of this journal (*R* 2.5).

Metternich, Prince Klemens Fürst von (1773–1859): **Austrian** minister of foreign affairs 1809–48; he arranged the **Congress of Vienna** (1814–15), a peace congress determining **European** boundaries and possessions, and **Napoleon**'s marriage to **Marie Louise** (*R* 2.248; Kinder 2.39). Shelley states, "as **Jehovah** hardened the heart of **Pharoah** for his own destruction, so does he soften the heart of Prince Metternich," who permitted **Italians'** scientific studies; Shelley implies that the Italians will use their discoveries for their own emancipation from external rule (*R* 2.116; Exodus 7.3). Shelley also mentions that Metternich is his **Bohemian** tenants' absentee ruler and that he assisted **Bologna** to resist **San Fedisti** but later occupied the city (*R* 2.14, 2.253–254).

Metz: French city on the **Moselle**, thirty-five miles east of **Verdun**. Shelley visited it June 1840 (*R* 1.13; *Letters* 3.1).

Meuse: French river; also town twenty miles southeast of **Chaumont**. Shelley mentions **Voltaire**'s 1740 meeting with **Frederic the Great** at Meuse castle near **Clêves** (*R* 1.227).

Mexico: North **American** country. **Victor Frankenstein** suggests that restraint of passion would have prevented the destruction of Mexico's empire (*Fr1* 84; *Fr3* 57). **Lionel Verney** asserts that **Raymond**'s safe return to **Athens** is a "treasure more invaluable than the wealth . . . piloted from Mexico" (*LM* 170). Plague lays Mexico waste (*LM* 232). **Gerard Neville** locates **Osborne** in Mexico, but **Hillary** cannot find him there (*F* 140, 268).

Meyerbeer, Giacomo (1791–1837): German composer and "central musical figure in **French** grand opera after 1831" (*NGD*). He wrote *Robert le Diable* [*Robert the Devil*] (1831), a five-act opera first performed in **Paris** (Rosenthal 420). Shelley mentions that an **Italian** version of it was presented in **Venice** October 1842 (*R* 2.128). In Paris, Meyerbeer's *Les Huguenots* (1836) was "one of the most memorable [premieres] in history" (*NGD*). Shelley was disappointed at seeing *La Dame Blanche* rather than *Les Huguenots* August 1842 (*R* 1.248).

"Mi manca la voce": See **Rossini, Gioacchino**.

Michelangelo Buonarroti (1475–1564): Italian sculptor, painter, and architect renowned for *David* (1501–1504) and the **Sistine Chapel**'s ceiling (1508–12) (Gowing 447–450). Shelley mentions Michelangelo repeatedly: she viewed **San Miniato Church**, for which Michelangelo designed protective measures during the 1529 siege of

Florence and which he described as "**La bella villanella**" ["the beautiful peasant"], and **Santa Maria degli Angeli Church**, which he built from **Baths of Diocletian** (1563) (*R* 2.135, 2.229; Moskal 300). Shelley terms him "great master" of "[p]erfection in drawing" and "most glorious example" of the Florentine school; she also praises the Sistine Chapel ceiling's "simple grandeur" (*R* 2.153, 2.231). [*R* 1.87, 2.144, 2.185, 2.219, 2.222].

Midas: *Midas*'s protagonist and **Phrygia**'s king.

Midas: Two-act verse drama Shelley adapted from **Ovid** 1820, eventually published 1922; influential editor Alaric Watts rejected it 1826 (*Journals* 316–317; Sunstein 275). **PBS** contributed two lyrics to it, and **Medwin** records the Shelleys' delight in the work (252). Shelley retains most details of various versions of the original **Greek** myth. When **Midas** chooses **Pan** as victor in a musical contest, the other competitor, **Apollo**, punishes Midas by giving him ass's ears. Some versions of the myth record that only the king's barber knows the secret and whispers it to the reeds, but Shelley casts prime minister **Zopyrion** in this role (Tripp 378). When Midas looks after **Silenus**, **Bacchus** grants the king his foolish request for the power to turn all he touches to gold as reward, but Midas, unable to eat, sleep, and so on, realizes his folly in the play's second act. He washes the power away in **Pactolus**.

Middleton, Thomas (1580–1627): English dramatist whose most famous work is tragedy *The Changeling* (written 1622). Shelley quotes Sir Oliver Twilight's speech to his wife in Middleton's *No Wit, No Help Like a Woman's* (wr. 1611; pub. 1657) as an epigraph to the *Lodore* chapter in which the **Villiers**es reunite in **London**: "O my reviving joy! thy quickening presence / Makes the sad night / Sit like a youthful spring upon my blood. / I cannot make thy welcome rich enough / With all the wealth of words" (*L* 2.263; Middleton 4.1.1–5).

Midsummer Night's Dream, A: Comedy **Shakespeare** wrote 1595 or 1596, first published 1600. Shelley describes **Castruccio** by adapting a line **Theseus** speaks about the lovers' strange tale, "'a habitation and a name'"; **Edmund Malville** uses the exact line, "'a local habitation and a name,'" to praise **Venice**'s power and beauty (*V* 2.146; *RI* 26; Shakespeare 5.1.17). Shelley also uses this line when considering **Pompeii**'s past (*R* 1.279).

Milan: Italian city seventy-five miles northeast of **Genoa**. Shelley spent three weeks there April 1818 and gives an in-depth description of Milan's opera and her affinity for the city (*Journals* 202; *Letters* 1.64). **Cincolo de' Becari** believes his visitor to be from Milan; the visitor claims to have seen **Corradino** there (*TP* 5, 7). **Castruccio** travels toward Milan en route to England and visits it on his return (*V* 1.67, 1.120, 1.129–132). Shelley refers to Milan throughout *Valperga*, since several political upheavals occur there; for example, **Scoto** "expelled the **Visconti** from Milan," **Louis of Bavaria** is crowned emperor there before Milan revolts, and **Galeazzo Visconti** later rules it (*V* 1.88–89, 1.98–99, 1.137, 1.143, 2.4, 2.36, 2.89, 2.122, 3.264). **Wilhelmina of Bohemia** lived there with **Magfreda**, who hides **Beatrice** with a leper just outside Milan (*V* 2.26, 2.35, 2.40). Wilhelmina was buried in Milan's church of **St. Peter** 1302 (*V* 2.27). The last four plague survivors winter in Milan's **Viceroy's Palace** (*LM* 430). **Caroline Frankenstein** first encounters **Elizabeth Lavenza** on **Lake Como**'s shores while **Alphonse Frankenstein** is in Milan (*Fr3* 41). **Flora Mancini** and **Count Fabian de' Tolomei** travel separately toward Milan searching for **Lorenzo Mancini**, who previously sent Flora a message that he had befriended the archbishop there (*Brother* 178–179, 184–186). Shelley visited Milan September 1840 (*R* 1.131–140).

Milan, Cathedral in: See **Duomo (Milan)**.

Milan, Duke of: See **Sforza**.

Milford Haven: Port and large estuary in southwest Wales, forty-eight miles west of Swansea. **Lewis Elmore** and **Horace Neville** intend to cross to **Ireland** from there (*Mourner* 96).

Miliorini, Il: Probably Shelley's Italian for "millionaire," the nickname of her driver from **Venice** to **Florence** 1842, who was known for his "stinginess" (*R* 2.131; Moskal 298).

Milton, John (1608–1674): Influential English author whose writings impressed Shelley greatly. Two epic poems in blank verse, *Paradise Lost* (1667) and *Paradise Regained* (1671), were especially important to her. Shelley draws extensively and frequently upon Milton's retelling of the **biblical** Fall in many of her works. **PBS** read *Paradise Lost* aloud to Shelley November 1816 and again April and August 1819 (*Journals* 146, 258, 294). Shelley takes *Frankenstein*'s epigraph from *Paradise Lost* and draws *Frankenstein*'s primary question regarding man's creation from Milton's work. Shelley also draws upon Milton's *Comus* (1634) in *Matilda* and upon his *Il Penseroso* (1645) in *Rambles*. Shelley takes *The Last Man*'s epigraph from *Paradise Lost*, and **Lionel Verney** compares wind whipping through sails to "such whir as may have visited the dreams of Milton, when he imagined the winnowing of the arch-fiend's van-like wings" (*LM* 297). Shelley notes **Lady Katherine Gordon** had "pleased the '**great Task Master**,'" the closing of Milton's sonnet, "On His being Arrived to the Age of Twenty-Four" (1632) (*PW* 3.15; Milton line 14; Fischer 274). **Lord Lodore** draws "his chief ideas from Milton's **Eve**" in educating his daughter, and Shelley quotes Milton to describe the **Villiers**es' **Eden** at **Mrs. Derham**'s (*L* 1.38, 2.271). Milton is one of few poets with whom **Elizabeth Falkner** is familiar before **Gerard Neville**'s instruction (*F* 236). Neville brings Elizabeth "the melodies of **Moore**, so '**married to immortal verse**,'" describing Moore's *Irish Melodies* with a line from *L'Allegro* (1645), in which Milton presents cheerful, social man enjoying life (*F* 236; Milton lines 135–137). Discussing **Florentine** painting, Shelley notes "the representation of such men and women as Milton and **Shakspeare** have embodied in verse, is not to be found in the works of these painters" (*R* 2.156–157). See individual works.

Minehead: English port on the **Bristol** Channel, twenty-one miles northwest of **Taunton**. **Lady Katherine Gordon** sees *Adalid* near Minehead (*PW* 3.51).

Minerva: **Roman** goddess of arts, crafts, and war, called Athena and **Pallas** in **Greek** (Tripp 380, 442; Howatson 366). **Valerius** kneels on **Tiber**'s banks and appeals, " 'Minerva protect thy Rome' " (*Val* 334).

Minories: Large **London** street leading to the **Tower**; it gains its name from the Minoresses, or nuns of St. Francis's second order, whose house still stands on it (Kent 411). **Lionel Verney** rides with **Adrian** "from **Hyde Park** even to where we now were in the Minories" (*LM* 333).

Minotaur: Legendary **Greek** monster, offspring of Queen Pasiphae and a bull. King Minos ordered **Daedalus** to construct a labyrinth to hide the minotaur, which **Theseus** eventually killed (Tripp 382). **Raymond** declares that "Daedalus never wound so inextricable an error round Minotaur, as madness has woven around [**Adrian**'s] imprisoned reason" (*LM* 70).

Mirabeau, Comte Honoré Gabriel Riqueti de (1749–1791): Controversial **French** politician and author. Shelley wrote Mirabeau's biography for *French Lives*. She attributes Mirabeau's youthful recklessness to his father's harsh treatment of him, his only son, and also characterizes Mirabeau's love for his married mistress, Sophie de Monnier, as true and inviolable. Imprisoned for debt after his marriage, Mirabeau composed *Essai sur la despotisme* [*Essay on Despotism*] (1767), which caused a sensation upon its publication; he also wrote *Essai sur les lettres de cachet* [*Essay on Lettres de cachet*] (1782) in prison, from which he was released 1780 (while his sentence was canceled 1782). Shelley admires Mirabeau's political speeches and principles, noting that his peculiar character was "the union of great genius with impetuous passions" (*FL* 2.257).

Miranda: See *Tempest, The*.

Mirandola, Giovanni Pico della [Conte della Concordia] (1463–1494): **Italian** philosopher. Shelley wrote Mirandola's biography for *Italian and Spanish Lives*. She records that he spent his life studying philosophy, learning several languages, and publishing "900 propositions—dialectic, moral, physical, mathematical, theological" in **Rome** 1487 (*ISPL* 1.161). Shelley notes that these documents sparked scholarly debates and that Mirandola was condemned as heretical, apologized, reformed his life, and devoted himself to theology and philosophy. Mirandola is now remembered for *Oratorio de hominis dignitate* [*Oration on Man's Dignity*] (comp. 1486; pub. 1495–96), a study of philosophy as the noblest human endeavor.

Miseno, Cape: North headland of **Naples**'s **Baiae**, called **Misenum** in **Roman** times; Shelley visited it March 1818 (*Journals* 242). "**Valerius the Reanimated Roman**" opens: "two strangers landed in the little bay formed by the extreme point of Cape Miseno" (*Val* 332, 339). Shelley describes the view from atop **Scaricatojo**, with Misenum to the west (*R* 2.283).

Misenum: See **Miseno, Cape**.

Miserere: One of the penitential **Psalms**, beginning in **Latin**, "Miserere mei Deus," meaning, "Have mercy upon me, Oh God" (Psalms 51). **Beaulieu** sings a miserere as **Richard of York** and his men arrive for protection (*PW* 3.166). Shelley enjoyed the Miserere at the **Sistine Chapel** in April 1843 (*R* 2.231).

Missy: Mrs. Baker gives **Elizabeth Falkner** this nickname (*F* 13).

Mitchell, Colonel John (1785–1859): Military officer (became major-general) and author, who published *Life of Wallenstein, Duke of Friedland* (1837), upon which Shelley relied for her account of **Wallenstein**; she footnotes the reference (*R* 2.7; Moskal 50; *DNB*).

Mithridates, Eupator (c. 108–63 B.C.E.): King Mithridates IV of Pontus conquered the **Black Sea**'s north coast; he declared war against **Rome** and invaded **Greece** 88 B.C.E., but was defeated 84 B.C.E. He declared war again 83–81 B.C.E., but **Sulla** defeated him, and **Pompey** defeated Mithridates's third attempt 66 B.C.E. (Kinder 1.89–91). With reference to Mithridates, **Lionel Verney** suggests that **Merrival**'s astronomical theories are discordant to the day's concerns: "if an old Roman of the period of the Republic had returned to life, and talked . . . of the last battle with Mithridates, his ideas would not have been more alien to the times" than Merrival's conversation (*LM* 290).

Mittenwald: See **Mittewald**.

Mittewald: Austrian village ten miles south of **Brenner**; Shelley spells it **Mittenwald** (*MSGE* 331). Shelley passed through it September 1842 (*R* 2.49).

Mivart's: Hotel founded 1815 on **Brook Street** in **London**'s exclusive West End; renamed Claridge's, it is now renowned for the exclusivity of its upper-class guest list (Leigh 408; Kent 466; Piper 79). **Lord** and **Lady Lodore** stay there immediately after marrying (*L* 1.114).

Modena: Italian city twenty-two miles northwest of **Bologna**. Shelley relates that **Carbonari** initially focused on Modena (*R* 2.250).

"Modern Italian Romances": Unsigned two-part critical piece that appeared in the *Monthly Chronicle* in November and December 1838; internal evidence strongly suggests it is Shelley's work. Sunstein first questionably attributed it to Shelley in 1989 (414). The article expresses, from an English speaker's perspective, a strong commitment to the **Italian Risorgimento** as it considers both "revolutionary" and "Christian" fiction, such as **Manzoni**'s I *Promessi Sposi* and **Guerrazzi**'s novels; Shelley considers these works in *Rambles*. The article concludes with the hope that the Italian people will strive to establish a government worthy of their culture and history, themes Shelley endorses in *Rambles*.

"Modern Italy": Shelley's review of Henry Digby Beste's *Italy as it Is* (1828) and Louis Simond's *A Tour in Italy and Sicily* (1828) first appeared in the July 1829 *Westminster Review*. Bennett suggests that several vague references in letters Shelley wrote to John Bowring refer to "Modern Italy"; Shelley returned the review's proofs June 1829 (*Letters* 1.31, 1.70, 1.78–79). Shelley discusses **Italy**'s current state—**Rome** "displays the ill-assorted marriage of ancient with modern"—before turning to Beste's *Italy as it Is*, which has "the absence of any thing like description" of Italian scenery (*ModIt* 129–130). Despite this fault, Shelley recommends it, especially to families planning to live in Italy; they "will derive considerable benefit from consulting him and following his directions" (*ModIt* 132). Of *Tour in Italy and Sicily*, Shelley states: "If all travellers wrote and described as [Simond] does, their productions would attain the highest places in the literary scale" (*ModIt* 132). The book details Simond's travels; though it contains no guide to artwork or political commentary, Shelley feels "gratitude towards its author" for this "picture of Italy" (*ModIt* 140). See **Sismondi**.

Moirae: **Greek** term also spelled "Moerae," which applies to the **Fates**, "divine beings who determined the course of events in human lives" (Tripp 246). **Zella Ziani** hears "the Moirae, the old Fates of her native Grecian soil, howled in [a storm's] breezes" (*EE* 110).

Mola di Gaeta: See **Gaeta**.

Moldau: River running through Czech Republic and converging with the **Elbe** twenty miles north of **Prague**. Shelley notes that Prague is on the Moldau (*R* 1.279).

Môle: **French** mountain twenty-five miles northeast of Bonneville and just south of **Lake Geneva** (*BSWI* 293). **Victor Frankenstein** discerns its peak through lightning flashes (*Fr1* 104; *Fr3* 72).

Molière (1622–1673): Stage and pen name of Jean-Baptiste Poquelin, popular **French** playwright and actor whose comedies influenced English Restoration drama. Shelley read Molière's *George Dandin; ou le Mari Confondu* [*George Dandin; or the Confused Husband*] (1668) 1817 and other plays 1818 (*Journals* 184, 203). **Lord Maristow** suggests that **Colonel Villiers**'s farcical relationship with **Miss Gregory** varies "the scene from a travestie of **Romeo and Juliet** to the comedies of **Plautus** or Molière" (*L* 2.225). Shelley wrote Molière's biography for *French Lives*, providing extensive extracts from many of his works, admiring *Tartuffe* (1667) and *Le Misanthrope* (1666) particularly. Shelley suggests that Molière's comedies, satirizing upper-class follies and pretensions, belong to all companies and ages and rise above much of French drama's frivolity in their earnest feeling and deep, passionate tones (*FL* 1.97–149).

Molinari, Louis Valeriani (1758–1828): **Italian** scholar who translated **Plutarch** and **Virgil** (Moskal 338). Shelley mentions that **Colletta** was friends with **Valeriani**, "translator of **Tacitus**" (*R* 2.209).

Moliterno, Prince (d. 1840): Nobleman who opposed **French** rule in **Italy** and attempted to enlist the British in this cause (Moskal 319). Shelley relates that he tried to persuade the **Carbonari** to drive **Murat** out of Italy (*R* 2.172).

Moncello: Minor *Valperga* character.

Moncenigo, Count: Venetian nobleman and **Faustina** and **Ludovico**'s father in "The Trial of Love."

Moncenigo, Countess: Count Moncenigo's wife who died giving birth to **Faustina** in "The Trial of Love."

Moncenigo, Faustina: Count and Countess Moncenigo's daughter, **Angeline**'s friend, and **Ippolito della Toretta**'s wife in "The Trial of Love."

Moncenigo, Ludovico: Ludovico Moncenigo's sister, **Count** and **Countess Moncenigo**'s son and **Faustina Moncenigo**'s brother in "The Trial of Love."

Moncenigo, Villa: **Moncenigo** house in the **Euganean Hills** and setting for parts of "The Trial of Love."

Mondolfo: Near **Sorrento** on a mountain overlooking the **Mediterranean**, Mondolfo family castle in "The Heir of Mondolfo" (*HM* 308).

Mondolfo, Lady Isabel: Prince Fernando Mondolfo's **Florentine** second wife and **Ludovico Mondolfo**'s mother in "The Heir of Mondolfo."

Mondolfo, Ludovico: Prince Fernando Mondolfo and his second wife Isabel's son, **Olimpio Mondolfo**'s brother, and male protagonist of "The Heir of Mondolfo." He marries **Viola Arnaldi**.

Mondolfo, Olimpio: Prince Fernando Mondolfo's older son with his first wife in "The Heir of Mondolfo."

Mondolfo, Prince Fernando: Antagonist in "The Heir of Mondolfo." Fernando has **Olimpio Mondolfo** with his first wife, a **Sicilian** princess, and **Ludovico Mondolfo** with **Florentine Isabel**, his second wife (*HM* 308).

Monna Lisabetta: **Cincolo de' Becari**'s unexpected early return home leads **Monna Gegia de' Becari** to speculate that he is Monna Lisabetta (*TP* 2).

Mont Anvert: See **Montanvers**.

Mont Blanc: Highest **Alpine** peak, where **Switzerland**, **France**, and **Italy** meet. The Shelleys viewed Mont Blanc 1816; **PBS** presents the mountain as a complex metaphor in "Mont Blanc" (1817) (*Letters* 1.20). Shelley admired "majestic Mont Blanc, highest and queen of all" (*H* 94). After **Justine Moritz**'s death, **Victor Frankenstein** retreats to **Chamonix**, from where he can view Mont Blanc (*Fr1* 123; *Fr3* 87). On his honeymoon voyage on **Lake Geneva**, Victor sees "Mont Blanc, and the assemblage of snowy mountains that in vain endeavour to emulate her" (*Fr1* 217; *Fr3* 161). As **Lionel Verney** and **Adrian** perform funeral rites for plague victims, they notice lightning flashes near Mont Blanc (*LM* 425). Shelley was disappointed when the weather during her 1840 stay in **Geneva** obscured Mont Blanc (*R* 1.141).

"Mont Blanc": PBS's poem, written 1816 and first published in *History* (1817). In this five-part meditation about a universal mind or power, PBS uses the **Arve** and Mont Blanc to represent the awe-inspiring natural unknown (White 1.454–455). See **Mont Blanc**.

Mont St. Gothard: Swiss mountain south of **Lucerne**. The Shelleys contemplated crossing St. Gothard August 1814 (*Journals* 20; *H* 46). **Dr. Hotham** discovers **Roger Dodsworth** in ice there (*RD* 43). **PFS** and his friends crossed St. Gothard while Shelley stayed in **Milan** September 1840 (*R* 1.126). Shelley again planned to take St. Gothard Pass May 1850, but snow rendered it impossible (*Letters* 3.378–379).

Mont Salève: Hill of limestone rock that Monnetier Valley separates into Petit and Grand Salève southeast of **Geneva**. At **Lake Geneva** summer 1816, Shelley saw Mont Salève and predicted that climbing it would afford "a delightful view of the course of the **Rhône** and **Arve**, and of the shores of the lake" (*H* 102–103). **Elizabeth Lavenza** and **Victor Frankenstein** view Mont Salève's peak during their honeymoon (*Fr1* 217; *Fr3* 161). Crashes of thunder echoing from Mont Salève accompany the storm Shelley terms **William Frankenstein**'s funeral dirge (*Fr1* 104; *Fr3* 72).

Montagu, Lady Mary Wortley (1689–1762): English author renowned for her letters; Shelley's variant is **Montague** (Barash 148). Shelley refers to **Nimeguen**'s "flying bridge," which Montagu saw August 1716 and compared to a flatboat slowly moving from one side of the river to the other (*H* 75; Montagu 1.200). When the **Villiers**es reunite at **Mrs. Derham**'s, Shelley notes, "Montague has recorded the pleasure to be reaped 'When we meet with champagne and a chicken at last,'" alluding to Montagu's "The Lover: A Ballad to Mr. Congreve" (1747) (*L* 2.270; Montagu 2.387, lines 25–26).

Montague, Lady: See **Montagu**.

Montague Square: Northeast of **Berkeley Square** in **London**'s Westminster district. The **Humphries** invite **Elizabeth Fitzhenry** to dine at their house there (*L* 2.142).

Montaigne, Michel Eyquem de (1533–1592): French philosopher and author, now chiefly remembered for *Essais* (1572–80, 1588), containing his moral formulations; Shelley read widely in *Essais* 1818 and 1819 while she was at **Bagni di Lucca**, which Montaigne also visited (*Journals* 663). Shelley wrote Montaigne's brief biography for *French Lives*. She draws information principally from Montaigne's own works, admiring his "enlightened and philosophical, though quaint and *naive* style, which renders him one of the most delightful authors in the world" (*FL* 1.1).

Montalègre: Section of **Lake Geneva**'s **Swiss** shore near **Cologny**. The Shelleys rented **Maison Chapuis** there summer 1816 (*Journals* 107). **Victor Frankenstein** and **Elizabeth Lavenza** enjoy viewing its "pleasant banks" at their honeymoon voyage's beginning (*Fr1* 217; *Fr3* 161).

Montani, Giuseppe (1789–1833): Italian writer (Petronio 4.42). Shelley lists him as an *Il Conciliatore* contributor (*R* 2.195).

Montanvers: Mountain on **Swiss-French** border and **Chamonix** Valley's

Montanvert

east side, renowned for its magnificent view of **Mont Blanc**'s glacier; Shelley's alternate spellings are **Mont Anvert**, **Montanvert**, and **Montenvers** (*BSWI* 299; *Journals* 116). Left of Chamonix's Hotel Royal lies a bridle path **Victor Frankenstein** evidently follows as he traverses Montanvers (*Fr1* 125; *Fr3* 88). Shelley draws from personal experience descriptions of the "sublime ecstasy" Victor experiences at the view of these mountains and glaciers (*Journals* 116). **Adrian** and **Lionel Verney** bury plague victims near Montanvers (*LM* 425).

Montanvert: See **Montanvers**.

Monte Aperto: The **Sienese** defeated **Florentines** at this 1260 battle fought just outside Siena (Villani 177). **Cincolo** and **Monna Gegia de' Becari**'s son died there; old men at **Euthanasia**'s court remember the battle (*TP* 4; *V* 1.249).

Monte Baldo: Mountain on **Lago di Garda**'s eastern shore (*MNIT* 258). Shelley saw it September 1842 (*R* 2.68).

Monte Catini: See **Montecatini**.

Monte Cavallo: **Quirinal**'s highest point; Shelley visited it several times April 1819 (*MROM* 13; *Journals* 263). **Lionel Verney** sleeps in **Colonna Palace** there (*LM* 461).

Monte San Giuliano: Mountain or hill near Bagni di San Guiliano, **Italian** town three miles northeast of **Pisa** (Green 73; Crook 2). The Shelleys moved to Bagni di San Giuliano's Casa Prini August 1820 (*Letters* 1.158–159; *Journals* 329; Sunstein 185–186). Shelley describes Pisa's revolt against **Uguccione della Fagguiola** that begins when he reaches Giuliano's summit (*V* 1.229; Green 73). **Orlando Quartezzani** occasionally views **Lucca** from San Giuliano (*V* 3.207).

Monte San Pelegrino: Apennine peak twenty-six miles northeast of **Florence**. In August 1820, **PBS** visited San Pelegrino, which inspired his *The Witch of Atlas* (1824) (*Journals* 328–329; White 2.214–216). Many religious travelers on pilgrimage to it visit nearby Castle **Valperga** (*V* 2.178–179).

Montecatini: Italian village fifteen miles east of **Lucca**; Shelley spells it **Monte Catini**. It was 14th-century **Val di Nievole**'s dominant village, later becoming a mineral spa; Shelley mentions it in an 1843 letter (Green 59; *Letters* 3.61). Shelley refers to **Uguccione della Faggiuola**'s 1315 siege of Montecatini's castle (*V* 1.209–211). [*V* 2.2, 3.250].

Montecchi e Capuletti: See **Bellini, Vincenzo**.

Montemayor, Jorge de (c. 1520–1561): Little is known about this **Portuguese** poet, whose name derives from that of his native town. Shelley wrote Montemayor's biography for *Italian and Spanish Lives*. His reputation rests upon his pastoral *Los siete libros de la Diana* [*Diana's Seven Books*] (c. 1559), of which Shelley gives an extensive plot summary while noting that "it sets history and chronology at defiance" (*ISPL* 3.89). Shelley considers *Diana's* style "particularly beautiful. Nothing can be more correct, yet less laboured; nothing more elegant, yet less exaggerated"; the "heartfelt truth of the sentiments, and the beauty of the descriptions" earned Montemayor an esteemed literary reputation (*ISPL* 3.91).

Montenvers: See **Montanvers**.

Monti, Vincenzo (1754–1828): **Italian** poet. Shelley wrote Monti's biography for *Italian and Spanish Lives*, asking Gabriele Rossetti for assistance with it April 1835 (*Letters* 2.238). Shelley claims Monti is "the greatest Italian poet that has appeared since the golden days of its poetry.... [H]e has a fervour, a power of imagery, an overflowing and redundance of ideal thought, that mark the genuine poet" (*ISPL* 2.303). Shelley admires Monti's tragedy *Aristodemo* [*Aristodemus*] (1787), which she first read May 1818, and notes the failure of his drama about jealousy, *Galeotto Manfredi* (1786–87), which she first read September 1818 (*ISPL* 2.312; *Journals* 210, 226). Monti's success as a poet truly began with his poem *In morte di Ugo Bassville* [*Hugo's Penance*] (1793–94), commonly known as *Basvilliana*, which details Hugh Basseville's murder. The poem is fiercely antirepublican in its discussion of the **French Revolution**; Shelley notes that it "at once raised Monti's reputation," but this poem caused Monti difficulty when the **French** invaded Italy 1797 (*ISPL* 2.317). Shelley notes Monti's tragedy *Caio Gracco* [*Caius Gracchus*] (1800) "is wanting in poetry," having first read it September 1818 (*ISPL* 2.326; *Journals* 226). Monti wrote "Bard" (1806) in honor of **Napoleon**'s **Egyptian** campaign (*ISPL* 2.328). Shelley discusses at length whether Monti's poems in Napoleon's honor were written for survival or from true feeling; she admires Monti's character while deploring his slavish submission to powerful figures. Shelley provides extensive extracts of Monti's letters and applauds his blank-verse translation of the *Iliad* (1810). While dicussing **Carbonari**, Shelley mentions that Monti is "by no means a pure political character" and subsequently notes, "under Monti's auspices, a great war of words began in Italy," referring to Monti's participation in the debate over the *National Dictionary* (*R* 2.163, 2.194).

Moore, Thomas (1779–1852): Musician and writer of patriotic and nostalgic songs who established himself as **Ireland**'s bard with *Irish Melodies* (1808–34). Moore's *Lalla Rookh* (1817) was also highly successful. Moore became Shelley's friend 1827, although she first met him 1824, and she assisted him in writing his life of **Byron** (published 1830). In 1827, Shelley recorded that Moore "reminds me delightfully of the past and I like him much—There is something warm & genuine in his feelings & manner which is very attractive ... & I never felt myself so perfectly at ease with anyone.... His singing is something new & strange & beautiful" (*Journals* 501–502). **Raymond** sings "the **Tyrolese song of liberty**," the subtitle of Moore's "Merrily Every Bosom Boundeth" (*LM* 63; Moore 363). As "**The False Rhyme**'s" epigraph, Shelley accurately quotes from Moore's "The Wonder": "**Come, tell me** where the maid is found / Whose heart can love without deceit, / And I will range the world around / To sigh one moment at her feet" (*TFR* 117; Moore 125). As first epigraph to the *Perkin Warbeck* chapter in which **Monina De Faro** nurses **Richard of York**, Shelley quotes from a song in the first part of Moore's *Evenings in Greece* (1826): "**Ah! where are they**, who heard in former hours / The voice of song in these neglected bowers? / They are gone!" (*PW* 2.222; Moore 338). As Feldman and Scott-Kilvert note, a copy of this poem in Moore's hand addressed to Shelley is in the Abinger collection (*Journals* 501). In *Lodore*, Shelley quotes from several of Moore's works, including *Lalla Rookh* and *Irish Melodies*. Crook suggests letter ten of Moore's *The Fudge Family in Paris* (1818), which Shelley read in 1818, as a probable source for Shelley's quotation, "No '**green spot**' of delight soothed [**Lord Lodore's**] memory" (*L* 1.97; Stafford 38; Crook 2; *Journals* 230). Shelley quotes the opening of Moore's "To—" (1806), which she first read 1817, as an epigraph to the chapter in which **Lady Lodore** gives up her fortune: "**The world had** just begun to steal / Each hope that led me lightly on, / I felt not as I used to feel, / And life grew dark and love was gone" (*L* 3.149; Moore 120; *Journals* 664). **Gerard Neville** gives **Elizabeth Falkner** some of Moore's melodies to learn and quotes from *Lalla Rookh* (*F* 236, 221). Neville brings Elizabeth "the melodies of Moore, so '**married to immortal verse**,'" describing Moore's *Irish Melodies* with a line from **Milton's** *L'Allegro* (*F* 236; *L'Allegro* lines 135–137). See "**Roger Dodsworth**."

Moors: North **African** ethnic and religious group that invaded and conquered most of **Spain** 711–714; **Granada** was the last Moor stronghold; **Ferdinand** and **Isabella I** took it 1492. Shelley consulted **Irving's** *Conquest of Granada* (1829) for her *Perkin Warbeck* scenes of Spanish-Moor wars (*Letters* 2.91; *PW* 1.159, 1.204–240). Shelley mentions that "Spanish annals of Moorish wars" celebrate **St. James** (*R* 2.46).

Moravia: Region that became part of **Bohemia** in the 11th century and is now in the Czech Republic. Shelley describes **Colletta's** imprisonment at **Brünn** there (*R* 2.207).

Moray, Earl of: Andrew Stuart, bishop of Moray; he was **James IV's** great-uncle (Fischer 221). In *Perkin Warbeck*, he opposes **Richard of York** and is James's uncle.

Mordecastelli, Vanni: Mordecastelli was an important **Lucchese** trade family 1308 and, like **Castruccio**, was expelled from the city; Vanni is Castruccio's advisor and officer in *Valperga* (Green 21, 38).

Morea: See **Peloponnese**.

Moréri, Louis (1653–1680): French historian renowned for *Grand dictionaire historique, ou mélange curieux de l'histoire sacrée et profane* [*Great Historical Dictionary, or Curious Miscellany of Sacred and Profane History*] (1674) (Hollier 382). *Valperga's* preface includes a translation of his account of **Castruccio**, which **William Godwin** added (*V* 1.iii; Crook 2).

Morgan, Lady [Sydney Owenson] (1776–1859): British author who customarily criticized oppressive governments in her works, such as *Italy* (1821) (Blain 762). Shelley notes that

Morgan's *Italy* is "dear" to **Italians** (*R* 1.x).

Moritz: Justine Moritz's deceased father; she was his favorite child.

Moritz, Justine: **Frankenstein** family's trusted servant; they treat her as family in *Frankenstein*. Shelley took "Moritz" from Carl Moritz's travel book, *Travels, Chiefly on Foot, through Several Parts of England in 1782* (1795), which she read 1816, and Justine is biographically resonant of **Fanny Godwin** (Sunstein 430; *Journals* 664).

Moritz, Madame: Justine Moritz's Roman Catholic mother in *Frankenstein*.

***Morning Herald*:** Daily **London** newspaper established 1782. Its circulation rivaled the *Times*'s, and in the early 19th century it was highly esteemed for its foreign correspondence and unbiased reporting (J. Grant 2.30, 2.32). **Lady Lodore** reads about a party at **Maristow Castle** in the *Morning Herald* (*L* 3.288).

***Morning Post*:** Daily **Tory London** newspaper established 1771; it chronicled high society (J. Grant 2.48, 2.52). **Longfield**'s inhabitants know **Lady Lodore** is active in London society, "as the Morning Post testified" (*L* 1.6). An "announcement in the Morning Post" marked Lady and **Lord Lodore**'s arrival in London after their marriage (*L* 1.114).

Morpheus: Son of the **Roman** god of sleep; he appears human in dreams (Ovid, *Metamorphoses* 11). Shelley describes **Brocklet** "as secluded, shadowy and still, as the abode of Morpheus" (*R* 1.195).

Morre: **French** village three miles southeast of **Besançon**; Shelley spells it **Mort**. Shelley stayed at this "miserable village" August 1814 (*H* 33; *Journals* 15).

Mort: See **Morre**.

"Mortal Immortal, The": Most anthologized of all Shelley's stories; it first appeared in the 1834 *Keepsake* as by "Author of **Frankenstein**," accompanied by an illustration titled *Bertha*, which Henry P. Briggs painted and Frederick Bacon engraved, illustrating the scene in which **Bertha** and her benefactress argue about **Albert Hoffer** (Robinson 390; *MI* 225). The story's title (drawn from **Keats**'s *Endymion* [1818]) refers to **Winzy**, the male protagonist who narrates this tale 16 July 1833, his 323rd birthday (Keats 1.844; *MI* 219). Winzy works as **Cornelius Agrippa**'s assistant, using money he earns to court Bertha, who is enraged when Winzy misses an arranged rendevous (*MI* 220–221). As revenge, Bertha goes hunting with Hoffer; this lovers' quarrel causes Winzy to drink secretly a magical liquid Agrippa concocted (claiming it would cure love) (*MI* 222). Winzy then visits Bertha to test this anti-love potion's effect. When Winzy visits Agrippa on his deathbed, he discovers the true power of the potion, which is the **Elixir of Immortality** (*MI* 224–226). Initially skeptical, Winzy begins to believe in it as wife Bertha ages while he stays youthful in appearance (*MI* 226). Neighbors call him **Scholar Bewitched** and shun him, so Winzy relocates to **France** with Bertha (*MI* 228).

Left alone after Bertha's death, Winzy worries about possible immortality but tries to believe that his having drunk only half the liquid has bestowed only half-eternity (*MI* 229). The tale concludes with Winzy's decision to test his immortality by facing "famine, toil, and tempest" (*MI* 230). Shelley's use of the alchemy and science theme and supernatural occurences is familiar due to *Frankenstein*, "**Valerius the Reanimated Roman**," and "**Roger Dodsworth**"; her inclusion of the Elixir of Immortality probably stems from **William Godwin**'s *St. Leon* (1799).

Mortimer: **Irish** family linking English and Anglo-Irish aristocracies; it asserted a claim to the throne **Edward IV** inherited (Connolly 369). **Richard of York** explains that he is royalty through **Plantagenet** and Mortimer; he also calls himself Mortimer's "descendant" (*PW* 1.284, 3.262).

Morton, John (1420–1500): Bishop of **Ely** and **Canterbury**'s archbishop; one of **Henry VII**'s counselors in *Perkin Warbeck* (*DNB*).

Mosaic: See **Horace**.

Moschus: See "**From Moschus**."

Moscow: **Russia**'s capital city. In 1814, Shelley saw **Nogent**, a town **Cossacks** "entirely desolated" as revenge for **Naples**'s 1812 attack on Moscow (*H* 19; Kinder 2.35). **Ludovico** and **Ferdinando Eboli** are in the army at Moscow together (*FE* 79). **Rupert Falkner** and **Elizabeth Falkner** travel there (*F* 38).

Mosè: See **Rossini, Gioacchino**.

Moselle: River flowing from northeastern **France** into **Germany**'s **Rhine**. Shelley sailed on it June 1840 (*R* 1.13). She viewed the Moselle-Rhine convergence July 1840 and passed this junction again 1842 (*R* 1.16–20, 1.25, 1.168).

Mosme: Small **Greek** village five miles north of **Zitza**. **Camaraz** and **Cyril Ziani** stay overnight there (*EE* 112).

Moulward: Place on Scotland's eastern coast, not further identified (Fischer 213). **Drummonds** burn eighty **Murrays** there (*PW* 2.194).

Mount's Bay: Bay of southern **Cornwall** between **Land's End** and the Lizard. **Lady Katherine Gordon** takes refuge in **Saint Michael's Mount** monastery near the bay (*PW* 3.173).

Mountcashel, Lady Margaret (1772–1835): Mary Wollstonecraft was governess to Margaret King in **Ireland** in 1786 before Margaret married Stephen Moore, Earl of Mountcashel, in 1791 (*Journals* 585; Seymour 24). Lady Mountcashel (sometimes Mount Cashell) took an active interest in English and Irish politics until she met **Tighe** in **Rome** 1804; she assumed the name **Mrs. Mason** (from a character in Wollstonecraft's *Original Stories from Real Life* [1788]) 1805 and left her husband and seven children (*Journals* 586). Lady Mountcashel then lived with Tighe in **London**, where her children's book, *Stories of Old Daniel* (1807), was published; they had two daughters, Nerina and **Laurette** (to whom Shelley dedicated "**Maurice**"). Lady Mountcashel was friends with **William God-**

win and his second wife (*Journals* 586–587). She and Tighe moved to **Italy** and settled in **Pisa** 1814, where Shelley first met them September 1819 (*Journals* 586–587). Shelley's *Letters* demonstrate that the two women remained in contact throughout much of the 1820s; Lady Mountcashel, a "towering nononsense *grande dame*," offered much practical advice (Sunstein 175). Lady Mountcashel was a supportive friend, especially of **Claire Clairmont**, and Shelley recorded "alas! all die" 24 February 1835 when she learned of Lady Mountcashel's death (*Journals* 545). See Appendix II of Shelley's *Journals* (585–588) and Edward C. McAleer's *The Sensitive Plant: A Life of Lady Mount Cashell* (1958).

Mountford, Sir Simon (d. 1495): Important Warwickshire gentleman executed February 1495 for supporting **Perkin Warbeck** (Arthurson 65, 79, 85). **Yorkist** since **Edward IV**, he supports **Richard of York**, especially in attacking **Hythe**, in *Perkin Warbeck*.

"Mourner, The": First published in the 1830 *Keepsake* as by "Author of 'Frankenstein'"; references to **Spain**, **Russia**, and the **Regent** suggest that Shelley sets the story 1813–14 (Robinson 379). Two illustrations, both titled *Virginia Water*, which **Turner** drew and Robert Wallis engraved, accompanied the story (*Mourner* 82, 84). Sunstein terms it "a story of excessive father-daughter love, patricide, and filial suicide" (34). Sunstein asserts that Shelley's reactions to a difficult period of her life were resolved through **Clarice Eversham**'s fictional suicide (297–298). The story opens with Shelley's lengthy and admiring description of **Virginia Water** and its vicinity (*Mourner* 81). Narrator **Horace Neville** asks his cousin **Juliet** to take care of an unmarked grave during his forthcoming absence and relates his encounter with **Ellen Burnet** (*Mourner* 81–83, 85). Horace met Ellen in **Windsor** Forest after running away from **Eton** (*Mourner* 86–87). Horace visited her while at school and prevented her intended suicide (*Mourner* 88–90). Horace returns home for Christmas, is injured in a hunting accident, and encounters **Lewis Elmore**, who describes his love for **Lord Eversham**'s daughter Clarice, as well as noting her excessive attachment to her father, whom she worships as "a guardian angel" (*Mourner* 91–92). Lewis and Clarice are engaged when Lewis enters the British army and goes to fight in Spain; during his absence, Clarice goes to the **West Indies** with her father to visit his estates there (*Mourner* 92). Lewis returns home wounded to learn that the *St. Mary*, upon which Lord Eversham and Clarice were returning from **Barbados** to **Liverpool**, had burned at sea and sunk (*Mourner* 93). Clarice's refusal to be rescued without her father perhaps inadvertently caused Lord Eversham's death; Clarice was ultimately saved but blames herself for his death (*Mourner* 94). Lewis traces Clarice to Liverpool but loses the trail (*Mourner* 95). When Lewis visits Horace, Lewis shows him a miniature of Clarice, and Horace realizes that Ellen is the same person (*Mourner* 96). They return to **Old Windsor**, only to find her unmarked grave in the churchyard (*Mourner* 96–97, 99). Ellen, who maintains her assumed identity and cannot bring herself even to write the word for the crime of which she believes herself guilty, welcomes death as a release from earthly suffering, as detailed in her last letter. "The Mourner" touches upon many themes with which Shelley had concerned herself during a similarly troubling time of her own life, when she wrote *Matilda* in 1819; the portrayal of Clarice's attachment to her father is autobiographical.

Mowbray, Anne (1472–1483): John and **Elizabeth Mowbray**'s daughter who married **Richard of York** 1478; he was murdered in the **Tower** before their marriage was consummated (*DNB*). Richard fondly remembers her in *Perkin Warbeck*.

Mowbray, Elizabeth (d. 1507): Duchess of Norfolk as John Mowbray's wife, John **Talbot**'s daughter, and **Anne Mowbray**'s mother (*DNB*). She reminisces with **Richard of York** at the **Surrey-Walden** marriage in *Perkin Warbeck*.

Mowbray, Thomas: Shelley mistakenly calls this first **Duke of Norfolk** the husband of **Elizabeth Mowbray** in *Perkin Warbeck*; her husband was John Mowbray (1444–76), fourth Duke of Norfolk (*DNB*). **Richard of York** remembers Thomas's death (*PW* 2.139).

Moyle, Sir Thomas (d. 1560): Shelley names this 1540s **House of Commons** speaker in passing but actually means his father, John (*DNB*; Fischer 396). **Lady Katherine Gordon** and **Elizabeth of York** stay overnight at his seat, **Eastwell Place** (*PW* 3.340).

Mozart, Wolfgang Amadeus (1756–1791): Austrian composer recognized as one of the greatest classical composers of all time (Bleiler 8, 14, 20, 28). Shelley greatly admired Mozart's work and frequently attended public and private performances in **London**. She saw *Don Giovanni* (subtitled *The Libertine's Punishment*) (1787) at **King's Theatre** May 1817 and again at the Haymarket Theatre January and February 1818 (*Journals* 170, 192, 194). She also saw Isaac Pocock's *The Libertine*, a play based on *Don Giovanni*, at London's Covent Garden March 1818 (*Journals* 196). Shelley saw *Figaro*, *Le Nozze di Figaro* [*The Marriage of Figaro*] (1786), in London February 1818; Figaro is Count Almaviva's valet (*Journals* 195). He plans to marry Susanna, but Almaviva attempts to seduce her. After Count and Countess Almaviva eventually reconcile, Figaro and Susanna marry. **Lionel Verney** seems to express Shelley's opinion: "Among the other transcendant attributes of Mozart's music, it possesses more than any other that of appearing to come from the heart; you enter into the passions expressed by him, and are transported with grief, joy, anger, or confusion, as he, our soul's master, chooses to inspire" (*LM* 139). Verney records "**Perdita** receded from the piano, for **Raymond** had joined in the trio of '*Taci ingiusto core*,' in Don Giovanni" (the **Italian** means "Be still, unreasonable heart!"); Donna Elvira, Giovanni's discarded love, sings it (*LM* 139; Mozart 2.1). **Idris** sings "that passionate and sorrowful air in *Figaro*, '*Porgi, amor, qualche ristoro*'"; Almaviva sings this appeal: "Pour, O love, sweet consolation, / On my lonely, my broken heart. / Give me back his lost affection, / Or, I beg you, let me die" (*LM* 139; Mozart 2.1–4). Shelley was disappointed at not seeing **Meyerbeer**'s *Hu-*

guenots in **Dresden**; she felt it superior to Mozart, "inasmuch as orchestral accompaniment is so wonderfully improved and extended since *Figaro*'s first performance" (*R* 1.248). She also mentions Mozart's *Zauberflaute*, her name for *Die Zauberflöte* [*The Magic Flute*] (1791) (*R* 1.177, 1.248; Scholes 593). Shelley arrived in **Salzburg** September 1842 during "the inauguration of the statue of Mozart and the anniversary of the century after his birth" and describes Mozart as "greatest of all composers" (*R* 2.33, 2.36).

Mr ——: Shelley mentions crossing **Lake of Como** with Mr.——, not further identified but possibly **Mr. F——** (*R* 1.84–85).

Muddy Creek: Several streams in North **America** bear this name. Shelley notes that "**Germans** know how to give the glory of spirit-stirring names to their valleys and their forests, very different from the **Little Woman**, or Muddy Creek, of America" (*R* 1.45).

Muhammad: Born in **Mecca**, **Arab** prophet and founder of **Islam**; Shelley calls him **Mahomet**. According to Islamic law, "a woman must not meet a man alone, nor should a woman travel alone" (Rasjidi 421). Strict restrictions about women's proper modest dress—which usually include veiling the face in public—also exist. **Safie**'s Christian Arab mother rejects Islamic principles about the position of women (*Fr1* 151; *Fr3* 108). This education enables Safie to disobey her father's command to return to **Turkey**, to travel with only one female companion during her flight to **Germany**, and to adjust to the **De La-**ceys' life. **Buzeccha** swears by Mahomet (*TP* 8).

Mülchen: Czech town ten miles north of **Tabor**. Shelley stayed there September 1842 (*R* 2.15–16).

Mullagh: See **Awbeg**.

Mumpf: **Swiss** town on the **Rhine**, five miles east of **Rheinfelden**; Shelley spells it **Mumph**. She traveled in a small canoe from **Laufenburg** to Mumph August 1814 (*H* 57–58; *Journals* 21).

Mumph: See **Mumpf**.

Munich: **German** city in **Bavaria**, 160 miles southeast of **Heidelberg**. Shelley mentions that **Mr. Wertheim** is from Munich (*R* 1.199). [*R* 2.46–47].

Munster: Southwestern **Irish** county. **Richard of York** spends time there, where **Desmond** rules; **O'Water** is respected throughout Munster (*PW* 1.274, 1.279, 1.288, 1.290–291).

Murano: Island in **Laguna** northeast of **Venice** (Littlewood 230). Shelley discusses **Bellini**'s masterpiece in **San Pietro Church** on Murano (*R* 2.93, 2.101).

Murat, Joachim (1767–1815): A marshal in **Napoleon**'s army; he married Napoleon's sister Caroline and became king of **Naples** 1808–15 (Morby 103; Kinder 2.35). "Ferdinando Eboli" takes place in Naples during Murat's reign; Shelley also uses **Gioacchino** (**Italian** version of his name) in this story. Shelley relates Murat's reaction to **Carbonarism** and discusses **Col-**

Muratori, Ludovico Antonio (1672–1750)

letta's *History of the Death of Murat* (*R* 2.170–174, 2.206–208).

Muratori, Ludovico Antonio (1672–1750): **Italian** historian; Shelley read his *Dissertazioni sopra le Antichità Italienne* [*Dissertations on Italian Antiquity*] (1751) 1820 and his twenty-eight volume *Rerum Italicarum scriptores* [*On Italian Writers*] (1723–51) 1821 (Cannon 293; *Journals* 329–332). His works were sources for *Valperga*.

Murcia: City in southeastern **Spain**, twenty-five miles inland from the **Mediterranean**. The Spanish army's concentration at Murcia and subsequent invasion near **Alcala** force **Herman De Faro** to leave Alcala (*PW* 1.209).

Murray, John (1778–1843): Publisher who built up the business his father established; it still exists in **London** today. Murray was a highly prosperous literary and commercial businessman, and his son continued his work with a successful series of travel books. Murray forwarded funds to writers he published (including assisting **William Godwin** with debts 1825), held literary gatherings at his house, and founded **Tory** *Quarterly Review* 1809 (*Journals* 472). **Byron** was Murray's most important client; **PBS** met Murray 1816 when he delivered the third canto of *Childe Harold's Pilgrimage* and "The Prisoner of Chillon" to him (*Journals* 134; Sunstein 134, 136; White 1.465). PBS also gave Murray *Frankenstein*'s manuscript, which the conservative Murray rejected 1817, though he liked it (*Journals* 171). **Moore** took Shelley to see Murray when she needed funds 1828; she valued his "prestige and high payments" but never provided the book she felt she owed him for his "check for a hundred pounds"—he refused *Perkin Warbeck* 1829 (Sunstein 287, 303). Shelley consistently offered to repay the debt by writing for Murray, but he refused to accept her work; November 1829, Shelley wrote to him, "I fear that my debt must stand over till better times—but be assured that I shall never forget it"; Feldman and Scott-Kilvert assert that Shelley repaid it (*Letters* 2.121; *Journals* 506, 513, 554). Shelley depended on Murray's travel books during her **European** tours: she praises their guidance, reports mistakes, and qualifies opinions (*R* 1.30, 1.49, 1.164, 1.195, 1.271, 1.278, 2.18, 2.39, 2.48, 2.61). Shelley quotes Murray's description of **Brocklet**, beginning " 'another watering-place' " (*R* 1.195; Moskal 175; *MSGE* 117). See Samuel Smiles's *A Publisher and His Friends. Memoirs and Correspondence of the Late John Murray* (1891).

Murrays: Scottish clan (Keay 718). **Drummonds** burn eighty of its members at **Moulward**; the clan is at peace during *Perkin Warbeck* (*PW* 2.194, 2.228).

Murrogh-en-Ranagh: Member of Scottish **O'Brien** clan, first Earl of **Thomond** 1543, and a minor *Perkin Warbeck* character (Connolly 397).

"Music": Fragment **PBS** wrote 1817. Shelley quotes the poem's opening when **Lionel Verney** finds music the " '**silver key** of the fountain of tears' " (*LM* 420; PBS line 1).

Muskerry: Land around Macroon in **Cork** (Connolly 334). Part of **Macarthy**

clan is called "Muskerry" in *Perkin Warbeck*.

"Mutability": Poem **PBS** published 1816. **Victor Frankenstein** quotes lines beginning " 'We rest.—a dream has power to poison sleep,' " as he climbs **Montanvert** (*Fr1* 126; *Fr3* 89; PBS lines 9–16). The **Creature** laments, " 'The path of my departure was free'; and there was none to lament my annihilation," a phrase Shelley adapts from PBS's poem (*Fr1* 156; *Fr3* 113; PBS line 14). Shelley adapts the poem's final stanza as an epigraph to the *Lodore* chapter in which **Lady Lodore** leaves **London**: "It is the same, for be it joy or sorrow, / The path of its departure still is free; / Man's yesterday can ne'er be like his morrow, / Nor aught endure save mutability" (*L* 3.170; PBS lines 13–16).

Myrrha*:** **Alfieri**'s tragedy, which Charles Lloyd translated from **Italian** 1815. It presents a version of the **Greek** myth in which **Aphrodite** punishes Myrrha for her beauty "with an incestuous infatuation for her father"; Myrrha contrives to become pregnant by her father, then flees, and the gods turn her into a tree (Tripp 387–388). In Alfieri's drama, Myrrha reveals to her father that she cannot marry since she loves him beyond all others; then she kills herself with his dagger. Shelley records reading Alfieri September 1818 and that she "translated Alfieri's *Mirra*," which may have helped her write ***Proserpine and ***Midas*** (*Journals* 226; Sunstein 155). **Matilda**'s expression of admiration for *Myrrha* as "best of Alfieri's tragedies" causes her father's frame to shake "with some concealed emotion that in spite of his efforts half conquered him" (*M* 165).

N

Naiad: Greek mythological nymph of a spring, lake, or brook (Tripp 399). **Hymera** is a naiad (*P* 53). **Lionel Verney** describes the magnificent **Alps**'s reflection in **Lake Geneva** as "palaces for the Naiads" (*LM* 80, 419).

Nancy: Minor characters in "The Mourner" and *Falkner*.

Nancy: French city on the **Moselle** about thirty miles south of **Metz**. Shelley mentions **Charles the Rash** "fell before Nancy" 1477 (*PW* 1.130). [*R* 1.16].

Nantes: French town on **Loire** about thirty-two miles east of St. Nazaire. **Chateau Villeneuve** is near Nantes, and **Henry IV** of France travels there (*D* 153, 159).

Naples: Port on southern **Italy**'s west coast about 150 miles south of **Rome**; its dialect and people are **Neapolitan**. The Shelleys visited Naples and saw historical spots such as **Virgil**'s tomb and **Vesuvius** December 1818 (*Journals* 241–249). **Valerius** and his friend row to Naples (*Val* 339). "**A Tale of the Passions**" relates events leading to **Conradin**'s execution in Naples (*TP* 1, 22). Shelley voices her favorable opinion of Naples through **Edmund Malville**; he calls the city "the real enchantress of Italy" (*RI* 28). "**The Heir of Mondolfo**" and "**Ferdinando Eboli**" are set near Naples (*HM* 308, 318; *FE* 65). *The Last Man* begins with the narrator's relation of Neapolitan guides' hesitation, fearing "spectres," to enter the cavern housing **Sibylline leaves** on 8 December 1818; the date corresponds with Shelley's own visit to Naples (*LM* 3–4). **Lionel Verney** plans to sail past Naples (*LM* 469). **Victor Frankenstein** is born in Naples (*Fr3* 40). **Countess de' Tolomei** visits Naples for **San Gennaro**'s feast (*Brother* 176, 182). **Lord Lodore** and **Ethel Villiers** plan to travel to Naples before Lodore's death, and Ethel actually travels there with her husband (*L* 1.251, 2.167). Neapolitan **Clorinda Saville** refuses to leave Naples for her husband's English home; **Lucy Saville** is prejudiced against

Clorinda because of race (*L* 2.176, 3.207, 3.210, 3.217). Shelley describes her June 1843 visit to Naples, recalling previous winter visits (*R* 2.262–263, 2.277). She also gives an account of Naples's **Carbonari** (*R* 2.164–165, 2.170, 2.177–178). [*V* 1.212; *SA* 55; *Trans* 122; *FE* 70, 73; *PW* 1.312; *L* 2.60, 2.187–188, 2.193, 3.199].

Naples, Bay of: See **Baiae**.

Naples, King of: See **Ferdinand II**.

Napoleon: See **Bonaparte**.

Napoli: **Italian** name for Nauplion, **Morean** port at gulf of Argolis's northern end. **Katusthius Ziani** asks **Cyril** and **Zella Ziani** to accompany him to Napoli, where Cyril had met Zella (*EE* 105, 107).

Narcissi: See **Narcissus**.

Narcissus: **Greek** mythological figure who fell in love with his own reflection in a pool and died because he could not turn away (Tripp 389). **Ino** carries "Star-Eyed Narcissi," flowers deriving their name from Narcissus (*P* 49). According to myth, **Zeus** promoted **Proserpine**'s abduction by causing "a narcissus with a hundred blooms" to grow as a distraction to assist **Pluto**'s abduction of her (Tripp 194).

Narni: **Italian** town about seven miles southwest of **Terni**. **Beatrice** passes through it (*V* 3.83).

Narrative of the Revolution of Naples in 1820: See **Colletta**.

Nassau: Popular central **German** holiday resort region, now called Siegerland (McLachlan 529). Shelley notes "*The Bubbles of the Brunnens* brought" Nassau's baths "into fashion with" the English (*R* 1.184).

National Air: British national anthem, "God Save the Queen"; **Germany**'s "Heil dir in Siegerkranz" is to the same tune (Moskal 173). Shelley heard the tune celebrating **Isabeau of Bavaria**'s birthday in **Kissingen** July 1840 (*R* 1.191).

National Dictionary: Following debate about which of **Italy**'s regional dialects should be the new nation's standard language, **Della Crusca Academy** published *Vocabolario* (1612) to standardize literary Italian as, essentially, the language of 14th-century **Tuscan** writers (*DIL* 428–432; Crook 2). Shelley mentions the academy and *Proposta* authors' "fierce battle" about language (*R* 2.163).

Navarre: Area north of the **Pyrennees** in southwest **France**, formerly an independent kingdom (Kinder 1.187; A. Grant 5). Shelley presents her fictional characterization of Navarre's historical **Queen Margaret** (*TFR* 117).

Naxos: Island of the **Cyclades** off **Greece**'s coast, famous for wine and associated with worshipping **Bacchus** (Tripp 391). **Ino** asserts **Enna**'s plains are more "fertile" and "verdant" than Naxos's "luscious vine" (*P* 45).

Nazarene: Variation of "Nazarite," one who has taken a vow of abstinence (Numbers 6). **Buzeccha** calls **Ricciardo**

Neapolitan

de' Rossini a Nazarene (*TP* 8). See **Saracen**.

Neapolitan: See **Naples**.

Neckar: River flowing through southwest **Germany** from the **Black Forest** to the **Rhine** at **Mannheim**. Shelley saw it July 1840 (*R* 1.33).

Nemi: Town and lake in Alban Hills about seventeen miles southeast of **Rome**. The Shelleys toured the area March 1819 (*Journals* 251). **French** troops fighting **banditti** in **Albano** came from **Naples** via Nemi (*SA* 55).

"Nepomuccidon": See **Percicus**.

Nepomuk, John: See **St. John Nepomuk**.

Neptune: Mythological **Roman** god of the sea. Shelley saw Jacopo Tatti Sansovino's Neptune statue (1567) in the main entrance to **Doge's Palace**'s courtyard September 1842 (*R* 2.84; Honour 43).

Neptune, Temple of: Ruins in **Paestum**; Shelley explored them in June 1843 (*R* 2.265).

Nereids: Sea nymphs to whom **Midas** will throw his unwanted gold (Tripp 395; *Midas* 153). Shelley calls **Venice** "favourite of **Amphitrite** and the Nereids," and she visited a "favourite grotto of the Nereids" in **Capri** June 1843 (*R* 2.123, 2.269).

Neri: Florentine **Guelph** faction (Crook 2). The Neri join the **Pulci** and **Buondelmonti** in celebrating Guelph victory (*TP* 4). Since Shelley lists the Neri with family names, she may have also been thinking of the Nerli, a Florentine Guelph family (Villani 71, 123). See **Bianchi**.

Nero (37–68 C.E.): **Roman** emperor 54–68 C.E., originally called Lucius Domitius Ahenobarbus (Howatson 383, 498). **Isabell Harley** calls " '**Caracalla** and Nero . . . mere workmen' " of Rome's monuments (*Val* 340).

Nessus: Greek mythological **centaur** who told Deïaneira that if she soaked a shirt in Nessus's blood, it would make her husband, Heracles, love her; instead, Heracles died a violent death from the poisoned shirt. "Shirt of Nessus" connotes an extreme torment, and Shelley uses this allusion to describe **Perdita** and **Raymond**'s lack of communication and **Gerard Neville**'s restricted freedom at his father's house (Tripp 395–396; *LM* 129; *F* 130). Shelley also refers to the shirt of Nessus in her November 1833 *Journals* entry (533).

Nestor: In **Greek** mythology, Pylos's king, esteemed for sagacity (Tripp 396). **Winzy** finds he makes "a sorry figure . . . among the Nestors of our village," since his youthful appearance contrasts greatly with those of village elders (*MI* 227).

Netherlands: See **Holland**.

Neu Markt: "New Market" **Dresden** section near the **Elbe** north of **Alt Markt** (Meras 154). Shelley stayed there August 1842 (*R* 1.232).

Neuchâtel: City (and canton) in western **Switzerland** on Lake Neuchâtel at the base of the **Jura**; Shelley spells it **Neufchâtel**. The Shelleys arrived there August 1814 (*Journals* 17; *H* 43–44).

Neuchâtel: See **Neuchâtel**.

Neumarkt: German name for **Egna**.

Neustadt: Prague's "New Town" section, which **Charles IV** founded 1348, laid out in spacious squares with wide streets, southeast of **Altstadt** (*BCSR* 295, 314). Shelley visited Neustadt August 1842 (*R* 1.280).

Neville, Alithea [née Rivers]: *Falkner* character; mystery about her disappearance lies at the novel's heart. Alithea is an idealized, faithful, traditional wife and mother.

Neville, Gerard: Major *Falkner* character; he is **Sir Boyvill** and **Alithea Neville**'s son and marries **Elizabeth Falkner**. Shelley perhaps draws Gerard's gentleness and care for Elizabeth and his education of her from her own somewhat idealized memories of **PBS**. Gerard's acceptance of **Rupert Falkner** without jealousy of the love Elizabeth bears him is a reconciliation Shelley never achieved between her own husband and father.

Neville, Horace: "The Mourner"'s protagonist, who narrates his encounter with **Ellen Burnet** to his cousin and fiancée **Juliet** (*Mourner* 86).

Neville, Sir Boyvill: Gerard Neville's father and **Alithea Neville**'s husband in *Falkner*.

Neville, Sir George: Yorkist supporter of **Richard III** who was banished to Scotland 1491; he joined **Perkin Warbeck** in **Paris** 1493 (Arthurson 7, 17, 54). **Richard of York** supporter in *Perkin Warbeck*.

"New-Created World": See **Haydn**.

New Forest: Wooded area west of **Southampton**, "new" 1079 when William the Conqueror transformed it into private hunting grounds (Hughes 134). **Clym of the Lyn** is supposed to guide **Robert Clifford** and his men through New Forest; **Richard of York** escapes from Clifford there (*PW* 3.139, 3.226). Clym calls himself the New Forest's King (*PW* 3.148). Shelley notes that before departing for **Europe** 1842, she and **PFS** stayed a week with a friend "on the skirts of the New Forest" (*R* 1.156). This friend could be Mr. Brett, with whom Shelley stayed at Exbury early June 1842 (Sunstein 356; Crook 2).

New Holland: Name given to Australia when a British colony, as it was in Shelley's day and would be until 1931 (Kinder 2.171). Plague rages there (*LM* 234).

New Museum: Museum Island in **Berlin** consists of five buildings, collectively called the Staatliche Museum zu Berlin [Berlin Museum]. Until 1859, "New Museum" [Neues Museum] applied to what is now Old Museum [Altes Museum], which Karl Friedrich Schinkel designed 1823 and inaugurated 1830 (Jackson 1.317–318). Shelley visited New Museum April 1843, and she describes its paintings (*R* 1.218–222).

New Orleans: Southern Louisiana port city. **Hillary** follows **Osborne** there but cannot find him (*F* 268).

New River Cut: Brenta section diverted 1510 to flow southeast into **Laguna** near Chioggia, **Italy** (Goy 68). "**Recollections of Italy**'s" narrator calls it an **Oronooko**, because of the inability of large ships to use it (*RI* 25).

New Town: See **Neustadt**.

New York: Major city and port on North **America**'s northeastern coast. **Lord Lodore** passes through it (*L* 1.24, 1.198). He and **Ethel Villiers** first meet **Fanny Derham**, **Mrs. Greville**, and **Edward Villiers** there, and **Mr. Hatfield** kills Lodore in a duel just outside the city (*L* 1.220, 1.260, 1.272). *Falkner* characters make inquiries for **Alithea Neville** in New York after her disappearance, **Hoskins** meets **Osborne** there, and **Gerard Neville** intends to sail there to begin searching for Osborne (*F* 113, 141, 281).

Newark-upon-Trent: English town about sixteen miles northeast of Nottingham. **Lord Lincoln**'s forces fight the troops of **Henry VII** of England there (*PW* 1.135).

Newbury: British town five miles west of **Reading**. **Lady Lodore** stays at an inn there while ill with scarlet fever, subsequently renting a villa during her recovery (*L* 3.192, 3.241, 3.285).

Newman's: Horatio Saville goes to Newman's while attempting to trace **Lady Lodore**'s departure from **London** (*L* 3.233). The context suggests that the reference is to a livery stable or a hotel with stables where post-horses were hired; Crook has speculated that Shelley may have been referring to Newman Mews, off Newman Street in London (Crook 2).

Newton, Sir Isaac (1642–1727): English mathematician, natural philosopher, and physicist renowned for discovering gravity, developing calculus, and constructing the first telescope. **Victor Frankenstein** compares his own quest to learn to Newton's attitude, in that in his studies "he felt like a child picking up shells beside the great and unexplored ocean of truth" (*Fr3* 44). Shelley probably paraphrased from an anecdote related by Joseph Spence (60).

Niagara Falls: Consisting of the **Canadian** or Horseshoe Falls and the **American** Falls, where the river drops about 160 feet, on Canada's border with the United States. **Lord Lodore** and **Edward Villiers** visit them (*L* 1.230, 2.45).

Niccolai, Otto (1810–1849): German composer who founded **Vienna** Philharmonic Society 1842 (Scholes 684). At **La Scala** September 1840, Shelley attended a performance of Niccolai's opera *Templario*, first performed 1840 and based on **Scott**'s *Ivanhoe* (1819) (*R* 1.111).

Niccolini, Giovanni Battista (1782–1861): Italian tragedian who taught at **Accademia delle Belle Arti (Florence)** after 1807 and was **Foscolo**'s friend. He is renowned for tragedies, such as *Beatrice Cenci* (1838), based on **PBS**'s *The Cenci*, *Arnaldo da Brescia* (1843), *Ino e Temisto*, and *Oedipus* (*DIL* 357–358; *R* 2.203). Shelley rates

Niccolini and **Manzoni** as the foremost Italian poets concerned with Italy's liberty (*R* 1.x). Niccolini also wrote *Polissena* [*Polixena*] (1810), a **Greek** tragedy modeled after **Alfieri** and winner of a **Della Crusca Academy** award; Shelley declares that "the beauty of the verses insured [its] success" (*DIL* 357; *R* 2.203). She describes objections to insults in Niccolini's "**Sicilian Vespers**," to which the **Austrian** minister stated, "Vous ne voyez pas que si l'addresse est à vous, le contenu est pour moi"—"You do not realize that while it may be addressed to you, the message is for me" (*R* 2.204; Moskal 336). Moskal suggests the reference is to Niccolini's *Giovanni da Procida* (1830) (336). Shelley also notes his *History of the House of Swabia* (*R* 2.205).

Niccolò de' Lapi: See **d'Azeglio**.

Nicholas, Emperor (1796–1855): Nicholas I, **Russian** tsar 1825–55. Shelley offers his desire to educate serfs as an example of the curious policy of "present arbitrary governments" (*R* 1.121).

Nicholas V, Pope (1397–1455): Pope 1447–55 (Kelly 244). Shelley mentions **Fra Angelico** refusing Nicholas's offer to be **Florence**'s archbishop (*R* 2.145). She also notes **Bologna** obtained papal protection during Nicholas's papacy (*R* 2.247).

"Night Scene, A": Poem signed "Mary S." in the 1831 *Keepsake*; Palacio discusses the text's attribution to Shelley (482–486). Its subject seems to apply to Shelley's friendship either with **Isabel Baxter Booth** or **Isabel Robinson**. The poem opens with the speaker exclaiming that she can neither see nor touch "gentlest Isabel," that "thy deep sighs, fraught with emotion bland, / Are to my sense the only outward signs / That on that couch my Isabel reclines" (lines 1, 10–12). The speaker pleads with Isabel to "darling, quick thine arms around me throw" and "one kiss, sweet heaven, 'tis Isabel indeed!" (39, 43).

Nijmegen: **Dutch** port on the **Rhine** about forty-five miles east of **Rotterdam**; Shelley spells it **Nimeguen**. The Shelleys passed through it September 1814 (*H* 74–75). See **Montagu**.

Nile: Large river originating in North **Africa** and flowing through **Egypt** into the **Mediterranean**. *The Last Man*'s narrator imagines the **Baiae**'s blue waters are so beautiful that **Cleopatra**'s Nile voyage would "more fitly" have been on the Baiae (*LM* 3). **Lionel Verney** reports plague on the Nile's shores; panic later spreads "from the banks of the Nile" after the sun's eclipse (*LM* 175, 224). Verney outlines his projected journey "passing the seven-mouthed Nile," referring to its delta (*LM* 469).

Nimeguen: See **Nijmegen**.

Nina Pazza per Amore: See **Paisiello**.

Niobe: In **Greek** mythology, the wife of Amphion of **Thebes**; her proud boasting about her fourteen children caused **Apollo** and Artemis to kill all or all but two of them, whereupon Niobe in her grief turned to stone (Tripp 397). Shelley saw a **Uffizi** chamber dedicated to "Niobe and her children"

January 1843; the Niobe sculpture had been excavated in **Rome** 1583 (*R* 2.155; Moskal 310).

Nion: See **Nyon**.

Nixon, Dame: **Margaret**'s grandmother, who owns a small cottage in Vale of **Bewling** where **Lady Lodore** lodges (*L* 3.249).

Noah: God's favorite in the **Bible**, whom he warns that a great flood will remove wicked humankind from earth and commands to build an ark to carry his family and two of each kind of animal to safety (Genesis 5.9–10.32). **Bindo** possesses "sawdust from Noah's sawpit when he clove the planks for the ark" (*V* 1.252).

Nods: French village about thirteen miles north of **Pontarlier**; Shelley spells it **Noé**. The Shelleys passed through it August 1814 (*Journals* 15; *H* 35).

Noé: See **Nods**.

Nogent: See **Nogent-sur-Seine**.

Nogent-sur-Seine: French town on the **Seine** about ten miles southeast of **Provins**; Shelley terms it **Nogent**. The Shelleys passed through it August 1814 (*Journals* 12). Shelley notes that **Cossacks** had "entirely desolated" Nogent (*H* 19; *Journals* 12; *STIE* 484).

Noll: Derogatory term meaning the top of the head, or crown, and nickname for "Oliver," used in reference to **Cromwell** (*OED*; Crook 2). Shelley speculates that the revived **Roger Dodsworth** "may be supposed to pass much of his time in [reverie], now and then interrupting himself with a royalist song against old Noll and the **Roundheads**" (*RD* 48).

Norfolk, Duchess of: See **Mowbray, Elizabeth**.

Norfolk, Duke of: See **Mowbray, Thomas**.

Norham Castle: Castle in Norham, English town about seven miles southwest of Berwick-upon-Tweed. **James IV** besieges Norham Castle, which the **Bishop of Durham** defends, and **Richard of York** demands that Scottish troops spare defeated English subjects there (*PW* 2.308, 2.310, 2.314).

North Pole: Northernmost point on earth. **Robert Walton** encounters **Victor Frankenstein** and the **Creature** while sailing toward it (*Fr1* 57; *Fr3* 33). Shelley was surprised at the planned route for her 1840 **European** tour—traveling to **Como** via **Frankfurt**: "this is something like going to the [equator] by the North Pole" (*R* 1.9).

North Sea: Body of water, also called **German Ocean**, separating England from **Belgium**, **Germany**, **Holland**, and Scandinavia. Returning to England from **Europe** September 1814, the Shelleys sailed across it (*Journals* 24). **Robert Walton** recounts working on several whaling expeditions there (*Fr1* 51; *Fr3* 27). **Hernan De Faro** plans to sail to the North Sea (*PW* 1.240). When **Ethel Villiers** walks over **Blackfriars Bridge** with her husband, "a bitter north-east wind swept up, bearing on its blasts the unthawed breath of the German Ocean" (*L* 3.29).

Northampton: English town forty miles northeast of **Oxford**. **Lady Brampton** is there when she hears of the **Yorkist** defeat at **Bosworth Field** (*PW* 1.37).

Northumberland: Northwestern English county on the Scottish border. For "**Roger Dodsworth**," Shelley draws from contemporary news furor about "**Dr. Hotham**, of Northumberland" (*RD* 43). **James IV**'s projected war against England would cause "groans from the Northumberland wilds" (*PW* 2.194). The **Raby** family lives there (*F* 147).

Norton, Caroline (1808–1877): **Sheridan**'s granddaughter who married George Norton 1827; their marriage was unhappy. Norton supported her family as a poet and novelist. She edited fashionable annuals. After the success of her first poetry volume, *The Sorrows of Rosalie: A Tale, with Other Poems* (1829), and of her first novel, *The Undying One* (1830), she became a leading and fashionable literary figure. Her husband caused public scandal 1837 when he initiated divorce proceedings and named prime minister Lord Melbourne in the case; Norton "vindicated her character" but was unable to obtain her children's custody (*Journals* 614). She subsequently published pamphlets regarding the injustices of women's societal position (*Journals* 614). Shelley seems to have agreed quietly with many of Norton's statements about the unfairness of laws regarding women's rights, and she remained faithful to her friend despite the social ostracism inflicted upon her; the two women were close for much of the 1830s, and Shelley relied on Norton's **parliamentary** influence for assistance (*Journals* 615–616). Shelley enjoyed Norton's '*The Wife*' and '*Woman's Reward*' (1835), considering these works to show "the Authoress to have the greatest sensibility joined to her acknowledged talent"; Shelley describes Norton as "a wonderful creature possessing— wit, beauty & sweetness at their highest grade" (*Letters* 2.243, 2.258). See Appendix III of Shelley's *Journals* and Jane Gray Perkins's *The Life of Mrs. Norton* (1909) (*Journals* 614–616).

***Notte, La*:** See **Correggio**.

Nourjahad: Protagonist of Frances Chamberlaine Sheridan's novel *The History of Nourjahad* (1767). The sultan of **Persia**, Schemzeddin, measures Nourjahad's suitability as his successor through several tests; in one he offers Nourjahad immense wealth, exacting only the penalty of extended periods of sleep. Nourjahad accepts eagerly and embarks initially upon a profligate course, but he later learns the error of his ways and reforms. **Matilda**'s father feels his sixteen-year absence from Britain has been like Nourjahad's sleep (*M* 162). **Winzy** reflects upon what he knows of immortality and before commencing his own tale declares "how happy was the fabled Nourjahad!" (*MI* 219).

Novara: Italian city about twenty-five miles west of **Milan**. Novara's lord submits to **Henry IV** of **Germany** (*V* 1.118).

Novello, Count Guido de' Guidi: **Florence**'s Podestà 1260; he made all Florentine citizens swear allegiance to **Manfred** and fled Florence when

Novello, [Joseph] Alfred (1810–1896)

Guelphs took it 1266 (Villani 182–183, 220–223). Minor character in "**A Tale of the Passions**."

Novello, [Joseph] Alfred (1810–1896): Vincent **Novello**'s son who sang bass and published music, printing cheap editions. Shelley footnotes that he published **Pearson**'s *Characteristic Songs of Shelley* (1840) (*R* 1.234).

Novello, Vincent (1781–1861): Musician and composer who founded **London**'s music publishing house Novello & Company 1828; it still exists today. Novello held musical evenings in his home and associated with many leading figures of the day, such as **Leigh Hunt** and **Lamb**; Shelley first met him March 1818 (*Journals* 196). She renewed the acquaintance on returning to England 1823, and, as her *Letters* demonstrate, she enjoyed musical evenings at his house frequently, as he heightened her appreciation for music and introduced her to **Haydn**'s works (*Letters* 1.392–393, 1.406–407; Sunstein 245, 251). Shelley was very affectionate toward Novello, but he curtailed their intimacy somewhat September 1824 (*Journals* 482). Shelley learned **Jane Williams** had spread rumors suggesting Shelley and Novello were lovers July 1827; Shelley sent Novello a lock of her mother's hair and concluded their friendship March 1828: "this gift then will remind you pleasantly of her who loves her friends forever—among whom she trusts always to find you although circumstances may divide us" (Sunstein 280; *Letters* 2.29). Shelley and Novello attended a regatta together June 1845, and she consulted him about a music teacher for her son the same year, but the intimacy of the 1820s was lost (*Letters* 3.187–188; Sunstein 368). Apparently, Shelley was also on cordial terms with Novello's wife, Mary Sabilla Hehl (c. 1787–1854) with whom she was still corresponding in 1846 (Crook 2; *Letters* 1.382; Bennett, "Newly Uncovered" 69). See Charles and Mary Cowden Clarke's *Recollections of Writers* (1878).

Nozzano: Castle five miles southwest of **Lucca**, across the **Serchio** from **Ripafratta**. Castruccio builds Nozzano tower in a forest near Lucca (*V* 3.147). Shelley viewed this site August 1820: "towards the west you will see a dark wood where they will tell you there are the ruins of a castle which Castruccio built" (*Letters* 1.364).

Nugent, Daniel: Character who discovers **Henry Clerval**'s body in *Frankenstein*. Crook suggests the name comes from Daniel Healey, **PBS**'s servant 1812–13, and Catherine Nugent, PBS's friend in **Ireland** (Crook 1.135; White 1.223–224).

Numa Pompilius: **Sabines**'s descendant and **Rome**'s ruler 715–673 B.C.E.; according to **Plutarch**, "during the whole reign of Numa, there was neither war, nor sedition" (*Lives* 1.111). The **Creature** learns about "peaceable lawgivers" like Numa from Plutarch's *Lives* (*Fr1* 156; *Fr3* 112).

Numantia: Ancient town (site in modern **Spain**) renowned for resisting the **Romans** for eight months in 113 B.C.E. Shelley claims that the siege of

Messina was equal to those at Numantia and **Saragossa** (*R* 2.210).

'Nunziata: Monna Gegia de' Becari's cousin in "**A Tale of the Passions**."

Nyon: **Swiss** town on **Lake Geneva**'s northwestern shore between **Côppet** and Rolle; Shelley spells it **Nion**. The Shelleys took the road from **Les Rousses** toward Nyon May 1816, but, to conform to the route listed on their passports, they had to travel through **Gex** instead (*H* 91).

Nysa: Mythical mountain where **Bacchus** was raised (Tripp 399). Bacchus refers to the "**nysian** impulse" when his foster-father returns to him, depicting their reunion as a fortuitous event (*Midas* 117).

Nysian: See **Nysa**.

O

"O listen while I sing to thee": Shelley's poem; its manuscript is in the Abinger collection, dated 12 March 1838 (Nitchie 210). The poem consists of four quatrains, in which the speaker states that her song "is meant for thee alone" and declares that her song's strengths depend upon the addressee's responses to her efforts (*O listen* lines 2 and 14). Nitchie reprints the manuscript text, which differs from the 1842 version of the poem set to music and printed "as a canzonet with accompaniment for harp or piano" (Nitchie 234–235; Sunstein 411).

O'Brien: **Thomond** kings in modern Clare county, **Ireland** (Connolly 397). **Murrogh-en-Ranagh** is an O'Brien, **Desmond**'s sister marries an O'Brien, and O'Briens support **Richard of York** (*PW* 1.291, 1.302).

O'Carrolls: **Irish** family from Ely (modern Offaly) county, hence an O'Carroll is **Prince of Ely** (Fischer 119). **Desmond** opposes them (*PW* 1.291, 1.298, 1.306).

O'Water, John: Shelley's variant for John Atwater, **Irish** "bourgeois, merchant and sometime mayor" of **Cork** (Arthurson 22–23). **Richard of York**'s ally in *Perkin Warbeck*.

Oakly: **Lady Cecil**'s home at **Hastings** (*F* 157).

Obizzi: The historical Obizi family assisted **Castruccio** in his ascendance to power in **Lucca**, then grew unhappy and joined a pro-**Florentine** faction with the Bernarducci to overthrow him (Green 52–53, 119). Shelley is historically accurate in portraying this family in *Valperga*; Castruccio bans them from Lucca (Green 193; *V* 2.149).

Obizzi, Galeotto: **Teresa Obizzi**'s powerful and proud husband in **Valperga**. Shelley probably alludes to Luto degli Obizi, who helped negotiate a treaty allowing **Guelph** exiles to return to their **Tuscan** lands (Green 83).

Obizzi, Randolfi: Minor character in *Valperga*.

Obizzi, Teresa: Minor character in *Valperga*.

Obizzo: Castruccio assists in restoring **Ferrara** to marquess Obizzo, connected to the **Este** family (*V* 2.6). Shelley probably refers to Ferrara's Opizo d'Este (Green 210).

"Ode on Napoleon": See **Manzoni**.

"Ode on Venice": Poem **Byron** wrote 1818 and published 1819; Shelley copied it for him September 1818 (Marchand 2.743, 2.754, 2.804; *Journals* 228). Shelley uses a line from Byron's poem to contrast 14th-century **Venice** with the Venice she knew, one where "degenerate inhabitants go '**crouching and crablike** through their sapping streets'" (*V* 1.58; Byron line 13).

"Ode to the West Wind": Poem PBS wrote October 1819, first published 1820 (*Journals* 299; White 2.193). Shelley quotes from it to describe **Castruccio**'s secret path to **Valperga** through woods where trees know "**His voice, and suddenly** grow grey with fear, / And tremble and despoil themselves" (*V* 2.229; PBS lines 41–42). **Euthanasia** describes weather with the line "**sapless foliage** of the ocean" (*V* 3.18; PBS line 40).

Odessa: Russian (today Ukrainian) **Black Sea** port. **Rupert Falkner** and **Elizabeth Falkner** arrive there in late autumn after traveling four years (*F* 37–38).

Oedipus: Figure in a well-known **Greek** myth with many variants. Strangers adopt Oedipus after his father Laius had turned him out in response to a warning that any son Laius fathered with Jocasta would kill him. Oedipus discovers his own destiny by consulting the **Delphic oracle**, flees his adoptive parents to avoid, as he thinks, acting out the prediction, and thus unwittingly fulfills the oracle by killing his own real father and marrying his mother. In Sophocles's play, *Oedipus at Colonus* (401 B.C.E.), Oedipus has discovered the nature of his transgression, blinded himself, and cast himself out of Thebes in remorse. Accompanied by loyal daughter **Antigone**, he finds himself on the **Eumenides**'s sacred wooded ground and asks the gods to grant him mercy and release him from his sufferings. **Matilda** compares herself to Oedipus, suggesting that she is full of remorse and wants to be shriven (*M* 151). As plague survivors prepare to cross from **Dover** to **Calais**, **Lionel Verney** quotes lines Shelley identifies from Sophocles's play (perhaps translated herself) beginning "'**As an unsheltered** northern shore'" (*LM* 372; Sophocles 295). As Verney ponders the future, he wishes for "some Oedipus to solve the riddle of the cruel **Sphynx**!" (*LM* 427). [*LM* 78].

Oedipus: See **Niccolini**.

Oerta: See **Oeta**.

Oes: See **Oos**.

Oeta: Greek mountain range north of **Athens** at Pindus mountains' base; Shelley spells it **Oerta**. **Lionel Verney** and **Perdita** ascend the Oeta with **Raymond**'s body (*LM* 208).

Offenberg: German town about thirty miles southwest of **Baden**. Shelley dined at **La Fortune** there July 1840 (*R* 1.42).

Old Ballad: See *Reliques*.

Old French Chronicle: See **Chastellain**.

Old Play: See *Laws of Candy, The* and **Fletcher**.

Old Reginald's Tower: Thirteenth-century circular tower on **Waterford** city wall, on site of Reginald the Dane's tower (1003), now a museum (Connolly 587; Fischer 283). During the siege, Waterford inhabitants supposedly said: "Old Reginald's tower... would have bled sooner than these **Sir Tristans**," admiring **Richard of York**'s and his followers' bravery (*PW* 3.38). Cannons there threaten the **Yorkist** siege (*PW* 3.42, 3.47).

Old Windsor: Small village on the **Thames** about three miles southeast of **Windsor** castle on **Great Park**'s edge (Hedley 9–10). **Ellen Burnet**'s unmarked grave is in "Old Windsor churchyard" (*Mourner* 85, 97).

Oldcraft, Mat: Richard of York supporter in *Perkin Warbeck*.

Olevano: See **Olevano Romano**.

Olevano Romano: Italian town about six miles southwest of **Subiaco**; Shelley calls it **Olevano** (*MROM* 405). Shelley mentions an English family who took refuge there during the 1837 **Roman** cholera epidemic; Shelley compares their situation to that in the *Decameron* (*R* 2.241).

Olivia, Lady: See *Twelfth Night*.

Ollier, Charles (1788–1859): Author who operated a publishing company 1817–23 and issued works by **Keats**, **Edward John Trelawny**, and **Leigh Hunt**, as well as publishing much of **PBS**'s work, though refusing *Frankenstein* (Sunstein 136; White 1.515; Seymour 190). Ollier did not profit from PBS's work, and the Shelleys' relationship with him became strained when he was not forthcoming with further publications or with funds; July 1820, Shelley wrote "Ollier is a ninny or worse" and, in January 1822 Shelley noted that Ollier "treats us infamously in every way" as she impatiently waited for news about *Valperga* (which Ollier did not publish) (*Letters* 1.153, 1.215; White 2.194). After PBS's death and as Ollier's publishing company failed, Shelley requested the return of her husband's manuscripts, receiving them October 1823 (*Letters* 1.261, 1.400–401; Seymour 188). Shelley complimented Ollier on his novel *Inesilla; or The Templar, A Romance; with Other Tales* (1824) February 1824 and remained in contact with him when he became Henry Colburn's and Richard Bentley's literary advisor (*Letters* 1.413–414). Shelley then applied to Ollier for help with obtaining books; for example, she asked for information about **Constantinople** when working on *The*

Last Man (*Letters* 1.431). Ollier was instrumental in getting both *Perkin Warbeck* and *Lodore* published; Shelley wrote: "thank you for your consideration & kindness ... interesting yourself in this matter is tenfold more valuable to me" (*Letters* 2.92, 2.206–207; Crook 2).

Olympus: **Asian** and **Greek** mountain range and home to the Greek gods, to whom **Midas** appeals when he feels his golden powers elevate him to their level (*Midas* 129).

Oman: Gulf separating modern Iran from the **Arabian** Sea's western end; Shelley spells it **Omar**, probably a typographical error. **Lionel Verney** records that panic caused by the solar eclipse spread "even to the sea of Omar" (*LM* 224).

Omar: See **Oman**.

Omega: See **Alpha**.

"On Ghosts": Essay Shelley published in the *London Magazine* (March 1824); it resulted from interesting ghost stories Shelley recorded in her *Journals* (Sunstein 254). Shelley quotes from **Wordsworth**'s "The Affliction of Margaret" as an epigraph, then relates several tales and her own experiences of dreaming of ghosts (*On Ghosts* 254). The essay's first ghost story describes the visits of a lover-ghost; **Thomas Jefferson Hogg** initially told it to Shelley December 1814 (*Journals* 54–55; *On Ghosts* 254). Shelley heard the second tale, about an **Italian** soldier and his friend who commits suicide, from Chevalier Angelo Mengaldo, the **Hoppners**' acquaintance, October 1818 (*On Ghosts* 255–256; *Journals* 230–232).

Shelley concludes by relating a ghost story that author Monk Lewis told **PBS** and **Byron** August 1816 (*Journals* 126–129; *On Ghosts* 256).

"On Reading Wordsworth's Lines on Peel Castle": Poem Shelley dated 8 December 1825, first published in Grylls's *Mary Shelley: A Biography* (1938) (302–303). **Wordsworth**'s "Elegiac Stanzas Suggested by a Picture of Peele Castle, In a Storm, Painted by Sir George Beaumont" (1807) is a commentary upon his past tranquil memory of the sea scene and of Beaumont's painting, and how the drowning death of his brother John changes his view of the sea. Hailing Wordsworth as "Nature's Chronicler," Shelley's speaker, too, comments upon how her view of the sea has been inexorably altered by her loss (**PBS**'s death by drowning) and her struggle to accept it (line 2).

"On this day I complete": Poem **Byron** wrote in **Greece** January 1824, "On This Day I Complete My Thirty-Sixth Year"; it was posthumously published October 1824 (Marchand 3.1163–1165; *Journals* 271–273). Shelley copied the text into her *Journals* September 1824, when she received a copy from **Pietro Gamba** (*Journals* 484). Shelley adapts a line from it to describe **Richard of York**: "a thousand times deceived, '**still he must love**' " (*PW* 3.201; Byron line 4).

Onias: High priest of the Jews c. 323-300 B.C.E. Shelley notes that **Heliodorus** was sent to obtain Onias's treasure (*R* 2.220; 2 Maccabees 3.7-40).

Oos: Small stream dividing **Baden** into its resort and residential areas;

Oracle, The

Shelley spells it **Oes** and terms it "a mere mountain torrent" (*R* 1.37).

Oracle, The: See **Winter**.

Oranienburg Gate: **Berlin** gate that stood until the late 19th century at the corner where Frederick Street becomes Chausee Street (Spritzer 165). Shelley visited **Eisengieserei**, "just outside the Oranienburg gate," July 1842 (*R* 1.228).

Orazio: See **Saville, Horatio**.

Orion: In **Greek** mythology, hunter and god placed in the stars after his death (Tripp 434). **Midas** asks **Bacchus** for the power of a golden touch, "That like Orion I could touch the stars!" (*Midas* 125). Arriving in **Rome** March 1843, Shelley saw "a comet.... [I]t loses itself among the stars of Orion" (*R* 2.215).

Orkney Islands: Scottish group of about seventy islands lying across Pentland Firth from the mainland. **Victor Frankenstein** chooses a remote island as the construction site for the **Creature**'s mate (*Fr1* 190; *Fr3* 138–139). Victor is acquitted of **Henry Clerval**'s murder because of proof that he was in the Orkneys when the body was found (*Fr1* 207; *Fr3* 153).

Orlando: Italian for Roland, hero of **Charlemagne** legends and title character of **Boiardo**'s *Orlando Innamorato* (1487) and **Ariosto**'s *Orlando Furioso* (1532). **Henry Clerval** writes plays celebrating Orlando (*Fr1* 66).

Orleans, Duke of: Louis I, duc d'Orléans (1372–1407); he was **French** **Charles VI**'s brother whom **Duke of Burgundy** assassinated; **Guido il Cortese** is in **Paris** at the time of this murder (*Trans* 122–123). Also **Charles VIII**'s son, Louis XII (1462–1515), who ruled France from 1498; he welcomes, then bids farewell to, **Richard of York** in Paris (*PW* 1.312, 1.317). [*R* 1.80]. See **Louis-Philippe**.

Ormond, Sir James (1420–1461): James Butler, fifth Earl of Ormond and **Ireland**'s Lord Deputy 1451 (*DNB*). The **Earl of Kildare** battles his enemy Ormond (*PW* 1.287, 1.304).

Orondates: Fictional hero of Gautier de Costes de la Calprenède's adventure romance novel, *Cassandre* (1642–50), first abridged and published in English as *Cassandra: the fam'd Romance* (1752) (Couprie 267). Orondates is an idealized heroic character, consistently exemplary in conduct both in battle and in love. Shelley notes that "there was something of the Orondates' vein" in **Ethel Villiers**'s ideas of love (*L* 1.59–60).

Oronooko: Large river (today Orinoco) flowing east from Venezuela's borders with Colombia and Brazil into the **Atlantic**. "**Recollections of Italy**'s" narrator includes in his list of **Italy**'s faults " 'that dirty **Brenta** (the **New River Cut** is an Oronooko to it)' " (*RI* 25). A man at **New York**'s coffee house recalls it was **Admiral Fitzhenry** who "took the Oronooko" during the **Revolutionary War**, probably Shelley's creation; Vargo suggests Shelley alludes to Aphra Behn's anti-slavery novel *Oroonoko* (1688) (*L* 1.258; Vargo 159).

Orpheus: In Greek mythology, **Thracian** minstrel whose playing and singing enchanted wild animals and made trees and rocks follow him (Tripp 435). Shelley recounts a friend's opinion that **Paganini**'s performance "realised the fables of Orpheus" (*R* 1.90).

Orseolo, Piero: Doge of **Venice** in 978. Shelley notes that he ordered the **Pala d'Oro** from **Constantinople** (*R* 2.122).

Osborne, James: *Falkner* character whose testimony is key to **Alithea Neville**'s disappearance.

Osimo: Italian town ten miles southwest of **Ancona**. In her account of the **French** occupation of Ancona, Shelley mentions that the pope ordered the provincial government be moved to Osimo (*R* 2.257).

Ossey-les-Trois-Maisons: French village about fourteen miles southeast of **Nogent**; Shelley calls it **Trois Maisons**. She stayed there August 1814 (*H* 21; *Journals* 12).

Ostend: **Dutch** port on the **North Sea** about forty-five miles northeast of **Calais**. **Castruccio** flees England by ship to Ostend (*V* 1.85, 1.88). **Hernan De Faro** moors the *Adalid* there when returning to **Flanders** to collect his family (*PW* 1.197–198). Throughout *Perkin Warbeck*, Shelley mentions Ostend, to and from which characters sail (*PW* 2.65–66, 2.69–70, 2.82).

Othello: **Shakespeare**'s *The Tragedy of Othello, the Moor of Venice* (1602), which the Shelleys read aloud August 1817 and which **Byron** proposed that they stage in **Pisa** in 1822 (*Journals* 179; *Letters* 1.470). Shelley saw the play in **London** February 1825 (*Letters* 1.469). Othello is a noble warrior whom the evil Iago tricks into extreme jealousy of his **Venetian** wife **Desdemona**. Othello's suspicions drive him to smother Desdemona; filled with remorse when he realizes her innocence and that his jealousy had been misplaced, he kills himself. **Edmund Malville** asserts that knowing " 'loving Moor [Othello]' " passed on a gondola in Venice before his journey there deepens his fondness for the city; he also mentions Desdemona (*RI* 26). **Lionel Verney** characterizes **Perdita** as dreaming " **'of moving accidents** by flood and field,' " a line Othello speaks (*LM* 16; *Othello* 1.3.137). Verney quotes from Othello's speech contemplating suicide in characterizing **Adrian** as "all mind; '**Man but a rush** against' his breast, and it would have conquered his strength" (*LM* 27; *Othello* 5.2.279–280). Verney later characterizes Perdita by suggesting "more truly than Othello she might say, '**To be once** in doubt, / Is—once to be resolved,' " lines Othello speaks in response to Iago's warning about jealousy (*LM* 121; *Othello* 3.3.191–194). Describing troops following **Heron**, Shelley notes they "in truth had '**never set a squadron** in the field / Nor the division of a battle knew / More than a spinster,' " lines Iago speaks about Cassio (*PW* 3.73; *Othello* 1.1.22–24). **Ethel Villiers** hopes her mother will "find a compensation for the higher destiny which might have been hers, but that, like the '**base Indian**,' she had thrown '**A pearl away**, / Richer than all his tribe' "; Shelley draws from Othello's final speech (*L* 2.280; *Othello* 5.2.356–358).

Rupert Falkner assures **Mrs. Baker** of financial reward and " 'Upon this hint she spake' " of **Elizabeth Falkner**'s history; Shelley adapts this line from *Othello* (F 23; Clemit 21; *Othello* 1.3.168). Shelley recalls seeing *Othello* as a ballet between opera acts in **Milan** 1818 (*R* 1.112). She describes **Vatican** galleries: "the eye is so fed by sights of beauty, 'that the sense aches at them,' " a line Othello speaks to Desdemona (*R* 2.217; *Othello* 4.2.71).

Otho (1815–1867): Second son of Ludwig I, **King of Bavaria**; he ruled **Greece** 1832–62 (Mobry 165). Shelley appears to regard Otho as a malignant version of his eccentric father (*R* 1.192; Crook 2).

Ottoman Empire: Established 1301, by 1800 the Ottoman Empire controlled a large area of western **Asia** and eastern **Europe**, including **Albania**, Bosnia, Bulgaria, Croatia, **Egypt**, **Greece**, Romania, **Syria**, and **Turkey**. Albanian **Mohammed Ali** usurped power in Egypt 1803 and gained Syria 1833, while Greece won its independence 1829. The empire subsequently declined as various subject states gained independence, and it could not maintain its influence as a world power (Kinder 2.87). Shelley refers to the empire's activities in *The Last Man* (161, 179).

Otway, Thomas (1652–1685): English dramatist best remembered for blank-verse tragedies, especially *The Orphan* (1680) and *Venice Preserved or a Plot Discovered* (1682). Shelley read Otway's comedy *Don Carlos* (1676) 1815 (*Journals* 665). **Belvidera**, heroine of *Venice Preserved*, marries the impoverished Jaffier against her father Priuli's wishes. She endures poverty and hardship to be with him, demonstrating consistently that her love for her husband outweighs all other concerns; Belvidera dies of grief after Jaffier commits suicide. **Edmund Malville** refers to these characters and asserts that knowing " 'gentle Belvidera' " passed on a gondola in **Venice** before his journey there deepens his fondness for the city (*RI* 26). Shelley quotes accurately from Belvidera's parting words to Jaffier when **Edward Villiers** arranges to meet his wife at midnight on Saturday (since bailiffs whom he is avoiding would be unable to arrest him on a Sunday): "adieu, till this evening;—and then, as Belvidera says, '**Remember twelve!**' " (*L* 3.3; Otway 3.2.211).

Ovid [Publius Ovidius Naso] (43 B.C.E.–17 C.E.): **Roman** author renowned for *Metamorphoses* (2 C.E.), which recounts **Greek** myths and Roman legends (Howatson 401–402). In April 1815, Shelley wrote to **PBS**: "I mean to construe some Ovid & to be very industrious"; she read widely in Ovid's *Metamorphoses* 1815 and 1820 (*Letters* 1.12; *Journals* 665, 316). **Isabell Harley** introduces **Valerius** to Ovid's works (*Val* 343). Shelley adapted *Midas* and *Proserpine* from Ovid. **Lord Lodore** finds "he could revel with Ovid in the imagery presented by a graceful, though voluptuous imagination" (*L* 1.25). Shelley describes **Brocklet** "as secluded, shadowy and still, as the abode of **Morpheus**, described by Ovid" in *Metamorphoses'* eleventh book (*R* 1.195).

Owyhee: Ship that **Bateman** commands, upon which **Gerard Neville** plans to sail to **America** (F 282).

Oxford: English city about fifty miles northeast of **London**, renowned for its university. In August 1815, the Shelleys, **Peacock**, and **Charles Clairmont** visited Oxford (Sunstein 104; Seymour 141). **Henry Clerval** and **Victor Frankenstein** relive Shelley's visit (Sunstein 104; *Fr1* 186; *Fr3* 136). "**Maurice's**" grandfather was a mathematics professor at Oxford University (*Maurice* 77). **Lewis Elmore** and **Horace Neville** rest in Oxford en route to **Bishopsgate** (*Mourner* 97). **Lord Lodore** attends Oxford University for two years, and **Richard Simon** is a priest in Oxford, where he finds **Lambert Simnel** (*L* 1.82, 1.84; *PW* 1.109–111). Shelley mentions that **Prague**'s university vied with Oxford's (*R* 2.2).

Oxford, Lord (1443–1513): John de Vere, **Oxford**'s thirteenth earl. **Lancastrian** who fought at **Bosworth Field**, **Stoke**, and Blackheath 1497, he was High Steward at the **Earl of Warwick**'s trial 1499 (*DNB*). In *Perkin Warbeck*, he condemns **Lord Stanley** and captures **Lady Katherine Gordon** at **St. Michael**'s **Chair**.

Oxydracae: Race of people **Plutarch** describes as "bravest people of **India**" in his "Life of **Alexander**" (*Lives* 2.513, 2.519). **Raymond** recalls: " 'Did not Alexander leap from the walls of the city of the Oxydracae, to shew his coward troops to victory, encountering alone the swords of its defenders?' " (*LM* 194; Plutarch, *Lives* 2.519).

P

P——: See **Shelley, Percy Florence**.

P——, Mr.: Shelley refers to a Mr. P——, who wanted to play the organ in the cathedral at **Trent**; not further identified (*R* 2.65).

Pacchiani, Francesco (1772–1835): Priest who became a **University of Pisa** professor 1801. A fascinating although eccentric man, his ecclesiastical superiors eventually recalled him to Prato, ten miles northwest of **Florence** (*Journals* 588–589). Shelley first met Pacchiani in **Pisa** 1820; he introduced her into society there. Initially, Shelley considered Pacchiani "the only **Italian** she had met who had a heart and soul," but she subsequently found him "a combination of **Machiavelli** and **Boccaccio**, for he talked like a **Lucifer**, shocked [PBS] with a dirty joke, and made a pass at **Claire [Clairmont]**" (Sunstein 191; *Letters* 1.165). Pacchiani introduced the Shelleys to **Mavrocordato**, **Taaffe**, and **Viviani**; although Shelley records frequent contact with Pacchiani 1820–21, both Shelleys avoided him after February 1821 (*Journals* 341–344, 349–351, 353). Sunstein suggests that Shelley portrays Pacchiani as **Benedetto Pepi** in *Valperga*, while Crook and Seymour see Pacchiani as **Tripalda** (Sunstein 191–192; Crook 3.xvi; Seymour 262). See Appendix II of Shelley's *Journals* and **Medwin**'s anecdotes in his *Life of Percy Bysshe Shelley* (1847) (*Journals* 588–589).

Pacific Ocean: **Robert Walton** admires past attempts to sail to the North Pacific Ocean via the Arctic Ocean, a route he hopes to complete (*Fr1* 50; *Fr3* 27). **Lionel Verney** asserts that **Raymond**'s return by sea to **Athens** is more valuable than treasure transported across the Pacific from **Mexico** (*LM* 170). **Hoskins** tells **Gerard Neville** that **Osborne** "wishes himself on the shores of the Pacific, to be far enough off" (*F* 282).

Pacini, Giovanni (1796–1867): **Italian** operatic composer who "modeled himself on **[Gioacchino] Rossini**"

(*NGD*). His ***L'Ultimo giorno di Pompei*** [*The Last Day of Pompeii*] (1825), which Shelley terms **Ultime Giorni di Pompeii**, achieved "immense popular success" when first performed at **Naples**'s **San Carlo**; it was subsequently performed in **London** 1831 (*NGD*). Shelley mistakes the opera's composer as Rossini in *Lodore* (*L* 3.204).

Pactolus: Gediz River tributary in eastern **Turkey**. **Midas** bathes away his golden touch in it (*Midas* 143; Tripp 439).

Padua: **Italian** city twenty miles southwest of **Venice**; Shelley visited it repeatedly 1818 (*Journals* 227, 229, 234). **Francesco de Guinigi** and **Castruccio** pass through and rest there (*V* 1.51–52, 1.58, 3.14). **Ludovico Moncenigo** lives there for his education (*Trial* 231). Shelley recorded her October 1842 visit there (*R* 2.116–117, 2.232).

Paesiello: See **Paisiello**.

Paestum: Ancient **Italian** city twenty-three miles southeast of **Salerno**, renowned for its **Greek** temple ruins; the Shelleys visited it February 1819 (*Journals* 249; *Letters* 1.87). **Viola Arnaldi** travels to Paestum, and **Villa Spina** has a view of it (*HM* 327; *FE* 66). Shelley mentions Paestum in her descriptions of Italy's coast (*R* 2.266, 2.270, 2.283).

Paganini, Nicolò (1782–1840): **Italian** violinist and composer (*NGD*). Shelley saw Paganini at **King's Theatre** July 1831 and recalls this "divine" performance in *Rambles* (*Journals* 522; *R* 1.91). **Payne** probably secured Shelley's tickets to the event, as she had requested May 1831 (*Letters* 2.136, 2.210).

Pagibonzi: Possibly Shelley's spelling of Poggibonsi, **Italian** town twenty-two miles south of **Florence**. **Monna Gegia de' Becari** mentions it being taken and **Agli**'s involvement (*TP* 3).

Paisiello, Giovanni (1740–1816): **Italian** opera composer whom Shelley calls **Paesiello** when referring to *Nina Pazza per Amore*, her name for his famous opera *Nina, o sia La pazza per amore* [*Nina, or One Made Mad By Love*] (1789) (Orrey 253, 266; *NGD*). Shelley enjoyed **Pasta** singing the opera's opening August 1840, an experience she had hoped for May 1825 (*R* 1.90; *Letters* 1.484).

Pala d'Oro: Tenth-century solid gold piece (made in **Constantinople**) exhibited behind **San Marco**'s high altar in **Venice** for church festivals (*Venice* 33). Shelley saw it October 1842 (*R* 2.122).

Palace: **Berlin** castle built mid-15th century; it served as the **Prussian** royal family's main palace and was destroyed 1950 (Spritzer 133). Shelley saw artwork displayed there July 1842 (*R* 1.225, 1.227).

Paladins: See **Ariosto**.

Palagio del Popolo: Florentine palace begun 1255 (Higson 125–126). **Buzeccha** tells **Ricciardo de' Rossini** about playing chess "before the *Palagio del Popolo*" (*TP* 8).

Palagio Reale: Seventeenth-century royal residence at **Naples** (*STIE* 286). **Despina Elisei** and **Guielmo Losten-**

Palamon

dardo remember their first encounter at it, when it was **Manfred**'s residence (*TP* 12).

Palamon: Theban knight who, after seven years' imprisonment, fights his cousin **Arcite** for the hand of Emily, **Theseus**'s sister-in-law. Arcite was freed from prison and then masqueraded at court as Philostrate in order to live near Emily. Arcite wins a duel with Palamon but dies by falling off his horse, and Theseus asks Palamon and Emily to marry. This story is in **Chaucer**'s "The Knight's Tale" (c. 1387), which Shelley read 1815, and Arcite and Palamon also appear in *Two Noble Kinsmen* (*Journals* 641). **William Borsiere** directs a performance of Palamon and Arcite for **Euthanasia**'s court (*V* 1.289).

Palatinate: See **Elector Palatine**.

Palatine: One of **Rome**'s **Seven Hills** and "seat of the earliest settlement"; it displays "the ruins of the Palace of the **Caesars**, in the midst of vineyards and gardens" (*MROM* 12). **Isabell Harley** asserts, "we have only to regret that the **Capitol** has not been neglected as Mount Palatine" (*Val* 340–341). **Lionel Verney** observes "sheep were grazing untended on the Palatine" (*LM* 463). Shelley admired the Palatine April 1843 (*R* 2.225, 2.229).

Palazzo Borghese: Large home, now a museum, on **Rome**'s Piazza Borghese; its construction began 1590 (*MROM* 273). Shelley visited it April 1843, particularly noting **Raphael**'s *Descent from the Cross* displayed there (*R* 2.222).

Palazzo Carega: Guido il Cortese's ancestral palace, where he and **Parisian** acquaintances hold nightly orgies (*Trans* 124). Shelley probably refers to Palazzo Carrega-Cataldi, built 1558–61 on **Genoa**'s Via Garibaldi (Howard 225).

Palazzo Manfrin: Palace housing a painting collection second only in **Venice** to that at the **Accademia delle Bella Arti** (*MNIT* 343). Shelley enjoyed its collection October 1842 (*R* 2.119, 2.157).

Palazzo Mocenigo: Four palaces on **Venice**'s **Canale Grande**, named after the noble Mocenigo family (Avery 649). Shelley mentions a **Tintoretto** piece in the palace **Byron** inhabited; Moskal points out that it is in Doge Mocenigo's palace (*R* 2.119; Moskal 292; Marchand 2.734).

Palazzo Pisani: Venetian palace with an 18th-century facade at Campo Morosini (Honour 184). Shelley visited it October 1842 (*R* 2.119–120).

Palazzo Pitti: Pitti Palace, Florentine palace begun in the 1450s that now houses an art gallery displaying about five hundred items of the **Medici** collection; above **Ponte Vecchio** a secret passageway, "Corridoio Vasarino" links Pitti Palace and the **Uffizi** (Chilvers 438). Shelley visited it January 1820; **Euthanasia** visits it (as a ducal residence) (*Journals* 305; *V* 2.124). Shelley believes that the Palazzo Pitti's art collection surpasses that of the Uffizi, excepting Uffizi's **Tribune** (*R* 2.156).

Palazzo Strozzi: Florentine palace **Euthanasia** visits (*V* 1.124; Forsyth 66–67).

Palazzo Verosposi: Lodgings at number 300 on the **Corso** in **Rome**. The Shelleys lived there March–May 1819 (*Journals* 251, 262).

Palermo: Capital of **Sicily**. Shelley footnotes that **Amari**'s account of the **Sicilian Vespers** was first published there (*R* 2.210; Moskal 340).

Palestine: Eastern **Mediterranean**'s coastal region, also called "The **Holy Land**." Objective of the Middle Ages' Crusades, it partly corresponds to modern Israel. **Gaspar de Vaudemont** declares his intention of becoming " 'a soldier of the cross' " there (*D* 156, 158).

Palikar: According to **Byron**'s "Notes" to *Childe Harold's Pilgrimage*, **Greek** term used as a "general name for a soldier amongst the Greeks and Albinese who speak **Romaic**—it means properly 'a lad' " (McGann 2.289). **Dmitri** admiringly calls **Constans Ziani** " 'brave Palikar' " (*EE* 111).

Palladian: See **Palladio**.

Palladio (1518–1580): **Vicenzan** architect; he built many of the city's buildings and palaces, in a style now known as **Palladian** (*MNIT* 287). According to Shelley, **Venice**'s **San Giorgio Maggiore Church** is modeled on a Palladian design (*R* 2.94; *RevB* 182). Shelley regretted having had only a brief, moonlit glance at Vicenza's Palladian palaces (*R* 2.77).

Pallas: See **Minerva**.

Palli, Georgio: Character who is "vice-admiral of the **Greek** fleet, a former friend and warm partizan of **Raymond**" (*LM* 215).

Palma Vecchio: See **Palma**.

Palma, Jacopo (1480–1528): Called **Palma Vecchio**, **Venetian** Renaissance painter. Shelley describes his *Three Sisters* (n.d.), which she saw in **Dresden**'s **Gallery** August 1840 (*R* 1.243). She also viewed several Palma pieces in an unnamed Venetian church September 1842 (*R* 2.97).

Palmyra: Small **Syrian** village; it was a city and state within Syria 267 C.E., but was destroyed 272 C.E. (Howatson 406; Volney 3–4). **PBS** refers to Palmyra's ruins in *Queen Mab* (1813) (lines 109–125). Shelley alludes to "sand-choked ruins of the desert temples of Palmyra" (*LM* 341).

Pan: In **Greek** mythology, shepherd-god of music famous for his amorous exploits. **Proserpine** compares **Ino**'s songs to those of Pan (*P* 35). **Midas** chooses Pan as winner of a musical contest between **Apollo** and Pan, since he is predisposed to favor his "guardian God, old-horned Pan, / The **Phrygian**'s God, who watches over our flocks" (*Midas* 97, 105).

Panagia: See **Mary**.

Pandemonium: **Satan**'s palace and **Hell**'s capital in **Milton**'s *Paradise Lost*. The **Creature** seeks shelter in a hut "as exquisite and divine a retreat as Pandemonium appeared to the demons of hell" (*Fr1* 134; *Fr3* 95; Milton, *Paradise Lost* 1.756–763).

Pandora: In **Greek** mythology, the first woman; her dowry was a chest filled with evils, which were released upon earth when she opened the box; only hope stayed inside. **Ceres** calls Pandora "Mother of mankind" (*P* 31). **Lionel Verney** feels that Pandora's gift cannot survive the plague: "Hope is dead!" (*LM* 313).

Pandur: One of two hot brine springs in **Kissingen** (*BGER* 164–65). Shelley describes taking the cure: Pandur water is "brought boiling in casks to the house.... The water made hot has the colour of iron rust, and is opaque" (*R* 1.188).

Pantheon: Literally **Greek** for "temple of all the gods," large domed temple built in **Rome** 128–18 B.C.E. Shelley visited it March 1819 (*Journals* 251; *Letters* 1.89). **Isabell Harley** shows **Valerius** the Pantheon at night, and **Euthanasia** visits it by moonlight, as the Shelleys did March 1819, seeing "the [moon's] yellow rays fall through the roof upon the floor of the temple" (*Val* 342; *V* 1.203; *Journals* 251). Shelley compares the eternal **Tiber** to decaying Pantheon (*SA* 51).

Paracelsus [Philippus Aureolus Theophrastus Bombastus von Hohenheim] (1493–1541): Radical **Swiss** physician and alchemist. His rejection of ancient philosophy and demand that medical and chemical studies be fused revolutionized science, while his doctrine of the "microcosm," emphasizing the atmosphere, evolved into a 17th-century belief in an "aerial saltpeter" that gives life (Debus 46–47, 53). **Victor Frankenstein** idolizes Paracelsus, calling himself a "disciple" of this man, one of the "lords of [his] imagination" (*Fr1* 68, 70, 179, 225; *Fr3* 44, 46, 130, 168).

***Paradise Lost*: Milton**'s epic poem, published 1667, based on the **biblical** account of the creation of the world, **Adam** and **Eve**'s exile from **Eden**, and **Satan**'s fall. Shelley records reading it 1815 (*Journals* 663). In *Frankenstein*, Shelley rewrites the fall with **Victor Frankenstein** as creator and the **Creature** as a miserable, unwanted, and lonely version of Adam; Shelley takes her novel's epigraph from *Paradise Lost*: Adam asks, "**Did I request thee**, Maker, from my clay / To mould me man? Did I solicit thee / From darkness to promote me?" (Milton 10.743–745). The Creature reads the **De Laceys**' copy of *Paradise Lost*, which makes him contemplate his own origin and recognize its differences (*Fr1* 157; *Fr3* 113). Shelley describes **Castruccio** as one "to whom, as to the fallen archangel, that line might be applied, '**Vaunting aloud**, though rack'd with deep despair'" (*V* 3.37–38; Milton 1.126). As *The Last Man*'s epigraph, Shelley quotes lines Adam speaks after a vision of the flood: "**Let no man seek** / Henceforth to be foretold what shall befall / Him or his children" (Milton 11.770–772). On the day of **Lady Katherine Gordon**'s birth, a seer had a vision of her brow encapsulated in "'**the likeness of** a kingly crown,'" a *Paradise Lost* line describing Satan's view of an evil spirit (*PW* 2.229; Milton 2.673). Lady Katherine later reflects "that '**death is the beginning** of life,'" an allusion to Adam's speech toward *Paradise Lost*'s close (*PW* 3.350; Milton 12.569–571). **Edward Villiers** feels **Ethel Villiers** is an "'**other half**,' towards whom he felt as if literally he had, to give her being, '**Lent / Out of** his side to her, nearest his heart; / Substantial life, to have her by his side, / Henceforth an individual solace dear' "; Shelley adapts these lines from Milton's passage in which Satan overhears Eve recalling how Adam asked her to accompany him (*L* 2.165; Milton 4.482–488). Shelley also describes the Villierses' happiness at being together with extensive reference to the *Paradise Lost* passage wherein Satan confirms himself in evil and leaps into Eden only to be tormented by the sight of Adam and Eve's happiness: " '**Imparadised**' by each other's presence. . . . No Eden was required to enhance their happiness; there needed no '**Crisped brooks**, / Rolling on orient pearls and sands of gold'; no '**Happy, rural seat,** with various view,' decked with '**Flowers of all hue**,' '**All trees of** noblest kind for sight, smell, taste';—nor '**cool recess**,' nor '**Vernal airs**, / Breathing the smell of field and grove' " (*L* 2.271; Milton 4.505–506, 4.215–217, 4.237–238, 4.247, 4.256–258, 4.264–265). Ethel has a difficult journey into **London** through fog, "the '**murky air**,' " a reference to Milton's description of Death smelling his work's results (*L* 2.258; Milton 10.280). Edward later admires the room at **Mrs. Derham**'s, remembering "when our carriage broke down on the **Apennines**, how glad we should have been if a room like this had risen, '**like an exhalation**' for our shelter!" a line taken from Milton's description of Satan's Palace, **Pandemonium** (*L* 3.18; Milton 1.710–711). She also uses this quotation to describe **Hastings**, perhaps imitating **Rogers**, who uses "like an exhalation" to describe **Venice** in his "*Italy*" (*R* 1.4; Moskal 77). Shelley emphasizes **Rupert Falkner**'s altered appearance after his confession with reference to Milton's description of Satan: "To say that he was '**not less than** archangel ruined,' is not to express the peculiar interest of Falkner's appearance" (*F* 237; Milton 1.591–594). At **Gmunden**, Shelley finds nature's beauty is such that she could "affirm, with Milton, that—'**Millions of spiritual** creatures walk the earth / Unseen, both when we wake and when we sleep,' " lines Adam speaks to Eve regarding God's omnipotence (*R* 2.27; Milton 4.677–678). Shelley subsequently describes the beauties of a visit to **Vallombrosa** with lines Milton uses to describe Satan's approach to the same region: " '**Thick as autumnal** leaves that strow the brooks / In Vallombrosa, where th' Etrurian shades / High over-arched embower' " (*R* 2.137; Milton 1.302–304). Shelley uses Satan's view of the heavenly city in describing **Linz**'s view of **Lake Como**, lines beginning " '**Obtains the brow** of some high-climbing hill' " (*R* 2.21; Milton 3.546–551). Shelley also uses Milton's phrase " '**darkness visible**' " to describe how **Venetian** prisoners would have seen dusk falling, and she uses Satan's impression of Adam and Eve " '**with native honour clad**' " to describe **David**'s figure in *The Killing of Goliath by David* (*R* 2.87, 2.95; Milton 1.63, 4.289). Shelley describes **Napoleon**'s court in **Dresden** as one "to which '**thrones, dominations**, princedoms' thronged" (*R* 1.253; Milton 5.600).

***Paradise Regained*:** **Milton**'s four-book poem, published 1671, based on Jesus's early life and serving as a short sequel to *Paradise Lost*. Shelley records reading it 1815 and 1820 (*Journals*

Paradiso

62, 319–320). She describes a mountain near **Linz** with lines from *Paradise Regained:* "**At whose verdant** feet / A spacious plain, outstretched in circuit wide, / Lay pleasant" (*Journals* 62, 319–320; *R* 2.19; Milton 3.253–255). Shelley draws a line from *Paradise Regained* to describe **Italian** Renaissance artists' desire to depict figures " '**Of good, wise, just**, the perfect shape,' " and refers to **Raphael** specifically as " '**high actions** and high passions best describing' " (*R* 2.141, 2.223; Milton 3.11, 4.266). Shelley also adapts a line to describe her March 1842 journey toward **Rome**: " '**Thought by thought**, and step by step led on' " (*R* 2.212; Milton 1.192).

Paradiso: See **Tintoretto**.

Paradiso: Third and final part of **Dante**'s *Divina Commedia*; it describes the delights of the earthly paradise at which the poet arrived at the end of *Purgatorio*, as **Beatrice** leads him through a world of song and light. Shelley read it 1819 (*Journals* 644). **Matilda**'s father compares his love for his daughter to Dante's love for Beatrice: "well may I say with [Dante] yet with what different feelings '**E quasi mi** perdei gli occhi chini,' " *Paradiso* lines describing how Dante turns away when Beatrice looks at him with love: "And, eyes downcast, I almost lost my senses" (*M* 178; *Paradiso* 4.142). Matilda later reads **Woodville**'s countenance as reflecting loving, even maternal, concern for her, just as Dante interprets Beatrice's expression: " '**Gli occhi drizzo** ver me con quel sembiante / Che madre fa sopra figlioul deliro,' " lines meaning "Settled her eyes on me with the same look / A mother casts upon a raving child" (*M* 198; *Paradiso* 1.101–102). Shelley quotes lines beginning " '**Non è poleggio**' " to describe "**Italy** and the Italians"; the lines translate: "this is no crossing for a little bark—/ the sea that my audacious prow now cleaves—/ nor for a helmsman who would spare himself" (*R* ix; *Paradiso* 23.67–69). In September 1840, Shelley noted "the soul is elevated and rapt by the sublime hymns to heavenly love, contained in the *Paradiso*. Nothing can be more beautiful than the closing lines" (*R* 1.96). In **Venice** September 1842, Shelley declared that **Titian**'s *Assumption*, "and the 'Paradiso' of Dante as a commentary, is the sublimest achievement of Catholicism" (*R* 2.91). Shelley quotes lines beginning "**Quale è colui**, che sognando vede" (meaning "As one who sees within a dream"), lines she also wrote in her *Journals* August 1840 and in a letter to **Leigh Hunt** (*R* 1.94; *Journals* 568–569; *Letters* 3.160–161; *Paradiso* 33.58–66). [*R* 2.231].

Parian marble: Fine white marble from **Cycladean** island of Paros. **Rupert Falkner** sees **Elizabeth Falkner**'s education under his own and **Miss Jervis**'s tutelage as "the moulding of a block of Parian marble into a muse" (*F* 44).

Paris: **France**'s capital city. Shelley and her party arrived there August 1814 (*H* 10). They found it expensive but visited many of its attractions during the week's stay, admiring **Tuileries** and **Saint Denis** gate especially (*H* 11–12). Shelley records a two-day delay in Paris en route to **Geneva** 1816 (*H* 86–87, 89). She returned to England through Paris 1823 after her husband's death, spending a month there 1828; having recovered from smallpox, "she was courted by a brilliant, sophisticated elite" and thoroughly enjoyed her stay (Sunstein 288). The **De Laceys** live in Paris, where they meet **Safie** and her father, and spend five months in prison there (*Fr1* 150–153; *Fr3* 107–110). **Castruccio** enjoys the "gaieties of the Parisian court" (*V* 1.93, 1.134). **Evadne Zaimi** leaves **London** for Paris, and English plague survivors stay there before beginning their search for safer, warmer lands; Paris is where the plague survivor groups splinter (*LM* 47, 399). Paris is initially a refuge for many **Yorkist** exiles after **Lancaster**'s victory, most importantly **Lady Brampton** and **Lord Barry** (*PW* 1.201–202, 1.229). **Richard of York** travels to Paris to enjoy "the utmost splendour and gaiety" of **Charles VIII**'s court (*PW* 1.308, 1.312). **Guido il Cortese** visits **Paris** during **Charles VI**'s reign (*Trans* 122–123). **Ludovico Moncenigo** travels there, and **Ippolito della Toretta** and **Faustina Moncenigo** "spent two or three years in Paris and the south of **Italy**" after marrying (*Trial* 234, 243). **Lady Lodore** intends to leave London for Paris, and the **Villiers**es hope to have enough money to travel there (*L* 2.77, 3.16). **Colonel Villiers** goes to Paris to avoid debts in England, and he is there at *Lodore*'s end, penniless, miserable, and alone (*L* 2.276, 3.308). Paris is a "transient, resting-place" for **Rupert Falkner** and **Elizabeth Falkner** (*F* 33). Shelley's first destination on her 1840 tour was Paris, where "there is a cheerfulness . . . that at once enlivens the visitor" (*R* 1.7). Shelley stayed several weeks visiting friends and sights such as **Versailles**; she passed through Paris again October 1840 and October 1842 (*R* 1.11, 1.146). [*Fr1* 211; *Fr3* 155, 157; *PW* 2.186, 2.198; *SP* 142, 145; *D* 158; *L* 1.138, 3.234, 3.262; *E* 301; *R* 1.145–146, 2.200].

Park Lane: Street in the wealthy and exclusive **London** Westminster district along **Hyde Park**'s eastern edge. The **Elmore** family's London residence is on **Stratton Street**, Park Lane (*Mourner* 90). **Lady Lodore**'s London residence is "a house in Park Lane" (*L* 3.92).

Park, Mungo (1771–1806): Surgeon who explored the Niger River and earned fame with *Travels in the Interior Districts of Africa Performed under the Direction and Patronage of the African Association in the Years 1795, 1796, and 1797* (1799), which the Shelleys read December 1814 (*Journals* 51–52). Shelley found the accounts "very interesting," although she notes "if [Park] was not so prejudiced they would be a thousand times more so" (*Journals* 52). When **Ethel Villiers** is alone at **Duke Street**, her isolation is such "as Mungo Park might have felt in central **Africa**" (*L* 2.284; Park 264–65).

Parliament: Britain's governmental system, consisting of a **House of Commons** and a **House of Lords** in **London** (the House of Lords no longer remains a hereditary privilege and will be dismantled). **Henry Clerval** and **Victor Frankenstein** contemplate **Charles I**'s problems with Parliament (*Fr1* 186; *Fr3* 136). The two houses are combined before events *The Last Man* records (*LM* 58). **Ethel Villiers** excitedly visits Parliament (*L* 2.210). **Lady Lodore** speaks to her daughter there for the first time since Ethel's childhood (*L* 2.214). *Perkin Warbeck*'s assembled army "rabble" plans to defeat the **Red Rose** and then "set fire to London and Parliament" (*PW* 3.75).

Parma: Italian city fifty-five miles northwest of **Bologna**. Shelley mentions that **Louis of Bavaria** crossed the **Apennines** at Parma when he invaded Italy (*V* 3.264).

Parnassus: Mountain northwest of **Athens** at the base of the Pindus range. **Greek** myth places the **Delphic oracle** a few miles south of Mount Parnassus, and the mountain was sacred to the muses and **Apollo** (Howatson 410). **Lionel Verney** and **Perdita** ascend Parnassus with **Raymond**'s body (*LM* 208).

Parry, Sir William Edward (1790–1855): In the *Hecla,* this British explorer discovered the entrance to the Northwest Passage in 1819; he struggled unsuccessfully to navigate the route (Baker 431–433). **Edmund Malville** discusses Parry's voyage (*RI* 25).

Parthian Pestilence: Parthia was formerly a district of western **Asia**, famous for its cavalry's "ability to shoot [arrows] backwards when retreating" (Howatson 411–412). **Lionel Verney** leads plague survivors from **Paris** but records that they cannot leave plague behind them: "We stood as marks, while Parthian Pestilence aimed and shot" (*LM* 398).

"Parvenue, The": Short story first published in the 1837 *Keepsake* as by "Mrs. Shelley" (Robinson 392–393). Alfred Gomersal Vickers drew and Robert Brandard engraved the accompanying illustration, a sea scene titled *Margate* (*Par* 272). **Fanny**'s poverty-stricken family, including her weak mother, crippled father, and numerous unnamed siblings, loses her when **Lord Reginald Desborough** marries her (*Par* 266–267). They spend two years abroad (*Par* 268–269). On returning to England, Lord Reginald tells his wife that her family has frequently asked for financial assistance but that he can no longer respond to their exorbitant requests (*Par* 270). Fanny travels alone to visit her family at **Margate** and is quickly dismayed when nearly every family member requests money (*Par* 270). Fanny applies to her husband by letter and then in person in **London**, even though she sees "his very heart closed on me as he wrote the cheque" (*Par* 273). Lord Reginald tires of Fanny's consistent requests to help her family and tells her she can have an allowance but must choose between her family and her husband (*Par* 273). Fanny chooses her family and spends three years at Margate, looking after her parents before their deaths (*Par* 273). She then writes to her husband that her duty is no longer divided, but he tells her it is too late—she learns he loves a lady of his own rank (*Par* 274). After receiving a letter from her sister **Susan** inviting her to **America** (where her husband **Lawrence Cooper** has totally reformed his former behavior), Fanny leaves England with a "desire to die" so as to facilitate her husband's happiness (*Par* 274). Sunstein notes this story is "uniquely revealing in painful autobiographical specificity," asserting that in it Shelley "condemned both father and husband" (331, 334). Shelley probably drew upon her and **PBS**'s financial difficulties with **William Godwin** for Fanny's character, and the father's consistent demands for money echo Godwin's; **Fanny Godwin** could be the source of the protagonist's name.

Pascal, Blaise (1623–1662): French mathematician whose first published work was his celebrated *Essay on Conic Sections* (1639). He also wrote two treatises that remained unpublished until after his death and then became famous: *On the Equilibrium of Liquids* (1653) and *On the Weight of the Atmosphere* (1653). Shelley wrote Pascal's biography for **French Lives**. She situates Pascal as an "example of the catholic principles of morality" and admires his *Lettres provinciales* [*Provincial Letters*] (1656–57) as a "book addressed to all classes" filled with "eloquence and beauty" (*FL* 1.184, 1.202). Shelley details Pascal's religious devotion to helping the poor and to following the gospels' dictates, concluding, however, that Pascal was a great mathematician who adhered "to the letter rather than the spirit" of Christianity, while admiring the carefully crafted refutation of atheism and the espousal of Christian truths evinced in his *Pensées* [*Thoughts*] (1669) (*FL* 1.213). Shelley cites Pascal as an example of an "enlightened" good Catholic for his deathbed request that two paupers receive the same medical care as he (*R* 2.235).

Pasha: **Ottoman** title indicating rank or honor, given to high military or civil officers. The pasha's troops are "in possession of many of the passes" when **Harry Valency** arrives in **Greece**, and the pasha's son imprisons **Euphrasia** in his harem (*E* 297, 303).

Pasha, Ali (1741–1822): Leader of a wild **Albanian** band; he established himself in **Ioannina** as principal commander of a large area of what is now **Greece** and southern Albania (*MGRE* 49). Pasha was hospitable to **Byron** during the latter's 1809 visit, but an unsuccessful rebellion against **Turkish** rule "ended in [Pasha's] ruin and death" 1822 (*MGRE* 396–397; Byron, *CHP* 2.418–423). **Dmitri** fights "under the banner of the renowned Ali" (*EE* 101). At **Milan**'s **La Scala** September 1840, Shelley attended a ballet based on Pasha's biography (*R* 1.112).

Passage: Probably name for waterway into Cork Harbor, perhaps referring to Passage West, **Irish** town six miles southeast of **Cork**. **Richard of York** arrives in Cork after "sail[ing] up Passage" (*PW* 1.273). During the invasion of **Waterford**, Richard positions his men near **Lumbard's Marsh**, close to Passage (*PW* 3.35).

Passeyr, Valley of: Northern **Italian** river flowing through **Hofer**'s native valley of Merano; **Tyrolese** peasants from there supported him 1809 (*R* 2.52, 2.55, 2.57).

Pasta, Madame Guiditta Maria Costanza (1797–1865): Italian soprano who debuted in **Milan** 1815 and subsequently performed in **Paris**, **London**, and all of Italy's major theaters in works by **Gioacchino Rossini**, among others; she also influenced and inspired **Vincenzo Bellini**, who created roles for her (*NGD*). In August 1824, Shelley wrote that she "heard Pasta & never was more affected by any scenic representation than by her acting of **Romeo**" (*Letters* 1.445). **Ethel Villiers** cannot suppress tears when she hears Pasta sing (*L* 1.294–295). Shelley records that "Madame Pasta has a villa" on **Lake Como**, noting, "never did any [voice] so move, so penetrate the human heart. In '**Giuletta**,' in '**Medea**,' and, above all, in the melting and pathetic tenderness of the opening air of the '**Nina Pazza per Amore**' of the divine **Paisiello**, she has in truth taken from the heart its last touch of hardness, and melted it into sweetest tears" (*R* 1.89–90).

Paterin: The Paterenes were members of a church reform movement in **Milan** during the 1050s; the term "became a general label for heretics" (McBrien 965). Shelley uses "Paterin" to describe **Beatrice**'s later religious beliefs and the man who befriends her when she escapes **Tripalda** (*V* 3.21, 3.40, 3.94, 3.154). Shelley probably shared Beatrice's Paterin beliefs after **Clara Shelley**'s death, and **Sismondi**'s account of **Albigensian** beliefs was probably an influence (Sunstein 162; *Letters* 1.85).

Patras: See **Lepanto**.

Paul Clifford: See **Bulwer-Lytton**.

Paul, Georgiana (1805-1847): **George** and **Aubrey Beauclerk**'s sister; she married banker John Dean Paul October 1826, and they had one son, **Sir Aubrey John Dean Paul** (*Journals* 506). Shelley first met Georgiana (familiarly called Gee) 1822, but they did not become close until the late 1820s and early 1830s (Sunstein 207, 286; *Journals* 522). While visiting her father 1830, Georgiana spoke so highly of Shelley and her son to her father's neighbor, **Sir Timothy Shelley**, that the latter sent PFS a sovereign (Sunstein 311). Shelley recorded she "did not like" Georgiana's lover, Sir F. Vincent, August 1831; Georgiana's husband discovered the affair, and the couple separated November 1831 (*Journals* 522; *Letters* 2.156). As Shelley records: "Poor Gee is sent to Norwood [outside **London**]—her child torn from her—cast away & deserted—My first impulse is to befriend a woman—I will do her all the good I can," and Shelley negotiated visiting rights for Georgiana (Sunstein 315–316; *Journals* 524). Georgiana signed a separation agreement February 1832 and traveled to **Ireland** for two years before settling in **Sussex**, but she and her husband never divorced; Shelley maintained their correspondence and visited her friend 1835, 1838, and 1839, having found Georgiana's "friendship & gratitude ... very soothing" October 1833 (Sunstein 316, 336, 347; *Journals* 524, 530; *Letters* 2.203). Georgiana visited **Claire Clairmont** 1838 and praised her to Shelley October 1843 (*Letters* 3.23, 3.100, 3.47, 3.117). Around 1843, Georgiana returned to live with her husband on London's **Strand**, "accommodated to her sorry marriage and worked in various charities"; Shelley was initially distrustful of Georgiana, but the two once again grew close (Sunstein 364, 368; *Journals* 524–525). Shelley and Georgiana spent summer 1847 together at **Brighton**; Shelley was with Georgiana during her final illness, writing December 1847 that Shelley had "lost my dear kind friend.... She shed a charm over my life by the lively & affectionate interest she took in all that belonged to me that I shall miss at every hour, in every act" (*Journals* 525; *Letters* 3.331, 3.373).

Paul, Sir Aubrey John Dean (1827–1890): John Dean and **Georgiana Paul**'s only son; he "succeeded his father to the baronetcy [1868] and became" **PFS**'s friend (*Journals* 506). When his parents separated 1832, Shelley negotiated with his father for Georgiana to visit her son (Sunstein 315–316). Aubrey was with PFS in Cowes August 1845, traveled in "the East" June 1848, and stayed with Shelley "for a few days" February 1849 (*Letters* 3.198, 3.340, 3.356). Shelley recorded his August 1850 engagement to Laura Kaye; he stayed with Shelley September 1850 and was married January 1851 (*Letters* 3.382, 3.385).

Paulet, Thomas: **Long Roger** recalls that Paulet was in the **Tower** when the **Duke of Clarence** was murdered (*PW* 3.301).

Pausilippo: See **Posilipo**.

Pavia: Italian city twenty miles south of **Milan**. Pavìa's lord submits to **Henry VII** of **Germany** (*V* 1.118). **Benedetto Pepi** asserts that Pavìa was "mart for all the rich merchandize [**Venetians**] brought from the East" during 8th–14th centuries (*V* 1.286).

Pavilion: Grand building in **Brighton**, which future **regent**, then Prince of Wales and **George III**'s eldest son, took "1786 to serve as his seaside residence"; now a museum and place of entertainment open to the public (Musgrave 11, 28, 38, 40). "**Euphrasia**'s" narrator frames **Harry Valency**'s relation of his **Grecian** tale by recording Christmas 1836's heavy snowfall, including the detail that "the Pavilion had no guests" (*E* 295).

Pavillon: See **Pavillon-Ste-Julie**.

Pavillon-Ste-Julie, Le: French village eight miles northwest of **Troyes**; Shelley terms it **Pavillon**. The Shelleys passed through it August 1814, noting villagers repairing houses **Cossacks** had destroyed (*Journals* 13; *H* 25).

Payne, John Howard (1791–1852): **American** actor and playwright whose first work was staged 1806; his most famous piece is the "operatic aria 'Home, Sweet Home'" (Sunstein 266). He wrote several successfully staged dramas and collaborated with **Irving**. Payne went to Britain 1813, was imprisoned for debt 1820, released 1821, and then settled in **Paris** before returning to **New York** 1832; he was subsequently American consul at Tunis 1842–45 and 1851–52 (*Letters* 1.432). Shelley first met him in Paris 1823 or in **London** 1824 and used his "free tickets" to see many plays; she was fascinated to learn more about Irving from Payne (Sunstein 256; *Letters* 1.347–353). They met again and became friends April 1825; as Sunstein notes, "much has been made of this episode" (266). Shelley seems to have fascinated Payne, and she enjoyed his company: June 1825, "Payne gave signs of declaring his love," but Shelley affirmed her devotion to her late husband and Payne left for Paris August 1825 (Sunstein 267; *Journals* 496). Bennett asserts that Payne then tried, unsuccessfully, to match Shelley with Irving late 1825 (*Letters* 1.493–494). Shelley maintained a correspondence with Payne "with genuine affection" for many years, and they met again briefly July 1826 and in London 1830, when Payne got Shelley tickets to see **Paganini** (Sunstein 268,

Paynim

310–311; *Journals* 496). Sunstein asserts that Payne, after returning to America, may have arranged for *Frankenstein*, *The Last Man*, and *Perkin Warbeck* to be published in **Philadelphia** (319–320). Franklin B. Sanborn, editing their correspondence in *The Romance of Mary W. Shelley, John Howard Payne, and Washington Irving* (1907), asserts that Shelley used Payne to try to orchestrate a marriage with Irving; Grace Overmyer's *America's First Hamlet* (1957) is more objective (Sunstein 398).

Paynim: Term given to a pagan or non-Christian, especially with reference to the Muslim faith. **Constance Villeneuve** dreams of "herself in Paynim land" and of **Gaspar de Vaudemont** as a miserable prisoner there (*D* 164).

Pays de Vaud: North of **Lake Geneva**, **Swiss** region containing the **Jura**. The Shelleys viewed its villages and scenery summer 1816 (*Journals* 111). **Henry Clerval** prefers **Rhine** scenery to Pays de Vaud's Jura (*Fr1* 183; *Fr3* 133).

Pazzi: Noble **Florentine** family who joined the **Guelphs** 1215 (Villani 41, 123, 125). They attend **Euthanasia**'s court (*V* 1.240, 1.256).

Peachy, Sir John: **Kent**'s sheriff 1495 (Arthurson 118). He marches to **Hythe** against **Richard of York** (*PW* 2.163–171).

Peacock Island: Lake Havel island in southwest **Berlin**, where Schloss Pfaueninsel [Peacock Island Castle] is located. During his reign (1797–1840), Frederick William III brought peacocks there (Tucker 114–115). Shelley wanted to visit it July 1842 (*R* 1.230).

Peacock, Thomas Love (1785–1866): British satirist, essayist, poet, and **PBS**'s friend (White 1.261). Peacock's novels include *Headlong Hall* (1816), *Melincourt* (1817), and *Nightmare Abbey* (1818); Shelley transcribed Peacock's poem *Rhododaphne; or, the Thessalian Spell* (1818) December 1817, and PBS wrote *A Defence of Poetry* (1821) in response to Peacock's *The Four Ages of Poetry* (1820) (*Journals* 186). Peacock was an independent man of letters and private scholar when he first met PBS 1812; both radicals, Peacock educated PBS in classical literature. Peacock was also **Harriet Shelley**'s friend, so that although he met and befriended Shelley September 1814, Peacock was never close to her (*Journals* 29–41, 58–60, 73). PBS's letters in *History* are addressed to Peacock, who was living in **Marlow** 1816. The Shelleys stayed with him there until their own house was ready; Shelley wrote to PBS September 1817 that "Peacock dines here every night to drink his bottle [*sic*] I have not seen him—he morally disgusts m[e]" (*Journals* 135, 165; *Letters* 1.23, 1.41). However, Shelley came to enjoy Peacock's "rapier wit, scholarship, literary gifts, and extraordinary ear for disputations" (Sunstein 105). **Claire Clairmont** refused Peacock's marriage proposal and, after joining the **East India Company** 1819, he married Jane Gryffydh 1820; they had three daughters, two of whom survived infancy (Sunstein 142; *Letters* 1.102). The Shelleys maintained correspondence with Peacock, and he became executor of PBS's estate, receiving sums of five hundred and two thousand pounds in trust for a lifetime annuity (*Letters* 3.165). Shelley found him "a ready, reliable executor," and he assisted her with various financial matters as well as, for example, helping her find a school for **PFS** 1827, but they maintained contact only regarding business affairs (Sunstein 246, 287). Shelley was anxious about Peacock's health 1835; Peacock became Examiner of India House 1837, a position he held until retiring 1856 (*Letters* 2.221–222). Peacock's *Memoirs of Percy Bysshe Shelley* (1858–60) implausibly claimed that PBS "had been happy with Harriet until he met" Shelley (Sunstein 391). See Carl Dawson's *Thomas Love Peacock* (1968).

Pearson, Henry Hugh [Henry Hugo Pierson] (1815–1873): English musician who moved to **Germany** and changed his name (*DNB*). He wrote songs for **Byron**'s *Thoughts of Melody* (1839) and for **PBS**'s verse, *Characteristic Songs of Shelley* (1840); Shelley considers "**Arethusa**" and "**Spirit of Night**" from the latter as Pearson's best (*NGD*; *R* 1.233). **PFS**'s college friend, Pearson joined Shelley's traveling party in **Dresden** August 1842 (Sunstein 357; *R* 1.233; *Letters* 3.34).

Pecchio, Giuseppe (1785–1835): Italian economist and author renowned for his *Vita di U. Foscolo* [*Life of Ugo Foscolo*] (1830) and *Storia della economia pubblica in Italia* [*History of Italian Public Economy*] (1802) (Petronio 4.301). Shelley mentions that he contributed to *Il Conciliatore* (*Letters* 1.531; *R* 2.195).

Pekin: See **Peking**.

Peking: **China**'s capital city, formerly called **Pekin** and now Beijing. **Lionel Verney** records that the sun's eclipse spreads fear all over the world, including Peking (*LM* 224).

Pelegrini, Hospital of: Sta Trinità de' Pellegrini, convalescent hospital for the poor in **Rome** (*MROM* 306). Shelley remarks on the crowds there April 1843 (*R* 2.232).

Pelissier: Bridge crossing the **Arve** near **Servox** (Crook 2). **Victor Frankenstein** passes "the bridge of **Pelissier**" after leaving Servox en route to **Chamonix** and the Mer de Glace (*Fr1* 123; *Fr3* 86).

Pellico, Silvio (1789–1854): Italian revolutionary and author renowned for *Francesca da Rimini* (1815) and *Le mie prigioni* [*My Prisons*] (1832), describing his time at **Spielberg** (*DIMH* 324). Shelley's guide at **Venice**'s **San Marco** prisons pointed out Pellico's former cell September 1842 (*R* 2.88). Shelley notes Pellico's *Francesca* and *Eufemio da Messina* (c. 1834); she credits him with founding *Il Conciliatore* 1818 (*R* 2.195–196).

Peloponnese: Peninsula forming **Greece**'s southern region, called **Morea** in Shelley's day. **Turkey**'s "stronghold in the Morea" provides a firm base for **Ottoman** invasions, and **Lionel Verney**, **Adrian**, and **Clara** intend to "run down the coast of the Morea" (*LM* 161, 439). **Katusthius Ziani** originates from Morea (*EE* 100). **Cyril** and **Zella Ziani** live there, so **Dmitri** abducts **Constans Ziani** there (*EE* 103, 105). **Elizabeth**

Falkner travels there to nurse **Rupert Falkner** (*F* 248). [*EE* 110].

Pendennis: Point overlooking Falmouth Bay in southwest **Cornwall**. Soldiers hiding near **Yeovil** joke about the king being there (*PW* 3.133).

Peneus: River south of **Parnassus** in **Thessaly**, renowned in **Greek** mythology for its beauty (Tripp 460). **Lionel Verney** and **Perdita** "coast the clear waves of the Peneus" as they return to **Athens** with **Raymond**'s body (*LM* 208).

Penseroso, Il: **Milton**'s 1645 poem celebrating melancholy and solitude. Shelley describes **Italian** gardens in which "Nature stands in place of *trimness*"; she provides a footnote to Milton's text: "**retired leisure** / That in trim gardens takes his pleasure" (*R* 1.78; Milton lines 49–50). She quotes *Il Penseroso* to describe discomfort at **Alt Markt**: "'in close covert, by some brook,' thirsting to betake myself to 'some wide-watered shore'" (*R* 1.258; Milton lines 139, 75). Shelley also uses Milton's text to describe chilly mornings in **Venice** as "'kerchiefed in a comely cloud'" (*R* 2.100; Milton line 125).

Pentheus: In **Greek** mythology, Theban king who imprisoned worshippers of his cousin **Bacchus** (here identified with Dionysus); "the prisoners' chains fell off and the jail doors were mysteriously 'opened'" (Tripp 461)." As revenge for his lack of respect, Bacchus caused Pentheus to be torn to bits as though he were a wild animal (see Euripedes's *Bacchae* (405 B.C.E.). Drunk **Silenus** tells Bacchus, "I might have fared more ill than you erewhile / in Pentheus' prisons, that death fated rogue" were it not for **Midas**'s assistance (*Midas* 119).

Pentland Hills: Range of hills southwest of **Edinburgh**. **Henry Clerval** enjoys the landscape (*Fr1* 189; *Fr3* 138).

Pepi, Benedetto: Fictional usurious **Cremonese** whom **Castruccio** rescues in the **Alps** (*V* 1.105–107). Sunstein asserts that Shelley based this character on **Francesco Pacchiani** (*Journals* 589; Sunstein 191).

Pera: Northern **European** section of **Constantinople** with **Golden Horn** to the southwest and Bosporus to the east (Coufopoulos 1). **Lionel Verney** records that **Greece**'s army already controls Pera before laying siege to **Stamboul** in the campaign to win Constantinople (*LM* 183).

Percicus: Sixteenth-century Jesuit poet who composed "**Nepomuceidon**" (1729) to honor **St. John Nepomuk** (*R* 2.6). See **Reeve**.

Perdita: **Lionel Verney**'s younger (by three years) sister in ***The Last Man***; her cottage is on **Windsor**'s grounds (*LM* 53). Her name could be drawn from **Shakespeare**'s *The Winter's Tale*, in which the lost princess Perdita grows up as a shepherdess. Shelley may also be alluding to Mary "Perdita" Robinson (1758–1800), an English novelist, poet, and actress who was mistress of the Prince of Wales and later retired to the Windsor area. **William Godwin** befriended her and attended her funeral; in 1815, **Peacock** escorted the Shelleys to "the tomb of the beautiful, vain, yet feeling & neglected Mrs. Robinson" (Crook 2; *Clairmont Correspondence* 1.14). Elements of Perdita's upbringing and her relationship with **Raymond** suggest that Shelley also draws from her own experiences (*Journals* 229).

Pericles (c. 495–429 B.C.E.): Leading **Athenian** statesman whose political ambition established him as Athens's most influential man after 461 B.C.E. (Howatson 420–421). **Isabell Harley** points out to **Valerius**: " 'if a man of the age of Pericles were to revive in Athens, how much more reason would he have to lament over her fall, than you over the age and decay of **Rome**' " (*Val* 342).

Perier, Casimir (1777–1832): **French** banker and politician who became Chamber of Deputies' President and Minister of the Interior 1831; Shelley spells his name **Perrier**. In describing France's occupation of **Ancona** and **Austria**'s occupation of **Bologna**, Shelley mentions that **Prince Metternich** impressed Perier (*R* 2.254).

Periodo delle Istorie Siciliane del secolo, Un: See **Amari**.

Perkin Warbeck: Shelley's historical novel, *The Fortunes of Perkin Warbeck: A Romance* (1830). By January 1827, Shelley had begun thinking about the "English Historical" subject (*Letters* 1.538). She wrote to **Jane Williams** September 1827 that she devoted an hour each morning to writing the work (*Letters* 2.6). As she wrote, Shelley continued to research her topic; **William Godwin** sent her information about **Edward IV**'s children September 1827, and she subsequently requested assistance from **Murray** (*Letters* 2.8). He provided her with several books she wanted, such as Thomas Leland's *The History of Ireland* (1773), Philipe de Comines's *Les Memoires* (1524), Thomas Crofton Croker's *The Fairy Legends and Traditions of the South of Ireland* (1825–28), and "some travels in **Andalusia**—*descriptive* of the *Scenery*" (*Letters* 2.56, 2.59). Shelley found these descriptions in **Irving**'s *A Chronicle of the Conquest of Granada* (1829), to which she directs readers (*PW* 1.203). Shelley contacted Croker for further information and details about **Irish** history (using his *Researches in the South of Ireland* [1824]), asked **Scott** for Scottish historical details, and wrote for assistance from **Mérimée**, who suggested Baron de Barante's *Histoire des ducs de Bourgogne de la maison de Valois, 1364–1477* [*History of the Bourgogne Dukes of the House of Valois, 1364–1477*] (1824–26) (*Letters* 2.65, 2.78; Sunstein 303; Fischer xvii). She also used the sources named in the novel's preface—**Hume, Bacon, Hall, Holinshed, Pinkerton,** and **Chastellain**—and had read **Shakespeare**'s *Henry VI* plays and *Richard III*, as well as **Ford**'s *Perkin Warbeck* (*PW* 1.v–vii; Fischer xiii). Shelley finished writing *Perkin Warbeck* November 1829 and began cutting the text from about five to three volumes (*Letters* 2.88). At that time, Murray declined to publish it even though he had loaned Shelley a hundred pounds that she considered an advance for the novel (*Letters* 2.89; Fischer xiv). Shelley felt that a historical subject "affords no scope for opinions," but her radical beliefs, such as support for the fallen **Jane Shore**, emerge in the text (Sunstein 309; *Letters*

2.27). After Murray's rejection, Shelley approached Henry Colburn, writing to him November 1829 that she thought *Perkin Warbeck* would be "far more popular" than *The Last Man* because "the story on which it is founded appears to me both beautiful and interesting" (*Letters* 2.89–90). Shelley sold him the manuscript for £150 January 1830 (*Letters* 2.98). The printer lost forty pages of volume three, and Shelley refused to change the title at Colburn's request; nonetheless, the novel came out 13 May; less than a dozen reviews resulted; they were not intensely negative, but *Perkin Warbeck* did not sell (*Letters* 2.108; Fischer xv; Sunstein 308). Like *Valperga*, *Perkin Warbeck* is historically accurate in most of its details, dates, and characters. The novel retells the life of **Richard of York**, one of **Edward IV**'s sons thought to have been murdered in the **Tower** in the 15th century; Shelley supposes that Richard of York survives to become **Perkin Warbeck**, an actual historical figure. Shelley's version begins at the **Yorkist** defeat at **Bosworth**, then follows Richard as he hides in **Flanders**, disguised as Perkin Warbeck while living at **Tournai** with **Madeline** and **Monina De Faro**. He and his cousin **Edmund Plantagenet** then fight in Andalusia's wars between the **Spanish** and the **Moors** before attempting to regain the English throne. He begins in Ireland, backed by **Desmond**, **Earl of Kildare**, **Lord Barry**, the **Bramptons**, **Margaret of Burgundy**, and **Stephen Frion**. Attacks on **Waterford**, **Exeter**, **Taunton**, **Stoke**, and **Norham** (which **James IV** leads primarily) fail, and Richard finally surrenders. His downfall is due in part to **Robert Clifford**'s and Frion's double-dealing; Clifford resents Richard because Monina (whom Clifford loves) supports him. Although Richard and Monina love each other, he marries **Lady Katherine Gordon**, a Scottish noblewoman related to James. At the novel's close, Richard has renounced his claim and is executed, which is historically accurate.

Perkin Warbeck: Ford's drama; *The Chronicle Historie of Perkin Warbeck. A Strange Truth* (1634). Shelley draws upon this play for her novel. As the first epigraph to *Perkin Warbeck*'s chapter in which **Richard of York** resides at the **French** court, Shelley quotes the Earl of Surrey's report of **Margaret of Burgundy**'s opinion of Richard in Ford's drama: "**She had styled him**—the fair **White Rose** of England" (*PW* 1.311; Ford 1.1.123–124). As an epigraph to the chapter in which **James IV** welcomes Richard to his Scottish court, Shelley quotes lines beginning " '**Cousin of York**, thus once more we embrace thee; / Welcome to James of Scotland!' " (*PW* 2.195; Ford 2.1.108–113). As an epigraph to the chapter in which Richard celebrates his marriage, Shelley quotes Richard's speech as he leaves **Lady Katherine Gordon** for battle in Ford's drama: " '**But these are chimes** for funerals: my business / Attends on fortune of a sprightlier triumph; / For love and majesty are reconciled, / And vow to crown thee Empress of the West' " (*PW* 2.254; Ford 3.2.159–162). As an epigraph to the chapter in which Richard prepares to leave Scotland, Shelley quotes from James's speech in Ford's drama, in which he refers to marriage with King Henry's daughter: " '**Yet, noble friends**, his mixture with our blood, / Even with our own, shall no way interrupt / A general peace' " (*PW* 2.318; Ford 4.3.44–46). As the first epigraph to the chapter in which Richard prepares to leave Scotland for **Ireland**, Shelley quotes from Katherine's speech to her husband in Ford's drama: " '**I am your wife**, / No human power can or shall divorce, / My faith from my duty' " (*PW* 3.1; Ford 4.3.101–103). As first epigraph to the chapter in which **Cornish** troops prepare to fight for Richard's cause, Shelley quotes from **Skelton**'s speech in Ford's drama: " '**Tis but going** to sea and leaping ashore, cut ten or twelve thousand unnecessary throats, fire seven or eight towns, take half a dozen cities, get into the market-place, crown him Richard the Fourth, and the business is finished' " (*PW* 3.72; Ford 4.2.61–66).

Perrier, Casimir: See **Perier**.

Persepolis: Formerly **Persia**'s capital, of which the ruins stand near Takht-e-Jamshid in southwestern Iran. Shelley mentions that **San Marco** owns "an antique porphyry vase with letters carved on it, such as are found in Persepolis" (*R* 2.122).

Perseus: See **Cellini**.

Persia: Ancient empire in southwest Asia, now called Iran. **Victor Frankenstein** studies the Persian language, which occupies **Henry Clerval** (*Fr1* 99; *Fr3* 68). **Matilda**'s father wanders through Persia during his absence from Britain (*M* 161). Plague sweeps through Persia (*LM* 225, 234, 324). **Lionel Verney** is concerned about exchanging "our temperate climate for the intolerable heats of a summer in **Egypt** or Persia" (*LM* 383).

"Personal Talk": Wordsworth's 1807 poem. Shelley quotes its opening as an epigraph to *Lodore*'s chapter in which **Elizabeth Fitzhenry** returns from **Maristow Castle**, lines beginning "**I am not One who** much or oft delights / To season my Fireside with personal talk" (*L* 3.245; Wordsworth lines 1–8). **Elizabeth Falkner** later reads about " '**The heavenly Una** with her milk-white lamb' " from the same text, reflecting on her love for **Gerard Neville** (*F* 157; Wordsworth lines 41–42).

Perth: Port on the Firth of **Tay** in east central Scotland, twenty miles southwest of **Dundee**. While visiting the **Baxters** 1812–13, Shelley probably visited Perth (Sunstein 61). **Henry Clerval** and **Victor Frankenstein** sail from **Edinburgh** to Perth (*Fr1* 186–190; *Fr3* 135, 138). From Perth, Clerval writes to Victor to request his company; he convinces Victor to return to Perth within two days (*Fr1* 196; *Fr3* 144). **Lionel Verney** travels via balloon to Perth to visit **Adrian** (*LM* 71). **Richard of York** and **James IV** travel from Perth to **Aberdeen** (*PW* 2.239–240).

Perticari, Count Giulio (1779–1822): **Monti**'s son-in-law and **Italian** writer who advocated a common Italian language in *Degli scrittori del trecento e dei loro imitatori* [*Of Thirteenth-Century Writers and Their Imitators*] (1818) and *Dell' amor patrio di Dante e del suo libro in torno il Volgare eloguio* [*Of Dante's Love of His Country and His Book about the Common Tongue*] (1820) (Steinberg 2.31). Shelley mentions his involvement in the reformation of the **National Dictionary** (*R* 2.163).

Peru: Country on central **South America**'s west coast. In the 16th century, **Spanish** explorers divided and destroyed the Incan empire there. **Victor Frankenstein** regretfully observes that obsessions like his, which "interfere with the tranquillity of [humankind's] domestic affections," caused the destruction of Peru's empire (*Fr1* 84; *Fr3* 57).

Perugia: **Italian** city thirty-five miles southwest of **Arezzo**. **Euthanasia** and **Beatrice** pass separately through it (*V* 1.207, 2.191, 3.83). **Battista Tripalda** is a canon of Perugia's **St. Ambrose** Cathedral; Shelley presents his banishment from that city as a false rumor (*V* 2.237, 2.240).

Perugino (1446–1524): Nickname of Pietro di Christofano Vanucci, **Italian** who painted several **Sistine Chapel** scenes (c. 1481) and was **Raphael**'s tutor 1499–1503 (Vasari 2.316, 2.329; Schmeckebier 262, 264). Shelley notes the folly of imitating other artists: "To imitate Perugino would be to write poetry in the obsolete language of **Chaucer**" (*R* 2.132). See **Umbria**.

Pescia: **Italian** town thirty miles northwest of **Florence**. Shelley correctly relates that **Galeazzo Visconti** died there 3 September 1328 (*V* 3.268; Green 252–253).

***Peter Bell the Third*:** Poem **PBS** wrote 1819 and Shelley copied October 1819 (*Journals* 300). **Wordsworth**'s *Peter Bell: a tale in verse* (1819) inspired PBS's poem, first published 1839 (*Journals* 560; White 1.168–169). Shelley quotes from the "Sin" section of her husband's poem as an epigraph to the **Lodore** chapter in which **Lord** and **Lady Lodore** first meet: "**Men oftentimes** prepare a lot, / Which ere it finds them, is not what / Suits with their genuine station" (*L* 1.93; PBS lines 270–272). Shelley also slightly alters lines to serve as an epigraph to the chapter in which Lady Lodore refuses to accompany Lord Lodore to **America**: "**Her virtue, like** our own, was built / Too much on that indignant fuss, / Hypocrite pride stirs up in us, / To bully out another's guilt" (*L* 1.179; PBS lines 289–292). She also quotes the section depicting Peter's verse as illuminating the world and effecting change as an epigraph to the chapter in which Lady Lodore sacrifices her wealth: "**Like gentle rains** on the dry plains, / Making that green which late was grey; / Or like the sudden moon, that stains / Some gloomy chamber's window panes, / With a broad light like day" (*L* 3.128; PBS lines 438–442).

Petrarca: See **Petrarch**.

Petrarch, Francesco (1304–1374): Popular **Italian** poet renowned for his sonnets, most of which are addressed to Laura de Sade, inspiration of his love poetry. Begun 1342–43, they are collected in *Rime Sparse* (1374). Shelley is familiar with many of Petrarch's sonnets and read his *Il trionfo della Morte* [*The Triumph of Death*] (c. 1360s) September 1819 and his *Works* September 1820; she calls him **Petrarca** (*Journals* 297, 333). *The Last Man*'s narrator records losing a companion while reconstructing the tale of the **sibyl**'s leaves and suggests that "with the selected and matchless companion of my toils, their dearest reward is also lost to me— '**Di mie tenere** frondi altro lavoro /

Credea mostrarte; e qual fero pianeta / Ne' nvidiò insieme, o mio nobil tesoro?'" (*LM* 6). Phyllis Zimmerman identifies these lines from Petrarch's sonnet 322, in which the speaker mourns a friend's premature death: "I thought I would show you other results / Of my frail branches. What star's evil ray / Hated us both, o my excellent treasure?" (Zimmerman 31–32; Petrarch lines 9–11). When **Idris** escapes the **Countess of Windsor**'s plans for her removal from England, **Lionel Verney** records that "not to excite fresh agitation in her, '*per non turbar* quel bel viso sereno,' I curbed my delight" (*LM* 88). Jean de Palacio identifies this line from Petrarch's sonnet 236: "Not to disturb the clear face I behold" (de Palacio 34; Petrarch line 5). Shelley describes **Ethel Villiers**'s happiness at spending the evening alone with her husband with a line, as Stafford notes, from number 341 of Petrarch's *Rime Sparse*: "not much was said, and their words were childish—words '**Intellete dar loro** soli ambedui'"; the line means, "Understood only by the two of us" (*L* 3.58–59; Stafford 230; Petrarch line 11). Describing **Lady Lodore**'s visit to her husband's grave, Shelley observes "Petrarch says, that he was never so young, but that he knew that he was growing old"; Petrarch celebrates old age in *Rerum senilium libri* [*Letters of Old Age*] (1501) (*L* 3.290; Petrarch 8.1–2). Shelley wrote Petrarch's biography for *Italian and Spanish Lives*. She admires Petrarch's translations of **Latin** texts and outlines the life of this "darling of the age" accurately, asserting that "the peculiar charm of Petrarch's character is warmth of heart, and a native ingenuousness of disposition" which, aligned with Christian principles, present noble characteristics belying his desire for popularity (*ISPL* 1.67–68). Shelley quotes from several of Petrarch's sonnets, admiring the depth of emotion she finds in his work, before concluding with the hope that her "brief and imperfect sketch" indicates Petrarch's "honest worth, his admirable genius, his high-toned feelings" (*ISPL* 1.115). Shelley completed this biography July 1834 (*Letters* 2.209). Shelley records her visit to the **Ambrosian Library**, where many materials were now kept "rigidly under lock and key: for some one, whose folly ought to have met with severe punishment, had endeavoured to purloin, and so mutilated, some of the relics of Petrarch" (*R* 1.111). While in **Florence**, Shelley, expressing her desire to explore the town and scenes so familiar to Petrarch, argues he was a "great" poet because he freely adhered to his mind's "genuine impulse"; she believes that **Manzoni**'s odes are second only to Petrarch's (*R* 2.134, 2.191, 2.200–201).

Pharoah: See **Bible**.

Pharsalia: See **Lucan**.

Phidias (c. 490–432 B.C.E.): Also spelled Pheidias, one of **Athens**'s greatest artists; he "was responsible for the adornment of Athens in the mid-fifth century [B.C.E.] . . . in particular for the construction of the Parthenon" (Howatson 429–430). Shelley saw some of Phidias's work at **London**'s British Museum February 1818 (*Journals* 193). **Lionel Verney** emerges after sleeping on **Mount Cavallo** to see "statues on each side, the works, as they are inscribed, of Phidias and Praxitiles, stood in undiminished grandeur, representing **Castor** and **Pollux**" (*LM* 461). The statue is indeed inscribed to Phidias, but it is doubtful it is his, since "the statues are evidently centuries older than the age of **Constantine**" (*MROM* 88). Shelley viewed "the *Rape of Ganymede* [which] is attributed to Phidias, and worthy of him" at **Venice**'s **Doge's Palace** September 1842 (*R* 2.86). See **Praxitilean**.

Philadelphia: Large port city on the Delaware River in southeastern Pennsylvania. **Lionel Verney** records that the *Fortunatus*, which sailed from Philadelphia, brings plague to England (*LM* 217).

Philip le Bel (1268–1314): **Charles of Valois**'s brother and **France**'s king 1285–1314. Philip used mercenary knights to occupy **Flanders** 1297 and transferred the papal residence to **Avignon** 1309 (Kinder 1.191). Philip hires exiled **Scoto** to aid him in France, and **Castruccio**'s military accomplishments against the **Flemish** impress him; Castruccio's involvement with Philip's war against Flemish rebels actually occurred 1303 (*V* 1.89, 1.92–93; Green 45). **Euthanasia**, explaining **Florentine** belief in mystical signs, refers to Philip's seizure of Florentine usurers (*V* 2.3). Shelley took this reference from **Villani**, who describes strife between Philip and Pope Boniface (Villani 344–350; Crook 3.122).

Philip of Macedon (382–336 B.C.E.): Also called Philip II, great military leader and **Alexander the Great**'s father who waged several wars in **Greece**, where he took Thebes and **Athens** 338 B.C.E. (Kinder 1.63). **Beatrice** refers to Philip (*V* 3.50).

Philistines: See **Samson**.

Philosopher's stone: See **Elixir of Immortality**.

Phoebus: See **Apollo**.

Phoenicia: Ancient **Mediterranean** kingdom in the area now comprising Israel, Lebanon, and **Syria**. **Benedetto Pepi** tells a story describing nobles wearing scarves made from Phoenician birds' feathers, emphasizing the nobility's extravagant, exotic taste (*V* 1.286).

Phrygia: Large area of **Asia** Minor; it is *Midas*'s setting.

Pia, Madonna: **Despina dei Elisei**'s mother and **Arrigo dei Elisei**'s wife in "A Tale of the Passions."

Piazza del Duomo [Florence]: Square that is **Florence**'s religious center (Higson 77–79). **Guelph** supporters assemble there to celebrate retaking Florence (*TP* 1–2).

Piazza del Duomo [Milan]: Square wherein **Milan**'s **Duomo** is located. Shelley enjoyed "a moonlight hour passed" there September 1840, finding it "a pleasure never to be forgotten" (*R* 1.113).

Piazza della Annunziata: **Florentine** square leading to the Foundling Hospital (*Florence* 167). Shelley visited the chapel in the square's hospital January 1843, seeing **Ghirlandajo**'s *The Adoration of the Magi* there (*R* 2.143).

Piazza della Signoria: Florentine square, an open-air museum, flanked by the **Uffizi** and Palazzo Uguccioni

(*Florence* 44). Shelley saw **Cellini**'s *Perseus* there January 1843 (*R* 2.155).

Piazza San Marco: St. Mark's Square in English, a city square that is the most popular sight for visitors to **Venice**; Shelley also refers to it as **Place of St. Mark**, **Piazza di San Marcos**, and **Piazza of San Marco** (*R* 2.104–105, 2.128). Its western end offers an incredible view of **San Marco**, and the square itself is beautiful, with its brick, marble, and mosaic designs (Honour 24, 28). Shelley passed through it when she visited the **Doge's Palace** October 1818 (Sunstein 158). **Edmund Malville** describes seeing the square while touring Venice by gondola at night (*RI* 26). Shelley detailed her April 1843 visits there, noting that "it is one of our amusements to visit the piazza of San Marco at two in the afternoon, when, on the striking of the hour on the great clock, the pigeons come down to be fed" (*R* 2.126). Shelley stayed at **Hotel d'Italia**, a three-minute walk from Piazza San Marco, September 1842 (*R* 2.128).

Piazza di San Marco: See **Piazza San Marco**.

Piazzetta: Square on the **Laguna** at **Venice**'s **San Marco**, marked by two huge granite pillars (1127) (*Venice* 20, 38). Shelley mentions viewing **San Giorgio Maggiore Church** from it September 1842 (*R* 2.94).

Piccadilly: Large street in **London**'s Westminster district, traditionally the center of fashionable shops and hotels. The **Villiers**es drop **Fanny Derham** off "in Piccadilly, not far from her own door" (*L* 3.72–73). **Edward Villiers** is later arrested there; **Ethel Villiers** finds it one of many "interminable suburbs" (*L* 3.83, 3.86). **Gerard Neville** takes the stagecoach from Piccadilly to **Liverpool** (*F* 125).

Piccol: See **Brentani**.

Piedmont: Northwestern **Italian** province that **France**, **Liguria**, **Lombardy**, and **Switzerland** border; its capital is **Turin**. "Piedmont" translates to "foot of the mountains" or "foothills." Shelley was interested in March 1821's "revolution of Piedmont," which ended 8 April (*Journals* 357–358). She describes Piedmont as a "wide landing place" near a "staircase of hills" (*Letters* 1.350). **Henry VII** of **Germany** stays there two months (*V* 1.128). Shelley mentions **Carbonarism** in Piedmont and notes **Azeglio** was from there (*R* 2.177, 2.201).

Pierre: See **Otway**.

Piesport: See **Pisport**.

Pieta: See **Titian**.

Pietro l'Eremita: See **Gioacchino Rossini**.

Pilnitz: Village on the **Elbe**, five miles southeast of **Dresden**. Shelley passed through it August 1842 (*R* 1.260–261).

Pincian: Notable hill in **Rome**. **Euthanasia** walks over Pincian while visiting her brother (*V* 1.206).

Pinkerton, John (1758–1826): Scottish historian who published *The History of Scotland from the Accession of the*

Piombi

House of Stuart to that of Mary, with Appendices of Original Documents (1797) (*DNB*). In **Perkin Warbeck**'s preface, Shelley directs readers to **Sir John Ramsay**'s letters to **Henry VII**, appended to Pinkerton's history (*PW* 1.vi). Shelley probably also read Pinkerton's *A General Collection of the best and most interesting Voyages and Travels in all parts of the world* (1807–14) November 1816 (*Journals* 146).

Piombi: "Sotto Piombi" is **Italian** for "under the leads," referring to apartments on **Doge's Palace**'s top floor; they served as **Venetian** prisons (early 19th century) (*MNIT* 335). Shelley describes her tour of these dungeons and mentions that her guide insisted Piombi prison never existed; she disbelieved him and cites **Pellico**'s description of the prison as evidence (*R* 2.87; Pellico 52).

Piombino: **Italian** city on a promontory across Canale di Piombino from **Elba**. The moon rose behind Piombino during Shelley's March 1843 voyage to **Rome** (*R* 2.213).

Piraeus: Natural harbor fortified to become **Athens**'s central port. **Lionel Verney** records, "the whole city poured out at the gate of Piraeus" to welcome **Raymond**'s return (*LM* 170).

Pisa: **Italian** city on the **Arno**, nine miles northeast of **Leghorn**. Shelley first visited Pisa May 1818 and then lived there and at the neighboring Baths of Pisa, four miles north, intermittently over the next three and a half years. Only in Pisa did the Shelleys really settle as residents of Italy with a circle of friends (Sunstein 191–192). Shelley treasured Pisa "as the perfection of Italy," even while she wished to "escape from one's house to the country without mingling with the inhabitants" (Sunstein 198; *Journals* 340). Shelley returned to Pisa in misery immediately after **PBS**'s death, so the city held both good and bad memories. **Corradino** returns to Pisa from **Germany** (*TP* 7, 20). Shelley recalls PBS's spirit in her memory of "Pisa's old pine wood" (*Ch* 131). **Edmund Malville** fondly relates a visit from " 'baths of Pisa to **Vico Pisano**' " (*RI* 29). A river overflows and destroys Pisa in **The Last Man** (*LM* 269). Shelley notes "Pisa was willing to abase **Florence**" when discussing **Carbonari**, and that **Amalfi** "was swallowed up by the kingdom of **Naples**, after having been pillaged by the Pisans in 1137" (*R* 2.162, 2.281). [*Brother* 167].

Pisces: Twelfth zodiacal sign, consisting of two fish. **Lionel Verney** notes the constellations' passage "from the short tyranny of watery Pisces . . . [to] **Taurus**" (*LM* 431).

Pisport: **German** village on the **Moselle** between **Trèves** and **Bernkastel**; Shelley spells it **Piesport** (*MCON* 307). She stayed there June 1840 (*R* 1.21–22).

Pistoia: **Italian** city twenty miles northwest of **Florence**. Shelley calls Pistoia "a town of some moment between Florence and **Lucca**" (*V* 1.2). **Castruccio** repeatedly conquers and visits Pistoia, where the **Bianchi** and **Neri** factions began (*V* 1.2, 3.109–110, 3.119, 3.172, 3.218). Shelley cites Castruccio's final siege of Pistoia as the cause of his death (*V* 3.267). **Euthanasia**'s mother's political interests include war with Pistoia, during which her oldest son dies (*V* 1.200, 1.206). **Beatrice**'s courage en route to **Valperga** castle fails in Pistoia (*V* 3.79–80).

Pitt, William, the Elder (1708–1778): First Earl of Chatham (**Lord Chatham**) 1761 and British statesman who pleaded in **Parliament** 18 November 1777 for sympathetic treatment of **Americans** during the **Revolutionary War** (*DNB*; Moskal 179). Shelley quotes from his 18 November 1777 **House of Lords** speech: "**If I were** an American, as I am an Englishman, while a foreign troop was landed in my country I never would lay down my arms, never—never—never!" (*R* 1.203; Moskal 179). She also quotes other sections of the speech beginning "**the mercenary sons**," "**devoted the Americans**," and "**traffic and barter**" (*R* 1.203).

Pitti Palace: See **Palazzo Pitti**.

Pius VII (1742–1823): Pope 1800–23 (Kelly 302–303). Shelley met Pius VII March 1819 (*Journals* 253). She describes Holy Week ceremonies and states that the ones she observed April 1843 were "less majestic" than those she experienced when Pius VII—"venerable and dignified old man"—was pope (*R* 2.230).

Place de la Concorde: **Champs Elysées** leads to this central **Parisian** square, constructed 1755–75. During the **French Revolution**, the guillotine stood in the square's northwest corner; an obelisk now stands in its center, placed there 1833 (*MIPA* 95). Shelley describes the view from **Tuileries**'s terrace, including Place de la Concorde (*R* 1.8). Although Shelley greatly admired its beauty, she thought **Berlin**'s Museum Island more impressive (*R* 1.227).

Place Vendôme: Octagonal square in **Paris**'s Opera region, begun during Louis XIV's reign (1643–1715) and completed 1701 (Jennett 26). A statue of the king was erected in the square but pulled down 1792 during the **French Revolution**; in 1810, **Napoleon** erected there a statue of himself, which was subsequently torn down and replaced by a statue of Henri IV, removed 1815 (Jennett 75–76; Kinder 2.37). In August 1814, the Shelleys "met at the Place Vendôme, a Frenchman who could speak English," and **PBS** records that the man proceeded to tell them "he had assisted in bribing the mob to overthrow the statue of Napoleon" (*Journals* 10). **Lionel Verney** records discord among parties of plague survivors "which at length proceeded so far, that the three divisions, armed, met in the Place Vendôme," where **Adrian** mediates the dispute 1 February (*LM* 376–377).

Plague: By the close of *The Last Man*, in which the plague quickly destroys the world's inhabitants, **Lionel Verney** assumes he is "the LAST MAN" alive on earth (*LM* 470). Shelley's accounts of plague seem to be drawn from a variety of documents, several of which she refers to in the novel itself; her interest in plague is evinced in her reading as early as 1817. Verney notes that he "peruse[s] **De Foe**'s account" and suggests that "pictures drawn in these books were so vivid, that we seemed to have experienced the results depicted by them" (*LM* 259). Verney later recommends the

Plainpalais

"accounts of **Boccaccio**, De Foe, and **Browne**" to readers who desire explicit details about daily death and accompanying rituals of plague; all of these authors' works influenced Shelley's novel (*LM* 267). Shelley describes plague as an "enemy to the human race," and it first occurs in her novel in **Constantinople**, aligning her text with Defoe's (*LM* 175). Shelley draws principally upon Defoe's physical descriptions of the disease and its effects; Verney personifies the plague as a feminine force, laughing and scorning humanity's efforts to avoid it (*LM* 316). Another source for some of the events in Shelley's text is John Wilson's "The City of the Plague" (1816), which Shelley read May 1817 (*Journals* 171). Shelley seems to have drawn upon Wilson's and Defoe's accounts of astrologers and prophets for her own inventions, and upon Wilson's "negro" character (Wilson 1.4.72–76, 3.4.132–135; *LM* 336–337). In her account of the 1837 cholera epidemic in **Rome**, Shelley alludes to those escaping the plague in the *Decameron* (*R* 2.241).

Plainpalais: **Geneva**'s southern section, along the **Arve**. Shelley visited Plainpalais summer 1816 (*H* 101; *Letters* 1.20). It is the site of **William Frankenstein**'s murder (*Fr1* 100; *Fr3* 69). [*Fr1* 103; *Fr3* 72].

Plantagenet: Name, adopted 1460, of the family that held England's throne 1154–1485 (*DNB*). Last male Plantagenet heir was Edward Plantagenet, **Earl of Warwick**, a *Perkin Warbeck* character, as were his cousins **Edmund Plantagenet** and **Richard of York**.

Plantagenet, Edmund: Shelley's fictional character, supposedly **Richard III**'s illegitimate son. **Richard of York**'s cousin and faithful supporter throughout *Perkin Warbeck*; **Lady Katherine Gordon** encounters him again at the novel's end.

Plantagenet, Richard: See **Richard of York**.

Plato (427–347 B.C.E.): Greek philosopher. He records his philosophy, the basis of Idealism, in *Dialogues* with **Socrates**; his *Epistles* are also important (Howatson 442–444). **PBS** read Plato's works repeatedly throughout his life, translated *Symposium* (c. 384 B.C.E.) July 1818 (Shelley having copied it for him), and subsequently translated others of Plato's works (*Journals* 217–218, 667; White 2.22–25; Holmes 429–438). **Lionel Verney** studies "the metaphysics of Plato" (*LM* 77). **Lord Lodore** finds that reading "Plato could elevate . . . his soul" (*L* 1.25). **Fanny Derham** "indulges in a thousand Platonic dreams," and Fanny later explains that she finds comfort in Plato's philosophy (*L* 1.224, 2.296, 3.9). **Horatio Saville** points "to some unexplained passage in Plato" as an example of his interest in academic studies (*L* 2.25).

Platz: Shelley refers to Lustgarten, a square now called Marx-Engels Platz since reunification, between **Berlin**'s **Unter den Linden** and Altes Museum (Tucker 61). Shelley praises the **Palace**'s view of it (*R* 1.227).

Plautus, Titus Maccius (c. 254–184 B.C.E.): Early **Roman** dramatist whose plays, about twenty of which survive of the 130 he is supposed to have written, are adapted from 4th-century B.C.E. "**Greek** New Comedy" (Howatson 444). **Lord Maristow** suggests that the farce of **Colonel Villiers**'s relationship with **Miss Gregory** varies "the scene from a travestie of **Romeo and Juliet** to the comedies of Plautus" (*L* 2.225).

Pleasures of Memory, The: See **Rogers**.

Plessis: Louis XI's chateau, Plessis-les-Tours, in the **Loire** Valley near Tours (Fischer 65). **Stephen Frion** travels from **Spain** to Plessis, arriving at the time of Louis XI's death (*PW* 1.151).

Pliniana: See **Pliny the Younger**.

Pliny the Elder [Gaius Plinius Secundus] (23–79 C.E.): Leading **Roman** writer and lawyer; his greatest work is *Naturalis Historia* [*Natural History*] (wr. 77 C.E.), first translated into English 1601 (Howatson 445–446). **Victor Frankenstein** reads his works (*Fr1* 71).

Pliny the Younger [Gaius Plinius Caecilius Secundus] (62–113 C.E.): **Pliny the Elder**'s nephew; he supported the Stoics and was a successful governor, as well as a landowner near **Rome**. Shelley read Pliny's *Letters* (c. 107–111 C.E.), consisting of ten books upon various subjects, March–May 1817 (*Journals* 166–169; Howatson 446–447). **Lionel Verney**, **Adrian**, **Clara**, and **Evelyn** fix their "summer residence" at **Pliniana** (*LM* 432). This villa, named after Pliny, is on **Lake Como** at Torno; the Shelleys visited it April 1818, but were unable to rent the villa as they had wished (*Journals* 204; Pliny, *Letters* 4.30.2–3; Paley 478–479). In August 1840, Shelley writes of her longing "to land at the Pliniana, which remained in my recollection as a place adorned by magical beauty" (*R* 1.89).

Plunket, Thomas: Lambert Simnel supporter whom Shelley casts as a **Lancastrian** promoted from chief justice to chancellor in **Ireland** (Fischer 112; *PW* 1.274, 1.287).

Plutarch (c. 46–120 C.E.): Greek biographer and moralist, best known for *Lives* of the Noble Grecians and Romans, also called *Parallel Lives*, a collection of biographies first translated into English 1579 (Hutchins v–vi). Shelley read *Lives* 1815 and frequently draws historical information from it (*Journals* 91). The **Creature** educates himself with a copy stolen from the **De Laceys** (*Fr1* 156–157; *Fr3* 112–113). **Lionel Verney** suggests that certain characters' early lives at **Windsor** "were a living comment on that beautiful sentiment of Plutarch, that 'our souls have a natural inclination to love, being born as much to love, as to feel, to reason, to understand and remember' "; Blumberg notes that a "similar sentiment is found" in Plutarch's "On Moral Virtue," in his *Moralia* (first English trans. 1603) (*LM* 92; Blumberg 75; Plutarch, *Moralia* 6.451C). **Adrian** finds that Greece ready to resist the **Turks** "and [that] the women, sacrificing their costly ornaments, accoutred their sons for the war, and bade them conquer or die with the spirit of the **Spartan** mother" (*LM* 161). The reference is to Plutarch's "Sayings of Spartan Women": "Another, as she handed her son his shield, exhorted him, saying, 'Either with this or upon this,' " mean-

Pluto

ing the son should fight with his shield or be borne home upon it after death in battle (*Moralia* 3.241F). Shelley recorded this phrase in an April 1822 letter (*Letters* 1.229).

Pluto: Roman name for Greek **Hades**, god of the Underworld. This "King of Hell" abducts **Proserpine**, draws her down into his world, and compels her to become his bride (*P* 65).

Plymouth: British port on **Devon**'s southern coast thirty-five miles southwest of **Exeter**. **Dame Smithson** lives there with **Maurice** for six months before her husband returns (*Maurice* 82).

Po: River running east from northern **Italy**'s **Alps** to the **Adriatic** on Italy's northwest coast. Severe winter rains cause the Po to overflow and ruin crops (*LM* 269). **Lionel Verney**, **Adrian**, and **Clara** "floated down the widening stream of the Po" en route to **Venice** (*LM* 438). Shelley's October 1842 journey to **Florence** was impeded since roads beside the Po had been "damaged by rain and flood" (*R* 2.131).

Pobratimo: Bond between **Dmitri** and **Katusthius Ziani**, which initiates "**The Evil Eye**'s" plot, formed after Katusthius rescued Dmitri "from the savage **Kakovougnis** of **Boularias**" (*EE* 102). Shelley provides a footnote: "In **Greece**, especially in Illyria and **Epirus**, it is no uncommon thing for persons of the same sex to swear friendship; the church contains a ritual to consecrate this vow. Two men thus united are called *pobratimi*, the women *posestrime*"; Shelley uses the singular form "pobratimo" (*EE* 100). Also mentioned in "**Illyrian Poetry—Feudal Scenes**."

Poccetti: See **Barbatelli**.

Podestà: During strife between **Ghibelline** and **Guelph** factions caused by their attempts to rule various cities, **Italian** city governments instituted this governmental position to replace the consul (Higson 110). **Cincolo de' Becari** travels to **Pisa** carefully, trying to avoid being seized and "carried before the *Podestà* of a village" (*TP* 19).

***Podestà*, Palace of the:** **Florence**'s government palace begun around 1250, also called Bargello and now the National Museum (*Artistic* 58). Shelley mentions **Giotto**'s portrait of **Dante** there (*R* 2.158).

Poésie Chrétienne, La: See **Rio**.

Poets of the Lakes: Group of British writers, such as **Wordsworth**, Robert Southey, and **Samuel Taylor Coleridge**, who lived in the Lake District in the early 19th century. Shelley notes that one of her Scottish traveling companions had visited the Poets of the Lakes (*R* 1.127).

Poictiers: See **Poitiers**.

Poitiers: 1356 battle fought 128 miles northeast of **Bordeaux**; English forces defeated the **French** and took King John II captive; Shelley spells it **Poictiers** (Cannon 750). **Richard of York** inspires supporters by referring to the defeat of the French by a small English force at Poitiers (*PW* 3.17).

Poland: Northeastern **European** country bordered by the **Baltic**, **Germany**, and **Russia**. **Lord Lodore** uses Polish farming practices he learned there during his youth; he also had an affair with **Theodora Lyzinski** there (*L* 1.14, 1.84, 1.136). **Elizabeth Falkner** claims that she and **Rupert Falkner** were traveling in Poland when **Alithea Neville** disappeared (*F* 161). Shelley notes that **France**'s 1830 revolution encouraged Poland to rebel against Russia (*R* 2.249).

Polenta, Guido della: Francesca of **Rimini**'s father (*V* 1.137; Ciardi 64).

Polidori, John William (1795–1821): As **Byron**'s physician, Polidori moved into **Villa Diodati** with Byron June 1816, and the Shelleys made his acquaintance summer that year (*Journals* 124, 126, 131). Polidori was fond of Shelley and "was clever, handsome, and interesting in regard to science and psychological phenomena, but so unstable and offensive that Byron was to fire him that fall" (Sunstein 121). **Murray** had asked Polidori to keep a record of his **European** travels with Byron; the resulting *Diary of Dr. John W. Polidori, 1816, Relating to Byron, Shelley, etc.* (1911) provides insight into Polidori's own character as well as into that summer's events. Polidori was a participant in the ghost-story competition as a result of which Shelley produced *Frankenstein*, and Shelley recalled that "poor Polidori had some terrible idea about a skull-headed lady who was so punished for peeping through a key-hole—what to see I forget" (*Fr3* 21). Polidori eventually published *The Vampyre: A Tale* 1819 in *New Monthly Magazine*; it was attributed to Byron (Sunstein 165). Polidori killed himself shortly thereafter. See D. L. MacDonald's *'Poor Polidori': A Critical Biography of the Author of 'The Vampyre'* (1991).

Poligny: **French** town twenty miles southeast of **Dôle**. Shelley passed through it 1814 (*H* 87–88).

Polixena: See **Niccolini**.

Poliziano, Angelo (1454–1494): An **Italian** author; Shelley wrote his biography for *Italian and Spanish Lives*. She admires Poliziano's poem, *Stanze di messere Angelo Poliziano cominciate per la giostra di Giuliano de' Medici* [*Angelo Poliziano's stanzas for Giuliano de' Medici's Tournament*] (1475–78), written partly in honor of his patron **Lorenzo de Medici**, and notes that Poliziano subsequently wrote in **Latin** and became a professor of **Greek** and Latin at **Florence** University 1483 (*ISPL* 1.165).

Pollux: See **Castor**.

Polynices: In **Greek** mythology, **Oedipus**'s son; he fulfilled his father's curse when he fought with his brother and both died. It was decreed he should remain unburied, but some versions of the myth record that his sister **Antigone** buried him anyway, even though it meant her death. **Lionel Verney** compares **Idris** to Antigone when she "discharged the funeral rites of Polynices" (*LM* 78).

Polyphemus: In **Greek** mythology, **Poseidon**'s son, a **Cyclops**, who lived on **Sicily**; he appears in works by **Euripides**, **Ovid**, and, most notably, in **Homer**'s *Odyssey* (Tripp 488–489). Shelley describes the cave beneath **Cocumella** as Polyphemus's (*R* 2.264).

Pomegranate seed

Starke also mentions Polyphemus in her descriptions of these caves, called the Caves of **Ulysses** (*STIE* 361).

Pomegranate seed: In **Greek** mythology, food of temptation for **Proserpine**. **Ascalaphus** reminds Proserpine that she has eaten "a pomegranate's seeds" in **Tartarus** and is thus irrevocably tied to **Hades** (*P* 75).

Pompeii: Ancient **Italian** city fifteen miles southeast of **Naples**; Mount **Vesuvius**'s eruption buried it 79 C.E. Shelley visited December 1818 and February 1819 (*Journals* 245, 249). **William Shelley** accompanied her through "Pompeii's **Roman** Market-place," located in the forum area in Pompeii's western quarter (*Ch* 79). **Horatio Saville** proposes a journey to Pompeii to the **Villiers**es, and Shelley compares **Fanny Derham**'s beauty to "calm-visaged, blue-eyed deities of the frescos of Pompeii" (*L* 2.212, 2.260). Shelley visited Pompeii June 1843 (*R* 2.279).

Pompey the Great (106–48 B.C.E.): **Roman** consul, general, and distinguished military leader who formed an informal triumvirate with Crassus and **Julius Caesar** 67–62 B.C.E. (Howatson 455, 107). Shelley probably learned about Pompey from **Plutarch**'s *Lives* (2.385–458). **Valerius** approaches Rome calling for Pompey to awake again (*Val* 334).

Pomptine Marshes: See **Pontine Marshes**.

Ponce de Leon, Don Rodrigo (b. c. 1442): Marquess of Cadiz who became his family's head 1469 and stormed the **Alhambra** 1482 (Blacker 74–80). Rodrigo is a minor *Perkin Warbeck* character (*PW* 1.205–206).

Ponente: Wind sweeping through southern **Italy**. Shelley describes this "west wind, brisk and fresh, which crisps the sea into sparkling waves," which she encountered at **Capri** June 1843 (*R* 2.267, 2.293).

Poniatowski, Józef Antoni (1763–1813): **Polish** soldier and marshal of **France**; he died at Battle of **Leipzig** (16–19 October 1813) attempting to cross the **Elster**. Shelley saw his place of death July 1840 (*R* 1.215).

Pontalier: See **Pontarlier**.

Pontarlier: **French** city ten miles west of the **Swiss** border; Shelley spells it **Pontalier**. The Shelleys caught up with their lost driver there August 1814 (*Journals* 16; *H* 39). Shelley calls Pontarlier a "frontier town of France," because it is near the village that houses a French frontier customhouse (*H* 37; *STIE* 564).

Ponte alle Grazie: Bridge over the **Arno** in **Florence**, built 1237 (*Florence* 80). Shelley crossed it to visit **San Miniato** October 1842 (*R* 2.135).

Ponte de' Sospiri: Venetian "Bridge of Sighs," connecting **Doge's Palace** with public prisons called the Carceri (*MNIT* 335–336). In September 1842, Shelley described the Doge's Palace, with a walled-up door that once led to Ponte de' Sospiri, and recalled a September 1818 visit (*R* 2.87; *Journals* 227–228).

Pontine Marshes: Large marshy area south of **Rome** bordering the

Mediterranean; Shelley sometimes writes "**Pomptine**" for Pontine. Traveling from Rome to **Naples** November 1818, Shelley crossed "the Pomptine Marshes," then reputed to be dangerous for travelers due to robbers (*Journals* 240). Writing December 1818, Shelley remarked that a companion on her journey, a "priest—a great strong muscular fellow was almost in convulsions with fear—to travel before daylight along the Pomptine Marshes" (*Letters* 1.83). **Horatio Saville** mournfully watches the **Villiers**es' carriage "as it skimmed along the level road of the Pontine Marshes" (*L* 2.196).

Pontremoli: Italian city eighteen miles north of **La Spezia**. Shelley includes Pontremoli in the list of territories under **Lucchese** control; **Castruccio** joins **Louis of Bavaria** there (*V* 2.174, 3.264).

Poole: English town twenty-eight miles southeast of **Yeovil**. **Swartz**'s men, hearing of **Yorkist** defeat, retreat to Poole until **Richard of York** leads them to battle (*PW* 3.127).

Pope, Alexander (1688–1744): Leading English literary figure, moral and satirical poet, and philosopher; his metrics and satires are still admired today. Shelley read Pope's translations of **Homer**'s *Iliad* (1715–20) 1815 and *Odyssey* (1725–26) August 1818 (*Journals* 668, 224). **PBS** read Pope's famous satirical poem *The Rape of the Lock* (1714) aloud May 1821 (*Journals* 368). **Lionel Verney** characterizes **Ryland**: "No man could crush a '**butterfly on the wheel**' with better effect" (*LM* 241–242). Paley identifies this quotation from Pope's "Epistle to Dr. Arbuthnot" (1727; rev. ed. 1735) (Paley 475; Pope lines 305, 307–308). As an epigraph to *Lodore*'s chapter introducing **Elizabeth Fitzhenry** in mourning for her brother, Shelley quotes from Pope's "Epistle to Robert, Earl of Oxford and Mortimer" (1722): "**Absent or dead**, still let a friend be dear, / A sigh the absent claims, the dead a tear" (*L* 1.1; Pope lines 13–14). Shelley read a poem by **Freyberg**'s valet de place, describing it as "in heroic measure, rhymed, meant to be in the style of Pope's didactic poems" (*R* 1.44–45). See "**Epistle to a Lady**," *Essay on Criticism*, and "**Essay on Man**."

Porro, Count Luigi (1780–1860): Milanese noble who employed **Pellico** as his sons' tutor; promoter of "literature and the arts"; Porro was condemned to death for **Carbonarism** (Pellico 241–42). Shelley mentions Porro supported and helped found *Il Conciliatore* (*R* 2.195).

Porta Ceresa: Mantua's southern city gate, at Corso Garibaldi's end. **Hofer** was executed near it 1810 (*R* 2.59).

Porta del Popolo: At the start of the **Corso**, major **Roman** gateway built 1561 to **Michelangelo**'s design (*MROM* 5). **Lionel Verney** enters Rome through it (*LM* 460).

Porta Molina: Mantua's northern gate, between Lago Superiore and Lago di Mezzo. Shelley describes **Hofer**'s Mantuan imprisonment, during which he blessed **Tyrolese** prisoners at the Porta's barracks (*R* 2.59).

Porta Romana: "Roman Gate" is **Florence**'s city gate facing **Rome**. **Cincolo de' Becari** observes people from **Guielmo Lostendardo**'s residence passing through it (*TP* 17).

Porta San Gallo: Northeastern **Florentine** city gate built 1284–1337 (*Florence* 144). Shelley traversed Florence from the gate "to **Schneiderff's Hotel**" October 1842 (*R* 2.133).

Porte: French term meaning "high gate," traditional term for the **Ottoman Empire**'s government; it derives from the elevated palace gate from which justice was dispensed. **Evadne Zaimi**'s "intrigues with **Russia** for the furtherance of her object, excited the jealousy of the Porte" (*LM* 114).

Portlester, Baron of: **Kildare**'s father-in-law, Rowland FitzEustace (Fischer 117). For supporting **Lambert Simnel**, he was forced to resign from his forty-year post as **Irish** treasurer (*PW* 1.286).

Portsmouth: English port ten miles southeast of **Southampton**; it was a major embarkation point for **Europe** in Shelley's day. **Lionel Verney** and **Perdita** travel from Portsmouth to **Greece**, and Verney later returns to the same port alone (*LM* 165, 216). The *Fortunatus*, bringing plague from **Philadelphia**, drifts "towards the harbour" at Portsmouth (*LM* 217). **Jahn Warbeck** suggests that **Madeline De Faro** take **Richard of York**, disguised as her son, to Portsmouth for transportation to Europe (*PW* 1.90). [*Fr1* 210].

Portugal: Southwestern European country bordered by the **Atlantic** and **Spain**. **Hernan De Faro** is "in the service of Portugal"; his reputation "stood foremost among those in the King of Portugal's employ" (*PW* 1.146, 1.207, 2.181). **Miss Jervis** travels through Portugal with the **Cecils** (*F* 73). Shelley wrote biographies of several Portuguese authors for *Italian and Spanish Lives*' third volume.

Posilipo: Hill west of **Naples** where "**Virgil** wrote the *Georgics* and the [*Aeneid*]"; Shelley spells it **Pausilippo** (Clement 261). **Horatio Saville** recovered from his passion for **Lady Lodore** when he "awoke again to life as he looked down from Pausilippo" onto Naples's **Baiae** (*L* 2.173).

Post: **Domodossola** inn where Shelley stayed October 1840 (*R* 1.133).

Potsdam: German town seventeen miles southwest of **Berlin**, **Frederic the Great**'s summer residence; Shelley spells it **Potzdam** (Meras 133). Shelley wanted to visit Potsdam in July 1842 but traveled to **Dresden** instead (*R* 1.230).

Potzdam: See **Potsdam**.

Poynings, Sir Edward (1459–1521): **Ireland**'s Lord Deputy 1494–96. **Henry VII** of **England** sent Poynings and **Doctor Warham** to **Flanders** July 1493 to refute **Perkin Warbeck**'s claim to the throne (Holinshed 3.506). Poynings arrived in Ireland 1494; he forcefully stopped the conspirators and enacted many harsh laws, commonly known as Poynings's Law, the worst of which subordinated Irish **Parliament** to the English Parliament (*DNB*). Poynings is a *Perkin Warbeck* character.

Poyns, Thomas: Yorkist supporter arrested at the 1439 conspiratorial meeting at **Robert Clifford**'s house (*PW* 2.50; Holinshed 3.507).

Poytron, Stephen (d. 1495): Yeoman from Meonstoke, Hampshire, executed 1495 for supporting **Perkin Warbeck**; he is a minor *Perkin Warbeck* character (Arthurson 1, 46, 220; *PW* 1.308).

Pozzi: Dark cells in **Venice**'s **Doge's Palace**'s lower two stories (*MNIT* 335). Shelley describes her September 1842 tour of these dungeons (*R* 2.87).

Prague: Large Czech city 175 miles south of **Berlin**. Shelley records arriving there August 1842 (*R* 1.279). She recounts Prague's history and describes the city's sights (*R* 1.279–280, 2.1–9). See **Altstadt**, **Graben**, **Hradschin**, **Klein Seite**, and **Neustadt**.

Prague, Archbishop of: See **John II**.

Praxitilean: Of or in reference to the **Athenian** sculptor Praxiteles (c. 400–340 B.C.E.), who "created the first monumental nude"; his reputation rests principally on his statue of **Aphrodite** of Knidos (Havelock 3, 48). Alone and depressed in England October 1824, Shelley recorded that "societies of men are numerous—surely there are amiable hearts—even as the marble contains in itself the statue before the Praxitilean hand removes its veil—so are there some whose internal natures fold up a treasure of affection which might make me at least for some brief moments happy? but I am alone!" (*Journals* 484–485). **Lionel Verney** admires a statue by Praxiteles in desolate **Rome** (*LM* 461). The statue is inscribed to Praxiteles, but it is doubtful the work is his (*MROM* 88). Shelley records that the passing years have not been marked with a "Praxitilean hand" on **Lord Lodore**'s face (*L* 1.215). Seeing **Osborne** after many years, **Rupert Falkner** notes "time, sickness, and remorse had used other than Praxitilean art, and had defaced the lines of grace and power which had marked him many years ago" (*F* 287). **Harry Valency** asserts that every element of **Chief Constantine** "reminded you of some Praxitilean shape" (*E* 297).

Prebisch Thor: Large natural rock arch near **Grosse Winterberg** in **Saxon Switzerland**; Shelley spells it **Prebischthor** (*MCON* 458). Shelley viewed it August 1842 (*R* 1.273–274).

Prebischthor: See **Prebisch Thor**.

Presburg, Treaty of: See **Pressburg, Treaty of**.

Presentation of the Virgin: See **Titian**.

Pressburg, Treaty of: Signed 26 December 1805 by **Austria** and **France** after **Napoleon**'s victories at Ulm and Austerlitz. It was severe for Austria; the French empire acquired Austria's **Italian** lands. Shelley mentions this treaty (spelled **Presburg**) as causing Austria to lose the **Tyrol** (*R* 2.42).

Prevesa: Small town on **Epirus**'s southwest coast fifty miles south of **Ioannina** at the Gulf of **Arta**'s entrance; now part of **Greece**, it was in southern **Albania** in Shelley's day. **Dmitri** "had just returned from an expedition beyond Prevesa" when **Katusthius Ziani** visits (*EE* 101).

Prince of Painters: See **Raphael**.

Prince of Poets: See **Shakespeare**.

Prior, Matthew (1664–1721): English poet and renowned diplomat who published *Poems on Several Occasions* (1719). In Prior's *Solomon on the Vanity of the World: A Poem in Three Books* (1708), Solomon considers knowledge, pleasures, and power, successively, concluding that all is vanity and ultimately submitting to God's will. **Lionel Verney** compares **Clara**'s devotion to **Idris** to servant Abra's devotion to Solomon: Clara "went beyond our desires, earnest, diligent, and unwearied,— '**Abra was ready** ere we called her name, / And though we called another, Abra came'" (*LM* 310; Prior 2.362–363). As an epigraph to *Lodore*'s chapter in which Shelley reveals **Lord Lodore**'s liaison with **Theodora Lyzinski**, she quotes: "**Amid two seas**, on one small point of land, / Wearied, uncertain, and amazed, we stand; / On either side our thoughts incessant turn, / Forward we dread, and looking back we mourn" (*L* 1.160; Prior 3.613–616).

Priory: See **Bethlem**.

"Prisoner of Chillon": **Byron**'s dramatic monologue about François Bonivard, 16th-century **Swiss** patriot, published 1816. The speaker describes being imprisoned with his brothers in **Chillon** Castle, where he watches them die and is then released. Shelley read "The Prisoner of Chillon" aloud August 1818 but had copied the poem earlier (*Journals* 131, 225). "**The Swiss Peasant**'s" frame-story narrator possesses "The Prisoner of Chillon" and claims to have read it three times within an hour (*SP* 136).

Procida: **Italian** island between **Naples** and **Ischia**. Shelley viewed it from **Scaricatojo** July 1843 (*R* 2.283).

Procrustes: Greek mythological scoundrel who, living on the road from **Eleusis** to **Athens**, invited travelers to spend the night. If they did not fit in his bed, "he would either stretch them or lop off their extremities until they did"; **Theseus** killed him (Tripp 498). **Lady Cecil** asserts that **Alithea Neville** felt like a traveler Procrustes had caught when she recognized she must alter her own nature and desires to conform to those of her husband (*F* 101).

Procter, Bryan Waller (1787–1874): English lawyer and poet who published under the pseudonym **Barry Cornwall**. Shelley first met him upon her 1823 return to England; she wrote that she found Procter "evidently vain, yet not pretending, and his ill health is for me an interesting circumstance.... Yet after all, except [*Dramatic Scenes, and Other Poems* (1819)] I do not like Procter's style—and, worst of all, have not read much that he has written" (*Letters* 1.384, 1.386–387). Shelley noted November 1823, however, that she had seen Procter "several times and I like him" as such "an enthusiastic admirer" of **PBS** and "moreover gentle & gentlemanly & apparently endued with a true poetic feeling" (*Letters* 1.403–404). In January 1824, Shelley showed Procter a tragedy she had written, and he "offered to help get it produced," but she subsequently abandoned the project (*Journals* 468, 474; Sunstein 255). Procter "served as an intermediary between [Shelley] and those who volunteered to guarantee the publishing expense" of PBS's poems (*Journals* 481; *Letters* 1.386). Shelley seems to have flirted briefly with Procter September 1823–April 1824 (*Journals* 481–482). In September 1824, Shelley "hoped or wished for friendly feeling" from this "Poet—who sought me first . . . Whose gentle manners were pleasing & who seemed to a degree pleased. . . . [A]ssociation, gratitude esteem made me take interest in his long tho' rare visits—they have ceased—it is four months since I have seen him" (*Journals* 481–482). Procter married Anne Skepper October 1824, and, according to Sunstein, since his wife refused to meet Shelley, Procter's and Shelley's interaction ended (*Journals* 482; Sunstein 263). Shelley wrote offhandedly October 1824, "of course I shall never see him again," admitting that this "pains" her (*Letters* 1.452). **Lionel Verney**, concerned over **Adrian**'s health, questions whether his "eyes, those '**channels of the soul**' [have] lost their meaning," a phrase probably derived from "The Broken Heart" in Procter's *Dramatic Scenes* (1819) (*LM* 43; Blumberg 37; Cornwall 27). See R. W. Armour's *Barry Cornwall: A Biography of Bryan Waller Procter* (1935).

***Profession of Eloisa*:** Painting **Marcott Alleyn** plans to create; he thinks visiting convent of **St. S——** will provide "some excellent hints for my picture" (*BMI* 36, 42).

***Promessi sposi*:** Manzoni's *I Promessi sposi* [*The Betrothed*] (1825–27); set in **Milan** and **Bergamo**, it relates the romance between **Lucia** and weaver **Renzo** (assisted by a **Capuchin**, Father **Cristofero** but complicated by **Lombard** lord **Don Rodrigo**) (*DIL* 314). **Innominato**, **Italian** for "Unnamed," is a villain who kidnaps Lucia but then repents; Shelley states that Innominato and Rodrigo represent "the nobility" (*DIL* 314; *R* 2.199). Shelley calls the lovers representatives of "the people," while Father Cristofero represents the "pious clergy" (*R* 2.199). Shelley planned to publish a translation of the novel, but **Murray** was not interested (Sunstein 290). Shelley viewed **Resegone**, "so frequently mentioned by Manzoni in the *Promessi Sposi*" (*R* 1.67). She later states that the novel "is an imitation of the romances of **Walter Scott**" and praises Manzoni's "grandeur of description" and "unity and nobility of purpose" (*R* 2.198).

Prometheus: In **Greek** mythology, divine being whose name means "forethought"; he created the human race out of clay and was its champion (Tripp 499). Prometheus stole fire from the Gods and gave it to humankind, so **Zeus** ordered him to be fastened to a cliff in **Caucasus** and that an eagle peck out his liver each day; it regrew every night. Promethean myth is a recurrent element in many of Shelley's major works and was also a favorite subject of other Romantic writers, such as **PBS** and **Byron**; PBS's *Prometheus Unbound* (1820) is perhaps most famous. Shelley reinvents the Promethean myth in *Frankenstein*, subtitled "or, The Modern Prometheus." **Matilda** compares **Woodville** to Prometheus and suggests that Woodville must experience life's pain to ennoble humankind through art as a poet (*M* 191). **Proserpine** asks **Ino** to sing of "How great Prometheus from **Apollo**'s car / Stole heaven's fire—a God-like gift for Man!" (*P* 33). **Idris** compares her fear of plague, a "gnawing of sleepless expectation of evil, to the vulture that fed on the heart of Prometheus" (*LM* 304). Shelley suggests that **Rupert Falkner** "might have served for a model of Prometheus—the vulture at his heart producing pangs and spasms of physical suffering" (*F* 258). The change from "liver" to "heart" is a variant on the myth found in both Shelleys' works and appears to be their own contribution (Crook 2).

Propontis: See **Marmora**.

Proposta [Proposal]: **Austrian** reform of **Italy**'s *National Dictionary*. **Monti** and **Perticari** wrote *Proposta di alcune correzioni ed aggiunte al vocablario della Crusca* [*Proposal of Corrections and Additions to the Della Crusca Dictionary*] (c. 1816–18), as Shelley notes in her discussion of **Carbonari** (*R* 2.163).

Propylaeum: Greek architectural entrance to sacred enclosures; the most famous is on **Athens**'s **Acropolis**. Shelley notes that the **Brandenburg Gate**'s **Car of Victory** is modeled on it (*R* 1.219).

Proserpine: Shelley records finishing this two-act verse drama, adapted from **Ovid**, 3 April 1820 (*Journals* 316). Shelley was initially unsuccessful in publishing her version of the myth of **Proserpine**'s abduction. Influential editor Alaric Watts rejected the drama 1826, but Shelley placed an altered version in *The Winter's Wreath* (1832), attributed to "the Author of *Frankenstein*" (Sunstein 275). **PBS** contributed two lyrics to his wife's drama, and **Medwin** records the couple's delight in the work (252). The drama's plot maintains most of the widely accepted aspects of Proserpine's myth. **Pluto** takes her when she wanders alone; Shelley glosses over whether she chose to eat or was tricked into eating **pomegranate seeds** that consign her to remain in the Underworld part of each year. Shelley's play focuses upon Proserpine's loving relationship with her mother: **Ceres**'s devotion to her daughter is such that she defies the gods. In view of the recent loss of two of her own children, Shelley's portrayal of the mother-daughter relationship may be autobiographical.

Proserpine: Protagonist of Shelley's *Proserpine*. In **Roman** mythology, Proserpine (called Persephone in **Greek** myth) disobeys the commands of her mother **Ceres** (Demeter in Greek) to wait for her in **Enna**, and **Pluto** (**Hades** in Greek) subsequently abducts her. As she has eaten **pomegranate seeds**, **Jove** (**Zeus** in Greek) rules in favor of Pluto's claim to her and decrees that Proserpine must spend six months of each year in the Underworld. In every version of the myth, Proserpine is resigned to reside in the Underworld part of the year, while her mother mourns and the vegetation dies; when Proserpine returns to the surface, vegetation blooms (Tripp 463–464). **Matilda** compares herself to Proserpine (*M* 164).

Proserpine's Song: First appears in print in *The Winter's Wreath* version.

Proserpine sings two stanzas when her attendants leave her alone (*P* 47; Crook 2). **PBS** composed the verses 1820 specifically for his wife's drama (White 2.565). She asks "Sacred Goddess, Mother Earth" to "Breathe thine influence most divine / On thine own child Proserpine," just as she does on all nature (*P* 47).

Prospero: See *Tempest, The*.

Protectoral Palace: In *The Last Man*, official **London** residence of the elected Protector of England (*LM* 105).

Proteus: In **Greek** mythology, minor sea god who could take several shapes; character in **Homer**'s *Odyssey* (4.410–420, 4.480–490). Shelley describes foreign customs as "never fully understood, Proteus-like" (*R* 2.181).

Protoklepht: **Greek** word meaning "robber leader." **Katusthius Ziani** "proceeded to **Patras** with the Protoklepht" after **Constans Ziani**'s abduction, and Shelley later calls **Dmitri** a Protoklepht (*EE* 106, 112).

Provence: Southeastern **French** region bordering the **Mediterranean** and **Italy**; its people are **Provençal**. **Despina dei Elisei** wants **Charles of Anjou** to "return to Provence, and reign" (*TP* 14). **Stephen Frion** lived in Provence when he worked for **René I** and still has a Provençal accent; various characters call him Provençal (*PW* 1.148–149, 1.183, 1.188, 2.280, 3.8).

Provence, King René of: See **René I**.

Provins: **French** town forty-five miles southeast of **Paris**. The Shelleys stopped there August 1814 (*Journals* 11; *H* 18).

Prussia: Northeastern **European** kingdom (1701–1871) with **Berlin** as its capital; after seizing parts of northern **Germany** and western **Poland** in the 18th and 19th centuries, it was dominant in the German Empire 1871–1919; it was dissolved 1947. Shelley entered Prussia's "frontier" June and again July 1840; she admired schools, currency, and government-managed carriages there but criticized its landscape of "sandy desarts" (*R* 1.16, 1.122, 1.166, 1.207, 1.217, 2.23).

Prussia, King of (1795–1861): Frederick William IV ruled Prussia 1840–61 (Morby 137; *BRHI* 122). Shelley saw **Stolzenfels Castle** and records that it was "restored by the present King of Prussia when Crown Prince" (*R* 1.171). [*R* 1.220].

Prussia, Queen of (1776–1810): Louisa of Mecklenburg-Strelitz, who married **Prussia**'s Frederick William III 1793. Shelley noted her portrait in **Berlin** July 1840 (*R* 1.226; Moskal 193).

Psalms: Biblical book. **Lionel Verney** questions humanity's superiority in a world raging with plague, recalling that "once man was a favourite of the Creator, as the royal psalmist sang, '**God had made him** a little lower than the angels, and had crowned him with glory and honour. God made him to have dominion over the works of his hands, and put all things under his feet'" (*LM* 316). Verney despairs at continuous death among plague survivors: "our name was written 'a little

Psyche

lower than the angels'; and, behold, we were no better than ephemera" (*LM* 398). Shelley adapts these passages from Psalms 8.4–6. Shelley describes **Lord Lodore**'s desire for his wife to turn away from **London** society in favor of a more at-home life with reference to "the Psalmist" who proclaims "**O for the wings** of a dove, that I might flee away and be at rest!" (*L* 1.239; Psalms 55.6). **Rupert Falkner** quotes "**as the hart panteth** for the water brooks" of Psalms when he meets **Mrs. Rivers** (*F* 171; Psalms 42.1–2).

Psyche: See **Cupid**.

Pugnano: Small **Italian** town three miles northwest of Bagni **San Giuliano**. The Shelleys often visited it while the **Williams**es lived there 1821 (*Journals* 360; *Letters* 1.263). Shelley recalls **PBS** standing beneath the shade of "Pugnano's trees" (*Ch* 130). **Euthanasia** passes through Pugnano (*V* 3.207).

Pulci: Once-powerful **Guelph** family of **Florence** mentioned in "**A Tale of the Passions**" (Villani 71, 124; *TP* 4).

Pulci, Bernardo: Shelley wrote Florentine Pulci's necessarily brief biography for *Italian and Spanish Lives*. This eldest of three brothers wrote an elegy for Cosimo de' Medici, "translated the *Eclogues* of **Virgil** into Italian, and wrote other pastoral poetry," but Shelley provides little additional information (*ISPL* 1.167).

Pulci, Luca (d. 1470): Minor Italian poet. Shelley wrote a necessarily brief biography of him for *Italian and Spanish Lives*. She remarks upon Luca's various poetic epistles and two longer poems: "Driadeo d'Amore," a pastoral concerned with mythological fables, and "Ciriffo Calvaneo," which she describes as a "romantic narrative poem, deficient in that interest and poetic excellence necessary to attract readers in the present day" (*ISPL* 1.167).

Pulci, Luigi (1432–1484): Most celebrated of the **Florentine** Pulci brothers; Shelley wrote a necessarily brief biography for *Italian and Spanish Lives*. She introduces the debate over whether Luigi's *Il Morgante* [*Morgante*] (1483) is a burlesque or serious poem and then provides a plot summary and excerpts (*ISPL* 1.168). Shelley admires this romantic narrative poem about **Charlemagne** (*ISPL* 1.179).

Purgatorio: Second part of **Dante**'s *Divina Commedia*, which describes Purgatory as a mountain on which sinners occupy different ledges in succession; the poet travels to the top with **Virgil** as his guide. Dante then arrives in the earthly paradise, where he meets **Beatrice**, who subsequently becomes his guide. Shelley was reading *Purgatorio* August 1819 as she started to write *Matilda* (*Journals* 294). **Matilda** compares her solitary wanderings in Scotland to Dante's *Purgatorio,* using the line "**Ond' era pinta** tutta la mia via"; when Dante enters **Eden**'s earthly paradise and encounters a lady singing in a wooded area near a river, he notes "the flowers that colored all of her pathway" (*M* 158; *Purgatorio* 28.42). Matilda later imagines being united with her father and **Woodville** in heaven: "I pictured to myself a lovely river such as that on whose banks Dante describes Matilda gathering flowers, which ever flows '—**bruna, bruna**, / Sotto l'ombra perpetua, che mai / Raggiar non lascia sole ivi, nè Luna"; these *Purgatorio* lines describe Dante's view of the water across which he sees Matilda picking flowers: "dark, dark, beneath / the never-ending shadows, which allow / no ray of sun or moon to reach those waters" (*M* 205; *Purgatorio* 28.31–33). Shelley noted September 1840, "I have read the *Purgatorio* and ***Paradiso***, with ever new delight.... The pathetic tenderness of the *Purgatorio*... wins its way to the heart" (*R* 1.96). Viewing **Giotto**'s portrait of Dante in the **Tribune** January 1843, Shelley recorded that Dante "himself confesses [pride] in the *Purgatorio*" (*R* 2.158).

Pyramids: Best known examples of this kind of structure, of which the four sides are equilateral triangles extending to a point above a square base, are the Great Pyramids near Giza in **Egypt**, constructed 26th century B.C.E. as tombs for **pharoahs**. *The Last Man*'s narrator finds that some of the **Sibylline** leaves contain writings of "Egyptian hieroglyphics, old as the Pyramids" (*LM* 5).

Pyrennees: Mountain range stretching from the Bay of Biscay eastward to the **Mediterranean**, thus forming **France**'s border with **Spain**. **Horatio Saville** suspects that **Lady Lodore** has gone to "**Bagnères de Bigorre** among the Pyrenees," and **Ethel Villiers** later informs her mother of Horatio's return from the Pyrenees (*L* 3.239, 3.303).

Pythagoras (c. 580–500 B.C.E.): Ancient **Greek** philosopher reputed to have miraculous powers; today he is associated with numerical theories and astronomy. His celebrated teachings include a theory of reincarnation, or "the transmigration of souls," in which the soul "is immortal, a fallen divinity imprisoned in the body as in a tomb" (Howatson 476–77). Having introduced **Virgil**'s discussion of reincarnation in the *Aeneid*, Shelley asserts, "Pythagoras, we are told, remembered many transmigrations of this sort" (*RD* 49).

Pythian maid: Prophetess of the **Delphic oracle** in **Greek** mythology (Tripp 193). **Lionel Verney** wishes for a "Pythian maid" to explain humanity's history when he and three others are the only plague survivors (*LM* 427).

Python: In **Greek** mythology, **Apollo** killed a huge serpent in **Delphi** at an early age and then took over the oracle there (Tripp 61–62). **Proserpine** asks **Ceres** to recount the tale of Apollo's combat with this creature (*P* 29).

Q

Quartezzani: Shelley's spelling of **Villani**'s "Quartigiani," powerful **Lucchese** family involved in the **Castruccio-Uguccione de Faggiuola** plot to take Lucca; after helping Castruccio 1327, they joined a **Florentine** conspiracy against him (Green 52, 97; *V* 3.197). In *Valperga*, Castruccio hears of the plot and executes the conspirators—he actually seized the Quartigiani and executed twenty-two of them (Green 97; *V* 3.221, 3.232).

Quartezzani, Orlando: Based on historical "Lando," conspirator against **Castruccio** in *Valperga* (Crook 3.302).

Quartezzani, Ugo: Based on historical figure, head conspirator in **Florentine** plot to overthrow **Castruccio** in *Valperga* (Crook 3.302).

Quartezzano, Cavaliere Pagano: Historically, Pagano Cristofani was joint commander of **Lucca** with **Castruccio** (Green 97). Castruccio shares his power with Cavaliere, whom he makes consul (*V* 1.231).

Queen: See **Wenceslaus IV** and **Isabeau of Bavaria**.

Queen of Beauty: Statue also called **Venus de' Medici**, sculptor unknown (Moskal 309). Shelley viewed it January 1843 at the **Uffizi**, where it has been since 1677 (*R* 2.152).

Quevedo y Villegas, Francisco Gómez de (1580–1645): Spanish author; Shelley wrote Quevedo's biography for *Italian and Spanish Lives*. He published a selection of poems under pseudonym Bachiller Francisco de la Torre, but many of his works were lost, and his reputation rests upon his prose works; Shelley characterizes his wit as "terse, pointed, bitter, and driven home with an unsparing hand" (*ISPL* 3.277). Shelley disapproves of Quevedo's participation in a 1618 plot to take **Venice** but admiringly asserts, "the vivacity and energy of his works display the unabated vigour of his soul" (*ISPL* 3.272). She records Quevedo's letters of *El Caballero de la Tenaza* [*Knight of the Pincers*] (c. 1606) "are very whimsical," but Quevedo's *Sueños* [*Visions*] (comp. 1605–1622; pub. 1627) are "novel, singular and striking," as well as "full of knowledge of human nature, vivacity, wit and daring imagination"; Shelley records reading *Visions* May 1819 (*ISPL* 3.275–76; *Journals* 262). She was impressed with Quevedo's wit (*Letters* 3.300).

Quirinal: One of **Rome**'s **Seven Hills** and a Roman papal palace (Wall 128). Shelley visited the Quirinal gardens March 1819 (*Journals* 253). **Euthanasia** walks on the Quirinal (*V* 1.205–206). Shelley refers to Rome's 1837 cholera epidemic, during which the pope shut himself in the Quirinal (*R* 2.238).

Quirinus: Roman god, associated with **Quirinal** hill, who disappeared after founding and developing Rome; also later identified with **Romulus** (Tripp 517; Howatson 479). **Valerius** finds all of Rome void, even " 'antient temples where I worshipped Quirinus' " (*Val* 341).

Quito: Ecuador's capital city. **Lionel Verney** records disasters spread throughout the world, including Quito, destroyed by earthquake (*LM* 232).

Quixotic: See **Don Quixote**.

R

Rabelais, Francis (c. 1483–1553): **French** monk who became professor of **Greek**. Shelley wrote Rabelais's biography for *French Lives*. *Great and Inestimable Chronicles of the Grand and Enormous Giant Gargantua* (1532) is no longer considered Rabelais's work, but sequel *Pantagruel* (1532) and *Gargantua* (1534) are undoubtedly his; their burlesque wit and satire ensure his reputation and achieved great success when they appeared. Shelley dismisses accounts of Rabelais's debts and drinking, asserting he was a victim of the common error of confounding a book's contents with its author's life; she admires his narrative and burlesque talents while deploring his grossness (*FL* 1.36).

Rabenau: German village seven miles northwest of **Dresden**. Shelley visited **Pearson** there August 1842 (*R* 1.232–235, 1.239–242). [*R* 1.256–257, 1.261].

Raby, Edwin: Raby family's twelve-year-old heir in *Falkner*.

Raby, Edwin: Elizabeth Falkner's father, who dies at *Falkner*'s beginning.

Raby, Elizabeth: See Falkner, Elizabeth.

Raby, Mrs.: Elizabeth Falkner's aunt in *Falkner*.

Raby, Mrs. Isabella: Elizabeth Falkner's mother in *Falkner*.

Raby, Oswi: Head of *Falkner*'s **Raby** family. Oswi's harsh attitude toward son **Edwin Raby** and his subsequent refusal to help **Elizabeth Falkner** unless she is given wholly into his care are probably based upon **Sir Timothy Shelley**'s attitude toward Shelley and **PFS** after **PBS**'s death.

Racine, Jean (1639–1699): French author. Shelley wrote Racine's biography for *French Lives*. He befriended **Boileau-Despréaux**, **La Fontaine**, and **Molière** before ensuring his own literary reputation as dramatist with *Alex-

andre le grand [*Alexander the Great*] (1665). Shelley asserts that Racine rivals **Corneille** as a dramatist and admires Racine's comedy *Les Plaideurs* (1668) for its satire of lawyers, *Athalie* (1691) as his best work with perfect versification, and *Phèdre* (1677) as the best of his heroic tragedies in its representations of human agony. Shelley also admires *Esther* (1689), a moral historical play suitable for ladies' recitation (*FL* 1.296–328).

Radcliffe, Ann (1764–1823): English Gothic novelist best known for *The Mysteries of Udolpho* (1794), which Shelley read 1815 (*Journals* 669). Shelley read Radcliffe's *The Italian* (1797) November 1814; many of the novel's scenes are set in and around a convent at the top of a mountain and a monastery, and the monks' movements are cast in shadows so as to appear almost supernatural (*Journals* 48). **Lionel Verney** remembers "the dark monk, and floating figures of '*The Italian*'" (*LM* 462).

Radnorshire: Former name of Powys, east central Welsh county bordering England. **Lord Lodore** first meets **Lady Santerre** and her daughter there, and **Ethel Villiers** later finds an advertisement for "a cottage to be let near **Rhyaider Gowy** in Radnorshire" (*L* 1.97, 3.242).

Raffaelle: See **Raphael**.

Ragozzi: **Kissingen** spring containing more iron than the **Pandur**; Shelley drank its water June 1842 (*R* 1.188; *Letters* 3.32).

Rainer: Schwaz innkeeper; Shelley notes he is a **Tyrolese** minstrel with clean rooms (*R* 2.45).

Rakehells, King of: Rogues' leader. **Henry VII** of England mockingly calls **Richard of York** the "King of Rakehells" (*PW* 3.102).

Ram: Zodiac's first sign, more commonly called Aries. **Lionel Verney** notes the constellations' passage "from the short tyranny of watery **Pisces** and the frigid Ram" (*LM* 431).

***Rambles*:** See *Rambles in Germany and Italy, 1840, 1842, and 1843*.

***Rambles in Germany and Italy, 1840, 1842, and 1843*:** Shelley's second book of travel-writing following *History* and her final publication; Edward Moxon brought it out in 1844. Due to financial hardship and to share proceeds with Ferdinando Gatteschi (a poor **Italian** writer whom she had met in **Paris**), Shelley contacted Moxon September 1843 about publishing two volumes recounting the recent **European** tours she had taken with her son and his university friends (Moskal 49; *Letters* 3.93). On 31 June 1840, Shelley accompanied **PFS**, **Defell**, **Ellis**, and **Julian Robinson** to **France**, **Germany**, and Italy, where they spent two months at **Lake Como** (*Journals* 566; Seymour 476–477). When PFS returned from **Milan** to **Cambridge** for exams, Shelley and her maid, **Henry**, traveled to Paris via **Switzerland**, completing this tour October 1840 (Sunstein 350; Seymour 477; *Journals* 568). The second European tour, June 1842–July 1843, included **Austria**, **Belgium**, Germany, Italy, and **Prussia**; **Pearson**, **Knox** (at

359

Shelley's expense), and possibly Ellis accompanied Shelley and PFS (*Letters* 3.29–30; Seymour 482–483; *Journals* 572). Relying on letters, such as those to her aunt **Everina Wollstonecraft**, and journal entries, Shelley wrote a quasi-epistolary travel memoir, with the first volume ready for press January 1844; *Rambles* was published late summer 1844 (Moskal 51; Seymour 489). In *Rambles*, Shelley's extensive commentary on cultural, artistic, literary, and political events accompanies her descriptions of the places she visited, such as **Baden-Baden**, **Berlin**, **Dresden**, **Florence**, **Kissingen**, Milan, Paris, **Prague**, **Rome**, and **Venice**. She nostalgically compares her middle-aged return to Europe, chiefly Italy, with her youthful life there with **PBS**. Shelley also critiques the advice and descriptions offered in popular travel guides of the day, which **Murray** published primarily. In her preface, Shelley refers to these guides ("Sometimes they inform, sometimes they excite curiosity") before alluding to the political aspect of *Rambles*: "in treating of [Italians] my scope grew more serious" (*R* 1.vii). Shelley recounts and supports the push for Italian independence; this serious political stance attracted the attention of reviewers, some of whom deemed such opinions improper for a woman (Moskal 52–53; Seymour 489). Overall, though, *Rambles* was reviewed favorably (Moskal 52–53).

Ramsay, Sir John (d. 1513): Lord of **Bothwell** and **Laird of Balmayne**, **Henry VII**'s informer; he arranged the failed kidnapping plot to take **Perkin Warbeck** 1496 (*DNB*). He opposes **Richard of York** in *Perkin Warbeck*.

Rape of Ganymede: See **Phidias**.

Raphael: Archangel who accompanies Tobias to Media in **apocryphal** book Tobit, which Shelley read March 1820 (*Journals* 633; Tobit 5.1–11.7). **Wilhelmina** claims Raphael announced that her pregnancy would yield the "incarnation of the Holy Spirit," whom she names **Beatrice** (*V* 2.26).

Raphael [Sanzio, Raffaello] (1483–1520): Great **Italian** High Renaissance painter; Shelley calls him **Prince of Painters** and **Raffaelle** (Turner 25.897–908; *R* 1.3, 2.220). She compares **Lady Katherine Gordon**'s appearance to one of Raphael's Madonnas (*PW* 3.256). Shelley viewed his *Cartoons* (c. 1515–16 series of nine tapestries intended to adorn the **Sistine Chapel**) at **Hampton** Court; seeing them increased her anticipation for her trip abroad to see more of his artwork (*R* 1.3; Gowing 563). Shelley praised Raphael paintings she viewed in **Europe**, comparing his *Adoration of the Magi* to his *Transfiguration*, Raphael's last major work, commissioned 1517 and left unfinished at his death (*R* 1.223–224). She cites the **Vatican**'s *Madonna di Foligno* (c. 1512) and **Palazzo Borghese**'s *Descent from the Cross* (Shelley's name for *Deposition* or *Entombment of Christ* [1507]) as Raphael's best work: "These pictures are the triumph of Christian art" (*R* 2.222; *MROM* 273–274). She viewed *Dispute of the Sacrament* (c. 1508), one of four frescoes in the Vatican's Stanza della Segnatura, April 1843 (*MROM* 223; *R* 2.20). In **Berlin** July 1842, Shelley admired Raphael's *Madonna di*

Casa Colonna, which she calls *Virgin and Child* (MCON 340; R 1.220). Shelley saw Raphael's *Madonna di San Sisto* at **Gallery in Dresden** August 1842; this *Sistine Madonna* (1512–14) is "doubtless the most famous single altarpiece of the entire Renaissance" (Schemeckebier 421; R 1.236). The painting was done for San Sisto's Black Friars, hence Shelley's title (Vasari 3.198). Shelley viewed Raphael's *Sposalizio* (c. 1504), calling it "*Marriage of the Virgin*," in **Brera** September 1840: it is "in his first and most chaste style; where beauty of expression and grace of design are more apparent, than when, in later days, his colouring grew more rich, his grouping more artificial" (R 1.110; Vasari 3.132). Shelley points to the **Farnesina** *Galatea* [*The Nymph Galatea*] (c. 1512–14) as exemplifying the excellence of Raphael's later style (R 2.223). [PW 1.8]. See also **Colonna Gallery, Colonna Palace, Cupid, Dante, Farnesina, Fornarina, Greece,** *Hamlet,* **Heliodorus,** *Ion,* **Joseph, Lanzi,** *Magi, Paradise Regained,* **Perugino, Pope Julius II, St. Peter's, Vatican, Wordsworth.**

Ratcliffe, Sir Robert (d. 1495): Lord **Fitzwater**'s cousin who lived disguised as a peasant after the **Battle of Stoke** and is arrested at the 1493 conspiratorial meeting at **Robert Clifford**'s house (PW 2.22–23, 2.50; Holinshed 3.507).

Ravello: Italian village two miles northeast of **Amalfi**. Shelley admired the "picturesque" view from it July 1843 and visited its 11th-century cathedral, built into a hill and dedicated to St. Panteleone (R 2.292–293; Moskal 384; Notestein 236).

Ravenglass: Small English town on **Cumbria**'s coast, thirty miles southwest of **Carlisle**. **Hoskins** is a Ravenglass native (F 138).

Ravenna: **Italian** town on the **Adriatic** forty miles east of **Bologna**. **Byron** lived there with **Teresa Guiccioli** and **Clara Allegra Byron** 1821; **PBS** visited August 1821 (*Journals* 376–377; White 2.306). **Guido della Polenta**, Ravenna's Lord, sees **Henry VII** of **Germany** crowned emperor (V 1.137). **Lionel Verney** is shipwrecked near Ravenna; he wanders through it for three days before becoming delirious (LM 449, 452).

Raymond, Lord: Ambitious character in *The Last Man*. Shelley learned of **Byron**'s death in **Greece** while writing the novel; Raymond is an idealized portrait of her friend (*Journals* 477).

Reading: **Berkshire** town thirty-five miles west of **London**. Lady **Lodore** spends a night there en route to **Newbury**, and **Edward Villiers** successfully traces her journey (L 3.189, 3.233–234, 2.238–239, 3.241).

Reali Uffizi: See **Uffizi Gallery**.

Rebecca at the Well: See **Giorgione**.

"Recollections of Italy": Published anonymously in the January 1824 *London Magazine*, Shelley's short story details the narrator's conversation about **Italy** with **Edmund Malville** as they sit in a **Henley-on-Thames** park (Robinson 375). Robinson suggests that Shelley's October 1823 reference to an article in progress intended for "the

Red Rose

London" may have been "Recollections" (Robinson 375; *Letters* 1.393). When the narrator disparages **Venice**, Malville defends it—"he loved Italy, its soil, and all that it contained, with a strange enthusiasm" (*RI* 25). Malville praises Venice and its sights, then offers favorable impressions of **Lombardy** and **Naples** (*RI* 26–28). He prefers **Tuscany** above all and concludes by describing a journey from **Pisa** to **Vico Pisano**, a trip that Shelley actually made September 1821 with **PBS** and the **Williams**es (*RI* 29–30; *Journals* 380). The story ends with Malville and the narrator attempting to enjoy a boat outing in rainy weather (*RI* 31). Robinson asserts that Malville "presents the author's own recollections of Italy"; the narrator reveals Shelley's negative view of it, as presented in her *Journals* (Robinson 375; Sunstein 160).

Red Rose: See **Lancaster**.

Red Sea: Body of water between **Arabia** and **Africa**. About **Adrian**'s love for **Evadne Zaimi**, **Lionel Verney** suggests "their track would be like the passage of the Red Sea" (*LM* 33). Shelley alludes to the **biblical** story of God parting the Red Sea for Moses and Israelites fleeing **Egypt** (Exodus 14.21–22, 14.30).

Reeve, Henry (1813–1859): British writer who contributed to several periodicals, met **William Godwin** 1831, and became the *Edinburgh Review*'s editor 1855 (*DNB*). Shelley notes that Reeve's version of **St. John Nepomuk** differs from the usual legend and quotes in footnotes a long section, beginning "**During the contests**," from his "**Sketches of Bohemia** and the Sclavonian Provinces of the **Austrian** Empire," published in *Metropolitan Magazine* (1837) (*R* 2.4–6; Moskal 230). She also quotes his description of **Wallenstein**'s palace in **Kleine Seite** from the same text: " '**coiled as it** were around the foot of imperial rock' " (*R* 2.6).

Reformation: Sixteenth-century religious revolution that became the basis for Protestantism; **Luther** and **Huss** led reform in **Europe**, and England's reformation began 1534. Shelley cites the Reformation as the cause for lack of charity in England, footnoting that it forced **Queen Elizabeth** to institute Poor Laws (*R* 2.234).

Regent's cottage: There is no direct record of this place in histories of **Windsor** or its vicinity, but in Shelley's day the term may have applied to the house now known as Royal Lodge. George IV (regent 1811–20) stayed at Royal Lodge, "his private home three miles away [from Windsor Castle] in the **Great Park**," during the 1820s while Windsor Castle was renovated (Hedley 168–169). "**The Mourner**'s" narrator recalls this royal residence's grounds as more accessible to the public during **George III**'s reign (*Mourner* 81).

Regent's Park: Large public park in northwest **London**, laid out 1811 and named in honor of the regent who became George IV 1820 (Cunningham 696). Shelley lived near Regent's Park April 1836–February 1837 (*Journals* xli). **Lady Lodore** rides through it (*L* 3.125).

***Relation of the Death of the Family of the Cenci*:** Translation of an **Italian** manuscript, *Relazione della morte della famiglia cenci seguita in Roma il di 11 Maggio 1599* [*Relation of the Cenci Family's Death in Rome on 11 May 1599*], which the Shelleys obtained from the **Gisbornes** May 1818 (*Journals* 211). This manuscript, "a history of **Beatrice Cenci**, copied from the archives of the Palazzo Cenci at **Rome**," derived from **Muratori**'s *Annali d'Italia* [*Annals of Italy*] (1762–70), is the basis for **PBS**'s *The Cenci* (1819) (*Journals* 211; Curran 40). Shelley copied the manuscript 23 May 1818, and PBS sent a translation to **Peacock** July 1819; both are lost (*Journals* 211). A translation in Shelley's handwriting exists in the Bodleian; it was first printed in the second edition of *The Poetical Works of Percy Bysshe Shelley* (1839–40). The translation opens by blaming Francesco Cenci for events described: he "not only occasioned his own ruin & death but also that of many others and brought down the entire destruction of his house" (C 174). Wealthy Francesco marries "an exceedingly rich lady," with whom he has seven children before her death; he subsequently marries Lucretia Petroni (C 175). *Relation* describes Francesco's crimes, of which "Sodomy was the least and Atheism the greatest" (C 175). His sons attempt to have him executed because he is so cruel—he sent his oldest sons, Giacomo, Cristofero, and Rocco, to Salamanca University but refused to maintain them financially. Francesco's bribery frustrates his sons' pleas to the pope; Francesco is freed from prison and returns home. When the eldest daughter escapes by convincing the pope to marry her to Carlo Gabrielli, Francesco fears his youngest daughter, Beatrice, will act similarly and thus imprisons her in his home (C 181). Beatrice and Lucretia complain about their "misery" to Monsignore Guerra, who agrees to assist with murdering Francesco (C 185–189). When the plan for **banditti** to kidnap Francesco during his journey to La Petrella fails, Beatrice and Lucretia pay Marzio and Olympio a thousand crowns to kill him (C 195). They murder him horrifically 9 September 1598 (C 197–199). Beatrice and Lucretia dispose of the body by throwing it from a balcony so his death will look accidental (C 199). The death is investigated, and Guerra has Olympio assassinated to prevent his confession (C 203). Marzio, who escapes an attempt on his life, confesses, thereby incriminating the Cenci family, who are thus imprisoned at Corte Savelli (C 203). The family suffers torture, especially after Olympio's assassin confesses and Guerra flees. However, the case against them is weak (due to the mitigating circumstance of their father's cruelty); advocates for their defense convince the pope to pardon them, which he plans to do until Paolo Santa Croce commits parricide in **Subiaco** (C 217). After marching through Rome, Giacomo, Lucretia, and Beatrice are decapitated; Bernardo is spared due to his youth (C 229–231). *Relation* is an important source for PBS's *The Cenci* (White 2.91). As Curran points out, it has "far greater value than simply that of enabling us to reconsider the charges of plagiarism lodged for many years so glibly and so speciously against [PBS's] tragedy. The source also gives us an uncommon insight into the workings of the poet's imagination," in that we are able to investigate his departures from the source;

Reliques

Curran details these differences in *Shelley's Cenci; Scorpions Ringed with Fire* (1970) (40–46). This account of the Cenci legend is valuable evidence that Shelley collaborated with PBS on his drama; he used her notes and consulted with her during its composition (Sunstein 164).

Reliques: Medieval to 17th-century ballads, songs, and sonnets that Thomas Percy collected as *Reliques of Ancient English Poetry*, first published 1765 and expanded 1767, 1775, and 1794. It played an important role in the Romantic era's ballad revival. Shelley noted 1834 that **PFS** "does not like any poetry except Percy's Ancient ballads" (*Letters* 2.209). **Dame Barnet** reads *Reliques'* opening ballad, "**Chevy Chase**," to neighborhood children (*Maurice* 62). Dame Barnet also reads from "**Babes in the Wood**," in which an uncle arranges for his niece and nephew to be taken into a wood and killed so the uncle can gain their inheritance (*Maurice* 62). One of the supposed murderers saves the children's lives, leaving them alone to search for help. Cold and hungry, they settle to sleep; squirrels bring nuts to their feet while birds cover them with leaves. After running away from **Eton**, **Horace Neville** "thought of the **Children in the Wood**, of their leafy shroud, gift of the pious robin" (*Mourner* 87; "Babes in the Wood" lines 127–128). As an epigraph to the *Perkin Warbeck* chapter in which **Stephen Frion** first appears, Shelley quotes an "Old Ballad," actually Percy's "Sir Aldingar": "**Our king he kept** a false stewarde, / Sir Aldingar they him call; / A falser stewarde than he was one, / Servde not in bower nor hall" (*PW* 1.140; *Reliques* 2.9.1–4). As an epigraph to the chapter in which Frion imprisons **Richard of York**, Shelley quotes the opening of "Gilderoy": "**Gilderoy was** a bonny boy, / Had roses tull his shoone; / His stockings were of silken soy, / With garters hanging doon" (*PW* 1.158; *Reliques* 1.12.1–4). As an epigraph to the chapter wherein **Robert Clifford**'s fascination with **Monina De Faro** grows, Shelley quotes lines beginning " '**His father was** a right good lord' " from "**The Heir of Lynne**" (*PW* 2.1; *Reliques* 2.5.5–12). As a first epigraph to the chapter in which Richard meets **Jane Shore**, Shelley quotes from Percy's "**Ballad of Jane Shore**": " '**So love did vanish** with my state, / Which now my soul repents too late; / Then, maids and wives, in time amend, / For love and beauty will have end' " (*PW* 2.130; *Reliques* 2.26.101–102, 149–150). As an epigraph to the chapter in which Richard and loyal followers take refuge at **Beaulieu**, Shelley quotes from "Adam Bell, Clym of the Clough, and William of Cloudesley": " '**He might have dwelt** in green forest, / Under the shadows green; / And have kept both him and us at rest, / Out of all trouble and teen' " (*PW* 3.150; *Reliques* 1.1.189–192).

Rembrandt van Rijn (1606–1669): **Dutch** Baroque artist. Shelley admired his portrait of **Duke Adolph of Gueldres** July 1840; Moskal identifies the painting as *Samson Threatening His Father-in-Law* (*R* 1.220; Moskal 189).

René I (1409–1480): Duke of Anjou and **Provence** and Count of **Piedmont**, as well as **Naples**'s titular king 1435–42 and **Margaret of Anjou**'s father. **Stephen Frion**'s illustrious career began when he copied poetry for René's court (*PW* 1.149, 1.151).

Renzo: See *Promessi sposi*.

Resegone: Italian mountain with **Lecco** at its base (*BSWI* 493). Shelley describes beautiful mountainous scenery near **Varenna**, specifically mentioning Resegone (the highest peak); **Manzoni** frequently refers to it in *Promessi Sposi* (*R* 1.67).

Reuss: Swiss river emptying into **Lake Lucerne**. Its water is deep green and "exceedingly rapid," with several falls, which the Shelleys sailed over 1814 (*H* 57). **Alphonse Frankenstein** finds poor, mournful **Caroline Frankenstein** in a house near the Reuss (*Fr1* 63; *Fr3* 38). Shelley's horse nearly washed away in the Reuss en route to **Altorf** October 1840 (*R* 1.152).

Reveley, Henry (c. 1788–1875): **Maria Gisborne** and her first husband's only son. "[A]n engineer trained by the famous John Rennie," he was "a remarkably submissive son" (Sunstein 154). The Shelleys first met Reveley 1819; Shelley wrote somewhat sarcastically that he "is the pattern of good boys. . . . [H]e is only thirty years of age and always does as he is bid," while conceding he "is very clever" (*Letters* 1.104). PBS was intrigued by Reveley's plans to build a steamboat, "which he hoped would revolutionize **Mediterranean** shipping," and joined in 1819 plans with enthusiasm, obtaining finances for the project, lost October 1820 due to technical difficulties (*Letters* 1.116–117; Sunstein 154; White 2.16–17, 2.164–165; Holmes 527). Reveley purportedly proposed marriage to **Claire Clairmont** September 1819 and did not share in the Gisbornes' estrangement from the Shelleys, for he visited them October 1820 and renewed his friendship with PBS thereafter (*Letters* 1.160; *Journals* 336; *Clairmont Correspondence* 1.469). Reveley bought a boat from **Leghorn** April 1821 and sailed with PBS at Bagni **San Giuliano** May 1821 (*Journals* 364–365). Reveley married 1824, then moved to Capetown, South **Africa**, before becoming the first architect and engineer in Australia, where he settled; little is known about his life after 1838 until his death in England (Clairmont, *Journals* 468–470; Crook 2). See his biographical sketch in Appendix C of Claire Clairmont's *Journals*.

"Review of *1572 Chronique du Temps de Charles IX*": Shelley's favorable review of **Prosper Mérimée**'s *Chronicle of the Times of Charles the Ninth* (1829) appeared in the 13 October 1830 *Westminster Review*. She compliments his earlier *Clara Gazul* (1825) and praises *Chronicle* (*Rev 1572* 495). This review is brief and gives several excerpts, with scant contextualization.

"Review of *Cloudesley; A Tale*": Shelley's unsolicited review of **William Godwin**'s novel *Cloudesley* (1830) appeared in the 27 May 1830 *Blackwood's Magazine* (Sunstein 295). Shelley praises the novel, mentions her father's prior three novels, compliments the didactic writing genre, and applauds her father's genius: "While other writers represent manners rather than passions, or passions at once vague and incomplete, he conceives, in its entireness, the living picture of an event with all its adjuncts; he sets it down in its vivid reality: no part is dim, no part is tame" (*RevC* 711).

"Review of *The Bravo; a Venetian Story*": Shelley's review of **James Fenimore Cooper**'s *The Bravo; a Venetian Story* (1831) appeared in the 16 January 1832 *Westminster Review*. Shelley notes Cooper's ability to describe effectively the **American** frontier and its colorful figures, then demonstrates that this talent is lacking in his attempt to paint **Venetian** life. She specifically criticizes *Bravo*'s dialogue and melodrama (*RevB* 191). The *Westminster Review*'s editor disliked Shelley's original complimentary conclusion, so she "inserted one of his suggested criticisms," which was a warning to Cooper not to stray from accustomed subjects and settings (Sunstein 315).

"Review of *The English in Italy*": Shelley's review of three works: Constantine Henry Phipps, first Marquis of Normanby's *The English in Italy* (1826), Charlotte Ann Eaton's *Continental Adventures* (1826), and **Jameson**'s *Diary of an Ennuyée* (1826). Shelley contemplated placing the review in *New Monthly Magazine*, but it appeared in the October 1826 *Westminster Review* (*Letters* 1.527). Shelley finds Normanby's book excellently planned, summarizes the stories constituting *The English in Italy*, and points to "Zingari" as "perhaps the best part of the book" (*RevEng* 327–328, 331). She recommends the book highly (*RevEng* 328). Shelley finds *Continental Adventures* "a worse plan" because "[i]t mixes real scenes with fictitious ones, not in the style of the *English in Italy*" but as a "common novel" (*RevEng* 337). Shelley also criticizes *Diary* because, as a fictional tale presented as fact, it "disturbs and confuses the reader" (*RevLoves* 474; *RevEng* 339). Shelley found it, however, to be "written with great spirit and great enthusiasm" (*RevEng* 340). About a year after publishing this review, Shelley cited it as a good example of her critical writing; she "received a good many Compliments about it" (*Letters* 2.115).

"Review of *The Loves of the Poets*": Shelley's review of **Jameson**'s *The Loves of the Poets* (1829) appeared in the October 1829 *Westminster Review* (*Letters* 2.85). Shelley describes the work, which presents various poets' amorous relationships—such as **Petrarch**'s with Laura—and asserts that "[p]erhaps the most interesting portion . . . is that dedicated to the commemoration of conjugal poetry—the poets being for the most part women" (*RevLoves* 475). Shelley uses Jameson's text for her own reflections on poetry and love; she writes two paragraphs about mourning, declaring that a "woman's love is tenderness, and may wed itself to the lost and dead" (*RevLoves* 476). Shelley criticizes Jameson for omitting Classical poets and fictionalizing accounts of contemporary, unnamed poets, but the review seems favorable overall.

Revolt of Islam, The: Poem **PBS** composed and published 1817, originally titled *Laon and Cythna; or The Revolution of the Golden City* and dedicated to Shelley with fourteen stanzas of verse, in which he calls her "Child of love and light" and "mine own heart's home" (*Journals* 167, 181; White 1.527–533; "Revolt" line 9, 2). He revised the poem to lessen its emphasis upon incest and its attacks upon religion before reissuing it as *The Revolt of Islam* (1818) (*Journals* 187; White 1.548–552). Shelley uses lines from it to describe **Monina De Faro**'s beauty: " 'sweet lips like roses, / With their own fragrance pale, which Spring but half uncloses' " (*PW* 2.157; PBS 6.33.8–9). As an epigraph to *Perkin Warbeck*'s chapter in which **Richard of York** and his wife travel to **Ireland**, Shelley quotes: "**One moment** these were heard and seen; another / Past, and the two who stood beneath that night, / Each only heard, or saw, or felt the other" (*PW* 3.20; PBS 6.24.1–3).

Revolution of 1830: French revolution organized by Adolphe Thiers in response to the July Ordinances, which censored the press, dissolved the Chamber of Deputies, and changed election laws. This revolution resulted in Charles X's abdication and Louis Philippe I's ascension (Kinder 2.49). Shelley criticizes French commoners' behavior and attributes to this revolution their loss "of that grace of manner which once distinguished them" (*R* 1.142–143, 2.249).

Revolutionary War: Fought 1775–83, resulting in **America**'s independence from Britain; Shelley calls it the **American war**, compares it to problems in **Italy**, and mentions the **Hessians** involved in it (*R* 1.203).

Reynolds, Sir Joshua (1723–1792): First president of the Royal Academy and leading 18th-century English portrait painter. Nineteenth-century art critics admired his *Discourses* (1769–90), lectures given at the Royal Academy supporting art's traditional values. Shelley went "to an exhibit of Reynolds's paintings" in **London** 1813 (Sunstein 58). She suggests that a Reynolds canvas depicting a beautiful orphan would always do more justice to **Elizabeth Falkner** than her pen could (*F* 29). Shelley recalls "Sir Joshua Reynolds, in his Lectures, mentions the boldness of [**Rubens**] in enveloping the dead body with a white cloth" (*R* 1.159). Discussing Rubens's *Descent from the Cross*, Reynolds notes "the greatest peculiarity of this composition is the contrivance of the white sheet, on which the body of Jesus lies. . . . [N]one but great colourists can venture to paint pure white linen near flesh"; Reynolds's discussion is actually located in *A Journey to Flanders and Holland* (1781) (280–281).

Rheinfelden: Swiss Rhine port between **Laufenburg** and **Basle** (*BSWI* 22). The Shelleys slept there August 1814 (*Journals* 21; *H* 59).

Rhine: River rising in the **Swiss Alps** and forming part of Switzerland's and **France**'s borders with **Germany**, then flowing north through Germany into **Holland**, entering the **North Sea** at **Rotterdam**. Shelley thought that "the river is exceedingly beautiful: the waves break on the rocks and the decents [sic] are steep and rapid" August 1814 (*Journals* 20). *History* records sailing "down the castled Rhine" (*H* v). Desperate for funds in Switzerland, the Shelleys saved money by returning to England along the Rhine, which was far cheaper than traveling by land; they departed from **Loffenburgh** August 1814 (*H* 54–55). The river journey was difficult, but Shelley admired the scenery, praising **Byron**'s description of it in Canto 3 of *Childe Harold's Pilgrimage*, and calling "this part of the Rhine ... the loveliest paradise on earth" (*H* 56, 62–63, 68–69). **Victor Frankenstein** and **Henry Clerval** journey from **Strasbourg** to Rotterdam on the Rhine (*Fr1* 181; *Fr3* 132). The **Villiers**es travel it en route to **Naples** (*L* 2.167). **Elizabeth Falkner** and **Rupert Falkner** return to England along the same Rhine route (from **Basle** to Rotterdam) the Shelleys took (*F* 82). Shelley again passed along the "blue mountain river, brawling and foaming among rocks" by steamer from **Coblentz** to **Mainz** 1840 (*R* 1.48, 1.27). She traveled along the Rhine from **Cologne** to Coblentz, expressing her desire to explore its banks further, June 1842 (*R* 1.167, 1.170–171).

Rhône: **Swiss** river flowing through **Lake Geneva** and **Lyons** to **Marseilles** and into the **Mediterranean**. Shelley compares blue Rhône waters to green **Reuss** waters (*H* 57). She suggests that hiking **Mont Salève** would provide a rewarding "view of the course of the Rhône" (*H* 103). **Victor Frankenstein** longs "to see once more the blue lake and rapid Rhône, that had been so dear to me in early childhood" and later tracks the **Creature** along it (*Fr1* 208, 227; *Fr3* 154, 169). **Elizabeth Falkner** and **Rupert Falkner** travel the Rhône from Marseilles (*F* 76). Shelley recorded "our road now lay along the valley of the Rhône, more picturesque far than the valley of the **Rhine** near **Coire**" October 1840 (*R* 1.137, 1.141).

Rhyaider Gowy: Shelley's name for a Welsh village in *Lodore*; she could be referring to **Radnorshire**'s Rhyader, twenty-five miles southeast of Aberystwyth, which **PBS** stayed near July 1811 (White 1.145–148). **Lord Lodore** travels there after returning from **Europe** (*L* 1.97). He meets **Lady Santerre** and her daughter there and marries **Lady Lodore** in Rhyaider Gowy's parish church (*L* 1.113). Lady Lodore intends to return to Rhyaider Gowy when she determines to leave **London** forever; **Ethel Villiers** finds an advertisement for a cottage there in Lady Lodore's London house, so **Edward Villiers** sets out to search for Lady Lodore there (*L* 3.151, 3.242).

Rialto: Originally name for **Venetian** islands, Rialto now refers to Venice's main market district, settled in the 7th century and formerly called **Rivo Alto**. Ponte di Rialto, the shop-lined bridge Antonio da Ponte built 1588–91, crosses **Canale Grande** and leads into the Rialto's markets (Honour 202). The Shelleys' October 1818 Canale Grande hotel offered a view of the Rialto bridge (Sunstein 160). **Edmund Malville** advises the narrator of "**Recollections of Italy**" to ignore Venice's defects, such as the fish market's smell in the Rialto, and to focus instead on "the simple beauty of the Rialto's single arch" (*RI* 26–27). In September 1842, Shelley reminisced about her time in Venice with **PBS** 1818: "Then I saw, as now I see, the bridge of the Rialto spanning the canal" (*R* 2.81). She also mentions that **Faliero**, **Candiano**, and **Dandolo** built the district (*R* 2.114).

Ricardo el Muchacho: See **Richard of York**.

Ricci, Luigi (1805–1859): Italian opera composer. Shelley saw Ricci's

Chi dura Vince; overro La luna di miel [*He who Endures Wins; or, the Honeymoon*] (1834) in **Venice** October 1842 (*R* 2.129).

Ricciardo: Ruggieri dei Antelminelli's **Ghibelline** companion and friend in *Valperga*. Also **Messer Tommaso de' Manelli**'s son in "**A Tale of the Passions**"; **Monna Gegia de' Becari** confuses **Ricciardo de' Rossini** with this Ricciardo.

***Richard II*:** **Shakespeare**'s tragedy, first published 1597, and probably one of the history plays the Shelleys read April 1819 (*Journals* 259). It records Richard's fall. Bolingbroke, later Henry IV, challenges Richard's misrule and takes the throne, disrupting the natural order. After Richard is murdered through misinterpretation of Bolingbroke's orders, Bolingbroke plans to go on a crusade. As an epigraph to the *Perkin Warbeck* chapter in which Shelley presents **Lord Lincoln**'s history, she quotes a passage in which Hotspur informs Bolingbroke that Richard has taken refuge and will not yield: "'**Yes, my good Lord**, / It doth contain a king; King Richard lies / Within the limits of yon lime and stone'" (*PW* 1.29; Shakespeare 3.3.24–26). As an epigraph to the novel's chapter in which **Richard of York** is wounded in battle at **Waterford**, Shelley uses a line indicative of Shakespeare's Richard II's cold ambition: "'**Now for our Irish wars**'" (*PW* 3.26; Shakespeare 2.1.155). As second epigraph to the chapter in which Richard arrives in **Cornwall** to limited support, Shelley draws from a passage in which Shakespeare's Richard, despite returning from **Ireland** with only limited support, reminds himself he is nonetheless England's ruler: "'**Am I not king**? / Awake, thou coward Majesty! thou sleepest. / Is not the king's name forty thousand names?'" (*PW* 3.72; Shakespeare 3.2.83–85). As an epigraph to the chapter in which Richard leads troops to attack **Yeovil**, Shelley draws from the Earl of Salisbury's speech bemoaning Richard II's downfall while witnessing his troops' desertion: "'**Ah! Richard**, with the eyes of heavy mind, / I see thy glory, like a shooting star, / Fall to the base earth from the firmament'" (*PW* 3.120; Shakespeare 2.4.18–20). **Lady Lodore** considers that her whole life will alter as she prepares to leave her fortune to her daughter: "'**I am too old** to fawn upon a nurse, / Too far in years to be a pupil now,'" but Shelley points out the change in circumstances will not necessitate removal to a foreign country where "'**My native English**, now I must forego,'" although her everyday language will alter when the "tongue becomes '**an unstrung viol**, or a harp, / . . . put into his hands, / That knows no touch to tune the harmony'" (*L* 3.165–166). Thomas Mowbray speaks these lines upon learning of his lifetime banishment from England (Shakespeare 1.3.159–165, 170–173).

***Richard III*:** Historical drama **Shakespeare** wrote 1592–93 and published 1597. It recounts **Richard III**'s bloody rise to power and his death at **Henry VII**'s hands. Shelley read it August 1814, and **PBS** read it aloud August 1818; *Richard III* was an important source for *Perkin Warbeck* (*Journals* 20, 222). As an epigraph to the novel's chapter introducing **Elizabeth of York**'s discontent in her marriage, Shelley quotes from a passage in which

Richard III (1452–1485)

newly widowed Queen Elizabeth bemoans her husband's loss: " **'Small joy have I** in being England's Queen' " (*PW* 1.50; Shakespeare 1.3.110). As a second epigraph to the chapter in which **Elizabeth Woodville** dies, Shelley quotes from Queen Margaret's speech: " **'Long die thy** happy days before thy death; / And, after many lengthened hours of grief, / Die neither mother, wife, nor England's queen!' " (*PW* 1.311; Shakespeare 1.3.206–208). Shelley describes noble friends accompanying the **Earl of Warwick** to **St. Paul's** under Henry's orders as " **'These cloudy princes**, and heart-sorrowing peers,' " a line adapted from Buckingham's speech (*PW* 1.129; Shakespeare 2.2.112–114). As an epigraph to the chapter in which **Richard of York** breaks into the **Tower** to visit Warwick, Shelley takes a line that Shakespeare's young Prince Edward speaks in response to Richard III informing him he is to reside in the Tower: " **'I do not like** the Tower, of any place' " (*PW* 2.89; Shakespeare 3.1.68). **Lady Lodore** feels a renewed delight after her decision to alleviate her daughter's poverty by sacrificing herself: "where her ennui, her repinings, her despair? **'In the deep bosom** of the ocean buried!' " quoting a line from the opening soliloquy (*L* 3.134; Shakespeare 1.1.3–4).

Richard III (1452–1485): Duke of Gloucester and king of England from 1483; he died at **Bosworth**, as Shelley recounts in *Perkin Warbeck* (*DNB*).

Richard of York: Also known as **Richard Plantagenet**, the hope of the **White Rose**, Duke of York, **Ricardo El Muchacho** (his **Spanish** nickname meaning "Richard the boy"), and **Perkin Warbeck**; *Perkin Warbeck*'s protagonist is **Edward IV**'s son, and the rightful English king. Modern historians accept that the historical Warbeck was an imposter (Sunstein 299).

Richford, William: Yorkist supporter arrested at the 1493 conspiratorial meeting at **Robert Clifford**'s house (*PW* 2.50; Holinshed 3.507).

Richmond: English town in **Yorkshire** eleven miles southwest of Darlington. **Matilda**'s family mansion is situated nearby, site of her parents' "youthful loves" (*M* 156, 166–167). Her father confesses his incestuous desire there.

Richmond: English town six miles east of **Egham**. **Henry VII**'s first palace at **Shene** burned down 1498, so near *Perkin Warbeck*'s beginning he holds council with chief supporters at newly constructed Richmond Palace, an example of Shelley's revision of historical dates (*PW* 1.122). Henry is "absent inspecting his new palace at Richmond" 1499 when his wife and **Lady Katherine Gordon** visit **Richard of York** in the **Tower** (*PW* 3.330). **Ethel Villiers** and her aunt move from **London** to Richmond, where **Edward Villiers** "came nearly every day" (*L* 2.82, 2.114). Shelley spent two months there before departing for **Europe** 1840 (*R* 1.2–3; *Journals* 564). [*L* 2.120, 2.147, 2.158].

Richmond, Countess of (1443–1509): Lady Margaret Beaufort, mother of **Henry VII** of England (*DNB*). She arranges Henry's marriage to **Elizabeth of York** and lives with

Elizabeth Woodville at **Winchester** in *Perkin Warbeck*.

Richmond, Earl of: Henry VII's hereditary title before his 1485 proclamation as England's monarch after **Bosworth Field**. Shelley calls Henry both Earl of Richmond and simply "Richmond" (*PW* 2.200, 3.111).

"Rime of the Ancient Mariner, The": Samuel Taylor **Coleridge**'s well-known poem, first printed in *Lyrical Ballads*' 1798 edition; eight-year-old Shelley heard him recite it to **William Godwin** (Sunstein 40). Shelley frequently alludes to the poem in her works and bases *Frankenstein*'s frame structure on it; **Robert Walton** mentions the poem explicitly: "I am going to unexplored regions, to '**the land of mist** and snow;' but I shall kill no albatross, therefore, do not be alarmed for my safety, or if I should come back to you as worn and woful [*sic*] as the 'Ancient Mariner'" (*Fr1* 55; *Fr3* 30; Coleridge line 49). **Victor Frankenstein** interrupts Walton's journey with a tale, just as the Mariner interrupts Coleridge's wedding guest. As the wedding guest does, Walton learns from another's experiences and proceeds on his way a wiser man. Victor's pursuit of knowledge at all costs parallels the Mariner's voyage and his sin in killing the albatross. After he gives the **Creature** life and subsequently flees in horror, Victor walks all night and uses lines from the poem to describe himself: "**Like one who**, on a lonely road, / Doth walk in fear and dread, / And, having once turned round, walks on, / And turns no more his head; / Because he knows a frightful fiend / Doth close behind him tread" (*Fr1* 88; *Fr3* 59; Coleridge lines 446–451). Describing **Richard of York**'s escape from his **London** imprisonment, Shelley notes it was in "the '**leafy month of June**'" (*PW* 3.243; Coleridge line 370). As "**Transformation**'s" epigraph, Shelley quotes the Mariner telling his story and how he subsequently wanders over earth retelling it, lines beginning "**Forthwith this frame** of mine was wrench'd / With a woful agony" (*Trans* 121; Coleridge lines 578–585). "Transformation's" narrator insists on the veracity of the Mariner's statement (*Trans* 121). Shelley quotes Coleridge's poem to describe the environment when voyaging to islands near **Venice**; she imagined her party "'**The first that ever** burst / Into that silent sea'" (*R* 2.101; Coleridge line 105). [*M* 187].

Rimini: Italian port sixty-five miles northwest of **Ancona**. Shelley implies that **Castruccio** passes through it en route to **Este** (*V* 1.42).

Rinaldo: See *Gerusalemme Liberata*.

Rio, Alexis-François (1797–1874): **French** art critic and author of *De la Poèsie chrètienne dans son principe, dans sa matière et dans ses formes* [*The Poetry of Christian Art, its Principles, Matter and Forms*] (1836), which Shelley references repeatedly in *Rambles* (*R* 1.154, 1.237, 1.245, 2.140, 2.152). Shelley toured **Rome**'s and **Dresden**'s galleries with Rio, and she directly quotes his assessment of art, occasionally in footnotes (*R* 2.93, 2.146; *Letters* 3.37, 3.62, 3.68–69). Moskal discusses Rio's influence on Shelley and provides citations for the long quotations beginning "'**It presents** the imposing seriousness'" and "'The compunction of man's heart'" (Moskal 50–51, 279, 305).

Ripafrata: See **Ripafratta**.

Ripafratta: In 1820, village on the **Lucca-Tuscany** border five miles southwest of Lucca, on the **Serchio**; Shelley passed through Lucca August 1820 (Clairmont, *Journals* 169). Shelley spells it **Ripafrata** when the **Pisan** governor secretly plots "to advance in a hostile manner" there against **Castruccio** (*V* 3.198). **Euthanasia** passes through it (*V* 3.207).

Ripamonti, Giuseppe (1573–1643): **Italian** historian whose *Historia ecclesial mediolanensis* [*Ecclesiastical History of Milan*] (1617–25) and *Historiarum patriae in continationem Tristani Calchi libri XXII* [*National History in Continuation of Tristani Calchi's Book 22*] (1641–43) provide Federigo **Borromeo**'s biography. Shelley relates that **Manzoni** based *Promessi sposi* on Ripamonti's historical accounts, which include **Innominato** and Borromeo's life (*R* 2.198). Ripamonti's *De peste quae fuit anno 1630* [*The Plague or Ruin of the Year 1630*] (1641) was Manzoni's source for *Promessi* (Petronio 4.563).

Risorgimento: Movement 1842–61 to unify **Italy** (*DMIH* 360). Shelley recounts its history in *Rambles* (*R* 2.161–181, 2.190–210).

Riva: Italian city at **Lago di Garda**'s northern tip. Shelley arrived there September 1842 (*R* 2.68, 2.72).

Rivers, Alithea: See **Neville, Alithea**.

Rivers, Captain: Alithea Neville's father in *Falkner*.

Rivers, Earl of (c. 1442–1483): Anthony Woodville (**Elizabeth Woodville**'s brother), second Earl of Rivers, fought on both sides in the **Wars of the Roses**. He became **Edward V**'s protector; **Richard III** executed him (*DNB*). He fights at **Loxa** then dies in **Brittany**; **Thomas Thwaites** wants to avenge his death (*PW* 1.211, 2.22).

Rivers, Mrs.: Alithea **Neville**'s idealized mother and maternal figure for **Rupert Falkner** in *Falkner*.

Rivo Alto: See **Rialto**.

Robert le Diable: See **Meyerbeer**.

Robert the Bruce (1274–1329): King Robert I of Scotland. **James IV** tells **Richard of York** stories about Robert awarding **Lord Huntley** his lands (*PW* 2.240, 2.248).

Robert's Hotel: **Calais** hotel; both **Murray** and **Starke** list it (*MCON* 102; *STIE* 469). Shelley enjoyed staying there June 1840 (*R* 1.5).

Robin Hood: Legendary English outlaw who robbed wealthy, authoritative people and gave the poor the spoils. Martin Parker's *True Tale of Robin Hood* appeared 1632. **Jonson**'s *The Sad Shepherd* (1641), which the Shelleys read 1819, is subtitled "A Tale of Robin Hood" (*Journals* 656). **Henry Clerval** composes plays about Robin Hood (*Fr1* 66). **Robert Clifford** asks **Clim of the Lyn** to track their way through **New Forest**, but Clim demands food, since "a thirty miles ride since matins, his fast unbroken, would have made Robin Hood a laggard" (*PW* 3.139).

Robinson, Isabel (1810–1869): "Dark, pretty with large dark eyes & hair curled in the neck," Isabel "had become pregnant by a lover who could not or would not marry her" 1826 when Shelley first met her and lent her assistance (Sunstein 273; *Letters* 1.540, 2.11). Shelley assisted Isabel in hiding her pregnancy from her family, and Isabel put the baby out to nurse; her family seemingly never learned the true circumstances of Adeline's birth, and Adeline's father may possibly have been an **American** adventurer, William Grenville Graham (Sunstein 273; Bennett, *Mary Diana Dods* 255). Shelley stayed with the Robinsons February 1827, and Isabel later told Shelley of July 1827 rumors **Jane Williams** circulated about Shelley's shortcomings as a wife (*Journals* 502). Shelley and Isabel went to Arundel together July–September 1827; there, Shelley nursed Isabel through severe asthma, marking Isabel's "matchless sufferings": they hatched an elaborate plan that would allow Isabel to reclaim and live with her child (Sunstein 280–281; *Journals* 503–504). The plan was successfully completed: **Dods** became "Mr. Sholto Douglas" and eloped to **Dieppe** with Isabel October 1827, Shelley accompanying them for a few days—Shelley's *Letters* detail their plan (Sunstein 280, 283; *Letters* 1.556–575, 2.7–8, 2.12–13; Bennett, *Mary Diana Dods* 26, 74–85, 245–252). In **Paris**, Isabel became "Mrs. Douglas," and she and Dods successfully masqueraded as husband and wife (Sunstein 283). Shelley visited them April–June 1828 but was uncomfortable with the couple's masquerade; Isabel played the "heartless coquette" in preparation for her planned separation from her "husband" after two years (*Journals* 507–508; Sunstein 287). After Dods's death, Isabel returned to **London** 1830 but was "no longer fascinating, and indifferent" to Shelley—she no longer needed Shelley's assistance (Sunstein 309). Sunstein suggests Shelley wrote "**A Night Scene**" for Isabel, but their former intimacy seems to have dissolved at this time (309). After 1840, Isabel lived in **Italy** with Reverend William Falkner as her husband until her death (Sunstein 446). See Betty T. Bennett's *Mary Diana Dods, A Gentleman and a Scholar* (1991) for a full account of the Robinson-Douglas affair.

Robinson, Julia: Shelley knew the Robinson family by 1827; she records visiting them February 1828, and Julia became a good friend while Shelley lived in **London** in the 1830s (*Journals* 506–507). Shelley took Julia with her to visit **Isabel Robinson** in **Paris** April 1828, and they stayed together in **Hastings** June and July 1828; when Julia fell ill in August, Shelley took her back to London and stayed with her until year's end (*Journals* 508; Sunstein 289, 291). Julia was "in love with a socially prominent Chester man" 1829, and Shelley assisted their relationship without passing judgment (Sunstein 305; *Journals* 514, 520–521). The two were very close: Julia spent "some weeks" with Shelley March 1833, and they visited Putney together September 1833 (*Journals* 529–533; Sunstein 319, 322). Julia went to **Brussels** December 1834 for two years, but the women reunited for an 1836 **Brighton** visit before Julia went to **Ireland** (*Journals* 541, 550; Sunstein 334). In December 1837, Shelley was "happy in the generosity, fidelity & inexpressive tenderness & sweetness of [Julia] who, tho' absent, does not forget" (*Journals* 551). Julia returned to live with Shelley 1838 and nursed her during a nervous illness March 1839, but Shelley seems to have felt financially burdened by both Julia and **Rosa Beauclerk** by this time; they returned to their father's house 1840 (*Journals* 563; Sunstein 340–341). Shelley took Julia to one of **Rogers**'s breakfasts February 1840 but broke their friendship January 1841 after Julia told **Claire Clairmont** "she and her sisters had given up brilliant society" for Shelley (Sunstein 339, 354). As Shelley noted in an October 1842 letter, such a statement "utterly prevents my ever associating with [Julia] again on terms of friendship—poor thing—what benefit can she see in covering the truth with false tinsel—one cannot guess—but it is nature with some people" (*Letters* 3.41).

Robinson, Julian (1818–1899): Joshua Robinson's son who attended **Cambridge** with **PFS**, became a chaplain, married Harriet, "a girl with some money," January 1844 and left for **India** 1845 (*Journals* 507; Sunstein 279; *Letters* 3.81). Julian met Shelley and her son in **Paris** June 1840 and accompanied them through **Germany** to **Como** on the journey described in *Rambles*; Shelley does not refer to Julian by name (Sunstein 349; *Letters* 2.346, 3.1; *R* 1.1, 1.146). Julian may have written the account of "the perilous journey" from **Milan** to **Lucerne** undertaken by PFS and his friends (*R* 1.146-152).

Robinson, Rosa Matilda: See **Beauclerk, Rosa**.

***Robinson Crusoe*:** See **Defoe**.

Rocco Giovane: Shelley's spelling of "Rocca Giovane," ruined village in Alban Hills (McGann 2.261). **Domenico** and his band's hideout; they die defending it against **French** troops in "**The Sisters of Albano**" (*SA* 61).

Roche: **Irish** baronial family. **Countess of Desmond** is "of the noble family of Roche" (*PW* 1.302, 1.304, 2.177).

Rochester: **Kent** town twelve miles southeast of **Dartford** on the main road from **London** to **Dover**; the Shelleys must have passed through it when eloping to **Europe** 1814. Plague survivors traveling to **France** are detained for a day there (*LM* 346). See **Lucy Martin** (*LM* 350–351).

Rodosto: **Thracian** port on **Marmora** ninety-five miles east of **Makri**; it was **Greek** in Shelley's day but is now Tekirdag in **Turkey**. **Lionel Verney** records the Turkish army's siege of Rodosto (*LM* 174). When Turks learn of **Raymond**'s approach, they retreat, but **Argyropylo** "had advanced, so as to be between the Turks and Rodosto; a battle, it was said, was inevitable" (*LM* 178).

"Roger Dodsworth: The Reanimated Englishman": Cyrus Redding, *New Monthly Magazine*'s 1820s editor, printed Shelley's article (attributed to "Mrs. Shelley") "in a volume of his reminiscences" 1863, although Shelley had submitted the story to the magazine 1826 (Robinson 377). Shelley composed the article September–October 1826, as evinced by references to **Mr. Sapio**'s contemporary performances in *The Oracle*, and as Robinson details in his 1975 article "Mary Shelley and the Roger Dodsworth Hoax." Shelley wrote it in response to an ongoing contemporary literary discussion; *Journal du Commerce de Lyon* first reported a story regarding **Roger Dodsworth**'s reanimation 28 June 1826 and, after many British newspapers reprinted the story in July, prominent British writers, such as **Moore** and **Rogers**, continued a discussion in print of the original story for the rest of 1826 (Robinson 377). Shelley briefly summarizes **Dr. Hotham**'s discovery of Dodsworth, frozen in frost in **Italy** 1654 while returning to England; she maintains facts original articles provided about this discovery while asserting her belief in the possibility of such "animation" (*RD* 43–44). Shelley then speculates that Dodsworth would find little familiar in the world over 170 years after his death (*RD* 44–45). Shelley provides a humorous imagined conversation between Hotham and Dodsworth, as Dodsworth struggles to fill in the historical gap through which he slept, proposing that supposedly **Tory** Hotham suspects Dodsworth of Radicalism (*RD* 45–48). Shelley concludes with speculation over theories about transmigration of souls (*RD* 48–50). As with *Frankenstein*, this tale testifies to Shelley's consistent interest in animation and, as in "**Valerius the Reanimated Roman**," to her interest in historical reincarnation. See **Pythagoras**.

Rogers, Samuel (1763–1855): Poet and banker who visited **William Godwin**'s house when Shelley was a child; **PBS** met him 1817 (Sunstein 40; *Journals* 553; White 1.541). He entertained many leading figures of his day at renowned breakfasts during which he promoted lively and provocative conversation. Sunstein notes: "June 1838 [Shelley] was particularly delighted when the ancient poet Samuel Rogers began inviting her to his famous select breakfasts," which she found "delightful—of such intellectual fascinating society" (Sunstein 339; *Journals* 553). Shelley attended breakfasts regularly and obviously enjoyed them, asking Edward Moxon 1843, "Where is Mr. Rogers? I will visit town to see him though for no one else" (*Letters* 3.93). **Rupert Falkner** describes **Mrs. Rivers**'s house as an "abode of tranquillity" that he associates "with the poet's wish: '**Mine be a cot** beside the hill—/ A beehive's hum shall sooth my ear; / A willowy brook, that turns a mill, / With many a fall shall linger here,'" the opening stanza of Rogers's "A Wish" (1786) (*F* 171–172; Rogers lines 1–4). Shelley dedicated *Rambles* to Rogers, author of *The Pleasures of Memory* (1792) (*R* 1.vi). She quotes from Rogers's *Italy, a Poem* several times, as well as referring readers to Rogers's description of **Salvator Rosa** (*R* 2.84, 2.155, 2.186, 2.284).

Roland de la Platière, Madame (1754–1793): Born Marie Jeanne Phlipon, this engraver's daughter married Jean Mari Roland de la Platière 1780; her **Parisian** drawing room became a popular meeting place for leading figures of the day, but she was denounced during the Reign of Terror, writing her unfinished *Memoirs* (published posthumously 1795) and bearing her fate nobly during five months' imprisonment 1793. Her husband, having escaped Paris, killed himself upon learning of her death. Shelley wrote Roland's biography for *French Lives*. She admires Roland's fortitude, noting that she remained reserved in Parisian company while privately supporting and advising her husband in his opinions that the king should be relieved of royal functions and writing some of her husband's official letters. Shelley refers readers to Roland's *Memoirs* for the best insights into this figure—a "noble-hearted woman, whose soul was devoted to the fulfilment of her duties" (*FL* 2.286).

Rollin, Charles (1661–1741): Author of eight-volume *The Ancient History of the Egyptians, Carthaginians, Assyrians, Babylonians, Medes & Persians, Macedonians, and Grecians* (1730–38) and **Paris** University's principal. **Matilda** finds the book on her aunt's shelves (*M* 158).

Romagna: North central **Italian** region bordering the **Adriatic**. **Tripalda** imprisons **Beatrice** there (*V* 3.157). [*R* 2.257].

Romagnosi, Gian Domenico (1761–1835): **Italian** journalist who collaborated on the *National Dictionary* and *Il Conciliatore*, as Shelley points out (Petronio 4.583; *R* 2.195).

Romaic: Modern **Greece**'s vernacular language. **Raymond** greets **Evadne Zaimi** in Romaic when they meet in **London** (*LM* 109). **Elizabeth Falkner** learns of **Rupert Falkner**'s illness when she receives a letter in Romaic from **Vasili** (*F* 64). **Miss Jervis** claims "to know a good deal of Romaic" and probably taught Elizabeth enough to understand it (*F* 73). **Harry Valency** studies Romaic (*E* 297).

Romani: Man whom **Clorinda Saviani**'s family wants her to marry in "**The Bride of Modern Italy**"; she does so at the story's conclusion.

Rome: **Italy**'s capital city, thirteen miles inland from the west coast and on the **Tiber**, constructed on the river's plain on the slopes of **Seven Hills**. The Shelleys first visited it November 1818, when Shelley "visited the [**Coliseum**] three times and fell in love with the city" (Sunstein 161). The Shelleys visited **Cestius**'s tomb beside the Protestant cemetery where **Keats**, **PBS**, and **William Shelley** were all to be buried (*Journals* 239). They returned to live in Rome March 1819, taking rooms on the **Corso**; Shelley was so delighted to see "the Holy City again" that "for three months she explored the city with supreme pleasure" (*Journals* 251; Sunstein 163). They left Rome for **Leghorn** immediately after William's death June 1819 (Sunstein 167). **Victor Frankenstein** compares Oriental poetry with Rome's "manly and heroical poetry," and the **Creature** learns "of the wars and wonderful virtue of the early Romans" from **Volney**'s *Ruins of Empires* (*Fr1* 97, 147; *Fr3* 67, 105). **Valerius** returns there in Shelley's day and contrasts it unfavorably with the glories of his 1st-century B.C.E. Rome (*Val* 333, 336–37). **Ricciardo de' Rossini** speaks hopefully of his wish to see **Corradino** crowned in Rome (*TP* 7, 22). Shelley recalls how William Shelley "Had gazed with infant wonder on the grace / Of stone-wrought deities, and pictured saints, / In Rome's high palaces" just before "His spoils were strewed beneath the soil of Rome," and she appeals to the city holding her husband's and son's tombs (*Ch* 80–82, 87, 113–116). **Edmund Malville** fondly asserts that " 'Rome is still the queen of the world' " (*RI* 28). Rome is the setting for "**The Bride of Modern Italy**" and home to the **Saviani** family; **Clorinda Saviani** is "one of the most highborn and loveliest girls in Rome" (*BMI* 33–34). **Lionel Verney** reads about Rome's history, and he and **Raymond** draw on it in preparation for their **Kishan** battle (*LM* 77, 178). Verney imagines the Tiber flooding Rome as plague spreads throughout **Europe**; **Adrian** proposes leaving England for "sacred and eternal Rome" (*LM* 269, 327). Verney ultimately arrives there alone, comforted by "that wondrous city, hardly more illustrious for its heroes and sages, than for the power it exercised over the imaginations of men" (*LM* 436, 456, 461). Verney finishes his narrative briefly detailing his year's residence there (*LM* 465, 462). **Countess Atanasia D——** tells "**Sisters of Albano**'s" story during the party's "last excursion before quitting Rome" (*SA* 51, 55, 63). The central female protagonists' mother dies at Rome's **Santa Chiara** convent, where youngest daughter **Anina** resides; elder daughter **Maria** was formerly a nun-nurse there (*SA* 54). **Guido il Cortese** visits Rome, and **Countess de' Tolomei** attends Rome's Easter festival (*Trans* 122; *Brother* 178). The **Villiers**es travel with **Clorinda** and **Horatio Saville** to visit Rome during Passion Week (*L* 2.192–193, 2.201–203, 2.206). When struggling with financial difficulties in **London**, the Villierses recall Rome affectionately (*L* 2.240). Shelley returned to Rome with **PFS** March 1843, witnessing a comet upon their arrival and remaining in the city until May; in *Rambles*, she describes her return to many of the sites she had formerly enjoyed (*R* 1.38, 1.80, 1.220, 1.229, 2.214–248).

Rome in the Nineteenth Century: See **Eaton**.

Romeo and Juliet: Shakespeare's tragedy (1597), recording two title protagonists' persistence in loving each other despite their families' mutual enmity. The play concludes with both protagonists' suicides; their families, the Montagues (or **Montecchi**) and **Capulets** (or **Capaletti**), subsequently repent of their hatred. Shelley read it April 1819 (*Journals* 256). **Lionel Verney** watches young dancers at **Alfred**'s birthday party, unable to escape thoughts of plague: "you fancy that you live: but frail is the '**bower of flesh**' that encaskets life" (*LM* 240). **Lady Katherine Gordon** states, " 'when my soul quits this 'bower of flesh,' these leaves and flowers . . . may decay and die' " (*PW* 3.153). Contemplation of innocence "within that lovely 'bower of flesh' " of **Ethel Villiers** comforts **Lord Lodore**, and he uses his concern for Ethel's "matchless 'bower of flesh' " as part of the reason to leave England for **America** (*L* 1.34, 1.175). Shelley compresses this line from those **Juliet** speaks, questioning why Romeo killed her cousin Tybalt (Shakespeare 3.2.80–82). Shelley compares "**The Brother and Sister**'s" family conflict to animosity between Capaletti and Montecchi (*Brother* 166). **Lord Maristow** suggests that the farce of **Colonel Villiers**'s relationship with **Miss Gregory** varies "the scene from a

Romford

travestie of *Romeo and Juliet* to the comedies of **Plautus** or **Molière**" (*L* 2.225). Shelley describes **Rupert Falkner**'s recovery with a line adapted from Romeo's speech: " '**His bosom's lord** sat lightly on its throne' " (*F* 311; Shakespeare 5.1.3). In September 1840, Shelley retired to **Villa Sommariva**, "where the hum of many thousand voices falls softened and harmless on my ear. '**Eyes, look your last!**' "; Romeo utters this phrase just before he kisses Juliet and drinks the poison that kills him (*R* 1.102–103; Shakespeare 5.3.112). Shelley praises **Germany** with a line Juliet speaks: " '**What's in a name**?'—You know the quotation" (*R* 1.174; Shakespeare 2.2.43). In **Verona** September 1842, Shelley saw a tomb not likely to be "**the tomb of** the Capulets"; her quote may come from Shakespeare, but is probably **Burke**'s reference (*R* 2.76; Shakespeare 4.1.111–112). [*R* 2.127, 2.129]. See **Vincenzo Bellini**.

Romford: **London** district nine miles northeast of the city's center. **Lord Lovel** leaves London through Romford (*PW* 1.48).

Romulus: Legendary cofounder of **Rome**, with brother Remus. The twins were thrown onto the **Tiber** in a basket, which floated to shore, where "a she-wolf" rescued and "suckled" them; they quarreled about building a city, and Romulus killed Remus before founding Rome (Tripp 514–515). The **Creature** prefers "peaceable lawgivers" over the type of leader Romulus represents (*Fr1* 156; *Fr3* 112). **Lionel Verney** characterizes himself during childhood in **Cumberland** "as uncouth a savage as the wolf-bred founder of old Rome," alluding to Romulus (*LM* 14).

Roncesvalles: Village and valley in **Spain**'s **Pyrenees** twenty miles northeast of Pamplona and legendary scene of **Charlemagne**'s defeat and the site of the death of his most famous knight, Roland. **Henry Clerval** convinces **Victor Frankenstein** to take part in childhood games celebrating "heroes of Roncesvalles" (*Fr3* 42).

Rosa, Salvatore: See **Salvator Rosa**.

Rosalind: See *As You Like It*.

"Rosalind and Helen: A Modern Eclogue": Poem **PBS** began late summer 1817 and completed 1818, published as title piece to his 1819 volume of poems (White 1.533, 1.739–40). It concerns two reunited sisters' different fates and includes many of the private and public issues with which PBS was concerned. Shelley copied the poem February 1818, liking it "since it was based in part on her friendship with **Isabel Booth**" (*Journals* 194). Each *Falkner* volume's epigraph comes from this poem: "**There stood, / In record** of a sweet sad story, / An altar and a temple bright, / Circled by steps, and o'er the gate / Was sculptured, 'To Fidelity!' " (PBS lines 1051–1055). Helen speaks these lines to her sister in describing her husband Lionel's carving of a veiled woman and her dog; the monument stands in honor of the dog that saved Lionel's mother's life by rescuing her from the sea.

Rose Blanche: See **White Rose**.

Rosina: Orphan whom **Sir Peter Vernon** raises in "The Invisible Girl." Rosina is the "Invisible Girl," so called for the tower light sailors see while her physical presence remains undiscovered. **Henry Vernon** hangs a portrait of her under this name in the tower (*IG* 202).

Ross, Duke of (c. 1476–1504): James Stewart, Archbishop of St. Andrews and Scotland's Lord High Chancellor; **James IV**'s brother, he refused to join Scotland's 1496 attack on England (Arthurson 13, 140–141). Shelley spells his name **Rosse**. Pretending to be Ross, **Richard of York** escapes from the **Tower** (*PW* 2.117).

Rosse: See *Macbeth*.

Rosse, Duke of: See **Ross**.

Rosselli, Cosimo (1439–1507): **Florentine** painter renowned for his **Sistine Chapel** frescoes (1482) and his **Saint Ambrosio's Church** fresco representing the Miracle of the Sacrament (1485–86) (Schmeckebier 213–215). Shelley describes the latter, complimenting its "truth of nature and ideal beauty" (*R* 2.142; *Florence* 176; Schmeckebier 215).

Rossini, Gioacchino Antonio (1792–1868): Italian opera composer and director of **Naples**'s **San Carlo** Theatre c. 1813–22 (Scholes 891). Shelley saw many Rossini operas there, but did not particularly like his works, writing that "nothing is heard in Italy now but Rossini & he is no favourite of mine—he has some pretty airs—but they say that when he writes a good thing he goes on copying it in all his succeeding operas for ever and ever" (*Letters* 1.89). The **Saville** sisters journey to **Pompeii**, where they "got up Rossini's opera of the *Ultime Giorni di Pompeii* among the ruins"; this opera is actually **Pacini**'s (*L* 3.204). In **Bergamo**, Shelley saw Rossini's *Pietro l'Eremita* [*Peter the Hermit*], the Italian version of *Mosé in Egitto* [*Moses in Egypt*] (1818) that was performed in **London** 1822, feeling "the music is the best of Rossini" (*R* 1.108; *NGD*). She found "**Mi manca la voce**," sung in *Mosé*'s second act, Rossini's "chef-d'oeuvre" (*R* 1.108). See *Barbiere di Siviglia*.

Rossini, Ricciardo de': In "A Tale of the Passions," **Despina dei Elisei** masquerades as the **Milanese** Ricciardo while in **Florence**.

Rotterdam: Seaport on **Holland**'s eastern coast where the **Rhine** flows into the **North Sea**. Shelley spent one September 1814 day there (*H* 76). **Victor Frankenstein** and **Henry Clerval** embark there for **London** (*Fr1* 181, 184; *Fr3* 132, 134). **Elizabeth Falkner** and **Rupert Falkner** return to England from Rotterdam (*F* 82).

Rouge et Noir: French card game, "Red and Black" or *Trente et Quarante* [*Thirty and Forty*], played principally at casinos. Shelley watched gamblers play it in **Baden-Baden** (*R* 1.40).

Round Table: Table that King Arthur received upon marrying Guinevere; its shape made all its seats equal. **Henry Clerval** initiates games centering around characters drawn from Round Table knights (*Fr3* 42).

Round Tower: Cork tower where residents meet **Richard of York** (*PW* 1.280).

Roundheads: Derogatory name for **Cromwell**'s **Parliamentary** or Puritan supporters during the English Civil War (1642–48), originating in distaste for their "closely cropped hair" (Kinder 1.267). Shelley imagines **Roger Dodsworth** singing "a royalist song against old **Noll** and the Roundheads" (*RD* 48).

Rousseau, Jean-Jacques (1712–1778): **Swiss** social and political philosophical author. Rousseau posited the superiority of the "natural man" to "civilized man" and argued that civilization had a corrupting rather than beneficial effect upon humankind in *Discours sur les sciences et les arts* [*Discourse on the Sciences and Arts*] (1750), which established his reputation. He continued his thesis in *Discours sur l'origine de l'inégalité* [*Discourse on the Origins of Inequality*] (1754). Author of several novels, autobiographical works, and a theory of politics, *Du contrat social* [*Of the Social Contract*] (1762), Rousseau is credited as a formative thinker behind the **French Revolution**. Threat of persecution for his daring ideas compelled him to flee Switzerland after publication of *Émile, ou Traité de l'éducation* [*Émile, or Treaty on Education*] (1762), which Shelley first read September 1816 and again January–February 1822 (*Journals* 136, 389–390, 394–397). **Mary Wollstonecraft** criticized Rousseau's educational scheme in *Émile*, because, even while it emphasized such innovations as the importance of physical education, it maintained women's inferiority. In **Plainpalais** 1816, Shelley viewed and noted "a small obelisk [which] is erected to the glory of Rousseau"; this memorial marks where **Genevese** magistrates were executed 1792 (*H* 101–102; Moskal 46). **Woodville** pleads with **Matilda** not to give up hope of life, by compelling her to consider how the world would be if Rousseau had despaired while so young (*M* 202). **Lord Lodore** undergoes a course of physical education upon which "Rousseau might have passed his approbation" (*L* 1.73). Shelley wrote Rousseau's biography for *French Lives*. She provides an accurate and detailed account of his early life while consistently referring readers to Rousseau's autobiography *Les Confessions* [*Confessions*] (1782–89), which Shelley read November 1817, considering its publication the act of an insane man (*Journals* 182–183). Shelley condemns Rousseau for giving five of his children to the foundling hospital, and she critiques *Discourse on the Sciences and Arts* for neglecting the strength of the affections. Shelley says of *Julie, ou la Nouvelle Héloîse* [*Julie, or the New Héloîse*] that its "success was unparalleled" upon its 1760 publication, finding the work, which she read June–July 1817 and again January–February 1820, "full of noble sentiments and elevated morality" (*FL* 2.150; *Journals* 175–176, 307–308). She also admires *Les Rêveries du promeneur solitaire* [*Reveries of a Solitary Walker*] (1782), read July–August 1816, as "the most finished, the most interesting, and eloquent of his works" (*FL* 2.169; *Journals* 121–123). Shelley asserts that Rousseau's "real defect was a want of moral courage to meet any menacing and uncertain evil" and concludes that he was a proud man who "had passed his existence in romantic reveries," and feels "*Émile* stands in the first rank for its utility: his theories however engendered some errors" (*FL* 2.121, 2.172–173).

Roveredo: Italian city on the **Adige**, twelve miles south of **Trent**. Shelley changed horses there September 1842 (*R* 2.66).

Rovigo: Italian city eighteen miles northeast of **Ferrara**. **Castruccio** passes through it as a boy (*V* 1.44). Rovigo later figures prominently in the plan to return Ferrara to Marquess **Obizzo**, as Castruccio and **Galeazzo Visconti** meet there to plan the attack; troops follow Castruccio from Rovigo to the secret passageway into Ferrarra (*V* 1.293, 2.13, 2.70).

Rubens, Peter Paul (1577–1640): Flemish painter of *Descent from the Cross* (1611–14), one of two large paintings in **Antwerp Cathedral** (Chilvers 491–492). Shelley viewed it June 1842 (*R* 1.159). She refers to **Reynolds's** opinion that *Descent* evinces Rubens's "boldness" (*R* 1.159).

Rubicon: Phrase "to cross the Rubicon," meaning to make a final and irrevocable decision, derived from **Julius Caesar's** 49 B.C.E. crossing of the Rubicon River in northern **Italy** to march on **Rome** even though it was illegal to bring troops south of the river, a law designed specifically to protect Rome from occupation (Howatson 502). **Rupert Falkner** "had passed the fatal Rubicon, placed by conscience between innocence and crime" when abducting **Alithea Neville** (*F* 35).

Rue Saint Honoré: Parisian street that "became a fashionable quarter" in the 18th century and is today one of Paris's oldest streets (Jennett 27). **Adrian** leaves his meeting with plague survivors opposing him by way of the Rue Saint Honoré (*LM* 382).

Ruines of Rome: **Spenser's** 1591 translation of Joachim Du Bellay's 1558 **French** edition of the text, celebrating all **Rome's** glories, especially its monuments, legends, and writers (Oram 381). **Edmund Malville** describes Rome with lines from Spenser's poem, which Shelley also recorded in her *Journals*: "**All that Athens** ever brought forth wise, / All that Afric ever brought forth strange, / All that which Asia ever had of prize, / Was here to see;—O, marvellous great change! / Rome living was the world's sole ornament, / And dead is now the world's sole monument" (*RI* 28; Spenser, *Ruines* 29.401–406; *Journals* 251). **Lionel Verney** uses Spenser's words in calling Rome "this '**world's sole monument**'" (*LM* 466; *Ruines* 29.406).

Ruins of Empires: See **Volney**.

Rupe de Noce: "Rock of Noce," Italian village in **Tuscany** (Crook 2). **Edmund Malville** passed it en route from **Pisa** to **Vico Pisano** (*RI* 30).

Russia: Northeastern **European** country with **Moscow** as its capital. Shelley wrote of her disappointment when Russia disapproved of **Greece's** revolt (*Letters* 1.189). **Claire Clairmont** lived in Russia March 1823–May 1828 (Clairmont, *Journals* 297–415). Shelley suggests **Cossacks'** destruction of **Nogent** was perhaps retribution for the burning of "Moscow and the destruction of the Russian villages" (*H* 19). **Napoleon** invaded Russia June 1812; his troops destroyed all they could find in the wake of the fleeing Russians who burned Moscow rather than conceding its fall (Kinder 2.35). Russia's forces pursued **French** troops back into France when they retreated in the depth of winter and caused widespread destruction. **Robert Walton** writes to his sister about Russia's climate, and **Victor Frankenstein** pursues the **Creature** through Russia toward *Frankenstein*'s end (*Fr1* 51, 54, 227; *Fr3* 27, 29, 169). **Evadne Zaimi**'s "intrigues with Russia" are part of the ambition leading to her downfall (*LM* 114). Plague destroys Russia in *The Last Man*, and plague survivors leaving **Paris** include Russian soldiers (*LM* 269, 400). Shelley provides indication of "The Mourner"'s time frame, since **Clarice Eversham** "would talk of Napoleon—Russia, from whence the emperor now returned overthrown" (*Mourner* 90). **Lord Lodore** travels in Russia in his youth and later dines at the Russian Ambassador's in **London** (*L* 1.84, 1.143, 1.166–167). **Rupert Falkner** cares for **Elizabeth Falkner** devotedly when she contracts measles "in a wild district of Russia" (*F* 38). Elizabeth later insists to **Gerard Neville** that she was with Falkner in Russia when **Alithea Neville** disappeared (*F* 161). Shelley saw "the monument [a fountain] erected by French vanity at the time of Napoleon's invasion of Russia" in **Coblentz** and later notes a Russian nobleman's death "under the operation of bathing in one" of **Soolen Sprudel**'s gas baths (*R* 1.169, 1.186). Shelley finds "the handsomest women are one or two Russians" at **Kissingen** baths and later expresses her fears that Russia's "unwritten story" may one day reveal acts of tyranny similar to those she notes in **Franconia**'s history (*R* 1.193, 1.205). [*L* 1.253, 1.258].

Ryland: Political "leader of the popular party, a hard-headed man, and in his way eloquent" (*LM* 55).

S

S. Tommaso's Church: Venetian church housing documents giving **Titian**'s death date and burial site; Shelley visited it September 1842 (*R* 2.93).

Sá de Miranda, Francisco (1481–1558): Portuguese poet recognized for bringing **Italian** verse forms into Portugal; Shelley spells his name **Saa**. She wrote his biography for *Italian and Spanish Lives* but provides very little information. Shelley writes that Miranda's "Spanish poems are bucolic, and more truly imbued with rural imagery" than many of his contemporaries' works, asserting that "none excels" Miranda "in the union of simplicity and grace" or in "charm of melancholy sentiment" and "vehemence of passion" (*ISPL* 3.88).

Saa de Miranda: See **Sá de Miranda**.

Saale: River rising in **Bavaria** and joining the **Elbe** near Barby. Shelley traveled from the **Main** valley to the Saale's June 1842 (*R* 1.179–180). She walked through **Kissingen**'s riverside meadows, which became barren plains intersected by the Saale, between **Weimar** and **Elster** July 1842 (*R* 1.185–186, 1.213).

Sabines: Tribes of **Apennine** people, apparently "ancestors of the warlike Samnites, who defied the later **Romans** from the mountains of southern **Italy**"; 290 B.C.E., **Curius** ended Roman wars with Sabines and Samnites (Tripp 518). **Lionel Verney** compares **Adrian** and **Idris** to Sabines when they visit him as he is "feasting on sorry fruits for supper" (*LM* 79). Shelley compares **Admiral Fitzhenry**'s return at the **Revolutionary War**'s conclusion to "the Sabine farm, of which he had, by course of descent, become proprietor" to Curius's retreat to his farm following victory (*L* 1.4). Shelley imagined "the cry of the Sabines" while looking over Rome; **Romulus**, while founding Rome, kidnapped Sabine women to furnish Romans with wives (*R* 2.227; Tripp 574).

Sacred Way: English translation of Italian "Sacre Via," **Rome**'s oldest street. **Lionel Verney** observes that "a buffalo stalked down the Sacred Way that led to the **Capitol**" (*LM* 463).

Sacrifice of Isaac: See **Titian**.

Safie: **Mahometan**'s beautiful daughter; **Felix De Lacey** assists her in escaping a **Parisian** prison in *Frankenstein*. The **Creature** benefits from Felix's tutoring of Safie.

Sagori: Mountains northeast of **Zitza** running east to west across **Epirus**; their inhabitants are **Sagorians**. Shelley describes Sagorians as "mild, amiable, social people; they are gay, frank, clever; their bravery is universally acknowledged" (*EE* 111–112). **Camaraz** and **Cyril Ziani** trace **Dmitri** to "an elevated peak" of Sagori, and Sagorians support **Katusthius Ziani** against Dmitri (*EE* 112–114).

Sailor: **Charles Harding**'s loyal dog in "**The Smuggler and His Family**"; he hails the return of his master's boat, which is depicted in the story's illustration (*S* 214, 217).

St. Albans: Large town thirty miles northwest of **London**. **Lionel Verney** and **Adrian** "first came upon a few stragglers of the **Irish** at St. Albans" (*LM* 300). The **Wars of the Roses** "erupted into conflict at the battle of St. Albans" when **Yorkist** forces captured **Henry VII** May 1455 (Sanders 80). **Robert Clifford** advises **Richard of York** against proclaiming his real identity to **Lord Fitzwater** because the latter would resent "'a name whose very echo would bring St. Albans...before him'" (*PW* 1.185). When Yorkists in England learn of Richard's favorable reception in **France**, "the days of St. Albans...passed in all their grim conclusions before their eyes" but do not deter them against continuing their struggle against Henry (*PW* 1.201, 2.15).

St. Ambrose (c. 340–97): Patron saint of learning and of **Milan** (Delaney 48–49). **Ambrosian Library** is named for him. **Battista Tripalda** is a member of a **Perugian** collegiate church dedicated to St. Ambrose (*V* 3.237).

Saint Ambrosio's Church: Florentine church in Piazza of S. Ambrogio on Via S. Ambrogio (*Florence* 175–176). Shelley discusses its paintings by **Rosselli** (*R* 2.142).

St. Andrew (d. c. 60): One of Jesus's apostles and Scotland's patron saint (Farmer 20–21). **James IV** swears by St. Andrew (*PW* 2.221).

St. Andrews: Scottish port eleven miles southeast of **Dundee**. While touring with the **Baxters** 1813, Shelley visited it (Sunstein 61). **Henry Clerval** and **Victor Frankenstein** pass through it (*Fr1* 189; *Fr3* 138). One of **James IV** and **Mary Boyd**'s children becomes Archbishop of St. Andrews (*PW* 2.189).

St. Anna, Convent of: Hospital in Ferrarra; Shelley refers to "the dark cell there where **Tasso** was confined for mental instability 1579 (*R* 2.263; Moskal 368).

St. Anthony: Patron saint of domestic animals, called **St. Antonio** in Italian (Delaney 601). **Francesco de Guinigi** notices some peasants performing the ceremony of St. Antonio blessing their oxen (*V* 1.52). **Euthanasia** explains to **Castruccio** the importance of **Bindo**, who oversees St. Anthony's blessing of the cattle (*V* 1.251).

St. Antonio: See **St. Anthony**.

St. Aubin: French village nine miles northwest of **Trois Maisons**; the Shelleys arrived there August 1814, to find that **Cossacks** had destroyed it (*Journals* 12; *H* 20).

St. Bartholomew's Hospital: Founded 1123 in **London**'s Smithfield district, St. Bartholomew's is the oldest English hospital. **Lionel Verney** meets a woman whose husband, **George**, had been taken ill the previous night and sent to St Bartholomew's (*LM* 279–280).

St. Beelzebub: See **Satan**.

St. Bernardin: **Alpine** pass between **Italy** and **Switzerland**. At **Splügen** July 1840, Shelley left with some "fellow travellers,—some were going over the St. Bernardin" (*R* 1.59). Shelley's reference could apply either to San Bernardino Pass, linking **Bellinzona**, Italy to **Chur**, Switzerland, or to Great St. Bernard Pass, connecting **Drance** and Kora Baltea Valleys (Moskal 106).

St. Bernard's Well: Edinburgh mineral spring, reputed to have medicinal benefits (Catford 219). **Henry Clerval** admires it (*Fr1* 189; *Fr3* 138).

St. Bridget (d. c. 525): Abbess of **Kildare**; Shelley refers to her as **Bridget**. **Desmond** warns that defeating the **Butlers** will require "white tooth'd Bridget['s]" aid (*PW* 3.31).

St. Catherine (d. c. 310): Little is known about this **Alexandrian** saint who was put to death after consistently converting people to Christianity; Joan of Arc heard her voice, and she is patron saint of maidens (Delaney 138). **Constance Villeneuve** undergoes the ritual of St. Catherine's couch, hoping that, " 'as I have heard, the saint deigns to direct her votaries in dreams' " (*D* 158). St. Catherine's bed or couch is "a narrow ledge overhanging the deep rapid **Loire**," and Constance completes all "the conditions of the spell," such as removing her cloak and shoes and loosening her hair, before spending the night on the ledge and experiencing "**The Dream**" of the story's title (*D* 160, 162). This episode seems to be Shelley's fictional creation, since there is no record of a St. Catherine directly connected to the ritual described. Shelley praises a **Barbatelli** fresco (in **Santa Maria degli Angioli Convent**'s cupola) that depicts **biblical** saints including St. Catherine, "the bride of Christ" (*R* 2.148).

St. Cecilia: Patron saint of musicians, singers, and poets (Delaney 602). **Ildone**'s singing is so beautiful "that, if you shut your eyes, you might have imagined that St. Cecilia herself had descended" (*V* 1.258). Shelley praises a **Barbatelli** fresco (in the cupola of the **Santa Maria degli Angioli Convent**) depicting **biblical** saints including St. Cecilia, "the musician" (*R* 2.148).

St. Clara (1194–1253): Also known as Clare, she became a nun 1212, founded the Minoresses of Poor Clares, and was instrumental in the **Franciscan** order's growth and spread (Delaney 148). Shelley praises a **Barbatelli** fresco (in **Santa Maria degli Angioli Convent**'s cupola) depicting **biblical** saints including St. Clara, "the nun" (*R* 2.148).

St. Columban (c. 540–615): **German** monk who founded a monastery between **Milan** and **Genoa** (Delaney 156). **Alberto Scoto** relates that **Matteo Visconti** lived in "his miserable castle of St. Columban among the **Euganean Hills**" after being chased out of Milan 1302 (*V* 1.98).

St. Declan (d. 5th century): Irish bishop in **Waterford**; he founded **Ardmore** church (Farmer 129–130). **Richard of York**'s supporters pray at St. Declan's shrine at Ardmore (*PW* 3.33).

Saint Denis: Named for **France**'s patron saint, central gateway into **Paris** and a "triumphal" arch erected during Louis XIV's reign (1643–1715) (Jennett 26). Plague survivors arrive there on a "serene morning" (*LM* 379). **Henry IV** swears by Saint Denis (*D* 159).

St. Dunstan (909–988): Benedictine monk and **Canterbury**'s archbishop (Farmer 137–139). **Trereife** swears by him (*PW* 3.69).

St. Finbar (c. 560–c. 610): **Cork**'s patron saint; he founded a monastery there (Farmer 178–179). **Richard of York** kneels in front of St. Finbar's shrine at Cork (*PW* 1.280).

St. George (d. c. 303): England's patron saint (Farmer 197). **Lord Fitzwater** swears by him (*PW* 2.10).

St. George: Ship carrying **Richard of York** at the time of **Meilar Trangmar**'s death (*PW* 1.262).

St. George's Chapel: Chapel at **Windsor** castle. **Edward IV** ordered its construction 1473; it was not completed until the following century; it subsequently served as tomb of English kings and queens (Hedley 57–58, 149–150). **Countess of Windsor** ensures that **Alfred** is "buried in the family vault, in St. George's Chapel," and **Lionel Verney** bears **Idris**'s body there (*LM* 355–56).

Saint Gingolph: Swiss town eleven miles east of **Evian** on **Lake Geneva**; Shelley terms it **Saint Gingoux** (*BSWI* 285). Shelley visited **Vevay** rather than Saint Gingolph October 1840 (*R* 1.138).

Saint Gingoux: See **Saint Gingolph**.

Saints Giovanni's and Paolo's Church: **Venetian** church called S. Zanipolo, begun late 13th century (Shelley states 1246) and consecrated 1430; **Gentile** and **Giovanni Bellini** are buried there (Honour 86). Shelley enjoyed visiting it September 1842 (*R* 2.97–98).

St. James: **Innsbruck**'s patron saint (*MIAU* 87). Shelley discusses how **Dietfurth** contributed to the legend that St. James "had appeared in person to guard [Innsbruck], placed under his especial protection" (*R* 2.46).

St. James's: Street south of **Piccadilly** in **London**'s Westminster district; it becomes **Duke Street**. **Mrs. Derham**'s house is on St. James's; **Ethel Villiers** arrives in London knowing only that her husband "lodged in Duke Street, St. James's" (*L* 2.257). A bailiff inquiring for **Edward Villiers** at **Union Club** can similarly learn only his address (*L* 2.286).

Saint Jean le Maurienne: See **Maurienne, La**.

St. John, Jane Gibson: See **Shelley, Jane**.

St. John Nepomuk: Saint born in Nepomuk, **Bohemia**, and canonized 1729 (Delaney 324). Several versions of his life exist. Shelley saw the St. John Nepomuk statue on the Charles Bridge connecting **Kleine Seite** with **Prague**. She relates how he was thrown into the **Moldau** for his refusal to betray his queen's confession to **Wenceslaus IV**. She also gives the "true history of this saint," from **Reeve**, who calls him Johanko von Pomuk and states that the incident causing his execution concerned church reform in 1381 (*R* 2.5–6).

St. John the Baptist (d. c. 30): Saint renowned for baptizing Jesus (Farmer 258–259). **Richard of York** arrives in **Ireland** 24 June 1492, St. John's feast day (*PW* 1.279; Farmer 258). [*R* 2.222].

St. Julian: Mythical saint known as Julian the Hospitaller; he was the subject of several paintings in **Flanders** (Farmer 273). Flemish servant **Bryan** swears by St. Julian (*PW* 1.192).

St. Leonard's-on-Sea: Village on England's southeast coast two miles west of **Hastings**. Shelley passed through it June 1840 (*R* 1.4).

St. Mark, Place of: See **Piazza San Marco**.

St. Mark's: See **San Marco**.

St. Maria degli Angioli's Church: Florentine church built 1615 on Via della Pergola (*Artistic* 154). Shelley visited it January 1843 (*R* 2.148).

St. Martin: Soldiers' patron saint (Delaney 603). **Castruccio** swears by him, and **Bindo** states that St. Martin has declared victory for forces protecting **Valperga** castle (*V* 2.150, 2.251).

St. Mary: See **Mary**.

St. Mary: Vessel upon which **Lord** and **Clarice Eversham** embark at **Barbados** for England; it is "destroyed by fire on the high seas," and Lord Eversham drowns (*Mourner* 90, 93).

St. Mary's: Abbey near **Colchester**; either St. Mary Magdalen or St. Mary-at-the-Walls church. **Sir Humphrey Stafford** plans to seek asylum there (*PW* 1.5).

St. Maurice: **Swiss** town on the **Rhône** ten miles north of **Martigny**. Shelley arrived there October 1840 (*R* 1.138).

St. Maurice, Abbot of: **Euthanasia**'s uncle in *Valperga*; she travels to **Rome** with him when her brother is ill.

St. Mauro: See **Santa Maura**.

St. Michael: Archangel; legend records that he appeared on **Saint Michael's Mount** 495 (Farmer 338–339). **Heron** and the army welcome **Richard of York**, crying, "Saint Michael and **Cornwall** for ever" (*PW* 3.74).

Saint Michael's Chair and Saint Michael's Mount: Island village including **Saint Michael's Chair** (where, according to legend, the archangel Michael appeared 495) and an 8th-century Celtic monastery five miles east of **Cornwall**'s Penzance. **Lady Katherine Gordon** climbs the Chair and takes refuge at the monastery there during the attack on **Exeter** (*PW* 3.174–176).

St. Michael's Church: Dating from 822, church in **Fulda** north of **Fulda Cathedral** (*BGER* 130). Shelley visted it July 1842 and toured the subterranean vaults where **Athanasius** reportedly lived (*R* 1.206).

St. Pancras: Now renowned for its station and the British Library, this **London** area also has the church where **Mary Wollstonecraft** and **William Godwin** were married and originally buried before **Jane Shelley** moved their remains to **Bournemouth**. Shelley's biographers note that Godwin took Shelley there (then north of the city) as a child to visit her mother's grave; construction of railway lines destroyed its original location later in the nineteenth century (Sunstein 26; Seymour 43, 540).

St. Patrick (c. 390–461): Ireland's patron saint (Farmer 379). **Desmond** swears by him (*PW* 2.120, 3.31, 3.51).

St. Paul's: Seventeenth-century, domed, Baroque **London** cathedral, built 1675–1710 on the site of its Gothic predecessor, destroyed in the Great Fire of London (1666). As a child, Shelley possibly accompanied her stepmother to St. Paul's (Sunstein 43, 32; Crook 2). **Henry Clerval** and **Victor Frankenstein** notice St. Paul's domination of London's skyline (*Fr1* 184; *Fr3* 134). **Lionel Verney** and **Adrian** pass St. Paul's on their final ride through London (*LM* 332). The **Villiers**es plan to meet at the northern side of St. Paul's churchyard (*L* 3.33). St. Paul's is the setting for several events in *Perkin Warbeck:* the **Duke of Warwick** appears at it after being imprisoned in the **Tower** for a year, and the cathedral serves as the rendevous point **Robert Clifford** designates for **Monina De Faro**, who is supposed to seek assistance from the **Dean of St. Paul's**, head of the cathedral (*PW* 1.128, 1.133, 2.7, 2.12). Imprisoned **Richard of York** rides in procession from **Westminster Palace** to St. Paul's; he escapes en route (*PW* 3.198–199, 3.222).

St. Paul's, Dean of: See **St. Paul's**.

St. Peter: Disciple of Jesus; he was martyred in **Rome** c. 67 C.E. Shelley mentions that he was imprisoned at the **Mamertine** (*R* 2.229).

St. Peter's: A basilica marking the spot where St. Peter's remains were deposited has stood in the **Vatican** since 90 C.E. (*MROM* 96). Julius II rejuvenated the old structure 1503, and successive popes continued its reconstruction; **Michelangelo** and **Raphael** worked on it until the new basilica, largest in the world, was dedicated 1626 (*MROM* 96–98). St. Peter's is recognized worldwide for stupendous architecture and as seat of the pope and center of the Roman Catholic Church. Shelley visited St. Peter's immediately after arriving in **Rome** November 1818 and recorded, "The outside of the church disappoints us—We do not think it so fine as **St. Pauls** [sic]" (*Journals* 237–238). Shelley attended a ceremony there "to see the feet of the pilgrims who have journeyed to Rome for the holy week" and saw the annual Easter Sunday illuminations April 1819 (*Journals* 257; *MROM* 112–113). **Valerius** looks out from the **Coliseum** over St. Peter's dome (*Val* 336). **Euthanasia** enjoys gazing at clouds floating over St. Peter's, where **Louis of Bavaria** is later crowned emperor (*V* 1.205, 3.265). *The Last Man*'s narrator compares reconstructing the **sibyl**'s leaves to artwork in St. Peter's (*LM* 6). Alone in Rome, **Lionel Verney** commemorates the new year: "On that day I ascended St. Peter's, and carved on its topmost stone the aera 2100, last year of the world!" (*LM* 467). Shelley passed St. Peter's when entering Rome March 1843, and, after seeing April 1843's Holy Week ceremonies, noted that the sight of "**Pope Gregory**, shutting his eyes as he is carried around St. Peter's, because the motion of the chair makes him sea-sick, by no means excites respect," while she enjoyed the "illumination of St. Peter's" signaling the celebrations' conclusion (*R* 2.214, 2.230, 2.232).

St. Peter's patrimony: Term for papal territorial acquisitions and **Vatican** finances. Shelley notes **Bologna**'s loss of independence when it became part of "the patrimony of St. Peter" due to the **Congress of Vienna** (*R* 2.248).

St. Petersburgh: Now St. Petersburg, **Baltic** seaport in northern **Russia**, 350 miles northeast of **Moscow**. **Robert Walton**'s first letter to his sister from St. Petersburg opens *Frankenstein* (*Fr1* 49; *Fr3* 25). **Elizabeth Falkner** nurses **Rupert Falkner** when he falls ill there, and **Miss Jervis** enters Falkner's employ after many years living in St. Petersburg (*F* 38–39).

St. S—— Convent: Clorinda Saviani and Teresa de' Tolomei live in this Roman convent (*BMI* 32). Shelley based it on Pisa's Santa Anna convent, where Emilia Viviani lived.

St. Sebastian's Church: Early-16th-century **Venetian** church (Honour 164). **Paul Veronese**, who is buried there, worked on the church 1555–70; Shelley mentions seeing his *Martyrdom of St. Mark* there September 1842 (*R* 2.99–100).

St. Sophia's: **Constantine** the Great began construction of **Constantinople**'s St. Sophia's church 326 C.E.; it became a mosque after Constantinople's fall to the **Turks** 1453 (Coufopoulos 54–56; Crook 2). **Raymond** asks **Lionel Verney** to stay with him until they "see the cross on St. Sophia," meaning until they have captured Constantinople (*LM* 184). Raymond later predicts his death and asks for a grave that outlasts St. Sophia (*LM* 187).

St. Stephen's: Westminster Palace chapel, named after founder King Stephen, who inherited England's throne 1135; an alternative name for the **House of Commons** in Shelley's day (Saunders 26). From 1547, the House of Commons used St. Stephen's Chapel as a meeting place until the November 1834 "great fire" destroyed it, after

St. Sulpice

which the chapel was quickly reconstructed (Saunders 39, 67, 123). Shelley witnessed the fire: "we saw it here from its commencement burning like a Volcano—it was dreadful to see" (*Letters* 2.215). *The Last Man*'s **parliamentary** House sits in St. Stephen's, and **Lionel Verney** and **Adrian** are present there with other "members of the state" when **Raymond** is elected Lord Protector (*LM* 101–102). As reports of plague spread and England awaits the election of a new Lord Protector after Raymond's death, "St. Stephen's did not echo with the voice which filled every heart" any longer (*LM* 221–222). Shelley speculates that **Roger Dodsworth** may "become whig or **tory** as his inclinations lead, and get a seat in the, even to him, once called chapel of St. Stephens" (*RD* 48). **Ethel Villiers** "visited once or twice the ventilator of St. Stephen's," which is the gallery "at the end of the house, facing the speaker's chair" in which visitors are "present by courtesy" (*L* 2.210; Leigh 57). For this scene, Shelley drew upon her own 1825 visit there (*Letters* 1.466, 1.470). **Lord Maristow** believes **Horatio Saville**'s "talents and eloquence would place him high among the legislators of St. Stephen's" (*L* 2.221).

St. Sulpice: Swiss Alpine village seventeen miles southwest of **Neuchâtel**. The Shelleys passed through it August 1814 (*H* 41; *Journals* 16).

St. Theodore Chapel: Chapel in San Marco; according to Shelley, it was built in 552 and incorporated into San Marco in 828 (*R* 2.121).

St. Theresa: King Sancho I's daughter, also known as Teresa of **Portugal**, who founded a Benedictine monastery in Lorvao, substituting nuns for monks, and who lived there as a nun after separating from her husband, King Alfonso IX of Leon (Delaney 543). **Bindo** possesses her tooth (*V* 1.252).

St. Thomas: First-century apostle renowned for doubting: he refused to believe in Jesus's resurrection until touching Jesus's wounds. **Richard of York** overhears someone (probably disbelieving **Lord Fitzwater**) swear by St. Thomas at **Lisle**, and Fitzwater later repeats this oath (*PW* 1.166, 2.9). **Robert Clifford** swears by St. Thomas (*PW* 2.32, 2.142).

St. Thomas Aquinas (c. 1225–1274): **Albert the Great**'s student and friend; Aquinas is renowned as Christianity's greatest teacher (Delaney 552–53). Shelley saw two painted tablets at **Florence**'s **Santa Maria Novella Church** January 1843, one of which shows disciples surrounding Aquinas (*R* 2.146).

St. Thomas à Beckett (1118–1170): Martyred Archbishop of **Canterbury**. **Monina De Faro** masquerades as a pilgrim to St. Thomas's shrine (*PW* 2.156).

St. Ursula: According to one legend, Ursula's ten ladies-in-waiting and one thousand maidens were killed in about 451 when they passed through **Cologne**, and Ursula subsequently refused to marry the Hun chief who led the murderous band (Delaney 465). **Euthanasia** sends a servant carrying refreshments to St. Ursula nunnery near castle **Valperga** (*V* 2.187–188).

St. Wolfgang Lake: Austrian Alpine lake eight miles west of Bad **Ischl**.

PFS and his friends bathed there September 1842 (*R* 2.31).

Saladin (c. 1137–1193): Muslim warrior from northern **Syria** who opposed the Crusades and defeated Christians in **Egypt**, where he ruled (Kinder 1.137). **Castruccio** compares himself to Saladin (*V* 2.9).

Salerno: **Italian** town thirty miles southeast of **Naples**; the Shelleys slept there February 1819 (*Journals* 249). **Viola Arnaldi** and her son are imprisoned there (*HM* 324, 326–327, 330–331). **Ferdinando Eboli**'s family estates are near Salerno, and **Villa Spina** is in the **Apennines** north of the city (*FE* 65–66). In July 1843, Shelley sailed to Salerno, finding it "less picturesquely situated than **Amalfi**" (*R* 2.287, 2.290, 2.294).

Salt Hill: Area at **Slough**'s western end five miles north of **Windsor**. Leaving **London** April 1815, the Shelleys "stayed for three days at the Windmill Inn, Salt Hill," then a separate village (*Journals* 76). **Lionel Verney** rides beyond **Eton** "towards Salt Hill" and visits "a little wood" nearby (*LM* 310–311). The **Villiers**es stay in "one of the inns at Salt Hill" (*L* 2.7). [*L* 3.72–73].

Salvator Rosa (1615–1673): Neapolitan painter who was a **PBS** favorite; the Shelleys saw some of his work in **London** February 1818 (*Journals* 193). Shelley remarked that **Lady Morgan**'s biography, *The Life and Times of Salvator Rosa* (1824), "is pronounced dull" March 1824 (*Letters* 1.416). Shelley notes: "the hardships and the dangers attendant on his pursuit, paints a smuggler in Salvator hues" (*S* 205). Shelley admired Rosa's seascape sunset at **Palazzo Pitti** January 1843, stating that he "best represents the peculiar beauty of the southern **Italian** coast" (*R* 2.156, 2.284).

Salvi, Lorenzo (1810–1879): Italian tenor who first performed in **Naples** 1830; he usually performed in **Donizetti**'s and **Bellini**'s operas (Rosenthal 436). Shelley saw Salvi, "a bad actor, but with a tenor voice of good quality and great sweetness," perform *Templario* at **Milan**'s **La Scala** September 1840 (*R* 1.112).

Salzburg: Austrian city and mountain on the **Salzer**, sixty-five miles southeast of **Munich**. Shelley found Salzburg "surpassed all" September 1842 (*R* 2.32). She arrived during a festival celebrating **Mozart**'s birth and stayed at **Erzherzog Carl** inn (*R* 2.34–35).

Salzer: River flowing along the **German-Austrian** border and meandering through **Salzburg**. Shelley viewed the "impetuous torrent, rushing at the foot of romantic crags" September 1842 (*R* 2.36).

Salzkammergut: Northeastern **Austrian** region near **Salzburg** known for its salt industry and many spa-villages popular during Shelley's day (*MIAU* 135). Shelley enjoyed her September 1842 tour of **Linz**, **Gmunden**, and **Ischl**, "the magic circle" of towns in Salzkammergut (*R* 2.33).

Samaritan: Inhabitant of Samaria, northern kingdom of the ancient **Hebrews**. When Shelley attended mass at the **Duomo** in **Milan**, she heard a sermon about the good Samaritan, who

Sampson

aided a stranger (*R* 1.112; Luke 10.25-37).

Sampson: See **Samson**.

Samson: Biblical figure in the book of Judges renowned for wisdom and physical strength, which he loses when Delilah cuts his hair; Shelley also spells it **Sampson** (Judges 13–16). **Lionel Verney** suggests that **Adrian**'s influence improves his own character: "My manly virtues did not desert me, for the witch **Urania** spared the locks of Sampson, while he reposed at her feet; but all was softened and humanized"; Shelley replaces Delilah's human love with Urania's heavenly love (*LM* 32). Verney refers to Samson again in comparing a gale's strength to Samson's destruction of the **Philistine** temple (*LM* 356; Judges 16.29–30).

San Carlo: **Neapolitan** theater built 1737, burned and then rebuilt 1816; Shelley saw an opera there December 1818 (Clement 141–142, 175; Collison-Morley 157; *Journals* 243). The **Savilles** appreciate **Clorinda Saville**'s musical talents: "music, heard in such perfection at the glory of Naples, the theatre of San Carlo" (*L* 2.190). **Edward Villiers** recalls its magnificence (*L* 2.240).

San Carlo Borromeo, statue of: See **Borromeo**.

San Fedisti: Italian troops, "half brigands, half soldiers, formed by the priests in opposition to" **Carbonari**; Shelley points to **Coletta**'s description of them (*R* 2.253).

San Francesco: Lucchese church Shelley visited August 1820; she wrote: "you can go to the church of San [Francesco].... [H]alf way up the aisle on the right hand side you will see on the wall a slab to the memory of **Castruccio** & underneath this newer one the little old one which contains the inscription I have quoted" at *Valperga*'s end (*Letters* 1.364). Castruccio is buried there (*V* 3.269).

San Frediano: Fourteenth-century **Lucca** district (Meek 7). **Castruccio** takes Lucca from the **Guelphs** by attempting to enter the city at its gate, making Lucca a **Ghibelline** stronghold (Green 53). Following the victory, **Uguccione della Faggiuola** sacks San Frediano church, which housed the pope's treasure (*V* 1.164–165). The account of the 1314 plunder at this church is historically accurate (Green 55). See **San Friano**.

San Friano: Section of **Florence**; Shelley terms it **San Frediano** in *Valperga* when **Castruccio** hears about its plans to present **Festa d'Inferno** (*V* 1.17). Shelley uses **Villani**'s *Chronicle*'s description (Villani 360).

San Gennaro (d. c. 305): Italian for Januarius, saint born in **Naples** (Delaney 210–211). **Countess de' Tolomei** views his feast celebration (September 19) in Naples (*Brother* 182).

San Geronimo: See **Domenichino**.

San Giorgio Maggiore Church: Venetian church (Shelley calls **Convent**) on San Giorgio Maggiore island at Giudecca Island's eastern point, first built 790 (*R* 2.94; Honour 107–109). Shelley notes that **Veronese**'s *Marriage at Cana* was moved from the church to

Accademia delle Belle Arti (Venice); *Marriage* was commissioned for the church (*R* 2.90; Moskal 277).

San Giorgio Maggiore Convent: See **San Giorgio Maggiore Church**.

San Marco: Well known **Venetian** landmark that became a "Cathedral church" 1807 although construction of a church there began in the 9th century; its most marked feature is a tall red tower situated on one side of **Piazza San Marco** (Honour 29). Shelley probably visited the church, **St. Mark's**, 1818 (*Journals* 229–234). **Lionel Verney** records that he, **Adrian**, and **Clara** "saw the ruins of [Venice] from the height of the tower of San Marco" (*LM* 439). Shelley provides a history and description of San Marco (*R* 2.121–122).

San Martino: Thirteenth-century **Lucchese** cathedral (Simon 84–85). **Bindo** presents many of his religious relics to its priest (*V* 1.252).

San Michele: Thirteenth-century **Lucchese** church (Delaney 408–409; Simon 79–80). **Beatrice** plans to enter the convent nearest **Castruccio**'s palace, where nuns are "dedicated to San Michele," the archangel Michael (*V* 3.106; Crook 2).

San Miniato: Florentine gate "under the hill of Oltr' Arno" near **San Miniato Church** (*Florence* 257). Shelley passed through it en route for San Miniato church November 1842 (*R* 2.135).

San Miniato Church: Eleventh-century **Florentine** church renowned for its basilica and named for a Florentine martyr beheaded and buried in its cemetery (Higson 96). Shelley visited it November 1842 (*R* 2.135).

San Paolo fuore delle Mura Cathedral: **Roman** church destroyed by fire 1823 and rebuilt 1854 (Moskal 347). Shelley noted **Severn**'s altarpiece there April 1843 (*R* 2.224).

San Pietro Church: Church at **Murano** (Honour 231). Shelley saw **Giovanni Bellini**'s masterpiece there September 1842 (*R* 2.93). The church contains two Bellini works: *Barbarigo Altarpiece* (1488) and *Assumption* (c. 1505–15) (Honour 231–232).

San Pietro d'Arena: **Genoa** suburb. **Marchese Torella** owns a villa there (*Trans* 124).

San Terenzo: Small **Italian** village four miles southeast of **Sarzana**. The Shelleys moved to **Casa Magni** there, sharing it with the **Williamses** April–September 1822 (*Letters* 1.237; *Journals* 410).

Sancho Panza: Don Quixote's squire, who regularly brings the visionary knight down to earth (Crook 2). The picnic at **Gros Bois** reminded Shelley of Don Quixote and Sancho (*H* 16). Shelley highlights Sancho's reliance on trite wisdom: "Every thing must have a beginning, to speak in Sanchean phrase, and that beginning must be linked to something that went before" (*Fr3* 22).

Sandra: Housekeeper at **Apennine Tolomei** villa where **Flora Mancini** lives while **Countess de' Tolomei** visits **Rome** in "The Brother and Sister."

Sanskrit: Indian upper-class language dating from the 3rd century and structurally similar to **Latin** and classical **Greek**. **Henry Clerval** and **Victor Frankenstein** endeavor to learn Sanskrit (*Fr3* 67).

Sant' Anna Convent: Este convent where **Angeline** boards and later takes the veil (*Trial* 231, 243).

Sant' Oreste: See **Soracte**.

Santa Chiara: Convent in **Rome** and convent near **Sorrento**. **Maria** and **Anina** are nuns in Rome's convent, and **Viola**'s cottage is quarter of a mile east of Sorrento's convent (*SA* 53; *HM* 320).

Santa Croce Church: Florentine church begun in 1294 (Moskal 313). Shelley viewed frescoes there January 1843 (*R* 2.160).

Santa Maria de' Frari Church: Venetian church begun 1340 and completed 1469 (Honour 56). Shelley saw **Giovanni Bellini**'s altarpiece of Madonna and saints (1488) there September 1842 (*R* 2.92–93).

Santa Maria de la Salute: Venetian church completed 1687 at **Canale Grande**'s entrance (Honour 143–148). In Venice October 1818, the Shelleys must have observed the church, prominent in the city's outline. **Edmund Malville** describes a nighttime gondola voyage during which he admired moonbeams illuminating its cupolas (*RI* 26). In September 1842, Shelley asserted that it was built "when architecture had degenerated, and a multiplicity of ornaments was preferred to that simple harmonious style" (*R* 2.95).

Santa Maria degli Angeli Church: **Michelangelo** built this church in **Rome** from the **Baths of Diocletian**'s ruins 1563; Shelley saw and admired it as "striking and majestic" in April 1843 (*R* 2.229).

Santa Maria degli Angioli Church: Florentine convent; Shelley praises a **Barbatelli** fresco in its cupola that depicts **biblical** saints (*R* 2.148).

Santa Maria Maggiore Church: Church on the Esquiline Hill in **Rome** (Moskal 355). Shelley mentions a procession on 15 August 1837, when the pope accompanied "a famous black Madonna" from the church to **St. Peter's** in order to combat the cholera epidemic (*R* 2.238).

Santa Maria Novella Church: Florentine church (facade begun 1350) northwest of **Duomo** (*Artistic* 100). Shelley visited it January 1843 (*R* 2.146).

Santa Maura: Italian name for Lesbos, **Ionian** isle north of **Cefalonia**, from which **Sappho** is supposed to have jumped to her death; Shelley calls it **St. Mauro** (*MGRE* 80). **Camaraz** and **Cyril Ziani** sail north of St. Mauro (*EE* 110).

Santa Reparata: Legendary saint denounced in 3rd-century **Palestine** for being Christian; she was tortured and thrown into a furnace but escaped unharmed; she was later beheaded (Delaney 490). **Monna Gegia de' Becari** reponds to **Marzio**'s death with, "Santa

Reparata is too good to us to allow such ill luck" (*TP* 4).

Santa Trinita Church: Ninth-century church in **Florence**'s Piazza S. Trinita; it was rebuilt in the 13th century and completely altered in the 16th century (*Florence* 19). Shelley admired **Ghirlandajo**'s *The Life of St. Francis* frescoes there (*R* 2.144).

Santerre, Cornelia: See **Lodore, Lady**.

Santerre, Lady: Sir **John Santerre**'s widow and **Lady Lodore**'s mother in *Lodore*; White suggests that she is modeled on Eliza Westbrook, **Harriet Shelley**'s sister (2.679).

Santerre, Sir John: **Lady Santerre**'s husband and **Lady Lodore**'s father in *Lodore*.

Santiago (d. 44): **Spanish** for St. James the Great, soldiers' patron saint (Farmer 250). **Hernan De Faro** swears by him (*PW* 3.84).

Santissima Annunziata Church: **Florentine** church built 1262 northeast of **Duomo** (*Artistic* 121–123). Shelley mentions that **Barbatelli**'s most renowned work is there (*R* 2.147).

Santissima Annunziata Convent: Servi di Maria founded this 13th-century church and convent of the Most Holy Annunciation northeast of **Florence**'s **Duomo** (Higson 284–287). Shelley especially notes **Barbatelli**'s fresco series in the convent's cloister (*R* 2.147).

Sapio, Mr.: Actor and opera singer who performed in *The Oracle* in London 7 August–30 September 1826, according to the *Times*. Shelley speculates **Dr. Hotham** would have regarded **Roger Dodsworth**'s dress like that of "Mr. Sapio's costume in **Winter**'s Opera of the Oracle" (*RD* 44).

Sappho: Seventh-century **Greek** lyric poet still closely associated with her island home Lesbos (**Santa Maura**); little is known about her life (Howatson 506–507). Shelley asserts, "the soul of our modern **Corinna** would have been purified and exalted by a consciousness that once it had given life to the form of Sappho" (*RD* 49). In "**The Death of Love**," Shelley asks if personified love died by leaping "with love: lorn [*sic*] Sapho from the steep, / Which o'ertops the dark and threat'ning sea?" (lines 5–6).

Saracen: Term originally referring to someone from the **Roman** Empire's **Syrian** borders and later a term for an **Arab** or Muslim. **Buzeccha**, also called **Nazarene**, is a Saracen (*TP* 8). [*R* 2.210, 2.228].

Saragossa: **Spanish** town 160 miles northwest of Barcelona, renowned for its resistance to a **French** siege (1808-1809) during the Peninsular War; **Byron** memorialized it in *Childe Harold's Pilgrimage*. Shelley claims that the siege of **Messina** was equal to those at **Numantia** and Saragossa (*R* 2.210).

Saramita, Andrea: **Magfreda**'s principal follower in *Valperga*; the **Inquisition** imprisons her.

Sardanapalus, a Tragedy: Drama **Byron** wrote, dedicated to **Goethe**, and published 1821 (Marchand 2.895, 2.908–

909, 2.918, 3.953, 3.966). Shelley read it January 1822 (*Journals* 392). King Sardanapalus, reflecting upon his baffled attempts to rule without war, yearns for a "green spot" of peace, a possible source for "No 'green spot' of delight soothed [**Lord Lodore**'s] memory"; Crook suggests letter ten of **Moore**'s *The Fudge Family in Paris* (1818), which Shelley read in 1818, as a more probable source (*L* 1.97; Stafford 38; Byron 4.1.514; Crook 2; *Journals* 230).

Sardinia: Italian Mediterranean island seven miles south of **Corsica**. Shelley notes **Carbonarism**'s rise there (*R* 2.169).

Sardinia, King of (1798–1849): Charles Albert ruled Sardinia-**Piedmont** 1831–49. Shelley traveled to the king's realm and criticizes him for neglecting the **Simplon** Pass (*R* 1.128, 1.132).

Sarto, Andrea del: See **Andrea del Sarto**.

Sarzana: **Italian** town six miles east of **La Spezia**. **Castruccio** controls Sarzana; he actually took it 1314 (*V* 2.174; Green 124).

Satan: Hebrew word meaning "adversary," referring to the serpent who tempted **Eve** in **Eden**, one identity of this fallen angel; he is sometimes termed **Arch Tempter** or **Belial** (a fallen angel in **Milton**'s *Paradise Lost*). According to Milton, the rebel angel Beelzebub is "in heaven called Satan" (1.82). The **Creature** sees himself as Satan rather than **Adam** because, like Satan, he often experiences envy (*Fr1* 157; *Fr3* 113; Milton 1.35). Unlike Satan, the Creature has no companions (*Fr1* 158; *Fr3* 113). The **Dwarf** swears by **St. Beelzebub** (*Trans* 127). **Winzy** sees **Cornelius Agrippa**'s exchange of gold for his services as Satan's temptation (*MI* 220). Young **Rupert Falkner** sees **Sir Boyvill Neville** as "incarnate Belial" (*F* 198). Shelley describes **Luther**'s room in **Wartburg Castle** July 1842; plaster from the wall is missing where Luther supposedly threw his ink stand at the Arch Tempter's head (*R* 1.208).

Saubach: The Czech town **Töplitz** is on the Saubach (meaning "pig's rivulet") River; **Murray** calls it "a small stream" (*MSGE* 498). Shelley saw it August 1842 (*R* 1.278).

Saunders: **Union Club** porter in *Lodore* who helps **Ethel Villiers** when bailiffs are looking for her husband.

Savanarola: See **Savonarola**.

Saviani: In "The Bride of Modern Italy," **Roman** family hoping to find a nobleman willing to accept a low dowry for daughter **Clorinda Saviani**.

Saviani, Clorinda: "The Bride of Modern Italy's" title character; Shelley based her on **Emilia Viviani**. Like Emilia, Clorinda cleverly plays suitors against one another in attempting to gain a favorable husband (Sunstein 193–195; *Journals* 596–597).

Saville, Clorinda: Passionate **Neapolitan** who marries **Horatio Saville** in *Lodore*. Shelley draws Horatio's meeting Clorinda in a convent, where her parents confine her to await their decree of an arranged marriage, from the Shelleys' 1821 encounter with **Emilia**

Viviani in Santa Anna convent (Sunstein 193; White 2.605, 2.679). Also name of only surviving child of Horatio and Clorinda Saville.

Saville, Harriet: Lord **Maristow**'s daughter, **Edward Villiers**'s cousin, and sister of **Lucy**, **Horatio**, **Sophia**, and **Mr. Saville** in *Lodore*.

Saville, Horace: See **Horatio Saville**.

Saville, Horatio: Lord **Maristow**'s second son, **Edward Villiers**'s cousin, **Clorinda Saville**'s husband, and later **Lady Lodore**'s husband at *Lodore*'s close. His family calls him **Horace**, and **Italians** call him **Orazio** (*L* 2.179, 3.211).

Saville, Lucy: Lord **Maristow**'s daughter, **Edward Villiers**'s cousin, and sister of **Sophia**, **Horatio**, **Harriet**, and **Mr. Saville** in *Lodore*.

Saville, Margaret: **Robert Walton**'s sister and correspondent in *Frankenstein*.

Saville, Mr.: Lord **Maristow**'s elder son, **Edward Villiers**'s cousin, and elder brother of **Horatio**, **Harriet**, **Sophia**, and **Lucy Saville** in *Lodore*. His death means Horatio inherits their father's title.

Saville, Sophia: Lord **Maristow**'s daughter, **Edward Villiers**'s cousin, and sister of **Lucy**, **Horatio**, **Harriet**, and **Mr. Saville** in *Lodore*.

Savonarola, Girolamo (1452–1498): **Italian** preacher, church reformer, and writer who became **San Marco**'s Prior 1490. He placed Republican **Florence** under strict rule after the **Medici** were exiled; his political and religious criticism, such as in *Trattato circa il reggimento e governo della città di Firenze* [*Treatise on Florence's Organization and Government*] (1498), led to his execution (*DIL*). Spelling his name **Savanarola**, Shelley mentions that the Florentines remember him (*R* 2.185).

Savoy Alps: Southeastern **Alpine** section of **France** named for Savoie, formerly a duchy adjacent to the **Swiss** and **Italian** borders; **Mont Blanc** is its highest peak. The Shelleys approached this area March 1818: "All the scenery of Savoy is beautiful & I know it well— This morning's ride was perfectly delightful" (*Journals* 200–201; *Letters* 1.357). A storm accompanied by thunder echoing from the **Jura** to the Savoy Alps occurs in *Frankenstein* (*Fr1* 103; *Fr3* 72).

Saxon Switzerland: Mountainous region beginning eight miles north of **Dresden** and extending into **Bohemia** (*MCON* 453). Shelley toured it August 1842 (*R* 1.256, 1.260).

Saxony: Central northeastern **German** region, formerly a separate kingdom that became part of the **Rhine** Confederation 1807 (Kinder 2.29, 2.51, 2.61). Saxon people invaded and settled in England in the 5th and 6th centuries, so British people's lineage is sometimes called Anglo-Saxon. **Corradino** has "round Saxon features" (*TP* 20). A young girl and her blind father in **Ferney** are "Germans from Saxony" (*LM* 421). Shelley describes some native **Irish** as dressed in "antique costume, tight truise, saffron tunics, and flowing

Scala, Cane della (c. 1288–1329)

robes [which] distinguished them from the Saxons" (*PW* 1.303). Shelley notes that Saxony's normal schools are "admirable" (*R* 1.122, 2.251). See **Elector of Saxony**.

Scala, Cane della (c. 1288–1329): Often called Can' Grande della Scala, historical figure who was **Dante**'s patron (Crook 2). **Sismondi** describes him as "the most able **Ghibelline** captain in **Italy**, the best soldier, the best politician, and the person whose services and attachment the [**German**] emperor **Henry VII** most valued"; della Scala ruled **Verona** 1312–29 (Sismondi 123, 139–140; Crook 2). In *Valperga*, della Scala leads the siege of **Cremona** September 1317; the city was actually taken 1311 (*V* 1.290, 2.105–106, 2.112, 2.117; Villani 401). Shelley saw his family's tomb "of the **Scalingers**" September 1843 (*R* 2.76).

Scala d'Oro: Built 1556–1557, staircase at top and left of **Scala dei Giganti** in **Venice**'s **San Marco** (*Venice* 43). Shelley saw it October 1842 (*R* 2.85).

Scala dei Giganti: Built 1485, staircase in **Venice**'s **San Marco**; its name refers to giant **Mars** and **Neptune** statues flanking it (*Venice* 42). Shelley saw it September 1842 (*R* 2.84).

Scaligers: Della Scala family, whose tomb Shelley saw in **Verona** September 1843, noting its lack of Gothic architecture (*R* 2.76; Moskal 268). The family owned **La Rocca** at **Lago di Garda** (*R* 2.69).

Scaricatojo: Shelley made the steep descent from Scaricatojo to the **Bay of Naples** by mule in July 1843; not further identified (*R* 2.283-284).

Schaffhausen: Swiss town on the **Rhine** twenty-five miles north of **Zurich**. Shelley stayed there July 1840 (*R* 1.49).

Schandau: Czech town on the **Elbe** twenty miles southeast of **Dresden** (Shelley spells it **Shandau**) (*MCON* 457). She rested there August 1842 (*R* 1.260, 1.267).

Scheherezade, Sultaness: See *Arabian Nights*.

Scheldt: River flowing from northern **France** across **Belgium** at **Antwerp** and into the **North Sea** from **Holland**. Shelley sailed the Scheldt to Antwerp June 1842 (*R* 1.157).

Schiller, Friedrich von (1759–1805): **German** writer whose most famous works are *Kabale und Liebe* [*Intrigue and Love*] (1784) and *Wallenstein* (1799), which **Samuel Taylor Coleridge** translated (1800). Shelley read Schiller's *Don Carlos* (1787) 1815 and "Schiller's armenian," a translation of *Der Geisterseher* (1789), 1816 (*Journals* 91, 94). Shelley quotes lines from *Wallenstein* as an epigraph for the *Perkin Warbeck* chapter in which **Stephen Frion** betrays **Richard of York**: "**With / My fortune** and my seeming destiny, / He made the bond, and broke it not with me. / No human tie is snapped betwixt us two" (*PW* 3.1; Schiller 3.7). Another Schiller epigraph prefaces the chapter in which **Elizabeth of York** asks English **Henry VII** to spare Richard: "**Oh, that stern** unbending man! /

In this unhappy marriage what have I / Not suffered—not endured!" (*PW* 3.98; Schiller 1.3). Shelley calls Germany the "land of Schiller and **Goethe**" and mentions attempting to learn German at **Kissingen** by reading a Schiller play aloud (*R* 1.175, 1.194). She also refers to Schiller's descriptions of **Hessians** in "*Cabal and Love*," criticizing using foreign mercenaries by recounting a scene from it, and records visiting Schiller's house and grave in **Weimar** July 1842 (*R* 1.203–204, 1.211; Schiller 2.1).

Schneider: **Strasbourg** university student who shared the Shelleys' boat from Strasbourg to **Mannheim** September 1814 (*Journals* 22; *H* 64).

Schneiderff's Hotel: Florentine hotel where Shelley stayed October 1842 (*STIE* 74; *R* 2.133).

Scholar Bewitched: See **Winzy**.

Schröder-Devrient, Wilhelmine (1805–1860): German soprano who performed in **Weber**'s *Der Freischütz* in **London** 1833 (*NGD*; Moskal 208). Shelley enjoyed her **Dresden** performance July 1842 (*R* 2.254).

Schwartz: See **Swartz**.

Schwarzenberg, Prince Felix (1800–1832): Austrian statesman. Shelley calls **Prince Swarzenberg** (her spelling) an absentee ruler (*R* 2.14).

Schwarzes Ross: **Prague** hotel on the **Graben**. Shelley stayed at **Drei Linden** since the Schwarzes Ross, **Starke**'s recommendation, was full (*R* 1.280; *SIDTC* 427).

Schwaz: **Austrian** town fifteen miles northeast of **Innsbruck**; Shelley spells it **Swartz**. She slept there September 1842 (*R* 2.45).

Schwitz: **Strasbourg** university student who shared the Shelleys' boat from Strasbourg to **Mannheim** September 1814 (*Journals* 22; *H* 64).

Scio: **Greek** island, now called Chios, off **Turkey**'s west coast in the **Aegean**; its native inhabitants are **Sciotes**. **Dmitri** spends "several years in Scio, the most civilized of the Greek islands," where he marries **Helena** (*EE* 101). Dmitri returns there from **Albania** to find that **Mainotes** have destroyed his home, killed his wife, and taken his child (*EE* 101). **Camaraz** later reveals that **Zella Ziani** is actually a Sciote (*EE* 114). [*EE* 115].

Scipios: Important **Roman** family whose most famous members are referred to as Scipio the Elder and Scipio the Younger, involved in the Second Punic War (218–201 B.C.E.) against **Hannibal** (Kinder 1.81, 1.83, 1.85). Shelley probably learned about Scipio from **Plutarch**'s description of **Cato** in *Lives* (1.519, 1.525, 1.541). **Valerius**'s companion persuades him to view monuments that the Scipios "planned and modified," and **Euthanasia** praises the **Tiber**, whose "waters flowed here when the Scipios and the **Fabii** lived on thy shores" (*Val* 340; *V* 1.202).

Sclavonia: See **Slavonia**.

Scoto, Alberto: Guelph military commander who helped run the **Viscontis** out of **Milan** 1302 before fighting as a mercenary in **France** (Sismondi

124). **Castruccio** joins Scoto's troops (*V* 1.88, 1.94, 3.171). Shelley is historically accurate, since Castruccio was fighting "under the leadership of Alberto Scotti of Piacenza," where Scoto was lord 1290–1313, by April 1303 (Green 45).

Scott, Sir Walter (1771–1832): Scottish author of poems *The Lay of the Last Minstrel* (1805) and *Marmion* (1808); after about 1814, Scott principally wrote historical novels and is renowned for works such as *Rob Roy* (1817) and *Ivanhoe* (1819). Scott reviewed *Frankenstein* enthusiastically for the March 1818 *Blackwood's*; Shelley consulted him about Scottish history for *Perkin Warbeck*; like Shelley, he contributed to **Lardner**'s *Cabinet Cyclopaedia* (Sunstein 156, 303, 323; *Letters* 1.71, 2.90). Shelley read many of Scott's novels 1814–21, and his *The Heart of Midlothian* (1818) (its title referring to **Edinburgh**'s Old Tolbooth prison) July 1842; this historical novel explores Jeanie Deans's attempts to obtain pardon for her sister Effie, held in prison for murder (*Journals* 671–672; *R* 1.217).

Scutari: In Shelley's day, name given to part of **Constantinople** on the Bosporus, **Asian** shore, now Üskürdar (Coufopoulos 1). The **Greek** army apprehends several **Janizaries** attempting to escape there during a siege (*LM* 191).

Scylla: In **Greek** mythology, six-headed female monster living in a cave opposite **Charybdis**, mythical whirlpool at the Strait of **Messina**'s northern end; Charybdis sucked down the sea, and Scylla could take sailors from ships as they crossed between **Sicily** and **Italy**'s southwestern tip (Homer, *Odyssey* 7.103–119). Shelley wrote about **John Taaffe**, who, figuratively, "got between Scylla and Charybdis, from which he has not yet extricated himself" (*Letters* 1.229). "**Recollections of Italy**'s" narrator disdainfully recalls " 'Venice, with its uncleaned canals and narrow lanes, where Scylla and Charybdis meet you at every turn' " (*RI* 26). **Lionel Verney** ultimately proposes to dare "twin perils of Scylla and Charybdis" (*LM* 469). Shelley notes about **Florentine** painting: "there is nothing theatrical nor affected, which is the Charybdis—nor anything constrained or inane, which may be termed the Scylla of the art" (*R* 2.142).

Sécheron: **Swiss** village just northeast of **Geneva**. The Shelleys stayed there May 1816 (*Journals* 107). **Victor Frankenstein** plans to spend the night there upon returning from **Ingolstadt** (*Fr1* 103; *Fr3* 72).

Seidlitz: According to Moskal, Seidlitz water is "an artificial aperient water, infused with magnesium sulphate and carbonic acid, of the same composition as the natural Seidlitz spring" (169). Shelley notes that the **Max Brunnen** water resembles Seidlitz water (*R* 1.183).

Seine: River flowing through **Paris** into the **English Channel** at Le Havre. The Shelleys viewed it in a pretty valley near **Charenton** 1816 (*H* 15). Shelley enjoyed Parisian sights along the Seine 1840 and traveled on it by steamer (*R* 1.8, 1.144).

Seleucus: King of **Syria** 187-175 B.C.E. Shelley notes that he sent **Heliodorus** to the Jewish temple to obtain

Onias's treasure (*R* 2.220; 2 Maccabees 3.7-40).

Semele: See **Zeus**.

Senate House: Otherwise known as Curia; **Rome**'s senate met there; it stood in the **Forum** (Howatson 516). **Valerius** recalls that political activities in Rome led him to live " 'in the Senate House' " (*Val* 333).

Seneca the Younger (c. 4 B.C.E.–65 C.E.): Influential **Roman** senator who served as Emperor Nero's advisor 54–62 C.E. A prolific writer, he expounded his Stoic philosophy in much of his work; **PBS** read Seneca May 1815 (Howatson 517; *Journals* 77–78). **Isabell Harley** introduces **Valerius** to Seneca's works (*Val* 343). Shelley quotes a passage beginning **"settled in some** secret nest" from **Marvell**'s "The Second Chorus from Seneca's Tragedy of Thyestes" (*L* 1.12). Seneca's *Thyestes* (n.d.) deals "with the gruesome revenge of Atreus against his brother" (Howatson 571).

Seni: See **Zenno**.

"Sensitive-Plant, The": Poem **PBS** wrote and published 1820. As an epigraph to the *Perkin Warbeck* chapter in which **Richard of York** first meets **Lady Katherine Gordon**, Shelley quotes: " '**A Lady, the wonder** of her kind, / Whose form was upborne by a lovely mind; / Which dilating had moulded her mien and motion, / Like a sea-flower unfolded beneath the ocean' " (*PW* 2.204; PBS 2.5–8).

Serapis: God of healing (sometimes associated with **Zeus**) who was a combination of **Egyptian** god Osiris with various **Greek** gods (Howatson 518). **Lionel Verney** characterizes the religious leader in **Paris** "as a patriarch, a prophet, nay a deity; such as . . . Serapis the lawgiver" (*LM* 386).

Serbelloni: Burgundian family, three brothers of which moved to **Spain**, **Naples**, and **Lombardy** in early 15th century. Shelley gives **Gabriel Serbelloni**'s history and mentions two Serbelloni brothers were still living in 1840, but both were childless (*R* 1.80–83). She also refers to Giovanni Baptista Serbelloni (d. 1778), who served **Charles VI**, fought in the **Seven Years' War**, and became **Governor of Lombardy** (*R* 1.82; Moskal 117).

Serbelloni, Gabriel (1508–1580): Knight of **Malta** who fought in **Charles V**'s service (Moskal 116). Shelley notes his part in **Battle of Lepanto** (*R* 1.80–81).

Serbelloni, Villa: At **Bellagio**, villa renowned for its extensive gardens and scenic view of **Lake Como**'s eastern bank (*BSWI* 490). Shelley declares that it was her favorite villa on the lake; she visited it repeatedly July-August 1840 (*R* 1.80–83, 1.91).

Serchio: Italian river stretching from near **Lucca** to the Ligurian Sea. Shelley lived near it while at Bagni **San Giuliano**, and she saw it overflow its banks October 1820 (*Journals* 338). **William Shelley** bathed in the Serchio (*Ch* 75). Shelley notes "the Serchio, taking life from [the sun's] smiles, sped down in his course, roaring and howling," and, since it winds throughout Lucca's plain, it is referred to repeatedly in

Serravalle

Valperga; its "murmurings" are audible in castle **Valperga,** which is built on a rock the Serchio borders to the north (*V* 1.164, 1.181, 1.265, 2.169, 2.203, 2.256, 3.215, 3.254). **Mandragola** claims to be able to control the Serchio (*V* 3.4, 3.126).

Serravalle: Northern **Italian** village eleven miles north of Conegliano (*MSGE* 386). Shelley regretted not seeing **Slovino di San Marco** near Serravalle (*R* 2.66).

Servi di Maria: Italian for "Servants of **Mary**," order founded by seven **Florentine** youths 1233 (McBrien 1186–1187). Shelley especially noted **Barbatelli**'s fresco series, depicting the seven founders, in **Santissima Annunziata Convent**'s cloister (*R* 2.147).

Servox: See **Cerveaux**.

Servox, Vale of: See **Cerveaux**.

Servoz: See **Cerveaux**.

Sesto: Section of an **Italian** city. **Monna Gegia de' Becari** believes **Ricciardo de' Rossini** is **Messer Tommaso de' Manelli**'s son, "he that lived o'th'**Arno**, and baked for all that Sesto"; Shelley refers to Sesto Oltrarno (*TP* 18).

Sesto Callende: Italian town on **Lake Maggiore**'s southern tip. Shelley met her Scottish traveling companions there September 1840 (*R* 1.126–127).

Seven Hills: **Rome** was developed upon seven hills: Aventine, **Caelian**, **Capitoline**, Esquiline, **Palatine**, Quirinal, and Viminal (*MROM* 12–13). Shelley records her visits to various places on many of these Seven Hills 1819 (*Journals* 251–265). **Valerius**'s " 'eyes wander over the seven hills, and all their glories are faded' " (*Val* 341).

Seven Sleepers: From Ephesus, ancient **Greek** city, "early Christians who slept in a cave for several centuries, initially to avoid the persecution of Decius" (Todd 215). **PBS** told Shelley and **Claire Clairmont** "the story of the seven sleepers to beguile the time" (*Journals* 13). **Matilda**'s father alludes to them when referring to past experiences as though they were dream recollections (*M* 162). Shelley points out "the story of the Seven Sleepers rests on a miraculous interposition—they slept," whereas **Roger Dodsworth** actually dies before being reanimated (*RD* 44). **Winzy** declares he has "heard of the Seven Sleepers—thus to be immortal would not be so burthensome," before commencing his own tale (*MI* 219).

Seven Towers: Now four towers remain of this palace on **Constantinople**'s walls, which, during the **Ottoman Empire**, "served as a place of detention for state prisoners" (Coufopoulos 136). **Raymond** sends **Lionel Verney** to Seven Towers to see **Karazza** (*LM* 197).

Seven Years' War: **French** and **British** war fought 1756–63 in North **America** and **India**; it ended with the Peace of **Paris**, which awarded several French and **Spanish** territories to Britain (Kinder 1.283). Shelley mentions a **Serbelloni** fighting in it (*R* 1.82).

Severn, Joseph (1793–1879): English painter remembered for his friendship with **Keats**, whom he accompanied to **Italy**. Shelley corresponded with him in 1825 and met him at **Rogers**'s home in August 1838 (Seymour 368-369, 459; *Journals* 552). Shelley notes that his painting, the altarpiece on the *Apocalypse*, in the **San Paolo fuore delle Mura Cathedral** is the first work by a Protestant to be exhibited in a **Roman** church; she claims he was held in high esteem in Rome (*R* 2.224).

Sévigné, Madame de (1626–1696): The *Letters* of this **French** noblewoman, Marie de Rabutin-Chantal before her 1644 marriage, first published 1725, were immensely popular. Written mainly to her daughter, they record her interaction with France's high society and were printed in many editions throughout the 18th and 19th centuries; Shelley read them 1819 (*Journals* 301–302). **Lady Cecil**, speaking of **Sir Boyvill Neville**'s visit, refers to de Sévigné's humor; Blumberg identifies the passage from de Sévigné's ninety-sixth letter to her daughter (*F* 98; Blumberg 91). Shelley wrote de Sévigné's biography for *French Lives* and admires her, noting the "delicacy and finesse of understanding that distinguish her letters," as well as the widow's exemplary conduct among leading **Parisian** circles (*FL* 1.216). In 1842, Shelley noted "de Sevigné sagely remarks, that '**nothing seems** to impede the exercise of our free will as much as not having a paramount motive to urge us one way or the other,'" not further identified (*R* 1.173).

Sèvre: See **Sèvres**.

Sèvres: Suburb ten miles southwest of **Paris**, renowned for porcelain since 1756. Shelley saw **Sèvre** (her spelling) vases at **Berlin**'s **Palace** July 1842 (*R* 1.226).

Seymour, Sir George (1797–1880): British diplomat who was minister-resident at **Florence** 1830; Shelley states that he disagreed with the pope's military occupation of provinces such as **Ancona**, **Romagna**, and **Bologna** (*R* 2.254; *DNB*).

Seymour Street: Running approximately west-east in **London**'s Westminster district just northeast of **Hyde Park**. **Elizabeth Fitzhenry** and **Ethel Villiers** stay there while visiting London (*L* 2.77).

Sfondrati, Francesco: **Siena**'s 16th-century governor and bishop, then cardinal of **Cremona**; Shelley recounts his history because the Sfondrati family owned **Villa Sommariva** (*R* 1.78–80).

Sforza, Francesco (1401–1466): The Sforza family ruled **Milan** for eighty-five years, beginning with Francesco I, **Bishop of Cremona**, who became duke 1450 (Ady v, 64). Shelley mentions Sforza employing a **Sfondrati** "in various negotiations" (*R* 1.79).

Shakespeare, William (1564–1616): Shelley frequently refers to the corpus of her favorite author, Shakespeare, occasionally spelling his name **Shakspeare**. Throughout her life she read and studied his works (Sunstein 59). **Robert Walton** writes to his sister about his former desire to be a poet like Shakespeare (*Fr1* 51; *Fr3* 27). In *Matilda*, Shelley refers to *As You Like It*, *The Tempest*, and *King John* (*M* 159, 186–187). When **Woodville** tries to per-

Shakespeare, William (1564–1616)

suade Matilda to cling to life, he challenges her to imagine the world without Shakespeare (*M* 202). In "**Recollections of Italy**," Shelley accurately quotes from *A Midsummer Night's Dream* (*RI* 26). In *The Last Man*, Shelley refers to *Antony and Cleopatra*, *Cymbeline*, *Hamlet*, *Henry VI*, *Julius Caesar*, *Macbeth*, *Othello*, *Romeo and Juliet*, and *Twelfth Night*, as well as several sonnets, and she calls Shakespeare **Prince of Poets**. **Lionel Verney** tells his balloon pilot the words of the "prince of poets": " '**Oh! human wit**, thou can'st invent much ill, / Thou searchest strange arts: who would think by skill, / An heavy man like a light bird should stray, / And through the empty heavens find a way?' " (*LM* 71). The lines are from **Heywood**'s "The Tale of Daedalus," mistakenly included in Shakespeare's poems between 1612 and 1780 (Blumberg 59; Heywood lines 25–28; Crook 2). Verney notes **Raymond**'s altered appearance after his imprisonment with reference to Shakespeare's second sonnet: "if care had besieged [Raymond's] brow, '**And dug deep** trenches in his beauty's field' " (*LM* 176; Shakespeare lines 1–2). When Verney buries **Evadne Zaimi**, he notes that her physical appearance has declined vastly, quoting Shakespeare's sixty-third sonnet: "**Crushed and o'erworn**, / The hours had drained her blood, and filled her brow / with lines and wrinkles" (*LM* 182; Shakespeare lines 2–4). Verney marvels at **Adrian**'s leadership as plague spreads: " '**Like to the lark** at break of day arising, / From sullen earth, sings hymns at heaven's gate,' " lines from Shakespeare's twenty-ninth sonnet (*LM* 247–248; Shakespeare lines 11–12). Shelley copied the opening lines of this sonnet in her *Journals* 30 January 1825, while grieving her recent losses and current isolation in England (489). Describing **Richard of York**'s recollection of dismal memories upon seeing the **Tower** again, Shelley again quotes the same lines (*PW* 2.90). Describing Richard's disappointment at motley troops supporting him near **Taunton**, Shelley notes "he felt, '**in disgrace with fortune** and men's eyes,' " another phrase taken from Shakespeare's twenty-ninth sonnet (*PW* 3.122; Shakespeare line 1). *Falkner*'s narrator describes **Elizabeth Falkner**'s steadfast devotion to **Rupert Falkner**, suggesting " '**Their state, / Like** to a lark at break of day arising / From sullen earth, sings hymns at heaven's gate,' " lines again taken from Shakespeare's twenty-ninth sonnet (*F* 62; Shakespeare lines 10–12). Verney mourns Adrian and **Clara** and wishes he could share their death, "so that '**If the dull substance** of my flesh were thought,' even now I had accompanied them to their new and incommunicable abode," the opening line of Shakespeare's forty-fourth sonnet (*LM* 452; Shakespeare line 1). Shelley uses the same sonnet as an epigraph to the *Perkin Warbeck* chapter in which the **Earl of Oxford**'s capture of **Lady Katherine Gordon** swiftly succeeds her fears for her husband's safety: "If the dull substance of my flesh were thought, / Injurious distance should not stop my way; / For then, despite of space, I would be brought / To limits far remote, where thou dost stay" (*PW* 3.169; Shakespeare lines 1–4). As an epigraph to the *Lodore* chapter in which the **Villiers**es are reunited, Shelley again quotes this sonnet's opening (*L* 3.1). Verney records he will sail from **Rome**

Shakespeare, William (1564–1616)

with "a few books; the principal are **Homer** and Shakespeare" (*LM* 469). Many characters in Shakespeare's history plays also appear in *Perkin Warbeck*; Shelley draws particularly from *Richard II*, *Richard III*, *1 Henry IV*, *Henry V*, and *King John*, as well as *Troilus and Cressida*, *Antony and Cleopatra*, *The Two Gentlemen of Verona*, and several sonnets. She also uses Shakespeare's collaborative play with **John Fletcher**, *Two Noble Kinsmen*. As the first epigraph to the *Perkin Warbeck* chapter in which Shelley outlines the downfall of many of Richard's followers due to **Robert Clifford**'s maneuverings, Shelley quotes from Shakespeare's "The Rape of Lucrece" (1594): " '**Oh, what excuse** can my invention make?' " (*PW* 2.38; Shakespeare line 225). As an epigraph to the chapter in which Richard confronts **James IV** about his Scottish troops plundering English villages, Shelley quotes the opening of Shakespeare's thirty-fourth sonnet: " '**Why didst thou** promise such a beauteous day, / And make me travel forth without my cloak, / To let base clouds o'ertake me on the way, / Hiding thy bravery in their rotten smoke?' " (*PW* 2.309; Shakespeare lines 1–4). As an epigraph to the chapter in which Richard escapes imprisonment in **London**, Shelley quotes Shakespeare's thirty-third sonnet, lines beginning " '**Full many** a glorious morning have I seen' " (*PW* 3.236; Shakespeare lines 1–6). As an epigraph to the chapter in which **Henry VII** permits Lady Katherine to see her husband, Shelley quotes from Shakespeare's 112th sonnet: " '**Your love and pity** doth th' impression fill, / Which vulgar scandal stamped upon my brow; / For what care I who calls me well or ill, / So you o'erskreen my bad—what good allow?' " (*PW* 3.251; Shakespeare lines 1–4). As an epigraph to *Perkin Warbeck*'s conclusion, Shelley quotes from Shakespeare's 151st sonnet: " '**Love is too young** to know what conscience is, / Yet who knows not, Conscience is born of Love? / Then, gentle cheater, urge not my amiss, / Lest guilty of my faults thy sweet self prove' " (*PW* 3.339; Shakespeare lines 1–4). In "**The Swiss Peasant**," **Ashburn** argues " 'no living being among us but could tell a tale of soul-subduing joys and heart-consuming woes, worthy, had they their poet, of the imagination of Shakspeare' "; Shelley also refers to Shakespeare in "**The Brother and Sister**" (*SP* 137; *Brother* 166). Shelley quotes from *Antony and Cleopatra* to describe **Ethel Villiers**'s delight at living with her husband, and the Villierses also read *Troilus and Cressida* to each other (*L* 2.197, 2.276, 3.1, 3.60, 3.67). Shelley notes **Roger Dodsworth** "had, as he crossed **Mount Saint Gothard**, mourned a father—now every being he had ever seen is '**lapped in lead**,' is dust, each voice he had ever heard is mute"; Robinson identifies this line from *The Passionate Pilgrim* (1599), which W. Jaggard published and misattributed to Shakespeare (*RD* 47; Robinson 47; Dowden xiii, line 7). Shelley uses "**and as good lost** is seld or never found" as an epigraph to the *Lodore* chapter wherein **Edward Villiers** meets **Lady Lodore** for the first time, misattributing it to "Shakspeare"; Stafford notes this line comes from a poem, "Beauty blemisht is beauty lost," author unknown, number thirteen in *The Passionate Pilgrim* (*L* 2.67; Stafford 129). Shelley uses the opening lines, beginning "**How like a winter** hath

Shakspeare, William

my absence been," of Shakespeare's ninety-seventh sonnet as an epigraph to the chapter in which Ethel is isolated from her husband (*L* 2.246; Shakespeare lines 1–4). Shelley quotes from Shakespeare's eighteenth sonnet as an epigraph to the chapter in which Ethel hears her mother's voice for the first time and sees her beauty closely: "**Shall I compare thee** to a summer's day? / Thou art more lovely and more temperate; / Rough winds do shake the darling buds of May, / And summer's lease hath all too short a date; / But thy eternal summer shall not fade" (*L* 2.197; Shakespeare lines 1–4, 10). Shakespeare is one of the few English poets with whom Elizabeth Falkner is familiar prior to **Gerard Neville**'s education of her, and Shelley specifically refers to *Hamlet* and *The Winter's Tale* (*F* 236). Shelley admires Shakespeare's characterization of **Constance**, and she compares **Florentine** paintings' depictions to Shakespearean characters (*R* 2.78, 2.141–142). Shelley describes "the glorious statue of **John of Bologna**" with reference to *Hamlet* and notes "the representation of such men and women as **Milton** and Shakspeare have embodied in verse, is not to be found in the works of these painters" (*R* 2.155–57). See individual plays.

Shakspeare, William: See **Shakespeare**.

Shandau: See **Schandau**.

Shawe: See **Andrew of the Shawe**.

"She dwelt Among the Untrodden Ways": Poem in **Wordsworth**'s Lucy series (1800). **Matilda** compares her own isolated childhood to Lucy's in Wordsworth's text: "**there were none** to praise / And very few to love" (*M* 157; Wordsworth lines 3–4). **Lionel Verney** compares **Perdita** to the violet and **Idris** to the star in Wordsworth's poem, " '**A violet by** a mossy stone / Half hidden from the eye, / Fair as a star when only one / Is shining in the sky,' " and states his impressions of the text: "Wordsworth has compared a beloved female to two fair objects in nature; but his lines always appeared to me rather a contrast than a similitude" (*LM* 52; Wordsworth lines 5–8). Recalling **Venice** in 1818 while there again September 1842, Shelley remembered **PBS**'s visits to **Byron** and notes, although the scene remains the same, " '**The difference to me!**' "—Wordsworth's concluding line (*R* 2.81; Wordsworth line 12).

Sheerness: Seaport on Sheppey island in the **Thames**'s mouth sixteen miles northwest of **Canterbury**. **Gerard Neville** plans to join a vessel sailing for **New York** there (*F* 158, 219).

Shelley, Charles Bysshe (1814–1826): Child born a month prematurely to **PBS** and **Harriet Shelley** after their separation; PBS accepted paternity (White 1.389). PBS first visited him 7 December 1814 (*Journals* 50). Charles was living with his mother's family, the Westbrooks, in Warwickshire when Harriet died and, 6 January 1817, PBS traveled to **London** to begin the court struggle with the Westbrooks for custody of Charles and **Ianthe Shelley** (*Journals* 152–153). The case lasted throughout 1817; PBS was refused custody but chose Dr. Thomas Hume as their guardian July 1818 (*Journals* 155; White 1.725–726). PBS subsequently contributed two hundred pounds a year to his children's care, until his death; Shelley expressed concerns about Charles's future care to **Maria Gisborne** September 1822 (*Letters* 1.261). **Sir Timothy Shelley** became Charles's guardian 1823, but Charles died of tuberculosis, and Shelley's finances thus improved, as she was mother of the Shelley family's sole male heir (Sunstein 273; Seymour 362). See Roger Ingpen's *Shelley in England: New Facts and Letters from the Shelley-Whitton Papers* (1917).

Shelley, Clara Everina (1817–1818): The Shelleys' third child. When Clara contracted dysentery, Shelley took immediate action, departing **Este** to meet **PBS** in **Padua** and then continuing to **Venice** for consultation with Dr. Francesco Aglietti, who declared the situation hopeless (White 2.35–39). Upon Clara's death, Shelley recorded, "This is the Journal book of misfortunes" (*Journals* 226). Shelley calls Clara "my sweet girl, whose face resembled *his*," PBS's (*Ch* 63). See **Brenta**.

Shelley, Elena Adelaide (1818–1820): Her true parentage is unknown, but, "apparently for the sake of an unknown English lady, [**PBS**] secretly undertook the charge of an illegitimate baby girl born December 27, 1818, to the lady or a connection of hers," arranged for foster parents at **Naples** and, February 1819, "had the infant baptized Elena Adelaide Shelley and illegally registered as his by his wife, 'Maria Padurin,' after the unwitting [Shelley's] **Paterin** philosophy" (Sunstein 163; White 2.71–83). In March 1820, PBS traveled to **Leghorn** concerning Elena, about whose existence he had alerted the **Gisbornes**, but it seems Shelley did not learn about her until June 1820, when **Paolo Foggi** attempted to blackmail the Shelleys about her (Sunstein 182; Seymour 225; *Journals* 311). On 18 June 1820, just eight days after Elena's death, Shelley wrote with obscure reference to "a variety of circumstances [which] have occurred not of the most pleasant nature," which worsened when **Byron** told PBS that **Elise Foggi** had informed the **Hoppners** that Elena was PBS's child by **Claire Clairmont** (*Letters* 1.147; Sunstein 201). There has been much speculation about the child's true parentage; Feldman and Scott-Kilvert provide extensive notes about the facts and debates concerning Elena's brief existence (*Journals* 249, 321; White 2.546–550).

Shelley, Harriet (1795–1816): PBS's first wife, née Westbrook. "[D]aughter of a prosperous **London** innkeeper," she eloped with and married PBS 1811 and tried to follow his radical politics; she subsequently wanted him to renounce his radical stance and accept his heritage (Sunstein 68; White 1.154–155). Their daughter, **Ianthe Shelley**, was born 1813 (Sunstein 69). Harriet and PBS undertook a second marriage ceremony March 1814; July 1814, Harriet pretended, while pregnant, to go along with their subsequent separation agreement, and there followed rumors about whether PBS fathered **Charles Shelley** (Sunstein 77; White 1.327). After PBS eloped to **Europe** with Shelley, Harriet demanded that he return to her; when he refused, she "spread a slander ... which she knew to be false"—that **William Godwin** had sold

Shelley, [Eliza] Ianthe (1813–1876)

Shelley and **Claire Clairmont** to PBS (Sunstein 87–88; White 1.376). Though he accepted paternity of Charles, PBS told Harriet he would support her but no longer considered her his wife (Sunstein 88). Shelley wrote April 1815 that Harriet "meant (if [PBS] did not make a handsome settlement on her) to prosecute [him] for atheism"; PBS arranged for two hundred pounds a year for his estranged wife May 1815 (*Letters* 1.13–15). Harriet's pregnant body was found in the Serpentine, **Hyde Park**, 10 December 1816, apparently a suicide by drowning, although accidental death was recorded (*Letters* 1.25; Seymour 175; White 1.481–482). Both Shelleys felt considerable guilt over Harriet's death, and PBS tried, albeit unsuccessfully, to gain custody of their two children (Sunstein 140). In December 1825, Shelley noted PBS and Harriet "did not part by mutual consent" (*Letters* 1.508). Sunstein asserts that **Cornelia Santerre** is a portrait of Harriet and thus evidence that by 1835 Shelley "saw Harriet as an estimable, spirited, misguided young woman" (320). Shelley published her husband's *Queen Mab* (1813) 1839 without its original dedication to Harriet, recording in her *Journals* February 1839: "Poor Harriet to whose sad fate I attribute so many of my own heavy sorrows as the atonement claimed by fate for her death" (Sunstein 343; *Journals* 560). See Richard Holmes's *Shelley: The Pursuit* (1974).

Shelley, [Eliza] Ianthe (1813–1876):

Harriet Shelley and **PBS**'s only daughter, christened Eliza Ianthe but called Ianthe (White 1.317). In her suicide letter, Harriet specified that she wished Ianthe to stay with her sister, Eliza Westbrook; PBS and the Westbrooks were refused custody after a court struggle, and Dr. Thomas Hume was appointed guardian July 1818 (*Journals* 155; *Letters* 1.26, 1.30, 1.227; White 1.481–482). PBS subsequently contributed two hundred pounds a year to her and **Charles Shelley**'s care until his death; Shelley expressed concern about Ianthe's future care to **Maria Gisborne** September 1822 (*Letters* 1.261). PBS left six thousand pounds in trust for Ianthe; **Sir Timothy Shelley** maintained his deceased son's payments until 1823, when Eliza and her father became Ianthe's guardians (*Letters* 1.263; White 1.725–727). Ianthe married Edward Jeffries Esdaile 1837, and they settled in **Devon**, where they had seven children, three of whom survived to adulthood (*Letters* 1.293). **PFS** visited his half-sister April 1842, December 1843, and April 1844 (*Letters* 3.24, 3.102, 3.120). Shelley expressed concern about Ianthe's health March 1844, and she appealed May 1846 to **Medwin** not to publish his planned biography of PBS, as it would damage Ianthe, "who is innocent of all blame" (*Letters* 3.116–117, 3.284). See Roger Ingpen's *Shelley in England: New Facts and Letters from the Shelley-Whitton Papers* (1917).

Shelley, Jane (1820–1899):

PFS's wife. Born illegitimate and raised as Jane Gibson in the Lake District after her father's 1832 death; she married Charles Robert St. John 1841 and was widowed 1844 (*Letters* 3.334–335). She was guardian of her first husband's illegitimate son, Charles Robert St. John II, whom she first met February 1849 and with whom she remained in contact throughout the 1860s (*Letters* 3.356–357). Jane met PFS 1847, and they were engaged 24 March 1848 (*Letters* 3.334–335; Sunstein 379). March–April 1848, Jane stayed with Shelley, who called her "the best & sweetest thing in the world," writing June 1848 that Jane "is in herself the sweetest creature I ever knew—so affectionate so soft—so gentle with a thousand other good qualities.... [S]he looks what she is all goodness & truth [*sic*]. She has no taste for society & will thus participate in Percy's taste for a domestic quiet life" (*Letters* 3.334, 3.337, 3.342). With a "fortune of £15,000," Jane married PFS 22 June 1848; she "idolized Mary, whom she described as tender, gentle, lovely, noble, suffering in silence and totally selfless" (*Letters* 3.334–335, 3.342; Sunstein 381). Shelley was concerned about Jane's health winter 1848–49; Jane and PFS bought Boscombe Manor, 105 miles southwest of **London**, 1849, and lived there with Shelley (*Letters* 3.353, 3.360–361). Shelley recorded Jane's improving health August 1849 and noted that Jane "is to me a beloved daughter," calling her a "very ideal of woman—gentle, soft—yet very vivacious" (*Letters* 3.370, 3.376). Concern over Jane's health led her, PFS, and Shelley abroad: they went to **Paris** September 1849, then Nice, **France**, for six months, and finally **Italy** May 1850, staying at **Como** for several weeks, before returning to England June 1850—Shelley recorded Jane was better August 1850, but she soon became ill again (*Letters* 3.380, 3.383). Jane and PFS had no children: they adopted Jane's brother's youngest child, Bessie Florence Gibson (c. 1852–1934), affectionately called Flossie, April 1855 (*Letters* 3.374). Jane insisted that Shelley be buried with her parents in **Bournemouth**, moving the bodies there, and was zealous to preserve Shelley's heritage: she controlled access to Shelley papers and "preserved the vast majority of the original manuscripts," although destroying some that reflected unfavorably upon Shelley (*Letters* 3.394–395; Sunstein 394; Seymour 540–542; White 2.625–626). Jane's *Shelley and Mary* (1882) provides a carefully censored view of Shelley's life; Jane left the Shelley papers to **Oxford**'s Bodleian Library and to family members, so access to Shelley papers remains restricted (Sunstein 397). See Maud Rolleston's *Talks with Lady Shelley* (1925).

Shelley, Mary (1797–1851): Mary **Wollstonecraft** and **William Godwin**'s daughter, **Mary Wollstonecraft Godwin**, born in **London** 30 August 1797; Shelley spent her earliest years in the care of relatives and friends following her mother's death. Godwin married **Mary Jane Clairmont** 1801, after which Shelley had a stable, though unhappy, home. She idolized Godwin, whose literary connections gave Shelley access to leading authors, such as **Samuel Taylor Coleridge** (Seymour 58). Shelley read and reread Godwin's and Wollstonecraft's works throughout her life. **PBS** visited Godwin 1812. Two years later (spring 1814), Shelley and PBS declared their love, and, 28 July 1814, against Godwin's wishes, eloped; **Claire Clairmont** joined them. They traveled across **France** and **Switzerland**, returning to London mid-September; Shelley details their journey in *History*. Godwin refused to see or communicate with Shelley, as did many former friends scandalized by her behavior. In February 1815, Shelley gave birth to a premature infant who died two weeks later. The

Shelleys set up house in **Bishopsgate** August 1815, where she gave birth to **William Shelley** January 1816. Although Godwin still refused to see Shelley, he demanded financial support from PBS. Departing for Switzerland May 1816, the Shelleys summered on **Lake Geneva** with **Byron** nearby at **Villa Diodati**. He suggested the ghost-story contest out of which came *Frankenstein*. The Shelleys returned to England August 1816, settling in **Bath** and marrying 30 December, after **Harriet Shelley**'s death. In March 1817, they moved to **Marlow**, where **Clara Shelley** was born September; she died September 1818 in **Italy** (the Shelleys having moved there March 1818), where William also died June 1819. After losing two children within a year, Shelley, again pregnant, became suicidal, depressed, and withdrawn. Shelley began writing *Matilda* August 1819 and gave birth to **PFS** in November; she wrote *Valperga* 1820–21. Pregnant again, Shelley miscarried June 1822; PBS drowned in July, leaving Shelley widowed with a son and no financial resources. She moved to **Genoa** and wrote "**The Choice**" before returning to London August 1823. To celebrate PBS's poetic genius, Shelley collected and edited his works, publishing *Posthumous Poems of Percy Bysshe Shelley* (1824). Still needing money, she applied to **Sir Timothy Shelley** for funds, receiving only a hundred pounds a year for her son. Turning to writing as a living, Shelley published many successful short stories as well as poetry and drama in the *London Magazine* and literary annuals, such as the *Keepsake*. In the 1830s, Shelley also made money by writing biographies for **Dionysius Lardner**'s *Cabinet Cyclopedia*. Shelley continued to write novels too, publishing ***The Last Man, Perkin Warbeck, Lodore, Falkner***, and a revised edition of *Frankenstein* with a new introduction. Shelley then returned to PBS's work, editing and adding biographical and critical notes to *The Poetical Works of Percy Bysshe Shelley* (1839) and publishing *Essays, Letters from Abroad, Translations, and Fragments* (1840). Shelley and her son toured **Europe** 1840 and 1842–43, travels she describes in *Rambles*. Shelley died of a brain tumor 1 February 1851; she is buried at **Bournemouth** with her parents. Recent biographies are Emily Sunstein's *Mary Shelley: Romance and Reality* (1989) and Miranda Seymour's *Mary Shelley* (2000); see also Betty T. Bennett's *Mary Shelley: An Introduction* (1998).

Shelley, Percy Bysshe (1792–1822): British Romantic poet and Shelley's husband. **Sir Timothy Shelley**'s son, he was expelled from **Oxford** after authoring with **Thomas Jefferson Hogg** a pamphlet about atheism. He married **Harriet Shelley** 1811, and they had two children, **Ianthe** and **Charles Shelley**; the pamphlet and marriage alienated him from his family. Admiring **William Godwin**, PBS first met Shelley in 1814 (or possibly briefly in 1812); they fell in love and eloped to **Europe**. Back in England, the Shelleys struggled with debt and subsequently with rumors about PBS's relationship with **Claire Clairmont**, who was part of their household; these rumors, economic circumstances, and PBS's radical beliefs led to their eventual exile from Britain. Shelley bore their first child, a premature daughter who quickly died, February 1815, and their second, **Wil-**

liam Shelley, January 1816; Shelley and PBS married 1816 after Harriet's death (PBS was denied custody of Ianthe and Charles). PBS's letters and poem "Mont Blanc" appear in *History*. The same year, his *Alastor* was published, and the Shelleys spent summer in Byron's company at Lake Geneva. PBS's *The Revolt of Islam* was published 1818, the year the Shelleys left England permanently to settle in Italy, where their children, William and Clara Everina Shelley, died, and where PFS, their only child to survive infancy, was born (1819). They stayed in various major cities, including Venice and Rome, before settling in Pisa (1820). PBS also registered himself as illegitimate Elena Adelaide Shelley's father in Naples 1819, a biographical mystery still to be solved. Although their marriage was undoubtedly strained by Claire's presence, by their childrens' deaths, and by PBS's infidelity (such as his 1820 affair with Teresa "Emilia" Viviani), both Shelleys were productive in Italy. They frequently visited Byron, while becoming friends with Edward and Jane Williams. In Italy, PBS wrote many of his now-renowned works: *Julian and Maddalo*, *Prometheus Unbound* (wr. 1818–19, pub. 1820), *The Cenci*, "The Mask of Anarchy," *Peter Bell the Third*, *Epipsychidion* (1821), and his important prose piece, *A Defence of Poetry*. Sailing back from Leghorn after meeting the Hunts there, PBS drowned 8 July 1822. Although their marriage had been frequently difficult, Shelley never forgot her husband and their love; October 1822, she recorded: "For eight years . . . I communicated with unlimited freedom with one whose genius, far transcending mine, awakened & guided my thoughts; I conversed with him; rectified my errors of judgement, obtained new lights from him, & my mind was satisfied. Now I am alone!" (*Journals* 429). Shelley always encouraged her husband's writing and believed in his talent; after his death, she idealized his memory and was active in establishing his reputation, initially arranging publication of his *Posthumous Poems* (1824). Shelley published his *Poetical Works* (1839), editing the texts and providing notes lending invaluable insight into the circumstances of the works' composition and their contextual histories. Unsurprisingly, Shelley's works abound with references to her husband's texts, and her *Journals* and *Letters* record their love and Shelley's continued devotion to his memory. She also fictionalizes incidents of their lives together; for example, 15 August 1822, Shelley wrote an account of one of PBS's visions: "he had seen the figure of himself which met him as he walked on the terrace & said to him—'How long do you mean to be content' " (*Letters* 1.245). **Lord Lodore** hears a voice, which "had spoken audibly to his senses," ask, "**How long will** you be at peace?" when he is nervously contemplating letters received from England (*L* 1.47). See Newman Ivey White's *Shelley* (1940) and Richard Holmes's *Shelley: The Pursuit* (1974). See individual works and "The Boat on the Serchio," "Charles the First," "Cyclops," "From Moschus," *Hellas*, "Hymn to Mercury," "The Indian Girl's Song," *Ion*, "Letter to Maria Gisborne," "Lift not the Painted Veil," "Music," "Mutability," "Ode to the West Wind," "Rosalind and Helen: A Modern Eclogue," "The

Sensitive-Plant," "The Sunset," and "To the Lord Chancellor."

Shelley, Percy Florence (1819–1889): Shelley and **PBS**'s only surviving child; his birth relieved Shelley's depression following **William Shelley**'s death (*Journals* 302). Shelley doted on her shy son; she was always extremely concerned about his health and his affinity, similar to his father's, for boating (*Letters* 3.44, 3.72, 3.74, 3.122; Sunstein 327). Although Shelley wanted him to attend **Eton**, like PBS, **Sir Timothy Shelley** refused, and PFS attended Harrow, then Trinity College, **Cambridge**, receiving an education similar to **Byron**'s (*Journals* 507, 528, 531). PFS accompanied Shelley on her 1840 and 1842–43 **European** tours recounted in *Rambles*; several of his college friends, such as **Ellis** and **Knox**, joined them. He requested and received an allowance from Sir Timothy 1841 and inherited the baronetcy and family home, Field Place, 1844. PFS's appearance at court disappointed Shelley, who blamed his shyness for his lack of friends and recognition (*Letters* 3.179; Sunstein 369). He also failed to get a seat in **Parliament** (Sunstein 372, 378). PFS married widow **Jane Gibson St. John** June 1848; Shelley approved of the match (Sunstein 378–379). They all moved to Field Place, then to **Bournemouth**, where PFS bought Boscombe Manor, 1850 (Sunstein 379–383). Shelley spent her final days with her son, and he buried her in St. Peter's Churchyard there (*Letters* 1.255–256). PFS and Jane had no children but adopted Bessie Florence (Flossie) Gibson, Jane's niece, after 1855 (*Letters* 3.374). Though PFS lacked his parents' ambition and accomplishments, he wrote plays, composed music, and painted scenery for two Bournemouth theaters, one that he built at Boscombe and one on Tite Street. He was buried with his father's heart in the family grave at Bournemouth. See Roger Ingpen's *Shelley in England* (1917).

Shelley, Sir Timothy (1753–1844): **PBS**'s father and Member of **Parliament**. PBS's relationship with his father was always strained by his own actions. After PBS's 1811 elopement with **Harriet Shelley**, Sir Timothy refused to have direct contact with his son. They communicated through the family lawyer, **Whitton**, and Sir Timothy would not allow his son's name to be spoken in his presence (White 1.155; Holmes 88, 110–111). When Sir Timothy gained his title and estates 1815, he settled many of his son's debts and subsequently pursued lawsuits against his son's creditors; by 1816, the two reached a satisfactory arrangement of the estates, and PBS attained a lump sum and yearly annuity (*SCGS* 382–383, 388; White 1.396–399; Holmes 284–285). When Shelley returned to Britain with **PFS** 1823, eventually "Sir Timothy, who detested Mary as much as he detested his dead son, did however reluctantly agree to pay her a small allowance" 1824 to help with PFS's education; their relationship was always tense (*SCGS* 472; Holmes 732). Sir Timothy was infuriated by the publication of PBS's *Posthumous Poems* (1824), as he did not want his son to be remembered as a poet; Shelley had to agree not to bring PBS's name before the public as a condition of the financial settlement (White 2.385–386;

Holmes 732). In August 1824, she noted that Sir Timothy "writhes under the fame of his incomparable son as if it were a most grievous injury done to him" (*Letters* 1.444). Shelley resented her father-in-law's constraints upon her but complied in consideration of her son's future, regretting December 1834 "that the cruelty of Percy's relations will obscure his existence as it has mine by their wickedness" (*Journals* 542). Shelley asked Sir Timothy July 1838 for permission to publish PBS's works, "on grounds that several pirated editions had already appeared"; he agreed but would not permit a biography (White 2.401; Sunstein 341–342). When Sir Timothy finally died, Shelley noted that she did "not blame Sir Tim so much as others for the great injustice he has done his grandson" (*Letters* 3.131). PFS's inheritance, though, was ensured, and this financial guarantee greatly eased the last years of Shelley's life, even though she had to pay Sir Timothy's widow and his two daughters back all the money "Sir Timothy had lent her, with interest, since 1823" (Sunstein 364). See Newman Ivey White's *Shelley* (1940), Richard Holmes's *Shelley: The Pursuit* (1974), and Shelley's *Letters* and *Journals*.

Shelley, William Godwin (1816–1819):

The Shelleys' first child to survive infancy, born 24 January 1816 (Sunstein 113). William was a source of delight and traveled with the Shelleys before unexpectedly dying, from either typhoid or cholera, in **Rome**, 7 June 1819 (*Journals* 265; *Ch* 65–86). He was buried near Tomb of **Cestius** in the Protestant cemetery, which would also become his father's burial place. When **PBS**'s remains were buried 21 January 1823, it was discovered that William's remains had been lost; the remains of an adult were found beneath the stone supposedly marking William's grave (Sunstein 237). Shelley wrote February 1823, "What matters it that they cannot find the grave of my William; that spot is sanctified by the presence of his pure earthly vesture & that is sufficient" (*Journals* 450). She also expresses these sentiments in "**The Choice**" (*Ch* 87–96).

Shene:
Fourteenth-century palace in Surrey; **Henry VII** rebuilt it and renamed it **Richmond** (Weinreb 782). Henry meets with advisors at Shene on several occasions (*PW* 1.122, 2.59, 2.114, 3.214). **Monina De Faro** meets **Sir William Stanley** there (*PW* 1.326, 3.271).

Sheridan, Richard Brinsley (1751–1816):
Irish author whose first play, *The Rivals* (1775), established him in fashionable society; he became manager and part owner of **Drury Lane Theatre** and a member of the Literary Club with Samuel Johnson and **Reynolds** before becoming a famous **House of Commons** orator. Shelley asserts, "former experiences of **Alcibiades** or even of the emasculated **Steeny** of **James I**. [*sic*] might have caused Sheridan to have refused to tread over again the same path of dazzling but fleeting brilliancy" (*RD* 49). *Falkner*'s narrator suggests that **Alithea Neville** "seemed the very object whom Sheridan addressed when he said '**For friends in every** age you'll meet, / And lovers in the young' "; Don Carlos speaks these lines to Louisa in Sheridan's *The Duenna: A Comic Opera* (1794)

(*F* 136; Sheridan 1.5.135–136). Shelley quotes from title protagonist **Dangle**'s speech in Sheridan's *The Critic, or a Tragedy Rehearsed* (1781) to describe her difficulty in understanding **Kissingen**'s travel advisor: "**Egad, I think** the interpreter is the hardest to understand of the two!" (*R* 1.180; Sheridan 1.2.31–32).

Sheriff Hutton: English town ten miles northeast of **York**. **Elizabeth of York** calls the **Earl of Warwick** her "fellow-prisoner of Sheriff Hutton" (*PW* 3.203). The two were held captive there when young (*PW* 1.24, 1.26, 1.54–55, 1.120; Holinshed 3.479).

Shield of Hercules: See **Hesiod**.

Shore, Jane (c. 1445–1527): Edward IV's mistress; minor character who assists **Richard of York** in *Perkin Warbeck*.

Shrewsbury, Earl of: See **Talbot**.

Shropshire: Central western English county bordering Wales. **Horace Neville**'s family home is there, and he contemplates "riding across the country from Shropshire to **Berks**" to see **Ellen Burnet** (*Mourner* 95).

Siberia: North **Asian** region stretching from the Ural Mountains to the Pacific. "**Euphrasia**" opens Christmas 1836 during a snowstorm transforming "**Brighton** into a town of Siberia" (*E* 295).

Sibilla, Queen: See **Sibylla, Queen**.

Sibyl: Prophetess in classical myth and important figure in *Aeneid*. The Shelleys visited the **Elysian Fields** and Lake **Avernus** near **Naples** 8 December 1818, but did not go to the nearby subterranean temple supposed to be that of **Cumae**'s sibyl, who wrote prophecies on leaves (*Journals* 242; Crook 3.170). Shelley refers to "sybilline leaves" (also the title of **Samuel Taylor Coleridge**'s 1817 volume of poetry) in *Valperga* (*V* 2.138). *The Last Man*'s narrator recreates the Shelleys' visit to the Elysian Fields at the novel's opening on the same date, and Shelley imagines a natural cave on the bank of Avernus as the Cumaean sibyl's cave wherein they find leaves on which are written the novel's story (*LM* 3). An old woman, known as a sibyl, helps **Richard of York** and others escape danger in **Caen Wood** (*PW* 2.128). **Gerard Neville** tells **Elizabeth Falkner** that the third time they meet will be the true test of their relationship "if sibyls' tales are true" (*F* 81). The Cumaean sibyl offered **Rome**'s last king the Sibylline Books of prophecies: the king refused the first two times, so the sibyl burned the books, but she "finally sold the last three [volumes] to him at the original price" (Howatson 521).

Sibylla, Queen: Sibylla of Acerra, **Sicily**'s 13th-century queen; Shelley spells it **Queen Sibilla** (Runciman 11). **Despina dei Elisei** remembers first meeting **Guielmo Lostendardo** at **Manfred**'s court when she was "an attendant on" Queen Sibylla, Manfred's wife (*TP* 12). Shelley incorrectly refers to Sibylla: Manfred was married to **Savoy**'s Beatrice and then to **Epirus**'s Helena Angelina (Runciman Table IV).

Sicilian Vespers: Massacre of **French** in **Palermo** on Easter Monday

1282 that began the **Sicilian** revolt; it is named for the riot outside a church at vespers. Shelley comments on this event, calling it "tremendous" and misunderstood; she relays **Amari**'s version (*R* 2.209).

"Sicilian Vespers": See **Niccolini**.

Sicily: Island at **Italy**'s southwest tip, identified as **Trinacria** in classical days (Tripp 577). **Corradino** escapes battle with **Charles d'Anjou** in a hired vessel sailing toward Sicily but is captured at sea (*TP* 22). **Prince Mondolfo**'s first marriage is to a Sicilian princess (*HM* 308). **Ferdinando Eboli**'s father follows **Ferdinand IV** in retreat to Sicily (*FE* 65). Trinacria is *Proserpine*'s setting (*P* 35, 59, 71). Shelley outlines the history of **Gabriel Serbelloni**, whom "the Vice-Royalty of Sicily" rewarded for bravery and skill in battle; Shelley later reflects on a young Englishman at **Bastei** who travels only "for the sake of saying" that he has traveled, using "his Sicily" as an example of his mode of expression (*R* 1.81, 1.265). Shelley also discusses Sicilian **Amari** (*R* 2.209).

Sidmouth: Port on **Devon**'s southern coast fifteen miles southeast of **Exeter**. The countryman relates **Maurice**'s story to his father en route there (*Maurice* 67).

Siege of Jerusalem: See **Tacitus**.

Siena: Italian city thirty-five miles south of **Florence**; Shelley's variant is **Sienna**. **Tadeo della Ventura** tells **Castruccio** Siena will not submit to **Henry VII** of **Germany** (*V* 1.118, 1.124). Later in the **Lombard** wars, Henry unsuccessfully attacks Florence, then retires to Siena, where he dies (*V* 1.157). Henry actually died at Buon Convento, twelve miles south of Siena (Sismondi 128). **Padre Lanfranco** goes to Siena on business (*V* 3.118). **Giacomo** and **Teresa de' Tolomei** are of the Siennese **Tolomei** family (*BMI* 33). Shelley gives a brief historical sketch of **Francesco Sfondrati**, whom **Charles V** named Siena's governor (*R* 1.79). Siena is setting for "**The Brother and Sister**"; both **Ugo** and **Lorenzo Mancini** are banished from it (*Brother* 168, 172). [*V* 2.4].

Sienna: See **Siena**.

Sierra: Reference to **Andalusian** mountains. Shelley describes **Alcala**'s "rugged Sierra" scenery (*PW* 1.208, 1.218, 1.231).

Sigismunda: See **Boccaccio**.

Signor ——: Acquaintance Shelley made in **Venice** September 1842 through Laura Galloni's introductory letter (Moskal 270; *Letters* 3.40; Sunstein 358; *R* 2.79–80, 2.128). Not further identified.

Silenus: Greek mythological figure who "represented the spirit of wild life in a creature half-man, half-animal" and was "expert at music and given to prophecy when captured," as well as having a reputation for drunkenness (Howatson 523; Tripp 524). Silenus is **Bacchus**'s foster father. Bacchus rewards **Midas** with a golden touch when Midas returns drunken Silenus safely to Bacchus's care. The narrator of "**Recollections of Italy**" sits on the **Thames**'s bank "to read the **Eclogue** of

Silenus," a reference to **Virgil**'s sixth *Eclogue,* detailing two shepherds' capture of Silenus and the "songs of ancient myths" he sang to them (*RI* 25; Howatson 523).

Sill: River in western **Austria** joining the **Inn** near **Brenner**. Shelley was on its banks September 1842 (*R* 1.49).

Simnel, Lambert (c. 1475–1525): Richard Simon's **Earl of Warwick** impersonator who was crowned **Edward VI** in **Dublin** 1487, arrested at **Stoke**, pardoned, and employed in **Henry VII**'s kitchen (*DNB*). He appears in *Perkin Warbeck*.

Simon, Richard: **Oxford** priest who led the **Lambert Simnel** conspiracy; he was arrested at **Stoke** (*DNB*). Shelley also spells his name **Symond**; he appears in *Perkin Warbeck*.

Simon: Prince Mattathias's second son and last remaining brother of the **Maccabees** family. Shelley notes that the story of **Heliodorus** was related by Simon (*R* 2.220; 2 Maccabees 3.7-40).

Simone: See **Limone**.

Simplon: **Swiss Alpine** town at the **Simplon Pass** on the Swiss-**Italian** border. Shelley breakfasted there October 1840 (*R* 1.135–36).

Simplon Pass: Road winding through the **Alps** at Mount Leone on the **Swiss-Italian** border. Shelley took it October 1840 (*R* 1.134–35).

Sinn: Central **German** river joining the **Saale** and **Main** rivers at Gmunden. Shelley describes it as "a brawling stream" at **Brükenau** (*R* 1.200).

Sion: **Swiss** city near the **Rhône** eighteen miles northeast of **Martigny**. Shelley slept there October 1840 (*R* 1.138).

Sir Tristans: See **Tristans, Sir**.

Sirmio: Former name of Sirmione, **Italian** village nineteen miles southeast of **Brescia**. Shelley saw it September 1840 (*R* 2.72).

Sismondi, Jean Charles Léonard Simonde de (1773–1842): Swiss historian who lived in England, then **Tuscany**, where he was imprisoned repeatedly during **Italian** political turmoil. He married in England 1819 and thereafter lived mainly in Switzerland. Shelley read his sixteen-volume *Histore des républiques italiennes du moyen âge* [*History of the Italian Republic in the Middle Ages*] (1809–18), which details Italian history from the **Roman** Empire's 5th-century fall until 1805, 1819 and 1820, using it as a primary source for *Valperga* (Cannon 380; *Journals* 247–248, 333–337; *V* 1.iii). She found **Castruccio** in it and compiled a chronology and list of additional sources from Sismondi (Sunstein 162, 176). She praised the work highly and recommended it to **Maria Gisborne**: "If you want to read a *true* picture of Italians read the two last Chapters of Sismondi's history" (*Letters* 1.88). She also favorably reviewed Sismondi's *A Tour in Italy and Sicily* (1828) in "**Modern Italy**" (Sunstein 296).

"Sisters of Albano, The": Published in the 1828 *Keepsake* as "By the author of '**Frankenstein**' "; Robinson believes this Shelley story to be the first specifically prepared for the annual (Robinson 377). This tale's events take place in and near **Albano**, and *Lake Albano* is the accompanying illustration, which **Turner** drew and Robert Wallis engraved (*SA* 52). The tale's frame story is about a traveling party viewing Albano's landscape (*SA* 51). **Countess Atanasia D——** then relates a sentimental, cautionary tale about **Andrea**'s daughters, **Maria** and **Anina**, and "mingling of love with crime" (*SA* 53). The story focuses on the relationship between fifteen-year-old Anina and **Domenico Baldi**, a **banditti** member. Despite Andrea's praise for **French** soldiers who have trapped banditti at **Rocco Giovane**, Anina attempts to take provisions to the starving criminals and is arrested (*SA* 58). Maria, a nun of **Rome**'s **Santa Chiara** convent, resolves to rescue her sister and wears her habit to elicit pity (*SA* 59). When Maria learns that the command to execute Anina is irreversible, she exchanges clothes with her sister, who then escapes while Maria faces death (*SA* 60). Frightened of discovery and fearing her father's reproaches, Anina roams the mountains until three criminals take her hostage and transport her to Rocco Giovane, where she encounters Domenico (*SA* 61). Enraged by the intention of the French soldiers to execute a peasant girl for providing aid to his gang, Domenico convinces his comrades to attack their oppressors (*SA* 62). He urges Anina to travel to the Roman convent, where she will be safe, and en route Anina encounters her father, who is worriedly searching for his daughters (*SA* 63). He sends Anina along as he climbs the mountain, only to meet a funeral procession (bearing Maria's corpse) amid a violent skirmish led by Domenico, also killed. Countess Atanasia D——'s sketch of Anina caring for an aged Andrea, wishing only "to find repose in the grave," concludes the story (*SA* 64). Sunstein interprets "The Sisters of Albano" autobiographically, as a restatement of Shelley's own love for "an outlaw that was forbidden by her father" (290). Two versions of "The Sisters of Albano" were performed on stage in **London** 1830 (Sunstein 308).

Sistine Chapel: **Vatican** chapel built 1473 and famous for its ceiling, which **Michelangelo** painted 1508–12. Shelley calls this work "sublime" (*R* 2.219, 2.231).

Sistine Madonna: See **Raphael**.

Six Months in the West Indies: See **Henry Nelson Coleridge**.

Skelton, Richard: **Cornish** tailor and **Yorkist** supporter in *Perkin Warbeck* (Holinshed 3.318).

"Sketches of Bohemia": See **Reeve**.

Skyllo: Cape Scyllaeum or Syllì is at **Morea**'s southwestern tip in the **Mediterranean** on the Gulf of Argolis, with a small island opposite that Shelley terms and spells Skyllo. In **Greek** mythology, this is where, after betraying her father, **Scylla** drowned herself or was drowned by Minos of **Crete** (Howatson 514). **Cyril** and **Zella Ziani** "weathered the islands of Skyllo and **Cerigo**" (*EE* 108).

Slavonia: Historical region between **Danube**, Drava, and Sava in eastern

Croatia; Shelley spells it **Sclavonia**. **Benedetto Pepi** wears a Slavonian cloak and wishes **Florentines** to be scattered over the world like Slavonians (*V* 1.107, 1.124). [*R* 2.1].

Slough: English town five miles northeast of **Windsor**. **Lionel Verney** receives a letter carried by "a man just come from Slough" (*LM* 350).

Slovino di San Marco: Rubble-filled area resulting from an earthquake, the "landslide of St. Mark," on the **Adige**, thirty-three miles north of **Verona**; **Dante** describes it in *Inferno* (Ciardi 115; Dante 12.4–6). Shelley regretted not viewing it September 1842 (*R* 2.66).

"Slumber Did My Spirit Seal, A": Poem in **Wordsworth**'s Lucy series (1800). With lines from Wordsworth's text, **Matilda** finally rejoices that she will become one with nature: "**Rolled round in** earth's diurnal course / With rocks, and stones, and trees" (*M* 207; Wordsworth lines 7–8). Shelley adjusts the same lines to show **Elizabeth Falkner**: "**Borne round in** earth's diurnal course / With rocks, and stones, and trees" (*F* 15; Wordsworth lines 7–8).

Smithson, Daddy: Sailor, **Dame Smithson**'s husband, and **Maurice**'s adoptive father in "**Maurice**."

Smithson, Dame: In "Maurice," woman who snatches two-year-old **Maurice** from his parents' nurse at **Ilfracombe** and pretends he is her child.

"Smuggler and His Family, The": Short story first appearing in *Original Compositions in Prose and Verse, Illustrated with Lithographic Drawings; to Which is Added Some Instrumental Music* (1833), attributed to "Mrs. Shelley" (Robinson 389). The accompanying illustration, which Louis Haghe drew, depicts the story's final scene and is titled with Shelley's prose, beginning *Struggling with wind and water* (*S* 216). Set in **Cornwall**, Shelley relates **Jem Harding**'s involvement with a band of smugglers and its effects upon his family. **Jane Harding** raises her eldest son **Charles Harding** in "guarded innocence," pleading with her husband not to involve their son in smuggling (*S* 206). Jem loves his wife, notwithstanding shame due to his occupation that makes him harsh toward her, and he resolves to adhere to her wishes until, at sea one day, he sees a signal from smugglers warning of immediate danger (*S* 209–210). Jem hastens to the cave containing stolen goods, and he and Charles then help the smugglers conceal them (*S* 210). Jem kills a revenue officer who attacks his son, but they both avoid capture and return home several days later (*S* 211–212). Jane subsequently blames herself as she witnesses her son's distress over the knowledge of his father's true profession (*S* 212–213). When Charles refuses to participate further in his father's trade, Jem forces Charles to leave home and angrily sets out to sea alone (*S* 212–213). Jane worries during both men's three-day absence, until Charles returns and informs her that the smugglers have been caught and either killed, taken, or escaped (*S* 214). Charles leaves alone to find his father, while Jane is again left to wait anxiously until, on the second day of waiting, she walks to the nearest town with her children **Tommy** and **Jenny Harding** (*S* 215). There she finds a letter from Charles informing her Jem has died in jail after forgiving Charles (*S* 215–216). **Sailor**'s howls alert her of Charles's return, and he lands safely from the stormy sea (*S* 217–218). Jane, in her overprotective love for her son and her fears for his life while at sea, is autobiographical.

Socrates (469–399 B.C.E.): Greek philosopher whose teaching methods **Plato** presents in his *Dialogues*. Socrates believed philosophy should investigate ethical questions and that knowledge is virtue. **Woodville** invokes Socrates as one who did not despair of life while young, thus benefitting the world immeasurably through his work (*M* 202).

Soldanieri: Historically, noble **Florentine Ghibelline** family; **Euthanasia** visits their tomb (Villani 81, 124; *V* 2.126).

Solomon: Biblical king renowned for knowledge and wealth (1 Kings 10.23–24). **Raymond** tells **Lionel Verney** of his aspiration to be king like " 'mightiest men of the olden times,' " including " 'Solomon, the wisest of men' " (*LM* 56).

Solomon: See **Prior**.

Solomon's Song: Usually Song of Solomon; **biblical** book. **Lionel Verney** celebrates spring's arrival in **Milan**: " '**For lo! winter** is past, the rain is over and gone; the flowers appear on the earth, the time of the singing of birds is come, and the voice of the turtle is heard in our land; the fig tree putteth forth her green figs, and the vines, with the tender grape, give a good smell' "; Shelley footnotes these lines as from "Solomon's Song" (*LM* 431; Solomon 2.11–12).

Solon (c. 638–558 B.C.E.): Athenian statesman known as a wise lawgiver due to his political and economic reforms (Hutchins 70). The **Creature** admires "peaceable lawgiver" Solon, whose biography **Plutarch** narrates in *Lives* (*Fr1* 156; *Fr3* 112; Plutarch 1.120–144).

Sommariva, Villa: Sfondrati family's villa on **Lake Como** between **Cadenabbia** and **Tremezzo**, renowned for its art collection, gardens, and Sommariva family cemetary (*BSWI* 490). Shelley visited it repeatedly July–August 1840 (*R* 1.78–80).

"Song of Apollo": **PBS** wrote these verses, which Holmes identifies as a version of the **Homeric** Hymn "Apollo," specifically for Shelley's *Midas* 1820; they were first published as "Hymn of Apollo" 1824 (Holmes 611; White 2.596). **Midas** judges a musical contest between Apollo and **Pan**, with Apollo performing his song first (*Midas* 97–99).

"Song of Pan": **PBS** wrote these verses, which Holmes identifies as a version of the **Homeric** Hymn "Pan," specifically for Shelley's *Midas* 1820; they were first published as "Hymn of Pan" 1824 (Holmes 611; White 2.596). **Midas** judges a musical contest between **Apollo** and Pan, with Pan performing second (*Midas* 99–103).

Soolen Sprudel: See **Soolensprudel**.

Soolensprudel: Artesian brine spring a mile north of **Kissingen**; Shelley spells it **Soolen Sprudel** (*MSGE* 113). Shelley visited it repeatedly July 1842 (*R* 1.186).

Soracte: Mountain twenty-five miles north of **Rome**. **Beatrice** mentions it when recounting her journey (*V* 3.84). Shelley also refers to it as **Sant' Oreste** when stating it recalls *Childe Harold's Pilgrimage* (*R* 2.227; Moskal 349).

Sorrento: Italian town on the peninsula between Bay of **Naples** and Gulf of **Salerno**, fifteen miles southeast of Naples. Shelley spent two "perfect" months there May–July 1843, writing to **Claire Clairmont**: "The place is wonderfully beautiful & we live in the midst of orange groves—the night's rain has filled the air with odours" (Sunstein 359; *Letters* 3.73). Most of "The Heir of Mondolfo's" action occurs at **Mondolfo** castle in mountains near Sorrento (*HM* 308). **Horatio Saville** promises "to take a house for [the **Villiers**es], for the summer, at **Castel à Mare**, or Sorrento" (*L* 2.196). Shelley enjoyed the beauty of houses on cliffs overlooking the bay while staying there June 1843 (*R* 2.262–267). Comparing Sorrento to **Castelammarre**, Shelley concludes that "Sorrento is in every way cheaper and more practicable for those who are not rich" (*R* 2.296).

Sorrows of Werter, The: **Goethe's** epistolary novel, *Die Leiden des jungen Werthers* [*The Sorrows of Young Werther*] (1774), caused a major stir in **Europe**, and many Romantics drew upon Goethe's example of a hero in conflict with the world and with himself; **Werter's** thwarted love for the engaged Charlotte leads him to shoot himself. Shelley read it 1815 (*Journals* 88). The **Creature** reads *Sorrows* and identifies with its sensitive artist (*Fr1* 155–156; *Fr3* 112). **Lionel Verney** is private secretary to the **Viennese** ambassador, just as Werther is (*LM* 36).

Soult, Nicolas-Jean de Dieu (1769–1851): Dalmatian duke who served as **France's** marshal general 1847; he commanded **Napoleonic** armies in several battles in the **French Revolutionary** and Napoleonic Wars, including **Waterloo**, and subsequently held various governmental posts (McLynn 545–546, 620). Shelley quotes Soult's 1830 comment in the **Chamber of Peers**: "The principle of non-intervention shall henceforth be ours; but on condition that it shall be respected by others" (*R* 2.249).

South America: The **Creature** pleads for a mate, promising **Victor Frankenstein** that he will subsequently remove to the "vast wilds of South America" (*Fr1* 173; *Fr3* 125).

South End: See **Southend-on-Sea**.

Southampton: Large British seaport twenty-five miles southwest of Salisbury. **Lord Lodore** travels to Southampton to sail for Le **Havre** (*L* 1.171, 1.176). **Fenton** passes through Southampton with letters and encounters **Lady Lodore** there (*L* 1.200). **Lord Lovel** concurs with **Lady Brampton's** suggestion that **Richard of York** should be taken to **Winchester** to see his mother before going to Southampton (*PW* 1.72). **Robert Clifford** later hails **Clim of the Lyn** "to track us through the **New Forest** to Southampton" (*PW* 3.139). **Shelley** spent the week before her departure to **Europe** 1842 "at the seat of a friend near Southampton" (*R* 1.156).

Southend-on-Sea: English town thirty-five miles east of **London** at the **Thames**'s mouth; Shelley calls it **South End**. After leaving **Jane Shore**, **Richard of York** passes Southend-on-Sea (*PW* 3.241, 3.247).

Southwark: **London** district south of the **Thames**. **Mat Oldcraft** reports bonfires in Southwark for **Richard of York** (*PW* 3.118).

Sovereign Pontiff: Former term, with sense of "bridge builder," for the pope. **Lionel Verney** uses this term with reference to a new year's ceremony (*LM* 467).

Spain: Country bordering **France** and **Portugal** and forming the majority of the Iberian Peninsula in southwestern **Europe**. **Napoleon** campaigned there from 1808, but British forces defeated him 1814 (Kinder 2.35). Ferdinand II then reigned as "absolute ruler," against whom the Spanish rose 1820 (Kinder 2.45). Shelley learned Spanish and, 1820, "was thrilled by the current Liberales uprising in Spain . . . which forced the king to grant a constitution" (Sunstein 178). **Prince Ferdinando Mondolfo** tries to separate **Viola Arnaldi** from his son by arranging for her to be " 'taken to a town in Spain' " (*HM* 323). **Lionel Verney** suggests that **Raymond**'s ship bringing him back to **Athens** is worth more than all the wealth "that was conveyed over [the ocean's] bosom to enrich the crown of Spain" (*LM* 170). Verney is also grateful that Spain stands between England and approaching plague (*LM* 231). **Lewis Elmore** is wounded in Spain soon after joining the army (*Mourner* 92–93). **Hernan De Faro** and his family are Spanish, and **Stephen Frion** spends time at **Ferdinand** and **Isabella I**'s Spanish court (*PW* 1.95, 1.150). De Faro takes his family and **Richard of York** to live in Spain, where **Edmund Plantagenet** joins them (*PW* 1.198–203, 1.207, 1.212). **Pedro d'Ayala**, "ambassador from Spain," brokers peace between **Henry VII** of England and Scottish **James IV** (*PW* 2.314, 3.92, 3.246). **Miss Jervis** travels through Spain with the **Cecils** (*F* 73). Shelley wrote biographies of several Spanish authors for *Italian and Spanish Lives*. She records **Gabriel Serbelloni**'s adventures in Spain and also notes disputes between France and Spain at the opening of her account of **Carbonari**, as well as the fact students at medical school in **Salerno** would travel to Spain to further their knowledge (*R* 1.80–81, 2.162, 2.294). [*Trans* 123].

Spanish Armada: 1588 **Spanish** naval force consisting "of a massive sea force of 130 of the largest naval and maritime ships in the world of that era" (Rasor 3). The English defeated the Spanish Armada in a series of naval battles. Seeing **Tilbury Fort** causes **Victor Frankenstein** and **Henry Clerval** to remember when British forces gathered at Tilbury to fight the Spanish Armada, which never reached the port (*Fr1* 184; *Fr3* 134).

Sparta: Dominant in ancient times, **Greek** town ninety miles southeast of **Patras**; its people are characterized as brave and disciplined (Tripp 534). **Rousseau** discusses Spartan women's education in *Émile*'s fifth book, which is possibly where Shelley learned about it; she terms **Lady Lodore** "a woman who in Sparta had formed a heroine" (Stafford 72; *L* 1.202). See **Plutarch**.

Spencer: See **Spenser**.

Spenser, Edmund (c. 1552–1599): Influential and much admired British poet best known for his long poem *The Faerie Queen* (1590, 1596). Shelley occasionally refers to Spenser as **Spencer** and refers to *The Faerie Queene* repeatedly, especially in *Perkin Warbeck* and *Lodore*. In December 1819, Shelley wrote, Spenser "is a favourite author of mine," further reflecting "perhaps it is not in pathos but in the simple description of beauty that Spencer excels" (*Journals* 48, 177; *Letters* 1.121–122). Shelley notes that the **Prior of Kilmainham** "appointed a meeting in a secluded dell, near the bank of the **Mullagh**, or **Awbeg**, the river which Spenser loves to praise" in several of his works (*PW* 1.293). **Gerard Neville** introduces **Elizabeth Falkner** to the work of "Spenser, of ancient date" (*F* 236). See *Ruines of Rome*.

Sphynx: In **Greek** mythology, female monster who would "ask a riddle of young Theban men"; when they could not answer her, "she would eat them" (Tripp 536). The riddle was, " 'What is it that goes on four legs in the morning, two at midday, and three in the evening?' " **Oedipus** eventually gave the answer: " 'Man, who crawls in infancy, walks upright in his prime, and leans on a cane in old age' " (Tripp 421–422). **Lionel Verney** marvels at humankind and its renewal despite the plague's threat: "Strange system! riddle of the Sphynx, most awe-striking! that thus man remains, while we the individuals pass away" (*LM* 228). Verney later feels he is left to solve humanity's mystery and appeals "for some Oedipus to solve the riddle of the cruel Sphynx!" (*LM* 427).

Spielberg: See **Spielburg**.

Spielburg: Eleventh-century castle in **Brünn** that was a political prison 1740–1855; Shelley uses both spellings: Spielburg and **Spielberg**. Shelley saw **Confalonieri** return to **Como** from imprisonment there September 1840; **Pellico** was also imprisoned there (*R* 1.121, 2.88).

Spina, Adalinda: Marchese Spina's daughter and **Ferdinando Eboli**'s wife in "Ferdinando Eboli."

Spina, Marchese: Adalinda Spina's father in "Ferdinando Eboli."

Spina, Villa: Spina family's house in **Naples** in "Ferdinando Eboli"; Adalinda and Marchese Spina live there (*FE* 66, 76).

Spini: Geri Spini lived just outside **Florence**'s walls 1325; Shelley noticed the name while researching material for *Valperga* (Green 177). **Euthanasia** explains her negative attitude toward **Castruccio**'s plans for Florence in terms of her political connection to and love for the Spini family (*V* 1.240).

"Spirit of Night": See **Pearson**.

Splügen: Swiss town seventeen miles north of **Chiavenna**. Shelley dined there July 1840 (*R* 1.59).

Spoleto: Small **Italian** town sixty miles northeast of **Rome**. **Euthanasia** and **Castruccio** trace **Beatrice** there (*V* 2.191). **Lionel Verney** passes through Spoleto (*LM* 457–460).

Sposalizio: See **Raphael**.

Spree: Northeastern **German** river meandering through **Berlin**. Shelley saw it July 1842 (*R* 1.228).

Spy, The: See **Cooper, James Fenimore**.

Stadt Rom: British travelers frequented this **Berlin** hotel on the **Unter den Linden** in Shelley's day (*STIE* 459). Shelley stayed there July 1842 (*R* 1.218).

Staël, Madame de (1766–1817): **French** writer **Byron** met 1816. Anne Louise Germaine Necker married Baron Eric Magnus of Staël-Holstein 1786, and her **Parisian** drawing room became a meeting place for many leading social and political figures. She published *Lettres sur Rousseau* [*Letters about Rousseau*] (1789), *Réflexions sur le procès de la reine* [*Reflections on the Queen's Trial*] (1793), and *Réflexions sur la paix intérieure* [*Reflections on the Interior Peace*] (1795). Her *Littérature et ses rapports avec les institutions sociales* [*Literature and its Relation to Social Institutions*] (1800), which **PBS** read 1815, restored her fading popularity somewhat (*Journals* 678). In the same year her husband died, the publication of *Delphine* (1802), a novel condemned as immoral, led **Napoleon** to rule that Staël must remain forty leagues from Paris. Her best-known novel is *Corinne; ou l'Italie* [*Corinne; or Italy*] (1807), which Shelley read February–March 1815, December 1818, and November 1820 (*Journals* 67–68, 243, 340). Staël visited **Germany** and wrote another admirable work, *De l'Allemagne* [*Of Germany*] (1810), which Shelley first read 1815 (*Journals* 678). A leading figure of the **European** Romantic movement, Staël's work, especially *Corinne*, evoked profound interest among her contemporaries and inspired many subsequent women writers. Shelley wrote Staël's biography for **French Lives**; she had previously suggested writing a biography for **Murray**'s *Family Library* 1829 and 1830 (*Letters* 2.89, 2.105, 2.113). Shelley emphasizes Staël's close relationship with her father and admires the posthumous *Dix Années d'exil* [*Ten Years of Exile*] (1821) and *Corinne* especially (*FL* 2.331). Shelley suggests that Staël's novels are somewhat lighthearted, while noting the impressive style and research evident in *De l'Allemagne*, concluding that Staël's novels provide accurate pictures of life even though they are devoid of moral courage (*FL* 2.343).

Stafford, Humphrey (1439–1469): **Devonshire** earl wounded at **St. Albans** (*DNB*). **Yorkist** *Perkin Warbeck* character.

Stafford, Thomas: Humphrey Stafford's brother and **Yorkist** supporter in *Perkin Warbeck*.

Staines: English town seven miles southeast of **Windsor**. **Lionel Verney** accompanies **Adrian** there (*LM* 84).

Stamboul: Constantinople's oldest section; **Golden Horn** separates it from **Pera**, and **Marmora** borders it (Coufopoulos 1). **Raymond** leads **Greeks** against Stamboul, and when some **Janizaries** are apprehended trying to escape from this section, they warn, " 'The curse of **Allah** is on Stamboul, share ye her fate' " (*LM* 191). The plague first occurs there (*LM* 193). Stamboul's falling ruins kill Raymond (*LM* 198, 206). **Katusthius Ziani** sails as master of his "father's vessels to Stamboul" and later visits **Cyril Ziani** to announce his journey there (*EE* 102, 105).

Stanley, William (d. 1495): Yorkist who refused to support **Richard III** at **Bosworth**, became **Henry VII**'s Lord Chamberlain, was denounced by **Robert Clifford**, and was beheaded on **Tower** Hill (*DNB*). Major character in *Perkin Warbeck*.

Stanwell: Small English village six miles east of **Windsor**. **Lionel Verney** intends to return from **Rochester** by way of Stanwell, but bad weather impedes the journey (*LM* 354).

"Stanzas for Music": Poem **Byron** published 1816. Shelley adopts a line from it: **Jane Harding** watches for her son's boat all day until "the moon rose as daylight faded, and '**wove her chain** upon the deep' " (*S* 208; Robinson 208; Byron lines 9–10).

"Stanzas: How like a star you rose upon my life": Poem Shelley first published in the 1839 *Keepsake*, as "By the Author of *Frankenstein*" (179). It consists of two octaves, in which a speaker recalls, "How like a star you rose upon my life," only to mourn the loss of the "you," who is "My heaven deserting for another sphere" (*Stanzas: How like* lines 1, 7). In the second stanza, the speaker mourns the loss of her **Hesperus**, since now, "You glad the morning of another heart" while the speaker has only dreams and memories (9–10).

"Stanzas: I must forget thy dark eyes' love-fraught gaze": Poem Shelley first published in the 1833 *Keepsake*; Sunstein suggests it was written summer 1832 (Sunstein 318). It consists of three octaves, which repeat the refrain, "I must forget," as though the speaker is trying to convince herself to "forget thy love" and continue her own life (*Stanzas: I must forget* line 13). But the speaker prefers death to forgetting and envies **Daphne**, who, "changed to leaves, / No more can weep, nor any longer moan" (17–18). The speaker also desires " a draught of that **Lethean** wave" but concludes, "Love, hope, and thee, I never can forget!" (21, 24).

"Stanzas: O, come to me in dreams, my love!": Poem Shelley first published in the 1839 *Keepsake*, as "By the Author of *Frankenstein*" (201). It consists of four stanzas, in which the speaker consistently desires "my love" to "come to me in dreams" (*Stanzas: O, come* line 1). The speaker compares herself to **Psyche** and insists that "gentle sleep shall veil my sight," so the speaker's lover will not be revealed and lost as Psyche's was (9).

"Stanzas: The Tide of Time Was at my Feet": See "La Vida es Sueño."

"Stanzas: To love in solitude and mystery": Poem published anonymously in the 1832 *Keepsake*, which Bennett confirmed as Shelley's in 1997 ("Newly Uncovered" 73). The poem's first sextet questions the purpose of love for one "who can ne'er be mine"; the second stanza declares an inability to resist love's "weapon of a smile" and the speaker's resignation to "dedicate my soul" to "worship" of love or the object of the speaker's desire (lines 2, 9, 12). Bennett notes that "To Is[ ]," written on "the reverse of the poem," suggests an intended dedication to **Isabel Robinson** ("Newly Uncovered" 73).

Star and Garter: Historic hotel in **Richmond** (Vargo 215). **Edward Villiers** suggests **Elizabeth Fitzhenry** and **Ethel Villiers** dine there (*L* 2.83).

Starke, Mariana (c. 1762–1838): English travel writer who lived in **India** as a child and later lived in **Italy**, where she died. Her guide-books, such as *Travels on the Continent* (1820), *Information and Directions for Travellers on the Continent* (1824), and *Travels in Europe for the use of Travellers on the Continent and likewise in the Island of Sicily* (1832), were used by Shelley and greatly influenced **Murray**'s handbook series (*DNB*; *Journals* 109; Seymour 219, 227). Shelley footnotes that Starke lived at the **Cocumella** and praises her "accurate and well written" description of southern Italy, for which "she is an excellent guide" (*R* 2.266).

Staudigl, Joseph (1807–1861): **Austrian** bass who performed in **London** 1842 and 1847 (*NGD*). Shelley praises his voice (*R* 2.177).

Steenie: **James I**'s nickname for his favorite, George Villiers (1592–1628), first Duke of **Buckingham** (Magnusson 224). Steenie negotiated **Charles I**'s marriage and remained in favor at court during the early 1620s, but his insolence and arrogance resulted in his assassination (Magnusson 224). Shelley's variant is **Steeny**. Shelley asserts that "the former experiences of ... emasculated Steeny of James I. might have caused **Sheridan** to have refused to tread over again the same path of dazzling but fleeting brilliancy" (*RD* 49).

Steeny: See **Steenie**.

Stelvio: Alpine northern **Italian** pass, fifty-four miles southeast of **Chur**. Shelley notes that it is a popular route (*R* 2.47).

Stern: German for "star" and name of Steig inn at **Hollenthal**'s southeastern end (*MCON* 551). Shelley stayed there July 1840 (*R* 1.46).

Sterne, Laurence (1713–1768): English author renowned for *The Life and Opinions of Tristram Shandy* (1759–1767) and *A Sentimental Journey Through France and Italy* (1768), both of which Shelley read 1818 (*Journals* 191–192). In September 1840, Shelley categorized changing guests in her **Milan** hotel's dining room as such types as **Curious Traveller** and **Knowing Traveller**, drawing on Sterne's satirical classification of travelers in his preface to *A Sentimental Journey* (*R* 1.120; Moskal 137).

Sterzinger Moos: **Austrian** marshy flat that was once a lake extending

Sterzinger Moss

from Sterzing, eight miles southwest of **Brenner**, to the gorge containing **Mittenwald**; Shelley translates it **Sterzinger Moss** (*MSGE* 331). She traversed it September 1842 (*R* 2.49).

Sterzinger Moss: See **Sterzinger Moos**.

Stirling: Twelfth-century fortress and city twenty-five miles northwest of **Edinburgh**; it was **James IV**'s residence (Donaldson 208). **Mary Boyd**, **Lady Jane Kennedy**, **Richard of York** and James enjoy a hawking expedition there (*PW* 2.189, 2.192).

Stockholm: Swedish port on the **Baltic Sea** 360 miles northeast of Copenhagen. **Rupert Falkner** and **Elizabeth Falkner** pass through it (*F* 38).

Stoke: Battle, 16 June 1487, four miles southwest of **Newark-upon-Trent**; **Lancastrians** defeated two thousand **German** mercenaries supporting **Lambert Simnel**. Several *Perkin Warbeck* characters die or are arrested there (*PW* 1.135–139).

Stolzenfels Castle: Neo-Gothic castle built 1836–42 on the **Rhine** south of **Coblentz** (*BGER* 167). Shelley passed it June 1840 (*R* 1.171).

Stony Stratford: Small English town thirty miles northeast of **Oxford**. **Elizabeth Falkner** and **Gerard Neville** reunite when she stops there for the night (*F* 250).

Storia del Reame di Napoli: See **Colletta**.

Strand: **London** street with **Charing Cross** at its western end and **Fleet Street** in the east. Her coach's slow progress along Fleet Street toward the Strand frustrates **Ethel Villiers** (*L* 2.258). A creditor looking for **Edward Villiers** claims that he "had been seen that very day in the Strand" (*L* 2.286). Ethel later passes along the Strand en route to rejoin her husband in prison (*L* 3.86).

Strangeways, Mat: **Tower** guard in *Perkin Warbeck*.

Strasbourg: French city sixty-five miles west of Stuttgart; Shelley also spells it **Strasburg** and **Strasburgh**. The Shelleys passed through it 1814 (*H* 63). **Alphonse Frankenstein** and **Elizabeth Lavenza** arrange for **Henry Clerval** to meet **Victor Frankenstein** there (*Fr1* 181; *Fr3* 132). Shelley and her party were determined not to visit Strasbourg, but two **Cantabs** who joined them at **Trèves** left them in **Mainz** to see it (*R* 1.29).

Strasburg: See **Strasbourg**.

Strasburgh: See **Strasbourg**.

Stratton Street: Street extending northwest from **Piccadilly** toward **Berkeley Square** in **London**'s Westminster district. **Lewis Elmore**'s London address is Stratton Street (*Mourner* 90).

Strozzi, Filippo (1498–1538): Italian noble who opposed the **Medicis** in **Florence** and committed suicide after receiving a death sentence (Petronio 5.205). Shelley mentions that Florentines read about him, referring to **Niccolini**'s drama *Filippo Strozzi* (1847) (*R* 2.185; Moskal 326).

Strub, Pass: Alpine pass, probably Steinpass, between **Salzburg** and **Tyrol**, east of Waidring. Shelley crossed it September 1842 (*R* 2.40).

Stuart: Scottish dynasty Robert II established 1371; it became England's 1603 when Scotland's James VI became **James I** of England. The **Commonwealth** 1649–60 and House of Orange 1689–95 interrupted Stuart rule, which ended with Queen Anne's death (1714) (Morby 70–71, 73). **Dr. Hotham** informs **Roger Dodsworth**, "the despicable race of the Stuarts, long outcast and wandering, is now extinct" because the Young Pretender (Charles Edward [1720–88]) died without legitimate issue after challenging **Hanoverian** rule 1745 and wandering around **Europe** (*RD* 46; Crook 2).

Stuart, Charles: See **Charles I**.

Stuhlingen: German town ten miles northwest of **Schaffhausen**. Shelley ate "the nastiest dinner" there July 1840 (*R* 1.48).

Styria: Austrian province on Slovenia's border, with capital Gräz. Shelley discusses Styrian **Alps**; **Gmunden**, **Ischl**, and **Linz** are in Styria (*R* 2.20, 2.33, 2.45).

Styx: In **Greek** mythology, this river formed **Tartarus**'s boundary, and gods drank its waters when swearing their highest oaths (Tripp 538–539). Underworld river and its goddess in *Proserpine* (*P* 71). **Zopyrian** thinks **Midas** will ask **Bacchus** to place his ears of an ass in the Styx as the reward for caring for **Silenus** (*Midas* 123).

Suabia: See **Swabia**.

Subiaco: Italian village thirty-two miles east of **Rome**. Fanny and **Louis Chaumont** live there (*SP* 137, 151–152).

Suir: River meandering through south central **Ireland** and emptying into **Waterford Harbor** at **Waterford**. After the first attack on Waterford, **Richard of York**'s fleet sails into the Suir (*PW* 3.40, 3.44).

Suli: Town and mountainous region in **Epirus** fifteen miles northwest of **Ioannina**; Shelley spells it **Sulli** (*MGRE* 390). Shelley describes Suli mountains south of **Zitza** (*EE* 111).

Sulla, Lucius Cornelius (c. 138–78 B.C.E.): General who became **Rome**'s consul 88 B.C.E. Like his predecessor **Marius**, Sulla killed his enemies and then introduced proscription, which was "the posting-up of the names of victims who might be killed without trial and their property confiscated" (Howatson 543). **Valerius** recalls Sulla's tyranny (*Val* 333, 336). Valerius's uncle, " 'who took care of me during my infancy, was proscribed by Sulla and murdered by his emissaries' " (*Val* 333).

Sulli: See **Suli**.

Sultana: Title of wife of the sultan, absolute monarch of the **Ottoman Empire** (Coufopoulos 20). **Evadne Zaimi** looked like a "Sultana of the East" (*LM* 182). [*PW* 1.150].

"Sunset, The": Poem **PBS** wrote 1816, according to Shelley. She quotes its opening lines as an epigraph to the *Lodore* chapter in which **Lady Lodore** and **Horatio Saville** develop their relationship: "One, within whose subtle being, / As light and wind within some delicate cloud, / That fades amid the blue noon's burning sky. / Genius and youth contended" (*L* 2.13; PBS lines 1–4).

Superior: Head of **St. S—— convent** in "The Bride of Modern Italy."

Surrey, Lord (1443–1524): Thomas Howard, first Earl of Surrey and second **Duke of Norfolk**; he fought at **Bosworth** and had seven daughters (*DNB*). **Richard of York** supporter in *Perkin Warbeck*; Richard attends a feast honoring Surrey's oldest daughter's marriage to **Lord de Walden**.

Susa: Italian town thirty miles northwest of **Turin**. The Shelleys passed through it March 1818, and Shelley visited again 1823 (*Journals* 202; *Letters* 1.352). **Benedetto Pepi** and **Castruccio** stay there with **Taddeo della Ventura** (*V* 1.110).

Susan: **Fanny**'s twin sister who marries **Lawrence Cooper** in "The Parvenue."

Sussex: Large southeastern English county. **Gerard Neville** reflects happily on times spent with **Elizabeth Falkner** at **Lady Cecil**'s residence there (*F* 226). The framework of "**Euphrasia**" is set there Christmas 1836 (*E* 295).

Suttil: Piazza San Marco café next to **Florian**; Shelley notes **Venetian** nobles frequent it (*R* 2.105).

Sutton, Dr. William: Yorkist supporter arrested at the 1493 conspiratorial meeting at **Robert Clifford**'s house (*PW* 2.50; Holinshed 3.507).

Swabia: Old southwestern **German** duchy the Hohenstaufens controlled 1079–1268; Shelley also uses the alternate spelling **Suabia** (Kinder 1.164–165). "A Tale of the Passions" details the history of **Manfred** and **Conradin**, of Suabia's house (*TP* 10, 21). Shelley also refers to **Pope Urban**, who "hated the house of Suabia" (*V* 1.3, 1.119).

Swartz: Martin Swartz's son in *Perkin Warbeck*; Shelley also spells it **Schwartz**.

Swartz: See **Schwaz**.

Swartz, Martin: German military commander who assists **Richard of York** in *Perkin Warbeck*.

Swartzwald: See **Black Forest**.

Swarzenberg, Prince: See **Schwarzenberg**.

Sweet Waters: Name given to the point where two streams converge into **Golden Horn** and separate **Galata** and **Pera** from **Constantinople**'s **Stamboul** side; its valley is renowned for its beauty (Coufopoulos 149). **Lionel Verney** notes that the **Greek** army blockades Constantinople "from the river **Kyat Kbanah**, near the Sweet Waters, to the Tower of **Marmora**" (*LM* 183). **Perdita** resides in luxury with **Raymond** and Verney at Sweet Waters' palace (*LM* 185, 195).

Swift, Jonathan (1667–1745): Irish satirical author, renowned for *Gulliver's*

Travels (1726), which Shelley first read 1816 (*Journals* 145). Lemuel **Gulliver**, a ship's surgeon, recounts his strange adventures: he is shipwrecked first in **Lilliput** and then in **Brobdignag**. Lilliput's inhabitants are only six inches tall; Swift satirizes English political parties and religious dissenters in his descriptions of Lilliputians' self-importance and petty civil squabbles, including Lilliputians' political opposition over which end of an egg to break. Brobdignag's inhabitants are twelve times taller than humans and belittle Gulliver for his society's follies. Shelley demonstrates her familiarity with this text in references to "flappers" (*Letters* 1.514). **Lionel Verney** refers to Gulliver, "toy of the Brobdignagians" (*LM* 231–232). **Lady Cecil** suggests that **Elizabeth Falkner** and **Gerard Neville** are alike in superiority of character, "thinking not of the petty circle of ideas that encompasses and presses down every other mind, so that they cannot see or feel beyond their own Lilliputian selves"; she also characterizes **Sir Boyvill Neville** as wholly "centred in his Lilliputian self" (*F* 86, 101). Shelley compares herself to Gulliver, who, "in the palm of the hand of the Brobdignagian reaper, could not have felt smaller" than she does from her want of money while traveling August 1842 (*R* 1.272). She also suggests that **Tuscany** and **Lombardy**'s debate over language "ended at last, as the question of big-endians and small-endians terminated in **Liliput**, by every one breaking his egg at whichever end he pleased" (*R* 2.163).

"Swiss Peasant, The": Story Shelley first published in the 1830 *Keepsake* as by "the Author of '**Frankenstein**'" (Robinson 382). The accompanying illustration, *The Swiss Peasant*, depicts a rustic woman carrying a child on her shoulders; Henry Howard painted and Charles Heath engraved it (*SP* 139). Shelley drew on her 1816 **Swiss** experiences, when **Byron** composed "**Prisoner of Chillon**," "the sole book" the tale's narrator possesses (*SP* 136). **Ashburn** bets the narrator that a Swiss woman that the two encounter can provide them with a romantic tale (*SP* 137). While seeking shelter at the woman's cabin, Ashburn and the narrator listen to her tale of **Fanny** and **Louis Chaumont**. The story's title refers to Fanny, a beautiful **Bernese** peasant girl who moves to the **Marville** family chateau when her own family is killed (*SP* 138). She is **Henry de Marville**'s childhood playmate; when he gradually falls in love with her, **Madame de Marville** disapproves of the match, while Fanny prefers Louis (*SP* 141). Jealous Henry's violent quarrel with Louis interrupts the blossoming relationship, and Louis is subsequently banished (*SP* 142). Fanny regretfully agrees to relinquish all contact with the exile and to stay at the Marvilles' chateau another year (*SP* 142–143). As the **French Revolution**'s sentiments spread throughout Switzerland, **Monsieur de Marville** violently disperses a mob, which causes Louis's return (*SP* 144). Acting as leader, Louis calls for the death of Monsieur, who departs in disguise from his home during the night and conceals himself at a mountain chalet (*SP* 145). Henry secretly returns from **Paris**, seeking refuge at his parents' home, and hides under straw in a wagon's bottom to escape with Fanny and Madame, who have been prom-

Switzerland

ised safe passage (*SP* 145–146). As the wagon moves through groups of commoners yelling at them, a wheel splinters, rendering the vehicle useless, and Henry emerges; the two Marvilles are taken prisoner (*SP* 148). Louis rushes to protect Fanny and obtains Madame's freedom while intending to allow the mob to murder Henry. Upon Fanny's defense of Henry—claiming he has ignored social stations and married her—Louis intervenes and obtains his release (*SP* 149). After hiding three weeks, the Marvilles safely return to their Berne chalet, but Fanny refuses to join them and moves to **Subiaco** (*SP* 150–151). Fanny does not again encounter Louis—"oblivion closed over Chaumont's name"—until he returns, aged and tired, from service in **France**'s army (*SP* 151). Fanny and Louis reunite, have a child, and live happily in Subiaco's hills.

Switzerland: Small central **European** country, formerly called **Helvetia**, which **Austria**, **France**, **Germany**, and **Italy** border. The Shelleys toured Switzerland 1814 and 1816 (*H* 40). Switzerland is **Victor Frankenstein**'s native country, and much of his narrative takes place there (*Fr1* 63, 104, 215; *Fr3* 42, 72, 154). English plague survivors spend a summer in "the icy vallies [sic] of Switzerland" (*LM* 383, 394, 401, 423, 428). Shelley's "**The Swiss Peasant**" is set there, and the **Villiers**es cross snow-capped Switzerland en route to Italy (*SP* 142; *L* 2.170). Shelley mentions that Germans passed through the **Black Forest** en route to Switzerland (*R* 1.45). She details her route through the country, including the **Lake Geneva** region; she began traveling through **Saxon** Switzerland August 1842 (*R* 1.259–260, 2.139–142).

Sybarite: Ancient **Greek** inhabitant of the colony of Sybaris on southern **Italy**'s Gulf of Táranto, "an important trading centre" whose "wealth and luxury became proverbial" 6th century B.C.E., but the settlement was destroyed around 510 B.C.E. (Howatson 544). **Lionel Verney** relates **Perdita**'s reliance upon **Raymond**'s "restored society, on his love, his hopes and fame, even as a Sybarite on a luxurious couch" (*LM* 177). Verney compares his isolation in **Rome** to **Robinson Crusoe**'s on a desert island: "who would not have preferred the Sybarite enjoyments I could command" (*LM* 448).

Symond, Richard: See **Simon**.

Syrens: Usually spelled sirens, bird-women who would lure sailors to their deaths with beautiful singing; **Ulysses** encounters them in book 12 of *The Odyssey*. Shelley refers to rocks near **Naples** as those of the sirens (*R* 2.266, 2.276, 2.283).

Syria: **Asian** country today bordered by Iraq, the **Mediterranean**, and **Turkey**. When **Raymond** is captured and believed to be dead, "even as the women of Syria sorrowed for **Adonis**, did the wives and mothers of **Greece** lament" him (*LM* 168). **Lionel Verney** includes Syria's coast in his forecasted journey (*LM* 469). **Katusthius Ziani** "wandered through Syria" (*EE* 102).

Syrinx: In **Greek** mythology, this nymph and virgin huntress fled from **Pan**'s advances. Unable to cross a river, she was turned into "a clump of sadly murmuring marsh reeds"; Pan cut some of these to different lengths, creating his "Pan pipes" or syrinx (Tripp 540). Pan plays this instrument in *Midas* (*Midas* 95). **Ceres** suggests that **Ino** entertain **Proserpine** with a song about Syrinx's "saddest change" (*P* 31).

T

Taaffe, John (c. 1787–1862): Irish author who settled in **Pisa** in 1816; **Pacchiani** introduced the Shelleys to him there in November 1820 (*Journals* 590, 593, 341). Sunstein suggests that, with "unconscious comic relief, Taaffe paid fussy court to" Shelley during her residence in Pisa, and, although she sarcastically termed Taaffe "poet laureate of Pisa," both Shelleys, especially **PBS**, enjoyed Taaffe's company (Sunstein 192–193; *Letters* 1.223). Shelley records reading Taaffe's "notes to **Dante**" March 1821; PBS proofread this work May 1821 and assisted Taaffe in getting it published by **Murray** as first (and only) volume of *A Comment on the Divine Comedy of Dante Alighieri* (1822) (*Journals* 357, 369; White 2.246). See Appendix II of Shelley's *Journals* and Clarence Lee Cline's *Byron, Shelley and their Pisan Circle* (1952) (*Journals* 590–593).

Tabor: Czech city fifty miles south of **Prague**. Shelley planned to stay overnight there September 1842, but the coach stopped in **Mulchen** instead (*R* 2.14).

Tacitus, Publius Cornelius (c. 56–117 C.E.): Little is known about this early **Roman** historian, but his works suggest that he saw military and diplomatic service; he was also a famous orator (Howatson 548–549). **PBS** read Tacitus's *Germania* (98 C.E.) August 1816; Shelley read Tacitus's *Annals* (c. 115–117 C.E.) summer 1817 (*Journals* 130–131, 679). PBS "read aloud the account of the **Siege of Jerusalem** from Tacitus" on **Lake Lucerne**'s shores August 1814, a reference to Tacitus's detailed account of Titus Caesar's 70 C.E. siege of **Jerusalem** in *Histories* (104–109 C.E.) (*H* 51; Tacitus, *Histories* 5.1–13; *Journals* 19). **Isabell Harley** introduces **Valerius** to Tacitus's works (*Val* 343). **Lionel Verney** imagines "heroes of Tacitus" (*LM* 462). Shelley refers to the eighth and ninth books of Tacitus's *Germania*, in which Tacitus depicts **Germany** as "a land of forest and heroes" (R 1.174–175). She also notes Tacitus's influence on **Colletta** (R 2.207–209).

Taenarus, Cape: Promontory that the Taygetus Mountains form, called the Taenarian Promontory, extending into **Cape Matapan** in southern **Maina**, a hundred miles southwest of **Corinth** (*MGRE* 23). Shelley notes that "dreaded and abhorred by the rest of the world as are the inhabitants of Cape Taenarus, they are celebrated for their domestic virtues and the strength of their private attachments" (*EE* 107). **Cyril** and **Zella Ziani** sail around Taenarus's "extreme point" (*EE* 108).

Tagliacozzo, Battle of: At the plain of Tagliacozzo, forty miles east of **Rome**, **Charles of Anjou**'s army defeated **Conradin**'s army 23 August 1268; Conradin attempted to escape but was apprehended forty-five miles away (Sismondi 94). In "**A Tale of the Passions**," the narrator describes Conradin's arrest: a **Frangipani** man seized him for being a "fugitive from the battle" (*TP* 22).

Taglioni, Marie (1804–1884): Italian ballerina. Shelley thought **Cerito** was "not comparable to Taglioni for an inexpressible something which renders her single in the poetry of the art" (R 1.108, 2.127).

Tagus: Portuguese river flowing through **Lisbon**. **Meilar Trangmar** finds the *St. George* on the Tagus and hires it to transport **Richard of York** (*PW* 1.255, 1.258).

Talbot, John (c. 1388–1453): Earl of **Shrewsbury**'s and **Elizabeth Mowbray**'s father (*DNB*). Shelley mentions he was "famous in the **French** wars," meaning the Hundred Years' War (*PW* 2.140; Fischer 193).

"Tale of the Passions, A": While researching **Italian** history for *Valperga*, Shelley became interested in **Manfred**'s story and planned to base her next long work on it (Sunstein 232). **William Godwin** objected to this topic, but Shelley subsequently wrote a short story about Manfred and **Conradin** (*Journals* 442; Sunstein 232). She had written most of it prior to **PBS**'s death, completing it 10 November 1822 (*Journals* 431, 442; Sunstein 232). It first appeared anonymously in January 1823's *The Liberal*, and as by Mrs. Shelley in 1839 under the title "A Tale of the Passions, or the Death of Despina" (Robinson 374–375; *Journals* 431). The story gives a romantic twist to the historical account of Conradin's execution in **Naples** 29 October 1268. Shelley uses **Florentine** names and creates a beautiful heroine who sacrifices her life by supporting the **Ghibelline** cause and Conradin. The tale opens with a sketch of an older couple; **Cincolo de' Becari** is a Ghibelline, and his wife **Monna Gegia de' Becari** is a **Guelph** (*TP* 2–3). When an unknown visitor, **Ricciardo de' Rossini** of **Milan**, arrives, the Becaris fail to see through the disguise of their foster-daughter, **Despina dei Elisei**, who has come to Florence to seek aid from **Guielmo Lostendardo**, who once loved her (*TP* 5). Cincolo escorts this visitor to a meeting with Guielmo, who imprisons Despina as revenge for her rejection of his advances years earlier (*TP* 10–15). When the visitor fails to return, Cincolo undertakes a dangerous trip to **Pisa** to deliver a message to Conradin, only then learning the stranger's true identity (*TP* 19–21). The story then focuses on Conradin's execution and adds that Guielmo shows Despina's corpse to Conradin immediately before his own execution (*TP* 22–23). Although the story met with negative reviews, Robinson recommends its concentrated narrative and especially notes the realistic dialogue and narrative sketch of Monna Gegia (Robinson 374; Sunstein 232).

Tantalus: Mythological **Greek** king tortured in **Hades** for stealing from the gods, telling mortals their secrets, and attempting to serve the gods a stew made from his own son; his torture consisted of being surrounded by water and fruit permanently just out of his reach (Tripp 542–543). Shelley describes **Edward Villiers**'s protracted meetings with **Mr. Gayland** regarding financial difficulties as "the alternations of total failure and suddenly renewed hopes, which are the Tantalus-food" (*L* 2.281). When the **Earl of Warwick** thinks he is free from captivity, "he rushed through the open door, intent to seize upon liberty, as Tantalus on his forbidden feast" (*PW* 3.308).

Tartar: Member of nomadic tribe renowned for military strength that controlled large parts of **Asia** in the 13th century (Kinder 1.179). **Lord Lodore** feels his wife's interest in **London** society leaves him isolated: "Home! A Tartar beneath his tent...may speak of home—I have none" (*L* 1.133).

Tartarus: Greek mythical region akin to hell, as far "beneath the surface of the earth, as heaven was above it" (Tripp 545). **Midas** describes gold as "Tartarian" (*Midas* 141). **Proserpine**'s fate is decided when she is "polluted by Tartarian food" (**pomegranate** seed) and thus cannot wholly resume life on earth (*P* 69, 71).

Tartary: Balkan state on the **Black Sea** northwest of the **Danube**'s mouth, made part of **Russia** 1791 (Robertson 23). **Victor Frankenstein** pursues the **Creature** from the Black Sea north through Tartary (*Fr1* 227; *Fr3* 169). **Benedetto Pepi** tells a story about **Charlemagne** resenting **Pavìan** courtiers' extravagant dress, including fur cloaks made from "skins of a thousand minute animals, brought from the wilds of Tartary"; Pepi later wears a Tartarian fur cloak (*V* 1.286, 2.118).

Tasso, Torquato (1544–1595): Italian Renaissance writer who lived for a period at **Ferrara**'s court; his works include the romantic epic *Rinaldo* (1562), *Aminta* (1573), *Gerusalemme Liberata* [*Jerusalem Delivered*] (1581), and *ReTorrismondo* (1587). Shelley read Tasso's *Aminta* April and July 1818 (*Journals* 203). For ***Italian and Spanish Lives***, Shelley wrote all of the entries except those for **Galileo** and Tasso; James Montgomery wrote Tasso's (*Letters* 2.257, 2.260). Shelley notes **Cadenabbia**'s scenery makes her think of **Rinaldo** in Tasso's *Gerusalemme Liberata* (*R* 1.95). She visited Tasso's **Sorrento** house June 1843 (*R* 2.263).

Tassoni, Alessandro (1563–1635): Italian author whose works contemporary literati consistently attacked. Shelley wrote Tassoni's biography for *Italian and Spanish Lives*. She admires Tassoni's early **Latin** work, "which displayed an extraordinary smoothness of versification and command of language" (*ISPL* 2.169). Tassoni's *Considerazioni sulle rime del Petrarca* [*Considerations on Petrarch's Poetry*] (1609) was the first of many works that engaged Tassoni in literary controversy, as did his *Dieci libri di pensieri diversi* [*Ten Books of Thoughts on Various Subjects*] (1620). Shelley particularly admires Tassoni's *La Secchia Rapita* [*The Rape of the Bucket*] (wr. 1585, pub. 1622), a burlesque poem of which she gives a lengthy plot summary (*ISPL* 2.170, 2.172).

Tätchen: Czech city on the **Elbe**, twenty-eight miles southeast of **Dresden**. Shelley arrived by boat and rested there for a few hours August 1842 (*R* 1.260, 1.275–276).

Taunton: English town twenty-nine miles northeast of **Exeter**. When the attack on Exeter fails, **Richard of York** decides to invade Taunton with his three thousand remaining troops (*PW* 3.110, 3.113, 3.120). Prior to the attack, one of **Henry VII**'s regiments enters the city to defend it (*PW* 3.122). Lost, Richard asks **Clym of the Lyn** to guide him to Taunton but finally reaches it only to surrender (*PW* 3.148, 3.186–188, 3.193–194).

Taurus: Constellation and zodiacal sign of a bull. **Lionel Verney** records, "Taurus high in the southern heavens shewed that it was midnight" (*LM* 202). Verney later notes the constellation's passage into "the radiant demesne of Taurus" (*LM* 431).

Tavernier, Madame: Louis Manoir's older, widowed fiancée in *Frankenstein*.

Tay: River and firth on Scotland's east coast, north of Firth of Forth; both **Perth** and **Dundee** are on its banks. En route to Dundee 1812, Shelley suffered from seasickness until the ship entered the Firth of Tay's calmer waters (Sunstein 56; Seymour 71–72). To cure an affliction of her left arm, Shelley bathed regularly in the Tay 1812 and 1813, when the arm healed completely (Sunstein 57, 59). **Henry Clerval** and **Victor Frankenstein** sail on the Tay (*Fr1* 189; *Fr3* 138). Shelley describes Scottish resistance to England as a "defiance [that] would be echoed in glad shouts from **Tweed** to Tay" (*PW* 2.194).

Taylor, Sir John: **Exeter** merchant and customs official who lived in **France** from 1491 (Arthurson 15). After supporting **Edward IV** and **Richard III**, he attempted to have **Earl of Warwick** crowned and then supported **Perkin Warbeck**, with whom he was arrested, then imprisoned in the **Tower** until after 1509 (Arthurson 16–18, 217). **Richard of York** supporter in *Perkin Warbeck*.

Teck, Frau Gräfinn von: See **Wurtemburg, Queen of**.

Tegrimi, Niccolò (1448–1527): **Lucchese** senator who wrote *Vita Castruccii Castracani* [*Life of Castruccio Castracani*] (1496) (Crook 3.5). Shelley notes this work in *Valperga*'s preface, with **Tegrino** for Tegrimi (viii).

Tegrino: See **Tegrimi**.

Tell, William: Legendary 13th–14th-century **Swiss** patriot forced to shoot an arrow through an apple placed upon his son's head for refusing to pay homage to Gessler, **Uri**'s **Austrian** governor (Sunstein 86–87). Some legends hold that the arrow killed Gessler. Shelley viewed the "chapel of Tell, and the village where he matured the conspiracy which was to overthrow the tyrant of his country" (*H* 49). "**The Swiss Peasant**'s" frame narrator is "beside the waters of Uri—where Tell lived" (*SP* 136).

***Tempest, The*:** **Shakespeare**'s last play (1611), thematically concerned with peace and reconciliation. Magician **Prospero** is **Milan**'s rightful duke who, having lost his throne, makes wise use of magic to serve and protect his daughter **Miranda** while they live on a deserted island. A storm initiates the play's complicated plot, of which the principal feature is Miranda's falling in love with Ferdinand, son of Alonso, king of **Naples**. Ultimately, Ferdinand and Miranda unite, and Prospero renounces magic when he is restored to his throne, having ensured his daughter's happiness and established peace with Naples. Shelley read Shakespeare's drama October 1818, and **PBS** read it aloud January 1820 (*Journals* 229, 305–306). **Matilda** conjures Miranda as a fictional companion in her childhood daydreams, and **Lionel Verney** endows heroines of all he reads with **Perdita**'s "beauty and matchless excellences," including "Miranda in the unvisited cave of Prospero" (*M* 159; *LM* 78). Shelley quotes an exchange between Miranda and Prospero in which he informs his daughter how they were removed from Milan, as an epigraph to the *Lodore* chapter in which Shelley details **Lord Lodore**'s close relationship with his daughter: "*Miranda.*—**Alack! what trouble** / Was I then to you! / *Prospero.*—O, a cherubim / Thou wast, that did preserve me!" (*L* 1.27; Shakespeare 1.2.151–153). Several times in *Lodore,* Shelley compares *The Tempest*'s father-daughter relationship to Lord Lodore and **Ethel Villiers**'s (*L* 1.70–71, 1.249; Shakespeare 1.2.38–39, 1.2.45, 5.1).

***Templario*:** See **Niccolai**.

Temple Bar: Gate marking the boundary between the cities of Westminster and **London**, located between **Fleet Street** and the **Strand** (Leigh 247). **Edward Villiers** and his wife pass "through Temple Bar" to prison (*L* 3.86).

"Tempo è ben di Morire": Shelley's irregular forty-eight line poem, dated 1833, which Nitchie first published in 1953 (Nitchie 231–233). The two-line title or epigraph, taken from **Petrarch**, means "It is a good time to die / And I have stayed longer than I wished." The poem's speaker recounts hearing a voice inviting the speaker to come "To our home!"; it is the voice of "my life's Lord," calling the speaker to join him in death since there is no joy or hope left for the speaker upon earth (lines 6–7).

Tenerani, Pietro da Torano (1798–1869): **Italian** sculptor with a **Roman** studio (*MROM* xlii). Shelley visited various Roman studios April 1843 and specifically praises Tenerani's "angel of the day of judgment" (*R* 2.224).

Tepeleni: Albanian town seventy-five miles northwest of **Ioannina**; Shelley terms it **Tepellenè**. **Ali Pasha** was born there, and **Byron** visited him there 1810, recreating his impressions in *Childe Harold's Pilgrimage* (*MGRE* 396; Byron, *CHP* 2.491–495). **Camaraz** and **Cyril Ziani** travel to Tepeleni (*EE* 110, 112).

Tepellenè: See **Tepeleni**.

Teplice: Czech town thirty miles south of **Dresden**; Shelley spells it **Töplitz**. Shelley bathed in this spa resort August 1842 (*R* 1.242).

Terni: Italian city fifty-five miles northeast of **Rome**. **Castruccio** and **Euthanasia** trace **Beatrice** "even to Terni; but there all trace was lost" (*V* 2.191, 3.83). Shelley compares **Rheinfelden** to Terni's falls, finding the latter "the finest cataract I have seen" (*R* 1.50).

Terrace of Bruhl: Popular promenade along the **Elbe**'s left bank in **Dresden** (*MCON* 435). Shelley enjoyed walking there summer 1842 (*R* 1.246).

Terracina: Italian seaport sixteen miles northwest of **Gaeta**. Shelley stayed there November 1818 and March 1819 (*Journals* 240, 251). The **Villiers**es witness **Clorinda Saville**'s excessive passion there (*L* 2.193, 2.196).

Thames: River running though **Oxford** and **London**. The Shelleys had their first home near the Thames and delighted in boating upon it; in 1815, "the lovers hired a shallow draft boat and rowed . . . to the source of the Thames and back" (Sunstein 104). Shelley described the Putney cottage to **Claire Clairmont**: "on the banks of the Thames—not *looking* on it—but the garden gate opens on the towing path" (*Letters* 3.87). **Victor Frankenstein** and **Henry Clerval** take the Thames to London (*Fr1* 184; *Fr3* 134). The framework of "**An Eighteenth-Century Tale**" depicts a party of friends residing at a **Buckinghamshire** house "on the river Thames" (*EC* 345). Guests at **Euthanasia**'s court enjoy exhibitions of tricks "known from the shores of the **Ganges** to those of the Thames" (*V* 1.269). "**Recollections of Italy**" takes place on the banks of the Thames, which the narrator feels is superior to the " 'muddy **Arno**' " (*RI* 25). Happy scenes at *The Last Man*'s opening take place at **Windsor** on the banks of the Thames (*LM* 80). **Lionel Verney** helps a party fleeing "up the Thames in a boat"; later he details the alterations that plague wrought upon formerly fertile fields beside the Thames (*LM* 258, 310). Verney and **Idris** look out at the Thames from Windsor for the last time with sadness before leaving for London (*LM* 329). **Horace Neville** swims across the Thames to Windsor forest while escaping from **Eton** (*Mourner* 87, 95). **Sir William Stanley** has a mansion in London with "a garden upon the Thames," which allows **Monina De Faro** to visit him there secretly (*PW* 2.55). **Yorkists** escape from London on the Thames several times in *Perkin Warbeck*, mainly because the **Tower** is on its banks (*PW* 2.79, 2.91, 3.226). **Sir Boyvill Neville** moves to a residence on the Thames (*F* 119). Shelley stayed two months prior to her 1840 departure to **Europe** at **Rich-**

mond, where she "spent many hours of every day on the Thames" (*R* 1.3). [*LM* 156; *L* 2.88].

"The Death of Love": Shelley's poem, dated 19 November 1831 and first published 1997 (Bennett, "Newly Uncovered," 72–73). The poem, in octaves with alternately rhyming lines, allegorically asks how love, personified as a "gentle boy" or **Cupid**, died (line 1). The speaker references several Classical deaths (such as **Sappho**'s) before concluding that "Death in pity gave eternal peace" to love within "this lorn heart" (lines 20, 26).

Themistocles (c. 525–460 B.C.E.): **Athenian** politician and military leader who had his greatest triumph 480 B.C.E., when **Greece**'s fleet destroyed **Persia**'s near Salamis; he ostracized political rival **Aristides** 483 B.C.E. (Kinder 1.57). The **Countess of Windsor**'s death breaks **Lionel Verney**'s ties with recent history, making it seem as remote as "the disputes of Themistocles and Aristides" (*LM* 416).

Thermopylae: Small town and pass at Mount **Oeta**'s northern foot, a hundred miles northwest of **Athens** (*MGRE* 218; Howatson 566). **Lionel Verney** and **Perdita** "pass the straits of Thermopylae" (*LM* 208).

Theseus: Legendary **Athenian** king who bravely chose to prove himself as a warrior and then reformed the government, forcing several townships to obey the commonwealth's authority; he performed many heroic feats including, with **Ariadne**'s assistance, killing the **Minotaur** in the Labyrinth (Howatson 566–567). The **Creature** reads **Plutarch**'s celebration of Theseus's accomplishments but prefers more "peaceable lawgivers" (*Fr1* 156; *Fr3* 112; Plutarch, *Lives* 1.1–27). In "**The Death of Love**," Shelley asks if personified love died from "the sharp pang he felt when Theseus fled," probably referring to rebellions that forced Theseus to leave Athens, so that he died away from the city he loved (line 3). See **Procrustes**.

Thessaly: **Greek** region bordered by **Albania**, **Macedonia**, and the **Peloponnese**. **Lionel Verney** learns, in an attempt to stop plague spreading from **Constantinople** through Greece, that "'a cordon has been drawn on the frontiers of Thessaly, and a strict quarantine exacted'" (*LM* 220). Many of *The Last Man*'s central Greek scenes are set there.

Thionville: **French** town on the **Moselle**, seventeen miles north of **Metz**. Shelley dined there June 1840 (*R* 1.16).

Thomas: Servant in *Perkin Warbeck*.

Thomond: Now County Clare in the middle of **Ireland**'s western (**Atlantic**) coast. **Desmond** ponders "the invasion of Thomond" (*PW* 1.303). [*PW* 1.298, 1.301, 2.120].

Thompson: Head servant at **Rupert Falkner**'s residence in *Falkner*.

Thonon: **French** city on **Lake Geneva**, three miles southwest of **Drance**. **Victor Frankenstein** tells **Robert Walton** about discovering **Cornelius Agrippa**'s theories at age thirteen while at a Thonon inn (*Fr1* 67; *Fr3* 44).

Thor: Norse mythological god of thunder; his weapon is a hammer. **Robert Clifford** denies his love for **Monina De Faro** by saying, "Thor's hammer could not knock a splinter from my hard heart" (*PW* 2.6).

Thrace: In Shelley's day, **Greek** region north of **Constantinople**; it now lies principally in **Turkey**. **Raymond** leads a battle resulting in Greek reclamation of Thrace (*LM* 161, 163). **Lionel Verney** joins "the army stationed at **Kishan** in Thrace" (*LM* 168, 177). Verney learns that plague has spread throughout Thrace (*LM* 208, 220). **Zella Ziani** fears that her husband has fallen "prey of some Thracian witchcraft" (*EE* 110).

Thrasymene: Italian lake, Trasimeno, ten miles west of **Perugia** (Crook 2). **Beatrice** recounts passing it (*V* 3.83)

***Three Ages of Man*:** See **Titian**.

Thuilleries: See **Tuileries**.

Thule: See *Ultima Thule*.

Thuringerwald: See **Thuringian Forest**.

Thuringian Forest: Hilly wooded district in central east **Germany** between **Fulda** and **Eisenach**, also called **Thuringerwald**. Shelley traveled there July 1842 (*R* 1.207–208).

Thwaites, Sir Thomas: Earl of **Rivers**'s friend who is arrested at the 1493 conspiratorial meeting at **Robert Clifford**'s house (*PW* 2.22, 2.50; Holinshed 3.507).

Tiber: Second-longest river in **Italy**, flowing from the **Apennines** east of **Florence** through **Rome** to its mouth on the Tyrrhenian Sea. In Rome 1819, Shelley encountered the Tiber on numerous walking tours of the city (*Journals* 262). **Padre Giuseppe** inspires **Valerius** to admire the Tiber, and **Euthanasia** also praises its beauty (*Val* 334; *V* 1.202, 1.205). Shelley contrasts the eternal Tiber with the decaying **Pantheon** and crumbling **Coliseum** (*SA* 51). Shelley viewed it from the **Capitol** April 1843 (*R* 2.227).

Tiberius, Palace of: Remnants of this palace's mosaics are on **Capri**'s eastern peak (*STIE* 373). Shelley visited it September 1843 (*R* 2.269–270).

Tibullus, Albius (c. 55–19 B.C.E.): **Roman** poet whose work is in *Corpus Tibullianum*. Shelley mentions that **Manzoni** read Tibullus "with delight" (*R* 2.199).

Ticino: Southern **Swiss** river emptying into **Italy**'s **Lago Maggiore**. The Ticino flooded **PFS**'s route September 1840 (*R* 1.150).

Tiel: Dutch port on the **Rhine**, twenty-five miles west of the **German** border. Shelley calls Tiel "**Triel**" when she records sleeping there September 1814 (*Journals* 23; *II* 75).

Tighe, George William (1776–1837): **Lady Mountcashel** met Tighe in **Rome** 1804; in 1805, she left her husband to be with him. They subsequently lived together in **London** until 1814, when they settled with their two daughters in **Pisa**, where Shelley first met them September 1819 (*Journals*

586–587). In spring 1820, Shelley asked the **Gisbornes** to recommend a residence in Casciano on Tighe's behalf, noting that "he had been confined the whole winter with an attack of rhumatism [*sic*]—he has been ordered the baths this May" (*Letters* 1.143). Sunstein notes "reclusive Tighe, an agronomist nicknamed 'Tatty' because he grew potatoes, was [Shelley's] model for **Guinigi** in *Valperga*" (186). See Edward C. McAleer's *The Sensitive Plant: A Life of Lady Mount Cashell* (1958).

Tilbury Fort: Fortification **Charles II** built in Tilbury, across the **Thames** from **Gravesend**. Sighting the fort, **Henry Clerval** and **Victor Frankenstein** recall **Queen Elizabeth I**'s encouraging speech to troops defending Tilbury from the **Spanish Armada** 1588, before the fort's construction (*Fr1* 184; *Fr3* 134; Crook 2).

Tiler, John: In *Perkin Warbeck*, English messenger who accompanies **Stephen Poytron** and **Stephen Frion** to Ardfinnan for **Charles VIII**.

Timon: Protagonist of **Shakespeare**'s *The Life of Timon of Athens* (1605–08), which Shelley read October 1818 (*Journals* 229). Timon is a generous **Athenian** host, but when his debts compel him to ask his frequent guests for financial assistance, it becomes apparent they are friends only when he has something to give them. Timon eventually invites his guests to a final feast consisting of stones and warm water, which Timon resentfully throws in guests' faces; he subsequently becomes a misanthrope and dies alone (Shakespeare 3.6). **Lionel Verney** relates the dream he has after an exhaustive and unsuccessful search for **Raymond**: "Methought I had been invited to Timon's last feast; I came with keen appetite, the covers were removed, the hot water sent up its unsatisfying steams, while I fled before the anger of the host, who assumed the form of Raymond" (*LM* 202).

"Tintern Abbey": Poem **Wordsworth** addressed to his sister Dorothy, who accompanied him on a return trip to the 12th-century abbey; its full title is "Lines composed a few miles above Tintern Abbey, on revisiting the banks of the Wye during a tour. July 13, 1798." First published in *Lyrical Ballads* (1798), the poem celebrates nature's restorative power. Shelley quotes from Wordsworth's poem to explain how **Henry Clerval** values nature: "**The sounding cataract** / Haunted him like a passion: the tall rock, / The mountain, and the deep and gloomy wood, / Their colours and forms, were then to him / An appetite; a feeling, and a love, / That had no need of a remoter charm, / By thought supplied, or any interest / Unborrow'd from the eye" (*Fr1* 183–184; *Fr3* 133; Wordsworth lines 76–83). **Horace Neville** is "eloquent in praise of English scenery" and admires the "river, winding '**with sweet inland** murmur,'" a further line from Wordsworth's text (*Mourner* 83; Wordsworth line 4). Shelley alludes to this line again in *Rambles* in describing **Oes** and **Amalfi** (*R* 1.37, 2.286; Wordsworth line 4).

Tintoretto, Jacopo Robusti (1518–1594): **Venetian** painter; Shelley admired his works in **San Marco** September 1842 (*R* 2.85). Shelley states that his *Paradiso* (1588) is in **Palazzo**

Mocenigo, but it is actually in the **Doge's Palace** (*R* 2.119; Moskal 292).

Tiresias: **Greek** myth relates that Tiresias experienced life as both man and woman; he "lived through at least seven generations" and became a famous prophet (Tripp 547–48). The narrator of "**The Mourner**" describes **Virginia Water**'s landscape, noting how the silence is broken by strains "more inspiring than the song of Tiresias which awoke **Alexander** to the deed of ruin"; Shelley mistakes "Tiresias" for "Timotheus" (*Mourner* 81; Crook 2).

Tirrel, James (d. 1502): He supposedly murdered the princes in the **Tower** (*DNB;* Holinshed 3.401). **Henry VII** of England tries to document the princes' deaths in *Perkin Warbeck* by interviewing Tirrel (*PW* 2.43–45).

Titans: In **Greek** mythology, after a ten-year war, **Zeus** and other gods defeated these immortals and imprisoned them in **Tartarus** (Howatson 573). **Proserpine** asks her mother to recount the "combat of the Titans and the Gods" (*P* 29).

Titi-See: **Alpine** lake near **Titisee**-Neustadt, eighteen miles southeast of **Freyberg**. Shelley learned its location July 1840 (*R* 1.47).

Titian, Tiziano Vecellio (c. 1485–1576): **Italian** painter who studied in **Venice** and produced numerous works before dying from plague. Titian's style developed throughout his career, but his paintings are distinguished by "the interplay of luminous color tones" (*Phaidon* 656). He was a friend of Ariosto, who celebrates Titian in *Orlando Furioso* (Vasari 4.269; Ariosto 33.2). Titian painted **Santa Maria della Salute**'s ceiling frescoes (1543–44), and his paintings are displayed in museums throughout **Europe**. Shelley viewed several Titian paintings, such as *The Assumption* (1516–18), an altarpiece at Venice's **Accademia delle Belle Arti**; Shelley saw it September 1842, finding the upper part "indeed glorious" (Chilvers 559–560; *R* 2.90). Shelley also saw Titian's *Death of St. Peter the Martyr* (1528–30) at the Accademia (she calls it *Martyrdom of St. Peter the Hermit*) (*R* 2.89). Fire destroyed the painting 1867 (Schmeckebier 480). The Accademia also displays Titian's *Pieta* (1573–76), which Shelley viewed September 1842, calling it *Mary Visiting the Tomb of Jesus* (*R* 2.90–91; Chilvers 559–560). Titian's *Presentation of the Virgin* (1534–38) is also displayed there (*Phaidon* 656). Shelley states that *Presentation* is "a picture I look at much oftener, and with far greater pleasure, than at the more celebrated *Martyrdom*" (*R* 2.90). Shelley thinks *Presentation*, accompanied by **Dante**'s *Paradiso* as commentary, is "the sublimest achievement of Catholicism" (*R* 2.91). Also in Venice, Shelley saw Titian's fresco *Cain Slaying Abel* (1543–44), in the series adorning the ceiling of Santa Maria della Salute (*Phaidon* 656). Shelley calls it *Death of Abel* and believes that it surpasses other frescoes (*R* 2.96). *Sacrifice of Isaac* (1542–44) also adorns the ceiling; Shelley thought it "the only representation of that tremendous act that ever pleased me" (*R* 2.95–96; Schmeckebier 474). She also admired *David and Goliath*, calling it *Killing of Goliath by David* (*R* 2.95). At **Palazzo Manfrin** Shelley viewed "*The Deposition from* the Cross," which is probably Titian's *Entombment* (mid-1520s) and *Repentant Magdalen*, which Shelley calls **Maddalena Scapigliata**; it is now in **St. Petersburg** (*R* 2.119; Moskal 292). At the **Gallery in Dresden**, Shelley viewed Titian's *Cristo della Moneta* [*Tribute Money*] (n.d.), which **Vasari** considered Titian's best work; Shelley calls it "[o]ne of the gems of the gallery" and mentions **Jameson**'s praise of it (*R* 1.243; Vasari 3.267–268). Shelley regretted being unable to see Titian's paintings that were destroyed by fire at the **Doges' Palace** 1577, but she did view a copy of his *Three Ages of Man* (c. 1514) housed there (*R* 1.243, 2.85, 2.89–91, 2.95–96, 2.119–120, 2.157). She also visited **Santa Maria de' Frari Church**, which contains Titian's tomb, at that time marked simply by a stone inscribed with his name (*R* 2.92–93). See **Barbarigo Palace**, **Bridgewater Collection**, **Giorgione**, **S. Tommaso Church**.

Titisee: See **Titi-see**.

Titus Flavius Vespasianus (d. 81 C.E.): **Vespasian**'s eldest son; he shared his father's rule until becoming **Rome**'s sole emperor 79–81 C.E. He is remembered "for the capture of **Jerusalem** in C.E. 70 after a long siege"; Arch of Titus commemorates this event, and Titus completed the **Coliseum**'s construction during his reign (Howatson 573). **Isabell Harley** names Titus as one of " 'the more virtuous' " of the Roman emperors but as inferior to the Roman republic's heroes (*Val* 340).

Tivoli: Italian city on the **Anio**, fifteen miles east of **Rome**. Marcott Alleyn spends time there to avoid **Giacomo de' Tolomei** (*BMI* 39).

Tmolus: Ancient **Greek** god of a hill who judges in **Apollo**'s favor in **Midas**'s musical contest.

"To Jane": Four-and-a-half-line fragment of Shelley's poem composed early 1826, first published in Grylls's *Mary Shelley: A Biography* (1938) (303). Shelley noted beside the title "(with the 'Last Man')," indicating that "thy Mary's offering" and "A tale of woe" may allude to her *The Last Man*, published just before the poem's composition (lines 2–3). Shelley terms Jane (probably **Jane Williams**) "dear solace of my life" (line 1).

"To the Lord Chancellor": Poem **PBS** wrote probably no earlier than 1820. **Lionel Verney** compares **Adrian** to "an inspired musician, who struck, with unerring skill, the '**lyre of mind**,' and produced thence divine harmony," a phrase taken from the poem (*LM* 26; PBS line 28).

Tobin, John (1770–1804): British playwright. Shelley compares the plot of his *The Honeymoon, or How to Rule a Wife* (1805) to that of *Chi Dura Vince* (*R* 2.129).

Todd, Sir Thomas: He attempted to kidnap **James IV** and **Duke of Rosse** 1491 for **Henry VII** of England; Todd is mentioned in *Perkin Warbeck* (Arthurson 13; *PW* 2.227).

Tolomei: **Mancini** family's enemy in "The Brother and Sister."

Tolomei, Count Fabian de': In "The Brother and Sister," Lorenzo Mancini's rival, Flora Mancini's guardian (and subsequent husband), and Countess de' Tolomei's son.

Tolomei, Countess de': In "The Brother and Sister," Count Fabian de' Tolomei's mother.

Tolomei, Giacomo de': Teresa de' Tolomei's brother, Clorinda Saviani's suitor, and Marcott Alleyn's friend in "The Bride of Modern Italy."

Tolomei, Teresa de': Giacomo de' Tolomei's sister and Clorinda Saviani's friend in "The Bride of Modern Italy."

Tom of Coventry: Character added to the Lady Godiva legend in the 17th century. To persuade her husband to lower taxes in Coventry, Lady Godiva rode naked on horseback through it. Peeping Tom was the only person who watched her ride and was struck blind instantly. Shelley describes Polidori's ghost story involving a "skull-headed lady" who looks through a keyhole and is punished by being "reduced to a worse condition than the renowned Tom of Coventry" (*Fr3* 21).

Top Kapou: Gate in walls surrounding Constantinople (Coufopoulos 141). Lionel Verney and Raymond ride "to the lofty mound, not far from the Top Kapou, (Cannon-gate)" (*LM* 183). Verney later sees Raymond and some soldiers through a telescope near Top Kapou, and he enters Constantinople there in search of Raymond (*LM* 197, 205).

Töplitz: See **Teplice**.

Torcello: Island northeast of Venice in the Laguna near Burano (Littlewood 234). Shelley visited Torcello September 1842 (*R* 2.101).

Torella, Juliet: Marchese Torella's daughter and Guido il Cortese's love interest in "Transformation."

Torella, Marchese: Juliet Torella's father and friend of Guido il Cortese's father in "Transformation."

Torella, Villa: Torella family's country retreat in San Pietro d'Arena. It is the scene of "Transformation's" violent acts, as Guido il Cortese attempts to kidnap Juliet Torella from it; the story's concluding fight scene occurs in its garden (*Trans* 131, 134).

Toretta, Camilla della: Ippolito's sister in "The Trial of Love"; this Bolognese lady befriends Angeline at Sant' Anna Convent.

Toretta, Ippolito della: Angeline's love interest in "The Trial of Love"; he marries Faustina Moncenigo.

Toretta, Marchese della: Camilla and Ippolito's father in "The Trial of Love"; he convinces Angeline and Ippolito to undergo the one-year separation trial.

Torquay: English seaside town twenty miles south of Exeter. In Shelley's time, Torquay was a popular resort for consumptives. The Shelleys stayed there June 1815 (Sunstein 99). Much of the action in "Maurice" takes place around Torquay: Barnet's brother is a shopkeeper there, and Barnet sells fish at Torquay's market (*Maurice* 59, 62, 68–69, 71, 73, 85). Shelley describes **Treby** in terms reminiscent of Torquay's actual appearance (*F* 5).

Torre, Guido della: The Della Torre family ruled **Milan** prior to **Visconti** but was expelled 1277 (Green 9, 26). The family was restored to power 1302, and Guidetto della Torre ruled until 1310 (Villani 343, 398–399). Shelley refers to Guido in *Valperga* (*V* 1.98–100, 1.118, 1.144).

Tory: Term applied to **Irish** outlaws in the 17th century, but after the 1689 Habeas Corpus Act, which gave "protection from arbitrary arrest and safeguarding of personal liberty," Tory was the name of a major political party in England's **Parliament** (Kinder 1.267). It was dominantly Anglican, consisted of members loyal to the throne, and subsequently became known as the Conservative Party. During her lifetime, Shelley witnessed repeated attempts to reform parliament and lived principally under Tory rule, but, raised in a Radical household, she was delighted at the prospect of a Whig Parliament and the accompanying Reform Bill in 1830 (*Letters* 2.133). Shelley notes, "we beg **Dr. Hotham**'s pardon if we wrong him in making him a high Tory" (*RD* 46).

Tossi, Betta: Frantic mother in "**The Sisters of Albano**."

Toulon: French city on the **Mediterranean**, thirty miles southeast of **Marseilles**. **Guido il Cortese** travels there (*Trans* 122).

Tournai: Province on **Belgium**'s Scheldt; Shelley spells it **Tournay**. **Richard of York** lives there with **Madeline De Faro**; **Perkin Warbeck** was from there (*PW* 1.143, 1.146, 1.148–149, 1.162, 1.199, 1.206, 1.336, 2.34).

Tournay: See **Tournai**.

Tower: Begun 1066, royal fortress on the north bank of the **Thames** in **London** and a royal residence until the 17th century. Shelley set many important *Perkin Warbeck* scenes at the Tower, where characters such as the **Earl of Warwick** and **Richard of York** are imprisoned (*PW* 1.53–54, 2.91–94, 3.282–285). See **Tower Yard**, **Traitor's Gate**, and **White Tower**.

Tower of the Capitol: See **Campidaglio**.

Tower Yard: Probably Shelley's name for Tower Green, east of Beauchamp Tower in the **Tower**. A small paved plot now marks the site where many prisoners were executed (Hibbert 166). **Robert Clifford** vows to save the **Earl of Warwick** from "having his head laid on the ungentle pillow in Tower Yard" (*PW* 1.177).

Towers, Matilda: Girl of "poor and humble birth" willing to be with **Sir Richard Gray** on his terms in "**The Elder Son**"; she is his mistress when **Clinton Gray** is born and becomes **Lady Gray** just before **Vernon Gray**'s birth (*ES* 261).

Traitor's Gate: Gate **Henry III** built under St. Thomas's Tower on the **Tower**'s south side; it was frequently used to hold prisoners who were to be executed (Hibbert 167). **Richard of York** and **Lord Barry** row on the **Thames** to Traitor's Gate (*PW* 2.91).

Tramore: Irish city eight miles south of **Waterford**. **Sir George Neville** and **Richard of York** must take the road to Tramore to return to their camp (*PW* 3.40).

Trangmar, Meiler: *Perkin Warbeck* character who works for **Henry VII** of England. Trangmar's history reveals his **Lancastrian** ties; he was **Henry VI**'s page, waited on **Edward, Prince of Wales**, loved **Queen Margaret**, and hates **Yorkists**, mainly because of his three sons' deaths at their hands (*PW* 1.247–248).

Transfiguration: See **Raphael**.

"Transformation": Published as "by the Author of '**Frankenstein**'" in the 1830 *Keepsake*, Shelley's short story has antecedents in **Byron**'s incomplete drama *The Deformed Transformed* (1824), which Shelley copied 1822 (Robinson 381; *Letters* 1.299). Both works are concerned with doubles and appearances. The accompanying plate *Juliet*, which J. C. Edwards engraved from Miss Sharpe's painting, depicts **Juliet Torella** looking out her window (*Trans* 133). In Shelley's story, Juliet and the handsome **Guido il Cortese** are raised together and exchange private betrothal vows (*Trans* 122). After his father's death, Guido squanders his wealth in **Paris** and returns to **Genoa** demanding his promised bride (*Trans* 123–124). When the fatherly **Marchese Torella** suggests altering the marriage contract since Guido is almost penniless, the enraged suitor attempts first to elope with, then to abduct, Juliet; as a result, he is banished (*Trans* 124–125). Wandering wildly by the sea, he encounters a loathsome **dwarf**, with whom he exchanges bodies for three days in return for treasure (*Trans* 129). The dwarf fails to reappear (Crook 2). The now hideous Guido journeys into Genoa, where he finds that Marchese Torella has pardoned the penitent Guido-esque form of the dwarf, who is on the point of marrying Juliet (*Trans* 125, 131). Guido and the dwarf fight, and Guido recovers his own body by falling on the dwarf's sword while mortally wounding him (*Trans* 134). Juliet nurses Guido back to health, Guido's rude and violent tendencies disappear, and the two marry; the grateful new husband credits this union to the incident with the dwarf (*Trans* 135). Sunstein suggests that Juliet is a "Maryish foster sister" whose refusal to willingly accompany Guido against her father's wishes is Shelley's self-criticism of her elopement with **PBS** (301). The supernatural occurrences in "Transformation" link it most prominently to Shelley's "**The Mortal Immortal**" and *Frankenstein*; the latter also contains the emphasis on doubles. Crook points out parallels between a shipwreck scene in **Calderón**'s *Magico Prodigioso* (1637) and "Transformation" (Crook 2).

Trarbach: German town on the **Moselle**, thirty-five miles southwest of **Coblentz**. Shelley passed through it June 1840 (*R* 1.23).

Traun: Deepest **Austrian** lake, between **Gmunden** and **Ebensee**. Traun River runs between the **Danube** and **Hallstadt**, flowing through Traun Lake

Traunstein

(*MIAU* 136–137). Shelley sailed on Traun Lake September 1842 and mentions falls on the river between **Lambach** and Gmunden (*R* 2.23, 2.28–29).

Traunstein: Alpine peak in **Austria**, overlooking the **Traun** at **Gmunden**. "The dark and gloomy" mountain "rose frowning" along Shelley's September 1842 route from **Lambach** to Gmunden (*R* 2.25–26).

Treasury: Room off the south transept of **San Marco** in **Venice**; it contains **Byzantine** art (*Venice* 34). Shelley visited it October 1842 (*R* 2.122).

Trebucci, Mount: Highest point of mountain range stretching along **Albania**'s southeastern edge into **Epirus**. **Dmitri** is a native of **Korvo** on Mount Trebucci, and **Cyril Ziani** and **Camaraz** climb Mount Trebucci when searching for **Constans Ziani** (*EE* 100, 112).

Treby: Fictional village on **Cornwall**'s coast that is *Falkner*'s opening setting. Shelley describes Treby in terms reminiscent of **Torquay**'s appearance, but she may also have adapted the name from Trebyan, Cornish village eight miles northwest of Fowey (*F* 5, 8–9, 20).

Treisam: German river; its valley, extending southeast from **Freiburg** to Steig, is called the **Hollenthal** (*MCON* 551). Shelley viewed it July 1840 (*R* 1.46).

Trelawny, Augusta Goring (d. 1875): Edward John Trelawny's third wife. While married to Harry Dent Goring (1801–59), Augusta began an affair with Trelawny 1838 (*Journals* 608). Augusta was an "enthusiastic friend" to Shelley November 1837, and "though they probably did not meet after 1838, they kept an interest in one another" (*Journals* 609; Seymour 461–463). Augusta returned to her husband temporarily March 1838, but she took a house close to Trelawny's at Putney 1839, where they remained for several years before marrying 1847 and settling at Usk (Augusta's first husband divorced her in 1841); they had three children before their marriage dissolved 1858, when Trelawny took a mistress (*Journals* 608–609; *Letters* 2.297, 2.319, 3.41, 3.152; Sunstein 354). Shelley kept up a slight correspondence with Augusta; she wrote to tell her of **PFS**'s marriage June 1848 and in February 1850 that she "had always, so to speak, a natural inclination for you" (*Letters* 3.339–340, 3.372–375). Shelley also requested Augusta to ask Trelawny to return a **Curran** portrait of her to her 1850; he did not comply with her request (*Letters* 3.376, 3.384; Seymour 535–536). See Appendix II of Shelley's *Journals* and Rosalie Glynn Grylls's *Trelawny* (1950) (*Journals* 608–609).

Trelawny, Edward John (1792–1881): British author and the Shelleys' friend. Trelawny served in the navy 1805–12, married Caroline Julia Addison (with whom he had two daughters), separated 1816, and divorced her for adultery 1819; he then moved to **Paris** and **Switzerland** (*Letters* 1.219, 1.338; *Journals* 526; Sunstein 206). His father's 1819 death left Trelawny with three hundred pounds a year (*Letters* 1.532). He met the **Williams**es and **Medwin** in **Geneva** 1820 and then met the Shelleys in **Pisa** January 1822; Shelley noted Trelawny "is extravagant.... [T]here is an air of extreme goodnature [sic] which pervades his whole countenance, especially when he smiles, which assures me that his heart is good. He tells strange stories of himself.... I am glad to meet with one who among other valuable qualities has the rare merit of interesting my imagination" (*Letters* 1.219; *Journals* 389, 391; Sunstein 206; White 2.340–341). His "strange stories" and tendency toward exaggeration were consistent in his writing career (Seymour 284). He drew upon his naval experiences for his romantic account of his early years, *Adventures of a Younger Son* (1831), which influenced *Falkner*; Shelley assisted him with publishing *Adventures* in Britain while Trelawny was living in **Florence** (*Letters* 2.73, 2.82–83). Trelawny declared his love to **Claire Clairmont** 1822, but she refused him (*Letters* 1.299; *Journals* 431). He informed Shelley of **PBS**'s death and was present at his cremation, preserving PBS's heart and giving it to **Leigh Hunt** (*Letters* 1.249, 1.251; White 2.380–383). Shelley wrote October 1822 that she entrusted "to the disinterested affection of [Trelawny] alone" and recorded December 1822 that Trelawny "was never more amiable or generous than now" (*Journals* 430; *Letters* 1.295). Trelawny provided Shelley with funds July 1823 (as he was later to do for Medwin's deserted wife) and went to **Greece** with **Byron** August 1823; Shelley was anxious about their temporarily disrupted correspondence (*Letters* 1.344, 1.310, 1.321, 1.368–369). Trelawny provided details of Byron's death to Shelley July 1824; he married thirteen-year-old Tersitza Androutsos 1825, and their daughter Zella was born 1826 (*Letters* 1.433–434, 1.470). They divorced 1828, and Trelawny returned to Britain before settling in **Italy** (*Letters* 1.470; *Journals* 509). Shelley refused to assist Trelawny with a PBS biography July 1829, and, although Trelawny apparently proposed to her summer 1831, he subsequently grew bitter toward her for her refusal to help him (*Letters* 2.82–83, 2.140–141). Trelawny visited Shelley summer 1832, but their close friendship came to an end, even though they continued to correspond. Shelley recorded that Trelawny "loves good sense, liberality & enthusiasm, beyond all things" but noted in her *Journals* Trelawny "is a strange yet wonderful being—Endued with genius—great force of character & power of feeling—but destroyed by *being nothing*—destroyed by envy & internal dissatisfaction" (*Letters* 2.170; *Journals* 526–527). Trelawny traveled to **America** March 1833–July 1835 and visited Shelley October 1836 (*Letters* 2.249–250; *Journals* 550). He formed a liason with **Augusta Goring** August 1838; after her 1841 divorce, they married 1847 and had three children together (*Journals* 608). The marriage broke up 1858 when Trelawny took another mistress (*Journals* 608–609; *Letters* 2.297). Trelawny's *Recollections of the Last Days of Shelley and Byron* (1858), based on his 1822 six-month friendship with PBS, depicted Shelley favorably (*Letters* 2.73). His growing resentment of Shelley is clearly evident in the revised and expanded edition, *Records of Shelley, Byron, and the Author* (1878), in which he indulges in a "brutal character assassination," fueled partially by his dislike of **Jane Shelley** (Sunstein 392). Trelawny's work damaged Shelley's posthumous reputation significantly, while his "recollections" and "records" are an exaggerated assortment of fact and fiction. Upon his death, Trelawny was buried next to PBS, as though they had been intimate friends (Sunstein 395). See William St. Clair's *Trelawny: The Incurable Romancer* (1977) and David Crane's *Lord Byron's Jackal: A Life of Edward John Trelawny* (1998).

Tremezzo: **Italian** town across **Lake Como**'s western arm from **Bellaggio**. Shelley hunted for lodgings there July 1840 before deciding to remain in **Cadenabbia** (*R* 1.64–65). She also describes sailing with **PFS** to Tremezzo August 1840 (*R* 1.84–85, 1.89).

Trent: **Italian** city on the **Adige**, twenty miles northeast of **Riva**. Shelley passed through it September 1842; she mentions the **Council of Trent** (1545–63), which the pope called "to safeguard the unity of the faith and the Church" (*R* 2.64–65; Kinder 1.239).

Trereife: Commoner fighting for **Richard of York** in *Perkin Warbeck*.

Trèves: French name for **German** city **Trier**, on the **Moselle** seventy-two miles southwest of **Mainz**. Shelley states it took her fourteen hours to travel the fifty-five miles from **Metz** to Trèves June 1840 (*R* 1.14). She stayed at **Hôtel de Trèves** (*R* 1.19).

Trevi: Fountain begun on **Rome**'s **Quirinal** 1735, completed 1762. Water falls over artificial rocks, and a large **Neptune** "attended by **Tritons**" stands in its center (*MROM* 91). Visitors to Trevi fountain today throw coins in its waters, believing this will ensure their return to Rome. Shelley visited it November 1818 (*Journals* 239). **Lionel Verney** notes "frost has suspended the gushing fountains—and Trevi has stilled her eternal music" (*LM* 467).

"Trial of Love, The": Shelley's story first appeared in the 1835 *Keepsake* as by "the author of **Frankenstein**" (Robinson 391). Its accompanying illustration, *The Letter,* which John Massey Wright drew and Charles Heath engraved, depicts a key scene (*Trial* 240). Shelley chose **Italy** for the setting of this complicated romance, the title of which refers to a test **Marchese della Toretta** devises when he learns of his son **Ippolito della Toretta**'s plans to wed lower-class, orphaned **Angeline** (*Trial* 233). The actual trial of love is a year-long separation, during which the lovers may not communicate. If they succeed, the Marchese promises to consent to their marriage, but he hopes his son will "form a more suitable attachment" during the year, even though he finds Angeline beautiful and gentle (*Trial* 234). The lovers accept these terms, and Ippolito travels to **Paris**, while Angeline secludes herself in **Este**'s **Sant' Anna Convent**, where the two first met when Ippolito visited his sister **Camilla della Toretta** there (*Trial* 233). Camilla is Angeline's only friend at the convent, since **Faustina Moncenigo** moved two years earlier to a celebrated **Venetian** convent (*Trial* 233). Her education completed, Faustina, accompanied by her father, returns to **Villa Moncenigo**, and the story opens with Angeline hurrying to greet her friend (*Trial* 231). Returning to the convent, Ippolito startles Angeline; he has returned to the area one month early (*Trial* 234). Angeline again encounters her lover as she and Faustina walk to the villa the following day, and Ippolito breaks his arm and bruises his leg while rescuing the two women from a buffalo (*Trial* 236). He recovers from his injuries while staying at Villa Moncenigo, where he becomes acquainted with and eventually engaged to Faustina (*Trial* 236, 241). Dedicated to observing the year-long trial, Angeline avoids the villa, thus remaining ignorant of these circumstances until too late. She attempts to write Ippolito a cautionary note, but Faustina is angry when she reads its contents, which are vague enough to keep secret the trial of love (*Trial* 241). After a month, on "the anniversary of the expiration of the year," Ippolito visits the convent, seeking forgiveness from Angeline, who refuses to see him (*Trial* 242). The story concludes with a "cheerful, if not happy" Angeline, who has become a nun and is relieved that she is not attached to such a "gay, inconstant, careless" man as Ippolito, whose wife Faustina is now extremely unhappy (*Trial* 243).

Tribune: **Uffizi** Gallery room where the museum's most precious items are kept (Berti 5). Shelley visited it January 1843 (*R* 2.152–155).

Triel: See **Tiel**.

Trier: See **Trèves**.

Trieste: Italian city northeast of **Venice**, across the Gulf of Venice. Shelley records the **Archduke** left Venice for Trieste October 1842 (*R* 2.129).

Trinacria: See **Sicily**.

Trinita de' Monti, La: Church (1494) overlooking Piazza di Spagna at the top of **Rome**'s Spanish steps (*MROM* 191). Shelley visited it April 1819 (*Journals* 260). **Lionel Verney** arrives in Rome alone to find "the near eminence of Trinita de' Monti appeared like fairy work" (*LM* 460).

Tripalda, Battista: Villainous fictional priest in *Valperga*.

Tristan, Sir: Allusion to Tristan, main character of medieval romance in which he goes to **Ireland** for Isolde, slays a dragon, and dies from wounds inflicted by a poisoned weapon. Various versions of this legend exist. During the siege of **Waterford**, the city's inhabitants supposedly said, "**Old Reginald's tower**... would have bled sooner than these Sir Tristans," admiring **Richard of York**'s and his followers' bravery (*PW* 3.38).

Triton: **Greek** mythological minor sea god. **Midas** will throw his unwanted gold to Tritons (*Midas* 153).

Troilus and Cressida: Troilus is son of King Priam of **Troy**; he loves **Cressida**, widowed daughter of Calchas, a priest who fled Troy during the Trojan War. **Boccaccio** tells their tragic love story in *Il filostrato* [*One Prostrated by Love*] (c. 1330s), which is the basis for **Chaucer**'s verse romance *Troilus and Criseyde* (1380s). Shelley read Chaucer's version 1820 and 1821, and Shakespeare's *Troilus and Cressida* (1609) 1818 (*Journals* 224, 333, 371). The Shelleys regarded *Troilus and Cressida* highly, praising its poetry and truth (Crook 2). **Borsiere** directs a performance of a version of the *Troilus and Cressida* story that concludes with the death of Cressida "deformed by dis-

Troilus

ease" (*V* 1.289). Crook points out that Shelley derived Cressida's diseased appearance from Robert Henryson's 15th-century *Testament of Cresseid* (3.117). Shelley describes **Richard of York** turning from "painful ideas" to "mightier objects, which gilded his mean estate, or were rather the '**gold o'erdusted**' by such extraneous poverty,' " an allusion to a phrase **Ulysses** uses in discussing time and honor in Shakespeare's drama (*PW* 2.131; Shakespeare 3.3.179). Shelley notes that despite their external union **Lord** and **Lady Lodore** are still separate: "there was no outpouring of the heart—no '**touch of nature**' " (*L* 1.115–116). Shelley later records that **Elizabeth Fitzhenry** would lay aside fears about the proposed journey to **Italy** if it were truly **Ethel Villiers**'s desire, since "the human heart for ever yearns for such demonstration [of affection] from another. What would this strange world be without that 'Touch of nature?' " (*L* 2.150). Shelley also used this phrase to describe **Pasta** in a May 1826 letter to the *Examiner*'s editor (*Letters* 1.518). In Shakespeare's drama, Ulysses speaks this phrase to comfort Achilles by suggesting that although memory is fickle, time immortalizes great deeds (Shakespeare 3.3.176–180). The **Villiers**es wait for **Fanny Derham** while reading scenes from Shakespeare's play; they discuss passages from it and compare their own lives to those of Troilus and Cressida (*L* 3.67–69). **Edward Villiers** stops reading after "having with difficulty decyphered the lines—'**She was beloved**—she loved;—she is, and doth; / But still sweet love is food for fortune's tooth,' " lines Troilus speaks as he informs Ulysses briefly of his love for Cressida (*L* 3.67; Shakespeare 4.5.293–294). Ethel encourages her husband to be like Troilus in his high estimation of love over worldly goods, to which Edward responds that she wants him to say " '**But, alas! / I am** as true as truth's simplicity, / And simpler than the infancy of truth,' " quoting lines in which Troilus pledges the truth of his love to Cressida (*L* 3.68; Shakespeare 3.2.167–169).

Troilus: See *Troilus and Cressida*.

Trois Maisons: See **Ossey-les-Trois-Maisons**.

Trollope, Mrs. Frances (1780–1863): British novelist who based *Domestic Manners of the Americans* (1832) on her 1827–30 experiences in **America** (*DNB*). Shelley describes the attitude of **French** common people as not genuinely courteous; instead "they go a step beyond, and remind one of Mrs. Trollope's description of the Americans" (*R* 1.143–144).

Troy: Ancient city in northwest **Asia** Minor near the Dardanelles; it figures prominently in **Homer**'s *Iliad* and *Odyssey*. **Castruccio** plays childhood military games in which he pretends to defend Troy (*V* 1.14). At **Euthanasia**'s court, *Troilus and Cressida*, set in Troy, is performed (*V* 1.289).

Troyes: **French** city eighty miles southeast of **Paris**. Shelley stayed there August 1814 (*H* 20, 26; *Journals* 13). French and **Russian** forces fought February–March 1814 at a battlefield just outside Troyes (*H* 27; McLynn 582–584).

Tudor, Henry: See **Henry VII** (1457–1509).

Tuileries: Parisian palace beside the Seine, first used in the late 16th century. Its construction began 1564, but "the garden, with the famous maze" and fountain had been completed 1476 (Okey 199, 269). Writing "**Thuilleries**" for Tuileries, Shelley records walking in the gardens August 1814, finding them "formal, in the **French** fashion, the trees cut into shapes, and without grass" (*H* 11). Plague survivors arrive from England to find Paris almost deserted, and only "a few pale figures were to be distinguished at the accustomed resort" at Tuileries (*LM* 374). The religious cult, which separates from **Adrian**'s party, bases itself in the Tuileries, and **Lionel Verney** "penetrate[s] the asylum of the Tuileries" in search of **Juliet** (*LM* 389). **Richard of York** receives "magnificent apartments in the Tuileries" when he first arrives in Paris (*PW* 1.312). Shelley notes that the "gravel of the **Tuilleries** [*sic*] and the **Champs Elysées** is not half so inviting as the sward of **Hyde Park**," but she finds no view more magnificent "than the view at high noon or sunset from the terrace of the Tuilleries, near the river, overlooking the Seine and its bridges" June 1840 (*R* 1.7–8).

Tuilleries: See **Tuileries**.

Tullia (c. 79–45 B.C.E.): **Cicero**'s daughter; at her death Cicero was "overwhelmed with grief" (Howatson 584, 131). **Valerius** tells his companion, "'Cicero did not love his Tullia as I do this divine creature,'" **Isabell Harley** (*Val* 339).

Tunbridge Wells: Large town fifty-five miles southeast of **London**. Mrs. **Raby** is there when she learns of **Rupert Falkner**'s imprisonment (*F* 242).

Turin: Italian city eighty miles northwest of **Genoa**; also a province in northwestern Italy's **Piedmont** region. The Shelleys were there briefly March–April 1818, and Shelley stayed there again July 1823 (*Journals* 202; *Letters* 1.351). Shelley describes Turin natives as "very ugly" and criticizes their clothing (*Letters* 1.352). **Castruccio** and **Benedetto Pepi** stay with Pepi's friend in Turin (*V* 1.128). **Amadeo** is from there (*R* 1.33).

Turkey: Formerly part of the **Ottoman Empire**, which included parts of northeast **Africa** around the **Mediterranean**, southwest **Asia**, and southeast **Europe**. In Shelley's time, the empire was far larger than the republic of Turkey is today and "Turk" referred to the ethnicity of the region's inhabitants. The **Greek**-Turkish wars raged throughout the 1820s, culminating 1829 in Greek independence. **Safie**'s father is a Turkish merchant who is unjustly imprisoned; Shelley refers to him as "the Turk" (*Fr1* 150; *Fr3* 107). **Matilda**'s father visits Turkey during his absence from Britain (*M* 156). Many of *The Last Man*'s protagonists participate with Greeks in war against Turkey (*LM* 170). When **Raymond** looks for the architect of plans for his proposed art gallery, a pair of Turkish slippers leads him to **Evadne Zaimi**, and she subsequently details her troubled marriage and the disruption Turks caused to her life in Greece (*LM* 109, 111–112). **Katusthius Ziani** does not "shrink at finding himself sole of his race among the savage mountaineers and despotic Turk" (*EE* 100). **Winzy** proclaims he is "jealous as a Turk" when **Bertha** plays the coquette (*MI* 221). **Harry Valency** relates his encounter with **Chief Constantine** as he recalls events he experienced during Greece's war against Turkey (*E* 297). Shelley details **Gabriel Serbelloni**'s military victories over Turks (*R* 1.80–81). She later notes she can obtain "luxuries—such as Turkish coffee" cheaply in **Venice** 1843, and she tells an **Italian** officer proud of his capture of a Turkish flag, "it gave me more pleasure than all the curiosities he was showing us" (*R* 2.103, 2.127). [*Fr3* 30].

Turner, Joseph Mallord William (1775–1851): British landscape painter (Chilvers 567). **William Godwin** introduced Shelley to him when she was a child; engravings of his works accompanied some of Shelley's stories, such as "The Sisters of Albano" (Sunstein 41). Shelley praises his illustrations in **Rogers**'s *Italy* (*R* 2.84).

Tuscany: North central **Italian** region containing the provinces **Arezzo**, Carrava, **Florence**, Grosseto, **Leghorn**, **Lucca**, Massa, **Pisa**, **Pistoia**, and **Siena**. Its chief rivers are the **Arno** and **Serchio**. While in Italy 1818–23, Shelley lived primarily there and was extremely interested in Italian politics: "What a glorious thing it will be if **Lombardy** regains its freedom—and Tuscany" (*Letters* 1.156). Shelley's "A Tale of the Passions" describes political events and battles that took place in 13th-century Tuscany (*TP* 1, 21). Shelley refers to "Tuscan fields" in enumerating cherished memories (*Ch* 123–124). She describes Tuscany as one of "the most civilized districts of Italy," but notes it was "torn to pieces by domestic faction, and almost destroyed by the fury of civil wars" (*V* 1.2). Most of *Valperga*'s action takes place in various Tuscan cities (*V* 1.88). Shelley voices her opinion of Tuscany through **Edmund Malville**, who states that for all "the delights of the south of Italy," he would choose to live in Tuscany because of its fertility and people (*RI* 28). He then recounts a journey through Tuscany, from Pisa to **Vico Pisano**, that the Shelleys and **Williams**es took September 1821 (*RI* 29; *Journals* 380). **Giacomo de' Tolomei** mentions translating an insult into "pure Tuscan" (*BMI* 42).

Tusculan Questions: See **Cicero**.

Tweed: River emptying into the **North Sea** at Scotland's southeast tip, on the border with England. **James IV** and **Richard of York** think an upcoming war with England will ease unrest between various Scottish clans, which will unite in "glad shouts from Tweed to **Tay**" (*PW* 2.194). "Crossing the Tweed" in Shelley frequently indicates transitions between England and Scotland (*PW* 2.278, 2.296, 2.319).

***Twelfth Night*:** **Shakespeare**'s comedy *Twelfth Night; or, what you will*, first performed 1602 and published 1623. **Lady Olivia**, the play's central character, is wholly self-absorbed until her love for the digiused Viola alters her perspective on life. **Raymond** denies wasting time in festivities by quoting Sir Toby Belch's jest to Feste in Shakespeare's drama: " '**Dost thou think** because thou art virtuous, there shall be no more cakes and ale?' " (*LM* 151; Shakespeare 2.3.113–115). Shelley notes that **Constance Villeneuve**, "like the

Lady Olivia in 'Twelfth Night,' vowed herself to loneliness and weeping" (D 155).

Twickenham: Town on the **Thames**, twelve miles southwest of **London**'s center. **Lady Santerre** and her daughter move to a villa there (L 1.157). [L 1.179, 1.200].

Twins: Zodiacal sign commonly known as Gemini; the constellation consists of two stars. **Lionel Verney** notes the constellation's passage into "the radiant demesne of **Taurus** and the Twins" (LM 431).

***Two Foscari. An Historical Tragedy, The*:** Drama **Byron** wrote and published 1821 concerning a **Jacopo Foscari** anecdote; Shelley read it January 1822 (Marchand 2.909, 3.953; *Journals* 392). With lines from Byron's drama, **Richard of York** questions what he has done to merit imprisonment: " '**I cannot charge** / My memory with much save sorrow—but / I have been so beyond the common lot / Chastened and visited, I needs must think / That I was wicked' " (PW 3.284; Byron 4.1.164–168).

***Two Gentlemen of Verona*:** Shakespeare's comedy, written 1594 or 1595 and first published 1623; Shelley read it October 1818 (*Journals* 229). As an epigraph to the *Perkin Warbeck* chapter in which **James IV** contrives **Richard of York**'s marriage to **Lady Katherine Gordon**, Shelley quotes from Valentine's speech about his love for Silvia: " '**She is mine own**; / And I as rich in having such a jewel, / As twenty seas, if all their sand were pearl, / Their water nectar, and the rocks pure gold!' " (PW 2.226; Shakespeare 2.4.165–168).

***Two Noble Kinsmen*:** Shakespeare's and **John Fletcher**'s collaborative play based on **Chaucer**'s "Knight's Tale" (c. 1387), written around 1612–13, first staged 1619, and first published 1634. As an epigraph to the *Perkin Warbeck* chapter in which **Richard of York** and his companions flee **London**, Shelley draws upon lines the jailer's daughter speaks: "**Let all the dukes** and all the devils roar, / He is at liberty! I've ventured for him; / And out I've brought him to a little wood / A mile hence" (PW 2.108; *Two Noble Kinsmen* 2.6.1–4). As an epigraph to the chapter in which **Lady Katherine Gordon** waits anxiously to learn if she is allowed to visit her imprisoned husband, Shelley quotes from lines the jailer's daughter speaks regarding the captive protagonists: " '**They are noble** sufferers. I marvel / How they'd have looked, had they been victors, that / With such a constant nobility enforce / A freedom out of bondage' " (PW 3.197; *Two Noble Kinsmen* 2.1.26–28). As an epigraph to the chapter in which the **Earl of Warwick** and Richard fail in their attempt to escape the **Tower**, Shelley quotes an exchange between **Arcite** and **Palamon**: " '**Gentle cousin**, / If you be seen, you perish instantly, / For breaking prison. / No, no, Cousin, / I will no more be hidden, nor put off / This great adventure to a second trial' " (PW 3.292; *Two Noble Kinsmen* 3.6.112–114, 117–119).

Typheus: In **Greek** mythology, earth god Ge and **Tartarus**'s child who "had a hundred burning snake heads and spoke with the voices of men and animals"; he attempted to overthrow the

Tyre

gods and to impose his own rule, but **Zeus** defeated him, and Typheus was crushed under a mountain and thrown into Tartarus (Tripp 594). **Ceres** fears her daughter may have been taken to "Earth-born Typheus['s] . . . dreary caverns" (*P* 57).

Tyre: **Lebanese** port fifty miles southwest of Beirut. Shelley alludes to **Fénelon**'s description of Tyre in *Télémaque*, comparing activity at **Amalfi**'s port to Tyre's (*R* 2.289).

Tyrol: **Alpine** province in western **Austria**. Shelley gives an account of Tyrol's 8 April 1809 uprising (*R* 2.38). She entered Tyrol September 1842 (*R* 2.37).

Tyrolese song of liberty: See **Moore**.

U

Ubaldo: Vanni Mordecastelli's secretary when he is **Lucca**'s acting governor during **Castruccio**'s absence (*V* 3.218–219).

Uffizi Gallery: **Florence**'s art museum, with the best **Italian** Renaissance painting collection; housed in the Uffizi Palace (1560–80), it opened to the public 1769. Shelley first visited it September 1819 (*Journals* 298; Sunstein 175). She returned January 1843 and wrote about its collection; she also calls it **Reali Uffizi** (*R* 2.152–156).

Ugolino (d. 1282): Count of Gherardesca who was named Captain-General of **Pisa** for ten years and achieved peace between **Ghibellines** and **Guelphs** but later became a hated tyrant who was finally imprisoned and starved to death (Sismondi 111–112). **Marco Lombardi** has worked for count Ugolino as a prophet prior to Ugolino's imprisonment in the tower where he starved (*V* 1.99, 3.45).

Ullswater: See **Ulswater**.

Ulswater: Also spelled **Ullswater**, **Cumbrian** lake twenty-five miles south of **Carlisle**. As a child, **Perdita** "dwelt in a cottage whose trim grass-plot sloped down to the waters of the lake of Ulswater," and **Lionel Verney** and Perdita become friends with **Adrian** during his year's residence there (*LM* 17, 36). When Perdita is miserable after **Raymond**'s departure, Verney tries to rejuvenate her spirits by a change of scene, including "native Ulswater" on their journey (*LM* 156).

Ultima Thule: **Latin** expression figuratively meaning "utmost point attainable." Literally, the phrase refers to mythical Thule, thought to be a land six days' sail north of Britain in ancient times (*OED*). **Isabell Harley** tells **Valerius** of her Scottish origin by saying, " 'I come from that *Ultima Thule* discovered by **Caesar**, but unknown in your days,' " a reference to Caesar's 55 B.C.E. invasion of Britain (*Val* 338;

455

Ultime Giorni di Pompeii

Howatson 570, 97). Shelley describes Scotland as a golden age dawning on "this tempestuous Thule of the world" (*PW* 2.187).

***Ultime Giorni di Pompeii*:** See **Pacini**.

***Ultime lettere di Jacopo Ortis*:** See **Foscolo**.

***Ultimo giorno di Pompei, L'*:** See **Pacini**.

Ulyse, Dan: See **Ulysses**.

Ulysses: In **Greek** mythology, **King of Ithaca** (**Ionian** island between **Cephalonia** and Greece) renowned "for his shrewdness and craft and by his eloquence" during the Trojan War; **Roman** name for Odysseus and protagonist of **Homer**'s *Odyssey* (Tripp 326, 404). Calypso detained Ulysses on Ogygia island on his return home, but instead of accepting her bribe of immortality, he spent each day sadly staring at the ocean, homesick (Homer 5.162–67). **Perdita**, frustrated at **Raymond**'s independence and activity, wishes she too could have a career but finds "adverse winds detain me on shore; like Ulysses, I sit at the water's edge and weep" (*LM* 163). **Richard of York** becomes enraged, then begs forgiveness for being "forgetful like **Dan Ulyse** of old in the **Lotus land**"; in the *Odyssey*, Ulysses visits this place, where inhabitants live upon the Lotus flower, making them forgetful and languid (*PW* 1.317; Homer 10.91–104). Shelley compares Richard to Ulysses (*PW* 3.326). In June 1843, Shelley noted "the rock [**Polyphemus**] flung to sink the vessel of Ulysses still lies a furlong from the mouth of the cavern" at the foot of **Sorrento**'s cliffs (*R* 2.264).

Umbria: Central **Italian** region including **Perugia** and **Terni**. Shelley praises Umbrian painters; **Perugino** and Pinturicchio are two famous painters of the Umbrian school (*R* 2.122).

Una: See *The Faerie Queen* and **Wordsworth**.

Uncle Thomas: Robert Walton and Margaret Saville's uncle in *Frankenstein*.

Union Club: At Trafalgar Square's southwest corner on Cockspur Street, Robert Smirke built the Union Club 1824; "containing some of the finest rooms" in **London**, it was "for the resort chiefly of mercantile men of eminence" (Leigh 256, 279; Cunningham 2.856). **Edward Villiers** is a club member, and **Ethel Villiers** locates his lodgings at **Mrs. Derham**'s by asking Union Club porter **Saunders** for directions (*L* 2.259, 2.285–286).

University of Berlin: Humboldt Unversity on the **Unter den Linden**, founded 1809 and housed in a 1753 palace (Tucker 54). Shelley describes the university as near the **Guard-house** and **Italian Opera** (*R* 2.218–219).

University of Pisa: Founded 1343. Shelley notes that its students were forbidden to dress as "illustrious men of **Italian** history" during Carnival (*R* 2.111).

University of Padua: Founded 1222. Shelley notes that **Wallenstein** met **Professor Argoli** there (*R* 2.7).

Unter den Linden: Berlin's wide promenade running east to west for the mile from modern Marx-Engels Platz to Pariser Platz. Shelley describes it as "the best street, which has a double avenue of lime-trees in the middle, running its whole length" July 1842 (*R* 1.218). See **Stadt Rom**.

Unter Innthal: Lower **Inn** valley, northeast from **Innsbruck**. Shelley traveled through it September 1842 (*R* 2.40).

"Untitled: 'Fair Italy!'": Shelley's poem, beginning "Fair **Italy**!" dated 10 September 1833 and first published 1997 (Bennett, "Newly Uncovered" 73–74). In regular rhymed quatrains, the speaker expresses a desire to return to Italy and its "light," since the speaker longs to be with the beloved buried there and "To sleep away my life beneath the sky" (lines 3, 10).

Uomini di Corte: Shelley translates this phrase as "men of court" and explains it as "story-tellers, minstrels, actors, or buffoons"; it occurs frequently in *Valperga* (*V* 1.97). **Alberto Scoto** teaches **Castruccio** how to use *Uomini di Corte* effectively in political intrigue, and several *Uomini di Corte* entertain guests at **Euthanasia**'s court (*V* 1.97–100, 1.256–258).

Urania: Heavenly muse introduced at the beginning of the seventh book of **Milton**'s *Paradise Lost*; her name means "heavenly one." **Greek** mythology also records her as one of the nine muses (Tripp 596). **Lionel Verney** suggests that **Adrian**'s influence improves his character: "My manly virtues did not desert me, for the witch Urania spared the locks of **Sampson**, while he reposed at her feet; but all was softened and humanized"; Shelley implies the superiority of heavenly love (replacing Delilah with Urania) (*LM* 32).

Uri, Lake: Southern arm of **Lake of Lucerne**, beginning at **Brunnen**, featured in **Godwin**'s *Fleetwood* (1805). The Shelleys visited it 1814, and **PBS** planned to read Shelley's early writings there (*Journals* 8–9; *H* 45; White 1.357). **Henry Clerval** declares the **Rhine** valley scenery more beautiful than **Swiss** Lake Uri's mountainous landscape (*Fr1* 182; *Fr3* 133). "**The Swiss Peasant**'s" frame narrator is "beside the water of Uri" (*SP* 136).

Urswick, Sir Christopher (1448–1522): Urswick negotiated English **Henry VII**'s 1483 marriage with **Elizabeth of York**; he subsequently became Henry's chaplain and confessor (*DNB*; Holinshed 3.490). Minor character in *Perkin Warbeck*.

Utopia: **Greek** word for "no place"; Thomas More depicts it as an ideal and harmonious political and social island country in *Utopia* (1516; trans. 1551), which Shelley read 1820 (*Journals* 311–312). **Lionel Verney** finds "poets of times so far gone by, that to read of them was to read of **Atlantis** and Utopia" (*LM* 431).

Uttervalde: See **Uttewalde**.

Uttewalde: **German** village a mile southeast of **Lohmen**; Shelley spells it **Uttervalde**. Shelley walked from it "through the valley to the **Bastei**" August 1842 (*R* 1.260).

V

Vado: Tower fifteen miles south of **Leghorn**, also setting for **PBS**'s *Mazenghi* (1824) (Crook 3.322). Vado sentinels find wreckage from **Euthanasia**'s ship (*V* 3.261).

Val di Nievole: River valley between **Lucca** and **Pistoia**. Seeing it August 1820, Shelley noted: "Passing through the plain of Lucca & the Val di Nievole you will see much of the scenery of **Valperga**" (*Letters* 1.364). Shelley accurately relates that **Castruccio** waged several battles in and near there (Green 59; *V* 2.203, 3.112).

Valdarno: Shelley's **Italian** for "valley of the **Arno**." Shelley traveled to **Vallombrosa** along a road winding "up the Valdarno" November 1842 (*R* 2.136).

Valdimagra: **Magra** valley in northwestern **Italy**. **Maroello Malespino** is from there (*V* 1.255).

Valdinera: Fortified **Apennine** village **Castruccio** controls (*V* 1.174). It was probably in the Nera River Valley near **Terni**.

Valency, Harry: Narrator of "Euphrasia: A Tale of Greece"; he relates his experiences during the **Greek** revolution to entertain fellow passengers while trapped by snow between **Brighton** and **Lewes** Christmas 1836. Shelley uses another narrator to give a third-hand account of Valency's story; only the tale's final section is in Valency's own voice.

Valeriani: See **Molinari**.

Valerius: Title protagonist of "Valerius the Reanimated Roman." A "**Roman** knight" in "'the time of **Cicero** and **Cato**,'" **Marius** killed his father, and **Sulla** proscribed his uncle, who cared for Valerius as a child; Shelley omits any explanation of how Valerius returns to Rome in her own day (*Val* 333). Valerius seems to be Shelley's own creation, although the name has antecedents in poet Valerius Gaius and compiler Valerius Maximus, 1st-century historical figures (Howatson 588). Valerius states: " 'I died when I was nearly forty-five, defending my country against **Catiline**,' " which situates his life approximately 108–62 B.C.E. (*Val* 333). Shelley draws Valerius's expressions of love for Rome, especially for the **Coliseum**, from emotions she recorded in her 1819 *Journals*.

"Valerius the Reanimated Roman": Although the exact date remains uncertain, both Nitchie and de Palacio argue that Shelley wrote this story during 1819; Robinson first published it 1976 (Robinson 397). Sunstein points out the story's "inter-century conceit" was fascinating for Shelley, "since it illuminated the divergent preoccupations of two periods" (164). The story's first part takes place in the **Elysian Fields**, where **Valerius** reveals his earlier life in **Rome** to an "Englishman of rank" before detailing his feelings upon returning to Rome in Shelley's day (*Val* 332). Shelley skims over the specifics of his return, noting only that Catholic priests, particularly **Padre Giuseppe**, cared for him (*Val* 334). Valerius explores Rome at night, much as the Shelleys did, realizing its altered state and finding comfort only in the **Coliseum**, which, in its state of magnificent ruin, seems to him to encapsulate his own emotions of despair while its existence maintains history's glory (*Val* 334–335). Valerius lives in the Coliseum for a year until **Isabell Harley** visits and persuades him to accompany her home so they can learn about each other (*Val* 336, 338). Valerius notes, " 'I cannot tell you how much I love her—how dear the sound of her voice,' " although Isabell invited him only to " 'consider me as your daughter' " (*Val* 339). Valerius concludes his narrative by stating his intention to travel to England (*Val* 339). Isabell's narrative details the relationship with Valerius further, as Isabell encourages Valerius to see Rome's glory in its ruins (*Val* 340–342). A nighttime visit to the **Pantheon** comforts Valerius, but only until he realizes its Christian consecration (*Val* 343). Despite Isabell introducing Valerius to esteemed authors and monuments, Valerius retains "a sadness of demeanour" (*Val* 343). Isabell states that while she "loved and revered" Valerius, she also felt "an involuntary uneasiness" when Valerius touched her hand (*Val* 343–344). Finally, Isabell owns "all the truth, my affection was increased" by such intimacy (*Val* 344).

Valley of Hell: See **Hollenthal**.

Vallombrosa: "Shady valley," now an **Italian** resort town about seventeen miles southeast of **Florence**; Shelley visited its scenic and secluded convent 1842 (*Florence* 282–283). A lay brother entertained her in the adjoining visitors' building, but being female she could not enter the convent itself (*R* 2.137–139; Crook 2).

Valois: See **Charles IV** (1294–1328).

Valperga: Fictional tiny state presided over by a castle of the same name northeast of **Lucca**, toward the Baths; **Euthanasia** inherits it from her mother and practices a benevolent feudalism, until such time as her vision of a Valperga merged within a united, peaceful, democratic, and republican **Tuscany** may be realized (*V* 1.9–10, 1.207, 1.179, 1.181–182). Euthanasia

Valperga

lives at Valperga, where she holds court, shelters relatives, and begins to love **Castruccio**, whose aggressive policies and tyrannical rule destroy Euthanasia's vision and independent domain (*V* 1.255, 2.208, 1.235–236). Accusing Euthanasia of complicity with his enemies, Castruccio storms the castle and razes it (*V* 2.217, 2.267, 2.285). Shelley would have known of the Abate Tommaso di Valperga, friend and dedicatee of **Alfieri**, and possibly had heard of the Piedmontese counts of Valperga; the name also appears to be derived from St. Walburga, after whom "*Walpurgisnacht*," or the "Witches' Sabbath" was named (*V* 2.3; Crook 2; Seymour 253).

***Valperga*:** Shelley's 1823 historical novel, subtitled *or the Life and Adventures of Castruccio, Prince of Lucca*. Shelley first thought about writing a historical romance while living in **Marlow** 1817; after reading **Dante**, **Staël**'s *Corinne*, **Livy**, and **Sismondi** in **Naples** 1819, she based her second novel upon historical **Castruccio** (Sunstein 138, 162). In Sismondi's *Histoire des républiques italiennes du moyen âge*, Shelley read about Castruccio; she began writing her novel 6 April 1820 (Sunstein 162, 178; *Journals* 268, 307). In addition to Sismondi, Shelley read and used the following works: **Machiavelli**'s *The Life of Castruccio Castracani of Lucca*, **Tegrimi**'s *Life of Castruccio*, **Villani**'s *Florentine Annals*, and Muratori's *Dissertazioni sopra le Antichità Italiane* [*Dissertations on Italian Antiquity*] (1765–66) (*Journals* 329–340; Crook 3.xi; *V* 1.iii). Shelley also visited **Lucca** August 1820 to familiarize herself with locations associated with Castruccio (*Journals* 328–329; Sunstein 185). She wrote most of the novel late 1820 while at Bagni **San Giuliano**, finished the rough transcript July 1821, and read part of it to **Maria Gisborne** 28 July 1821 (Sunstein 185; *Journals* 372, 375). Drawing on her study of 14th-century **Italian** history and firsthand knowledge of Italian art, architecture, and scenery, Shelley captures, with surprising accuracy and imaginative descriptions, the story of Castruccio, a **Ghibelline** exiled from his native Lucca as a young boy. Left an orphan, he lives in the **Euganean Hills** with **Francesco de Guinigi** for a year before traveling to England, where he becomes involved in the politics of **Edward II**'s court and has to flee the country after killing a noble. Castruccio returns to **France** and joins **Alberto Scoto**'s forces, learning the art of war and the benefits of espionage and political deception. Returning to Italy, Castruccio distinguishes himself in the Imperial army and returns a hero to Lucca, where a successful Lucchese revolt makes Castruccio the city's leader. Castruccio's love interest is **Euthanasia**, who has inherited **Valperga**; she refuses to join either the **Guelph** or Ghibelline side, due to her support of **Florence**. Despite their opposed political beliefs, Euthanasia and Castruccio become engaged, but his political aspirations take him to **Ferrarra**, where he meets and has an affair with prophetess **Beatrice**. When Castruccio leaves Beatrice for Euthanasia, Beatrice is inconsolable and abandons prophecy. Castruccio travels to Florence to meet Euthanasia, but **Galeazzo Visconti** has poisoned Euthanasia's mind against Castruccio—not because of his infidelity but because of his plans for her beloved Florence. Euthanasia rationally ignores her desire for Castruccio, who then turns his attention to military conquest. Castruccio and Euthanasia meet again after a conspiracy against Castruccio fails; he discovers that it was planned at Valperga Castle. Euthanasia refuses to relinquish the castle, so Castruccio takes it by force and razes it. While a prisoner in Lucca, Euthanasia meets Beatrice, whom the **Inquisition** has arrested for her **Paterin** beliefs. Euthanasia befriends Beatrice, whom, after she relates her story of false love, deceit, imprisonment, and torture, **Bindo** and **Mandragola** seduce with supernatural powers. The shock of seeing Castruccio with **Battista Tripalda** induces a fit from which Beatrice dies. When Euthanasia travels to Florence, she becomes embroiled in another plot against Castruccio, but only to save his life. When the plot fails, Castruccio exiles her to **Sicily**, but a storm destroys her ship, and Euthanasia drowns. In his remaining years, Castruccio continues to control Lucca and the surrounding territory; **Louis of Bavaria** knights him before he dies from illness after the siege of **Pistoia**. Shelley concludes *Valperga* by quoting the epitaph she found inscribed on an old slab marking Castruccio's grave in **San Francesco**. Beginning "**en vivo vivamque**," it may be translated as "Behold I live and will live, the fame of Italian history, the splendor of war, the glory of Lucca, the ornament of **Etruria**, Castruccio from the line of Gerius and **Antelminelli**. I have lived, I have sinned, I have grieved. I have yielded to demanding nature. You who wish well, come to the aid of a pious soul. You who are about to die, for a brief moment remember me" (*V* 3.269; *Letters* 1.365). Shelley completed *Valperga*'s fair copy 1 December 1821, and **PBS** sent the novel to **William Godwin** January 1822, since **Ollier** had refused an advance (*Journals* 384). Finally, G. and W. B. Whittaker published the novel February 1823, as "By the Author of *Frankenstein*," after Godwin changed the title (he inserted "*Valperga*") and made other minor revisions (Sunstein 162, 235; Seymour 320). As Godwin explained these changes in a letter to Shelley, although he had taken "great liberties with it," he affirmed that "all the merit of the book is exclusively your own. The whole of what I have done is nearly confined to the taking away things that must have prevented its success" (*Letters* 1.323). *Valperga* made Godwin four hundred pounds and was reviewed favorably.

Valperga, Count of: Euthanasia's maternal grandfather in *Valperga*; **Antonio dei Adimari** married his only daughter.

Valperga, Countess of: Antonio dei Adimari's wife and Euthanasia's mother in *Valperga*. Euthanasia assumes the title when her mother dies.

Van Diemen's Land: Its discoverer, Tasman, originally named Tasmania (1642) after Anthony van Diemen (1593–1642), governor of the **Dutch** East Indies; this island south of Australia became Tasmania while part of the British colony Australasia, as it was known in Shelley's day. Plague causes a decline in commerce there (*LM* 234).

Van Dyck, Sir Anthony (1599–1641): **Flemish** painter renowned for Baroque portraits of aristocrats. Shelley mentions that **Berlin**'s **New Museum** contains several Van Dyck portraits but does not list them as **Murray** does (*R* 1.220; *MCON* 342). She especially notes Van Dyck portraits of **Charles I** and his queen displayed at **Berlin**'s **Palace** July 1842 (*R* 1.225).

Vandamme, Dominique-René (1770–1830): **French** general in the **French Revolution** and **Napoleonic** Wars. Shelley describes **Arbesau** surroundings as the site of his defeat, referring to his 1813 surrender at Kulm (*R* 1.277).

Vandeuvre: See **Vendeuvre-sur-Barse**.

Vardarelli: Gaetano Vardarelli led "I Vardarelli," a group of bandits in **Naples** (c. 1810–1817) (Moskal 338). Shelley recommends the best sections of **Colletta**, including his description "of the tragical fate of the Vardarelli," who were murdered at **Ferdinand II**'s request (*R* 2.208).

Varenna: Italian town across **Lake Lecco** from **Bellaggio**. Shelley describes its beauty July 1840 (*R* 1.62, 1.67, 1.78).

Vasari, Giorgio (1511–1574): Italian painter who, 1547, began writing biographies of Italian artists, *Le vite de'piu eccelenti pittori, scultori e architetti* [*Lives of the Best Painters, Sculptors and Architects*] (1550). Vasari's most famous paintings are murals in **Rome**'s Palazzo della Cancellaris (1546), **Florence**'s Palazzo Vecchi (1554), and the **Uffizi** (1560) (*DIL* 274). *Rambles* reveals Shelley's acquaintance with Vasari's biographies; she repeatedly refers to his opinions of various artists and relies on his biographical sketches as sources for her own commentaries on several Renaissance Italian artists' lives (*R* 2.142, 2.145, 2.158). Shelley criticizes Vasari's own art as "inane, expressionless" (*R* 2.155). She gives her translation of his description of **Fra Angelico**, beginning "**It appears, from**" (*R* 2.145–146; Vasari 2.31–48). She also includes from Vasari **Michelangelo**'s phrase for **San Miniato**: "**La bella villanella**," meaning "The beautiful peasant" (*R* 2.135; Moskal 300; Vasari 4.30–254). Shelley quotes Vasari's description of **Ghirlandajo**'s *Death of St. Francis*; her translation begins, "**there is one** friar who kisses his hand" (*R* 2.144; Vasari 2.170–171).

Vasili: In *Falkner*, an **Albanian** of **Greek** lineage who follows **Rupert Falkner** during the Greek war. **Ali Pasha** gave **Byron** an Albanian soldier, Vassily, during Byron's 1809 visit; Shelley may draw her character's name from this association (Eisler 222).

Vasilico: See **Basilika**.

Vathek: See **Beckford**.

Vatican: Central **Roman** cathedral complex, with a palace and other holy buildings, on the **Tiber**'s bank. The popes made it their permanent residence 1377 and founded the Museum of the Vatican in early 16th century (*MROM* 193–194). Vatican City, constituted 1929, is an independent papal state within Rome (Kinder 2.152). The Shelleys frequently visited there 1819, and Shelley greatly admired the museum's art and sculptures, especially **Raphael**'s work (*Journals* 251–255). The crowning of **Henry VII** of **Germany** occurs in the **Lateran** because **Guelphs** control the Vatican (*V* 1.158). **Lionel**

Verney "haunted the Vatican" (*LM* 465). Shelley records that the **Berlin** museum gallery "surpasses in elegance and space anything I have ever seen, except in the Vatican" (*R* 1.219). Staying in Rome April 1843, Shelley declares that "a visit to the Vatican [is] a step out of every-day life into a world adorned by the works of the highest genius of all countries and all times" (*R* 2.216–217, 2.219–224).

Vaudemont, Gaspar de: Only survivor of his family; he loves **Constance Villeneuve** in "The Dream" and disguises himself as **Dan Apollo**.

Vedro: **Alpine** river in **Italy** joining Toce River north of **Duomo d'Ossola**. Shelley traveled beside it to **Simplon** October 1840 (*R* 1.136).

Vega: Plain surrounding **Granada**; it "spread out to a circumference of thirty seven leagues, surrounded by lofty mountains" (Irving 6). *Perkin Warbeck*'s **Spanish** scenes take place on the Vega, and when **Monina De Faro** leaves Spain, she misses "fertile laughing Vega" (*PW* 1.224, 1.227, 1.239, 2.21, 2.92).

Velino: **Italian** river joining Nar River near **Terni** via man-made channels formed 671; the confluence is a waterfall called *Caduta delle Marmore*, "Falls of Marble" (*STIE* 435). Shelley calls Velino's cascade the "grandest in **Europe**" (*R* 1.50).

Velletri: **Italian** town in Alban Hills, twenty-one miles southeast of **Rome**. **French** troops exterminated **banditti** there, where **Andrea** occasionally visited (*SA* 55).

Vendeuvre-sur-Barse: **French** village ten miles west of **Bar-sur-Aube**; Shelley calls it **Vandeuvre**. The Shelleys enjoyed its natural surroundings August 1814 (*Journals* 14; *H* 28).

Venice: Located two and a half miles off **Italy**'s northeastern coast, Venice comprises 120 islands in the northern **Adriatic**, from which the **Lido** separates it. Beginning 1818, **Clara Allegra Byron** lived with **Byron** in Venice, and **PBS** traveled there with **Claire Clairmont** August 1818 to see her (*Journals* 207, 224). Shortly thereafter, Shelley joined them in **Este**, but then traveled on to Venice with PBS to obtain medical aid for **Clara Shelley**, who died and is buried there (*Journals* 227). After Shelley's second visit, October 1818, she wrote that Venice is "a pleasant town to visit—it's [*sic*] appearance is so new and strange: but the want of walks and variety must render it disagreeable for a continuous residence" (*Letters* 1.81). **Francesco de Guinigi** takes **Castruccio** "to lovely Venice" to meet **Ethelbert Atawel** (*V* 1.51, 1.58, 1.63, 1.67, 1.286). Shelley calls the Adriatic "Venetian seas" (*Ch* 64). **Edmund Malville** admires Venice, "Queen of the sea, the city of gondolas and romance," but his friend makes derogatory comments; Shelley held both views (*RI* 25–26; *R* 2.78–80, 2.117). **Adrian**, **Clara**, and **Lionel Verney** stay in Venice briefly (*LM* 437–439). **Count Moncenigo** lives in Venice, while **Faustina Moncenigo** is educated at a convent there (*Trial* 231–233). Shelley struggled with her desire to revisit Venice but finally did so September 1842, detailing her experiences in *Rambles* (*R* 1.102, 1.109, 2.78; Seymour 484). [*Trans* 134; *Brother* 166].

Ventura, Tadeo della: Benedetto Pepi's friend who lives in Susa in *Valperga*.

Venus: Name given to the brightest planet, second from the sun, also known as morning star (**Lucifer**) and evening star (**Hesperus**). Also **Roman** fertility goddess associated with **Aphrodite**; she fell in love with mortal **Anchises** and bore him a son, Aeneas (Tripp 597, 58). **Matilda's** father attempts to explain his incestuous desire for her by comparing it to love Anchises might have had if Aeneas had been female (*M* 179). **Castruccio** dines under a faded sunset, the moon, and Venus (*V* 1.55). A castle **Valperga** ceiling exhibits "Venus and her **Cupids**" (*V* 1.184). **Lionel Verney** notes that "Venus lingered in the warm sunset" as he returns to **Windsor** (*LM* 219). The narrator of "**The Mourner**" hears "strains more sweet than those that lull Venus to her balmy rest" (*Mourner* 81). Shelley records distaste for "**Canova's** women," including his Venus (*R* 1.92). She admires **Venus de' Medici** in **Florence's Tribune** and **Rome's** *Venus of the Capitol* (*R* 2.152, 2.230).

Venus de' Medici: See *Queen of Beauty*.

Venus of the Capitol: Pentelic marble statue of **Venus** in **Rome's Capitol** Museum (*MROM* 260). Shelley admired it April 1843 (*R* 2.230).

Venus, Temple of: Part of **Rome's** Forum. In April 1843, Shelley enjoyed the view from the **Coliseum**, with the temple in the foreground (*R* 2.256).

Vercelli: Italian town forty miles northeast of **Turin**. **Tadeo della Ventura** mentions that **Lucca** joined Vercelli in surrendering to **Henry VII** of Germany (*V* 1.118).

Verdun: See **Verdun-sur-Meuse**.

Verdun-sur-Meuse: French city forty miles west of **Metz**; Shelley terms it **Verdun**. Shelley traveled through it June 1840 (*R* 1.12).

Vere, Sir Harry de: *Perkin Warbeck* character who, with a troop of royal guards, approaches **Richard of York** as **Clym of the Lyn** releases him. See **Veres**.

Veres: Noble British family that possessed an earldom for over five centuries; mentioned in *Perkin Warbeck* (*DNB*; *PW* 3.82).

Verney, Evelyn: **Lionel Verney** and **Idris's** younger child in *The Last Man*.

Verney, Lionel: *The Last Man's* first-person narrator and title figure. Sunstein calls Verney Shelley's "narrating alter-ego"; he gives Shelley's opinions and faithfully records events (103). Verney minutely details the fatal shipwreck that takes **Adrian** and **Clara** and leaves him "the LAST MAN" (*LM* 446, 448, 452). Verney then discovers writing materials and composes the novel, wanting to "leave a monument of the existence of Verney, the Last Man" (*LM* 466). Biographers suggest that Shelley directly aligns herself with Verney at her novel's close: "thus, through her fiction, Shelley ends as one unresigned to fate, refusing to live in the past, and launching out" (Sunstein 271; Seymour 357).

Vernon, Henry: Sir Peter Vernon's only son and **Rosina**'s beloved in **"The Invisible Girl."**

Vernon, Lord (1803–1866): George John Warren, fifth Baron Vernon; **Parliamentary** member and scholar who privately printed **Dante**'s works, such as *Inferno* (1858-1865). He was also a correspondent of the **Della Crusca Academy**. Shelley footnotes that **Kirkup** illustrated Vernon's editions (*R* 2.157).

Vernon, Sir Peter: "The Invisible Girl's" widower, who spoils his only son **Henry Vernon** and raises orphaned **Rosina**.

Vernon-Place: Henry Vernon and Rosina live at Sir Peter Vernon's family home in ——shire in **"The Invisible Girl"** (*IG* 196).

Verona: Italian city forty-five miles west of **Padua**. **Cane della Scala** rules Verona, and **Benedetto Pepi** visits him there (*V* 1.137, 2.105, 2.118). The Scala family controlled Verona 1262–1369 (Green 10). Shelley compares strife between **Siennese Tolomei** and **Mancini** to the hatred of Verona's **Montecchi** and **Capalletti** (*Brother* 166). [*R* 2.7?]

Veronese, Paul (c. 1528–1588): Name for Paolo Caliari, **Italian** artist named "Veronese" for the town in which he was born. In **Venice**'s **Doge's Palace** September 1842, Shelley saw an oil of **Catherine Cornaro** that she attributes to Veronese, but none of his works matches this description (*R* 2.85; Moskal 273–274). She saw his *Marriage Feast at Cana* (1562–63), calling it *Marriage at Cana*, at **Accademia delle Belle Arti (Venice)** September 1842, although Moskal notes that Shelley may be confusing this painting with another (*R* 2.90; Moskal 277). Shelley saw his *Martyrdom of St. Mark* (1558), calling it his *"chef d'oeuvre,"* at **St. Sebastian's Church** September 1842 (*R* 2.99–100; *Venice* 166). She viewed Veronese's *Family of Darius before Alexander* (c. 1570), which Shelley calls *Family of Darius at the Feet of Alexander*, at **Palazzo Pisani** October 1842 (*R* 2.119–120; *Phaidon* 677). See **Bonifazio**, **Veronese**.

Versailles: French town ten miles southwest of **Paris** and site of a palace built 1624–1708 (Kinder 1.261). After the **French Revolution**'s start and Louis XVI's 1793 execution, the palace ceased to be a royal residence and fell into disrepair; the French government restored it in the 20th century, making it a major tourist attraction. The Shelleys visited Versailles August 1816, but **PBS** recorded "people who shewed us the palace obstinately refused to say anything about the Revolution" (*Journals* 133; White 1.462). Shelley spent several days in Versailles August 1823 (*Journals* 468). **Adrian**'s party resides in Versailles's **Grand Trianon** (*LM* 382).

Vespasian [Titus Flavius Sabinus Vespasianus] (9–79 C.E.): Roman general who became Rome's emperor 69 C.E.; he began construction of the **Coliseum**, which his son **Titus** completed (Howatson 499, 593). **Padre Giuseppe** informs **Valerius** that the Coliseum " 'is the renowned Circus, built by Vespasian' " (*Val* 335). **Isabell Harley** later tells Valerius that when she visits the Coliseum, " 'I do not think of Vespasian who built it' " (*Val* 340).

Vesuvius

Vesuvius: Active volcano ten miles southeast of **Naples**. Traveling to Naples December 1818, the Shelleys recorded seeing "the flame of Vesuvius as we drive along," and they ascended the volcano December 1818 to "see the rivers of Lava gush from its sides" (*Journals* 241, 244; Seymour 222). Just before his execution, **Corradino** looks at Vesuvius's intermittent "flashing light" (*TP* 22). **Euthanasia** compares **Castruccio** to Vesuvius (*V* 3.206). **Edmund Malville** fondly remembers Naples's " 'festive appearance . . . mingled strangely with the insecurity with which one is inspired by the sight of Vesuvius' " (*RI* 28). **Ludovico Mondolfo** enjoys hunting on "the plain at the foot of Vesuvius" while the volcano "groaned heavily" (*HM* 311). **Lionel Verney** describes sunset at **Dover**: "the sea burned like a furnace, like all Vesuvius a-light, with flowing lava beneath" (*LM* 370). **Horace Neville** compares his anger to Vesuvius (*Mourner* 86). The **Villiers**es arrive at Naples to see "a blood-red flash shot up now and then from Vesuvius" (*L* 2.178). Shelley notes "by the moonlight we can perceive the smoke ascend from the crater of Vesuvius" and that "Vesuvius rises up immediately from the shore" when viewed June 1843 from the sea (*R* 2.263, 2.267, 2.277, 2.283).

Vettici: Hamlet of **Amalfi** (Moskal 381). In July 1843, Shelley mentions the laborers who carried travelers' luggage were from Vettici (*R* 2.288).

Vevai: See **Vevay**.

Vevay: Swiss city ten miles southeast of **Lausanne** on **Lake Geneva**'s northern bank; Shelley spells it **Vevai**. In *History*'s preface, Shelley states that her route includes Vevay (*H* v). Shelley traveled by steamer from Vevay to **Geneva** 1840 (*R* 1.138).

Via Mala: Road following the Hinterrhein River through the **Alps** from Reichenau to **Splügen**, near the **Swiss-Italian** border. Shelley took Via Mala July 1840 (*R* 1.57).

***Vicar of Wakefield, The*:** See **Goldsmith**.

Vicenza: **Italian** city seventeen miles northwest of **Padua**. Shelley may have stayed overnight there September 1842 (*R* 2.77). See **Palladio**.

Viceroy's Palace: Probably a reference to Palazzo Reale, near **Milan**'s **Duomo** (Noyes 255). **Lionel Verney**, **Adrian**, **Clara**, and **Evelyn** live there during winter (*LM* 430).

Vico: Vico Equesne, **Italian** town five miles northeast of **Sorrento**. Shelley passed it in July 1843 (*R* 2.296).

Vico Pisano: **Italian** town ten miles east of **Pisa**. The Shelleys visited it October 1820 and September 1821 with the **Williams**es (*Journals* 334, 380). Shelley evokes the 1821 journey in **Edmund Malville**'s description of Vico Pisano (*RI* 30).

Vienna: **Austria**'s capital city, one hundred miles southeast of **Budweis**; **Charles Clairmont** settled there 1830 (Seymour 398). **Lionel Verney** becomes ambassador of Vienna's private secretary (*LM* 36, 38, 41). **Countess of Windsor** leaves Vienna to return to England (*LM* 291). **Ellen** is "glad" Clinton Gray "was at Vienna" (*ES* 246). At his father's deathbed, **Lord Lodore** informs his sister he plans to return "immediately to Vienna" (*L* 1.85). **Elizabeth Falkner** and **Rupert Falkner** plan to visit Vienna (*F* 33). In 1842, Shelley recorded that her enthusiasm for **Italy** infected **Pearson**, who "intended repairing to Vienna in the winter" but altered his plans to pass through **Venice** first (*R* 1.235). Shelley regretted she was unable to visit Vienna September 1842; the city figures prominently in her history of the **Tyrol** (*R* 2.23, 2.60–61, 2.104).

Vienna, Congress of: Five powers, **Austria**, **Prussia**, **Russia**, Great Britain, and **Bourbon France**, met in **Vienna** (1814–1815) to reorganize **Europe** after the **Napoleonic** wars. Shelley recounts **Bologna**'s history, including the fact that its loss of independence resulted from the Congress of Vienna, as the Papal states were returned to the pope (*R* 2.248).

Villach: Austrian town sixty-five miles north of **Trieste**. Shelley mentions a route that includes Villach (*R* 2.35).

Villamarina, Principe: Clorinda **Saville**'s father, a "**Neapolitan** nobleman of the highest rank" (*L* 2.60).

Villani, Giovanni (c. 1275–1348): Florentine historian. He wrote twelve volumes of Florentine history from the time of the Tower of **Babel** to 1346. Shelley read Villani's *Cronica* (1537, 1554) in **Italian** 1820–21 while doing research for *Valperga*, and she critiques it in her essay "**Giovanni Villani**" (*Journals* 332, 681). In *Valperga*'s preface, Shelley acknowledges consulting Villani (*V* iii). In *Rambles*, Shelley lists Villani as a renowned Italian historian (*R* 2.205).

Villegas, Esteban Manuel de (1595–1669): Shelley includes Villegas in her brief discourse upon minor **Spanish** poets for *Italian and Spanish Lives*. Villegas's **Horace** translations and "original anacreontics" are published in *Eróticas o Amatorias* [*Erotic and Amatory Poems*] (1618) (*ISPL* 3.240). Shelley admires particularly his translation of *Anacreon* in *Eróticas* (*ISPL* 3.241). She esteems Villegas's poetry highly, asserting "he has more natural facility, added to classical correctness, than almost any other Spanish poet" (*ISPL* 3.241).

Villeggiatura: Custom of spending the summer at **Italian** country villas. Shelley noted that she was prevented from touring the country residences October 1843 by higher-ranking **Venetians** residing there (*R* 2.104).

Villeneuve, Chateau: Constance **Villeneuve**'s family home, on the **Loire** near **Nantes**, and setting for "The Dream" (*D* 153, 159).

Villeneuve, Countess Constance de: Heroine of "The Dream"; she loves **Gaspar de Vaudemont**.

Villeneuve-la-Guiard: See Villeneuve-la-Guyard.

Villeneuve-la-Guyard: French town twenty miles east of **Fontainebleau**; Shelley spells it **Villeneuve-la-Guiard**. **Lionel Verney** leads plague survivors there en route to **Switzerland** (*LM* 403–408).

Villiers, Colonel: Edward Villiers's monetarily reckless and selfish father in *Lodore*.

Villiers, Edward: Colonel Villiers's only son in *Lodore*; he marries **Ethel Villiers**. In the Villierses' fictional relationship, Shelley depicts her own 1814 experiences with **PBS** in **London**, when the couple were forced to live separately while PBS avoided bailiffs trying to arrest him for debt.

Villiers, Ethel: **Lord** and **Lady Lodore**'s only child and a central female protagonist of *Lodore*; she marries **Edward Villiers**. Sunstein suggests that Shelley depicts elements of herself in the "dependency and need for love in gentle Ethel" (49, 153). Seymour notes additional autobiographical elements (431–432).

Virgil, Publius Vergilius Maro (70–19 B.C.E.): **Roman** poet whose major works are *Eclogues* (37 B.C.E.), *Georgics* (29 B.C.E.), and the mythical epic *Aeneid* (c. 18 B.C.E.). The Shelleys enjoyed reading Virgil's *Works* together (*Journals* 681). **Euthanasia** learns "the polished language of **Cicero** and Virgil" (*V* 1.28). The **Latin poet** to whom Shelley refers in *The Last Man* could be Virgil (*LM* 6). **Lord Lodore** finds he can "hang enchanted over the majesty and elegance of Virgil" (*L* 1.25). Discussing **Italian** literature, Shelley notes that **Manzoni** read Virgil (*R* 2.199).

Virgin and Child: See **Raphael**.

Virgin in Glory Worshipped by Six Saints: See **Francia**.

Virginia Water: Artificial lake south of **Windsor**'s **Great Park**. Shelley recorded **PBS**'s walk there from **Marlow** July 1817 (*Journals* 177). **Lionel Verney** enjoys exploring "the grove of Virginia Water," and the lake's proximity to Windsor ensures its frequent mention in *The Last Man* (*LM* 41). "**The Mourner**" opens with a long description of Virginia Water's "fair expanse," and Shelley asserts that her story is set prior to the "iron gates enclosing the plantations and Virginia Water," which reserve the area "for the royal possessor"; Shelley thus links her story to **Turner**'s accompanying illustrations (*Mourner* 81, 83). [*Mourner* 86, 95].

Visconti, Azzo (d. 1339): One of **Galeazzo Visconti**'s sons; he controlled **Milan** until 1328 (Sismondi 142). He was involved in the 1325 battle of **Altopascio**; he traded **Castruccio** about eight hundred knights for a large, disputed amount of money (Green 170–175). In *Valperga*, this **Ghibelline** noble is Galeazzo's younger brother and marries **Fiametta dei Adimari** (*V* 2.122–123, 2.136).

Visconti, Galeazzo (1277–1328): Matteo Visconti's eldest son; he took control of **Milan** a few weeks prior to his father's June 1322 death (Sismondi 131). **Louis of Bavaria** imprisoned Galeazzo until **Castruccio** intervened 1327 (Sismondi 137). Throughout his rule, Galeazzo aided Castruccio in military endeavors, and the favor was returned; Shelley depicts Galeazzo as Castruccio's close friend and ally in *Valperga* (Green 140–141). Shelley includes the historical account of Louis's imprisonment of Galeazzo and Castruccio's involvement in his release, as well as

Galeazzo's subsequent death from the same fever that kills Castruccio (*V* 3.264, 3.266, 3.268).

Visconti, House of: Milanese family powerful in 13th–15th centuries. Shelley mentions that a **Sfrondati** married into this family (*R* 1.79).

Visconti, Matteo (1255–1322): Following Matteo's 1302 exile from **Milan**, **Henry VII** of **Germany** restored this **Ghibelline** noble to power 1310 (Villani 342–344, 397). Upon his return, Matteo exiled **Guido della Torre**, who had controlled Milan during his absence (Sismondi 124). Matteo ruled Milan for twelve years and abdicated in favor of his son **Galeazzo Visconti** a few weeks prior to his death (Sismondi 131). In *Valperga*, Shelley refers to Matteo and **Alberto Scoto**'s connection (*V* 1.88–89). Shelley also relates an anecdote from **Villani**, who describes Guido sending an entertainer to spy on exiled Matteo (Villani 342–344; *V* 1.98–100).

Visdomini: Noble **Guelph** family of **Florence** who attends **Euthanasia**'s court (Villani 125; *V* 1.256).

Vishnou: Hindu god known as "the Preserver" in several incarnations. **Lionel Verney** characterizes the religious leader in **Paris** as "a prophet, nay a deity; such as . . . Vishnou the preserver" (*LM* 386).

"Visit to Brighton, A": Article Shelley published in the December 1826 *London Magazine*. Shelley and **Jane Williams** lived in **Brighton** August 1826, and their experiences there served as a source for this article about "the worst place in the world" (*Letters* 1.527, 1.530; Sunstein 274). Shelley praises **London** life, then offers her travel experiences to ground her opinion of Brighton. While disparaging the town, which she warns travelers to avoid, she criticizes Brighton's chief landmarks: the beaches, park, libraries, and **Pavilion**. Shelley denounces Brighton by ironically complimenting such things as "little carriages," which are "most delightful," because "they are ever at hand to convey one from this seat of barrenness" (*Visit* 465).

Viterbo: Italian city forty miles north of **Rome**. Before **Conradin**'s 1268 execution, **Pope Clement IV** offended the Romans by moving from Rome to Viterbo (Sismondi 94). "**A Tale of the Passions**" mentions the pope's move (*TP* 21).

***Vita Nuova*:** See **Dante**.

Viviani, Teresa ["Emilia"] (b. 1802): In November 1820, **Pacchiani** introduced the Shelleys to Teresa Viviani, the **Pisan** governor's nineteen-year-old daughter, who was confined to **Sant' Anna Convent**; they nicknamed her Emilia (*Journals* 595; Sunstein 193; Seymour 266). Shelley was sympathetic to Emilia's situation—awaiting an arranged marriage—and **PBS** fell in love with her; he attempted to obtain her freedom and wrote the love poem *Epipsychidion* (1821) to her (Sunstein 193–194; *Letters* 1.165–166; White 2.247–269). Shelley visited Emilia until May 1821; Emilia married Luigi Biondi later that year (*Journals* 596–597; *Letters* 1.223). Although Shelley remained relatively silent about the PBS-Emilia situation, she made it the basis for "The Bride of Modern Italy," in which **Clorinda Saviani** represents Emilia. See Enrica Viviani della Robbia's *Vita di una donna* [*Life of a Lady*] (1936) and Appendix II in Shelley's *Journals* (595–597).

Volney, Constantin François de Chasseboeuf, comte de (1757–1820): French politician, traveler, and author. He published *Travels in Egypt and Syria* (1787) but is better known for *The Ruins, or Meditation on the Revolutions of Empires* (1791), which Shelley calls *Ruins of Empire* (and which **PBS** read 1812–13) (Daru xxii; White 1.277). A philosophical text, *Ruins* relates an educational tour conducted by Genius; he "will reveal to [Volney] the science of ages and the wisdom of the tombs" (14). Throughout, Volney encourages humans to learn from history to avoid repeating mistakes (41). Volney's *Ruins* serves as the textbook from which **Felix De Lacey** teaches **Safie** about history; the **Creature** also benefits from it (*Fr1* 146–147; *Fr3* 105).

Voltaire (1694–1778): French author born François-Marie Arouet. He gained literary fame with successful performances of the epic tragedy *Oedipe* (1718), thereafter adopting the name Voltaire, under which all his future works appeared. He is renowned for *Candide* (1759), which **PBS** read 1814 (*Journals* 682). Voltaire remains the acknowledged Enlightenment literary figure, and Shelley read many of his works (*Journals* 682). Shelley's Voltaire biography in *French Lives* provides a lengthy and detailed description, in which certain of her assertions are inaccurate and indicate personal bias against him. Shelley acknowledges that Voltaire wanted "to liberate his country from priestly thraldom and antique prejudices" through his works, but she criticizes the lack of morals she perceives in his writings and condemns him especially for his attack on **Rousseau** (*FL* 2.19). Shelley asserts that Voltaire "scarcely ever penned a line that is not instinct with spirit and life and genius," even while she feels he "will always receive a larger share of attention and praise than his intrinsic merits deserve" (*FL* 2.109–110). Shelley mentions **Frederic the Great** meeting Voltaire at **Meuse** castle (*R* 1.227).

Volterra: Italian town thirty-five miles southwest of **Florence**. **Louis of Bavaria** makes **Castruccio** duke of an area including Volterra (*V* 3.264–265). Louis actually conferred this title on Castruccio 17 November 1327 (Green 221).

Vorarlberg: Austrian state between **Bavaria**, Liechtenstein, **Switzerland**, and **Tyrol**, linked with Tyrol 1523–1918. Shelley mentions the inhabitants' desire in 1809 for freedom (*R* 2.49).

Vulcan: **Roman** god of fire; Hephaestus in **Greek** mythology (Tripp 598). **Midas** thinks his golden touch will bring Vulcan under his command (*Midas* 129–131).

W

Wagram, Battle of: Napoleon's forces defeated **Austria** on a plain eleven miles northeast of **Vienna** 5–6 July 1809. Shelley describes the defeat as crushing **Tyrolese** hopes for freedom (*R* 2.49).

Waidring: Austrian town twenty-eight miles southwest of **Salzburg**; Shelley spells it **Waidringen**. She stayed there September 1842 (*R* 2.40).

Waidringen: See **Waidring**.

Walbrook, Parish of: London district where the **Tower** is located. Upon **Elizabeth of York**'s arrival in London, she first goes to Walbrook (*PW* 1.60). **Desmond** suggests that **Digby** meet him there (*PW* 2.118).

Walden, Lord de: Richard of York attends the marriage feast given when Lord de Walden marries **Lord Surrey**'s oldest sister (*PW* 2.139).

Waldman: Victor Frankenstein admires this chemistry professor at **Ingolstadt** University in *Frankenstein*.

Walen: Austrian lake southeast of **Lake Zurich** and town on lake's eastern point; Shelley calls it **Wallenstadt**. She traveled by steamboat on this "gloomy" lake July 1840 (*R* 1.54).

Wales, Prince of: See **Arthur, Prince of Wales**.

Wallachia: Southern region of Romania since 1861; in Shelley's day, a principality under **Russian** control (Kinder 2.69, 2.81). Shelley was acquainted with "Prince Caraja, the former Ospadaro of Wallachia & his daughter the Princess Argiropoli" in **Pisa** 1821 (*Letters* 1.188). **Evadne Zaimi** "aimed at the title and power of Princess of Wallachia" (*LM* 113–114). See **Argyropylo**.

Wallenstadt: See **Walen**.

Wallenstein [Albrecht Eusebius Wenzeslaus von Waldstein] (1583–1634)

Wallenstein [Albrecht Eusebius Wenzeslaus von Waldstein] (1583–1634): Bohemian Catholic noble, created Duke of Friedland 1624. This **Habsburg Austrian** general rose to power in the Thirty Years' War, but following his defeat by **Gustavus Adolphus** in 1632, Wallenstein retired from public life and was subsequently assassinated (Kinder 1.253–255). Shelley discusses Wallenstein, including his dependence upon astrological predictions, in her history of **Prague** (*R* 2.6–9). See "**Death of Wallenstein, The**."

Walpole, Horace (1717–1797): Fourth Earl of **Oxford** who was a Member of **Parliament** as well as historian, scholar, and witty correspondent. He initiated the English Gothic tradition with *The Castle of Otranto* (1764). Shelley quotes loosely from a Walpole letter to Sir Horace Mann as an epigraph to the *Lodore* chapter in which **Lord Maristow** advises **Edward Villiers** not to trouble himself too much over **Colonel Villiers**'s behavior: "**I choose to** comfort myself by considering, that even while I am lamenting my present uneasiness, it is passing away" (*L* 2.220; Walpole 2.170; *Letters* 2.195).

Walter, Archbishop of Dublin [Walter Fitzsimmons] (d. 1511): After becoming archbishop 1484, Walter supported **Lambert Simnel** 1487; he subsequently renewed his allegiance to **Henry VII** of England and gained pardon. He became **Ireland**'s Lord Deputy 1492 (*DNB*). Shelley mentions him in *Perkin Warbeck* (*PW* 1.286).

Walter of Hornbeck: Skelton's customer who did not pay for "his misshapen suit" (*PW* 3.68, 3.70).

Walton, Robert: Sea captain and polar explorer in *Frankenstein*; his expedition through the Arctic Ocean brings him into contact with **Victor Frankenstein** and the **Creature**, whose tales he records in letters (the novel's frame) to his sister, **Margaret Saville**. "Walton's ambition for knowledge and glory parallel" young Victor's (Sunstein 126).

Wandering Jew: Legendary **Ahasuerus** urged Jesus to hasten as he carried the cross to Calvary; he was condemned to wander the earth until Jesus's second coming. **Winzy** refers to the Wandering Jew legend but claims he is not that condemned figure (*MI* 219).

Warbeck, Jahn (d. c. 1498): Perkin Warbeck's father. Shelley's character is a **Flemish** moneylender who gives **Richard of York** into his sister **Madeline De Faro**'s protection (*PW* 1.44–48, 1.87–90).

Warbeck, Perkin (c. 1474–1499): Pretender to England's throne who emerged 1491; **Margaret of Burgundy**, **James IV**, **Maximilian I**, French **Charles VIII**, and important **Irish** and English people variously supported him. Impersonating **Edward IV**'s younger son, he invaded England against **Henry VII** 1495, 1496, and 1497, when he was finally captured at **Beaulieu** and subsequently executed. Shelley believed Perkin really was **Richard of York**, despite his confession to being an impostor (Sunstein 299). *Perkin Warbeck* is Shelley's fictional version of various historical accounts; she consistently refers to the historical Perkin as Richard of York.

Warham, Doctor William (c. 1450–1532): Archbishop of **Canterbury**. **Henry VII** of England sent Warham and **Sir Edward Poynings** to **Flanders** to investigate the **Perkin Warbeck** conspiracy July 1493; **Holinshed** records Warham's speech to **Margaret of Anjou** (Holinshed 3.506). Warham was again connected to Perkin 1497, when he demanded **James IV** relinquish Perkin (*DNB*). Warham, mistaken as **Wattam**, is a minor character in *Perkin Warbeck*.

Wars of the Roses: War **Lancaster** and **York** Houses (represented by **red** and **white roses** respectively) fought over England's throne 1455–85; battles fought included those at **Stoke** and **St. Albans**. **Richard III** claimed England's throne 1483, after having murdered his nephews and **Edward IV**'s sons, Edward V and Richard; a Lancastrian, **Henry VII** defeated Richard III at **Bosworth Field** 1485 and took the throne for the **Tudors** (Kinder 1.189). Shelley revises history in *Perkin Warbeck* by exploring the life of **Richard of York**, Edward IV's son who was supposedly murdered in the **Tower**, and his struggle to regain his rightful throne; her novel, which opens immediately after **Bosworth Field**, refers to these wars repeatedly.

Wartburg Castle: Ludwig I founded this castle near **Eisenach** 1607 (McLachlan 868). It was renowned as **Luther**'s 1521 haven in which he translated the **Bible**'s New Testament from **Greek** into **German** (McLachlan 868). Shelley visited it July 1842 (*R* 1.207).

Warwick, Earl of (1475–1499): Edward Plantagenet, knighted 1483, Edward IV's nephew through George, **Duke of Clarence**. Richard III imprisoned him at **Sheriff Hutton** until 1485, when he moved to the **Tower**. **Henry VII** beheaded him for conspiracy (*DNB*). **Elizabeth of York** loves this *Perkin Warbeck* character.

Washington: Founded 1791 and incorporated 1802, capital city of the United States; Congress and the president have resided there since 1800. **Mrs. Greville**'s husband is in Washington when **Lord Lodore** meets her, and friends arrive at her house from Washington (*L* 1.227, 1.252). **Horatio Saville** remains in Washington while **Edward Villiers** travels to **New York** (*L* 2.45). **Hillary** meets **Osborne** in Washington, and **Gerard Neville** plans to meet Osborne there also (*F* 158, 266).

Waterford: Irish, fortified city and harbor eighty-five miles southeast of **Dublin**. **Keating** and **Desmond** decide to begin their conquest of Ireland with Waterford, a town that refuses to acknowledge **Richard of York** (*PW* 2.31–32). Soldiers enter Waterford county to attack the town July 1495, but the attack ultimately fails and Richard flees on the *Adalid* (*PW* 2.35–48, 3.40, 3.66, 3.74; *DNB*).

Waterford Harbor: See **Waterford**.

Waterloo, Battle of: British forces defeated **Napoleon** at this battle, fought three miles south of Waterloo, **Belgium**, 18 June 1815; it ended the Napoleonic Wars. Shelley mentions that the **Brandenburg Gate**'s car of Victory was returned to **Berlin** after the battle (*R* 2.219).

Wattam, Doctor: In the first edition of *Perkin Warbeck*, apparent error for **Warham**; hand-corrected by Shelley in her personal copy (Fischer 152, 401; Crook 2).

Weber, Carl Maria Friedrich Ernst (1786–1826): German widely regarded as the 19th century's leading composer (Warrack 365–66). Weber's *Abu Hassan* (1811) (Shelley uses *Abon Hassan*) is a one-act comic opera; first performed in England 1825, its plot is drawn from *Arabian Nights* (Warrack 122, 112–115). The band at **Alfred**'s birthday party "played the wild eastern air of Weber introduced in" *Abu Hassan* (*LM* 240). Shelley saw Weber's *Der Freischütz* [*The Marksman*] (1821) upon its first **London** production (August 1824) and expressed her admiration for Weber's work (*Letters* 1.445; Seymour 367). Some of the second act's scenes are set in **Wolf**'s **Glen**, "legendary abyss in the depths of the *Urwald* where lurks everything vile and horrifying and evil" (Warrack 216–18). At **Versailles**, **Lionel Verney** suggests that music cannot help him escape present misery, since music to him is "but as the demoniac chorus in the Wolf's Glen, and the caperings of the reptiles that surrounded the magic circle" (*LM* 384). Shelley enjoyed *Der Freischütz* in **Dresden**, especially the **Bridesmaid**'s role (that she terms **Linda**), despite "shabby and meagre" scenery July 1842 (*R* 1.254–255).

Weimar: Late-18th and early-19th-century intellectual center of **Germany**, twelve miles east of **Erfurt**; home to **Goethe** and **Schiller**. Shelley visited it July 1842 (*R* 1.210–213).

Weise Frau, Die: See **Boieldieu**.

Welford: English town sixteen miles southeast of **Leicester**. Knights defeated at **Bosworth Field** cross the **Avon** to avoid Welford (*PW* 1.2).

Wells, Lord (d. 1499): English Henry VII's uncle, sixth Baron Welles and first Viscount Welles (Fischer 340). Henry's cousin in *Perkin Warbeck*, ordered to apprehend **Richard of York** (*PW* 3.191–192).

Wenceslaus IV (1361–1419): Crowned **Bohemia**'s king 1363 and **Germany**'s 1378; he had **St. John Nepomuk** "slain by drowning" (Kinder 1.197). Shelley notes this legendary event, which occurred when Nepomuk refused "to betray ... secrets confided to him by his **Queen** in the confessional"; Wenceslaus was married to Lower **Bavaria**'s Joanna (d. 1386) and Bavaria's Sophia 1389 (*R* 2.4). [*R* 2.5].

Werner; or, The Inheritance: A Tragedy: Drama **Byron** began December 1821 and completed and published 1822; Shelley copied it January 1822 (Marchand 3.965, 3.1048; Sunstein 204; *Journals* 382–383, 390). After witnessing Stralenheim's murder and hearing a bell toll the hour, Gabor speaks lines that **Perdita** uses in writing to **Raymond** about her "fragile heart, every pulse of which knells audibly, 'The funeral note / Of love, deep buried, without resurrection'" (*LM* 143; Byron 3.3.8–9). **Guido il Cortese** watches the sun rise as "**day began to grizzle** its dark hair," a paraphrase of Ulric's line urging Werner to flee before sunrise (*Trans* 130; Byron 3.4.152–153).

Werter: See *Sorrows of Werter*.

Wertheim, Mr.: German language instructor from **Munich** whom Shelley hired at **Kissingen**. He helped her obtain transportation to **Leipzig** July 1842 (*R* 1.199).

West Indies: North **Atlantic** island group between North and South **America**; Shelley calls it the **Western Isles** and the **Western Indies**. **Monina De Faro** agrees to accompany her father there, but illness prevents her (*PW* 3.53). They later plan the same expedition, but Monina dies in (presumably) **Portugal**, and **Hernan De Faro** is "never heard of more" after sailing there (*PW* 3.281, 3.344).

Westbrook, Harriet: See **Shelley, Harriet**.

Western Indies: See **West Indies**.

Western Isles: See **West Indies**.

Westminster Abbey: Founded by Edward the Confessor in the 11th century. Every British monarch since 1066 has been crowned in this cross-shaped **London** church; the Abbey houses most British monarchs' tombs as well as those of other leading British historical figures (Saunders 21). In 1808, Shelley's "eleventh birthday treat was a visit to Westminster Abbey, where [**William**] **Godwin** gave the youngsters the first of several history lessons from the tombs" (Sunstein 39–40). **Lionel Verney**'s distress over the spread of the plague drives him near Westminster Abbey, where he "was attracted by the deep and swelling tone of the organ . . . which spoke peace and hope to the unhappy" (*LM* 283–284).

Richard of York refuses to accept the title of king "until at Westminster he received his paternal crown" (*PW* 1.286, 1.319). **Lady Katherine Gordon** hears Westminster Abbey's bells from her apartments in **Westminster Palace**, and Richard escapes imprisonment during a storm that breaks during his visit to Westminster Abbey (*PW* 3.202, 3.218). **Henry VII** of England displays Richard as a prisoner to London's citizens near Westminster Abbey (*PW* 3.257–259). Shelley declares that the interior of the **Duomo** in **Milan** "is not of course to be compared to Westminster Abbey," and she terms **Santa Maria de' Frari** church **Venice**'s Westminster Abbey (*R* 1.116, 2.92). Arriving at **Antwerp** Cathedral June 1842, Shelley noted how, "with a rudeness of gesture and tone that far surpassed Westminster, the door was pushed to, and held jealously ajar, till we had paid" to get in (*R* 1.159).

Westminster Palace: Edward the Confessor built **London**'s Westminster Palace in the 11th century, along with a monastery and abbey on the site; **Henry III** rebuilt much of it in the 13th century; since then, **Parliament** has sat in the Palace's Great Hall (Saunders 21, 28, 30, 55, 22). An 1834 fire destroyed much of Westminster Palace, although the Great Hall was saved; the New Palace of Westminster, which now houses Parliament, was constructed by 1847 (Saunders 298). **Lionel Verney** and **Adrian** visit Westminster Palace (*LM* 252–254). **Henry VII** of England resides and holds court there before relocating to the **Tower** (*PW* 1.124, 2.80, 3.148). **Lady Katherine Gordon** is held prisoner at Westminster Palace, and **Richard of York** is also held there before he escapes (*PW* 3.195, 3.199, 3.222). Richard is tried for treason "by the common courts, in Westminster Hall" of the palace at *Perkin Warbeck*'s close (*PW* 3.321).

Westmoreland: See **Cumbria**.

Wheel of Fortune: See **Cumberland**.

White Cliffs: Chalk cliffs at **Dover** characterizing Britain's shoreline along the strait connecting the **North Sea** and the **English Channel**. **Victor Frankenstein** observes the cliffs (*Fr1* 184; *Fr3* 134).

White Knight: Geraldine warrior and minor character in *Perkin Warbeck*.

White Opera Dancer: Strange, supernatural figure whom English plague survivors encounter in **France** in *The Last Man*.

White Rose: House of **York**'s emblem; **Lancaster**'s was the red rose, hence the name **Wars of the Roses** for the prolonged conflict between the families. Many characters struggle "to raise again the White Rose to its rightful supremacy" (*PW* 1.18). Shelley alludes to the White Rose repeatedly throughout *Perkin Warbeck*.

White Sand Bay: Small bay off **Cornwall**'s western coast between **Land's End** and Cape Cornwall. **Richard of York** arrives in England 3 September 1497, when the *Adalid* enters the bay (*PW* 3.63).

White Surrey: Horse in *Perkin Warbeck*.

White Tower: Tower's central tower. Begun 1078, it is the oldest part; its name results from a 17th-century whitewashing ordered by **Henry III** (Hibbert 165). The **Earl of Warwick** threatens to commit suicide by jumping from White Tower into the **Thames** if **Richard of York** escapes without him (*PW* 3.299).

Whitelock: English stranger who aspires to **Lord Lodore**'s fortune in **America** by pretending to love **Ethel Villiers** in *Lodore*.

Whitton, William (d. 1832): Shelley family's lawyer who assisted **PBS** in arranging his finances and inheritance 1815 (Sunstein 67; *Journals* 63; White 1.396–399; Seymour 68). After PBS's death, **Byron**'s solicitor approached Whitton about funds for Shelley, but he rejected her request January 1823, perhaps due to his own personal interests because his daughter had married **Sir Timothy Shelley**'s illegitimate son (Sunstein 234; Seymour 321). On returning to England, Shelley visited the "balding, thin-lipped, long-winded, cautious Whitton" and found him sympathetic to her financial difficulties even as he carried out Sir Timothy's instructions (Sunstein 244). Sir Timothy felt Whitton was almost too sympathetic to Shelley; her own relationship with him was businesslike but friendly. Whitton advised Shelley June 1824 about her annuity, and he lent her funds when Sir Timothy stopped her allowance (in 1826, for example) (Sunstein 258, 272). Until his death, Whitton remained in Sir Timothy's employ (Sunstein 315; Seymour 422). See Roger Ingpen's *Shelley in England: New Facts and Letters from the Shelley-Whitton Papers* (1917).

Wiatt: Robert Clifford's alias in *Perkin Warbeck*.

Wicherly, Adam: Fictional character in *Perkin Warbeck* (Fischer 313).

Wieland, Christoph Martin (1733–1813): German writer who published translations of Shakespeare's plays 1762–66 and founded German periodical *Der teutsche Merkur* [*The German Mercury*] 1773. Shelley read several translations of Wieland's works 1818, including *Aristipp und einige seiner Zeitgenossen* [*Aristippus and Some of His Contemporaries*] (1800–1802), *Geheime Geschichte des Philosophen Peregrinus Proteus* [*Private History of Philosopher Peregrinus Proteus*] (1791), and *Geschichte der Abderiten* [*History of the Abderite, Democritus*] (1781) (*Journals* 683). Shelley had previously read Wieland's *Geschichte des Agathon* [*History of Agathon*] (1766–67) December 1814, noting, "Wieland displays some most detestable opinions—he is one of those men who alter all their opinions when they are about 40 and then thinking that it will be the same with every one think themselves the only proper monitors of youth" (*Journals* 49, 51). Shelley visited Wieland's home and grave in Weimar July 1842 (*R* 1.211–212).

Wiesbaden: German city seven miles north of Mainz. In Coblentz in June 1842, Shelley left companions who were headed there (*R* 1.169).

Wilberforce: Steamer named for William Wilberforce (1759–1833), British politician, philanthropist, and slavery abolitionist. Shelley departed England 12 June 1842 on board the *Wilberforce*, bound for Antwerp (*R* 1.157).

"Wilhelm Meister": See Goethe.

Wilhelmina: Beatrice's mother in *Valperga*. Shelley probably based this fictitious character on Joanna Southcott, famous in England for her religious fanaticism; she died "1814, following a hysterical pregnancy that was supposed to deliver Shiloh, the second Christ" (Sunstein 53).

William the Conqueror's stone: Stone that served as William the Conqueror's breakfast table when he dined in Hastings prior to the Battle of Hastings (1066) (Hadfield 191). Shelley mentions seeing Hastings when the town was small and situated only around William's stone (*R* 1.3).

William of Apulia: See Gibbon.

Williams, Edward Ellerker (1793–1822): Retired naval officer who drowned with PBS. During a naval tour in India, Edward met Medwin, who introduced him and his "wife" Jane Williams (with whom he had two children) to the Shelleys in Pisa January 1821; Shelley described him as "the picture of good humour and obligingness" (*Letters* 1.180; White 2.282–283). Edward shared PBS's love of boating and was sailing *Don Juan* with him on the voyage that ended their lives (Sunstein 196; Seymour 303–305). This accident was doubly tragic for Shelley, because it not only deprived her of her husband but also claimed her closest friend: "Edward was genuinely devoted to Mary.... [t]hey exchanged locks of hair, had confidential conversations.... After [PBS] she loved him better than anyone" (Sunstein 198–199). In "**The Choice**," Shelley mourns Edward's death (*Ch* 156). See Appendix II in Shelley's *Journals* (597–599).

Williams, Jane (1798–1884): Born Jane Cleveland, **Edward Williams**'s and **Thomas Jefferson Hogg**'s "wife." She married John Edward Johnson 1814 and then met Edward; though details of their initial meeting are speculations, the two were probably together by 1817 (Rees 39–40; Seymour 270–271). The couple's first child, Edward Medwin Williams, was born February 1820 (*Journals* 598). **Medwin** introduced the couple to the Shelleys in **Pisa** 1821. Jane, "a lovely brunette," was seven months pregnant with their second child; Shelley attended Jane during Rosalind's birth March 1821 and became the daughter's godmother (Sunstein 196; *Journals* 357). The Shelleys and Williamses became close; they lived together and also separately at Pisa. Although Shelley "counted her a true friend" and corresponded with her throughout their lives, Jane "was vain, envious of Mary, and devoted to [PB]S," who wrote love poems to her (Sunstein 198, 213, 217; *Journals* 393; *Letters* 1.263, 1.566, 2.147, 3.286; White 2.364). The 1822 drowning deaths of PBS and Edward formed a special bond between Shelley and Jane: they traversed the **Genoan** Gulf searching for their husbands and comforted each other after their loss (Sunstein 718–720). Shelley and Jane departed Pisa for Genoa in September 1822, and Jane continued to **London** via **Geneva** (*Journals* 429). In England, Jane spread rumors about Shelley's shortcomings and told Hogg she had been PBS's "true platonic love" (Sunstein 239). Jane subsequently accompanied Shelley on her first public outing, to see the *Frankenstein*-based play *Presumption*, August 1823, and convinced **Leigh Hunt** to give PBS's heart to Shelley (Sunstein 242; *Journals* 444, 468). Shelley and Jane lived close to each other in Kentish Town for about three years, during which time Shelley spoke of herself as "wedded" to Jane (Sunstein 255, 258, 268; *Letters* 1.491). Jane undertook her own literary pursuits: she completed a play Edward had begun, wrote children's stories, responded in verse to Shelley's poetry to her, and began a story about the Shelleys and Edward (Sunstein 268–269, 271). However, unknown to Shelley, for much of this period Hogg and Jane were lovers; they began living together as man and wife in summer 1827 (*Letters* 1.544n). Jane also continued defaming Shelley; when **Isabel Robinson** heard rumors of this, she told Shelley, who nonetheless continued a close friendship with Jane until a February 1828 confrontation: "She is horror struck & miserable at losing my friendship & yet how unpardonably she trifled with my feelings & made me all falsely a fable to others" (*Journals* 506; Sunstein 281). The two slowly became friends again, and Shelley became godmother to Prudentia, Jane and Hogg's daughter, 1836 (Sunstein 302, 322, 229; Seymour 388). Although Jane's husband died 1840, she and Hogg did not marry. In "**The**

Choice," Shelley terms Jane "My dearest widowed friend" (*Ch* 143). See Joan Rees's *Shelley's Jane Williams* (1985).

Wilmot: Elizabeth Fitzhenry's maid for twenty years in *Lodore*.

Wilson, John (1720–1789): Scottish poet who wrote "Clyde, A Poem" (1767) (Wilson 1.190). Shelley notes bells " '**salute mine ear**' " in **Cadenabbia**; she may have taken this line from Wilson's text or from **Anstey** (*R* 1.103; Moskal 128; Wilson line 630).

Wimbledon: Southeastern **London** district. **Lady Lodore** learns of her daughter's attachment to **Edward Villiers** through an anonymous acquaintance who has seen the couple "together perpetually in **Richmond** Park and on Wimbledon Common" (*L* 2.120). **Elizabeth Falkner** and **Rupert Falkner** live in "a pleasant villa on Wimbledon Common," so many of *Falkner*'s central scenes take place there (*F* 83).

Winchelsea: Small English coastal resort nine miles northeast of **Hastings**. Winchelsea is visible from **Lady Cecil**'s house near Hastings (*F* 88).

Winchester: English cathedral city ten miles northeast of **Southampton**. **Elizabeth Woodville** holds court there when **Lady Brampton** visits (*PW* 1.67, 1.72). **Richard of York** and Elizabeth Woodville briefly reunite in Winchester Cathedral before he departs for **Flanders** (*PW* 1.99–103).

Windsor: William the Conqueror ordered construction of Windsor's first castle, twelve miles east of **Reading**, 1066 (Hedley 10). Situated on top of a hill overlooking the **Thames** west of **London**, the castle subsequently became a royal residence. **Queen Charlotte**'s fondness for Windsor led to the royal family's adoption of it as their summer residence in the 1770s (Hedley 145, 168). The royal family's affection for the residence led George V, 17 July 1917, to declare "Our House and Family shall be styled and known as the House and Family of Windsor" (Hedley 225). The Shelleys lived at **Bishopsgate** near Windsor August 1815–April 1816 (*Journals* 103–104; Seymour 137). **Henry Clerval** and **Victor Frankenstein** visit Windsor (*Fr1* 186; *Fr3* 135). **Maurice**'s father owns a house near Windsor park (*Maurice* 86). Shelley eerily foretells the royal family's adoption of the name of Windsor, since *The Last Man*'s last king of England "received the title of Earl of Windsor, and Windsor Castle, an ancient royalty, with its wide demesnes were a part of his allotted wealth" when England becomes a republic 2073 (*LM* 20). The king's children, **Adrian** and **Idris**, grow up at the castle, setting for many of the novel's important scenes (*LM* 33, 41). **Perdita**'s cottage is on Windsor's grounds, and family members are buried in **St. George's Chapel** (*LM* 53, 355). Part of "The Mourner" is set in Windsor's neighborhood, as **Clarice Eversham** has a cottage in Windsor Forest (*Mourner* 87, 97). **Lord Lodore** avoids punishment at **Eton** by running away to Windsor Forest (*L* 1.79–80). **Edward Villiers** guides **Ethel Villiers** around Windsor (*L* 2.5–8).

Windsor, Countess of: **Adrian** and **Idris**'s mother and England's last queen in *The Last Man*.

Winter, Peter von (1754–1825): German composer of many operas and dramatic ballets; "his first decisive success" was *Das unterbrochene Opferfest* [*The Oracle*] (1796) in Vienna (*NGD*). It was performed at London's English Opera House August–September 1826, and Shelley saw the opera during September (Robinson, "Mary Shelley" 26). Shelley compares Roger Dodsworth's appearance to "Mr. Sapio's costume in Winter's Opera of the Oracle" (*RD* 44).

***Winter's Tale, The*:** Shakespeare's drama, first staged 1611 and printed 1623; PBS read it aloud to Shelley October 1818 (*Journals* 229). Lady Cecil quotes lines that Leontes speaks describing his son's reaction to Leontes's accusation of his wife's infidelity in order to convey Gerard Neville's reaction to his mother's possible infidelity: "At the thought his heart grew sick within him:—'To see his nobleness! / Conceiving the dishonour of his mother, / He straight declined upon't, drooped, took it deeply; / Fastened and fixed the shame on't in himself; / Threw off his spirit, his appetite, his sleep, / And downright languished'" (*F* 111; Shakespeare 2.3.12–17).

Winzy: Protagonist and narrator of "The Mortal Immortal." His name seems comic, "but the Scottish word 'winze' means curse and is here used to emphasize the tragic curse of eternal life" (Robinson 390). Neighbors call him Scholar Bewitched because of his youthful appearance (*MI* 226).

Wittgenstein, Count Ludwig Adolf Peter (1769–1843): Russian soldier who helped suppress Hofer's rebellion but later fought against Napoleon (Moskal 256). Shelley describes his involvement at the Battle of Brenner in the Tyrol (*R* 2.55).

Wolf's Glen: See Weber.

Wollstonecraft, Everina (1765–1843): Mary Wollstonecraft's youngest sister; she ran a school in Dublin, and Shelley first met her 1806 when she visited London "on family business" (Sunstein 25; Seymour 115). Shelley was delighted to learn more about her mother from her aunt during this visit and a subsequent one September 1816 (Sunstein 37). Shelley named her daughter Clara Everina Shelley after her aunt; the two women exchanged letters December 1816 at the time of Fanny Godwin's death, continuing their correspondence in subsequent years (*Journals* 148–149, 172, 205; Seymour 477). Everina settled in London May 1833, where she "supported herself by hack writing"; Shelley "paid duty calls on her aunt . . . who was devoted to her and whom she helped support" throughout the 1830s (*Journals* 536; Sunstein 324, 339). Writing August 1834, Shelley notes "Everina was never a favourite with anyone—& now she is the most intolerable of God's creatures. The worst is, that being poor & friendless, it is on my conscience to pay her attention," while asserting "she can be amusing & means well—but her queerness—her assumption" annoyed Shelley (*Letters* 2.213; Seymour 485). Shelley wrote to her cousin Elizabeth Berry August 1839 to inform her Everina "is infirm—but is tolerable health [*sic*]—she is with very good people & well taken care of"

(*Letters* 2.321). After her aunt's death, Shelley discharged her remaining debts (Sunstein 361).

Wollstonecraft, Mary (1759–1797): Novelist, educational writer, and Shelley's mother. Her first published work was *Thoughts on the Education of Daughters* (1787); as a governess in **Ireland**, she wrote her first novel, *Mary: A Fiction* (1788). Subsequently living in **London**, Wollstonecraft wrote essays for the liberal *Analytical Review* and entered literary circles there while writing children's books and translations. She published *Vindication of the Rights of Men* (1790) in response to **Burke's** *Reflections on the Revolution in France* (1790), and her *A Vindication of the Rights of Woman* (1792) was well received and is still admired today for its feminist reasoning. Following a brief passion for married **Swiss** painter Henry Fuseli, Wollstonecraft traveled to revolutionary **France** with her lover **Gilbert Imlay** 1792; their daughter, **Fanny Godwin**, was born there 1794 (*SCGS* 160; Sunstein 14). Wollstonecraft's *History and Moral View of the Origin and Progress of the French Revolution* (1794) maintains the revolution's basic principles while condemning many of its events. Learning of Imlay's infidelities during a brief return to London, Wollstonecraft attempted suicide and then visited Scandinavia alone 1795 in an attempt to assist Imlay in his business; her trip resulted in *Letters Written During a Short Residence in Sweden, Norway, and Denmark* (1796) (Sunstein 14; *SCGS* 159–160). Upon their 1795 reunion, it was clear that Imlay wished to have no more to do with Wollstonecraft, and she again attempted suicide before recovering from the affair and resuming her literary career (*SCGS* 159–160). She then met and loved **William Godwin**, and, after she became pregnant, they married 1797 but maintained separate households; Wollstonecraft died 10 September 1797, eleven days after Shelley's birth (Sunstein 19; Seymour 18–20). Godwin published *Memoirs* of his wife (including her letters to Imlay) as well as her last novel, *Maria; or, The Wrongs of Woman* 1798; Godwin's open disclosure of Wollstonecraft's affairs and suicide attempts caused her reputation to sink. Shelley never knew her mother but felt her loss profoundly throughout her life, visiting her tomb repeatedly and reading and rereading her works (*Journals* 684). See Wollstonecraft's *Collected Letters* (1979), Claire Tomalin's *The Life and Death of Mary Wollstonecraft* (1974), and Janet Todd's *Mary Wollstonecraft: A Revolutionary Life* (2000).

Woods, Samuel: Minor character acquainted with **Lucy Martin** in *The Last Man*.

Woodville: Poet in *Matilda*, modeled on **PBS**; **Matilda** first meets Woodville after her father's suicide; she directs her narrative toward him, to be read after her death as an explanation for her isolation and sorrows. Matilda's proposal of a suicide pact is a gender reversal of PBS's proposal to Shelley (*M* 201; Sunstein 77–78). Shelley draws Woodville's "last lessons" directly from PBS's poetic philosophy: Woodville tells Matilda to have faith in the "refreshing bliss of Love" curing her pain (*M* 204–205).

Woodville, Elizabeth (1437–1492): Edward IV's wife (married 1464). She gave her children to **Richard III**, who presumably murdered **Edward V** and **Richard of York** in the **Tower**; her daughter **Elizabeth of York** married **Henry VII** to become queen of England. Woodville withdrew to a convent 1487 due to treasonable activities (*DNB*). Richard of York's mother in *Perkin Warbeck*.

Woolwich: London district. **Henry Clerval** and **Victor Frankenstein** visit it (*Fr1* 184; *Fr3* 134).

Worcester: English cathedral city twenty-five miles southwest of Birmingham. **Yorkist** factions advanced toward Worcester 12 October 1459 but quickly retreated when faced by **Henry VI**'s large army. The **Staffords** unsuccessfully attempt to take Worcester (*PW* 1.67, 1.83).

Wordsworth, William (1770–1850): British poet and **William Godwin**'s friend and, for a time, ardent admirer. Wordsworth's *Lyrical Ballads* (1798), written with **Samuel Taylor Coleridge**, broke new ground in poetic tradition, and his mature exploration of the transcendent in nature and good in humankind ensured his lasting popularity. Wordsworth gradually abandoned his youthful idealism and radical politics and became more conservative, especially following his 1843 appointment as poet laureate. Shelley encountered him during her childhood and by age thirteen "was becoming a devotee of Wordsworth's nature poetry" (Sunstein 49). As she matured, she was troubled by his loss of liberality and his growing conformity. **Matilda** begins her life of solitude after her father's suicide with lines, "**Before I see** another day / Oh, let this body die away!" from "The Complaint of the Forsaken Indian Woman" (1798) (*M* 189; Wordsworth lines 9–10). **Woodville** remembers **Elinor** as "**a sylvan Huntress** by his side," a line adapted from "Ruth" (1800) (*M* 194; Wordsworth line 95). Shelley uses nine lines, beginning "**Thou, thrush**," from poem XIII of *Poems founded on the Affections* (1800), to convey **Euthanasia**'s sentiment when she realizes **Castruccio**'s true character (*V* 2.193; Wordsworth lines 25–32). **Lionel Verney** wants to help **London**'s inhabitants combat plague but points out that "men are used to '—**move all together**, if they move at all,'" from "Resolution and Independence" (1807) (*LM* 271; Wordsworth lines 75–77). **Horace Neville** floats on **Virginia Water** "'**In that sweet** mood when pleasant thoughts / Bring sad thoughts to the mind,'" lines from the opening of "Lines Written in Early Spring" (1798) (*Mourner* 83; Wordsworth lines 3–4). Shelley quotes from "**The Hermit's Cell**" for several *Lodore* chapter epigraphs (*L* 1.82, 1.111, 1.126, 1.247). She adopts a line from "My Heart Leaps Up" (1807), "**The boy is father** of the man," as an epigraph to the *Lodore* chapter in which she introduces **Lord Lodore**'s childhood (*L* 1.66; Wordsworth lines 7–9). Shelley quotes accurately the closing lines of the thirtieth sonnet of *The River Duddon: A Series of Sonnets* (1820) as an epigraph to the *Lodore* chapter in which the **Villiers**es marry: "**Sure, when the separation** has been tried, / That we, who part in love, shall meet again" (*L*

2.144; Wordsworth lines 13–14). Shelley quotes from "She was a Phantom of delight" (1807) as epigraph to *Lodore*'s chapter opening with **Ethel Villiers** isolated in **Duke Street**: "I saw her upon nearer view, / A Spirit, yet a Woman too! / A Creature not too bright or good / For human nature's daily food; / For transient sorrows, simple wiles, / Praise, blame, love, kisses, tears, and smiles" (*L* 2.283; Wordsworth lines 11–12, 17–20). Shelley quotes accurately from *Peter Bell: a Tale in Verse* (1819), which **PBS** read October 1819 and to which he responded in *Peter Bell the Third*, as an epigraph to the *Lodore* chapter in which **Lady Lodore** remembers her dead husband: "**Repentance is** a tender sprite; / If aught on earth have heavenly might, / 'Tis lodged within her silent tear" (*Journals* 684; *L* 3.284; Wordsworth lines 148–50). *Falkner* is set in " '**the sweet shire** of Devon,' " a line adapted from "Simon Lee, the Old Huntsman" (1798) (*F* 5; Clemit 5; Wordsworth line 1). Shelley adapts lines from "The Fountain: A Conversation" (1800), " '**They talked** with open heart, and tongue / Affectionate and true, / A pair of friends,' " to emphasize **Elizabeth Falkner**'s mutual affection and respect for **Rupert Falkner** (*F* 63; Wordsworth lines 1–3). Considering **Raphael**'s paintings, Shelley recalls "Wordsworth's theory, that we enter this world bringing with us '**airs from heaven**,' memories of a divine abode and angelic fellowship which we have just left," a reference to Wordsworth's "Ode: Intimations of Immortality" (1807) as well as to a line in *Hamlet* (*R* 1.223; Wordsworth lines 63–64; *Hamlet* 1.4.41). While staying at **Brixen**, Shelley bought "a tiny figure of **Hofer** . . . who, as Wordsworth well expresses it, was '**Murdered, like one** ashore by shipwreck cast, / Murdered without relief,' " lines from Wordsworth's sonnet, "The martial courage of a day is vain" (1815), one of a series of six sonnets he wrote about the 1809–10 **Tyrolean** uprising (*R* 2.62; Wordsworth lines 12–13). Shelley also notes her belief that certain scenes are always indelibly linked with a certain time of life, and she observes that "Wordsworth, as many years ago I remember hearing Coleridge remark, illustrates the same fact, when he makes an insane and afflicted mother exclaim,— '**The breeze I see** is in the tree; / It comes to cool my babe and me,' " lines from "Her Eyes are Wild" (1798) (*R* 2.78; Wordsworth lines 39–40). See also "**Hermit's Cell**," "**Personal Talk**," "**She Dwelt Among the Untrodden Ways**," "**Slumber Did My Spirit Seal, A**," "**Tintern Abbey**," and "**World Is Too Much With Us, The**."

***Works and Days*:** See **Hesiod**.

"World Is Too Much With Us, The": Wordsworth's 1807 sonnet; Shelley requested it from **Ollier** November 1825 (*Letters* 1.504). **Lionel Verney** finds himself filled with life's spirit and beauties despite plague: "I '**Had sight of Proteus** coming from the sea; / And heard old **Triton** blow his wreathed horn,' " lines concluding Wordsworth's sonnet (*LM* 308; Wordsworth lines 13–14). Shelley quotes the sonnet's opening line accurately as an epigraph to the *Lodore* chapter in which **Edward Villiers** expresses love for **Ethel Villiers** and **Lady Lodore**

learns of their relationship (*L* 2.103). Describing **Gmunden**, Shelley notes she "could, while looking '**On that pleasant** lea, / Have glimpses that would make me less forlorn,'" drawing again from Wordsworth's text (*R* 2.27; Wordsworth lines 11–12).

Worseley, Sir William (c. 1435–1499): Dean of **St. Paul's** from 1478; for supporting **Richard of York**, **Henry VII** of England arrested Worseley and sentenced him to death 1495 but subsequently pardoned him (Arthurson 83, 85; *DNB*). Worseley is a minor *Perkin Warbeck* character.

Wurtemburg: Southeastern **German** region containing the **Black Forest**; **Stuttgart** is its capital. Shelley easily procured rooms at **Kissingen**'s **Kurhaus**, despite the establishment's preparations for the **Queen of Wurtemburg**'s arrival (*R* 1.180). She also states that German schooling, particularly in **Prussia**, Wurtemberg, and **Saxony**, is better than England's approach to educating the poor (*R* 1.122).

Wurtemburg, Queen of (1811–1888): Augusta of Saxe-Weimar-Eisenach, King William I's wife, married 1829 (Tschudi 53). Her July 1840 stay in **Kissingen**, under the alias **Frau Grafinn von Teck**, coincided with Shelley's (*R* 1.180, 1.190).

Wurzburg: Renowned for its castle, **German** city sixty miles east of **Darmstadt**. Shelley wanted to sail the **Main** there June 1842, but Wurzburg was too far removed from the arranged route to **Kissingen** (*R* 1.179).

Wye: River with several branches flowing from the central Welsh Cambrian mountains into the **Bristol** Channel. **Rhyaider Gowy** lies "in immediate vicinity to a cataract of the Wye" (*L* 1.97).

Yannina: See **Ioannina**.

Yeovil: Southwestern English town thirty-five miles south of **Bristol**. **Richard of York** travels toward Yeovil to present himself to **Schwartz**, but **Robert Clifford** takes him prisoner a few miles east of there (*PW* 3.128, 3.131).

York: Large northeastern English cathedral city in **Yorkshire** county, seventy miles east of **Lancaster**. **Lionel Verney** records that plague is "in all the more populous towns of England," including York (*LM* 268). In *Perkin Warbeck*, Shelley details familial conflicts between "long rival houses of Lancaster and York," represented by **Red** and **White Roses** respectively; **Elizabeth of York** and the **Earl of Warwick** are imprisoned at **Sheriff Hutton** in Yorkshire (*PW* 1.24, 1.31, 1.54–55). **Henry VII**'s "first ruling feeling of his heart was hatred of the **House of York**," aware that "his right of succession, even through the **House of Lancaster**, was ill-founded," but he solidifies his claim to the throne by marrying **Elizabeth of York** (*PW* 1.50–51, 1.60). References to York abound throughout *Perkin Warbeck*.

York, Duke of: See **Edward IV** and **Richard of York**.

Youghal Bay: Body of water on **Ireland**'s southern coast between **Cork** and **Waterford**; Shelley terms it **Youghall Harbour**. **Richard of York** departs Ireland from Youghal Bay to garner **Parisian** support (*PW* 1.310).

Youghall Harbour: See **Youghal Bay**.

Young, Edward (1683–1765): British poet and dramatist. **Lionel Verney** mourns **Raymond**'s death with a line adapted from Young's *The Complaint, or Night Thoughts* (1745), remarking that "life becomes doubly "**the desart and** the solitude" (*LM* 204; Blumberg 161; E. Young 1.114).

Ypsilanti, Prince Alexander (1792–1828): **Greek** general who, while in **Russia**'s service, invaded **Wallachia** 1821 and initiated Greece's war of independence; **Mavrocordato** told Shelley of these events (Sunstein 197; Kinder 2.45; *Letters* 1.188). In 1821, Ypsilanti's "Cry of War to the Greeks" was translated, probably collaboratively by both Shelleys, and sent to *The Examiner* and *The Morning Chronicle* (Sunstein 197; Crook 2). Ypsilanti is the Greek army's "warlike" leader in **The Last Man** (*LM* 185).

Z

Zaimi, Evadne: Greek ambassador to England's daughter in *The Last Man*; this beautiful eighteen-year-old quickly captures **Adrian**'s heart and later loves **Raymond**.

Zaimi, Prince: Evadne Zaimi's father and the **Greek** ambassador to England in *The Last Man*.

Zante: Short form of Zakinthos, **Ionian** island west of **Greece**. **Elizabeth Falkner** stays there while **Rupert Falkner** fights in mainland Greece; the islands were under the British government's protection during Greece's war of independence (*F* 60).

Zauberflaute: See **Mozart**.

Zenno, Gian Battista (1759–1797): 16th–17th century **Genoese** astrologer who saw "impending danger" in the stars just prior to **Wallenstein**'s death; Shelley, following **Samuel Taylor Coleridge**, spells it **Seni** (Mitchell 328; Crook 2). Shelley mentions Zenno fed Wallenstein's imagination "with dreams of yet higher glory" (*R* 2.7).

Zeughaus: Baroque armory in **Berlin**, completed 1706 on the **Unter-den-Linden**; it "is the oldest public building on the avenue"; Shelley terms it the **Arsenal** (Tucker 56). Shelley mentions it as near the **Guard-house** and **Italian Opera**, declaring that "the whole forms a splendid assemblage of buildings" July 1842 (*R* 1.219).

Zeus: Chief of **Greek** gods, playing an active role in many myths. **Lionel Verney** observes that **Adrian** is renewed by battling plague, so "the weakness of his physical nature seemed to pass from him, as the cloud of humanity did, in the ancient fable, from the divine lover of **Semele**" (*LM* 246). Semele was one of many of Zeus's mortal lovers; at her request, Zeus revealed himself to her in his full glory and thus inadvertently killed her (Tripp 525).

Ziani, Constans: Cyril and Zella Ziani's three-year-old son in "The Evil Eye."

Ziani, Cyril: Katusthius Ziani's brother, Zella Ziani's husband, and Constans Ziani's father in "The Evil Eye."

Ziani, Katusthius: Cyril Ziani's antagonist brother in "The Evil Eye."

Ziani, Zella: Female protagonist Camaraz raises as a Mainote in "The Evil Eye," perhaps named for Edward John Trelawny's Greek daughter; she marries Cyril Ziani, and they have a son, Constans Ziani. Dmitri is Zella's true father.

Zingarelli, Niccolò Antonio (1752–1837): Italian composer renowned for *opera seria* (*NGD*). Shelley praised Madame Pasta's performance in "Giulietta," Shelley's reference for Zingarelli's opera *Giulietta e Romeo* (1796), based on Shakespeare's *Romeo and Juliet* but with a happy ending (*R* 1.89–90).

Ziska, John (c. 1360–1424): Soldier who successfully led Hussites in battle at Kuttenberg 1419 and Nebovid 1422 (Kohn 211). Shelley refers to Prague as "savage" Ziska's native city (*R* 2.8).

Zitza: Greek village twelve miles northwest of Ioannina on a slope above Kalamas (*MGRE* 382). Byron passed through it 1809 and admired the monastery there, recording the visit and impressions in *Childe Harold's Pilgrimage* (Byron 2.424–468). Shelley quotes "**monastic Zitza**" from Byron's text before providing her own appreciative description of the scene through Cyril Ziani's eyes, and at Zitza Cyril learns of Dmitri's onward journey with Constans Ziani (*EE* 110–112; Byron, *CHP* 2.48.1).

Znaim: German name for Czech city of Znojmo, twenty-one miles southeast of Prague; Shelley spells it Znaym. After French troops defeated Austrians at Wagram 1809, they signed an armistice there (*R* 2.50).

Znaym, Armistice of: See Znaim.

Zopyrion: Midas's prime minister and close ally in *Midas*.

Zoumerkas: Epirus mountains north of Zitza; their inhabitants are Zoumerkians. Shelley describes how "the far blue mountains of Zoumerkas" frame the view from Zitza and terms Zoumerkians "uncivilized mountaineers" (*EE* 111, 113).

Zubia: Spanish town five miles southeast of Granada. Isabella I views a Moorish battle there (*PW* 1.225).

Zurich: Swiss lake and city twenty-five miles northeast of Lucerne. Shelley visited Zurich July 1840; she mentions it in a letter to Everina Wollstonecraft (*R* 1.52–53; *Letters* 3.2). Shelley finds Lake Zurich pales in comparison to both Lake Geneva and Lake Lucerne, but that it is nonetheless "a beautiful lake" (*R* 1.53).

Appendix I
Quotations Attributed to Their Authors

"Abra was ready": See Prior.
"Absent or dead": See Pope.
"Ah now": See Leigh Hunt.
"Ah! Richard": See *Richard II*.
"Ah! where are they": See Moore.
"Ahi, Costantin!": See *Inferno*.
"Ahi, la vedete": See *Arnaldo da Brescia*.
"airs from heaven": See Wordsworth and *Hamlet*.
"Alack! what trouble": See *Tempest, The*.
"Alas! he knows": See Fletcher.
"Alas, for man!": See *Lalla Rookh*.
"Alas, poor country": See *Macbeth*.
"All meaner things": See "Essay on Man."
"All my pretty": See *Macbeth*.
"All rose to do": See "Boat on the Serchio, The."
"All that Athens": See *Ruines of Rome*.
"All the regions": See Addison.
"All trees of": See *Paradise Lost*.
"also was an Arcadian": See *Eclogues*.
"Am I not king?": See *Richard II*.
"Amid two seas": See Prior.
"And all": See Maccabees.
"And as good lost": See Shakespeare.

"And bare, at once": See "The Lament of Tasso."
"And dug deep": See Shakespeare.
"And hooting at": See Coleridge, Samuel Taylor.
"And many rose": See "Boat on the Serchio, The."
"And so farewell": See Heywood.
"And then, with you": See "Cyclops: A Satiric Drama, The."
"Another watering-place": See Murray.
"Arcadian, also was an": See *Eclogues*.
"Art thou he": See *Faerie Queen, The*.
"As a rainbow": See *Childe Harold's Pilgrimage*.
"As an unsheltered": See Oedipus.
"As flowers beneath": See "Mask of Anarchy, The."
"As one / In some": See *Brides' Tragedy, The*.
"As the hart panteth": See Psalms.
"As the waters": See Bible.
"At seventeen years": See *As You Like It*.
"At whose verdant": See *Paradise Regained*.
"base Indian": See *Othello*.
"Bavarians, the": See Alison.
"Before I see": See Wordsworth.

Appendix I

"Better have loved": See **Fletcher**.
"blasts from hell": See *Hamlet*.
"blue sky, the": See "Christabel."
"Bones of the world, the": See *Letters Written During a Short Residence in Sweden, Norway, and Denmark*.
"bonny brent brow": See **Burns**.
"Borne round in": See "Slumber Did My Spirit Seal, A."
"bower of flesh": See *Romeo and Juliet*.
"boy is father, the": See **Wordsworth**.
"breeze I see, the": See **Wordsworth**.
"broad and garish": See *Cenci, The*.
"bruna, bruna": See *Purgatorio*.
"But if for me": See *Lalla Rookh*.
"But these are chimes": See **Ford's** *Perkin Warbeck*.
"But, alas! / I am": See *Troilus and Cressida*.
"but the mysteries": See **Lanzi**.
"But, when the roar": See "From Moschus."
"But when they": See Appendix II.
"Butterfly on the wheel": See **Pope**.
"by purple sails": See *Antony and Cleopatra*.
"Cada piedra": See **Calderón**.
"cannibal of her": See **Bacon**.
"cannibals of their": See **Bacon**.
"carried with it": See **Burke**.
"castled crags": See *Childe Harold's Pilgrimage*.
"chain is loos'd, the": See "Boat on the Serchio, The."
"channels of the soul": See **Procter**.
"Chi Dice Mal": See Appendix II.
"coiled as it": See **Reeve**.
"Come, tell me": See **Moore**.
"coming events": See **Campbell**.
"compunction, the": See **Rio**.
"Content to dwell": See "Epistle to a Lady."
"cool recess": See *Paradise Lost*.
"Corinthian capital": See **Burke**.
"Could you so": See **Jonson**.
"Cousin of York": See **Ford's** *Perkin Warbeck*.
"created a language": See *Defence of Poetry, A*.

"creation was good": See **Genesis**.
"crimson leaves": See *Cenci, The*.
"crisped brooks": See *Paradise Lost*.
"Crouching and crablike": See "Ode on Venice."
"Crushed and o'erworn": See **Shakespeare**.
"darkness visible": See *Paradise Lost*.
"day began to grizzle": See *Werner*.
"day we, The": See *Italy*.
"day will come, A": See *2 Henry VI*.
"dead earth upon": See *Hellas* and "Mask of Anarchy, The."
"death is the beginning": See *Paradise Lost*.
"desart and, the": See **Young**.
"devoted the Americans": See **Pitt**.
"Di mie tenere": See **Petrarch**.
"Did I request thee": See *Paradise Lost*.
"difference to me, the": See "She Dwelt Among the Untrodden Ways."
"discourse excellent": See *Hamlet*.
"Do you not think": See *Custom of the Country, The*.
"Does not the sun": See **Cleveland**.
"Dost thou hear": See *Antony and Cleopatra*.
"Dost thou think": See *Twelfth Night*.
"drag a slow": See *Essay on Criticism*.
"drink deep": See *Essay on Criticism*.
"dry land for": See **Genesis**.
"during the contests": See **Reeve**.
"E quasi mi": See *Paradiso*.
"Egad, I think": See **Sheridan**.
"En cor gentil": See **March**.
"En vivo vivamque": See *Valperga*.
"England, farewell": See "Charles the First."
"every nook": See *Macbeth*.
"Excellent creature!": See *Custom of the Country, The*.
"Eyes, look your last!": See *Romeo and Juliet*.
"falling from, The": See **Bacon**.
"Farewell, Erin!": See *Irish Melodies*.
"Farewell, kind lord": See *Henry V*.
"Farewell, sad Isle": See **Cleveland**.

Quotations Attributed to Their Authors

"Fears! What are they?": See "Hermit's Cell."
"Few people know": See Fitzgerald.
"first that ever, the": See *Rime of the Ancient Mariner.*
"Flowers of all hue": See *Paradise Lost.*
"For deeds of violence": See *Italy.*
"For friends in every": See Sheridan.
"For lo! winter": See Solomon's Song.
"For O, you stood": See "Death of Wallenstein, The."
"for what should": See Beaumont and Fletcher.
"For, when Cymocles": See *Faerie Queen, The.*
"Forests, ancient as the hills": See Samuel Taylor Coleridge.
"Forthwith this frame": See *Rime of the Ancient Mariner.*
"fortuna, la": See Calderón.
"From Ireland thus": See *2 Henry VI.*
"Full many": See Shakespeare.
"Funeral note, the": See Werner.
"generous, brave, and gentle": See *Alastor.*
"Gentle cousin": See *Two Noble Kinsmen.*
"Gilderoy was": See *Reliques.*
"Gli occhi drizzo": See *Paradiso.*
"God had made him": See Psalms.
"God sends down, the": See Elton.
"gold o'erdusted": See *Troilus and Cressida.*
"golden opinions": See *Macbeth.*
"grasshopper, the": See Ecclesiastes.
"great Task Master": See Milton.
"green spot": See Moore and *Sardanapalus.*
"grow with his growth": See Pope.
"habitation and, a": See *Midsummer Night's Dream, A.*
"Had sight of": See "World Is Too Much With Us, The."
"Happy, rural seat": See *Paradise Lost.*
"Has floated down": See *Italy.*
"He might have dwelt": See *Reliques.*
"He seemed breathless": See *Faerie Queen, The.*
"He would fight": See Alison.
"heavenly Una, the": See "Personal Talk."

"Heaves like": See *Childe Harold's Pilgrimage.*
"Her dear heart's confessor": See Lamb.
"Her virtue, like": See *Peter Bell the Third.*
"herald Mercury": See *Hamlet.*
"Herein / Shall my": See *Laws of Candy, The.*
"hero of unwritten": See "Mask of Anarchy, The."
"high actions": See *Paradise Regained.*
"high-born necessities": See *Cenci, The.*
"His bosom's lord": See *Romeo and Juliet.*
"His father was": See *Reliques.*
"His voice, and suddenly": See "Ode to the West Wind."
"Hopes, what are they?": See "Hermit's Cell."
"How like a winter": See Shakespeare.
"how long will": See PBS.
"I am not One who": See "Personal Talk."
"I am too old": See *Richard II.*
"I am your wife": See Ford's *Perkin Warbeck.*
"I cannot charge": See *Two Foscari, The.*
"I choose to": See Walpole.
"I do arrest ye": See *2 Henry VI.*
"I do not like": See *Richard III.*
"I have ten": See Goldsmith.
"I never felt": See Appendix II.
"I saw her upon": See Wordsworth.
"I would not": See "Death of Wallenstein, The."
"If I am": See *1 Henry IV.*
"If I were": See Pitt.
"If the dull substance": See Shakespeare.
"If you were": See Appendix II.
"Il gran peccato": See *Arnaldo da Brescia.*
"Imparadised": See *Paradise Lost.*
"in all bodies": See Burke.
"In all her": See *Italy.*
"in close covert": See *Il Penseroso.*
"in disgrace with fortune": See Shakespeare.
"In his eye": See *Childe Harold's Pilgrimage.*
"in sin and fear?": See *Heaven and Earth.*
"In that sweet": See Wordsworth.
"In the deep bosom": See *Richard III.*

491

Appendix I

"In the great pool": See *Cymbeline*.
"In the high chamber": See *Corsair, The*.
"In the midst": See Appendix II.
"In the turmoil": See Ford.
"In this dear work": See "Hymn to Mercury."
"in to-day already": See "Death of Wallenstein, The."
"In vagabond pursuit": See Ford.
"Inland": See "Tintern Abbey."
"Intellete dar loro": See Petrarch.
"It appears, from": See Vasari.
"It does much": See Fletcher.
"It is our will": See *Julian and Maddalo*.
"It is the same": See "Mutability."
"It is thy merit": See "Hymn to Mercury."
"It presents": See Rio.
"Its pride": See *Macbeth*.
"J'ai veu filz": See Chastellain.
"kerchiefed in": See *Il Penseroso*.
"know the pleasures": See Appendix II.
"La bella Villanella": See Michelangelo and Vasari.
"Lady, the wonder, a": See "Sensitive-Plant, The."
"land of mist, the": See *Rime of the Ancient Mariner*.
"lapped in lead": See Shakespeare.
"Lasciate ogni": See *Inferno*.
"late remorse": See *Childe Harold's Pilgrimage*.
"leafy month of June": See *Rime of the Ancient Mariner*.
"Lent / Out of": See *Paradise Lost*.
"les concierges": See Custine.
"Les deserts sont faits": See Kock.
"Let all the dukes": See *Two Noble Kinsmen*.
"Let me / Awake": See *Laws of Candy, The*.
"Let no man seek": See *Paradise Lost*.
"Let the poet": See Goethe.
"Li ruscelletti": See *Inferno*.
"Lifts its sweet": See Keats.
"Lifted the painted veil": See "Lift not the painted veil."
"Like a burnished": See *Antony and Cleopatra*.

"like an exhalation": See *Paradise Lost*.
"Like gentle rains": See *Peter Bell the Third*.
"Like one lost": See *3 Henry VI*.
"Like one who": See *Rime of the Ancient Mariner*.
"Like to the lark": See Shakespeare.
"Likeness of, the": See *Paradise Lost*.
"lilies glorious": See "Charles the First."
"little lower, a": See Psalms.
"Lo! the vast scene": See Camoens.
"local habitation, a": See *Midsummer Night's Dream, A*.
"lofty and magnificent": See Cicero.
"Long die thy": See *Richard III*.
"Lord of, the": See Maccabees.
"Love is too young": See Shakespeare.
"love of pleasure": See "Epistle to a Lady."
"low ambition": See "Essay on Man."
"low-thoughted care": See *Comus*.
"lyre of mind": See "To the Lord Chancellor."
"Ma la fede": See Metastasio.
"Man but a rush": See *Othello*.
"Man wants but": See Goldsmith.
"Married to immortal": See Milton, Moore, and *Irish Melodies*.
"Marry, this is": See *Hamlet*.
"Men oftentimes": See *Peter Bell the Third*.
"mercenary sons, the": See Pitt.
"Methinks I see": See Jonson.
"Millions of spiritual": See *Paradise Lost*.
"mind's eye": See *Hamlet*.
"Mine be a cot": See Rogers.
"mode of existence, the": See Burke.
"monastic Zitza": See *Childe Harold's Pilgrimage* and Zitza.
"moon is behind, the": See "Christabel."
"more in sorrow": See *Hamlet*.
"mousing owls": See *Macbeth*.
"move all together": See Wordsworth.
"Murdered, like one": See Wordsworth.
"murky air": See *Paradise Lost*.
"music / Of man's, the": See Ford.

Quotations Attributed to Their Authors

"music breathing": See *Bride of Abydos, The*.
"My heart is": See **Lamb**.
"My native English": See *Richard II*.
"My noble Queen": See *3 Henry VI*.
"Nathelesse, / I checked": See "Hymn to Mercury."
"Nelle chiese": See *Arnaldo da Brescia*.
"never set a squadron": See *Othello*.
"new-sprung race": See **Blamire**.
"Non è poleggio": See *Paradiso*.
"None, I trust": See **Ford**.
"Not less than": See *Paradise Lost*.
"nothing seems": See **Sévigné**.
"Now for our Irish wars!": See *Richard II*.
"Nulla Magis": See **Gibbon**.
"nursing her wrath": See **Burns**.
"O best of": See **Leigh Hunt**.
"O for the wings": See **Psalms**.
"O my reviving": See **Middleton**.
"O vedovate": See *Arnaldo da Brescia*.
"O, where have": See **Beaumont** and **Fletcher**.
"Obtains the brow": See *Paradise Lost*.
"Odio il": See Appendix II.
"Of good, wise, just": See *Paradise Regained*.
"of moving accidents": See *Othello*.
"Oh, Clifford!": See *3 Henry VI*.
"Oh! human wit": See **Heywood** and **Shakespeare**.
"Oh, it grieves": See *King John*.
"Oh that my": See **Bible**.
"Oh, that stern": See **Schiller** and "Death of Wallenstein, The."
"Oh, what excuse": See **Shakespeare**.
"Old familiar": See **Lamb**.
"On that pleasant": See "World Is Too Much With Us, The."
"Once more unto": See *Henry V*.
"Ond' era pinta": See *Purgatorio*.
"One fatal remembrance": See *Irish Melodies*.
"One moment": See *Revolt of Islam, The*.
"One, within whose": See "Sunset, The."
"open as day": See *2 Henry IV*.

"other half": See *Paradise Lost*.
"ounce of, an": See Appendix II.
"Our king he kept": See *Reliques*.
"our souls have": See **Plutarch**.
"overleaping": See *Macbeth*.
"painted scene": See *Cenci, The*.
"painted veil": See "Lift Not the Painted Veil."
"palaces of nature": See *Childe Harold's Pilgrimage*.
"Paragon of animals": See *Hamlet*.
"Pareamo aver qui": See **Ariosto**.
"path of, The": See "Mutability."
"pearl away, a": See *Othello*.
"Per aver pace": See *Inferno*.
"*Per non turbar*": See **Petrarch**.
"Perchè I Pisan": See *Inferno*.
"piece of heaven": See *Italy*.
"Pietosi a": See **Ariosto**.
"pin's fee": See *Hamlet*.
"Pisando la": See **Calderón**.
"Poor orphan!" See *Faerie Queen, The*.
"*Porgi, amor*": See *Figaro*.
"proud Keep, the": See **Burke**.
"pure, the open, the": See *Lalla Rookh*.
"Quale è colui": See *Paradiso*.
"Quel, ch'ella": See **Dante**.
"Quelle triste": See **Genlis**.
"quiet to quick": See *Childe Harold's Pilgrimage*.
"Quintessence of dust": See *Hamlet*.
"Remember twelve!": See **Otway**.
"remorse of love, the": See *Childe Harold's Pilgrimage*.
"Repentance is": See **Wordsworth**.
"retired leisure": See *Il Penseroso*.
"rich storehouse, a": See **Bacon**.
"Roll on": See **Markham**.
"Rolled round in": See "Slumber Did My Spirit Seal, A."
"sacred and home-felt, a": See *Comus*.
"Sad and troubled?": See **Fletcher**.
"sad immunities": See **Burke**.

493

Appendix I

"salute mine ear": See **Anstey** and **Wilson**.
"sapless foliage": See "Ode to the West Wind."
"serious and profound, a": See **Goethe**.
"Settled in some": See **Marvell** and **Seneca the Younger**.
"Severe in youthful": See Appendix II.
"Shall I be": See *Cenci, The*.
"Shall I compare thee": See **Shakespeare**.
"She had styled him": See **Ford's** *Perkin Warbeck*.
"She is mine own": See *Two Gentlemen of Verona*.
"She to a window": See *Faerie Queen, The*.
"She was beloved": See *Troilus and Cressida*.
"She was in her nature": See **Henry Nelson Coleridge**.
"She was most beautiful": See "Christabel."
"shook lions into": See *Antony and Cleopatra*.
"silver cord, the": See **Ecclesiastes**.
"silver key": See "Music."
"Sisters, I from": See "Fire, Famine, and Slaughter."
"Small joy have I": See *Richard III*.
"small still voice, the": See *Hellas*.
"Snatching their pleasures": See **Marvell**.
"snow fall": See **Burns**.
"So easy is": See *Faerie Queen, The*.
"So loth we part": See *Irish Melodies*.
"So Love did vanish": See *Reliques*.
"So young": See *Cenci, The*.
"sober certainty, a": See *Comus*.
"some wide-watered": See *Il Penseroso*.
"sounding cataract, The": See "Tintern Abbey."
"Souvent femme varie": See Appendix II.
"Souvent homme varie": See Appendix II.
"Speak!—What door": See "Cyclops: A Satiric Drama, The."
"stale and unprofitable": See *Hamlet*.
"Stands Scotland where": See *Macbeth*.
"Sterile promontory": See *Hamlet*.
"still he must love": See "On this day I complete."

"such morsels sweet": See "Hymn to Mercury."
"Such when as Archimago": See *Faerie Queen, The*.
"Sure, when the separation": See **Wordsworth**.
"Suso in Italia": See *Inferno*.
"sweet inland": See "Tintern Abbey."
"sweet lips like roses": See *Revolt of Islam, The*.
"sweet regard, a": See *Faerie Queen, The*.
"sweet shire, the": See **Wordsworth**.
"sylvan Huntress, a": See **Wordsworth**.
"Taci ingiusto core": See **Mozart**.
"Talk of green": See **Lamb**.
"Tell him his soul": See **Jonson**.
"Tempestuous Fortune": See *Faerie Queen, The*.
"teque, Fluctibus": See *Georgics*.
"that a man's": See **Burns**.
"that golden chain": See *Ion*.
"that the sense aches": See *Othello*.
"that there is": See *Hamlet*.
"Their state, / Like": See **Shakespeare**.
"Then Paridell": See *Faerie Queen, The*.
"There's a bliss": See *Lalla Rookh*.
"There's a divinity": See *Hamlet*.
"There are many": See **Bible**.
"There is no struggle": See **Alfieri**.
"There is no work": See **Ecclesiastes**.
"There is one": See **Vasari**.
"There stood, / In record": See "Rosalind and Helen: A Modern Ecloque."
"There was a spirit": See "Indian Girl's Song, The."
"There was no": See **Maccabees**.
"there were none": See "She Dwelt Among the Untrodden Ways."
"Therefore shall": See **Bible**.
"These are their": See *Julius Caesar*.
"These cloudy princes": See *Richard III*.
"They are noble": See *Two Noble Kinsmen*.
"They built a wall": See **Beddoes**.
"They talked": See **Wordsworth**.

"Thick as autumnal": See *Paradise Lost*.
"Thief that comes, a": See Bible.
"Think but whither": See Fletcher.
"This friar boasteth": See Chaucer.
"Thou, God": See *Faerie Queen, The*.
"Thou, thrush": See Wordsworth.
"thought by thought": See *Paradise Regained*.
"thrones, dominations": See *Paradise Lost*.
"Through the flesh": See Elton.
"Thy mountain": See Knox.
"Time and Change": See Landon.
"'Tis but going": See Ford's *Perkin Warbeck*.
"'Tis too late": See Browne.
"To be once": See *Othello*.
"to drink Antipodean": See *Brides' Tragedy, The*.
"To England": See *King John*.
"to keep it warm": See Burns.
"to paint the lily": See *King John*.
"To see his nobleness": See *Winter's Tale, The*.
"tomb of, the": See Burke and *Romeo and Juliet*.
"touch of nature": See *Troilus and Cressida*.
"Towards the North": See *Julian and Maddalo*.
"traffic and barter": See Pitt.
"Traitor, what hast": See *Faerie Queen, The*.
"Try to conceive": See Appendix II.
"Turn back": See Hesiod.
"Tyrol, the": See Beckford.
"Un dia llama": See Calderón.
"unclouded by": See "Lament of Tasso, The."
"unhouseled, unanointed": See *Hamlet*.
"unpledged bowl, the": See *Italy*.
"unstringed viol": See *Richard II*.
"upon this hint": See *Othello*.
"Urbs Latii": See Gibbon.
"Valley of beauty": See Knox.
"Vaunting aloud": See *Paradise Lost*.
"Veggo pur troppo": See Metastasio.
"Vernal airs": See *Paradise Lost*.
"very form and": See *Hamlet*.

"very poetry": See Leigh Hunt.
"very shoal of time": See *Macbeth*.
"Village chimes": See Appendix II.
"violet by, a": See "She Dwelt Among the Untrodden Ways."
"Vous ne": See Niccolini.
"We cannot hope": See Browne.
"We are many": See "Mask of Anarchy, The."
"We could not": See *Antony and Cleopatra*.
"We rest—a dream": See "Mutability."
"Welcome this evil": See *Don Quixote*.
"What are fears": See "Hermit's Cell."
"What if some": See *Faerie Queen, The*.
"What is peace?": See "Hermit's Cell."
"What is youth?": See "Hermit's Cell."
"What scene:" See *3 Henry VI*.
"What's in a name?": See *Romeo and Juliet*.
"When we meet": See Montagu.
"When winds": See "From Moschus."
"Where is now": See Job.
"Where the gigantic": See *Italy*.
"where the wicked": See Job.
"Wherever the Catholic": See Eaton.
"Whispered so and so": See "Fire, Famine, and Slaughter. A War Eclogue."
"Who then to frail": See Bacon.
"Whose house": See "From Moschus."
"Whose narrow fire": See *Cenci, The*.
"Why didst thou": See Shakespeare.
"Why, it cannot": See *1 Henry IV*.
"wild Albanian, the": See *Childe Harold's Pilgrimage*.
"will move / in hearts": See *Childe Harold's Pilgrimage*.
"windowless, deformed, a": See *Julian and Maddalo*.
"With / My fortune": See Schiller and "Death of Wallenstein, The."
"With ills the land": See Elton.
"with native honour": See *Paradise Lost*.
"with sweet inland": See "Tintern Abbey."
"Within these ten": See Fletcher.

Appendix 1

"Women think that": See **Lytton**.
"world's sole": See *Ruines of Rome*.
"world had just, the": See **Moore**.
"World is too, The": See "**World Is Too Much With Us, The**."
"wove her chain": See "**Stanzas for Music**."
"Yes, my good lord": See *Richard II*.

"Yet I would not": See "**Death of Wallenstein, The**."
"Yet, noble friends": See **Ford's** *Perkin Warbeck*.
"You are now": See "**Letter to Maria Gisborne**."
"Your love and pity": See **Shakespeare**.

Appendix II:
Unidentified Quotations

"**An ounce of**": Shelley describes the English as luckier than **Italians**, who may ignore their climate and surroundings, by "an ounce of sweet be worth a pound of sugar" (*RI* 24).

"**but when they**": As **Elizabeth Falkner** rushes to imprisoned **Rupert Falkner**, Shelley notes: "A philosopher not long ago remarked, when adverting to the principle of destruction latent in all works of art, and the overthrow of the most durable of edifices: 'but when they are destroyed, so as to produce only dust, Nature asserts an Empire over them; and the vegetative world rises in constant youth, and in a period of annual successions, by the labors of man, providing food, vitality and beauty adorn the wrecks of monuments, which were once raised for purposes of glory' " (*F* 249–50).

"**Chi Dice mal**": For "**The Dream**'s" epigraph, Shelley uses lines from an **Italian song**: "Chi dice mal d'amore / Dice una falsità!" (*D* 153). The Italian lines translate: "Who speaks evil of love / Tells a lie!"

"**in the midst**": **Lionel Verney** records plague survivors' struggle to continue living in England: " 'in the midst of despair we performed our tasks of hope' " (*LM* 316).

Italian song: For "**The Dream**'s" epigraph, Shelley uses lines beginning "**Chi dice mal**," attributing them to an Italian song (*D* 153).

"**know the pleasures**": Shelley describes **Ethel Villiers** as content to be alone: "she was one of those who 'know the pleasures of solitude, when we hold commune alone with the tranquil solemnity of nature' " (*L* 3.61).

"**odio il**": Shelley's description of **Tuscany**'s political climate includes an **Italian**'s assessment; he alludes to "a **Florentine** poet": "odio il tiranno che col sonno uccide," which translates "I hate the tyrant who kills with sleep" (*R* 2.188; Moskal 328).

"**severe in youthful**": Shelley describes **Mary** in **Raphael**'s *Madonna di San Sisto* as " 'severe in youthful beauty' " (*R* 1.236).

"**Souvent femme varie**": **Francis I** engraves "Souvent femme varie, / Bien fou qui s'y fie" on a window; these **French** lines translate to "woman often changes, / Mad the man who trusts her" and form "**The False Rhyme**" of the story of that name (*TFR* 117).

"**Souvent homme varie**": Queen Margaret changes the subject of **Francis I**'s rhyme from women to men: "Souvent homme varie, / Bien folle qui s'y fie" (*TFR* 119). These **French**

497

Appendix II

lines translate: "man often changes, / Mad the woman who trusts him!"

"**Try to conceive**": Referring to **Gerard Neville**'s desire to be alone, Shelley notes: "An eloquent author has said, in contempt of such a being: 'Try to conceive a man without the ideas of God and eternity; of the good, the true, the beautiful, and the infinite' " (*F* 234).

"**Village chimes**": **Jane Harding** asserts **Charles Harding** is "out of hearing of 'village chimes' " and so receives none of the benefits of civilized life" (*S* 204).

Bibliography

AA 1998 Road Atlas of Europe. 3rd ed. Basingstoke: AA, 1997.

AA Road Atlas of France. Basingstoke: AA, 1998.

Ady, Cecilia M[ary]. *A History of Milan under the Sforza.* London: Methuen, 1907.

Alfieri, Vittorio. "Myrrha." *The Tragedies of Vittorio Alfieri.* Trans. Charles Lloyd. Vol. 3. London: Longman, 1815.

Alighieri, Dante. *The Divine Comedy of Dante Alighieri: A Verse Translation.* Trans. Allen Mandelbaum. 3 vols. Toronto: Bantam, 1986.

———. *Vita Nuova.* Trans. Dino S. Cervigni and Edward Vasta. Notre Dame, Ind.: University of Notre Dame Press, 1995.

Alison, Archibald. *History of Europe: From the Commencement of the French Revolution in 1789, to the Restoration of the Bourbons in 1815.* 4 vols. New York: Harper, 1843.

Angeli, Helen Rossetti. *Shelley and His Friends in Italy.* New York: Haskell, 1973.

Arabian Nights. Ed. Andrew Lang. London: Longman, 1951.

Argan, Giulio Carlo, and Bruno Contardi. *Michelangelo Architect.* Trans. Marion L. Grayson. New York: Abrams, 1993.

Ariosto, Lodovico. *Orlando Furioso (The Frenzy of Orlando): A Romantic Epic by Ludovico Ariosto, Part One.* Trans. Barbara Reynolds. London: Penguin, 1975.

Armour, Richard W. *Barry Cornwall: A Biography of Bryan Waller Procter, with a Selected Collection of Hitherto Unpublished Letters.* Boston: Meador, 1935.

Arnold, Bruce. *The Art Atlas of Britain & Ireland.* London: Viking, 1991.

Arnold, Denis, gen. ed. *The New Oxford Companion to Music.* 2 vols. Oxford: Oxford University Press, 1983.

Arthurson, Ian. *The Perkin Warbeck Conspiracy, 1491–1499.* Stroud, Eng.: Sutton, 1994.

Artistic Guide to Florence and Its Surroundings, with Historical and Artistical Notes on the Principal Monuments, Illustrations, Topographical Maps, Catalogues of the Galleries, Etc. 3rd ed. Florence: Societa Editrice Fiorentina, 1930.

Attwater, Donald, ed. *A Catholic Dictionary, The Catholic Encyclopaedic Dictionary.* 3rd ed. New York: Macmillan, 1958.

Avery, Catherine B., ed. *The New Century Italian Renaissance Encyclopedia.* New York: Meredith, 1972.

Bacon, Francis. "Of Friendship." *The Essayes or Counsels, Civill and Morall.* Ed. Michael Kiernan. Cambridge, Mass.: Harvard University Press, 1985. 80–87.

Bibliography

———. "Of Marriage and Single Life." *The Essays: 1625*. Menston, Eng.: Scolar, 1971. 36–39.

———. *The Advancement of Learning*. The Advancement of Learning *and* New Atlantis. Ed. Arthur Johnston. Oxford: Clarendon, 1974. 3–212.

———. "The world's a bubble." *Florilegium Epigrammatum Graecorum, Eorum Que Latino Versu à Variis redditorum*. Ed. Thomas Farnabio. London: Passenger, 1671. 8–11.

Baedeker, Karl. *Switzerland and the Adjacent Portions of Italy, Savoy, and Tyrol: Handbook for Travellers*. 19th ed. Leipsig: Baedeker, 1901.

Bagley, John J. *Lancashire*. London: Batsford, 1972.

Baines, Edward. *Baines's Lancashire: History, Directory and Gazatteer of the County Palatine of Lancaster*. 2 vols. New York: Kelley, 1968.

Baker, Daniel B., ed. *Explorers and Discoverers of the World*. Detroit: Gale, 1993.

Balteau, J., et al., eds. *Dictionnaire de Biographie Française*. 19 vols. to date. Paris: Librairie Letouzey et Ané, 1961–.

Barash, Carol. "Lady Mary Wortley Montagu." *Dictionary of Literary Biography*. Vol. 95. Ed. John Sitter. Detroit: Gale, 1990. 145–158.

Bargellini, Piero. *Florence: An Appreciation of Her Beauty; Historical and Artistic Guide with 172 Plates, 18 Plans, 8 Coloured Plates and a Map of the City*. Florence: Arnaud, 1960.

Barnhart, Clarence L., ed. *The New Century Handbook of English Literature*. New York: Appleton, 1956.

Baumgarten, Monica I. *Baedeker's Rhine*. Trans. James Hogarth. Gen. Ed. Peter Baumgarten. Englewood Cliffs, N.J.: Prentice-Hall, 1985.

Baumgarten, Peter, gen. ed. *Baedeker's Austria*. 3rd ed. Trans. James Hogarth. Englewood Cliffs, N.J.: Prentice-Hall, 1988.

———, gen. ed. *Baedeker's Germany*. Trans. James Hogarth. 2nd English ed. New York: Macmillan, 1996.

———, gen. ed. *Baedeker's Czech/Slovak Republics*. Englewood Cliffs, N.J.: Prentice-Hall, 1994.

Bayne-Powell, Rosamond. *Eighteenth-Century London Life*. London: Murray, 1937.

Beaumont, Francis, and John Fletcher. *The Dramatic Works in the Beaumont and Fletcher Canon*. Fredson Bowers, gen. ed. 10 vols. Cambridge: Cambridge University Press, 1966–.

Beckford, William. *Italy: With Sketches of Spain and Portugal*. 2 vols. London: Bentley, 1834.

———. *Vathek: An Arabian Tale, 1786*. Trans. Samuel Henley. Menston, Eng.: Scolar, 1971.

Beddoes, Thomas Lovell. "The Brides' Tragedy." *The Complete Works of Thomas Lovell Beddoes*. Ed. Edmund Gosse. Vol. 2. London: Fanfrolico, 1928. 401–479.

Bennett, Betty T. *Mary Diana Dods, A Gentleman and a Scholar*. New York: Morrow, 1991.

———. *Mary Wollstonecraft Shelley: An Introduction*. Baltimore: Johns Hopkins University Press, 1998.

———. "Newly Uncovered Letters and Poems by Mary Wollstonecraft Shelley: ('It was my birthday and it pleased me to tell the people so—')." *Keats-Shelley Journal* 46 (1997): 51–74.

Bethmann, Freiherr Moritz von. "Das Bethmannsche Museum: Ariadne." *Guide to the Cultural Institutions of Frankfurt am Main*. Ed. Richard Oehler. Frankfurt: Verlag Moritz Diesterweg, 1936.

Betti, Franco. *Vittorio Alfieri*. Ed. Anthony Oldcorn. Twayne World Authors Ser. 732. Boston: Twayne, 1984.

Bible. New Revised Standard Version. New York: Oxford University Press, 1989.

Blacker, Irwin R., ed. *Prescott's Histories: The Rise and Decline of the Spanish Empire. The Essence of Ferdinand and Isabella. The Conquest of Mexico. The Conquest of Peru, and Philip II*. By William Hickling Prescott. New York: Viking, 1963.

Blackwell, Richard J. *Galileo, Bellarmine, and the Bible: Including a Translation of Foscarini's*

Letter on the Motion of the Earth. Notre Dame, Ind.: University of Notre Dame Press, 1991.

Blackwell, Thomas. *An Enquiry into the Life and Writings of Homer, 1735*. Menston, Eng.: Scolar, 1972.

Blain, Virginia, Patricia Clements, and Isobel Grundy. *The Feminist Companion to Literature in English: Women Writers from the Middle Ages to the Present*. New Haven, Conn.: Yale University Press, 1990.

Blainey, Ann. *Immortal Boy: A Portrait of Leigh Hunt*. London: Croom Helm, 1985.

Blamire, Susanna. *The Poetical Works of Miss Susanna Blamire, "The Muse of Cumberland."* Ed. Patrick Maxwell. Edinburgh: Menzies, 1842.

Bleiler, Ellen H. Introduction. *Don Giovanni*. By Wolfgang Amadeus Mozart. Trans. Ellen H. Bleiler. Dover Opera Guide and Libretto Ser. New York: Dover, 1964. 5–64.

Blumberg, Jane, ed. *The Last Man*. By Mary Shelley. Vol. 4 of *The Novels and Selected Works of Mary Shelley*. Gen. Ed. Nora Crook. 9 vols. London: Pickering, 1996.

Blunden, Edmund. *Leigh Hunt: A Biography*. London: Cobden-Sanderson, 1930.

Boccaccio, Giovanni. *The Decameron*. Trans. J. M. Rigg. Everyman ed. 2 vols. London: Dent, 1973.

Boia, Lucian, ed. *Great Historians from Antiquity to 1800: An International Dictionary*. 2 vols. New York: Greenwood, 1989.

Bolt, Rodney. *Bavaria*. London: Cadogan, 1995.

Bondanella, Peter, and Julia Conaway Bondanella, eds. *Dictionary of Italian Literature*. Rev. ed. Westport, Conn.: Greenwood, 1996.

Bowker, John, ed. *The Oxford Dictionary of World Religions*. Oxford: Oxford University Press, 1997.

Bowle, John. *Charles I: A Biography*. London: Weidenfeld, 1975.

Bratchel, M. E. *Lucca, 1430–1494: The Reconstruction of an Italian City-Republic*. Oxford: Clarendon, 1995.

Brogan, Hugh. *The Penguin History of the United States of America*. London: Penguin, 1990.

Brown, Charles Brockden. *Arthur Mervyn; or, Memoirs of the Year 1793*. Ed. Warner Berthoff. New York: Holt, 1962.

Browne, Thomas. *Hydriotaphia. The Major Works*. Ed. C. A. Patrides. London: Penguin, 1977. 261–316.

Browning, W. R. F. *A Dictionary of the Bible*. London: Oxford University Press, 1996.

Brunelli, Bruno, ed. *Tutte le Opere di Pietro Metastasio*. By Pietro Metastasio. 5 vols. Milan: Mondadori, 1951–65.

Bryan, Michael. *Bryan's Dictionary of Painters and Engravers*. Ed. George C. Williamson. 4th ed. 5 vols. London: Bell, 1903.

Burke, Edmund. *The Writings and Speeches of Edmund Burke*. Gen. Ed. Paul Langford. 9 vols. Oxford: Clarendon, 1981–91.

Burnell, Frederic [Spencer]. *Rome*. New York: Longman, 1930.

Burns, Robert. *The Poems and Songs of Robert Burns*. Ed. James Kinsley. 3 vols. Oxford: Clarendon, 1968.

Byron, George Gordon. *Lord Byron: The Complete Poetical Works*. Ed. Jerome J. McGann. 7 vols. Oxford: Clarendon, 1980–93.

Calderón de la Barca, Pedro. *Six Plays*. Trans. Denis Florence Mac-Carthy. New York: Las Américas, 1961.

Cameron, Kenneth Neill, ed. *Shelley and His Circle, 1773–1822*. Vols. 1–4. Cambridge, Mass.: Harvard University Press, 1961–70.

Campbell, Thomas. *Gertrude of Wyoming; A Pennsylvanian Tale. And Other Poems*. London: Longman, 1809.

———. *The Complete Poetical Works of Thomas Campbell*. Ed. J. Logie Robertson. Oxford ed. London: Frowde, 1907.

Campbell, Thomas Joseph, ed. *Richard Cumberland's* The Wheel of Fortune: *A Critical Edition*. By Richard Cumberland. New York: Garland, 1987.

Caneva, Caterina, Alessandro Cecchi, and Antonio Natali. *The Uffizi: Guide to the Collections and Catalogue of All Paintings*. Boston: Sandak, 1992.

Cannon, John, ed. *The Oxford Companion to Brit-

Bibliography

ish History. Oxford: Oxford University Press, 1997.

Carlton, Charles. *Charles I: The Personal Monarch*. London: Routledge, 1983.

Catford, E[dwin]. F[rancis]. *Edinburgh: The Story of a City*. London: Hutchinson, 1975.

Cavalli, Gian Carlo, ed. *Guido Reni: Chronologia della Vita e delle Opere, Catalogo Ragionato, Antologia Critica e Bibliografia*. Florence: Vallecchi, 1955.

Cervantes Saavedra, Miguel de. *Don Quixote*. Wordsworth Classics ed. Ware, Eng.: Wordsworth, 1994.

Chaucer, Geoffrey. *The Student's Chaucer, Being a Complete Edition of His Works*. Ed. Walter W. Skeat. New York: Oxford University Press, 1900.

Chilvers, Ian, and Harold Osborne, eds. *The Oxford Dictionary of Art*. New ed. Oxford: Oxford University Press, 1997.

Ciardi, John, trans. and ed. *The Inferno*. By Dante Alighieri. New York: Mentor, 1982.

Cicero, [Marcus Tullius]. *De Finibus Bonorum et Malorum*. Trans. H. Rackham. 2nd ed. Cambridge, Mass.: Harvard University Press, 1951.

Clairmont, Clara Mary Jane. *The Clairmont Correspondence: Letters of Claire Clairmont, Charles Clairmont, and Fanny Imlay Godwin*. Ed. Marion Kingston Stocking. 2 vols. Baltimore: Johns Hopkins University Press, 1995.

———. *The Journals of Claire Clairmont*. Ed. Marion Kingston Stocking. Cambridge, Mass.: Harvard University Press, 1968.

Clarke, Charles Cowden, and Mary Cowden Clarke. *Recollections of Writers*. New York: Scribners, 1878.

Clarke, John. "The House of Hanover." *The Lives of the Kings and Queens of England*. Ed. Antonia Fraser. New York: Knopf, 1975. 259–308.

Clement, Clara Erskine. *Naples, The City of Parthenope and Its Environs*. London: Gay, 1894.

Clemit, Pamela, ed. *Falkner*. By Mary Shelley. Vol. 7 of *The Novels and Selected Works of Mary Shelley*. Gen. Ed. Nora Crook. 9 vols. London: Pickering, 1996.

Cleveland, John. *Poems, with Additions, Never Before Printed*. 1653. Menston, Eng.: Scolar, 1971.

Cline, C[larence]. L[ee]. *Byron, Shelley and Their Pisan Circle*. Cambridge, Mass.: Harvard University Press, 1952.

Cochrane, Eric. *Historians and Historiography in the Italian Renaissance*. Chicago: University of Chicago Press, 1981.

Coleridge, Henry Nelson. *Six Months in the West Indies, in 1825*. 2nd ed. London: Murray, 1826.

Coleridge, Samuel Taylor. "The Death of Wallenstein." *Complete Poetical Works of Samuel Taylor Coleridge, Including Poems and Versions of Poems Now Published for the First Time*. Ed. Ernest Hartley Coleridge. Vol. 2. Oxford: Clarendon, 1912. 726–811.

———. *Samuel Taylor Coleridge*. Ed. H. J. Jackson. Oxford Authors Ser. Oxford: Oxford University Press, 1985.

Collinge, William J. *Historical Dictionary of Catholicism: Historical Dictionaries of Religions, Philosophies, and Movements, No. 12*. Lanham, Md.: Scarecrow, 1997.

Collison-Morley, Lacy. *Naples Through the Centuries*. New York: Stokes, 1924.

Connolly, S. J., ed. *The Oxford Companion to Irish History*. Oxford: Oxford University Press, 1998.

Cook, Petronelle. *Queen Consorts of England: The Power Behind the Throne*. New York: Facts On File, 1993.

Cook's Tourist's Handbook for the Rhine (South-Western Germany) and the Black Forest. New York: Cook, 1906.

Coppa, Frank J., ed. *Dictionary of Modern Italian History*. Westport, Conn.: Greenwood, 1985.

Cornwall, Barry. "The Broken Heart." *The Poetical Works of Milman, Bowles, Wilson, and Barry Cornwall*. Paris: Galignani, 1800. 24–27.

Cosgrove, Art, ed. *A New History of Ireland*. 10 vols. Oxford: Clarendon, 1993.

Cotterill, H[enry]. B[ernard]. *Italy from Dante to

Tasso (1300–1600): Its Political History as Viewed from the Standpoints of the Chief Cities with Descriptions of Important Episodes and Personalities and of the Art and Literature of the Three Centuries. London: Harrap, 1919.

Coufopoulos, Demetrius. A Guide to Constantinople. 4th ed. London: Black, 1910.

Couprie, A. "Cassandre." Dictionnaire des Oeuvres Littéraires de Langue Franşe. Ed. Jean-Pierre de Beaumarchais and Daniel Couty. Vol. 1. Paris: Bordas, 1994. 267.

Cowper, William. Table Talk. Cowper: Verse and Letters. Ed. Brian Spiller. Cambridge, Mass.: Harvard University Press, 1968. 183–204.

Crane, David. Lord Byron's Jackal: A Life of Edward John Trelawny. London: Flamingo, 1999.

Crook, Nora, ed. Frankenstein. By Mary Shelley. Vol. 1 of The Novels and Selected Works of Mary Shelley. Gen. Ed. Nora Crook. 9 vols. London: Pickering, 1996.

———, ed. Valperga. By Mary Shelley. Vol. 3 of The Novels and Selected Works of Mary Shelley. Gen. Ed. Nora Crook. 9 vols. London: Pickering, 1996.

Cumberland, Richard. Memoirs of Richard Cumberland, Written by Himself: Containing an Account of His Life and Writings, Interspersed with Anecdotes and Characters of Several of the Most Distinguished Persons of His Time, with Whom He Has Had Intercourse and Connexion. 2 vols. London: Lackington, 1807.

Cunningham, Peter. Handbook for London, Past and Present. 2 vols. London: Murray, 1849.

Curran, Stuart. Shelley's Cenci; Scorpions Ringed with Fire. Princeton, N.J.: Princeton University Press, 1970.

Daru, Count. "Life of Volney." The Ruins, or Meditation on the Revolutions of Empires, and the Law of Nature. By Constantine Francis Volney. New York: Eckler, 1926. xv–xxii.

Dawson, Carl. Thomas Love Peacock. London: Routledge, 1968.

Debus, Allen G. The Chemical Philosophy: Paracelsian Science and Medicine in the Sixteenth and Seventeenth Centuries. Vol. 1. New York: Science History, 1977.

Deecke, W. Italy: A Popular Account of the Country, Its People, and Its Institutions (Including Malta and Sardinia), with Numerous Maps and Illustrations. Trans. H. A. Nesbitt. London: Swan, 1904.

Defoe, Daniel. A Journal of the Plague Year, Being Observations or Memorials of the Most Remarkable Occurrences, as Well Publick as Private, Which Happened in London During the Last Great Visitation in 1665. Ed. Louis A. Landa. London: Oxford University Press, 1969.

———. The Life and Strange Surprizing Adventures of Robinson Crusoe. London: Penguin, 1985.

Delaney, John J. Dictionary of Saints. Garden City, N.Y.: Doubleday, 1980.

The Dictionary of National Biography. Ed. Leslie Stephen and Sidney Lee. 22 vols. London: Oxford University Press, 1949–50.

Dircks, Richard J. Richard Cumberland. Twayne English Author Ser. 196. Boston: Twayne, 1976.

Donaldson, Gordon, and Robert S. Morpeth. Who's Who in Scottish History. Oxford: Blackwell, 1973.

Dowden, Edward. Introduction. The Passionate Pilgrim, the First Quarto, 1599, a Facsimile in Photo-Lithography by William Griggs. Facsimile ed. 10. London: Griggs, 1883. i–xx.

Drabble, Margaret, and Jenny Stringer, eds. The Concise Oxford Companion to English Literature. Oxford: Oxford University Press, 1987.

Dryden, John. Fables Ancient and Modern. London: Scolar, 1973.

Dupuy, R[ichard]. Ernest, and Trevor N. Dupuy. The Harper Encyclopedia of Military History, from 3500 B.C. to the Present. 4th ed. New York: HarperCollins, 1993.

Durán, Manuel. Luis de León. Twayne World Authors Ser. 136. New York: Twayne, 1971.

Eagle, Dorothy, and Meic Stephens, eds. The Oxford Illustrated Literary Guide to Great Brit-

Bibliography

ain and Ireland. 2nd ed. Oxford: Oxford University Press, 1992.

Eaton, Charlotte. *Rome, in the Nineteenth Century; Containing a Complete Account of the Ruins of the Middle Ages, and the Monuments of Modern Times.* 3 vols. Edinburgh: Constable, 1820.

Edwards, Gwynne, trans. and ed. Introduction. *Plays: One.* By Pedro Calderón de la Barca. Methuen World Dramatists Ser. London: Methuen, 1991. i–xxxi.

Eisler, Benita. *Byron: Child of Passion, Fool of Fame.* London: Hamish Hamilton, 1999.

Elliott, J. K. *The Apocryphal New Testament: A Collection of Apocryphal Christian Literature in an English Translation.* Oxford: Clarendon, 1993.

Elton, Charles Abraham. "Dissertation on the Life, Writings, and Aera of Hesiod." Introduction. *The Remains of Hesiod, Translated from the Greek into English Verse; with a Preliminary Dissertation on the Life, Writings, and Aera of Hesiod and Illustrative Notes.* By Hesiod. Trans. Charles Abraham Elton. London: Lackington, 1812. 1–64.

Famiglietti, R. C. *Royal Intrigue: Crisis at the Court of Charles VI, 1392–1420.* New York: AMS, 1986.

Farmer, David [Hugh]. *The Oxford Dictionary of Saints.* 3rd ed. Oxford: Oxford University Press, 1992.

Fellows, Otis E., and Stephen F. Milliken. *Buffon.* Twayne World Authors Ser. 243. New York: Twayne, 1972.

Fenwick, Hubert. *Scotland's Castles.* London: Hale, 1976.

Fernau, Joachim. *The Praeger Encyclopedia of Old Masters.* Trans. James Cleugh and Monica Brooksbank. New York: Praeger, 1958.

Fielding, Henry. *Joseph Andrews.* Ed. Martin C. Battestin. Wesleyan ed. Middletown, Conn.: Wesleyan University Press, 1967.

Fischer, Doucet Devin, ed. *The Fortunes of Perkin Warbeck.* By Mary Shelley. Vol. 5 of *The Novels and Selected Works of Mary Shelley.* Gen. Ed. Nora Crook. 9 vols. London: Pickering, 1996.

Fitzgerald, Edward. "To Dearest Mother." 9 July 1789. In *The Life and Death of Lord Edward Fitzgerald.* By Thomas Moore. Vol. 1. New York: Harper, 1831. 114–16.

Ford, John. *The Broken Heart.* Ed. T. J. B. Spencer. Manchester, Eng.: Manchester University Press, 1980.

———. *The Works of John Ford.* Ed. Alexander Dyce. New ed. 3 vols. New York: Russell, 1965.

Forman, H[arry]. Buxton, ed. *The Choice. A Poem on Shelley's Death by Mary Wollstonecraft Shelley.* London: Privately printed, 1876.

Forsyth, Joseph. *Remarks on Antiquities, Arts, and Letters, During an Excursion in Italy in the Years 1802 and 1803.* London: Murray, 1835.

Foscolo, Ugo. *Ultime lettere di Jacopo Ortis.* Trans. Douglas Radcliff-Umstead. Chapel Hill, N.C.: University of North Carolina Press, 1970.

Foster, R[obert]. F[itzroy]. *Modern Ireland, 1600–1972.* London: Penguin, 1988.

France, Peter, ed. *The New Oxford Companion to Literature in French.* Oxford: Clarendon, 1995.

Fullard, Harold, ed. *Philips' Modern School Atlas.* 78th ed. London: Philip, 1981.

Gianakaris, C. J. *Plutarch.* Twayne World Authors Ser. 111. New York: Twayne, 1970.

Gibbon, Edward. *The Decline and Fall of the Roman Empire.* Vol. 1. of *Great Books of the Western World.* Ed. Robert Maynard Hutchins. Chicago: Encyclopedia Britannica, 1952.

Giebel, Wieland, ed. *Dresden.* Trans. David Ingram and Susan Bollans. Boston: Houghton Mifflin, 1993.

Gisborne, Maria, and Edward E. Williams. *Maria Gisborne & Edward E. Williams, Shelley's Friends: Their Journals and Letters.* Ed. Frederick L. Jones. Norman: University of Oklahoma Press, 1951.

Gittings, Robert. *John Keats.* London: Penguin, 1979.

Gittings, Robert, and Jo Manton. *Claire Clair-*

mont and the Shelleys, 1798–1879. Oxford: Oxford University Press, 1992.
Godwin, William. *St. Leon.* Ed. Pamela Clemit. World's Classics ed. Oxford: Oxford University Press, 1994.
Goethe, Johann Wolfgang von. *Gedenkausgabe der Werke, Briefe und Gespräche.* Ed. Ernst Beutler. 24 vols. Zurich: Artemis-Verlag, 1948–50.
———. *The Sufferings of Young Werther and Elective Affinities.* Ed. Victor Lange. The German Library 19. New York: Continuum, 1991.
Goldsmith, Oliver. *Edwin and Angelina. A Collection of Poems, Containing Goldsmith's Deserted Village, and Edwin and Angelina.* Bath, Eng.: Hazard, 1796.
———. *The Vicar of Wakefield.* Reading, PA: Spencer, 1936.
Gould, Cecil. *The Paintings of Correggio.* Ithaca, N.Y.: Cornell University Press, 1976.
Gowing, Lawrence, gen. ed. *A Biographical Dictionary of Artists.* Rev. ed. New York: Facts On File, 1995.
Goy, Richard J[ohn]. *Chioggia and the Villages of the Venetian Lagoon: Studies in Urban History.* Cambridge: Cambridge University Press, 1985.
Grahame, George. *Claude Lorrain: Painter & Etcher.* London: Seeley, 1895.
Grant, A[rthur]. J[ames]. *The French Monarchy (1483–1789).* Vol. 1. New York: Fertig, 1970.
Grant, James. *The Great Metropolis.* New York: Saunders, 1837.
Green, Louis. *Castruccio Castracani: A Study on the Origins and Character of a Fourteenth-Century Italian Despotism.* Oxford: Clarendon, 1986.
Gregorovius, Ferdinand. *History of the City of Rome in the Middle Ages.* Trans. Annie Hamilton. Rev. 2nd ed. 8 vols. London: Bell, 1909.
Grylls, R[osalie]. Glynn. *Mary Shelley: A Biography.* New York: Haskell House, 1969.
———. *Trelawny.* London: Constable, 1950.
Hadfield, John. *The Shell Guide to England.* London: Rainbird, 1977.

Hall, Ivan. "Gillow." *Dictionary of English Furniture Makers, 1660–1840.* Ed. Geoffrey Beard and Christopher Gilbert. Leeds, Eng.: Furniture History Society, 1986. 341–43.
A Handbook for Travellers in Central Italy, Including the Papal States, Rome, and the Cities of Etruria. 7th ed. London: Murray, 1867.
Handbook for Travellers in Greece: Describing the Ionian Islands, the Kingdom of Greece, the Islands of the Aegean Sea, with Albania, Thessaly, and Macedonia. New ed. London: Murray, 1854.
A Handbook for Travellers in Northern Italy: States of Sardinia, Lombardy and Venice, Parma and Piacenza, Modena, Lucca, Massa-Carrara, and Tuscany, as Far as the Val d'Arno. London: Murray, 1842.
A Handbook for Travellers in Southern Germany, Being a Guide to Bavaria, Austria, Tyrol, and the Danube from Ulm to the Black Sea. 15th ed. London: Murray, 1890.
A Handbook for Travellers in Switzerland and the Alps of Savoy and Piedmont, Including the Protestant Valleys of the Waldenses. London: Murray, 1838.
A Handbook for Travellers on the Continent, Being a Guide through Holland, Belgium, Prussia, and Northern Germany, and Along the Rhine, from Holland to Switzerland. London: Murray, 1836.
A Handbook of Rome and Its Environs. 7th ed. London: Murray, 1864.
Hardcastle, Daniel, Jr. *Banks and Bankers.* 2nd ed. London: Whittaker, 1843.
Hare, Augustus J. C. *Florence.* 8th ed. London: Kegan Paul, 1914.
———. *Venice.* 3rd ed. London: Allen, 1891.
Harvey, Leonard. *Islamic Spain, 1250 to 1500.* Chicago: University of Chicago Press, 1990.
Havelock, Christine Mitchell. *The Aphrodite of Knidos and Her Successors: A Historical Review of the Female Nude in Greek Art.* Ann Arbor: University of Michigan Press, 1995.
Haydn, J[oseph]. *The Creation: An Oratorio, in*

Bibliography

Vocal Score. Novello's Original Octavio ed. London: Novello, n.d.

Headlam, Cecil. *The Story of Naples*. London: Dent, 1927.

Hecht, Henry J. *The Motor Routes of Germany: Through North-Eastern France and Holland, to the Rhine, the Moselle, the Black Forest, the Thuringian Forest, the Taunus, and Bavaria*. Ed. Gordon Home. London: Black, 1914.

Hedley, Olwen. *Windsor Castle*. London: Hale, 1967.

Hesiod. *The Remains of Hesiod, Translated from the Greek into English Verse; with a Preliminary Dissertation on the Life, Writings, and Aera, of Hesiod and Illustrative Notes*. Trans. Charles Abraham Elton. London: Lackington, 1812.

———. *Theogony, Works and Days, Shield*. Ed. and trans. Apostolos N. Athanassakis. Baltimore: Johns Hopkins University Press, 1983.

Heywood, Thomas. *A Woman Killed with Kindness*. Ed. R. W. Van Fossen. Cambridge, Mass.: Harvard University Press, 1961.

———. "The Tale of Daedalus." *The Passionate Pilgrim, the First Quarto, 1599, a Facsimile in Photo-Lithography by William Griggs*. Facsimile ed. 10. London: Griggs, 1883.

Hibbert, Christopher. *Tower of London*. New York: Newsweek, 1971.

Higson, John W., Jr. *A Historical Guide to Florence*. New York: Universe, 1973.

Hobhouse, J[ohn]. C[am]. *A Journey Through Albania, and Other Provinces of Turkey in Europe and Asia, to Constantinople, During the Years 1809 and 1810*. 2 vols. Philadelphia: Carey, 1817.

Holinshed, Raphael. *Holinshed's Chronicles of England, Scotland, and Ireland*. 6 vols. New York: AMS, 1965.

Hollier, Denis, ed. *A New History of French Literature*. Cambridge, Mass.: Harvard University Press, 1989.

Holmes, Richard. *Shelley: The Pursuit*. London: Penguin, 1987.

Holt, Edgar. *Risorgimento: The Making of Italy 1815–1870*. London: Macmillan, 1970.

Homer. *The Iliad of Homer*. Trans. Ennis Rees. New York: Oxford University Press, 1991.

———. *The Odyssey*. Trans. Robert Fagles. New York: Viking, 1996.

Honour, Hugh. *The Companion Guide to Venice*. Englewood Cliffs, N.J.: Prentice-Hall, 1983.

Howard, Deborah. *The Architectural History of Venice*. New York: Holmes, 1981.

Howatson, M. C., ed. *The Oxford Companion to Classical Literature*. 2nd ed. Oxford: Oxford University Press, 1995.

Hudson, Derek. *Sir Joshua Reynolds: A Personal Study*. London: Bles, 1958.

Hughes, Holly, ed. *Fodor's '96 Great Britain*. New York: Fodor's, 1995.

Hume, David. *The History of England: From the Invasion of Julius Caesar to the Revolution in 1688*. 6 vols. New York: LibertyClassics, 1983.

Hunt, Leigh. "The Story of Rimini." *Selected Writings*. Ed. David Jesson-Dibley. Manchester, Eng.: Carcanet, 1990. 19–45.

Huscher, Herbert. "Alexander Mavrocordato, Friend of the Shelleys." *Keats-Shelley Memorial Bulletin* 16 (1965): 29–38.

Hutchins, Robert Maynard, ed. *Plutarch*. Vol. 14 of *Great Books of the Western World*. 54 vols. Chicago: Encyclopedia Britannica, 1952.

Ingpen, Roger. *Shelley in England: New Facts and Letters from the Shelley-Whitton Papers*. London: Kegan Paul, 1917.

Irving, Washington. *A Chronicle of the Conquest of Granada*. Boston: Twayne, 1988.

Italy '96. Berkeley Guides Ser. London: Fodor's, 1996.

Italy, in One Volume. G. R. Martineau, gen. ed. Guide Bleu Ser. Paris: Nagel, 1949.

Jackson, Virginia, ed. *Art Museums of the World*. 2 vols. New York: Greenwood, 1987.

Jameson, Anna. *Sketches of Art, Literature, and Character*. Boston: Houghton, 1881.

Jennett, Seán. *Paris*. London: Batsford, 1973.

Johnston, William M. *In Search of Italy: Foreign Writers in Northern Italy Since 1800*. University Park: Penn State University Press, 1987.

Jonson, Ben. "Catiline His Conspiracy." *Ben Jonson*. Vol. 5. Ed. C. H. Herford and Percy and Evelyn Simpson. 11 vols. Oxford: Clarendon, 1954. 409–549.

———. "The Sad Shepherd." *Ben Jonson*. Vol. 7. Ed. C. H. Herford and Percy and Evelyn Simpson. 11 vols. Oxford: Clarendon, 1963. 1–50.

Keats, John. *Keats: Poetical Works*. Ed. H. W. Garrod. Oxford Standard Authors ed. Oxford: Oxford University Press, 1987.

Keay, John, and Julia Keay, eds. *Collins Encyclopedia of Scotland*. London: HarperCollins, 1994.

Kelly, J[ohn]. N[orman]. D[avidson]. *The Oxford Dictionary of Popes*. Oxford: Oxford University Press, 1986.

Kent, William, ed. *An Encyclopaedia of London*. New York: Macmillan, 1951.

Kinder, Herman, and Werner Hilgemann. *The Penguin Atlas of World History*. Trans. Ernest A. Menze. Updated ed. 2 vols. London: Penguin, 1995.

Klein, Elaine. *Hippocrene Insider's Guide to Paris*. New York: Hippocrene, 1991.

Knight, David. *Humphrey Davy: Science & Power*. Oxford: Blackwell, 1992.

Knox, Andrew Alexander. *Giotto and Francesca, and Other Poems*. London: Edward Bull, 1842.

Kock, Charles-Paul de. *The Barber of Paris. The Masterpieces of Charles-Paul de Kock*. Trans. George Burnham Ives. Vol. 9. Philadelphia: Barrie, 1903. 3–431.

Kohn, George C. *Dictionary of Wars*. New York: Facts On File, 1986.

Lamb, Charles. *John Woodvil: A Tragedy. The Works of Charles and Mary Lamb*. Ed. E. V. Lucas. Vol. 5. London: Methuen, 1903. 131–76.

Landon, Letitia Elizabeth. *Poetical Works of Letitia Elizabeth Landon, "L.E.L."* Ed. F. J. Sypher. Scholars' Facsimiles and Reprints Ser. 443. Delmar, N.Y.: Scholars' Facsimiles and Reprints, 1990.

Lanzi, Abate Luigi. *The History of Painting in Italy, from the Period of the Revival of the Fine Arts, to the End of the Eighteenth Century*. Trans. Thomas Roscoe. 6 vols. London: Simpkin, 1828.

Leigh, Samuel. *Leigh's New Picture of London; or, A View of the Political, Religious, Medical, Literary, Municipal, Commercial, and Moral State of the British Metropolis: Presenting a Luminous Guide to the Stranger, on all Subjects Connected with General Information, Business, or Amusement*. New ed. London: Leigh, 1824–25.

Levine, Dan. *Frommer's Prague*. New York: Prentice, 1994.

Littlewood, Ian. *Venice: A Literary Companion*. London: Murray, 1991.

Loesser, Arthur. *Men, Women, and Pianos: A Social History*. New York: Dover, 1990.

Lovell, Ernest J[ames]., Jr. *Captain Medwin: Friend of Byron and Shelley*. Austin: University of Texas Press, 1962.

Low, David, ed. *Fodor's Berlin*. New York: Fodor's, 1993.

Levy, Alan. *Treasures of the Vatican Collections*. New York: Art Press, 1983.

Lucan. *Pharsalia*. Trans. Jane Wilson Joyce. Masters of Latin Literature Ser. Ithaca, N.Y.: Cornell University Press, 1993.

Lucretius, [Carus Titus]. *On the Nature of the Universe*. Trans. Ronald Melville. Oxford: Clarendon, 1997.

Lyles, William H. *Mary Shelley, an Annotated Bibliography*. New York: Garland, 1975.

Lytton, Edward Bulwer. *Paul Clifford*. London: Routledge, 1866.

MacDonald, David Lorne. *"Poor Polidori": A Critical Biography of the Author of* The Vampyre. Toronto: University of Toronto Press, 1991.

Machiavelli, Niccolo. *The Life of Castruccio Castracani of Lucca. The Chief Works and Others*. Trans. Allan Gilbert. 3 vols. Durham, N.C.: Duke University Press, 1965. 533–559.

———. *Mandragola*. Trans. Anne and Henry Paolucci. New York: Liberal Arts, 1957.

Mackey, Sampson Arnold. *The Mythological Astronomy of the Ancients Demonstrated, by*

Bibliography

Restoring to their Fables and Symbols Their Original Meanings. Minneapolis: Wizards Bookshelf, 1973.

Magnusson, Magnus, ed. *Cambridge Biographical Dictionary*. New York: Cambridge University Press, 1990.

March, Ausias. *Ausias March: Selected Poems*. Ed. and trans. Arthur Terry. Edinburgh Bilingual Library Ser. 12. Edinburgh: Edinburgh University Press, 1976.

Marchand, Leslie A. *Byron: A Biography*. 3 vols. New York: Knopf, 1953.

———, ed. *Byron's Letters and Journals: The Complete and Unexpurgated Text of All the Letters Available in Manuscript and the Full Printed Version of All Others*. London: Murray, 1973–81.

Markham, Gervase, and Lewis Machin. *The Dumbe Knight. A historicall comedy, acted sundry times by the children of his Maiesties Reuels*. London: Nicholas Okes, 1608.

Marshall, Peter H. *William Godwin*. New Haven, Conn.: Yale University Press, 1984.

Marvell, Andrew. *The Poems and Letters of Andrew Marvell*. Ed. H. M. Margoliouth. 2nd ed. 2 vols. Oxford: Clarendon, 1952.

Mather, Frank Jewett, Jr. *A History of Italian Painting*. New York: Holt, 1923.

McAleer, Edward C. *The Sensitive Plant: A Life of Lady Mount Cashell*. Chapel Hill: University of North Carolina Press, 1958.

McBrien, Richard P., ed. *The HarperCollins Encyclopedia of Catholicism*. San Francisco: HarperCollins, 1995.

McGann, Jerome J., ed. *Lord Byron: The Complete Poetical Works*. 7 vols. Oxford: Clarendon Press, 1980–93.

McLachlan, Gordon. *Germany: The Rough Guide*. Ed. Jo Mead. 3rd ed. London: Rough Guides, 1995.

McLynn, Frank. *Napoleon: A Biography*. London: Pimlico, 1998.

McRae, Stuart Gordon, and C. P. Burnham. *The Rural Landscape of Kent*. Wye, Eng.: Wye College, 1973.

Medwin, Thomas. *The Life of Percy Bysshe Shelley*. New ed. Ed. H. Buxton Forman. London: Oxford University Press, 1913.

Meek, Christine. *Lucca, 1369–1400: Politics and Society in an Early Renaissance City-State*. New York: Oxford University Press, 1978.

Meras, Phyllis. *Eastern Europe: A Traveler's Companion*. Boston: Houghton Mifflin, 1991.

Metastasio, Pietro. *Tutte le Opere di Pietro Metastasio*. Ed. Bruno Brunelli. 5 vols. Milan: Mondadori, 1951–65.

Michelin Motoring Map: Ireland. Paris: Michelin, 1996.

Michelin Tourist Guide: Austria. London: Michelin, 1994.

Michelin Tourist Guide: Italy. 4th ed. Watford, Eng.: Michelin, 1995.

Michelin Tourist Guide: Paris. 3rd ed. Watford, Eng.: Michelin, 1996.

Michelin Tourist Guide: Rome. London: Michelin, 1995.

Michelin Tourist Guide: Switzerland. London: Michelin, 1996.

Middleton, Thomas. *No Wit, No Help Like a Woman's*. Ed. Lowell E. Johnson. Lincoln: University of Nebraska Press, 1976.

Milton, John. "L'Allegro." *The Poetical Works of John Milton*. Ed. Egerton Brydges. New York: Mason, 1876. 717–25.

———. *"Comus" and Other Poems*. Ed. F. T. Prince. Oxford: Oxford University Press, 1968.

———. Paradise Lost *and* Paradise Regained. Ed. Christopher Ricks. Signet Classic Poetry Ser. New York: Penguin, 1982.

Mitchell, John. *The Life of Wallenstein, Duke of Friedland*. New York: Greenwood, 1968.

Montagu, Mary Wortley. *The Letters and Works of Lady Mary Wortley Montagu*. Ed. Lord Wharncliffe. 2 vols. Philadelphia: Carey, 1837.

Moore, Frank. *The Life of Oliver Goldsmith*. New York: Dutton, 1911.

Moore, Thomas. *The Life and Death of Lord Edward Fitzgerald*. 2 vols. New York: Harper, 1831.

———. *The Poetical Works of Thomas Moore, with Explanatory Notes, Etc.* New York: Hurst, n.d.

Morby, John E. *The Wordsworth Handbook of*

Kings and Queens. Ware, Eng.: Wordsworth, 1989.

Moskal, Jeanne, ed. *Travel Writing*. By Mary Shelley. Vol. 8 of *The Novels and Selected Works of Mary Shelley*. Gen. Ed. Nora Crook. 9 vols. London: Pickering, 1996.

Mossiker, Frances. *Madame de Sévigné: A Life and Letters*. New York: Knopf, 1983.

Mozart, Wolfgang Amadeus. *The Great Operas of Mozart; Complete Librettos in the Original Language*. Trans. W. H. Auden, et al. New York: Norton, 1962.

———. *Don Giovanni*. Trans. Ellen H. Bleiler. Dover Opera Guide and Libretto Ser. New York: Dover, 1964.

Muntz, Eugène. *Raphael: His Life, Works, and Times*. Trans. Walter Armstrong. London: Chapman, 1896.

Musgrave, Clifford. *Royal Pavilion: A Study in the Romantic*. Brighton, Eng.: Bredon, 1951.

Myers, Bernard S., ed. *McGraw-Hill Dictionary of Art*. 5 vols. London: McGraw-Hill, 1969.

Nauert, Charles G., Jr. *Agrippa and the Crisis of Renaissance Thought*. Urbana: University of Illinois Press, 1965.

Niccolini, G[iovanni]. B[attista]. *Arnold of Brescia: A Tragedy*. Trans. Theodosia Garrow. London: Longman, 1846.

Nicol, Donald M. *The Immortal Emperor: The Life and Legend of Constantine Palaiologos, Last Emperor of the Romans*. Cambridge: Cambridge University Press, 1992.

Nitchie, Elizabeth. *Mary Shelley: Author of Frankenstein*. New Brunswick, N.J.: Rutgers University Press, 1953.

Nolhac, Pierre de. *Versailles and the Trianons*. London: Heinemann, 1906.

Notestein, Lucy Lilian. *Hill Towns of Italy*. Boston: Little, 1963.

Noyce, Wilfrid. *The Alps, with Descriptive Essays by Karl Lukan*. Trans. Margaret Shenfield. London: Thames, 1963.

Noyes, Ella. *The Story of Milan*. London: Dent, 1908.

Okey, Thomas. *The Story of Paris*. London: Dent, 1906.

Oram, William A., et al., eds. *The Yale Edition of Shorter Poems of Edmund Spenser*. By Edmund Spenser. Yale ed. New Haven, Conn.: Yale University Press, 1989.

Orieux, Jean. *Voltaire*. Trans. Barbara Bray and Helen R. Lane. Garden City, N.Y.: Doubleday, 1979.

Origo, Iris. *The Last Attachment: The Story of Byron and Teresa Guiccioli as Told in Their Unpublished Letters and Other Family Papers*. London: Murray, 1971.

Orrey, Leslie, ed. *The Encyclopedia of Opera*. New York: Scribners, 1976.

Otway, Thomas. *Venice Preserved or a Plot Discovered*. Ed. Malcolm Kelsall. Lincoln: University of Nebraska Press, 1969.

Ousby, Ian, ed. *The Wordsworth Companion to English Literature*. Ware, Eng.: Wordsworth, 1994.

Overmyer, Grace. *America's First Hamlet*. New York: New York University Press, 1957.

Ovid. *The Metamorphoses of Ovid*. Trans. Allen Mandelbaum. New York: Harcourt, 1993.

Oxford English Dictionary. 2nd ed. 20 vols. Oxford: Clarendon, 1989.

Palacio, Jean de. *Mary Shelley dans son Oeuvre*. Paris: Klincksieck, 1969.

Paley, Morton D., ed. *The Last Man*. By Mary Shelley. World's Classics ed. Oxford: Oxford University Press, 1994.

Park, Mungo. *Travels in the Interior Districts of Africa: Performed under the Direction and Patronage of the African Association, in the Years 1795, 1796, and 1797*. Philadelphia: Humphreys, 1800.

Parry, Melanie, ed. *Larousse Dictionary of Women*. New York: Larousse, 1996.

Paul, C. Kegan. *William Godwin: His Friends and Contemporaries*. 2 vols. New York: AMS, 1970.

Pellico, Silvio. *My Prisons (I mie prigioni)* and *Francesca da Rimini, a Tragedy in Five Acts*. Trans. Florence Kendrick Cooper. New York: National Alumni, 1907.

Percy, Thomas. *Reliques of Ancient English Poetry, Consisting of Old Heroic Ballads, Songs, and Other Pieces of Our Earlier Poets Together with Some Few of Later Date*. Ed.

Bibliography

Henry B. Wheatley. 3 vols. New York: Dover, 1966.

Perkins, Jane Gray. *The Life of Mrs. Norton*. London: Murray, 1909.

Petrarca, Francesco. *Petrarch: Sonnets and Songs*. Trans. Anna Maria Armi. New York: Pantheon, 1946.

———. *Letters of Old Age: Rerum senilium libri I–XVIII*. Trans. Aldo S. Bernardo, Saul Levin, and Reta A. Bernardo. Vol. 1. Baltimore: Johns Hopkins University Press, 1992.

Petronio, Giuseppe, ed. *Dizionario Enciclopedico della Letteratura Italiana*. 6 vols. Rome: Laterza, 1966–70.

Phaidon Encyclopedia of Art and Artists. New York: Dutton, 1978.

Piper, David. *The Companion Guide to London*. New York: Harper, 1965.

Pliny. *Letters and Panegyricus in Two Volumes*. Trans. Betty Radice. Vol. 1. Cambridge, Mass.: Harvard University Press, 1969.

———. *Natural History, with an English Translation in Ten Volumes*. Trans. H. Rackham. Vol. 3. Cambridge, Mass.: Harvard University Press, 1940.

Plutarch. *Plutarch's Lives: (The Dryden Plutarch)*. Ed. Arthur Hugh Clough. Everyman ed. 3 vols. London: Dent, 1932.

———. *Moralia*. Trans. Frank Cole Babbitt. 14 vols. Cambridge, Mass.: Harvard University Press, 1949.

Pollin, Burton R. "Mary Shelley as the Parvenue." *Review of English Literature* 8.3 (1967): 9–21.

Pope, Alexander. *The Complete Poetical Works of Alexander Pope*. Ed. Henry W. Boynton. Cambridge ed. Boston: Houghton Mifflin, 1903.

Poston, Carol H., ed. Introduction. *Letters Written During a Short Residence in Sweden, Norway, and Denmark*. By Mary Wollstonecraft. Lincoln: University of Nebraska Press, 1976. vii-xxi.

Prance, Claude A. *Companion to Charles Lamb: A Guide to People and Places 1760–1847*. London: Mansell, 1983.

Prescott, William Hickling. *Prescott's Histories: The Rise and Decline of the Spanish Empire*. Ed. Richard J. Blackwell. New York: Viking, 1963.

Prior, Matthew. *The Literary Works of Matthew Prior*. Ed. H. Bunker Wright and Monroe K. Spears. 2nd ed. 2 vols. Oxford: Clarendon, 1971.

Radcliff-Umstead, Douglas. *Ugo Foscolo*. Twayne World Authors Ser. 115. New York: Twayne, 1970.

Radice, Betty. *Who's Who in the Ancient World: A Handbook to the Survivors of the Greek and Roman Classics*. London: Blond, 1971.

Rae, Gordon, and Charles E. Brown. *A Geography of Scotland: General and Regional*. London: Bell, 1959.

Raitt, A(lan). W(illiam). *Prosper Mérimée*. New York: Scribner, 1970.

Rasjidi, Mohammad. "Unity and Diversity in Islam." *Islam—The Straight Path: Islam Interpreted by Muslims*. Ed. Kenneth W. Morgan. New York: Ronald, 1958. 403–30.

Rasor, Eugene L. *The Spanish Armada of 1588: Historiography and Annotated Bibliography*. Westport, Conn.: Greenwood, 1993.

Rees, Joan. *Shelley's Jane Williams*. London: Kimber, 1985.

Reiman, Donald H., ed. *Shelley and His Circle, 1773–1822*. Vols. 5–8. Cambridge, Mass.: Harvard University Press, 1973–86.

Reynolds, Joshua. *A Journey to Flanders and Holland in the Year 1781. The Literary Works of Sir Joshua Reynolds, Late President of the Royal Academy; Containing His Discourses, Papers in the* Idler, *the Journal of a Tour through Flanders and Holland, and Also His Commentary on Du Fresnoy's Art of Painting*. Ed. Edmund Malone. 5th ed. Vol. 2. London: Cadell, 1819. 247–427.

Ricci, Corrado. *Beatrice Cenci*. Trans. Morris Bishop and Henry Longan Stuary. 2 vols. New York: Boni, 1925.

Richter, George Martin. *Giorgio da Castelfranco, Called Giorgione*. Chicago: University of Chicago Press, 1937.

Riggs, Arthur Stanley. *France from Sea to Sea*. New York: McBride, 1931.

Rippy, Frances Mayhew. *Matthew Prior.* Twayne World Authors Ser. 418. Boston: Twayne, 1986.

Road Atlas: Britain. Edinburgh: Bartholomew, 1990.

Road Atlas of Ireland. Dublin: Ordnance Survey, 1993.

Robertson, C. Grant, and J. G. Bartholomew. *An Historical Atlas of Modern Europe from 1789 to 1922 with an Historical and Explanatory Text.* London: Oxford University Press, 1924.

Robinson, Charles E. "Mary Shelley and the Roger Dodsworth Hoax." *Keats-Shelley Journal* 24 (1975): 20–28.

———, ed. *Collected Tales and Stories.* By Mary Shelley. Baltimore: Johns Hopkins University Press, 1990.

Roeder, Ralph. *The Man of the Renaissance: Four Lawgivers: Savonarola, Machiavelli, Castiglione, Aretino.* New York: Viking, 1933.

Rogers, Samuel. *Italy, A Poem.* London: Cadell, 1836.

———. *Poems.* London: Cadell, 1834.

Rolleston, Maud. *Talks with Lady Shelley.* London: Harrap, 1925.

Rollin, Charles. *The Ancient History of the Egyptians, Carthaginians, Assyrians, Babylonians, Medes & Persians, Macedonians, and Grecians.* 8 vols. New York: Duyckinck, 1812.

Rosenthal, Harold, and John Warrack. *The Concise Oxford Dictionary of Opera.* 2nd ed. New York: Oxford University Press, 1980.

Ross, Steven T. *Historical Dictionary of the Wars of the French Revolution.* Lanham, Md.: Scarecrow, 1998.

Rossington, Michael, ed. *Valperga, or, The Life and Adventures of Castruccio, Prince of Lucca.* By Mary Shelley. Oxford: Oxford University Press, 2000.

Runciman, Steven. *The Sicilian Vespers: A History of the Mediterranean World in the Later Thirteenth Century.* Cambridge: Cambridge University Press, 1958.

Sadie, Stanley, ed. *New Grove Dictionary of Music and Musicians.* 20 vols. London: Macmillan, 1980.

Sadleir, Michael. *Bulwer and His Wife: A Panorama, 1803–1836.* New ed. London: Constable, 1933.

St. Clair, William. *The Godwins and the Shelleys: The Biography of a Family.* London: Faber, 1989.

———. *Trelawny: The Incurable Romancer.* New York: Vanguard, 1977.

Salvatorelli, Luigi. *A Concise History of Italy, from Prehistoric Times to Our Own Day.* Trans. Bernard Miall. New York: Oxford University Press, 1939.

Sanborn, Franklin B. *The Romance of Mary W. Shelley, John Howard Payne and Washington Irving.* Boston: Bibliophile Society, 1907.

Sanders, Andrew. *The Short Oxford History of English Literature.* Oxford: Clarendon, 1994.

Saunders, Hilary St. George. *Westminster Hall.* London: Joseph, 1951.

Schiller, Friedrich von. *Love and Intrigue, or Louisa Miller.* Trans. Frederick Rolf. Great Neck, N.Y.: Barron's, 1959.

Schmeckebier, Laurence. *A New Handbook of Italian Renaissance Painting.* Rev. 2nd ed. New York: Hacker, 1981.

Scholes, Percy A. *The Oxford Companion to Music.* 10th ed. Rev. by John Owen Ward. Oxford: Oxford University Press, 1995.

Scott, Winifred. *Jefferson Hogg.* London: Cape, 1951.

Seltzer, Leon E., ed. *The Columbia Lippincott Gazetteer of the World.* New York: Columbia University Press, 1962.

Seymour, Miranda. *Mary Shelley.* London: John Murray, 2000.

Seward, Desmond. *The Bourbon Kings of France.* New York: Barnes, 1976.

Shakespeare, William. *The Complete Works of Shakespeare.* Ed. David Bevington. 4th ed. New York: HarperCollins, 1992.

———, and John Fletcher. *The Two Noble Kinsmen.* Ed. Eugene M. Waith. Oxford: Clarendon, 1989.

Shelley, Mary. "Absence." *Keepsake for 1831.* Ed.

Bibliography

Frederic Mansel Reynolds. London: Longman, 1831. 39.

———. "A Dirge." *Keepsake for 1831.* Ed. Frederic Mansel Reynolds. London: Longman, 1831. 85.

———. *The Choice. A Poem on Shelley's Death by Mary Wollstonecraft Shelley.* Ed. H. Buxton Forman. London: Privately printed, 1876.

———. *Collected Tales and Stories.* Ed. Charles E. Robinson. Baltimore: Johns Hopkins University Press, 1990.

———. "Defense of Velluti." *The Examiner* 958 (1826): 372–73.

———. *Falkner. A Novel.* New York: Harper, 1837.

———. *The Fortunes of Perkin Warbeck, A Romance.* 3 vols. London: Colburn, 1830.

———. *Frankenstein.* 1831. Ed. Johanna M. Smith. Case Studies in Contemporary Criticism Ser. Boston: Bedford, 1992.

———. *Frankenstein.* 1818. Ed. D. L. Macdonald and Kathleen Scherf. Peterborough, Ont.: Broadview, 1994.

———. "Giovanni Villani." *The Liberal* 4 (1824): 281–97.

———. *History of a Six Weeks' Tour Through a Part of France, Switzerland, Germany, and Holland; with Letters Descriptive of a Sail Around the Lake of Geneva, and of the Glaciers of Chamouni.* London: Hookham, 1817.

———. "Illyrian Poems—Feudal Scenes." Rev. of *La Guzla, ou Choir de Poésies Illyriques recueillies dans la Dalmatie, la Vosnie, la Croatie et l' Hervegowine, La Jaquerie; Feudal Scenes,* and *Le Théâtre de Clara Gazul, Comédienne Espagnole,* by Prosper Mérimée. *Westminster Review* 10 (1829): 71–81.

———. *The Journals of Mary Shelley: 1814–1844.* Ed. Paula R. Feldman and Diana Scott-Kilvert. Baltimore: Johns Hopkins University Press, 1995.

———. "La Vida es Sueño." In *Mary Shelley: Author of* Frankenstein. By Elizabeth Nitchie. New Brunswick, N.J.: Rutgers University Press, 1953. 231–33.

———. *The Last Man.* Ed. Morton D. Paley. World's Classics ed. Oxford: Oxford University Press, 1994.

———. *The Letters of Mary Wollstonecraft Shelley.* Ed. Betty T. Bennett. 3 vols. Baltimore: Johns Hopkins University Press, 1980–1988.

———. *Lives of the Most Eminent Literary and Scientific Men of France.* 2 vols. London: Longman, 1838–39.

———. *Lives of the Most Eminent Literary and Scientific Men of Italy, Spain and Portugal.* 3 vols. London: Longman, 1835–37.

———. *Lodore.* Ed. Lisa Vargo. Peterborough, Ont.: Broadview, 1997.

———. "Madame d'Houtetôt." *The Liberal* 3 (1823): 67–83.

———. *Matilda.* In *Mary Wollstonecraft: Mary, Maria; Mary Shelley: Matilda.* Ed. Janet Todd. London: Penguin, 1992.

———. *Maurice; or, The Fisher's Cot.* Ed. Claire Tomalin. London: Viking, 1998.

———. "Modern Italian Romances." *Monthly Chronicle* 2 (November and December 1838): 415–28, 547–57.

———. "Modern Italy." Rev. of *Italy as it Is,* by Henry Digby Beste, and *A Tour in Italy and Sicily,* by Louis Simond. *Westminster Review* 11 (1829): 127–40.

———. *Mythological Dramas:* Proserpine *and* Midas. *Bod MS. Shelley d.2.* Ed. Charles E. Robinson. Vol. 10 of *The Bodleian Shelley Manuscripts.* Gen. Ed. Donald H. Reiman. Facsimile ed. Garland Ser. New York: Garland, 1992.

———. "A Night Scene." *Keepsake for 1831.* Ed. Frederic Mansel Reynolds. London: Longman, 1831. 147–148.

———. *The Novels and Selected Works of Mary Shelley.* Gen. Ed. Nora Crook. 9 vols. London: Pickering, 1996.

———. "O listen while I sing to thee." In *Mary Shelley: Author of* Frankenstein. By Elizabeth Nitchie. New Brunswick, N.J.: Rutgers University Press, 1953. 234–35.

———. "On Ghosts." *London Magazine* 9 (1824): 253–56.

———. "On Reading Wordsworth's Lines on Peel Castle." In *Mary Shelley: A Biography.*

By R. Glynn Grylls. New York: Haskell House, 1969. 302–03.

———, trans. *Relation of the Death of the Family of the Cenci. Bodleian MS.Shelley adds.e.13.* Ed. Betty T. Bennett. Vol. 10 of *The Bodleian Shelley Manuscripts.* Gen. Ed. Donald H. Reiman. Facsimile ed. Garland Ser. New York: Garland, 1992.

———. Rev. of *1572 Chronique du Temps de Charles IX,* by Prosper Mérimée. *Westminster Review* 13 (1830): 495–502.

———. Rev. of *The Bravo; a Venetian Story,* by James Fenimore Cooper. *Westminster Review* 16 (1832): 180–92.

———. Rev. of *Cloudesley; A Tale,* by William Godwin. *Blackwood's Edinburgh Magazine* 27 (1830): 711–16.

———. Rev. of *The English in Italy,* by Constantine Henry Phipps, *Continental Adventures. A Novel,* by Charlotte Ann Eaton, and *Diary of an Ennuyée,* by Anna Brownell Jameson. *Westminster Review* 6 (1826): 325–41.

———. Rev. of *The Loves of the Poets,* by Anna Brownell Jameson. *Westminster Review* 11 (1829): 472–77.

———. "Stanzas: 'How like a star.' " *Keepsake for 1839.* Ed. Frederic Mansel Reynolds. London: Longman, 1839. 179.

———. "Stanzas: 'I must forget.' " *Keepsake for 1833.* Ed. Frederic Mansel Reynolds. London: Longman, 1833. 52.

———. "Stanzas: 'O, Come to me in dreams.' " *Keepsake for 1839.* Ed. Frederic Mansel Reynolds. London: Longman, 1839. 201.

———. "Stanzas: The Tide of Time Was at my Feet." In *Mary Shelley dans son Oeuvre.* By Jean de Palacio. Paris: Klinckslieck, 1969. 634.

———. "Stanzas: 'To love in solitude and mystery.' " In "Newly Uncovered Letters and Poems by Mary Wollstonecraft Shelley: ('It was my birthday and it pleased me to tell the people so—')." By Betty T. Bennett. *Keats-Shelley Journal* 46 (1997): 73.

———. "Tempo è ben di Morire." In *Mary Shelley: Author of* Frankenstein. By Elizabeth Nitchie. New Brunswick, N.J.: Rutgers University Press, 1953. 231–33.

———. "The Death of Love." In "Newly Uncovered Letters and Poems by Mary Wollstonecraft Shelley: ('It was my birthday and it pleased me to tell the people so—')." By Betty T. Bennett. *Keats-Shelley Journal* 46 (1997): 72–73.

———. "To Jane." In *Mary Shelley: A Biography.* By R. Glynn Grylls. New York: Haskell House, 1969. 303.

———. "Untitled: 'Fair Italy!' " In "Newly Uncovered Letters and Poems by Mary Wollstonecraft Shelley: ('It was my birthday and it pleased me to tell the people so—')." By Betty T. Bennett. *Keats-Shelley Journal* 46 (1997): 73–74.

———. *Valperga: or, the Life and Adventures of Castruccio, Prince of Lucca.* 3 vols. London: Whittaker, 1823.

———. *Valperga: or, the Life and Adventures of Castruccio, Prince of Lucca.* Ed. Stuart Curran. New York: Oxford University Press, 1997.

———. *Valperga: or, the Life and Adventures of Castruccio, Prince of Lucca.* Ed. Tilottama Rajan. Peterborough, Ont.: Broadview, 1998.

———. *Valperga; or, The Life and Adventures of Castruccio, Prince of Lucca.* Ed. Michael Rossington. Oxford: Oxford University Press, 2000.

———. "A Visit to Brighton." *London Magazine* 16 (1826): 460–66.

Shelley, Percy Bysshe. *Shelley's Poetry and Prose.* Ed. Donald H. Reiman and Sharon B. Powers. Norton Critical ed. New York: Norton, 1977.

Sheridan, Frances Chamberlaine. *The History of Nourjahad.* London: Dodsley, 1767.

Sheridan, Richard Brinsley. *Plays.* Ed. Cecil Price. London: Oxford University Press, 1975.

Simon, Kate. *Italy: The Places in Between.* New York: Harper, 1970.

Simond, Louis. *A Tour in Italy and Sicily.* London: Longman, 1828.

Sismondi, J. C. L. Simonde de. *History of the Italian Republics; or, the Origin, Progress, and*

Bibliography

    Fall of Italian Freedom. Philadelphia: Carey, 1832.

Smiles, Samuel. *A Publisher and His Friends: Memoir and Correspondence of the Late John Murray, with an Account of the Origin and Progress of the House, 1768–1843*. 2 vols. London: Murray, 1891.

Somerset Fry, Plantagenet. *The Kings & Queens of England & Scotland*. New York: Grove, 1990.

Sophocles. *The Three Theban Plays:* Antigone, Oedipus the King, Oedipus at Colonus. Trans. Robert Fagles. New York: Viking, 1982.

Soukup, Vladimaír. *Prague*. Gen. Ed. Heather Jones. Eyewitness Travel Guide Ser. New York: DK, 1996.

Spence, Joseph. *Anecdotes, Observations and Characters of Books and Men: Collected from the Conversation of Mr. Pope and Other Eminent Persons of His Time*. 1820. Ed. Bonamy Dobrée. Carbondale: Southern Illinois University Press, 1964.

Spencer, Edmund. *Travels in Circassia, Krim Tartary, &c., Including a Steam Voyage Down the Danube, From Vienna to Constantinople and Round the Black Sea, in 1836*. 2 vols. Westmead: Gregg, 1971.

———. *The Works of Edmund Spenser*. Ed. Edwin Greenlaw et al. Variorum ed. 10 vols. Baltimore: Johns Hopkins University Press, 1932–57.

———. "Ruines of Rome." *The Shorter Poems of Edmund Spenser*. Yale ed. Ed. William A. Oram et al. New Haven, Conn.: Yale University Press, 1989.

Spritzer, Lois, ed. *Birnbaum's '94 Berlin*. New York: HarperCollins, 1993.

Staël, Madame de. *Corinne, or Italy*. Trans. Avriel H. Goldberger. New Brunswick, N.J.: Rutgers University Press, 1987.

Stafford, Fiona, ed. *Lodore*. By Mary Shelley. Vol. 6 of *The Novels and Selected Works of Mary Shelley*. Gen. Ed. Nora Crook. 9 vols. London: Pickering, 1996.

Starke, Mariana. *Information and Directions for Travellers on the Continent*. 5th ed. London: Murray, 1824.

———. *Travels in Europe: For the Use of Travellers on the Continent and Likewise in the Island of Sicily: to Which is Added an Account of the Remains of Ancient Italy and Also of the Roads Leading to Those Remains*. 8th ed. Paris: Galignani, 1833.

Steinberg, S. H., ed. *Cassell's Encyclopedia of World Literature*. 3 vols. London: Cassell, 1973.

Sterne, Laurence. *A Sentimental Journey through France and Italy*. In *Sterne*. Ed. Douglas Grant. Cambridge, Mass.: Harvard University Press, 1970. 525–629.

Stories from the Thousand and One Nights: The Arabian Nights' Entertainments. Trans. Edward William Lane. Rev. by Stanley Lane-Poole. New York: Collier, 1909.

Storti, Amedeo. *A Practical Guide of Venice: With Brief Notes on the Pilings, the Mosaics, the Architectural Styles*. Venice: Storti, 1962–63.

Sunstein, Emily W. *Mary Shelley: Romance and Reality*. Baltimore: Johns Hopkins University Press, 1989.

Sweetman, John. *A Dictionary of European Land Battles: from the Earliest Times to 1945*. London: Hale, 1984.

Swift, Jonathan. *Gulliver's Travels*. Ed. Paul Turner. World's Classics ed. Oxford: Oxford University Press, 1996.

Tacitus. *The Complete Works of Tacitus*. Trans. Alfred John Church and William Jackson Brodribb. Ed. Moses Hadas. Modern Library ed. New York: Random, 1942.

Tasso, Torquato. *Jerusalem Delivered*. Trans. Ralph Nash. Detroit: Wayne State University Press, 1987.

Terry, Arthur. Introduction. *Ausias March: Selected Poems*. By Ausias March. Ed. and trans. Arthur Terry. Edinburgh Bilingual Library Ser. 12. Edinburgh: Edinburgh University Press, 1976. 1–25.

Timbs, John. *Abbeys, Castles, and Ancient Halls of England and Wales; Their Legendary Lore and Popular History*. Ed. Alexander Gunn. 3 vols. London: Warne, 1872.

———. *Curiosities of London; Exhibiting the Most Rare and Remarkable Objects of Interest in* the Metropolis, with Nearly Fifty Years' Personal Recollections. London: Virtue, 1867.

Todd, Janet. *Mary Wollstonecraft: A Revolutionary Life*. New York: Columbia University Press, 2000.

———, ed. *Matilda*. By Mary Shelley. In *Mary Wollstonecraft: Mary, Maria; Mary Shelley: Matilda*. London: Penguin, 1992.

Tomalin, Claire. Introduction. *Maurice, or the Fisher's Cot*. By Mary Shelley. Ed. Claire Tomalin. London: Viking, 1998. 1–54.

———. *The Life and Death of Mary Wollstonecraft*. London: Weidenfeld, 1974.

Tomes, John. *Scotland*. 7th ed. Chicago: Rand McNally, 1977.

Trevelyan, Raleigh. *Princes under the Volcano*. London: Macmillan, 1972.

Tripp, Edward. *The Meridian Handbook of Classical Mythology*. New York: Meridian, 1974.

Tschudi, Clara. *Augusta, Empress of Germany*. Trans. E. M. Cope. London: Swan, 1900.

Tucker, Alan, gen. ed. *The Berlitz Travellers Guide: Berlin*. New York: Berlitz, 1993.

Turner, Jane, ed. *The Dictionary of Art*. 34 vols. New York: Macmillan, 1996.

Untermeyer, Louis. *Blue Rhine, Black Forest: A Hand- & Day-book*. London: Harrap, 1930.

Vargo, Lisa, ed. *Lodore*. By Mary Shelley. Peterborough, Ont.: Broadview, 1997.

Vasari, Giorgio. *Lives of Seventy of the Most Eminent Painters, Sculptors and Architects*. Ed. E. H. and E. W. Blashfield and A. A. Hopkins. 4 vols. London: Bell, 1897.

Villani, Giovanni. *Villani's Chronicle: Being Selections from the First Nine Books of the Chroniche Fiorentine of Giovanni Villani*. Ed. Philip Wicksteed. Trans. Rose E. Selfe. London: Constable, 1906.

Virgil, Publius Vergilius Maro. *Aeneid*. Trans. Michael Oakley. London: Dent, 1964.

———. *The Eclogues and Georgics of Virgil*. Trans. C. Day Lewis. Garden City, N.Y.: Anchor, 1964.

———. *The Eclogues of Virgil*. Trans. A. J. Boyle. Melbourne: Hawthorn, 1976.

Viviani della Robbia, Enrica. *Vita di una donna (l'Emily di Shelley)*. Florence: Sansoni, 1936.

Volney, C[onstantine]. F[rancis]. *The Ruins, or, Meditation on the Revolutions of Empires: and the Law of Nature*. New York: Eckler, 1926.

Wall, Bernard. *Italian Art, Life and Landscape*. New York: Harper, 1964.

Walpole, Horace. "To Sir Horace Mann." 30 May 1751. Letter 228 of *Letters of Horace Walpole, Earl of Oxford, to Sir Horace Mann, British Envoy at the Court of Tuscany*. Ed. George James Welbore Agar-Ellis Dover. 2 vols. New York: Dearborn, 1833.

Warner, Charles Dudley, ed. *Biographical Dictionary and Synopsis of Books Ancient and Modern*. Detroit: Gale, 1965.

Warrack, John. *Carl Maria von Weber*. 2nd ed. Cambridge: Cambridge University Press, 1976.

Weinreb, Ben, and Christopher Hibbert, eds. *The London Encyclopaedia*. London: Macmillan, 1983.

White, Newman Ivey. *Shelley*. 2 vols. New York: Octagon, 1972.

Williamson, George C., ed. *Bryan's Dictionary of Painters and Engravers*. By Michael Bryan. Rev. 4th ed. 5 vols. London: Bell, 1903.

Wilson, James. *The Poets and Poetry of Scotland: From the Earliest to the Present Time Comprising Characteristic Selections from the Works of the More Noteworthy Scottish Poets with Biographical and Critical Notices*. 2 vols. London: Blackie, 1876.

Wilson, John. *The City of the Plague and Other Poems*. Ed. Donald H. Reiman. Garland Facsimile ed. New York: Garland, 1979.

Wollstonecraft, Mary. *Collected Letters of Mary Wollstonecraft*. Ed. Ralph M. Wardle. Ithaca, N.Y.: Cornell University Press, 1979.

———. *Letters Written During a Short Residence in Sweden, Norway, and Denmark*. Ed. Carol H. Poston. Lincoln: University of Nebraska Press, 1976.

Woodford, Susan. *The Art of Greece and Rome*. New York: Cambridge University Press, 1982.

Woolf, Stuart. *A History of Italy, 1700–1860: The Social Constraints of Political Change*. London: Methuen, 1979.

Bibliography

Wordsworth, William. *Poetical Works*. Ed. Thomas Hutchinson. Oxford: Oxford University Press, 1985.

Young, Edward. *The Complaint: or, Night-Thoughts on Life, Death, and Immortality*. Philadelphia: Jacobs, 1894.

Young, George, trans. *The Dramas of Sophocles Rendered in English Verse, Dramatic & Lyric*. By Sophocles. London: Dent, 1906.

Young, Peter, and Michael Calvert. *A Dictionary of Battles 1816–1976*. London: New English Library, 1977.

Zimmerman, Phyllis. "Some Lines of Italian Poetry in the Introduction to *The Last Man*." *Notes and Queries* 235 (1990): 31–32.

Zorzi, Alvise. *Venetian Palaces*. New York: Rizzoli, 1990.

Index

Pages in **bold** indicate the location of the main entry.

Addison, Joseph, **4**
Adriatic Sea, **5**
Aegean Sea, **5**
Aesop, 231
Africa, **6**, 325; Barbary, **33**; Carthage, **72**; Golden Coast, **176**; Good Hope, Cape of, **70**; Libya, **247**
Agrippa von Nettesheim, Cornelius, **6**
Albani, Cardinal Guiseppe, **7**
Albania, **7**; Acroceraunia, **4**; Argyro-Castro, **21**; Arnaout, **22**; Butrinto, **62**; Korvo, **232**; Tepeleni, **437**; Trebucci, Mount, **446**
Albert, Prince, **7**
Albert the Great, **7**
Albertus Magnus, **7**
Albigenses, **7**
Alcibiades, **8**
Alexander the Great, **8–9**, 338
Alfieri, Vittorio, **9**, 305; *Myrrha*, 9, **299**
Ali, Mohammed, **9–10**
Alison, Archibald, **10**; *History of Europe*, 10
Allah, **10**
Allori, Alessandro, **10**
Alpha, **10–11**
Alps, **11**; Dazio Grande, **109**; Julian Alps, **226**; Jura, **227**; Ligurian Alps, **248**; Montanvers, **289–90**; Mont Blanc, 78, **288**; St. Bernardin, **385**; Simplon Pass, **416**; Stelvio, **425**; Strub Pass, **427**; Titi-See, **441**
Altissimo, Cristofano, **11**
Amari, Michele, **12**; *Guerra del Vespro Sicilianno*, 12; *Un Periodo delle storie Siciliane*, 12
America, **12–13**, 92, 367; Niagara Falls, **304**. *See also* individual countries
Andrea del Sarto, **14–15**; *Andrea senza Errori*, 15
Andryane, Alexandre Philippe, **15**
Angelico, Fra [Guido di Pietro], **15**, 305, 462; *Deposition*, 15; Fra Giovanni of Fiesole, 15
Anspach, Margrave of, **15**
Anstey, Christopher, **15**
Antonello of Messina, **16**
Antoninus: Marcus, **16**; Pius, **16**
Antony, Marc, 16–17
Arabia, **18–19**
Arabian Nights, **19**, 474; Ahmed, Prince, 19; Aladdin, 19; Ali, Prince, 19; Badroulboudour, Princess, 19; Barmecide, 19; Houssain, Prince, 19; Scheherazade, 19
Araby, 18
Argiropoulo, Prince and Princess, 21
Ariosto, **21–22**, 43, 48, 92, 314; **441**; *Orlando Furioso* (Angelica, 21)

517

Index

Aristides, 22
Aristotle, 22
Arius, **21**
Armenia, 22
Arrivabene, Count Giovanni, **23**
Artemesia, 23
Arthur, Prince of Wales, **23**
Asia, **24–25**, 450; Asiatics, 24; Caspian Sea, **73**; Lydian, **261**; Ottoman Empire, **316**; Parthian Pestilence, **326**; Phrygia, **338**. *See also* individual countries
Aspern, Battle of, **25**
Athanasius, **25**
Atlantic Ocean, **26**
Atlantis, **26**
Auber, Daniel François Esprit, **26–27**; *Masaniello*, 26–27
Aurelius, Marcus, **27**
Australia, New Holland, **303**
Austria, **27**; Ampezzo, **13**; Bad Gastein, **31**; Berg Isel, **41–42**; Brenner, **54**; Brenner Pass, **54**; Ebensee, **124**; Eisach, **127**; Gmunden, **172**; Gmunden Lake, **172**; Hall, **188**; Hallstadt, Lake, **188**; Innsbruck, **214**; Ischl, **218**; Lambach, **238**; Linz, **249** (Goldener Lowe, **176**); Mittewald, **286**; St. Wolfgang Lake, **390–91**; Salzburg, **391** (Erzherzog Carl, **133**); Salzer, **391**; Salzkammergut, **391**; Schwaz, **399**; Sill, **416**; Sterzinger Moos, **425–26**; Styria, **427**; Traun, **445–46**; Traunstein, **446**; Tyrol, 27, **454**; Unter Innthal, **457**; Vienna, **466–67**; Villach, **467**; Vorarlberg, **470**; Waidring, **471**; Waidringen, **471**; Walen, **471**; Wallenstadt, **471**; Zurich, **488**
Austria, Don John of, **27–28**

B——, Prince, **30**
Bacon, Francis, **30–31**, 333
Baden, Grand Duke of, **31**
Baldelli, Giovanni Battista, **32**
Baltic Sea, **32**
Bandello, Matteo, **32**
Banditti, **32**
Barbarossa, Frederic, **33**
Barbatelli, Bernardino, **33**, 385
Basle, Council of, **34**
Bassano, Jacopo, **34**

Baxter: William Thomas, **36**, 50; Christina, 36
Bayard, Pierre Terrail, **36**
Beaumarchais, Augustin Caron de, 33
Beauclerk: Aubrey William, **37**, 328; George Robert, **37**; Rosa Matilda, **37–38**, 374
Beaumont, Sir Francis, **38**; *Custom of the Country*, **103**
Beccaria, Cesare, **39**
Beckford, William, **39**
Beddoes, Thomas, **39**
Belgium, **39–40**; Antwerp, **17**; Audenarde, **27**; Brabant, **53**; Brussels, **58**; Malines, **268**; Tournai, **444**
Bell, Andrew, 40
Bellini: Gentile, **40**; Giovanni, **40**, 391, 394; Vincenzo, **40**, 328
Berchet, Giovanni, **41**, 94; *Leonora of Burgher*, 41
Berkeley, George, **42**
Berni, Francesco, **42–43**, 48
Berthier, Louis Alexandre, **43**
Beste, Henry, 286
Bethmann, Simon Moritz von, **43**
Bianchi, **43–44**, 341
Bianco, Carlo, **44**
Bible, **44**; Abel, 66; Absalom, 3; Adam, 4, 322; Agnus Dei, 6; Ahasuerus, 134; Ancilla Dei, 14; Apocrypha, 18; Ave Maria, 28; Babel, 30; Cain, 66; David, 109; De Profundis, 110; Ecclesiastes, 124–25; Eden, 125; Elias, 129; Esther, 134; Eve, 136–37, 322; Gabriel, 162; Genesis, 165; Gospel, 178; Hagar, 187; Heliodorus, 194, 313; Holy Land, 203, 321; Joachim, 224; Job, 224; Joseph, 225; Lamentations, 238; Maccabees, 313, 264; Magi 266; Mary, 274; Miserere, 286; Noah, 30, 306; Onias, 313; Psalms, 109; **353–54**; Raphael, 360; Red Sea, 362; Samaritan, **391–92**; Samson, 392; Satan, 260, 322, 396; Seleucus, **400–401**; Simon, 416; Solomon, 109, **419**; Solomon's Song, **419**; Wandering Jew, 472
Biscay, Bay of, **45**
Black Sea, **45**
Blamire, Susanna, **46**
Blondel, **46**
Blücher, Gebhard Leberecht von, **46**

518

Boccaccio, Giovanni di, **47**, 271, 318, 342, 449; *Decameron*, 52, 240
Bohemia, 31, **47–48**
Boieldieu, François-Adrien, **48**; *Die weise Frau*, 48; *La Dame Blanche*, 48, 282
Boileau-Despréaux, Nicholas, **48**, 358
Bojardo, Matteo Maria, 42–43, **48**, 314
Bologna, John of, **48**
Bonaparte: Lucien, 30; Napoleon, 25, 30, 40, 43, **49**, 54, 98, 99, 122, 127, 159, 225, 271, 291, 297, 341, 350, 423, 467, 471, 473, 480
Bonifazio, Veronese, **49**
Booth: Catherine, 51; David, 36, **50**; Isabel Baxter, **50–51**, 305, 378; Margaret, 50
Borromeo, **51**; Cardinal Carlo, **51**; Federigo, 52
Boscán, Almugáver, Mosen Juan, **52**
Botta: Carlo, **52**; Giuseppe, **52**; Guglielmo, **52**
Bourbons, **53**
Brambilla, Teresa, **53**
Brennus, **54**
Brentani, **54–55**; Battista, 54; Bernardo, 54; Giovanni, 54; Luigi, 54; Paolo, 54; Peppina, 54
"Bride of Modern Italy, The" (Shelley), **55**, 469; Alleyn, Marcott, **10**; Eusta, **136**; Magni, Cieco, **266**; *Profession of Eloisa*, **351**; Romani, **367**; St. S——Convent, **389**; Saviani, **396** (Clorinda, **396**); Superior, **428**; Tolomei (Giacomo de', **443**; Teresa de', **443**)
Bridgewater Collection, **55–56**
Brockedon, William, **56–57**
"Brother and Sister, The" (Shelley), **57**; Mancini, **268** (Flora, **268–69**; Lorenzo, **269**; Ugo, **269**); Sandra, **393**; Tolomei, **442** (Count Fabian de', **443**; Countess de', **443**)
Brown, Charles Brockden, **57–58**; *Arthur Mervyn*, 58
Browne, Sir Thomas, 58, 342
Brutus: Lucius Junius, **58**; Marcus Junius, **59**
Buffon, Comte George-Louis Leclerc de, **59**
Bulwer-Lytton, Edward George, **59–60**; *Paul Clifford*, 59–60
Burchiello, **60**
Burghersh, Lord, **61**
Burgundy, **61**; Duke of, **61**; Mary of, **61**
Burke, Edmund, **61–62**, 378, 481
Burns, Robert, **62**
Byron, Clara Allegra, **63**, 84, 87, 89, 151, 204, 361, 463

Byron, **63–64**, 87, 95, 151, 153, 157, 163, 184, 200, 204, 207, 219, 276, 279, 291, 298, 313, 315, 327, 331, 345, 352, 361, 408, 410, 411, 412, 423, 429, 437, 445, 447, 462, 463; Albé, 64; *Bride of Abydos, The*, **55**, 63; *Childe Harold's Pilgrimage*, 63, **82–83**, 321, 368, 396, 488; *Corsair*, **98**, 63; "Darkness," 240; *Don Juan*, 63 (Haidée, **187**); *Heaven and Earth*, 63, **192–93**; "Lament of Tasso, The," 63, **238**; *Mazeppa*, 63, **277**; "Ode on Venice," 63, **311**; "On this day I complete," **313**; "Prisoner of Chillon," 63, 83, **350**; *Sardanapalus*, 63, **395–96**; "Stanzas for Music," 63, **424**; *Two Foscari, The*, 63, 153, **453**; *Werner*, **474**; Villa Diodati, 41, **115**, 345
Byzantine, **64**

C——, Lord, **65**
Cadmus, Dan, **65**
Caesar: Julius, **65–66**, 346, 381; Octavius, 66
Calderón de la Barca, Pedro, **67**, 236, 446
Caloyer, **67**
Calvin, John, **67**
Calvinist, **67–68**
Camillus, Marcus Furius, **68**
Camoens, Luis Vaz de Diaresis, **68**
Campbell, Thomas, **68–69**, 240
Canada, **69**; Niagara Falls, 304
Canal, Giovanni Antonio, **69**
Candiano, Tommaso, **69**
Canosa, Prince of, **70**
Canova, Antonio, **70**; *Cupid and Psyche*, 70; *Hebe*, 70
Cantabs, **70**
Capponi, Gino, **71**
Capuchin, **71**
Caracalla, Marcus Aurelius, **71**
Carbonari, 66, 70, **71**, 74, 98, 269, 297, 340, 347; Buoni Cugini, 60; Giovane Italia, La, **170**
Caroccio, **72**
Caroline, Queen, **72**
Carracci, Annibale, **72**; *Angel of Fame*, 72
Cassius, Gaius Longinus, **73**
Castelbarco, Guglielmo da, **73**
Castillejo, Cristóbal, **74**
Catiline, Lucius Sergius, **74**
Cato, Marcus Porcius, **74–75**

Index

Catullus, Gaius Valerius, **75**; "Ad Sirmionem Peninsulum," 75
Caucasus, Mount, **75**
Cavalcanti, Guido, **75**
Cellini, Benvenuto, **75**; *Perseus*, 75
Celt, **75**
Cenci, Beatrice, **76**, 185, 304, 363
Cerito, Fanny, **77**, 433
Cervantes Saavedra, Miguel de, **77**; *Don Quixote*, 77 (Don Quixote, **118–19**; Dulcinea, 118; Sancho Panza, 118, **393**)
Chaldee, **78**
Chamber of Peers, **78**
Charlemagne, **79**, 314, 354
Charles I, **79**
Charles II, **79**
Charles IV (France), **79**
Charles IV (Germany), **79**
Charles V, **79**
Charles VI, **79–80**
Charles VIII, **80**
Charles of Anjou, **80**, 433
Charles the Bold, **80**, 300
Charlotte Sophia, Queen, **80–81**, 479
Chastellain, Georges, 61, **81**, 333
Chaucer, Geoffrey, **81**, 320, 336, 450, 453
Chiabrera, Gabbriello, **82**
Chiaro Oscuro, **82**
China, **83**; Peking, **331**
Chiverton Park, **83–84**
Cicero, Marcus Tullius, **84–85**, 451; Cicerone, Villa di, 84, 162; Tusculan Questions, 85
Cincinnatus, Lucius Quinctius, **85**
Cinderella, **85–86**
Cleopatra, 16–17
Clairmont, Charles Gaulis, **86**, 172, 173, 317, 466
Clairmont, Claire [Jane], 8, 51, 63, 86, **87–88**, 103, 151, 152, 172, 173, 200, 204, 219, 232, 294, 318, 328, 330–31, 365, 374, 381, 403, 408, 410, 411, 447, 463
Claude Gellée Lorrain, **88**
Clement IV, Pope, **89**
Cleveland, John, **89**
Coleridge, Henry Nelson, **90**; *Six Months in the West Indies*, 90
Coleridge, Samuel Taylor, **90–91**, 173, 344, 399, 410, 482, 487; "Christabel," 84, 91; "Death of Wallenstein, The," **110–11**; "Fire, Famine, and Slaughter," 91, **148**; "Rime of the Ancient Mariner, The," 90, 371
Colletta, Pietro, 66, 70, **91**, 122, 269, 297, 433; *History of the Death of Murat*, 91; *History of the Kingdom of Naples*, 91; *Narrative of the Revolution of Naples*, 91; *Storia del reame di Napoli*, 91
Colonna, Vittoria, **92**
Columbus, Christopher, **92**
Combes, Colonel Michel, **93**
Compagni, Dino, **93**
Condorcet, Marquis Marie Jean Antoine, **94**
Confalonieri, Federico, **94**
Conradin, **94**, 433
Constance, **94–95**
Constantine XI Palaiologos, **95**
Cooper, James Fenimore, **96**, 366; *Bravo, The*, 96; *Excursions in Italy*, 96; *Spy, The*, 96
Coriolanus, **97**
Cornaro, Catherine, **97**
Corneille, Pierre, **97**, 358
Cornwall, Barry, 350
Correggio, Allegri Antonio, 82, **98**, 266; *Io*, 98; *La Notte*, 98; *Leda and the Swan*, 98
Cosimo I, **99**
Council of Ten, **99**
Count——, **99**
Coutts' *lettre d'indication*, **99–100**
Cowper, William, **100**
Cromwell, Oliver, **101**, 306, 380
Cumberland, Richard, **101–2**; *Wheel of Fortune, The*, 102
Cupid and Psyche, **102**
Curius Dentatus Manius, **103**
Curran, Amelia, **103**
Curran, John, 103
Custine, Astolphe Marquis de, **103**
Cyprus, **104**
Czech Republic: Baths of Bohemia, 30; Bohemia, 31, **47–48**; Brünn, **58** (Spielburg, 331, **422**); Budweis, **59** (Goldene Sonne, **176**); Doxan, **120**; Herrnsdretschen, **198**; Kamnitz, **228**; Laurenzi Berg, **243**; Lovosice, **259**; Moldau, **287**; Moravia, **292**; Mulchen, **297**; Prague, 349 (Altstadt **12**; Bridge, **179**; Drei Linden, **121**; Graben, **178**; Green Chamber, **181**; Hradschin, **207**; Kleine

Seite, **231**; Neustadt, **303**; Schwarzes Ross, **399**); Saubach, **396**; Schandau, **398**; Tabor, **432**; Tätchen, **435**; Teplice, **437**; Znaim, **488**

D——, **106**
d'Azeglio, Massimo Taparelli, **106**; *Ettore Fieramosca*, 106; *Niccolò de'Lapi*, 106
d'Hembyza, Antoine Ghislain, **86**
d'Hilliers, Baraguay, **106**
Dandolo, Cenone, **107**
Dannecker, Johann Heinrich von, 43, **107**; *Ariadne*, 107
Dante, 75, 81, **107**–**8**, 170, 278, 441, 460; Beatrice, **37**, 324, 354; *Divine Comedy*, 107, **116** (*Inferno*, 52, 107, 147, 155, **213**–**14**; *Paradiso*, 107, **324**, 441; *Purgatorio*, 107, **354**–**55**)
Danube, **108**
Darwin, Erasmus, **108**–**9**
Dauphin, **109**
Davy, Sir Humphry, **109**, 157
Deffell, George, **111**, 359
Defoe, Daniel, **112**, 240, 342; *Robinson Crusoe*, 112
Del Carretto, Marchese Francesco Saverio, **112**
Della Crusca Academy, **112**, 301, 305
Deo, Emanuel de, **113**
Despans de Cubières, **114**
Diet of Worms, **115**
Dietfurth, **115**
Diorama, **115**
Dods, Mary Diana, **116**–**17**, 373
Dogana, **117**
Dolci, Carlo, **117**
Domenchino, **118**; *Last Communion of St. Jerome*, 118
Dominican, **118**
Domitian, Titus Flavius, **118**
Don Pedro II, **118**
Donatello, **119**; *David*, 119
Donizetti, Gaetano, **119**, 391; *Elisir d'Amore*, 119; *Lucia di Lammermoor*, 119 ("Bell' Alma innamorata," 119)
Donna Estatica, **119**
Doric, **119**–**20**
Douglas, Mr. Sholto. *See* Dods, Mary Diana
Douglas, Mrs. *See* Robinson, Isabel
Draco, **120**

"Dream, The" (Shelley), **121**; Manon, **269**; Paynim, **330**; St. Catherine, **385**; Vaudemont, Gaspar de, **463**; Villeneuve (Chateau, **467**; Countess Constance, **467**)
Duc d'Enghien, **122**
Dutch, **123**

East India Company, **124**, 331
Easterlings, **124**
Eaton, Charlotte, **124**, 366; Rome in the Nineteenth Century, 124
Edwards, Dr., **126**
Egypt, **126**–**27**; Aegyptian Day **5**; Alexandria, **9**; Nile, **305**; Pyramids, **355**
"Eighteenth-Century Tale, An" (Shelley), **127**: Graham, Maria Langley, **178**
Elba, **127**
Elbe, **127**
"Elder Son, The" (Shelley), **127**–**28**; Beech Grove, **39**; Ellen, **130**; Gray (Clinton, **179**; Lady, **180**; Marianne, **180**; Sir Richard, **180**; Vernon, **180**); Hythe (Lady Caroline, **210**; Lord, **210**); Towers, Matilda, **444**
Elector of Saxony, **128**
Elector Palatine, **128**–**29**
Elixir of Immortality, **129**
Elizabeth of England, **129**
Elizabeth, Queen, **130**, 362
Ellis, Robert Leslie, 70, 106, **130**, 359
Elton, Charles Abraham, **130**
Embrun, Lady of, **131**
England: Albion, **7**; Avon **28**–**29**; Bath, **35**; Beaulieu, **38**; Bishopsgate, 45, 479; Berkshire, **42**; Bodmin, **47**; Bolter's Lock, **48**; Bosworth Field, **52**; 370, 473; Bournemouth, **53**, 388; Boxhill, **53**; Bracknell, **53**; Brentford, **54**–**55**; Brighton, **56**, 469, (Pavilion, **329**); Bristol, **56**; Buckingham, **59**; Buckinghamshire, **59**; Burford Bridge, **60**; Cader Idris, **65**; Camberwell, **68**; Cambridge, **68** (Cantabs, **70**); Canterbury, **70**; Carlisle, **71**; Cheltenham, **82**; Chester, **82**; Colchester, **90**; Commonwealth, **93**; Cornwall, **97**–**98**; Coventry, **100**; Cumbria, **102**; Dalston, **107**; Dartford, **108**; Datchet, **109**; Dawlish, **109**; Derby, **113**; Devonshire, **114**; Dolgellau, **118**; Dover, **120**; Downs, **120**; Eastwell Place, **124**; Egham, **126**; Ely, **130**;

521

Index

Englefield Green, **131**; English Channel, **131**–32; Essex, **133**; Exeter, **139**; Fairlight Bay, **141**–42; Flodden Field, **150**; Frogmore Gate, **160**; Gravesend, **179**; Great Park, **180**; Greenwich, **182**; Hampshire, **190**; Hampton, **190**, 360; Harwich, **191**; Hastings, **191**–92, 477; Henley-on-Thames, **194**; Hinckley, **200**; Holyhead, **203**; Hythe, **210**; Ilfracombe, **211**; Isis, **218**; Kent, **229**; Lancashire, **238**; Lancaster, **238**–39; Land's End, **239**; Launceston, **243**; Lea, **244**; Leicester, **245**; Lewes, **247**; Lincoln, **248**; Little Marlow, **249**; Liverpool, **250**; Luton, **261**; London, **255**–56 (Almack's, **10**; Barnes, **33**–34; Berkely Square, **42**; Bermondsey, **42**; Bethlem, **43**; Bishopsgate, **45**; Blackfriars, **45**–46; Blackheath, **46**; Blackwall, **46**; Brixton, **56**; Brook Street, **57**; London Bridge, **256**; Charing Cross, **79**; Cheapside, **81**; Chelmsford, **81**; Chelsea, **81**–82; Drury Lane Theatre, **121**–22; Duke Street, **122**; Edgware, **125**; Fleet, **149**; Fleet Street, **149**; Grosvenor Square, **183**; Hammersley's Bank, **189**; Hampstead, **190**; Holborn, **202**; Hyde Park, **209**–10; Kennington, **229**; Kenwood, **229**; King's Theatre, **231**; London Coffee House, **256**–57; Lothbury, **258**; Ludgate, **260**; Minories, **285**; Mivart's, **286**; Montague Square, **289**; Park Lane, **325**; Piccadilly, **339**; Regent's Park, **362**; Romford, **378**; St. Bartholomew's Hospital, **385**; St. James's, **386**–87; St. Pancras, **53**, 255, **388**; St. Paul's, **388**; St. Stephen's, **389**–90; Seymour Street, **403**; Southwark, **421**; Strand, **426**; Stratton Street, **426**; Temple Bar, **436**; Tower of London, **444**; Tower Yard, **444**; Traitor's Gate, **444**–45; Union Club, **456**; Walbrook, Parish of, **471**; White Tower, **476**; Whitelock, **476**; Westminster Abbey, **475**; Westminster Palace, **475**–76; Wimbledon, **474**; Woolwich **482**); Manchester, **268**; Margate, **271**; Marlow, **272**–73, 468; Matlock, **276**; Milford Haven, **284**; Minehead, **284**–85; Mount's Bay, **294**; New Forest, **303**; Newark-upon-Trent, **304**; Newbury, **304**; Norham Castle, **306**; Northampton, **307**; Old Windsor, **312**; Oxford, **317**; Pendennis, **332**; Fouldrey, Pile of, **154**; Plymouth, **344**; Poole, **347**; Portsmouth, **348**; Putney, **437**; Radnorshire, **359**; Ravenglass, **361**; Reading, **361**; Regent's Cottage, **362**; Richmond, **370**, (Star and Garter, **425**); Rochester, **374**; St. Albans, **384**, 473; St. Leonard's-on-Sea, **387**; St. Mary's, **387**; Saint Michael's Chair/Mount, **388**; Salt Hill, **391**; Sheerness, **406**; Sheriff Hutton, **414**; Shropshire, **414**; Sidmouth, **415**; Slough, **418**; Southampton, **420**–21; Southend-on-Sea, **421**; Staines, **423**; Stanwell, **424**; Stoke, **361**, **426**, 473; Stony Stratford, **426**; Sussex, **428**; Taunton, **435**; Thames, **437**; Tilbury Fort, **440**; Torquay, **443**–44; Tunbridge Wells, **451**; Twickenham, **453**; Ulswater, **455**; Virginia Water, **468**; White Cliffs, 120, **476**; White Sand Bay, **476**; Welford, **474**, Winchelsea, **479**; Windsor, **479** (Chapel Wood, **78**; Little Park, **249**; Long Walk, **257**; St. George's Chapel, **386**); Worcester, **482**; Wye, **484**; Yeovil, **485**; York, **485**; Yorkshire, **485**

Epictetus, **132**

Epicharis, **132**

Equador: Quito, **357**

Ercilla y Zúniga, Alonso de, **132**

Erin, **133**

Espinel, Vicente Martinez, **133**

Eton, **134**

"Euphrasia: A Tale of Greece" (Shelley), **135**–36; Constantine, Chief, **95**; Euphrasia, **135**; Pasha, **327**; Valency, Henry, **458**

Euripedes, 346

Europe, **136**; Flanders, **149** (Ghent, **169**); Scheldt, **398**. *See also* individual countries

"Evil Eye, The" (Shelley), **137**–38; 212: Belouk-Bashee, **41**; Boularias, **52**; Camaraz, **68**; Codja-Bashee, **70**; Dmitri, **116**; Fanar, **144**; Fanariote, **144**; Helena, **194**; Kakaboulia, **228**; Klephts, **231**; Pobratimo, **344**; Protoklepht, **353**; Ziani (Constans, **488**; Cyril, **488**; Katusthius, **488**, Zella, **488**)

F——, Mr., **139**, 296

F——, Mrs., **139**

Fabii, **139**

Fabricius Luscinus Gaius, **139**

Faliero, Alberto, **142**

Falkland, **142**

Falkner (Shelley), 128, **142**, 174, 410; Ashley, Mr., **24**; Baker, Mrs., **32**; Bateman, Captain, **35**; Belleforest, **40**; Carter, Mr., **72**; Cecil (Lady Sophia, **75**; Lord, **75**); Colville, Mr. **93**; Dromore, **121**; Falkner (Elizabeth, **142**; John, **142–43**; Rupert John, **143**); G——, Earl of, **162**; Glenfell, Lady, **172**; Gray, Thomas, **180**; Hillary, **200**; Hoskins, Gregory, **205**; James, **222**; Jervis, Miss, **224**; John Adams, **225**; Julius, **226**; Missy, **286**; Nancy, **300**; Neville (Alithea, **303**; Gerard, **303**; Sir Boyvill, **303**); Oakly, **310**; Osborne, James, **315**; Owyhee, **316**; Raby (Edwin, **358**; Mrs., **358**; Mrs. Isabella, **358**; Oswi, **358**); Rivers (Captain, **372**; Mrs., **372**); Thompson, **438**; Treby, **446**; Vasili, **462**

"False Rhyme, The" (Shelley), **143**; Francis I, **156**; Lagny (Emile de, **236**; Sire Enguerrard de, **236**); Leroux, Robinet, **246**; Margaret, Queen, **271**

famiglia Vianesi, **143**

Fane, John, 61

Fantasmagoriana, 157

Fantozzi, Federigo, **144**; *Nuova Guida*, 144

Father Rhine, **144**

Fénelon, **144–45**, 454; *Les aventures de Télémaque*, 144

Ferdinand II, **145**

Ferdinand III, **145**

Ferdinand IV, **145**

"Ferdinando Eboli: A Tale" (Shelley), **145–46**; Eboli (Count, **124**; Ferdinando, **124**; Ludovico, **124**); Spina (Adalinda, **422**; Marchese, **422**; Villa, **422**)

Ferrara, Cieco da, **146–47**

Ferruccio, Francesco, **147**

Festa d'Inferno, **147**

Ficino, Marsiglio, **147**

Fielding, Henry, **147**; Adams, Parson Abraham, 147

Filicaja, Vincenzo da, **148**

Fitzgerald, Lord Edward, **148**

Fletcher, John, 38, **149–50**; *Custom of the Country*, **103**; *Laws of Candy, The*, **243**; *Two Noble Kinsmen*, 320, **453**

Foggi, Elise, **151–52**, 204, 408

Foggi, Paolo, 151, **152**, 407

Ford, John, **153**; *Lover's Melancholy, The*, **258–59**; *Perkin Warbeck*, 333, **334–35**

Fornarina, **153**

Foscari, Jacopo, **153–54**

Foscolo, Ugo, **154**, 304, 331; *Ultime lettere di Jacopo Ortis*, 154

Fox, Charles James, **154**

France, **154–55**; Aix-la-Chapelle, **3**; Alsatian Hills, **11**; Amiens, **13**; Arve, **24**; Arvéron, **24**; Aube, **26**; Auxerre, **28**; Avignon, **28**; Bagnères de Bigorre, **31**; Bar-sur-Aube, **32–33**; Besançon, **43**; Bordeaux, **51**; Boulogne, **52–53**; Brittany, **56**; Burgundy, **61**; Calais, **66** (Robert's Hotel, **372**); Cenis, Mount, **76**; Cerveaux, **77**; Chablais, **78**; Chalons-sur-Marne, **78**; Chamonix, **78**; Champagnole, **78**; Champlitte, **78**; Charenton-le-Pont, **78**; Chaumont, **81**; Clermont, **89**; Corsica, **98**; Côte d'Or, **99**; Crécy, **100**; Dieppe, **115**; Dijon, **115**; Dôle, **117–18**; Douai, **120**; Echemines, **125**; Evian, **137**; Ferney, **146**; Fountainebleau, **152**; Gex, **168**; Gray, **179**; Guignes, **185**; Havre, **192**; La Maurienne, **234**; Lac Leman, 165, Langres, **239**; Les Rousses, **246**; Liège, **247** (Aigle Noire, **6**); Lille, **248**; Loire, **255**; Lyons, **261–62**; Maison Neuve, **267**; Marseilles, **273**; Metz, **282**; Meuse, **282**; Môle, **287**; Morre, **293**; Moselle, **294**; Nancy, **300**; Nantes, **300**; Navarre, **301**; Nods, **306**; Nogent-sur-Seine, **306**; Ossey-les-Trois-Maisons, **315**; Paris, **324–25** (Avenue des Champs Elysées, **78**; Barrière de l'Etoile, **34**; Bastille, **34**; Boulevards, **52**; Gros Bois, **182**; Hôtel Chatham, **205**; Place de la Concorde, **341**; Place Vendôme, **341**; Rue Saint Honoré, **381**; Saint Denis, **386**; Tuileries, **451**); Pavillon-Ste-Julie, Le, **329**; Plessis, **343**; Poligny, **345**; Pontarlier, **346**; Provence, **353**; Provins, **353**; St. Aubin, **385**; Savoy Alps, **397**; Seine, **400**; Sèvres, **403**; Strasbourg, **426**; Thionville, **438**; Thonon, **438–39**; Toulon, **444**; Trèves, **448**, (Hôtel de Trèves, **205**); Troyes, **450**; Vendeuvre-sur-Barse, **463**; Verdun, **464**; Verdun-sur-Meuse, **464**; Versailles, **465** (Grand Trianon, **179**; Hall of Hercules, **188**); Villeneuvre-la-Guyard, **467**

Francesca da Rimini, **155–56**

523

Index

Francia, Francesco Raibolini, **156**
Francis, Emperor, **156**
Francis I, **156**
Franciscan, **156**
Franconia, **156**
Frankenstein (Shelley), 146, **157–58**, 293, 352, 375, 410, 445: Biron, Louisa, **44**; Clerval, Henry, **89**; Creature, **100**; De Lacey, **110** (Agatha, **110**; Felix, **110**); Duvillard, **123**, 152; Frankenstein (Alphonse, **156**; Caroline, **156–57**; Ernest, **157**; Victor, **157**; William, **157**); Kirwin, **231**; Krempe, **232**; Lavenza (Elizabeth, **243**; Villa, **243**); Manoir, Louis, **269**; Mansfield (Manon, **269**; Miss, **269**); Melbourne, John, Esq., **280**; Moritz, **293** (Justine, **293**; Madame, **293**); Nugent, Daniel, **308**; Safie, **384**; Saville, Margaret, **397**; Tavernier, Madame, **435**; Uncle Thomas, **456**; Waldman, **471**; Walton, Robert, **472**
Franks, **159**
Frederic the Great, **159**
Frederics, **159**
Freemasons, **159**
French Empire, **159**
French Revolution, 34, **159–60**, 341, 462, 465
Fries: Herr, **160**; Madame, **160**
Fulda, Prince-Bishops of, **161**

Galignani, Giovanni, **162–63**
Galileo, **163**, 434
Gallois, Captian Thomas, **163**
Galloni, Laura, 99
Gamba, Pietro, **163**, 184, 313
Garcilaso de la Vega, **164**
Gascon, **164**
Gatteschi, Ferdinando, 359
Gauls, **164**
Gazzaniga, Marietta, **165**
Genlis, Madame de, **166**
George III, **166**
Germany, **167–68**; Aachen, **3**; Aix-la-Chapelle, **3**; Alsatian Hills, **11**; Bad, **31**; Baden-Baden, **31** (Kurhaus, **232–33**); Bastion, **34**; Bavaria, **35–36**; Berlin, **42** (Brandenburg Gate, **54**, 352; Eisengieserei, **127**; Guardhouse, **183**; Italian Opera, **219**; New Museum, **303**; Oranienburg Gate, **314**; Peacock Island, **330**; Platz, **342**; Stadt Rom, **423**; University of, **456**; Unter den Linden, **457**; Zeughaus, **487**); Bernkastel, **43**; Black Forest, **45**; Bonn, **49**; Botenlaube, **52**; Brocklet, **57**; Brükenau, **58** (Hotel of the Post, **205**); Brünn, **58**; Buttlar, **62**; Carlsruhe, **71**; Clêves, **89**; Coblentz, **90** (Geant, **165**; Hôtel Bellevue, **205**); Cochem, **90**; Cologne, **92**; Darmstadt, **108**; Dresden, **121** (Alt Markt, **11**; Gallery in Dresden, **163**; Green Vaults, **181**; Grosse Garten, **182**; Hôtel de Pologne, **205**; Japanese Palace, **224**; Neu Markt, **302**; Terrace of Bruhl, **437**); Ehrenbreitstein, **127**; Eisenach, **127**; Elster, **130**; Ems, **131**; Erfurt, **133**; Ettenheim, **134**; Frankfurt, **158** (Hôtel de Russie, **205**); Freyberg, **160**; Fulda, **161** (St. Michael's Church, **388**); German Ocean, 306; Gotha, **178**; Grosse Winterberg, **182–83**; Hamburg, **188**; Hammelburg, **189**; Heidelberg, **193** (Hall of Knights, **188**; Dwarf, **123**); Hohnstein, **202**; Hollenthal, **203**; Ingolstadt, **214**; Jena, **224**; Karlsbad, **228**; Kissingen, **231** (Kurhaus, **232–33**; Max Brunnen, **277**); Leipzig, **245**; Lenzkirch, **245**; Lohmen, **255**; Lohr, **255**; Main, **267**; Mainz, **267** (Mayence Catherdal, **277**); Mannheim, **269**; Munich, **297**; Nassau, **301**; Neckar, **302**; Offenberg, **312** (La Fortune, **234**); Oos, **313–14**; Pandur, **322**; Pilnitz, **339**; Pisport, **340**; Potsdam, **348**; Prebisch Thor, **349**; Rabenau, **358**; Ragozzi, **359**; Rhine, **367–68**; Saale, **383**; Saxony, **397–98**; Sinn, **416**; Soolensprudel, **420**; Spree, **423**; Stern, **425**; Stolzenfels Castle, **426**; Stuhlingen, **427**; Thuringian Forest, **439**; Trarbach, **445**; Treisam, **446**; Trier, **448**; Uttewalde, **457**; Wartburg Castle, **473**; Weimar, 175, **474**, 477; Weisbaden, **477**; Wurtemburg, **484**; Wurzburg, **484**
Ghibelline, **169**, 183, 344
Ghirlandajo, **169**, 339, 462; *Adoration of the Magi, The*, 169; *Death of St. Francis*, 169; *Life of St. Francis, The*, 169
Gibbon, Edward, 157, **169**
Gibson, John, **169**
Gillows, **169–70**
Gioja, Melchiore, 94, **170**

524

Giorgione, 40, **170**; *Rebecca at the Well*, 170
Giornico, **170**
Giotto, 37, 69, **170**, 355
Giovio, Paolo, **171**
Gisborne: John, **171**, 363, 409; Maria, **171**, 219, 363, 365, 407, 409
Godiva, Lady, 443
Godwin, Fanny [Imlay], 144, 157, 171, **172**, 173, 212, 327, 480, 481
Godwin, Mary Jane Clairmont, 86, 87, 171, **172–73**, 175, 410
Godwin, William (Shelley's father), 50, 53, 59, 69, 86, 87, 90, 103, 116, 122, 128, 157, 158, 171, 172, **173–75**, 202, 212, 243, 275, 292, 293, 294, 298, 327, 333, 362, 365, 371, 375, 388, 408, 410, 411, 433, 452, 461, 475, 481, 483; *Cloudesley*, 365–66
Godwin, William (Shelley's half-brother), 173, **175**
Goethe, Johann Wolfgang von, 107, **175–76**, 270, 396; *Faust*, 175; Goethe House, 175; *Sorrows of Young Werter, The*, 175, **420**; "Wilhelm Meister," 175
Goldoni, Carlo, **176**
Goldsmith, Oliver, **176–77**; "Goody Two-shoes," 177; *Vicar of Wakefield, The*, 176–77
Góngora y Argote, Luis de, **177**
Gordian knot, **177**
Goring: George, **178**; Ida, 37
Gracchi, **178**
Granville, Augustus, **179**
Greece, **180–81**; Acarnania, 3–4; Aegina, 5; Athens, 25–26 (Acropolis, 4; Piraeus, **340**; Propylaeum, **352**); Antiparos, 16; Arcadia, **20**; Arta, **23**; Athos, Mount, 26; Attica, 26; Basilika, **34**; Boeotian, **47**; Cefalonia, **75**; Cerigo, **77**; Corinth, **96–97**; Crete, **101** (Ida, **211**); Cyclades, **104**; Eleusis, **129**; Epirus, **132**; Férrai, **146**; Haemus, **187**; Hebrus, **193**; Hymettus, **210**; Ioannina, **215**; Ionian Isles, **215**; Isthmus of Corinth, **218**; Kalamas, **228**; Kardamyla, **228**; Larissa, **240**; Lepanto, **246**; Macedonia, **264**; Maina, **267** (Mainotes, 267); Makri, **267**; Marathon, **270**; Mosme, **294**; Naxos, **301**; Oeta, **312**; Parnassus, **326**; Peloponnese, **331–32**; Peneus, **332**; Prevesa, **349–50**; Rodosto, **374**; Sagori, **384**; Santa Maura, **394**; Scio, **399**; Sparta, **421–22**; Suli, **427**; Sybarite, **430**; Taenarus, Cape, **433**; Thermopylae, **438**; Thessaly, **438**; Thrace, **439**; Zante, **487**; Zitza, **488**; Zoumerkas, **488**
Greek mythology. *See* Mythology
Greenland, **181**
Gregory VII, Pope, **182**
Gregory XIV, Pope, **182**
Gregory XVI, Pope, **182**
Gregory, Doctor, **182**
Grossi, Tommaso, 94, **183**; *Fuggitiva*, 183; *Ildegonda*, 183; *Marco Visconti*, 183
Guarini, Battista, **183**
Gueldres, Duke Adolph of, **183**
Guelph, **183–84**, 302, 344, 354
Guerazzi, Francesco Domenico, 147, **184**, 286; *L'Assedio di Firenze*, 184; *La Battaglia di Benevento*, 184
Guglielmus Apulus, 169
Guicciardini, Francesco, **184**
Guiccioli, Teresa Countess, 63, **184**, 361
Guido Reni, **185**; *Angel of Annunciation*, 185
Guiscard, Robert, **185**
Gustavue Adolphus, **186**

Hardian, **187**
Hall, Edward, **188**, 333
Hampden, John, **190**
Handel, George Frederic, **190**
Hannibal, 69, **190**
Hans, **190**. *See also* Easterlings
Habsburg, **187**
Hasdrubal, **191**
Haspinger, Joseph Hastings, **191**
Haydn, Franz Joseph, **192**, 308; "New-Created World," 192
Hayward, Abraham, **192**
Head, Sir Francis Bond, **192**; *Bubbles of the Brunnens, The*, 301
Hebrew, **193**
"Heir of Mondolfo, The" (Shelley), **193–94**; Arnaldi, Viola, **22**; Mondolfo, **288** (Lady Isabel, **288**; Ludovico, **288**; Olimpio, **288**; Prince Fernando, **288**)
Henry III, **196**, 475
Henry IV (French), **196**
Henry IV (German), **196**
Henry, Mary Ann, **197**, 359

Index

Henryson, Robert, 450
Herrera, Fernando de, **198**
Herz, Henri, **198**
Hesiod, 130, 167, **199**; *Shield of Hercules*, 130, 199; *Works and Days*, 130, 199
Hesse Cassel (Duke of, **199**; Prince of, **199**)
Hessians, **199**
Heywood, Thomas, **199**
History of a Six Weeks' Tour (Shelley), 154, 167, **200**, 203, 359, 367, 410, 411
Hobhouse, John Cam, **200–201**
Hofer, Andreas, 42, 43, 106, **201**, 327, 347, 348, 483
Hoff, **201**
Hogg, Thomas Jefferson, **201–2**, 313, 411, 478
Holcroft, Thomas, 166, **202**
Holinshed, Raphael, **202**, 333
Holland, **202–3**; The Hague, **187**; Maaslius, **263**; Nijmegen, **305**; Ostend, **315**; Rotterdam, **379**; Tiel, **439**
Homer, 86, **203**, 346, 349, 353, 450; Cimmerian, **85**; Ulysses, 346, **456**
Hookham, Thomas, 200, **203**
Hoppner: Isabella, **203–4**, 313, 408; Richard, 203, **204**, 313, 408
Horace, **204–5**, 467
Hormayer, General, 10, **205**
Hughes, Professor, **207**
Huguenots, **207**
Hume, David, **207**, 333
Hungary, **207**
Hunt: Leigh, 155, 190, **207–8**, 229, 274, 280, 308, 311, 411, 447, 478; Marianne, 207, **208–9**, 411
Hurtado de Mendoza, Diego, b*209*
Huss, John, **209**, 362, 488

Il Conciliatore 41, **94**, 347
Imlay, Gilbert, 173, b*212*, 481
India, **212–13**; Bengal, **41**; Delhi, **112**; East India Company, **124**; Ganges, **163**; Indus, **213**; Hindostan, **200**; Kashmir, **229**; Oxycracae, **317**
Inquisition, **214**
"Invisible Girl, The" (Shelley), **214–15**; Bainbridge, Mrs., **32**; Rosina, **379**; Vernon (Henry, **465**; Lord, **465**; Sir Peter, **465**); Vernon-Place, **465**

Ionic, **215–16**
Iran: Ispahan, **218**; Persepolis, **335**; Persia, **335**
Ireland, **216**; Ardfinnin, **20**; Ardmore, **20**; Awbeg, **29**; Ballahourah, **32**; Ballybeg, Abbey of, **32**; Belfast, **39**; Buttevant, **62**; Clare, **88**; Connaught, **94**; Coollong, **96**; Cork, **97** (Garth, **164**; Round Tower, **380**); Drum, **121**; Dublin, **122**; Enniscorthy, **132**; Irish Channel, **217**; Kilbarry, **230**; Kilnemullagh, **62**; Killarney, **230**; Leinster, **245**; Lismore, **249**; Lumbard's Marsh, **261**; Mallow, **268**; Meath, **278**; Munster, **297**; Muskerry, **298–99**; Passage, **327**; Thomond, **438**; Tramore, **445**; Waterford, **473** (Little Island, **249**; Old Reginald's Tower, **312**); Youghal Bay, **485**
Irving, Washington, 179, b*217*, 329, 333
Isabeau of Bavaria, **217–18**
Islam, **218**; Allah, **10**; Heathenesse, **192**; Houris, **205–6**; Mahomet **297**; Mahometan, **267**; Muhammad, **297**
Italy, **219–21**; Abruzzi, **3**; Adda, **4**; Adige, **5**; Albano, **7**; Albaro, **7**; Alessandria, **8**; Altopascio, **11–12**; Amalfi, **12**; Ampezzo, **13**; Ancona, **14**; Anio, **15**; Apennines, **17**; Aquobuona, **18**; Arezzo, **20**; Arno, **22–23**; Arpino, **23**; Assisi, **25**; Astura, **25**; Bagni di Lucca, **31–32**; Baveno, **36**; Bellagio, **40** (Serbelloni, Villa, **401**); Benevento, **41**; Bergamo, **42**; Bisagno, **45**; Bologna, **48**; Bolvedro, **48–49**; Bolzano, **49** (Eppan Castle, **132**); Brescia, **55**; Brixen, **56** (Elephant, **129**); Brundisium, **58**; Cadenabbia, **65** (Albergo Grande, **7**; Grande Albergo, **179**); Calabria, **66**; Calmaldoli Convent, **67**; Campagna, **68**; Campo Morto, **69**; Cannae, **69–70**; Capo del Monte, **70**; Capraia, **71**; Capri, **71** (Grotto Azzuro, **183**); Capuan, **71**; Carate, **71**; Carrara, **72**; Casentino, **73**; Castello Lizzana, **73**; Catanzaro, **74**; Cava, **75**; Cenis, Mount, **76**; Chiavenna, **82**; Cisalpine, **86**; Civita Vecchia, **86**; Colico, **91**; Colli di Fontanelle, **91**; Como, **93** (Comasque, **93**); Como, Lake, **93**; Cortona, **98**; Crema, **100**; Cremona, **100**; Divedro, **116**; Domodossola, **118** (Post, **348**); Egna, **126**, 303; Elysian Fields, **131**, 271; Empoli, **131**; Eraclea, **132**; Este, **133–34** (Sant' Anna Convent, **394**); Etruria, **134**; Euganean

526

Index

Hills, **134–35**; Ferrarra, **147** (St. Anna, Convent of, **384**); Fiesole, **147**; Fiume Latte, **149**; Florence, **150–51** (Accademia delle Belle Arti, **4**, 304; *Arti Minori*, **23–24**; Batistero, **35** [Gates of, **164**]; Campanile, **68**; Carraia, **72**; Cascine, **73**; Duomo, **122–23**; Mercato Nuovo, **280**; Podestà, Palace of the, **344**; Palagio del Popolo, **319**; Palazzo Pitti, **320**; Palazzo Strozzi, **320**; Piazza del Duomo, **338**; Piazza della Annunziata, **338**; Piazza della Signoria, **338–39**; Ponte alle Grazie, **346**; Porta Romana, **348**; Porta San Gallo, **348**; Saint Ambrosio's Church, **384**; St. Maria degli Angioli's Church, **387**; San Friano, **392**; San Miniato, **393** [Church, **393**]; Santa Croce Church, **394**; Santa Maria degli Angioli Church, **394**; Santa Maria Novella Church, **394**; Santa Trinita Church, **395**; Santissima Annunziata [Church, **395**; Convent, **394**]; Schneiderff's Hotel, **399**; Tribune, **449**; Uffizi Gallery, 99, 306, 320, 356, **455**); Foligno, **152**; Forlí, **153**; Fosdinovo, **154**; Friuli, **160**; Fucecchio, **160–61**; Fusina, **161**; Gaeta, **162**; Genoa, **166** (Palazzo Carega, **320**, San Pietro d'Arena, **393**); Giulia, Villa, **171**; Guisciana, **185**; Ischia, **218**; Iselle, **218**; Isola Bella, **218**; Isola Madre, **218**; Isola Madre, **266**; La Spezia, **235**; La Verna Convent, **236**; Lago di Garda, **236**; Lago di Massaciucuoli, **236**; Lago Maggiore, **236**; Lago Scuro, **237**; Lasise, **240**; Lecco, **244** (Melzi, Villa, **280**); Lecco, Lake, **244**; Leghorn, **244–45**; Limone, **248**; Lodi, **252**; Lombardo-Veneto, **255**; Lombardy, **255**; Lombardy, Plains of, **255**; Lucca, **259** (San Francesco, **392**; San Frediano, **393**; San Martino, **393**; San Michele, **393**); Lungo l'Arno, **261**; Lunigiana, **261**; Magna Grecia, **366**; Magra, **266**; Malamocco, **267**; Mantone, **269**; Mantua, **269** (Porta Ceresa, **347**; Porta Molina, **347**); Marches, **270**; Mare Morto, **270–71**; Maremma, **271**; Mazzorbo, **278**; Menaggio, **280**; Mestre, **281**; Milan **283–84** (Ambrosian Library, **12**, 52, 337; Brera, **55**, 361; Hôtel de la Ville, **205**; La Scala, **235**; Duomo, **123**; La Scala, **304**; Piazza del Duomo, **338**; Viceroy's Palace, **466**); Miseno, Cape, **285**; Modena, **286**; Monte Aperto, **290**; Monte Baldo, **290**; Monte San Giuliano, **290**; Monte San Pelegrino, **290**; Montecatini, **290**; Murano, **297** (San Pietro Church, **393**); Naples, **300–301** (Baiae, **32**; Bauli, **35**; Chiaja, **82**; Palagio Reale, **319–20**, San Carlo, **392**) ; Napoli, **301**; Narni, **301**; Nemi, **302**; New River Cut, **304**; Val di Nievole, **458**; Novara, **307**; Nozzano, **308**; Olevano Romano, **312**; Osimo, **315**; Padua, **319** (University of, **456**); Paestum, **319** (Neptune, Temple of, **302**); Pagibonzi, **319**; Parma, **326**; Passeyr, Valley of, **327**; Pavia, **329**; Perugia, **336**; Pescia, **336**; Piedmont, **339**; Piombino, **340**; Pisa, **340** (University of, 318, **456**); Pistoia, **340–41**; Po, **344**; Pompeii, **346**; Pontine Marshes, **346–47**; Pontremoli, **347**; Posilipo, **348**; Procida, **350**; Pugnano, **354**; Ravello, **361**; Ravenna, **361**; Resegone, 351, **365**; Rimini, **371**; Ripafratta, **372**; Riva, **372** (La Rocca, **235**); Rocco Giovane, **374**; Romagna, **376**; Rome, **376–77** (Arch of Constantine, **20**; Barberini Palace, **33**; Baths of Caracalla, **35**; Baths of Diocletian, **35**; Borghese Gardens, **51**; Caelian Hill, **65**; Campidoglio, **69**; Capitol, **70**; Capitoline, **70**; Castel Sant' Angelo, **73**; Cestius, Tomb of, **77–78**; Coliseum, **91**; Colonna Gallery, **92**; Column of Antoninus, **92**; Corso, **98**; Farnesina, **144**; Forum, **153**; Janicular Hill, **223**; Jesuits, Church of, **224**; Jupiter Stator, **227**; Lateran, **242**; Mamertine, **268**; Monte Cavallo, **290**; Palatine, **320**; Palazzo Borghese, **320**; Palazzo Verosposi, **321**; Pantheon, **322**; Pelegrini, Hospital of, **331**; Pincian, **339**; Porta del Popolo, **347**; Quirinal, **357**; San Paolo fuore delle Mura Cathedral, **393**; Santa Chiara, **394**; Santa Maria degli Angeli Church, **394**; Santa Maria Maggiore Church, **394**; Sacred Way, **384**; Senate House, **401**; Seven Hills, **402**; Tower of the Capitol, **444**; Trevi, **448**; Trinita da Monti, La, **449**; Venus, Temple of, **464**); Roveredo, **381**; Rovigo, **381**; Rupe de Noce, **381**; Salerno, **391** (Gulf of, **185**); San Terenzo, **393**; Sardinia, **396**; Sarzana, **396**; Scaricatojo, **398**; Serchio, **401–2**; Serravalle, **402**; Sesto Callende, **402**; Siena, **415**;

Sirmio, **416**; Slovino di San Marco, **418**; Sommariva, Villa, **419**; Soracte, **420**; Sorrento, **420** (Cocumella, **90**); Spoleto, **423**; Subiaco, **427**; Susa, **428**; Terni, **437**; Terracina, **437**; Thrasymene, **439**; Tiber, **439**; Tivoli, **442**; Torcello, **443**; Tremezzo, **448**; Trent, **448**; Trieste, **449**; Turin, **451**; Tuscany, **452**; Umbria, **456**; Vado, **458**; Valdarno, **458**; Valdinera, **458**; Valdimagra, **458**; Vallombrosa, **459**; Varenna, **462**; Vatican, 360; **462–63** (St. Peter's, **388–89**; Sistine Chapel, 282, 336, 360, 379, **417**); Vedro, **463**; Velino, **463**; Velletri, **463**; Venice, 315, **463–64** (Accademia delle Belle Arti, **4**; Armenian Convent, **22**; Barbarigo Palace, **33**; Beppo, **41**; Brenta, **54**; Burano, **60**; Canal Orfano, **69**; Canale della Giudecca, **69**; Doge's Palace, **117**; Fenice, **145**; Florian, **151**; Fondamenti Nuovi, **152**; Grand Canal, **179**; Hôtel d'Italia, **205**; Laguna, **236**; Leone Bianco, **246**; Library of St. Mark, **247**; Lido, **247**; Merceria, **280**; Pala d'Oro, **319**; Palazzo Mangrin, **320**; Palazzo Mocenigo, **320**; Palazzo Pisani, **320**; Piazza San Marco, **338**; Piazzetta, **339**; Piombi, **340**; Place of St. Mark, **339**; Ponte de' Sospiri, **346**; Pozzi, **349**; Rialto, **368**; San Giorgio Maggiore Church, **392–93**; San Marco, **393** (St. Theodore Chapel, **390**; Scala d' Oro, **398**; Scala dei Giganti, **398**); Santa Maria de' Frari Church, **394**; Santa Maria de la Salute, **394**; S. Tommaso's Church, **383**; Saints Giovanni's and Paolo's Church, **386**; St. Sebastian's Church, **389**; Suttil, **428**; Treasury, **446**); Vercelli, **464**; Verona, **465** (Gran Parigi, **179**); Vesuvius, 300, 346, **466**; Vicenza, **466**; Vico, **466**; Vico Pisano, **466**; Vettici, **466**; Viterbo, **469**; Volterra, **470**

Jacobins, **222**
Jaggernaut, **222**
James I, **222–23**
Jameson, Anna Brownell, **223**, 366
Jenzenstein, John II of, **224**
Jerusalem, **224**
Johnson, Samuel, **228**
Jonson, Ben, **225**

Joseph II, **225**
Josephine, **225–26**
Julius II, Pope, **226**

Keats, John, 207, **229**, 293, 311, 376, 403
Keepsake, 3, 57, 121, 135, 143, 145, 214, **229**, 293, 295, 305, 326, 410, 418, 424, 425, 429, 445, 448
King Log, **230–31**
Kirkup, Mr. Seymour Stocker, **231**
Knights of Malta, **231–32**
Knox, Alexander Andrew, **232**, 360
Kock, Charles-Paul de, **232**; *Le Barbier de Paris*, 232

L'Hôte, Madame, **234**
l'Ouverture, François, **234**
La Fontaine, Jean de, **234**, 358
La Motte Fouque, **234–35**; *Magic Ring*, 235
La Noue, Monsieur de, **235**
La Place, Pierre Simon, **235**
La Rochefoucauld, François, **235**
Lablache, Luigi, **236**
Lamb: Charles, **237–38**, 107, 130, 308 (Elia, 237); Mary, 237
Lancaster, House of, **238**, 473, 476, 485
Lancaster, Joseph, 40
Landon, Letitia Elizabeth, **239**
Landor, Walter, **239**
Lanti, Duke of, **239**
Lanzi, Luigi, **239–40**
Lardner, Dionysius, 240, 250, 410
Lario, 240
Last Man, The (Shelley), 69, 163, 201, **240–42**, 410; Adrian, **5**; Alfred, **9**; Argyropylo, **21**; Athol, Duke of, **26**; Black Spectre, **45**; Clara, **88**; Cumaean Sibyl, **101**; Duke of——, **122**; Florio, **151**; Fortunatus, **153**; George, **166**; Idris, **211**; Juliet, **226**; Karazza, **228**; L——, Duke of, **234**; Lion, **249**; Martha, **273**; Martin, Lucy, **274**; Merrival, **281**; Palli, Georgio, **321**; Perdita, **332–33**; Protectoral Palace, **353**; Raymond, Lord, **361**; Ryland, **382**; Verney (Evelyn, **464**; Lionel, **464**); Viceroy's Palace, **466**; White Opera Dancer, **476**; Windsor, Countess of, **479**; Woods, Samuel, **481**; Ypsilanti, Alesander, **486**; Zaimi (Evadne, **487**; Prince, **487**)

Latin, 241–42
Latini, Brunetto, 242
Laurette, 243
Lawrence, Sir Thomas, 243
Lazzarini, Colonel, 243–44
Lebanon, 244; Tyre, 454
Lefebvre, General Pierre, 244
León, Luis de, 245
Leonardo da Vinci, 245–46
Leopold I, 246
Leopold, II, 246
Levant, 247
Lewis, Monk, 313
Ligne, Prince de, 248
Lions, 249
Lives of the Most Eminent Literary and Scientific Men of France (Shelley), 94, 97, 144, 240, 257, 285, 287, 289, 327, 234, 235, **250**, 358, 376, 380, 403, 423, 470
Lives of the Most Eminent Literary and Scientific Men of Italy, Spain and Portugal (Shelley), 9, 52, 60, 67, 68, 74, 77, 82, 92, 132, 133, 147, 148, 154, 164, 176, 177, 183, 184, 208, 240, 245, **250–52**, 265, 271, 278, 281, 285, 290, 337, 345, 348, 354, 356, 383, 434, 435, 467
Livy, Titus Livius, **252**, 460
Lodore (Shelley), 128, 163, **252–54**, 410; Bessy, Aunt, **43**; Bewling, **43**; Bewling, Vale of, **43**; C——, Marquess of, **65**; Chilverton Park, **84**; Craycroft, **100**; D——, Earl of, **106**; Derham (Fanny, **113**; Francis, **113**; Mrs., **113**; Sarah, **113**; Sir Gilbert, **113**); Fenton, **145**; Fitzhenry, **148** (Admiral, **148**; Elizabeth, **148**; Henry, **149**); G——, Countess of, **162**; Gayland, Mr., **165**; Gregory (Miss, **182**; Mrs., **182**); Hatfield, Mr., **192**; Humphries (Mr., **207**; Mrs., **207**); Laurie, **243**; Lodore (Lady, **254**; Lord, **254**); Longfield, **257**; Lyzinski (Count Casimir, **262**; Countess Theodora, **262**); Maristow (Castle, **277**; Lady, **277**; Lord, **272**; Viscount, **272**; Viscountess, **272**); Margaret, **271**; Markham, Captain, **272**; Newman's, **304**; Nixon, Dame, **306**; Rhyaider Gowy, **368**; Santerre (Lady, **395**; Sir John, **395**); Saunders, **396**; Saville (Clorinda, **396–97**; Harriet, **397**; Horatio, **397**; Lucy, **397**; Mr., **397**;

Sophia, **397**); Villamarina, Principe, **467**; Villiers (Colonel, **468**; Edward, **468**; Ethel, **468**); Wilmot, **479**
Louis XIV, **258**
Louis-Philippe, **258**
Lucas, Louis, **259**
Lucan, 75, **259**; *Pharsalia*, 259
Lucretius, Titus Carus, **260**
Lucullus, Lucius Licinius, **260**
Luini, Bernardino, **260–61**
Luther, Martin, 80, 115, 128, **261**, 362, 473
Luxembourg, **261**
Lycurgus, **261**
Lyndsay, David. *See* Mary Diana Dods

Machiavelli, **264–265**, 318, 460; Life of Castruccio Castracani of Lucca, The, 185, 265
Mackey, Sampson Arnold, **265**
Madonna del Soccorso, **266**
Magdalen, The, **266**
Malta, **268**; Knights of, **231–32**
Manfred, **269**
Manhes, General, **269**
Manzoni, Alessandro, 39, 46, 52, 94, 108, 176, 183, **269–70**, 286, 304, 365, 439; Adelchi, 270; Carmagnola, 270; "Cinque Maggio," 270; Ermengarda, 270; "Ode on Napoleon," 270; Promessi sposi, 270, **351**, 372 (Don Rodrigo, 351, Father Capuchin, 351, Innominato, 351, 372, Lucia, 351, Renzo, 351)
March, Ausias, **270**
Margaret, Queen, **271**
Marie Louise, **271**
Marini: Giambattista, **271–72**; Ignazio, **272**
Markham, Gervase, **272**; *The Dumb Knight*, 272
Marmara, **273**
Martello, **273**
Marvell, Andrew, **274**
Mason, Mrs. *See* Mountcashel
Massinger, Philip, 38, 243
Matilda, **275**
Matilda (Shelley), 128, 144, 147, 174, **275–76**, 295, 410; Diana, **114**; Elinor, **129**; Gaspar, **164**; Matilda, **275**; Woodville, **481**
Matthias, **276**
"Maurice" (Shelley), **276**: Barnet, **34** (Dame, **34**; Gregory, **34**); Benson, **41**; Betsy, **43**; Henry,

529

Index

194; Jackson, 222; Maurice, 276; Smithson (Daddy, 418; Dame, 418)
Mavrocordato, Alexander, 180, 194, **276–77**, 318, 486
Maximilian II, **277**
Mayr, Simon, **277**; *Medea*, 277
Medici, **278**; Lorenzo de, **278**, 345
Mediterranean Sea, **278–79**
Medwin, Thomas, 61, 201, **279–80**, 283, 352, 409, 447, 477, 478
Mehmed II, **280**
Mérimée, Prosper, 212, **280–81**, 333, 365
Merlin, **281**
Metastasio, Pietro, **281**
Methodius, **281**
Metropolitan Magazine, **282**, 362
Metternich, Prince Klemens Fürst von, **282**, 333
Meyerbeer, Giacomo, **282**; *Les Huguenots*, 282; *Robert le Diable*, 282
Mexico, **282**
Michelangelo, 70, 226, **282–83**; 348, 389, 394, 462
Midas (Shelley), **283**, 299, 316; Asphalion, **25**; Evoe, **138**; Lacon, **236**; Marsyas, **273**; Midas, **283**; Phrygia, **338**; Tmolus, **442**; Zopyrion, **488**
Middleton, Thomas, **283**
Milbanke, Annabella, 63
Miliorini, Il, **284**
Milton, 170, **284**, 292; *Comus*, **93–94**; *Paradise Lost*, 157, **322–23** (Adam, 322; Demogorgon, **113**; Eden, **125**; Eve, **136–37**; 322; Mammon, **268**; Pandemonium, **321**; Satan, 322, **396**; Urania, **457**); *Paradise Regained*, **323–24**; *Penseroso, Il*, 332
Mirabeau, Comte Honoré Gabriel, **285**
Mirandola, Giovanni Pico della, **285**
Misenum, **285**
Mitchell, Colonel, **286**
Mithridates, Eupator, **286**
Molière, **287**, 358, 378
Molinari, Louis Valeriani, **287**
Moliterno, Prince, **287**
Montagu, Lady Mary Wortley, 170, **289**
Montaigne, Michel, **289**
Montani, Giuseppe, 94, **289**
Montemayor, Jorge de, **290–91**
Monti, Vincenzo, **291**, 335, 352

Moore, Thomas, 201, 250, 284, **291–92**, 298, 375, 396; *Irish Melodies*, **217**, 291; *Lalla Rookh: An Oriental Romance*, **237**, 291; "Tyrolese song of liberty," 291
Moors, **292**
Moréri, Louis, **292**
Morgan, Lady (Sydney Owenson), **292–93**
Morning Herald, **293**
Morning Post, **293**
Morea, Nauplion, 301
"Mortal Immortal, The" (Shelley), **293–94**, 445; Agrippa, **6**; Bertha, **43**; Hoffer, Albert, **201**; Winzy, 480
Mountcashel, Lady Margaret, **294–95**, 439–40
"Mourner, The" (Shelley), 174, **295–96**; Bellerophon, **40**; Burnet, Ellen, **62**; Cooke, Mr. **96**; D——, Earl of, **106**; Elmore (Lewis, **130**; Park, **130**); Eversham (Clarice, **137**; Lord, **137**); Nancy, **300**; Neville, Horace, **303**; *St. Mary*, **387**
Mozart, Wolfgang Amadeus, **296–97**; Almaviva, **296**; *Die Zauberflöte*, 296; *Don Giovanni*, 296; *Figaro*, 296
Mr.——, **297**
Murat, Joachim, **297–98**
Muratori, Ludovico Antonio, **298**, 363
Murray, John, 57, 63, 75, 144, 176, 179, 181, 205, **298**, 333, 345, 351, 360, 432
Mythology: Actaeon, **4**; Adonis, **5**; Alpheus, **11**; Amalthea, **12**; Amphion, 306; Amphitrite, **13–14**, 302; Anchises, **14**, 464; Antaeus; Antigone, **16**, 311, 345; Aphrodite, **18**, 102, 299, 349, 464; Apollo, **18**, 306, 326, 355; Arethusa, **20**; Ariadne, **21**, 438; Artemis, 306; Ascalaphus, **24**; Atlas, **26**; Aurora 27; Bacchus, **30**, 301, 309, 332; Bellerophon, **40**; Bellona, **41**; Boreas, **51**; Cassandra, **73**; Castor, **74**, 338; Centaur, **76**, 302; Cerberus, **77**; Ceres, **77**; Charon, **81**; Circean Stye, **86**; Cumaean Sibyl, **101**; Cupid, **102**, 438, 464; Cybele, **104**; Cyclopes, **104**, 346; Daedalus, **107**; Daphne, **108**; Delphic Oracle, **112–13**, 326, 355; Demeter, **77**; Deucalion, **114**; Diana, **114**; Dionysus, 30, 332; Dodona, **116**; Echo, **125**; Elysian Fields, **131**; Eos, **27**; Erebus, **132**; Eumenides, **135**, 311; Euterpe, **136**; Fates, **287**; Galatea, **162**; Ganymede, **163**; Ge, **454**; Gorgon, **178**, 279;

530

Hades, 132, 344; Hebe, **193**; Hecate, **193**; Hercules, **197–98**; Hesperus, **199**, 464; Hyacinth, **209**; Icarus, **211**; Io, 98; Isis, **218**; Janus, **223–24**; Jove, **226**; Juno, **227**; Jupitor, **227**; Latona, **242**; Leander, **244**; Lethe, **246**; Lucifer, **260**, 464; Mars, **272**; Medea, **278**; Medusa, **279**; Mercury, **280**; Minerva, **285**; Minotaur, **285**, 438; Moirae, **287**; Morpheus, **293**; Naiad, **300**; Narcissus, **301**; Neptune, **302**; Nereids, **302**; Nessus, **302**; Nestor, **302**; Niobe, **305–6**; Oedipus, **311**, 345; Olympus, **313**; Orion, **314**; Pan, **321**; Pandora, **321–22**; Peneus, **332**; Pentheus, **332**; Perseus, 75; Pluto, **344**; Polynices, **345**; Polyphemus, **345–46**; Pomegranate seed, **346**; Pollux, 74, 338; Procrustes, **350**; Prometheus, **351–52**; Proserpine, **352**; Proteus, **353**; Psyche, 102; Pythian maid, **355**; Python, **355**; Quirinus, **357**; Remus, **378**; Rhea, 104; Romolus, 357, **378**; Scylla, **400**; Semele, **487**; Serapis, **401**; Sibyl, **414**; Silenus, **415–16**; Skyllo, **417**; Sphynx, 311, **422**; Styx, **427**; Syrens, **430**; Syrinx, **430–31**; Tantalus, **434**; Tartarus, 132, **434**, 454; Theseus, 320, 350, **438**; Thor, **439**; Tiresias, **441**; Titans, **441**; Triton, **449**; Typheus, **453–54**; Ulysses, **456**; Urania, **457**; Vulcan, **470**; Venus, **464**; Zeus, 351, **487**;

National Air, **301**
National Dictionary, **301**, 336
Nazarene, **301–2**
Neri, 183, **302**, 341
Nero, **302**
Newton, Sir Isaac, **304**
Nicaea, Council of, 21
Niccolai, Otto, **304**; *Templario*, 304
Niccollini, Giovanni Battista, 31, **304–5**, *Arnaldo da Brescia*, **22**, 304; *Giovanni da Procida*, 305; *History of the House of Swabia*, 305; *Ino e Temisto*, 304; *Oedipus*, 304; *Polixena*, 305; "Sicilian Vespers," 305
Nicholas, Emperor, **305**
Nicholas V, Pope, **305**
Noll, **306**
Normanby (Constantine Henry Phipps), 366
Norse mythology. *See* Mythology
North Pole, **306**

North Sea, **306**
Norton, Caroline, 192, **307**
Nourjahad, **307**
Novello: Count Guido de' Guidi, **307–8**; Joseph Alfred, 190, **308**; Vincent, **308**
Numa Pompilius, **308**
Nysa, **309**

Ollier, Charles, 194, 200, 229, **312–13**, 461, 483
Oman, **313**
Omega, 10–11
Orlando, **314**
Orleans, Duke of, **314**
Orondates, **314**
Oronooko, **314**
Orpheus, **315**
Orseolo, Piero, **315**
Otho, **316**
Ottoman Empire, 207, **316** (Porte, **348**); Janizaries, **223**
Otway, Thomas, **316**; Belvidera, 316
Ovid, 283, 293, **316**, 346, 352; Morpheus, 316

P——, Mr. **318**
Pacchiani, Francesco, 277, **318**, 332, 432, 469
Pacific Ocean, **318**
Pacini, Giovanni, **318–19**, 379; *L'Ultimo giorno di Pompei*, 319
Paganini, Nicolò, 315, **319**
Paisiello, Giovanni, **319**, 328; *Nina Pazza per Amore*, 319
Palamon, **320**
Palestine, **321**; Holy Land, **203**, 321
Palikar, **321**
Palladio, **321**
Palma Vecchio, **321**
Palma, Jacopo, **321**
Paracelsus, **322**
Parian marble, **324**
Park, Mungo, **325**
Parliament, 307, **325–26**, 341, 444, 475; House of Commons, **206**; House of Lords, **206**
Parry, Sir William Edward, **326**
"Parvenue, The" (Shelley), **326–27**; Cooper, Lawrence, 96; Fanny, 144; Susan, **428**
Pascal, Blaise, **327**
Pasha, Ali, **327**, 437, 462
Pasta, Madame Guiditta, 319, **327–28**

Index

Paul, Georgiana, **328**
Paul, Sir Aubrey John Dean, 328, **329**
Payne, John Howard, 319, **329–30**
Peacock, Thomas Love, 87, 111, 200, 203, 317, **330–31**, 333, 363
Pearson, Henry Hugh, 308, **331**, 358, 360; "Arethusa," 331; "Spirit of the Night," 331
Pecchio, Giuseppe, **331**
Pellico, Silvio, 94, 122, **331**, 340, 347; *Eufemio da Messina*, 331
Percicus, **332**; "Nepomuceidon," 332
Percy, Thomas: *Reliques*, **364** ("Babes in the Woods," 364; "Ballad of Jane Shore," 361; "Chevy Chase," 364; "Heir of Lynne, The," 364; "Sir Aldingar," 364)
Pericles, **333**
Perier, Casimir, **333**
Perkin Warbeck (Shelley), 174, 217, **333–34**, 410; Abbot **3**; Adalid, **4**; Alcalde, **8**; Algerines, **9**; Andrew of the Shawe, **15**; Astley, John, **25**; Astwood, **25** (Thomas, **25**); Audley, Lord, **27**; Ayala, Don Pedro de, **29**; Ayza, Sultana, **29**; Barley, William, **33**; Barretts, **34**; Barry, Lord, **34**; Barrymores, **34**; Barrys, **34**; Bedford, Duke of, **39**; Berkeley, **42**; Bess, **43**; Beverem, Sire de, **43**; Blewit, Abel, **46**; Boabdil El Chico, **46**; Bolingbroke, **48**; Bonshaw, Laird of, **50**; Boyd, Mary, **53**; Brakenbury, Sir Robert, **53**; Brampton (Lady, **53**; Sir Edward, **53**); Brittany, Anne of, **56**; Broke, Lord, **57**; Broughton, Sir Thomas, **57**; Bryan, **59**; Buchan, **59**; Buckingham, Duke of, **59**; Burgh, Hubert, **61**; Butler, **62** (Lady Eleanor, **62**); Cassils, Earl of, **73**; Cheney (Lady, **82**; Sir John, **82**); Clan Cartie Reagh, **88**; Clarence, Duke of, **88**; Clifford (Lady, **89**; Robert, **89**; Sir Roger, **88**); Clim of Tregothius, **89–90**; Clim of the Lyn, **90**; Concressault, Lord of, **94**; Courcy, de, **99**; Courtney (Sir John, **99**; William, **99**); Cressenor, Thomas, **101**; d'Ayala, Don Pedro, **106**; Dacre (Lord, **106**; Randal of, **107**); Daraxa, **108**; Daubeney (Giles, **109**; William, **109**); Daubeny, Gilbert, **109**; De Courcy, **110**; De Faro (Hernan, **110**; Madeline, **110**; Monina, **110**); Desborough, Lord Reginald, **113**; Desies, **114**; Desmond (Countess of, **114**; Earl Maurice of, **114**); Devon, Earl of, **114**; Devonshire, Earl of, **114**; Diaz, Bartholomew, **114–15**; Dick, **115**; Dickon, **115**; Diego, **115**; Digby, Sir John, **115**; Donegans, **119**; Dorset, Lord, **120**; Douglas, Archibald, **120**; Dragon, **120**; Drummonds, **121**; Eastwell Place, **296**; Edward III, **126**; Edward IV, **126**; Edward VI, **126**; Edward, Prince, **126**; El Zagal, **127**; Elizabeth of York, **129–30**; Empson, Richard, **131**; Errol, Earl of, **133**; Father Piers, **144**; Ferdinand, **145**; Fermoy, Lord, **146**; Fitzwater, Lord John, **149**; Fitzwilliam, **149**; Floeur-de-Luce, **150**; Floyer, Adam, **151**; Fountain of Myrtles, **154**; Fox, Bishop Richard, **154**; Frion, Stephen Etienne, **160**; Garthe, Thomas, **164**; Geraldine, Thomas, **167**; Geraldines, **167**; Gitani, **171**; Gloucester, Duke of, **172**; Gomelez, Almoradi, **177**; Gordon (Castle, **178**; Lady Katherine, **178**); Gray, John, **180**; Hamilton, Sir Patrick, **188**; Harry, **191**; Henry V, **196**; Henry VI, **196**; Henry VII, **196**; Heron, **198**; Hobler, **201**; Homes, **203**; Howard (John, **206**; Lady Anne, **206**; of Effingham, **207**); Howards, **207**; Huntly, Earl of, **209**; Isabella I, **218**; Jack of the Wynd, **222**; James, **222**; Jame III, **223**; James IV, **223**; Keating, James, **229**; Kennedy, Lady Jane, **229**; Kern, **230**; Kerry, Knight of, **230**; Kildare, Earl of, **230**; Knight of the Glen, **231**; Lackland, **236**; Lalayne, Sire Roderick de, **237**; Langborne, Robert, **239**; Lavalan, John, **243**; Lennox, **245**; Lessey (Sir Richard, **246**; Sir William, **246**); Lincoln, Earl of, **248**; Lion-Heart, **249**; Lisle, Sir Edward, **249**; Long Roger, **257**; Louis XI, **258**; Lovel, Lord Francis, **258**; Luttrel, Sir Hugh, **261**; Mac Swiney, **263**; Macarthy of Muskerry, **263**; Macarthy Reagh, **263**; MacCarthys, **264**; March, Earl of, **270**; Margaret, **271**; Margaret of Anjou, **271**; Margery, Mistress, **271**; Martin, **274**; Maximilian I, **277**; Meath, Bishop of, **278**; Moray, Earl of, **292**; Mortimer, **294**; Morton, John, **294**; Mountford, Sir Simon, **295**; Mowbray (Anne, **296**; Elizabeth, **296**; Thomas, **296**); Moyle, Sir Thomas, **296**; Murrays, **298**; Murrogh-en-Ranagh, **298**;

Neville, Sir George, **303**; O'Brien, **310**; O'Carrolls, **310**; O'Water, John, **310**; Oldcraft, Mat, **312**; Ormond, Sir James, **314**; Oxford, Lord, **317**; Paulet, Thomas, **329**; Peachy, Sir John, **330**; Plantagenet, **342** (Edmund, **342**); Plunket, Thomas, **343**; Ponce de Leon, Don Rodrigo, **346**; Portlester, Baron of, **348**; Poynings, Sir Edward, **348**; Poyns, Thomas, **349**; Richard of York, **370**; Richard Plantagenet, **370**; Richford, William, **370**; Richmmond (Countess of, **370–71**; Earl of, **371**); Rivers, Earl of, **372**; Roche, **374**; Ross, Duke of, **379**; Poytron, Stephen, **349**; Rakehells, King of, **359**; Ramsay, Sir John, **360**; Ratcliffe, Sir Robert, **361**; St. George, **386**; Shore, Jane, **414**; Simnel, Lambert, **416**; Simon, Richard, **416**; Skelton, Richard, **417**; Stafford (Humphrey, **423**; Thomas, **423**); Stanley, William, **424**; Strangeways, Mat, **426**; Surrey, Lord, **428**; Sutton, Dr. Willliam, **428**; Swartz, Martin, **428**; Talbot, John, **433**; Taylor, Sir John, **435**; Thomas, **438**; Thwaites, Sir Thomas, **439**; Tiler, John, **440**; Tirrel, James, **441**; Todd, Sir Thomas, **442**; Trangmar Meiler, **445**; Trereife, **448**; Urswick, Sir Christopher, **457**; Vere, Sir Harry de, **464**; Veres, **464**; Walden, Lorde de, **471**; Walter, Archbishop of Dublin, **472**; Walter of Hornbeck, **472**; Warbeck, John, **472**; Warbeck, Perkin, **472**; Warham, Doctor William, **473**; Warwick, Earl of, **473**; Wattam, Doctor, **474**; White Surrey, **476**; Wells, Lord, **474**; White Knight, **476**; Wiatt, **477**; Wicherly, Adam, **477**; Woodville, Elizabeth, **482**; Worseley, William, **484**

Persia, **335**
Perticari, Count Giulio, **335**, 352
Peru, **336**
Perugino, **336**
Petrarch, Francesco, 106, 278, 281, **336**, 366, 436
Phidias, **337–38**
Philip of Macedon, **338**
Phoenicia, **338**
Pinkerton, John, 333, **339–40**; *History of Scotland*, 340
Pitt, William, the Elder, **341**

Pius VII, **341**
Plague, 58, 112, **341–42**; Parthian Pestilence, 326
Plato, 147, 215, **342**
Plautus, Titus Maccius, **342–43**, 378
Pliny the Elder, **343**
Pliny the Younger, **343**
Plutarch, 178, 287, 308, 317, **343–44**; *Lives*, 343
Podestà, **344**
Poets of the Lakes, **344**
Poitiers, **344**
Poland, **344–45**
Polidori, John William, 62, 157, **345**
Poliziano, Angelo, **345**
Pompey the Great, **346**
Ponente, **346**
Poniatowski, Józet Antoni, **346**
Pope, Alexander, **347**; "Epistle to a Lady," **132**; *Essay on Criticism*, **133**; "Essay on Man," **133**
Porro, Count Luigi, **347**
Portugal, **348**; Lisbon, **249**; Madeira, **266**; Tagus, **433**
Praxitilean, **349**
Pressburg, Treaty of, **349**
Presumption, 158
Prior, Matthew, **350**
Procter, Bryan Waller, **350–51**
Proposta, 301, **352**
Proserpine (Shelley), 299, 316, 346, **352**; Hymera, **210**; Ino, **214**; Iris, **216**; Proserpine, **352**, "Proserpine's Song," **352–53**
Prussia, **353**; King of, **353**; Queen of, **353**
Pulci: Bernardo, **354**; Luca, **354**; Luigi, **354**
Pyrennees, **355**
Pythagoras, **355**

Queen of Beauty (Venus de'Medici), **356**
Quevedo y Villegas, Francisco Gómez, **356–57**

Rabelais, Francis, **358**
Racine, Jean, **358–59**
Radcliffe, Ann, **359**; *Italian, The*, 359
Rainer, **359**
Rambles in Germany and Italy (Shelley), 155, 168, 192, 220, **359–60**, 368, 371, 411, 412
Raphael, 55, 162, 226, 239, 320, 336, **360–31**, 389, 462; *Adoration of the Magi*, 360; *Car-*

toons, 360; *Dispute of the Sacrament*, 108, 360; *Entombment of Christ*, 360; *Madonna di Casa Colonna*, 361; *Madonna di Foligno*, 360; *Madonna di San Sisto*, 361; *Nymph Galatea, The*, 361; Prince of Painters, 360; Raffaelle, 360; *Sistine Madonna*, 361; *Sposalizio*, 361; *Transfiguration*, 153, 360

"Recollections of Italy" (Shelley), **361–62**; Malville, Edmund, **268**

Red Sea, **362**

Reeve, Henry, 282, **362**, 387; "Sketches of Bohemia," 362

Reformation, **362**

Red Rose, 238, 326, **485**

Rembrandt van Rijn, 183, **364**

René I, **364–65**

Reveley, Henry, 171, **365**

Revolution of 1830, **367**

Revolutionary War, 341, **367**

Reynolds, Sir Joshua, **367**, 381

Rhine, **367–68**

Ricci, Luigi, **368–69**; *Chi dura Vince*, 369

Richard III, **370**

Rio, Alexis-François, **371–72**; *De la Poèsie chrètienne*, 371

Ripamonti, Giuseppe, **372**

Risorgimento, 71, **372**

Robert the Bruce, **372**

Robin Hood, **372–73**

Robinson, Isabel, 117, 305, **373**, 478

Robinson, Julia, 38, **373–74**

Robinson, Julian, 359, **374**

Robinson, Mary, 332

"Roger Dodsworth: The Reanimated Englishman" (Shelley), 174, 293, **374–75**; Dodsworth (Mr. Roger, **117**; Roger, **117**); Fairfax, Lord Thomas, **141**; Hotham, Dr., **205**; Sapio, Mr., **395**

Rogers, Samuel, 374, **375**; *Italy*, **221**, 375 ("Como," 221; "Florence," 221; "Geneva," 221; "Naples," 221); *Pleasures of Memory, The*, 375

Roland de la Platière, Madame, **375–76**

Rollin, Charles, **376**

Romagnosi, Gian Domenico, 94, **376**

Romaic, **376**

Romania, Wallachia, **471**

Roman mythology. *See* Mythology

Rosselli, Cosimo, **379**

Rossini, Gioacchino Antonio, 318, 328, **379**; *Mosè* 272, 379, ("Mi manca la voce," 379; *Pietro l'Eremita*, 379)

Rouge et Noir, **379**

Round Table, **379**

Roundheads, **380**

Rousseau, Jean-Jacques, 157, 170, **380–81**

Rubens, Peter Paul, 367, **381**; *Descent from the Cross*, 381

Rubicon, **381**

Russia, **381–82**, 471; Archangel, **20**; Circassia, **86**; Cossacks, **99**; Courland, **99**; Georgia, **166**; Moscow, **294**; Odessa, **311**; St. Petersburgh, **389**; Siberia, **414**; Tartary, **434**

Sá de Miranda, Francisco, **383**

Sabines, **383**

St. Ambrose, **384**

St. Andrew, **384**

St. Anthony, **384–85**

St. Bridget, **385**

St. Catherine, **385**

St. Cecilia, **385**

St. Clara, **385–86**

St. Colomban, **386**

St. Declan, **386**

St. Dunstan, **386**

St. Finbar, **386**

St. George, **386**

St. James, **386**

St. John Nepomuk, 332, 362, **387**, 474

St. John the Baptist, **387**

St. Julian, **387**

St. Martin, **387**

St. Michael, **387**

St. Patrick, **388**

St. Peter, **388**

St. Peter's patrimony, **389**

St. Theresa, **390**

St. Thomas, **390**

St. Thomas Aquinas, **390**

St. Thomas à Beckett, **390**

St. Ursula, **390**

Saladin, **391**

Salvator Rosa, **391**

Salvi, Lorenzo, **391**

San Fedisti, **392**

San Gennaro, **392**
Sanskrit, **394**
Santa Reparata, **394–95**
Santiago, **395**
Sapio, Mr., **395**
Sappho, **395**, 438
Saracen, **395**
Sardinia, King of, **396**
Saudia Arabia: Mecca, **278**, 297
Savonarola, Girolamo, **397**
Saxon Switzerland, **397**; Kleine Winterburg, **231**; Kuhstall, **232**
Scaligers, **398**
Schiller, Friedrich von, 107, **398–99**; *Cabal and Love* 107
Schneider, **399**
Schröder-Devrient, Wilhelmine, **399**
Schwarzenberg, Prince Felix, **399**
Schwitz, **399**
Scipios, **399**
Scotland: Aberdeen, **3**; Athol, **26**; Ben Nevis, **41**; Berwick, **43**; Birnam Hill, **44**; Carse of Gowrie, **72**; Dundee, **122**; Dunkeld, **122**; Edinburgh, **125–26**, (Arthur's Seat, **23**; Edinburgh Castle, **126**; Fife, **147**; Grampians, **178–79**; Greenock, **182**; Highland, **200**; Holyrood, **203**; Leith, **245**; Loch Katrine, **252**; Loch Lomond, **252**; Lothians, **258**; Lowlands, **259**; St. Bernard's Well, **385**); Moulward, **294**; Northumberland, **307**; Orkney Islands, **314**; Pentland Hills, **332**; Perth, **335**; St. Andrews, **384**; Stirling, **426**; Tay, **435**; Tweed, **452**
Scott, Walter, 48, 119, 250, 304, 333, 351, **400**; *Heart of Midlothian, The*, 400
Seidlitz, **400**
Seneca the Younger, **401**
Serbelloni, **401**; Gabriel, **401**; Villa, **401**
Servi di Maria, **402**
Seven Sleepers, **402**
Seven Years' War, **402**
Severn, Joseph, **402–3**
Sévigné, Madame de, **403**
Seymour, Sir George, **403**
Sfondrati, Francesco, 182, **403**
Sforza, Francesco, **403**
Shakespeare, William, 97, 157, **403–6**, 450, 488; *Antony and Cleopatra*, **16–17**; *As You Like It*, 24 (Rosalind, 24; Adam, 24); *Cymbeline*, **104**; *Hamlet*, **188–89**, 483; *1 Henry IV*, **194–95**, 333; *2 Henry IV*, **195**, 333; *2 Henry VI*, **195**; *3 Henry VI*, **195–96**; *Henry V*, **196**; *Julius Caesar*, 66, **226–27**; *King John*, **230** (Constance, **94–95**); *Life of Timon of Athens, The* (Timon, **440**); *Macbeth* 45, 193, **263–264** (Malcolm, 263; Macduff, 263; Rosse, 263); *Merry Wives of Windsor, The* (Falstaff, **143**); *Midsummer Night's Dream, A*, **283**; *Othello*, **315–16** (Desdemona, 315); *Richard II*, **369**; *Richard III*, 333, **369–70**; *Romeo and Juliet*, 343, **377–78** (Capulets, 377; Juliet, 377; Montecchi, 377); *Tempest, The*, **436** (Miranda, 436; Prospero, 436); *Twelfth Night*, **452–53** (Lady Olivia, 453); *Two Gentlemen of Verona*, **453**; *Two Noble Kinsmen*, 320, **453**; *Winter's Tale, The*, 332, **480**
Sheridan, 307; *Critic, The*, **102**
Shelley, Charles Bysshe, 157, **406–7**, 408, 411
Shelley, Clara Everina, 8, 37, 54, 84, 88, 275, **407**, 410, 411, 463, 480
Shelley, Elena Adelaide, 152, **407**, 411
Shelley, Harriet, 157, 202, 203, 330, 395, 407, **407–8**, 410, 411, 413
Shelley, (Eliza) Ianthe, 157, 407, **408**, 411
Shelley, Jane, 53, 202, 388, **408–9**, 412, 448
Shelley, Mary, **409–10**; "Absence," **3**; Albion House, **8**; Casa Magni, **72–73**; Casa Prini, 290, "Choice, The," **89**, 115, 410, 414, 478, 479–80; "Death of Love, The," 115, 243, 396, 438; "Defense of Velluti," **111**; "Dirge, A," **115–16**, 125; *Fields of Fancy, The*, **147**, 275; "Giovanni Villani," **170–71**, 467; "Hate," **192**; "Illyrian Poems—Feudal Scenes," 212, 281; "La Vida es Sueño," **236**; "Madame d'Houtetôt," **265–69**; Maison Chapuis, 267, 289; "Modern Italian Romances, " **286**, "Modern Italy," **286–87**; "Night Scene, A, 51, **305**, 373; "O listen while I sing to thee," **310**; "On Ghosts," **313**; "On Reading Wordsworth's Lines on Peel Castle," **313**, 340; Palazzo Verospusi, **321**; *Relation of the Death of the Family of the Cenci*, **363–64**; "Review of *1572 Chronique du Temps de Charles IX*," 281, **365**; "Review of *Cloudesley; A Tale*," 174, **365–66**; "Review of *The Bravo; a Venetian Story*," **366**;

"Review of *The English in Italy*," 223, **366**; "Review of *The Loves of the Poets*," 223, **366**; "Stanzas: How like a star you rose upon my life," **424**; "Stanzas: I must forget thy dark eyes' love-fraught gaze," **424**; "Stanzas: O, come to me in dreams, my love!" **424**; "Stanzas: The tide of time was at my feet," 235; "Stanzas: To love in solitude and mystery," **425**; "Tempo è ben di Morire," **436**; "To Jane," **442**; "Untitled: Fair Italy," **457**; "Visit to Brighton, A," **469**. *See also* individual titles of longer works
Shelley, Percy Bysshe, 24, 50, 53, 58, 59, 63, 67, 76, 78, 79, 80, 84, 87, 89, 94, 98, 103, 104, 107, 108, 113, 116, 119, 122, 134, 136, 151, 152, 157, 166, 167, 172, 174, 192, 200, 202, 203, 204, 207, 216, 219, 226, 229, 231, 247, 252, 256, 268, 274, 275, 277, 278, 279, 283, 283, 290, 298, 303, 313, 315, 316, 318, 327, 330, 340, 341, 347, 351, 352, 358, 360, 361, 362, 365, 375, 376, 391, 402, 407, 410, **410–12**, 413, 432, 433, 447, 461, 467, 468, 469, 470, 477, 478, 481, 483; *Alastor*, **6–7**; "Aziolo, The," **29**; "Boat on the Serchio, The," **46–47**; *The Cenci*, **76**, 304, 363; "Charles the First," 79, **80**; "Cyclops, The," **104**; *Defence of Poetry, A*, **111**; "From Moschus," **160**; "Hymn to Mercury," **210**; "Indian Girls's Song, The," **213**; *Ion*, **215**; *Hellas*, **194**; *Julian and Maddalo*, **226**; "Letter to Maria Gisborne, **246–47**; "Lift not the painted veil," **248**; "Lines Written Among the Euganean Hills," **134**; "Mask of Anarchy, The," **274–75**; *Mazenghi*, **458**; "Mont Blanc," 78, 200, **288–89**; "Music," **298** ; "Mutability," **299**; "Ode to the West Wind," **311**; *Peter Bell the Third*, **336**, 483; "Proserpine's Song," **352–53**; *Revolt of Islam, The*, **366–67**; "Rosalind and Helen," 51, **378**; "Sensitive-Plant, The," **401**; "Song of Apollo," **419**; "Song of Pan," **419**; "Sunset, The," **428**; "To the Lord Chancellor," **442**
Shelley, Percy Florence, 50, 51, 53, 71, 73, 111, 130, 136, 202, 232, 347, 328, 329, 331, 358, 359–60, 364, 374, 391, 409, 410, 411, **412–13**, 413, 439

Shelley, Sir Timothy, 328, 358, 407, 409, 410, 411, 412, **413**, 476
Shelley, William Godwin, 11, 37, 84, 78, 103, 133, 151, 157, 174, 275, 376, 410, 411, 412, **413**
Shene, **413**
Sheridan, Richard Brinsley, **413–14**; *Critic, The*, 414
Sibylla, Queen, **414**
Sicilian Vespers, **414–15**
Sicily, **415**; Enna, **132**; Etna, Mount, **134**; Messina, **281**, 309; Palermo, **321**
Sierra, **415**
Signor ——, **415**
Simond, Louis, 286
Sismondi, Jean Charles Léonard Simonde de, 250, 398, **416**, 460; *Histore des républiques italiennes du moyen âge*, 416
"Sisters of Albano, The" (Shelley), **416–17**; Andrea, **14**; Anina, **15**; Baldi, Domenico, **32**; D——, Countess Atanasia, **106**; Maria, **271**; Tossi, Betta, **444**
Slavonia, **417–18**
"Smuggler and His Family, The" (Shelley), **418–19**; Harding (Charles, **191**; Jane, **191**; Jem, **191**; Jenny, **191**; Tommy, **191**); Sailor, **384**
Socrates, **419**
Solon, **419**
Sophocles, 311
Soult, Nicolas-Jean de Dieu, **420**
South America, **420**; Andes, **14**
Southcott, Joanna, 36
Southey, Robert, 344
Sovereign Pontiff, **421**
Spain, **421**; Alcala, **8**; Alhambra, **9**; Almeria, **10**; Andalusia, **14**; Aragon, **19**; Baza, **36**; Cadiz, **65**; Cardela, **71**; Granada, **179**; Jaén, **222**; Loxa, **259**; Malaga, **267**; Murcia, **298**; Numantia, **308–9**; Roncesvalles, **378**; Saragossa, 309, **395**; Vega, **463**; Zubia, **488**
Spanish Armada, **421**
Spenser, Edmund, **422**; *Faerie Queen*, **139–141**; *Ruines of Rome*, **381**
Staël, Madame de, **423**, 460; Corinna, **96**
Starke, Mariana, **425**
Staudigl, Joseph, **425**
Steenie, **425**
Sterne, Laurence, **425**

Index

Strozzi, Filippo, **426–27**
Stuart, **427**
Suir, **427**
Sulla, Lucius Cornelius, **427**
Sultana, **427**
Swabia, **428**
Swartz, **428**
Sweden, Stockholm, **426**
Swift, Jonathan, **428–29**; Brobdignagians, 429; Gulliver, 429; Lilliput, 429
"Swiss Peasant, The" (Shelley), **429–30**; Ashburn, 24; Chaumont (Fanny, 81; Louis, 81); Marville (Henry de, 274; Madame de, 274; Monsieur de, 274)
Switzerland, **430**; Airolo, 6; Altdorf, 11; Amstag, 14; Andermatt, 14; Arbesau, 20; Basle, 34; Bellinzona, 40–41; Belrive, 41; Berne, 42; Bissone, 45; Brig, 56; Brunnen, 58; Chillon, 83, 350; Chur, 84; Clarens, 88; Cologny, 92; Côppet, 96; Côte d'Or, 99; Dottingen, 120; Drance, 120–21; Faido, 141; Falls of the Rhine, 143; Fluelen, 151; Geneva, 165 (Chêne, 82; Hôtel des Bergues, 205; Plainpalais, 342); Geneva, Lake, 165–66; Hôtel du Lac, 205; La Valais, 235; Laufenburg, 242–43; Lausanne, 243; Lucerne, 259; Lucerne, Lake, 259–60; Lugano, 260; Lugano, Lake, 260; Martigny, 273–74; Mont Salève, 289; Mont St. Gothard, 289 (Devil's Bridge, 114); Montalègre, 289; Mumpf, 297; Neufchâtel, 302–3; Nyon, 309; Pays de Vaud, 330; Pelissier, 331; Reuss, 365; Rheinfelden, 367; Rhône, 368; Saint Gingolph, 386; St. Maurice, 387; St. Sulpice, 390; Sécheron, 400; Simplon, 416; Sion 416; Schaffhausen, 398; Splügen, 423; Ticino, 438; Uri, Lake, 457; Vevay, 466
Syria, **430**; Damascus, 107; Palmyra, 321

Taaffe, John, 318, **432**
Tacitus, **432–33**; *Siege of Jerusalem*, 432
Tagliacozzo, Battle of, **433**
Taglioni, Marie, **433**
"Tale of the Passions, A" (Shelley), 259, **433–34**; Agli, Messer Giani dei, 6; Becari (Cincolo de', 38; Monna Gegia de', 39); Bosticchi, Giuseppe de', 52; Buzeccha, 63; Conradin, 94; Doneratico, Count Gherardo, 119; Elisei 129 (Arrigo dei, **129**; Despina dei, **129**); Elizabeth, Countess, **129**; Frangipani, **156**; Frederic, Duke of Austria, **159**; Gargalandi, Ubaldo de', **165**; Giudi, Count Guido Novello de', **171**; Lanfranchi, **239**; Lostendardo, Guielmo, **258**; Manelli, Messer Tommaso de', **269**; Monna Lisabetta, **288**; 'Nunziata, **309**; Pia, Madonna, **338**; Pulci, **354**; Ricciardo, **369**; Rossini, Ricciardo de,' **379**; Sesto, **402**
Tartar, **434**
Tasso Torquato, **434**; *Gerusalemme Liberata*, 168, 434; *Rinaldo*, 434
Tassoni, Alessandro, **434–35**
Teck, Frau Grafinn von, **434**
Tegrimi, Niccolò, **434–35**, 460; *Life of Castruccio*, 434
Tell, William, **436**
Tenerani, Pietro, **436–37**
Themistocles, **438**
Tiberius, Palace of, **439**
Tibullus, Albius, **439**
Tighe, George William, 294, **439–40**
Tighe, Laurette, 243, 276, 294
Tintoretto, 286, **440–41**
Titian, 33, **441–42**; *Assumption, The*, 441; *Cain Slaying Abel*, 441; *Cristo della Moneta*, 442; *David Slaying Goliath*, 441; *Death of St. Peter the Martyr*, 441; *Entombment*, 442; *Pieta*, 441; *Presentation of the Virgin*, 441; *Repentent Magdalen*, 442; *Sacrifice of Isaac*, 441; *Three Ages of Man*, 56, 442
Titus Flavius Vespasianus, **442**
Tobin, John, **442**; *Honeymoon, The*, 442
Tom of Coventry, **443**
Torre, Guido della, **444**
Tory, 298, **444**
"Transformation" (Shelley), 146, **445**; Carega, 71; Dwarf, 123; Guido Il Cortese, 185; Torella (Juliet, 443; Marchese, 443; Villa, 443)
Trelawny, Augusta Goring, **446**, 447
Trelawny, Edward John, 61, 63, 87, 98, 163, 231, 279, 311, 446, **446–48**, 488
Trelawny, Zella, 87
Trent, Council of, **448**
"Trial of Love, The" (Shelley), **448**; Angeline, 15; Caterina, 74; Moncenigo (Count, 288; Countess, 288; Faustine, 288; Ludovico,

537

288; Villa, **288**); Sant' Anna Convent, **394**; Toretta (Camilla della, **443**; Ippolito della, **443**; Marchese della, **443**)
Tristan, Sir, **449**
Troilus and Cressida, **449–50**
Trollope, Frances, **450**
Troy, **450**
Tullia, **451**
Turkey, **451–52**; Ararat, **19**; Constantinople, **95–96** (Khiyat Haneh, **230**; Pera, **332**; Scutari, **400**; Seven Towers, **402**; Stamboul, **424**; Sweet Waters, **428**; Marmora, Tower of, **273**, St. Sophia's, **389**; Top Kapou, **443**); Cydnus, **104**; Golden Horn, **176**; Hellespont, **194**; Kesan, **230**; Marmora, **273**; Rodosto, **374**
Turner, Joseph Mallord William, 295, **452**

Ultima Thule, **455–56**
United States: Boston, **52**; Charlestown, **80**; Illinois, **211**–12; Little Woman, **249**; Muddy Creek, **297**; New Orleans, **304**; New York, **304**; Philadelphia, **338**; Washington, **473**
Utopia, **457**

"Valerius: The Reanimated Roman" (Shelley), 293, 375, **459**; Giuseppe, Padre, **172**; Harley (Isabell, **191**; Lord, **191**); Marius, Gaius, **272**; Valerius, **458–59**
Valperga (Shelley), 128, 174, 254, 334, 410, **460–61**; Adimari (Antonio dei, **5**; Euthanasia, **136**, Fiammetta dei, **5**; Lauretta dei, **5**); Alberti, **7**; Albinois, **7**; Alderigo, **8**; Aldiani, **8**; Aldino, **8**; Alviani, **12**; Andreuccio, **15**; Antelminelli (Castruccio **74**, Dianora dei, **16**; Ruggieri dei, **16**); Atawel, Ethelbert, **25**; Avogadii (Berta, **28**; Nicola dei, **28**); Beatrice, **36–37**; Bergamino, **42**; Bernardi, **42**; Bindo, **44**; Bonconti, **49**; Bondelmonti, **49** (Bondelmonte de', **49**; Francesco, **49**); Borsiere, William, **52**; Cardona, Raymond de, **71**; Casaregi, Radolfo di, **73**; Castel Tealdo, **73**; Castellana, **73**; Castle Valperga, **459–60**; Castiglione, Giovanni da, **74**; Donati, **119**; Edward I, **126**; Edward II, **126**; Ezzelino, **139**; Faggiuola (Francesco della, **141**; Ranieri della, **141**; Uguccione della, **141**); Fairy's Fountain, **142**; Farinata, **144**; Filippini, **148**; Fondi, Ludovico de, **152**; Francesco, **156**; Frederick III, **159**; Gaveston, Piers, **164**; Gianfigliazi, **169**; Goffredo, Count, **176**; Grimaldi, **182**; Guarino, **183**; Guinigi, **185**, 440 (Arrigo de, **185**; Francesco de, **185**; Leodino de, **185**); Ildone, **211**; La Valle, **235**; Lanfranco, Padre, **239**; Langusco, **239**; Ligi, Fior de, **248**; Lorenzo, **257**; Louis, IV, **258**; Magfreda, **266**; Malespino (Calista de, **267–68**; Maroello, **268**); Malvezzi (Viscount di, **268**; Viscountess di, **268**); Malvoglio, **268**; Mandragola, Fior di, 265, **269**; Manfred, **269**; Marchesana, Madonna, **270**; Marco, **270**; Marsilio, **273**; Moncello, **288**; Mordecastelli, Vanni, **292**; Obizzi (Galeotto, **310–311**; Randolfi, **311**; Teresa, **311**); Obizzo, **311**; Paterin, 37, **328**; Pazzi, **330**; Pepi, Benedetto, 318, **332**; Philip le Bel, **338**; Polenta, Guido della, **345**; Quartezzani, **356** (Orlando, **356**; Ugo, **356**); Quartezzano, Cavaliere Pagano, **356**; Ricciardo, **369**; St. Maurice, Abbot of, **387**; Saramita, Andrea, **395**; Scala, Cane della, **398**; Scoto, Alberto, **399–400**; Soldanieri, **419**; Spini, **422**; Tripalda, Battista, **449**; Ubaldo, **455**; Ugolino, **455**; Uomini di Corte, **457**; Valperga (Count of, **461**; Countess of, **461**); Ventura, Tadeo della, **464**; Visconti (Azzo, **468**; Galazzo, **468–69**; House of, **469**; Matteo, **469**); Visdomini, **469**; Wilhelmina, **477**
Van Diemen's Land, **461**
Van Dyck, Anthony, **461–62**
Vandamme, Dominique-Renè, **462**
Vardarelli, **462**
Vasari, Giorgio, **462**
Venus of the Capitol, **464**
Veronese, Paul, **465**; *Family of Darius before Alexander*, 465; *Marriage Feast at Cana*, 465; *Martyrdom of St Mark*, 465
Vespasian, 118, **465**
Via Mala, **466**
Vienna, Congress of, **467**
Villani, Giovanni, 170, 338, 460, **467**
Villegas, Esteban Manuel de, **467**
Villeggiatura, **467**
Villeneuve-la-Guyard, **467–68**
Virgil, 287, 300, 348, **468**; *Aeneid*, **5–6**, 241, 355,

468 (Dido, **114–15**, Sibyl, **414**); *Ecologues*, **125**, 354, 468; *Georgics*, **167**, 468
Vishnou, **469**
Viviani, Teresa, 55, 318, 389, 411, **468–69**
Volney, Constantin François de Chasseboeuf, comte de, **470**; *Ruins of Empires*, 470
Voltaire, 89, **470**

Wagram, Battle of, **471**
Wallenstein, 110, 286, 456; Burgau, Margraf of, **60**
Walpole, **472**
Wars of the Roses, 384, **473**, 476
Waterloo, Battle of, **473**
Weber, Carl; 399, **474**; *Abon Hassan*, 474; Bridesmaid, 474; *Der Freischütz*, 474; Linda, 474; Wolf's Glen, 474
Wenceslaus IV, **474**
Wertheim, Mr., **475**
West Indies, **475**: Barbados, **33**; Jamaica, **220**
White Rose, 238, **476**, 485
Whitton, William, 413, **476–77**
Wieland, Christoph, **477**
William of Apulia, 169
William the Conqueror: stone, **477**
Williams, Edward Ellerker, 84, 98, 219, 279, 354, 362, 411, 447, **477–78**
Williams, Jane, 56, 84, 87, 116, 202, 219, 308, 333, 354, 362, 373, 411, 447, 469, 477, **478–79**
Wilson, John, **479**
Winter, Peter von, **480**; *Oracle, The*, 480
Wittgenstein, Count Ludwig, **480**
Wollstonecraft, Everina, 122, 143, 360, **480–81**
Wollstonecraft, Mary, 53, 61, 170, 172, 173, 212, 216, 294, 380, 388, 410, 480, **481**; *Letters Written During a Short Residence in Sweden, Norway, and Denmark*, 212, **247**, 481
Wordsworth, William, 173, 189, 313, 336, 340, 344, **482–83**; *The Hermit's Cell*, **198**, 482; "Personal Talk," **335**; "She dwelt Among the Untrodden Ways," **406**; "Slumber Did My Spirit Seal, A," **418**; "Tintern Abbey," **440**; "World Is Too Much With Us, The," **483–84**
Wurtemburg, Queen of, **484**

York, House of, 238, 473, 476, **485**
Young, Edward, **483**
Ypsilanti, Alexander, **486**

Zenno, Gian Battista, **487**
Zingarelli, Niccolò, **488**; *Giuletta*, 488
Ziska, John, **488**
Zodiac: Bear, **36**; Pisces, **340**; Ram, **359**; Taurus, **435**; Twins, **453**

About the Authors

LUCY MORRISON is an Assistant Professor of English at Salisbury University. She has published articles in *Studies in Philology*, *Studies in Short Fiction*, and the *Keats-Shelley Review*.

STACI STONE is the Director of Humanities and Assistant Professor of English at Murray State University. She is the author of *Instructor's Manual for Understanding Race, Class, Gender, and Sexuality: A Conceptual Framework* and has supplied entries on Maria Edgeworth and Margaret Veley in the *Encyclopedia of the Essay* and the *Dictionary of Literary Biography*.

PR
5398
.A2
M67